REMEMBERING THEIR SACRIFICE
IN THE SECOND WORLD WAR

NORTH DOWN AND ARDS

Compiled by Barry Niblock

Published 2014 by
Barry Niblock
www.barryniblock.co.uk

First Edition
First Impression

Designed by April Sky Design, Newtownards
Tel: 028 9182 7195
Web: www.aprilsky.co.uk

Printed by W&G Baird Ltd, Antrim

ISBN 978-0-9570627-2-6

Dedication and Thanks

This Book of Honour is dedicated to the memory of all those men and women with North Down and Ards connections who died in service, or as a result of enemy action, during the Second World War – Air Force, Army, Royal Navy, Merchant Navy and Nursing Personnel together with Civilians. More than 650 people are commemorated.

The people from North Down and Ards who died in the First World War are commemorated in my two Great War Books of Honour which were published on 11 November 2011 (11/11/11):

Remembering Their Sacrifice in the Great War – Ards
Remembering Their Sacrifice in the Great War – North Down

During the First World War, Chaplain to the Forces the Revd Geoffrey Studdert Kennedy MC – also known as Woodbine Willie – said:

'The brutality of war is literally unutterable
There are no words foul and filthy enough to describe it'

In 1914 the author H.G. Wells wrote a series of articles that subsequently appeared as a book entitled *The War That Will End War*. This title evolved into the common catchphrase *The War To End All Wars*. But of course it didn't. During the Second World War General Dwight D. Eisenhower said:

'I hate war as only a soldier who has lived it can, only as one who has seen its
brutality, its futility, its stupidity'

Use of the poppy as a symbol of remembrance of those who died in war was inspired by the First World War poem *In Flanders Fields* written in May 1915 by the Canadian physician Lieutenant Colonel John McCrae after he witnessed the death of a fellow soldier on the battlefield. This is the first verse:

In Flanders fields the poppies blow
Between the crosses, row on row,
That mark our place; and in the sky
The larks, still bravely singing, fly
Scarce heard amid the guns below

In 1918 an American Young Women's Christian Association (YWCA) worker named Moina Michael campaigned to have the poppy adopted as the national symbol of remembrance in America and in 1920 the National American Legion adopted it. When the British Legion was founded in 1921 (the Royal prefix was granted in 1971) it too adopted the poppy as its symbol of remembrance, as did veterans' groups in Australia, Canada and New Zealand.

In September 1914 the British poet Robert Laurence Binyon (1869-1943) wrote the poem *For The Fallen* and the fourth verse has come to be widely used in remembrance ceremonies commemorating the Fallen in the First and Second World Wars and Other Conflicts. In 1939 Binyon said it was the fourth verse that came to him first:

> *They shall not grow old, as we that are left grow old:*
> *Age shall not weary them, nor the years condemn.*
> *At the going down of the sun and in the morning*
> *We will remember them*

Sir Winston Churchill once said about the Second World War:

> *'Never in the field of human conflict was so much owed by so many to so few'*

And so today it behoves us all to remember the Sacrifice of those who died:

> *Greater love hath no man than this,*
> *that a man lay down his life for his friends*
> *St. John 15:13*

This Book of Honour could not have been written without help from a great many people and a list of acknowledgements is included towards the back of the book. Here, at the outset, I want to put on record my particular thanks to **Heather Lyons** for all her time-consuming work and painstaking effort in helping me to gather information about those who died; her genealogical expertise; her diligence in following up leads; her patience and persistence in leaving no stone unturned and her willingness to always go the extra mile – not only in collecting information but taking photographs in cemeteries and other places throughout Northern Ireland and further afield. Thank you Heather for all that you have done; words are really not enough.

Also at the outset I want to thank **my wife Anne** for her encouragement; her patience; her help with research and proof-reading and her support in countless other ways throughout the project. Without your help Anne I couldn't have done it.

For our grandchildren Ella, Sophie, Jason, Brugh and Rowan

May they and children everywhere be able to live in peace

Author's Preface – A Tribute

Lists of names on War Memorials are a poignant reminder of lives lost but on their own the lists do not convey the human tragedy behind each death. A woman once said of the war memorial in her home village, 'How I hated it. I knew so many of the lads whose names were engraved there – warm, vital, laughing people – no connection with the lifeless, cold thing which commemorates them'. This Book of Honour seeks to establish the context of the deaths and in so doing to pay tribute to all those people with North Down/Ards connections who died during the Second World War.

There has been extensive publicity during the information-collecting stage of this project and exhaustive efforts have been made to ensure that the list of names is as complete as possible. That said, it is accepted that some names may yet be missing. If that is the case and, where evidence is provided to support their inclusion, such names will be included in any future edition of this book. New names, together with additional information collected about people already listed in this book, will be added to the *War Dead of North Down and Ards* website which may be found at www.barryniblock.co.uk This website is interactive and readers are invited to use it to provide new information.

It will be noticed that there is more information in this book about some people than others. That is simply a reflection of the data available at the time of writing and the objective is to increase the amount of information in those cases where there is currently very little known. That said, space constraints in this book dictate that not everything known about some of those who died has been included. In such cases additional information may be included on the website and it is hoped that the details published there, and in this book, will provide a useful starting point for family historians and others wishing to pursue additional research.

In this book we remember the sacrifice of those who died and the impact on generations of their families left behind – grandparents; parents, uncles and aunts; brothers, sisters and cousins; spouses and children and in some cases grandchildren. It is beyond the scope of this book to pay tribute to all of the other North Down/Ards heroes who fought and survived the Second World War. Some information about them may be added to the *War Dead of North Down and Ards* website on an ongoing basis.

BARRY NIBLOCK

Contents

Introduction

Where a casualty's name is **emboldened,** more details can be found in the *Names in Alphabetical Order* Section of this book.

Geographical Area

The geographical area covered by this Book of Honour is the area currently defined by the combined North Down and Ards Borough Council area as it is in 2014. Some of the people who are included are commemorated on the War Memorials in more than one town or village. For example, Able Seaman **George Victor Lowry** is listed on both Bangor and Groomsport War Memorials; Leading Aircraftman **Norman McReynolds** is listed on both Bangor and Newtownards War Memorials.

Several instances have also been found where casualties are commemorated in more than one church, for example, Able Seaman **George Victor Lowry** is commemorated in First Bangor Presbyterian Church and in Groomsport Parish Church of Ireland Church.

Criteria for Inclusion

Criteria for including names in this Book of Honour have been set so that they are as inclusive as possible. Anyone who died in service or as a result of enemy action during the Second World War and who had a demonstrable association with the North Down/Ards area has been included:

- Those who were born in the area, including those who subsequently moved away from the area
- Those who were born elsewhere but came to work/reside in the area
- Those who married into local families
- Those who had strong family connections with the area
- Those who died in the area and/or were buried in the area
- Those who died while they were stationed in the area

Sources of Information

In compiling the material for this Book of Honour a wide range of information sources has been tapped. Names have been collected from Cenotaphs, Royal British Legion and Church Memorial Plaques, together with the Memorial Plaques and Rolls of Honour in Loyal Orange Halls, Masonic Halls, Public Buildings, Schools, Sports Clubs, and Workplaces. Provincial and local newspapers published during and after the war years have been very informative, particularly the *County Down Spectator* and *Newtownards Chronicle*.

Information has been collected from a range of websites and databases including Church Records, the 1901 Census (taken on 31 March 1901), the 1911 Census (taken on 2 April 1911), Regimental Museums, the National Archives in Britain together with Military Archives in Australia, Canada, New Zealand, South Africa and the United States of America. War diaries and attestation papers have also been useful.

A series of public appeals for information generated a good response from surviving relatives of people who died. That said, and as has already been stated, it is not possible to say beyond all doubt that the list of names included in this Book of Honour has no omissions. Furthermore, to date it has not been possible to find definitive information about some of the people whose names are listed on War Memorials in the North Down/Ards area. This book contains a lengthy list of acknowledgments and amongst them are many experts who have given advice on the interpretation of data. In cases where it has not been possible to corroborate information they have helped me to draw conclusions. That said, any errors in the book are mine and mine alone.

Military Installations in North Down and Ards

During the Second World War there were a great many military installations in the North Down and Ards area. In some cases there remain visible traces of them to the present day and in other cases there is nothing left to indicate where they were located. In the paragraphs that follow, some *examples* are provided to give an indication of the range of installations in the area; the list is illustrative and not definitive. The military installations in North Down and Ards included defensive positions designed to protect people, property and/or military sites from attack by the enemy, along with search and rescue, hospital, billeting, Prisoner-of-War and other facilities.

Belfast was vulnerable because of its position at the head of Belfast Lough. This made it relatively easy to locate from the air. For this reason Light and Heavy Anti-Aircraft gun emplacements and bunkers were situated in many places including Ballyrainey near Comber and Ballymacormick Point near Groomsport. Shipping in Belfast Lough was vulnerable to attack by enemy submarines and there were other defensive installations along the North Down coastline. At Orlock, between Groomsport and Donaghadee, there was a Submarine Refuelling Station and also at Orlock – at Sandeel Bay – there was one end of a Submarine Indicator Loop. This was a cable laid on the seabed across Belfast Lough from Orlock to Blackhead in County Antrim and it was designed to detect a submarine passing over it by means of an induced current caused by the submarine's magnetism. Once detected, action could then be taken to detonate electrically operated mines. Also at Orlock was one of the Coastal Defence Batteries equipped with a Searchlight Position.

Pilot Boats

Pilot Boats berthed in Bangor were deployed to escort both naval and merchant shipping coming into Belfast Lough. Crewed by civilians under Naval direction, both the boats and the crew were the responsibility of the Admiralty Berthing Officer. Three men from Donaghadee along with one man from Bangor were drowned on Saturday 8 May 1943 in what became known locally as the 'Bangor Bay Disaster'. They died when the Pilot Launch *Miss Betty* capsized and sank while returning to port after responding to a call from a ship entering Belfast Lough. The three men from Donaghadee who died were **Harry Aiken, William George Nelson** and **William White.** The Bangor man who died was **William Sloan Anderson.**

SS *Troutpool*

From time to time enemy aircraft dropped mines in Belfast Lough and it is believed to have been this type of mine that sank the SS *Troutpool*. On route from Rosario in Argentina to Britain with a cargo of grain, the SS *Troutpool* had put into Belfast Lough for degaussing – a process designed to reduce the likelihood of any magnetic mines in the water being attracted by the ship's hull. After re-starting her engines she was struck by two mines around 2.00 pm on 20 July 1940 and sank about a mile off the coast near Bangor. Eleven crew members were killed in the explosions and five of them were buried in the North Down/Ards area; Fireman and Trimmer **Shief Ahmed** (buried in Bangor Cemetery) and Carpenter **Thomas Smith Beckett** (buried in Movilla Cemetery, Newtownards) were the only two whose bodies were identified. Three unidentified sailors from the SS *Troutpool* were buried in Movilla Cemetery (one on 1 August 1940, one on 24 August 1940 and one on 26 August 1940). At low tide the superstructure of SS *Troutpool* was visible and, because it was a hazard to shipping, the wreckage was dispersed with explosives.

The nine crew members whose bodies were either not identified or not found are commemorated on the Tower Hill Memorial in London (Panel 112):

- Ali Abdul (aged 39); Fireman and Trimmer; British Arab; 216 Bute Road, Cardiff
- Mohamed Awled (aged 40); Fireman and Trimmer; British Arab; 216 Bute Road, Cardiff
- Muckele Caleb (aged 43); Fireman and Trimmer; British Arab; 216 Bute Road, Cardiff
- Alexander Connell (aged 19); Mess Room Boy; Son of Alexander Connell of 356 Argyle Street, Glasgow
- Salek Ahmed Demari (aged 41); Fireman and Trimmer; British Arab; 291 Hope Street, Glasgow
- Donald Andrew MacDougall (aged 17); Ordinary Seaman; Son of Donald and Theresa MacDougall, of Castlebay, Isle of Barra
- **John McGrath** (aged 53); Able Seaman; Son of Hugh and Margaret McGrath, Portaferry
- Donald McNeill (aged 41); Able Seaman; Son of Neil McNeill and Catherine McNeill of Main Street, Port Charlotte, Isle of Islay
- William George Murray (aged 25); Ordinary Seaman; Son of William and Annie Murray of 28 Drummuir Street, Hopeman, Morayshire

At the time it was speculated that the mines which sank the SS *Troutpool* were dropped by a long-range German Focke-Wulf Fw Condor 200 aircraft of the type that crashed into Belfast Lough on 25 July 1940 killing two of its five crew members. The two men who died that day were named as Unteroffizier Willi Andreas and Unteroffizier Rudolf Wagner and their bodies were never recovered. The three survivors who managed to climb aboard a life raft and were subsequently captured by the anti-submarine trawler HMS *Paynter* were named as Hauptmann Volkmar Zenker, Unteroffizier Heinz Hoecker and Gefreiter Hohmann.

There are records of German Luftwaffe aircraft being shot down over Northern Ireland during the Second World War, for example, a Heinkel He 111 aircraft was shot down east of Downpatrick during the 7/8 April 1941 air raid on Belfast and a Junkers Ju 88 aircraft was brought down near Ardglass on 6 May 1941. Both of these aircraft crashed into the sea.

There are two other CWGC headstones in Movilla Cemetery that commemorate Merchant Navy seamen whose bodies were found but not identified, and neither was their ship identified. One unknown casualty was buried on 10 March 1945 in one of the graves and in the other grave three unknown casualties were buried together (one was buried on 2 January 1941, one on 6 February 1941 and one on 3 May 1942). Unidentified soldiers buried in battlefield cemeteries had similar inscriptions on their headstones. In all cases they were:

Known Unto God

On 4 September 1940 Anastasios Noytakion, a 33 year old Greek seaman, died in Bangor Hospital as a result of an accident and he was buried two days later in Bangor Cemetery (Grave 5W 172).

MV *Santa Lucia*

On 1 November 1940 this Dutch motor coaster struck a mine and sank in Belfast Lough with the loss of four crew members. Two who were buried in Bangor Cemetery were named as Johannes de Jong aged 21 (Grave 5X 22) and Guitje S. van Dyke aged 33 (Grave 5X 23a).

MV *Karanan*

On 20 January 1942 this Dutch motor coaster was on route from Liverpool to Belfast with a general cargo when she was in collision with the steam tanker *British Engineer* near Mew Island (one of the Copeland Islands) and she sank with the loss of two crew members.

Prisoners-of-War

There were several Prisoner-of-War camps in Northern Ireland at various locations including Newtownards, Rockport, Seahill and Jackson Road in Holywood. HMS *Al Rawdah* (built in 1911) was requisitioned by the Ministry of Shipping in 1940 for use as prison ship. HMS *Al Rawdah* was moored in Strangford Lough off Killyleagh and some of the prisoners held there were later transferred to Crumlin Road Gaol in Belfast. The *Al Rawdah* remained in use as a prison ship until 1946 and she was scrapped in 1953.

Grey Point Fort

Grey Point Fort at Helen's Bay was an important Coastal Defence Battery Gun Emplacement comprising Ammunition Magazine, Gun Batteries, Shelters, Observation Post, Fire Command, Radar Platform and three Searchlight Emplacements. During the Second World War the Fort was the Operations Headquarters for all Northern Ireland coastal defences and it was used specifically to protect Belfast Lough. As part of this role, when a ship entered Belfast Lough it was contacted by coastal defence personnel and required to make itself known. If there was no response the ship was signalled to 'heave to or be sunk'. Gunners stationed at Grey Point Fort carried out regular shooting practice using a target on a barge towed one mile behind a Clyde tug. The still-visible War Department Boundary Stone for Grey Point Fort bears the markings WD No. 1 to HWM in line with BS 1 & 2.

Pillboxes and Air Raid Shelters

A great many Pillboxes and Air Raid Shelters were constructed throughout the North Down and Ards area. A Type 22 Pillbox (a hexagonal guard post with rifle ports) was constructed on the course at Bangor Golf Club. Pillboxes were so-called because their shape was similar to that of the boxes in which medical pills were dispensed. During the war all of the shrubbery near the pillbox was removed to ensure an unobstructed line of fire. A Nazi bomb that fell onto the first fairway of Bangor Golf Course exploded harmlessly. To prevent any air landing attempts, steel posts were driven into the second fairway and the Golf Club's commitment to the war effort included a Tillage Order in 1940 for 18 acres of the course to be used to grow food crops. An anti-landing obstruction was constructed in the north east corner of Strangford Lough by driving lines of posts into the sandy foreshore. Nearby there were airfield defensive structures known as Seagull Trenches (reinforced 'W' shaped trenches said to look like a seagull's wings).

Pillboxes were built on the shore of Strangford Lough between Comber and Newtownards and at Ballyvester between Millisle and Donaghadee. The remains of Air Raid Shelters can still be seen at Ballyvester and Helen's Bay. After the war some Air Raid Shelters along the coastline were demolished and the remains used to shore up sea defences, for example, at Groomsport and Ballyholme.

The Air Raid Shelter constructed in the middle of the road at the top of Main Street in Bangor was demolished and all the debris removed. The Public Air Raid Shelter in Ward Park, Bangor still stands. Air Raid Shelters built for use by hospital staff and patients were located at Ards Hospital and Air

Raid Shelters built for use by RAF personnel were located at the Quarter, Ardkeen. Guard posts were constructed in residential areas too, for example, at the corner of Maxwell Road and Bryansburn Road in Bangor West.

General Dwight D. Eisenhower

In the build-up to the D-Day landings in Normandy in June 1944, Belfast Lough was filled with all types of naval and other shipping, including the United States battleships USS *Arkansas*, USS *Nevada* and USS *Texas* and the United States Cruisers USS *Quincy* and USS *Tuscaloosa*. General Dwight D. Eisenhower had a temporary headquarters in Bangor and he addressed Allied troops in Bangor before they departed. On 9 July 2005, his granddaughter, Mary Jean Eisenhower, came to the town to rename Bangor Marina's North Pier as the Eisenhower Pier. The plaque on the Eisenhower Pier bears the following inscription:

'From here started the long hard march to Allied victory'
Dwight D Eisenhower
Opposite this point was the gathering area for a massive convoy of mixed
ships which sailed to arrive at the beaches of Normandy on D-Day
6 June 1944

SS *Empire Tana*

The remains of the wreck of the SS *Empire Tana* lie in Ballyhenry Bay, Strangford Lough (near Portaferry). Built in 1923 as the *Carso* by shipbuilders Stabilmento in Trieste, Italy she was scuttled by the Italians in Kisamayu, Italian Somaliland in 1941 when this port was captured by British Forces. Subsequently salvaged by the Allies, *Carso* was renamed the SS *Empire Tana* and used as a cargo ship until February 1944 when she was damaged in a collision off Casablanca in Morocco. The SS *Empire Tana* was used as part of the Gooseberry Breakwater (ships sunk to create an area of sheltered water) during the D-Day landings on Sword Beach in Normandy on 6 June 1944. After the war the ship was purchased by the John Lee Breakers Yard at Ballyhenry Bay and the intention was to beach her at high tide but she hit a rock and broke into two pieces. The forward section was later cut away and salvaged.

Cloughey Lifeboat

During the Second World War the Cloughey lifeboat *Herbert John* was involved in some noteworthy rescues. On 28 January 1941 the Dutch steamer SS *Alhema* became grounded on the North Rock off Cloughey. On route from Liverpool to Port Said in Egypt the SS *Alhema* was carrying supplies for the British Eighth Army. Forty-five men had to be taken off and all of the cargo was lost. On 21 January 1942 the Motor Coaster *Cairngorm* went aground off Ballyquintin Point. The *Cairngorm* had fired distress flares which were seen by HMS *Montbretia*, a Royal Navy corvette which was escorting a convoy northwards from the Mersey. When HMS *Montbretia* approached to investigate the flares the convoy followed and the corvette, along with four freighters from the convoy – SS *Asiatic*, SS *Bronxville*, SS *Browning* and SS *Orminster* – together with another small coaster, the *Dorian*, all got stuck on the rocks between Kearney Point and Ballyquintin Point.

Royal Air Force Air Sea Rescue Units were based at Portaferry (No. 56) and Donaghadee (No. 57). Their motto was *The sea shall not have them*. There was a Lookout Post above Millin Bay, Portaferry.

Bombing Range at South Island

A practice Bombing Range was operated at South Island in Strangford Lough, north of the village of Greyabbey. One of the practices was to Skip Bomb a line of old military vehicles positioned on the island. Skip Bombing was a low-level bombing technique whereby bombs dropped onto the water skipped across the surface. On one occasion a Supermarine Seafire aircraft was struck by debris from a bomb dropped by the aircraft flying ahead of it and this caused the Seafire to crash into the Lough near Kircubbin. At Mount Stewart there was a Bombing Range Quadrant Tower (usually two quadrant towers and the target itself formed three points of a triangle and the purpose was to score the accuracy of practice bombing). Military Personnel based at Palace Barracks in Holywood were transported to Greyabbey for shooting practice at a range which was known locally as *The Long Shot*.

Munitions – Manufacture and Disposal

On Coyle's Lane in the townland of Ballyrobert there was a munitions factory in which shell casings were produced. Other items that were made locally included recoil gear for Bofors Guns together with aircraft components at Glencraig. There were reports that in June 1943 Belfast Lough was the disposal site selected when some 50,000 rounds of 'K' Class ammunition (this contained both explosive and toxic chemical agents) were dumped.

Military Hospitals and Service Personnel Billets

Bangor Central Primary School was used as a Military Hospital during the Second World War and personnel who worked in the Hospital were billeted at the Pickie and Strand Hotels in Bangor. American troops were billeted at Ballyholme and the Pickie Hotel was used as an Officer's Club. Landing

Craft exercises were carried out by the US forces at Ballyholme Beach and the American big band musician Glenn Millar played at Caproni's Ballroom, Ballyholme. While travelling to France to entertain US troops Glenn Millar's aircraft disappeared on 15 December 1944 in bad weather over the English Channel and his body was never recovered.

From 25 December 1943 until 29 April 1944 Clandeboye Estate was the headquarters of the 277th Army Band of the United States Army, and American forces with responsibility for vehicle storage and issue were stationed at Camp Pinetum in Clandeboye Estate. In Comber the Old Mill was used to accommodate both British and American forces. One of the Units billeted there was the Staffordshire Regiment. During the Second World War there was a tremendous demand for metal to smelt down for making munitions and Comber made an important contribution. After the First World War the town was presented with a captured German Field Gun as a memorial to Second Lieutenant Edmund de Wind who was awarded the Victoria Cross. During the Second World War this memorial gun was cut up and smelted down – as were the railings round the First World War Memorial Garden in Newtownards. Second Lieutenant Edmund de Wind is commemorated on Page 184 in the Book of Honour *Remembering Their Sacrifice in the Great War – Ards* compiled by Barry Niblock.

At Mount Stewart near Greyabbey, attic rooms connected to the main house were used as a Convalescent Ward during the Second World War. Following the deployment of 231 Squadron RAF to Newtownards Airfield in 1940 soldiers from 106 Field Squadron (Air Support) Royal Engineers (Volunteers) arrived to work on the airfield to make it suitable for RAF operations. Headquarters Company of the Royal Engineers was based at Mount Stewart with their Officer Commanding (Major Fulton) being billeted in the House while junior ranks were housed in the buildings around the Coach House and Stables.

During the Second World War, Redburn House in Holywood was acquired by the Air Ministry and used as accommodation for Women's Royal Air Force (WRAF) personnel. Also on the site there was a Military Hospital. Redburn House was once the home of the Dunville family and during the First World War Second Lieutenant John Spencer Dunville was awarded the Victoria Cross. Second Lieutenant Dunville is commemorated on Page 143 in the Book of Honour *Remembering Their Sacrifice in the Great War – North Down* compiled by Barry Niblock.

Kinnegar Base Depot in Holywood was an Army Ordnance Depot during the Second World War and it was also where detachments of British and

American forces were billeted. There was an Anti-Aircraft Battery on site and another at Ballysallagh, Craigantlet. Palace Barracks in Holywood also provided accommodation for several different Battalions of British and American forces. In Groomsport, 515 Field Survey Company, Royal Engineers were billeted in Groomsport House. The stable block and outbuildings on the Dunleath Estate at Ballywalter were used by military personnel including the Royal Ulster Rifles and the Royal Berkshire Regiment.

Killynether House, Newtownards was requisitioned by the British Army during the Second World War. Situated below Scrabo Golf Club, Killynether House was a large building with considerable grounds. The building was not released by the Ministry of Defence until 31 May 1949. Killynether House has since been demolished and the Nissan Huts removed. Several Units of American forces were billeted in Donaghadee, including Portavoe House and also in Killyleagh Castle which is located just outside the geographical area covered by this Book of Honour.

Craigdarragh House at Helens Bay was used as an Army Camp with a large number of soldiers living in the grounds; later the same camp was used to house Prisoners-of-War. There was an Army Camp at Crawfordsburn House.

Campbell College Belfast

When Campbell College was evacuated in 1940 and relocated in Portrush the buildings in Belfast became Number 24 (London) General Hospital. On the night of 4/5 May 1941 the Hospital was bombed and 19 medical staff and patients were killed. In February 1946 Campbell College was returned to civilian use as a school and in 2001 the last of the Nissan Huts which had been erected in the grounds as wards were removed. Amongst those with a North Down/Ards connection who died there was Wilhelm Dalbeck (aged 33). He was a German Prisoner-of-War (A 438606) being held at Jackson Road, Holywood and he died at Number 24 (London) General Hospital on 23 July 1945.

Refugee Children Movement

The Kindertransport, also known as the Refugee Children Movement (RCM), was a rescue mission that brought to Britain around 10,000 predominantly Jewish children from Nazi Germany, Austria, Czechoslovakia, Poland and the Free City of Danzig. Ballyrolly House in Millisle became a Kinderfarm where the refugee children grew vegetables. There was a synagogue on site and the children attended Millisle Primary School. At the entrance to the school there is now a Safe Haven Holocaust Memorial Garden and Memorial Plaque. Recently plans have been announced to preserve the farm and outbuildings.

Chain Home Stations

There was a Chain Home Station at Ganaway Road, Millisle and another one at Roddans Road, Ballywalter. Chain Home was the code name for a ring of coastal early warning radar stations built before and during the Second World War. Also known as Air Ministry Experimental Stations (AMES), there were two types – Type 1 Stations provided for the long-range detection of aircraft and Type 2 Stations detected aircraft at lower altitudes. Situated in the Craigantlet Hills between Holywood and Newtownards was a Medium Frequency Direction Finding (MF/DF) Radio Station associated with the airfield at Sydenham.

Bogus Airfields and Starfish Sites

There was a bogus airfield located at Kearney, Portaferry. At the commencement of the Second World War the Air Ministry formed a secret department to oversee ways of misleading German Luftwaffe bombers by using decoys and other means of deception. Colonel Sir John Turner was in charge. Decoy Sites included bogus airfields constructed on open ground and equipped with dummy aircraft, vehicles and buildings. These 'K' Sites were designed to deceive the enemy during daylight hours. To simulate airfields at night 'Q' Sites were equipped with dummy flare paths and other airfield lights.

In order to draw enemy bombers away from towns and cities, dummy towns known as Starfish Sites were set up on open land. At night specially made 'fireworks' could be ignited to simulate bomb explosions and fires in a town under attack. On Starfish Sites QL lights were designed to simulate welding flashes from factories, railway signals and lights not complying with blackout regulations. There was a Starfish Site at Creighton's Wood near Holywood.

George Best Belfast City Airport

Sydenham Airport was established by Short Brothers (Shorts) in 1937 and from 1938 to 1939 it was known as Belfast Harbour Airport – Belfast's main civilian airport. At the start of the Second World War the airport became RAF Sydenham (RAF Belfast) and was used for training purposes by both the Air Force and Fleet Air Arm of the Royal Navy who took control of the Royal Naval Air Yard Belfast (HMS *Gadwall*). On 5 May 1941 the airfield was bombed and left temporarily unusable. There is a Memorial Plaque at the airport bearing the words:

In memory of the men of 804 and 702 Naval Air Squadrons, based at Sydenham, Belfast between March 1941 and July 1942 which operated Fairey Fulmar and Hawker Sea Hurricane Fighter aircraft from CAM-ships (Catapult Armed Merchantmen) on convoy defence duties during the Battle of The Atlantic.

Newtownards Airfield

Before the outbreak of the Second World War, Newtownards Airfield was the second of Northern Ireland's two civil aerodromes. Opened on 31 August 1934 by the Duke of Abercorn it was constructed on 50 acres of land provided by the 7th Marquess of Londonderry. After the outbreak of war this airfield was requisitioned and used as a Satellite Landing Ground (SLG) for de Havilland Tiger Moths and Miles Magisters from RAF Sydenham. In July 1940 Royal Air Force 416 Flight, which was equipped with Westland Lysanders, moved from Aldergrove to Newtownards and was re-designated 231 Squadron.

In December 1941 Newtownards airfield came under the control of RAF Fighter Command. Target towing aircraft such as Westland Lysanders, Miles Master Mark IIs and Boulton Paul Defiants were used to facilitate air-to-air gunnery practice by fighter pilots based at Ballyhalbert Airfield. RAF Ballyhalbert was one of more than 20 new airfields constructed in Northern Ireland during the Second World War and will be referred to again later in this Section.

290 Squadron

290 Squadron was formed at RAF Newtownards on 1 December 1943 and provided training for anti-aircraft defences in Northern Ireland. 290 Squadron moved to RAF Long Kesh on 25 March 1944 and to RAF Turnhouse near Edinburgh on 28 August 1944. In January 1945 290 Squadron went to Belgium and on 27 October 1945 it was disbanded.

On 15 July 1944 two aircraft from 290 Squadron Royal Air Force based at Long Kesh crashed while they were entertaining a crowd of spectators at Warrenpoint during a Civil Defence Demonstration. The aircraft involved were a Miles Martinet TT1 (MS626) with a crew of two and an Airspeed Oxford (LX 598) with a crew of three. While one aircraft was climbing over the town the other was approaching from the direction of Carlingford Lough. The pilots saw each other at the last minute and, although both took evasive action, the two planes made contact and crashed. All five men aboard the two aircraft were killed.

Aboard the Oxford were:

- WO Lucien Arthur W.J. Eccles aged 21 from Hindley Green, Wigan.
- FS Dennis Myers aged 21 from Boroughbridge Yorkshire.
- Sergeant Peter Sturdy from Willesden, Middlesex.

Aboard the Martinet were:

- WO Albert Gordon Gibb aged 28 from Huyton, Lancashire.
- Sgt George William Mosey aged 26 from Hamsterley Colliery, Durham.

Long Kesh Airfield

During the Second World War several buildings that were part of the Long Kesh Airfield complex were situated very close to All Saints Church of Ireland Church, Eglantine, Lisburn. In the graveyard adjoining that church there are 21 CWGC headstones including one for Flying Officer **Gordon Elgin Vance** who died along with Squadron Leader **Thomas George Westlake** when their Airspeed Oxford aircraft crashed into the sea on 15 April 1944 close to the Copeland Islands, Donaghadee. Airspeed Ltd., was founded by the aeronautical engineer Nevil Shute Norway who later became famous as the novelist Nevil Shute.

Ballyhalbert and Kirkistown Airfields

Construction of an airfield at Ballyhalbert commenced in 1940 and Royal Air Force Station Ballyhalbert opened officially on 26 June 1941. It was designed to be a Fighter Airfield and Sector Station with one satellite at Kirkistown, some five miles to the south west. Fighter defence of Belfast and the east coast of Northern Ireland was a top priority and the first Station Commander was Wing Commander H.D. McGregor DSO. Ballyhalbert's satellite airfield, RAF Kirkistown, opened in July 1941. Aircraft based at Ballyhalbert included Hawker Hurricanes, Boulton Paul Defiants, Supermarine Spitfires, Bristol Beaufighters and de Havilland Mosquitoes.

The first operational unit arrived at Ballyhalbert on 15 July 1941 – 'A' Flight of 245 Squadron RAF with their Hawker Hurricane aircraft – and on 30 July 1941 Wing Commander F.L. White replaced Wing Commander H.D. McGregor DSO as Station Commander. The information contained in the following paragraphs provides an overview of operations at RAF Ballyhalbert during the Second World War with the objective of putting into context the accidents and deaths that occurred there. What follows is not intended to be a definitive historical account.

On Tuesday 26 August 1941, as senior officers at Ballyhalbert awaited the arrival of 504 (County of Nottingham) Squadron, they witnessed what became known locally as the Battle of Ballyhalbert. A very strong wind was blowing as the 18 Hawker Hurricane aircraft flew in from RAF Chilbolton in Hampshire. Most of the aircraft were brand-new and many of the pilots were fresh from their Operational Training Units. Crowds of local people turned out to see the Hurricanes land. At that stage the Station at Ballyhalbert wasn't completely finished and only one runway was serviceable. To either side of this runway was a quagmire of mud because of the ongoing construction work. The 18 aeroplanes flew in low over the airfield in close formation and then Squadron Leader Philip Trevor Parsons made the first approach to land with all the other pilots lining up behind him. The intention was for each aeroplane to touch down after crossing the Glastry Road and then taxi to the dispersal area.

There was just one minor shunt as 'A' Flight landed and then it was the turn of 'B' Flight, led in by Flight Lieutenant 'Bindle' Barnes. Flight Lieutenant Barnes landed safely but the pilot following him was too close and, to avoid a collision, he veered off the runway into the mud and overturned. Other aircraft that day suffered a similar fate and accounts vary as to the number of aircraft (between eight and twelve) destroyed or damaged. Only minor injuries were sustained by the pilots. A little over a year later, on 2 October 1942, Squadron Leader Philip Trevor Parsons was killed at Colerne in Wiltshire, England while serving with 264 Squadron. Aged 25 he was a son of Squadron Leader W.W. Parsons and Madge Parsons and the husband of Vera Parsons of Exeter. He was buried in Colerne (St. John the Baptist) Churchyard.

On 11 August 1941, 712 Defence Squadron was formed at Ballyhalbert and on 11 September, 280 defence personnel arrived to undertake guard duties at both Ballyhalbert and Kirkistown. On 15 September the GOC General Majendie visited Ballyhalbert, Kirkistown and Tubber na Carrig House, Kircubbin to inspect the defences at those Stations. It was in the grounds of Tubber na Carrig House that the Royal Air Force Air Operations Block for Ballyhalbert Airfield was located.

John Andrews, Prime Minister of Northern Ireland, paid a visit on 17 September 1941 and 504 Squadron put on a display of formation flying. It is recorded in the Operations Record Book that on 25 September 'Operations' moved from Aldergrove to Kircubbin. On 19 November 1941 Pilot Officer **Frederick Hugh Anderson** was killed in a flying accident. His funeral service in Ballyhalbert Parish Church of Ireland at Ballyeasborough was conducted by Squadron Leader Revd T.A. Jenkins MA, the Station Chaplain.

504 Squadron moved to RAF Kirkistown on 12 January 1942 and 25 Night-Fighter Squadron arrived at Ballyhalbert with their Bristol Beaufighters. In February 1942 Wing Commander H.P. Pleasance replaced Wing Commander F.L. White as Station Commander and later in the month Group Captain K.S. Brake assumed command.

Not all of the aircraft crashes at RAF Ballyhalbert had fatal consequences. On 25 February 1942 a Supermarine Spitfire aircraft (AA906) overshot the runway and cart-wheeled onto its nose. The pilot was Sergeant K.G. Brookes (No. 1202898) and he was uninjured. However, there was a fatal outcome on 15 April 1942 when Leading Aircraftman **John Connell Cowan** died after being shot during manoeuvres. 25 Night-Fighter Squadron left Ballyhalbert and on 19 June 1942, 504 Squadron returned to Ballyhalbert from Kirkistown. In August 1942 United States Army Air Forces (USAAF) 5th Fighter Squadron arrived at Ballyhalbert with their Spitfires.

In October 1942, 504 Squadron left Ballyhalbert and 501 Squadron arrived. On 4 November 1942 **Frederick Strutt**, a 31 year old civilian died at Ballyhalbert Airfield. He was working with the Drem Lighting System at the airfield and he was killed when a Bristol Beaufort aircraft piloted by Sergeant G.B. Swift ran off the runway and struck him. The Drem Lighting System was devised by Wing Commander Richard Llewellyn Roger Atcherly at RAF Drem Station in East Lothian, Scotland. It took the form of a circle of lights around the runway and its purpose was to guide pilots safely home (the Spitfire had a long nose and sometimes this impeded a pilot's vision). Along the beach at Ballyhalbert an Approach Lighting System was constructed.

In December 1942 and January 1943 there were adverse reports about the deplorable state of the buildings at Ballyhalbert Airfield. Water ran into many of the buildings during periods of heavy rain. In addition to the buildings on the airfield site there were several dispersed sites nearby with buildings for housing personnel and other purposes. At times there were more than 1,300 service personnel stationed at Ballyhalbert including RAF, WAAF, Army and Navy personnel.

On 17 January 1943 a local couple, Dave and Hannah Donnan, were on the seashore south of Portavogie when they witnessed a fatal accident. Two Spitfires of 501 Squadron were engaged in a practice dogfight when they collided. One plane landed safely at Ballyhalbert but the other was seriously damaged and crashed. The pilot, Flying Officer **Philip Kenneth Woodsend,** baled out but his parachute failed to open and he plummeted onto the beach, not far from where Dave and Hannah Donnan were standing.

During March 1943 District Courts Martial were held to try airmen from Ballyhalbert on charges of stealing public property. Sentences ranged from 40 days detention to six months hard labour. On 28 March 1943 a Church Parade was held to celebrate the 25th anniversary of the formation of the Royal Air Force in 1918. It is recorded in the Operations Record Book for Ballyhalbert Station that at the end of March 1943 an invasion exercise for the training of aircrew personnel was begun but, owing to a fatal accident, the exercise was not completed.

On 30 April 1943 501 Squadron departed and 130 Squadron arrived with their Spitfires. 2707 Squadron arrived from Ballykelly on 1 July 1943. On 4 July 1943 Sir Herbert Emerson, former Governor of the Punjab, presented 130 Squadron with their crest. 130 Squadron left on 5 July 1943 and 315 (City of Deblin) Polish Fighter Squadron arrived with their Spitfires, as did 26 Squadron RAF with their North American P-51 Mustangs. At that time these two squadrons shared the Station. General Kazimierz Sosnkowski, Inspector General of Polish Armed Forces, visited Ballyhalbert in August 1943.

On 22 August Pilot Officer **Jerzy Ryszard Tuczemski** of 315 Squadron died when he crashed during a training exercise. On 15 September Wing Commander Charles Ronald Hancock OBE DFC assumed command of the Station at Ballyhalbert and during October the first Fleet Air Arm Squadron arrived with Supermarine Seafires, Grumman Wildcats, Grumman Hellcats, Chance Vought Corsairs, Fairey Fulmars, Miles Martinets and Fairey Barracudas. In November 1943, 315 (City of Deblin) Polish Fighter Squadron was replaced by 303 (Kosciuszko) Polish Fighter Squadron and 125 Squadron Bristol Beaufighters took over night defence.

On 29 December Wing Commander **Charles Ronald Hancock OBE DFC** was killed in a flying accident and on 11 January 1944 Group Captain Richardson assumed command. On 17 March 1944 two de Havilland Mosquitoes of 125 Squadron collided in mid air and crashed into the sea. No trace was ever found of any of the four crew members and they are all commemorated on the Runnymede Memorial:

- Flying Officer **Donald Maldwyn Griffiths**
- Flying Officer **Frederick John Reid**
- Pilot Officer **Horace James Rich**
- Flight Lieutenant **Eric Augustus Snow**

On 21 March 1944 RAF Kirkistown ceased to be a satellite of Ballyhalbert and its administration was transferred to Royal Air Force Northern Ireland Headquarters. In April 1944 it was reported that a Naval Rating who had been transferred from Ballyhalbert to 25th General Hospital with acute appendicitis died of peritonitis following an operation.

On 19 May 1944 General Eisenhower, Supreme Commander Allied Forces, paid a brief visit to Ballyhalbert Airfield. On 25 October 1944 the Air Ministry authorised transfer of RAF Station Ballyhalbert from Fighter Command to Royal Air Force Northern Ireland Headquarters. On 3 November 1944 Commander V.W.L. Proctor took over command as Senior Naval Officer at Ballyhalbert and on 13 January 1945 Group Captain C.J. Collingwood OBE DFC assumed command of Ballyhalbert Station.

Other Squadrons stationed at Ballyhalbert included 784 Naval Squadron with Fairey Fulmars, 1840 Naval Squadron with F6F Hellcats and 808/885 Naval Squadrons with Supermarine Seafires (the naval version of Supermarine Spitfires adapted for operation from aircraft carriers). On 14 July 1945 Ballyhalbert Airfield was handed over to the Royal Navy and commissioned on 17 July as HMS *Corncrake*. Kirkistown Airfield was commissioned as HMS *Corncrake II*. On 13 November 1945 Ballyhalbert Airfield was returned to the Royal Air Force and closed. It was abandoned in 1947 and sold to developers in March 1960.

Ballywalter Airfield

Some of the new airfields built after the start of the Second World War were designated as Satellite Landing Grounds (SLGs) and used to store aircraft including Avro Ansons, Bristol Blenheims, Vickers Wellingtons, Westland Lysanders, Handley Page Hampdens, Handley Page Herefords, Armstrong Whitworth Whitleys, Fairey Battles, Blackburn Bothas and Chance Vought Corsairs. They were outstations of No. 23 Maintenance Unit (MU) at Aldergrove and the grass-strip airfield at Ballywalter was known officially as 16 SLG. The first test landing at Ballywalter was by an Avro Anson on 25 April 1941 and because of cross winds the runway was extended by some 250 yards for operational use. The site officially opened on 1 June 1941 and Vickers Wellingtons were among the aircraft stored there. It closed on 14 March 1945. Ballywalter House stands across the main road from what was Ballywalter Airfield and aircraft were hidden among trees in the grounds of Dunleath Estate.

Millisle Airfield

Construction of an airfield for the United States Army Air Force (USAAF) was commenced but not finished. Part of the runway still remains and some of the buildings situated on the Killaughey Road are used at the present time by small businesses.

Luftwaffe Raid on Newtownards Airfield

Between 10.45 pm and 4.30 am during the night of Easter Tuesday 15 April 1941 and Wednesday 16 April 1941 there was a large-scale German air raid on the City of Belfast. That night the Luftwaffe also bombed other targets including Newtownards Airfield. The airfield was guarded by soldiers of the 70th (Young Soldiers) Battalion, Royal Inniskilling Fusiliers. Some of these soldiers were too young for front line service and were deployed instead on home defence.

Newtownards Airfield was attacked with a considerable number of incendiary bombs and some high-explosive bombs. One high-explosive bomb that fell on the hutments of 'A' Company Headquarters killed 13 men, all of whom served with the 70th Battalion, Royal Inniskilling Fusiliers. Most were killed instantly and the remainder died the following day as a result of their injuries. The casualties were all taken to Newtownards Hospital.

- Fusilier **William Bellamy**
- Fusilier **Samuel Burke**
- Lance Corporal **Alexander Carlisle**
- Fusilier **Andrew Copling**
- Fusilier **Hugh Fulton**
- Fusilier **George Graham**
- Fusilier **Daniel Higgins**
- Fusilier **Leslie Love**
- Fusilier **Samuel McFarland**
- Company Quartermaster Sergeant **William McMurray**
- Fusilier **Ernest McNeill**
- Warrant Officer Class II **Alfred Penfold**
- Fusilier **Matthew Wright**

On Monday 5 March 2012 a Memorial to the 13 soldiers of the 70th Battalion Royal Inniskilling Fusiliers who were killed during the air raid on Newtownards aerodrome on the night of 15/16 April 1941 was unveiled and dedicated in the War Memorial Garden, Newtownards.

Also during the night of 15/16 April 1941 there was another casualty with a North Down/Ards connection. Flight Lieutenant **Wilfrid Mark Hamilton Brookes** of 231 Squadron who was in Belfast at the time, was killed during the air raid.

North Down/Ards Civilians Killed on 15/16 April 1941

In addition to the deaths in Belfast and at Newtownards Airfield due to enemy action on 15/16 April 1941 there were other deaths as well. Nearby towns and villages, including Bangor and Newtownards, were also attacked. Areas of Bangor where bombs fell included Ashley Gardens, Bangor Golf Clubhouse, Baylands, Farnham Road, Hazeldene Gardens, Knockmore Park and Ranfurly Avenue. Fires blazed on Scrabo Hill, Newtownards and bombs fell on Green Road, Conlig and on Comber Road, Newtownards. At least 14 civilians with North Down and Ards connections were killed, including five in Bangor:

- **Matilda Grattan** together with her daughters **Angeline Grattan** and **Shelagh Grattan** died at 40 Ashley Gardens, Bangor
- **Margaret Byers Watt** died at 5 Hazeldene Gardens, Bangor
- **Robert Wright** of 32 Baylands, Bangor died of his injuries in Bangor Hospital

The other nine died in Belfast:

- **Edith, Henry, Isabella** and **William Dunwoody**
- **Nancy Simms Gribbin**
- **Thomas Morton**
- **Ellen, Bessie** and **Evelyn Tate**

The attack on 15/16 April 1941 was not the first enemy attack on Bangor. Incendiary bombs were dropped on Bangor on Friday 13 September 1940 and, although there was damage to property, there were no casualties. There is also on record an instance of Bangor being hit by 'friendly fire'. This happened on Tuesday 2 January 1940 during a Royal Navy training exercise. There was damage to property but again no casualties. One of the houses damaged on that occasion was occupied by the Holland family and some six months later, on 23 July 1940, Sergeant Observer **Charles Julius Holland** was killed in action.

At other times civilians with North Down/Ards connections died as a result of enemy action, for example, **Margaret Kate McGowan** (aged 21) from Kinlough in County Leitrim died at Moneyreagh on 17 December 1942. She was engaged in Air Raid Precautions (ARP) work.

Polish Airmen Buried in Northern Ireland (Six in North Down/Ards Area)

After the invasions of Czechoslovakia and Poland by Nazi Germany in 1939 many Czech and Polish airmen and airwomen came to Britain and joined the Royal Air Force. Fourteen RAF Squadrons were predominantly Polish and two of these Polish Squadrons were stationed at RAF Ballyhalbert airfield – 315 *(City of Deblin)* Squadron from July until November 1943 and 303 *(Kosciuszko)* Squadron from November 1943 until April 1944. Records show that airmen and airwomen of other nationalities were also stationed at Ballyhalbert and these included American, Australian, Canadian, Dutch, Free French (including Lieutenant Jacques Andrieuz), Newfoundlander and New Zealander.

In addition to the predominantly Polish Squadrons, Polish airmen also served in other RAF Squadrons and some of these Squadrons were based in Northern Ireland for varying lengths of time. By the end of the Second World War it was recorded that the bodies of 15 Polish airmen were buried in Northern Ireland, six of them in graveyards in the North Down/Ards area. Eight of the 15 Polish airmen were based in Northern Ireland when they were killed and seven were based elsewhere at the time of their deaths.

Sergeant Franciszek Pretkiewicz served with 245 Squadron based at RAF Aldergrove in County Antrim. On 30 November 1940 he was on a training exercise when the engine of his Hurricane fighter aircraft seized and he crashed near Cushendall in County Antrim. He was buried in Glenavy Roman Catholic Graveyard, Co. Antrim.

Six Polish airmen serving with 304 (Polish) Squadron, RAF Coastal Command based at RAF Predannack in Cornwall, England comprised the crew of a Vickers Wellington bomber which crashed on the slopes of Mount Brandon in the Republic of Ireland during the night of 20/21 December 1943. They were returning to base from a patrol over the Bay of Biscay and all six men were killed on impact:

- Flight Sergeant Klemens Adamowicz
- Sergeant Stanislaw Czerniawski
- Sergeant Pawel Kowalewicz
- Sergeant Kazimierz Lugowski
- Sergeant Wincentry Pietrzak
- Sergeant Naftali Pawel Kuflik

Their bodies were handed over to the British authorities near Middletown in County Armagh. Sergeant Kuflik was buried in Carnmoney Jewish Cemetery, Co. Antrim and the other five were buried in Milltown Roman Catholic Cemetery, Belfast.

Sergeant **Jozef Antoni Pudelko** served with 6 Anti-Aircraft Co-operation Unit (AACU) and he was based for a time at RAF Newtownards. On 23 April 1942 he was the pilot of a Lysander communications and target-towing aircraft which crashed on take-off from RAF Belfast (now the George Best Belfast City Airport). He and Sergeant Norman Elcock were both killed.

Sergeant **Edward Lewandowski** also served with 6 Anti-Aircraft Co-operation Unit (AACU) and he was based for a time at RAF Newtownards. He was killed on 30 April 1942 during a training flight when the Lysander aircraft he was piloting hit a balloon cable at RAF Belfast and spun to the ground.

Based at RAF Jurby in the Isle of Man, Wing Commander **Wladyslaw Eugeniusz Heller** was navigator on board an Avro Anson aircraft from No. 3 School of General Reconnaissance at Squire's Gate airfield, Blackpool and he died when the aircraft crashed on Knocklayd Mountain in County Antrim during the course of a navigation exercise on the night of 18 October 1943. He was buried in Movilla Cemetery, Newtownards, Co. Down.

Sergeant **Henryk Andrzej Flegier** served with 315 (Polish) Squadron, based at RAF Ballyhalbert and he was killed on 5 October 1943 when the Spitfire fighter aircraft he was piloting crashed 1½ miles northwest of Ballyhalbert airfield as he was carrying out a practice interception. He was buried in Movilla Cemetery, Newtownards, Co. Down.

Sergeant **Henryk Komenda** served with 256 Squadron, RAF and he was on temporary attachment at RAF Newtownards as a member of a special flight of Boulton Paul Defiant night fighters. He was killed on 9 July 1942 when the Defiant aircraft he was piloting crashed at Woodburn in County Antrim and he was buried in Movilla Cemetery, Newtownards, Co. Down. Sergeant (Air Gunner) **Peter Charles Hunter Phillips** was also killed in the crash and he too was buried in Movilla Cemetery, Newtownards, Co. Down.

On 11 September 1943 Warrant Officer **Stanislaw Grondowski** of 315 Squadron based at RAF Ballyhalbert was leading a flight of three Spitfires for practice formation flying. In bad weather over the hills immediately to the west and north of Belfast the three aircraft became separated and, in the course of trying to find each other, they crashed in various places. Warrant Officer Grondowski died when his Spitfire flew into the ground near Plantation House, close to Lisburn. Sergeant **Wladyslaw Kolek**, who had joined 315 Squadron only two days beforehand, was killed when his Spitfire flew into high ground at Ballyutoag in County Antrim. The third pilot was Sergeant Zygmund and, although he was seriously injured, he survived his crash. Both Warrant Officer Grondowski and Sergeant Kolek were buried in Ballycranbeg (Mount St. Joseph) Roman Catholic Graveyard, Co. Down.

Pilot Officer **Jerzy Ryszard Tuczemski** served with 315 Squadron and he was killed on 22 August 1943 in the course of a low flying navigational training exercise. His Spitfire was seen to be experiencing engine trouble prior to flying into the ground on Long Mountain, north-north-east of Rasharkin in County Antrim. Pilot Officer Tuczemski was buried in Ballycranbeg (Mount St. Joseph) Roman Catholic Graveyard, Co. Down.

Other Polish airmen who were based in Northern Ireland during the Second World War and who died in service were not buried in Northern Ireland. It was reported in the press that on 14 December 1943 Flying Officer **Stanislaw Podobinski** of 303 Squadron had been lost while returning to Ballyhalbert from Toome in County Antrim. In adverse weather he crashed his Supermarine Spitfire aircraft two miles south of Snaefell Mountain in the Isle of Man and he was buried in Jurby (St. Patrick) Churchyard in the Isle of Man.

Aircraft Crashes in the Mourne Mountains

During the Second World War a number of aircraft crashed in the Mourne Mountains, for example:

On 16 March 1942 a Vickers Wellington Bomber (X3599) crashed near the Black Stairs close to the Glen River at Grid Reference 363 293. There were at least four fatalities including 24 year old Assistant Section Officer Barbara Blakiston-Houston (WAAF), a passenger, who was buried in Seaforde Parish Church of Ireland Graveyard. Also killed was the Revd James Dawson Crawford of 14 King Street, Thetford, Norfolk. He was a son of Joseph H. Crawford, of Drum, Newbliss, Co. Monaghan and the husband of E.E. Crawford.

On 19 July 1942 a Bristol Beaufighter aircraft X7822 of 153 Squadron crashed on Shanlieve Mountain at Grid Reference 250 214. The aircraft was totally destroyed and both crew members were killed – Pilot Officer **John Peter Sadd** and Sergeant **Marks Wayne**.

On 12 September 1943 there were three fatalities when a Vickers Wellington Bomber (X9820) crashed on the Northwest face of Slieve Commedagh at Grid Reference 343 286, approximately 150 feet from the summit. They were Flight Sergeant John Sherlock Price aged 33 (RNZAF); Sergeant Harold Thomas Arthur Walters aged 21 from Hendon, Middlesex and Sergeant Thomas Brewin aged 20 from Leicester.

On 10 April 1944 a Martin B-26 Marauder aircraft (41-18150) crashed on the South-western side of Chimney Rock Mountain at Grid Reference is 362 255, just below the summit. Five American crewmen on board were killed – 2nd

Lt Howell C. Osborne from Arkansas, 2nd Lt Chester M. Turner from Kansas, Staff Sgt Roy R. Cappe from Pennsylvania, Staff Sgt William J. Devenney from Pennsylvania and Sgt Jimmie Gyovai from West Virginia.

There were two fatalities when a de Havilland Mosquito aircraft (NS996) crashed on 12/13 January 1945 just above the Castles on Slieve Commedagh at Grid Reference 345 281. They were Flight Lieutenant Robert MacKenzie aged 22 from Edinburgh and Flying Officer John Gordon Faragher aged 21 from Sale, Cheshire. Their bodies weren't found until 3 March 1945.

The British Commonwealth Air Training Plan (BCATP)

Under an agreement signed in December 1939, Canada provided training facilities for airmen from all parts of the British Commonwealth. Training began in the spring of 1940 and by the end of 1943 more than 3,000 students were graduating every month. By the end of the war the BCATP had produced more than 131,500 aircrew including pilots, wireless operators, air gunners and navigators.

Ferry Command

There was also a need in Europe for war planes built in North America and so RAF Ferry Command was established to coordinate the arrangements for these aircraft to be flown from Gander in Newfoundland to the United Kingdom. In all some 9,340 aircraft were flown across the Atlantic with the loss of 74 aircraft and around 500 airmen. The first flight of seven aircraft from Gander arrived at Aldergrove on 11 November 1940.

War-Related News Items

Earlier in this Section both the *County Down Spectator* and the *Newtownards Chronicle* were acknowledged as valuable sources of information about North Down/Ards casualties in the Second World War. Included for interest at this point are some other war-related news items that were reported in the local press. The deaths of casualties from just outside the North Down/Ards area boundary were reported, for example, Sergeant John Edward Redmond Sharvin from Strangford who served with the RAF was killed on 24 October 1940. Sergeant (Wireless Operator/Air Gunner) Samuel Hugh Albert Jess (aged 19) from Killyleagh served with the RAF and he died on 13 March 1941.

Leading Writer Robert Victor (Rob) Berner aged 22 from Shrigley, Killyleagh served with the Royal Navy aboard HMS *Hood* and he was one of more than 1,410 men who died on 24 May 1941 when HMS *Hood* was shelled and sunk in the Denmark Strait. Born on 23 May 1919 he was a son of Robert Victor

Berner and Catherine Berner (nee Mullan) and as a Leading Writer his duties encompassed administration and accountancy. Out of the entire ship's company there were only three survivors – William Dundas, Robert Tilburn and Edward Briggs. HMS *Hood* casualties are all commemorated in a Book of Remembrance in St. John the Baptist Church, Boldre, Hampshire. Marine Charles Telford (Downpatrick), Lieutenant Commander **John Gordon Morrison Erskine** (Holywood) and Ordinary Seaman **Lambert Charles Shepherd** (Bangor) also died aboard HMS *Hood*. In 2012 an unsuccessful attempt was made to retrieve the bell from HMS *Hood*. It had been intended to put the bell on display at the National Museum of the Royal Navy in Portsmouth.

Fusilier Harry Atkinson aged 23 from Grimsby, Lincolnshire served with the 4th Battalion, Royal Welch Fusiliers and was stationed in Northern Ireland when he died on 9 May 1941. He was buried in Killyleagh Church of Ireland Churchyard. Sergeant (Wireless Operator/Air Gunner) Harry Crawford from Castlerock served with the RAFVR and he died on 15 May 1941. Harry Crawford was a noted table tennis player in Northern Ireland and he often competed in Newtownards. Fusilier John Henry McNeilly aged 25 from Crossgar served with the Royal Inniskilling Fusiliers and he saw service in North Africa, Sicily and Italy. Fusilier McNeilly was invalided home with shell shock and he spent time recuperating in the military hospital in Bangor. Shortly before he was scheduled to go back on duty he was found dead in a London street on 15 April 1945. He had sustained multiple stab wounds to his thigh and it was concluded that he had been murdered. He was buried in Killyleagh Roman Catholic Cemetery.

Wartime Romances

Both wartime and post-war weddings involving service personnel were reported in the local press and below are a few examples. In 1940 Sadie McKeag of 123 Mill Street Newtownards married Canadian soldier Albert Cromwell and they had four children. After the war Sadie and her four children left Newtownards for the United States to join her husband Albert who had settled in Seattle after demobilisation. Madge Croan of 23 Frederick Street, Newtownards married US Army infantryman Charles Leopold when he was stationed in Northern Ireland and they had a son named Joseph. After the war Madge and Joseph left for South Carolina in the United States to join Charles when he was demobilised.

In May 1946 Eileen Joan McBlain WAAF from Bangor married Flight Sergeant Basil de Beauvoir Marsh RAF from Newtownards. In June 1946 ex-Sergeant James (Jimmie) Graham RAF of Southwell Road, Bangor married Margaret Ashton Eccles from New Zealand. Jimmie Graham was captured at the fall of Singapore and held in a Japanese Prisoner-of-War camp for 3½ years. He and Margaret Eccles met in Auckland at a luncheon given for released Prisoners-of-War.

In September 1946 Lieutenant (A) Basil L.T. Boyd of Donaghadee married Audrey M. Hankin (left) who had been a Voluntary Aid Detachment (VAD) nurse attached to the Royal Navy. In November 1946 Captain J.N. Boal Royal Engineers from 20 Manse Road, Bangor married Gertrude Elaine Houston from Groomsport. In April 1947 Georgina Stevenson from 4 West Street, Newtownards married Herbert C. Nieto of Jersey City, USA. They met when Herbert was stationed in Northern Ireland. In November 1947 Joan Henrietta Wallace of Church Street Newtownards married Clifford Samuel Gamble of Gouverneur, New York. Their romance began when he was stationed in Northern Ireland.

Year By Year Chronology of News Items

During 1941 it was reported that soldiers stationed in outlying parts of the Ards District had made requests for musical instruments; there were reports too about older men enlisting. A Comber old soldier joined up in South Africa where he had established a very successful business. John Wright was a great-grandfather who had recently celebrated his golden wedding anniversary when he answered the call for ex-servicemen up to the age of 60 years who had been engineers in the First World War to enlist. He had four grandsons and three grandsons-in-law already serving when he was accepted after understating his age (he said that he was 59 years and 5 months old).

In September 1941 Gunner Sammy Wright from Newtownards was able to broadcast a message from the North African desert on the BBC Forces programme to his wife Jean at 39 Frederick Street: 'This is Sammy calling. It must be two years since you heard my voice. Tell wee Sammy I am sorry I missed his birthday but I hope you got my telegram. Good night and God bless you'.

Sometimes after a serviceman or woman was reported as *missing in action* it came as a relief when news came through that he or she was being held as a Prisoner-of-War. In 1942 this was the case for the family of Flight Lieutenant William Herbert Thallon of 80 Brunswick Road, Bangor.

In June 1942 there was widespread concern throughout Newtownards and the surrounding district when word came through that Tobruk had fallen. Back in 1939 a considerable number of young men from the area had joined the ranks of 5 Battery 2 Light Anti-Aircraft Regiment, Royal Artillery based at Movilla Camp in Newtownards and it was in Libya that many of them were subsequently killed, wounded or taken prisoner. One such man who was taken prisoner was Robert Adair from Newtownards; he managed to escape after being held for eleven months in Italy and was then in hiding for a further fifteen months before making contact with Allied Forces and being repatriated.

Julian (Jules) Dorrian of 89 Movilla Street, Newtownards joined the Battery on 7 October 1939 and he was at Tobruk when the Allied garrison was overrun by the German Army. Some 30,000 prisoners were taken. When the order was given 'every man for himself' Jules Dorrian managed to escape but in the process he had to leave behind all his personal possessions, including precious letters from his family in Newtownards. There was one from his mother dated 9 March 1942 in which she expressed the hope that it wouldn't be long before Jules was back home again. Jules Dorrian's personal possessions were found by a German Afrika Corps soldier named Werner Posselt and Werner held on to them as war souvenirs.

After the Second World War ended Werner Posselt lived in East Germany and it wasn't until after the dismantling of the Berlin Wall in 1990 that he was able to begin the process of finding Jules Dorrian. Some 52 years after the fall of Tobruk the two former enemies met in 1994 and Werner handed back to Jules his precious letters. Werner Posselt died on 5 August 2005. Jules Dorrian died on 5 August 2010.

In 1942 it was reported that 21 year old Francis Millar from Ballyhalbert had been torpedoed twice within three days and, along with 16 companions, had spent 28 days in a 24-foot open boat in the South Atlantic. Francis Millar first went to sea when he was 14 years old and on 5 November 1940 he was serving aboard the SS *Kenbane Head* when that ship was sunk in what became known as the 'Jervis Bay Incident'. One of the men who died was Francis Millar's close friend **David John (Dave) Pritchard** from Ballyhalbert. Other local men who lost their lives aboard the SS *Kenbane Head* were **James McNeilly Belshaw** from Ballywalter, **George McClelland Leckey** from Holywood and **Reginald John Primmer** from Portaferry. Francis Millar survived that sinking and was tossed about on a raft for 36 hours before being picked up and landed at a Canadian port.

In the summer of 1942, far out in South Atlantic, the ship that Francis Millar was serving on was torpedoed and seven men were killed. The survivors took to a lifeboat and were picked up after 36 hours. Then their rescue ship was torpedoed and sunk and Francis Millar was one of 16 survivors who took to a lifeboat. This lifeboat's radio transmitter was damaged and the boat ran out of fuel. With very little food on board there had to be strict rationing and it was very hot during the day and very cold at night. Relief came after 28 days when they were rescued and brought ashore on the east coast of Africa. Francis Miller was 52 years old when he died on 14 May 1973 and he was buried in Ballyhalbert Cemetery.

In April 1943 it was reported that a Court Martial was held in Bangor. Sergeant Harold Potter, a Canadian pilot, was found guilty of performing unauthorised aerobatics over Bangor on 8 November 1942. His aircraft crashed at 29 Ashley Drive and as a result Sergeant Potter was reduced in rank.

Able Seaman Henry Clarke from Belfast served with the Royal Naval Volunteer Reserve aboard HMS *Lagan* and he was 24 years old when he was killed on 20 September 1943. HMS *Lagan* was struck by a torpedo fired from the German submarine *U-270*. It was noted in the press that his father Jeremiah, his mother Lavinia, six of his brothers, a sister and her husband and child had all been killed when their home at 4 Ballynure Street, Belfast took a direct hit during the air raid on Easter Tuesday 1941.

When Prisoners-of-War were repatriated they came home to joyous scenes and a tumultuous reception and this was the case in May 1943 when Gunner Alexander Murphy returned to his home at 82 Mill Street, Newtownards. He said he was looking forward to a plate of bacon and eggs. Gunner Murphy was one of a group repatriated in exchange for Italian Prisoners-of-War and the exchange took place in Lisbon, Portugal. He had been serving with 5 Battery 2 Light Anti-Aircraft Regiment, Royal Artillery at Tobruk and he said that around 2.00 am on 20 June 1942 word came through that German tanks were approaching. With five other men Gunner Murphy was in an advanced gun pit that took a direct hit during the subsequent fighting. Four men in the pit were killed – Lieutenant (Acting Captain) **John Malcolmson Gibson**, Sergeant **Alexander Davidson** and Gunner **David McClinton** all from Newtownards and Gunner George Alfred Rayner from Glastonbury in Somerset. Only Gunner Murphy and Bombardier Orr from Scotland survived.

Gunner Murphy was injured in the attack and he reported that, as a Prisoner-of-War in Italy, he had been treated well by the Germans but he said that while he was in the prison hospital the Italian orderlies stole his clothes, his new boots and his false teeth. When he was being repatriated he asked for his false teeth to be returned but this request was refused. He commented, 'When you are getting hard biscuits to eat you need all the teeth you've got!'

Another Prisoner-of-War to return home safely in 1943 was Gunner James Wilson of Springhill, Bangor. He too served with the Royal Artillery and was taken prisoner in January 1942 in Libya. Gunner Wilson escaped from an Italian Prisoner-of-War Camp and after 28 days he reached the British lines in southern Italy. There was an added poignancy to his homecoming because his brother, Aircraftman First Class **Robert Logan (Bobby) Wilson**, had died in an aircraft accident on 28 June 1942.

Sergeant Reginald Charles Bracewell of Moira Drive, Bangor served with the King's Royal Rifle Corps and he was awarded the DCM for gallantry. It was reported that in the action he got his arm blown off.

Sister Betty Makepeace was a former pupil of Glenlola School in Bangor and she was serving on a hospital ship off the coast of Italy when it was sunk by German Luftwaffe dive bombers – despite having the unmistakable Red Cross markings prominently displayed. Sister Makepeace and Sister Warnes from Morningthorpe, Norwich scrambled into a lifeboat but the boat capsized and sank. Despite having a broken leg Betty managed to swim to a raft and she clung to it until she was picked up by a British ship.

Sometimes there were happy reunions overseas to report. In 1944 brothers George and Joseph McGrath of the Shore, Portaferry met in Africa while they were both on leave. They hadn't seen each other for four years. In other cases there were lucky escapes. Flight Lieutenant O.C. Cochrane of 108 Groomsport Road, Bangor served with Coastal Command and before the war he was a 22 year old divinity student at Trinity College Dublin. He was the navigator aboard a Bristol Beaufighter aircraft taking part in a raid on the Den Helder anchorage in the Netherlands. One engine stopped working completely after taking a direct hit and the pilot brought his aircraft home safely on one damaged engine – a journey of some 130 miles – and then landed the aircraft on flat tyres.

Letters pages in newspapers provided a platform for an increasing number of ex-soldiers and their families to voice concerns that, after the sacrifice they had made, they were unable to find work and unable to get a house. Others sought to re-establish contact with relatives. George Vance was being held in a Prisoner-of-War Camp in Germany when he placed a letter seeking the address of his half sisters Sadie, Mollie, Annie and Lily Norris who formerly resided in Church Terrace, Newtownards.

Often when service personnel came home on leave they were honoured in some way. Fusilier John Smyth of Greengraves, Newtownards was given a monetary gift and for Gunner R.J. Finlay the Local Comforts Committee arranged a party in the Roden Hall, Kircubbin.

On 10 January 1945 nineteen men were killed on the Bangor to Belfast railway line when a train crashed into the back of a workmen's train that was stopped at a signal near Ballymacarrett Junction. Fourteen of the men were from Bangor and among the other victims was George Dempster from Hall Street, Conlig. He had served with the Royal Inniskilling Fusiliers during the Great War and been awarded the DCM. During the Second World War he served with the Royal Engineers before he was discharged because of his age. After that he worked as a labourer in Belfast.

It was reported that Lady Margaret Stewart, daughter of the Marquess and Marchioness of Londonderry, who worked as a war correspondent had been injured in a road accident that claimed the life of William Ewart Rippon of *The Peterborough Citizen*. William Rippon was buried in Venray War Cemetery in the Netherlands. It was also noted that the Marquess of Londonderry had provided land for the aerodrome at Newtownards which opened on 31 August 1934. Early in 1936 Lord Londonderry had visited Hitler in Germany and on 26 May 1936 Hitler's Foreign Minister, Joachim von Ribbentropp, landed at Newtownards when he visited Mount Stewart. In 1947 while piloting a glider out of Newtownards Lord Londonderry sustained serious back injuries when the towrope of his glider broke and the glider crashed to the ground. After that he suffered a series of strokes and died in 1949.

Convalescent servicemen recuperating in North Down/Ards were sometimes entertained by local communities and it was reported that one such event took place on 7 April 1945 in the Masonic Hall, Millisle.

In April 1945 Portavogie fisherman William Donnan was drowned off Kearney. He was working aboard the fishing boat *Britannia* skippered by Hugh Warnock when he disappeared. Since the incident did not involve enemy action he was not recorded as a war casualty.

Norman Clarke, a minor, from 191 Mill Street Newtownards was severely injured when he picked up a hand grenade in an old quarry at Scrabo and it exploded. It had been left there accidentally by the Home Guard.

It was reported that LAC Robert Scott RAF aged 71 from Kilkeel who had served in three wars and the RUC and who had won a VC at Ladysmith was the first man to pass through the Ulster RAF Personnel Dispersal Centre at Long Kesh on 25 June 1945. Born on 4 June 1874 in Haslingden, Lancashire Robert Scott died on 21 February 1961 (aged 86) and he was buried in Christ Church Cemetery, Kilkeel. Others who passed through the Ulster RAF Personnel Dispersal Centre at Long Kesh on 25 June 1945 included Flight Lieutenant T.H. Herriott MBE from Portaferry and LAC Robert McCandless from Mill Street, Newtownards.

A Merchant Seaman from Newtownards was fined at Derry Petty Sessions for assaulting Mrs Matilda Armstrong Kelly of Holybush, Culmore in County Londonderry. He and another sailor called at her house at midnight asking for a drink of water which she gave them. When she refused them permission to come into her house the seaman from Newtownards punched her. Matilda Armstrong Kelly's husband, Petty Officer Stoker Robert Kelly (aged 41), had been a casualty on HMS *Hood*.

With the lifting of censorship after the war a previously untold story was reported. On 2 March 1941 Samuel Thompson from High Street, Ballyhalbert was the sole survivor when his ship, the SS *Castlehill*, was bombed by two German Luftwaffe aircraft off Minehead in County Waterford. Samuel Thompson was 18 years old at the time and he was taken to the Waterford County and City Infirmary. The SS *Castlehill* was a collier owned by John Kelly and Son Belfast and she was sailing in ballast to England having discharged 800 tons of coal at Cork. The German planes dropped high explosive bombs on the SS *Castlehill* and her bridge was blown away. Samuel Thompson was blown into the water and while he was clinging to some wreckage he was fortunate to survive when his position was machine-gunned from the air as the two planes flew low over him. Some time later he was picked up by a passing trawler. In all, ten men aboard the SS *Castlehill* were lost. Samuel Thompson attained the rank of Captain and he died on 8 September 2002 aged 80 years. He was buried in Ballyhalbert Cemetery and on his headstone there is a tribute to his *Castlehill* crewmates who were lost.

In August 1945 Lieutenant-Colonel Blair 'Paddy' Mayne was awarded a third bar to his DSO and there follows a summary of the recommendation that was approved. On Monday 9 April 1945 he was ordered to infiltrate the German lines and advance towards the city of Oldenburg. His objective was to clear a path for Canadian armoured cars and tanks and 'to cause alarm and disorganisation behind the enemy lines'. The complete success of this operation was attributed to the brilliant leadership and cool, calculating courage of Lt-Col Mayne who, 'by a single act of supreme bravery, drove the enemy from a strongly held key village'. In December 1945 Blair Mayne set off on an expedition to the South Pole but the recurrence of an old war injury forced him to return home. On 16 December 1947 he was decorated by His Majesty the King at a ceremony in Buckingham Palace and this was described in the 27 December 1947 edition of the *County Down Spectator*. Lieutenant Colonel Robert Blair 'Paddy' Mayne was killed in a road traffic accident in Mill Street, Newtownards on 14 December 1955 and was buried in Movilla Cemetery. His uncle, Andrew McCutcheon Mayne, died on 9 February 1917 and is commemorated on Page 348 in the Book of Honour *Remembering Their Sacrifice in the Great War – Ards* compiled by Barry Niblock.

Problems concerning the lack of housing for ex-servicemen continued to feature in the news and there were several 'vigilante cases' reported in Newtownards where ex-servicemen took possession of vacant dwelling houses. One serviceman's wife's whose husband was soon to be demobilised made a plea for a house; she said that she'd be content with just one room and a kitchen. She said that she had lost her home in a fire four years previously and since then had been living in a barn with her teenage daughter at a rent of six shillings per week. She gave her name as K. Gregory of Ballydavey, Craigavad.

When soldiers who were recuperating at Rathgael Convalescent Camp undertook route marches through Newtownards they generally stopped off for refreshments at the YMCA Canteen in the Town Hall in Conway Square.

Towards the end of 1945 three German prisoners escaped from Holywood Camp and they were later recaptured in a hayshed belonging to Hugh Brown of Killaughey, Donaghadee. In 1946 the ongoing removal of air raid shelters from the streets of Newtownards was reported and the static water tank in Conway Square was dismantled. In March 1946 a young Merchant Navy seaman named Hugh Bennett (aged 23) of Mill Lane in Comber drowned in what was known locally as the Starch Mill Pond.

Ex-soldier Wilfred Kerr (aged 23) from Greengraves, Newtownards died in April 1946 after the bicycle he was riding was in collision with a car on the Old Belfast Road. He had been discharged from the Army a year previously after being seriously wounded in Burma.

Some 1,250 people including Naval ratings and RAF personnel were rescued on 1 May 1946 when the US troopship *Georgetown* went aground near Ballyhornan. The Cloughey and Donaghadee lifeboats both attended.

In October 1946 John Martin (aged 24) of 14 King Street, Bangor died after a short illness. He had been employed during the war on the patrol boats in Belfast Lough.

In 1947 a story concerning Fred Booth who lived in Court Street, Newtownards was carried in the local press. At one time Fred's brother Jack had lived in Enniskillen and, after Jack Booth and Harriet Wilson from Ballinamallard were married, they moved to the United States. During the First World War Jack Booth served with the North Irish Horse and he was awarded the Military Medal for gallantry. Jack and Harriet Booth had nineteen children – eighteen boys (one died in infancy) and one girl. Jack Booth and all 17 of his sons worked for the Ford Motor Company in the United States; they all served in the Second World War and they all survived.

The Designated War Years

The Commonwealth War Graves Commission (CWGC) commemorates civilians who died as a result of enemy action during the Second World War together with service personnel who died during the designated war years:

- While they were in Commonwealth military service *or*
- Of causes attributable to service

The designated war years are:

- 4 August 1914 to 31 August 1921 for the First World War and
- 3 September 1939 to 31 December 1947 for the Second World War

The end date for the First World War is an official date determined by the British Parliament. As the end date for the Second World War the Commission selected a date approximately the same period of time after VE Day as the official end of the First World War was after the 1918 Armistice. That means that some servicemen and servicewomen who died after 31 December 1947 of causes attributable to service are not officially commemorated. In some cases church committees decided to commemorate individuals who died after 31 December 1947, for example, **Robert Totton Senior** who died on 27 October 1948 is commemorated in Wesley Centenary Methodist Church, Bangor.

During the Second World War Terence Munro (Terry) Ferguson served with the Royal Air Force and he was 25 years old when he died of a pulmonary embolism on 16 January 1948, following an appendicectomy operation. Terry was educated at Regent House School, Newtownards, he played rugby at Ards Rugby Football Club and he was commemorated on a memorial plaque in the grounds of the Rugby Club.

Sapper George Galway was 19 years old when he died of meningitis on Friday 13 February 1948 in the 29th Military Hospital, Germany. He had joined the Army as a Boy Soldier aged 14. During the Second World War James McNeilly Douglas of 1 Portaferry Road, Newtownards served with the Royal Navy and in 1945 he was invalided out. He died on Sunday 29 May 1949 (aged 28). It was reported in the press that Robert Campbell who had served with the 5 Battery 2 Light Anti-Aircraft Regiment Royal Artillery, and had been held as a Prisoner-of-War, died on 3 July 1950.

In Bangor Cemetery there is a headstone commemorating Norman Leslie Matson DSM who died on 1 September 1950 'as a result of war wounds'. There is an inscription on his headstone:

Thy will be done

Other local men died in conflicts fought soon after the Second World War ended, for example, Private Sharman Douglas who served with the 21st Infantry Regiment of the American Army was killed in July 1950 during the Korean War. Aged 24, he was the youngest son of Mr and Mrs William Douglas of 1 Portaferry Road, Newtownards – and a brother of James McNeilly Douglas (mentioned above) who died on 29 May 1949 William Adair RUR (aged 31) from Newtownards was killed on 3 January 1951 at Happy Valley, Korea and he is commemorated on the UN Wall of Remembrance, Busan, Korea.

Medals and Awards

For the Second World War two types of medal were awarded – those awarded for gallantry and those awarded for service:

Gallantry Medals Awarded to North Down/Ards Casualties

The highest military decoration for gallantry was the Victoria Cross and during the Second World War there were none awarded to any of the casualties with North Down/Ards connections.

Distinguished Service Order (DSO)

One casualty with North Down/Ards connections was awarded the Distinguished Service Order (DSO). This was the second highest military decoration for gallantry, originally awarded to commissioned Army officers for distinguished service or acts of gallantry against the enemy. The DSO was also made available to officers of the Royal Air Force and the Royal Navy. After a review of the honours system in 1993, the DSO ceased to be awarded for gallantry and was replaced by the new all services, all ranks Conspicuous Gallantry Cross at the level below the Victoria Cross.

Brigadier Robert Dermot Barnes Perrott

Distinguished Conduct Medal (DCM)

One casualty with North Down/Ards connections was awarded the Distinguished Conduct Medal (DCM). Equivalent to the DSO for commissioned officers, this military decoration was instituted during the Crimean War to recognise gallantry in 'other ranks' of the British Army. From 1942 members of the Royal Navy and the Royal Air Force were also entitled to receive the award. After the 1993 review the DCM was discontinued and replaced by the Conspicuous Gallantry Cross.

Warrant Officer Class II (Company Sergeant Major) Edward Potts

Distinguished Flying Cross (DFC)

Eight casualties with North Down/Ards connections were awarded the Distinguished Flying Cross (DFC). Instituted in 1918, the DFC was the third highest military decoration for gallantry and was awarded to warrant officers and officers of the RAF for acts of valour while flying in operations against the enemy. It was later made available to equivalent ranks in the Royal Navy and Army for acts of valour in the air. The equivalent award for other ranks was the Distinguished Flying Medal (DFM). Following the 1993 review, the DFM was discontinued and the DFC became available to all ranks of all services for exemplary gallantry in the air in the presence of the enemy. It is at a level below the Conspicuous Gallantry Cross and it is at the equivalent level to the Distinguished Service Cross (for exemplary gallantry at sea) and the Military Cross (for exemplary gallantry on land).

Commander Eduard Bakker
Flight Lieutenant Desmond Wallace Ferguson Barker
Squadron Leader George Crawford
Flight Lieutenant Robert Aubrey Alexander Doherty
Wing Commander Charles Ronald Hancock
Flight Lieutenant Hugh Raymond Harrison
Flight Lieutenant Wilfred Ronald Maitland
Flying Officer (Navigator) William Watson Miller

Distinguished Service Cross (DSC)

One casualty with North Down/Ards connections was awarded the Distinguished Service Cross (DSC). Instituted in 1901, this award was originally known as the Conspicuous Service Cross and was awarded for gallantry in the presence of the enemy to warrant and subordinate officers of the Royal Navy who were ineligible (on account of their rank) for the Distinguished Service Order. Renamed the Distinguished Service Cross in 1914, it also became available for award to junior Navy officers. In 1940, it also became available to Army and RAF officers serving aboard naval vessels. The equivalent award for other ranks for gallantry at sea in presence of the enemy was the Distinguished Service

Medal (DSM). Following the 1993 review, the DSM was discontinued and the DSC became available to all ranks of all services for exemplary gallantry at sea in presence of the enemy. It is at a level below the Conspicuous Gallantry Cross and is at the equivalent level to the Military Cross (for exemplary gallantry on land) and the Distinguished Flying Cross (for exemplary gallantry in the air).

Lieutenant Commander William Robert Patterson

Military Cross (MC)

Three casualties with North Down/Ards connections were awarded the Military Cross (MC). The Military Cross was the third level military decoration awarded to officers and (since 1993) other ranks of the British Armed Forces.

Lieutenant Ernest Basil Snell Hewitt
Brigadier Robert Dermot Barnes Perrott
Major Herbert Noel Wallace

Military Medal (MM)

Three casualties with North Down/Ards connections were awarded the Military Medal (MM). The Military Medal was the third level military decoration awarded to other ranks and (since 1993) has been discontinued with the Military Cross being awarded to all ranks of the British Armed Forces.

Rifleman Hugh Henry McGlennon
Lieutenant Owen Shanks
Lance Corporal Alexander Richard Day Vinycomb

Officers of the Order of the British Empire (OBE)

Three casualties with North Down/Ards connections received awards under the Most Excellent Order of the British Empire. These awards were for outstanding services of a non-combatant nature. All three were made Officers of the Order of the British Empire (OBE).

Wing Commander Charles Ronald Hancock
Lieutenant Commander William Robert Patterson
Brigadier Robert Dermot Barnes Perrott

Air Force Cross (AFC)

One casualty with North Down/Ards connections was awarded the Air Force Cross. This decoration was awarded to all ranks of the RN, RM, Army and RAF in recognition of exemplary gallantry in the air on non-active operations.

Squadron Leader George Crawford

Mentioned in Despatches (MID)

Sixteen casualties with North Down/ Ards connections were Mentioned In Despatches. This happened when a more senior officer mentioned a subordinate who performed some noteworthy action.

Marine **William Thomas Anderson**
Lieutenant **James Craig (2 bars)**
Captain **Samuel David Corry**
Chaplain 4th Class **The Revd James Arthur Douglas**
Signalman **Arthur Donald Field**
Flight Sergeant (Pilot) **Herbert Hannay**
Captain **David Alexander Hynes Hodgett**
Petty Officer Stoker **James Jamfrey**
Lieutenant Colonel **Francis John Leland**
Wing Commander **Victor Edwin Maxwell (2 bars)**
Wing Commander **Malcolm Morgan McMullan**
Sister **Edith Doreen Pedlow**
Major **Edward Douglas Rea**
Pilot Officer (Wireless Operator/Air Gunner) **Gerald Cecil William Stone**
Corporal **Matthew Wilson**
Captain **Robert Neville Desmond Young**

Croix de Guerre avec Palme (with Palm)

One casualty with North Down/Ards connections was awarded the Croix de Guerre with Palm. Created in 1915, this French military decoration was awarded to individuals or to units of foreign military forces allied to France whose men performed heroic deeds in combat with the enemy. Awards to units were *avec Palme*.

Lieutenant Colonel Francis John Leland

Purple Heart

One casualty with North Down/Ards connections was awarded a Purple Heart. The Purple Heart is a United States military decoration awarded in the name of the President to those who were wounded or killed while serving with the US military.

Private Leland Truesdale Pentz

Service Medals and Awards

It is beyond the scope of this book to list all of the medals, campaign stars, bars, clasps and emblems awarded to Imperial troops for service during the Second World War. Nor is there room to describe the precise qualifications for their award to Navy, Army, Air Force, Merchant Navy, Nursing and Civilian personnel. Examples and broad guidelines only are outlined below.

War Medal

The War Medal was awarded to all full-time personnel of the armed forces wherever they were serving, so long as they had served for at least 28 days between 3 September 1939 and 2 September 1945. It was granted in addition to the Campaign Stars and the Defence Medal.

Defence Medal

The Defence Medal was awarded to service personnel for three years service in a non-operational area or six months service overseas in territories subjected to air attack or otherwise closely threatened. Personnel of Anti-Aircraft Command, RAF ground crews, Dominion forces stationed in the UK, the Home Guard, Civil Defence, National Fire Service and many other civilian units qualified for the medal.

Campaign Stars and Clasps

Initially, eight different campaign stars were issued for the Second World War. The maximum number of stars that could be earned by any one person was five, while those who qualified for more received a clasp to be sewn on to the ribbon of the appropriate star. Only one clasp per ribbon was permitted – the first to be earned after qualifying for the star. The eight stars are listed below with the associated clasps in brackets:

1939-45	(Battle of Britain)
Atlantic	(Air Crew Europe or France and Germany)
Air Crew Europe	(Atlantic or France and Germany)
Africa	(North Africa 1942-43, 8th Army or 1st Army)
Pacific	(Burma)
Burma	(Pacific)
Italy	(None)
France and Germany	(Atlantic)

 A ninth Campaign Star – the Arctic Star – was announced in 2012. The Arctic Star is a retrospective award for any length of service above the Arctic Circle by members of the British Armed Forces and the Merchant Navy between 3 September 1939 and 8 May 1945.

North Down and Ards Second World War Casualties

652 Second World War casualties with North Down/Ards connections were positively identified of whom 22 were women. At the time of writing it has not been possible to find definitive information about seven of the names that are inscribed on war memorials in North Down/Ards – **R.G. Gibson, George E. Lowry, William Martin, Thomas Shipcott, D.R. Weir, George McKee** and **William Shaw**. There is evidence *in some cases* that names may have been inscribed in error and this is discussed in more detail in the

Names in Alphabetical Order Section of this book.

Army	246	(Canadian 8; Australian 3; Indian 3; USA 2)
Air Force	231	(Canadian 9; NZ 8; Polish 8; Australian 2; Dutch 1)
Navy	76	(NZ 3; Canadian 1; South African 1; USA 1)
Merchant Navy	64	(Australian 1; Canadian 1; USA 1)
Civilian	32	
Nursing	3	

The causes of death were many and varied. Some 40% of casualties were killed on active service, either killed in action or dying later as a result of their wounds. A further 18% (mostly merchant seamen and civilians) died as a direct result of enemy action. Around 11% died of illness in service, two individuals dying after medical operations. Eight North Down/Ards casualties died in Prisoner-of-War Camps, two were murdered and others died by suicide. More than 25% of casualties died as a result of injuries sustained in accidents involving aircraft, motor vehicles, motorcycles, trains and sleep-walking; others accidentally drowned. Of those casualties who died accidentally, some 120 were killed in aircraft accidents (more than half of all the Air Force casualties died in aircraft accidents).

Age Profile of North Down/Ards Fatalities

It has been possible to determine the age of 646 of the casualties. The youngest (aged 14) and the oldest (aged 74) were both civilians. Two-thirds of the casualties were less than 30 years of age.

19 and under	56	8.7 %
20 to 29	372	57.6 %
30 to 39	134	20.7 %
40 to 49	45	7.0 %
50 to 59	24	3.7 %
60 to 69	11	1.7 %
70 and over	4	0.6 %

North Down/Ards Fatalities by Month/Year

It has been possible to establish the date of death for 650 of the casualties. The second quarter of 1941 had the highest number of casualties with 60; a contributory factor was the Belfast Blitz. The year with the highest number of casualties overall was 1942 with 141 (22%).

	Quarter 1	Quarter 2	Quarter 3	Quarter 4	Total
1939				13	13
1940	4	33	11	33	81
1941	15	60	16	18	109
1942	44	37	32	28	141
1943	29	28	33	26	116
1944	24	29	40	20	113
1945	28	24	4	6	62
1945					8
1947					6
1948					1
Total					650

Erection of Second World War Memorial Plaques

After the war ended churches, towns and villages set up committees to oversee the compilation of lists of names of the men and women who served and died, and to organise the erection of memorials to commemorate them. In North Down and Ards this process spanned a period of some fifty years and, to illustrate this, some examples follow in chronological order. The examples are illustrative and not exhaustive.

On Sunday 7 November 1947 a memorial tablet was unveiled by the Revd J. Millar Craig in Hamilton Road Presbyterian Church, Bangor.

On Sunday 9 May 1948 a 1939/45 war memorial plaque was added to the War Memorial in Ballywalter. This plaque was dedicated by the Revd George Heron while Canon C.T. Jackson and the Revd S.J. McIlveen participated in the ceremony.

On Sunday 26 September 1948 a pipe organ and communion table were dedicated by the Right Revd A.W. Neill DD (Moderator of the General Assembly) in Ballygilbert Presbyterian Church in memory of the members of the congregation who gave their lives in two world wars. Two memorial tablets, one for each war, were unveiled by Lieutenant Colonel Sir Walter Smiles CIE DSO MP. Lieutenant-Colonel Smiles lost his life in the sinking of the MV *Princess Victoria* on 31 January 1953.

On Sunday 7 November 1948 four oak doors presented in thanksgiving for victory and in memory of the men who gave their lives in two world wars were unveiled by Vice-Admiral Sir Wilfred Patterson in Groomsport Parish Church of Ireland Church. Sir Wilfred's family resided in Groomsport for some years and his nephew was one of those commemorated. The doors were dedicated by the Right Revd Dr William Shaw Kerr, Bishop of Down and Dromore.

On Sunday 13 November 1949 a brass memorial tablet was unveiled in Trinity Presbyterian Church, Bangor by James Templeton, Member of Kirk Session, and dedicated by Lieutenant Colonel the Revd D.C. Henderson, Deputy Assistant Chaplain General.

On Tuesday 31 January 1950 a memorial plaque to commemorate the former pupils of Regent House School Newtownards who were killed in the Second World War was unveiled by Lieutenant Colonel Blair Mayne DSO and dedicated by the Revd Henry Savage – both former pupils.

On Saturday 13 May 1950 Mrs Mary Gibson unveiled the list of names of Second World War casualties that had been added to Newtownards and District War Memorial. Her only son, Lieutenant **John Malcomson Gibson**, had been killed in action at Tobruk in June 1942. The prayer of dedication was said by the Revd T.R. Johnston.

On Sunday 11 November 1951 a memorial tablet in Wesley Centenary Methodist Church, Bangor was unveiled by Samuel Connolly, Chairman of the Bangor Branch of the British Legion, and dedicated by the Revd J.B. Jameson.

Shops and other businesses in Donaghadee closed on Monday 13 August 1951 and people turned out in great numbers to greet Vice-Admiral Earl Mountbatten of Burma when he arrived to perform the opening ceremony on the new headquarters of the Donaghadee branch of the British Legion on Shore Street.

On Friday 27 June 1952 Comber's new Garden of Remembrance was officially opened. It was dedicated to the memory of the men from Comber and District who gave their lives in the Second World War and it was Lieutenant Colonel Lord Glentoran who unveiled the memorial plaques. The prayer of dedication was said by the Venerable Archdeacon Charles Campbell Manning who had been an Army Chaplain during the First World War. Among the principal guests were officers from an American Navy ship lying off Bangor.

The Second World War Memorial Plaque on Bangor and District War Memorial was not unveiled until November 1967 and this accounts for some of the omissions and inaccuracies in the list of inscribed names. The process by which the list of names was compiled is described under the name **Lowry, G.E.** in the *Names in Alphabetical Order* Section of this book. The plaque was unveiled by Councillor Bertie McConnell who had been blinded whilst on active service in the Second World War and the plaque was dedicated by the Revd W.J. McKinstry-Wallace.

On Sunday 7 May 1995 a Memorial Plaque in Bangor Parish Church of Ireland Church (St. Comgall's) was dedicated by the Right Revd Brian Hannon, Bishop of Clogher – in memory of all those from Bangor Parish who died in the Second World War. (At the beginning of the Second World War Bangor Parish included all of Bangor and had two churches – Bangor Parish Church (St. Comgall's) and Bangor Abbey. Plans for another church – the Church of St. Columbanus at Ballyholme – were under consideration).

Names in Chronological Order

In this Section, the names of servicemen, servicewomen, nursing personnel and civilians with North Down/Ards connections who died in the Second World War are presented chronologically within the context of the War. It is beyond the scope of this book to provide details about all of the battles in each of the Theatres of War; the objective in this Section is simply to put the deaths of men and women with Ards/North Down connections into context by giving an overview of the overall conflict and where it was fought across the globe.

The Inter-War Years

On Armistice Day, 11 November 1918, the guns fell silent on the Western Front and the Great War ended with more than 10,000,000 dead and twice that number wounded. The League of Nations was founded after the Paris Peace Conference and the signing of the Treaty of Versailles on 28 June 1919. Four nations dominated the negotiations – Britain represented by Prime Minister David Lloyd George, France represented by Prime Minister Georges Clemenceau, the United States of America represented by President Woodrow Wilson and Italy represented by Prime Minister Vittorio Orlando. Although membership of the League of Nations was advocated strongly by President Wilson, the US Congress did not ratify American participation. One of the League's objectives was to maintain world peace – but this it proved unable to do.

After the Great War ended, Corporal Adolf Hitler joined the German Workers' Party (DAP), which later became the National Socialist German Workers' Party (NSDAP) or Nazi Party, and in 1921 Hitler took over as its leader. By 1933 the Nazi Party was the largest party in Germany and the German President, Paul von Hindenburg, appointed Adolf Hitler as Reich Chancellor. When Hindenburg died in 1934 Hitler became Führer – the head of the German nation – and in 1935 the British-occupied Saar region was restored to Germany. Hitler introduced conscription and in 1936 German troops re-occupied the demilitarised zone of the Rhineland. At the same time Fascist movements were gaining power elsewhere, including Italy where Benito Mussolini assumed control. Already ruling Eritrea and Somaliland, Italy attacked and gained control of Abyssinia (Ethiopia) in 1936, thus creating the Colony of Italian East Africa. Emperor Haile Selassie went into exile. Spain was gripped by civil war and, when Generalissimo Francisco Franco prevailed – with help from German and Italian troops

– the Spanish Government became aligned to the Fascist group. In 1932 Franklin Delano Roosevelt was elected President of the USA and in 1936 he was re-elected.

Militarists in Japan led by General Hideki Tojo rose to power in the early 1930s and in 1931 Japan invaded Manchuria. When censured by the League of Nations, Japan withdrew from membership in 1933. Later Italy, Germany and Spain also withdrew from membership of the League of Nations. The mid-1930s saw the emergence of the Axis Powers when Nazi Germany, Japan and Italy signed an anti-communist tripartite treaty (the Anti-Comintern Pact) that included military objectives. The Second Sino-Japanese War fought between 7 July 1937 and 9 September 1945 was a military conflict fought primarily between the Republic of China and the Empire of Japan. In December 1937 the Imperial Japanese Army captured the Chinese city of Nanking and there were reports of widespread rape, murder and looting. In the Soviet Union, Joseph Stalin conducted a 'purge' of the Soviet Armed Forces and several high ranking officers were executed.

In May 1938 Neville Chamberlain became British Prime Minister. Nazi Germany occupied and annexed Austria and in September 1938 Government representatives from Britain and France met with Adolph Hitler in Munich. They reached an agreement that Germany would make no further territorial demands if given Sudetenland – the predominantly German-speaking portion of Czechoslovakia. However, in March 1939 the German Army invaded Czechoslovakia, recognised the independence of Slovakia and made the rest of the nation a Protectorate. Hitler then demanded control of the free city of Danzig (Gdansk) in Poland and German access to it through the Polish Corridor – the narrow Polish strip that separated Germany from Prussia. When that demand was refused, Hitler abrogated a 1934 anti-war pact with Poland and on 23 August 1939 signed a non-aggression pact with the Soviet Union which had been formed in 1922 in the aftermath of the Russian Revolution. This pact – the Molotov Ribbentrop Pact – included protocols for the partition and annexation of countries including Estonia, Finland, Latvia, Lithuania, Poland and Romania and it remained in force until 22 June 1941 when Germany invaded the Soviet Union. Britain and France pledged support for Poland and offered military assistance to any country that felt menaced by Germany (these included Romania and Greece). On 7 April 1939 Italy invaded and occupied Albania. During this time Nazi Germany was expanding its military strength, intensifying its oppression of Jews and building the defensive Siegfried Line. French Forces established the fortified Maginot Line. Conscription in Britain (for 20 to 22 year-old men) was introduced in April 1939.

The Outbreak of the Second World War

On Friday 1 September 1939 the German Army invaded Poland and legislation in Britain was enacted for the conscription of all men aged between 18 and 41. On 3 September 1939 Britain, France, India, Australia and New Zealand declared war with Nazi Germany. Estonia, Finland, Ireland, Italy, Latvia, Lithuania, Norway and Switzerland declared their neutrality. On 3 September 1939 the German submarine *U-30* sank the British passenger ship SS *Athenia* on its way from Glasgow to Montreal with the loss of more than 100 lives (including Civilian Margaret Lennon from Donaghadee). So began the Second World War which lasted some 2,194 days and claimed the lives of more than 55,000,000 people. Neville Chamberlain appointed Winston Churchill as First Lord of the Admiralty and Britain revived the convoy system for merchant shipping; the Battle of the Atlantic was fought throughout the war. Australia, Canada, Newfoundland and South Africa (under Prime Minister Jan Smuts) declared war with Nazi Germany while both Japan and the United States declared their neutrality in the European conflict. The first British offensive of the Second World War was a raid by the Royal Air Force (RAF) on the German fleet in the Heligoland Bight. The first units of the British Expeditionary Force (BEF) left for France in September 1939 and were deployed along the Belgian-French border.

By 17 September 1939 the German Army had reached the city of Brest-Litovsk (now Brest, Belarus) and the Soviet (Red) Army invaded Poland. That day the British aircraft carrier HMS *Courageous* was sunk by the German submarine *U-29*. On 21 September 1939 General Reinhard Heydrich, a leading Nazi official, announced that all Jews in Poland were to be imprisoned in ghettos and on 27 September 1939 the Polish Army surrendered in Warsaw. In the weeks that followed, Hitler annexed western Poland into the German Reich and Stalin annexed eastern Poland into the Soviet Union. The German Schutzstaffel (SS) established the first Jewish ghetto in Piotrkow, Poland.

On 14 October 1939 the German submarine *U-47* penetrated the naval base at Scapa Flow in the Orkney Islands and sank the British battleship *Royal Oak*. Marine William Thomas Anderson from Newtownards was killed. The first air attack on British territory took place on 16 October 1939 near the Forth Bridge in Scotland. On 27 October 1939 Belgium proclaimed its neutrality and on 30 November 1939 the Red Army invaded Finland. The 1940 Olympic Games which were to have been held in Finland were cancelled and Denmark, Sweden and Norway declared their neutrality in the Russian-Finnish war. In December 1939 Hitler held a meeting with Vidkun Quisling, founder of the National Union which was a Norwegian pro-Nazi movement, and on 14 December the Soviet Union was expelled from the League of Nations. The first Canadian and the first Indian troops arrived in Europe.

During the Battle of the River Plate in South America the German battleship *Admiral Graf Spee* was damaged and later scuttled. On Christmas Eve 1939 Pope Pius XII made an appeal for peace and on 28 December meat rationing was introduced in Britain. Hitler delivered a New Year message in which he said 'The Jewish-capitalistic world will not survive the twentieth century'.

In the fourth quarter of 1939 thirteen people with North Down/Ards connections died.

03 September 1939	Civilian **Margaret Lennon**
17 September 1939	Able Seaman **William Jordan Cooke**
17 September 1939	Able Seaman **John Sturgeon**
27 September 1939	Leading Aircraftman **Ritson Finlay Petts**
28 September 1939	Private **Leonard Stanley Reid**
14 October 1939	Marine **William Thomas Anderson MID**
24 October 1939	Sergeant **Reginald Austin Bigger**
23 November 1939	Lieutenant **Thomas Hugh Cecil Hickland Fee**
02 December 1939	Bombardier **Thomas Wesley Boyd**
12 December 1939	Ordinary Seaman **Harold McMeekin**
22 December 1939	Warrant Officer Class II (CSM) **Douglas Holden Johnston**
28 December 1939	Policeman **Frederick James Woods**
31 December 1939	Rifleman **William Fox**

1940

In January 1940 Herman Goering, a fighter pilot in the Great War and founder of the Gestapo in 1933, took control of all German war industries; the Soviet Union signed a treaty with Bulgaria and General Semyon Timoshenko took command of Soviet Forces in Finland. In Britain food rationing was extended to include bacon, butter and sugar and in February Britain announced that all merchant ships were to be armed. Germany declared that all British merchant ships would in future be regarded as warships and also began work to transform the town of Auschwitz in Poland into a concentration camp. On 12 March 1940 Finland accepted Soviet terms and signed a peace treaty with the Soviet Union. Mussolini declared that Italy was ready to join Germany in the fight against Britain and France. On 20 March 1940 Paul Reynaud replaced Edouard Daladier as Prime Minister in France.

In the first quarter of 1940 four people with North Down//Ards connections died.

06 February 1940	Private **Alfred Hayes**
17 February 1940	Chief Officer **Hugh Bell**
02 March 1940	Private **Samuel Kirham**
14 March 1940	Able Seaman **Robert George Hamilton**

Norwegian coastal waters were vital for the transport of Swedish iron ore to the German blast furnaces and Hitler gave orders for the invasion of Norway and Denmark on 9 April 1940. Britain laid minefields in Norwegian territorial waters to hinder German shipping and landed troops at Namsos on 8 April. The German Army invaded Denmark and Norway and Vidkun Quisling seized power in Norway. In view of these attacks Britain and France requested permission from Belgium for their troops to enter Belgian territory but this request was refused. While Denmark accepted a German ultimatum, King Haakon of Norway repudiated the puppet government of Vidkun Quisling. Allied troops landed at Narvik and Andalsnes in Norway and German Forces continued to march northwards, forcing Allied troops to withdraw.

On 10 May 1940 Hitler launched his Western Offensive and attacked the Netherlands, Belgium, Luxembourg and France. It was the Blitzkrieg or 'Lightning War'. Neville Chamberlain resigned as British Prime Minister and was replaced by Winston Churchill. On 14 May 1940 Secretary of State for War Anthony Eden announced plans for the formation of the Home Guard. The Dutch Army surrendered and Queen Wilhelmina fled to England. The German Army pierced French defences in the Battle of Sedan leaving Paris vulnerable to attack and Winston Churchill flew to Paris for talks. The German Army captured Saint Quentin, Cambrai, Brussels and Antwerp. Rommel occupied the heights around Arras, and Amiens was taken. A breach in the Allied Line was opened and, having reached the sea, the Germans surrounded the Allied divisions in Flanders and France.

German Forces moved towards Boulogne and Calais and the Allies fell back to Dunkirk. On 27 May 1940 the evacuation of the British Expeditionary Force from Dunkirk (*Operation Dynamo*) began. Belgium surrendered to the German Army on 28 May 1940 and King Leopold III was arrested. The Germans entered Ypres, Ostend and Lille. Stafford Cripps was appointed British Ambassador to the Soviet Union on 30 May 1940 and the evacuation from Dunkirk ended on 4 June 1940. Many lives were saved but a huge amount of equipment had to be left behind. As a result, British troops were left severely under-equipped. Paris was bombed by the Luftwaffe and on 5

June the Battle of France began with heavy bombardment along the line of the Somme and the Aisne.

On 7 June King Haakon left Norway bound for London and, two days later, Allied troops left Norwegian soil. On the Western Front the Nazi German Army occupied Rouen, Dieppe and Compiegne and crossed the Marne and the Seine. On 10 June 1940 Italy, under Benito Mussolini, declared war with Britain and France. That night Italy attacked Malta from the air and soon thereafter the RAF bombed Turin and Genoa. On the Western Front Rheims was taken by the Germans and on 14 June the German Army occupied Paris. The Red Army occupied the Baltic states of Lithuania, Estonia and Latvia (later annexing them as autonomous republics within the USSR). The Germans took Verdun and the USA agreed to send war materials to France but not to enter hostilities. Dijon fell to the Germans as did Caen, Cherbourg, Rennes, Briare, Le Mans, Nevers and Colmar. Meanwhile the RAF bombed Hamburg and Bremen. Brest and Nantes fell to the Germans as did Samur and Lyons.

In France Philippe Petain became Prime Minister after the resignation of Reynaud's government and General de Gaulle formed a French government in exile. Petain asked both Italy and Germany for an armistice and the armistice with Nazi Germany was signed on 22 June 1940 in the same railway carriage in which the Germans surrendered at the end of the Great War. France formally surrendered on 25 June 1940 and Britain recognised General de Gaulle as leader of the Free French – the French resistance organisation formed to continue the struggle against the Axis powers. Vichy France (the name given to the surrendered French State) was divided into two zones – the northern 'occupied zone' and the southern 'free zone' headed by Marshal Philippe Petain.

Towards the end of June the Red Army occupied Romanian Bessarabia and Bukovina and the Germans landed in Jersey and Guernsey. At the beginning of July the Royal Navy destroyed several French Navy vessels at Mers-el-Kebir to prevent their use by the Germans.

In the second quarter of 1940 thirty-three people with North Down/Ards connections died.

08 April 1940	**Leading Aircraftman Norman McReynolds**
09 April 1940	**Leading Aircraftman Frederick Armand Morrison**
09 April 1940	**Driver Hugh Erin Reid**
12 April 1940	**Corporal Matthew Wilson MID**
14 April 1940	**AC2 Ernest Alfred Raymond Llewellyn Jones**

14 April 1940	Second Lieutenant **Robert Arnold Thompson**
24 April 1940	Flying Officer **Anthony Alexander Talbot Bulloch**
02 May 1940	Telegraphist **Jacob Walter Coulter**
14 May 1940	Flying Officer **Robert Lawrie Lorimer**
18 May 1940	Gunner Trevor **Maynard Watt McVitty**
18 May 1940	Sergeant **Herbert Reginald Megarry**
21 May 1940	Corporal **Henry Heaven**
23/26 May 1940	Corporal **James Frederick Young**
25 May 1940	Pilot Officer **James Hamilton Gordon**
27 May 1940	Second Lieutenant **Robert Norman Cecil Scott**
28 May/02 June 1940	Corporal **William Nolan**
29 May 1940	Fusilier **George Young**
01 June 1940	Warrant Officer Class III (TSM) **Walter Stanley Smith**
01 June 1940	Pilot Officer **Alan Lancelot Treanor**
01 June 1940	Private **Leslie Waite**
01/02 June 1940	Rifleman **John Robert Gilpin**
04 June 1940	Mate **John Cully**
04 June 1940	Chief Engineer Officer **John Gibson**
04 June 1940	Fireman **Francis Maginness**
04 June 1940	Ordinary Seaman **James McMaster**
06/08 June 1940	Private **John Gracey McNeilly**
08 June 1940	Able Seaman **Alexander Doak**
08 June 1940	Able Seaman **Hugh Alexander Eagleson**
08 June 1940	Ordinary Seaman **Alfred George McDowell**
08 June 1940	Ordinary Seaman **David Scott**
19 June 1940	Lance Corporal **James Charles McCaul**
25 June 1940	Leading Aircraftman **Alexander James Donaghy**
29 June 1940	Lieutenant Commander (E) **Robert Pollock Beattie**

It was Hitler's intention to destroy British air power and coastal defences prior to an invasion of Britain and on 10 July 1940 the Luftwaffe launched an air attack on Britain with an assault by 70 aircraft on docks in South Wales. This was the start of the Battle of Britain and by 13 August up to 1,500 aircraft per day were attacking targets in Britain. Italian aeroplanes bombed naval bases in Alexandria in Egypt and Haifa in Palestine. Britain attacked and destroyed the French Navy to prevent it falling into German hands and in retaliation the Vichy French Air Force bombed Gibraltar. On 23 July the British Home Guard was officially established and the use of radar proved crucial in the defence of Britain from air attack.

At the beginning of August 1940 Hitler set 15 September as the date for *Operation Sealion* – the invasion of Britain. The Italian Army advanced into British Somaliland in East Africa and on 13 August the Luftwaffe launched a sustained and systematic attack on targets in Britain – in preparation for the planned invasion, which was later postponed. Targets included RAF Fighter Command aircraft, airfields and installations. Britain decided to send forces to the Middle East and the Italians attacked Gibraltar. Later that month the Luftwaffe carried out the first all-night bombing raid on London and in a retaliatory raid the Royal Air Force bombed Berlin. Civilian casualties in Britain during August 1940 exceeded 1,000 (by the end of the war more than 60,000 British civilians had been killed). The Blitz on London and other cities in Britain had begun. British ships left Scapa Flow to support an intended Free French landing at Dakar in French West Africa.

German Luftwaffe air attacks on targets in Britain, including London, continued through September. Buckingham Palace was damaged. The Italians attacked Tel Aviv in Palestine and began an offensive in Egypt. On 13 September the Italians occupied Sollum and three days later Sidi Barrani. Between 13 August and 22 September 1940 at least 15,000 tons of bombs were dropped on Britain. On 23 September King George VI instituted the George Cross and George Medal as civilian awards. Towards the end of the month Japan occupied Vietnam; Vidkun Quisling was installed by the Germans as Head of State in Norway; British aircraft raided the port of Tobruk in Libya; the British ships under attack off Dakar were ordered to withdraw to Freetown, capital of the British Colony of Sierra Leone; Japan signed a tripartite pact with Nazi Germany and Italy – the Axis Powers. British civilian casualties from German air attacks during September totalled almost 7,000. In Romania General Ion Antonescu forced King Carol II to abdicate and Romania signed the Tripartite Pact.

In the third quarter of 1940 eleven people with North Down/Ards connections died.

11 July 1940	Pilot Officer **Ian Milne Hossack**
12 July 1940	Sergeant **Sydney Ireland**
20 July 1940	Fireman and Trimmer **Shief Ahmed**
20 July 1940	Carpenter **Thomas Smith Beckett**
20 July 1940	Able Seaman **John McGrath**
23 July 1940	Sergeant **Charles Julius Holland**
25 July 1940	Captain **Thomas Oswald Corrin**
07 August 1940	Lance Corporal **William Young Brown**
12 August 1940	Gunner **William Hugh Murphy**

| 22 August 1940 | Constable **William Oscar Thompson** |
| 11 September 1940 | Pilot Officer **Alexander William Valentine Green** |

At the beginning of October 1940 Britain refused a request from Japan to close the Burma Road – the mountainous road from Burma to China by which western supplies reached the army of Chiang Kai-shek. German Forces entered Romania. Later in the month Hitler met Francisco Franco to try to persuade Spain to join the war and the Italian army invaded Greece from Albania. British civilian casualties from German air attacks during October totalled more than 6,000, at least 600 of them children under 16.

During November the RAF bombed Berlin, Naples, Brindisi, Lecce, Munich, Danzig and Dresden. On 5 November Franklin Delano Roosevelt was re-elected President of the United States of America for a third term. The Royal Navy attacked the Italian Navy at Taranto and on 14 November 1940 the Luftwaffe 'carpet bombed' Coventry. The Royal Air Force bombed Hamburg and the Skoda works at Pilsen in Czechoslovakia. Heavy fighting continued on the Italian (Albanian) Greek front and both Hungary and Romania signed the Tripartite Pact with Germany, Italy and Japan. The RAF attacked Libyan bases at Benghazi, Berka and Benina. The Greeks captured Koritsa in Albania and then Sarande and Permet in early December.

In North Africa the British Western Desert Offensive began on 9 December and in Egypt British Forces broke through the Italian lines at Sidi Barrani. There, British Forces took many thousands of prisoners, and also at Sidi Omar and Sollum. Luftwaffe air attacks on various towns and cities in Britain continued and the RAF bombed Dusseldorf, Mannheim and Turin.

In the fourth quarter of 1940 thirty-three people with North Down/Ards connections died.

01 October 1940	Sergeant **Alfred White**
02 October 1940	Radio Officer **Edward George Mee**
09 October 1940	Sapper **Henry Houghton**
17 October 1940	Driver **Eric Joseph Heyes**
19 October 1940	Captain **Maurice Evelyn Beale**
19 October 1940	Second Lieutenant **William Edward David Paul**
23 October 1940	Pilot Officer **Frederick Eustace Stronge**
25 October 1940	Leading Aircraftman **Henry Dougan Sandford**
30 October 1940	Civilian **George Holden Baird**
31 October 1940	Pilot Officer **Basil Pollock Erskine**

05 November 1940	**Third Engineer Officer John George Briggs Baxter**
05 November 1940	**Carpenter James McNeilly Belshaw**
05 November 1940	**Second Officer George McClelland Leckey**
05 November 1940	**Assistant Steward Reginald John Primmer**
05 November 1940	**Sailor David John Pritchard**
16 November 1940	**Leading Stoker Charles Archibald Morrison**
21 November 1940	**Driver George William Evens**
21 November 1940	**Fusilier George Leslie Gell**
21 November 1940	**Private Derek Rodney Swift**
21 November 1940	**Driver Sidney John Wren**
02 December 1940	**Sub-Lieutenant (E) James Gordon Barre**
02 December 1940	**Marine Samuel Clydesdale**
02 December 1940	**Able Seaman Douglas Collister**
02 December 1940	**Able Seaman John Ferris Deveney**
04 December 1940	**Lieutenant (A) Richard Ridley**
06 December 1940	**Fusilier Frederick Bloomfield**
08 December 1940	**Third Officer William Ian Muir McMullan**
09 December 1940	**Gunner John Cecil Beresford Harris**
10 December 1940	**Pilot Officer Frederick William McMurray**
11 December 1940	**Leading Aircraftman Thomas Henderson Watson**
13 December 1940	**Fusilier James Graham**
16 December 1940	**Corporal Hugh Kennedy**
20 December 1940	**First Radio Officer Robert George Wylie Irwin**

1941

At the beginning of January 1941 British Naval and Air Forces mounted a bombardment on the major Italian fortification at Bardia in Libya and on 5 January Bardia fell to a combined British and Australian Force. Many thousands of prisoners were taken but General Bergonzoli managed to withdraw with a few thousand men to Tobruk. Later in the month Hitler decided to send German Forces to support the Italian Forces in Libya and the German Forces were led by General Erwin Rommel – the Desert Fox.

During January, fighting continued along the Greek-Albanian front and there were several engagements in the Mediterranean. Italian and German aircraft carried out a series of heavy raids on Malta. British aircraft from Malta attacked the airfield at Catania in Sicily. Hitler demanded that King Boris of Bulgaria should join the Axis powers and open her borders for German troops to attack Greece. Greece requested help from Britain. In East Africa British Forces in the Sudan began an offensive against Italian Forces in Eritrea and Italian Somaliland.

Following attacks by British and Australian Forces the Italian garrison at Tobruk surrendered on 22 January 1941. Many thousands of prisoners were taken. One of the first tank battles of the North African War took place near Mechili in Libya. Italian troops evacuated Derna in Libya and formed a new line of defence at El-Agheila. The Greek Prime Minister, General Ioannis Metaxas, died and was replaced by Alexandros Korizis (he committed suicide on 18 April 1941 after Greece surrendered).

At the beginning of February 1941 Australian troops entered Benghazi and the whole of the Cyrenaica region of Libya was held by Allied Forces. Germany and Spain signed an agreement and on 12 February Rommel arrived in Tripoli. Hitler met with the Yugoslavian Prime Minister Dragisa Cvetkovich and pressed him to sign the Tripartite Pact. In Italian East Africa the Allied Forces took Mogadishu and in Libya the British and German Forces had their first engagement. On 1 March 1941 Bulgaria signed the Tripartite Pact and joined forces with Germany, Italy and Japan. On 4 March 1941 the first convoy of British cargo ships and warships left Alexandria in Egypt with cargo and troops bound for Piraeus and Volos in Greece. The US Senate passed the Lend-Lease Bill – the programme under which the USA supplied the Allies with materials for the war effort. It would be a further nine months before the USA entered the war.

Heavy bomb attacks on Britain continued and British troops invaded Italian-controlled Ethiopia from British Somaliland. In North Africa General Gariboldi succeeded Marshal Graziani in command of Italian Forces. On 24 March 1941 General Erwin Rommel mounted his first attack in the Desert War and retook El Agheila. The following day Yugoslavia signed the Tripartite Pact and this was followed by a revolution led by a group of air force officers. The son of the murdered King Alexander took over as King Peter II and Yugoslavia left the Pact. Hitler ordered the immediate liquidation of Yugoslavia. The biggest naval battle of the war to date took place off Cape Matapan in Greece. By the end of March 1941 it was estimated that almost 29,000 British civilians had been killed and air attacks continued on cities and towns in Britain on an almost nightly basis.

In the first quarter of 1941 fifteen people with North Down/Ards connections died.

17 January 1941	**Lieutenant (A) John Carr**
23 January 1941	**Assistant Steward Ronald Wilson Baker**
09 February 1941	**Private Frank Mason**
12 February 1941	**Flt Lt Desmond Wallace Ferguson Barker DFC**
19 February 1941	**Fusilier Edward Francis Owen**
24 February 1941	**Able Seaman James Smiley Logan**
01 March 1941	**Sergeant Joseph Gerald Earley**
01 March 1941	**Master John Frazer Jefferson**
01 March 1941	**Ordinary Seaman Robert Joseph Shaw**
01 March 1941	**Master Arthur Hill Coates Waterson**
08 March 1941	**Third Engineer Officer Joseph Gerald Foster**
11 March 1941	**Sergeant Victor Hall Skillen**
13 March 1941	**Corporal Andrew Ennis**
14 March 1941	**Driver Patrick Hynds**
25 March 1941	**Barber William James Canavan**

In early April 1941 Bulgaria, Italy and Germany invaded Yugoslavia and Greece. The Italian Army in Ethiopia evacuated Addis Ababa and surrendered to Allied Forces. Japan signed a non-aggression pact with the Soviet Union. Rommel launched a heavy attack on Tobruk. On 15 April the Luftwaffe attacked Belfast. On 17 April Yugoslavia surrendered to the German Army and four days later Greece surrendered to the German Army. General Rommel and his army entered Egypt on 25 April 1941. British, Dutch and American representatives met in Singapore to draw up a defence plan in the event of a Japanese attack. British Forces were forced to evacuate Greece. On 30 April Rommel mounted another heavy attack on Tobruk as part of the Siege of Tobruk which lasted for 240 days between April and November 1941.

On 2 May the Anglo-Iraqi War began and on 4 May the Luftwaffe attacked Belfast again. On 5 May 1941, the fifth anniversary of the Italian occupation of Addis Ababa, Emperor Haile Selassie of Ethiopia returned to his capital in triumph. On 10 May 1941 Rudolph Hess, deputy leader of the Nazi Party, parachuted into Britain and was immediately arrested. He said that his mission was to make peace with Britain. (He was held prisoner until 1945 when he faced trial at Nuremberg with other Nazi war criminals). That night the Houses of Parliament and Westminster Abbey were bombed – the last air attack on Britain until July. Hitler appointed Martin Bormann as Hess's successor. German attacks on Malta continued and attacks on Crete began. On 27 May the German battleship *Bismarck* was sunk.

By the beginning of June 1941 all remaining British troops were evacuated from Crete. On 8 June British and Free French Forces invaded Syria and Lebanon (mandated to France by the League of Nations after the First World War and the partitioning of the Ottoman Empire) where they attacked French garrisons loyal to the Vichy government under Marshal Philippe Petain. Germany and the Soviet Union were ideologically at variance and, despite the Non-Aggression Pact of 1939, on 22 June 1941 Germany invaded the Soviet Union (*Operation Barbarossa*). Again using the Blitzkrieg technique, over four million Axis soldiers invaded the USSR along an 1,800 mile front. Albania, Finland, Hungary, Italy and Romania also declared war with the Soviet Union. Meanwhile, the USA took an increasingly pro-China stance in the Japan-China war.

In the second quarter of 1941 sixty people with North Down/Ards connections died.

04 April 1941	Sergeant **William Francis Ernest Gault**
04 April 1941	Corporal **James Harvey Rowan**
05 April 1941	Engineer Commander **Leslie Henry Willis Mauger**
08 April 1941	Civilan **Thomas Gardener Ferguson**
10 April 1941	Sergeant **David Francis Henderson**
14 April 1941	Flight Sergeant **Alexander Magowan McVea**
15 April 1941	Flight Lieutenant **Wilfrid Mark Hamilton Brookes**
16 April 1941	Fusilier **William Bellamy**
16 April 1941	Fusilier **Samuel Burke**
16 April 1941	Lance Corporal **Alexander Carlisle**
16 April 1941	Fusilier **Andrew Copling**
16 April 1941	Civilian **Edith Dunwoody**
16 April 1941	Civilian **Henry Dunwoody**
16 April 1941	Civilian **Isabella Dunwoody**
16 April 1941	Civilian **William Dunwoody**
16 April 1941	Fusilier **Hugh Fulton**
16 April 1941	Fusilier **George Graham**
16 April 1941	Civilian **Angeline Grattan**
16 April 1941	Civilian **Matilda Grattan**
16 April 1941	Civilian **Shelagh Grattan**
16 April 1941	Civilian **Nancy Simms Gribbin**
16 April 1941	Fusilier **Daniel Higgins**
16 April 1941	Fusilier **Leslie Love**

16 April 1941	Fusilier **Samuel McFarland**
16 April 1941	Fusilier **Ernest McNeill**
16 April 1941	Civilian **Thomas Morton**
16 April 1941	Warrant Officer Class II (CSM) **Alfred Penfold**
16 April 1941	Civilian **Elizabeth Tate**
16 April 1941	Civilian **Ellen Ogle Tate**
16 April 1941	Civilian **Evelyn Tate**
16 April 1941	Civilian **Margaret Byers Watt**
17 April 1941	Company Quartermaster Sergeant **William McMurray**
17 April 1941	Fusilier **Matthew Wright**
17 April 1941	Civilian **Robert Wright**
23 April 1941	Aircraftman 2nd Class **Arthur James King**
26 April 1941	Gunner **Hugh Gamble**
26 April 1941	Gunner **William Graham**
26/27 April 1941	Gunner **Edward Adam Moore**
01 May 1941	Lance Bombardier **Robert Orr Thompson**
02 May 1941	Lt Cdr **William Robert Patterson OBE DSC**
05 May 1941	Gunner **John Brown**
05 May 1941	Gunner **Henry Corry**
05 May 1941	Second Lieutenant **John Nelson Hamilton**
05 May 1941	Private **Archibald Joseph Adolphus Holt**
05 May 1941	Civilian **James Thompson**
06 May 1941	Civilians **William and Bertha McGowan**
10 May 1941	Lieutenant **James Craig MID and 2 Bars**
11 May 1941	Sergeant **Robert Richardson**
21 May 1941	Leading Aircraftman **Clifford Samuel Ferguson**
22 May 1941	Able Seaman **James Francis Bailie**
24 May 1941	Lt Cdr (E) **John Gordon Morrison Erskine**
24 May 1941	Ordinary Seaman **Lambert Charles Shepherd**
06 June 1941	Boatswain **John Hawthorne**
06 June 1941	Chief Steward **William McKinley Rae**
06 June 1941	Third Engineer Officer **James Skillen**
12 June 1941	Flight Sergeant **Herbert Hannay MID**
16 June 1941	Fusilier **William Fox**
18 June 1941	Sergeant **Alexander Campbell**
19 June 1941	Flying Officer **William Howard Corbett**

In July 1941 the Eastern Front had three distinct sectors – north-western under Voroshilov, western under Timoshenko and south-western under Budenny – and initially the German Army advanced swiftly. At the same time bombardment of Tobruk by Axis aircraft and artillery continued. Germany announced the end of the Yugoslav nation and redrew the map of the country, establishing Croatia and dividing territory between Germany, Hungary and Italy. An armistice was signed in Syria and thereafter Syria and Lebanon came under Allied control. Britain and the Soviet Union signed an agreement of mutual aid, the Luftwaffe raided Moscow and the German Army advanced towards Leningrad. Marshal Josip Broz Tito led partisan resistance in Yugoslavia and Montenegro against the occupying Italians and Germans. Besieged since 22 June, the Soviet garrison at Brest-Litovisk surrendered to the Germans. British convoys reached Malta and Japanese Forces occupied southern Indo-China. In South America, Peru invaded Equador.

In August 1941 American aid reached the USSR and Joseph Stalin took over as Commander-in-Chief of the Soviet Armed Forces. Winston Churchill and Franklin D. Roosevelt met in Newfoundland. Nazi plots were discovered in Argentina, Chile and Cuba. Heavy fighting continued on the Eastern Front and British and Soviet Forces invaded Iran. Soviet Forces headed for Teheran from the north and, approaching from the south, British Forces occupied the Abadan oilfields. An armistice with a newly appointed Iranian Government was signed on 27 August. Another Enigma machine was captured (this cipher machine was invented by the German engineer Arthur Scheribius and during the war British code-breakers were able to decrypt large numbers of messages which provided vital intelligence).

At the beginning of September 1941 the Germans began shelling Leningrad and, in the Mediterranean, the US merchant ship *Steel Seafarer* was sunk by German aircraft in the Gulf of Suez. Finnish Forces cut the Leningrad-Murmansk railway and, with the first snow on the Eastern Front, the situation in Leningrad became increasingly desperate as people died of cold and starvation. British aircraft attacked Sicily and the German Army captured Kiev, the Ukrainian capital in the Soviet Union. Convoys continued to sail from Gibraltar to Malta.

In the third quarter of 1941 sixteen people with North Down/Ards connections died.

04 July 1941	Sergeant **John Cecil Brandon Irwin**
08 August 1941	**Flight Sergeant Edward Carson Thompson**

17 August 1941	Sergeant **Samuel John Luke**
24 August 1941	Driver **James Walter Hubbard**
26 August 1941	Sergeant **John Patterson MacIlwaine**
28 August 1941	Pilot Officer **William Moody MacDonald**
01 September 1941	FO **Alexander Arthur Fenwich Towry Steavenson**
11 September 1941	Lance Bombardier **William Ward Phillips**
15 September 1941	Private **Archibald Crozier**
15 September 1941	Aircraftman 1st Class **John Harold Maxwell**
20 September 1941	Flight Lieutenant **Patrick Joseph Anthony Byers**
20 September 1941	Junior Engineer Officer **William Lough**
25 September 1941	Gunner **Joseph Dalzell**
25 September 1941	Gunner **Samuel Graham**
25 September 1941	Bombardier **William John McNeilly**
25 September 1941	Gunner **James Meredith**

In October 1941 the German Army advanced on Moscow and the Royal Air Force bombed Nuremburg and other towns in Germany. In Japan Prince Konoe resigned and General Hideki Tojo became Prime Minister. The US destroyer *Reuben James* was torpedoed and sunk by a German submarine. In early November 1941 American warships escorted a convoy transporting Canadian troops from Halifax in Nova Scotia to the Far East. On the Eastern Front soldiers suffered terribly from frostbite. The British aircraft carrier *Ark Royal* was sunk off Gibraltar and in Libya heavy fighting continued around Tobruk. The remaining Italians in Gondar, Ethiopia laid down their arms and Italian East Africa ceased to exist.

At the beginning of December 1941 Britain declared war with Finland, Hungary and Romania and the upper age limit for conscription was raised to 51. On 7 December 1941, without any previous declaration of war, Japanese Forces attacked the US air and naval base at Pearl Harbour in Hawaii. More than 2,000 people were killed. Japan declared war with USA and Britain and then Japanese Forces invaded Malaya, Thailand and the Philippines. Soon thereafter the USA, Britain, the Netherlands, New Zealand, China, Australia and India, together with many Central and South American countries, declared war with Japan. Japanese Forces bombed Singapore and landed on Hong Kong Island. On the Eastern Front there was a Soviet counteroffensive and Hitler announced the end of the winter offensive against Russia. Soviet Forces had halted the German advance. In Libya, British Forces retook Sidi Rezagh and restored a supply corridor to Tobruk, thus relieving the besieged garrison. Germany and Italy declared war with the United States of America.

Japan signed a treaty with Thailand. In Britain, Parliament passed the National Service Act and this provided for the conscription of unmarried women the following year. The Japanese Army captured Manila, capital of the Philippines and, on 25 December 1941, Hong Kong surrendered to the Japanese. The Japanese launched a series of air attacks against Rangoon in Burma. British commandos attacked German bases on the Norwegian islands. The USA and Britain declared war with Romania, Bulgaria and Hungary.

In the fourth quarter of 1941 eighteen people with North Down/Ards connections died.

02 October 1941	**Master William Johnston Meek**
23 October 1941	**Sergeant William Des Brisay Gilmour**
23 October 1941	**Rifleman John McFarlane**
08 November 1941	**Pilot Officer George Marshall McCombe**
19 November 1941	**Pilot Officer Frederick Hugh Anderson**
27 November 1941	**Sergeant Robert Samuel Carson**
05 December 1941	**Sergeant Thomas Leonard Kirk**
10 December 1941	**Able Seaman David Cowan**
10 December 1941	**Able Seaman Samuel Smith**
14 December 1941	**Captain Humphrey Barron Thomson**
19 December 1941	**Petty Officer Stoker Albert Parr Cole**
19 December 1941	**Marine Robert Lyttle Harrison**
19 December 1941	**Able Seaman Crawford Henderson**
22 December 1941	**Pilot Officer Richard Percival William Barker**
22 December 1941	**Ordinary Seaman William James Tweed**
24 December 1941	**Sergeant Eric Ritchie Bowman**
25 December 1941	**Private Robert Conway**
28 December 1941	**Second Lieutenant Robert James Reid**

1942

In early January 1942 there was heavy fighting in the Crimea on the Eastern Front; in North Africa the German and Italian Forces consolidated in the area of Agedabia, later abandoning it and consolidating at El Agheila. Japanese Forces took Jesselton in British North Borneo and later in the month the whole of British North Borneo surrendered to the Japanese. German and Italian aircraft continued to bombard Malta; Japanese aircraft continued to bombard Singapore; there was heavy fighting on the Baatan Peninsula in the Phillipines and on 11 January the Japanese Army captured Kuala Lumpur, capital of Malaya, as well as strategically important islands in Borneo and the Celebes Sea.

In China, Chiang Kai-shek became Commander-in-Chief of all Allied troops operating there. German submarines in the Atlantic targeted shipping along the eastern coast of the USA. Japan declared war with the Netherlands and Dutch East Indies and also attacked British Forces and military installations in Burma. On 17 January the Axis garrisons at Sollum and Halfaya in North Africa surrendered. Throughout the month, and in terrible weather conditions, there was heavy fighting along the Eastern Front. German troops were ordered not to give any food to civilians or Prisoners-of-War and the death toll of civilians in Leningrad continued to rise. Rommel launched a counter-offensive in North Africa and by the end of the month had taken Benghazi. The first large naval battle in the Pacific Theatre of War took place in the Strait of Makassar, between Borneo and the Celebes. Thailand declared war with Britain and the United States of America. Australia ordered full mobilisation and the first contingents of American troops landed in Northern Ireland. British Forces in Malaya withdrew to Singapore and blew up the causeway connecting the island to the mainland. So began the siege of Singapore with Japanese Forces shelling from Johore in Malaya. Britain and the USSR signed a treaty with Iran and the 'Persian corridor' became an important supply route from the Western Front to the Eastern Front.

In February 1942 Vidkun Quisling was appointed Minister-President of Norway as Hitler wound down the German administration in that country and transferred power. In the Pacific, the Americans attacked Japanese air bases in the Marshall and Gilbert Islands. Fighting continued along the Eastern Front and Malta suffered further heavy bombardment. In North Africa Rommel continued to advance and German Forces captured Derna in Libya. British Forces were ordered to hold the Tobruk fortress at all costs. Japanese Forces invaded Java, they made further progress in Burma and they landed on the island of Singapore. Japanese suicide squads made repeated attacks on many fronts. In the English Channel German warships forced a passage through the British fleet and made for Norway. On 15 February 1942 Singapore surrendered to the Japanese. Some people were evacuated but 70,000 prisoners were taken. In the Dutch East Indies the Japanese invaded Bali, east of Java, and on 19 February the Japanese Air Force bombed Darwin in Australia and Mandalay in Burma. The civilian population in Rangoon was evacuated. Allied aircraft bombed Benghazi and Tripoli in Libya and a naval battle in the Java Sea ended with a Japanese victory. This opened a supply route to the Sunda Islands which included Borneo, Java, Sumatra, Sulawesi, Bali and Timor.

In March 1942 Japanese Forces entered Rangoon in Burma, they took Java and controlled the whole of the Dutch East Indies and they began bombardment of New Guinea. They also landed on Buka in the Solomon Islands and continued heavy bombardment of the Philippines. The RAF bombed the Renault works on the outskirts of Paris and also carried out raids on air and naval installations at Benghazi. The RAF also bombed the Krupp armament works at Essen. With the fall of Rangoon, Allied HQ in Burma was relocated to Maymyo near Mandalay. On the Eastern Front there were significant Soviet advances. Malta suffered ongoing heavy bombardment and in *Operation Save Malta* a British convoy of four ships was sent from Alexandria to replenish supplies. This convoy came under attack by Axis Forces and all four ships were sunk. The Royal Air Force bombed Lubeck in Germany and destroyed many ancient buildings. Germany retaliated with raids on the historic British cities of Exeter, York and Canterbury. That the RAF had air superiority in Europe was to some extent due to the demands of the Eastern Front on Luftwaffe resources. Japanese troops landed on Christmas Island, south of Java and in Burma they took the Toungoo area.

In the first quarter of 1942 forty-four people with North Down/Ards connections died.

04 January 1942	Bombardier **Francis Eric Sheals**
07 January 1942	Pilot Officer **Walter Bartholomew McManus**
10 January 1942	Sergeant **Robert Wilkinson Foreman**
10 January 1942	Sergeant **Ralph Henry John Winter**
14 January 1942	Flight Sergeant **Gordon Wemyss Reid**
17 January 1942	Gunner **James Cartner Dixon**
17 January 1942	Able Seaman **Robert John Warden**
19 January 1942	Gunner **Herbert Walter Kemp**
19 January 1942	Civilian **Julie Maude Macoun**
19 January 1942	Civilian **Leslie Stuart Macoun**
24 January 1942	Driver **John Hutchinson**
25 January 1942	Pilot Officer **Kenneth Duncan Adams**
25 January 1942	Sergeant **Ross Wellesley Lindeman**
25 January 1942	Flight Sergeant **Robert Low**
26 January 1942	Leading Aircraftman **Frederick James Miley**
29 January 1942	Captain **David Alexander Hynes Hodgett MID**
29 January 1942	Telegraphist **Albert George MacFarlane**
08 February 1942	Private **Gerald Mavor Bell**
08 February 1942	Aircraftwoman 2nd Class **Jean Dibby Wright**

09 February 1942	Corporal **Campbell Allen**
09 February 1942	Captain **Robert James Bleakley**
09 February 1942	Flight Sergeant **Edward Dennis Cannon**
09 February 1942	Able Seaman **William Charles Woods**
11 February 1942	Flight Sergeant **George Johnston Cheatley**
11 February 1942	Sergeant **Anthony Wilson Lavender**
11 February 1942	Sergeant **Nagu Ranganatha**
14 February 1942	Sailor **William Patton**
17 February 1942	Civilian Nursing Sister **Ida M. Nelson**
18 February 1942	Flight Sergeant **Cecil Thomas Deane**
18 February 1942	Flight Sergeant **John Robert Lucas**
20 February 1942	Sister **Edith Doreen Pedlow MID**
24 February 1942	Sergeant **Joseph Mercer**
27 February 1942	Leading Aircraftman **Robert Reid McClean**
02 March 1942	Able Seaman **George Victor Lowry**
04 March 1942	Private **Robert Byers**
06 March 1942	Flying Officer **Hubert Stanley Sheals**
07 March 1942	Gunner **John Madden**
11 March 1942	Engine Room Artificer 4th Class **Norman Crothers**
14 March 1942	Private **Barry John Stubbings**
15 March 1942	Seaman **Hugh Conway Campbell**
17 March 1942	Pilot Officer **Derek Alfred Cook**
23 March 1942	Lance Corporal **Henry Cromie**
28 March 1942	Flight Sergeant **John Thompson Graham**
31 March 1942	Able Seaman **James White**

On 3 April 1942 the Japanese bombed Mandalay in Burma and launched an attack on the Bataan Peninsula in the Philippines where they went on to take Mount Samat. In the Indian Ocean they attacked Colombo in Ceylon. German air attacks on Malta continued and the island was awarded the George Cross by King George VI for 'heroism and devotion'. Luzon (the largest island in the Philippines) surrendered and as the Battle of Bataan ended so began the 'March of Death' by captured Filipino and American soldiers towards San Fernando; many died of disease, malnutrition and ill-treatment along the way. On 18 April 1942 the Americans attacked Tokyo from the air and Pierre Laval became Head of Government in Vichy France under Chief of State Philippe Petain. In the Philippines, Japanese Forces captured Cebu Island and Panay Island and on 24 April the Luftwaffe bombed Exeter – part of the ongoing campaign to bomb historic cities in

Britain. Japanese Forces captured Mandalay in Burma and closed the Burma Road at Lashio. British Forces retired behind the Irrawaddy River, across the Ava Bridge.

In May 1942 Axis air attacks on Malta continued and the Battle of the Coral Sea began when Japanese Forces landed on Tulagi and Guadalcanal in the Solomon Islands. Britain invaded Madagascar and, in the Philippines, Corregidor Island surrendered to the Japanese. On 16 May 1942 the US 1st Armoured Division arrived in Northern Ireland and on 20 May the Japanese conquest of Burma was complete. Mexico declared war with the Axis Powers and in North Africa Rommel began his spring offensive. On 30 May the first 'Thousand Bomber' raid (*Operation Millennium*) by the RAF took place; the target for more than 1,000 Allied bomber aircraft that night was Cologne.

At the beginning of June 1942 the 150th Brigade of British 50th Infantry Division was overwhelmed in Libya and a Japanese submarine sank a merchant ship in Sydney Harbour. Japanese Forces attacked Alaskan territory during the Aleutian Islands Campaign when they invaded Attu and Kiska. In the Battle of Midway in the Pacific Ocean the US Navy decisively defeated the Imperial Japanese Navy. In North Africa Rommel captured Tobruk on 21 June and, pursued by Rommel, British Forces had to retreat into Egypt. Mersa Matruh fell on 28 June and an Allied defence line was established at El Alamein. In a 'Thousand Bomber' attack on Bremen the RAF suffered heavy losses. On the Eastern Front German Forces were victorious at Kharov and at the end of the month the battle for Sevastopol in the Crimea was virtually over. The Mediterranean was dominated by the Italian Navy and Axis Air Forces.

In the second quarter of 1942 thirty-seven people with North Down/Ards connections died.

05 April 1942	Marine **Robert John O'Neill**
09 April 1942	Leading Cook (S) **Thomas Wilson**
13 April 1942	Sergeant **William Matchett Mahaffy**
15 April 1942	Leading Aircraftman **John Connell Cowan**
18 April 1942	Fusilier **William John Shields**
18 April 1942	Lance Corporal **George Henry Young**
19 April 1942	Fusilier **Albert John Young**
23 April 1942	Leading Aircraftman **Francis John Noel Gorman**
23 April 1942	Sergeant **Josef Antoni Pudelko**
25 April 1942	Gunner **William James Martin**

27 April 1942	Lieutenant (Paymaster) **John Lyle Taggart Glass**
30 April 1942	Sergeant **Edward Lewandowski**
30 April 1942	Lieutenant (E) **John Moir**
05 May 1942	Second Lieutenant **Desmond Robert King**
11 May 1942	Aircraftman Second Class **Ronald Hodgson**
17 May 1942	Sergeant **Cyril Johnson Crozier**
21 May 1942	Flight Sergeant **Edmund Verner Shaw**
26 May 1942	Flight Sergeant **Gordon Charles Edwards**
26 May 1942	Sergeant **William Richard Willis**
26 May 1942	Flight Sergeant **Stanley Donald Wills**
30 May 1942	Flight Lieutenant **Wilfred Ronald Maitland DFC**
30 May 1942	Leading Aircraftman **Leslie Frederick Williams**
31 May 1942	Sergeant **Richard Sweet Cruise**
05 June 1942	Private **Thomas Newell**
09 June 1942	Flight Lieutenant **Harold Abraham McCaghey**
10 June 1942	Bombardier **Harold Johnston**
13 June 1942	Able Seaman **David Orr**
14 June 1942	Colour Sergeant **Nathaniel Robert Smith**
20 June 1942	Gunner **William Robert Bailie**
20 June 1942	Gunner **Robert Cromie**
20 June 1942	Lance Bombardier **Edward James Flynn**
20/21 June 1942	Lieutenant **John Malcomson Gibson**
21 June 1942	Sergeant **Alexander Davidson**
21 June 1942	Gunner **David McClinton**
28 June 1942	Aircraftman 1st Class **Robert Logan Wilson**
29 June 1942	Fireman **James Clegg**
29 June 1942	Brigadier **Robert Dermot Barnes Perrott DSO OBE MC**

The First Battle of El Alamein began on 1 July 1942 and that same day Sevastopol fell to the Germans. Guadalcanal was securely in the hands of the Japanese and the American Air Force flew its first missions in Europe. At the end of the month the Royal Air Force mounted a heavy attack on Hamburg and the Japanese took Kokoda in Papua New Guinea. Axis bombers continued to bombard Malta.

In August 1942 German Forces continued to advance towards Stalingrad and convoys to Malta were decimated. 'Wolf Packs' of German submarines operated in the Atlantic Ocean. American Forces invaded Guadalcanal and established the Henderson Airfield. General Bernard Montgomery was appointed Commander of the British Eighth Army in North Africa and Rommel made an unsuccessful attempt to break through the British lines at Alam Halfa. In *Operation Jubilee* British and Canadian Forces mounted an unsuccessful raid on Dieppe. Brazil declared war with the Axis countries. The Indian Congress asked for independence from Britain and Mahatma Ghandi was arrested. British Air Forces attacked Japanese Forces at Milne Bay on Papua New Guinea while inland the Japanese advanced on Port Moresby.

In September 1942 the Irish Republican Army initiated a campaign in Belfast. On the Eastern Front the Germans continued to attack Stalingrad, Novorossiysk and Grozny. Australian and US Forces defeated Japanese Forces at Milne Bay and fighting continued on Guadalcanal. British aircraft bombed Tobruk.

In the third quarter of 1942 thirty-two people with North Down/Ards connections died.

08 July 1942	Lieutenant **William Henry Lowry Andrews**
08 July 1942	Flying Officer **Neville Stuart King**
09 July 1942	Leading Aircraftman **Henryk Komenda**
09 July 1942	Sergeant **Peter Charles Hunter Phillips**
15 July 1942	Sailor **Patrick Joseph Gibson**
15 July 1942	Fifth Engineer Officer **Thomas McMahon Houston**
15 July 1942	Able Seaman **John Joseph Kennedy**
17 July 1942	Wing Commander **Malcolm Morgan McMullan MID**
19 July 1942	Pilot Officer **John Peter Sadd**
19 July 1942	Sergeant **Marks Wayne**
24 July 1942	Sergeant **Maxwell Warnock Apperson**
25 July 1942	Flight Lieutenant **Ephraim Hugh Brown**
27 July 1942	Pilot Officer **Thomas Andrew McCann**
29 July 1942	Flight Sergeant **Angus Campbell Kelly**
07 August 1942	First Officer **Robert Hughes**
12 August 1942	First Radio Officer **William James McCrory**
13 August 1942	Sixth Engineer Officer **Hugh Longueville Price**
19 August 1942	Private **Hugh Boal**
19 August 1942	Sub-Lieutenant **Colin William Horner Haslett**
19 August 1942	Lance Corporal **James Keenan**
20 August 1942	Captain **Samuel David Corry MID**
25 August 1942	Sergeant **Robert Henry Harper**

27 August 1942	Pilot Officer **Gerald Cecil William Stone MID**
31 August 1942	Leading Aircraftman **Alan Brown**
07 September 1942	Major **Hilton David Proctor**
12 September 1942	Corporal **William James Hunter**
14 September 1942	Sgt **John Edwin Charles Averell Steele-Nicholson**
15 September 1942	Sergeant **Ernest Watson**
20 September 1942	Second Lieutenant **Bernard Wakeford**
26 September 1942	Flight Sergeant **William Benjamin Fry**
27 September 1942	Flight Sergeant **David Harrison Freeland**
30 September 1942	Second Lieutenant **David Morrow**

In October 1942 fierce fighting continued in Stalingrad and the German Army progressed towards Grozny. American aircraft bombed Japanese installations in the Solomon Islands and America sent further supplies to the Soviet Union. American aircraft bombed Lille. In North Africa General Montgomery ordered an attack at El Alamein and the RAF stepped up attacks on Axis installations. The second Battle of El Alamein began on 23 October with a surprise artillery attack on the Italian and German positions. Rommel was in Germany at the time and the acting commander, General Stumme, died of a heart attack. American and Japanese aircraft fought in the Battle of Santa Cruz Islands (in the Solomon Islands).

On 2 November 1942 in North Africa the British Army launched the opening attacks of *Operation Supercharge* and two days later the Axis Forces were in full retreat from El Alamein in Egypt. Initially heavy rain hampered pursuit by the Allied Forces but some days later they took the Halfaya Pass and then occupied Bardia in Libya. *Operation Torch* began on 7 November when Allied Forces landed in Algeria, Morocco and Tunisia. Initially Philippe Petain vowed to resist the Anglo-American landings and his deputy in the French Vichy Government, Pierre Laval, agreed to the German demand that French airports in Tunisia be opened to German aircraft. Then, on 10 November 1942, Admiral Jean Darlan, High Commissioner in Algiers announced the surrender of Vichy French Forces in Algeria and Morocco and he crossed over to the Allied side.

On 11 November 1942 Hitler invaded Vichy France and Benito Mussolini ordered the occupation of Corsica. American and Japanese Forces fought the Battle of Guadalcanal and the British Army recaptured Tobruk. There was heavy fighting between Allied and Axis Forces in Tunisia. On the Eastern Front the Red Army launched a huge and successful counter-offensive against the German Forces at Stalingrad. In Libya the Eighth Army took

Benghazi and Agedabia and, in Senegal in West Africa, Dakar was occupied by the Allies. In French Somaliland some of the garrison loyal to the Vichy Government crossed over into British Somaliland and joined the Allied Forces. On 27 November 1942 the French fleet was scuttled at Toulon.

At the beginning of December 1942 German Forces took Tebourba in Tunisia. The RAF bombed Tripoli in Libya and the Axis Forces withdrew from El Agheila and Buerat. On 24 December Admiral Jean Darlan, at one time Marshal Petain's right hand man, was assassinated by a young student in Algiers.

In the fourth quarter of 1942 twenty-eight people with North Down/Ards connections died.

02 October 1942	Signalman **Hans Calvert**
02 October 1942	Petty Officer Stoker **James Jamfrey MID**
04 October 1942	Private **Andrew Leebody**
07 October 1942	Lieutenant **James Sinclair Adair**
24 October 1942	Surgeon **William Errol Charles McCullough**
26 October 1942	**Patrick Edward Doran**
28 October 1942	Corporal **Albert Charles Tyler**
02 November 1942	Sailor **William Joseph Mehegan**
02 November 1942	Gunner **John White**
03 November 1942	Trooper **Thomas Shillington**
04 November 1942	Civilian **Frederick Strutt**
06 November 1942	Sergeant **Thomas James McCloud**
14 November 1942	Trooper **George Griffith Griffiths**
14 November 1942	Third Radio Officer **Charles Knox McCune**
18 November 1942	Private **Alexander McCullough**
20 November 1942	Aircraftman First Class **Hugh Craig**
24 November 1942	Sub-Lieutenant (A) **William Foster**
25 November 1942	Sub-Lieutenant (A) **John Richard Mathers**
30 November 1942	Sergeant **Robert Valentine Ievers**
01 December 1942	Flight Sergeant **George Francis Grattan**
02 December 1942	Engine Room Artificer 4th Class **Donald McClement**
03 December 1942	Aircraftman 1st Class **Francis Meredith**
15 December 1942	Sergeant **George Stewart Crossan**
15 December 1942	Lieutenant **Anthony Godby**
17 December 1942	Civilian **Margaret Kate McGowan**

22 December 1942	**Civilian Gladys Doreen Merrison**
22 December 1942	**Leading Aircraftman Joseph Frederick Merrison**
28 December 1942	**Cook Robert Crone**

1943

In January 1943 fierce fighting continued on the Eastern Front (including Leningrad, Kurst and Stalingrad), in New Guinea, in Burma and in Guadalcanal. The ten-day Casablanca Conference was convened to discuss strategic issues and was attended by Franklin D. Roosevelt and Winston Churchill. Joseph Stalin was unable to attend because of military operations in Moscow. At the conference, Allied landings in France and Sicily (*Operation Husky*) were agreed, together with an intensification of bombing raids on Germany to destroy industrial installations and communications. For the first time since 1941 Allied aircraft bombed Berlin and the Luftwaffe attacked London. The USAAF attacked Wilhelmshaven. In North Africa the British Army entered Tripoli and advanced towards Tunisia. Admiral Karl Doenitz was appointed Commander-in-Chief of the German Navy.

In February 1943 British and US aircraft carried out heavy bombing raids across Germany and Sicily and the Soviet Army took Stalingrad, Rostov, Kharkov, Slavyansk and Sumy. Generalissimo Chiang Kai-shek agreed to the deployment of Chinese troops in the campaign to recapture Burma. US Forces defeated Japanese Forces on the island of Guadalcanal. Allied Forces advanced into Tunisia and there was fierce fighting; Axis Forces took Sidi Bouzid and Allied Forces occupied the city of Kasserine. In the Pacific Theatre of War the US made plans for an advance on the Philippines (*Operation Reno*). The RAF began a round-the-clock air offensive over Europe and in one 48 hour period they made 2,000 sorties.

In March 1943 the Red Army re-took more German-occupied Soviet towns and in Burma a route was opened for Allied supplies to get to China. Bombing ferocity in Europe intensified and it was reported that in one 40-minute attack on Essen more than 150 4,000-pound bombs were dropped. Many thousands of people were left homeless. In the Battle of the Bismarck Sea, to the north of Papua New Guinea, US Forces destroyed a Japanese supply convoy heading for New Guinea. Japanese aircraft attacked Allied installations at Wau in New Guinea. The Soviet Army suffered a reverse when German Forces retook the city of Kharkov. Allied bombers attacked Palermo in Sicily. In Tunisia Allied Forces took Gafsa and blocked the Tebaga Pass. Fierce fighting ensued and Indian troops overran the system of fortifications known as the Mareth Line.

In the first quarter of 1943 twenty-nine people with North Down/Ards connections died.

06 January 1943	Leading Aircraftman **Robert Stanley Hegan**
07 January 1943	Convoy Signalman **Hugh Douglas Cole**
07 January 1943	Sapper **Joseph William Ogram**
09 January 1943	Fireman **Donald Gordon Reid**
10 January 1943	Apprentice **William Edward Trimble**
17 January 1943	Flying Officer **Philip Kenneth Woodsend**
20/21 January 1943	Rifleman **Joseph Smyth**
21 January 1943	Captain **Hubert Henderson**
21 January 1943	Flight Sergeant **John Stewart Hill**
31 January 1943	Private **Norman Strahan McKee**
04 February 1943	Sergeant **Arthur Moore Templeton**
06 February 1943	Private **Hugh Young**
08 February 1943	Signalman **Arthur Donald Field MID**
14 February 1943	Sergeant **James Ernest Nicholls**
17 February 1943	Sergeant **Henry Walter Stanley**
18 February 1943	Second Lieutenant **William Laurence Megaw**
18 February 1943	Fusilier **Edwin Appleby Record Watson**
23 February 1943	Third Radio Officer **George Barry Neville Bewley**
03 March 1943	Lieutenant **Edward Victor Polley**
09 March 1943	Sergeant (Pilot) **David John Goodchild**
11 March 1943	Sergeant (Air Gunner) **Robert Moore**
12 March 1943	Sergeant (Air Gunner) **Eric Shaw**
13 March 1943	Able Seaman **William Harper**
13 March 1943	Able Seaman **John White**
14 March 1943	Carpenter **John Alexander McNeilance**
18 March 1943	Lieutenant **Terence Michael Scott Hadow**
21 March 1943	SQMS **Alexander Scott Brown**
26 March 1943	Flight Sergeant **John McCalla Tait**
30 March 1943	Guardsman **Norman McKimm**

In April 1943 there was heavy fighting on the Leningrad front. Antwerp, Naples, Sicily and Sardinia were heavily bombed. Japanese Forces prepared for an air offensive in the South Pacific and concentrated all available aircraft in Papua New Guinea. From there, Japanese Forces attacked airfields and shipping in New Guinea and the Solomon Islands area. Mid-month Admiral Yamamoto died when the aircraft he was travelling in was shot down in a planned operation following the deciphering of a coded message. Fighting on the Eastern Front was halted temporarily because of the thaw. Hitler and Mussolini met in Salzburg to discuss strategy. In Tunisia, British and US Forces continued to advance as the Axis Forces retreated towards Enfidaville. The massacre of Jews in the Warsaw ghettos began.

In May there was further heavy fighting on the Eastern Front and in Tunisia the Allied Forces captured Tunis. By 11 May Allied Forces controlled the whole country and the Germans there surrendered unconditionally. Air attacks on Germany and Italy by the RAF continued, including the Zeppelin factory at Friedrichshafen where radar equipment was manufactured. Japanese troops evacuated Kiska Island in the Aleutians and, in the Mediterranean, Allied Forces captured the Italian islands of Pantelleria, Lampedusa, Linosa and Lampione. Bombing raids on Sicily continued in preparation for the invasion of Sicily – *Operation Husky*. The RAF introduced the 'shuttle' system whereby aircraft that completed a bombing mission in Europe flew on to North Africa and then undertook a further bombing mission on their way back to Britain. In May 1943 there came a turning point in the Battle of the Atlantic when U-boats were withdrawn from the north Atlantic following a series of heavy losses. On 30 June a major Allied offensive began in the South Pacific – *Operation Cartwheel*.

In the second quarter of 1943 twenty-eight people with North Down/Ards connections died.

06 April 1943	Major **Herbert Noel Wallace MC**
10 April 1943	Lance Sergeant **John Boocock**
11 April 1943	Warrant Officer **Samuel Nicholl Beckett**
12 April 1943	Sergeant **Peter Murray Rogerson**
19 April 1943	Galley Boy **William James Morrow**
21 April 1943	Sergeant (Navigator) **Peter Tristan Smith**
24 April 1943	Lance Corporal **Alexander Richard Day Vinycomb MM**
25 April 1943	Fusilier **Joseph Nixon**
27 April 1943	Sergeant **James Douglas Marr**
27 April 1943	Lieutenant **Patrick Edmund Charles Nugent**
06 May 1943	Private **Thomas Charles Deville**
06 May 1943	Driver **William Graham**
06 May 1943	Rifleman **Charles Smart**
08 May 1943	Deck Hand **Harry Aiken**
08 May 1943	Engineer **William Sloan Anderson**
08 May 1943	Coxwain **William George Nelson**

08 May 1943	Pilot **William White**
04 June 1943	Sergeant **Alexander L. Quillan**
12 June 1943	Lieutenant (A) **George Leslie Werts**
12 June 1943	Flying Officer (Pilot) **Douglas Williams**
14 June 1943	Sergeant **Thomas Ernest Victor Doherty**
18 June 1943	Corporal **Francis Neville Sloss**
20 June 1943	Lieutenant **William Harold Graham**
22 June 1943	Sergeant **David Stuart Donaldson**
22 June 1943	Pilot Officer **Hugh Conn Thompson**
24 June 1943	Third Radio Officer **James McMurtry Corbett**
25 June 1943	Private **James Kerr**
26 June 1943	Flying Officer **Arthur Buckby Sinton**

In July 1943 intense Allied bombing of southern Italy, Sardinia and Sicily continued prior to the invasion. On the Eastern Front there was heavy fighting in the Kursk region and Soviet troops mounted attacks across that entire Theatre of War. General Sikorsky, leader of the Polish Government in exile, died when his plane crashed near Gibraltar. American aircraft mounted a series of attacks in the Solomon Islands. On 9 July a fleet of some 3,000 boats set sail from Tunisia for the invasion of Sicily the following day. The boats suffered difficulties in strong winds and rough seas but American and British troops began a speedy advance. By 23 July all of western Sicily was under Allied control. The RAF made a massive night raid on Hamburg in Germany and US bombers attacked targets in Norway.

On 25 July the Fascist Grand Council in Italy passed a vote of no confidence in Mussolini and invited the King of Italy, Victor Emmanuel III, to assume control of the Italian Armed Forces. Mussolini was arrested and sent to the island of Ponza. Later he was imprisoned on Maddalena Island (off Sardinia) before being taken to Abruzzi in Italy. The King invited Marshal Pietro Badoglio to form a new Government, which he did, omitting all Fascists. Immediately Hitler sent eight German divisions then in Germany and France to occupy the alpine passes between Italy and Austria, France and Switzerland and he stated his intention to restore the Fascist regime in Italy.

In August fierce fighting continued in Sicily as Allied Forces advanced. US bombers bombed the oil refineries at Ploesti in Romania. Burma declared itself independent of Great Britain. Soviet Forces continued their advance all along the Eastern Front and they retook Kharkov as well as Glukhov, Orel, Taganrog and Yelnya. In the Solomon Islands the Americans took Munda Airfield on New Georgia Island. Allied Forces bombed cities in the north of Italy including Genoa, Milan and Turin. US aircraft bombed Rome and also Wiener Neustadt in Austria. By 17 August all of Sicily was under Allied control. Italy requested an armistice but the Allies insisted on unconditional surrender. The King of Bulgaria, King Boris III, died and was succeeded by his six-year old son Prince Simeon.

On 3 September 1943 Allied Forces invaded southern Italy, landing on the Calabrian coast between Reggio and Villa San Giovanni. Soviet troops continued to advance along the Eastern Front taking many cities including Stalino. On 8 September Italy surrendered unconditionally to the Allies and it was announced that all Italians who helped to eject German Forces from Italian soil would have support from the United Nations. King Victor Emmanuel III and his Cabinet left Italy, leaving the Italian Royal Army without orders. Italian and German soldiers ceased to be allies and became enemies.

In *Operation Avalanche*, Allied troops landed on the Italian coast near Salerno. On the Eastern Front, Soviet troops continued to advance and German troops continued to retreat. Germany took control of Croatia, Greece and part of Yugoslavia. Iran declared war with Germany. German troops occupied Rome and clashed with Italian troops. The Italian fleet formally surrendered to Admiral Cunningham. In Italy the British Airborne Division took Brindisi and later Bari. A German commando unit rescued Mussolini from his prison on Gran Sasso and took him to Munich in Upper Bavaria and then to Rastenburg – the Wolf's Lair – Hitler's headquarters. German troops evacuated Sardinia and moved to Corsica.

Mussolini, under direction from Hitler, declared an Italian Social Republic – essentially a puppet state of Nazi Germany. On the Eastern Front, Soviet soldiers recaptured Smolensk, Roslavl and Temruk. In Italy, Allied troops entered Foggia and occupied the airport. The people of Naples rose up against the Germans who were plundering their city. Avellino was taken by the Allies.

In the third quarter of 1943 thirty-three people with North Down/Ards connections died.

04 July 1943	Sergeant **Richard Mailey**
10 July 1943	Corporal **Andrew Eccles**
15 July 1943	Private **Harold William Calvert**
15 July 1943	Flying Officer **Francis Raymond Moore**
19 July 1943	Lieutenant **Brian Thomas Stewart Rothwell**
21 July 1943	Flying Instructor **Deryk Jay Bleakley**

22 July 1943	Flying Officer **Robert Henry Rutherford**
26 July 1943	Pilot Officer **John Stanley Smyth**
28 July 1943	Sergeant **Henry Victor Hawkins**
29 July 1943	Driver **Kenneth Herbert Andow**
30 July 1943	Pilot Officer **Wallace Robert Smyth**
01 August 1943	Sergeant **Albert Abraham Goldstone**
05 August 1943	Sapper **John Bowen**
06 August 1943	**Sydney Murray**
08 August 1943	Major **Walter Raleigh Draper**
08 August 1943	Fusilier **John Matthews**
08 August 1943	Flying Officer **Thomas George Rodgers**
10 August 1943	Flight Lieutenant **Harold Anthony Kidd-May**
13 August 1943	Fusilier **Edward Graham**
21 August 1943	Flight Lieutenant **John McCrory**
22 August 1943	Pilot Officer **Jerzy Ryszard Tuczemski**
23 August 1943	Flight Sergeant **Robert Angus Moore**
23 August 1943	Sergeant **Newtown Hunter Middleton Williams**
28 August 1943	Pilot Officer **Thomas Norman Stockdale**
03 September 1943	Flight Sergeant **George Wilson**
04 September 1943	Sergeant **Robert McKeag**
09 September 1943	Third Engineer Officer **Albert Sandfield**
10 September 1943	Stoker 1st Class **David Cromie**
11 September 1943	Flight Sergeant **Stanislaw Grondowski**
11 September 1943	Sergeant **Wladyslaw Kolek**
11 September 1943	Gunner **William McBlain**
15 September 1943	Sub Lieutenant (A) **David Francis Apperson Hollywood**
25 September 1943	Lance Corporal **Thomas Dickson**

On 1 October Allied Forces entered Naples. In Austria, Allied Forces bombed Vienna and, in Italy, Allied commandos captured Termoli, Benevento and Capua. German Forces captured the island of Kos in the Mediterranean. The Portuguese Government agreed to provide Britain with naval facilities in the Azores. There was intense fighting in Italy and on 13 October Italy declared war with Germany; at the end of the month Allied Forces captured Teano and Cantalupo.

At the beginning of November, Soviet troops captured Armyansk in the Crimea and Kakhovka on the Lower Dniepr. On 6 November they captured Kiev, third largest city in the USSR. Mid-month, Army commanders suspended the Allied offensive in Italy to give soldiers an opportunity to consolidate their positions. In Greece, German Forces occupied the island of Leros while Berlin suffered immense damage in a series of Allied bombing raids. In one raid more than 2,000 tons of bombs were dropped in 30 minutes. Churchill, Roosevelt and Chiang Kai-shek met in Cairo and later, in November, Churchill, Roosevelt and Stalin met in Teheran.

During the night of 2 December 1943 the Germans caused extensive loss of life and destruction of ships when they attacked Bari. In India, Japanese bombers attacked Calcutta harbour. On 27 December the German battleship *Scharnhorst* was sunk off the North Cape. The year ended with significant Allied progress on several fronts – Stalingrad, Kursk (at that time the Eastern Front extended over a distance of more than 1,300 miles), the Pacific and Italy. Some military historians have commented that it was the events of 1943 that determined the ultimate outcome of the war. General Dwight D. Eisenhower was appointed Supreme Allied Commander of the Allied Expeditionary Force (in advance of the planned Normandy Landings – *Operation Overlord*).

In the fourth quarter of 1943 twenty-six people with North Down/Ards connections died.

03 October 1943	**Flight Lieutenant William Thomas Irwin**
05 October 1943	**Sergeant Henryk Andrzej Flegier**
16 October 1943	**Group Captain John Evelyn Matier MacCallum**
18 October 1943	**Wing Commander Wladyslaw Eugeniusz Heller**
25 October 1943	**Commander Eduard Bakker DFC**
03 November 1943	**Lieutenant Ernest Basil Snell Hewitt MC**
03 November 1943	**Lance Corporal Andrew McVeigh**
04 November 1943	**Captain Charles Arthur Rea**
05 November 1943	**Warrant Officer Thomas Francis Jefferson**
12 November 1943	**Sergeant Robert Trevor Gibson**
13 November 1943	**Chief Engineer (Marine) John James Tait**
15/16 November 1943	**Fusilier James McMaster**
17 November 1943	**Rifleman Ernest Oscar Thompson**
18 November 1943	**Flight Sergeant William Barraclough**
18 November 1943	**Sergeant Walter Edward Fern**
18 November 1943	**Flight Sergeant Andrew Greenwell Gibbison**
18 November 1943	**Flight Sergeant Raymond Farquhar Simpson**
02 December 1943	**Rifleman Desmond Hull**
02 December 1943	**Lance Corporal John Mawhinney**

02 December 1943	**Second Officer Leonard Whiston**
05 December 1943	**Captain Robert Patrick Perceval-Maxwell**
09 December 1943	**Flying Officer Ian Alexander Calthrop Campbell**
14 December 1943	**Flying Officer Stanislaw Podobinski**
18 December 1943	**Flying Officer Norman Edmond Hanna**
29 December 1943	**Wing Commander Charles Ronald Hancock OBE DFC**
31 December 1943	**Chief Engineer John Gilkenson Nicholson**

1944

In January 1944 the RAF began another intense bombing campaign over Berlin. On the Eastern Front Soviet Forces captured Radovel and Olevsk, close to the Polish border. The Soviet advance continued and communications between Leningrad and Moscow were restored when the Leningrad siege ended. On 22 January Allied Forces landed at Anzio and Nettuno in Italy and captured the harbours. Allied aircraft dropped two million leaflets on Rome announcing the imminent arrival of liberation forces.

In the Pacific Theatre of War, US Forces invaded the Marshall Islands on 31 January. There was heavy fighting in Italy and, in an Allied attack the Benedictine Abbey on Monte Cassino was destroyed. In the Pacific, Truk (now Chuuk) Lagoon in the Caroline Islands, which was Japan's main base for operations in New Guinea and the Solomon Islands, was destroyed by US Forces on 18 February.

By mid-March 1944 the German Army had been driven back on the Eastern Front to the line it held in 1941, a few days after the invasion. War continued to be waged in Europe and in other countries across the world including Burma, China, New Guinea and India together with islands such as the Admiralty and St. Matthias Islands (Bismarck Archipelago, Papua New Guinea), Bougainville (Solomon Islands), Green Islands (Papua New Guinea), Mariana Islands (Philippine Sea), New Britain and New Ireland (Papua New Guinea). At the end of March 1944 Hollandia (now Jayapura) in New Guinea was heavily shelled by US Forces.

In the first quarter of 1944 twenty-four people with North Down/Ards connections died.

04 January 1944	**Flight Sergeant Hugh Baird**
09 January 1944	**Bombardier Thomas McCutcheon**
16 January 1944	**Civilian David Garfield Logie**
21 January 1944	**Private Stewart Courtney**
21 January 1944	**Sergeant Rudolph Angel Antonio Forte**

07 February 1944	**Staff Sergeant Thomas Anthoney**
08 February 1944	**Guardsman William Pollock**
12 February 1944	**Junior Engineer Officer John Corbett Hall**
12 February 1944	**Sister Muriel Emily Leckey**
13 February 1944	**Sergeant Thomas Adair**
13 February 1944	**Sub-Lieutenant (A) John Esmond Marshall**
18 February 1944	**Able Seaman Thomas Gould**
23 February 1944	**Wing Commander Victor Edwin Maxwell MID and Bars**
23 February 1944	**Captain Robert Neville Desmond Young MID**
12 March 1944	**Sub-Lieutenant (A) Francis Graham Reid**
13 March 1944	**Private John George Benson**
16 March 1944	**Sergeant William Duncan Irwin**
17 March 1944	**Flying Officer Donald Maldwyn Griffiths**
17 March 1944	**Flying Officer Frederick John Reid**
17 March 1944	**Pilot Officer Horace James Rich**
17 March 1944	**Flight Lieutenant Eric Augustus Snow**
22 March 1944	**Flight Sergeant John Cameron Keith Webb**
23 March 1944	**Flying Officer John Finlay Mitchell**
24 March 1944	**Flight Sergeant Ian Gordon Campbell**

On 12 April in Italy King Victor Emmanuel III abdicated and his son Umberto became Regent and during the second quarter of 1944 heavy fighting continued on all fronts. In France, Allied Forces mounted air attacks on German gun emplacements and airfields in Normandy and in China the Japanese launched an offensive in Henan Province. In New Guinea US Forces occupied Hollandia. On the Eastern Front there was intense fighting in the Ukraine where the Soviet Army took Odessa and in the Crimea where they took Sevastopol. Finland rejected a peace offer extended by the Soviet Union. At 11.00 pm on 11 May in Italy, Allied Forces opened fire along a line that extended from the mountains east of Cassino to the sea. The Americans expanded their control in the Pacific.

On 4 June 1944 the US Army captured Rome and on D-Day, 6 June 1944, Allied Forces landed in Normandy on the north coast of France. The date was decided on the basis of detailed meteorological calculations. The beaches where the landings took place were named Omaha and Utah (American Forces) and Gold, Juno and Sword (Commonwealth Forces). A great many lives were lost in the process and in the subsequent fighting.

In Italy, Marshal Pietro Badoglio resigned and was replaced by Ivanoe

Bonomi. On 13 June the first German V1 flying bombs (V for Vergeltung meaning reprisal) were directed towards England. US Forces attacked the island of Iwo Jima in the Japanese Volcanic Islands. Allied Forces advanced in France and US Forces attacked Cherbourg which surrendered at the end of the month. US and Japanese Forces fought the Battle of the Philippine Sea and US Forces emerged victorious. US Forces were victorious too at Saipan in the Mariana Islands (Philippine Sea) and they planned an attack on Guam in the same island group.

In the second quarter of 1944 twenty-nine people with North Down/Ards connections died.

01 April 1944	Chief Engine Room Artificer **Christopher Vivash**
12 April 1944	Sergeant **William John Morrison**
13 April 1944	Lieutenant **James Gilmore Scott**
15 April 1944	Flying Officer **Gordon Elgin Vance**
15 April 1944	Squadron Leader **Thomas George Westlake**
23 April 1944	Lieutenant **Noel Montgomery Neely**
27 April 1944	Leading Aircraftman **Richard George Yeaman**
30 April 1944	Sub-Lieutenant **Samuel McMaster Boyd**
04 May 1944	Sergeant **Margaret King**
06 May 1944	Leading Aircraftman **Stanley Mynett**
06 May 1944	Sergeant **Victor Wadmore**
12 May 1944	Private First Class **James Polley**
17 May 1944	Corporal **John Williams**
21 May 1944	Flying Officer **Geoffrey Alexander Bowman**
25 May 1944	Sergeant **James Shields**
03 June 1944	Rifleman **Charles Maxwell**
07 June 1944	Squadron Leader **George Crawford DFC AFC**
07 June 1944	Rifleman **John Chapman Oliver**
12 June 1944	Flight Lieutenant **Geoffrey Austin Harrison**
13 June 1944	Lieutenant **Simon Denis St. Ledger Fleming**
15 June 1944	Flying Officer **James Kenneth Weir**
17 June 1944	Flying Officer **Hugh Francis Morrow**
18 June 1944	Private **Harold Lamb**
18 June 1944	Private **Frederick George Wright**
19 June 1944	Rifleman **William Johnston**
19 June 1944	Private **Robert James Major**
19 June 1944	Lance Sergeant **Andrew Robert Stewart**

28 June 1944	Flight Sergeant **Ronald Nelson**
29 June 1944	2nd Engineer Officer **Reginald William Dudley Gibbs**

Between D-Day, 6 June and 1 July 1944 the Allies landed more than 900,000 men, around 600,000 tons of equipment and more than 175,000 vehicles in Normandy. In that period more than 60,000 men were killed or wounded. During July, fighting continued in Burma (Chinese and American Forces took Myitkyina), in China, on the Eastern Front (Soviet Forces took cities including Brest-Litovsk, Minsk, Pinsk and Vilna), in France, in Italy, in India, in the Mariana Islands (including Guam and Tinian), in New Guinea (including Numfoor Island), in the Volcano and Bonin Islands. The US Government recognised the Provisional Government of the French Republic headed by General de Gaulle. On 20 July there was an attempt to assassinate Hitler in the Wolf's Lair at Rastenburg (*Operation Valkyrie*). The attempt failed and in the months that followed some 5,000 people were tried and executed (including one of the leaders, Colonel Claus von Stauffenberg, on 21 July 1944). Others who had supported the attempt committed suicide, including Hans von Kluge on 18 August 1944 and Erwin Rommel on 14 October 1944.

In August the Finnish president Risto Ryti resigned and he was replaced by Marshal Karl Gustav Mannerheim. US Forces took Guam and Tinian and, operating from Soviet bases, US aircraft raided airfields in Romania. Allied Forces landed in the south of France and by the end of the month they controlled the coast line between the Rhone Delta and Nice. They marched inland taking towns and cities including Avignon, Marseilles and Toulon. In the South West Pacific, Allied Forces invaded Morotai Island in the Northern Moluccas. In New Guinea the Allied operations on Biak Island were completed. In Northern France the whole Allied Line continued to march forward and, on 23 August, Paris was liberated by the French Forces of the Interior (FFI). That day in Romania the pro-German Premier Ion Antonescu was deposed. King Michael I asked Constantin Sanatescu to form a Government and Romania accepted the unconditional surrender demanded by the Russians. As a reprisal, German aircraft raided Bucharest and Romania declared war with Germany. In Italy, Allied Forces entered Florence and advanced towards the Gothic Line – the last major Axis line of defence along the summits of the Apennine Mountains.

During September 1944 many towns and cities in Northern France were liberated, including Brest, Boulogne, Calais, Dunkirk and Verdun, together with many towns and cities in Belgium, including Antwerp (the battle for the port continued), Bruges, Brussels and Liege. In Southern France the city of Lyons was liberated. On 4 September, Finnish Forces called a ceasefire and an armistice was signed between Finland and the Soviet Union. The Soviet Union declared war with Bulgaria and within a few hours forced that country to capitulate. On 8 September the first of the V2 flying bombs fell on London. The Belgian Government of Hubert Pierlot (which took sanctuary in London when Belgium was occupied by the Germans in May 1940) returned to Brussels.

On 15 September 1944 Allied Forces entered Germany and then, two days later, they entered Holland (near Arnhem). This latter operation (*Operation Market Garden*) failed in the face of stiff German resistance and Allied Forces suffered heavy casualties in an unsuccessful attempt to hold the bridge at Arnhem. In Greece, German Forces evacuated Mitilini and the Ionian Islands.

In the third quarter of 1944 forty people with North Down/Ards connections died.

03 July 1944	Fusilier **David Francis Prosser**
04 July 1944	Sub-Lieutenant (A) **Frederick Robert Akister**
07 July 1944	Corporal **Edward Dempster**
07 July 1944	Pilot Officer **William Maxwell Henry**
08 July 1944	Lieutenant **Denis Harold Smallman**
09 July 1944	Private **Robert Hoey**
10 July 1944	Rifleman **John Harold Blythe**
17 July 1944	Fusilier **William Radcliffe Partridge**
18 July 1944	Private **George Boyling**
20 July 1944	Sergeant **James Campbell**
22 July 1944	Sergeant **Terence John McQueen**
24 July 1944	Flight Lieutenant **Hugh Raymond Harrison DFC**
26 July 1944	Flying Officer **George Stanley Corry**
30 July 1944	Fusilier **John Kavanagh McHugh**
31 July 1944	Corporal **James H. Whelan**
03 August 1944	Private **Samuel McBride**
05 August 1944	Chaplain 4th Class **The Revd James Arthur Douglas MID**
07 August 1944	Trooper **John Bennett Campbell**
11 August 1944	Stoker 1st Class **Robert James Hoy**
14 August 1944	Driver **Ronald James Buckingham**
14 August 1944	Flying Officer **George Desmond Hamilton**
16 August 1944	Sergeant **Benjamin Beeby**

17 August 1944	**Lance Sergeant Ronald Chapman**
20 August 1944	**Sergeant Kennedy Boyd Black**
20 August 1944	**Sergeant Frank Bennett Bloor**
20 August 1944	**Flight Sergeant Thomas Charles Crisp**
20 August 1944	**Flying Officer Raymond Hodgson**
20 August 1944	**Sergeant George William Thomas Walker**
23 August 1944	**Flying Officer Donald Stanley Ashton Monard**
26 August 1944	**Pilot Officer Hugh Wilson**
31 August 1944	**Lieutenant William Ernest Watson**
01 September 1944	**Leading Seaman Frederick Caulfield**
08 September 1944	**Cabin Boy Thomas Crawford Barbour**
08 September 1944	**Fireman Garner Wilson**
12 September 1944	**Sergeant Stanley Minnis**
13 September 1944	**Second Lieutenant William James Neely Pinkerton**
13 September 1944	**Private Herbert Anthony White**
16 September 1944	**Flight Sergeant Alan McDonald Wilson**
22 September 1944	**Sergeant Patrick Leslie Whitehouse**
23 September 1944	**Captain John Frederick Smellie**

During October 1944 Allied Forces created breaches in the Siegfried Line. The original Siegfried Line was a line of defensive forts built by Germany during the First World War as part of the Hindenburg Line. During the Second World War the Siegfried Line was a 390-mile long defence system stretching from Kleve (on the border with the Netherlands) to Weil am Rhein (on the border with Switzerland). It comprised bunkers, tunnels and 'dragon's teeth' tank traps. Allied Forces landed on the Greek mainland and took Athens, Corinth, Piraeus and Thessaloniki; German Forces evacuated the Greek islands and by the beginning of November all of Greece was freed from German occupation.

As well as in Western Europe, fighting continued in Italy where persistent rain hampered the Allied advance. Preparations were made to consolidate positions during the inevitable delays caused by winter weather. In Holland, Allied Forces liberated Breskens, Esschen and Venray. In the Philippines, US Forces invaded Leyte and captured Tacloban airport. There were intense naval and air engagements during the Battle of Leyte Gulf. Kamikaze ('divine wind') units of suicide pilots were deployed by the Japanese. General Douglas MacArthur reinstalled the Government of the Philippines under the presidency of Sergio Osmena. US Forces took the islands of Leyte and Samar. In Hungary the Germans were driven out of Debrecen and, in Yugoslavia,

Belgrade and Dubrovnik were liberated. In Germany, Aachen was taken. On the Eastern Front, Soviet Forces occupied the whole of Transylvania.

In November 1944 the first British minesweeper reached Antwerp and began to clear the Scheldt estuary. Walcheren Island was captured. Allied bombers bombed German cities day and night. Franklin D. Roosevelt was elected President of the United States for a fourth term. In Tromso Fjord, Norway RAF bombers sank the German battleship *Tirpitz*. The Norwegian Government in exile announced that Norwegian units serving under Colonel Arne Dahl would operate against the Germans. German Forces evacuated Albania, Serbia, Bosnia and Herzegovina.

In December 1944 the Germans launched a counter-offensive in the Ardennes (the Battle of the Bulge), US aircraft attacked Luzon in the Philippines and in Hungary there was intense street fighting in Budapest. Hungary declared war with Germany and, in Germany, Allied Forces reached Remagen.

In the fourth quarter of 1944 twenty people with North Down/Ards connections died.

02 October 1944	Lieutenant **John Andrew Nugent**
03 October 1944	Trooper **Aaron Smyth**
06 October 1944	Private **John Wray**
09 October 1944	Fusilier **Spencer Jones**
09 October 1944	Corporal **Thomas Paterson Muckle**
13 October 1944	Sergeant **Thomas Carnduff**
13 October 1944	Able Seaman **Thomas John Cochrane**
21 October 1944	Major **Edward Douglas Rea MID**
22 October 1944	Aircraftman 2nd Class **Cyril Charles Cameron**
01 November 1944	Able Seaman **Stanley Geddis**
02 November 1944	Lance Corporal **William Murray McKelvey**
04 November 1944	Captain **David Martin Bailie**
12 November 1944	Rifleman **Robert Warden**
16 November 1944	Flying Officer **Robert Keith James**
21 November 1944	Sergeant **David Corry**
16 December 1944	Private **Thomas Stewart**
16 December 1944	Marine **Robert Totton**
22 December 1944	Civilian **Sally Moir**
25 December 1944	Gunner **Hector Black**
31 December 1944	Flight Sergeant **Alex Joseph Bell**

1945

On 1 January 1945 Luftwaffe bombers carried out surprise raids on airfields in Belgium, Holland and France destroying many Allied aircraft. Meanwhile, the Allied counterthrust against the German Army in the Ardennes and elsewhere along the Western Front continued. There was a lull in fighting along the Italian Front and, because of the defeats sustained by the German Army on the Eastern Front, that front had been substantially reduced in length. A little over three million German soldiers faced more than double that number of Soviet soldiers. In Romania there was heavy fighting around Bucharest and, in the Philippines, convoys of ships transporting US troops assembled in the Gulf of Leyte in preparation for the invasion of Luzon on 9 January. US aircraft attacked Japanese ships and aircraft in Formosa (Taiwan) and the Ryukyu Islands. In Burma, British Forces invaded Akyub Island. On 17 January on the Eastern Front, Soviet Forces gave the Polish Army the honour of being the first to enter Warsaw, by then reduced to a pile of rubble (after crushing the Warsaw uprising the Germans had deported most of the population of 600,000 to concentration camps). Soviet Forces advanced through Poland towards the German border. On 27 January 1945 Soviet troops liberated the Nazi concentration camp at Auschwitz. Just five days earlier the Nazis took some 60,000 prisoners out of the camp on a 35-mile death march to Wodzislaw Slaski to be taken from there by freight train to other camps. More than 25% of these prisoners died on the journey.

In February, Soviet Forces continued their advance in East Prussia, Poland, Germany and Hungary. US Forces in the Philippines advanced towards Manila. On the Western Front, Allied Forces continued their offensive operations against the Siegfried Line and they attacked the Schwammenauel Dam. In France, most of the west bank of the Rhine south of Strasbourg was liberated. At the Yalta Conference in Crimea, Winston Churchill, Franklin D. Roosevelt and Joseph Stalin met to discuss Europe's post-war reorganisation. On the Eastern Front, German troops in Budapest surrendered. In the Philippines, the Bataan Peninsula was liberated and Japanese Forces in the Zigzag Pass area were overcome. Between 13 and 15 February 1945 more than 700 RAF bombers and more than 500 USAAF bombers attacked the city of Dresden dropping around 4,000 tons of high explosive bombs and incendiary devices. It was reported that a 'cyclone of fire raged for four days and four nights'. In the Volcano Islands, US Forces prepared for a landing on Iwo Jima on 19 February and American precision bombing of Tokyo continued. On the Eastern Front, Soviet Forces continued to advance in Poland and Pomerania. All resistance in Manila was overcome and intense fighting on Iwo Jima continued. On 23 February US Forces raised the American flag on the summit of Mount Suribachi as they continued to eliminate the remaining pockets of Japanese resistance on the island. In Burma a bridgehead across the Irrawaddy River was consolidated.

In March 1945 the town of Venlo in Holland was taken by Allied Forces, as was Mönchengladbach in Germany. Turkey declared war with Germany and Japan; Finland declared war with Germany. US aircraft began carpet bombing Tokyo while, in Germany, boys born in 1929 (aged 15/16) were being enrolled in the regular armed forces. On the Eastern Front, Soviet Forces captured Grudziadz (a key point in the German defensive system in the lower Vistula in Poland) and advanced towards Danzig (taken on 30 March). In Germany, US Forces were able to secure the bridge over the Rhine at Remagen before the Germans could destroy it and Allied Forces took Xanten. In Burma, apart from a few enemy strongholds such as Fort Dufferin, Allied Forces took much of the city of Mandalay. They also took Ava Fort on a bend of the Irrawaddy River south of Mandalay. By the end of the month Mandalay was in Allied hands.

In Germany, Allied Forces crossed the Moselle and the Wied rivers. The bridge at Remagen finally collapsed but by that time Allied Forces had other river crossings in place. On 24 March, some 3,000 aircraft dropped around 14,000 British paratroopers for an Allied crossing of the Rhine. The German town of Wesel was taken. In the Japanese Ryukyu Islands, US Forces prepared to invade Okinawa. Argentina declared war with Germany. General Eisenhower modified plans for the final assault on the Western Front – Leipzig became the target instead of Berlin, which the Russians were rapidly approaching from the east. The Germans were in general retreat and Frankfurt was taken.

In the first quarter of 1945 twenty-eight people with North Down/Ards connections died.

06 January 1945	Sergeant **Ernest Henry Mackenzie Barr**
07 January 1945	Sergeant **William McLean**
07 January 1945	Flight Lieutenant **Frederick Watson Ritchie**
22 January 1945	Sergeant **David Burrows George**
08 February 1945	Lieutenant **Owen Shanks MM**
09 February 1945	Private **Leland Truesdale Pentz Purple Heart**
16 February 1945	Private **Frank William Braisher**
17 February 1945	Master **Robert Ernest Kyle**
19 February 1945	Pilot Officer **Samuel Irwin Taylor**

23 February 1945	**Ft Lt Robert Aubrey Alexander Doherty DFC**
24 February 1945	**Flying Officer William Watson Miller DFC**
26 February 1945	**Gunner Joseph Shanks**
01 March 1945	**Lieutenant Richard John Michael Harrison**
07 March 1945	**Flight Sergeant Thomas Watters Doggart**
08 March 1945	**Sergeant Thomas Norman Dunlop**
08 March 1945	**Pilot Officer Ian Lindsay Munce**
14 March 1945	**Leading Aircraftman David Lindsay**
19 March 1945	**Flight Lieutenant Brian Kenneth Levinge Fuge**
20 March 1945	**Lieutenant Maurice Edward Young**
21 March 1945	**Sergeant Thomas Torney**
22 March 1945	**Sergeant William Cummins**
24 March 1945	**Private Hugh Robert Hewitt**
24 March 1945	**Corporal James McLean**
24 March 1945	**Rifleman Robert James Miskimmin**
25 March 1945	**Captain Basil Sheridan Hamilton-Temple-Blackwood**
25 March 1945	**Rifleman Joseph McCullough**
25 March 1945	**Able Seaman Francis Robinson**
29 March 1945	**Corporal John Hardy**

On 1 April 1945 US Forces landed on Okinawa. Canadian troops moved out from the Nijmegan bridgehead and advanced on Arnhem. In Hungary, Soviet troops captured the town of Nagykanizsa in the centre of the Hungarian oilfields (the Germans had deployed a lot of resources in an effort to hold on to the oilfields). Soviet troops reached Vienna and by mid-month captured it. On the Western Front, the garrison at Kessel surrendered. In East Prussia, Königsberg surrendered and the fortress commander was sentenced to death (in absentia) by Hitler. Fighting continued on the Italian Front as Allied Forces moved steadily forward and took places like Carrara, Argenta, Bologna, Modena, Verona, Genoa and Vicenza. Bridgeheads were established over the River Po. Italian partisans took control of Milan. In Moscow, the USSR and Yugoslavia signed a treaty of collaboration while US aircraft carried out massive raids on Tokyo. On the Western Front, places like Bamberg, Arnhem, Groningen, Soltau, Ulzen, Halle, Liepzig, Nuremburg, Stuttgart, Ulm, Bremen and Munich were taken. Franklin D. Roosevelt died on 12 April and Harry S. Truman became the 33rd President of the USA. On 15 April, British Forces liberated the Nazi concentration camp at Bergen-Belsen in northwest Germany where they found over 50,000 starving and seriously ill prisoners together with some 13,000 unburied corpses. US Forces entered

the town of Colditz and captured the Castle on 16 April. After delays caused by bad weather, US Forces began their final offensive against German troops in Italy. Japanese suicide aircraft continued to attack American warships. On the Eastern Front, Soviet Forces began to bombard Berlin on 16 April. Hitler issued an order, 'He who gives the order to retreat is to be shot on the spot'.

On 20 April 1945 Hitler celebrated his 56th birthday in his bunker at the Reich Chancellery in Berlin. On 22 April Heinrich Himmler met Count Bernadotte of the Swedish Red Cross and offered German surrender to the Western Allies but not to the Russians. This offer was rejected and unconditional surrender on all fronts was demanded. The Allied advance in Germany continued and Hitler assumed personal command of the defence of Berlin. In Burma, Japanese Forces withdrew from Rangoon and went into retreat.

Mussolini was captured as he attempted to leave Italy and he and his mistress, Clara Petacci, were executed by Italian partisans near Dongo on Lake Como. Their bodies were taken to Milan and hung upside down for public viewing. On 29 April, Colonel Viktor von Schweinitz signed a document for the unconditional surrender of all German troops in Italy with effect from 1.00 pm (GMT) on Wednesday 2 May 1945. That same day Hitler appointed Joseph Goebbels as Reich Chancellor and Grand Admiral Karl Donitz as Reich President. In a civil ceremony Hitler married his mistress Eva Braun and the following day, 30 April 1945, they committed suicide together at 3.30 pm.

On 1 May Joseph Goebbels instructed General Hans Krebs to meet the Soviet General Vasily Chuikov and request a ceasefire. Chuikov demanded unconditional surrender. The Berlin garrison commander General Weilding decided to surrender unconditionally and Krebs committed suicide. Goebbels had his six children killed before he and his wife committed suicide together. After the surrender was announced there continued to be pockets of resistance in Berlin and over the days that followed German Forces elsewhere in Germany, in Denmark, in Austria and in the Netherlands surrendered.

On 7 May 1945 in Reims, France (in an act of military surrender) and then on 8 May 1945 in Berlin (in an act of unconditional surrender), Nazi German military representatives signed an Instrument of Surrender. Victory in Europe Day (VE Day) was celebrated on 8 May. Because it was just after midnight Moscow time when the Instrument was signed, Victory Day in the Soviet Union was celebrated on 9 May. Allied Forces remained in Germany as an Army of Occupation. During May and June 1945, US aircraft continued to bomb Tokyo and other Japanese cities. Fighting continued along parts of the Eastern Front, in the Philippines (the Luzon campaign ended on 30

June), in Okinawa (captured on 22 June), in Burma, in Malaya, in China and in New Guinea.

In the second quarter of 1945 twenty-four people with North Down/Ards connections died.

02 April 1945	Lieutenant **Brian Beven Russell**
06 April 1945	Corporal **Martin Ryan**
10 April 1945	Sergeant **William Anderson**
10 April 1945	Sub-Lieutenant (A) **Edmund John Hoy**
11 April 1945	Petty Officer **Hugh McNally**
12 April 1945	Lt Col **Francis John Leland MID Croix de Guerre**
12 April 1945	Warrant Officer Class II (CSM) **Edward Potts DCM**
13 April 1945	Corporal **John Ancham**
16 April 1945	Second Lieutenant **Michael Kenny Pendlebury**
18 April 1945	Sergeant **Robert Clarke**
18 April 1945	Lance Sergeant **John Meredith**
20 April 1945	Sub-Lieutenant (A) **George Henry Crawford Lowden**
23 April 1945	Flight Sergeant **John Herbert Hamilton**
26 April 1945	Rifleman **Hugh Henry McGlennon MM**
27 April 1945	Stoker 1st Class **Thomas Murray**
30 April 1945	Lance Bombardier **Francis Xavier Mulligan**
02 May 1945	Lance Bombardier **James Murphy Mair**
07 May 1945	Lieutenant Commander (S) **George Ellis**
03 June 1945	Squadron Leader **Robert William Stanley Marshall**
10 June 1945	Corporal **Albert Edward Reuben**
14 June 1945	Bombardier **William Montgomery**
20 June 1945	Lance Bombardier **Edward Martin**
27 June 1945	Corporal **James Darragh**
28 June 1945	Gunner **John Thomson**

On 1 July 1945 the Chinese liberated Liuchow Airfield at Liuzhou which had been held by the Japanese since 7 November 1944 when it was captured during the Battle of Guilin-Liuzhou. On 13 July Italy declared war with Japan. On 16 July the first atomic bomb was successfully tested by the Americans at Alamogordo in New Mexico. Winston Churchill resigned on 26 July 1945 after being defeated in the 1945 General Election; he was succeeded as British Prime Minister by Clement Attlee. The Potsdam Conference (Potsdam was a city bordering Berlin) held during July/August 1945 was attended by British, US and Soviet representatives and on 26 July the Allies issued a proclamation

demanding unconditional surrender by Japan. If this was refused the Allies threatened 'complete destruction'. Japan's response was to reject the Potsdam ultimatum and to deploy yet more kamikaze aircraft. On 6 August 1945 the United States dropped an atomic bomb on the Japanese city of Hiroshima (population 300,000). Headlines in British newspapers included *Hiroshima Obliterated in a Massive Ball of Fire; Most Terrifying Weapon in History* and *Japan Given 48 Hours to Surrender.*

As had been agreed at the Teheran Conference in November 1943, and at the Yalta Conference in February 1945, the Soviet Union entered the Pacific Theatre of War within three months of the end of the war in Europe. The USSR declared war with Japan on 8 August 1945 and invaded Manchukuo (Manchuria). The next day the United States dropped an atomic bomb on the Japanese city of Nagasaki. At that point Emperor Hirohito was prepared to surrender unconditionally but the military leaders in Japan refused. On 14 August Emperor Hirohito made a radio broadcast accepting unconditional surrender but this was not accepted by all sections of the military and some refused for months, even years, to surrender. On 24 August the USSR and China signed a Treaty of Alliance and on 29 August in Singapore, Admiral Lord Mountbatten received the surrender of the Japanese Forces in South East Asia. US Forces began to occupy Japan.

Japan signed an Instrument of Capitulation on 2 September 1945 (VJ Day or Victory over Japan Day) aboard the US Navy battleship USS *Missouri* in Tokyo Bay. The Second Sino-Japanese War ended on 9 September 1945 (the conflict between the Republic of China and the Empire of Japan which began on 7 July 1937). The state of war between Japan and the Allies formally ended when the Treaty of San Francisco (signed on 8 September 1951 in the War Memorial Opera House) came into force on 28 April 1952. Four years later, on 19 October 1956, Japan and the Soviet Union signed the Soviet-Japanese Joint Declaration of 1956 which formally brought to an end their state of war.

After the defeat of Nazi Germany that country was divided into four military occupation zones administered by Britain, France, the United States and the Soviet Union. Then, in 1949, two German states emerged – the Federal Republic of Germany (West Germany) which was a capitalist parliamentary democracy and the German Democratic Republic (East Germany) which was a totalitarian communist dictatorship. Building of the Berlin Wall by the GDR began on 13 August 1961 and formed a barrier until 9 November 1989 when the East German Government announced that all GDR citizens could visit West Germany. The Treaty of Peace with Germany (Treaty on the Final Settlement with Respect to Germany) was signed in Moscow on 12

September 1990 and this paved the way for German reunification which was formally concluded on 3 October 1990.

The Commonwealth War Graves Commission (CWGC) commemorates service personnel who died during the designated war years:

- While they were in Commonwealth military service or
- Of causes attributable to service

The designated war years are:

- 4 August 1914 to 31 August 1921 for the First World War and
- 3 September 1939 to 31 December 1947 for the Second World War

The end date for the First World War is an official date determined by Parliament. As the end date for the Second World War the Commission selected a date approximately the same period after VE Day as the official end of the First World War was after the 1918 Armistice. The CWGC also commemorates civilians who died as a result of enemy action during the Second World War.

In the third quarter of 1945 four people with North Down/Ards connections died.

12 July 1945	Major **Robert Henry Cutler**
18 August 1945	Sergeant **Hugh Blackwood Price**
08 September 1945	Sapper **William Coffin**
08 September 1945	Lieutenant **Frank Wilfred McGarry**

In the fourth quarter of 1945 six people with North Down/Ards connections died.

10 October 1945	Sub Lieutenant (A) **John Samuel Hornby**
12 October 1945	Sub Lieutenant **Samuel Jamieson Fitchie**
12 November 1945	Signalman **Ronald Victor Joseph Martin**
23 November 1945	Sergeant **Robert Keith Eston**
05 December 1945	Sergeant **Leslie Tom Measday**
24 December 1945	Leading Aircraftwoman **Annie Irvine**

During 1946 eight people with North Down/Ards connections died.

07 February 1946	Corporal **Henry Oliver**
05 May 1946	Seaman First Class **Harry Hanna Shipcott**
21 May 1946	Warrant Officer **William Gallagher Gordon**

29 June 1946	Craftsman **Wilfred Leitch**
19 August 1946	Sapper **Morrison Woods**
20 August 1946	Leading Stoker **Robert Duff**
15 September 1946	Surgeon **William Elliot Fraser**
19 December 1946	Captain **Edward E Lee**

During 1947 six people with North Down/Ards connections died.

20 April 1947	Gunner **John Edmonds**
22 May 1947	Able Seaman **Eugene Hector McSweeney**
01 June 1947	Aircraftman 2nd Class **James McBride**
26 June 1947	Ordinary Seaman **John Johnston**
11 September 1947	Sergeant **Henry Garrett Burrows**
19 October 1947	Private **Robert Richard Lacey**

Some local communities and some Churches took the decision to commemorate people who died after 31 December 1947.

27 October 1948	**Robert Totton (Senior)**

Names in Alphabetical Order

In this Section, the names of servicemen, servicewomen, nursing personnel and civilians with North Down/Ards connections who died in the Second World War are presented alphabetically by surname. Casualties whose names are **emboldened** in the text have their own individual entries in this Section. For names marked with an asterisk (*) some additional information may be found in the Section beginning on Page 899.

Adair Family: James Sinclair (father) and Thomas (son)

James Sinclair Adair and his son Thomas both died in service during the Second World War. James Sinclair Adair's brother, John Thomas Adair, died on active service during the First World War. Before the First World War John Thomas Adair was a factory manager and during the war he served as a Lieutenant with the 10th Battalion, Bedfordshire Regiment *attached* to the 1st Battalion, Border Regiment. He died on 22 August 1915 (aged 31) and was buried at sea. Lieutenant John Thomas Adair is commemorated on the Helles Memorial, Gallipoli, Turkey; on Page 1 in the *Belfast Book of Honour – Journey of Remembering* compiled by Derek Smyth and on James Sinclair Adair's CWGC headstone in Belfast City Cemetery (where his age is inscribed as 26).

A

Adair, James Sinclair
Lieutenant
No. 127083, 6th Battalion, Royal Ulster Rifles
Died of illness in service on Wednesday 7 October 1942 (aged 52)
Belfast City Cemetery
(Section H Grave 471; not the Glenalina Extension)

James Sinclair Adair was born on 23 March 1890 in Belfast and he was a son of Henry William Thomas Adair and Elizabeth (Lizzie) Adair (nee McKnight). Henry William Thomas Adair was a mechanic and he and Elizabeth (Lizzie) McKnight were married on 24 December 1881 in Eglinton Street Presbyterian Church, Belfast. They had at least six children – John Thomas (born 20 February 1884); Mary Ann (born 1 February 1887); James Sinclair (born 23 March 1890); Victor (born 13 September 1891); Albert (born 29 April 1894) and Herbert (born 7 October 1895).

101

Records show that the Adair family lived at a number of different addresses in Belfast, including 49 Snugville Street in 1884, 190 Agnes Street in 1887, 9 Jaffa Street in 1901 and 2 Century Street in 1911. Henry William Thomas Adair died on 4 November 1910 (aged 53) and Elizabeth Adair died on 8 October 1927 (aged 67). In both cases their last place of residence was 2 Century Street, Belfast and both were buried in Belfast City Cemetery (Section H Grave 471).

James Sinclair Adair worked as a rent agent's assistant and he was described as a Civil Servant when he and Jane Elizabeth Wooster from Kent were married on 25 February 1920 in Ballygilbert Presbyterian Church. They had at least two children, Thomas (born 9 June 1923 in Belfast) and Dorothy Kathleen (born 16 July 1931, baptised in Shore Street Presbyterian Church, Donaghadee). James Sinclair Adair and his family lived in Princess Gardens, Donaghadee and later at *Laurington*, Millisle Road, Donaghadee.

A

During the Second World War Lieutenant James Sinclair Adair served with the Royal Ulster Rifles on the Home Front and he was 52 years old when he died on 7 October 1942 as a result of a duodenal ulcer. He was buried in Belfast City Cemetery in the same grave as his parents. His effects amounted to some £440 and probate was granted to his widow. Lieutenant James Sinclair Adair is commemorated on Donaghadee and District War Memorial and in Shore Street Presbyterian Church, Donaghadee. His wife, Jane Elizabeth Adair, died on 25 October 1980 (aged 87) and she was buried in Belfast City Cemetery in the same grave as her husband and parents-in-law. James Sinclair Adair's son, **Thomas Adair**, also died in service during the Second World War.

Adair, Thomas (Tom)
Sergeant (Wireless Operator/Air Gunner)
No. 1531154, 458 Squadron, Royal Air Force Volunteer Reserve
Killed on active service on Sunday 13 February 1944 (aged 20)
Malta Memorial, Valetta, Malta (Panel 14 Column 2)

Thomas Adair was born on 9 June 1923 in Belfast and he was the only son of James Sinclair Adair and Jane Elizabeth Adair (nee Wooster) who moved from Belfast to Donaghadee. **James Sinclair Adair** died in service during the Second World War. Thomas Adair attended Donaghadee

Public Elementary School and then Regent House School, Newtownards from 1936 until 1938. After leaving school Thomas Adair worked in the linen business before joining the Royal Air Force Volunteer Reserve.

Sergeant Thomas Adair was 20 years old when he was killed on 13 February 1944 and John Rodgers, Headmaster of Regent House School, commented that Tom had lost his life 'when his bomber was brought down off the coast of Italy'. Tom was one of a crew of six aboard a Vickers Wellington Mark XIII aircraft (JA104) that took off from RAF Bone in Algeria on an anti-submarine patrol off Ghisonaccia, Corsica and later ditched in Pinarello Bay, Corsica. Two crew members survived, Flying Officer Robert Henry Male and Flight Sergeant Henry William Baines. In addition to Thomas Adair, three other crew members died:

- Flight Sergeant Harry William Brandon aged 31 from Ealing, Middlesex
- Flight Sergeant William McIver Mounsell Lipscomb aged 22 (RAAF)
- Flight Sergeant Sydney Neam Campbell aged 29 (RAAF)

There were also three members of ground crew aboard the aircraft and one survived – Sergeant Cecil Francis Arty Percy. The two who died were:

- Corporal Kieran Kenny aged 24 (RAAF)
- LAC Gordon George Parkin MID aged 30 (RAAF)

Sergeant Thomas Adair's body was never recovered. Within a 16 month period Thomas Adair's mother lost her husband and her son; Dorothy Kathleen Adair lost her father and her brother. Sergeant Thomas Adair is commemorated on the Malta Memorial; on Donaghadee and District War Memorial; in Shore Street Presbyterian Church, Donaghadee; in Regent House School and on his father's CWGC headstone in Belfast City Cemetery.

Adams, Kenneth Duncan (Kenneth)
Pilot Officer (formerly Captain Royal Artillery)
No. 106212, Royal Air Force Volunteer Reserve
Killed on active service on Sunday 25 January 1942 (aged 31)
Lisbon (St. George) British Churchyard, Portugal
(Plot G1 Front Row Grave 16)

Kenneth Duncan Adams was born on 2 August 1910 and he was a son of William George Duncan Adams and Wilhelmina (Mina) Adams (nee Stafford) who were married on 27 April 1904 in Osborne Park Methodist Church, Belfast. The Adams family lived in Belfast at 15 Windsor Park and later at *The Hill*, Newforge, Malone Road. William George Duncan Adams was a linen merchant and his business was in Adelaide Street, Belfast. William and Mina Adams had at least three children – Arthur William Stafford (born 4 April 1906); Margaret Kathleen (born 10 April 1909) and Kenneth Duncan (born 2 August 1910).

Kenneth Duncan Adams attended Rockport School, Craigavad and Campbell College, Belfast. His older brother, Arthur William Stafford Adams, also attended Campbell College. Kenneth's father, William George Duncan Adams, died at *The Hill*, Newforge on 3 August 1940 (aged 61) and was buried in Belfast City Cemetery (Glenalina Extension Grave H 88). His mother, Mina Adams, was living in *Rock Cottage*, Quintin, Portaferry when she died on 15 February 1973 (aged 97) and she was buried in the same grave. Kenneth's brother, Arthur William Stafford Adams, died on 8 November 1988 and was buried with his parents.

A

Before he joined the Royal Air Force Volunteer Reserve, Kenneth Duncan Adams was a Captain in the Royal Artillery. He and Patricia Harrison of Kings Worthy, Winchester in Hampshire were married in St. Mary's Church, Kings Worthy on 7 January 1942 – less than three weeks before Kenneth was killed. Patricia Adams lived in Prestbury, Cheshire. Pilot Officer Kenneth Duncan Adams was 31 years old when he died on 25 January 1942. He was one of a crew of six aboard a Vickers Wellington IC aircraft (Z9098) that was on its way from RAF Portreath in Cornwall to Gibraltar. As they were flying over the British Armed Boarding Vessel (ABV) HMS *Loch Oskaig* near Cape Carvoeiro in Portugal, shots fired in error from the ship's anti-aircraft guns hit the aircraft. When they tried to land on a beach near Sesimbra, four of the crew were killed. Sergeant John Kevin Evans and Sergeant Leonard Francis James Harris were severely wounded. In addition to Pilot Officer Kenneth Duncan Adams the other three crew members who died were:

- Sergeant Noel Arnold Graystone aged 25 from Purley, Surrey
- Sergeant Hugh Berry aged 21 from Fishponds, Bristol
- Sergeant Thomas Patrick McBride aged 24 from Bexleyheath, Kent

Sergeant Harris recovered from his injuries but was subsequently killed on 15 April 1943 and was buried in Durnbach War Cemetery in Germany.

Pilot Officer Kenneth Duncan Adams is commemorated in Rockport School and in Campbell College. There is an inscription on his CWGC headstone in Lisbon (St. George) British Churchyard, Portugal:

Let no man forget the supreme sacrifice made for freedom
Rest in Peace

Adams, Samuel L.
Died on Monday 5 April 1943

> ADAMS—Treasured memories of a loving husband and father, Samuel L. Adams, who died April 5, 1943.
> Always remembered by all at 29 May Avenue, Bangor.

Samuel L. Adams was **not** a casualty of war but his name is included in this Book of Honour as an example of someone whose name was wrongly listed in a newspaper *Roll of Honour* column for Second World War casualties. Three names: Samuel L. Adams, William Beggs and Kennedy (forename not given) were included in the *Roll of Honour* column in the 7 April 1945 edition of the *County Down Spectator* and there was a memorial notice for Samuel L. Adams which read:

Adams – Treasured memories of a loving husband and father, Samuel L.
Adams who died April 5, 1943.
Always remembered by all at 29 May Avenue, Bangor.

> Death of Mr. Samuel Adams.—Many friends in Bangor will learn with sincere regret of the death of Mr. Samuel Adams, which occurred at his residence, 29 May Avenue, on Monday. Mr. Adams, who was about sixty years of age, passed away with startling suddenness having been out only a short time previously. The deceased gentleman was actively associated with First Bangor Presbyterian Church, and was a member of the choir and keenly interested in music. He is survived by his wife and a grown-up family, and to them deep sympathy will be offered in their loss. At the funeral, which took place on Wednesday, the officiating clergyman was the Very Rev. Dr. W. J. Currie. The arrangements for the funeral were carried out by Messrs. James Russell & Co., rear of Ulster Bank, Bangor.

The previous year, in the 8 April 1944 edition of the *County Down Spectator*, there was a similarly worded memorial notice in the *In Memoriam* column.

The death of Samuel L. Adams on 5 April 1943 was reported in the 10 April 1943 edition of the *County Down Spectator*. The report indicated that Samuel L. Adams was about sixty years of age and that he had 'passed away with startling suddenness' at his residence, 29 May Avenue, Bangor. The report stated that he was actively associated with First Bangor Presbyterian Church, a member of the choir and 'keenly interested in music'. He was survived by his wife and grown-up family.

Desk searches and public appeals for information have confirmed that these three men who were listed in the *Roll of Honour* column in the 7 April 1945 edition of the *County Down Spectator* did **not** die in service during the Second World War. Their names were inserted in error in that edition's *Roll of Honour* column.

Ahmed, Shief
Fireman and Trimmer
SS *Troutpool* (West Hartlepool), Merchant Navy
Died as a result of enemy action on Saturday 20 July 1940 (aged 46)
Bangor Cemetery, Co. Down (Section 5 X Grave 23 B)

A

Described in the Register of Deceased Seamen as a British Arab, Shief Ahmed was born in 1894 in Aden, Yemen and he was the husband of Margaret Ahmed of 6 McAlpine Street, Glasgow. He was 5 feet 4 inches tall with brown eyes, black hair and a swarthy complexion and during the Second World War he served in the Merchant Navy as a Fireman and Trimmer aboard the SS *Troutpool*. Owned by the Pool Shipping Company, the SS *Troutpool* was built in 1927 by William Gray and Company Ltd., West Hartlepool and in 1940 she was on a voyage from Rosario in Argentina to Great Britain with a cargo of grain when she sank in Belfast Lough after being struck by two magnetic mines.

Burial of Arab Seaman.—The remains of Shief Ahmed, an Arab seaman, whose body was washed ashore at Bangor on Sunday, were interred in Bangor New Cemetery on Tuesday afternoon. A short committal service was conducted by Rev. Dr. M. W. Beatty, a retired missionary from India, who was accompanied by Mr. J. D. Gamble, O.B.E., representing the British Sailors' Society. The funeral arrangements were carried out by Mr. R. J. Hooke, undertaker, Main Street, Bangor.

The SS *Troutpool* had put into Belfast Lough for degaussing – a process involving the passing of an electric current through a cable round the ship's hull (designed to reduce the possibility of magnetic mines in the sea being attracted by the ship's hull). After re-starting her engines she was struck by two mines around 2.00 pm on 20 July 1940 and sank about a mile off the coast near Bangor. Eleven crew members were killed in the explosions. At low tide the superstructure was visible and, because it was a hazard to shipping, the wreckage was dispersed with explosives. At the time it was speculated that the mines which sank the SS *Troutpool* were laid by a long range Focke-Wulf Fw 200 Condor aircraft known to have been operating in the area.

Fireman and Trimmer Shief Ahmed was buried in Bangor Cemetery, as was **Thomas Smith Beckett** who was the Ship's Carpenter aboard SS *Troutpool*. Three unidentified sailors from SS *Troutpool* were buried in Movilla Cemetery, Newtownards – one on 1 August 1940, another on 24 August 1940 and the third on 26 August 1940. Able Seaman **John McGrath** from the SS *Troutpool* whose body was never recovered is commemorated on the Tower Hill Memorial in London.

There is an inscription on Shief Ahmed's headstone in Bangor Cemetery:

A token of love and remembrance of one we will never forget

Fireman and Trimmer Shief Ahmed was 46 years old when he died.

Aiken, Harry
Deck Hand
Miss Betty, Pilot Launch
Drowned on Saturday 8 May 1943 (aged 21) (Bangor Bay Disaster)
Donaghadee Parish Church of Ireland Graveyard, Donaghadee, Co. Down

Three men from Donaghadee along with one man from Bangor were drowned on Saturday 8 May 1943 in what came to be known locally as the 'Bangor Bay Disaster'. There were no survivors. The four men died when the Pilot Launch *Miss Betty* capsized and sank while returning to port after responding to a call from a ship entering Belfast Lough. The four men who died worked on the pilot boats that were based in Bangor. These pilot boats were in constant service, not only for merchant shipping coming into Belfast, but also for many of the naval vessels using Belfast Lough. At the outbreak of war *Miss Betty* was requisitioned by the Admiralty from Jim Davidson, Donaghadee.

The three Donaghadee men who died were **Harry Aiken, William George Nelson** and **William White**. The Bangor man who died was **William Anderson**. Aboard *Miss Betty* on the day they died, William White was the pilot and William George Nelson was the coxswain. William Anderson was the engineer and Harry Aiken was the deck hand. Harry Aiken had been doing this type of work for 2½ years.

AICKEN—May, 1943 (by drowning), Harry, dearly-loved youngest son of Agnes and the late Henry Aicken. Interred in Donaghadee Churchyard. Deeply regretted by his sorrowing Mother, Brothers and Sisters, Sister-in-law and little Niece, Lorna; also his Friend, Hugh Bennett. Cumberland papers please copy.

Harry Aiken was a single man who lived with his widowed mother Agnes at 4 Bow Street, Donaghadee. Harry was her youngest son. Harry's uncle, Private Maxwell Aiken, who had served with the Border Regiment, died on active service on 23 April 1918 during the First World War. Private Maxwell Aiken is commemorated on Page 85 in the Book of Honour *Remembering Their Sacrifice in the Great War – Ards* compiled by Barry Niblock.

A

Harry Aiken was born in Silloth, Cumberland (now part of Cumbria), his birth was registered in the fourth quarter of 1921 in Wigton and he was baptised in Carlisle Cathedral. He was a son of Henry and Agnes Aiken (nee McCaw) who were married on 12 February 1915 in Donaghadee Parish Church of Ireland Church. Henry Aiken was born on 21 July 1891 in Donaghadee and he worked as a painter. Agnes McCaw was born on 7 May 1891 and she was a daughter of Joseph McCaw of Ballymacruise, Carrowdore. After their marriage Henry and Agnes moved to Silloth where Henry worked as a gasworks stoker. Henry and Agnes Aiken had six children all of whom were born in Cumberland – Agnes (Peggy, born 1916); Maxwell Lens (born 7 June 1917); Joseph (Joe, born 13 November 1919); Harry (born 1921); Madeline H. (born 1923) and Sheila M. (born 1928, died 1930).

During the First World War Henry Aiken served in the Army and he was admitted to Whitby Sanatorium with pneumonia after time spent in the Yorkshire Fells on trench testing operations. After Henry died of tuberculosis on 19 June 1931 Agnes and her five surviving children moved to 4 Bow Street, Donaghadee.

The Pilot Launch *Miss Betty* was around 40 feet long and the disaster was witnessed by Bangor Harbour Master John H. Corry and Customs Officer G.A. Coppard. *Miss Betty* was owned by the Admiralty but crewed by civilians under naval direction and she left Bangor in moderate weather conditions at 8.55 am on 8 May 1943. During the trip the weather deteriorated and on the way back to Bangor the crew had to contend with a strong north-easterly gale and a heavy breaking sea. At 11.40 am, when they were only about 60 to 70 yards from the safety of Bangor harbour, the disaster happened. The boat successfully negotiated a number of strong waves before being overwhelmed by a broadside hit on the port side. *Miss Betty* capsized, turned over in the water and remained upside down.

Harry Aiken's body was washed ashore at Bangor about 7.00 pm on the day of the disaster and his funeral service was held in Donaghadee Parish Church the following Tuesday. Naval ratings acted as pall bearers and senior naval officers were in attendance. Harry Aiken was 21 years old when he died and he was buried in Donaghadee Parish Church of Ireland Graveyard. At the inquest on Harry Aiken which was held in Bangor before the Coroner, Dr. Wallace, District Inspector Gerald Cullen appeared for the police, Mr M. Harper appeared for the Admiralty and Mr D.H. Smyth appeared for the next-of-kin. Lieutenant Commander Hans Dane stated that in his capacity as Admiralty Berthing Officer he was in charge of civilian Admiralty pilots and a number of civilians as crew for the Pilot Launch *Miss Betty*. It was by orders from his office that *Miss Betty* left the pier at 8.55 am in response to the call for a pilot ship and he confirmed that she was seaworthy. The Coroner's verdict was that Harry Aiken's death was caused by asphyxia due to accidental drowning.

Along with Coxswain William George Nelson and Pilot William White, Deck Hand Harry Aiken is commemorated on a separate plaque on Donaghadee and District War Memorial. Harry's mother Agnes died on 29 October 1985 (aged 94) and she was buried in the same grave as her son.

Akister, Frederick Robert

Sub-Lieutenant (A)

800 Squadron, Royal Naval Volunteer Reserve, HMS *Emperor*
Killed in an aircraft accident on Tuesday 4 July 1944 (aged 20)
Rawdon (St. Peter) Churchyard, Yorkshire, England (Section D Grave 578)

Frederick Robert Akister's birth was registered in the first quarter of 1924 in Prestwich, Lancashire and he was a son of Frederick and Mary Akister (nee Farrer) whose marriage was registered in 1923 in Chorlton, Lancashire.

During the Second World War Frederick Robert Akister served with the Royal Naval Volunteer Reserve. On 28 June 1944, No. 800 (Fleet Air Arm) Squadron arrived at Ballyhalbert from HMS *Emperor*. This Ruler-Class Escort Aircraft Carrier was built by the Seattle-Tacoma Shipbuilding Corporation in the USA and was transferred to the Royal Navy in August 1943 under the Lend-Lease Agreement between the USA and Britain. Less than a week after he arrived in Ballyhalbert, Sub-Lieutenant (A) Frederick Robert Akister was killed when his Grumman F6F Hellcat aircraft (JV146) crashed. He was making a steep turn at an altitude of about 1,000 feet when his aircraft spun to the ground between Ballywalter and Greyabbey. When he was buried on 11 July 1944 in Rawdon (St. Peter) Churchyard, Yorkshire his last home address was recorded as *Egerton House, Town Street, Rawdon.*

A

Sub-Lieutenant (A) Frederick Robert Akister was 20 years old when he died and he is commemorated on Rawdon War Memorial and on a (now very faded) brass memorial plaque near the crash site. The plaque is screwed to a wooden fence-post at the side of the Tullykevin Road, Greyabbey and it bears the inscription (unedited):

In memory of Sub Lt (A) F R Akister 800 Squadron RNVR aged 20
Killed when his Hellcat GU146 crashed on 4th of July 1944
He is not forgotten

Sub-Lieutenant Akister's father Frederick died on 16 October 1950 (aged 56) and his mother Mary died on 21 March 1951 (aged 58). They had lived at 14 First Avenue, Rawdon.

Allen, Campbell
Corporal
No. T/100575, 15 Infantry Brigade Group Company,
Royal Army Service Corps
Killed on active service on Monday 9 February 1942 (aged 23)
Kranji War Cemetery, Singapore (Special Memorial 24 E 16)

Campbell Allen was born on 17 February 1918 at 5 Gainsborough Drive, Belfast and he was a son of William and Sarah Allen (nee Hillis). William Allen worked as a ship's caulker and he and Sarah Hillis were married on 24 December 1913 in Whitehouse Parish Church of Ireland Church, Newtownabbey.

Campbell Allen's paternal grandparents were Robert and Jane Allen (nee Campbell) who were both born in County Antrim. Robert Allen was a traction engine driver and he and Jane Campbell were married in Govan, Scotland on 29 November 1883. They had eight children including – William (born 1885); Jane (born 1886); John (born 1888) and David (born 12 October 1896) who were all born in Scotland and then James (born 21 September 1898) and Robert (born 26 December 1899) who were born in Belfast.

During the Second World War Corporal Campbell Allen served with 15 Infantry Brigade Group Company, Royal Army Service Corps in the South-East Asian Theatre of War and he died on 9 February 1942. During the previous day Japanese Forces had crossed the Johore Straits from Malaya and landed on Singapore Island at the mouth of the Kranji River and on 9 February they launched an attack on Singapore Island. Campbell Allen was 23 years old when he died and he is commemorated on Bangor and District War Memorial (as Allan. C.) and in Trinity Presbyterian Church, Bangor. The Revd W.G. Wimperis said that Campbell Allen was 'a sincere Christian youth, lovable and intelligent above average'. He had been a Sunday School teacher and a collector at the Sabbath evening services. He worked in the Civil Service and 'had the promise of a successful future'.

During the First World War a Private Campbell Allen (No. 350466) who served with the 18th Battalion (4th Glasgow) Highland Light Infantry was

A

killed in action on 26 October 1917 and is commemorated on the Tyne Cot Memorial in Belgium and on Page 8 in the *Belfast Book of Honour – Journey of Remembering* compiled by Derek Smyth. At the time of writing no definitive connection has been established between this First World War casualty and Corporal Campbell Allen who was killed in the Second World War.

Ancham, John (Jack)
Corporal
No. 4193876, 1st Battalion, Hampshire Regiment
Killed on active service on Friday 13 April 1945 (aged 24)
Becklingen War Cemetery, Soltau, Niedersachsen, Germany
(Grave 4 K 11)

A

John Ancham's birth was registered in the third quarter of 1920 in Forden, Montgomeryshire and he was a son of James Lewis Ancham and Edith Emily Ancham (nee Edwards). James Lewis Ancham worked as a waggoner and he and Edith Emily Edwards were married on 31 July 1920 in Forden Parish Church.

ANCHAM—April, 1945, Killed in Action in Germany, Corporal John Ancham, the Hampshire Regiment, son-in-law of William and Jane Gabbie, 14, William Street, Newtownards.

John Ancham was the husband of Violet Ancham (nee Russell) and they had a daughter called Edith. On 17 July 1929 Violet's mother Jane married William Gabbie in Ballygilbert Presbyterian Church and they lived at 14 William Street, Newtownards. During the Second World War Violet and Edith Ancham lived with Violet's mother and stepfather, Jane and William Gabbie. John Ancham served with the Royal Welch Fusiliers and in 1944 he was wounded in action in Normandy. When he returned to service he was transferred to the 1st Battalion, Hampshire Regiment and he was 24 years old when he was killed on 13 April 1945 during the latter stages of the Allied invasion of Nazi Germany. In a letter to John's widow, John's Commanding Officer wrote, 'Your husband was a very fine leader and a popular member of the company. We shall all miss him very much indeed'. Corporal John Ancham's daughter Edith was three years old on 22 April 1945, the day after news came through about her father's death. John Ancham's father, James Lewis Ancham, died on 12 December 1953 in St. Asaph, Montgomeryshire.

Anderson, Frederick Hugh*
Pilot Officer (Pilot)
No. 404880, 153 (RAF) Squadron, Royal New Zealand Air Force
Killed in a aircraft accident on Wednesday 19 November 1941 (aged 22)
Ballyhalbert (St. Andrew's) Church of Ireland Churchyard, Co. Down
(Grave 1)

Frederick Hugh Anderson was born on 1 April 1919 and he was a son of Hugh Alexander Anderson and Ruby Eleanor Anderson (nee Pemberton) of Wanganui, Wellington, New Zealand. Hugh Alexander Anderson was a farmer and during the First World War he served as a Private (No. 12543) with 'J' Company in the Wellington Infantry Battalion. Hugh Alexander and Ruby Eleanor Anderson had three sons – Frederick Hugh (born 1919); James Pellew (born 1920) and Geoffrey Pemberton (born 1924). Hugh Alexander Anderson died on 21 April 1969 (aged 81) and Ruby Eleanor Anderson died in 1987 (aged 92).

From 1934 until 1937 Frederick Hugh Anderson attended Wanganui Collegiate School where he was a member of Marris House and a Prefect. After leaving school he took up farming. During the Second World War Frederick Hugh Anderson served with the Royal New Zealand Air Force in 153 Squadron. On 14 October 1941 a flight from 256 Squadron arrived at RAF Ballyhalbert to form 153 Squadron and they began flying the following day. 153 Squadron was officially formed on 24 October and they flew Boulton Paul Defiant aircraft on night patrols. The motto of the Squadron was *Noctividus* – seeing by night – and their badge comprised a bat (flying mammal) in front of a six-pointed star. Pilot Officer Frederick Hugh Anderson was killed on 19 November 1941 when the Boulton Paul Defiant aircraft (N1645) he was flying, undershot as it was landing at RAF Ballyhalbert. The Air Gunner on board was injured but survived.

A

Pilot Officer Frederick Hugh Anderson was buried in Ballyhalbert (St. Andrew's) Church of Ireland Churchyard at Ballyeasborough and he is also commemorated in St. Andrew's Church. His second cousin, Sub-Lieutenant (A) **John Samuel Hornby**, was killed in an aircraft accident on 10 October 1945 and was buried in the same graveyard. John Samuel Hornby is also commemorated in St. Andrew's Church. Both men are commemorated in

113

Wanganui Collegiate School; on the New Zealand National War Memorial in Wellington and on the New Zealand Cenotaph Database in Auckland War Memorial Museum.

Three other relatives of Pilot Officer Frederick Hugh Anderson were also killed on active service during the Second World War. His brother, Lance Corporal James Pellew Anderson (No. 276577), served with the 25th Battalion, New Zealand Infantry in Italy and he died on 2 August 1944. Lance Corporal Anderson was buried in Florence War Cemetery (Grave VII D 3).

In addition to John Samuel Hornby, two other cousins died. Both were sons of Frederick Hugh Anderson's aunt, Helen Margaret Anderson, who was married to George Le Heup Marshall. Corporal Hugh Roger Marshall (No. 1252) served with the Divisional Cavalry Regiment, New Zealand Armoured Corps and he died on 24 May 1941. He was buried in Suda Bay War Cemetery, Greece (Grave 2 C 7).

A

Flying Officer George Montgomerie Marshall (No. 391841) served with 258 (RAF) Squadron, Royal New Zealand Air Force and he died on 30 July 1941. He was buried in Ipswich Old Cemetery, Suffolk (Section X H Grave 436 C).

Anderson, William Sloan (Billy)
Engineer
Miss Betty, **Pilot Launch**
Drowned on Saturday 8 May 1943 (aged 28) (Bangor Bay Disaster)
Bangor Cemetery, Co. Down (Section 4 U Grave 12)

Three men from Donaghadee along with one man from Bangor were drowned on Saturday 8 May 1943 in what came to be known locally as the 'Bangor Bay Disaster'. There were no survivors. The four men died when the Pilot Launch *Miss Betty* capsized and sank while returning to port after responding to a call from a ship entering Belfast Lough. The four men who died worked on the pilot boats that were based in Bangor. These pilot boats were in constant service, not only for merchant shipping coming into Belfast, but also for many of the naval vessels using Belfast Lough. At the outbreak of war *Miss Betty* was requisitioned by the Admiralty from Jim Davidson, Donaghadee.

The three men from Donaghadee who died were **Harry Aiken**, **William George Nelson** and **William White**. The Bangor man who died was William Anderson. Aboard *Miss Betty* on the day they died, William White was the pilot and William George Nelson was the coxswain. William Anderson was the engineer and Harry Aiken was the deck hand.

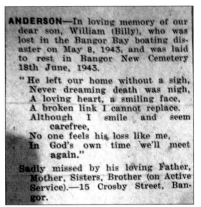

ANDERSON—In loving memory of our dear son, William (Billy), who was lost in the Bangor Bay boating disaster on May 8, 1943, and was laid to rest in Bangor New Cemetery 18th June, 1943.

"He left our home without a sigh,
Never dreaming death was nigh,
A loving heart, a smiling face,
A broken link I cannot replace.
Although I smile and seem carefree,
No one feels his loss like me,
In God's own time we'll meet again."

Sadly missed by his loving Father, Mother, Sisters, Brother (on Active Service).—15 Crosby Street, Bangor.

The Pilot Launch *Miss Betty* was around 40 feet long and the disaster was witnessed by Bangor Harbour Master John H. Corry and Customs Officer G.A. Coppard. *Miss Betty* was owned by the Admiralty but crewed by civilians under naval direction and she left Bangor in moderate weather conditions at 8.55 am on 8 May 1943. During the trip the weather deteriorated and on the way back to Bangor the crew had to contend with a strong north-easterly gale and a heavy breaking sea. At 11.40 am, when they were only about 60 to 70 yards from the safety of Bangor harbour, the disaster happened. The boat successfully negotiated a number of strong waves before being overwhelmed by a broadside hit on the port side. *Miss Betty* capsized, turned over in the water and remained upside down.

A

William Sloan (Billy) Anderson's birth was registered in the third quarter of 1914 and he was a son of William John and Martha Anderson (nee Sloan) of 15 Crosby Street, Bangor. William John Anderson was a stoker and he and Martha Sloan were married on 11 July 1911 in Wesley Centenary Methodist Church, Bangor. Billy Anderson's body was washed ashore at Portpatrick in Scotland on Tuesday 15 June 1943, some 38 days after the accident. His funeral to Bangor Cemetery took place at 6.30 pm on Friday 18 June 1943 and the inscription on his gravestone reads:

Anderson
In Loving Memory of our Dear Son
William (Billy)
Who Lost His Life in Bangor Bay Boating Disaster
8th May 1943
Aged 28 years

Engineer William Sloan (Billy) Anderson is commemorated on Bangor and District War Memorial and in Wesley Centenary Methodist Church, Bangor.

Anderson, William (Bill)
Sergeant
No. 3131578, 4/5th Battalion, Royal Scots Fusiliers
Killed in action on Tuesday 10 April 1945 (aged 26)
Rheinberg War Cemetery, Kamp Lintfort, Nordrhein-Westfal, Germany (Grave 13 C 7)

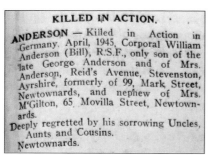

KILLED IN ACTION.

ANDERSON — Killed in Action in Germany, April, 1945, Corporal William Anderson (Bill), R.S.F., only son of the late George Anderson and of Mrs. Anderson, Reid's Avenue, Stevenston, Ayrshire, formerly of 99, Mark Street, Newtownards, and nephew of Mrs. M'Gilton, 65 Movilla Street, Newtownards.
Deeply regretted by his sorrowing Uncles, Aunts and Cousins.
Newtownards.

William (Bill) Anderson was the only son of George and Mary Anderson (nee Perry) of 4 Reid's Avenue, Stevenston in Ayrshire and before that, 99 Mark Street, Newtownards. George Anderson worked as a clerk in an explosives factory and he and Mary Perry were married on 31 January 1912 in Ballygrainey Presbyterian Church.

A

Their daughter Mabel was born in Newtownards on 18 February 1913. Bill's paternal grandparents, William and Elizabeth Anderson (nee Greer), were married on 23 September 1876 in Newtownards Parish Church of Ireland Church (St. Mark's) and they had nine children – George (born 28 December 1876); Mary (born 24 August 1878); William (born 17 April 1881); Jane (Jeannie, born 28 October 1883); Eliza (Lizzie, born 17 July 1886); Catherine (Cassie, born 6 November 1888); Roberta (Robina, born 25 August 1891); William (born 18 January 1894) and Martha (born 25 June 1897). Bill's grandfather, William Anderson, died on 24 February 1931 and his grandmother, Elizabeth, died on 7 March 1932.

During the Second World War Sergeant William (Bill) Anderson served with the Royal Scots Fusiliers (in civilian life he had been a joiner) and on 29 August 1942 he and Jane Turner McKay of 6 Main Street, Callander, Perthshire were married in St. Kessog's Church of Scotland, Callander. Sergeant Anderson was 26 years old when he was killed on 10 April 1945 during the latter stages of the Allied invasion of Nazi Germany. His aunt Robina McGilton (nee Anderson) placed a *Killed in Action* notice in the 28 April 1945 edition of the *Newtownards Chronicle*. Robina Anderson and James McGilton were married on 25 September 1918 in Ballygrainey Presbyterian Church and they lived at 65 Movilla Street, Newtownards.

Anderson, William Thomas
Mentioned in Despatches
Marine
No. PO/X 2917, HMS *Royal Oak*, Royal Marines
Died as a result of enemy action on Saturday 14 October 1939 (aged 19)
Portsmouth Naval Memorial, Hampshire (Panel 36 Column 1)

OUR HEROES—IN MEMORIAM.

ANDERSON—In loving memory of my dear son, and our dear brother, William Thomas Anderson, who lost his life through the sinking of H.M.S. "Royal Oak" in Scapa Flow on 14th October, 1939.

Though land and sea divide the spot
   Where our beloved lies sleeping,
Yet in our hearts he's not forgotten,
   But in the Saviour's keeping.

Ever remembered by his loving Father, Mother, Brothers, Sisters and Grandmother: also his Brother Samuel in the R.N.

17, Raceview Terrace, Newtownards.

William Thomas Anderson was a son of Samuel and Georgina Anderson (nee Dempster) of 17 Raceview Terrace, Comber Road, Newtownards. They were married on 22 December 1920 in Second Newtownards Presbyterian Church. William Thomas Anderson served with the Royal Marines and he died in the early hours of 14 October 1939 when the battleship HMS *Royal Oak* was sunk at around 1.30 am by torpedoes fired from the German submarine *U-47*. This submarine had penetrated the British Navy's main anchorage at Scapa Flow in Orkney and more than 830 men lost their lives that night in the icy, oil-covered waters. Many of them were Boy Seamen not yet 18 years old.

A

HMS *Royal Oak* was a Dreadnought battleship built at the Devonport Dockyard and commissioned in May 1916. She first saw action during the First World War, on 31 May 1916 at the Battle of Jutland. When Queen Maud of Norway (a grand-daughter of Queen Victoria and the wife of King Haakon VII of Norway) died of heart failure in London on 20 November 1938 her body was returned to Norway on 24 November 1938 aboard HMS *Royal Oak* for her state funeral in Oslo.

Marine William Thomas Anderson was 19 years old when he died and he is commemorated on Newtownards and District War Memorial; on Portsmouth Naval Memorial in Hampshire and also in a Book of Remembrance and on a Memorial Plaque in St. Magnus's Cathedral in Kirkwall, Orkney (the ship's bell from HMS *Royal Oak* was recovered in the 1970s and added to this display).

Andow, Kenneth Herbert
Driver
No. T/59946, 1 Field Ambulance, Royal Army Service Corps
Died as a result of a motorcycle accident on Thursday 29 July 1943
(aged 23)
Bone War Cemetery, Annaba, Algeria (Grave VIII B 3)

> Mrs. K. H. Andow, 15, Belfast Road, Bangor, received word at the week-end that her husband, Driver H K. Andow, R.A.S.C., died on 29th July, as the result of injuries received in a motor cycle accident in North Africa.

Kenneth Herbert Andow's birth was registered in the second quarter of 1919 in Ormskirk, Lancashire and he was a son of Edward and Elizabeth Andow (nee Mawdesley). Edward Andow worked as a gardener and his marriage to Elizabeth Mawdesley was registered in the second quarter of 1912 in Ormskirk. They had at least five children – Mary E. (born 1913); Lydia (born 1915); George E. (born 1917); Kenneth Herbert (born 1919) and Donen (born 1921).

Kenneth Herbert Andow was the husband of Maureen Andow of Bangor. During the Second World War he served with 1 Field Ambulance, Royal Army Service Corps and he was 23 years old when he died on 29 July 1943 as a result of injuries received in a motorcycle accident in North Africa. He was buried in Bone War Cemetery, Annaba, Algeria.

Andrews, William Henry Lowry (Lowry)
Lieutenant
No. 143809, 32 Field Regiment, Royal Artillery
Died of wounds on Wednesday 8 July 1942 (aged 23)
El Alamein War Cemetery, Egypt (Grave XXIX A 9)

William Henry Lowry Andrews was born on 8 December 1918 and he was the only son of Joseph Moody (Joe) Andrews and Levina (Ina) Hatrick Andrews (nee Graham) who lived at 9 College Avenue, Bangor and later at 23 Ashley Park, Bangor. Joe Andrews and Ina Graham were married on 10 January 1917 in Windsor Presbyterian Church, Belfast and they had two children – Lowry and Hilda. Lowry Andrews attended Inchmarlo (Royal Belfast Academical Institution Preparatory Department) from 1927 until 1929 and Bangor Grammar School from 1929 until 1936.

At Bangor Grammar School Lowry Andrews won prizes for French, English and Woodwork. In Sixth Form he won a prize in Bangor Borough Council's

A

essay competition. He was a school Prefect and passed the Ulster Bank's Clerkship Examination. He played rugby for the school and won the Barker Mitchell Cup for cross-country running. Of Lowry Andrews, the Headmaster wrote, 'he had the splendid qualities of energy and decision, and the priceless gift of fluent, clear and well-phrased speech'.

LIEUTENANT
W. H. L. ANDREWS
ROYAL ARTILLERY
8TH JULY 1942 AGE 23

After leaving school Lowry Andrews worked in the Head Office of the Ulster Bank in Belfast and he became a member of the Officers' Training Corps at Queen's University. At the outbreak of the Second World War he enlisted and was called up in December 1939. He obtained his commission in August 1940, went first to India and later to Iraq. Lowry Andrews served as a Lieutenant with the Royal Artillery and his sister Hilda served as a Leading Aircraftwoman in the Women's Auxiliary Air Force (WAAF).

On 8 July 1942, aged 23, Lieutenant William Henry Lowry Andrews died of wounds sustained during the Western Desert Campaign and he is commemorated on Bangor and District War Memorial; in Trinity Presbyterian Church, Bangor; on the Ulster Bank War Memorial (this memorial was unveiled on 19 November 1948 and is now located in Ulster Bank Head Office, Donegall Square East, Belfast); in RBAI and in Bangor Grammar School.

Anthoney, Thomas
Staff Sergeant
No. 7259952, Royal Army Medical Corps
Died on active service on Monday 7 February 1944 (aged 32)
Taukkyan War Cemetery, Myanmar (Grave 12 K 17)

Thomas Anthoney's birth was registered in the first quarter of 1912 in Mansfield, Nottinghamshire and he was a son of Arthur Burton (Tony) Anthoney and Mary Ann Anthoney (nee Pitchfork) whose marriage was registered in the second quarter of 1889 in Basford, Nottinghamshire. Tony Anthoney was a coal miner and he and Mary Ann had at least ten children including Arthur Burton, Albert, Elizabeth, Herbert, Charles, Ernest, Lilly and Thomas.

Thomas Anthoney was a soldier stationed at Palace Barracks, Holywood when he and Alice May Herron of 6 Hill Street, Holywood were married on 17 October 1936 in Holywood Non-Subscribing Presbyterian Church. Alice May Herron was a daughter of Robert and Mary Anne Herron (nee Quee) who were married on 12 April 1898 in Holywood Non-Subscribing Presbyterian Church. They had at least nine children – Ellen (born 15 February 1899); Thomas (born 9 September 1900); Robert (born 24 July 1902); John (born 21 June 1904); Jane (born 10 May 1906); William (born 9 October 1908); Amelia (born 23 June 1910); Georgina (born 24 May 1912) and Alice May (born 24 March 1914). Three Herron men (Robert, Alex and John) and four Quee men (James, Robert, Thomas and John) who were members of Holywood Non-Subscribing Presbyterian Church served during the Second World War. Thomas Anthoney was a brother-in-law of **Harry Heaven** who died on 21 May 1940.

A   Thomas and Alice May Anthoney had a son called Leonard. During the Second World War Thomas Anthoney served with the Royal Army Medical Corps and he was 32 years old when he died on 7 February 1944. Staff Sergeant Thomas Anthoney is commemorated on Holywood and District War Memorial as T. Anthony and in Holywood Non-Subscribing Presbyterian Church as Thomas Anthony RAMC.

Apperson, Maxwell Warnock (Max)
Sergeant
No. 534437, 405 (RCAF) Squadron, Royal Air Force
Killed in an aircraft accident on Friday 24 July 1942 (aged 24)
Barmby-on-the-Moor (St. Catherine) Churchyard, Yorkshire, England (Row F Grave 1)

Maxwell Warnock (Max) Apperson's birth was registered in the first quarter of 1918 in Newtownards and, before joining the Royal Air Force around 1936, he lived at 12 Marquis Street, Newtownards. Max was a son of James and Margaret Apperson (nee Wilson) who were married on 15 August 1901 in Glastry Presbyterian Church. James Apperson worked as a bread server and he and Margaret had at least seven children – Jane (born 29 June 1902); John (born 26 June 1905); Elizabeth (born 8 September 1907, married Joseph Elwood on 24 August 1927); Annie (born 15 August 1910); Agnes (born 8 March 1913); James and then Maxwell Warnock who was born after his father

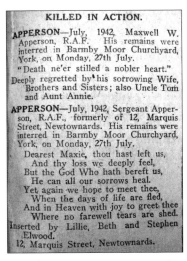

died). James Apperson Senior was 39 years old when he died on 26 October 1917.

On 15 June 1940 Max Apperson and Joyce Evelyn Calver of 44 Bristol Road, Ipswich were married in St. John the Baptist Church, Ipswich. The birth of their son, Alan Maxwell Warnock Apperson, was registered in the second quarter of 1943 in Ipswich, Suffolk. Joyce Apperson died in 1983.

During the Second World War Sergeant Maxwell Warnock Apperson served with the Royal Air Force in Bomber Command and he was 24 years old when he died on 24 July 1942. He was one of a crew of eight aboard a Handley Page Halifax Mark II aircraft (W7769) that took off from RAF Pocklington in Yorkshire at 37 minutes past midnight on 24 July 1942 on a mission to bomb Duisburg. All eight men were killed when their aircraft crashed at 4.53 am as it was returning to base. While circling the airfield for the second time in readiness for landing, an engine failed and the aircraft crashed into New Street in the village of Pocklington. It demolished part of a house before crashing into a school and bursting into flames. The other seven crew members who died that night were:

- Pilot Officer Robert Baker Albright aged 26 (RCAF)
- Pilot Officer George Frederick Strong aged 21 (RCAF)
- Warrant Officer Class II William Charles Thurlow aged 22 (RCAF)
- Sergeant William Colloton aged 22 from Birkenhead
- Flight Sergeant Robert William Hexter aged 22 (RCAF)
- Flight Sergeant Thomas Reid Owens aged 21 (RCAF)
- Sgt Albert James Western aged 25 from Brampford Speke, Devon

Three days after the crash, Sergeant Max Apperson was buried in Barmby-on-the-Moor (St. Catherine) Churchyard, Yorkshire. His wife, brothers and sisters, together with his uncle Tom and aunt Annie placed a death notice in the 1 August 1942 edition of the *Newtownards Chronicle* and it contained the text:

Death ne'er stilled a nobler heart

In 1942 and subsequent years there were *In Memoriam* notices inserted by his sister Lillie, Beth and Stephen Elwood of 12 Marquis Street, Newtownards, his brother and sister-in-law James and Mabel Apperson of 17 Hazelbrook Avenue, Bangor, his brother John in England and his sister Mrs Young also in England. One of the notices contained the verse:

> *Duty called, and he was there, to do his bit and take his share,*
> *His heart was good, his spirit brave, his resting place a hero's grave.*

Sergeant Maxwell Warnock Apperson is commemorated on Newtownards and District War Memorial.

Bailie, David Martin (David)
Captain
United States of America Merchant Vessel *Robert Watchorn*
Died of illness on Saturday 4 November 1944 (aged 64)
National Memorial Cemetery of the Pacific, Honolulu, Hawaii
(Plot P Row O Grave 509)

A
B

> **KILLED ON ACTIVE SERVICE**
>
> **BAILIE** (by cable)—Captain David Martin Bailie, only son of the late Captain David Bailie and Ann Bailie (late of Ballyhalbert), died at sea. Buried at Calcutta on November 6, 1944.
> Deeply regretted by his Sister, Mary Thompson, and his Nephew and Nieces.—15 Thornhill Drive, Belfast.

In the *Killed On Active Service* column in the 25 November 1944 edition of the *County Down Spectator* there was a death notice which stated that David Martin Bailie, only son of the late Captain David Bailie and Ann Bailie (late of Ballyhalbert), had died at sea and been buried at Calcutta on 6 November 1944. His death was deeply regretted by his sister Mary Thompson and his nephew and nieces at 15 Thornhill Drive, Belfast.

David Martin Bailie was born on 1 May 1880 (in some maritime records the year of David Martin Bailie's birth is stated to be 1883 and in others 1886) and he was a son of David Bailie, a sailor from Ballyhalbert, and Ann Bailie (nee Martin) of Belfast. Ann Martin was a daughter of Jervis Martin who was also a sailor. David Bailie and Ann Martin were married on 30 July 1863 in Eglinton Street Presbyterian Church, Belfast and they lived in Ballyhalbert. They had at least seven children and six of them were baptised in Glastry Presbyterian Church – Margaret Ann (born 21 May

1866); Jane (born 12 April 1870, died in infancy); Jane (born 12 April 1872); Mary (born 9 February 1875); David (born 1 May 1880) and Lizzie (born 29 October 1883). Lillian (Lily) Bailie was born around 1887/88 and in April 1911 she and her brother David were living in Ardenlee Avenue, Belfast. Lillian Bailie and Arthur Thompson were married on 17 October 1912 in Belmont Presbyterian Church, Belfast.

David Martin Bailie's father, Captain David Bailie, was born about 1831 and he died in April 1894 aged 63. There is evidence to suggest that he died aboard the *Machrihanish*. This ship was a British 3-masted sailing barque built in 1883 by Robert Duncan and Company, Glasgow. In 1908 she was purchased by a Norwegian company, renamed SV *Avance* and on 1 June 1911 she ran aground and foundered off Lobos de Tierra, Peru. David Martin Bailie's mother Ann died on 22 May 1898 and David erected a headstone in Ballyhalbert Graveyard in memory of his mother. It bears the inscription:

Bailie
In loving memory of my dear mother Ann, wife of the late Captain David Bailie, who fell asleep 22 May 1898.
Also my dear sister Lillian Thompson who died 24 Nov 1928
Asleep in Jesus
Erected by David M. Bailie

B

Maritime records indicate that David Martin Bailie was 5 feet 9 inches tall with fair hair and blue eyes. He had an anchor tattoo on his right hand and he cited his sister Lily Thompson of Rosetta Park, Belfast as his next of kin. On 13 May 1901 he was granted his Second Mate Certificate of Competency:

By the Lords of the Committee of Privy Council for Trade
Certificate of Competency as Second Mate of a foreign-going ship

To David Bailie
Whereas it has been reported to us that you have been found duly qualified to fulfil the duties of Second Mate on a foreign-going ship in the Merchant Service, we do hereby, in pursuance of the Merchant Shipping Act, 1894, grant you this Certificate of Competency.

By order of the Board of Trade
This 13th day of May 1901
Signed by one of the Assistant Secretaries to the Board of Trade
Countersigned by the Registrar General
Registered at the Office of the Registrar General of Shipping and Seamen

During his long career as a seaman there are records of David Martin Bailie serving aboard various ships, for example, *Holkar* from 9 May 1896 to 21 May 1900, *Hardwick Hall* from 22 May 1900 to 3 August 1900, *Bolivar* from 23 October 1900 to 11 February 1901, *Prada* from 26 February 1901 to 11 April 1901, *Balmore* from 13 July 1901 to 10 June 1902 and *Glenericht* from 8 August 1902 to 1 February 1904. On 1 August 1918 he arrived in London aboard the *Buruta* from Lagos in West Africa and it is recorded that his country of last permanent residence was Nigeria. This journey was made during the period of time when his application for naturalisation as a citizen of the USA was pending. For naturalisation purposes his Certificate of Arrival in the United States was dated 15 June 1912, the date he arrived at Ellis Island, New York aboard *Windermere*. He had left Cardiff on 15 May 1912. In his Petition for Naturalisation dated 6 October 1920 he described himself as a longshoreman and his address was 175 Hicks Street, Brooklyn, New York. This was one of the documents where his date of birth is recorded as 1 May 1886. He had declared his intention to become a US citizen on 7 July 1915 and so had completed the five years residency requirement. David Martin Bailie became a naturalised citizen of the United States of America on 6 January 1921 at the US District Court in Brooklyn, New York.

B

He continued his career as a Master Mariner and in March 1943 he was Captain of the *Molly Pitcher*, an American Steam Merchant Ship completed in February 1943 at the Bethlehem Fairfield Shipyards Inc., Baltimore, Maryland. She was on her maiden voyage from Baltimore to Casablanca, Morocco via New York with a general cargo of sugar, coffee, explosives, coal, tractors, trucks and ambulances. At 8.34 pm on 17 March 1943, some 500 miles west of Lisbon, Portugal the *Molly Pitcher* was hit by a torpedo fired from the German submarine *U-167*. The order was given to abandon ship and the *Molly Pitcher* sank after being hit by another torpedo, this one fired from the German submarine *U-521*. Four men died and 66, including Captain Bailie, survived that attack.

Captain David Martin Bailie aged 64 died aboard the *Robert Watchorn* on 4 November 1944, sometime between 7.40 am and 9.00 am. At the time of his death the vessel was near Calcutta in the Hooghly River, India. He was found dead and a US Army Medical Officer who boarded the vessel at Calcutta pronounced that he had suffered a heart attack. The official cause of death was 'coronary occlusion with myocardial infarction' and it was reported afterwards that Captain Bailie had been interred at Lower Circular Road Cemetery, Calcutta, India (Plot CRCE, Row 5 East, Grave 4 South). His effects were taken into custody by the Master (formerly the Chief Mate) of the *Robert Watchorn* which was operated by the Black Diamond Steam

Ship Company. The inventory of his effects included cash ($69), clothing and some miscellaneous items. Buried with him were one full dress uniform, one shirt, one tie, one pair of socks and one pair of shoes.

Captain David Martin Bailie's body was later exhumed and reinterred on 15 December 1949 in the National Memorial Cemetery of the Pacific, Honolulu, Hawaii in Plot P Row O Grave 509. The interment report indicates that his body was brought there from Barrackpore Cemetery in India. Captain Bailie is commemorated in the American Battle Monuments Commission (ABMC) Memorial Website and Second World War Registry.

Bailie, James Francis (Jim)
Able Seaman
D/SSX 24182, HMS *Gloucester*, Royal Navy
Killed in action on Thursday 22 May 1941 (aged 21)
Plymouth Naval Memorial, Devon (Panel 46 Column 2)

James Francis (Jim) Bailie was born on 13 December 1919 and he was a son of James Francis Bailie, who farmed in the townland of Ballyboghilbo, Greyabbey, and Sarah Eleanor Bailie (nee Campbell) from the townland of Ballyfrenis, Carrowdore. His parents were married on 25 April 1918 in Ballyfrenis Presbyterian Church and they had eight children – James Francis (born 13 December 1919); George (born 28 May 1922); Leona (born 21 April 1924, died of diabetes aged 16 when the family lived in the townland of Ballyherly, Portaferry); David John (born 3 December 1925, died in a tractor accident aged 13); Samuel (born 16 October 1927); Henry (born 5 May 1932); Robert (born August 1936, Robert's twin brother Andrew died in infancy when the family lived in the townland of Kilnatierny, Greyabbey).

During the Second World War Jim Bailie served with the Royal Navy aboard the light cruiser HMS *Gloucester*. Built in the Devonport Dockyard, Plymouth, HMS *Gloucester* was completed in January 1939. The ship was first deployed in the Indian Ocean and then in the waters off South Africa before joining the Mediterranean Fleet in May 1940. On 22 May 1941, during the German invasion of Crete, HMS *Gloucester* was sunk by German Junkers Ju 87 (Stuka) dive-bombers and Ju 88 fighter-bombers off the island of Kythera in the Eastern Mediterranean. More than 700 men lost their lives.

Able Seaman James Francis Bailie was 21 years old when he died and he is commemorated on Plymouth Naval Memorial in Devon and on Greyabbey and District War Memorial which is mounted on the outside wall of Greyabbey Parish Church of Ireland Church (St. Saviour's).

Bailie, William Robert
Gunner
No. 1484268, 5 Battery, 2 Light Anti-Aircraft Regiment, Royal Artillery
Killed in action on Saturday 20 June 1942 (aged 31)
Knightsbridge War Cemetery, Acroma, Libya (Grave 1 D 16)

William Robert Bailie was born on 9 July 1910 and he was a son of Robert Bailie (alias Patterson) and Martha Bailie (nee Graham) of 169 Greenwell Street, Newtownards. Robert Bailie worked as a fowl plucker and he and Martha Graham were married on 18 January 1909 in First Donaghadee Presbyterian Church. William Robert Bailie and his brother Thomas, who was born on 13 January 1913, were baptised in Greenwell Street Presbyterian Church, Newtownards.

ARDS SOLDIER KILLED.

WAS PREVIOUSLY REPORTED MISSING.

Mr. and Mrs. Robert Bailie, of 169, Greenwell Street, Newtownards, have been officially notified that their son, Gunner W. R. Bailie, R.A., who was reported missing in June last, following the fall of Tobruk, must now be presumed killed in action. The young soldier, who joined up soon after the outbreak of war, went to the Middle East a short time afterwards.

William Robert Bailie enlisted shortly after the outbreak of the Second World War. He served with the Royal Artillery and he was reported missing in action after the fall of Tobruk. Later it was officially confirmed that he must be presumed killed in action near Tobruk port. His aunts Annie and Eileen who lived at 50 Talbot Street, Newtownards placed an *Our Heroes – In Memoriam* notice in the 19 June 1943 edition of the *Newtownards Chronicle*, as did his father, mother, brother and sister-in-law. Their notice contained the verse:

> *May the heavenly winds blow softly o'er that sweet and hallowed spot;*
> *Though the seas divide us from your grave, you will never be forgot*

Gunner William Robert Bailie was 31 years old when he was killed and when his body was recovered he was buried in Knightsbridge War Cemetery, Acroma, Libya. He is commemorated on Newtownards and District War Memorial.

B

Baird, George Holden (George)
Civilian War Dead
SS *Rutland*
Died as a result of enemy action on Wednesday 30 October 1940
(aged 39)

ROBERT BAIRD,
BORN 28TH MAY 1860. DIED 10TH JANUARY 1924
ALSO HIS BELOVED WIFE ELIZA
BORN 12TH JULY 1860. DIED 27TH OCTOBER 1944
ALSO THEIR SON GEORGE HOLDEN,
LOST AT SEA OCTOBER 1940.
AND THEIR SON ROBERT HENRY BAIRD,
DIED 26TH MARCH 1953.

George Holden (George) Baird was born on 10 August 1901 in Bangor and he was a son of Robert and Eliza (Lizzie) Baird (nee McCay) of 15 Farnham Park, Bangor. Robert Baird was from Letterkenny in County Donegal, he was born on 28 May 1860 and he worked as a tea agent. Lizzie Baird (nee McCay) was from Londonderry and she was born on 12 July 1860. Robert and Lizzie were married on 10 April 1883 in Carlisle Road Presbyterian Church, Londonderry and they had nine children – John James (born 6 March 1884, died 26 April 1885); Kathleen (born 27 March 1885); Robert Henry (born 4 April 1888, died 26 March 1953); Lizzie Christina (born 10 July 1890, died 2 October 1895); Ethel (born 29 May 1892); Albert Ernest (born 20 June 1894, died 25 October 1894); William (born 4 August 1895); Gertrude (Lillie, born 22 November 1896) and George Holden (born 10 August 1901). Robert Baird died on 10 January 1924 and Lizzie Baird died on 27 October 1944.

B

Mrs. L. D. Baird, 6 Osborne Drive, Bangor, has received a communication from the War Graves Commission with reference to her husband, Mr. George Holden Baird, who was lost at sea while returning from a colonial appointment in South America in October, 1940. The late Mr. Baird had almost completed a three years' engagement as radiographer in a hospital at Georgetown, British Guiana. There were no survivors from the ship in which he travelled.

It was reported in the press that George Baird attended Bangor Grammar School and later played rugby for the Bangor Club. He was a member of Bangor Operatic Society and he worked as a radiographer in the Royal Victoria Hospital, Belfast and also in Bangor Hospital. George Holden Baird and Lily Downing Moores, who was born in 1911 in Prestwich, Lancashire, were married in 1933 in Manchester and they lived at 24 Osborne Drive, Bangor. Their daughter, Valerie Lillian Baird, was born in 1935 and on 22 April 1938 the Baird family boarded ship in London bound for British Guiana (now Guyana) in South America where George was going to take up a three-year engagement as a radiographer in a hospital in Georgetown. The Baird family lived at 67 Camp Street, Georgetown and in February 1939 George's wife and daughter returned to Bangor. They lived at 6 Osborne Drive and, after the outbreak of war, Lily Baird held the position of Deputy Food Officer for Bangor.

When war was declared, George Holden Baird decided to return to the United Kingdom some six months before the scheduled end of his colonial appointment and he was a passenger aboard the *SS Rutland* when he died on 30 October 1940. Some records give 31 October 1940 as the date of the sinking. The *SS Rutland* was a cargo steamer built in 1935 by the Caledon Shipbuilding and Engineering Company Ltd., Dundee and owned by the Leith, Hull and Hamburg Line. While on route from Demerara in South America via Bermuda to Larne with a cargo of charcoal bauxite, the *SS Rutland* (a straggler from Convoy HX-82) was torpedoed and sunk southwest of Rockall by the German submarine *U-124*. There were no survivors.

Of the many civilians of the Commonwealth whose deaths were due to enemy action in the Second World War, the names of some 67,092 are commemorated in the Civilian War Dead Roll of Honour, located near St. George's Chapel in Westminster Abbey, London. George Holden Baird was 39 years old when he died and he is commemorated on the family grave headstone in Bangor Cemetery, Co. Down. It bears the inscription:

Fear not, for I have redeemed thee, I have called thee by name, thou art mine
Isaiah 43.1

B

Baird, Hugh
Flight Sergeant
No. 415181, 487 Squadron, Royal New Zealand Air Force
Killed in action on Tuesday 4 January 1944 (aged 21)
Runnymede Memorial, Surrey, England (Panel 263)

Hugh Baird was born on 13 May 1922 in Greyabbey and he was a son of Hugh and Eliza Jane Baird (nee Taylor) of Ballyvester, Donaghadee. Hugh Baird Senior was a farmer and he also owned *The Northern Bar*, a public house in Greyabbey. Hugh Baird and Eliza Jane Taylor were married on 25 June 1913 in Ballygrainey Presbyterian Church and they had four children – Agnes Jane (Jeannie, born 28 January 1914); Elizabeth (Lily, born 10 February 1916); Dorothy (Dolly, born 21 September 1919) and Hugh (born 13 May 1922). In the mid-1920s the Baird family moved from North Street Greyabbey to Matangi which is situated between Hamilton and Cambridge in North Island, New Zealand. Hugh Baird Senior was a dairy farmer and when he died he was buried in Hamilton East Cemetery, New Zealand.

Hugh Baird was educated at Matangi Primary School and Hamilton Technical

College. After leaving school he worked on his father's dairy farm until he joined the Royal New Zealand Air Force (RNZAF). He first applied to join the RNZAF in November 1940 when he was 18 years old. On 7 September 1941 he arrived at the Initial Training Wing, RNZAF Levin, to begin his Air Force training. On 18 October 1941 Hugh proceeded to RNZAF Bell Block to begin flying training with No. 2 Elementary Flying Training School.

Following this course he left for Canada on 17 December 1941. He was posted for further training to No. 3 Service Flying Training School at Calgary in Alberta. He trained there on the twin-engined Cessna Cranes of the Royal Canadian Air Force. On 24 April 1942 he was awarded his flying badge (his wings) and promoted to the rank of Sergeant. On 19 May 1942 he was posted to No. 6 Bombing and Gunnery School, Mountain View, Ontario. There he trained on Avro Anson and Fairey Battle aircraft. He completed this phase of his training on 17 August 1942 and moved on to No. 34 Operational Training Unit at Pennfield Ridge, New Brunswick. He trained there on Lockheed Ventura medium bombers.

On finishing this course, Hugh Baird spent a short period of waiting at No. 1 'Y' Depot, Halifax in Nova Scotia, before crossing the Atlantic to Britain in December 1942. In February 1943 Hugh was posted to No. 487 (New Zealand) Squadron at RAF Feltwell in Norfolk, where this bomber squadron was flying Venturas. He did a short course with No. 1508 Beam Approach Training Flight at Horsham St. Faith in March 1943, and was promoted to Flight Sergeant on 1 May 1943. On 23 May 1943 he piloted a Ventura on a mission to bomb enemy targets at Zeebrugge in Belgium. In June he and his crew bombed targets in Caen and Cherbourg, both in France. In September 1943 Hugh Baird and his Squadron converted to de Havilland Mosquito aircraft, and over the next three months he took part in several raids over enemy territory.

At 9.20 am on 4 January 1944 Flight Sergeant Hugh Baird took off in de Havilland Mosquito FB VI aircraft (LR331/W) from RAF Hunsdon in Hertfordshire. As a member of 487 (NZ) Squadron, he was taking part in an attack against a Noball (V-1 rocket) site in Northern France. Though seen by other crews over the target and thought to be under normal control, Hugh Baird's Mosquito never returned to base. The conclusion reached was that his aircraft crashed over the English Channel during its return. The body of his Canadian navigator, Flying Officer John Frederick Parker, was washed up three days later at Plage-St Cecile, Pas de Calais in France but Hugh Baird's body was never recovered.

Flight Sergeant Hugh Baird was 21 years old and he had accumulated 667 flying hours when he died on 4 January 1944. He is commemorated on the Runnymede Memorial in Surrey; on the New Zealand National War Memorial in Wellington and on the New Zealand Cenotaph Database in Auckland War Memorial Museum.

Baker, Ronald Wilson
Assistant Steward
SS Lurigethan (Belfast), Merchant Navy
Died as a result of enemy action on Thursday 23 January 1941 (aged 21)
Tower Hill Memorial, London (Panel 66)

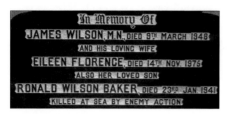

Ronald Wilson Baker was born in Belfast on 30 November 1919 and he was a grandson of Edward and Martha Baker (nee Wilson) who were married on 24 December 1887 in Fortwilliam Park Presbyterian Church, Belfast. He was a son of John Samuel Baker and Eileen Florence Baker (nee Aiken) who were married on 11 July 1918 in Duncairn Presbyterian Church, Belfast. John Samuel Baker worked as a brass finisher and in the CWGC Debt of Honour it is recorded that the Baker family lived in Comber.

Ronald Wilson Baker went to sea as a Galley Boy and during the Second World War he served in the Merchant Navy as Assistant Steward aboard the SS *Lurigethan*. This ship was built as the Dutch cargo steamer *Celaeno* by the Rotterdam Dry Dock in 1916 and then in 1933 she was renamed *Lurigethan* when she was sold to G. Heyn and Sons (Ulster Steamship Company Ltd.), Belfast.

In 1941 the SS *Lurigethan* was sailing unescorted from Africa to Great Britain (she was a straggler from Convoy SLS-61) with a cargo of cotton seeds and general goods when she was bombed at 11.15 am on 23 January 1941 by a German Focke-Wulf Fw 200 aircraft some 280 miles west of Galway. Of the 51 people who were on board the ship, sixteen died – including Assistant Steward Ronald Wilson Baker. The survivors abandoned ship in lifeboats but the SS *Lurigethan* did not sink immediately. She sank after being torpedoed by the German submarine *U-105*.

Assistant Steward Ronald Wilson Baker was 21 years old when he died and he is commemorated on the Tower Hill Memorial in London and on the Wilson family grave headstone in Bangor

Cemetery. James Wilson MN died on 9 March 1948 and his wife Eileen Florence (formerly Baker, nee Aiken) died on 14 November 1975.

Bakker, Eduard (Eddy)
Distinguished Flying Cross
Commander
320 (Netherlands) Squadron, Royal Air Force
Killed in action on Monday 25 October 1943 (aged 34)
Orry-la-Ville Dutch War Cemetery, Senlis, Oise, France (Section C Row 1 Grave 9)

Commander Eduard Bakker's death was reported in the 30 October 1943 edition of the *County Down Spectator*. His death had been announced by Lieutenant-Admiral J. Furstner who was the Dutch Minister for Naval Affairs in London. Commander Bakker's wife, Dorothy Margaret Bakker (nee Tyrrell, born 25 September 1918), was the elder daughter of Herbert and Dorothy Tyrrell (nee Kirkpatrick) of *Marathon*, Seacliff Road, Bangor and she was a grand-daughter of the late John Tyrrell JP, former High Sheriff of Belfast. She was also a niece of Air Vice-Marshal William Tyrrell DSO MC. Margaret Bakker's uncles, Captain John Marcus Tyrrell and Captain Walter Alexander Tyrrell MC were killed in action during the First World War and they are commemorated on Page 340 in the Book of Honour *Remembering Their Sacrifice in the Great War – North Down* compiled by Barry Niblock.

The Netherlands Naval Aviation Service (Marine-Luchtvaartdienst; MLD) was the Naval Aviation Branch of the Royal Netherlands Navy and was formed in 1914. Germany invaded the Netherlands on 10 May 1940 and MLD aircraft were redeployed to France, later going to Britain where Dutch personnel formed 320 (Netherlands) Squadron, initially in the Royal Air Force Coastal Command and later Bomber Command. Commander Eduard Bakker came to England in 1940 and he met Dorothy Margaret Tyrrell at Pembroke where she was serving as a commissioned officer of the Women's Auxiliary Air Force (WAAF). They were married on 3 January 1941 in Helen's Bay Presbyterian Church. The newspaper report indicated that Commander Bakker was one of the first Dutch airmen to be awarded the Distinguished Flying Cross and that he had 'a career of unusual distinction'. 'He had active service in France and Belgium and he helped to rebuild the Netherlands East Indies Air Force'.

After his marriage Eduard Bakker was tasked with advising the Dutch Government as to what type of war planes they needed and in this capacity he and his wife paid an official visit to Santiago in California to evaluate American aircraft. During 1941 they made further trips to the United States; on 6 September 1941 they travelled from Glasgow to New York aboard the SS *Port Dunedin* (their daughter, Wilhelmina Dorothy Margaret, was born on 9 October 1941 in San Diego, California). From California the Bakker family travelled to the Dutch East Indies, now Indonesia, arriving just a few days before the attack on Pearl Harbour (7 December 1941). Eduard Bakker served throughout the Japanese invasion and he was evacuated to Australia with his wife and baby daughter on one of the last planes to leave. From Melbourne, the Bakker family returned to the United States in April 1942 aboard the SS *Mariposa* and early in 1943 they travelled from New York to the United Kingdom aboard the *Rimutaka*. Initially Eduard was engaged in administrative work before being transferred, at his own request, to operational flying. He had accumulated more than 5,000 hours of flying time.

Born on 28 March 1909 in Rotterdam, Commander Eduard Bakker was 34 years old when the North American B-25 Mitchell II bomber (FR178) he was flying was shot down over Brest on 25 October 1943. That day 24 aircraft of 98 and 320 Squadrons RAF had been despatched to bomb the Lanevoc-Poulmic airfield. Commander Bakker was buried in Orry-la-Ville Dutch War Cemetery in France. The Dutch National Second World War Monument is located in Dam Square, Amsterdam.

Barbour, Thomas Crawford (Crawford)
Cabin Boy
SS Empire Heritage (Cardiff), Merchant Navy
Died as a result of enemy action on Friday 8 September 1944 (aged 18)
Tower Hill Memorial, London, England (Panel 42)

Thomas Crawford Barbour was born in Bangor on 9 April 1926 and in the Register of Deceased Seamen his last place of abode is recorded as 25 Stanley Road, Bangor. He went to sea and during the Second World War he served as a Cabin Boy aboard the SS *Empire Wordsworth*. All of the *Empire* ships were owned by the Ministry of War Transport. Thomas Crawford Barbour was six feet tall and he had a tattoo on his right forearm when he signed on in Liverpool on 21 November 1943. He was one of 73 'Distressed British Seamen' (DBS) aboard the SS *Empire Heritage* when he died on 8 September 1944. Distressed British Seamen were survivors of previous sinkings or men who had been discharged from ships abroad because of illness and were being given passage back to Britain.

The SS *Empire Heritage* was completed in 1930 by Armstrong Whitworth and Company Ltd., Newcastle-upon-Tyne as the SS *Tafelberg* – a South African whale factory-ship built for the Kerguelen Sealing and Whaling Company Ltd., Capetown, South Africa. On 28 January 1941 the *Tafelberg* was damaged by a mine and beached at Porthkerry in Wales. A year later the ship was refloated and taken to Whitmore Bay. She was rebuilt as the steam tanker *Empire Heritage* by the Ministry of War Transport and returned to service in February 1943. The SS *Empire Heritage* was torpedoed and sunk about 15 miles northwest of Malin Head, Co. Donegal when on route from New York to Liverpool in Convoy HX-305. At around 6.00 am on 8 September 1944 she was struck by a torpedo fired from the German submarine *U-482* and an hour later she was hit by a German Navy Acoustic Torpedo (GNAT). The rescue ship *Pinto* stopped to pick up survivors and at around 6.40 am the *Pinto* was torpedoed and sunk by *U-482*. *Pinto* survivors were picked up by the trawler HMS *Northern Wave* and taken to Londonderry. Thus it was that some of the DBS who had been aboard the SS *Empire Heritage* survived three separate sinkings during one crossing of the Atlantic. In addition to its passengers, the *Empire Heritage* was carrying a cargo of 16,000 tons of fuel oil and almost 2,000 tons of deck cargo. The deck cargo included a number of Sherman tanks that are now strewn over the seabed around the wreck site.

 Cabin Boy Thomas Crawford Barbour aged 18 and Fireman **Garner Wilson** from Newtownards were two of those aboard the *Empire Heritage* who were presumed drowned. Cabin Boy Thomas Crawford Barbour is commemorated on the Tower Hill Memorial in London and on Bangor and District War Memorial (as Barbour C.).

Barker Brothers, Desmond Wallace Ferguson and Richard Percival William

Desmond Wallace Ferguson Barker and Richard Percival William Barker were sons of Richard Barker and Honey Sheilagh Hall Barker (nee Ferguson), of Gisborne, Auckland, New Zealand. Their father, Richard Barker, and their paternal grandfather, Percival Barker, were New Zealand sheep farmers. Their maternal grandfather, John Ferguson, was a linen manufacturer and he and his wife Harriette Shillington Ferguson (nee Hall) from Glenavy were married on 6 November 1865 in May Street Presbyterian Church, Belfast. They had nine children including John (born 9 February 1868); William (born 27 August 1870); Harriet (born 21 September 1872); Anna Maria Hall (born 7 August 1874); Honey Sheilagh Hall (born 1878); Elese Hall (born 1879); Robert (born 1880); and Joseph Hall (born 1885). The Ferguson family lived in the townland of Ballykillare, Crawfordsburn and John Ferguson died sometime before the end of March 1901.

Richard Barker and Honey Sheilagh Hall Ferguson were married on 2 September 1908 in First Bangor Presbyterian Church. Sheilagh's brother William Ferguson and Kathleen J.H. Ferguson were their witnesses. William Ferguson lived at *The Craig*, Carnalea. The deaths of Desmond Wallace Ferguson Barker and Richard Percival William Barker were reported in the *County Down Spectator* and their uncle William Ferguson placed *Killed in Action* and *In Memoriam* notices in the same newspaper. Desmond was the first of the two brothers to die. Their father, Richard Barker, died on 24 January 1942 aged 74, one month after the death of his second son. Their mother, Sheilagh Barker, died on 27 September 1946 (aged 68) and both parents were buried in Taruheru Cemetery, Gisborne, New Zealand.

B

Barker, Desmond Wallace Ferguson (Desmond)
Distinguished Flying Cross
Flight Lieutenant
No. 70043, 83 Squadron, Royal Air Force
Killed in an aircraft accident on Wednesday 12 February 1941 (aged 27)
Finningley (Holy Trinity and St. Oswald) Churchyard Extension, Nottinghamshire, England (Row H Grave 1)

BARKER—Killed in action, Flight-Lieut. Desmond Wallace Ferguson Barker, D.F.C., R.A.F., elder son of Mr. and Mrs. Richard Barker, Gisborne, New Zealand, and nephew of Mr. William Ferguson, The Craig, Carnalea, County Down.

Desmond Wallace (in some records spelt Wallis) Ferguson Barker was born on 27 February 1914 at Gisborne in New Zealand and he was the elder son of Richard and Sheilagh Ferguson. He was educated at Cambridge University in England and before the outbreak of the Second World War he practised as a barrister. He joined the Royal Air Force in November 1939 and during the Second World War he attained the rank of Flight Lieutenant in 83 Squadron.

In August 1940 it was reported that 'an unusual experience' had befallen Flight Lieutenant Barker one night when he was returning from an attack on the

Dortmund-Ems canal. The port engine of his Handley Page Hampden aircraft was hit and shortly afterwards, while flying over the Dutch coast, the damaged propeller fell off. The bomber dropped some 2,000 feet before he regained control. Then, about ten miles from the English coast, the other engine began to falter, but by coaxing it along he was able to make a landing in the sea just a few yards from the shore. The crew escaped without serious injury.

Flight Lieutenant Desmond Barker was based at RAF Scampton in Lincolnshire (now the base of the RAF Aerobatic Team, otherwise known as the Red Arrows). He was one of a crew of four aboard a Handley Page Hampden Mark I aircraft (AD722) when he died on 12 February 1941. They had been on air operations over Bremen and their aircraft crashed after hitting a building while trying to land at Finningley in Yorkshire. Sergeant George Targett was injured and the other two crew members who died were:

- Sgt William Harry Lowson aged 20 from Weldon, Northamptonshire
- Flying Officer Frank Selby Wilson aged 34 from Stockwell, London

Flight Lieutenant Desmond Barker was 27 years old when he died, his effects amounted to some £1,065 and probate was granted to Frederick William Newton Weston, Lieutenant HM Army and Valerie Percival Kathleen Barker, spinster.

Barker, Richard Percival William (Richard)
Pilot Officer
No. 41464, Royal New Zealand Air Force
Killed in an aircraft accident on Monday 22 December 1941 (aged 25)
Grantham Cemetery, Lincolnshire, England (Section 17 Row M Grave 11)

BARKER—Killed in action, Pilot-Officer Richard P. W. Barker, New Zealand Air Force, younger and only surviving son of Mr. and Mrs. Richard Barker, Gisborne, New Zealand, and brother of Flight-Lieut. Desmond Barker, D.F.C., R.A.F. (killed in action in February, 1941), and nephew of Mr. William Ferguson, The Craig, Carnalea, Co. Down.

Richard Percival William Barker was the younger son of Richard and Sheilagh Ferguson and during the war he served as a Pilot Officer in the Royal New Zealand Air Force. He died on 22 December 1941 at Terrace Hills, Lincolnshire, some ten months after the death of his brother Desmond. It was reported in the press that Richard died 'in an incident similar to his brother'.

Richard was one of eight men aboard a Handley Page Halifax Mark I aircraft (L9522) of 28 Conversion Flight that took off at 10.25 am from its Heavy Conversion Unit at RAF Leconfield in Yorkshire on a Ferry flight to the Handley Page factory at Radlett, Hertfordshire. Weather conditions were described as 'extremely adverse'. The aircraft, which was captained by Flight Lieutenant Owen, was seen about 40 minutes later flying low over Lincolnshire, in the vicinity of Knipton, heading towards Barkston Woods in poor visibility. The aircraft crashed a few minutes later into a wooded area on the top of a high ridge known as Terrace Hills. All eight men on board were killed and in addition to Pilot Officer Richard Percival William Barker (aged 25) the others who died that morning were:

- Flt Lt Robert Fenwick Owen DFC aged 25 from St. Albans, Hertfordshire
- Pilot Officer William Stuart Beattie aged 24 (RNZAF)
- Sergeant Leslie Merrifield aged 23 from Horwich, Lancashire
- FO Eric Arthur Fawns Gibb DFM aged 22 from Edinburgh
- Sgt Stanley Robert Mayston DFM aged 21 from Thornton Heath, London
- Sergeant James Albert Denning
- Corporal James Anthony Hancock aged 21 from Blackburn, Lancashire

Flight Lieutenant Desmond Wallace Ferguson Barker and Pilot Officer Richard Percival William Barker are both commemorated on the New Zealand National War Memorial in Wellington and on the New Zealand Cenotaph Database in Auckland War Memorial Museum.

Barr, Ernest Henry Mackenzie (Mac)
Sergeant (Air Gunner)
No. 1796037, 158 Squadron, Royal Air Force Volunteer Reserve
Killed in action on Saturday 6 January 1945 (aged 21)
Durnbach War Cemetery, Bad Tolz, Bayern, Germany (Grave 5 D 20)

DIED ON ACTIVE SERVICE

BARR—Reported missing after bombing operations over Hanau, Germany, January 6, 1945, Sergeant Ernest Henry Mackenzie Barr (Mac), aged 22, Navigator-Bomber, R.A.F., son of Mr. and Mrs. E. Barr, Beech-Erne, Londonderry. Body recovered after tragic search by father in an unknown grave in Grossheim, Germany. Ever remembered by his Uncle and Aunt, J. H. Freel, 29 Southwell Road, and Mrs. Mackenzie, 5 Somerset Ave., Bangor.

Ernest Henry Mackenzie (Mac) Barr was a son of Ernest David and Eileen May Barr (nee Freel), of *Beech-Erne*, Londonderry and his death on active service was reported in the 5 October 1946 edition of the *County Down Spectator*. His uncle, J.H. Freel, lived at 29 Southwell Road and his aunt, Mrs Mackenzie, lived at 5 Somerset Avenue,

Bangor. The story of his death was reported under the headline *Father Finds Body Interred in Unknown Person's Grave.*

Ernest David Barr was a chemist with premises in William Street, Londonderry and, during the First World War, he served with the Royal Flying Corps. He and Eileen May Freel were married on 6 September 1922 in St. Macartin's Church of Ireland Church, Enniskillen. Mac worked with his father before he joined the Royal Air Force Volunteer Reserve in 1943. At the time of his death on 6 January 1945 he was serving with 158 Squadron.

Following a 2,000 bomber raid on Frankfurt in Germany during the night of 6 January 1945 Sergeant Ernest Henry Mackenzie (Mac) Barr was reported missing over Hanau. Despite persistent enquiries, Mac's father was unable to get definitive information as to his son's fate so, after the war ended, he decided to go to Germany himself and pursue his investigations personally. In July 1946 he obtained permission to travel to Paris to interview the American authorities who controlled the zone in which his son had been reported missing. In September he travelled by train from Paris to Frankfurt (a 14-hour journey) and there he spoke to Red Cross personnel who provided motor transport, a driver and an interpreter.

B

For two days in Frankfurt he tried without success to get information about the fate of his missing son. He moved on to Hanau and interviewed people who remembered the raid on 6 January 1945 but they could give him no information about the fate of his son. Then he travelled to Grossheim where he spoke to the Commandant and a number of people in a displaced person's camp nearby. A young lady living in the camp remembered the night of the raid and the spot where an aircraft had crashed. She remembered that seven bodies had been recovered from the wreckage and when she saw Mac's photograph she confirmed that he was one of the seven. Then Mac's father returned to Hanau to speak to Herr Wenzel who was the Registrar of births and deaths for the district. He too recognised Mac's picture and he remembered that Mac's identity disc had been missing so he was buried along with others in an unknown person's grave. Herr Wenzel took Mac's father to see the grave. Having located the grave Mac's father obtained permission to have it opened and his son's body exhumed. He identified his son by his hair, teeth and the shape of his head. Sergeant Ernest Henry Mackenzie Barr's body was placed in a coffin and reinterred in Durnbach War Cemetery. The seven airmen were aboard a Handley Page Halifax Mark III aircraft (NR195) and the other six who died were:

- Flight Lieutenant John Julius Krefter aged 29 (RAAF)
- Flying Officer Kenneth Roy Nerney aged 19 (RAAF)

- Sgt Alexander Thomas Clyde aged 34 from Woodford Bridge, Essex
- Flight Sergeant Leslie Gilbert Morgan aged 22 from Enfield, Middlesex
- Sergeant James Gore aged 23 from Knotty Ash, Liverpool
- Sgt Peter Samuel Cotterell aged 21 from Broadway, Worcestershire

Sergeant Ernest Henry Mackenzie Barr was 21 years old when he died and he is commemorated in Foyle College, Londonderry.

Barraclough, William
Flight Sergeant (Navigator/Bomber)
No. 1083474, Royal Air Force Volunteer Reserve
Killed in an aircraft accident on Thursday 18 November 1943 (aged 22)
Chorley Cemetery, Lancashire, England (Section E E C Grave 921)

William Barraclough's birth was registered in the second quarter of 1921 in Bradford, Yorkshire and he was a son of Willie and Phyllis Anne Barraclough (nee Mather) whose marriage was registered in the fourth quarter of 1917 in North Bierley, Yorkshire. They had at least three children – Tyson (born 1918); William (born 1921) and Victor (born 1924). William Barraclough's marriage to Marion Tootell was registered in the fourth quarter of 1942 in Chorley, Lancashire. During the Second World War William Barraclough served with the Royal Air Force Volunteer Reserve.

Flight Sergeant William Barraclough was 22 years old when he died on 18 November 1943 along with the other three crew members when their Lockheed Hudson Mark V aircraft (AE653) of No. 5 (Coastal) Operational Training Unit based at RAF Long Kesh, crashed into Strangford Lough just south of Chapel Island (off Greyabbey). They were on a rocket-firing exercise using the submarine target at South Island in Strangford Lough.

The other three men who died in the crash were the pilot, Sergeant **Walter Edward Fern** (RAFVR); Flight Sergeant **Raymond Farquhar Simpson** (RNZAF) and Flight Sergeant **Andrew Greenwell Gibbison** (RNZAF).

Flight Sergeant William Barraclough was buried in Chorley Cemetery, Lancashire, England just a few months before his daughter Elaine was born. Her birth was registered in the third quarter of 1944 in Chorley. There is an inscription on Sergeant Barraclough's CWGC headstone:

Glorious re-union, our abiding hope

His effects amounted to some £119 and probate was granted to his widow Marion who was living at 20 Bolton Street, Chorley. He is commemorated on Chorley War Memorial.

Barre, James Gordon (Gordon)
Sub-Lieutenant (Engineer)
HMS *Forfar*, Royal Naval Volunteer Reserve
Killed in action on Monday 2 December 1940 (aged 23)
Liverpool Naval Memorial, Lancashire (Panel 4 Column 1)

James Gordon Barre was born on 7 May 1917 and he was the second son of Robert John and Esther Calvert Barre (nee MacClean) of 7 Ballinacurra Terrace, Limerick. They were married on 26 January 1911 in Rostrevor Parish Church of Ireland Church and James Gordon Barre was baptised in Limerick Presbyterian Church. The Barre family lived at 11 Hamilton Road in Bangor where Robert Barre conducted business as a chemist. Later the Barre family moved to 18 Parkside Drive, Barrie in Ontario, Canada. Gordon Barre was educated at Trinity Public Elementary School, Bangor and, from 1929 until 1930, at Bangor Grammar School. His brother, Robert Frederick Barre, also attended Bangor Grammar School. After he left school Gordon Barre worked as an engineering apprentice at the Mackie Engineering Works in Belfast. He was an active member of the Boys' Brigade Company of Hamilton Road Presbyterian Church, Bangor and he was also a member of Ballyholme Yacht Club.

Gordon Barre joined the Canadian Pacific Line, a company under the Canadian Pacific Railway Line and he sailed in many of their ships. He also participated in the evacuation of British Forces from Dunkirk. HMS *Forfar* was formerly the passenger ship SS *Montrose* built by the Fairfield Shipbuilding and Engineering Company Ltd., Govan, Glasgow. Launched in 1920, the SS *Montrose* was operated by Canadian Pacific Steamships Ltd., until she was requisitioned by the Admiralty, converted to an armed merchant cruiser in November 1939 and renamed HMS *Forfar*. On 2 December 1940 HMS *Forfar* was on her way to join Convoy OB-251 when she was torpedoed and sunk by the German submarine *U-99* some 500 miles west of Ireland. The convoy was on route from Liverpool to New York. Sub-Lieutenant (E) James Gordon Barre was one of more than 170 men who lost their lives.

Maurice Wilkins was Headmaster of Bangor Grammar School for 24 years from 1923 until 1947 and it was his custom to write *In Memoriam* articles for ex-pupils of the school who died on active service during the Second World

War. These articles were published in the *County Down Spectator*. Of the 39 boys of Bangor Grammar School who fell in the Second World War, 36 had attended during his headmastership and he wrote articles about 30 of them.

Concerning the six for whom no articles appeared he later wrote, 'Reasons for omission may have been – uncertainty as to the fate of men posted as missing (J.T. Graham), pressure of work or my absence on vacation (J. Holland, H. Hannay, W. Mahaffy), delay in news reaching Bangor when a family had gone away (T. Kidd-May) or where a boy had left school at an early age (G. Barre)'. In 1965, for a compilation of the *In Memoriam* articles, Maurice Wilkins added his recollections for five of the six boys for whom no articles had been written. In the case of Gordon Barre he wrote, 'Of G. Barre I can recall only the name which I remember I had entered myself in the School Registers, as my practice was. He was in the Junior School and only with us for a short while'. Gordon Barre's last visit to Bangor was two months before he died.

B

Sub-Lieutenant (E) James Gordon Barre was 23 years old when he died and he is commemorated on Liverpool Naval Memorial in Lancashire; on Bangor and District War Memorial; in Hamilton Road Presbyterian Church, Bangor and in Bangor Grammar School. Gordon's elder brother Robert Frederick Barre was a farmer in Canada and after Gordon died Fred joined the Royal Canadian Air Force. Fred Barre visited Bangor when he was on leave in 1943 and, early in 1944, he was taken prisoner while engaged in air operations over enemy territory. He was held for 17 months in Stalag 4 until he was released by the Russians in May 1945. Gordon and Fred Barre had another brother whose name was Maurice.

Baxter, John George Briggs
Third Engineer Officer
***SS Beaverford* (London), Merchant Navy**
Died as a result of enemy action on Tuesday 5 November 1940 (aged 57)
Tower Hill Memorial, London, England (Panel 15)

John George Briggs Baxter was born in Portaferry on 14 September 1883 and his birth was registered in Downpatrick. He was the only son of Henry and Mary Baxter (formerly Jefferson, nee Briggs). Henry Baxter worked as an estate agent and rate collector and he and Mary Jefferson were married on

29 December 1881 in Derriaghy Church of Ireland Church, Lisburn. Mary already had a daughter whose name was Arminella Jefferson (Mary Briggs and Redmond Jefferson were married on 2 February 1866 in Lisburn Church of Ireland Cathedral).

Portaferry Seaman Missing.—Mrs. Nellie Baxter, Rock-Angus. Portaferry, has been officially informed that her husband, Engineer Officer John G. B. Baxter, missing since November 5 last, is now presumed lost at sea.

In 1911 John George Briggs Baxter was a marine engineer in the Mercantile Marine and he was boarding with the Jones family who lived in Bootle cum Linacre in Lancashire. On 4 October 1915 he was living at 36 Oxford Road, Putney when he and Madge Amelia Clarkson (born 1892 in Cupar, Fife; daughter of publican Henry Clarkson) were married in St. Stephen's Church of England Church, Wandsworth, Surrey. They subsequently divorced and on 17 November 1930 John George Briggs Baxter was living at 19 Clifford Street, Govan, Glasgow when he and Ellen Elizabeth (Nellie) McFadden from Portaferry were married in Langside Old Church of Scotland, Glasgow. Nellie was a daughter of Robert and Annie McFadden (nee Gowan) from Portaferry where Nellie's father, by then deceased, had been a master draper.

During the Second World War John George Briggs Baxter served with the Merchant Navy as Third Engineer Officer aboard the SS *Beaverford*. This ship was built in 1928 by Barclay, Curle and Company Ltd., Whiteinch, Glasgow and owned by the Canadian Pacific Steamship Company. In November 1940 the SS *Beaverford* was sailing from Halifax in Nova Scotia to Great Britain in Convoy HX-84 with more than 30 other merchant vessels escorted by the armed merchant ship HMS *Jervis Bay*. The convoy was intercepted by the German battle cruiser *Admiral Scheer* which had been commissioned in November 1934. Hopelessly outgunned, HMS *Jervis Bay* engaged the enemy and was sunk in the process. However, this gave the convoy time to scatter and the *Admiral Scheer* was only able to sink six other ships, five from the convoy (*Beaverford*, *Fresno City*, *Kenbane Head*, *Maidan*, *Trewellard*) and one sailing independently (*Mopan*). The SS *Beaverford* sank off the coast of Greenland with the loss of 77 men. The tanker *San Demetrio* was set on fire by the *Admiral Scheer* but didn't sink and was later salvaged. The *Admiral Scheer* capsized in Kiel harbour in Germany when struck by RAF bombs dropped during a raid on 9 April 1945.

Third Engineer Officer John George Briggs Baxter was 57 years old when he died and Nellie was living at *Rock-Angus,* Portaferry when she received the news of his death. Nellie Baxter died on 13 July 1975 and she was buried in the McFadden family grave in Ballymanish Graveyard, Portaferry:

> *In loving memory of Robert McFadden died 5th August 1925*
> *And his Wife Annie McFadden died 24th Oct.1933*
> *Also their beloved Son Hugh G. McFadden died 12th September 1965,*
> *Interred in Sydney, Australia*
> *Also his Daughter Nellie Baxter (nee McFadden) died 13th July 1975*

Third Engineer Officer John George Briggs Baxter is commemorated on the Tower Hill Memorial in London.

Beale, Maurice Evelyn (Jimmy)
Captain
No. 56229, 4th Battalion, Royal Welch Fusiliers
Accidentally drowned on Saturday 19 October 1940 (aged 28)
Killyleagh Church of Ireland Churchyard, Co. Down (Section A Grave 470)

B

BODY WASHED ASHORE AFTER FIVE MONTHS.

On 19th October, 1940, two military officers, Captain Maurice Evelyn Beale and Second Lieutenant W. E. D. Paul went out for a sail in Strangford Lough off Killyleagh, and failed to return, and late that evening the empty boat was washed ashore. Extensive search was carried out, but without result, and the affair had no solution until Wednesday of this week when the body of Captain Beale, who was 28 years of age and single, and whose home address was Hiltress, Stamford Brooke Avenue, London, W.6, was picked up by Petty Officer B. D. Ebsworh off Portaferry. It was brought ashore and an inquest was held in the Boardroom of the Ards District Hospital on Thursday evening by Dr. R. A. M'C. Wallace.

Maurice Evelyn (Jimmy) Beale's birth was registered in the third quarter of 1912 in Brentford, Middlesex and he was a son of Maurice Octavius Beale and Evelyn Gladys Georgina Beale (nee Saunders) of Stamford Brook Avenue, Hammersmith, London. Maurice Octavius Beale was born in 1877 in Lutterworth, Leicestershire and in 1881 he and his older brother, Ernest Septimus Beale, were living in the Infant Orphan Asylum, Wanstead, Essex. Maurice Octavius Beale became a chartered accountant and on 3 April 1907 he and Evelyn Gladys Georgina Saunders, who was a schoolteacher, were married in Christ Church, Turnham Green, Middlesex. They had at least three children, Marjorie, Stanley and Maurice Evelyn (Jimmy). Maurice Octavius Beale of 47 Beechwood Avenue, Kew Gardens in Surrey died on 24 March 1933. His effects amounted to some £6,504 and probate was granted to his widow Evelyn Beale.

Maurice Evelyn (Jimmy) Beale was educated at Bloxham School, Banbury in Oxfordshire where he played rugby for the school. He became a teacher and was an Assistant Master at Oriel House School, St. Asaph, Denbighshire in Wales. During the Second World War he served with the Royal Welch Fusiliers. Until his death he was Adjutant of the 4th Battalion while this Battalion was stationed in Northern Ireland (from December 1939 until November 1941 headquartered at Banbridge and then Keady). At the time of his death he was stationed in Killyleagh. On 19 October 1940, along with Second Lieutenant **William Edward David Paul** of Chester, he borrowed a 14-foot centre-board sailing boat from Benjamin Bennett of Killyleagh to go sailing in Strangford Lough. A heavy sea was running as they left Killyleagh harbour and some hours later the boat, badly holed, was washed ashore at Holm Bay. There was no trace of either of the two bodies. Exactly five months later, on 19 March 1941, Captain Beale's body was found floating in the water and brought ashore at Portaferry. From the remnants of the jacket he was wearing his remains were identified by Major Wilfred James Hutton. At the inquest the Coroner returned a verdict of 'found drowned' and Captain Beale was buried at 10.00 am on Sunday 23 March 1941 in Killyleagh Parish Church of Ireland Churchyard, Co. Down. His effects amounted to some £4,533 and probate was granted to his widowed mother, Evelyn Beale. She died in 1960.

Second Lieutenant Paul's body was never recovered and he is commemorated on Brookwood Memorial, Surrey, England. Another Second World War casualty who was buried in Killyleagh Church of Ireland Churchyard was Fusilier Harry Atkinson (No. 4199802) who served with the 4th Battalion, Royal Welch Fusiliers and who died on 9 May 1941 aged 23. He was a son of Arthur and Sarah Atkinson of Grimsby in Lincolnshire and the husband of Winifred Thelma Atkinson, also of Grimsby.

Beattie, Robert Pollock
Lieutenant Commander (Engineer)
HMS *Willamette Valley*, Royal Naval Reserve
Killed in action on Saturday 29 June 1940 (aged 40)
Liverpool Naval Memorial, Lancashire (Panel 1 Column 2)

In the 31 August 1940 edition of the *County Down Spectator* the death of Lieutenant Commander (E) R.P. Beattie was reported under the headline

Bangor Naval Officer's Death. It was reported that the Misses Beattie of *Knocklofty House*, Hamilton Road, Bangor had received intimation about the death of their brother on 29 June 1940. Before the war he had served with the Royal Mail Line.

Robert Pollock Beattie was born on 9 June 1900 in Belfast and he was a son of James Boal Beattie, who was born in County Donegal, and Margaret Sarah Beattie (nee Pollock), who was born in County Monaghan. Margaret Sarah Pollock was James Boal Beattie's second wife and they were married on 10 October 1894 in Ballyalbany (Second Monaghan) Presbyterian Church. They lived at 20 Titania Street in Belfast and later in *Bell-vue*, Cregagh Road, Belfast. James Boal Beattie was a policeman and later he worked as a coroner's registrar. James and Margaret Beattie had seven children – Elizabeth (born 5 July 1895 and baptised in St Enoch's Presbyterian Church, Belfast); Mary (born 10 January 1897); Matilda (born 8 January 1899); Robert Pollock (born 9 June 1900); James Boal (born 11 April 1902) and William (born 25 March 1904, died 26 July 1905 aged 16 months). William Beattie was buried in the City Cemetery (Grave H 4 80), as were his parents. James Boal Beattie died on 13 January 1917 aged 60 and Margaret Sarah Beattie died at 1 Knocklofty Park, Belfast on 7 April 1937 (aged 73).

During the Second World War Lieutenant Commander (E) Robert Pollock Beattie served in the Royal Naval Reserve aboard the Q-ship HMS *Willamette Valley* (with the Royal Fleet Auxillary cover name HMS *Edgehill*). Q-ships (also sometimes called decoy vessels, special service vessels or mystery ships) were small merchantmen armed with concealed guns that could be deployed quickly if they came under attack by an enemy submarine. Such decoy ships had been used in the First World War and in September and October 1939, at the beginning of the Second World War, at least nine were commissioned immediately for use in the North Atlantic. Built in 1928 by Napier and Miller Ltd., Old Kilpatrick, Glasgow as *West Lynn* and renamed *Willamette Valley* in 1931, she was requisitioned in September 1939 by the Royal Navy and converted to a decoy ship. Commissioned as Special Service Vessel (SSV) HMS *Edgehill (X 39)* she was torpedoed and sunk by the German submarine *U-51* on 29 June 1940. Lieutenant Commander (E) Robert Pollock Beattie was 40 years old when he died and he is commemorated on the Liverpool Naval Memorial. His effects amounted to some £326 and probate was granted to his sister Elizabeth.

Beckett, Samuel Nicholl
Warrant Officer
No. 970018, 429 (RCAF) Squadron, Royal Air Force Volunteer Reserve
Killed in action on Sunday 11 April 1943 (aged 25)
Rheinberg War Cemetery, Kamp Lintfort, Nordrhein-Westfal, Germany
(Collective Grave 8 K 12-17)

Bangor Warrant Officer Believed Killed.—Warrant-officer Samuel Nicholl Beckett, R.A.F.V.R., 39 Rugby Avenue, Bangor, reported missing in April, is now believed killed on air operations. A son of Mr. S. N. Beckett, 45 Edgecombe Gardens, Belfast, he was an old Belfast Academical Institution boy and joined the R.A.F. at the outbreak of war.

In some records, including the CWGC Debt of Honour, Samuel's second forename is spelt Nicoll. Samuel Nicholl Beckett was born on 2 September 1917 and he was a son of Samuel Nicholl Beckett and Elizabeth Beckett (nee Swanton) of 13 Thorndale Avenue, Belfast and, later, *Greenways*, 45 Edgecumbe Gardens, Belfast. Samuel Nicholl Beckett Senior worked as an Insurance Manager with the Prudential Assurance Company Ltd., and he and Elizabeth Swanton were married on 9 December 1902 in University Road Methodist Church, Belfast. For a time the Beckett family lived in Lurgan and they had at least five children – Eileen Anna (born 9 January 1905); John (born 14 March 1906); James (born 1 July 1908); William (born 8 May 1912) and Samuel Nicholl (born 2 September 1917).

Samuel Nicholl Beckett was educated at Antrim Road Public Elementary School, Belfast and the Royal Belfast Academical Institution (RBAI) from 1928 until 1933. He left school aged 16 to join the British Tanker Company Ltd., part of the Anglo-Persian Oil Company Ltd., as an Apprentice Officer. He joined the Royal Air Force Volunteer Reserve shortly after the outbreak of war and on 19 March 1942 he and Victoria Maud Carson of 39 Rugby Avenue, Bangor were married in Helen's Bay Presbyterian Church. A little over a year later Warrant Officer Samuel Nicholl Beckett aged 25 was killed in action on 11 April 1943. Initially he was reported missing in action and later it was officially confirmed that he must be presumed killed. He was one of a five man crew aboard a Vickers Wellington Mark X aircraft (HE636) that took off at 11.21 pm from RAF East Moor in Yorkshire on a mission to bomb Frankfurt. The aircraft crashed and, in addition to Warrant Officer Samuel Nicholl Beckett, the other four crew members who died that night were:

- WO Douglas William Jefferis aged 23 from Taunton, Somerset
- Flying Officer Leslie Sidney Knott aged 27 from Houndslow, Middlesex
- Flight Sergeant Alun Gwyn Lewis
- Flight Sergeant Kleon Donald Franklin aged 31 from Poole, Dorsetshire

All were buried in Rheinberg War Cemetery and Warrant Officer Samuel Nicholl Beckett is commemorated in RBAI. On Sunday 2 September 2011 a commemorative church service was held in Baronscourt Parish Church in County Tyrone to dedicate a plaque to the memory of the eighteen scouts from 74ᵗʰ Belfast (RBAI) Scout Group who lost their lives in the Second World War, many of whom had camped on the Baronscourt Estate in the years immediately prior to the outbreak of hostilities. The plaque commemorated the 70ᵗʰ anniversary of the first building of a memorial cairn by RBAI scouts on the nearby hill known as Bessy Bell. In addition to Warrant Officer Samuel Nicholl Beckett the plaque bears the names of Captain **Samuel David Corry**, Sergeant **Sydney Ireland** and Bombardier **Francis Eric Sheals**.

Beckett, Thomas Smith (Thomas)
Carpenter
SS *Troutpool* (West Hartlepool), Merchant Navy
Died as a result of enemy action on Saturday 20 July 1940 (aged 32)
Bangor Cemetery, Co. Down (Section 5 X Grave 21)

Thomas Smith Beckett was born on 19 July 1908 and he was a son of Archibald and Margaret (Minnie) Beckett (nee Smith) of 2136 Dumbarton Road, Yoker, Glasgow. Archibald Beckett worked as a rigger and he and Minnie Smith were married on 14 August 1903 in Nitshill, Glasgow. During the Second World War Thomas Beckett served in the Merchant Navy as a Carpenter aboard the SS *Troutpool*. Owned by the Pool Shipping Company, the SS *Troutpool* was built in 1927 by William Gray and Company Ltd., West Hartlepool and in 1940 she was on a voyage from Rosario in Argentina to Great Britain with a cargo of grain when she sank in Belfast Lough after being struck by two magnetic mines. The SS *Troutpool* had put into Belfast Lough for degaussing – a process involving the passing of an electric current through a cable round the ship's hull (designed to reduce the possibility of magnetic mines in the water being attracted by the ship's hull). After re-starting her engines she was struck by two mines around 2.00 pm on 20 July 1940 and sank about a mile off the coast near Bangor. Eleven crew members were killed in the explosions. At low tide the superstructure was visible and, because it was a hazard to shipping, the wreckage was dispersed with explosives. At the time it was speculated that the mines which sank the SS *Troutpool* were laid by a long range Focke-Wulf Fw 200 Condor aircraft known to have been operating in the area.

Carpenter Thomas Smith Beckett died the day after his 32nd birthday and he was buried in Bangor Cemetery, as was **Shief Ahmed** who was the Ship's Fireman and Trimmer. Three unidentified sailors from SS *Troutpool* were buried in Movilla Cemetery, Newtownards – one on 1 August 1940, another on 24 August 1940 and the third on 26 August 1940. Able Seaman **John McGrath** from Portaferry, whose body was never recovered, is commemorated on the Tower Hill Memorial in London.

Beeby, Benjamin
Sergeant
No. 3596582, 2nd Battalion, Royal Scots Fusiliers
Died of illness in service on Wednesday 16 August 1944 (aged 40)
Holywood Cemetery, Co. Down (Protestant Ground Grave 1393)

Benjamin Beeby's birth was registered in the third quarter of 1905 in Basford, Nottinghamshire. His father William was a coal miner and in the 1911 census it is recorded that William Beeby was 46 years old, he had been married for 24 years and he and his wife had 20 children, 13 of whom were still living. Benjamin Beeby was a Corporal in the 1st Battalion, Border Regiment stationed in Palace Barracks, Holywood when he and Martha Forde of 21 The Strand, Holywood were married in Belfast Registry Office on 7 November 1936. Martha's father Samuel was a brass moulder and he and Lily Kidd were married on 23 June 1910 in St. Augustine's Church of Ireland Church, Londonderry.

B

Benjamin Beeby was promoted to the rank of Sergeant, he was transferred to the 2nd Battalion, Royal Scots Fusiliers and he developed cancer of the stomach. He was 40 years old when he died at 21 The Strand, Holywood on 16 August 1944. He was buried in Holywood Cemetery on 19 August 1944 and there is an inscription on his CWGC headstone:

At rest
Always remembered by his loving wife and sons Benny and Raymond

Bell, Alex Joseph
Flight Sergeant (Wireless Operator/Air Gunner)
No. 1580819, Royal Air Force Volunteer Reserve
Killed in an aircraft accident on Sunday 31 December 1944 (aged 20)
Wellingborough (Doddington Road) Cemetery, Northamptonshire, England (Section N Grave 65)

Alex Joseph Bell was born around 1924 and he was the youngest son of Alexander and Mary Bell of 9 Raceview Terrace, Comber Road, Newtownards. The marriage of Alex Joseph Bell and Mavis Hilda Jarvis (born 15 September 1925, daughter of Mark and Ellen Jarvis) was registered in the second quarter of 1944 in Wellingborough, Northamptonshire.

During the Second World War Alex Joseph Bell served with the Royal Air Force Volunteer Reserve and he was 20 years old when he was killed in an aircraft accident on 31 December 1944. He was buried in Wellingborough (Doddington Road) Cemetery, Northamptonshire and there is an inscription on his CWGC headstone:

Tho' you are gone from us you remain in our fondest memories ever

Mavis Hilda Bell (nee Jarvis) and Charles Keith Underwood were married on 20 March 1948 in Wellingborough Congregational Church.

Bell, Gerald Mavor (Gerald)
Private
No. NX41008, 2/18th Battalion, Australian Infantry, Australian Imperial Force
Killed in action on Sunday 8 February 1942 (aged 35)
Singapore Memorial, Singapore (Column 119)

ROLL OF HONOUR
BELL—Gerald Mavor Bell, Australian Imperial Force, third son of the late Mr. and Mrs. Francis Bell, Bangor. Killed in action at Malaya, 8th February, 1942.
Proudly remembered by his Sisters and Brothers.

Gerald Mavor Bell was born on 29 December 1906 and he was the youngest son of Francis and Agnes Jane Bell (nee McKay) who lived at 16 Hamilton Road, Bangor and then at *Strathmavor*, Baylands, Bangor. Francis Bell worked as a textile designer and he and Agnes Jane McKay were married on 30 August 1887 in Ballymacarrett Presbyterian Church, Belfast. They had seven children – Selina Caroline (Lena, born 20 February 1888); William Rosslyn (born 31 August 1890); Catherine Jeffrey (Kitty, born 11 March 1893); Francis Somerset (born 6 March 1898); Margaret Jane (Rita, born 11 April 1901); Eileen Agnes (born 13 January 1904) and Gerald Mavor (born 29 December 1906). At least three of the children (including Gerald) were baptised in First Bangor Presbyterian Church.

Gerald Mavor Bell was just three weeks short of his ninth birthday when his mother Agnes Jane died on 10 December 1915. His father Francis married Elizabeth Jane Craig and they had one son – Leighton Bell who became a surgeon. Francis Bell died on 14 May 1926 and Elizabeth Jane Bell died in 1969. Gerald's brother, Captain William Rosslyn Bell MC, died on 9 March 1976 (Captain Bell served during the First World War with the Royal Irish Rifles and he was awarded the Military Cross on 4 October 1918 for conspicuous gallantry and devotion to duty during operations south of Dadizeele).

Gerald Mavor Bell attended Bangor Grammar School from 1920 until 1923 and on 7 November 1923 he left London aboard the SS *Themistocles* bound for Australia. His last address in the UK was *Glenfaba*, 5 College Avenue, Bangor. In Australia he worked as an agricultural labourer and he lived in East Moree, New South Wales. He enlisted on 10 July 1940 in Tamworth, New South Wales and cited his brother William as his next-of-kin. Gerald Bell served with the 2/18th Battalion, Australian Infantry and he was 35 years old when he was killed in action on 8 February 1942. The 2/18th Battalion had been assigned to defend the northwest coast of Singapore Island against the invasion by Japanese Forces on 8 February and by dawn on 9 February 1942 more than half their number had been killed or wounded.

B

BELL G. M.   Private Gerald Mavor Bell's body was never recovered and he is commemorated on the Australian War Memorial (Panel 40); on the Singapore Memorial; on Bangor and District War Memorial and in Bangor Grammar School.

Bell, Hugh
Chief Officer
SS *Cheldale* (Newcastle-on-Tyne), Merchant Navy
Killed in a shipping accident on Saturday 17 February 1940 (aged 47)
Tower Hill Memorial, London, England (Panel 27)

Hugh Bell was born on 8 September 1892 in Cloughey, Co. Down and he was a son of William and Rachel Bell (nee Bailie). William Bell worked as a labourer and he and Rachel Bailie were married in Glastry Presbyterian Church. Rachel Bailie worked as a seamstress and she was a daughter of Hugh Bailie who was a sailor. William and Rachel Bell had two children, Hugh (born 8 September 1892) and James (born 26 April 1895).

Hugh Bell was 5 feet 6½ inches tall with dark hair and blue eyes when he obtained his certificate of competency as First Mate on 1 February 1915. During the Second World War he served with the Merchant Navy aboard the SS *Cheldale*. This cargo ship was built in 1925 by John Priestman and Company Ltd., Southwick (Sunderland) and on 17 February 1940 she sank in the Indian Ocean 24 miles off the coast of Durban, South Africa following a collision with the motor vessel MV *Greystone Castle*. Some 16 of the 35 SS *Cheldale* crew members were lost.

B

Chief Officer Hugh Bell was 47 years old when he died and he is commemorated on the Tower Hill Memorial in London and on the family grave headstone in Cloughey Presbyterian Churchyard:

Erected by William Bell in loving memory of
His wife Rachel Bell died on 18 April 1933
Also the above William Bell died 7 February 1942
Also his son Hugh Bell Master Mariner lost at sea 17 February 1940
Also his daughter-in-law May died 20 February 1949
Captain James A. Bell MBE died 30 May 1972
And his son William Bell MN died 31 January 1998

Bellamy, William (Billy)
Fusilier
No. 6983155, 70th Battalion, Royal Inniskilling Fusiliers
Died as a result of enemy action on Wednesday 16 April 1941 (aged 28)
Sutton-in-Ashfield Cemetery, Nottinghamshire, England
(Section C Grave 7629)

William (Billy) Bellamy's birth was registered in the second quarter of 1912 in Mansfield, Nottinghamshire and he was a son of William and Mary Ellen Bellamy (nee Beasley). William Bellamy was a boot and shoe maker and his marriage to Mary Ellen Beasley was registered in the fourth quarter of 1899 in Mansfield. They had at least three children – Albert Edward, Ethel May and William (Billy).

Fusilier William (Billy) Bellamy was one of 13 soldiers serving with the 70th Battalion, Royal Inniskilling Fusiliers who died as a result of an air raid on Newtownards aerodrome during the night of 15/16 April 1941. Fusilier **Daniel Higgins** who also died that night was buried in Newtownards (Movilla) Cemetery and under his name in this Book of Honour there is a summary of all the people with North Down or Ards connections who died that night.

Fusilier William (Billy) Bellamy was buried in Sutton-in-Ashfield Cemetery, Nottinghamshire on 21 April 1941 and in the burial register his address was recorded as 56 St. Michael Street, Sutton-in-Ashfield. On his CWGC headstone there is an inscription:

Deep in our hearts a memory is kept of one we loved and will never forget

Billy's friends from Eastfield Side (an area of Sutton-in-Ashfield also known as Sutton Forest Side) placed a separate plaque on his grave as a token of their respect. There were no other family members buried in the grave. Fusilier William (Billy) Bellamy was 28 years old when he died and he is commemorated on Sutton-in-Ashfield War Memorial.

Belshaw, James McNeilly (Jim)
Carpenter
SS *Kenbane Head* (Belfast), Merchant Navy
Died as a result of enemy action on Tuesday 5 November 1940 (aged 36)
Tower Hill Memorial, London (Panel 60)

James McNeilly (Jim) Belshaw was born on 10 September 1904 and he was the second son of John and Jane Belshaw (nee McNeilly). Both of his parents came originally from East Street in Newtownards and they were married on 10 January 1899 in Newtownards Parish Church of Ireland Church (St. Mark's). John

B

151

Belshaw was a Petty Officer in the Coastguards at Ballywalter and he and Jane had two children while he was stationed there – Thomas McNeilly (born 10 July 1900) and James McNeilly (born 10 September 1904). Both were baptised in Ballywalter Presbyterian Church. Their third son, Samuel McNeilly, was born in July 1908 when John was stationed in Donegal and at that time the Belshaw family lived in Portnoo, Lackagh, Glenties. During the First World War John Belshaw had served with the Royal Navy.

James Belshaw was the husband of Jane (Nettie) Belshaw (nee Kerr). Jane Kerr was 2½ when her mother Adelaide died on 1 January 1911 and she was brought up by her grandparents, Henry and Eliza Jane Beggs, who had 18 children. Jane's father Thomas remarried. James Belshaw and Jane Kerr were married on 25 June 1930 in Belfast Registry Office and they lived at 2 Dunleath Terrace, Ballywalter. James Belshaw was a carpenter in Ballywalter and he and Jane had two children, Jean and Sheila. James Belshaw went to sea and during the Second World War he served in the Merchant Navy as a carpenter aboard the SS *Kenbane Head*. This ship was built in 1919 by Workman, Clark and Company and owned by G. Heyn and Sons Ltd., who operated the Ulster Steamship Company (Head Line).

B

> **BELSHAW**—Lost at sea, through enemy action, November, 1940, James M'Neilly, loving husband of Nettie, dear Daddy of Jean and Sheila.
> 2, Dunleath Terrace, Ballywalter.

In November 1940 the SS *Kenbane Head* was sailing from Halifax in Nova Scotia to Great Britain in Convoy HX-84 with more than 30 other merchant vessels escorted by the armed merchant cruiser HMS *Jervis Bay*. The convoy was intercepted by the German battlecruiser *Admiral Scheer* which had been commissioned in November 1934. Hopelessly outgunned, HMS *Jervis Bay* engaged the enemy and was sunk in the process. However, this gave the convoy time to scatter. The *Admiral Scheer* was only able to sink six other ships, five from the convoy (*Beaverford, Fresno City, Kenbane Head, Maidan, Trewellard*) and one sailing independently (*Mopan*). The SS *Kenbane Head* went down off the coast of Greenland with the loss of 23 men. The tanker *San Demetrio* was set on fire by the *Admiral Scheer* but later salvaged. Other crew members with local connections who lost their lives aboard the SS *Kenbane Head* were **George McClelland Leckey** from Holywood, **Reginald John Primmer** from Portaferry and **David John Pritchard** from Ballyhalbert. On 9 April 1945 the *Admiral Scheer* was capsized in Kiel harbour, Germany by RAF bombs dropped during a raid.

Carpenter James McNeilly Belshaw is commemorated on Tower Hill Memorial in London; on Ballywalter and District War Memorial and in

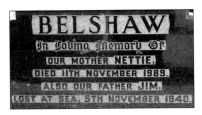

Ballywalter Presbyterian Church. He is also commemorated on two headstones in Whitechurch Cemetery Ballywalter. One was erected by his daughters who were aged 8 and 6 when their father died and it bears the inscription:

BELSHAW
In loving memory of our mother Nettie died 11 November 1989.
Also our father Jim lost at sea 5 November 1940.

One of the survivors of the sinking, Dave Fullerton, told Jim's family afterwards how Jim had bought slippers for his two daughters and, because Jim Belshaw was colour blind, he had asked Dave for his advice about the colour.

The other headstone in Whitechurch Cemetery bears the inscription:

BELSHAW
In loving memory of John Belshaw died 19 May 1939.
Also his wife Jane Belshaw died 10 April 1947.
Also their sons
James McNeilly, lost at sea through enemy action 5 November 1940
Samuel McNeilly died at sea 3 March 1965. Interred at Gibralter
Thomas McNeilly died at sea 20 June 1965. Cremated at Ceylon

B

All three of John and Jane Belshaw's sons died at sea. Sammy was a Radio Officer and had just gone back to sea when he died of coronary heart disease. Tom was a Chief Engineer and went back to sea after his wife Edith died. He too died of coronary heart disease and his ashes were brought back to Newcastle-on-Tyne to be scattered in the same Garden of Remembrance where Edith's ashes had been scattered.

Benson, John George (John)
Private
No. 13014845, Pioneer Corps
Died of illness on Monday 13 March 1944 (aged 60)
Drumcree Church of Ireland Churchyard, Co. Armagh
(New Ground Grave 325)

John George Benson was a nephew of the late William H. Willis of 75 Victoria Avenue, Newtownards and after John died on 13 March 1944 his

DIED ON ACTIVE SERVICE.

BENSON—13th March, 1944, at Glasgow, Private John G. Benson, Pioneer Corps, nephew of the late Wm. H. Willis, 75, Victoria Avenue, Newtownards. Sincerely regretted by his sorrowing Cousins.

cousins placed a *Died on Active Service* notice in the 18 March edition of the *Newtownards Chronicle*. John George Benson was born on 22 March 1885 and he was a son of John and Jane Benson (formerly Trueman, nee Willis, daughter of Thomas Willis) of Cannagola More, Portadown. Both were widowed when they got married on 8 March 1870 in Tartaraghan Church of Ireland Church (St. Paul's), Co. Armagh. Jane had previously been married to Samuel Trueman (11 October 1866 in St. Paul's, Tartaraghan).

John Benson Senior (son of James Benson) was a farmer and he and Jane Benson (formerly Trueman, nee Willis) had at least eight children – Elizabeth (born 15 January 1871); Ann (born 8 October 1872); Margaret (born 4 June 1875); Teresa (born 12 September 1877, died in infancy); Thomas William (born 17 January 1880); Teresa (born 15 October 1882); John George (born 22 March 1885) and James (born 7 February 1889 although he declared 8 February 1891 in his attestation papers). Two of John George Benson's sisters died in infancy; his father John died on 19 October 1913 (aged 71 although 85 is inscribed on his headstone); his brother James died on active service in Belgium during the First World War; his mother Jane died on 22 January 1929 (aged 87) and his sister Elizabeth died on 6 September 1931 (aged 60).

Private James Benson (No. 55571) enlisted in Toronto, he served with the 19th Battalion, Canadian Infantry and he was 27 when he died on 25 July 1916. He was buried in Bedford House Cemetery, West-Vlaanderen, Belgium (Enclosure No. 41 G 2).

During the Second World War John George Benson served with the Pioneer Corps and he was 60 years old when he died of a stroke at 1.30 am on 13 March 1944 in a Military Hospital in Glasgow. At the time of his death he was stationed in Bellahouston Camp, Glasgow and his home address was 12 Gaffikin Street, Belfast. He was a single man and in civilian life he worked as a clerk. Private John George Benson was buried in Drumcree Church of Ireland Churchyard, Co. Armagh.

Bewley, George Barry Neville (Barry)
Third Radio Officer
MV *Eulima* (London), Canadian Merchant Navy
Died as a result of enemy action on Tuesday 23 February 1943 (aged 18)
Halifax Memorial, Nova Scotia, Canada (Panel 23)

George Barry Neville (Barry) Bewley was born on 27 April 1924 in Montreal and he was the eldest son of John (Jack) Neville Bewley and Sarah (Sally) Bewley (nee Stokes). Jack Bewley was an Englishman, Sarah Stokes was from Belfast (her father James was a mineral water manufacturer) and they met in Canada where Jack was working for a biscuit making company. Sarah Bewley brought Barry, her infant son, to Belfast in 1925 and her husband Jack followed soon thereafter. The Bewley family lived in Primrose Street, Bangor and George Barry Neville Bewley was baptised in Millisle Church of Ireland Church (St. Patrick's). Jack Bewley joined the Civil Service and he worked in the Law Courts. He and Sarah had three more children – Kenneth; Margaret Helen Joyce (born 7 February 1929) and Patricia Rosalind (born 4 March 1931). The two girls were baptised in Carrowdore Church of Ireland Church (Christ Church). Barry Bewley was educated at Bangor Central Public Elementary School, Bangor Technical College and Belfast Mercantile College. In July 1937, aged 13, he was selected to go with other pupils to the King's Hall in Belfast to meet King George VI and Queen Elizabeth.

During the Second World War George Barry Neville Bewley served with the Canadian Merchant Navy aboard the motor vessel MV *Eulima*. Built in 1937 by Wilton Feijenoord, Schiedam, Netherlands and owned by the Anglo-Saxon Petroleum Company Ltd., London she operated as a fuel tanker. In February 1943 she was on route from Liverpool to New York in Convoy ON-166. The ship was in ballast and on 23 February 1943 she was torpedoed by the German submarine *U-186* and sank around 10.30 am in the North Atlantic, some 300 miles south of Cape Race in Newfoundland. More than 60 men aboard were killed. Less than three months later, on 12 May 1943, *U-186* was depth-charged and sunk by the Royal Navy destroyer HMS *Hesperus*.

Initially Third Radio Officer George Barry Neville Bewley was reported as missing and so for a time his family hoped that he might be found alive. Later it was officially confirmed that he must be presumed dead.

B

 Barry Bewley was 18 years old when he died and he is commemorated on the Halifax Memorial in Nova Scotia and on Bangor and District War Memorial.

Bigger, Reginald Austin
Sergeant
No. 580320, 77 Squadron, Royal Air Force
Killed in action on Tuesday 24 October 1939 (aged 24)
Runnymede Memorial, Surrey, England (Panel 1)

 Reginald Austin Bigger was born on 27 July 1915 and he was a son of William Austin Bigger and Mary Clark Bigger (nee Gray) of 3 Anchor Lodge, Kinnegar, Holywood, Co. Down. They were married on 15 July 1914 in Belfast Registry Office. Reginald Austin Bigger attended Lower Sullivan Public Elementary School and then Sullivan Upper School, Holywood from 3 September 1928 until 28 March 1933. After leaving school he joined the Royal Air Force.

B

 During the Second World War he served in Bomber Command and on 24 October 1939 he was one of a crew of five aboard an Armstrong Whitworth Whitley Mark V aircraft (N1358). They took off at 6.50 pm from RAF Driffield in Yorkshire on a Nickel raid (dropping propaganda leaflets) and their targets were Hamburg and Wilhelmshaven in Germany. A wireless telegraphy signal was intercepted at 11.15 pm but nothing further was heard from the aircraft. No trace of the aircraft was ever found and the other crew members who died that night were:

- PO Philip Edwin William Walker aged 23 from Kentish Town, London
- Sergeant George Jonathan Burrell aged 28 from Hitcham, Suffolk
- Aircraftman 1st Class Alexander Bernard Bogle MacDonald
- AC1 James Alfred Topham aged 18 from Bromley Cross, Lancashire

Sergeant Reginald Austin Bigger was 24 years old when he died and he is commemorated on the Runnymede Memorial in Surrey; on Holywood and District War Memorial and in Sullivan Upper School.

Black, Hector Alexander (Hector)
Gunner
No. 1472337, 447 Battery, 66 (4th Battalion the Gloucestershire Regt)
Searchlight Regiment, Royal Artillery
Died in service on Monday 25 December 1944 (aged 41)
Ballygowan Presbyterian Churchyard, Co. Down
(Section E Row 6 Grave 63)

Hector Alexander Black was born in Belfast on 2 November 1903 and he was a son of John and Isabella Black (nee Boyd), both of whom were born in Scotland. John was from Kirkinner and Isabella was from New Luce, both in Wigtownshire. They were married on 13 October 1882 in New Luce Church of Scotland Church. The Black family moved to Ireland sometime after 1898 and in 1901 they were living at 2 Skegoniel Avenue in Belfast. In 1911 they were living in Whitehouse, Co. Antrim. John Black worked as a dairyman and gardener and he and Isabella had at least seventeen children including Agnes (born Scotland, 1886); John (born Scotland, 1887); Mary Anderson Forsythe (born Scotland, died 25 January 1909 aged 17); Thomas (born Scotland, died 16 October 1907 aged 13 years six months); Jemima (born Scotland 1898); Hector Archibald McDonald (born 28 June 1900, died 25 December 1900); stillborn and unnamed child (buried in Grave A2 255, Belfast City Cemetery) and Hector Alexander (born 2 November 1903). By 1911 fourteen of John and Isabella Black's seventeen children had died and only three remained alive.

B

Hector Black and Margaret McQuade of Dundonald were married on 11 July 1930 in Comber Non-Subscribing Presbyterian Church and during the Second World War Hector served with 447 Battery, 66 (4th Battalion the Gloucestershire Regiment) Searchlight Regiment, Royal Artillery. This Battery formed part of the anti-aircraft defences around Bristol. Gunner Hector Black was 41 years old when he died on Christmas Day 1944 and he was buried in Ballygowan Presbyterian Churchyard. There is an inscription on his CWGC headstone:

The eternal God is thy refuge
And underneath are the everlasting arms

Black, Kennedy Boyd (Boyd)
Sergeant (Flight Engineer)
No. 1130432, Royal Air Force Volunteer Reserve
Killed in an aircraft accident on Sunday 20 August 1944 (aged 22)
Balteagh Presbyterian Churchyard, Co. Londonderry

Kennedy Boyd Black was born on 10 September 1921 and he was a son of Joseph Douglas and Maude Black (nee Love) of Drumsurn, Limavady. Joseph Black was a farmer and he and Maude Love were married on 2 December 1909 in Mageramason Presbyterian Church, Co. Tyrone. They had seven children – Alexander Douglas Moorehead (born 21 August 1910, died 11 July 1971); James Stewart Pattison (born 17 March 1912, died 16 February 1984; he was a Presbyterian Minister); Joseph Victor McDonald (born 30 September 1913, died 1993); Gilbert Louis Houston (born 12 March 1915, died 6 December 1981); Samuel Arthur Oliver (born 30 July 1916, died 1981); Agnes Wilhelmina Elizabeth (born 11 February 1918, died 12 May 2003) and Kennedy Boyd (born 10 September 1921). Kennedy Boyd Black's grandmother, Jane Black, died on 10 October 1928 (aged 85); his mother, Maude Black, died on 28 March 1943 (aged 55) and his father, Joseph Douglas Black, died on 3 January 1947 (aged 70). During the Second World War Kennedy Boyd Black served with the Royal Air Force Volunteer Reserve.

On 20 August 1944 an Avro Anson aircraft (LT658) from No. 12 Air Gunners School based at Bishops Court was on an air gunnery exercise when it broke up in mid-air as a result of a structural failure. Wreckage fell to the ground over a wide area centred on Ballygalget Roman Catholic Church, Portaferry and all five crew members on board were killed – Flying Officer (Pilot) **Raymond Hodgson**, Sergeant (Flight Engineer) Kennedy Boyd Black, Sergeant (Flight Engineer) **Frank Bennett Bloor**, Flight Sergeant (Flight Engineer) **Thomas Charles Crisp** and Sergeant (Air Gunner) **George William Thomas Walker**. All five deaths were registered in Downpatrick.

Sergeant (Flight Engineer) Kennedy Boyd Black was 22 years old when he died and he was buried in Balteagh Presbyterian Churchyard, Limavady, Co. Londonderry and he is commemorated on a Memorial Plaque in the Church.

B

Bleakley Brothers, Robert James and Deryk Jay

The deaths of Robert James Bleakley and Deryk Jay Bleakley are commemorated on the Bleakley family grave headstone in Clandeboye Cemetery, Bangor. Both were born in Colombo, Ceylon (now Sri Lanka) and they were sons of James and Jane Bleakley (nee Simpson). James Bleakley was born on 1 June 1883 and Jane Simpson was born on 12 July 1886. Both James and Jane were born in Darwen, Lancashire and they were married there, in Holy Trinity Church, in 1910. James Bleakley was a physics lecturer and their son John was born in Manchester on 5 January 1912. The Bleakley family moved to Colombo in Ceylon where James became Vice-Principal of the Government Teacher-Training College and Jane became Secretary for Trinity College of Music *in the East*. Three more children were born in Colombo – Robert James on 25 October 1914, Mabel Joyce on 19 December 1919 and Deryk Jay on 30 May 1923.

B

Shortly after the outbreak of the Second World War John Bleakley, who had recently qualified as a doctor, joined the Royal Army Medical Corps and was posted to Thiepval Barracks in Lisburn. He had frequent occasion to send injured officers to *Seacourt*, Princetown Road, Bangor, then a house being run as a convalescent home by its owner, Mrs Kathleen Hadow, for officers after they were discharged from hospital prior to their return to their Units. After he sustained a motor-cycle injury John referred himself to *Seacourt* where he met Mrs Hadow's daughter Kathleen Nancy Hadow whom he married on 13 September 1941 in Mountpottinger Non-subscribing Presbyterian Church, Belfast. He was posted to the south of England and attached to the 53rd Welsh Division. He landed on the Normandy Beaches on 27 June 1944 and travelled 2,000 miles on to Hamburg and Belsen, arriving there the day after it was liberated. After being demobilised, Major John Bleakley settled at *Seacourt* in Bangor where he entered general medical practice.

Seacourt had been the home of Captain James Samuel Davidson who was killed in action on 1 July 1916 and who is commemorated on Page 131 in the Book of Honour *Remembering Their Sacrifice in the Great War – North Down* compiled by Barry Niblock. Mrs Kathleen Hadow was Captain Davidson's younger sister.

Mabel Joyce Bleakley and Wendell Bryan Anderson, a lawyer who was working in the UK Legal Department of the United States Army Air Forces (USAAF), were married in London on 3 April 1944. Joyce and their infant son travelled aboard a US troopship to America in 1945, to be joined later by Wendell after his discharge. They lived in Logan, Utah. Mabel Joyce Anderson (nee Bleakley) died on 22 December 2012.

James and Jane Bleakley moved from Ceylon to *Seacourt* in Bangor and at the age of 76 James died at sea aboard the *Loch Ryan* on 5 December 1959 on the return journey from a visit to their daughter whom they had not seen for 20 years. Jane Bleakley died on 29 March 1985 (aged 98) and their son John died on 8 April 1992 (aged 80).

Bleakley, Robert James (Bob)
Captain
Straits Settlements Volunteer Force
Died on active service on Monday 9 February 1942 (aged 28)
Singapore Memorial, Singapore (Column 391)

B

Robert James Bleakley was a classical scholar at Peterhouse, Cambridge, an athlete and a pianist. He joined the Imperial Civil Service with a posting to Malaya for which he was required to learn Arabic and Chinese. He wrote an English-Chinese primer (dictionary). He was first posted to Singapore then assigned to Kuala Lumpur in Malaya, with periods spent in China where he witnessed at first hand Japanese brutality against the Chinese. During the war, as the Japanese Forces were approaching Kuala Lumpur, Bob Bleakley was evacuated to Singapore where he served as a Captain in the Straits Settlements Volunteer Force. When he was leading his men through a rubber plantation outside Singapore on 9 February 1942 he believed that some of them had become separated from the main group and he returned to search for them. He never returned and was later presumed to have been killed or captured by the Japanese Forces that had invaded the island the previous day.

Captain Robert James Bleakley aged 28 was engaged to fellow-student Dorothy Whitehouse but he died before they could be married. He is commemorated on the Singapore Memorial; on the Malayan Civil Service Memorial in St. Andrew's Cathedral, Singapore and on the Bleakley family grave headstone in Clandeboye Cemetery, Bangor.

Bleakley, Deryk Jay (Deryk)

Pilot Officer (Flying Instructor)
No. 145409, Royal Air Force Volunteer Reserve
Killed in an aircraft accident on Wednesday 21 July 1943 (aged 20)
Bloemfontein (Hamilton) War Cemetery, South Africa
(European Block Grave 7)

Deryk Jay Bleakley was an enthusiastic ice-skater and he played the clarinet in a jazz band. He joined the Royal Air Force Volunteer Reserve straight from Berkhamsted School and trained as a pilot. He said that his main objective was 'to stop the Germans strafing England'. He

was posted to South Africa to complete his training and then he was appointed Pilot Officer (Flying Instructor). On 21 July 1943 the Tiger Moth bi-plane that he and his trainee-pilot were flying went into a spin and crashed. Despite breaking his back, the trainee-pilot survived the crash. Flying Instructor Deryk Jay Bleakley was 20 years old when he was killed and he is commemorated on the Bleakley family grave headstone in Clandeboye Cemetery, Bangor.

Bloomfield, Frederick

Fusilier
No. 7044877, 6th Battalion, Royal Inniskilling Fusiliers
Died as a result of an accident on Friday 6 December 1940 (aged 27)
Holywood Cemetery (Protestant Ground Collective Grave 1263)

Frederick Bloomfield's birth was registered in the first quarter of 1913 in Birmingham, Warwickshire and he was a son of carpenter Frederick James Bloomfield and Jennie Bloomfield (nee Johnson). Their marriage was registered in the third quarter of 1906 in Tynemouth, Northumberland and they had at least five children – Robert James (born 1908); Frederick (born 1913); Franklin (born 1915); Albert (born 1922) and Dennis (born 1929).

The marriage of Frederick Bloomfield and Eileen Brown was registered in the fourth quarter of 1937 in Birmingham, Warwickshire and they lived at 52 Sandringham Road, Great Barr, Birmingham. During the Second World War Fusilier Frederick Bloomfield served with the Royal Inniskilling Fusiliers and he was 27 years old when he died on 6 December 1940 as a result of an accident at Palace Barracks Holywood. His effects amounted to some £70 and probate was granted to his widow, Eileen Bloomfield.

Fusilier Frederick Bloomfield was buried in a collective grave in Holywood Cemetery and the other two men buried in this collective grave were Rifleman **John McFarlane** and Driver **Sidney John Wren**.

Bloor, Frank Bennett (Frank)
Sergeant (Flight Engineer)
No. 980285, Royal Air Force Volunteer Reserve
Killed in an aircraft accident on Sunday 20 August 1944 (aged 24)
Carlton Cemetery, Nottinghamshire, England
(Section A Row M 6 Grave 190)

B

Frank Bennett Bloor's birth was registered in the fourth quarter of 1919 and he was a grandson of Joseph and Ellen Elizabeth Bloor (nee Butler). He was a son of Frank Lancelot Bloor and Annie Bloor (nee Bennett) who were married on 22 December 1918 in Netherfield Church, Nottingham. Frank Lancelot Bloor was born on 7 November 1891 at Bulwell, Nottingham and he and Annie had two children – Frank Bennett (born 1919) and Bernard John (born 1 January 1929, died 15 June 2013).

Before the outbreak of the Great War Frank Lancelot Bloor worked as a storekeeper for a bat manufacturer and he was one of the first people in the area to have a driving licence and a motor vehicle; his driving licence was printed on parchment. He volunteered for the army and served with the Royal Horse Artillery. Gunner Frank Bloor (No. 67804), 'L' Battery, Royal Horse Artillery, Mediterranean Expeditionary Force left for Gallipoli on the cattle boat SS *Haverford* on 16 March 1915. They encountered very rough seas and many of the horses and men were ill with sea sickness. Gunner Bloor suffered many privations and witnessed harrowing scenes of death and suffering before he became so ill with dysentery that he was sent to a hospital in Cairo. In October 1915 he returned to England and reached Sheffield Hospital on 31 October. He was then stationed near Brighton and served as chauffeur for an army officer before being demobilised. He was then chauffeur for Lord Alfred Eden Browne before Lord Browne returned to France where he was killed on 27 August 1918. After the war Frank Lancelot Bloor was a Haulage Contractor before working as a driver for Trent Buses.

He then worked at the Royal Ordnance Factory before he and his wife bought their own newsagent's shop.

From an early age Frank Bennett Bloor was interested in motor bikes and cars. His first job was at the local Meadow Lane Dairy as a general errand boy and he made deliveries on his push bike. He then went to work at Truman's Garage as a trainee mechanic before joining the RAF. His marriage to Marjorie J. Jackson was registered in the fourth quarter of 1942 in York; they had no children and, after Frank died, Marjorie later remarried.

On 20 August 1944 an Avro Anson aircraft (LT658) from No. 12 Air Gunners School based at Bishops Court was on an air gunnery exercise when it broke up in mid-air as a result of a structural failure. Wreckage fell to the ground over a wide area centred on Ballygalget Roman Catholic Church and all five crew members on board were killed – Flying Officer (Pilot) **Raymond Hodgson**, Sergeant (Flight Engineer) **Kennedy Boyd Black**, Sergeant (Flight Engineer) Frank Bennett Bloor, Flight Sergeant (Flight Engineer) **Thomas Charles Crisp** and Sergeant (Air Gunner) **George William Thomas Walker**. All five deaths were registered in Downpatrick.

Sergeant Frank Bennett Bloor was 24 years old when he died and he was buried in Carlton Cemetery, Nottinghamshire, England. His mother Annie died on 8 April 1965 aged 69 and his father, Frank Lancelot, died in March 1974 aged 83. They were buried in the same grave as their son. Frank's brother, Bernard John Bloor, served with the Royal Signals from 1947 until 1949, for part of that time in Malaya, and he was *Mentioned in Despatches* in recognition of gallant and distinguished service whilst under fire.

Blythe, John Harold (known as Jack, sometimes as Norris)*
Rifleman
No. 7019887, 1st (Airborne) Battalion, Royal Ulster Rifles
Killed in action on Monday 10 July 1944 (aged 23)
Ranville War Cemetery, Calvados, France (Grave IVA B 19)

John Harold Blythe was born at 11.30 am on 3 November 1920 in Saltcoats, Ayrshire and he was a son of Ellen Blythe (nee Bennett) who was the widow of Alfred Blythe who was killed in action on 1 July 1916 and who is commemorated on Page 115 in the Book in Honour *Remembering Their Sacrifice*

in the Great War – Ards compiled by Barry Niblock. Alfred Blythe worked as a labourer and in 1911 he was living at 24 Thomas Street, Newtownards with his widowed mother, Agnes Blythe. Later he lived at 54 Mark Street, Newtownards. Alfred Blythe and Ellen Bennett were married on 13 July 1911 in Newtownards Parish Church of Ireland Church (St. Mark's) and they had two children – Henry Murray Blythe (born 28 January 1912, served with No. 5 Field Ambulance during the Second World War) and Winifred Blythe (born 30 November 1913).

7019887 RIFLEMAN
J. BLYTHE
THE ROYAL ULSTER RIFLES
AIRBORNE
10TH JULY 1944

B

John Harold (Jack) Blythe married Mary Josephine Bridget Young who was born on 15 October 1923 in County Antrim and, after Jack was killed, his widow married Jack Donat Landry. Mary Landry died on 9 March 2008 in Longueuil, Quebec, Canada.

Jack Blythe was a keen footballer and he was goalkeeper for the East End team in the Newtownards summer league. After he enlisted in 1940 he was the goalkeeper for his Battalion team. He went to France soon after the Normandy invasion and was home on leave in January 1944. Six months later he was killed in action on 10 July 1944.

KILLED IN ACTION.

BLYTHE—July, 1944, Jack (Norris) Blythe, Royal Ulster Rifles, Airborne, late of Newtownards (aged 23 years).
Although we're in a far-off land,
And your grave we cannot see,
As long as life and memory last
We shall remember thee.
Ever remembered by his Friends.
MR. and MRS. CAIRNS and FAMILY,
9, Zion Place, Newtownards.

There was one *Killed in Action* notice in the 29 July edition of the *Newtownards Chronicle*. It was inserted by his friends, Mr and Mrs Cairns of 9 Zion Place, Newtownards and it contained the verse:

Although we're in a far-off land,
And your grave we cannot see,
As long as life and memory last
We shall remember thee.

Rifleman John Harold Blythe was 23 years old when he died and he is commemorated on Newtownards and District War Memorial.

Boal, Hugh Brown (Hugh)
Private
No. H/19475, Queen's Own Cameron Highlanders of Canada,
Royal Canadian Infantry Corps (RCIC)
Died on active service on Wednesday 19 August 1942 (aged 37)
Dieppe Canadian War Cemetery, Hautot-sur-Mer, Seine-Maritime,
France (Special Memorial No. 7)

 Hugh Brown Boal was born on 20 March 1905 and he was a son of Ellen Boal of Granshaw, Bangor. Ellen Boal had three children – Isabella (born 24 December 1900); Hugh Brown (born 20 March 1905) and Isaac (born 15 May 1911, died 26 October 1911). All three were baptised in Ballygrainey Presbyterian Church. Ellen Boal and Samuel Mawhinney from Drumawhey, Donaghadee were married in First Donaghadee Presbyterian Church on 2 August 1912 and they lived at 27 Bangor Road, Newtownards. Hugh Boal and his sister Isabella lived with their maternal grandparents Robert and Mary Boal in the townland of Granshaw, Bangor. Robert Boal worked as an agricultural labourer. On 28 March 1924 Hugh Boal travelled to Canada aboard the SS *Doric* and declared his intention to settle there and work as a farm labourer.

B

 At attestation Hugh Boal stated that his date of birth was 3 June 1906. He served with the Queen's Own Cameron Highlanders of Canada, Royal Canadian Infantry Corps (RCIC) and he was 37 years old when he died during the Dieppe Raid on 19 August 1942. Allied Forces sustained heavy losses during this attack on the German-occupied port of Dieppe in northern France. Private Hugh Boal was buried in Dieppe Canadian War Cemetery and his CWGC headstone bears the inscription:

Buried elsewhere in this Cemetery

Private Hugh Boal is commemorated on the Canadian Virtual War Memorial (Internet) and on Page 59 of the Canadian Second World War Book of Remembrance.

Boocock, John
Lance Sergeant
No. 1605531, 199 Battery, 81 Light Anti-Aircraft Regiment, Royal Artillery
Killed in a motorcycle accident on Saturday 10 April 1943 (aged 30)
Gateshead (Saltwell) Cemetery, Durham (Division 1 Grave 381)

John Boocock's birth was registered in the fourth quarter of 1913 in Gateshead, Durham and he was a son of John Henry Boocock who was born in 1873 in Halifax, Yorkshire, and Edith Louise Boocock (nee Hunt) who was born in 1877 in Woolwich, Kent. John Henry Boocock served with the Royal Garrison Artillery (No. 87471) and he and Edith Hunt were married in Halifax Parish Church of England Church, Yorkshire on 20 August 1902. They had at least four children – Norman (born in Bombay on 13 June 1903); Maude (born in St. Helena on 20 November 1904); Winifred (born in the Isle of Wight on 28 February 1907) and John (born in Gateshead in 1913). John Henry Boocock was discharged on 10 November 1912 at Pembroke Dock at the end of his second period of engagement. On 12 September 1914 he rejoined the colours and served with the Royal Garrison Artillery during the First World War until he was discharged on 24 March 1916 because his services were no longer required.

During the Second World War John Boocock served with 199 Battery, 81 Light Anti-Aircraft Regiment, Royal Artillery and in the 17 April 1943 edition of the *Newtownards Chronicle* under the headline *Tragic Accident Near Ballywalter – Lance Sergeant Burned To Death* the death of John Boocock was reported. Lance Sergeant Boocock was burned to death in a motorcycle crash which happened about 11.00 pm on Saturday 10 April 1943 in the Roddens district when he was travelling from the RAF site at Ballywalter to RAF Ballyhalbert. Close to The Cosy Café his motorcycle skidded onto the bank, travelled a short distance along the grass, struck a stone and overturned onto the road. John Boocock was pinned beneath the machine which burst into flames. Andrew Gilmore who lived at *The Warren*, Roddens together with a passing airman, LAC Joseph Waite, extinguished the flames but when John Boocock was extricated he was dead.

The Coroner's verdict was that death was caused by multiple severe burns. Aged 30 and from Gateshead, Lance Sergeant John Boocock was buried in Gateshead (Saltwell) Cemetery, Durham.

Bowen, John
Sapper
No. 2119186, 38 Field Company, Royal Engineers
Killed on active service on Thursday 5 August 1943 (aged 25)
Catania War Cemetery, Sicily, Italy (Grave I E 34)

In the CWGC Debt of Honour it is recorded that John Bowen was a son of Mr and Mrs Patrick John Bowen of Portaferry. In the Army Roll of Honour it is recorded that John Bowen was born in Lanarkshire, Scotland and his place of residence is recorded as Motherwell and Wishaw in Lanarkshire.

In 1901 Patrick John Bowen aged 13 was living on the family farm in the townland of Ballyridley, Portaferry. He was a son of William and Veronica Bowen (nee O'Connor) and after he left school he moved to Scotland where he worked as a boiler fireman in a colliery. He lived at 64 Chapel Street and then at 91 Muir Street, Hamilton in Lanarkshire. On 5 July 1911 Patrick John Bowen and Margaret Steed Henderson were married in Hamilton Roman Catholic Church. Margaret Steed Henderson was a daughter of John and Margaret Henderson (nee Steed) of 2 Clydeford Drive, Uddingston, Lanarkshire and she worked as a domestic servant. Their son, John Bowen, was born in 1918 in Hamilton and during the Second World War he served with 38 Field Company, Royal Engineers.

On 10 July 1943 a combined Allied force of Commonwealth and American troops invaded Sicily and Sapper John Bowen (aged 25) was one of many who died in the heavy fighting just short of the town of Catania which was taken by the Allied Forces on 5 August 1943. Sapper John Bowen was buried in Catania War Cemetery, Sicily.

Bowman Brothers, Eric Ritchie and Geoffrey Alexander

Eric Ritchie and Geoffrey Alexander Bowman were sons of Hugh Bowman MBE and Annie Edwards Bowman (nee McAreavey) who were married on 26 December 1912 in Cliftonville Presbyterian Church, Belfast. The Bowman family lived in Belfast before they moved to Bangor where they lived in *Casaeldono*, 22 Bryansburn Road. Their father Hugh was an official in the Ministry of Agriculture and their uncle, Robert Ritchie Bowman, was Permanent Secretary to the Ministry of Labour. Eric and Geoffrey Bowman had four siblings – Flight Sergeant Hugh Bowman who was stationed in Imphal, India with South East Asia Command; Petty Officer Rosaleen Bowman (later Mrs Douglas Wood) who served with the Women's Royal Naval Reserve; Helen (later Mrs Desmond Burland) and Edgar. Their father Hugh died in 1965 and their mother Annie died in 1967.

Bowman, Eric Ritchie (Eric)
Sergeant (Pilot)
No. 1500548 (1500448 on headstone), Royal Air Force Volunteer Reserve
Killed in an aircraft accident on Wednesday 24 December 1941 (aged 25)
Bangor Cemetery, Co. Down (Section 4 V Grave 82)

Eric Bowman, the eldest son, was born on 4 August 1916 and he was educated at Royal Belfast Academical Institution (RBAI) from 1929 until 1934. He entered the Civil Service and worked in the Ministry of Agriculture. He enrolled in the RAF before the outbreak of war and held a commission in the Reserve of Officers. He was called up on the outbreak of hostilities and in the 30 December 1939 edition of the *County Down Spectator* it was reported that he had been seriously injured on Christmas Eve in a flying crash in Scotland. He suffered concussion and multiple injuries and then, with his parents at his bedside, he regained consciousness four days later. At the time his brother Geoffrey, also in the RAF, was at home on Christmas leave.

DIED ON ACTIVE SERVICE.
BOWMAN—December, 1941, killed in action, Sergeant-Pilot Eric Ritchie, eldest and much-loved son of Hugh and Annie E. Bowman, "Casaeldono," 22 Bryansburn Road, Bangor. Interred in Bangor New Cemetery.

As a result of his injuries Eric was passed unfit for flying and in November 1940 he resigned his commission and returned to civilian life. Then, following the Blitz on Belfast in April 1941, he applied for another medical examination and was passed fit for service. Some eight months later, Sergeant Eric Bowman was killed on Christmas Eve (exactly two years to the day after his previous crash) when the Short Stirling aircraft on which he was a crew member crashed in the Bedfordshire countryside while on training manoeuvres. He had been based at RAF Waterbeach, north of Cambridge, and five other RAF personnel were also killed in the crash:

- Pilot Officer Henry Barrymore Rowland aged 22 (RAAF)
- Sergeant Gerald Harry Savoy aged 21 from Bradfield Combust, Suffolk
- Sgt Edward C. Welsh aged 34 from Kingwilliamstown, South Africa

- Sergeant Reginald John Clark aged 21 from Wyke Regis, Weymouth
- Sergeant Vernon Charles Akes aged 23 (RAAF)

Three crew members survived the crash and returned to active service – Corporal Jack Mainwaring from Hale, Lancashire; Corporal John William Dawson from Keighley, Yorkshire and Corporal Sam Hawley Atkinson from Wetherby, Yorkshire. All three subsequently lost their lives on active service during 1942.

Sergeant Eric Ritchie Bowman was 25 years old when he died, he was buried on 31 December 1941 in Bangor Cemetery and he is commemorated on Bangor and District War Memorial; in First Bangor Presbyterian Church and in RBAI.

Bowman, Geoffrey Alexander (Geoffrey)
Flying Officer
No. 149526, 53 Squadron, Royal Air Force Volunteer Reserve
Killed in action on Sunday 21 May 1944 (aged 24)
Runnymede Memorial, Surrey, England (Panel 204)

Geoffrey Bowman was born on 1 June 1919 and, after attending Bangor Public Elementary School, he attended Bangor Grammar School from 1932 until 1935. He played both rugby and cricket for the school and was a member of the Dramatic Society. The headmaster wrote later that Geoffrey had taken first place in the 1932 entrance scholarship competition with his close friend Bertie Hannay coming second. The headmaster went on, 'they were together in their work and play; together in their love of fun and abounding vitality; together in their examination successes, in their time of leaving school and choice of a career; together in their voluntary self-dedication to the hazards of air-warfare and now, beyond death's mystery, together they wear the crowns of immortality'. Flight Sergeant **Bertie Hannay** was killed in action on 12 June 1941.

B

After leaving school, Geoffrey Bowman worked for the Friends' Provident and Century Insurance Company in Belfast. In 1938 he joined the Royal Air Force Volunteer Reserve and when the Bangor ATC was founded he gave talks to the boys about his experiences. In the 11 April 1942 edition of the *County Down Spectator* it was reported that a British bomber had made a forced landing on the coast of Portugal, near Cape Espichel, and the crew of four (including Geoffrey Bowman) all survived.

In May 1944 Geoffrey was reported as missing in action and, one year later, his death was reported in the 2 June 1945 edition of the *County Down Spectator*. It was noted that he was 'officially presumed to have lost his life on anti-submarine operations'. Flying Officer Bowman and eight other crew members died when their Consolidated B-24 Liberator aircraft crashed into the sea. The other men who died were:

- Warrant Officer Frederick William Atherton aged 29 from Liverpool
- Flying Officer William McTaggart DFM aged 26 from Glasgow
- FS Robert Dougall Christie aged 23 from West Derby, Liverpool
- Flight Sergeant George Harrison aged 29 from Macclesfield, Cheshire
- Flying Officer Herbert William Watkins aged 23 (RAAF)
- Flight Sergeant Walter William Moore aged 25 (RAAF)
- Flight Sergeant Jack Kenneth Richards aged 25 (RAAF)
- Flight Sergeant John Thomas Kerr aged 21 (RAAF)

Flight Sergeant George Harrison's body was the only one to be recovered and he was buried in the British Cemetery at Bilbao in Spain. Flying Officer Geoffrey Alexander Bowman was 24 years old when he died and he is commemorated on the Runnymede Memorial in Surrey; on Bangor and District War Memorial; in First Bangor Presbyterian Church; on the family grave headstone in Bangor Cemetery and in Bangor Grammar School.

Boyd, Samuel McMaster (Samuel)
Sub-Lieutenant (E)
No. R145084, HMRT *Advantage*, Royal Naval Reserve
Died on active service on Sunday 30 April 1944 (aged 24)
Bermuda Royal Naval Cemetery, Bermuda (Grave 427)

Samuel McMaster Boyd was born on 18 March 1920 and he was a son of William and Margaret (Maggie) Boyd (nee McMaster) of 3 Clementine Terrace, Ballyhalbert. They were married on 16 May 1919 in Ballyhemlin Non-Subscribing Presbyterian Church and at that time William described himself as a Private in the Machine Gun Corps (Reserve). Maggie Boyd died on 23 January 1973.

Samuel McMaster Boyd served aboard His Majesty's Rescue Tug (HMRT) *Advantage*. The function of such ships was to escort convoys and then tow to the nearest point of land any ships that were attacked by U-boats and severely damaged but not sunk. Launched in September 1942 and commissioned in April 1943, HMRT *Advantage* was a Favourite Class tug built by the Levingston Shipbuilding Company, Orange, Texas, USA and supplied to the Admiralty under the Lend-Lease Agreement. Samuel was 24 years old when he died on 30 April 1944 and he was buried in Bermuda Royal Naval Cemetery. There is an inscription on his CWGC headstone:

At the going down of the sun and in the morning we remember him

DIED ON ACTIVE SERVICE.
BOYD—April, 1944, at Bermuda, Lieut. Samuel McMaster Boyd, R.N.R., dearly-loved son of Margaret Boyd, 3 Clementine Terrace, Ballyhalbert. Deeply regretted by his sorrowing Mother and Sister; also his Grand-mother, Aunt Minnie and Uncle John, in U.S.A.; also Uncle John Whitla.

DIED ON ACTIVE SERVICE.
SHAMROCK MASONIC LODGE 354, KIRCUBBIN.
BOYD—The Officers and Brethren of above Lodge desire to express their deep sorrow at the death at a Naval Hospital in Bermuda of their highly-esteemed brother, Lieut. Samuel McMaster Boyd, R.N.R., Ballyhalbert, and convey their sincere sympathy to his parents and relations.
A. G. MAXWELL, W.M.
J. SINCLAIR, Sec.

There were three *Died on Active Service* notices in the 6 May 1944 edition of the *County Down Spectator*: one from his mother and sister, grandmother, aunt Minnie and uncle John in the USA and his uncle John Whitla; one from his aunt Christina and uncle Robert Bailie of 3 Clementine Terrace, Ballyhalbert and one from the Merchant Navy Club. Two weeks later there was a notice from Shamrock Masonic Lodge 354 in Kircubbin of which Samuel had been a member. Sub-Lieutenant (E) Samuel McMaster Boyd is commemorated on the McClement family grave headstone in Ballyhalbert Cemetery.

In loving memory of Margaret McClement died 18 November 1915
Also her son John Whitla died 15th May 1952
Also his niece Margaret Boyd born 22 December 1891 died 23 January 1973
Also her son Samuel Boyd (RNR) born 18 March 1920 died 30 April 1944

Boyd, Thomas Wesley
Bombardier
No. 1542601, 316 Battery, 102 Heavy Anti-Aircraft Regiment, Royal Artillery
Died of illness on Saturday 2 December 1939 (aged 48)
Holywood Cemetery, Co. Down (Grave 1397)

Thomas Wesley Boyd was born on 19 August 1891 in Belfast and he was a son of Robert and Anne Jane Boyd (nee Perry) of 265 Conway Street, Belfast (1901 census) and 14 Glenvale Street, Belfast (1911 census). Robert Boyd worked as a planer in a foundry and he and Anne Jane Perry were married on 30 November 1874 in St. Mary's Church of Ireland Church, Belfast.

Robert already had a daughter from his first marriage – Margaret Anne (born 1861) – and he and Anne Jane had ten children: Anne Jane (born 6 April 1876); Sarah (born 22 September 1878); Martha (born 23 July 1880); Mary (born 13 October 1882); John (born 9 October 1884); Emily (born 20 April 1887); Jessie (born 30 May 1889); Thomas Wesley (born 19 August 1891); Jane (born 26 November 1893) and George (born 17 August 1897). Robert Boyd died between 1901 and 1911.

Thomas Wesley Boyd enlisted on 14 April 1909 and he served as a Private in the 2nd Battalion, Royal Inniskilling Fusiliers (No. 9637). In 1911 he was stationed in Mandora Barracks, Stanhope Lines, Aldershot where he served under Major General H.M. Lawson. During the First World War he served overseas before being transferred to the Military Foot Police (No. P17899). Thomas Wesley Boyd and Margaret Taylor of Cliftonville, Belfast were married on 9 September 1918 in St. Anne's Church of Ireland Cathedral, Belfast and he was discharged from the MFP on 25 March 1919.

During the Second World War Thomas Wesley Boyd served with the Royal Artillery. He was 48 years old when he died of a gastric ulcer in Holywood Military Hospital on 2 December 1939 and he was buried on 5 December in Holywood Cemetery. There is an inscription on his CWGC headstone:

At the going down of the sun and in the morning we will remember him

Boyling, George
Private
No. 4035295, 4th Battalion, King's Shropshire Light Infantry
Killed in action on Tuesday 18 July 1944 (aged 23)
Bayeux Memorial, Calvados, France (Panel 16 Column 2)

George Boyling was born in Birkenhead and his birth was registered in the second quarter of 1921. He was a son of George and Olive Boyling (nee Dowley) whose marriage was registered in the second quarter of 1919 in Atcham, Shropshire. In the CWGC Debt of Honour it is recorded that George Junior was the husband of Mary Patricia Boyling of Bangor, Co. Down.

During the Second World War Private George Boyling served with the 4th Battalion, King's Shropshire Light Infantry and he was 23 years old when he was killed on 18 July 1944. His body was never recovered. This Battalion was mobilised at the outbreak of war and had intensive training in Northern Ireland. The Battalion landed at Normandy on 14 June 1944 ('D-Day plus 8') and was in action at the River Odon and in *Operation Epsom* which did not achieve its objective of capturing Caen. Caen was eventually taken on 9 July in *Operation Charnwood* and from there further advances were planned. On 18 July 1944, Allied bombers and fighters attacked targets to the east of Caen but the advance southwards by Allied ground forces was impeded by minefields and limited availability of bridges over the waterways.

Private George Boyling is commemorated on the Bayeux Memorial in France.

Braisher, Frank William (Frank)
Private
No. 5343796, 5th Battalion, Dorsetshire Regiment
Died on active service on Friday 16 February 1945 (aged 29)
Reichswald Forest War Cemetery, Kleve, Nordrhein-Westfalen, Germany (Grave 57 A 7)

Frank William Braisher's birth was registered in the third quarter of 1915 in London and he was a son of Frank William and Alice Maud Braisher (nee Ellen). He was a grandson of Abraham and Ellen Braisher who lived at 12 Weimar Street, Putney and who had two sons – George (born 1888) and Frank William (born 1891). Frank William Braisher Senior lived in Wandsworth, London where he worked as a carpenter. On 31 May 1914 he and Alice Maud Ellen, a daughter of William John Ellen, were married in the Church of St. John the Evangelist in Putney.

Frank William Braisher Junior was a soldier when he and Kathleen Florence Murray (daughter of John Murray, a labourer) were married on 12 July 1943 in First Bangor Presbyterian Church. During the Second World War Frank served with the 5th Battalion, Dorsetshire Regiment and he was 29 years old when he died on 16 February 1945 during the Allied invasion of Nazi Germany.

Private Frank William Braisher is commemorated on Bangor and District War Memorial and in First Bangor Presbyterian Church. His father was 74 years old when he died in London in 1965.

Brookes, Wilfrid Mark Hamilton (Mark)
Flight Lieutenant
No. 37846, 231 Squadron, Royal Air Force
Died as a result of enemy action on Tuesday 15 April 1941 (aged 23)
Sannox Old Churchyard, Kilbride, Isle of Arran (West Extension)

Wilfrid Mark Hamilton (Mark) Brookes was born on 3 November 1917 and he was a son of the Revd Wilfrid Stanley Brookes and Jane MacNaught Brookes (nee Brown) of Corrie, Ayrshire in Scotland. They were married on 1 June 1909 in Hillhead United Free Church in Glasgow. Before becoming a Presbyterian Minister Wilfrid Stanley Brookes was a commercial traveller. The Brookes family lived for a time in Canada and in 1920 they were living at 25 Willowbank Street in Glasgow, which had been Jane's home address. They had four children – Margaret Winifred (Greta); Edwin (Ted); Mark (born 3 November 1917) and Janet Sheila. The Brookes family also lived at 35 Hyde Park Terrace in Leeds (Revd Wilfrid's home town) and also for a time in Jamaica where Revd Brookes was a missionary. Wilfrid Mark Hamilton Brookes attended Fulneck School in Leeds from April 1931 until December 1934 and during the Second World War he served with the Royal Air Force in France, Belgium and Northern Ireland. His brother Ted also served in the RAF and after the war became a doctor.

Between 10.45 pm and 4.30 am during the night of Easter Tuesday 15 April and Wednesday 16 April 1941 there was a large-scale German Luftwaffe air raid on the City of Belfast. Other nearby towns and villages, including Bangor and Newtownards, were also attacked. At least five civilians with North Down and Ards connections were killed. That night the aerodrome at Newtownards, which was the Headquarters of 231 Squadron, Royal Air Force, was attacked and 13 soldiers serving with the Royal Inniskilling Fusiliers were killed. Fusilier **Daniel Higgins** was buried in Newtownards (Movilla) Cemetery and under his name in this Book of Honour there is a summary of all those people with North Down or Ards connections who died that night.

Flight Lieutenant Wilfrid Mark Hamilton Brookes (aged 23) of 231 Squadron, who was in Belfast at the time, was killed during the air raid and he was buried in Sannox Old Churchyard, Kilbride on the Isle of Arran, Scotland. There is an inscription on his CWGC headstone:

B

Why seek ye the living among the dead?
He is not here, but is risen
St. Luke XXIV 5.6

His father died on 16 May 1956 and was buried beside his son. There is an inscription on his headstone:

In loving memory of the Reverend Wilfrid Stanley Brookes
Died 16th March 1956 aged 74 years
Faithful Minister of this Parish for 19 years
He is not dead, he doth not sleep
He hath awakened from the dream of life
Also his wife Margaret died 7th July 1967

Sources in Kilbride have confirmed that Mark's mother, Jane McNaught Brookes, was always known as Margaret. Jane McNaught Brookes was 82 years old when she died in 1967 and her death was registered in Aberdeen. Flight Lieutenant Wilfrid Mark Hamilton Brookes is commemorated on Corrie War Memorial, Isle of Arran and in Fulneck School. A tribute was published in the July 1941 edition of the Fulneck School Magazine:

B

'It was with the deepest regret that we received information of the death on active service of Flight Lieutenant W.M.H. Brookes, who had been serving in the Royal Air Force for five years and had seen service in France and Belgium and was subsequently posted to Northern Ireland. His Wing Commander writes of him: "He was one of the world's best. Cheerful but unassuming, he always showed a very keen and active interest in his profession. He was my best flight commander and the most experienced pilot in the squadron. The service and the country can ill afford to lose such a valuable officer. He will be greatly missed in the Mess, as he was without any doubt the most popular member of it. He leaves behind him a host of friends in the service." We remember with affection the many fine qualities which W.M.H. Brookes possessed and we offer our sympathy to his relatives.'

Brown, Alan
Leading Aircraftman
No. 1479901, Royal Air Force Volunteer Reserve
Killed in an aircraft accident on Monday 31 August 1942 (aged 19)
Miami (Grand Army of the Republic) Cemetery, Oklahoma, USA
(Block 14 Row 1 Grave 3)

BROWN—August, 1942, on Active Service, Leading Aircraftman Alan Brown, younger son of Mr. and Mrs. Samuel Brown, 3, Hunt's Park, Donaghadee. Deeply regretted.

Born on 17 January 1923, Alan Brown was the younger son of Samuel and Jane Brown (nee McCance) of 3 Hunt's Park, Donaghadee. Samuel Brown was a merchant and he and Jane McCance were married on 16 September 1914 in Ballygrainey Presbyterian Church. Their elder son, John McCance Brown, was born on 10 June 1915 and baptised in First Donaghadee Presbyterian Church.

During the Second World War Alan Brown served with the Royal Air Force Volunteer Reserve and he was killed in a flying accident while undergoing flight training at Miami, Ottawa County, Oklahoma, USA. He was buried in the British Block of Miami (Grand Army of the Republic) Cemetery. Fourteen other British servicemen are also buried there.

B

In Loving Memory of
SAMUEL DIED 8TH JUNE 1971 AGED 85 YEARS
ALSO HIS WIFE JANE DIED 1ST OCTOBER 1972 AGED 85 YEARS
ALSO THEIR SON ALAN KILLED ON ACTIVE SERVICE IN U.S.A.
31ST AUGUST 1942 AGED 19 YEARS BURIED AT MIAMI, OKLAHOMA

Leading Aircraftman Alan Brown was 19 years old when he died on 31 August 1942 and he is commemorated on Donaghadee and District War Memorial; in First Donaghadee Presbyterian Church and on the Brown family grave headstone in Ballyvester Cemetery, Donaghadee. His father Samuel died on 8 June 1971 (aged 85); his mother Jane died on 1 October 1972 (aged 85); his elder brother John died on 18 July 1984 (aged 69) and his eldest sister Jean (wife of Jack Acklam of Silsden, Yorkshire) died on 14 February 1992 (aged 71).

Brown, Alexander Scott (Alexander)
Squadron Quartermaster Sergeant
No. 7897764, North Irish Horse, Royal Armoured Corps
Killed in action on Sunday 21 March 1943 (aged 27)
Medjez-el-Bab Memorial, Tunisia (Face 4)

Alexander Scott Brown was born in 1915 in Polemont, Stirlingshire and he was a son of Alexander and Mary Brown (nee Scott, daughter of John and Mary Duff Scott). Alexander Brown Senior was a colliery inspector from Polemont when he and Mary Scott from Belfast were married on 17 July 1914 in Crescent Presbyterian Church,

Belfast. In the 17 April 1943 edition of the *County Down Spectator* it was reported that SQMS Alexander S. Brown was a son of Mr and Mrs Thomas Stockdale of 33 Princetown Road, Bangor and he was 'missing believed killed on active service' (he was Thomas's step-son).

Thomas Stockdale of 5 Geoffrey Street, Belfast worked as a labourer and Hannah Coey of 1 Keswick Street, Belfast worked as a reeler when they were married on 14 December 1913 in St. Silas's Church of Ireland Church in Belfast. They had at least four children – Elsie (born 1915); Mary (Molly); Iris (born 1920) and Thomas Norman (born 1922). They lived at *Clonfin*, Ballymaconnell, Bangor and Hannah Stockdale died there on 8 February 1926. Hannah Stockdale was buried in Belfast City Cemetery – Glenalina Extension (Grave J 120). Also buried in that grave were Ellen Stockdale of 16 Harrybrook Street, Belfast who died on 2 March 1946 and Mary Stockdale of 107 Clandeboye Road, Bangor who died on 18 February 1970. Ellen Stockdale was Thomas Stockdale's mother and Mary Stockdale was his second wife. After Hannah died, Thomas Stockdale married Alexander Scott Brown's mother, Mary Brown (nee Scott). Thomas and Mary were married on 24 September 1927 in Ballygilbert Presbyterian Church.

B

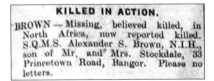

KILLED IN ACTION.

BROWN — Missing, believed killed, in North Africa, now reported killed. S.Q.M.S. Alexander S. Brown, N.I.H., son of Mr. and Mrs. Stockdale, 33 Princetown Road, Bangor. Please no letters.

Before joining the North Irish Horse at the outbreak of war Alexander Brown was employed by Messrs Norman McNaughton and Sons in Corporation Street, Belfast. The press report pointed up the fact that Alexander had a brother serving in the RAF and two sisters in the ATS. In the 29 May 1943 edition of the *County Down Spectator* there was a *Killed in Action* notice which repeated that he was a son of Mr and Mrs Stockdale of 33 Princetown Road, Bangor. Alexander Brown's half-brother was **Thomas Norman Stockdale** and he died some five months later, on 28 August 1943.

Alexander Brown's sister Mary (Molly) was married to Gunner **John Thomson** (No. 1560614), Royal Artillery and John was 29 years old when he died on 28 June 1945 at Palace Barracks, Holywood. Brothers-in-law, Thomas Norman Stockdale and John Thomson were buried in the same grave in Belfast (Dundonald) Cemetery.

NORTH IRISH HORSE
SQDN. QMR-SJT.
BROWN A.S.

On 2 February 1943 the North Irish Horse landed in Algiers and marched 17 miles to their camp. Thereafter they were involved in various actions and on 21 March 1943 Alexander Brown aged 27 was one of two men who were killed when the lorry they were travelling in was mortar bombed near Beja in Tunisia. Squadron Quartermaster Sergeant Alexander Scott Brown was buried in an unknown grave and he is commemorated on the Medjez-el-Bab Memorial; on Bangor and District War Memorial; in Wesley Centenary Methodist Church, Bangor and on the Scott family grave headstone in Belfast (Dundonald) Cemetery. Alexander Scott Brown and Thomas Norman Stockdale were grandsons of John and Mary Duff Scott. Mary Duff Scott died on 10 April 1933 (aged 66) and John Scott died on 11 November 1942 (aged 79).

Brown, Ephraim Hugh (Hughie)
Flight Lieutenant
No. 41777, 230 Squadron, Royal Air Force Volunteer Reserve
Killed on active service on Saturday 25 July 1942 (aged 24)
Alamein Memorial, Egypt (Column 247)

B

Ephraim Hugh (Hughie) Brown was born in Portaferry on 9 February 1918 and he was a son of Ephraim Hugh (Ephriam) and Elizabeth (Elsie) Brown (nee Brown) of Westgate, Portaferry. Ephriam Brown ran the family business (William Brown) in Ferry Street, Portaferry selling agricultural merchandise. He and his wife Elsie were second cousins and they were married on 17 June 1914 in St. Paul's Church of Ireland Church, Belfast. They had five children – Thomas (Tommy, born 11 October 1915); Ephriam Hugh (Hughie, born 9 February 1918); Olive Christine (Olive, born 22 July 1919); William Price (Billy, born 25 April 1921) and Richard Percival (Dickie, born 22 January 1933). During the Second World War Tommy served as an ARP Warden, Olive served with the WAAF at Ballykinlar and Billy served with the Fleet Air Arm.

Hughie Brown attended the Royal Belfast Academical Institution (RBAI) from 1930 until 1934 and after he left school he worked in the family business in Portaferry. A keen sailor, he was also an active member of the local Young Farmers' Club. In 1938 he applied to join the Royal Air Force Volunteer Reserve and travelled across to Strangford by boat for tutoring for the entrance examination. He went to Glasgow for his medical examination. Hughie was home on leave for a few days in early April 1939 before leaving for Prestwick, and then the RAF Depot at Uxbridge. He sailed to Egypt on 12 April 1939. He wrote letters home from wherever he was stationed and these letters have been preserved by his family. In one of his letters from the Flight

School in Prestwick he said that he was earning 16 shillings and sixpence (16/6) per day. His service officially commenced on 29 May 1939 and in August 1939 he wrote from No. 4 Flying Training School when he was in Abu Sueir, Egypt. He was with 33 Squadron flying Gloster Gladiator aircraft and he concluded the letter by saying that he was going to Iraq. This letter was censored and it wasn't delivered until 1946, four years after Hughie's death. In December 1939 he was with 102 Maintenance Unit in Egypt and he was being paid £1 per day. In August 1940 he was with 33 Squadron in Habbaniya (55 miles west of Baghdad) and he said that it was so hot they flew in shirts and shorts, rather than wearing flying overalls. On 30 October 1940 he was posted to 112 Squadron as a Pilot Officer and he took part in the Greek campaign, again flying Gloster Gladiators. On Christmas Eve 1940 he and some others flew from Egypt to Jerusalem and stayed in the King David Hotel at a cost of 36 shillings per day. On Christmas Day he went by taxi to Bethlehem.

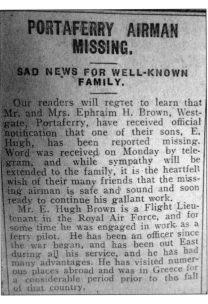

PORTAFERRY AIRMAN MISSING.

SAD NEWS FOR WELL-KNOWN FAMILY.

Our readers will regret to learn that Mr. and Mrs. Ephraim H. Brown, Westgate, Portaferry, have received official notification that one of their sons, E. Hugh, has been reported missing. Word was received on Monday by telegram, and while sympathy will be extended to the family, it is the heartfelt wish of their many friends that the missing airman is safe and sound and soon ready to continue his gallant work.

Mr. E. Hugh Brown is a Flight Lieutenant in the Royal Air Force, and for some time he was engaged in work as a ferry pilot. He has been an officer since the war began, and has been out East during all his service, and he has had many advantages. He has visited numerous places abroad and was in Greece for a considerable period prior to the fall of that country.

On 13 March 1941, still with 112 Squadron based at Sidi Haneish in Egypt and flying a Gloster Gladiator, he shot down an enemy plane in a dogfight with Italian Forces over the Kelcyre area in Albania. Two days earlier he had been credited with damaging an enemy plane. He was transferred to 230 Squadron on 14 April 1941 where he operated as a Flight Lieutenant piloting Sunderland Flying Boats. On 3 August 1942 his family received a telegram informing them that, during the night of 25/26 July, Hughie and his crew were missing in action over the Mediterranean, off the Egyptian coast. They left RAF Aboukir in Egypt aboard a Short Sunderland aircraft (L5806) to carry out an anti-submarine patrol but failed to return. Searches over the next two days found nothing. Later it was officially confirmed that Flight Lieutenant Hughie Brown (aged 24), and all the other members of the crew, must be presumed dead:

- Flight Lieutenant William Arthur Hargreaves Chapman
- Flying Officer Jack Edward Sedgwick Bentley aged 28 (RNZAF)
- Flying Officer Albert Gordon Boswell Williams aged 25 (RNZAF)

- PO Eric Ernest Thomas Cattemull aged 22 from Teddington, Middlesex
- Pilot Officer Kenneth Frederick Harding aged 28 from Gravesend, Kent
- Pilot Officer Herbert Reginald Nash aged 22 from Brockley, London
- Flight Sergeant Leonard Blashill
- Flight Sergeant Roland Lionel Manley aged 29 (SAAF)
- Sergeant William Bulman aged 26 from Aspatria, Cumberland
- Sergeant Alastair Hugh Macdonald aged 24 from Glasgow
- Sergeant Amon Riding aged 21
- Sgt Eric Sutherland Clutton Williams aged 26 from Whitstable, Kent

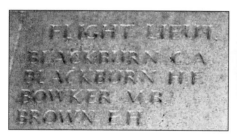 

B Flight Lieutenant Ephraim Hugh Brown is commemorated on the Alamein Memorial in Egypt; on the Valetta Memorial in Malta for airmen with no known grave; in RBAI and on a memorial plaque on one of the pews in Portaferry Methodist Church. The Brown family burying ground is in Ballymanish Cemetery, Portaferry.

Brown, John
Gunner
No. 1465501, 175 Battery, 66 Light Anti-Aircraft Regiment, Royal Artillery
Died as a result of enemy action on Monday 5 May 1941 (aged 28)
Newtownards (Movilla) Cemetery, Co. Down (Section 23 Grave 111)

John Brown was born on 21 May 1913 and he was a son of William and Ellen Brown (nee Cassidy) of 37 Greenwell Street, Newtownards. They were married on 10 October 1896 in Newtownards Parish Church of Ireland Church (St. Mark's). William Brown worked as a general labourer and he and Ellen had at least ten children including Bessie (born 20 January 1895); Hugh (born 27 November 1897, died in infancy); Margaret (Maggie, born 29 January 1899); William (born 6 April 1901); Hugh (born 23 July 1903); Matthew (born 18

June 1906); Robert (born 26 September 1910); Annie (born 18 November 1912) and John (born 21 May 1913).

John Brown and Sarah (Sadie) Wallace were married on 12 October 1934 in Newtownards Parish Church (St. Mark's), they lived at 80 East Street, Newtownards and they had three children: Edna, Wallace and Joan.

During the Second World War Gunner John Brown served with the Royal Artillery and he and Gunner **Henry Corry** died at Twin Islands, Belfast during the German Luftwaffe air raid on 5 May 1941. They were buried with military honours in Newtownards (Movilla) Cemetery on 8 May 1941.

There were *Death Notices* in the 10 and 17 May 1941 editions of the *Newtownards Chronicle* from John Brown's wife and family; his parents-in-law and family of 105a East Street, Newtownards; his father, sister and brother-in-law Maggie and William Curragh and Wee Bill of 39 Greenwell Street, Newtownards; his brothers Matthew and William (both on active service); his brother and sister-in-law Hugh and Maggie Brown of Kettering, North Hants, England; his aunt Martha in Canada; his sister and brother-in-law Bessie and William John Johnston and family of 46 Movilla Street, Newtownards; his brother and sister-in-law Robert and Eileen Brown and niece Ellen of 63 Greenwell Street, Newtownards and from the members of Lord Londonderry's CLB Flute Band, Newtownards.

B

Gunner John Brown was 28 years old when he died and he is commemorated on Newtownards and District War Memorial and in Newtownards Parish Church (St. Mark's). His wife Sadie died on 2 July 1997.

Brown, William Young (William, sometimes Billy)
Lance Corporal
No. 7686313, Intelligence Corps
Died as a result of enemy action on Wednesday 7 August 1940 (aged 24)
Brookwood Memorial, Surrey, England (Panel 21 Column 1)

William Young Brown and his twin sister Mary Young Brown were born in Dublin on 20 February 1916. William was the younger son of Thomas Watters Brown and Mary Elizabeth Brown (nee Hadden) of *Ben Ingan*, Warren Road, Donaghadee. They were married on 12 August 1913 in Rosemary Street Presbyterian Church, Belfast. In 1918 Thomas Watters Brown was elected Member of Parliament for North Down and in June 1921 he was appointed Solicitor General for

Ireland. In August 1921 he was promoted to the position of Attorney General for Ireland. He resigned that post in December 1921 and served as a Judge of the High Court of Justice in Northern Ireland from 1922 until his death on 7 October 1944. William Young Brown's mother, Mary Elizabeth Brown, died on 11 May 1976 and his twin sister Mary died in October 2005.

During the Second World War William Young Brown's older brother, James Alexander Brown, served as a Captain with the Royal Ulster Rifles (6th Airborne Division) and from 1967 until 1978 he was a County Court Judge in Co. Down. From 1978 until 1982 he was Recorder of Belfast.

DIED ON ACTIVE SERVICE.

BROWN—7th August, 1940, the result of enemy action, Lance-Corporal William Young Brown, Field Security Police, younger son of Mr. Justice and Mrs. Brown. Ben Ingan, Donaghadee.

William Young Brown was educated at Mourne Grange School, Kilkeel; at Campbell College, Belfast from 1930 until 1933; in the Sillig Institution, Vevey, Switzerland and in France. There was a short biography in the December 1940 edition of *The Campbellian*:

'Billy Brown was an outstanding example of the boy, unsuccessful at school, who does well later. Owing to an illness while at his preparatory school, he was exceptionally backward when he arrived at Campbell. He left the school at the age of 17 from the Upper Fourth and went to a school in Switzerland. There he developed a passion for languages, though previously he had been unable to put two French words together.

Returning to Ireland he served his apprenticeship in the Rope Works, but found time and energy to attend language classes four nights a week. As a result, upon leaving the Rope Works, he obtained a good post with Messrs Combe, Barbour and Company and did so well that, shortly afterwards, he was promoted to a post carrying much greater responsibility and salary than that enjoyed by the average young man of his age. He continued language studies and actually delivered a lecture in Spanish to the Spanish Society in Leeds, being billed as Senor Don W.Y. Brown.

His eyesight, which was bad, would have debarred Billy from active service, but his linguistic qualifications, due entirely to his own efforts, procured him admission to the Field Security Police, and he died by enemy action whilst serving in this Force. He would have asked no better.

Billy's attractiveness, which all who knew him felt strongly, was mainly due to the fact that he was essentially unselfish. Added to this was a quiet but very strong sense of humour. It will be long before we cease to be conscious of the gap he has left.'

Soon after returning to duty following a short period of home leave spent in Donaghadee, Billy was reported missing on 7 August 1940 after the sinking of the SS *Mohamed-Ali El-Kebir* about 250 miles west of Malin Head. This military transport ship was on route from Avonmouth to Gibraltar when she was hit by a torpedo fired from the German submarine *U-38*. Later Billy was officially presumed dead, one of around 120 who died.

Lance Corporal William Young Brown was 24 years old when he died and he is commemorated on the Brookwood Memorial in Surrey; on Donaghadee and District War Memorial; in Shore Street Presbyterian Church, Donaghadee and on the family grave headstone in Movilla Cemetery, Newtownards.

Buckingham, Ronald James (Ronald)
Driver
No. T/217710, Royal Army Service Corps
Died on active service on Monday 14 August 1944 (aged 30)
Assisi War Cemetery, Italy (Grave III C 12)

B

Ronald James Buckingham's birth was registered in the third quarter of 1914 in Edmonton, Middlesex and he was a son of Albert Ernest and Sarah Buckingham (nee Jakes) who lived at 8 Church Lane, Silver Street, Enfield, Middlesex. Albert Ernest Buckingham worked as a carter on the Great Northern Railway and his marriage to Sarah Jakes was registered in the first quarter of 1902 in Caxton, Cambridgeshire. They had at least four children – Ernest Reginald, Albert George, Frank Irvine and Ronald James. The marriage of Ronald James Buckingham and Edith Molly Kirkwood was registered in the second quarter of 1940 in Edmonton, Middlesex.

> **ROLL OF HONOUR**
>
> BUCKINGHAM—In loving memory of my husband, Driver Ronald Buckingham, R.A.S.C., killed in Italy, August 14, 1944.
> Ever remembered by his loving Wife, Molly Buckingham. —30 Osborne Park, Bangor.

During the Second World War Ronald James Buckingham served as a driver with the Royal Army Service Corps and he was 30 years old when he died in Italy on 14 August 1944 as German forces tried to stop the Allied advance. In 1946 his wife Molly was living at 30 Osborne Park, Bangor and she placed a *Roll of Honour* notice in the 17 August 1946 edition of the *County Down Spectator*.

Bulloch, Anthony Alexander Talbot (Anthony)
Flying Officer
No. 33224, 224 Squadron, Royal Air Force
Killed in action on Wednesday 24 April 1940 (aged 23)
Runnymede Memorial, Surrey, England (Panel 5)

> **Missing Ulster Air Force.**—Flight-Lieut. Anthony Bulloch, whose father, Mr. John Bulloch, resides at Orchard Hill, Craigavad, has been reported to be missing. Flight-Lieutenant Bulloch joined the R.A.F. at the age of 18, and has been serving for the past five years. His sister is the wife of District-Inspector R. E. G. Shillington, R.U.C.

Anthony Alexander Talbot Bulloch was a son of John Lytle Bulloch and Agnes Marion Evelyn Bulloch (nee Forde) of *Orchard Hill*, Craigavad. They were married on 31 December 1912 in St. Columba's Church of Ireland Church, Knock, Belfast. In 1935 Anthony's sister Mary (Peggy) married District Inspector Robert Edward Graham Shillington, Royal Ulster Constabulary (later Chief Constable Sir Graham Shillington).

Anthony Bulloch was 18 years old when he joined the Royal Air Force in 1935 and during the Second World War he served in Coastal Command. On 24 April 1940 he was one of a crew of four aboard a Lockheed Hudson Mark I aircraft (N7283). They took off from RAF Leuchars in Scotland at 5.04 am on an anti-submarine patrol and at 7.30 am they were shot down off Haakonshellen in Norway. The other crew members who died that morning were:

- Pilot Officer Robert George Meadows Harmston aged 19; his was the only body to be recovered and he was buried in Bergen (Mollendal) Church Cemetery, Norway
- Leading Aircraftman Alfred William Hallam
- Leading Aircraftman Stanley Lane

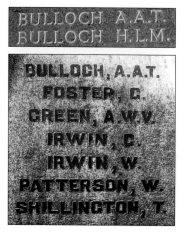

Flying Officer Anthony Alexander Talbot Bulloch was 23 years old when he died on 24 April 1940 and he is commemorated on the Runnymede Memorial in Surrey and in Glencraig Parish Church of Ireland Church, Craigavad. He was related to Trooper **Thomas Shillington** and also to Flying Officer Hugh Larmor McLearn Bulloch (No. 37788) who attended Inchmarlo Preparatory School and who is commemorated in RBAI. Flying Officer H.L.M. Bulloch served with 149 Squadron, he was killed on 2 January 1940 and he too is commemorated on the Runnymede Memorial.

Burke, Samuel

Fusilier
No. 6982708, 70ᵗʰ Battalion, Royal Inniskilling Fusiliers
Died as a result of enemy action on Wednesday 16 April 1941 (aged 18)
Londonderry City Cemetery, Co. Londonderry
(Section S Class B Grave 1218)

Fusilier Samuel Burke was a son of George and Annie Burke (nee Moore) of Braehead, Londonderry whose marriage was registered in the fourth quarter of 1917 in Londonderry. Fusilier Burke was one of 13 soldiers serving with the 70ᵗʰ Battalion, Royal Inniskilling Fusiliers who died as a result of an air raid on Newtownards aerodrome during the night of 15/16 April 1941. Fusilier **Daniel Higgins** who also died that night was buried in Newtownards (Movilla) Cemetery and under his name in this Book of Honour there is a summary of all those people with North Down or Ards connections who died that night.

B

Fusilier Samuel Burke was 18 years old when he died as a result of enemy action and there is an inscription on his CWGC headstone:

Thy purpose Lord we cannot see but all is well that's done by Thee

Burrows, Henry Garrett (Harry)

Sergeant
No. B/74471, Royal Canadian Armoured Corps
Died of illness on Thursday 11 September 1947 (aged 39)
North Toronto (St. James's) Cemetery, Ontario, Canada (Block T Lot 181)

Henry Garrett Burrows was born on 4 April 1908 and he was a son of Robert and Maggie Burrows (formerly McConnell, formerly Burrows, nee Ritchie) of 47 North Street, Newtownards. Both of his parents had previously been married; his mother Maggie's first marriage had been to his uncle (his father's brother), William Burrows.

William Burrows (a servant, full age, bachelor, son of John Burrows, Ballyhaskin, Carrowdore) and Maggie Ritchie (full age, spinster, daughter of Hamilton Ritchie, Kilbright, Carrowdore) were married on 7 May 1886 in Ballycopeland Presbyterian Church. Maggie had six children before

William died – Mary Elizabeth (born 17 June 1883); Margaret Jane (born 17 November 1887); James Charles (born 1 August 1890, died of wounds on 29 March 1918 and commemorated on Page 133 in the Book of Honour *Remembering Their Sacrifice in the Great War – Ards* compiled by Barry Niblock); Robert (born 31 December 1892); Sarah (born 14 April 1895) and Agnes McConnell (born 22 June 1897). On 22 March 1897, three months before Agnes was born, William Burrows was found drowned in Spencer Basin, Dufferin Dock, Belfast. He was 36 years old.

In 1901 the widowed Maggie Burrows (aged 35 and working as a hand embroiderer) was living in Ballyfrenis with five of her children – Mary Eliza, James Charles, Robert, Sarah and Agnes. All belonged to the United Free Church of Scotland. Also living in the townland of Ballyfrenis in 1901 was William Burrows's brother Robert Burrows (a labourer aged 47), his wife Maggie (nee Menagh, a seamstress aged 42) and six of their children – William John, David, Robert, James, Mary (Minnie) and Charles. All belonged to the United Free Church of Scotland. Robert Burrows and Margaret (Maggie) Menagh were married on 13 December 1880 in Newtownards Registry Office and they had nine children – Eliza (born 19 December 1881); William John (born 1884); David (born 7 August 1886); Robert (born 26 August 1888); James (born 15 July 1890); Mary (Minnie, born 9 March 1893); Charles (born 31 August 1895); Maggie (born 10 May 1899) and Samuel (born 27 September 1903). Maggie Burrows (nee Menagh) died on 12 March 1905 (aged 46).

Robert Burrows (a labourer, full age, widower, living at 108 Jocelyn Street, Belfast, son of John Burrows) and Maggie McConnell (full age, widow, living at 108 Jocelyn Street, Belfast, daughter of Hamilton Ritchie) were married on 12 February 1906 in St. Patrick's Church of Ireland Church, Ballymacarrett, Belfast. They had three children – Matilda (born 10 August 1906), Henry Garrett (Harry, born 4 April 1908, birth registered 25 January 1927) and Ethel (born 31 July 1910).

In 1911 Robert Burrows (a labourer aged 59) and his wife Maggie (a hand embroiderer aged 46), were living in Ballyfrenis with ten children. Four were children of Robert and Maggie Burrows (nee Menagh) – David, James, Minnie and Samuel; three were children of William and Maggie Burrows (nee Ritchie) – Maggie Jane, Sarah and Agnes; three were children of Robert and Maggie Burrows (formerly McConnell, formerly Burrows, nee Ritchie) – Matilda, Harry and Ethel May. All belonged to the United Free Church of Scotland.

On 27 March 1926 half-brothers Samuel and Harry Burrows sailed from Belfast to Halifax, Nova Scotia aboard the SS *Alaunia*. They arrived on

B

4 April 1926 on their way to Toronto to live and work. Harry's father, Robert Burrows, died on 18 February 1929 (aged 75) and his mother, Maggie Burrows, died on 17 September 1949 (aged 85). Maggie's daughter, Ethel Beattie of 47 North Street, Newtownards, was present at her death.

Henry Garrett (Harry) Burrows was the husband of Margaret Burrows (nee Harper) of 204 First Avenue, Toronto. During the Second World War Sergeant Henry Garrett (Harry) Burrows served with the Royal Canadian Armoured Corps and he was 39 years old when he died of 'a metastatic carcinoma due to service' on 11 September 1947. He was buried in North Toronto (St. James's) Cemetery and when his wife died in 1981 she was buried there too. Their headstones lie flat on the grave and both bear the inscription:

Some day we will understand

Sergeant Henry Garrett (Harry) Burrows is commemorated on the Canadian Virtual War Memorial and on Page 594 in the Canadian Second World War Book of Remembrance.

B

Byers, Patrick Joseph Anthony (Pat)
Flight Lieutenant
No. 40078, 451 (RAAF) Squadron, Royal Air Force
Killed on active service on Saturday 20 September 1941 (aged 25)
Benghazi War Cemetery, Libya (Grave 8 E 17)

KILLED ON ACTIVE SERVICE.

BYERS—Previously reported wounded, prisoner of war, Middle East, Flight Lieutenant Pat. J. A. Byers, only and dearly-loved son of John A. and Lily Byers (nee Boyd), Capetown, South Africa, died September last, Interred at Derna.
Deeply regretted.

Patrick Joseph Anthony Byers was born in South Africa and he was the only son of John Alexander Byers and Elizabeth Jane (Lily) Byers (nee Boyd). In accordance with a special licence granted by the Revd John Macmillan, Moderator of the General Assembly of the Presbyterian Church in Ireland, they were married on 11 December 1911 in the house of the bride's father, Anthony Boyd, who farmed in the townland of Ballyhaskin, Carrowdore. John Alexander Byers was a commercial traveller (wholesale drapery) from East Street in Newtownards (his mother Euphemia was widowed; his father, James had been a contractor).

John Alexander Byers travelled regularly to South Africa in connection with his work and, from 1902 onwards, there are records of his voyages, mostly from and to Southampton, aboard various ships including SS *Guscon*, SS *Briton* and SS *Balmoral Castle*. He arrived in Southampton on 10 June 1911 and, after his marriage on 11 December 1911, he and his wife travelled to Capetown aboard SS *Kenilworth Castle* on 16 December 1911. They settled in Cape Town and when they came back to Britain, as they did regularly, they stayed at *Hillside*, Ballyhaskin. In the 1920s Patrick was with them when they travelled aboard various ships including SS *Balmoral Castle*, SS *Kenilworth Castle*, SS *Windsor Castle*, SS *Dunbar Castle* and SS *Carnarvon Castle*.

In the 1930s Patrick Joseph Anthony Byers joined the RAF and he was promoted to the rank of Pilot Officer on 14 August 1938. In the 22 November 1941 edition of the *Newtownards Chronicle* it was reported that Flight Lieutenant Patrick Joseph Anthony Byers had been wounded and was being held as a Prisoner-of-War. In 1940 he had visited his uncles and aunts in the Ards area – Joseph Byers of Newtownards, Mrs T.H. Kerr of Newtownards, Alexander Boyd of Ballyhaskin, Andrew Boyd of Ballyhaskin and Mrs William Boyle of Mountpleasant, Ganaway, Millisle. In January 1942 it was confirmed that he had been killed on active service and his family placed a *Killed on Active Service* notice in the 24 January 1942 edition of the *Newtownards Chronicle*. His effects in England amounted to some £377 and his last address was recorded as Capetown. He was 25 years old when he died.

B

Byers, Robert
Private
No. 5335137, 2nd Battalion, Royal Berkshire Regiment
Died as a result of an accident on Wednesday 4 March 1942 (aged 27)
Kirkee War Cemetery, India (Grave 7 B 8)

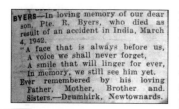

BYERS—In loving memory of our dear son, Pte. R. Byers, who died as result of an accident in India, March 4, 1942.
"A face that is always before us,
A voice we shall never forget,
A smile that will linger for ever,
In memory, we still see him yet.
Ever remembered by his loving Father, Mother, Brother and Sisters.—Drumhirk, Newtownards.

Robert Byers was a son of Andrew and Agnes Byers (nee Murdock) of Thomastown, Portaferry and later Drumhirk, Newtownards. Andrew Byers worked as a labourer and he and Agnes Murdock were married on 23 February 1909 in Newtownards Registry Office. Their first child was a daughter named Isabella who was born in 1910.

Robert Byers was a career soldier and he was 27 years old when he died in India on 4 March 1942 as a result of an accident. His father, mother, brother and sisters placed a *Died on Active Service* notice in the 6 March edition of the *Newtownards Chronicle* and *In Memoriam* notices in subsequent years. The one in 1944 contained the verse:

A face that is always before us, a voice we shall never forget,
A smile that will linger for ever, in memory, we still see him yet

Cairnduff, Thomas (see Carnduff, Thomas)
Callister, Douglas (see Collister, Douglas)

Calvert, Hans
Signalman
D/JX 229549, HMS *Tamar*, Royal Navy
Killed on board the SS *Lisbon Maru* on Friday 2 October 1942 (aged 26)
Plymouth Naval Memorial, Devon (Panel 67 Column 3)

Hans Calvert's birth was registered in the first quarter of 1916 in Belfast and he was a son of Thomas Matthews Calvert and Sarah Jane Calvert (nee Lappin). Thomas Matthews Calvert was born on 30 December 1890 and baptised in Raffrey Presbyterian Church. The Calvert family lived in the townland of Tullyveery, Killyleagh and Thomas worked as a grocery assistant before he moved to 44 Glencollyer Street in Belfast to work as a bread server. Sarah Jane Lappin lived at 267 Skegoniell Avenue, Belfast and she and Thomas Calvert were married on 3 December 1913 in Jennymount Methodist Church, Belfast. Later Thomas and Sarah Calvert lived in Killinchy Street, Comber and they had at least four children – Thomas, Hans, Grace and Alex.

Hans Calvert joined the Royal Navy in 1940 and it was reported in the press that he had been home on leave in April/May 1941. At that time his brother Alex was serving with the RAF in India. Signalman Hans Calvert was stationed for a time at HMS *Tamar* which was the Royal Navy's shore base in Hong Kong from 1897 until 1997.

The *Lisbon Maru* was a Japanese freighter used by Japanese Forces as a troopship and Prisoner-of-War transport ship between China and Japan. When she was sunk in the China Sea by USS *Grouper* on 1 October 1942 the *Lisbon Maru* was carrying Japanese Army personnel and around 1,800 British Prisoners-of-War from Hong Kong – including Signalman Hans Calvert. The *Lisbon Maru* was not displaying appropriate markings to indicate that she was carrying Prisoners-of-War and more than 800 of those on board perished. USS *Grouper* was an American submarine built in Connecticut, commissioned in February 1942 and sold for scrap in 1970.

Signalman Hans Calvert was 26 years old when he died and he is commemorated on Plymouth Naval Memorial; on Comber and District War Memorial and in Second Comber Presbyterian Church. A reunion of *Lisbon Maru* survivors was held on 2 October 2007 aboard HMS *Belfast,* a museum ship moored on the River Thames in London and operated by the Imperial War Museum.

Calvert, Harold William
Private
No. K/93200, Veterans Guard of Canada
Died of illness on Thursday 15 July 1943 (aged 50)
Somenos (St. Mary's) Church Cemetery, British Columbia, Canada

In the CWGC Debt of Honour it is recorded that Harold William Calvert was a son of Isabel Calvert of Bangor. He was born on 15 December 1892 in Belfast (in attestation records the year of his birth is recorded in one place as 1888 and in another as 1889) and he was a son of Leonard and Isabella (Isabel) Calvert (nee Creaney) who were married on 6 October 1871 in Moira Methodist Church, Co. Down. Leonard Calvert was a Civil Engineer and he worked as a Land Surveyor and Valuer. He and Isabella had 13 children – two daughters born 18 September 1872 and 24 April 1874; Rebecca (born 26 February 1876); Frederick (born 5 March 1878); Florence (born 10 February 1880); Helen Victoria (born 1882); James Edward (born 1884); Albert Leonard (born 1 November 1885); Thomas (born 3 December 1887); George Walter born 20 October 1889); Edith Isabel (born 3 November 1891); Harold William (born 15 December 1892) and Edwin Arthur Peel (born 2 January 1895). The Calvert family lived at *Polnoon,* Strandtown, Co. Down and Leonard Calvert died on 21 July 1899 (aged 50). He was buried in Belfast City Cemetery (Grave L 1 387) and probate of his will was granted to his widow Isabella. Later Isabella Calvert moved to 18 Clifton Road, Bangor where she died on 17 February 1950 aged 99. She was buried in Belfast City Cemetery in the same grave as her husband.

In 1901 the Calvert family was living in Holywood Road, Belfast and in 1911 Harold William Calvert was living in Coleraine Road, Portstewart. When he moved to Canada in 1912 he sailed from Glasgow to St. John aboard the SS *Athenia* and he recorded his occupation as an insurance

C

clerk. In September 1914 he joined the Canadian Army. He and Edith Annie Johnston (born in Ireland and living in Duncan, British Columbia) were married in Dublin in the fourth quarter of 1914 and they had a son named John Harold Knowles (Jack) Calvert (born 3 May 1916 in London, England). On 24 July 1919 Edith and her three year old son travelled from Liverpool to Halifax, Nova Scotia aboard the White Star Liner *Adriatic*. Jack was educated at the University School in Victoria, British Columbia where he was a keen sportsman.

During the Second World War Lieutenant John Harold Knowles (Jack) Calvert (No. 72794) served with 59 Field Company, Royal Engineers and he died on 10 October 1940 (aged 24) at Brompton Barracks, Chatham. His home address was recorded as Bishops Waltham, Hampshire and his effects amounted to some £616. His cremated remains were buried in Belfast City Cemetery (Section I Grave 53) on 26 October 1940 alongside William McVicker of 17 Claremont Street, Belfast (died 7 March 1914 aged 53). Buried in the adjacent grave (Grave 54) were William Robert McVicker (born 1 September 1883, died 24 August 1950 aged 62) and Hilda Sismey McVicker (died 3 February 1977 aged 94). In the CWGC Debt of Honour it is recorded that Jack Calvert's wife was Hilda Sismey Calvert. Her maiden name was McVicker, she was born in Belfast in 1916 and she was a daughter of William Robert and Hilda Sismey McVicker (nee Mundell) who were married on 27 December 1913 in Bishop Auckland, Co. Durham.

C

During the First World War Private Harold William Calvert (No. 28898) served with the 16th Battalion, Canadian Scottish, 1st Division, Canadian Expeditionary Force (CEF) from 1914 until he was demobilised at the Canadian Discharge Depot in Buxton, Derbyshire in July 1919. While serving in France he contracted rheumatic fever. He re-enlisted in August 1919 and during the Second World War Private Calvert served until 22 April 1943 in Canada only. He was discharged as medically unfit and was 50 years old when he died of heart block and pneumonia on 15 July 1943. It was officially confirmed that his death was due to service. He was awarded service medals from both World Wars – the War Medal 1939-45, the Canadian Volunteer Service Medal and Clasp, the 1914-15 Star, the British War Medal and the Victory Medal.

Private Harold William Calvert is commemorated on the Canadian Virtual War Memorial (Internet) and on Page 143 of the Canadian Second World War Book of Remembrance (his son Jack on Page 11).

Cameron, Cyril Charles (Cyril)
Aircraftman 2nd Class (Pilot U/T)
No. 3225065, Royal Air Force Volunteer Reserve
Died as a result of an accident on Sunday 22 October 1944 (aged 19)
Bangor Cemetery, Co. Down (Section 4 V Grave 86)

The youngest of four brothers, Cyril Charles Cameron was born on 4 July 1925 and he was a son of Hugh and Alice Eleanor Cameron (nee Dodd) of 22 Donaghadee Road, Bangor. Hugh Cameron from Belfast was a warehouseman and he and Alice Eleanor Dodd from Bangor were married on 20 February 1918 in Broadway Presbyterian Church, Belfast. After attending Bangor Central Public Elementary School, Cyril Cameron attended Bangor Grammar School from 1938 until 1943. In his final year he won the special prize awarded annually by Lord Bangor, Chairman of the Board of Governors, to the best all-round boy in character, work and games. He was a fine athlete and captained the 1st XV rugby team. He was a member of 4th Bangor (Trinity) Boy's Brigade and he was a member of the Bangor Flight ATC where his prowess in the art of gliding won him the distinction of being the first ATC cadet in Northern Ireland to get his wings as a glider pilot.

> CAMERON—October 22, 1944, at Grimsby, Cadet Cyril Charles Cameron, youngest son of Mrs. Alice E. Cameron and the late Mr. Hugh Cameron, 22 Donaghadee Road, Bangor. Funeral from above address to Bangor New Cemetery, on Saturday, 28th October, at 3 p.m. House strictly private. No flowers.

Cyril Cameron joined the Royal Air Force Volunteer Reserve straight from school in September 1943 and he was undergoing training in England when he was killed. He was 19 years old when he died in Grimsby Hospital on 22 October 1944 from injuries sustained in the accidental explosion of an incendiary bomb. At the inquest a verdict of death due to misadventure was recorded. Giving evidence, Air Cadet Ladzris said that he (Ladzris) had picked up an incendiary bomb in the bombing dump, intending to put it on the stock. It slipped and, when it hit the ground, ignited. Cadet Ladzris picked up the bomb, carried it out of the hut, placed it on the road and placed a container over it. The container ignited and, not being aware that the bomb was explosive, Cyril Cameron used a stick to turn over the container and rake the burning bomb into it – with the intention of moving the bomb into the field. He had just lifted the container when the bomb exploded and he was blown bodily into the air. A doctor pronounced the cause of death to be 'shock due to the injuries received'.

Aircraftman 2nd Class Cyril Charles Cameron was buried in Bangor Cemetery and the mourners at his funeral included RAF personnel, teaching staff and boys from Bangor Grammar School, his brothers Hugh, W. and S.E. Cameron, his uncles S. and C. Cameron and his cousin W.G. Wilson. There is an inscription on his CWGC headstone:

In loving memory of Cyril
Died on active service

Aircraftman 2nd Class Cyril Cameron is commemorated on Bangor and District War Memorial; in Trinity Presbyterian Church, Bangor and in Bangor Grammar School. His brother Hugh was serving with the RAFVR in England.

Campbell Brothers, Alexander and James (Jimmy)

The deaths of Alexander and James Campbell on active service during the Second World War are commemorated on the Campbell family grave headstone in Comber Cemetery. Alexander and James Campbell were sons of James and Jane Seeds Campbell (nee Martin) of 24 Woodlee Street, Belfast and then 25 Brownlow Street, Comber. Jane Seeds Martin was born on 12 August 1883 and she was a daughter of Moses and Jane Martin (nee Seeds) who were married on 30 March 1878. James Campbell was a hackle maker and he and Jane Martin were married on 30 April 1904 in Woodvale Presbyterian Church, Belfast. They had at least six children – Jane (born 20 December 1904); James (born 20 May 1906); John Samuel (born 28 December 1907); Sarah (born 26 December 1909); Ellen (born 3 March 1912) and Alexander (born around 1922). Other Campbell deaths are also commemorated on the headstone in Comber Cemetery: Elsie died on 10 April 1929 (aged 0); Margaret died on 24 November 1932 (aged 22) and Albert died on 28 May 1945 (aged 20). James Campbell Senior died on 31 March 1952 (aged 70) and Jane Seeds Campbell died on 28 January 1969.

Campbell, Alexander
Sergeant (Wireless Operator/Air Gunner)
No. 974217, 50 Squadron, Royal Air Force Volunteer Reserve
Killed in an aircraft accident on Wednesday 18 June 1941 (aged 19)
Hatfield (Woodhouse) Cemetery, Yorkshire, England (Row EE Grave 20)

On 18 June 1941 Alexander Campbell was one of a crew of five aboard a Handley Page Hampden Mark I aircraft (P4389) that took off from RAF Lindholme in Yorkshire at 6.50 pm to carry out an air test. Almost immediately after take-off the aircraft crashed into a field beyond the airfield and everyone on board was killed. The other crew members who died that day were:

- Sergeant Lawrence Rex Hinde aged 20 from Lymington, Hampshire (his brother Michael Dounis Hinde also died in service)
- Corporal Morris Ernest Balkin from Langside, Glasgow
- Leading Aircraftman Harry Barton aged 26 from Bacup, Lancashire
- AC2 Class Percy Charles Kemp aged 26 from Worthing, Sussex

Sergeant Alexander Campbell was 19 years old when he died and he was buried in Hatfield (Woodhouse) Cemetery, Yorkshire. There is an inscription on his CWGC headstone:

> *Just two little words*
> *They mean so much*
> *Our Son*

Campbell, James (Jimmy)
Sergeant
No. K/53057, General List, Canadian Army
Killed in action on Thursday 20 July 1944 (aged 38)
Bretteville-sur-Laize Canadian War Cemetery, Calvados, France (Grave X D 4)

James Campbell was born on 20 May 1906 in Belfast and he lived in Comber with his parents until 6 April 1929 when he moved to Canada. He travelled from Belfast to Halifax, Nova Scotia aboard the Cunard liner SS *Scythia* and after living for a time in Winnipeg he moved to the United States. In his Petition for Naturalisation dated 21 March 1938 in which he sought permanent residency in the United States he declared that he was a utility worker living at 3415½

Bellevue Avenue, Los Angeles, California and he was the husband of Alice Leah Mary Campbell (nee Byrd). In 1929 he had declared his occupation to be a hackle setter – he set and maintained the pins in a hackle (comb) which was a toothed instrument used in linen making. Alice Byrd was a daughter of John Henry and Sarah Hannah Byrd (nee Roper), she was born on 13 June 1911 in Winnipeg and she and James Campbell were married on 26 September 1936 in Eagle Rock, California. Alice had entered the United States on 18 September 1936 at Noyes, Minnesota and at the time of the Petition they had no children. James Campbell entered the United States on 9 November 1929 at Blaine in Washington State from Vancouver in British Columbia, Canada.

James Campbell enlisted on 20 February 1940 in Vancouver and he served with the Canadian Army. He was 38 years old when he was killed during the Allied thrust southwards from Caen to close the Falaise Gap and he was buried in Bretteville-sur-Laize Canadian War Cemetery in France. James was awarded the following service medals – the 1939-1945 Star, the France and Germany Star, the Italy Star, the Defence Medal, the War Medal (1939-45) and the Canadian Volunteer Service Medal. He is commemorated on the Canadian Virtual War Memorial (Internet); on Page 266 of the Canadian Second World War Book of Remembrance and there is an inscription on the Campbell family grave headstone in Comber Cemetery:

My peace I give unto you

Campbell, Hugh Conway (Hugh)
Captain
SS *Miriam Thomas*, Merchant Navy
Lost at sea, supposed drowned, on Sunday 15 March 1942 (aged 53)

Hugh Conway Campbell was born on 17 May 1889 (in some records, 16 May) at Ballycopeland, Co. Down and he was a son of William John and Grace Campbell (nee Fitzsimmons). William John Campbell from Ballybarnes, Newtownards worked as a labourer and he and Grace Fitzsimmons (aged 19) were married on 31 August 1886 in Newtownards Registry Office. They had four children – Hugh Conway (born 17 May 1889); Mather (born 22 January 1891); David (born 28 October 1893) and a male child (born 11 May 1899). William John Campbell died and on 7 June 1913 Grace Campbell (nee Fitzsimmons) married James Mennis (a widower from Mill Street, Newtownards who worked as a labourer) in Newtownards Registry Office.

Hugh Conway Campbell and District Nurse Zillah O'Neill (nee Gunning) were married on 23 June 1923 in Christ Church, Carrowdore. Zillah's first husband John O'Neill was killed in action during the First World War and he is commemorated on Page 489 in the Book of Honour *Remembering Their Sacrifice in the Great War – Ards* compiled by Barry Niblock. John and Zillah O'Neill had two daughters, Mary Jane (Molly, born 23 October 1911) and Johnina (Joan, born 17 October 1915).

Hugh Conway Campbell was a Master Mariner and he and Zillah had two daughters, both of whom were born in Bangor – Dorothy (born 9 June 1925) and Rhoda (born 21 August 1926, died 8 May 2004). Hugh and Zillah Campbell and their children moved to Ballywalter. Hugh's stepdaughter, Molly O'Neill, died of pulmonary infection and heart failure on 31 December 1930 aged 19; his wife Zillah died of influenza on 13 May 1931 aged 40 and his other stepdaughter, Joan O'Neill, died of pulmonary tuberculosis on 18 September 1931 aged 15. Within a period of nine months Hugh Campbell lost his wife and both of his stepdaughters. All three were buried in the same grave in Whitechurch Cemetery, Ballywalter. After their mother's death, Dorothy and Rhoda Campbell lived with relatives in Denbigh in Wales.

C

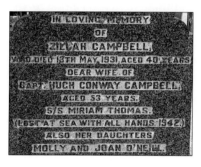

Hugh Conway Campbell was 5 feet 7 inches tall and he had an anchor tattooed on his left hand. During the Second World War he served in the Merchant Navy as Captain aboard the SS *Miriam Thomas*. Built in 1920 by Colby Brothers Ltd., Lowestoft, this cargo ship was owned by the Carriers Shipping Company, Liverpool. On the night of 15 March 1942 Captain Hugh Conway Campbell was one of at least seven men who lost their lives when the SS *Miriam Thomas* sank some seven miles south of Chicken Rocks. She sank after a collision with the Admiralty Hospital Ship *Vasna* which was on route from Barry Roads in Wales to Ponta Delgado in Portugal. A subsequent enquiry into the sinking held that the *Vasna* alone was to blame. There was no negligence on the part of the *Miriam Thomas*.

In the Register of Deceased Seamen seven men who were aboard the SS *Miriam Thomas* were listed as 'supposed drowned' – Hugh Campbell (Master), Harry Owen Roberts (Mate); Joseph Balmer (Engineer), Tommy Hill (Second Engineer), John Mulhall (Fireman), Howell Roberts (AB) and Cornelius Glavin (AB). These seven men who died aboard the SS *Miriam*

Thomas are not included in the CWGC Debt of Honour. Captain Hugh Conway Campbell was 53 years old when he died and he is commemorated on the family grave headstone in Whitechurch Cemetery, Ballywalter. His effects amounted to some £35 and probate was granted to the journalist David Edward Pryce Roberts and his wife Annie Ruby Roberts.

Campbell, Ian Alexander Calthrop (Ian)
Flying Officer (Pilot)
No. 127887, 111 Squadron, Royal Air Force Volunteer Reserve
Died attempting to escape on Thursday 9 December 1943 (aged 21)
Sangro River War Cemetery, Italy (Grave XI C 7)

Ian Alexander Calthrop (Ian) Campbell was born in Bengal, India on 2 November 1922 and he was the younger son of Major General James Alexander Campbell DSO (born 3 December 1886) and Violet Constance Madeline Campbell (nee Calthrop). James Alexander Campbell was divorced when he and Violet Calthrop were married on 16 July 1920 in Lansdowne, Bengal. James Campbell had been in the Suffolk Regiment when he and Freda Massingberd Leith-Hay Clark were married on 1 June 1911 in the Parish Church of St. Peter, Pimlico in London. James and Violet Campbell had two sons – Gordon Thomas Calthrop (born 8 June 1921 in Quetta, India) and Ian Alexander Calthrop (born 2 November 1922). Major General James Alexander Campbell DSO retired in 1944 and he died on 3 February 1964. Violet Constance Madeline Campbell died in 1978.

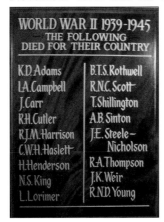

Ian Campbell and his brother Gordon both attended Rockport School, Craigavad and at that time the family address was Rush Park in Whitehouse, Co. Antrim. After leaving Rockport, Ian Campbell attended Wellington College in Berkshire where he won the Gibson Medal for physical training and the Pender Prize for Natural History. He became a Prefect, he played hockey for the school and when he left he was Second-in-Command of the ATC. In 1936 he went to RAF Valley in Anglesey and he trained at Cambridge and in the United States. He served in Malta and Italy.

Gordon Thomas Calthrop Campbell MC also served during the Second World War and after a bullet severed his sciatic nerve he was partially disabled for the rest of his life. He followed a diplomatic and then a political career becoming Secretary of State for Scotland in Prime Minister Edward Heath's Conservative Government. He was appointed to the House of Lords as Baron Campbell of Croy and he died in 2005.

Flying Officer Ian Alexander Calthrop Campbell was a Spitfire pilot and he died on 9 December 1943 after being shot while trying to escape from his German captors. He had been captured after he baled out of his aircraft when it was burning out of control over Italy. Flying Officer Ian Alexander Calthrop Campbell was 21 years old when he died and he is commemorated in Rockport School.

Campbell, John Bennett (John)
Trooper
No. 7012451, 43rd (2/5th Battalion Gloucestershire Rgt.) Regiment, Reconnaissance Corps, RAC
Died of wounds on Monday 7 August 1944 (aged 28)
La Bigne Churchyard, Calvados, France

C

John Bennett (John) Campbell's birth was registered in the first quarter of 1917 in Newtownards and he was a son of James and Margaret Campbell of Newtownards. John's father James was killed in action during the First World War when John was only six months old. James Campbell is commemorated on Page 144 in the Book of Honour *Remembering Their Sacrifice in the Great War – Ards* compiled by Barry Niblock. James Campbell aged 23 of Clandeboye (he was in the Army) and Margaret (Maggie) Reid of Newtownards were married on 21 May 1915 in Newtownards Parish Church of Ireland Church (St. Mark's). Family sources have indicated that Maggie had previously been married to George McAlpine and they had a son named George. James and Maggie Campbell had two children, John Bennett and Frederick, and, after James died, Maggie married John Graham and they lived at 13 West Street, Newtownards. Maggie and John Graham had eight children – James (born 1920, died in infancy); Matilda (born 1921); James (born 1923); Agnes (born 1925); Hugh (born 1927); Martha (born 1929; William (Bill, born 1932) and Daniel (Danny, born 1933).

John Bennett Campbell was the husband of Olive Campbell (nee Hutton) of Cowper Road, Harpenden in Hertfordshire. Their marriage was registered in the first quarter of 1941 in St. Albans, Hertfordshire and they had one child, Margaret R., whose birth was registered in the fourth quarter of 1941 in St. Albans.

John Bennett Campbell joined the Royal Ulster Rifles in 1934 and when he died he was with the 43rd (2nd/5th Battalion Gloucestershire Regiment) Regiment, Reconnaissance Corps, RAC. Having seen service in China, Palestine and elsewhere, Trooper John Bennett Campbell died of wounds just ten days before completion of ten years service. He was 28 years old when he was killed during the Allied thrust southwards from Caen to close the Falaise Gap.

There were three *Killed in Action* notices in the 2 September 1944 edition of the *Newtownards Chronicle,* one from his wife Olive and his mother Maggie Graham of 13 West Street, Newtownards; one from his aunt Lily and uncle Robert McCandless and his three cousins (all on active service) and one from his cousins Ruby and John Hamilton (Merchant Navy) and family of 203 Mill Street, Newtownards. They bore the following verses:

> *A silent thought, a hidden tear keeps his memory ever dear*
> *We shall always remember him smiling*

Trooper John Bennett Campbell is commemorated on Newtownards and District War Memorial; in Newtownards Parish Church (St. Mark's) and in Harpenden Methodist Church.

Campbell, John Gordon (known as Ian)

Flight Sergeant (Navigator)
No. 1489683, 619 Squadron, Royal Air Force Volunteer Reserve
Killed in action on Friday 24 March 1944 (aged 30)
Berlin 1939-1945 War Cemetery, Berlin, Germany
(Collective Grave 8 J 11-12)

John Gordon (Ian) Campbell was born on 7 September 1913 and he was the younger son of Samuel and Jane Moffet Campbell (nee Armstrong) of 106 Seacliff Road, Bangor. Samuel Campbell was a draper whose business was at 36/38 Main Street, Bangor. Samuel Campbell and Jane Armstrong from Ballysallagh were married on 5 October 1910 in Conlig Presbyterian Church. Jane Armstrong's brother, William Wilberforce Armstrong, was killed in action during the First World War and he is commemorated on Page 79 in the Book of Honour *Remembering Their Sacrifice in the Great War – North Down* compiled by Barry Niblock.

John Gordon (Ian) Campbell's elder brother, William Armstrong Campbell (Billy, born 26 September 1911), was a well-known swimmer and his sister Elsie married Captain Alastair Leggat who served with the Royal Artillery. John Gordon Campbell was enrolled in Bangor Grammar School as Ian

Gordon Campbell and he was described by the Headmaster as 'a bright and apt pupil'. He attended the School from 1923 until 1929 when he passed the Northern Ireland Junior Certificate with three credits. Before joining the Royal Air Force Volunteer Reserve in 1940 he worked in Short and Harland's in Belfast. He was well-known in amateur radio circles and he was a member of Ballyholme Yacht Club.

After joining up, John Gordon (Ian) Campbell went to England and from there to Canada for training. On 24 March 1944 he was one of a seven man crew that took off at 6.53 pm from RAF Coningsby in Lincolnshire in an Avro Lancaster Mark I aircraft (DV328) on a mission to bomb Berlin. The aircraft crashed south of Teltow (part of the agglomeration of Berlin) and all aboard were killed. They were all buried in Berlin 1939-1945 War Cemetery. In addition to Flight Sergeant John Gordon (Ian) Campbell the other six crew members who died were:

- Pilot Officer Paul Thompson aged 29 (RNZAF)
- Sergeant Bernard Francis Gratwicke
- FO Joseph Vincent Leyland aged 21 from Preston, Lancashire
- Sergeant John Desmond Pedley
- Sergeant Leonard Minshull aged 29 from Liverpool
- Flight Sergeant James Hay aged 32 (RAAF)

C

More than 70 British aircraft were lost that night.

 Flight Sergeant John Gordon (Ian) Campbell was 30 years old when he died and he is commemorated on Bangor and District War Memorial; in Trinity Presbyterian Church, Bangor; in Bangor Grammar School and on the family grave headstone in Bangor Cemetery. His mother Jane died on 20 June 1946 and his father Samuel died on 27 February 1976 (aged 93).

Canavan, William James
Barber
SS *Britannia* (Glasgow), Merchant Navy
Died as a result of enemy action on Tuesday 25 March 1941 (aged 47)
Tower Hill Memorial, London (Panel 19)

William James Canavan was born on 10 March 1894 in Belfast and he was a son of James and Mary Canavan (nee Convery). In the CWGC Debt of Honour he is described as a nephew of Sarah M. Mullan of Portaferry. James

Canavan of 28 Institution Place, Belfast worked as a labourer; Mary Convery of 48 Raglan Street, Belfast worked as a printer and they were married on 15 April 1893 in St. Peter's Roman Catholic Church, Belfast. As a child, William James Canavan lived with his widowed maternal grandmother Mary Convery and his aunt Sarah Convery in New Row, Portaferry.

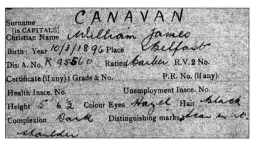

Described in maritime records as being 5 feet 6½ inches tall with hazel eyes, black hair, a dark complexion and having a scar on his right shoulder he worked as a barber and during the Second World War he served aboard the passenger vessel SS *Britannia*. Built by Alexander Stephen and Sons, Glasgow, this ship of the Anchor Line was launched in December 1925. During the Second World War SS *Britannia* operated as a troop ship and on 11 March 1941 she set sail from Liverpool with both service personnel and paying passengers aboard. They were headed initially for Freetown in Sierra Leone. Some 750 miles west of Freetown, SS *Britannia* was intercepted and sunk by the German auxiliary cruiser *Thor*. There were approximately 500 passengers and crew members aboard and Barber William James Canavan aged 47 was one of around 250 people who died. One of the SS *Britannia* lifeboats reached the coast of Brazil after some 23 days at sea.

In the Register of Deceased Seamen William James Canavan's last place of abode is recorded as 147 Reidvale Street, Glasgow and he is commemorated on the Tower Hill Memorial in London.

Cannon, Edward Dennis
Flight Sergeant (Pilot)
No. 403424, 504 (RAF) Squadron, Royal New Zealand Air Force
Killed in an aircraft accident on Monday 9 February 1942 (aged 25)
Stoneykirk Cemetery, Wigtownshire, Scotland (Section C Grave 134)

Edward Dennis Cannon's birth was registered in the second quarter of 1916 in Kaponga, Taranaki, North Island, New Zealand. He was married in New Zealand in 1941. During the Second World War Edward Dennis Cannon from Stratford, Taranaki served with the Royal New Zealand Air Force.

On 9 February 1942 Flight Sergeant (Pilot) Edward Dennis Cannon of 504 (RAF) Squadron based at RAF Ballyhalbert took off from RAF Kirkistown in a Supermarine Spitfire aircraft (P8576) which developed an engine cooling problem and had to be abandoned over the sea west of Stranraer. Flight Sergeant Edward Dennis Cannon baled out but did not survive. His body was later washed ashore and he was buried south of Stranraer in Stoneykirk Cemetery, Wigtownshire. He was 25 years old when he was killed and he is commemorated on the Taranaki Roll of Honour; on the New Zealand Fighter Pilots' Roll of Honour; on the New Zealand National War Memorial in Wellington and on the New Zealand Cenotaph Database in Auckland War Memorial Museum.

Carlisle, Alexander
Lance Corporal
No. 6984668, 70th Battalion, Royal Inniskilling Fusiliers
Died as a result of enemy action on Wednesday 16 April 1941 (aged 19)
Brookwood Memorial, Surrey, England (Panel 11 Column 2)

Lance Corporal Alexander Carlisle was one of 13 soldiers serving with the 70th Battalion, Royal Inniskilling Fusiliers who died as a result of an air raid on Newtownards aerodrome during the night of 15/16 April 1941. Fusilier **Daniel Higgins** who also died that night was buried in Newtownards (Movilla) Cemetery and under his name in this Book of Honour there is a summary of all those people with North Down or Ards connections who died that night.

Lance Corporal Alexander Carlisle was 19 years old when he died on 16 April 1941 in Ards District Hospital. He died of shock and haemorrhage resulting from his multiple injuries and he is commemorated on the Second World War Memorial in Ballymena Memorial Park.

Carnduff, Thomas
Sergeant
No. 1021210, Royal Air Force Volunteer Reserve
Died as a result of an accident on Friday 13 October 1944 (aged 22)
Ramleh War Cemetery, Israel and Palestine (including Gaza) (Grave 5 H 13)

In some records his surname is spelt Cairnduff. Thomas Carnduff was born on 18 October 1921 and he was the second son of Thomas and Elizabeth Carnduff (nee Cummings) of 90 East Street, Newtownards. Thomas Carnduff worked as a gardener and he and Elizabeth Cummings were married on 16 March 1912 in Newtownards Parish Church of Ireland Church (St. Mark's). Thomas Carnduff Senior was on active service throughout the Great War and he and Elizabeth had at least five children including William (born 25 August 1912); twins John and Maggie (born 1919) and Thomas (born 18 October 1921).

During the Second World War Thomas Carnduff served with the Royal Air Force Volunteer Reserve and he was home on leave in July 1944. He died of injuries on 13 October 1944 in Ramleh, Israel just five days before his 23rd birthday. He had five years' service, almost two of which were spent in India.

There were Died on Active Service notices in the 28 October 1944 edition of the *Newtownards Chronicle* from his parents, brothers and sisters at 90 East Street, Newtownards; his brother and sister-in-law John and Ellie Carnduff of 24 South Street, Newtownards and one from the members of Lord Londonderry's Own CLB Flute Band, Newtownards.

Thomas Carnduff is commemorated on Newtownards and District War Memorial and in Newtownards Parish Church (St. Mark's).

Carr, John
Lieutenant (A)
HMS *Goshawk*, Royal Naval Volunteer Reserve
Died as a result of enemy action on Friday 17 January 1941 (aged 33)
Lee-on-Solent Memorial, Hampshire, England (Bay 2 Panel 6)

John Carr was born on 16 May 1908 and he was a son of Thomas James and Mary Carr (nee Workman) of *Blythswood*, 16 Deramore Drive, Belfast. Thomas James Carr worked as a stockbroker and he and Mary Workman were married on 4 June 1907 in Fitzroy Avenue Presbyterian Church, Belfast. They had at least three children – John (born 16 May 1908); Thomas James (born 21 September 1909) and Samuel (born 4 July 1913). John and Thomas James Junior were educated at Rockport School, Craigavad. Thomas James Carr Senior died on

20 December 1956 (aged 83) and Mary Carr died on 12 November 1974 (aged 91). Both were buried in Belfast City Cemetery (Glenalina Extension).

During the Second World War Lieutenant John Carr was assigned to HMS *Goshawk* which was a Royal Naval Air Station at Piarco in Trinidad and he was killed when travelling to Piarco aboard the SS *Almeda Star*. The SS *Almeda Star* was built in 1926 by Cammell Laird and Company, Birkenhead and owned by the Blue Star Line in London. The SS *Almeda Star* was torpedoed on 17 January 1941 by the German submarine *U-96* about 350 miles west of the island of Lewis in the Outer Hebrides when on route from Liverpool to Buenos Aires via Trinidad.

At 7.45 am on 17 January 1941 the SS *Almeda Star* stopped after being hit amidships. The submarine fired two further torpedoes and then surfaced to shell the ship. Another torpedo fired at 9.55 am hit the fore section of the SS *Almeda Star* causing her to sink. The master, 136 crew members, 29 gunners and 194 passengers were lost. Among the passengers were 21 officers and 121 ratings of 749, 750 and 752 Fleet Air Arm Squadrons. There were no survivors.

Lieutenant John Carr was 33 years old when he died and he is commemorated on the Lee-on-Solent Memorial in Hampshire and in Rockport School.

C

Carson, Robert Samuel (Bertie)
Sergeant
No. 1062319, Royal Air Force Volunteer Reserve
Killed in an aircraft accident on Thursday 27 November 1941 (aged 22)
Omagh (Dublin Road) Cemetery, Omagh, Co. Tyrone
(Section B Grave 444)

Robert Samuel (Bertie) Carson was born on 8 January 1919 in Castlederg and he was a son of James and Margaret Isabella Carson (nee McKinley) of *Holmview*, Campsie, Omagh, Co. Tyrone. James Carson was a creamery manager and he and Margaret McKinley were married on 27 March 1918 in Westbourne Presbyterian Church, Knockbreda, Belfast. They had at least two children – Robert Samuel (born 8 January 1919) and Margaret Isabella Joyce (born 7 August 1920). Robert Samuel Carson was educated at Omagh Academy and, before joining the Royal Air Force Volunteer Reserve, he was a member of staff of Messrs W.W. Cleland Ltd., Printers and Stationers, in Belfast. For some five years he lived in Bangor with his aunt Mrs Meara and his cousin Mrs H.D. Bailie. He was a member of Trinity Presbyterian Church, Bangor where he was a Sunday School teacher, Boys' Brigade officer and leader of the Life Boys.

ROLL OF HONOUR.

CARSON—In proud and grateful memory of Bertie, who gave his life in the R.A.F. on November 27th, 1941. "He counted his life not dear unto the end."

During the Second World War Sergeant Robert Samuel Carson served with the Royal Air Force Volunteer Reserve and he was 22 years old when he was killed on Thursday 27 November 1941. His death was registered in Melton Mowbray, Leicestershire. At his funeral in Omagh on Tuesday 2 December, two service aircraft circled overhead and dipped in salute. It was recorded that he died while engaged in non-operational flying duties. Sergeant Robert Samuel (Bertie) Carson is commemorated on Bangor and District War Memorial and in Trinity Presbyterian Church, Bangor. There is an inscription on his CWGC headstone:

I have fought a good fight, I have finished my course, I have kept the faith
2 Timothy 4, 7

Caulfield, Frederick

C

Leading Seaman
LT/JX 183819, HM Motor Minesweeper *117*, Royal Naval Patrol Service
Killed in action on Friday 1 September 1944 (aged 28)
Lowestoft Naval Memorial, Suffolk (Panel 14 Column 1)

Frederick Caulfield was born on 14 October 1915 at 26 Charlotte Street in Stranraer, Wigtownshire and in the CWGC Debt of Honour it is recorded that he was a son of Frederick and Agnes Caulfield. Agnes Caulfield worked as a domestic servant. Frederick Caulfield Junior was the husband of Mary Caulfield (nee Boyd) of 17 Clandeboye Place, Bangor. Before the war Frederick Caulfield worked as a waiter in Antrim and Mary Boyd worked as a servant. They were married on 1 November 1936 in St Patrick's Roman Catholic Church, Lisburn. During the Second World War, Frederick Caulfield served in the Royal Naval Patrol Service aboard HMMM *117*. When the Royal Naval Reserves were mobilised in August 1939 Lowestoft became the Central Depot for the Royal Naval Patrol Service and the RNPS depot became known as HMS *Europa*. The importance of small ships for minesweeping had first been recognised during the First World War.

Built in 1942 by J.S. Doig Ltd., Grimsby, HMMM *117* was sunk by a mine off Civitavecchia, Italy on 1 September 1944. Leading Seaman Frederick Caulfield was one of some 17 men who were killed and he is commemorated on Lowestoft Naval Memorial in Suffolk. He was 28 years old when he died and his death was reported in the 21 October 1944 edition of the *County Down Spectator* under the headline *Bangor Seaman Presumed Killed*. After Frederick died his wife Mary moved to Scarborough in Ontario, Canada and she died there in 1980.

Chapman, Ronald
Lance Sergeant
No. 2027589, 1st Battalion, East Lancashire Regiment
Killed in action on Thursday 17 August 1944 (aged 30)
Banneville-La-Campagne War Cemetery, Calvados, France
(Grave IV E 23)

Ronald Chapman's birth was registered in the third quarter of 1914 in London and he was a son of William Thomas and Elizabeth Chapman (nee Harragan). William Chapman worked as a cellarman in a tavern and he and Elizabeth Harragan were married on 23 December 1894 in St. Thomas's Church of England Church, Bethnal Green, Middlesex.

Ronald Chapman was the husband of Violet Chapman of Holywood, Co. Down and during the Second World War he served with the 1st Battalion, East Lancashire Regiment. He was 30 years old when he was killed on 17 August 1944. After the Normandy Landings in June 1944 and the taking of Caen in July 1944 the Allied Forces thrust southwards to close the Falaise Gap – a corridor of land that the Germans sought to maintain to allow their escape. The Battle of the Falaise Pocket was fought from 12 to 21 August 1944 and it was on 17 August that the German Forces began to withdraw. There is an inscription on his CWGC headstone:

He liveth in our hearts, beloved and unforgotten

Cheatley, George Johnston (George)*
Flight Sergeant
No. 748222, 269 Squadron Royal Air Force Volunteer Reserve
Killed in action on Wednesday 11 February 1942 (aged 24)
Runnymede Memorial, Surrey, England (Panel 73)

C

George Johnston Cheatley was born on 25 March 1917 in Dromore, Letterkenny, Co. Donegal and he was a son of David Gallagher Cheatley and Sarah Cheatley (nee Johnston). One of 13 children, David Gallagher Cheatley was a son of William and Jane Cheatley who farmed in Dromore. William Cheatley died on 23 November 1906 and probate was granted to his wife Jane. On 7 June 1913 William's son, David Gallagher Cheatley, married Sarah Johnston in Milford, Co. Donegal (she was from Gortnavern, Co. Donegal) and he continued to work the family farm in County Donegal until the farm was sold.

On 5 March 1921 David and Sarah Cheatley and their four children, Jane (Jean); William (born in 1915); George Johnston (born 25 March 1917) and Charlotte (Molly), moved to Wanganui in New Zealand. They sailed aboard the SS *Remuera*. The Cheatley family returned to Northern Ireland in 1923 aboard the SS *Tainui*. By then they had five children, Mathena having been born in New Zealand. At that stage they declared their proposed place of abode to be 9 Shankill Road, Belfast. The story is told that when sailing up Belfast Lough David asked Sarah which side of the Lough she wanted to live on. Thus it was that the Cheatley family settled at *Brookmount Farm* near Crawfordsburn. The land, some 37 acres, was owned by the Marquess of Dufferin and Ava.

C

George Johnston Cheatley attended Ballymullen Public Elementary School and in 1930 he won a prize of 5 shillings in a *Belfast Telegraph* children's drawing competition. His mother Sarah died at *Brookmount Farm* on 21 June 1939 and probate was granted to her husband. The marriage of George Johnston Cheatley and Hughedna Doreen Shanks was registered in the fourth quarter of 1939 in Brentford, Middlesex and they had a son named David.

During the Second World War George Johnston Cheatley served with the Royal Air Force Volunteer Reserve and he was 24 years old when he died on 11 February 1942. He was one of a four man crew aboard a Lockheed Hudson Mark III aircraft (V9054) based at RAF Kaldadarnes in Iceland which failed to return to base from convoy escort duty. An SOS signal was picked up but no trace of the aircraft and its crew was ever found. The other three crew members who died were:

- FS Godfrey Middleton James Mayes aged 19 from Duncton, Sussex
- Flight Sergeant Francis Ernest Daking aged 26

• Sergeant Tom Parkinson

Flight Sergeant George Johnston Cheatley is commemorated on the Runnymede Memorial in Surrey and in Ballygilbert Presbyterian Church. After he died his widow and son moved to Canada where Doreen remarried. During the war Mathena Cheatley served with the WRNS.

Clarke, Robert
Sergeant
No. 619994, Royal Air Force
Died as a result of an accident on Wednesday 18 April 1945 (aged 41)
Madras War Cemetery, Chennai, India (Grave 5 C 13)

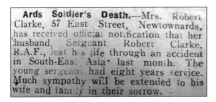

Ards Soldier's Death.—Mrs. Robert Clarke, 57 East Street, Newtownards, has received official notification that her husband, Sergeant Robert Clarke, R.A.F., lost his life through an accident in South-East Asia last month. The young sergeant had eight years service. Much sympathy will be extended to his wife and family in their sorrow.

Robert Clarke was born on 30 October 1903 (in some records 31 October 1903) and he was a son of Robert and Isabella Clarke (nee McCutcheon) who lived at 27 Frederick Street, Newtownards before they moved to Irish Street, Downpatrick. Robert Clarke worked as a shoemaker and sewing machine agent and he and Isabella McCutcheon were married on 9 February 1897 in First Newtownards Presbyterian Church. They had at least seven children – Maggie (born 5 March 1898); John Wellbran (born 22 February 1900); William Alexander (born 21 May 1902); Robert (born 31 October 1903); James McClenaghan (born 21 March 1905); Hugh McCutcheon (born 21 November 1906; died 7 June 1907) and Hugh McCutcheon (born 16 April 1909). The six youngest children were baptised in Greenwell Street Presbyterian Church, Newtownards.

Robert Clarke Junior was working as a fitter when he and Wilhelmina Stratton were married on 9 October 1924 in Newtownards Parish Church of Ireland Church (St. Mark's). Wilhelmina Stratton was a daughter of Henry Stratton who served with the 13th Battalion, Royal Irish Rifles during the First World War. Rifleman Henry Stratton was severely wounded and died in Ards Hospital on 10 November 1929. His name is inscribed on Newtownards and District War Memorial and he is commemorated on Page 621 in the Book of Honour *Remembering Their Sacrifice in the Great War – Ards* compiled by Barry Niblock.

During the Second World War Robert Clarke served with the Royal Air Force and he was 41 years old when he died as a result of an accident in South-East Asia on 18 April 1945. He had eight years service. His mother who lived at 7 West Street, Newtownards and three brothers placed a *Died on Active Service* notice in the 28 April 1945 edition of the *Newtownards Chronicle* and the following week there was a *Killed on Active Service* notice from his wife and family who lived at 57 East Street, Newtownards.

Sergeant Robert Clarke is commemorated on Newtownards and District War Memorial and in First Newtownards Presbyterian Church.

Clegg, James
Fireman
SS *Empire Mica* (Middlesborough), Merchant Navy
Died as a result of enemy action on Monday 29 June 1942 (aged 37)
Tower Hill Memorial, London, England (Panel 44)

James Clegg was born in Donaghadee on 8 September 1904 and he was a son of Thomas and Frances Agnes (Fanny) Clegg (nee Purvis) of Union Street, Donaghadee and later 9 Castle Street, Donaghadee. Thomas Clegg was a seaman and he and Frances Agnes (Fanny) Purvis were married on 25 August 1897 in Donaghadee Methodist Church. Thomas and Fanny Clegg had at least nine children – Robert John Purvis (born 20 June 1900); Thomas (born 14 December 1902); James (born 8 September 1904); Philip Delacherois (born 6 July 1905); Florence Evelyn (born 15 April 1908); John (born 12 November 1910); Frances Agnes (born 22 February 1912); Francis (born 14 October 1913) and Elizabeth (born 24 June 1915). Eight were baptised in Donaghadee Methodist Church. For a time Fanny Clegg lived with her unmarried aunt Margaret Purvis. In April 1911, when the census was taken, Thomas Clegg was in Bootle, Lancashire working aboard the SS *Ida*.

During the First World War Thomas Clegg served with the Merchant Navy. He was a son of James Clegg, a seaman from Union Street, Donaghadee, and Elizabeth Clegg (nee Thompson). They were married on 30 September 1873 in Newtownards Parish Church of Ireland Church (St. Mark's). They had at least six children, four of whom were baptised in Donaghadee Methodist Church – Thomas (born 29 September 1874); John (born 7 December 1875); Eliza Jane (born 8 July 1877); Mary Anne (born 5 September 1879); Elizabeth (born 12 August 1888) and James (born 24 October 1890). Thomas Clegg died on 9 December 1916 and he was buried in Donaghadee Parish Church of Ireland Graveyard. He is commemorated on Donaghadee and District War Memorial and in Donaghadee Methodist Church.

During the Second World War Thomas Clegg's son, James Clegg, served with the Merchant Navy aboard the SS *Empire Mica* and he died on 29 June 1942. The SS *Empire Mica* was a steam tanker built in 1941 by the Furness Shipbuilding Company Ltd., Haverton Hill, Middlesborough and owned by the Anglo-American Oil Company Ltd. On 29 June 1942 she was sailing unescorted from Houston, Texas to the United Kingdom via New Orleans, Louisiana with a cargo of 12,000 tons of vaporising oil when she was hit on the port side by two torpedoes fired from the German submarine *U-67*. The attack happened at around 8.00 am in the Gulf of Mexico, southwest of Cape St. George, Florida. The tanker caught fire, exploded and sank. Two of the launched lifeboats were engulfed by flaming oil on the surface of the water, killing all those who were aboard. Fireman James Clegg was one of more than thirty men who died that morning. Around 15 survivors were rescued and landed at Panama City, Panama.

 Fireman James Clegg is commemorated on the Tower Hill Memorial in London; on Donaghadee and District War Memorial and on the family grave headstone in Donaghadee Parish Church of Ireland Graveyard. The inscription reads:

C

Erected by Thomas Clegg in memory of his daughter:
Frances Agnes Clegg born 22 February 1912 died 2 November 1912.
Also the above named Thomas Clegg died 9 December 1916 aged 42 years.
Also his beloved wife Frances Agnes Clegg died 14 July 1938 aged 63 years.
Also his son John Clegg died 12 May 1939 aged 28 years.
Also his son James lost at sea through enemy action 29 June 1942.

Clydesdale, Samuel
Marine
No. PLY/13833, HMS *President III*, Royal Marines
Died as a result of enemy action on Monday 2 December 1940 (aged 50)
Plymouth Naval Memorial, Devon, England (Panel 43 Column 1)

Samuel Clydesdale was born on 31 August 1890 in Ballyward, Co. Down and he was a son of Ellen Clydesdale. Marine Samuel Clydesdale died on 2 December 1940 and is commemorated on the Stevenson family grave headstone in Holywood Cemetery, Co. Down:

In loving memory of
Sarah Clydesdale died 11 January 1937
Samuel Clydesdale, Royal Marines lost at sea December 1940
Margaret Stevenson beloved wife of William Stevenson 7 April 1947

Also the above William Stevenson died 31 January 1956
Their son Samuel Clydesdale Stevenson died 31 October 1969
Alice, wife of Samuel Clydesdale Stevenson died 29 January 1995

Sarah Clydesdale was 82 when she died and Margaret Stevenson (nee Clydesdale) – Samuel's sister – was 63 when she died. Margaret Clydesdale (born 8 March 1884 in Ballyward) and William Stevenson, a painter from Holywood, were married on 9 April 1912 in Fountainville Presbyterian Church, Belfast. Margaret's father's name was recorded as Alexander Clydesdale. Ellen Clydesdale died on 30 November 1903.

Samuel Clydesdale served during the First World War and was awarded the 1914-15 Star, the Victory Medal and the British War Medal. He and Kate Fryer of Devonport were married on 6 May 1920 in Eastney Registry Office, Portsea Island, Portsmouth, Hampshire. During the Second World War Samuel Clydesdale was attached to HMS *President III* which was the shore-based accounting base for the naval gunners on Defensively Equipped Merchant Ships (DEMS). Marine Samuel Clydesdale was the naval gunner serving aboard the MV *Lady Glanely* when he was killed and in the Register of Deceased Seamen his last place of abode is recorded as 2 Strand Street, Stonehouse, Plymouth.

Built in 1938 by William Doxford and Sons Ltd., Sunderland the MV *Lady Glanely* was on route from Vancouver in Canada via Panama and Bermuda to London with a cargo of wheat and lumber when she was torpedoed and sunk by the German submarine *U-101* about 400 miles west of the Bloody Foreland in County Donegal. Marine Samuel Clydesdale aged 50 was one of more than 30 men who died and he is commemorated on the Plymouth Naval Memorial in Devon.

Cochrane, Thomas John (Tom)
Able Seaman
C/JX 375555, HM LCT (A) *2454*, Royal Navy
Accidentally drowned on Friday 13 October 1944 (aged 20)
Chatham Naval Memorial, Kent (Panel 75 1)

Thomas John Cochrane was born on 30 October 1923 and he was the eldest son of Joseph and Elizabeth Helene Cochrane (nee Gracey) of 108 Scrabo Road, Newtownards. Joseph Cochrane and Elizabeth Gracey were married on 23 December 1921 in Hillsborough Presbyterian Church. It was reported in the *Newtownards Chronicle* that the Cochrane family moved to Newtownards in 1936 from Dromore, Co. Down and that Tom joined the Royal Navy in 1942 after a year in the Ulster Home Guard (formerly

the Ulster Defence Volunteers). Prior to active service he worked for James Mackie and Sons Ltd., Belfast. Able Seaman Thomas James Cochrane aged 20 died on 13 October 1944 when HM LCT (A) *2454* ran ashore on Chesil Beach in Dorset. HM LCT (A) *2454* was a Mark 5 version of His Majesty's Landing Craft Tank (Armoured) which was used as an amphibious assault ship for landing tanks on beachheads.

HM LCT (A) *2454* was caught in a force 9 gale whilst on route from Dartmouth to Portland. Her engine failed and, despite attempts to anchor, the vessel was swept onto the shingle bank at Chesil Beach where her back was broken. The local Coastguard Rocket Lifesaving Company from Wyke Regis was quickly at the scene and managed to get lines onto the vessel, but eleven of the crew were washed overboard by the 30ft waves, together with the lines. Two coastguard officers, Commander Legh and Coastguardsman Robert Henry Treadwell ran into the surf in an attempt to pass the lines by hand but both were swept away and drowned. Both men were posthumously awarded the Silver Sea Gallantry Medal. A further attempt was made by another three coastguards who were swept back ashore. In what was described as 'an amazing feat of endurance' Auxiliary Coastguard George Brown stayed in the surf for over 30 minutes and managed to get aboard and pass the lines to the two remaining crew. He and one of the crew were hauled ashore but the remaining line broke before the final crewman could be rescued. Albert Oldfield, another Auxiliary Coastguard, succeeded in passing a line to the final crewman and he was subsequently saved.

Nine of the thirteen Royal Navy crew died along with two Coastguard officers. There were only four survivors. Auxiliary Coastguard George Brown also received the Silver Sea Gallantry Medal together with the Royal Humane Society Silver Medal and the Stanhope Gold Medal for 'the bravest successful rescue in 1944'.

Able Seaman Thomas John Cochrane is commemorated on Chatham Naval Memorial in Kent; on Dromore (Co. Down) War Memorial and on Newtownards and District War Memorial. One of the *Killed on Active Service* notices inserted by his family in the *Newtownards Chronicle* included the text:

He was only one, but he was ours

Coffin, William (Willie)
Sapper
No. 1951203, Royal Engineers
Killed in a motorcycle accident on Saturday 8 September 1945 (aged 38)
Bangor Cemetery, Co. Down (Section 5 W Grave 95)

William Coffin was born on 20 September 1906 and he was the eldest son of Philip and Agnes (Hannie) Mason Coffin (nee Kelly) who lived in Ravenhill Avenue, Belfast and later at 38 Railwayview Street, Bangor. Philip Coffin worked as a painter and he and Hannie Kelly were married on 19 September 1905 in Donegall Street Congregational Church, Belfast. They had at least six children including William (born 20 September 1906); George (born 1 March 1910); Joan; Maureen and Phyllis.

William Coffin worked as a ship's painter and he and Winifred May Wright from Drumgavlin, Dunmore, Dromara, Co. Down (born 16 May 1907, daughter of William Wright who was a scutcher) were married on 28 November 1927 in Magherahamlet Parish Church of Ireland Church, Ballynahinch. After they were married William and Winifred lived in Hull and they had four children, one of whom they named Philip.

COFFIN—September 8, 1945, at military hospital, Southampton (as result of an accident), William (sapper), dearly-loved husband of Winifred Coffin, Hull. Funeral from his mother's residence, 38 Railway-view Street, Bangor, on Friday, at 4 p.m., to Bangor New Cemetery. Deeply regretted by his sorrowing Wife and Family.

Sapper William Coffin aged 38 died on 8 September 1945 in a Military Hospital in Southampton and it was reported in the 22 September 1945 edition of the *County Down Spectator* that he died as a result of a motorcycle accident in Southampton and that the funeral took place from his mother's residence in Bangor. His late father had been a local Councillor. Military honours were conferred for the funeral which was conducted by Pastor David Burrows, a former minister in Bangor Baptist Church. Amongst the mourners were William's son Philip; his brother George; his sister and brother-in-law Joan and Fred Lindsay of 44 Victoria Road, Bangor; his sister and brother-in-law Maureen and Corporal Walter Richardson; his sister and brother-in-law Phyllis and Charlie Fulton of 77 Church Street, Newtownards, and his brother-in-law Lance Corporal Stuart Wright.

Sapper William Coffin is commemorated on Bangor and District War Memorial and in First Bangor Presbyterian Church. There is an inscription

on his CWGC headstone:

The day Thou gavest, Lord is ended

In 1950 William's widow, Winifred May Coffin, married John L. Schultz in Hull, Yorkshire and her death was registered there in the first quarter of 1982.

Cole, Albert Parr (Albert)
Petty Officer Stoker
D/KX 82617, HMS *Stanley*, Royal Navy
Killed in action on Friday 19 December 1941 (aged 27)
Plymouth Naval Memorial, Devon (Panel 51 Column 3)

C

Albert Parr Cole was the only son of Albert Charles and Margaret Frances Cole. Albert Charles Cole was a policeman and in the 1920s he, Margaret and their children Albert and Maud moved from Cottage Grove, Stockwell in London to South Africa. When Albert Parr Cole died the Cole family was living at 14 Primrose Avenue, Bangor.

Albert Parr Cole served in the Royal Navy aboard HMS *Stanley*. Originally named USS *McCalla*, this destroyer was built by the Bethlehem Shipbuilding Corporation of Quincy, Massachusetts in the USA and was commissioned in May 1919. USS *McCalla* was decommissioned in June 1922 and then, after the outbreak of the Second World War, she was re-commissioned and handed over to Britain in October 1940 at Halifax in Nova Scotia. As HMS *Stanley* she became a ship of the Royal Navy and on 19 December 1941, when she was on station at the rear of a convoy in the North Atlantic, she exploded and sank after being hit by a torpedo fired from the German submarine *U-574*. More than 130 crew members died. Twelve minutes later *U-574* was sunk by HMS *Stork*.

Albert Parr Cole aged 27 had nine years service in the Royal Navy and his two brothers-in-law were also on active service – Alex McDougall and Stanley Went (Maud's husband). In the years after Albert died his mother Margaret and his two sisters placed *In Memoriam* notices in the *County Down Spectator* and one of them contained the verse:

Too good in life to be forgotten
O why was he taken so soon?

Petty Officer Stoker Albert Parr Cole is commemorated on Plymouth Naval Memorial in Devon and in Bangor Parish Church of Ireland Church (St. Comgall's).

Cole, Hugh Douglas
Convoy Signalman
No. C/JX 234034, SS *Benalbanach*, Royal Navy
Died as a result of enemy action on Thursday 7 January 1943 (aged 20)
Chatham Naval Memorial, Kent, England (Panel 70 3)

LOST AT SEA.
COLE—Convoy Signaller HUGH DOUGLAS COLE, R.N. (20), eldest son of Mr. and Mrs. S. D. COLE, 27 Spencer Street, Holywood.— Deeply regretted by his Father and Mother, Brothers, Frederick and Dennis; Mr. Hugh Patty, Grandfather. Isobel Patty and Mrs M'Knight. Aunties, and his Chums, William Cowling and Jack Stevenson.
Gone to be with Christ.

Hugh Douglas Cole was born in 1923 and he was the eldest son of Samuel Douglas Cole (born 1902 in Pontypridd, Glamorganshire) and Madeline Margaret Cole (nee Patty, daughter of Hugh Patty who worked as a gardener) of 27 Spencer Street, Holywood. They were married on 16 August 1922 in Holywood Non-Subscribing Presbyterian Church and they had three children – Hugh Douglas, Frederick and Dennis. During the Second World War Hugh Douglas Cole's father Samuel and his brother Fred were also on active service.

C

Hugh Douglas Cole served in the Royal Navy and he was aboard the SS *Benalbanach* when he died on 7 January 1943. Built in 1940 by Charles Connell and Company Ltd., Scotstoun, Glasgow for use as a passenger/cargo ship, the SS *Benalbanach* was owned by Ben Line Steamers Ltd. – William Thomson and Company. In 1941 she was taken over by the Royal Navy as an Auxiliary Transport Ship and in November 1942 she took part in the landing at Oran in the North Africa campaign. It was on her second trip to the Allied landing area that she sank. The SS *Benalbanach* left the Clyde on 24 December 1942 bound for Bone in North Africa with more than 350 Motor Transport officers and men together with a cargo of tanks, motor vehicles, ammunition, petrol and general military stores. Shortly after 6.00 pm on 7 January 1943 the SS *Benalbanach* sank north-west of Algiers after being hit by two torpedoes fired from an enemy aircraft. The water was very cold and Convoy Signalman Hugh Douglas Cole aged 20, along with Sapper **Joseph William Ogram** from Donaghadee, were among more than 400 men who died.

 Convoy Signalman Hugh Douglas Cole is commemorated on Chatham Naval Memorial in Kent; on Holywood and District War Memorial and in Holywood Non-Subscribing Presbyterian Church.

Collister, Douglas
Able Seaman
SS *Victoria City* (Bideford), Merchant Navy
Died as a result of enemy action on Monday 2 December 1940 (aged 29)
Tower Hill Memorial, London (Panel 114)

> **Bangor Men Lost at Sea.**—The names of two Bangor men appear in a list published on Wednesday of members of the Merchant Navy and fishing fleets who have died as a result of enemy action. They are Douglas Collister, A.B., of 4 King Street, Bangor, and John Ferris Deveney, A.B., of Upper Balloo.

In some records the surname is spelt Callister. Douglas Collister came from Cronkbourne Village, Douglas in the Isle of Man and he was a son of William (son of Daniel) and Margaret Winifred Collister (nee Teare, daughter of James). They were married on 1 November 1911 in the Parish of Braddan, Isle of Man. William Collister worked as a collier in Lancashire before he joined the Army. Douglas Collister was born on 18 August 1912 in Atherton, Lancashire (in the baptismal register his surname is spelt Callister) and his brother Daniel was born on 17 December 1913.

Douglas Collister and Annie Reid McCracken of Bangor were married on 24 February 1932 in Bangor Abbey and they lived at 4 King Street, Bangor. Maritime records show that Douglas was 5 feet 8½ inches tall with brown hair, grey eyes and a pale complexion. He had the word *Mizpah* tattooed on his left forearm. This Biblical word signifies an emotional bond between people who are separated and comes from Genesis 31:49 – *May the Lord keep watch between you and me when we are away from each other* (New International Version).

 Douglas Collister served in the Merchant Navy aboard the SS *Victoria City* and he died on 2 December 1940 aged 29 when this ship was torpedoed by the German submarine *U-140* in the North Atlantic during a voyage from Halifax, Nova Scotia to Great Britain. More than 40 men died, including Able Seaman **John Ferris Deveney** from Bangor. The SS *Victoria City* was a cargo steamer built in 1929 by William Gray and Company Ltd., West Hartlepool and owned by Sir William Reardon Smith and Sons Ltd., Cardiff.

Able Seaman Douglas Collister is commemorated on the Tower Hill Memorial in London; on Bangor and District War Memorial (as Callister D.); on Douglas War Memorial, Isle of Man and in Bangor Parish Church of

Ireland Church (St. Comgall's). Douglas Collister's wife Annie was 49 years old when she died of heart disease on 4 October 1959 and she was buried in Bangor Cemetery.

Conway, Robert

Private
No. 1302489, Pioneer Corps
Accidentally drowned on Thursday 25 December 1941 (aged 41)
Bangor Cemetery, Co. Down (Section 6 P Grave 21 C)

Robert Conway was a son of Samuel and Agnes Conway (nee McGuinness) of Castle Square, Bangor. They were married on 13 July 1891 in First Donaghadee Presbyterian Church. Samuel Conway worked as a general labourer and he and Agnes had at least eleven children including John (born 30 October 1891); Eliza Jane (born 26 April 1893); Anna Mary (born 11 February 1895); James Andrew (born 13 September 1896); William Charles (born 19 July 1898); Robert (born 3 September 1900); Thomas (born 6 March 1902); Rachel (born 31 August 1903); Samuel (born 25 June 1905) and David (born 6 March 1907). John and Eliza Jane were baptised in First Donaghadee Presbyterian Church, the rest in Trinity Presbyterian Church, Bangor.

Robert Conway worked as a labourer and he and Elizabeth (Lillie) Burns of 12 Main Road, Conlig were married on 29 December 1920 in Conlig Presbyterian Church. Lillie's brother, George Burns, was killed in action during the Great War and he is commemorated on Page 132 in the Book of Honour entitled *Remembering Their Sacrifice in the Great War – Ards* compiled by Barry Niblock.

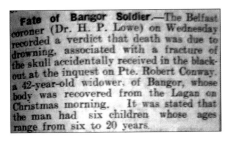

Fate of Bangor Soldier.—The Belfast coroner (Dr. H. P. Lowe) on Wednesday recorded a verdict that death was due to drowning, associated with a fracture of the skull accidentally received in the black-out at the inquest on Pte. Robert Conway, a 42-year-old widower, of Bangor, whose body was recovered from the Lagan on Christmas morning. It was stated that the man had six children whose ages range from six to 20 years.

Robert Conway enlisted after the outbreak of hostilities and during the Second World War he served with the Pioneer Corps in the United Kingdom Theatre of War. His wife Lillie was 45 years old when she died of nephritis on 28 January 1941 in Ards District Hospital and she was buried in Bangor Cemetery (Section 6 P Grave 21 C). Private Robert Conway died on Christmas Day 1941 and the findings of the inquest following his death were reported in the 31 January 1942 edition of the *County Down*

Spectator under the headline *Fate of Bangor Soldier*. At the inquest the Belfast Coroner, Dr H.P. Lowe, recorded a verdict that death was due to drowning associated with a fracture of the skull accidentally received in the blackout. Robert Conway was described as 'a widower from Bangor whose body was recovered from the River Lagan on Christmas morning 1941'. It was reported that he left six orphaned children whose ages ranged from six to 20 years. Private Robert Conway was 41 years old when he died and he was buried in Bangor Cemetery in the same grave as his wife.

Cook, Derek Alfred (Dick)
Pilot Officer (Pilot)
No. 68173, 49 Squadron, Royal Air Force Volunteer Reserve
Killed in an aircraft accident on Tuesday 17 March 1942 (aged 21)
Bangor Cemetery, Co. Down (Section 3 L Grave 1 B)

Derek Alfred (Dick) Cook was born on 5 April 1920 in Guernsey and he was a son of Herbert John and Elsie May Cook (nee Williams). Herbert John Cook was from Chippenham in Wiltshire and Elsie May Williams was from Salisbury in Wiltshire. They were married in 1909 in Salisbury Cathedral. Herbert John Cook worked for the Great Western Railway and he and Elsie May lived in Slough when he was based at Paddington Station. He was transferred to Guernsey in the Channel Islands and there he had responsibility for the transportation of cargo. Herbert John and Elsie May Cook had two children – Joan Margaret (born around 1913) and Derek Alfred (Dick, born 5 April 1920). The Cook family moved to Belfast in 1923 when Herbert John was appointed Railway Cargo Transportation Officer for Ireland. Initially accommodated in a hotel, the Cook family moved to 12 Prospect Road, Bangor and later 47 Gransha Road, Bangor. Dick Cook was a choirboy in Bangor Parish Church of Ireland Church (St. Comgall's) and he was also confirmed there in 1936.

Dick Cook was educated at Bangor Central Public Elementary School and then Bangor Grammar School from 1933 until 1936. He played rugby for the school and was described by the headmaster as, 'a quiet, manly type of boy, well built and athletic, of natural and unassuming manners, his face strong and full of character.' He was the fourth member of the 1936 Junior Certificate class in Bangor Grammar School to die on active service, the others being **Frank Gault**, **Julius Holland** and **William MacDonald**. A keen golfer, Dick Cook was a member of Bangor Golf Club. On leaving school he worked on the clerical staff of the Great Western Railway in England before joining the Royal Air Force Volunteer Reserve and getting his commission in May 1941.

Dick Cook took part in many operational flights and it was reported that, on one occasion, he was injured when piloting a bomber over Cologne. He was wounded with shrapnel in the shoulder and, although suffering great pain and weakness, he landed his plane safely at the home aerodrome. Pilot Officer Dick Cook died at 11.30 am on 17 March 1942 when his Handley Page Hampden Mark I aircraft (P1226) crashed at Derry Farm, Branscombe, Devon and official intimation of his death reached his parents on 18 March 1942. At that time his brother-in-law, Edward Magowan Lawson, was serving in the Merchant Navy. There were two men aboard the aircraft which took off from Exeter in poor visibility on a training exercise. They headed out towards the sea and when they came back over the coast they crashed into a fog-shrouded hillside. The other crew member who died that morning was:

- Pilot Officer Robert Emmett Manders (RCAF)

Pilot Officer Dick Cook's remains were brought home to his parent's residence at 47 Gransha Road and then taken for interment in Bangor Cemetery. The officiating clergy included the Revd Walter Horatio Good and the Revd James Hamilton. Dick Cook was 21 years of age when he died and he is commemorated on Bangor and District War Memorial (as Cooke D.A.); in Bangor Parish Church (St. Comgall's); in Bangor Golf Club and in Bangor Grammar School. Dick's father died on 21 November 1963 and his mother died on 11 September 1989, three months after her 100th birthday.

Cooke, William Jordan (Jordan)
Able Seaman
No. D/SSX 13584, HMS *Courageous*, Royal Navy
Killed in action on Sunday 17 September 1939 (aged 27)
Plymouth Naval Memorial, Devon, England (Panel 33 Column 2)

William Jordan Cooke was born on 31 May 1913 in Moneyreagh, Co. Down and he was a son of Joseph and Elizabeth (Lizzie) Cooke (nee Todd) of Ballyloughan, Comber. Joseph Cooke worked as a labourer and he and Elizabeth Todd were married on 7 November 1902 in Granshaw Presbyterian Church, Castlereagh, Belfast. They had at least five children – Martha Prudence (born

1 June 1903, died 1904); John (born 10 June 1905); Harry (born 6 March 1908); Joseph (born 1 July 1910) and William Jordan (born 31 May 1913).

During the Second World War William Jordan Cooke served in the Royal Navy aboard HMS *Courageous*. This ship was launched in 1916 as a battle cruiser and then converted into an aircraft carrier in the 1920s. Aged 27, Jordan Cooke died on Sunday 17 September 1939 when HMS *Courageous* was torpedoed by the German submarine *U-29* south west of Ireland in the Western Approaches (the sea-area due west of the English Channel). HMS *Courageous* sank at 7.40 pm, within 15 minutes of being hit, and more than 500 lives were lost. Able Seaman William Jordan Cooke is commemorated on Comber and District War Memorial, in First Comber Presbyterian Church and on the Plymouth Naval Memorial in Devon. His brother Joseph and sister-in-law Ina were living in Comber Road, Ballygowan.

Copling, Andrew (Andy)
Fusilier
No. 6984669, 70ᵗʰ Battalion, Royal Inniskilling Fusiliers
Died as a result of enemy action on Wednesday 16 April 1941 (aged 16)
Dromore Cathedral Churchyard, Dromore, Co. Down

C

Andy Copling was born on 22 July 1924 at 17 Shipbuoy Street, Belfast, his mother's family home. When signing up for the Army he gave his date of birth as 22 July 1922 (two years older than his true age). He was the eldest child of Ernest Victor Copling (who was born in London) and Jane Copling (nee McCloy, who was born in Belfast) and they lived at 5 Riverside Terrace, Dromore, Co. Down. Ernest Victor Copling and Jane McCloy were married on 12 March 1923 in St. John's Church of Ireland Church, Laganbank, Belfast and they had eight children – Andrew (Andy); Ernest (Ernie); Jean; Violet; Edward (Ted); Rosetta (Rose); Robert (Bob) and Andrew (Andy, born in 1945 and named after his brother who died).

Andy Copling was educated at Dromore Primary School (then in Church Street, Dromore) and after leaving school he worked for a short time at McVeigh's Dairy in Church Street before he joined the Army. During the Second World War Andy's father Ernest also served as a soldier. Ernest was a Sergeant Major, he served in France and was involved in the evacuation at

Dunkirk. When Ernest Copling was demobilised he got a job as a chauffeur with John Graham (Building Contractor), Dromore.

Fusilier Andrew Copling was one of 13 soldiers serving with the 70th Battalion, Royal Inniskilling Fusiliers who died as a result of an air raid on Newtownards aerodrome during the night of 15/16 April 1941. Fusilier **Daniel Higgins** who also died that night was buried in Newtownards (Movilla) Cemetery and under his name in this Book of Honour there is a summary of all those people with North Down or Ards connections who died that night.

Andy Copling was buried in Dromore Cathedral Churchyard, Co. Down and he is commemorated on a brass plaque on one of the Cathedral pillars near the lectern. He is also commemorated on Dromore and District War Memorial. The photograph of Andy reproduced in this book was inscribed on the back with the words, 'To Dad with love' and signed 'Andy'. Andy's father Ernest died on 19 December 1952 and his mother Jane died on 30 March 1974. Both were buried beside their son. There is an inscription on his CWGC headstone:

C

Our proudest possessions are memories of your smile

Corbett, James McMurtry (Jimmy)
Third Radio Officer
SS *British Venture* (London), Merchant Navy
Died as a result of enemy action on Thursday 24 June 1943 (aged 22)
Tower Hill Memorial, London, England (Panel 21)

James McMurtry Corbett's birth was registered in the first quarter of 1921 in Newtownards and he was the sixth son of Thomas Henry and Margaret Anne Corbett (nee Robinson) who lived in Portallo Street, Belfast, then at 67 Weir Street, Belfast and later at 97 Victoria Road, Bangor. Thomas Henry Corbett worked as a meter inspector and he and Margaret Robinson were married on 16 September 1897 in Rosemary Street Presbyterian Church, Belfast. They had at least ten children – David Robinson (born 10 September 1898); Thomas Dennison (born 9 April 1900); Robert Henry Parsons (born 12 August 1901); Grace (born 17 October 1903, died in infancy); Wilhelmina Anna (born 3 August

1905); Thomasina (born 5 September 1907); Harriet Nora (born 16 September 1909); Grace (born 10 September 1911); Annie (born 8 December 1913) and James McMurtry.

During the Second World War James McMurtry Corbett served with the Merchant Navy aboard the British Steam Tanker SS *British Venture*. This ship was built in 1930 by Lithgows Ltd., Port Glasgow for the British Tanker Company and on 24 June 1943 she was torpedoed by the Japanese submarine *I-27* in the Indian Ocean, about 300 miles south of Reunion Island. She was not in convoy and more than 40 men were killed. Initially Jimmy Corbett aged 22 was posted as missing as a result of enemy action and about one month later his death by drowning was officially presumed.

In the 17 July 1943 edition of the *County Down Spectator* there were death notices from his family (father, mother, brothers, sisters, brothers-in-law, sisters-in-law, nieces, nephews, aunt and uncle) and also from the manager and staff of Belfast Co-operative Society. The family notice contained the text:

A perfect son, a unique brother

Third Radio Officer James McMurtry Corbett is commemorated on Bangor and District War Memorial and in Hamilton Road Presbyterian Church, Bangor.

Corbett, William Howard Woodward (William)
Flying Officer
No. 82974, Royal Air Force Volunteer Reserve
Killed in an aircraft accident on Thursday 19 June 1941 (aged 32)
Upper Heyford Cemetery, Oxfordshire, England (Section B Grave 87)

William Howard Woodward Corbett was the younger son of Howard Newton Corbett and Agnes Margaret Corbett (nee Woodward) of 18 Montrose Road, Sheffield in Yorkshire. Howard Newton Corbett was a bank clerk before he became a journalist and his marriage to Agnes Margaret Woodward was registered in the first quarter of 1903 in Cardiff, Glamorgan. They had at least three children – Lawrence Woodward (born 1906); Ellaine Harriet Woodward (born 1907) and William Howard Woodward (born 1908). William's birth was registered in the fourth quarter of 1908 in Barnet, Middlesex and he was baptised on 31 January 1910 in St Oswald's Church, Bannerdale Road, Sheffield.

The Corbett family moved to the USA but they didn't all travel together. On 26 July 1924 Agnes and her three children Lawrence (a journalist), Ellaine and William travelled from Liverpool to New York aboard the Cunard steamship *Laconia*. Then, on 20 January 1929, Howard, Agnes and Ellaine returned to England aboard the SS *Arabic*. Howard Newton Corbett died on 22 August 1938.

During the Second World War William Howard Corbett served with the Royal Air Force Volunteer Reserve and at that time his widowed mother was living at Castleavery, Newtownards. On 26 August 1940 he was promoted from Acting Pilot Officer on probation to Pilot Officer on probation. He was home on leave in Newtownards at the beginning of May 1941 and some five weeks later he died as a result of a flying accident. On 19 June 1941 he was one of a crew of four aboard a Handley Page Hampden aircraft (AD831) belonging to 16 OTU (Operational Training Unit) based at RAF Upper Heyford and they were on a training exercise when their aircraft crashed at Baynards Green near the airfield. All four crewmen died in the crash and were buried in Upper Heyford Cemetery. In addition to Flying Officer William Howard Corbett the other three men who died were:

- Sergeant Joseph Jossie Goldman aged 22 from Bloemfontein, Orange Free State, South Africa
- Sergeant Charles William Davis aged 23 from Freshwater, Carbonear, Newfoundland
- Sergeant Patrick Lally aged 23 from Kilbeg, Co. Galway, Irish Republic

At the time of his death, which was registered in Ploughley, Oxfordshire, Flying Officer William Howard Corbett's brother Lawrence was serving as a Captain with the Royal Army Service Corps. Along with his widowed mother, Captain Corbett attended his brother's funeral in Oxfordshire.

Corrin, Thomas Oswald (Thomas)
Captain
No. 101649, 316 Battery, 100 HAA Regiment, Royal Artillery
Died in service on Thursday 25 July 1940 (aged 48)
Buried in Great Marsden (St. John) Churchyard, Blackburn, Lancashire
and commemorated on a Special Memorial in Nelson Cemetery,
Lancashire, England.

Thomas Oswald Corrin was born on 25 June 1892 in Briercliffe, Lancashire and he was a son of Samuel Wilberforce Corrin and Ellen Corrin (nee Halstead) whose marriage was registered in the fourth quarter of 1887 in Burnley, Lancashire. Samuel Corrin worked as a joiner and the Corrin family lived at 20 Jubilee Street, Briercliffe with Extwistle and then Cotton Row, Burnley before they moved to 16 Ayr Street, Barrow-in-Furness. Thomas had an older brother whose name was Sydney William Corrin.

During the First World War, Thomas Corrin served with 1/4th Border Regiment and then as a Captain with the 31st Punjabis in the British Indian Army. Thomas Corrin and May Chisholm from Knock, Belfast were married in 1914 in the British Consulate, Mesopotamia, Iraq. Thomas Corrin studied Music at Trinity College Dublin and was Organist in Holywood Parish Church of Ireland Church (St. Philip and St. James) from June 1929 until July 1940. The Corrin family lived at 28 Hawthornden Road, Belfast.

Captain Thomas Oswald Corrin was 48 years old when he died on 25 July 1940 at Skelmorlie Road, Largs, Ayrshire and his effects amounted to some £6,500. Probate was granted to his widow May. Thomas Corrin is commemorated on Holywood and District War Memorial; on memorial plaques in Holywood Parish Church (St. Philip and St. James) and in Christ Church, Oxford.

Corry Brothers, David and Henry

David and Henry Corry were sons of David Corry (son of Robert Corry, a linen weaver) and Margaret (Maggie) Corry (nee Irvine, daughter of Samuel Irvine, a linen weaver). The Corry family lived at 46 East Street and later at 6 James Street, Newtownards. David Corry Senior worked as a linen weaver and he and Maggie Irvine were married on 14 October 1893 in Regent Street Methodist Church, Newtownards. They had at least nine children – Robert

John (born 14 February 1894); Mary (born 3 September 1895); Thomas (born 1 January 1897); Henry (born 29 January 1899); Annie (born 12 May 1901, died in infancy); William Morris (born 25 June 1902); David (born 17 June 1906); James (born 8 March 1908) and Wyndham (born 22 February 1914).

Robert John and Thomas Corry died in service during the First World War and they are commemorated on page 169 in the Book of Honour *Remembering Their Sacrifice in the Great War – Ards* compiled by Barry Niblock. David and Henry Corry died in service during the Second World War; Henry was the first of these two brothers to die. Overall, four Corry brothers died in service in two world wars.

Corry, Henry
Gunner
No. 1544177, 175 Battery 66 Light Anti-Aircraft Regiment, Royal Artillery
Died as a result of enemy action on Monday 5 May 1941 (aged 42)
Newtownards (Movilla) Cemetery, Co. Down (Section 23 Grave 40)

Henry Corry was born on 29 January 1899, he worked as a labourer and on 29 March 1920 he and Margaret Heaney were married in Newtownards Parish Church of Ireland Church (St. Mark's). They lived at 87 East Street, Newtownards and their daughter Ena and son-in-law Robert Snow (on active service) lived in England. During the Great War Henry Corry had served with the 13th Battalion, Royal Irish Rifles and he was held as a Prisoner-of-War in Germany for nine months. He was a member of the Newtownards Branch of the British Legion. During the Second World War Gunner Henry Corry served with the Royal Artillery and he and Gunner **John Brown** died at Twin Islands, Belfast during the Luftwaffe air raid on 5 May 1941. They were buried with military honours in Movilla Cemetery on 8 May 1941.

Gunner Henry Corry is commemorated on Newtownards and District War Memorial and in Newtownards Parish Church of Ireland Church (St. Mark's). There is an inscription on his CWGC headstone:

He died a hero
At the going down of the sun and in the morning we will remember him

Corry, David
Sergeant
No. 3126332, Royal Scots Fusiliers
Died of illness on Tuesday 21 November 1944 (aged 38)
Newtownards (Movilla) Cemetery, Co. Down (Section 23 Grave 131)

David Corry was born on 17 June 1906 and, like his father David and his grandfather Robert, David Corry Junior worked as a linen weaver. He and Sarah Gunning (daughter of Samuel Gunning, Tubber Road, Kircubbin who was a farmer) were married on 2 October 1936 in Newtownards Registry Office. They lived at 71 Church Street, Newtownards and during the Second World War David Corry served with the Royal Scots Fusiliers. He was 38 years old when he died of tuberculosis on 21 November 1944 and was buried in Movilla Cemetery. Sergeant David Corry is commemorated on Newtownards and District War Memorial and in Newtownards Parish Church (St. Mark's).

Corry, George Stanley (Stanley)
Flying Officer
No. 49879, 225 Squadron, Royal Air Force
Killed on active service on Wednesday 26 July 1944 (aged 23)
Florence War Cemetery, Italy (Grave XII E 4)

George Stanley Corry was born on 6 May 1921 and he was the elder son of Herbert Finlay Corry and Isobella (Isabel) Corry (nee Kirkland) of 22 Cardigan Drive, Belfast, then 113 Wandsworth Road, Knock and later 27 Bryansburn Road, Bangor. Herbert Finlay Corry was a linen merchant and he and Isobella Kirkland were married on 25 February 1920 in Fisherwick Presbyterian Church, Belfast. George Stanley Corry was educated at Royal Belfast Academical Institution (RBAI) from 1933 until 1940 and he was a member of the Queen's University OTC. He played rugby at RBAI and won prizes for swimming and life-saving. He was 19 when he joined the Royal Inniskilling Fusiliers in 1940 and in April 1941 he received a cadetship to Sandhurst. In July 1941 he was commissioned in the North Irish Horse and in 1942 he was transferred to the Royal Air Force. He trained in Southern Rhodesia, got his wings and was promoted Flying Officer in June 1943.

At the evening service in Trinity Presbyterian Church, Bangor on Sunday 30 July 1944 the Revd W.G. Wimperis informed the congregation that Flying Officer George Stanley Corry had been killed on active service. He was 23 years old and the congregation paid tribute by standing in silence. A short time before Stanley died his younger brother Geoffrey, then aged 18, joined the Royal Irish Fusiliers.

Flying Officer George Stanley Corry is commemorated on Bangor and District War Memorial; in RBAI; in Trinity Presbyterian Church, Bangor and on the family grave headstone in Bangor Cemetery.

Corry, Samuel David (Samuel)
Mentioned in Despatches
Captain
No. 119736, Royal Army Medical Corps and No. 3 Commando
Died of wounds on Thursday 20 August 1942 (aged 28)
St. Sever Cemetery Extension, Rouen, Seine-Maritime, France
(Block 'S' Plot 4 Row R Grave 14)

C

Samuel David Corry was born on 2 October 1913 and he was the second son of Samuel Corry and Anna Corry (nee Stoupe) of 14 Victoria Avenue, Newtownards and later Bangor, Co. Down. Samuel Corry Senior owned a hemstitching factory and he and Anna Stoupe were married on 12 August 1908 in Wesley Centenary Methodist Church, Bangor. Later Samuel Corry Senior was awarded the OBE. Samuel David Corry's elder brother, Robert (Bob) Corry, was born on 21 March 1910 and his younger brother, Joseph Stoupe (Stoupe) Corry, who was born on 22 April 1916, served with the Royal Artillery during the Second World War. Samuel David Corry attended the Model School, Newtownards and then the Royal Belfast Academical Institution (RBAI) from 1926 until 1932. He studied medicine at Queen's University Belfast and played rugby for the university team. After qualifying as a doctor he was appointed to the medical staff of the Down Infirmary. He was an all-round athlete winning both junior and senior inter-provincial honours in rugby and, while he was at Queen's, he won the light-heavyweight university boxing championship of Ireland. He was also a keen golfer and cricketer.

Dr Samuel David Corry joined the Army shortly after the outbreak of war and he was with the Monmouthshire Regiment when he volunteered for the Special Service Battalion which fought in Norway. At the end of the Norwegian campaign in 1940 he was attached to the Commandos and he took part in several raids against German positions including the Norwegian Lofoten Islands, Vaagso Island and Port Maaloy. It was reported in the 3 April 1942 *Supplement to the London Gazette* that he had been Mentioned In Despatches 'in recognition of gallant and distinguished services in successful combined operations against the enemy at Vaagso and Maaloy'.

He was posted as missing in action after the raid on the German-occupied port of Dieppe in France which began at 5.00 am on 19 August 1942. There were very heavy casualties that day and later it was officially confirmed that Captain Samuel David Corry had died of wounds sustained during the fighting.

C

Captain Samuel David Corry is commemorated on Newtownards and District War Memorial; in RBAI and on the family grave headstone in Movilla Cemetery Newtownards. His mother Anna died on 23 September 1965 aged 83 and his father Samuel died on 23 March 1972 aged 90. His brother, Joseph Stoupe Corry, died on 26 July 2006. There is an inscription on Captain Corry's CWGC headstone:

He saved others
Himself he could not save

On Sunday 2 September 2011 a commemorative church service was held in Baronscourt Parish Church, Co. Tyrone to dedicate a plaque to the memory of the eighteen scouts from 74th Belfast (RBAI) Scout Group who lost their lives in the Second World War, many of whom had camped on the Baronscourt Estate in the years immediately before the outbreak of hostilities. The plaque commemorated the 70th anniversary of the first building of a memorial cairn by RBAI scouts on the nearby hill known as Bessy Bell. In addition to Captain Samuel David Corry the plaque bears the names of Warrant Officer **Samuel Nicholl Beckett**, Sergeant **Sydney Ireland** and Bombardier **Francis Eric Sheals**.

Coulter, Jacob Walter (Jackie)
Telegraphist
No. D/J 109264, HMS *Maori*, Royal Navy
Died of wounds on Thursday 2 May 1940 (aged 31)
Plymouth Naval Memorial, Devon, England (Panel 39 Column 3)

> KILLED ON ACTIVE SERVICE.
> COULTER — May 2, 1940, on active service on H.M.S. Maori, Jacob Walter Coulter, telegraphist, dearly-loved husband of Christina Coulter, 10 Croft Street, Bangor.
> "The Harbour lights are gleaming bright,
>   The gales and storms are o'er,
>   And safe at last, all danger past,
>   At anchor by the shore."
> Deeply regretted by his sorrowing wife; also his father-in-law and mother-in-law, Robert and Christina Brown, 10 Croft Street; brothers-in-law and sisters-in-law, Wm. and Lydia Truesdale, 37 Belfast Road, and John and Lily Conway, 63 Elmwood Avenue; and Robert Brown, jun., 10 Croft St.

Jacob Walter (Jackie) Coulter was born on 22 September 1908 in Belfast and he was a son of Samuel and Ethel Coulter (nee Keenan) who lived at 18 Lendrick Street and later 24 Albert Street, Belfast. Samuel Coulter worked as a labourer and he and Ethel Keenan were married on 25 August 1908 in Belfast Registry Office. Jacob Walter Coulter's paternal grandparents were Samuel and Louisa Coulter (nee Morrison). Samuel Coulter worked as a labourer and he and Louisa Morrison were married on 24 December 1886 in Donegall Pass Presbyterian Church, Belfast. They lived at 13 Mayne Street, Belfast and they had four children including Samuel (Jackie's father, born around 1887) and Robert (born around 1889). Two other children died in infancy. Louisa Coulter was widowed sometime before 1901 and when she died on 1 April 1923 aged 72 she was living at 13 Ardoyne Village, Belfast. Louisa Coulter was buried in Belfast City Cemetery, Glenalina Extension (Grave H 20).

C

Jacob Walter Coulter's mother Ethel was a daughter of Jacob Walter and Letitia Keenan (nee Jellie) of *Glenburn House*, Belfast. Jacob Walter Keenan worked as a shipbroker – a specialist broker who negotiated between would-be charterers and the owners of cargo ships and also between the buyers and sellers of ships. Jacob Walter Keenan was born in County Roscommon and he and Letitia Jellie were married on 2 June 1887 in Sandys Street Presbyterian Church, Newry. They had at least three children – Lamont (born around 1890); Emily and Ethel (born around 1893). After Letitia Keenan died Jacob Walter Keenan remarried. He and Emily Graham (also born in County Roscommon) were married on 19 March 1901 in Trinity Church of Ireland Church, Belfast. Jacob Walter Keenan of Clara Park, Neill's Hill, Belfast died on 29 September 1917 and he was buried in Dundonald Cemetery (Grave E5 838). Emily Keenan moved to Brunswick Road in Bangor.

Jacob Walter Coulter's parents, Samuel and Ethel, had three other children all of whom died in infancy and were buried in the Public Ground of Belfast

City Cemetery – Ethel Louise died on 20 November 1909 aged 4 weeks; an unnamed child died on 18 October 1910 aged 8 hours and Samuel Maurice died on 21 November 1911 aged 12 weeks.

Jacob Walter Coulter lived with his maternal step-grandmother Emily Keenan in Brunswick Road, Bangor and he joined the Royal Navy around 1924. On 5 August 1937 he married Christina (Teenie) Brown in Bangor Abbey and during the Second World War Teenie lived with her parents, Robert and Christina Brown, at 10 Croft Street, Bangor. Jackie Coulter served as a Telegraphist on board HMS *Maori* and he had 16 years of service in the Royal Navy when he died on 2 May 1940 from shrapnel wounds in the neck following a bomb explosion during a German air attack. HMS *Maori* was a Tribal-class destroyer built by the Fairfield Shipbuilding and Engineering Company Ltd., at Govan in Scotland. She was commissioned in 1939 and saw service with the Home Fleet and the Mediterranean Fleet. Following an attack by German aircraft on 12 February 1942 HMS *Maori* sank at her moorings in Malta Grand Harbour. She was subsequently raised and scuttled off Malta in July 1945.

C

After Telegraphist Jackie Coulter died, his wife Teenie placed a death notice in the *County Down Spectator* and it contained the verse:

> *The Harbour lights are gleaming bright*
> *The gales and storms are o'er*
> *And safe at last, all danger past*
> *At anchor by the shore*

There were newspaper tributes from Teenie's parents, Robert and Christina Brown, and also from his brothers-in-law and sisters-in-law: William and Lydia Truesdale of 37 Belfast Road, Bangor; John and Lily Conway of 63 Elmwood Avenue, Bangor and Robert Brown Junior of 10 Croft Street. A later tribute to Jackie included the verse:

> *Afar he sleeps – the ocean's roar*
> *Disturbs his calm repose no more*
> *What though no voice of home was near*
> *To soothe with love his dying ear*
> *The cloud is passed from that clear brow*
> *It glows in Heaven's own brightness now*

Telegraphist Jacob Walter Coulter is commemorated on Bangor and District War Memorial and in Bangor Parish Church of Ireland Church (St. Comgall's).

Courtney, Stewart

Private

No. 2699016, 4th Battalion, The Parachute Regiment, Army Air Corps
Killed in action on Friday 21 January 1944 (aged 30)
Bari War Cemetery, Italy (Grave VI D 20)

 Stewart Courtney was born on 30 April 1913 in Belfast and he was a son of Thomas and Elizabeth (Eliza) Courtney (nee Ferguson) of 7 Collingwood Avenue, Belfast, then Greencastle Street, Belfast and then Princetown Road, Bangor. Thomas Courtney was a master plumber and later a water inspector. He and Elizabeth Ferguson (born in Bolton, Lancashire) were married on 11 July 1898 in Crescent Presbyterian Church, Belfast. They had at least six children – James (born 26 May 1899); John (born 22 October 1901); Thomas (born 20 June 1905); William (born 19 June 1907); Charles (born 29 November 1910) and Stewart (born 30 April 1913).

Stewart Courtney was the husband of Annie Courtney (nee Johnson) of Old Trafford, Manchester. Their marriage was registered in the third quarter of 1934 in Manchester and they had two children – Ann E. (her birth was registered in the first quarter of 1937) and Brian (his birth was registered in the fourth quarter of 1937).

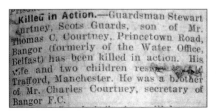

In the 19 February 1944 edition of the *County Down Spectator* there was a report under the headline *Killed in Action* which stated that Guardsman Stewart Courtney, Scots Guards, son of Thomas C. Courtney, Princetown Road, Bangor (formerly of the Water Office, Belfast) had been killed in action on 21 January 1944. His wife and two children lived in Old Trafford, Manchester and he was a brother of Charles Courtney, Secretary of Bangor Football Club. Stewart Courtney was 30 years old when he died.

The Allied invasion of the Italian mainland began on 3 September 1943 near Reggio Calabria in the south followed by the Gulf of Salerno. The invasion coincided with an armistice made with the Italians who then re-entered the war on the Allied side. The town of Bari on the Adriatic Sea was an important supply base and hospital centre.

Cowan, David
Able Seaman
No. P/UD/X 1415, HMS *Repulse*, Royal Naval Volunteer Reserve
Killed in action on Wednesday 10 December 1941 (aged 24)
Portsmouth Naval Memorial, Hampshire, England (Panel 60 Column 3)

David Cowan was born on 13 June 1917 and he was a son of David and Mary (Minnie) Cowan (nee Carroll). David Cowan and Minnie Carroll were married on 5 February 1915 in First Bangor Presbyterian Church and they had two children, both of whom were baptised in First Holywood Presbyterian Church – James (born 26 November 1915) and David (born 13 June 1917).

During the Second World War David Cowan served with the Royal Naval Volunteer Reserve aboard HMS *Repulse*. HMS *Repulse* was a battle cruiser built by John Brown & Company at Clydebank, Scotland and completed in 1916. She operated in the North Sea during the Great War and then underwent an extensive refit that was completed in 1922. HMS *Repulse* was further modernised in the early 1930s and she operated in the North Sea and Atlantic Ocean during the first two years of the Second World War. Later in 1941 she was sent to the Far East and accompanied the new battleship HMS *Prince of Wales* to Sembawang Naval Dockyard in Singapore. They became part of Force Z and sailed from Singapore on 8 December 1941. While returning to Singapore on 10 December 1941 HMS *Repulse* and HMS *Prince of Wales* were attacked by Japanese bombers and torpedo planes. The two ships sank off the coast of Malaya within an hour of each other. Able Seaman **Samuel Smith** from Newtownards who was aboard the *HMS Prince of Wales* was also killed.

Able Seaman David Cowan (aged 24) was one of more than 500 men who died and he is commemorated on Portsmouth Naval Memorial in Hampshire; on Holywood and District War Memorial and in First Holywood Presbyterian Church.

Cowan, John Connell
Leading Aircraftman
No. 1349530, 2712 Squadron, Royal Air Force Regiment,
Royal Air Force Volunteer Reserve
Died after a shooting accident on Wednesday 15 April 1942 (aged 19)
Arngask New Cemetery, Perthshire, Scotland (Section 4 Grave 342)

YOUNG AIRMAN KILLED.

SHOT WHILE ON MANŒUVRES.

The story of the tragic manner in which a nineteen-years-old member of the R.A.F. by being shot by another airman during manœuvres was told at an inquest held on Thursday, 16th April, by Dr. R. A. McC. Wallace, Coroner. The deceased was L.A.C. John Connell Cowan, whose home address was given as Durnzie Farm, Glenfarg, Perthshire. Head-Constable Cooke conducted the proceedings on behalf of the police.

John Connell Cowan was born in 1923 and he was a son of Ronald McDonald Cowan and Joan Murray Cowan (nee Connell) of Bridge of Earn, Perthshire, Scotland. Ronald Cowan worked as a ploughman and he and Joan Connell were married on 28 April 1922 in Hilton of Gask Church of Scotland in the parish of Findo Gask, Perthshire.

During the Second World War John Connell Cowan served with the Royal Air Force Volunteer Reserve and in 1942 he was stationed at Ballyhalbert in 2712 Squadron, Royal Air Force Regiment. The function of this Regiment was to secure the airfield from attack.

The death of Leading Aircraftman John Connell Cowan at Ballyhalbert on 15 April 1942 was reported in the 25 April 1942 edition of the *Newtownards Chronicle* under the headline *Young Airman Killed – Shot While on Manoeuvres*. An inquest was held on 16 April 1942 by the Coroner, Dr R.A.McC. Wallace. Corporal W.R.D. Davies said that he was in charge of the guard on the previous evening. The guard consisted of twelve men and when each man went on duty he was issued with five rounds of ammunition. Each man was personally responsible for the ammunition issued to him and it was the rule that no cartridge should be 'up the spout'. When not actually on guard the men were allowed to sleep but they had to keep their rifles handy. The system was 'two hours on and four hours off'. When the men came off duty they reported at the guardroom to hand over their ammunition.

C

On the morning of the shooting, when the twelve men were going off duty, one of them complained of feeling unwell and asked to be excused to report himself sick. He went for breakfast first and then found that he was too late for the sick parade so he returned to his billet. Corporal W.R.D. Davies said that he thought everyone had handed in their ammunition but he must have 'muddled the count' because he did not notice that he was five rounds short. Later in the day, at around 2.45 pm, Leading Aircraftman John Connell Cowan was shot during manoeuvres and it was found that one of the men had live cartridges in his rifle. The man was placed under close arrest and he and others were called to give evidence at the inquest about the circumstances of the shooting. The Medical Officer stated that he had found a bullet wound in the left upper side of LAC Cowan's chest. The bullet entered from the rear and exited from the front. Death was due to shock and haemorrhage and the Coroner found that the gunshot wounds were 'caused by the accidental discharge of a rifle by LAC George Garry'. LAC Cowan was 19 years old when he died.

Craig, Hugh
Aircraftman First Class
No. 1082514, Royal Air Force Volunteer Reserve
Died of illness on Friday 20 November 1942 (aged 23)
Singapore Memorial, Singapore (Column 417)

Hugh Craig was born on 19 April 1919 and he was baptised in First Saintfield Presbyterian Church. He was the third son of John and Catherine Craig (nee Wightman) of Ravara, Ballygowan. John Craig was a farmer and he and Catherine were married on 4 June 1913 in Ballygowan Presbyterian Church. They had seven children – William (born 28 March 1914); Robert John; Hugh; Jane Wightman; Kathleen; Margaret Jane and Isabella.

Hugh Craig attended Carrickmannon Public Elementary School and when he left school he drove a lorry for Minnis Brothers (General Merchants), Main Street, Saintfield. Hugh Craig and Margaret Carse were married on 3 October 1940 in Ballygowan Presbyterian Church and they lived in the townland of Ballynichol between Ballygowan and Comber. Their only son Hugh was born in May 1941 and Hugh Craig Senior never saw his son.

Hugh Craig joined the Royal Air Force Volunteer Reserve in late 1940 and in February 1941 he sailed from Belfast to Heysham on his way to Blackpool for posting. He was stationed at RAF Catterick in Yorkshire and in June 1941 he moved to RAF West Kirby in the Wirral Peninsula, Cheshire. In September 1941 he was posted to RAF Kuantan Pahang in Malaya where he used his skills in lorry driving and maintenance.

Aircraftman First Class Hugh Craig was captured by the Japanese and, aged 23, he died of colitis aboard a Prisoner-of-War transport ship on 20 November 1942. It wasn't until June 1943 that Hugh's family received confirmation of his death through the International Red Cross Committee. Many of Hugh's letters to family members arrived after he died and all of them were full of reassurances as to how well he was and how concerned he was for the safety and wellbeing of his family at home.

CRAIG H.

THEIR GRANDSON L/AG HUGH CRAIG R.A.F.
KILLED ON ACTIVE SERVICE 18TH NOVEMBER 1942 AGED 23 YEARS

Hugh Craig is commemorated on the Singapore Memorial; on the Craig family grave headstone in First Saintfield Presbyterian Church Graveyard and on a memorial plaque in First Saintfield Presbyterian Church which bears the inscription:

He died as a prisoner of war in the Far East

Hugh Craig's father John died on 27 June 1958 and his mother Catherine died on 23 October 1967.

Craig, James
Mentioned in Despatches with 2 Bars
Lieutenant
No. 115186, 7th Battalion, Royal Ulster Rifles
Died of illness on Saturday 10 May 1941 (aged 46)
Belfast City Cemetery, Northern Ireland (Section G 2 Grave 593)

James Craig was born on 29 September 1894 and he was a son of Richard James Craig and Mary Craig (nee Anderson) of *Breda House*, Randalstown. They were married on 19 May 1891 in St Anne's Church of Ireland Church, Belfast. Richard James Craig worked as a rate collector and auctioneer and he and Mary had at least five children – Lavinia (born 2 September 1891); James (born 29 September 1894); Jessie Campbell (born 6 April 1897); William Charles and John Campbell (born 22 August 1900). James Craig attended Royal Belfast Academical Institution (RBAI) from 1908 until 1912 and in civilian life he worked as a solicitor. James Craig was on active service during the First World War and on 11 May 1921 he and Kathleen Maud Cairns Northey were married in Macrory Memorial Presbyterian Church, Belfast. They lived at *Ivacraig*, Craigavad.

James Craig's father died on 31 March 1930 and his effects amounted to some £1,086. Probate was granted to his widow Mary and his son James. During the Second World War James Craig served with the Royal Ulster Rifles and he was 46 years old when he died on 10 May 1941 in Holywood Military Hospital. His effects amounted to some £1,793 and probate was granted to his widow Mary and Hector Francis Northey who was a medical doctor.

Lieutenant James Craig is commemorated on the memorial plaque in the Royal Courts of Justice, Belfast and in RBAI.

Crawford, George
Distinguished Flying Cross
Air Force Cross
Squadron Leader
No. 72986, 53 Squadron, Royal Air Force Volunteer Reserve
Killed on active service on Wednesday 7 June 1944 (aged 29)
Runnymede Memorial, Surrey, England (Panel 200)

CRAWFORD G.,D.F.C.,A.F.C. In the CWGC Debt of Honour it is recorded that George Crawford aged 29 was the husband of Leslie Crawford of Marino, Co. Down. George Crawford was the only son of Mr and Mrs Hugh Crawford of *Mulberry Cottage*, Ham, Richmond in Surrey. Hugh Crawford had been a Captain in the Indian Army and in 1901 he got married in Bombay.

During the Second World War George Crawford served with the Royal Air Force Volunteer Reserve and on 3 September 1941 he was promoted from Flying Officer to Flight Lieutenant. He was awarded the Air Force Cross in 1942/43 and on 7 January 1944, as Acting Squadron Leader with 53 Squadron in Coastal Command, he was awarded the Distinguished Flying Cross. His citation read:

'This officer was the Captain of an aircraft detailed for an anti-submarine patrol recently. In spite of difficulties Squadron Leader Crawford persisted in his mission and eventually a U-boat was sighted. Coolly and skilfully Squadron Leader Crawford pressed home his attack with great determination. Undeterred by accurate and concentrated anti-aircraft fire he made two runs over the vessel straddling it with his depth charges on the second run. In this action Squadron Leader Crawford displayed skill, courage and resolution of a high order'.

On 7 June 1944 Squadron Leader George Crawford was one of a crew of ten aboard a Consolidated B-24 Liberator aircraft (BZ778/M) that took off on an anti-submarine patrol. They were hit by flak when they attacked a surfaced U-boat and their aircraft crashed with the loss of all on board. In addition to Squadron Leader George Crawford the other nine crew members who died that day were:

- Flying Officer Douglas Gordon Biggs (RCAF)
- Pilot Officer Robert John Martin aged 29 from Headington, Oxfordshire
- Flying Officer John Geoffrey Smith
- FO H. Richardson DFM aged 26 from Weston-super-Mare, Somerset
- Sergeant Ronald Stoten aged 22 from Haywards Heath, Sussex

C

- Warrant Officer Bruce George Barton aged 21 (RNZAF)
- Sergeant Kenneth Vaughan Jones
- Warrant Officer Harry Ashley Corns
- Warrant Officer Robert Alexander O'Kane aged 23 (RNZAF)

The body of Squadron Leader George Crawford DFC AFC was never recovered and he is commemorated on the Runnymede Memorial. His effects amounted to some £10,376 and probate was granted to his father. Four months after her husband died Leslie Crawford (nee Boyd) gave birth to a son in Johnston House, Royal Victoria Hospital in Belfast. Her son was born on 29 October 1944 and she named him George David Hugh Crawford.

Crisp, Thomas Charles
Flight Sergeant (Flight Engineer)
No. 1464893, Royal Air Force Volunteer Reserve
Killed in an aircraft accident on Sunday 20 August 1944 (aged 29)
Nunhead (All Saints) Cemetery, London, England
(Screen Wall Panel 5 Square 5 Collective Grave 41286)

Thomas Charles Crisp's birth was registered in the third quarter of 1914 in St. Olave, Bermondsey, London and he was a son of Thomas John and Elizabeth Charlotte Crisp (nee North) of Bermondsey. Their marriage was registered in the second quarter of 1911 in Bermondsey.

C

Thomas Charles Crisp was the husband of Maud Lillian Crisp (nee Greenaway) and their marriage was registered in the second quarter of 1936 in St. Olave, Bermondsey. During the Second World War Thomas Charles Crisp served with the Royal Air Force Volunteer Reserve.

On 20 August 1944 an Avro Anson aircraft (LT658) from No. 12 Air Gunners School based at Bishops Court was on an air gunnery exercise when it broke up in mid-air as a result of a structural failure. Wreckage fell to the ground over a wide area centred on Ballygalget Roman Catholic Church and all five crew members on board were killed – Flying Officer (Pilot) **Raymond Hodgson**, Sergeant (Flight Engineer) **Kennedy Boyd Black**, Sergeant (Flight Engineer) **Frank Bennett Bloor**, Flight Sergeant (Flight Engineer) Thomas Charles Crisp and Sergeant (Air Gunner) **George William Thomas Walker**. All five deaths were registered in Downpatrick.

Flight Sergeant (Flight Engineer) Thomas Charles Crisp was 29 years old when he died and he was buried in Nunhead (All Saints) Cemetery, London.

Cromie, David
Stoker 1ˢᵗ Class
No. D/KX 152720, HMS *Abdiel*, Royal Navy
Died as a result of enemy action on Friday 10 September 1943 (aged 19)
Plymouth Naval Memorial, Devon, England (Panel 82 Column 1)

David Cromie was born in 1924 and he was the eldest son of Albert and Agnes (Aggie) Cromie (nee Blair) of 36 Well Road, Ballywalter. They were married on 24 September 1923 in Newtownards Registry Office. David's uncle, David Cromie, died of wounds in the First World War and he is commemorated on Page 174 in the Book of Honour *Remembering Their Sacrifice in the Great War – Ards* compiled by Barry Niblock. David's uncles Thomas and Robert Cromie were also on active service and they survived the First World War. Albert and Aggie Cromie had four children – David; Maureen (married John Lemon who served in the Royal Air Force during the Second World War and died on 19 December 1978); Elizabeth (died 7 February 1935 aged 2½) and William.

C

During the Second World War David Cromie served with the Royal Navy aboard the minelayer HMS *Abdiel*. HMS *Abdiel* was built by J.S. White and Company (Cowes), commissioned in 1941 and she served successively with the Mediterranean Fleet (1941), the Eastern Fleet (1942), the Home Fleet (1942/43) and the Mediterranean Fleet (1943). HMS *Abdiel* was sunk by mines in Taranto harbour, Italy on 10 September 1943. The mines had been laid a few hours earlier by the German torpedo boats *S-54* and *S-61* as they left the harbour. HMS *Abdiel* was carrying troops of the 1ˢᵗ Airborne Division (6ᵗʰ Welch Parachute Battalion) and Stoker 1ˢᵗ Class David Cromie aged 19 was among more than 100 soldiers and sailors who were killed when two mines detonated beneath the ship. His cousin **Harry Cromie** and his second cousin **Robert (Bobby) Cromie** also died in the Second World War.

Stoker 1ˢᵗ Class David Cromie is commemorated on Plymouth Naval Memorial, Devon; on Ballywalter and District War Memorial; in Ballywalter Presbyterian Church and on the family grave headstone in Whitechurch Cemetery, Ballywalter. David's father Albert died on 1 March 1983 and his mother Aggie died on 3 February 1993.

Cromie, Henry (Harry)
Lance Corporal
No. 1888355, 3 Field Squadron, Royal Engineers
Died on active service on Monday 23 March 1942 (aged 30)
Knightsbridge War Cemetery, Acroma, Libya (Collective grave 8 C 12-14)

Henry (Harry) Cromie was born on 10 December 1911 in Ballywalter and he was a son of Thomas and Eva Cromie (nee Brennan) who lived in Ballywalter. Thomas Cromie worked as an agricultural labourer and he and Eva Brennan were married on 17 March 1909 in Ballywalter Church of Ireland Church.

Harry Cromie's nickname was *Majury*. He moved to England and he was married in Cheshire. During the Second World War he served with 3 Field Squadron, Royal Engineers. In a letter dated 17 February 1942 to his aunt May Cromie (nee McMath and wife of his uncle Robert), Harry was looking forward to the end of the war and returning to England where he said the prospects for work were good. A month later, on 23 March 1942, he died and was buried in Knightsbridge War Cemetery at Acroma in Libya. There was an airfield and advance fuelling station at Acroma which was an important point on the Eighth Army supply route. His cousin **David Cromie** and his second cousin **Robert (Bobby) Cromie** also died in the Second World War. Robert and May Cromie's son David John was on active service and survived the Second World War.

Lance Corporal Henry Cromie was 30 years old when he died and he is commemorated on Ballywalter and District War Memorial (as Sapper Harry Cromie R.E.) and in Ballywalter Presbyterian Church (as Harry Cromie).

Cromie, Robert (Bobby)
Gunner
No. 1476595, 5 Battery 2 Light Anti-Aircraft Regiment Royal Artillery
Died of wounds on Saturday 20 June 1942 (aged 33)
Tobruk War Cemetery, Libya (Grave 10 D 6)

Robert (Bobby) Cromie was born on 2 March 1908 and he was the only son of Robert and Martha Cromie (nee Semple) of 24 Well Road, Ballywalter and before that they lived in the townland of Ballaghbeg, Kilcoo, Newcastle, Co. Down. Robert Cromie Senior worked as a labourer and he and Martha

239

Semple were married on 13 February 1903 in Ballycopeland Presbyterian Church, Millisle. Robert (Bobby) Cromie was baptised in Ballywalter Presbyterian Church.

Robert (Bobby) Cromie and Edith A. Gibson of Ballywalter Park, Ballywalter were married on 15 April 1936 in Glastry Presbyterian Church and they had a daughter named Sylvia (born 2 July 1937). During the Second World War Gunner Robert (Bobby) Cromie served with the Royal Artillery and he died on 20 June 1942 at Tobruk when Axis Forces led by Erwin Rommel attacked and captured the garrison. Afterwards, the Chaplain who was with him when he died said that Bobby's final words were:

In peace let me resign my breath and Thy salvation see
I was a guilty sinner, but Jesus died for me

His second cousins **David Cromie** and **Harry Cromie** also died during the war. Gunner Robert (Bobby) Cromie is commemorated on Ballywalter and District War Memorial and in Ballywalter Presbyterian Church. After the war Edith and Sylvia Cromie both moved to Canada. Sylvia was a comptometer operator and on 14 August 1957 she travelled from Liverpool to Montreal on board the Cunard steamship *Carinthia*.

C

Crone, Robert (Bobby)
Cook
SS *Melmore Head* (Belfast), Merchant Navy
Died as a result of enemy action on Monday 28 December 1942 (aged 28)
Tower Hill Memorial, London (Panel 69)

Robert (Bobby) Crone was born on 28 November 1913 and he was a son of Robert and Ellen Crone (nee Sinnerton) who lived with Robert's parents, Henry and Elizabeth Crone at 174 Grosvenor Road, Belfast before they moved to Springfield Road, Belfast and later to 34 Albert Street, Bangor. Bobby's father Robert was a turf accountant and his grandfather Henry was a hairdresser. Robert Crone and Ellen Sinnerton were married on 27 January 1909 in St Anne's Church of Ireland Cathedral, Belfast and they had twelve children including Henry (Harry, born 24 June 1909); Herbert (born 30 January 1911); Ernest; Robert (Bobby, born 28 November 1913); William; Jenny; Eileen; Margaret (Peggy); Ella and Evelyn. Bobby's mother Ellen died in November 1971 and his father Robert died in August 1975.

Bobby Crone attended school in Belfast before the family moved to Bangor. In 1929 he was confirmed in Bangor Parish Church of Ireland Church (St. Comgall's) and after he left school he worked as a cook before going to sea. He completed the Shipping Federation School of Nautical Cookery Course in Glasgow in 1940. On 9 May 1941 Bobby Crone was serving aboard the cargo ship SS *Bengore Head* and he was rescued after that ship was torpedoed by the German submarine *U-110* and sank east of Cape Farewell, Egger Island, Greenland. The SS *Bengore Head* was built in 1922 by Irvine's Shipbuilding, West Hartlepool, she was owned by the Ulster Steamship Company, Belfast and she was on route from Belfast to Montreal with a cargo of coal and agricultural binder twine when she sank.

In December 1942, with more than ten years of service, Bobby Crone was serving as a Cook in the Merchant Navy aboard the ship SS *Melmore Head* when this ship was torpedoed. The SS *Melmore Head* was a steam merchant ship built by Workman, Clark and Company Ltd., Belfast in 1918 and was also owned by the Ulster Steamship Company Ltd. Bobby was lost in the North Atlantic Ocean, north of the Azores, at 10.00 pm on 28 December 1942 when his ship was blown up by two torpedoes fired from the German submarine *U-225*. Fourteen of the 49 crew members were killed and Bobby Crone's body was never recovered. One of the newspaper tributes to Bobby Crone included the verse:

C

Beyond the sea of death love lives
Yesterday, today and for ever

Cook Robert Crone was 28 years old when he died and he is commemorated on the Tower Hill Memorial in London; on Bangor and District War Memorial and in Bangor Parish Church (St. Comgall's).

Crossan, George Stewart
Sergeant
No. 648044, 119 Squadron, Royal Air Force
Died in service on Tuesday 15 December 1942 (aged 21)
Runnymede Memorial, Surrey, England (Panel 80)

George Stewart Crossan's birth was registered in the second quarter of 1921 in Bawnboy, Co. Cavan and he was a son of Joseph and Sarah Crossan (nee Creighton). Sarah Creighton was born in County Fermanagh, Joseph Crossan worked as a postman and their marriage was registered in the fourth quarter of 1910 in

Bawnboy, Co. Cavan. In 1911 Joseph and Sarah Crossan were living in Dring, Bilberry, Co. Cavan with Joseph's parents, George and Catherine Crossan.

During the Second World War Sergeant George Stewart Crossan served with the Royal Air Force in 119 Squadron which was formed in March 1941 as part of Coastal Command. In April 1942 the Squadron moved to RAF Lough Erne at Castle Archdale in County Fermanagh where they flew Consolidated PBY-5A Catalina Mk IIIA aircraft. In August 1942 they returned to RAF Pembroke Dock and flew Short Sunderland aircraft.

Sergeant George Stewart Crossan was 21 years old when he died on 15 December 1942 and in the CWGC Debt of Honour it is recorded that his parents, Joseph and Sarah Crossan, lived in Holywood, Co. Down. Sergeant Crossan's body was never recovered and he is commemorated on the Runnymede Memorial in Surrey.

Crothers, Norman
Engine Room Artificer 4th Class
No. C/MX 50923, HMS *Naiad*, Royal Navy
Killed in action on Wednesday 11 March 1942 (aged 23)
Chatham Naval Memorial, Kent, England (Panel 60 2)

C

Norman Crothers was born on 21 February 1919 and he was the only son of Josiah and Agnes Graham Crothers (nee Kerr). Josiah Crothers was an Army Sergeant serving in Alexandria when he and Agnes Kerr were married on 19 February 1908 in Belmont Presbyterian Church, Belfast. Later the Crothers family lived at 99 Victoria Road in Bangor and they had six children – Margaret Kerr (born 16 January 1909 in Belfast); Catherine (born 12 April 1910 in Enniskillen); Agnes (Peggy, born 1 May 1913); Kathy; Maisie and Norman. Josiah Crothers died on 2 November 1930 and at the time of his death he was working as a barrack warden.

Having gained a Junior Down Regional Scholarship, Norman Crothers attended Bangor Grammar School from 1931 until 1934. He obtained one distinction and six credits in the Junior Certificate examination. His ambition was to join the Royal Navy and he was successful in passing the special Royal Navy examination. Described by the headmaster as 'tall and straight and strongly built with a grave expression and the unusual combination of dark eyes with curling fair hair', he played rugby for the school.

During the Second World War Norman Crothers served aboard the Dido-

OUR DEATHLESS DEAD

W.H.L.ANDREWS	S.J.LUKE
J.G.BARRE	T.A.McCANN
G.M.BELL	W.E.C.McCULLOUGH
G.A.BOWMAN	W.M.McDONALD
C.C.CAMERON	F.W.McMURRAY
J.G.CAMPBELL	T.J.MacQUEEN
D.A.COOKE	W.M.MAHAFFY
N.CROTHERS	W.J.MEEK
W.F.E.GAULT	F.J.MILEY
R.T.GIBSON	W.W.MILLER
J.T.GLASS	R.A.MOORE
D.J.GOODCHILD	D.MORROW
J.T.GRAHAM	L.T.PENTZ
J.N.HAMILTON	E.V.POLLEY
N.E.HANNA	J.H.ROWAN
H.HANNAY	R.H.RUTHERFORD
D.F.HENDERSON	J.S.SMYTH
J.C.C.HOLLAND	H.C.THOMPSON
H.A.KIDD-MAY	M.E.YOUNG
G.H.C.LOWDEN	

class light cruiser HMS *Naiad* in the Royal Navy. Prior to that there had been two other ships bearing the name HMS *Naiad*, the first having been commissioned in 1798 (the name comes from Greek mythology where the Naiads were water nymphs) and seeing action in the Napoleonic wars. The second HMS *Naiad* saw action in the Great War. The third HMS *Naiad* was laid down in 1937 by R. and W. Hawthorn, Leslie and Company Ltd., Hebburn-on-Tyne, launched in 1939 and completed on 24 July 1940. Completion was delayed because of damage from air raids. On 9 March 1942 HMS *Naiad* sailed from Alexandria as flagship of an attack force and it was during the return voyage on 11 March that she sank in the eastern Mediterranean, north of Sidi Barrani in Egypt, after being torpedoed by the German submarine *U-565*. More than 80 members of the crew were lost. Norman's last shore address was 46 Lawson Road, Colwyn Bay, Denbighshire. His effects amounted to some £262 and probate was granted to his widowed mother.

Engine Room Artificer Norman Crothers was 23 years old when he died and he is commemorated on Chatham Naval Memorial, Kent; on Bangor and District War Memorial; in First Bangor Presbyterian Church; in Bangor Grammar School and on the family grave headstone in Bangor Cemetery.

Crozier, Archibald*
Private
No. 13011578, Pioneer Corps
Died of illness on Monday 15 September 1941 (aged 32)
Bangor Cemetery, Co. Down (Section 1 B Grave 97)
Brookwood Memorial, Surrey, England (Panel 20 Column 3)

Archibald Crozier was born on 31 July 1909 and he was a grandson of William James and Henrietta Crozier (nee Neill) and a son of Walter Henry and Annie Crozier (nee Nelson) who were married on 23 September 1902 in St. Anne's Church of Ireland Church, Belfast. Walter Crozier served as a drill instructor at Clandeboye Camp during the First World War and Walter's brother, Rifleman William Crozier (Archibald's uncle), died in the First World War. Rifleman William Crozier is commemorated on Page 126 in the Book of Honour *Remembering Their Sacrifice in the Great War – North*

Down compiled by Barry Niblock. Walter and Annie Crozier had at least five children – William (born 13 January 1903); Hugh (born 28 April 1905); Walter (born 8 January 1907); Archibald (born 31 July 1909) and Frederick (born 7 August 1912).

Archibald Crozier worked as a labourer and he and Alice Josephine Rice (aged 23, daughter of Owen Rice, a farmer) were married on 24 January 1933 in Newtownards Registry Office. Archibald and Alice Crozier lived at 14 Victoria Road, Bangor and later at 11 Hazelbrook Avenue, Bangor. During the Second World War Private Archibald Crozier served with the Pioneer Corps and he was 32 years old when he died of pulmonary tuberculosis at 11 Hazelbrook Avenue on 15 September 1941. He was buried on 18 September 1941 in Bangor Cemetery in the same grave as his paternal grandparents and he is commemorated on the Brookwood Memorial in Surrey. Henrietta Crozier died on 9 November 1923 aged 64 and William James Crozier died on 22 January 1926 aged 80. Their son William who died in the First World War is commemorated on their headstone but their grandson Archibald is not.

Crozier, Cyril Johnson (Cyril)
C
Sergeant
No. 1061583, 86 Squadron, Royal Air Force Volunteer Reserve
Killed in action on Sunday 17 May 1942 (aged 29)
Sola Churchyard, Norway (British Plot E 9)

> **DIED ON ACTIVE SERVICE**
> CROZIER.—May, 1942, formerly reported missing, now reported killed in action, Sergeant-Observer Cyril J. Crozier, R.A.F., husband of Meta Crozier, 18 Farnham Road, Bangor, and only son of Mr. and Mrs. W. J. Crozier, 13 Fourth Avenue, Bangor. Interred in military cemetery, Sola, Stavanger, Norway, May, 1942.

Cyril Johnston Crozier was born in Londonderry on 11 February 1913 and he was the only son of William John and Ada Crozier (nee Johnson). William John Crozier was a school teacher and he and Ada Johnson were married on 9 April 1912 in Coleraine Methodist Church. They lived in Coleraine and Cyril attended Coleraine Academical Institution from 1923 until 1926. He also attended Queen's University, Belfast where he studied languages. He obtained an MA degree and a Higher Diploma in Education and until the outbreak of war he was on the staff of Lisburn Technical High School for Boys where he taught French and English. After Cyril died a colleague said that, 'though he was a scholar he did not parade his learning. He was an authority on the French language and to him education was more than a profession'.

The Crozier family moved from Coleraine to Bangor where they lived at 13 Fourth Avenue. Cyril Crozier and Meta Wilson of 18 Farnham Road,

Bangor were married on 12 November 1941 in Queen's Parade Methodist Church, Bangor. Both were well-known in musical circles in Bangor and at the wedding Meta's sister Betty played the organ. Her sister Molly was bridesmaid. Cyril and Meta Crozier honeymooned in the Republic of Ireland and just six months later Cyril was killed in action. He served with the Royal Air Force Volunteer Reserve and initially he was reported missing in action. In October 1942 it was officially confirmed that he had been killed and was buried in Norway. His effects amounted to some £95 and probate was granted to his widow Meta.

Sergeant Cyril Johnson Crozier was 29 years old when he died and he is commemorated on Bangor and District War Memorial; in Coleraine Academical Institution and in Queen's University, Belfast.

Cruise, Richard Sweet (Richard)
Sergeant
No. 523187, 214 Squadron, Royal Air Force
Died on Sunday 31 May 1942 (aged 26)
Reichswald Forest War Cemetery, Kleve, Nordrhein-Westfalen, Germany (Collective Grave 14F 7-14)

C

> **ROLL OF HONOUR**
>
> CRUSE—In loving memory of my dear grandson, Sergt. Richard S. Cruse, Flight Engineer, who lost his life over Cologne, May 31, 1942.
> Fondly remembered.
> Mrs. Ballantine, 29 Mount Street, Donaghadee.

In some records the surname is spelt Cruse and in others Creuse. Richard Sweet Cruise's birth was registered in the fourth quarter of 1915 in Newtownards and he was a son of William John Sweet Cruise and Elizabeth Cruise (nee Ballantine) of Parker Street, Newtownards Road, Belfast. Richard's death was reported in the 13 February 1943 edition of the *Newtownards Chronicle* under the headline *Young Airman Presumed Dead*. His father William served with the Royal Engineer Signals Service during the Great War and before that he had worked as a tramway motorman.

Richard Sweet Cruise's great-grandfather, Richard Sweet Cruise, was a lighthouse keeper who was stationed at Ballygrot, Greypoint and Donaghadee. His grandfather, William Sweet Cruise (born 1836), married Elizabeth Austin on 4 January 1870 in Bangor Abbey and he was harbour master in Donaghadee. William died on 6 January 1896 and Elizabeth died on 7 October 1901. Richard Sweet Cruise's uncle, also called Richard Sweet Cruise (born 5 June 1873 at Orlock), was a coastguard officer.

Richard's parents, William John Sweet Cruise and Elizabeth Ballantine, were married on 23 October 1909 in Donaghadee Parish Church of Ireland Church and they had at least four children – William (born 1 October 1909); Stanley (born 10 December 1911); Alexander (born 24 February 1913) and Richard Sweet (born 1915).

Richard Cruise was brought up by his maternal grandmother Annie Ballentine of 29 Mount Street (then the lower part of Moat Street), Donaghadee and before joining the Royal Air Force around 1935 he worked for the Strangford Knitting Company in Newtownards. His uncle Edward Ballantine lived at 4 Patricia Gardens, Donaghadee Road, Newtownards. The marriage of a Richard Sweet Cruise and Ruth Lloyd was registered in the third quarter of 1940 in Wirral, Cheshire.

Sergeant Richard Cruise was reported missing in May 1942 during air operations over Germany and some nine months later he was officially reported to have been killed. He was one of an eight man crew aboard a Short Stirling Mark I aircraft (W7534) that took off from RAF Stradishall in Suffolk on a mission to bomb Cologne. The aircraft crashed near Monchengladbach and everyone on board was killed. They were all buried in Reichswald Forest War Cemetery, Germany. The other seven crew members who died were:

- Pilot Officer Harry Dent aged 23 from Marylebone, London
- Sergeant Clarence Henry Muir aged 22 (RAAF)
- PO Sydney Stephen Dimond aged 32 from Enfield Town, Middlesex
- Sergeant Geoffrey Charles Bunning
- Sergeant John Henry Munday
- Pilot Officer William Davies aged 31 from Edinburgh
- Sergeant Patrick Gerald McGrath

Sergeant Richard Sweet Cruise was 26 years old when he died and he is commemorated on Donaghadee and District War Memorial.

Cully, John Hughes (Jack)
Mate
SS *River Humber* (Bristol), Merchant Navy
Died as a result of a collision at sea on Tuesday 4 June 1940 (aged 33)
Tower Hill Memorial, London, England (Panel 87)

Jack Cully was born on 20 October 1905 and he was a son of Samuel and

Margaret (Maggie) Cully (nee Hughes) who were married on 8 May 1899 in Glastry Presbyterian Church. Samuel Cully worked as a fisherman and he and Margaret had at least eight children, all of whom were baptised in Cloughey Presbyterian Church – James Hughes (born 4 July 1901); Hugh (born 6 November 1903); John Hughes (Jack, born 20 October 1905); Kathleen (born 4 May 1907, died 28 February 1909); Kathleen Isabella (born 27 June 1910); Bertha Kennedy (born 1 July 1913); Samuel (born 5 May 1916) and Alice Kirkpatrick (born 2 July 1919).

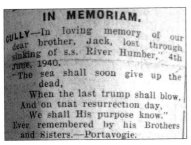

IN MEMORIAM.

CULLY—In loving memory of our dear brother, Jack, lost through sinking of s.s. River Humber," 4th June, 1940.
"The sea shall soon give up the dead,
When the last trump shall blow,
And on that resurrection day,
We shall His purpose know."
Ever remembered by his Brothers and Sisters.—Portavogie.

Jack Cully and Martha Stevenson of Belfast were married on 16 May 1928 in St. John's Church of Ireland Church, Laganbank, Belfast. Jack Cully's father Samuel died on 9 July 1929 (aged 56) and his mother Margaret died on 22 August 1941.

During the Second World War Jack Cully served with the Merchant Navy aboard the SS *River Humber*. Built in 1920 by Hepple and Company Ltd., South Shields and owned by Charles Neill Ltd., Bangor, the SS *River Humber* was on passage from Dublin to Preston in ballast when she sank after a collision with HMS *Folkestone* in the Irish Sea east-north-east of Skerries, Dublin. Ordinary Seaman **James McMaster** and Fireman **Frank Maginnis** died in the same incident. The fourth man who died was Chief Engineer Officer John Gibson aged 32 from Gardenstown in Banffshire, Scotland. **John Gibson*** was born in Pennan, Aberdeenshire in Scotland although he did live for a time at 26 Primrose Street, Bangor. Jack Cully's shore address at the time of his death was 77 Roseberry Road, Belfast.

CULLY

In Loving Memory Of

KATHLEEN
DIED 28TH FEBRUARY 1909

SAMUEL DIED 9TH JULY 1929

JACK LOST AT SEA 4TH JUNE 1940

MARGARET DIED 22ND AUGUST 1941

After Jack Cully died the Worshipful Master of Portavogie LOL 552, John McMullan, and the Secretary, W.H. Mawhinney, placed a notice in the 8 June 1940 edition of the *County Down Spectator*: 'The officers and members of Portavogie LOL 552 desire to tender sincere and heartfelt sympathy to the relatives of Brother Jack Cully and Mr John McMaster who lost their lives in the sinking of the SS *River Humber*.'

Mate Jack Cully was 33 years old when he died and he is commemorated on the Tower Hill Memorial in London; on the Cully family grave headstone in Ballyhalbert Cemetery and in Portavogie Loyal Orange Lodge No. 552.

Cummins, William (Billy)
Sergeant (Flight Engineer)
**No. 1881267, 166 Squadron, Royal Air Force Volunteer Reserve
Died on active service on Thursday 22 March 1945 (aged 30)
Rheinberg War Cemetery, Kamp Lintfort, Nordrhein-Westfal, Germany
(Grave 6 D 7)**

William (Billy) Cummins was born on 25 January 1915 and baptised in Bangor Parish Church of Ireland Church (St. Comgall's) on 21 February 1915. He was the only son of Samuel and Ellenor Jane (Nellie) Cummins (nee Carter) who lived in Bangor. Samuel Cummins was 24 years old, a widower and he was working as a plater for Harland and Wolff in Belfast when he and Nellie Carter were married on 28 December 1910 in the Mariner's Church of Ireland Church, Belfast. Samuel's first wife was Mary Adair and they were married on 24 December 1907 in Lisburn Methodist Church.

Billy Cummins's uncle Chris Carter lived at 12 Prospect Road, Bangor and Billy was seven years old when his mother Nellie died in March 1922 aged 36. When Billy's father Samuel moved to England to work for Swan Hunter at Birkenhead Billy stayed on in Bangor because of his job and his ties with local scouting. Billy worked as a car mechanic in W.H. Alexander's Garage in Belfast and he was Assistant Scoutmaster to Sandy Dalzell in First Bangor Scout Troop. Billy Cummins joined the Royal Air Force Volunteer Reserve and sometime during the Second World War, according to family sources, he got married.

> **DIED ON ACTIVE SERVICE.**
> CUMMINS—Missing since March 22, 1945, now presumed to have lost his life during air operatons over enemy territory, Sergt. (Flight Eng.) W. Cummins (Billy), son of the late Mrs. Cummins and of Mr. S. Cummins, Birkenhead (formerly of Bangor, Co. Down), and nephew of C. Carter, 12 Prospect Road, Bangor.

Sergeant William Cummins served with 166 Squadron in Bomber Command and on 22 March 1945 he was one of a seven man crew aboard an Avro Lancaster Mark I aircraft (PD365) that took off at 11.27 pm from RAF Kirmington in Lincolnshire on a mission to bomb the railway yards at Hildesheim in Germany. Their aircraft failed to return and the other six airmen who died that night were:

- FS Richard Ernest Moore aged 29 from Thornton Heath, Surrey
- Sergeant John Hanlon aged 21
- FS John Marrinan aged 22 from Copster Green, Lancashire
- Warrant Officer Laurence Reed aged 23 from Leeds
- Sergeant Frank Hume aged 23 from Foulness, Essex
- Flight Sergeant Clifford Theodore Johnson aged 19 (RCAF)

Sergeant Billy Cummins was 30 years old when he died and he is commemorated on Bangor and District War Memorial and in Bangor Parish Church (St. Comgall's). At the time of Billy's death his father Samuel was living in Bebington, Birkenhead, Cheshire.

Cutler, Robert Henry (Tabby)*
Major (demobilised)
King's African Rifles
Died as a result of an aircraft accident on Thursday 12 July 1945 (aged 41)
City Park Cemetery, Nairobi, Kenya (Section 3 Lot 75)

Robert Henry Cutler was born in Belfast on 21 June 1904 and he was the only son of Henry Albert Cutler (born 1861) and Frances Mabel Cutler (nee Atkinson, born 1876) of 7 Shandon Park, Belfast. Both of his parents were born in England and his father was a Civil Engineer. His sister, Nora Mabel Cutler, was born on 28 November 1905.

The Cutler family lived in Groomsport during the summer months and in 1913 Robert Henry Cutler attended Rockport School, Craigavad as a day boy. He was a keen yachtsman. Later he obtained an MA degree from Cambridge University and he lived in London until 1928 when he moved to Tanganyika (now Tanzania) in East Africa to take up the post of Superintendent of Education. In 1930 he and Ruth Wyckham Hewlet-Cooper were married in Dar es Salaam, Tanganyika and they had two children.

At the outbreak of the Second World War Robert Henry Cutler joined the Army and served with the King's African Rifles in Abyssinia (now Ethiopia) before assuming special training duties with the askari (local soldiers). Major Robert Henry Cutler was demobilised in January 1944 and he received a letter from General Sir Bernard Paget who was General Officer Commanding-in-Chief, East Africa Command. The letter included the paragraph, 'It having been found necessary in the general interest of the War Effort that you should return to civil life and duty, I wish to tell you how much I regret the severance of your connection with the troops of the East

Africa Command and, at the same time, thank you very sincerely for your valuable services with the Army'. It may be of interest to note that Sir Bernard Paget's younger son, Lieutenant Tony Paget, died on 5 March 1945 as a result of wounds received while serving with the 1st Battalion, Oxfordshire and Buckinghamshire Light Infantry (the 43rd) during the Battle of Reichswald.

After he was demobilised in January 1944 Major Robert Henry Cutler was appointed Director of Training in Tanganyika's demobilisation scheme and he died in Nairobi, Kenya on 12 July 1945. In the 13 July 1945 edition of the Tanganyika Standard it was reported that there were no survivors when an aeroplane crashed in attempting to take off from Eastleigh Aerodrome, Nairobi the previous day. 'Amongst the eleven people who died was Mr R.H. Cutler, Director of Training in Tanganyika's demobilisation scheme and formerly Education Officer'.

In January 1946 Major Cutler's colleagues presented eight Provincial Challenge Shields as a tribute to his memory:

'We, the colleagues of R.H. 'Tabby' Cutler including past and present members of the Headquarters Staff, European, Asian and African, and the staffs of the Dar es Salaam, Mpwapwa, Mwanza, Tanga, Tabora, Malangali, Moshi, Kashasha and Southern Province schools, present, as a tribute to his memory eight Provincial Challenge Shields for Handicrafts, to be known as the Cutler Memorial Shields. We wish these shields to be open for competition each year by the African schools of each Province in Tanganyika Territory, and we hope that the resulting Annual Handicrafts Competitions and Exhibitions, either by themselves or through the development of similar competitions open to the schools of each District, will do much to foster the practical side of Education in which Mr Cutler took so great an interest'.

Major Robert Henry Cutler is commemorated on Groomsport and District War Memorial; in Groomsport Parish Church of Ireland Church and in Rockport School, Craigavad.

Dalzell, Joseph (Joe)
Gunner
No. 1476588, 5 Battery, 2 Light Anti-Aircraft Regiment, Royal Artillery
Died of wounds on Thursday 25 September 1941 (aged 36)
Tobruk War Cemetery, Libya (Grave 6 K 9)

Joseph (Joe) Dalzell was born on 5 March 1905 and he was a son of William and Agnes Dalzell (nee Gordon) who were married on 18 September 1896 in Newtownards Parish Church of Ireland Church (St. Mark's). They lived at 60 Movilla Street, Newtownards. William Dalzell worked as a wool weaver and general labourer and he and Agnes had thirteen children including Martha (born 22 June 1898); Agnes (born 6 February 1900); James (born 1901); Hugh (born 1 September 1903); Joseph (born 5 March 1905); David (born 11 September 1906); Robert (born 22 January 1908); Jane (born 6 May 1910) and Emily (born 10 December 1911). Four of their children died in infancy.

Joseph Dalzell worked as a labourer before he joined the Army and he and Ellen McLarty (aged 20, daughter of Duncan McLarty) were married on 14 July 1931 in Newtownards Registry Office. They lived at 5 George Street and later 8 Upper Movilla Street, Newtownards and they had three children.

Joe Dalzell's parents-in-law lived at 27 Upper Movilla Street, Newtownards as did his sister-in-law and brother-in-law Margaret and James Cardy (Royal Navy). During the Second World War Gunner Joseph Dalzell served with the Royal Artillery and he died on 25 September 1941 during the siege of Tobruk along with three other men from Newtownards – **Samuel Graham**, **William John McNeilly** and **James Meredith**. Gunner Dalzell was 36 years old when died of wounds in No. 4 Australian General Hospital, Tobruk. His wife Ellen placed a *Killed in Action* notice in the 11 October 1941 edition of the *Newtownards Chronicle* and it contained the verse:

Why what we long for most of all,
Eludes so oft our eager hand;
Why hopes are crushed and castles fall,
Up there sometime we'll understand.

Gunner Joseph (Joe) Dalzell is commemorated on Newtownards and District War Memorial. His brother-in-law James Woods and his nephew Gordon were both on active service. Joe's wife Ellen died on 26 November 1985.

D

Darragh, James
Corporal
No. 6977528, Royal Army Medical Corps
Died of illness on Wednesday 27 June 1945 (aged 32)
Bangor Cemetery, Co. Down (Section 5 X Grave 9)

James Darragh was born on 1 May 1913 in the townland of Tamlaght, Ballymoney and he was a son of Richard and Elizabeth (Lizzie) Darragh (nee Weir) of Rasharkin, Co. Antrim. Richard Darragh was a farmer in the townland of Tamlaght and Richard's parents were Henry and Mary Jane Darragh. After Richard Darragh's first wife died he lived with his widowed mother Mary Jane, his son Henry and his brother James.

Richard Darragh and Elizabeth Weir were married on 22 February 1912 in Dirraw Roman Catholic Church, Ballymoney and their son James was born on 1 May 1913. During the Second World War, James Darragh served with the Royal Army Medical Corps. Corporal James Darragh was 32 years old when he died of peritonitis in Bangor Military Hospital on 27 June 1945. He was buried in Bangor Cemetery on 30 June and there is an inscription on his CWGC headstone:

Queen of the Most Holy Rosary Pray for Him R I P

Davidson, Alexander (Alex)
Sergeant
No. 7007149, 5 Battery, 2 Light Anti-Aircraft Regiment, Royal Artillery
Died of wounds on Sunday 21 June 1942 (aged 40)
Knightsbridge War Cemetery, Acroma, Libya (Grave 2 F 5)

Alexander Davidson was born around 1902 and he was a son of Hugh James and Julia Isabel Davidson who lived at 3 William Street, Newtownards. Hugh James Davidson served in the First World War and he and Julia had at least five children – Alexander; Francis (Sandy, moved to Canada); Robert (served with the Royal Irish Rifles and then as a bomb disposal sergeant with the Royal Air Force); Thomas (served for 28 years with the Royal Air Force) and William (served with the Royal Irish Rifles and died aged 22). Alexander Davidson joined the Royal Irish Rifles when he was 16 years old and served for ten

D

years. He spent four years in India. Then he worked as a bricklayer before joining the Royal Artillery in 1937/38.

Alexander Davidson (aged 22) and Agnes Kennedy Arnold (aged 21) were married on 18 March 1927 in Newtownards Registry Office and they lived at 13 Wallace's Street No. 2, Newtownards. Alexander and Agnes Davidson had six children – James Arnold (Jim, served with the RAF); Julia Elizabeth; Rita Kennedy; Alexander; Margaret White and Joseph Arnold (Joe). Postwar Joe Davidson served with the Royal Air Force Regiment and then the Parachute Regiment.

OUR HEROES—IN MEMORIAM.

DAVIDSON—In loving memory of my dear husband, and our dear father, Sergeant Alexander Davidson, who died of wounds received at Tobruk on 21st June, 1942.

Fond is the link that is broken,
Dear is the one that is gone,
But in memory we shall keep him
As year after year passes on.

Always remembered by his Wife and Family.
AGNES DAVIDSON.
13, Wallace Street No. 2,
Newtownards.
Also his Brother-in-law, Gnr. Joseph Arnold (prisoner of war in Italy).

During the Second World War Alexander Davidson served with the Royal Artillery, as did other family members – his wife's brother, Joseph Arnold from Greenwell Street, Newtownards; Davy Savage (his wife's sister May's husband) and his wife's cousin Julius (Jules) Dorrian of Movilla Street, Newtownards. Gunner **William James (Billy) Martin** who died on 25 April 1942 was one of the Gunners who served under Sergeant Alexander Davidson.

D

Sergeant Alexander Davidson died of wounds on 21 June 1942, along with three of his comrades, after being hit by shell-fire at Tobruk the previous day. Their gun position was sited some 2¼ miles south of Tobruk docks, on a broad plateau above an escarpment and about a thousand yards east of the road running almost due south out of Tobruk. Their Navy, Army and Air Force Institutes (NAAFI) Building was on the same plateau but slightly further north. The Axis Forces (21 Panzer Division) swept through their gun position some time between 2.30 and 5.00 pm on Saturday 20 June and reached the harbour area shortly afterwards. The other men who died were Lieutenant (Acting Captain) **John Malcolmson Gibson** from Newtownards, Gunner **David McClinton** from Newtownards and Gunner George Alfred Rayner from Glastonbury in Somerset.

Alexander Davidson's wife Agnes placed a notice in the 9 January 1943 edition of the *Newtownards Chronicle* and it contained the verse:

May the heavenly winds blow softly
O'er that sweet and hallowed spot,
Though the sea divides us from your grave,
You will never be forgot

Sergeant Alexander Davidson was 40 years old when he died and he is commemorated on Newtownards and District War Memorial; in Newtownards Parish Church of Ireland Church (St. Mark's) and on the family grave headstone in Movilla Cemetery Newtownards. His wife Agnes died on 10 March 1960 and their son James died on 1 December 1982. Alexander's mother Julia died on 26 April 1946 and was buried in Movilla Cemetery.

Deane, Cecil Thomas (Cecil)
Flight Sergeant (Air Gunner)
No. 904963, 153 Squadron, Royal Air Force Volunteer Reserve
Killed in an aircraft accident on Wednesday 18 February 1942 (aged 25)
Mortlake Crematorium, Surrey, England

Cecil Thomas Deane's birth was registered in the first quarter of 1917 in Hammersmith, London and he was a son of Albert George and Alice Margaret Deane (nee Carter) of Shepherd's Bush, London. Their marriage was registered in the third quarter of 1913 in Brentford, Middlesex. Cecil Deane was a renowned international swimmer, he swam in the European Games in Paris in September 1938 and he held long distance championship records in England, Belgium and Holland.

Cecil Thomas Deane and Queenie Stocks of Farnsfield, Nottinghamshire were married on 30 November 1940 in Mansfield Registry Office and during the Second World War Cecil served with the Royal Air Force Volunteer Reserve. On 18 February 1942 a Boulton Paul Defiant aircraft (T3914) with 153 Squadron based at RAF Ballyhalbert spun into the sea off Kearney, Co. Down after the pilot appeared to lose control. There were unconfirmed reports that he had been attempting to avoid another aircraft. Both crew members were killed and four days later their bodies were recovered from the sea near Burial Island to the north of Portavogie. The two men who died were Flight Sergeant (Pilot) **John Robert Lucas** and Flight Sergeant (Air Gunner) Cecil Thomas Deane (aged 25).

Dempster, Edward (Eddie)
Corporal
No. 7012285, 1st (Airborne) Battalion, Royal Ulster Rifles
Died of wounds on Friday 7 July 1944 (aged 30)
Hermanville War Cemetery, Calvados, France (Grave 2 A 3)

Edward Dempster was a son of James and Elizabeth (Lizzie) Byers Dempster

KILLED IN ACTION.

DEMPSTER—Corporal Edward (Eddie) Dempster, Royal Ulster Rifles, died of wounds received in action on July, 1944. Formerly of Donaghadee.

Deeply regretted by his sorrowing Sister and Brother-in-law.—Mary and Vic. Also the Hull Family. Sister Mary, 142 High Street, North Fleet, Kent.

(nee Stewart) of 11 Meetinghouse Lane, Donaghadee. They were married on 14 March 1910 in St. Anne's Church of Ireland Cathedral, Belfast. James Dempster worked as a general labourer and he and Lizzie had at least six children – James (born 23 June 1910); Hugh (born 22 June 1911, died 21 September 1911); Thomas (born 11 September 1912); Edward (born 22 November 1913); Mary (married Vic Hull and lived at 142 High Street, North Fleet, Kent) and Hugh Stewart (born 30 April 1919 and baptised 13 May 1919 in Donaghadee Methodist Church).

7012285 CORPORAL
E. DEMPSTER
THE ROYAL ULSTER RIFLES
AIRBORNE
7TH JULY 1944 AGE 30

The marriage of Eddie Dempster and Betty Watkins of Westfields, Hereford was registered in the third quarter of 1941 in Hereford and during the Second World War Eddie served with the 1st (Airborne) Battalion, Royal Ulster Rifles. On 6 June 1944 this Battalion landed by glider near Ranville in Normandy and was initially deployed to extend the bridgehead south of the River Orne. Corporal Eddie Dempster was 30 years old when he died of wounds on 7 July 1944 and he is commemorated on Donaghadee and District War Memorial. There is an inscription on his CWGC headstone:

D

In loving memory, the night is ended, I have heard reveille on the other side

Deveney, John Ferris (Jack)
Able Seaman
SS *Victoria City* (Bideford), Merchant Navy
Died as a result of enemy action on Monday 2 December 1940 (aged 35)
Tower Hill Memorial, London (Panel 114)

John Ferris (Jack) Deveney was born on 14 June 1905 and he was a son of George and Mary Ann Deveney (nee Ferris) who lived at 94 Castle Street, Bangor. They were married on 13 April 1899 in St. Thomas's Church of Ireland Church, Belfast and they had five children – Walter (born 30 August 1901); twins John Ferris and Elizabeth (born 14 June 1905); Margaret (Peggy, born 16 September 1907) and Martha (born 11 January 1910, later married Allen

Hedley). John Ferris Deveney was baptised on 9 July 1905 in Bangor Parish Church of Ireland Church (St. Comgall's). Jack's father, George Deveney, was a seaman for over 30 years and for part of that time he worked as a cook on various ships belonging to Messrs John Kelly Ltd. George Deveney died on 6 February 1925, Mary Ann died on 17 July 1966, Peggy died on 22 April 1999 and they are all commemorated on the family grave headstone in Bangor Cemetery.

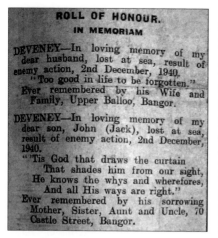

ROLL OF HONOUR.

IN MEMORIAM

DEVENEY—In loving memory of my dear husband, lost at sea, result of enemy action, 2nd December, 1940.
"Too good in life to be forgotten."
Ever remembered by his Wife and Family, Upper Balloo, Bangor.

DEVENEY—In loving memory of my dear son, John (Jack), lost at sea, result of enemy action, 2nd December, 1940.
"'Tis God that draws the curtain
That shades him from our sight,
He knows the whys and wherefores,
And all His ways are right."
Ever remembered by his sorrowing Mother, Sister, Aunt and Uncle, 70 Castle Street, Bangor.

Jack Deveney served in the Merchant Navy for more than ten years and before going to sea he worked as a haulage contractor between Bangor and Belfast. Jack Deveney of 70 Castle Street, Bangor and Anne (Annie) Orchard of Osborne Drive, Bangor were married on 4 July 1929 in Ballygrainey Presbyterian Church. Both of their fathers were deceased sailors. Jack and Annie Deveney had four children – Kathleen, John Ferris, Margaret and Thomas. Jack Deveney served aboard the SS *Victoria City* and he died on 2 December 1940 when this ship was torpedoed by the German submarine *U-140* in the North Atlantic during a voyage from New York via Halifax in Nova Scotia to London. At the time the SS *Victoria City* was a straggler in Convoy HX-90. The SS *Victoria City* was a cargo steamer built in 1929 by William Gray and Company Ltd., West Hartlepool (Sunderland) and owned by Sir William Reardon Smith and Sons Ltd., Cardiff. More than 40 men died, including Able Seaman **Douglas Collister** who also lived in Bangor.

At the time of Jack's death his wife Annie and their children lived at Upper Balloo, Bangor and his mother Mary Ann, his sister Peggy and his aunt, Ellie Alexander, lived at 70 Castle Street, Bangor. During the First World War Jack's brother Walter served as an Air Mechanic 2nd Class in the Royal Air Force. Walter joined the Royal Naval Air Service on 29 January 1917 and on 1 April 1918 this service was merged with the Royal Flying Corps to form the Royal Air Force. Walter and Annie Deveney lived at 29 Castle Mount, Bangor and Allen and Martha Hedley (nee Deveney) lived at 8a Thomas Street, Newtownards.

After Jack Deveney died several family members placed *Roll of Honour* notices in the *County Down Spectator* and these included the following verses:

He answered his country's call
Too good in life to be forgotten now
Tis God that draws the curtain that shades him from our sight
He knows the whys and wherefores and all His ways are right

Able Seaman John Ferris Deveney was 35 years old when he died and he is commemorated on the Tower Hill Memorial in London; on Bangor and District War Memorial (as Devenney J.) and in Bangor Parish Church (St. Comgall's).

Deville, Thomas Charles (Thomas)
Private
No. 7020517, Pioneer Corps
Died of illness on Thursday 6 May 1943 (aged 35)
Bangor Cemetery, Co. Down (Section 5 X Grave 1)

Thomas Charles Deville was born on 2 April 1907 in Fulham, London and in the CWGC Debt of Honour he was described as a foster-son of James George Deville and Emily Deville who lived in Middlesex. Thomas Charles Deville's parents were James George Deville who was born on 5 March 1871 at 4 Leyborne Street, St. Pancras, Kentish Town, Middlesex and Jane Deville (nee Adkins) who was born on 8 July 1872 at 10 Alpha Place, West Kilburn, Middlesex. Jane Adkins was 17 when she and James George Deville were married on 15 March 1890 in Fulham, London.

D

James George and Jane Deville had at least 15 children including George (born 9 February 1891); Lily (born 18 October 1892); Henry (born 24 March 1894); Dorothy (born 9 April 1895); Jane Eliza (born 4 June 1896); Robert (born 14 October 1897); Percy (born 18 May 1899); Clara (born 1 September 1900); Violet (born 21 October 1901); Minnie (born 22 December 1902); William (born 6 March 1905); Thomas Charles (born 2 April 1907); Frederick (born 5 May 1909); Richard (born 1 October 1910) and Joseph Benjamin (born 17 October 1913). Jane Deville was 41 when she died of tuberculosis on Christmas Day 1913 in Fulham Infirmary. After Jane died James George Deville remarried and he and Emily had at least one child – Emily Frances (born in 1916). James George Deville died in 1925 in Kensington, Middlesex.

During the Second World War Private Thomas Charles Deville served with the 113th Company, Pioneer Corps and he was stationed in Antrim. He was

35 years old and married when he died on 6 May 1943 in Bangor Hospital as a result of pancreatic cancer. He was buried in Bangor Cemetery and there is an inscription on his CWGC headstone:

He was away three years but a day
He has been called to where he will stay RIP

Dickson, Thomas (Tommy)*
Lance Corporal
No. 7019627, 2nd Battalion, Royal Ulster Rifles
Died as a result of an accident on Saturday 25 September 1943 (aged 25)
Bangor Cemetery (Section 5 W Grave 79)

Thomas Dickson was born on 23 July 1918 and he was baptised in Bangor Parish Church of Ireland Church (St. Comgall's) on 11 August 1918. He was the eldest son of James and Eileen Dickson (nee Watt) who lived at 8 King Street, Bangor. During the First World War James Dickson served as a Rifleman with the Royal Irish Rifles and his address was Victoria Barracks, Holywood when he and Eileen Watt of 52 Chadolly Street, Belfast were married in St. Anne's Church of Ireland Cathedral, Belfast on 30 November 1917. They had at least four children – Thomas, James (Jimmy), Mary Frances and Kathleen.

Prior to the outbreak of the Second World War Thomas Dickson worked as a green keeper at Bangor Municipal Golf Links, Carnalea. During the war the upper nine holes of this golf course came under the plough as part of the *Dig for Victory* campaign. The greens were spared and part of the 12th fairway was used by members of the forces for recreational purposes. Thomas Dickson was a member of Bangor Racing Pigeon Club and on 12 April 1941 he and Elsie Barr from 57 Central Avenue, Bangor were married in Bangor Abbey.

During the Second World War Thomas Dickson served with the Royal Ulster Rifles and he died on 25 September 1943 as a result of an accident. His wife Elsie lived at 32 Clandeboye Road, Bangor and his aunt Kathleen Watt lived at 22 May Avenue, Bangor. Later Elsie Dickson moved to 13 Scrabo Road, Newtownards and then to 5 Arundel Terrace, Newcastle, Co. Down.

Military honours were accorded for Lance Corporal Thomas Dickson's funeral to Bangor Cemetery which took place on 30 September 1943.

Comrades from the Royal Ulster Rifles acted as pall bearers and the services were conducted by the Revd James Hamilton. A tribute included the verse:

We who loved him miss him most
For every pain that we must bear
For every sorrow, every care
God knows the reason

Lance Corporal Thomas Dickson was 25 years of age when he died and he is commemorated on Bangor and District War Memorial and in Bangor Parish Church (St. Comgall's). His younger brother James also served with the Royal Ulster Rifles and his sister Mary served with the Auxiliary Territorial Service (ATS). There is an inscription on his CWGC headstone:

The fittest place where man can die is where he dies for man

His sister Kathleen died on 8 July 1953 aged 23, his father James died on 29 November 1969, his mother Eileen died on 29 April 1977 and his brother Jimmy died on 16 January 1988.

Dixon, James Cartner (James)   D
Gunner
No. 3599804, 5/3 Maritime Regiment, Royal Artillery
Killed in action at sea on Saturday 17 January 1942 (aged 21)
Chatham Naval Memorial, Kent, England (Panel 67 Column 2)

Gunner James Cartner Dixon is commemorated on the Dixon family grave headstone in Redburn Cemetery (Plot 380), Holywood. He was born in the second quarter of 1920 in Workington, Cumberland (his mother's maiden name was Stephenson), he lived in Workington and during the Second World War he served with 5/3 Regiment, Royal Artillery. He was 21 years old when he was killed in action at sea on 17 January 1942. His body was never recovered and he is commemorated on the Chatham Naval Memorial in Kent. His wife Rose (34 Church Road, Holywood) was 88 years old when she died on 23 December 1989 and the headstone in Redburn Cemetery (only the one burial in the grave) bears the inscription:

RIP Sweet Jesus have mercy on their souls

Gunner James Cartner Dixon is listed as having been aboard the British steam merchant ship SS *Culebra* when he was killed. This ship was built in

1919 as the SS *War Mirage* by Irvine's Shipbuilding and Dry Dock Company Ltd., West Hartlepool, later renamed SS *Riposto* and then SS *Culebra*. The SS *Culebra* was on route from London to Jamaica via Bermuda carrying a general cargo that included aircraft parts when she was attacked and sunk by shells fired from the German submarine *U-123*. She was dispersed from Convoy ON-53, her position in the North Atlantic was east-northeast of Bermuda and 45 lives were lost. Records vary as to the date of the sinking with both 17 January 1942 (CWGC and Deaths at Sea Register) and 25 January 1942 (uboat.net) being reported.

Doak, Alexander
Able Seaman
D/SSX 24183, HMS *Glorious*, Royal Navy
Killed in action on Saturday 8 June 1940 (aged 20)
Plymouth Naval Memorial, Devon (Panel 37 Column 2)

Alexander Doak's birth was registered in the first quarter of 1920 and he was a son of William and Annie Doak who lived at 83 Mark Street, Newtownards. During the Second World War Alexander Doak served with the Royal Navy aboard the aircraft carrier HMS *Glorious*. This ship was originally built as a battle cruiser by Harland and Wolff in Belfast and completed in 1917. During the late 1920s she was converted to an aircraft carrier.

The evacuation of Allied Forces from Norway (*Operation Alphabet*) was carried out between 5 and 8 June 1940. On the afternoon of 8 June 1940 HMS *Glorious* and her escorting destroyers HMS *Acasta* and HMS *Ardent* were proceeding independently to Scapa Flow when they were intercepted in the Norwegian Sea by the German battle cruisers *Gneisenau* and *Scharnhorst*. At around 6.00 pm the three British ships were sunk by sustained and heavy gunfire with the loss of more than 1,500 lives. In addition to Able Seaman Doak, two other men from Newtownards also died – Able Seaman **Hugh Alexander Eagleson** and Ordinary Seaman **David Scott**.

Able Seaman Alexander Doak was 20 years old when he died and he is commemorated on Plymouth Naval Memorial in Devon; on a stained glass window in the Church of St. Peter, Martindale in Cumbria; on a memorial plaque in Harstad, Norway and on Newtownards and District War Memorial. His father William died on 25 January 1950 (aged 66).

Doggart, Thomas Watters (Thomas)
Flight Sergeant
No. 1821642, 44 Squadron, Royal Air Force Volunteer Reserve
Died on active service on Wednesday 7 March 1945 (aged 20)
Runnymede Memorial, Surrey, England (Panel 270)

Ardsman's Son Missing.—News has been received by Mr. Thomas Doggart, Maryhill Road, Glasgow, that his only son, Thomas Watters Doggart, who was serving with the Royal Air Force, is missing from recent operations. The young airman is a grandson of the late Mr. T. W. Doggart, Newtownadrs, and a nephew of Mr. W. Lamont Doggart, Frances Street, of Mrs. Amberson, Pound Street, Newtownards, and of Mr. H. J. Doggart, Bangor.

When Flight Sergeant Thomas Watters Doggart went missing in action it was reported in the 24 March 1945 edition of the *Newtownards Chronicle* under the headline *Ardsman's Son Missing*. Thomas Watters Doggart was a grandson of the late Thomas Watters and Alice Doggart (nee Lamont), Newtownards and a nephew of William Lamont Doggart, Frances Street, Newtownards, Agnes Jane Amberson (nee Doggart), Pound Street, Newtownards and Horatio James Doggart, Bangor.

Flight Sergeant Thomas Watters Doggart was born on 14 January 1925 in Hutchesontown, Glasgow and he was a son of Thomas Watters Doggart and Mary McDonald Doggart (nee Munro) of Maryhill Road, Glasgow. Thomas Watters Doggart Senior worked as an engine fitter and he and Mary McDonald Munro were married on 19 May 1915 in the Augustine United Free Church, Glasgow. They had three children – Mary Munro (born 2 January 1916); Thomas Watters (born 14 January 1925) and Alexander Lamont (born 28 September 1929). Flight Sergeant Thomas Watters Doggart's grandfather, Thomas Watters Doggart, had worked as a postman in Newtownards and he and his wife Alice had nine children including David Hutchinson, James MacDonald, William Lamont, Horatio James, Alice, Agnes Jane and Thomas Watters.

During the Second World War Thomas Watters Doggart Junior served with the Royal Air Force Volunteer Reserve in Bomber Command and he died on 7 March 1945. Flight Sergeant Doggart was one of a seven man crew aboard an Avro Lancaster Mark I aircraft (NG396) that took off at 6.31 pm from RAF Spilsby in Lincolnshire on a mission to bomb harbour facilities at Sassnitz in Germany. Their aircraft was lost over the Baltic and the other six crew members who died that night were:

- Flying Officer Bernard Francis Boyle (RCAF)
- Sgt William Christopher Thornton aged 28 from Cashel, Co. Tipperary
- PO James Pickup aged 32 from Ashton-under-Lyne, Lancashire
- Flight Sergeant William James Cruse Turner

D

- FS John C. Smith aged 20 from Chalfont St. Peter, Buckinghamshire
- Sergeant Charles James Hance aged 20 from Heston, Middlesex

During the First World War six of Flight Sergeant Thomas Watters Doggart's relations were killed. His great-grandfather Arthur Doggart was a brother of John Doggart who had eight children including Hugh and Horatio. Hugh Doggart had eight children and three of his sons were killed in the Great War – James Neil, Thomas Maddock and Alexander. They are commemorated on Page 194 in the Book of Honour *Remembering Their Sacrifice in the Great War – Ards* compiled by Barry Niblock. Hugh's brother, Horatio Doggart, had five children and three of his sons were also killed in the Great War – James, Hugh and William. They are commemorated on Page 137 in the Book of Honour *Remembering Their Sacrifice in the Great War – North Down* compiled by Barry Niblock.

Flight Sergeant Thomas Watters Doggart's body was never recovered and he is commemorated on the Runnymede Memorial in Surrey.

Doherty, Robert Aubrey Alexander (Aubrey)
Distinguished Flying Cross
Flight Lieutenant
No. 102594, 608 Squadron, Royal Air Force Volunteer Reserve
Killed in action on Friday 23 February 1945 (aged 27)
Runnymede Memorial, Surrey, England (Panel 265)

D

Robert Aubrey Alexander Doherty was born on 2 August 1917 and he was the only son of Robert John and Sarah Doherty (nee Press) of *Maureen*, Cabin Hill Gardens, Knock, Co. Down. Robert John Doherty was an engineering draughtsman and he and Sarah Press were married on 4 April 1912 in St. Mark's Church of Ireland Church, Dundela. Aubrey Doherty attended St. Columba's School, Knock and then Regent House School, Newtownards from 1927 until 1934. After leaving school he went to Queen's University Belfast to study electrical engineering. He was employed by Victor Ltd., Car Dealers and he played rugby for CIYMS. Aubrey joined the Royal Air Force Volunteer Reserve in July 1939 and was called up in August 1939.

During the Second World War Aubrey Doherty served as a Sergeant Pilot and completed 14 operational sorties with 102 Squadron. In April 1941 he was posted to 104 Squadron and he completed a further 10 successful sorties including a daylight raid on Brest. Wing Commander Simonds of 104 Squadron wrote, 'He has consistently pressed home his attacks with courage, zeal and determination and has proved himself to be an outstanding example of a Sergeant Pilot. These qualities were recognised in him and the recommendation for his appointment to commissioned rank was approved. His keenness and devotion to duty have been a sterling example to the other non-commission officer pilots and crews in the Squadron. I have no hesitation in recommending Pilot Officer Doherty very strongly for the award of the Distinguished Flying Cross'. Aubrey Doherty was appointed to commissioned rank on 7 August 1941 and the award of his DFC was reported in the Third Supplement to *The London Gazette* of 21 October 1941 (published by authority on 24 October 1941).

On 23 February 1945 Flight Lieutenant Aubrey Doherty was one of a two man crew aboard a de Haviland Mosquito Mark XX aircraft (KB350) in the Path Finder Force. They took off at 6.16 pm from RAF Downham Market in Norfolk and their mission was to fly in ahead of the bombers and pinpoint targets in Berlin. Their aircraft was lost without trace and the other crew member who died was:

- Flying Officer Leonard Moore aged 21 from Blyth, Northumberland.

Flight Lieutenant Robert Aubrey Alexander Doherty had completed more than 65 operational sorties when he died at the age of 27 and he is commemorated on the Runnymede Memorial in Surrey; in Regent House School and in Queen's University Belfast.

D

Doherty, Thomas Ernest Victor
Sergeant
No. 1081823, Royal Air Force Volunteer Reserve
Killed in action on Monday 14 June 1943 (aged 20)
Runnymede Memorial, Surrey, England (Panel 147)

Thomas Ernest Victor Doherty was a son of Ernest and Jane Doherty (nee Bowman) of Newtownards. They were married on 8 July 1920 in Duncairn Gardens Methodist Church, Belfast. During the Second World War Thomas Ernest Victor Doherty served with the Royal Air Force Volunteer Reserve and he was based at RAF Turnberry in Ayrshire when he was killed on 14

June 1943. Sergeant Thomas Ernest Victor Doherty's body was never recovered and he is commemorated on the Runnymede Memorial in Surrey and on the Turnberry War Memorial. He was 20 years old when he died.

Donaghy, Alexander James
Leading Aircraftman
No. 544946, Royal Air Force
Died as a result of enemy action on Tuesday 25 June 1940 (aged 26)
Runnymede Memorial, Surrey, England (Panel 22)

Local Airman Reported Missing.—Mr. and Mrs. C. Donaghy, "Rutland," Donaghadee Road, Bangor, have been officially informed that their son, Leading Aircraftman A. J. Donaghy, has been reported missing since 25th June. The young airman, who was educated at Coleraine Academical Institution and carried on a business in Southwell Road, Bangor, for a time, joined the R.A.F. some five years ago and was making good progress in the Service. He has a fine flying record. A young man of splendid talents, the official intimation that he is reported missing will be received with deep regret by his many friends, who will join with us in extending sympathy to his parents and the other relatives in the time of acute anxiety through which they are passing and the hope that more reassuring tidings may soon come to hand.

Alexander James Donaghy was born on 7 February 1914 in Killybegs, Co. Donegal and he was a son of Arthur Donaghy (born 1880 in Sixmilecross, Co. Tyrone) and Alice F. Donaghy (nee King, born 1889 in London). Arthur Donaghy was a Constable in the Royal Irish Constabulary when his marriage to Alice King was registered in the third quarter of 1908 in Glenties, Co. Donegal. Their daughter Minnie Florence Donaghy was born on 29 December 1911 in Killybegs. When the Donaghy family moved to Portrush they lived in Princes' Terrace and Alexander James attended the Irish Society's School in Coleraine. Then he studied at Coleraine Academical Institution from 1929 until 1933. When the Donaghy family moved to Bangor they lived at *Rutland*, Donaghadee Road and Alexander James Donaghy carried on a business in Southwell Road. He joined the Royal Air Force in 1935.

In November 1940 Leading Aircraftman Alexander James Donaghy's parents were informed that he had been reported missing in action on 25 June 1940 and later it was officially confirmed that he must be presumed killed. He is commemorated in Coleraine Academical Institution and his name is included on the Victim List for the Lancastria Association of Scotland compiled by Brian Crabb. There is evidence to suggest that Leading Aircraftman Alexander James Donaghy aged 26 was one of an estimated 4,000 people who died when His Majesty's Troopship HMT *Lancastria* was bombed by German aircraft and sunk off the French port of St. Nazaire while taking part in *Operation Ariel*, the evacuation of British nationals and troops from France two weeks after the Dunkirk evacuation. HMT *Lancastria* had embarked an unknown number of passengers (some estimates put the total as high as 9,000) and, after she sank, news of the disaster was suppressed. Leading Aircraftman Alexander James Donaghy is commemorated on the Runnymede Memorial in Surrey. His father Arthur died in Bangor in 1972 and his mother Alice died in 1976.

Donaldson, David Stuart (David)
Sergeant
No. 1127694, 7 Squadron, Royal Air Force Volunteer Reserve
Killed on active service on Tuesday 22 June 1943 (aged 20)
Runnymede Memorial, Surrey, England (Panel 147)

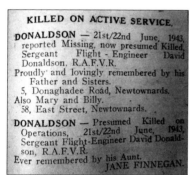

> **KILLED ON ACTIVE SERVICE.**
>
> DONALDSON — 21st/22nd June, 1943, reported Missing, now presumed Killed, Sergeant Flight - Engineer David Donaldson, R.A.F.V.R.
> Proudly and lovingly remembered by his Father and Sisters.
> 5, Donaghadee Road, Newtownards.
> Also Mary and Billy.
> 58, East Street, Newtownards.
>
> DONALDSON — Presumed Killed on Operations, 21st/22nd June, 1943, Sergeant Flight-Engineer David Donaldson, R.A.F.V.R.
> Ever remembered by his Aunt.
> JANE FINNEGAN.

David Stuart Donaldson was a son of David Stuart Donaldson and Louisa Nelson Donaldson (nee Finnegan) of Ballyharry, Newtownards. David Stuart Donaldson Senior was a blacksmith and he and Louisa Nelson Finnegan were married on 31 March 1920 in Ballyblack Presbyterian Church.

During the Second World War David Stuart Donaldson Junior served with the Royal Air Force Volunteer Reserve and he was reported missing during air operations on 22 June 1943. He was officially presumed to have been killed in action and in the 23 June 1945 edition of the *Newtownards Chronicle* there were *Killed on Active Service* notices from his father and sisters at 5 Donaghadee Road, Newtownards; from Mary and Billy at 58 East Street and from his aunt Jane Finnegan.

Sergeant David Stuart Donaldson was one of a seven man crew aboard a Short Stirling Mark I aircraft (R9272) that took off at 11.40 pm on 21 June 1943 from RAF Oakington in Cambridgeshire on a mission to bomb Krefeld in Germany. The aircraft was shot down by a German night fighter and crashed at Gilze in Noord-Brabant, Netherlands. Two crew members survived the crash and were taken Prisoner-of-War – Pilot Officers J.H. Ross and M.P. Ellis. The body of Sergeant F.J.B. Dukes was recovered and buried in Bergen-Op-Zoom War Cemetery. All of the others are commemorated on the Runnymede Memorial in Surrey. In addition to Sergeant David Stuart Donaldson the other four crew members who died that night were:

- Flt Lt James S. Watt DSO DFC aged 21 from Buenos Aires, Argentina
- Flt Lt Frederick Arthur G. Tompkins DFC aged 28 from Morden, Surrey
- Sergeant Arnold John Sutton aged 22 from Long Eaton, Derbyshire
- Sergeant Frederick James Benjamin Dukes aged 21 from Hull

 Sergeant David Stuart Donaldson was 20 years old when he died and he is commemorated on Newtownards and District War Memorial.

Doran, Patrick Edward

Civilian War Dead
Died of illness on Monday 26 October 1942 (aged 56)
Bangor Cemetery, Co. Down (Section 1A Grave 33)

Patrick Edward Doran was born on 19 November 1885 and he was a son of James and Isabella Doran (nee Darragh) of Annette Street, Belfast. They were married on 26 January 1875 in St. Joseph's Roman Catholic Church, Belfast. Patrick Edward Doran worked as a labourer and on 8 May 1909 he and Kathleen Young were married in St. Matthew's Church of Ireland Church, Belfast. They had a son named John and they lived at 22 Kingston Street, Belfast before moving to 106 High Street, Bangor.

During the Second World War Patrick Edward Doran was a member of the Royal Marine Police Special Reserve. He died of tuberculosis at 106 High Street, Bangor on 26 October 1942 and was buried in Bangor Cemetery the following day. In the CWGC Debt of Honour he is described as a Civilian. Of the many civilians of the Commonwealth whose deaths were due to enemy action in the Second World War, the names of some 67,092 are commemorated in the Civilian War Dead Roll of Honour, located near St. George's Chapel in Westminster Abbey, London.

The Royal Marine Police was created by an Order in Council and came into being on 13 October 1922. It was administered by the Adjutant General, Royal Marines and for records, pay, clothing and discipline purposes it was attached to the three Royal Marine Divisions at Chatham, Portsmouth and Plymouth (Devonport). All members of the Royal Marine Police were sworn in as Special Constables under the Special Constables Act 1923 but originally they were serving and retired members of the Royal Corps of Royal Marines. They were subject to military law under the provisions of the Army Act. Pensioners from the Royal Navy were subsequently accepted.

Initially, members of this new Police Force were recruited according to their previous ranks in the Armed Forces. This created a semi-military force as men in the lower ranks served under men who had commanded them in the Royal Marines or the Royal Navy. After the outbreak of the Second World War recruitment dried up because of the practice of recruiting only pensioners from the Royal Marines and the Royal Navy. Men who were expecting to retire from these Forces were retained for the duration of the War. For this reason the rules were amended to permit ex-servicemen from any branch of the Armed Forces to enlist in a new section of the force known as the Royal Marine Police Special Reserve. This still failed to achieve target numbers and a third force, the Admiralty Civil Police was formed. Anyone, regardless of former military service, could join and some men joined the Admiralty Civil Police as an alternative to joining the Armed Forces.

As a result, at the end of the War in 1945, the Admiralty found itself with three police forces, each with different conditions of service and discipline, but all under the same Chief Constable. In October 1949 the three forces were disbanded and the Admiralty Constabulary was formed.

Patrick Edward Doran was 56 years old when he died and he is commemorated on the family grave headstone in Bangor Cemetery. His wife Kathleen died on 19 December 1973.

Douglas, Revd James Arthur (James)
Mentioned in Despatches
Chaplain 4th Class
No. 244123, Royal Army Chaplains' Department *attached* **5th Battalion Wiltshire Regiment**
Died on active service on Saturday 5 August 1944 (aged 34)
Tilly-sur-Seulles War Cemetery, Calvados, France (Grave VII C 3)

D

> **Chaplain's Death on Active Service.**
> —Rev. James Douglas, chaplain to the British Army, whose death on active service has been reported, was curate at Colebrooke, Co. Fermanagh, before his military appointment. He was married to Miss Harte, daughter of Rev. F. E. Harte, M.A., Helen's Bay, ex-President of the Irish Methodist Church, by whom and three children he is survived.

James Arthur Douglas was born on 9 March 1910 in Waterford and he was the second son of John Douglas (born in County Antrim) and Kathleen Douglas (nee Walshe, born in Dublin). They were married on 10 August 1904 in Trinity Church of Ireland Church, Waterford and they lived at 12 South Parade, Waterford. Both John and Kathleen Douglas were National School Teachers and they had at least two children – John Henry (born 10 July 1905) and James Arthur (born 9 March 1910).

James Arthur Douglas attended Newtown School in Waterford (a co-educational school run by a Board of Management but owned by the Religious Society of Friends). He gained a BA degree from Trinity College Dublin in

1932 and entered Holy Orders. In 1935 he married Annie Hildegarde Harte. Annie Harte was born on 12 April 1907 in South Circular Road, Dublin and she was a daughter of the Revd Frederick Edward Harte MA (a Methodist Minister) and Annie Humphrey Harte (nee Guards) who lived in Helen's Bay, Co. Down.

Prior to the outbreak of the Second World War the Revd James Douglas was Church of Ireland Curate at Colebrooke in County Fermanagh and during the war he served with the Royal Army Chaplains' Department *attached to* the 5th Battalion Wiltshire Regiment and he died on 5 August 1944 during the fighting to capture Mont Pincon. The Revd James Arthur Douglas left a widow and three children and he is commemorated in Trinity College Dublin. His death was reported in the 19 August 1944 edition of the *County Down Spectator*.

D
Draper, Walter Raleigh (Walter)
Major
No. 135233, Royal Army Ordnance Corps
Died of illness on Sunday 8 August 1943 (aged 54)
Holywood Cemetery, Co. Down (Grave 1189)

Walter Raleigh Draper was baptised on 4 November 1888 in Bebington Parish Church, Cheshire and he was a son of Hugh William and Alice Kate Draper (nee Noble) of New Bebington, Cheshire. Hugh William Draper worked as a 'leather and hide factor' and he and Alice Kate had at least three children – Arnold Inman, Charles Noble and Walter Raleigh.

Walter Raleigh Draper and Alice Marion Augusta (Alice) Glazebrook (daughter of Alfred Percy and Alice Fanny Glazebrook) were married on 10 July 1918 in Bebington. They subsequently divorced and both remarried. Alice's marriage to George H.L. Dobree was registered in the fourth quarter of 1929 in Kensington, London and Walter's marriage to Marjorie A. Plumpton was registered in the second quarter of 1932 in Bristol, Gloucestershire.

During the Second World War Major Walter Raleigh Draper served with the Royal Army Ordnance Corps and he was 54 years old when he died of a pulmonary embolism on 8 August 1943 in the Royal Victoria Hospital, Belfast. He was buried on 11 August in Holywood Cemetery and his address was recorded as *Wanaragh*, Demesne Road, Holywood.

Duff, Robert Heyburn (Robert)
Leading Stoker
No. D/KX94612, HMS *Meteor*, Royal Navy
Died of illness on Tuesday 20 August 1946 (aged 28)
Bangor Cemetery, Co. Down (Section 5 X Grave 35)

Robert Heyburn Duff's birth was registered in the fourth quarter of 1918 in Newtownards and he was a son of Robert and Jeannie Duff (nee Heyburn) of 82 Argyle Street, Belfast. Robert Duff was a motor driver and he and Jeannie Heyburn from Groomsport were married in Ballygilbert Presbyterian Church. Jeannie's sister Hannah and James Coey, also a motor driver, were married in Ballygilbert Presbyterian Church on 23 October 1913. Robert and Jeannie Duff had at least two children – Robert Heyburn (born about 1918) and Betty Heyburn (born about 1921).

During the Second World War Robert Heyburn Duff served with the Royal Navy aboard HMS *Meteor*. HMS *Meteor* was a Marne-class Destroyer built by Alex Stephens, Linthouse, Govan in Scotland and after completion she began operational service in September 1942. She was the eighth ship of the Royal Navy to be named HMS *Meteor*. HMS *Meteor* survived the Second World War and afterwards she was transferred to the Reserve Fleet. Later she was sold to the Turkish Navy and formally handed over at Portsmouth on 26 September 1959. She was renamed *Piyale Pasha*.

Leading Stoker Robert Heyburn Duff (aged 28) died of tuberculosis in Ards District Hospital on 20 August 1946 and he is commemorated on Groomsport and District War Memorial; in Groomsport Presbyterian Church and on the Duff family grave headstone in Bangor Cemetery. His grandmother, Mary Heyburn, died on 15 February 1957 (aged 89); his mother Jeannie died on 12 September 1978; his aunt, Mary Heyburn, died on 27 July 1979 and his father Robert died on 21 September 1983.

D

Dunlop, Thomas Norman (Norman)
Sergeant
No. 1798048, 57 Squadron, Royal Air Force Volunteer Reserve
Died on active service on Thursday 8 March 1945 (aged 19)
Runnymede Memorial, Surrey, England (Panel 274)

DUNLOP T. N. Thomas Norman Dunlop was born on 17 May 1925 in Newtownards and he was a son of William and Margaret Dunlop (nee Dunlop). William Dunlop worked as an upholsterer and he and Margaret Dunlop were married on 23 January 1918 in Regent Street Methodist Church, Newtownards. William's parents lived at 30 Delaware Street, Belfast and Margaret's parents lived at 37 Court Street, Newtownards. William and Margaret Dunlop had at least four children including Jim, Norman and Molly. During the Second World War Jim Dunlop served with the Royal Navy.

Norman Dunlop was a founder member of 1901 (Cregagh) Air Training Corps Squadron and he was an apprentice electrician before he joined the Royal Air Force Volunteer Reserve on 22 June 1943. He served in Bomber Command and on 7 March 1945 he was one of a seven man crew aboard an Avro Lancaster Mark I aircraft (PB852) that took off at 6.25 pm from RAF East Kirkby in Lincolnshire on a mission to bomb oil installations at Harburg in Germany. Their aircraft was lost without trace and the other six men who died that night were:

- FO Charles William Baush aged 30 from Muswell Hill, Middlesex
- Flight Sergeant Norman Cooper
- Flight Sergeant John Ernest Thompson aged 22 from Hoole, Cheshire
- Flight Sergeant Donald Stuart Whitehouse from Sheffield
- Flight Sergeant John Leslie Stone
- Warrant Officer Donald Forbes aged 21 from Chiswick, Middlesex

Sergeant Thomas Norman Dunlop is commemorated on the Runnymede Memorial in Surrey and on Page 156 in *Ireland's Aviator Heroes of World War II* by John C. Hewitt.

Dunwoody Brothers and Sisters:
Edith, Henry, Isabella and William

Edith, Henry, Isabella and William Dunwoody lived at 13 Lincoln Avenue, Belfast and it was there that they died during the blitz on Wednesday 16 April 1941. They were sons and daughters of the late Matthew and

Elizabeth Dunwoody (nee Barrett) and they were buried on 23 April in Holywood Cemetery, Co. Down. Matthew Dunwoody (in some records spelt Dunwoodie) and Elizabeth Barrett were married on 4 February 1876 in Holywood Parish Church of Ireland Church (St. Philip and St. James).

Matthew Dunwoody worked as a carpenter and he and Elizabeth had ten children – William (born 20 January 1877); Thomas (born 24 May 1878, died in infancy); Matthew (born 14 October 1879); Isabella (Isabel, born 10 October 1881); twins Henry and Thomas (born 31 July 1883, Thomas died in infancy); Edith (born 28 July 1885); Elizabeth (born 26 April 1888, died in infancy); Louisa (born 8 November 1889, died in infancy) and Louisa Millicent (born 29 June 1893). Four of Matthew and Elizabeth Dunwoody's children died in infancy and four were killed during the Second World War.

Dunwoody, Edith
Civilian War Dead
Died as a result of enemy action on Wednesday 16 April 1941 (aged 55)
Holywood Cemetery, Co. Down (Grave New 1372)

D

Edith Dunwoody worked as a housekeeper and she was 55 years old when she was killed during the Blitz on Wednesday 16 April 1941.

Dunwoody, Henry
Civilian War Dead
Died as a result of enemy action on Wednesday 16 April 1941 (aged 57)
Holywood Cemetery, Co. Down (Grave New 1371)

Henry Dunwoody worked as a linen lapper and he was 57 years old when he was killed during the Blitz on Wednesday 16 April 1941.

Dunwoody, Isabella (Isabel)
Civilian War Dead
Died as a result of enemy action on Wednesday 16 April 1941 (aged 59)
Holywood Cemetery, Co. Down (Grave New 1372)

Isabella Dunwoody worked as a housekeeper and she was 59 years old when she was killed during the Blitz on Wednesday 16 April 1941.

Dunwoody, William
Civilian War Dead
Died as a result of enemy action on Wednesday 16 April 1941 (aged 64)
Holywood Cemetery, Co. Down (Grave New 1371)

William Dunwoody was a painter and he was 64 years old when he was killed during the Blitz on Wednesday 16 April 1941.

Of the many civilians of the Commonwealth whose deaths were due to enemy action in the Second World War, the names of some 67,092 are commemorated in the Civilian War Dead Roll of Honour, located near St. George's Chapel in Westminster Abbey, London.

Eagleson, Hugh Alexander (Hugh)
Able Seaman
D/SSX 20113, HMS *Glorious*, Royal Navy
Killed in action on Saturday 8 June 1940 (aged 23)
Plymouth Naval Memorial, Devon (Panel 37 Column 2)

D

Hugh Alexander Eagleson was the fourth son of Hugh Alexander and Margaret (Maggie) Eagleson (nee McCullough) who lived at 110 East Street, Newtownards. Hugh Eagleson Senior worked in a public laundry and he and Maggie McCullough were married on 10 November 1900 in Ballyblack Presbyterian Church. They had at least seven children including Mary (Minnie, born 9 January 1901); Ann (born 7 March 1905, died in infancy); William John (born 19 April 1907); Robert (born 28 March 1911); Thomas (born 25 July 1913) and Hugh Alexander.

Hugh Alexander Eagleson joined the Royal Navy and during the Second World War he served aboard the aircraft carrier HMS *Glorious*. This ship was built as a battle cruiser by Harland and Wolff in Belfast and completed in 1917. During the late 1920s she was converted to an aircraft carrier.

The evacuation of Allied Forces from Norway (Operation Alphabet) was carried out between 5 and 8 June 1940. On the afternoon of 8 June 1940 HMS *Glorious* and her escorting destroyers HMS *Acasta* and HMS *Ardent* were proceeding independently to Scapa Flow when they were intercepted in the Norwegian Sea by the German battle cruisers *Gneisenau* and *Scharnhorst*. At around 6.00 pm the three British ships were sunk by sustained and heavy gunfire with the loss of more than 1,500 lives. These included Able Seaman

Hugh Alexander Eagleson aged 23 together with Able Seaman **Alexander Doak** and Ordinary Seaman **David Scott**, both also from Newtownards.

Able Seaman Hugh Alexander Eagleson is commemorated on Plymouth Naval Memorial in Devon; on a stained glass window in the Church of St. Peter, Martindale in Cumbria; on a memorial plaque in Harstad, Norway; on Newtownards and District War Memorial; in Newtownards Parish Church of Ireland Church (St. Mark's) and on the family grave headstone in Movilla Cemetery, Newtownards. His mother Margaret died on 7 March 1934 (aged 54); his father Hugh died on 22 May 1960 (aged 82) and his sister Minnie died on 5 May 1965.

Earley, Joseph Gerald
Sergeant
No. 970686, 78 Squadron, Royal Air Force Volunteer Reserve
Died on active service on Saturday 1 March 1941 (aged 21)
Runnymede Memorial, Surrey, England (Panel 42)

Joseph Gerald Earley was a son of Michael Early (born County Mayo) and Margaret Mary Earley (nee Donohoe) of 13 Brunswick Road, Bangor. Their marriage was registered in the third quarter of 1913 in Loughrea, Co. Galway where Constable Michael Earley, Royal Irish Constabulary (RIC), was stationed. Joseph Gerald Earley joined the Royal Air Force Volunteer Reserve and during the Second World War he served with 78 Squadron as a wireless operator and air gunner. On 1 March 1941 he was one of a crew of five aboard an Armstrong Whitworth Whitley Mark V aircraft (N1525) that took off from RAF Dishforth in Yorkshire at 7.01 pm on a mission to bomb Cologne. After reporting a successful attack, the aircraft and its crew disappeared without trace. The other crew members who died were:

• Pilot Officer Mervyn James David aged 23 from Birmingham
• Sergeant James William Quincey aged 26 from Hatfield, Hertfordshire
• Sergeant Raymond Clark aged 21 from Monmouth
• Sergeant Roy Bradbury aged 25 from Great Barr, Staffordshire

Sergeant Joseph Gerald Earley was 21 years old when he died and he is commemorated on the Runnymede Memorial in Surrey; on Bangor and District War Memorial and on the family grave headstone in Bangor

EARLEY J.G.

Cemetery. His father Michael was a retired RIC Sergeant when he died at 13 Brunswick Road, Bangor on 18 December 1936 (aged 62). Joseph Gerald Earley's mother Margaret was 59 years old when she died at the same address on 27 January 1948. Her daughter Jean was present when she died.

Eccles, Andrew
Corporal
No. 3709614, 1ˢᵗ (Airborne) Battalion, Border Regiment
Killed in action on Saturday 10 July 1943 (aged 28)
Cassino Memorial, Italy (Panel 7)

Andrew Eccles's birth was registered in the third quarter of 1914 in Barrow in Furness, Lancashire and he was a son of Andrew and Mary E. Eccles (nee Richardson). Andrew Eccles Senior worked as a labourer and his marriage to Mary Richardson was registered in the fourth quarter of 1910 in Barrow in Furness.

Andrew Eccles enlisted in 1932 and he was a Private in the 1ˢᵗ Battalion, Border Regiment based at Palace Barracks, Holywood when he and Sarah (Sadie) Irvine Brine (aged 18, daughter of John Brine, 22 Spring Street, Belfast) were married on 29 June 1936 in Belfast Registry Office. During the Second World War Corporal Andrew Eccles served with the 1ˢᵗ (Airborne) Battalion, Border Regiment and he was reported missing in action on 10 July 1943 during the Allied invasion of Sicily (*Operation Husky*). In November 1943 it was officially confirmed that he must be presumed killed in action. He was 28 years old, his body was never recovered and he is commemorated on the Cassino Memorial in Italy. His wife Sadie and their little son were living at 3 High Street, Ballyhalbert, Co. Down.

Edmonds, John
Gunner
No. 1469241, 5 Battery, 9 Heavy Anti-Aircraft Regiment, Royal Artillery
Died of illness on Sunday 20 April 1947 (aged 35)
Newtownards (Movilla) Cemetery, Co. Down (Section 24 Grave 158)

John Edmonds was born at his parents' home on 25 March 1912 and he was a son of David John and Sarah Maria (Mary) Edmonds (nee Magilton) of 114 Mill Street, Newtownards. David John

Edmonds worked as a labourer and he and Sarah Maria Magilton were married in Newtownards Registry Office. Eliza Jane Edmonds of Back Shuttlefield, Newtownards was present at the birth. David John and Sarah Maria (Mary) Edmonds had at least three children – John (born 25 March 1912); Dina (born 3 January 1916) and Mary Agnes (born 10 December 1919). The two girls were baptised in Greenwell Street Presbyterian Church, Newtownards.

John Edmonds worked as a labourer and he and Florence McBriar (aged 18, daughter of David McBriar of 91 John Street, Newtownards) were married on 23 December 1937 in Newtownards Registry Office. They lived in Mill Street, Newtownards. During the Second World War John Edmonds served as a Gunner with the Royal Artillery and he was 35 years old when he died of tuberculosis on 20 April 1947. There is an inscription on his CWGC headstone in Movilla Cemetery:

Gone to be with Christ which is far better

His parents were buried beside him.

Edwards, Gordon Charles

Flight Sergeant (Observer)
No. 777621, 153 Squadron, Royal Air Force Volunteer Reserve
Killed in an aircraft accident on Tuesday 26 May 1942 (aged 25, CWGC)
Harbledown (St. Michael) Churchyard, Kent, England (North of Church)

Sergeant Observer Gordon Charles Edwards was based at RAF Ballyhalbert and he was killed when his Bristol Beaufighter aircraft (X7573) crashed in the townland of Moneyneagh near Loughguile in County Antrim on 26 May 1942 during a training flight. He was unmarried and his death was registered in Ballymoney (his age was recorded as 27). All three crew members on board were killed.

The pilot was **Stanley Donald Wills** aged 20 (Royal Australian Air Force) who was buried in Ballyhalbert (St. Andrew's) Church of Ireland Churchyard, Ballyeasborough, Co. Down. The other Sergeant Observer aboard was **William Richard Willis** aged 22 (Royal Air Force Volunteer Reserve) who was buried in Ballycranbeg (Mount St. Joseph's) Roman Catholic Churchyard, Co. Down.

Flight Sergeant Gordon Charles Edwards is commemorated on the Marandellas

War Memorial in Southern Rhodesia (now Marondera, Zimbabwe). It is likely that he had farmed in Southern Rhodesia for a time.

Ellis, George
Lieutenant Commander (S)
Royal Navy, HMS *Caroline*
Died of illness on Monday 7 May 1945 (aged 68)
Bangor Cemetery, Co. Down (Section 4U Grave 112)

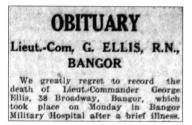

OBITUARY

Lieut.-Com. G. ELLIS, R.N.,
BANGOR

We greatly regret to record the death of Lieut.-Commander George Ellis, 38 Broadway, Bangor, which took place on Monday in Bangor Military Hospital after a brief illness.

Lieutenant Commander George Ellis lived at 38 Broadway, Bangor and he died on 7 May 1945 in Bangor Military Hospital after a short illness. He was born on 13 March 1877 in Balbriggan, Ireland and he was the eldest son of the late William and Julianna (Julia) Ellis (nee Marsh) who lived in Hamilton Road, Bangor. William Ellis and Julia Marsh were married on 6 June 1876 in Balrothery, Balbriggan. George's paternal grandfather, Edmund Ellis had been a farmer. William Ellis was a coastguard officer and he and Julia had at least eight children including Eleanor, George, Julia, William, James Blake, Harriet Martha and Sarah Anne (born 10 April 1892).

George Ellis's sister Julia married David Ewing Gardiner on 18 June 1900 in Bangor Parish Church of Ireland Church (St. Comgall's) and his sister Sarah Anne married William Brown on 15 April 1922 in Bangor Abbey. George Ellis attended the Royal Hospital School, Greenwich, London and he entered the Royal Navy as a boy. He rose to commissioned rank and was on active service during the Great War. George Ellis's first wife died and he and Beatrice Annie Holdnall, who was born in 1881, were married on 22 June 1907 in the Parish Church, Stoke Damerel, Plymouth. They had at least one child – William George Ellis who was born on 1 March 1909 in Stoke Damerel. The Ellis family lived at 62 Whittington Street, Pennycomequick, Plymouth.

George Ellis was recalled to service at the beginning of the Second World War and he was placed in charge of the supply base at Pollock Dock in Belfast. HMS *Caroline* was a C-class light cruiser built in 1914 by Cammell Laird of Birkenhead and during the Second World War HMS *Caroline* served as the Royal Navy's headquarters in Belfast harbour.

A keen bowler, George Ellis was Vice-President of Bangor Bowling Club. He was survived by his wife, his brother William and three sisters: Mrs Eleanor McClure, Belfast; Miss Harriet Ellis, Bangor and Mrs William Brown, Glasgow. It was reported in the 12 May 1945 edition of the *County*

Down Spectator that Lieutenant Commander George Ellis's only son, Dr William George Ellis, who before the war was a zoology lecturer at Liverpool University, had died on active service early in the war. Dr William George Ellis is commemorated on the University of Liverpool Second World War Memorial Plaque. William George Ellis and Rachel Iris Kithuga Crawhall (born 30 July 1919 in Bavaria) were married on 4 April 1936 in Bangor Registry Office, Caernarvonshire, Wales. Her death was registered in the third quarter of 1974 in Taunton, Somerset.

Lieutenant Commander (S) George Ellis was 68 years old when he died and he was buried in Bangor Cemetery, Co. Down. His widow, Beatrice Annie Ellis, died on 29 November 1957 at Woodlands Road, Sparkhill, Birmingham.

Ennis, Andrew
Corporal
No. 7013181, Reconnaissance Corps, Royal Armoured Corps
Died in a motor accident on Thursday 13 March 1941 (aged 23)
Ballycranbeg (Mount St. Joseph's) Roman Catholic Churchyard
(Plot 3 Row D Grave 4)

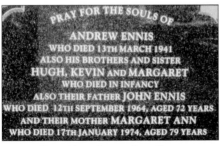

Andrew Ennis was born on 10 January 1918 and he was a son of John and Margaret Ann Ennis (nee McMullan) of Gransha, Kircubbin. He was a grandson of James and Mary Ennis (nee Dougherty). Andrew's father John worked as a labourer and he and Margaret Ann McMullan (daughter of William McMullan, a shoemaker) were married on 3 November 1914 in Mount St. Joseph's Roman Catholic Church, Ballycranbeg. John and Margaret Ann Ennis had thirteen children – William James (born 1 February 1915); John (born 25 February 1916); Andrew (born 10 January 1918); Henry (born 24 March 1920); Brian (Bernard, born 11 August 1923); Cecilia (born 16 February 1925); Hugh (born 7 November 1926; a previous child also named Hugh died in infancy); Tommy (born 23 September 1928); Boniface (born 5 June 1930); Kevin (born 30 October 1931; died in infancy); Catherine (born 27 June 1934) and Margaret (born 3 April 1936; died in infancy).

Andrew Ennis joined the Royal Ulster Rifles and during the Second World

War he served with the Reconnaissance Corps, Royal Armoured Corps. His death was reported in the 22 March 1941 edition of the *Newtownards Chronicle* under the headline *Kircubbin Soldier Killed*. It was reported that he had been killed in a motor accident in Wales. Corporal Ennis was one of a party travelling in a motor car which struck a telegraph pole near Abergavenny. The driver of the car, Private James Leonard Vickers escaped uninjured but Private James Farrell (aged 21) of Chelsea, London was also killed. At the inquest a verdict of accidental death was returned.

Andrew Ennis's brother William James lived and worked in England and during the Second World War he served with the Royal Norfolk Regiment. After the war he told family members that he had been one of the first into Belsen concentration camp when it was liberated on 15 April 1945 and he was sickened by the mountains of bodies and the smell. They found 53,000 starving and seriously ill prisoners and 13,000 corpses lying unburied in the camp. Andrew's brother Henry joined the Royal Navy in 1937 aged 17 and, like William James, he also survived the war.

Corporal Andrew Ennis was 23 years old when he died and he is commemorated on the family grave headstone in Ballycranbeg Roman Catholic Churchyard. His father John died on 12 September 1964 (aged 72) and his mother Margaret Ann died on 17 January 1974 (aged 79).

E

Erskine Brothers, Basil Pollock and John Gordon Morrison

Basil Pollock Erskine and John Gordon Morrison Erskine were sons of Robert Magill Erskine JP and Eleanor Erskine (nee Pollock) of *Donnybrook*, Holywood. Robert Magill Erskine was a 'travelling goods manufacturer' and he and Eleanor Pollock were married on 15 April 1902 in High Street Presbyterian Church, Holywood. They had at least four children – Robert Colin Erskine (born 25 June 1903, died in an accident in 1950); John Gordon Morrison (born 20 December 1907); Margaret (born 26 April 1911) and Basil Pollock (born 28 September 1921). Basil Pollock Erskine was the first of the two brothers to die in the Second World War.

Erskine, Basil Pollock (Basil)
Pilot Officer (Pilot)
No. 44190, 233 Squadron, Royal Air Force
Killed in action on Thursday 31 October 1940 (aged 19)
Sola Churchyard, Norway (British Plot B 4)

Pilot Officer Basil Pollock Erskine was born on 28 September 1921 and he was the third son of Robert and Eleanor Erskine. He attended Campbell College from 1935 until 1939 and a short biography was published in the December 1940 edition of *The Campbellian*:

'Basil Erskine's most striking characteristic was the concentrated drive which he applied to anything he undertook. As a small boy he constructed single-handed and in term time, an excellent canoe, a work requiring unremitting labour and infinite patience; as a Cadet at Cultra Yacht Club he was ready for his tests before the examiner had quite learnt them himself; as a Scout he obtained his First Class Badge within four months of joining the Troop, a record at Campbell – and possibly anywhere. When he joined the Air Section of the Officers' Training Corps he rapidly became its senior NCO.

But it was as a Scout in camp that you saw Basil at his best. The woods seemed to be his native place. His remarkable native ingenuity found full scope in devising the shifts and gadgets that make camp a home-from-home; the lashings and knots were the joy of his skilful hands. His cooking done over a wood fire made the mouth water. We shall always remember with pride his excellent running of his Patrol in camp at Mourne Park, and with affection his cheery, vivid presence, his shrewd jokes, and his good company around the camp fire. His life was short, but he lived every minute of it'.

During the Second World War Basil Erskine served with the Royal Air Force in Coastal Command and he was killed in action on 31 October 1940 during an offensive patrol operation. He was one of a crew of four aboard a Lockheed Hudson Mark II aircraft (T9377) that took off at 10.20 am from RAF Leuchars in Fife, Scotland. They reached the Norwegian coast in formation with two other aircraft and attacked a cargo vessel. Their plane was shot down by fire from a German minesweeper and crashed at 12.55 pm north of Lister in Norway. The other crew members who died that day were:

- Pilot Officer William Owen Weaber
- Sergeant Henry Dean aged 20 from Stoke-on-Trent
- Sergeant James Andrew Wallace

Sergeant Dean has no known grave and is commemorated on the Runnymede Memorial in Surrey. The other three men were buried in Sola Churchyard, Norway. Pilot Officer Basil Pollock Erskine was 19 years old when he died and he is commemorated on Holywood and District War Memorial and in Campbell College, Belfast.

Erskine, John Gordon Morrison (John)
Lieutenant Commander (E)
HMS *Hood*, Royal Navy
Killed in action on Saturday 24 May 1941 (aged 33)
Portsmouth Naval Memorial, Hampshire, England (Panel 45, Column 2)

John Gordon Morrison Erskine was born on 20 December 1907 and he was the second son of Robert and Eleanor Erskine. He attended Campbell College from 1919 until 1925 and he played cricket for the school. In 1925 he joined the Royal Navy (Special Entry) and attended Keyham Royal Naval Engineering College in Plymouth. He became Lieutenant (E) in 1930 and Lieutenant Commander (E) in 1939. A short biography was published in the July 1941 edition of *The Campbellian*:

'By the death on service of Lieutenant Commander J.G.M. Erskine the Navy has lost an officer of great ability and promise. After passing second into the Engineering branch of the Royal Navy at the Special Entry examination in 1925, he passed out first from Keyham and followed this up by a distinguished record in the Dagger course at the Royal Naval College, Greenwich. Most of his subsequent service till the outbreak of war was at the Admiralty. He lost his life on HMS *Hood* in the recent battle in the Atlantic'.

John Gordon Morrison Erskine and Nancy Brown were married on 15 April 1933 in Holywood Parish Church of Ireland Church and they lived in Holywood. During the Second World War Lieutenant Commander John Erskine served aboard HMS *Hood*. Nicknamed the *Mighty Hood*, HMS *Hood* was an Admiral-class battle cruiser built by John Brown and Company, Clydebank and she was commissioned in May 1920. On 24 May 1941 HMS *Hood* and HMS *Prince of Wales* were in the Denmark Strait between Greenland and Iceland when they intercepted the German warships *Prinz Eugen* and *Bismarck*. HMS *Hood* was hit by shells fired from both ships but it was a shell fired from *Bismarck* which triggered the magazine explosion that destroyed the aft part of the ship. With her back broken she sank in less than three minutes. More than 1,410 men lost their lives including John Gordon Morrison Erskine and **Lambert Charles Shepherd** (Bangor).

Lieutenant Commander John Gordon Morrison Erskine was 33 years old when he died and he is commemorated on Portsmouth Naval Memorial in Hampshire; on Holywood and District War Memorial; in the

HMS *Hood* Book of Remembrance in St. John the Baptist Parish Church, Boldre in Hampshire and in Campbell College, Belfast.

Eston, Robert Keith (Keith)
Sergeant
No. 408709, 14th/20th King's Hussars, Royal Armoured Corps
Died as a result of an accident on Friday 23 November 1945 (aged 31)
Staglieno Cemetery, Genoa, Italy (Grave III A 28)

Robert Keith Eston was born on 7 February 1914 and he was the only son of Robert James Eston and Florence Eston (nee Keith) of 45 Frances Street, Newtownards. Robert James Eston was a National School Teacher and he and Florence Keith (she was a daughter of Hutchinson Keith) were married on 5 July 1911 in Duncairn Presbyterian Church, Belfast. Florence Keith's witness was her sister Helen who married David Freeland on 9 April 1913 and their only son, **David Harrison Freeland**, died on active service on 27 September 1942.

Robert Keith Eston attended Newtownards Public Elementary School No. 1 and then Regent House School, Newtownards from 1927 until 1929. School records indicate that after leaving school he 'went into business'. Robert Keith Eston married Doris Eston (nee O'Neill) of Pelaw, Gateshead, Co. Durham and their marriage was registered in the third quarter of 1944 in Durham.

E

 During the Second World War Keith Eston served with the 14th/20th King's Hussars, Royal Armoured Corps and his father Robert James died on 12 May 1945. Sergeant Robert Keith Eston was 31 years old when he died as a result of an accident in Italy on 23 November 1945 and he is commemorated in Regent House School and on the family grave headstone in Holywood Cemetery. His mother Florence died on 15 May 1963.

Evens, George William
Driver
No. T/82775, 6 Corps Ammunition Park, Royal Army Service Corps
Died as a result of an accident on Thursday 21 November 1940 (aged 23)
Brookwood Memorial, Surrey, England (Panel 16 Column 2)

George William Evens was born on 6 March 1917 and he was a son of Ernest Doman Evens and Gladys Irene Evens (nee Crossing) who were married on 2 April 1913 in Plympton St. Mary Anglican Church in Devon. Gladys lived at Haye Farm in Devon with her father and sisters and Ernest Evens ran the farm. George William Evens was baptised in Plympton St. Mary Church and in some records his surname is spelt Evans. During the Second World War he served with the Royal Army Service Corps.

EVENS. G. W. The death of Driver George William Evens was reported in the 30 November 1940 edition of the *County Down Spectator* under the headline *Tragic Death of Three Soldiers*. Three young soldiers were killed in Clandeboye Camp, Ballyleidy when, during a violent storm, a large tree fell across the hut in which they were sleeping. They were Driver George William Evens (aged 23) from 39 Regent Street, Plymouth; Private **Derek Rodney Swift** from Blackpool and Driver **Sydney John Wren** from Stansted in Essex. The roof of the hut in which Private Swift was sleeping caved in and pinned him to the bed. To release him his comrades used a heavy jack to raise the fallen roof and hacksaws to cut down the bed. He suffered severe internal injuries and he was dead when his comrades got him out. Both Driver Wren and Driver Evens were crushed by fallen debris; Driver Wren died from 'asphyxia due to crushing' and Driver Evens died from 'laceration of the brain'. Their deaths were registered in Newtownards and Driver Evens was buried in Plympton St. Mary Churchyard on 26 November 1940. His father was buried there on 5 November 1947 and his mother died in 1980.

Driver George William Evens is commemorated on the Brookwood Memorial in Surrey, England.

Fee, Thomas Hugh Cecil Hickland
Lieutenant (E)
HMS *Rawalpindi*, Royal Naval Reserve
Killed in action on Thursday 23 November 1939 (aged 28)
Liverpool Naval Memorial, Lancashire, England (Panel 2 Column 1)

Thomas Hugh Cecil Hickland Fee was born on 1 January 1911 and he was the only son of David Alfred Fee JP and Josephine Margaretta Fee (nee Beck) of *Baythorpe*, Holywood. David Fee worked as an Estate Agent and Government Valuer and before moving to Holywood the Fee family lived in Cregagh, Belfast. David Fee and Josephine Beck were married on 10 July 1906 in St. George's Church of Ireland Church, Belfast.

Thomas Hugh Cecil Hickland Fee attended Campbell College from 1920 until

1921 and then the University School, Hastings in Sussex. After leaving school he worked as an apprentice manager in Harland and Wolff Ltd., Belfast and at that time he lived at 8 Pretoria Street, Stranmillis Road. Later he went to sea to gain engineering experience and he served aboard the SS *Rawalpindi*.

Built by Harland and Wolff Ltd., Greenock, Scotland and launched on 26 March 1925, the SS *Rawalpindi* was a passenger ship operating on the London to Bombay route by the P&O Steam Navigation Company Ltd. She was requisitioned by the Admiralty in August 1939, converted to an Armed Merchant Cruiser (AMC) and renamed HMS *Rawalpindi*. Thomas Hugh Cecil Hickland Fee was given commissioned rank.

While patrolling north of the Faroe Islands on 23 November 1939, HMS *Rawalpindi* investigated a possible enemy sighting, only to find that she had encountered two of the most powerful German warships, the battleships *Scharnhorst* and *Gneisenau* conducting a sweep between Iceland and the Faroes. In his book, *The Sinking of the Kenbane Head*, Sam McAughtry asserts that the Armed Merchant Cruiser HMS *Jervis Bay* had originally been assigned to the Northern Patrol but, at the last minute her windlass was damaged and her place was taken by HMS *Rawalpindi*. A year later, on 5 November 1940, HMS *Jervis Bay* was sunk when escorting Convoy HX-84 and three local men who were serving aboard the SS *Kenbane Head* (one of the ships in the convoy) were killed. They were **James McNeilly Belshaw** from Ballywalter, **George McClelland Leckey** from Holywood and **David John Pritchard** from Ballyhalbert.

F

HMS *Rawalpindi* was able to signal back to base the location of the German battleships *Scharnhorst* and *Gneisenau*. Despite being hopelessly outgunned, 60-year old Captain Edward Coverley Kennedy decided to fight, rather than surrender as demanded by the Germans. He was heard to say, 'We'll fight them both, they'll sink us, and that will be that; good-bye'. The two German warships shelled HMS *Rawalpindi* and she sank within 40 minutes. Lieutenant Thomas Hugh Cecil Hickland Fee was one of more than 230 men who died. Captain Kennedy (father of the broadcaster and writer Ludovic Kennedy) was posthumously Mentioned in Despatches. Less than 50 men were rescued. *Scharnhorst* was sunk on 26 December 1943 during the Battle of the North Cape and *Gneisenau*, heavily damaged in an air raid on Kiel Harbour in Germany on 26/27 February 1942, was sunk by the Germans on 23 March 1945 as a blockship (to prevent access) at Gotenhafen in Poland.

A letter from Lieutenant Commander (E) B.J. Dyer, Royal Naval Reserve, was published in the December 1945 edition of The Campbellian: 'Lieutenant Fee was in charge of the stokehold during the *Rawalpindi* action and was shut off from the rest of the ship by water-tight doors. Early in the action there was a hit in the after-stokehold. This caused a slow leak, so that the boilers were slowly put out of action. At the same time the engine room was badly knocked about, with great loss of life and machinery put out of action. So you can see that Lieutenant Fee had a job on his hands. However, when I paid a visit, the oil lamp was giving enough light to keep things going, so everybody was calm and collected. Of course, the gunfire was making a terrific din.

The next I saw of Lieutenant Fee was when he reported to me that the stokeholds were flooded, fires all out and that he had shut all the emergency oil valves and ordered all hands out of the stokeholds. No loss of life up to now. Well done, Fee. What to do now? I told him to take over his boat, get it ready and put all the badly wounded in the bottom. A little later I had a minute to spare to give a hand there and we noticed some blood dripping on the deck. This led to a discovery of a big hole in the bottom of the boat. It did not matter though as a shell burst just below and blew the boat to pieces shortly after.

By this time things were in a pretty bad state, fires all over the place and a great number of casualties. But your friend was still full of beans, certainly showing no signs of the weak heart he was supposed to have. So I told him to get in one of the other boats and clear out. There were not many left alive by then and not many boats either. It was very cold and a heavy sea running and just starting to get dark. I did not see what actually happened but I heard that the boat which carried your friend out of danger was overloaded, being one of the last boats left and a sea caught her and turned her right over, and drowned everybody in her. Wasn't that rotten luck after missing everything else?

FEE T.H.C.H. So you can rest assured that Engineer Lieutenant Fee was one of those that showed them that we still know how to die. I expect you have heard that there were no decorations for anybody on the *Rawalpindi*, but I expect that was because everybody there deserved a VC, with Lieutenant Fee right on the front line'.

Lieutenant Thomas Hugh Cecil Hickland Fee was 28 years old when he died and he is commemorated on the Liverpool Naval Memorial in Lancashire and in Campbell College, Belfast.

Ferguson, Clifford Samuel
Leading Aircraftman (Pilot U/T)
No. 1109099, Royal Air Force Volunteer Reserve
Killed in an aircraft accident on Wednesday 21 May 1941 (aged 19)
Holywood Cemetery, Co. Down (Grave 1217)

Clifford Samuel Ferguson was born on 5 March 1922 and he was the eldest son of Frederick William and Eva Ferguson (nee Hollywood) who lived in Ardlee Avenue, Holywood. Frederick Ferguson was a salesman/commercial traveller and he and Eva Hollywood were married on 5 January 1921 in Knock Methodist Church, Belfast. Clifford Samuel Ferguson was educated privately before going to Sullivan Upper School, Holywood on 1 September 1931. He left school in June 1939 and joined the Royal Air Force Volunteer Reserve.

Leading Aircraftman Clifford Samuel Ferguson was 19 years old and unmarried when he died on 21 May 1941 as a result of an aircraft accident at RAF Little Rissington in Gloucestershire and he was buried in Holywood Cemetery. He is commemorated on Holywood and District War Memorial (as C.S.F. Ferguson) and in Sullivan Upper School, Holywood. Below his name which is inscribed on the surround of the Ferguson family grave there is an inscription:

Young, strong and free

Also buried in the Ferguson family grave were his paternal grandparents, Samuel James and Elizabeth Ferguson who lived at 27 Church View, Holywood. Samuel Ferguson was a grocer and general merchant and he died on 18 March 1939. Elizabeth Ferguson died on 6 February 1941 so neither knew about the death of their grandson. Samuel and Elizabeth Ferguson had three children two of whom died in infancy – their daughter Evelyn died on 2 March 1894 and their son Norman died on 22 October 1895.

Leading Aircraftman Clifford Samuel Ferguson was a second cousin of **David Francis Apperson Hollywood** who died in service on 15 September 1943.

Ferguson, Thomas Gardiner
Civilian War Dead
Died as a result of enemy action on Tuesday 8 April 1941 (aged 54)
Belfast City Cemetery (Grave K2 145)

In some records his second forename is spelt Gardener. Thomas Gardiner Ferguson was born on 23 October 1886 in Ballymena, Co. Antrim and he was the younger son of William James and Sarah Kellan Ferguson (nee Mann, daughter of Gardiner Mann). William James Ferguson worked as a labourer and he and Sarah Mann were married on 12 April 1884 in Wellington Street Presbyterian Church, Ballymena. They had two children, James (born 1 April 1885) and Thomas Gardiner (born 23 October 1886). Sarah Ferguson died on 3 August 1891 and William James, then working as a joiner, married Elizabeth Jackson on 26 August 1896 in Agnes Street Presbyterian Church, Belfast. The Ferguson family moved from Cloughfern, Whitehouse to 38 Percy Street, Belfast and William James worked as a joiner in Harland and Wolff Shipyard.

Thomas Gardiner Ferguson also worked as a joiner in the shipyard and he lived at 7 Primrose Avenue in Bangor. He was 54 years old when he died as a result of enemy action on 8 April 1941 at the Harland and Wolff Shipyard, Queen's Island in Belfast and he was buried in Belfast City Cemetery on 15 April 1941. Also buried in the same grave were his mother Sarah Ferguson (died 3 August 1891 aged 27); Edith Louisa Mann (died 12 December 1893 aged five weeks) and Francis Ferguson (died 24 February 1900 aged 52).

Of the many civilians of the Commonwealth whose deaths were due to enemy action in the Second World War, the names of some 67,092 are commemorated in the Civilian War Dead Roll of Honour, located near St. George's Chapel in Westminster Abbey, London.

Fern, Walter Edward

Sergeant
No. 1434201, Royal Air Force Volunteer Reserve
Killed in an aircraft accident on Thursday 18 November 1943 (aged 20)
Runnymede Memorial, Surrey, England (Panel 149)

F

Walter Edward Fern's birth was registered in the first quarter of 1923 in Doncaster, Yorkshire. He was a son of Walter and Nora Fern (nee Jackson) whose marriage was registered in the third quarter of 1914 in Doncaster. They had at least three children – George R. (birth registered in 1915), Nora (birth registered in 1917) and Walter Edward (birth registered in 1923).

During the Second World War Sergeant Walter Edward Fern served with the Royal Air Force Volunteer Reserve and he died on 18 November 1943 along with the other three crew members when their Lockheed Hudson Mark V aircraft (AE653) of No. 5 (Coastal) Operational Training Unit based at RAF Long Kesh, crashed into Strangford Lough just south of Chapel Island (off Greyabbey). Sergeant Fern was the pilot and they were on a rocket-firing exercise using the submarine target at South Island in Strangford Lough.

The other three men who died in the crash were Flight Sergeant **William Barraclough** (RAFVR); Flight Sergeant **Raymond Farquhar Simpson** (RNZAF) and Flight Sergeant **Andrew Greenwell Gibbison** (RNZAF).

Sergeant Walter Edward Fern's body was never recovered and he is commemorated on the Runnymede Memorial in Surrey. He was 20 years old when he died.

Field, Arthur Donald
Mentioned in Despatches
Signalman
No. P/LD/X 4414, HMS *Bredon*, Royal Naval Volunteer Reserve
Killed in action on Monday 8 February 1943 (aged 24)
Portsmouth Naval Memorial, Hampshire, England (Panel 80 Column 2)

Arthur Donald Field's birth was registered in the third quarter of 1918 in Barnet, Middlesex and he was a son of Sidney and Henrietta Field (nee Smith). Arthur Donald Field lived in North Finchley, London before he joined the Royal Naval Volunteer Reserve in 1938 and he was stationed in Belfast prior to his marriage. He was the husband of Janette Kathleen Field (nee McDowell) of 57 University Street, Belfast and during the Second World War he served aboard HMS *Bredon*.

HMS *Bredon* was a Naval Trawler of the Anti-Submarine Warfare (ASW) type. A Naval Trawler was a ship built along the lines of a fishing trawler but fitted out for naval purposes. HMS *Bredon* was built by Cook, Welton and Gemmell Ltd., Beverley and Hull and commissioned on 29 April 1942. Less than a year later, at around 8.00 am on 8 February 1943, HMS *Bredon* was torpedoed and sunk off the Canary Islands by the German submarine *U-521*. Signalman Field was posthumously Mentioned in Despatches for his bravery and devotion to duty after the ship had been torpedoed: 'Though the order to abandon ship had been given, Signalman Field remained on the bridge in an attempt to attract attention with his night-signalling lamp. Heedless of the danger of the fast sinking ship, he made no endeavour to save his own life while there was a chance of getting a signal through and he was still engaged in this gallant act when HMS *Bredon* sank and he went down with the ship'. His effects amounted to some £187 and probate was granted to his widow.

Signalman Arthur Donald Field is commemorated on the Cotter/ McDowell family grave headstone in Holywood Cemetery, Co. Down – along with his brother-in-law, Ordinary Seaman **Alfred George McDowell**. On the gravestone they are both described as grandsons of Margaret Cotter McDowell. Arthur Donald Field was 24 years old when he died.

Fitchie, Samuel Jamieson
Sub-Lieutenant
HMS *Arawa*, Royal Navy
Died of illness on Friday 12 October 1945 (aged 28)
Killinchy Non-Subscribing Presbyterian Churchyard (Row 2 Grave 22)

Samuel Jamieson Fitchie's birth was registered in the second quarter of 1917 in Newtownards and he was a son of Robert Henry M. Fitchie and Agnes Fitchie (nee Bowman) of Ballyminstra, Kilmood, Co. Down. Robert Henry M. Fitchie was a carpenter and he and Agnes Bowman from the townland of Magherascouse were married on 27 July 1910 in Ballygowan Presbyterian Church. Their first child, James, was born on 24 August 1913.

During the Second World War Samuel Jamieson Fitchie served with the Royal Navy aboard HMS *Arawa*. HMS *Arawa* was built as the *Esperance Bay* in 1921 by William Beardmore and Company Ltd., Dalmuir, Scotland and in 1936 she was renamed *Arawa*. Owned by the Shaw, Savill and Albion Company Ltd., London this passenger ship was requisitioned by the Admiralty and converted to an Armed Merchant Cruiser in 1939. She operated in the China, East Indies and South Atlantic Stations until 1941 when she was used as a troopship by the Ministry of War Transport (MOWT) and later as a repatriation ship for prisoners. HMS *Arawa* was returned to her owners in 1945.

Sub-Lieutenant Samuel Jamieson Fitchie was 28 years old and unmarried when he died of pulmonary tuberculosis on 12 October 1945 in Musgrave Park Hospital, Belfast. His father, who lived at *Stormont View*, Lower Castlereagh, was with him when he died. Sub-Lieutenant Samuel Jamieson Fitchie was buried in Killinchy Non-Subscribing Presbyterian Churchyard and there is an inscription on his CWGC headstone:

Worthy of everlasting remembrance

Three Fitchie deaths are commemorated on the family grave headstone – Phoebe Fitchie (died 10 March 1935); Samuel J. Fitchie (died 12 October 1945) and Robert M. Fitchie (died 31 December 1984).

Flegier, Henryk Andrzej

Sierz (Sierzant equivalent to Sergeant)
No. P780038, 315 (City of Deblin) Polish Fighter Squadron
Killed in an aircraft accident on Tuesday 5 October 1943 (aged 30)
Newtownards (Movilla) Cemetery, Co. Down
(RC Plot Section 18 Grave 24)

Henryk Andrzei Flegier was born on 21 December 1912 and during the Second World War he served with the Polish Fighter Squadron. On 9 September 1943 Sergeant Henryk Andrzej Flegier survived when the Supermarine Spitfire Mark V aircraft (W3937) he was flying was written off following an accident during a training flight. Less than a month later, Sergeant Flegier was killed when his Supermarine Spitfire Mark V aircraft (BL922) lost power and crashed 1½ miles northwest of Ballyhalbert during a low-flying training exercise. Sergeant Henryk Andrzej Flegier was 30 years old when he died and he is commemorated on Panel 15 of the Polish War Memorial at Northolt in London.

F

Fleming, Simon Denis St. Ledger (Simon)

Lieutenant
No. 166084, Royal Artillery and Long Range Desert Group
Killed in action on Tuesday 13 June 1944 (aged 23)
Foiano Della Chiana War Cemetery, Italy (Grave I G 1)

Simon Denis St. Ledger Fleming was born in Bangor Castle on 6 January 1921 and he was baptised on 7 February 1921 in Bangor Parish Church of Ireland Church (St. Comgall's). Simon's father was Captain Harold Murray Fleming of the First Dragoon Guards and his mother was the Honourable Eleanor Clare Alice Bingham, daughter of John George Barry Bingham (the Baron Clanmorris), Bangor Castle. His parents were married in Bangor Parish Church (St. Comgall's) on 15 September 1915. Subsequently the Fleming family lived in Great Barton, Suffolk. Simon Denis St. Ledger Fleming was educated at Harrow and he joined the Royal Artillery in 1939.

In June 1944 it was reported in the press that the Clanmorris family had been bereaved. The report stated that Lieutenant Simon Denis St. Ledger Fleming had been killed in action in Italy and that previously he had been

Clanmorrie Family Bereaved

Lieut. S. D. St. L. FLEMING
KILLED IN ACTION

Lieut. Simon D. St. L. Fleming, R.H.A., a grandson of the 5th Lord Clanmorris and nephew of the present Lord Clanmorris, Bangor Castle, reported missing a year ago, is now officially reported to have been killed in action in June, 1944, while on special operations. Aged 23, he was born in Bangor Castle and educated at Harrow. He enlisted in the Royal Artillery in 1939 and gained his commission in 1940. He volunteered for service in the Middle East in 1941 and served with the 8th Army in North Africa. He was wounded in action in July, 1942, but rejoined his regiment in June to take part in the advance from El Alamein. In 1943 he was seconded to the Long Range Desert Group, C.M.F.

serving with the Eighth Army in North Africa He obtained his commission in 1940 and was wounded in action in 1942. He rejoined his regiment to take part in the advance from El Alamein and in 1943 he was seconded to the Long Range Desert Group. Aged 23, Lieutenant Simon Denis St. Ledger Fleming died in Italy when his parachute failed to open during a descent on 13 June 1944.

Simon Denis St. Ledger Fleming was a grandson of the Fifth Lord Clanmorris and a nephew of the then Lord Clanmorris of Bangor Castle. His grandmother Maude, Lady Clanmorris, was 82 years of age when she died on 14 February 1941 and she was buried in private burying ground in the Castle Demesne. Maude was the only child of Robert Edward Ward DL of Bangor Castle and from him she inherited the Bangor estate. She married the Fifth Baron Clanmorris in 1878 and they had seven sons and three daughters. Bangor Castle, with 129 acres of land, was purchased by Bangor Borough Council in 1952.

Simon Denis St. Ledger Fleming is commemorated in Bangor Parish Church (St. Comgall's) as are two of his uncles – Second Lieutenant the Hon. Richard Gerald Ava Bingham who was killed in action during the First World War and Commander the Hon. Edward Barry Stewart Bingham who was awarded the Victoria Cross for gallantry during the Battle of Jutland in 1916. Second Lieutenant the Hon. Richard Gerald Ava Bingham is commemorated on Page 96 in the Book of Honour *Remembering Their Sacrifice in the Great War – North Down* compiled by Barry Niblock.

Flynn, Edward James (Eddie)
Lance Bombardier
No. 1473912, 5 Battery, 2 Light Anti-Aircraft Regiment, Royal Artillery
Killed in action on Saturday 20 June 1942 (aged 25)
Alamein Memorial, Egypt (Column 33)

Edward James Flynn's birth was registered in the fourth quarter of 1916 in Newtownards and he was a son of Edward P. and Janice (Jeanie) Flynn (nee Mayne) of 15 Belfast Road, Bangor and formerly of Newtownards. Edward P. Flynn was a tailor and he and Janice Mayne were married on 2 March 1914 in Newtownards Registry Office. During the First World War

Edward Flynn Senior served with the Royal Irish Rifles and he was wounded at Mons.

During the Second World War Lance Bombardier Edward James Flynn served with the Royal Artillery and on 20 June 1942 he was reported as missing in action at Tobruk. His body was never recovered and a little over a year later, in August 1943, he was officially presumed to have been killed in action. His parents placed an *Our Heroes In Memoriam* notice in the 21 August 1943 edition of the *Newtownards Chronicle* and in 1944 the *In Memoriam* notice contained the verse:

> *You are standing near in memory,*
> *And the month of June is here,*
> *How we think of that sad message,*
> *We had lost a son so dear.*

 Ten days before Lance Bombardier Edward James Flynn died, his brother-in-law, Bombardier **Harold Johnston** of Thomas Street, Newtownards was also killed in action at Tobruk. In October 1944 Lance Bombardier Edward James Flynn's younger brother, Private Hugh Flynn who served with the Royal Ulster Rifles Airborne Division, was reported to be missing in action at Arnhem and then a month later it was reported that Hugh was a Prisoner-of-War. Lance Bombardier Edward James Flynn was 25 years old when he died and he is commemorated on Newtownards and District War Memorial.

F

Foreman, Robert Wilkinson (Robert)
Sergeant
No. 1052298, 153 Squadron, Royal Air Force Volunteer Reserve
Killed on active service on Saturday 10 January 1942 (aged 20)
Runnymede Memorial, Surrey, England (Panel 97)

 Robert Wilkinson Foreman was born on 22 January 1921 and he was a son of John T. Foreman and Hilda Foreman (nee Wilkinson) of 19 St. Helen's Street, Corbridge, Northumberland. Their marriage was registered in the fourth quarter of 1920 in Hexham, Northumberland and they had at least four children – Robert W. (born 22 January 1921); Ann W. (born 1922, she married Cyril G. Edgar in 1943); Monica (born 1925) and Barbara (born 1928). Robert Foreman was educated at the Queen Elizabeth Grammar School in Hexham and he played both rugby and cricket for the school. After leaving school he worked for Strachan and Company, Accountants in

Newcastle and he was actively involved with youth work including Corbridge Church Lad's Brigade, Corbridge Boys' Club and the Junior Imperial League.

 Robert Wilkinson Foreman joined the Royal Air Force Volunteer Reserve in 1940, he obtained his wings in October 1941 and he served with 153 Squadron based at Ballyhalbert. He died on 10 January 1942 (12 days short of his 21st birthday) when his Boulton Paul Defiant aircraft (T3931) failed to return from a night patrol over the Irish Sea. The two crew members on board were declared missing and their bodies were never recovered. Sergeant Robert Wilkinson Foreman was the Pilot and Sergeant **Ralph Henry John Winter** was his Air Gunner. Both men are commemorated on the Runnymede Memorial in Surrey.

Forshaw, John Matthew
Private
No. 3386277, 1st Battalion, East Lancashire Regiment
Died of illness on Tuesday 3 May 1938 (aged 18)
Holywood Cemetery, Co. Down (Grave 1264)

F

Private John Matthew Forshaw was not a casualty of war but his name is included in this Book of Honour as an example of a soldier who died while he was stationed in North Down during the inter-war years. During the First World War the 1st Battalion of the East Lancashire Regiment served on the Western Front and between the two world wars they served in several countries including the West Indies, Malta, Egypt, India, China, Germany and Northern Ireland (from 1935 until 1939). Private John Matthew Forshaw was stationed at Palace Barracks in Holywood and he was 18 years old and unmarried when he died of cerebro-spinal fever in Purdysburn Fever Hospital on 3 May 1938. Three days later he was buried in Holywood Cemetery.

Forte, Rodolfo Angelo Antonio
Served as: Forte, Rudolph Angel Antonio (Rudolph)
Sergeant (Air Gunner)
No. 1565064, 76 Squadron, Royal Air Force Volunteer Reserve
Killed on active service on Friday 21 January 1944 (aged 21)
Berlin 1939-1945 War Cemetery, Germany (Collective Grave 6 A 13-16)

Rudolph Forte's uncle who lived at 12 High Street, Newtownards placed

a *Killed in Action* notice in the 8 April 1944 edition of the *Newtownards Chronicle* and in the same edition there was a report on Rudolph's death under the headline *Ards Man's Nephew Killed*. Rudolph Angel Antonio Forte was born in 1923 in Hawick and he was a son of Masimino and Maria Pacetta Forte who lived in Galashiels, Selkirkshire after moving there from Mortale in Italy. Rudolph spent much of his boyhood living in Bangor and he joined the Royal Air Force Volunteer Reserve in 1941.

Ards Man's Nephew Killed.—News has been received that Rudolph Forte has died in action while flying over enemy territory. The young airman, whose parents reside in Scotland, spent much of his boyhood in Bangor. He had about three years' service with the Royal Air Force. He is a nephew of Mr. P. Forte, 12 High Street, Newtownards.

Sergeant Rudolph Forte was 21 years old when he was killed in action on 21 January 1944 while flying over enemy territory. He was one of a seven man crew aboard a Handley Page Halifax Mark V aircraft (LK922) that took off at 8.06 pm from RAF Holme-on-Spalding-Moor in Yorkshire on a mission to bomb factories near Magdeburg in Germany. The aircraft was shot down over Helmstedt and three of the crew survived and were taken prisoner – Sergeant (Navigator) T. Fraser, Flying Officer (Air Bomber) D.H. McVie and Sergeant (Wireless Operator) C.M. Bennett. The four crew members who were killed were buried in Collective Grave 6 A 13-16 in the Berlin 1939-1945 War Cemetery. In addition to Sergeant Rudolph Forte the other crew members who died that night were:

F

- Flight Sergeant Henry Boyes
- Sergeant James McCurry
- Sgt Reginald Sydney Western aged 21 from Stanmore, Middlesex

Foster, Joseph Gerald (Gerald)
Third Engineer Officer
SS *Dunaff Head* (Belfast), Merchant Navy
Died as a result of enemy action on Saturday 8 March 1941 (aged 30)
Tower Hill Memorial, London, England (Panel 36)

Joseph Gerald Foster was born on 6 October 1910 and he was a son of James Scott Foster and Helen Louise Foster (nee Spratt) of *Ivydene*, Cable Road, Whitehead, then 31 Godfrey Avenue, Ballyholme, Bangor and then Church Road, Helen's Bay. James Scott Foster worked as a clerk and he and Helen Spratt were married on 13 December 1906 in St. Columba's Church of Ireland Church, Belfast. Joseph Gerald Foster attended

Royal Belfast Academical Institution (RBAI) from 1920 until 1926. During the Second World War he served in the Merchant Navy aboard the SS *Dunaff Head* and it was recorded that he was 6 feet 1 inch tall with brown eyes and fair hair.

The SS *Dunaff Head* was built in 1918 by Workman, Clark and Company Ltd., Belfast and was owned by the Ulster Steamship Company. At 1.09 am on 8 March 1941 the SS *Dunaff Head* was on route from Glasgow to St. John, New Brunswick in Convoy OB-293 (she was in ballast) when she was torpedoed and sunk by the German submarine *U-A* south of Iceland. Third Engineer Officer Joseph Gerald Foster aged 30 was one of the five crew members who were lost. The master, 34 crew members and four gunners were picked up by HMS *Verity* and landed at Loch Ewe on the northwest coast of Scotland.

Third Engineer Officer Joseph Gerald Foster is commemorated in Glencraig Parish Church of Ireland Church; in RBAI and on the family grave headstone in Bangor Cemetery. Gerald's mother died on 20 April 1960 and his father died on 16 November 1965. His sister Muriel (born 20 November 1907, married Dr Hugh Wallace OBE) is also commemorated on the family grave headstone.

Foster, William
Sub-Lieutenant (A)
HMS *Daedalus*, Royal Naval Volunteer Reserve
Killed in an aircraft accident on Tuesday 24 November 1942 (aged 22)
Belfast City Cemetery (Glenalina Extension Section D Joint Grave 22)

William Foster's birth was registered in the fourth quarter of 1920 in Hendon, Middlesex and he was a son of Herbert William Foster and Martha Higginson Foster (nee Barker). Herbert William Foster worked as a cashier for a public works contractor and his marriage to Martha Higginson Barker was registered in the third quarter of 1905 in Chapel-en-le-Frith, Derbyshire. In the CWGC Debt of Honour it is recorded that Herbert William Foster and Martha Higginson Foster lived in Chislehurst, Kent.

During the Second World War Sub-Lieutenant (A) William Foster served with the Royal Naval Volunteer Reserve and in November 1942 he was based at RAF Kirkistown. On 24 November 1942 a Fairey Fulmar aircraft (BP821) of 887 Squadron, Fleet Air Arm, based at Kirkistown made a steep turn when approaching the airfield, went out of control and spun into the ground near the airfield. Both crew members were killed. They were the Pilot, Sub-Lieutenant (A) **John Richard Mathers** who died the following day in Bangor Military Hospital and his Observer, Sub-Lieutenant (A) William Foster aged 22 who died on the day of the crash. On 28 November 1942 both men were buried together in Belfast City Cemetery (Glenalina Extension Section D Joint Grave 22). Sub-Lieutenant (A) William Foster is commemorated on Chislehurst War Memorial.

Fox, William
Rifleman
No. 7015254, Royal Ulster Rifles
Died of illness on Sunday 31 December 1939 (aged 29)
Belfast City Cemetery (Glenalina Extension Section U1 Grave 214)

William Fox was born on 24 August 1910 and he was a son of John and Charlotte Fox (nee Purcell) of 7 Melbourne Street, Woodvale, Belfast. John Fox worked as a bricklayer's labourer and he and Charlotte Purcell were married in St. Stephen's Church of Ireland Church, Belfast. They had at least seven children – Ellen (born 18 January 1898); Hannah (born 10 August 1899); Annie (born 18 March 1902, died 1 December 1902); John (born 4 March 1904); Charlotte (born 5 May 1906); William (born 24 August 1910) and George (born 19 May 1912).

William Fox and Ada Peacocke Miller (born 12 March 1912) were married on 14 September 1935 and they had two children – Margaret Irene and William (Billy). William Fox joined the Royal Ulster Rifles and he died on 31 December 1939 in the Military Hospital, Knocknagoney, Belfast following an operation. He was buried on 3 January 1940 in Belfast City Cemetery (Glenalina Extension) and some six weeks later his wife Ada was laid to rest beside him. Ada Fox died on 15 February 1940 after a short illness and their two children were cared for by their maternal grandparents, Robert and Margaret Miller, at 3 Castle Street, Bangor. Irene Fox was four years old and Billy Fox was just over a year old when their parents died. Five years later their uncle Billy Miller was killed.

Flying Officer **William Watson (Billy) Miller DFC** who was Ada Fox's brother (and Rifleman William Fox's brother-in-law) died on 24 February 1945.

Fox, William
Fusilier
No. 6985086, 70th Battalion, Royal Inniskilling Fusiliers
Died of illness on Monday 16 June 1941 (aged 18)
Holywood Cemetery, Co. Down (RC Ground Collective Grave 1042)

It is recorded in the Army Roll of Honour 1939-1945 that William Fox was born in the Republic of Ireland and he lived at 28 Phibsborough Road, Dublin. His birth was registered in the fourth quarter of 1922 in Dublin North. During the Second World War Fusilier Fox served with the Royal Inniskilling Fusiliers and he was 18 years old and unmarried when he died of tubercular meningitis on 16 June 1941 in the 24th (London) General Hospital, Belfast. This hospital was also known as Campbell College Military Hospital. Two days later Fusilier William Fox was buried in Holywood Cemetery.

Fraser, William Elliot
Surgeon
SS *Peshawar* (Glasgow), Canadian Merchant Navy
Died of illness on Sunday 15 September 1946 (aged 67)
Bangor Cemetery, Co. Down (Section 4 R Grave 158)

William Elliott Fraser was a son of James Harshaw Fraser and Sophia Robinson Fraser (nee Elliott). They were married in London, Middlesex County, Ontario, Canada on 5 June 1871. James Harshaw Fraser was a lawyer and political figure in Ontario and he died in Gravenhurst, Ontario on 28 July 1899. During the Second World War Gravenhurst (previously called Sawdust City) was the site of a training camp for Norwegian Air Service personnel and also the site for a German Prisoner-of-War Camp.

The marriage of William Elliott Fraser and Caroline Champion was registered in the first quarter of 1917 in Marylebone, London. Later the Fraser family moved to Bangor. Their daughter Sophie, who was a nurse, was 24 years old when she died of tuberculosis on 10 December 1940 and she was buried in Bangor Cemetery. During the Second World War Surgeon William Elliott Fraser MD served with the Canadian Merchant Navy and he was 67 years old when he died of heart disease on 15 September 1946. Two days later he was buried alongside his daughter in Bangor Cemetery. Surgeon William Elliott Fraser is commemorated on the Canadian Virtual War Memorial (Internet) and on Page 138 in the Canadian Merchant Navy Book of Remembrance displayed in the Memorial Chamber of the Peace Tower in Ottawa.

Freeland, David Harrison (Harry)
Flight Sergeant
No. 979399, 138 Squadron, Royal Air Force Volunteer Reserve
Killed in action on Sunday 27 September 1942 (aged 26)
Merville Communal Cemetery Extension, Nord, France
(Plot 2 Row B Grave 15)

David Harrison Freeland was born on 26 February 1916 and he was the only son of David and Helen Freeland (nee Keith) of *Jackson Hall*, Craigavad. David Freeland worked as a clerk and he and Helen Keith were married on 9 April 1913 in Duncairn Presbyterian Church, Belfast. Helen Keith's sister Florence married Robert James Eston on 5 July 1911 and their only son, **Robert Keith Eston**, died in service on 23 November 1945.

David Harrison Freeland was educated at Sullivan Upper School, Holywood which he attended from 1926 until 1929 and then at Coleraine Academical Institution. He played rugby at school and afterwards for the North of Ireland club. He played tennis for the Norwood Tennis Club, Holywood and badminton for the Belfast Commercial Boat Club. He was the founder and captain (1938 to 1940) of the 70th Belfast Company (Ballygilbert) Boys' Brigade.

On leaving school Harry Freeland worked for Messrs McMullan's of Ireland Ltd., Petrol and Oil Distributors, Linenhall Street, Belfast. He joined the Royal Air Force Volunteer Reserve immediately after the outbreak of war and was called up in February 1941. Harry Freeland and Sarah (Peggy) McDowell of *Windermere*, 2 Brunswick Road, Bangor were married on 15 May 1942 in Ballygilbert Presbyterian Church.

During the Second World War Flight Sergeant Harry Freeland served in Bomber Command and he was one of a five man crew aboard an Armstrong Whitworth Whitley Mark V aircraft (Z9275) that took off from

KILLED IN ACTION.

FREELAND—Flight-Sergeant-Pilot David Harrison (Harry) Freeland, R.A.F., beloved husband of Sergeant Peggy Freeland, W.A.A.F.

FREELAND—Flight-Sergeant-Pilot David Harrison (Harry) Freeland, R.A.F., only son of David and Helen Freeland, Jackson Hall, Craigavad.

FREELAND—The 70th Belfast Company (Ballygilbert) Boys' Brigade. A Memorial Service to Flight-Sergeant-Pilot Harry Freeland, R.A.F. (our late Captain), killed in action, will be held in Ballygilbert Presbyterian Church, Craigavad, on Sunday, 1st November, 1942, at 5.30 p.m. All friends welcome. We mourn the loss of a gallant leader.

RAF Tempsford in Bedfordshire on a Special Operations Executive (SOE) operation. The purpose of SOE operations was to link up with local resistance movements. Their aircraft crashed near Merville in France and two crew members were taken Prisoner-of-War – Sergeant J.H. Cox and Sergeant P.G. Moore. Flight Sergeant David Harrison Freeland was killed and the other two crew members who died that day were:

- FS Edmund George Hayhoe aged 19 from Harrow Weald, Middlesex
- Flight Sergeant Frederick George Green aged 21 from Liverpool

Flight Sergeant David Harrison Freeland was 26 years old when he died on 27 September 1942 and there were three *Killed in Action* notices in the 31 October 1942 edition of the *County Down Spectator*. There was one from his widow, Sergeant Peggy Freeland WAAF (they had been married for just over four months) and another from his parents. The 70th Belfast Company (Ballygilbert) Boys' Brigade placed a notice announcing a memorial service to be held in Ballygilbert Presbyterian Church at 5.30 pm on Sunday 1 November 1942. Boys' Brigade Companies from Belfast (Ballygilbert), Bangor, Holywood and Ballymiscaw attended the service.

Flight Sergeant David Harrison (Harry) Freeland is commemorated on Holywood and District War Memorial; in Ballygilbert Presbyterian Church and in Sullivan Upper School, Holywood. Harry's father, David Freeland MBE, presented the Harry Freeland Perpetual Championship Trophy in Harry's memory, to be awarded annually at Balmoral Agricultural Show for the champion bird in the poultry classes at the Show.

Fry, William Benjamin
Flight Sergeant (Pilot)
No. R/98031, 504 (RAF) Squadron, Royal Canadian Air Force
Killed in an aircraft accident on Saturday 26 September 1942 (aged 22)
Drumachose (Christ Church) Church of Ireland Churchyard, Co. Londonderry (Grave 8)

William Benjamin Fry was born on 9 December 1919 and he was a son of William Benjamin and Bessie Bryant Fry (nee Johnston) who lived at 119

North Bonham Street, San Benito, Cameron County, Texas, USA. William Benjamin Fry Senior was born in 1894 in Oklahoma and he worked as a manager in a loan office; Bessie Bryant Johnston was born on 14 August 1896 in Albertha, Randolph County, Arkansas and they were married on 22 February 1919 in Corpus Christi, Nueces County, Texas. They had at least four children – William Benjamin (born 9 December 1919); Norman (born 1924); Bessie Lee (born 1928) and Jennie Mae (born 1929).

William Benjamin Fry was the husband of Mildred Harris Fry and they lived in San Benito. He joined the Royal Canadian Air Force and during the Second World War he served in 504 (RAF) Squadron. On 26 September 1942 a Supermarine Spitfire aircraft (AB135) of No. 504 (RAF) Squadron based at RAF Ballyhalbert hit the ground half a mile south of Dungiven in County Londonderry. This aircraft was carrying out low level manoeuvres while taking part in *Exercise Punch*. The pilot, Flight Sergeant William Benjamin Fry, was killed and he was buried in Drumachose (Christ Church) Church of Ireland Churchyard, Limavady, Co. Londonderry. His father, William Benjamin Fry Senior, died in 1969 and his mother, Bessie Bryant Fry, died on 12 June 1985 at San Antonio in Texas.

Flight Sergeant William Benjamin Fry was 22 years old when he died and he is commemorated on the Canadian Virtual War Memorial (Internet) and on Page 75 of the Canadian Second World War Book of Remembrance.

Fuge, Brian Kenneth Levinge
Flight Lieutenant
No. 41394, 541 Squadron, Royal Air Force
Killed in action on Monday 19 March 1945 (aged 28)
Runnymede Memorial, Surrey, England (Panel 265)

Brian Kenneth Levinge Fuge was born in 1918 in India and he was a son of Captain Thomas Marshall Llewellyn Fuge who served with the Indian Army and Frances Ellen Fuge (nee Levinge). His parents were married in December 1917 and they had at least two children – Brian Kenneth Levinge (born 1918) and Patricia Evelyn Margaret (born 1919). The Fuge family travelled regularly between India and Britain; on 6 June 1920 they landed at Plymouth after a voyage from Karachi and on 27 September 1922 they landed at London after a voyage from Calcutta.

On 8 December 1934 Brian Kenneth Levinge Fuge was appointed as a Probationary Midshipman in the Royal Naval Volunteer Reserve and he was attached to HMS *Caroline* in the Ulster Division of the RNVR. During the Second World War he served with the Royal Air Force and was promoted to the rank of Flight Lieutenant. He was killed in action on 19 March 1945 and his body was never recovered.

Brian Kenneth Levinge Fuge was the husband of Olive Maureen Fuge of Bangor. They were married in 1944 and in 1945 their daughter Rosemary Maureen was born. Flight Lieutenant Fuge's last home address was 55 Station Road, Wallingford, Berkshire and his effects amounted to some £234. Probate was granted to his widow. Olive Maureen Fuge re-married and her husband, Cornelius McClean, worked as a Civil Servant. They lived at 5 Shandon Park, Bangor and on 26 October 1948 they moved to Canada. Brian Kenneth Levinge Fuge's mother, Frances Ellen Fuge, died on 17 August 1955 and his father, Captain Thomas Marshall Llewellyn Fuge, died on 20 November 1965. Brian Kenneth Levinge Fuge was 28 years old when he died and he is commemorated on the Runnymede Memorial in Surrey.

Fulton, Hugh
Fusilier
No. 6984727, 70th Battalion, Royal Inniskilling Fusiliers
Died as a result of enemy action on Wednesday 16 April 1941 (aged 17)
Belleek (St. Luke's) Church of Ireland Churchyard, Co. Armagh

Hugh Fulton was born in 1924 and he was a son of William Moffet Fulton and Julia Fulton (nee Chambers) of Tandragee Road, Markethill, Co. Armagh. William Moffet Fulton was trained by his father James as a bootmaker and he and Julia Chambers were married on 23 May 1912 in Belleek (St. Luke's) Church of Ireland Church, Co. Armagh. They had eleven children – Thomas (born 1 September 1912): David George (born 5 February 1914); Mary; William; John (died in childhood); Hugh; Martha; Walter; Julia; Noel and Albert.

Aged 16 and against his parents' wishes Hugh Fulton enlisted in Armagh. His brother David was already serving with the Royal Inniskilling Fusiliers and his brother William was in the Fleet Air Arm. Although Hugh was underage his parents decided not to sign him out – because of his absolute determination to enlist. That decision compounded their grief when Hugh died aged 17. He

F

looked a much older man in uniform than he did before he enlisted. Fusilier Hugh Fulton was one of 13 soldiers serving with the 70th Battalion, Royal Inniskilling Fusiliers who died as a result of an air raid on Newtownards aerodrome during the night of 15/16 April 1941. Fusilier **Daniel Higgins** who also died that night was buried in Newtownards (Movilla) Cemetery and under his name in this Book of Honour there is a summary of all those people with North Down or Ards connections who died that night.

Fusilier Hugh Fulton's body was brought to Markethill, Co. Armagh by military transport and he was buried in St. Luke's Church of Ireland Churchyard, Carrickananny Road, Belleek, Co. Armagh. There is an inscription on his CWGC headstone:

On the tearless shore to part no more
We shall meet our loved ones there

F

G

Hugh Fulton's father, William Moffat Fulton, was 51 years old when he died of cancer in 1942. His mother Julia was 64 years old when she died in 1957 and both were buried in the family plot in St. Luke's Church of Ireland Churchyard.

Gamble, Hugh
Gunner
No. 1476586, 5 Battery, 2 Light Anti-Aircraft Regiment, Royal Artillery
Killed in action on Saturday 26 April 1941 (aged 28)
Athens Memorial, Greece (Face 2)

Hugh Gamble was born on 4 December 1912 and he was a son of David and Jane Gamble (nee Dempster) who lived at 80 East Street, and later in Corry Street, Newtownards. During the First World War David Gamble served with the Royal Irish Fusiliers and he died in a German Prisoner-of-War Camp on 25 August 1916 at the age of 32. Private David Gamble is commemorated on Page 235 in the Book of Honour *Remembering Their Sacrifice in the Great War – Ards* compiled by Barry Niblock. Prior to the outbreak of the First World War David Gamble worked as a general labourer and he and Jane

Dempster were married on 1 January 1909 in Newtownards Registry Office. Jane Dempster already had two children – Georgina Dempster born in 1899 and David Dempster born in 1900. David and Jane Gamble had at least four children – James (born 2 September 1910); Hugh (born 4 December 1912); William John (born 1 July 1914) and Samuel. The first three of these children were baptised in Greenwell Street Presbyterian Church, Newtownards. After Hugh's father David died in 1916 his widowed mother Jane moved to Whitespots, Newtownards.

Hugh Gamble and Mary Ann Miskimmins Melville were married on 17 June 1938 in Groomsport Parish Church of Ireland Church and they lived in Murdoch's Lane, Cottown, Bangor. Hugh worked on Murdoch's Farm and he and Mary Ann had two children, Ella and Jean. Ella was two years old when her father died and Jean was just six months old. Hugh never saw his daughter Jean and she died of rheumatic fever when she was 16 years old.

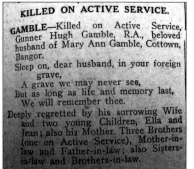

KILLED ON ACTIVE SERVICE.

GAMBLE—Killed on Active Service, Gunner Hugh Gamble, R.A., beloved husband of Mary Ann Gamble, Cottown, Bangor.

Sleep on, dear husband, in your foreign grave,
A grave we may never see,
But as long as life and memory last,
We will remember thee.

Deeply regretted by his sorrowing Wife and two young Children, Ella and Jean; also his Mother, Three Brothers (one on Active Service), Mother-in-law and Father-in-law; also Sisters-in-law and Brothers-in-law.

G

Gunner Hugh Gamble was already in the Army before the outbreak of the Second World War. During the war he served with the Royal Artillery and initially he was reported as missing in action in Greece. Some seven months later it was officially confirmed that he must be presumed killed in action on 26 April 1941. His widow placed a *Killed on Active Service* notice in the 22 November 1941 edition of the *Newtownards Chronicle* and then *Our Heroes – In Memoriam* notices each year thereafter in an April edition of the same newspaper. The 1943 notice contained the verse:

> *A loving husband, true and kind, missed by those he left behind;*
> *Forget him, no, I never will, as time rolls on I love him still.*
> *We lost our best and dearest friend, dear Daddy, when we lost you.*

Gunner Hugh Gamble was 28 years old when he died and he is commemorated on Donaghadee and District War Memorial and on Newtownards and District War Memorial.

Gault, William Francis Ernest (Frank)
Sergeant (Pilot)
No. 950326, 245 Squadron, Royal Air Force Volunteer Reserve
Killed in an aircraft accident on Friday 4 April 1941 (aged 20)
Bangor Cemetery (Section 4 V Grave 39)

William Francis Ernest (Frank) Gault was born on 4 November 1920 and he was the elder son of John Ernest Gault (born in Dungannon, Co. Tyrone) and Isabella Gault (nee Johnston, born in Howth, Co. Dublin). John Ernest Gault was a commercial traveller and he and Isabella Johnston were married in Castleblayney, Co. Monaghan. Later they lived at 1 Farnham Road, Bangor and they had five children – William Francis Ernest (Frank), Dorothy, Audrey, John (Jack) and Maureen. During the Second World War Dorothy Gault served with the Women's Royal Naval Service (WRNS).

Frank Gault was baptised in Bangor Parish Church of Ireland Church (St. Comgall's), he was a member of the church choir and he was confirmed in Bangor Parish Church in 1936. Frank attended Bangor Grammar School from 1933 until 1939 and he was described by the Headmaster as 'universally beloved and utterly and completely loyal to his duty.' He played rugby for the school and was prominent in the Debating and Dramatic Societies. At school he and **Norman Edmond Hanna** were close friends. He was selected to represent the school to speak about *What I Think about Life* at a Bangor Rotary Club Luncheon in 1939. He was also described as a clever footballer and in everything he did he 'showed initiative, dependability and powers of leadership'. Frank joined up immediately after leaving school.

G

Sergeant Pilot Frank Gault served with the Royal Air Force Volunteer Reserve and he was 20 years old when he died on 4 April 1941. Based at RAF Aldergrove, Frank was returning to base after escorting a convoy of ships out of Belfast Lough. In low cloud, the Hawker Hurricane aircraft (V7678) he was flying crashed into the hills above Carrickfergus. His funeral to Bangor Cemetery on Monday 7 April 1941 followed 'an impressive service held in Bangor Parish Church.' Tributes to Frank Gault included the verses:

Always in our thoughts
Precious memories to cherish in an aching heart, like fadeless flowers

Sergeant William Francis Ernest Gault is commemorated on Bangor and District War Memorial, in Bangor Parish Church (St. Comgall's) and in Bangor Grammar School. His parents were buried with him in the same grave and there is an inscription on his CWGC headstone:

Went the day well? I died and never knew
Well or ill, freedom I died for you

Geddis, Stanley
Able Seaman
No. D/JX 138939, HMS *Whitaker*, Royal Navy
Killed in action on Wednesday 1 November 1944 (aged 26)
Plymouth Naval Memorial, Devon, England (Panel 86 Column 2)

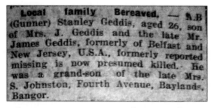

Stanley Geddis's birth was registered in the first quarter of 1918 in Newtownards and he was a son of James and Jeanie Berry Geddis (nee Johnston). James Geddis was an electrician and he and Jeanie Berry Johnston were married on 4 February 1911 in St. Clement's Church of Ireland Church, Knockbreda, Belfast. They had two children – Sarah Sheila (born 27 February 1912) and Stanley (born 1918). The Geddis family lived at 1 Glendower Street, Belfast and then for a time in Bangor with Jeanie's mother at 4 Fourth Avenue, Baylands. On 1 July 1922 they sailed from Liverpool to New York aboard the SS *Cedric* and they lived there before moving to Manasquan, New Jersey in the United States of America and it was there that James Geddis died on 11 May 1930. In June 1930 the widowed Jeanie Geddis and her two children, Sheila and Stanley, returned to Belfast aboard the SS *Samaria* and they moved back to 4 Fourth Avenue, Baylands, Bangor.

During the Second World War Stanley Geddis served with the Royal Navy aboard HMS *Whitaker* and when he was killed in action on 1 November 1944 his mother was living in Beeston, Nottinghamshire. Under the headline *Local Family Bereaved*, the death of Able Seaman Stanley Geddis was reported in the 2 December 1944 edition of the *County Down Spectator*.

HMS *Whitaker* was a frigate of the Captain class and she was built by the Bethlehem-Hingham Shipyard Inc., Hingham, Massachusetts, USA. The Captain class was a designation given to 78 frigates of the Royal Navy constructed in the United States of America, launched in 1942/1943 and delivered to the United Kingdom under the provisions of the Lend-Lease agreement – the programme under which the United States of America supplied the United Kingdom and other Allied nations with military material between 1941 and 1945. Commissioned by the Royal Navy on 28 January 1944, HMS *Whitaker* was torpedoed off Malin Head, Co. Donegal some nine months later when Convoy SC-159 was attacked by the German submarine *U-483*. Hit by two torpedoes shortly after 2.00 am on 1 November 1944, her whole bow section was destroyed due to an explosion in the forward magazine. More than 90 men were killed. Surviving crew members extinguished the fires and stopped the ship from flooding. HMS *Whitaker* was towed to Londonderry, and subsequently to Belfast. She was returned to the US Navy in March 1945, sold for scrap in 1947 to John Lee, Belfast and broken up in 1948.

Initially Able Seaman Stanley Geddis (aged 26) was reported as missing in action and then it was reported that he must be presumed killed. His body was never recovered and he is commemorated on the Plymouth Naval Memorial in Devon. The death of his mother, Jeanie Berry Geddis, was registered in the third quarter of 1964 in Nottingham.

Gell, George Leslie
Fusilier
No. 4200582, 7th Battalion, Royal Welch Fusiliers
Died as a result of a road accident on Thursday 21 November 1940 (aged 24)
Kingsway New Cemetery, Nottinghamshire, England
(Section A Row L Grave 1254)

> Fusilier George Leslie Gell, aged 23 years, who belongs to Nottngham, died in the Ards District Hospital on Thursday, 21st November, as the result of injuries sustained in an accident in which he was involved while motor cycling on the Killinchy-Comber Road on 15th November. The young soldier sustained fractures of both arms and both legs, one of the latter having to be amputated. A blood transfusion was given by Constable S. Hamill in the hope of saving the young man's life, and hopes were entertained that that would be accomplished when his condition improved, but he had a turn for the worse on Thursday and died.

George Leslie Gell's birth was registered in the fourth quarter of 1916 in Basford, Nottinghamshire and he was a son of Leslie Victor Horsley Gell and Amelia Gell (nee Baker) of East Kirkby, Nottinghamshire. Their marriage was registered in the fourth quarter of 1915 in Mansfield, Nottinghamshire. Leslie Victor Horsley Gell was a son of Ernest and Sarah Gell and as a 14-year old boy in 1911 Leslie Victor Horsley Gell had worked as a pony driver and gang lad in a coal pit.

Fusilier George Leslie Gell's death was reported in the 23 November 1940 edition of the *Newtownards Chronicle* (in the *County Down Spectator* report his surname was spelt Gill). Fusilier Gell died as a result of a head-on collision between his military motor cycle and a saloon motor car which occurred on the main road on the Comber side of Lisbane Post Office at 6.25 pm on Friday 15 November 1940. Both of Fusilier Gell's arms and both of his legs were broken in the accident and one of his legs was so badly shattered that it

G

had to be amputated in Ards District Hospital.

Fusilier Gell was travelling towards Comber and the motor car was travelling towards Killinchy. It was being driven by Lieutenant Colonel Grove-Raines who lived at *Ardview*, Killinchy. Dr B.R. Henry of Comber was called to the scene of the accident and he dressed Fusilier Gell's injuries. Later, at Ards District Hospital, Constable Hamill of the Royal Ulster Constabulary donated a pint of blood for Fusilier Gell to have a blood transfusion. Afterwards Constable Hamill commented that 'the giving of a quantity of blood does not interfere with the donor's life'. The newspaper reported that 'after a short rest and a cigarette, Constable Hamill returned to the barracks and the following morning he was back on duty as though nothing out of the ordinary had taken place'.

Initially Fusilier Gell's condition seemed to be improving. Then, at 12.45 am on Thursday 21 November, his condition began to deteriorate and he subsequently died at 3.15 am. The cause of death was 'pulmonary embolism following multiple injuries'. An open verdict was returned at the inquest which was held that evening by Dr R.A. Wallace, Coroner for the district. The Revd R. Emrys Evans BA, Chaplain to the deceased's Battalion, and the Revd W.T. Dennison, Minister of Newtownards Methodist Church, conducted a brief service at the hospital before Fusilier Gell's remains were removed to RAF East Kirkby, Lincolnshire for interment in Kingsway New Cemetery, Nottinghamshire. There is an inscription on his CWGC headstone:

Beautiful memories never fade of one we loved but could not save

Fusilier George Leslie Gell was 24 years old when he died and he is commemorated on Kingsway War Memorial, Nottinghamshire. Amelia Gell was 67 when she died and she was buried on 28 January 1961 beside her son. Leslie Victor Horsley Gell remarried and his marriage to Annie E. Dyson was registered in the first quarter of 1962 in Basford, Nottinghamshire. Leslie Victor Horsley Gell was 91 when he died and he was buried on 23 December 1987 in the same grave as his son. At the time of writing Fusilier Gell's CWGC headstone is the only headstone on the grave.

George, David Burrows (David)
Sergeant (Flight Engineer)
No. 1796593, 153 Squadron, Royal Air Force Volunteer Reserve
Killed on active service on Monday 22 January 1945 (aged 22)
Venray War Cemetery, Limburg, Netherlands (Grave VII B 4)

David Burrows George was the youngest child of James and Ellen George (nee Stewart) who were married on 25 September 1907 in Bangor Abbey and lived at 6 Dufferin Avenue, Bangor. James George was a shoemaker and he had his own business at 6 Dufferin Avenue. Ellen George (daughter of Edmund Stewart, a postman) was a dressmaker and she and James had six children – Edmund (born 19 March 1909, died aged four days); Sarah Nelson (Sadie, born 8 January 1911, died of tuberculosis 1937); Anne (Annie, born 11 February 1913, died 2012 aged 99); James (Jim, died aged 78); Elizabeth (Elsie, born 8 April 1921, died aged 87) and David Burrows (born 1922). David was 8 when his mother Ellen died on 11 May 1931 and after that it was his sister Annie who cared for her brothers and sisters. On 14 March 1933 James George married Lydia Jackson in Cregagh Presbyterian Church, Belfast and Lydia became the children's stepmother. James George died on 20 July 1948.

David George was educated at Bangor Central Public Elementary School and on leaving school he worked in the engineering department of the Post Office at Telephone House, Belfast. He joined the Royal Air Force Volunteer Reserve in December 1943 and on completion of his training in England he led the cadet parade of his unit and was recommended for a commission after achieving a high percentage in his examinations. David spent Christmas 1944 at home in Bangor with his family who at that time lived at 8 Donaghadee Road.

> **KILLED ON ACTIVE SERVICE**
>
> GEORGE—January 21-22, 1945, on air operations at Duisburg, Germany, Flight - Engineer - Sergeant David Burrows George, R.A.F., younger son of James George, 8 Donaghadee Road, Bangor, and the late Ellen George.
>
> "At the rising of the sun, and the going down thereof, we will remember him."
>
> Deeply regretted by his Sisters and Brother, Annie (Mrs. Daniels), Quorn, Leicester; Elsie (Mrs. Orr), Springfield Avenue, Bangor; Jim, Airdre, Scotland.

On 22 January 1945 Sergeant David George was one of a crew of seven aboard an Avro Lancaster Mark I aircraft (NG185) that took off at 4.40 pm from RAF Scrampton in Lincolnshire on a mission to bomb Duisburg. The aircraft crashed over Germany and initially Sergeant David George was posted as missing in action. After his death was officially confirmed his family placed a *Killed in*

Action notice in the 17 November 1945 edition of the *County Down Spectator*. He was deeply regretted by his sister Mrs Annie Daniels in Quorn, Leicester; his sister Mrs Elsie Orr in Springfield Avenue, Bangor and his brother Jim George in Airdrie, Scotland.

The other six crew members who were killed were:

- FO Kenneth William Winder aged 33 from Stamford, Lincolnshire
- Sergeant Alfred Jack Rabin aged 22 from Kentish Town, London
- Flying Officer Matthew Arnold Smith (RCAF)
- Sergeant Robert Evans aged 21 from Liverpool
- Flight Sergeant Gerald Burton Hamilton aged 18 (RCAF)
- Sergeant Thomas O'Gorman

G

Their bodies were found by US forces and taken to the Netherlands for interment in the American Cemetery at Margraten. Later their remains were transferred to Venray War Cemetery. There is an inscription on Sergeant George's CWGC headstone:

Death is swallowed up in victory
1 Corinthians XV 54

Sergeant (Flight Engineer) David Burrows George was 22 years old when he died and he is commemorated on Bangor and District War Memorial and in Wesley Centenary Methodist Church, Bangor.

Gibbison, Andrew Greenwell
Flight Sergeant (Wireless Operator/Air Gunner)
No. 424976, Royal New Zealand Air Force
Killed in an aircraft accident on Thursday 18 November 1943 (aged 22)
Eglantine Church of Ireland Cemetery, Co. Down (Section E Grave 36)

Andrew Greenwell Gibbison was a son of Francis B.M. Gibbison and Coralie Gibbison (nee Carr) of Kauroa, Auckland, New Zealand. During the Second World War Flight Sergeant Andrew Greenwell Gibbison served with the Royal New Zealand Air Force and he died on 18 November 1943, along with the other three members of the crew, when their Lockheed

Hudson Mark V aircraft (AE653) of No. 5 (Coastal) Operational Training Unit based at RAF Long Kesh, crashed into Strangford Lough just south of Chapel Island (off Greyabbey). They were on a rocket-firing exercise using the submarine target at South Island in Strangford Lough.

The other three men who died in the crash were the pilot, Sergeant **Walter Edward Fern**; Flight Sergeant **Raymond Farquhar Simpson** and Flight Sergeant **William Barraclough**. Flight Sergeant Andrew Greenwell Gibbison was 22 years old when he died and he was buried in Eglantine Church of Ireland (All Saints) Cemetery, Lisburn, Co. Down (CWGC designation).

Gibbs, Reginald William Dudley
Second Engineer Officer
No. 1111732, SS *Empire Portia* (Newcastle-upon-Tyne), Merchant Navy
Died as a result of enemy action on Thursday 29 June 1944 (aged 42)
Gosport (Ann's Hill) Cemetery, Hampshire, England (Plot 189 Grave 13)

Reginald William Dudley Gibbs was born on 10 October 1901 in South Stoneham, Southampton, Hampshire and he was a son of William and Antoinette Gibbs. William Gibbs was a coachman and cab proprietor and he and Antoinette had at least five children – Frederick A., Mabel Antoinette, Reginald William Dudley, Victor and Percy.

G

Reginald William Dudley Gibbs and Grace Wallace Legge were married on 27 July 1933 in Second Holywood (High Street) Presbyterian Church and during the Second World War he served with the Merchant Navy aboard the SS *Empire Portia*. The SS *Empire Portia* was built by Swan, Hunter and Wigham Richardson Ltd., Wallsend-on-Tyne and she was completed in 1943 for the Ministry of War Transport (MOWT). She was operated by Common Brothers Ltd., Newcastle-upon-Tyne. At about 4.00 pm on 29 June 1944 the SS *Empire Portia*, sailing in Convoy FTM-22 from the Normandy beaches to Portsmouth, was badly damaged by an explosion off Selsey Bill (a headland in West Sussex extending into the English Channel). The vessel was taken in tow by the British landing ship HMS *LST-416* but the tow parted and she ran aground with a broken back on Peel Bank near Ryde, Isle of Wight. The forward section was towed to Falmouth in Cornwall and the aft section to Briton Ferry in South Wales. The captain and 41 crew members were saved but five of the crew were lost. The German submarine *U-988* was known to be in the area but it did not return from patrol and, in the absence of a report, it was not clear whether the SS *Empire Portia* had been torpedoed or mined.

One of the survivors later recalled that the SS *Empire Portia* accommodated around 500 troops in the main hold along with equipment and cargo on deck. They were returning from their third trip to the beachhead at Arromanches, northwest of Caen, on the stretch of coastline designated Gold Beach during the Normandy Landings. At Arromanches there was a mulberry harbour – a portable temporary harbour built to facilitate the rapid offloading of cargo. After the explosion, survivors took to the lifeboats and the ship that picked them up took them to Gosport. Second Engineer Officer Reginald William Dudley Gibbs was 42 years old when he died aboard the rescue ship on 29 June 1944 and he was buried in Gosport (Ann's Hill) Cemetery on Monday 3 July 1944.

 In the Register of Deceased Seamen his last place of abode was recorded as 1 Seaview Terrace, Holywood, Co. Down and the cause of death was 'due to mine explosion'. Second Engineer Officer Reginald William Dudley Gibbs is commemorated on Holywood and District War Memorial (as D.W. Gibbs).

Gibson, John Malcomson (John)
Lieutenant (Acting Captain)
No. 126704, 5 Battery, 45 Light Anti-Aircraft Regiment, Royal Artillery
Killed in action between Saturday 20 and Sunday 21 June 1942 (aged 30)
Knightsbridge War Cemetery, Acroma, Libya (Grave 2 F 1)

G

> **LIEUT. J. M. GIBSON REPORTED MISSING, BELIEVED KILLED.**
>
> Newtownards people, and many outside our immediate neighbourhood, will learn with regret that official news was received on Thursday that Lieutenant John M. Gibson, R.A., is missing, believed killed, while serving with the Middle East Forces. Lieutenant Gibson was with the battery composed for the most part of men from Newtownards and Bangor, many of whom have been reported missing.

John Malcomson (in some records spelt Malcolmson) Gibson was born on 29 March 1912 in Newtownards and he was a son of James Gibson who worked as a carpenter and Mary Elenor Gibson (nee Malcomson) of Kimberley Buildings, Newtownards and later *Glenside*, Ballystockart, Comber. They were married on 13 August 1908 in Conlig Presbyterian Church and they had at least three children – Mary Ann (born 25 May 1909), Elizabeth Malcomson (born 28 July 1910) and John Malcomson (born 29 March 1912). These three children were baptised in First Newtownards Presbyterian Church.

John Gibson attended Castle Gardens Public Elementary School, Newtownards and then Regent House School, Newtownards from 1927 until 1932. Then he went to Teacher Training College. Shortly before the outbreak of the Second World War he was appointed Principal of Ballystockart Public

Elementary School and, while he was there, he and his mother and sister worshipped in First Comber Presbyterian Church. He was an accomplished all-round sportsman – a successful sprinter, he played rugby for Ards Rugby Club and soccer for the Drones in the Summer League. He was a keen tennis player and he also played hockey.

During the Second World War John Gibson served in the Royal Artillery, initially with the Battery composed for the most part of men from Newtownards and Bangor. He joined the Battery before the outbreak of war and became a Sergeant. Then he was posted to England where he obtained his commission. He served with the Middle East Forces and initially he was reported missing believed killed during heavy fighting on 20/21 June 1942. Later it was confirmed that he had died. John Gibson and three of his comrades died on 20/21 June 1942 after being hit by shell-fire at Tobruk – Sergeant **Alexander Davidson** from Newtownards, Gunner **David McClinton** from Newtownards and Gunner George Alfred Rayner from Glastonbury in Somerset. Their gun position was sited some 2¼ miles south of Tobruk docks, on a broad plateau above an escarpment and about a thousand yards east of the road running almost due south out of Tobruk. Their Navy, Army and Air Force Institutes (NAAFI) Building was on the same plateau but slightly further north. The Axis Forces (21 Panzer Division) swept through their gun position some time between 2.30 and 5.00 pm on Saturday 20 June and reached the harbour area shortly afterwards.

G

Lieutenant John Malcomson Gibson was 30 years old when he died and he is commemorated on Newtownards and District War Memorial; in First Newtownards Presbyterian Church; in Regent House School; on the Queen's University War Memorial; on the Stranmillis College Roll of Honour; on the family grave headstone in Bangor Abbey Graveyard and in First Comber Presbyterian Church (as Captain John Gibson).

Gibson, Joseph Patrick (served as Patrick Joseph Gibson)
Sailor
MV *Empire Attendant* (Glasgow), Merchant Navy
Died as a result of enemy action on Wednesday 15 July 1942 (aged 30)
Tower Hill Memorial, London, England (Panel 38)

Joseph Patrick Gibson was born on 29 June 1911 and he was a son of William and Isabella Gibson (nee Glenn) who lived at 59 Castle Street, Bangor. They were married on 12 July 1901 in St. Anne's Church of Ireland Church, Belfast. William Gibson was a night watchman and railway porter and he and Isabella had at least five children – William (born 27 September 1901);

Robert (born 5 February 1903); John Glenn (born 21 October 1906); Annie (born 13 August 1908) and Joseph Patrick (born 29 June 1911). Isabella Gibson died on 3 October 1911 (aged 33) and she was buried in Bangor Cemetery.

Joseph Patrick Gibson was a sailor and he lived at 38 High Street, Carnlough in County Antrim. During the Second World War he served as Patrick Joseph Gibson with the Merchant Navy aboard the MV *Empire Attendant*. This passenger cargo vessel was launched in December 1920 as *Magnava* and completed as *Domala* in 1921 by Barclay, Curle and Company, Whiteinch, Glasgow. She was owned by the British India Steam Navigation Company. Following damage sustained in an air attack in 1940, *Domala* was requisitioned by the Ministry of War Transport, rebuilt and renamed MV *Empire Attendant*. She was placed under the management of Andrew Weir and Company (Bank Line). On 1 July 1942 she sailed from Liverpool as part of Convoy OS-33 with a cargo of stores, vehicles and a quantity of explosives bound for Freetown in Sierra Leone. On 10 July 1942 the escort vessel, HMS *Pelican*, signalled the Admiralty that MV *Empire Attendant* had broken down for the seventh time and was out of contact. At 3.30 am on 15 July 1942, when she was south of the Canary Islands and off the west coast of Africa, the MV *Empire Attendant* sank after being torpedoed by the German submarine *U-582*. All 59 men aboard the MV *Empire Attendant* were presumed drowned; there were no survivors. In addition to Sailor Patrick Joseph Gibson (aged 30), Fifth Engineer Officer **Thomas McMahon Houston** and Able Seaman **John Joseph Kennedy** also died. They are commemorated on the Tower Hill Memorial in London.

Gibson, R.G.

The name Gibson, R.G. is commemorated on Bangor and District War Memorial. Desk searches and public appeals to date have produced no further information and, at the time of writing, it has not been possible to determine whether R.G. Gibson was a casualty of war or if the name R.G. Gibson was inscribed on the plaque in error. The Second World War Memorial Plaque on Bangor and District War Memorial was not unveiled until November 1967 and this accounts for some of the omissions and inaccuracies in the list of inscribed names. **Gibson, R.T.** (immediately below) is *not* commemorated on Bangor and District War Memorial. The process used to compile the list of names for Bangor and District War Memorial is outlined under the name **Lowry, G.E.** in this Book of Honour.

Gibson, Robert Trevor
Sergeant (Flight Engineer)
No. 1036711, Royal Air Force Volunteer Reserve
Killed in an aircraft accident on Friday 12 November 1943 (aged 21)
Belfast City Cemetery (Glenalina Extension Section B Grave 68)

Robert Trevor Gibson was born on 28 October 1922 and he was the only son of Edward Stanley Gibson and Elizabeth Jane (Isa) Gibson (nee Beasant) of 44 Ballyholme Esplanade, Bangor. They were married on 27 March 1922 in Knockbreda Church of Ireland Church, Belfast. Robert Trevor Gibson attended Bangor Grammar School from 1932 until 1938 and, after his mother died on 19 August 1936 at the age of 35, his father moved to Huntly in Aberdeenshire. During the Second World War Robert Trevor Gibson served with the Royal Air Force Volunteer Reserve and he was 21 years old when he died in an aircraft accident on 12 November 1943 whilst in training at RAF Halfpenny Green (previously RAF Bobbington and now Wolverhampton Airport – then in Worcestershire, now in Staffordshire).

The funeral took place to-day from the residence of his aunt, Mrs. O'Neill 171 University Street, Belfast, of Sergeant R. Trevor Gibson, R.A.F., only son of Mr. E. Stanley Gibson and the late Mrs. Isa Gibson, of Bangor, who was killed on active service.

Sergeant Gibson was an old Bangor Grammar School boy, and many of his old classmates attended the funeral. Bangor Swimming Club was also represented.

Sergeant Robert Trevor Gibson's funeral at 11.00 am on Wednesday 17 November was from 171 University Street, Belfast (the home of his aunt, Mrs O'Neill) to Belfast City Cemetery (Glenalina Extension). Former classmates from Bangor Grammar School and members of Bangor Swimming Club attended the funeral and six RAF Sergeants acted as pall bearers. A bugler sounded the Last Post. The service was conducted by the Revd H.H. McClure from Second Islandmagee Presbyterian Church, Co. Antrim and the Revd J. Martin of Sinclair Seamen's Presbyterian Church, Belfast. Mourners included

his father Stanley, his uncle George Gibson and his cousin Leo Gibson.

In his tribute to Sergeant (Flight Engineer) Robert Trevor Gibson the Headmaster of Bangor Grammar School, Maurice Wilkins MA, said that he would be remembered for his drawing skills and his excellence in map making. He excelled at rugby and athletics and won the Brent Harris Challenge Cup for the high jump in 1935. He was an enthusiastic member of the school's Dramatic Society.

Sergeant (Flight Engineer) Robert Trevor Gibson is commemorated in Bangor Grammar School and on his CWGC headstone in Belfast City Cemetery (Glenalina Extension). He was buried in the same grave as his mother and his maternal grandparents – Hugh Charles Beasant who died on 11 February 1923 and Mary Beasant who died on 20 December 1938.

Gilmour, William Des Brisay
Sergeant (Pilot)
No. 1073643, 504 Squadron, Royal Air Force Volunteer Reserve
Killed in an aircraft accident on Thursday 23 October 1941 (aged 20)
Cappagh (St. Eugenius) Church of Ireland Churchyard, Co. Tyrone

G

William Des Brisay Gilmour's birth was registered in the first quarter of 1921 in Brentford, Oxfordshire and he was a son of Dr George Van Barneveld Gilmour from London and Sara Johnston Gilmour (nee Kyle) whose family home was *Knockmoyle House*, Omagh, Co. Tyrone. They were married on 6 June 1916 in Cappagh (St. Eugenius) Parish Church of Ireland Church, Co. Tyrone and they lived at 25 Ormond Road, Rathmines, Dublin.

During the Second World War Sergeant William Des Brisay Gilmour served with the Royal Air Force Volunteer Reserve and he was with 504 Squadron based at RAF Ballyhalbert when he died. On 23 October 1941 he was flying a Hawker Hurricane aircraft (Z5204) when he crashed in the townland of Knockmoyle, three miles north of Omagh. At the time he was carrying out low flying aerobatics in the vicinity of his maternal grandmother's house. Sergeant (Pilot) William Des Brisay Gilmour was 20 years old when he died and he was buried in the Kyle family plot in Cappagh (St. Eugenius) Church of Ireland Churchyard. The others commemorated there are:

- William Hazlett Kyle died 26 January 1913 (aged 53)
- His wife Sara died 13 April 1945 (aged 80)
- Robert Hazlett Kyle died 15 January 1927 (aged 31)
- Jane, wife of Robert Hazlett Kyle, died 24 September 1963 (aged 68)

- William Hazlett, son of Robert Hazlett and Jane Kyle, died 21 July 1966 (aged 46)
- Marion Elizabeth Kyle died 23 January 1980 (aged 87).

William Des Brisay Gilmour's father, George Van Barneveld Gilmour, died in Dublin on 22 August 1962.

Gilpin, John Robert*
Rifleman
No. 7013792, 2nd Battalion, Royal Ulster Rifles
Killed in action between Saturday 1 and Sunday 2 June 1940 (aged 19)
Dunkirk Memorial, Nord, France (Column 129)

In the CWGC Debt of Honour it is recorded that John Robert Gilpin was a stepson of Mary Gilpin of Cultra, Co. Down. He was born on 18 December 1920 in County Leitrim in the Republic of Ireland and he was a son of William and Esther Gilpin (nee White). William Gilpin worked as a labourer and he and Esther had at least two children – Esther (born 1 November 1918) and John Robert (born 18 December 1920). Esther Gilpin (nee White) died when she was 26 years old and her death was registered in the third quarter of 1926 in Mohill, Co. Leitrim. William Gilpin remarried and he and his second wife Mary lived at Dalchoolin, Cultra.

During the Second World War Rifleman John Robert Gilpin served with the Royal Ulster Rifles and he was reported missing at Dunkirk. Later it was officially confirmed that he must be presumed killed on either 1 or 2 June 1940. He was 19 years old when he died, his body was never recovered and he is commemorated on the Dunkirk Memorial in France.

Glass, John Lyle Taggart (Lyle)
Lieutenant (Paymaster)
HMS *Corfu*, Royal Naval Reserve
Died during a medical operation on Monday 27 April 1942 (aged 27)
Mombasa (Mbaraki) Cemetery, Kenya
(Prot. Service Plot Row D Grave 22)

John Lyle Taggart (Lyle) Glass was born on 11 June 1914 and he was the second son of George Francis Glass (a linen salesman), and Mamie Anderson Glass (nee Taggart) of 10 Farnham Park, Bangor. He was baptised on 23 September 1914 in Bangor Parish Church of Ireland Church (St. Comgall's).

George Francis Glass and Mamie Anderson Taggart were married on 1 September 1909 in Bushmills Presbyterian Church, Co. Antrim and they had four children – Thomas Francis (born 3 March 1912, died 1992); John Lyle Taggart (born 11 June 1914); Mamie Elizabeth (born 1920, died 2000) and Eileen May (born 1924, died 2011).

It was reported that Lyle Glass was 'the thirteenth old boy of Bangor Grammar School to make the supreme sacrifice'. He came to Bangor Grammar School from Bangor Collegiate School in January 1924 at the age of nine. He was described by the Headmaster as, 'straight, tall and graceful in build and he gave of his best in everything.' He played cricket for the school and in his final season he won the prize for the highest batting average. He also played rugby for the school, his last match being in January 1931, on the eve of his sailing to England for an interview with P&O Directors. Lyle Glass loved the sea and from an early age he had an ambition to sail to distant parts of the world; his favourite book was said to be *Westward Ho* by Charles Kingsley.

G

Despite the worldwide slump in 1931, he was accepted by P&O as a Cadet Officer at the age of 16 and he sailed the Pacific and China seas. When on leave he always returned to visit Bangor Grammar School. After he died the Headmaster said, 'Always the fatal harvest of war seems to take away our very best – the brave, the modest, the manly and the unselfish.' One of his best friends at school was Pilot Officer **Frederick William McMurray** who was killed on 10 December 1940.

During the Second World War Paymaster Lieutenant Lyle Glass served with the Royal Naval Reserve and on 13 April 1941 he was one of some 280 survivors when the ship on which he was serving – HMS *Rajputana* – sank after being torpedoed by the German submarine *U-108* in the waters between Greenland and Iceland. Survivors were picked up by HMS *Legion* and around 40 men died. Launched on 6 August 1925 the SS *Rajputana* was a passenger ship operated by the P&O Steam Navigation Company, London and on 14 September 1939 she was requisitioned by the Admiralty and converted to an armed merchant cruiser.

After a short period of home leave following the sinking of HMS *Rajputana* Lyle Glass returned to sea and served aboard HMS *Corfu*. Launched on 20 May 1931 SS *Corfu* was a passenger ship operated by the P&O Steam Navigation Company, London and, on 14 September 1939, she was requisitioned by the Admiralty and converted to an armed merchant cruiser. She was returned to her owner on 31 July 1947.

DIED ON ACTIVE SERVICE.
GLASS—April, 1942, died on active service, Paymaster-Lieut. John L. T. Glass, R.N.R., beloved second son of George F. and Mamie Glass, Farnham Park, Bangor.

On 27 April 1942 Lyle Glass died of heart failure during a tonsillectomy operation in Mombasa Hospital, Kenya. Lyle was 27 years old and his mother Mamie was said to be 'broken-hearted' after his death. Her grief was compounded by the fact that he was buried in Mombasa. She said, 'No body, no funeral, no grave.' Mamie Glass died suddenly on 21 May 1945, just 13 days after the German surrender on 8 May 1945.

Paymaster Lieutenant Lyle Glass is commemorated on Bangor and District War Memorial; in Bangor Parish Church (St. Comgall's) and in Bangor Grammar School. Lyle's elder brother, Thomas Francis Glass, was a solicitor by profession and during the war he served with the Army in the Middle East. Lyle's father, George Francis Glass, died in 1965.

Godby, Anthony (Tony)
Lieutenant
No. 135000, 1st Northamptonshire Yeomanry, Royal Armoured Corps
Died as a result of an accident on Tuesday 15 December 1942 (aged 27)
Chislehurst Cemetery, Kent, England (Section A Grave 128)

G

In the CWGC Debt of Honour it is recorded that Anthony Godby was the husband of Daphne Mary Godby of Donaghadee, Co. Down. Anthony Godby's birth was registered in the third quarter of 1915 in Lewisham, London and he was a son of John Christopher Godby who was born on 28 January 1881 and Mary Eleanor (Eileen) Godby (nee Martin-Smith) who was born on 24 October 1880. John Christopher Godby was a stock exchange clerk and their marriage was registered in the fourth quarter of 1907 in Kensington, London. They had at least three children – Mary V. (born 1910); John M. (born 1913) and Anthony (Tony, born 1915). For a time the Godby family lived at 28 Halons Road, Etham in Kent.

Tony Godby was the husband of Daphne Mary Godby (nee Pannell) of Bromley, Kent. Daphne was born in 1916 and their marriage was registered in the third quarter of 1939 in Woolwich, London. At the outbreak of war Tony Godby was with the Inns of Court Regiment, Royal Armoured Corps and on 8 June 1940 he obtained his commission as a Second Lieutenant from the Officer Cadet Training Unit, Sandhurst. During the Second World War Lieutenant Anthony Godby served with the 1st Northamptonshire

Yeomanry, Royal Armoured Corps and he was 27 years old when he died as a result of an accident on 15 December 1942. At the time of his death his wife Daphne was living at 6 Mottingham Road, Mottingham, London. His effects amounted to some £678 and probate was granted to his widow. His brother John was serving with the Royal Regiment of Artillery. His father died on 6 November 1955 and his mother died on 23 January 1970.

Goldstone, Albert Abraham
Sergeant
No. 979911, 143 Squadron, Royal Air Force Volunteer Reserve
Killed in action on Sunday 1 August 1943
Runnymede Memorial, Surrey, England (Panel 150)

It was reported in the press that Albert Abraham Goldstone's mother lived in Glen Road, Craigavad. Albert Abraham Goldstone was educated at Chorlton High School, Manchester and he joined the Royal Air Force Volunteer Reserve in 1939. It was also reported that he had two brothers serving with the RAF. One of them, Flying Officer Jack Goldstone, was Irish table tennis champion in 1940 and he also held the Ulster championship.

In June 1941, 143 Squadron was formed at RAF Aldergrove as a long-range fighter unit in Coastal Command. Equipped with Bristol Beaufighter aircraft, the Squadron moved to north-east England and then to Scotland for convoy patrols along the east coast. In December 1941, 143 Squadron became a training unit. In August 1942, the Squadron moved to East Anglia for convoy patrols and air-sea rescue missions and in November 1942 became operational on anti-shipping raids. In August 1943, 143 Squadron moved to Cornwall to provide fighter support for anti-submarine aircraft operating over the Bay of Biscay.

GOLDSTONE A.A. Sergeant Albert Abraham Goldstone was killed in action on 1 August 1943, his body was never recovered and he is commemorated on the Runnymede Memorial. The other man who died was:

• Sergeant Cyril Henry William Watts aged 23 of Stratford, Essex

Student records in Chorlton High School do not go back as far as the Second World War and the school does not have a war memorial.

Goodchild, David John (David)
Sergeant (Pilot)
No. 1795195, Royal Air Force Volunteer Reserve
Killed in an aircraft accident on Tuesday 9 March 1943 (aged 19)
Streatham Park Cemetery, Surrey, England (Square 6B Grave 19215)

David John Goodchild was born on 2 August 1923 and he was the elder son of Thurlow and Mary Goodchild (nee Irwin). During the First World War

Thurlow Goodchild (No. 367552) served as a Sergeant with the RASC. His attestation was on 20 June 1916 and he was discharged on 5 May 1920.

The marriage of Thurlow Goodchild (born 1878) and Mary Irwin was registered in the second quarter of 1922 in St. George Hanover Square, London and David's younger brother, Richard T. Goodchild, was born in 1927 in London. The Goodchild family moved from London to Bangor, Co. Down where they lived at 133 Belfast Road.

David John Goodchild was educated at Bangor Central Public Elementary School and then at Bangor Grammar School from 1936 until 1940 where he excelled in French, Latin and Chemistry. In 1940 he gained the Cambridge School Certificate and qualified to pass London University Matriculation. At that point, aged 17, he opted to relinquish his final year at school, resigned his scholarship and began an industrial career combined with evening study at the Technical Institute. In sport he played rugby for the school and he excelled at athletics. The Headmaster said of him that 'he had a brilliant and versatile brain, an athletic constitution and a resolute character'. In 1941 David joined the Royal Air Force Volunteer Reserve through the Queen's University Air Squadron and went to Georgia in the United States of America for training. He was with No. 7 Elementary Flying Training School (EFTS) at RAF Desford in Leicestershire when he died on 9 March 1943 aged 19. He was flying a de Havilland Tiger Moth aircraft (N6753) which went into a spin at 2,500 feet during a training flight and crashed to the ground. He was buried in Streatham Park Cemetery, Surrey.

Sergeant (Pilot) David John Goodchild is commemorated on Bangor and District War Memorial; in Ballygilbert Presbyterian Church; in the annals of Helen's Bay Presbyterian Church and in Bangor Grammar School.

G

Gordon, James Hamilton
Pilot Officer (Air Gunner)
No. 43157, 15 Squadron, Royal Air Force
Killed in action on Saturday 25 May 1940 (aged 30)
St. Inglevert Churchyard, Pas de Calais, France (Collective Grave)

James Hamilton Gordon was born on 16 September 1909 in Donaghey, Stewartstown, Co. Tyrone and he was the only son of James and Matilda Gordon (nee Hardie). James Gordon Senior worked as a book-keeper and he and Matilda Hardie were married on 2 October 1901 in Stewartstown (St. Patrick's) Church of Ireland Church, Donaghendry.

James Hamilton Gordon and Virtue Olive Musgrave (born 1914) were married on 2 June 1937 in First Holywood Presbyterian Church. During the Second World War James Hamilton Gordon served with the Royal Air Force in Bomber Command and on 25 May 1940 he was one of a crew of three aboard a Bristol Blenheim Mark IV aircraft (P6913). They took off at 10.27 am from RAF Wyton in Cambridgeshire on a bombing mission and their aircraft was shot down near St. Inglevert (between Calais and Marquise) in France. The other crew members who died that day were:

- Pilot Officer Douglas Sidney Reeve Harriman aged 20 from London
- Sergeant Peter Bloomer aged 22 from Tottenham, Middlesex

All three were buried together in a collective grave in St. Inglevert Churchyard, Pas de Calais, France. Peter Bloomer's brother Charles served with the Royal Navy aboard HMS *Hebe* and he was killed on 22 November 1943. Families react to tragedy in different ways; after Charles and Peter Bloomer died, their father destroyed all photographs of his two sons and family members were forbidden from ever mentioning their names again.

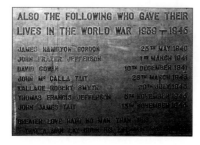

Pilot Officer James Hamilton Gordon was 30 years old when he died on 25 May 1940 and he is commemorated on Stewartstown and District War Memorial, Co. Tyrone; in Stewartstown (St. Patrick's) Church; on Holywood and District War Memorial; in First Holywood Presbyterian Church and on Page 317 in *Cookstown's War Dead* compiled by Cookstown District Council.

Gordon, William Gallagher
Warrant Officer (Observer)
No. 1682131, Royal Air Force Volunteer Reserve
Killed in an aircraft accident on Tuesday 21 May 1946 (aged 26)
Newtownards (Movilla) Cemetery, Co. Down (Section 1 Grave 6)

William Gallagher Gordon was born on 22 June 1919 and his birth was registered in Belfast. He was a grandson of John Gordon (a teacher) and Sarah (Sally) Gordon (nee Gallagher) who were married on 29 July 1856 in Watton-on-the-Hill Parish Church, Lancaster. William Gallagher Gordon was a son of Thomas Craig Gordon and Annie Margaret Gordon (nee Robinson) of 51 Clovelly Street and later *Thornhill*, Upper Newtownards Road, Belfast. Thomas Craig Gordon worked in the shipyard as a plater's helper and he and Annie Margaret Robinson were married in 1906. They had at least four children – Sarah (born 1907); Dorothea (born 28 May 1908, died in infancy); Dorothea Robinson (born 21 November 1910) and William Gallagher (born 1919).

William Gallagher Gordon was a Pilot Instructor and he was 26 years old when he died in an aircraft accident on 21 May 1946. His address was recorded in the burial register as 60 Moss Lane, Pinner in Middlesex. He died at RAF South Cerney near Cirencester in Gloucestershire and his effects amounted to some £391. Probate was granted to his widowed mother.

Warrant Officer William Gallagher Gordon was buried in Movilla Cemetery (Section 1 Grave 6) and other family members commemorated there include his paternal grandfather John Gordon (born 27 May 1824, died 26 September 1899); his paternal grandmother Sally Gordon (born 20 February 1837, died 22 August 1909); his uncle James Campbell Gordon (born 6 May 1873, died 22 January 1877); his aunt Helen Edith Gordon (born 21 February 1861, died 13 January 1901); his father Thomas Craig Gordon (born 15 April 1879, died 5 October 1932) and his mother Annie Margaret Gordon (died April 1959).

Gorman, Francis John Noel (Frankie)
Leading Aircraftman
No. 647105, 274 Squadron, Royal Air Force
Died in service on Thursday 23 April 1942 (aged 20)
El Alamein War Cemetery, Egypt (Grave XXXI D 17)

KILLED ON ACTIVE SERVICE.

GORMAN—Frankie, L.A.C., 7 Beatrice Avenue, Bangor, killed in Middle East, April, 1942. Inserted by his sorrowing Mother and Brother Jim.

Francis John Noel (Frankie) Gorman was a son of Albert and Isabella Gorman (nee Johnston) of 7 Beatrice Avenue, Bangor. Albert Gorman was on active service during the Great War and he and Isabella Johnston were married on 19 March 1918 in Wesley Centenary Methodist Church, Hamilton Road, Bangor. They had at least two children – Jim (born 1920) and Frankie (born 1922).

Frankie Gorman was educated at Main Street and Central Public Elementary Schools in Bangor. He was a keen swimmer and a member of the 2nd Bangor (Hamilton Road Methodist) Boys' Brigade Company. He played football for 2nd Bangor BB and in 1932/33 he won the Junior Drill Award. Frankie joined the Royal Air Force when he was 17 and spent a year in England before he was drafted to the Middle East. In RAF sports competitions he won prizes for discus and javelin throwing and for swimming.

Leading Aircraftman Francis John Noel Gorman was 20 years old when he died in Egypt on 23 April 1942 and he is commemorated on Bangor and District War Memorial and in Queen's Parade Methodist Church, Bangor.

G

Gould, Thomas
Able Seaman
No. P/JX283876, HMS *Penelope*, Royal Navy
Killed on active service on Friday 18 February 1944 (aged 25)
Portsmouth Naval Memorial, Hampshire, England (Panel 82 Column 2)

GOULD T.

The death of Able Seaman Thomas Gould was commemorated in a series of *Killed In Action* notices published in the 10 March 1944 edition of the *Belfast Telegraph*. The notices stated that Thomas Gould was the third son of David Gould of Hall Street, Conlig and the late Ann Jane Gould and his death was deeply regretted by his father, his stepmother, his brother Harry on active service, his stepsisters and stepbrothers, Jack on active service, his aunt Lily and uncle Harry Carson and family of Abbey Street, Bangor, his sister and brother-in-law Lily and Jack Browne of 25 Belgrave Street, Belfast, his brother David who was serving in the Royal Navy and his sister-in-law Bessie and their children David and Jim of 89 Bristol Street, Belfast and his brother and sister-in-law Alex and Eleanor Gould of 22 Christopher Street, Belfast.

Thomas Gould's father David was born on 13 May 1889 and he was a son of

Robert Gould who worked as a rougher (flax dresser) and Jane Gould (nee Hamilton). David Gould was a 23 year-old bachelor living at 29 Malvern Street, Belfast when he and Annie (Ann) Jane Mills were married on 8 April 1912 in St. Anne's Church of Ireland Cathedral, Belfast. Ann Jane was a 22 year-old spinster and a daughter of tinsmith Hugh Mills. David and Ann Jane Gould had five children – Alexander Mills (born 17 February 1913); David (born 28 May 1914); Elizabeth (Lily born 13 March 1916); Thomas (born 1 July 1918) and Henry Carson (Harry born 24 April 1920). Ann Jane Gould was 34 years old and her address was Ballymagee, Bangor when she died on 10 June 1925. She was buried in Belfast City Cemetery (Glenalina Extension Grave O 309).

During the Second World War Thomas Gould served with the Royal Navy aboard HMS *Penelope*. HMS *Penelope* was an Arethusa-class light cruiser built by Harland and Wolff, Belfast, launched in 1935 and commissioned in 1936. At the outbreak of war HMS *Penelope* was in the Mediterranean and she joined the Home Fleet in 1940. In 1941 she joined Force 'K' operating out of Malta against Italian ships carrying supplies to the Axis Forces in North Africa. HMS *Penelope* was holed so many times by bomb fragments that she was nicknamed 'HMS *Pepperpot*'. After extensive repairs she operated in home waters until 1943 when she went to the western Mediterranean. In September that year she was part of Force 'Q' involved with the Allied landings at Salerno in Italy. She took part in operations throughout the Mediterranean and on 18 February 1944 HMS *Penelope* was on route from Naples to Anzio when she was torpedoed by the German submarine *U-410*. Able Seaman Thomas Gould aged 25 was one of more than 400 men who died. His body was never recovered and he is commemorated on the Portsmouth Naval Memorial in Hampshire.

G

Graham Brothers, Samuel and William

Samuel and William Graham were born in Newtownards and they were sons of William and Agnes Graham (nee McCormick) of 28 Frances Street, Newtownards. William Graham Senior worked as a car driver and his father, Hugh Graham, operated the transport service between Bangor and Newtownards. William Graham and Agnes McCormick were married on 3 September 1901 in Ballyblack Presbyterian Church and they had at least seven children – Hugh (born 9 June 1902, died 14 January 1905); William (born 27 December 1903); James (born 16 August 1905); Elizabeth (born 13 June 1907); Samuel (born 30 January 1909); George (born 4 February 1911) and Thomas. Their father, William, died on 26 March 1927. During the Second World War brothers Samuel and William Graham both served with the Royal Artillery and their brother James served with the Royal Ulster Rifles. Their brother George also served. Samuel was the first of the two Graham brothers to die during the Second World War.

Graham, Samuel
Gunner
No. 1483918, 5 Battery, 2 Light Anti-Aircraft Regiment, Royal Artillery
Died of wounds on Thursday 25 September 1941 (aged 32)
Tobruk War Cemetery, Libya (Grave 6 K 11)

Samuel Graham was born on 30 January 1909 and he was the husband of Greta Graham (nee Johnston) of 15 Queen Street, Newtownards. Samuel Graham was a mill worker from Greenwell Street when he and Greta Johnston (aged 18) were married on 3 December 1932 in Newtownards Registry Office. Gunner Samuel Graham was 32 years old when he died on 25 September 1941 during the siege of Tobruk and there were three *Killed in Action* notices in the 11 October 1941 edition of the *Newtownards Chronicle*. The combined notice from his wife Greta, their three sons and his parents-in-law who lived at 5 Canal Row, Newtownards included the verse:

G

> *The news was sad, the blow was hard, God's will it shall be done;*
> *With a manly heart he did his part, and a crown of victory won*

> GRAHAM—Killed on Active Service, Gunner Samuel Graham, R.A., beloved husband of Greta Graham, 15, Queen Street, Newtownards.
> The news was sad, the blow was hard, God's will it shall be done; With a manly heart he did his part, And a crown of victory won.
> Deeply regretted by his sorrowing Wife and Children; also his Mother-in-law and Father-in-law and Family, 5 Canal Row. Newtownards

The second notice was from his brother and sister-in-law James (Jim) and Annie Graham of 135 Frances Street, Newtownards, also his brother Thomas. The third was from his aunts Lizzie and Hannah Graham of 95b South Street, Newtownards. The following week there was a notice from his brother William (Willie) and sister-in-law Sarah of 142 Greenwell Street, Newtownards and it included the verse:

> *Times have changed in many ways, but one thing changeth never,*
> *The memory of those happy days when we were all together*

Gunner Samuel Graham died of wounds on 25 September 1941 in No. 4 Australian General Hospital, Tobruk along with three other men from Newtownards – **Joseph Dalzell**, **William John McNeilly** and **James Meredith** – and he is commemorated on Newtownards and District War

Memorial. A little over a year and a half later **William Graham** died of wounds sustained in action.

Graham, William (Willie)
Driver
No. T/1475605, Royal Army Service Corps, previously Royal Artillery
Died of wounds on Thursday 6 May 1943 (aged 39)
Suez War Memorial Cemetery, Egypt (Grave 2 G 12)

William Graham was born on 27 December 1903 and he was the husband of Sarah Graham (nee Hamilton) of Carrowdore. William Graham from Frances Street, Newtownards was working as a motorman when he and Sarah Hamilton (aged 19) were married on 8 December 1924 in Newtownards Registry Office. They lived in Greenwell Street, Newtownards before moving to Carrowdore. Having played for the Thistle Football Club and for Boyne Rovers Football Club, William was well-known locally as a goal-keeper. William served with the Royal Artillery before being transferred to the Royal Army Service Corps and he was 39 years old when he died of wounds in a military hospital on 6 May 1943.

G

> **DIED ON ACTIVE SERVICE.**
> GRAHAM — At a Military Hospital, Middle East, 6th May, 1943, Private William Graham, beloved husband of Sarah Graham.
> "We were not there at time of death
> To hear his last faint sigh,
> We only know he passed away
> And never said good-bye."
> Sadly missed by his sorrowing Wife and two little Sons, George Arthur and Hugh, Carrowdore, Greyabbey; also his Mother-in-law, Sarah Hamilton, and Niece, Sadie Gregory, Carrowdore; also his Sister-in-law and Brother-in-law and Family, Agnes Anna & Thomas Gregory, 11 George's St., Newtownards; also his Brother-in-law and Sister-in-law and Family, G. A. and Matilda Hamilton, Ballyhaskin, Millisle.
> "He sleeps in a foreign land."

After William died there were two *Died on Active Service* notices in the 29 May 1943 edition of the *County Down Spectator*. The combined notice (from his wife Sarah and two sons George Arthur and Hugh of Carrowdore, Greyabbey; his mother-in-law Sarah Hamilton and niece Sadie Gregory of Carrowdore; his sister-in-law and brother-in-law Agnes Anna and Thomas Gregory of 11 George's Street, Newtownards and his brother-in-law and sister-in-law G.A. and Matilda Hamilton of Ballyhaskin, Millisle) included the verse:

> *We were not there at time of death to hear his last faint sigh,*
> *We only know he passed away and never said good-bye*

The other notice was from his sister-in-law and brother-in-law Isabella and Stanley Edmunds of 9 Chamberlain Street, Belfast. His brothers James and Thomas Graham lived at 135 Frances Street, Newtownards and his sister Mrs Cree lived in Bangor. Driver William Graham is commemorated on

Newtownards and District War Memorial as Wm. Graham *Greenwell St.*

Graham, Edward
Fusilier
No. 4451503, 1st Battalion, Royal Irish Fusiliers
Killed in action on Friday 13 August 1943 (aged 31)
Cassino Memorial, Italy (Panel 11)

Edward Graham was born on 18 July 1912 in the mining village of Chopwell, County Durham. He was the only son of Sarah Ann Graham and his grandfather, uncles and cousins were all engaged in the mining industry. Aged 22, Edward Graham joined the 9th Battalion, Durham Light Infantry (Territorial Army) on 2 May 1935. After being called up for military service on 1 September 1939 he was transferred to the Royal Irish Fusiliers and posted to Ballykinler in County Down. It was while he was stationed there that he met Eveline McBride from Portaferry and they were married on 25 January 1941 in Ballyphilip Church of Ireland Church, Portaferry. Their home address was 31 High Street, Portaferry and their first son, John Joseph Graham, was born on 1 December 1941. He died the same day.

G

In November 1942 the Regiment was posted to North Africa and subsequently took part in the Allied landings in Sicily. The Fusiliers were at the forefront of intense fighting as the Allies fought their way up the East Coast of Sicily against fierce resistance from the enemy. On 13 August 1943 the Regiment cleared the village of Maletto and was preparing to advance towards the town of Randazzo in the foothills of Mount Etna. Fusilier Edward Graham was one of several soldiers killed by enemy machine gun fire when they were sent out to reconnoitre the area. His body was never recovered and he is commemorated on the Cassino Memorial. The following day the town of Randazzo was taken and the Royal Irish Fusiliers were withdrawn to rest and regroup.

On 22 July 1943 Eveline Graham gave birth to twin boys, Edward and Sydney Graham and it is highly unlikely that Fusilier Edward Graham ever received this news. Fusilier Edward Graham was 31 years old when he died and he is commemorated in Ballyphilip Church Portaferry and on the rood screen in St. John's Church, Chopwell, Co. Durham.

Graham, George
Fusilier
No. 6982035, 70th Battalion, Royal Inniskilling Fusiliers
Died as a result of enemy action on Wednesday 16 April 1941 (aged 24)
Belfast (Dundonald) Cemetery, Co. Down (Section E 1 Grave 490)

 Fusilier George Graham was one of 13 soldiers serving with the 70th Battalion, Royal Inniskilling Fusiliers who died as a result of an air raid on Newtownards aerodrome during the night of 15/16 April 1941. Fusilier **Daniel Higgins** who also died that night was buried in Newtownards (Movilla) Cemetery and under his name in this Book of Honour there is a summary of all those people with North Down or Ards connections who died that night.

Fusilier George Graham was 24 years old when he died, he was buried in Belfast (Dundonald) Cemetery and there is an inscription on the Graham family grave headstone:

G

Graham
In loving memory of my dear daughter Christina died 3 February 1939
Also my daughter-in-law Minnie Graham died 20 April 1939
Also my dear son Fusilier George Graham
Died result enemy action 16 April 1941
Also our dear mother Mary A. Dickie died 8 January 1960
At rest

Christina Graham of 88 Glenmachan Street, Belfast was 15 when she died; Minnie (Mary) Graham of 1a Stranmillis Street was 32 when she died; George Graham's home address was 34 Laganvale Street, Belfast and Mary Dickie of 6 Silvergrove Street, Belfast was 77 when she died. On 25 December 1916 Archibald Graham (a labourer aged 30 from Lower Broughshane, Co. Antrim) and Martha Dickie (aged 36, also from Broughshane) were married in Kirkinriola Church of Ireland Church, Ballymena.

Graham, James (Jimmy)
Fusilier
No. 3129435, 1st Battalion, Royal Scots Fusiliers
Died as a result of a road accident on Friday 13 December 1940 (aged 24)
Newtownards (Movilla) Cemetery, Co. Down (Section 12 Grave 127)

James Graham was the youngest son of Samuel and Sophia Graham (nee

Barr) of 19 Movilla Street, Newtownards. Samuel Graham was a fish dealer and he and Sophia Barr were married in St. Anne's Church of Ireland Church, Belfast. They had at least eleven children – William (born 1 April 1897); Mary (born 1899); Jane (born 1901); Sophia (born 1902); Edith (born 1904); Martha (born 1906); Ellen (born 1907); Samuel (born 19 April 1909); Thomas (born 1910); Elizabeth (Lizzie died 11 July 1919) and James (born 1916). For a time around 1901 the Graham family lived in Paisley, Scotland.

DIED ON ACTIVE SERVICE.

GRAHAM—13th December, 1940 (suddenly), in England, Fusilier James Graham, dearly-loved youngest son of Sophia and the late Samuel Graham. Funeral, with Military Honours, from his mother's home, 19, Movilla Street, Newtownards, to Movilla Cemetery today (Saturday), at 3 p.m.

He gave his strength for England that Britain yet unborn
May grow in greener pastures and greet a fairer dawn.
He gave his life for England, that from his lowly bed
That flowers of fuller freedom may blossom where he bled.

Sadly missed by his sorrowing Mother, Brothers and Sisters.

James Graham joined the Army in 1933 when he was 17 and spent five years in India, returning home in August 1940. He died on 13 December 1940 following a road accident in Steyning, Sussex and his family placed a *Died on Active Service* notice in the 21 December 1940 edition of the *Newtownards Chronicle*. It included the verse:

G

He gave his strength for England that Britain yet unborn
May grow in greener pastures and greet a fairer dawn.
He gave his life for England, that from his lowly bed
Flowers of fuller freedom may blossom where he bled

Jimmy Graham's funeral was with military honours and it took place on 21 December 1940 from his mother's house. Two of his brothers were also on active service – Thomas serving with the Royal Scots Fusiliers and Samuel serving with the Colonial Police in Singapore. Before that Samuel had served with the Gordon Highlanders.

Fusilier James Graham was 24 years old when he died and he is commemorated on Newtownards and District War Memorial and on the family grave headstone in Movilla Cemetery. His father Samuel died on 5 May 1927 and his mother Sophia died on 23 March 1946.

Graham, John Thompson (John)
Flight Sergeant
No. 968335, 7 Squadron, Royal Air Force Volunteer Reserve
Killed in action on Saturday 28 March 1942 (aged 29)
Runnymede Memorial, Surrey, England (Panel 74)

John Thompson Graham was born on 21 December 1912 and he was a son of Joseph and Elizabeth (Bessie) Isabel Graham (nee Workman) who lived in the townland of Ballysallagh Major, Bangor. Later the Graham family moved to *Ardmore House* in Newtownards. Joseph Graham was a farmer and butcher and he and Bessie Isabel Workman were married on 1 January 1908 in Belfast Registry Office. Joseph already had a daughter by his first wife Catherine (nee McGuckien). His daughter's name was Elizabeth (Lily) and she was born on 11 July 1898. Joseph and Bessie Isabel Graham had at least four children – Josephine A. (born 3 March 1909); John Thompson (born 21 December 1912); Edmund and Ross.

John Thompson Graham was educated at Clandeboye Public Elementary School and from 1925 until 1929 at Bangor Grammar School where he played rugby for the school. A foundation member of Newtownards Young Farmers' Club, he was keenly interested in cattle judging and won several prizes in Young Farmers' Club competitions. He was also a member of the Newtownards Chamber of Trade.

OUR HEROES—IN MEMORIAM.

GRAHAM—In loving memory of Flight Sergeant J. T. Graham, Missing on Operational Flight over Lubeck, 28th/29th March, 1942.
Sadly missed.
Father, Mother, Brothers and Sisters. Ardmore, Newtownards.

John Graham joined the Royal Air Force shortly after the outbreak of war. His brother Edmund also served with the RAF and his brother Ross was a veterinary surgeon attached to the Home Guard in London. It was reported in the 4 April 1942 edition of the *Newtownards Chronicle* that John Thompson Graham was missing in action and later it was officially confirmed that he must be presumed dead. Flight Sergeant John Thompson Graham was one of seven men aboard a Short Stirling Mark I aircraft (W7501) that took off from RAF Oakington in Cambridgeshire at 7.38 pm on 28 March 1942 on a mission to bomb Lubeck. At 10.05 pm their plane was shot down by a German night-fighter and crashed into the North Sea north of Terschelling in the Dutch Frisian Islands. None of their bodies was ever recovered and they are all commemorated on the Runnymede Memorial. The other six crew members who died that night were:

- Flight Lieutenant Jeffrey Hugh Edwards
- Sergeant Ronald Philip Cale
- Sergeant Leonard Reil Eagle aged 20 from Southsea, Hampshire
- Sergeand Louis Robert Martin Norris aged 24 from Burtle, Somerset
- Sergeant John Charles Lyon Banks aged 22 from Heathfield, Sussex
- Sergeant Desmond Edwin Sproule Sidney-Smith aged 20 from Sydenham, Co. Down

G

Desmond Edwin Sproule Sidney-Smith was a son of Tredgar Sidney-Smith (who served in India during the First World War) and Irene Helen Margaret Sarah Sidney-Smith (nee Sproule). They were married on 16 November 1916 in Fintona Presbyterian Church, Co. Tyrone.

Flight Sergeant John Thompson Graham was 29 years old when he died and he is commemorated on Bangor and District War Memorial; on Newtownards and District War Memorial; in First Newtownards Presbyterian Church and in Bangor Grammar School.

Graham, William (Topsy)
Gunner
No. 148427, 5 Battery, 2 Light Anti-Aircraft Regiment, Royal Artillery
Killed in action on Saturday 26 April 1941 (aged 35)
Athens Memorial, Greece (Face 2)

G

GRAHAM—In proud and loving memory of my dear son, and our dear brother, Gunner William ("Topsy") Graham, R.A. Killed in Action in the Middle East 26th April, 1941.
"Ubique."
May the heavenly winds blow softly O'er that sweet and hallowed spot, Though the seas divide us from your grave,
You will never be forgot.
Sadly missed by his sorrowing Mother, Sisters and Brothers Jim (Prisoner of War).
MARY GRAHAM.
30, Mark Street, Newtownards.

William Graham was born on 11 February 1906 and he was the eldest son of Robert and Mary Graham (nee Cardy) of 30 Mark Street, Newtownards. Robert Graham was a factory labourer and he and Mary Cardy were married on 8 October 1904 in Newtownards Parish Church of Ireland Church (St. Mark's). They had at least three children – William (born 11 February 1906); Margaret (Maggie, born 12 March 1909) and James (born 28 February 1912). Robert Graham served with the Royal Irish Rifles during the Great War and two of Mary Graham's brothers, James and William Cardy, were killed. James and William Cardy are commemorated on Page 147 in the Book of Honour *Remembering Their Sacrifice in the Great War – Ards* compiled by Barry Niblock.

William Graham joined the Army on the day that war was declared and served with the Royal Artillery. Initially he was reported as missing in action on 26 April 1941 and later it was officially confirmed that he must be presumed killed. In the 29 November 1941 edition of the *Newtownards Chronicle* there were four *Killed in Action* notices, including one from his sorrowing mother, brothers (including Jim who was on active service with the Royal Artillery) and sisters and one from his brother Robert and sister-in-law Agnes of 42 Movilla Street, Newtownards. The one from his mother included the verse:

When last we saw him smiling, he looked so strong and brave,
We little thought how soon, he'd be laid in a hero's grave

William Graham was 35 years old when he died and he is commemorated on Newtownards and District War Memorial as Wm. Graham *Mark St.* and in Newtownards Parish Church (St. Mark's).

Graham, William Harold (Harold)
Lieutenant
No. EC/1767, Royal Indian Army Service Corps
Killed in service on Sunday 20 June 1943 (aged 33)
Suez War Memorial Cemetery, Egypt (Grave 3 B 6)

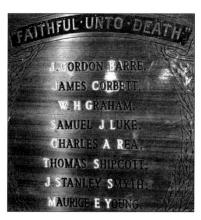

William Harold Graham was born on 17 August 1909 and he was a son of William Samuel and Martha E. Graham (nee King) who were married on 7 July 1903 in Kingsmills Presbyterian Church, Co. Armagh. William Samuel Graham worked as a bricklayer and farmer and he and Martha lived in the townland of Derrycughan, Co. Armagh. William Samuel and Martha Graham had at least three children – Eleanor Agnes (born 4 May 1904); Samuel Thomas (born 25 May 1906) and William Harold (born 17 August 1909).

William Harold Graham trained to be a Missionary and for a time he lived in Bangor, Co. Down. When he was in Dublin he lived at 318 North Circular Road. On 11 November 1933 he left Southampton bound for Bombay, India and it was his intention to work there as a Missionary. He sailed aboard the SS *Naldera*. In December 1935 he and Margaret Mitchell Bell, then aged 25, were married in Bombay. Margaret Mitchell Bell was born on 3 July 1910 in England and she was a daughter of Robert and Jane Bell (nee Bell) who were married on 13 June 1901 in Claggan Presbyterian Church, Cookstown, Co. Tyrone. Margaret Mitchell Bell also trained to be a Missionary and she had been living at 12 St. Andrew's Drive, Pollokshields, Glasgow when she left London on 8 November 1935 bound for Bombay. She sailed aboard the SS *Carthage*.

During the Second World War William Harold Graham served with the Royal Indian Army Service Corps in Egypt and on 3 June 1940 his wife,

Margaret Mitchell Graham, left Liverpool (her UK address was 3 Conan Road, Hampstead, London) bound for the Federated Malay States. She sailed aboard the SS *Hakusan Maru*. Lieutenant William Harold Graham was killed on 20 June 1943 in Egypt and in the Letters of Administration associated with his will his former connection with Church House in Belfast was duly noted.

Lieutenant William Harold Graham was 33 years old when he died and he is commemorated on Bangor and District War Memorial and in Hamilton Road Presbyterian Church Bangor. Margaret Mitchell Graham's death was registered in August 1995 in Islington, London.

Grattan Family: Matilda Grattan, her daughters Angeline Grattan and Shelagh Grattan and her son George Francis Grattan

Matilda Grattan (nee McDonald) was the wife of Andrew Francis (Andrew) Grattan and they lived at 40 Ashley Gardens, Bangor. Andrew Grattan was born in March 1875 in Rathdowney, Co. Laois, Republic of Ireland (then Queen's County, Ireland) and he was a son of Robert and Catherine Grattan who lived in Moore Street, Rathdowney. On 14 July 1893 aged 18 he enlisted in Birr, Co. Offaly, Republic of Ireland (then King's County, Ireland) and served with the 4th Battalion, Leinster Regiment (No. 3908). Before that Andrew had worked as a labourer. Over the next 18 years Andrew Francis Grattan served in many places throughout the world – Home 1893, Malta 1894, Bermuda 1895, Canada 1897, Home 1900, South Africa 1901, Home 1901, South Africa 1904, Mauritius 1906 and Home 1911.

Grattan, Matilda
Civilian War Dead
Died as a result of enemy action on Wednesday 16 April 1941 (aged 54)
Bangor Cemetery, Co. Down (Unmarked grave) (1 A 164)

Grattan, Shelagh
Civilian War Dead
Died as a result of enemy action on Wednesday 16 April 1941 (aged 20)
Bangor Cemetery, Co. Down (Unmarked grave) (1 A 164)

Grattan, Angeline
Civilian War Dead
Died as a result of enemy action on Wednesday 16 April 1941 (aged 18)
Bangor Cemetery, Co. Down (Unmarked grave) (1 A 164)

Matilda Grattan (née McDonald) was born sometime between 1883 and 1887 (records vary) in Birr and on 9 September 1902 she and Andrew Grattan were married in Birr. Between then and 1911 four children were born – Robert born on 23 June 1903 in Birr (Robert became a seaman and in 1930 was aboard the SS *Markland*); Mary Kathleen born on 19 December 1905 in Middleburg, Transvaal, South Africa; Hilda Geraldine born on 12 October 1907 in Birr and George Francis born on 22 March 1910 in Devonport. In 1911 the Grattan family was living in married quarters in Granby Barracks, Devonport where Andrew was serving as a Colour Sergeant with the 1st Leinster Regiment. On 22 November 1911 he was discharged from the Army at his own request at Devonport and he stated that his intended place of residence was Moore Street, Rathdowney.

The Grattan family moved to Canada and on 13 December 1915 Andrew joined the Canadian Overseas Expeditionary Force. In 1916 he was promoted to Regimental Sergeant Major. He broke his tibia and was later discharged from the Army. On 22 July 1918, at the age of 43, he joined the Royal Air Force as an Assistant Armourer (No. 276443) and was promoted to the rank of Sergeant. He was discharged on 7 February 1919 after 201 days of service because he was no longer physically fit – a stiff knee resulting from his broken leg. Andrew and Matilda Grattan had at least three more children – Andrew; Shelagh (born in 1921) and Angeline (born in 1923). The Grattan family moved to Bangor where they lived at 40 Ashley Gardens.

G

Between 10.45 pm on Easter Tuesday 15 April 1941 and 4.30 am on Wednesday 16 April 1941 there was a large-scale German Luftwaffe air raid on the City of Belfast. Other nearby towns and villages, including Bangor and Newtownards, were also attacked. Areas of Bangor where bombs fell included Ashley Gardens, Bangor Golf Clubhouse, Baylands, Farnham Road, Hazeldene Gardens and Ranfurly Avenue. Fires blazed on Scrabo Hill, Newtownards and bombs fell on Green Road, Conlig and Comber Road, Newtownards. At least 28 people with North Down and Ards connections were killed that night, including 14 civilians.

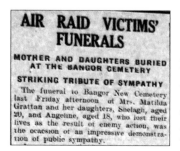

AIR RAID VICTIMS' FUNERALS

MOTHER AND DAUGHTERS BURIED AT THE BANGOR CEMETERY

STRIKING TRIBUTE OF SYMPATHY

The funeral to Bangor New Cemetery last Friday afternoon of Mrs. Matilda Grattan and her daughters, Shelagh, aged 20, and Angeline, aged 18, who lost their lives as the result of enemy action, was the ocaesion of an impressive demonstration of public sympathy.

Matilda Grattan, together with her daughters Shelagh and Angeline, were killed on 16 April 1941 when their home in Ashley Gardens was hit by a bomb during the German air raid. **Margaret Byers Watt** aged 60 died at 5 Hazeldene Gardens, Bangor and **Robert Wright** aged 41 of 32 Baylands, Bangor died of his injuries in Bangor Hospital. That night the aerodrome at Newtownards, which was the

Headquarters of 231 Squadron, Royal Air Force, was attacked and 13 soldiers serving with the Royal Inniskilling Fusiliers were killed. Fusilier **Daniel Higgins** was buried in Newtownards (Movilla) Cemetery and under his name in this Book of Honour there is a summary of all those people with North Down or Ards connections who died that night.

The funeral of Matilda, Angeline and Shelagh Grattan to Bangor Cemetery was reported in the 26 April 1941 edition of the *County Down Spectator*. A service was held in St. Comgall's Roman Catholic Church, Brunswick Road, Bangor on 18 April 1941 and then a hearse containing Matilda Grattan's remains proceeded to Bangor Cemetery. The hearse returned twice to the Church for the bodies of her daughters. The chief mourners were Major Andrew Grattan, husband and father of the deceased, together with his daughters, Kathleen Grattan and Mrs George O'Connell from Salthill in County Galway. Three of Andrew and Matilda's sons, Andrew, George and Robert Grattan, were abroad. The Mayor of Bangor, Councillor W.H. McMillan, and the Town Clerk, Mr R.M. Moore, represented the Council and residents of the town. No headstone was erected on their grave (1A 164).

G

Of the many civilians of the Commonwealth whose deaths were due to enemy action in the Second World War, the names of some 67,092 are commemorated in the Civilian War Dead Roll of Honour, located near St. George's Chapel in Westminster Abbey, London.

After his wife and daughters were killed, Andrew Francis Grattan moved to Brunswick Road, Bangor and, some eight months after their deaths, army pensioner Andrew Francis Grattan died on 23 December 1941. He suffered from diabetes and he died in a hyperglycaemic coma. Andrew Francis Grattan was 63 years old when he died in the townland of Ballaghanery, Annalong and he was buried in Bangor Cemetery. His effects amounted to some £762 and probate was granted to his daughter Kathleen. One year later, on 1 December 1942, Andrew's son, Flight Sergeant George Francis Grattan, died in a Japanese Prisoner-of-War Camp.

Grattan, George Francis (George)
Flight Sergeant
No. 521645, Royal Air Force
Died in a Prisoner-of-War Camp on Tuesday 1 December 1942 (aged 32)
Yokohama Cremation Memorial, Japan (Panel 5)

George Francis Grattan was born on 22 March 1910 in Devonport during the time that his father was stationed there. Flight Sergeant George Francis

Grattan was the husband of Daisy Evangeline Grattan (nee Griffiths) and their marriage was registered in Surrey. They had at least two children – Robin Francis (born 28 June 1936, died May 1996) and Moira M. (born 1 December 1937). Moira Grattan worked as a typist and she lived at 6 Edinburgh Road, Highfields, Chesterfield, Derbyshire before moving to Southern Rhodesia.

During the Second World War Flight Sergeant George Francis Grattan served with RAF Seletar in Singapore and his death was reported in the 31 July 1943 edition of the *County Down Spectator* under the headline *Died of Wounds while Prisoner of Japs*. He was taken prisoner at the fall of Singapore on 15 February 1942 and it is recorded that he died of acute colitis on 1 December 1942 at Fukuoka No. 4 Branch Camp in Moji, Japan where he was assigned prison number 5043. There is evidence to suggest that he arrived at Moji on 28 November 1942 having been transported on the Japanese 'hell ship' *Dainichi Maru*. Aircraftman 1st Class **Francis Meredith** also died at Fukuoka No. 4 Branch Camp in Moji. George Francis Grattan's effects amounted to some £107 and probate was granted to his widow Daisy Evangeline. His address in England was recorded as 68 Thomas Road, Gosport, Portsmouth. Daisy E. Grattan later remarried and her marriage to Gorrell A. Wheatcroft was registered in the fourth quarter of 1946 in Chesterfield, Derbyshire. Flight Sergeant George Francis Grattan was 32 years old when he died and he is commemorated on the Yokohama Cremation Memorial in Japan.

Green, Alexander William Valentine (known as Peter)
Pilot Officer
No. 78082, 235 Squadron, Royal Air Force Volunteer Reserve
Killed in action on Wednesday 11 September 1940 (aged 21)
Runnymede Memorial, Surrey, England (Panel 8)

Alexander William Valentine Green (known as Peter) was born on 14 February 1919 and he was a son of Alexander and Marjory Green (nee Watson) of *Seamount*, Craigavad, Holywood. Before that the Green family lived in Belfast in Windsor Park and also in Cherryvalley Park. Alexander

335

Green Senior was a Lieutenant in the 16th Battalion, Royal Irish Rifles when he and Marjory Watson were married on 5 March 1918 in Magheralin Church of Ireland Church. Alexander William Valentine (Peter) Green attended Campbell College from 1932 until 1937 and then the De Haviland Aeronautical School in Hatfield.

During the Second World War Peter served with the Royal Air Force Volunteer Reserve in Coastal Command and he died on 11 September 1940. He was one of a three man crew aboard a Bristol Blenheim Mark IV aircraft (L9396) which took off at 3.55 pm from RAF Thorney Island in Sussex and their mission was to escort Fleet Air Arm Fairey Albacore aircraft raiding Calais. Their aircraft was shot down at 5.30 pm and crashed into the sea. None of the bodies was recovered and they are commemorated on the Runnymede Memorial. The others who died were:

- PO Peter Claude Wickings-Smith aged 22 from Bedford, Bedfordshire
- Sgt Reginald Douglas Haig Watts aged 35 from Far Cotton, Northamptonshire

G

Pilot Officer Alexander William Valentine Green's effects in England amounted to some £108 and probate was granted to his father. There was a short tribute in the December 1940 edition of *The Campbellian*:

'We regret to announce the death of Peter Green. Apparently the bomber of which he was navigator was shot down in action and all the crew killed. Its occupants had, before this, managed to bring down a German bomber. Peter, from his earliest youth, displayed a keen interest in aviation. On leaving school he became a student in the de Havilland Technical School. Rejected as a pilot for physical reasons, he qualified as a navigator. Since the beginning of the War, when on leave, he never neglected a chance of visiting the school. We shall miss him very much'.

Pilot Officer Alexander William Valentine (Peter) Green was 21 years old when he died and he is commemorated on the Battle of Britain Memorial in Westminster Abbey; in Glencraig Parish Church of Ireland Church, Craigavad; in the annals of Helen's Bay Presbyterian Church and in Campbell College Belfast.

Gribbin, Nancy Simms (Nancy)
Civilian War Dead
Died as a result of enemy action on Wednesday 16 April 1941 (aged 74)
Holywood Cemetery, Co. Down (Grave 479)

Nancy Simms Gribbin was born on 24 July 1866 in Belfast and she was a daughter of the late James and Sarah Gribbin (nee Simms) who lived in Percy Street, Belfast and before that, Christopher Street, Belfast. James Gribbin was a National School teacher and he and Sarah Simms were married on 25 August 1858 in Belfast Registry Office. They had at least four children – Ellen Mary (born 1859); John (born 1863); Nancy Simms (born 24 July 1866) and James (born 16 October 1868).

Nancy Gribbin worked as a linen winder and she was 74 years old when she died on 16 April 1941 at 25 Percy Street, Belfast. During the Blitz an air raid shelter in Percy Street received a direct hit and around 70 people were killed when it collapsed. Nancy Gribbin was buried on 23 April 1941 in Holywood Cemetery.

Of the many civilians of the Commonwealth whose deaths were due to enemy action in the Second World War, the names of some 67,092 are commemorated in the Civilian War Dead Roll of Honour, located near St. George's Chapel in Westminster Abbey, London.

Griffiths, Donald Maldwyn (Maldwyn)
Flying Officer
No. 148008, 125 Squadron, Royal Air Force Volunteer Reserve
Killed in an aircraft accident on Friday 17 March 1944 (aged 22)
Runnymede Memorial, Surrey, England (Panel 206)

G

Donald Maldwyn Griffiths's birth was registered in the first quarter of 1922 in Cardiff, Glamorganshire. He was a son of Maldwyn and Irene Grace Griffiths (nee Williams) of 8 Upper Kincraig Street, Roath. Maldwyn Griffiths Senior was an engineer and he and Irene Grace Williams were married on 7 February 1921 in Roath Parish Church, Cardiff. They lived at 58 Thornhill Road, Llanishen, Cardiff. During the Second World War Maldwyn Griffiths (Junior) served with the Royal Air Force Volunteer Reserve.

On 17 March 1944 two de Havilland Mosquito aircraft (HK 261 and HK 326) of No. 125 Squadron based at RAF Ballyhalbert were airborne over the Irish Sea on a night practice interception exercise from which they failed to return. Based on Ground Controlled Interception (GCI) radar evidence from Ballywooden, Bishopscourt it was presumed that the two aircraft had collided, resulting in the deaths of both crews. Each crew comprised two men and their bodies were never recovered. They were Flight Lieutenant **Eric Augustus Snow** (Pilot of HK261); Flying Officer Donald Maldwyn Griffiths

(Navigator aboard HK261); Flying Officer **Frederick John Bartlett Reid** (Pilot of HK326) and Pilot Officer **Horace James Rich** (Navigator aboard HK326). Flying Officer Donald Maldwyn Griffiths was 22 years old when he died and he is commemorated on the Runnymede Memorial in Surrey. His effects amounted to some £112 and probate was granted to his mother.

Griffiths, George Griffith (George)
Trooper
No. 3763227, 7th Battalion, the King's Regiment (Liverpool),
Royal Tank Regiment, Royal Armoured Corps
Lost in the SS *Scillin* sinking on Saturday 14 November 1942 (aged 37)
Alamein Memorial, Egypt (Column 24)

George Griffith Griffiths was born on 21 September 1905 in Bootle, Lancashire and he was a son of David and Jane Griffiths (nee Prescott) who lived at 32 Holywell Street, Bootle. He was baptised on 3 October 1905 in St. Leonard's Parish Church, Bootle. David Griffiths, who was born in 1876, was a dock labourer and his marriage to Jane Prescott (born 1878) was registered in the fourth quarter of 1899 in Liverpool. David and Jane Griffiths had at least eight children – John David (born 1901); Jane (born 1902); Charles (born 1904); George (born 1905); Elizabeth (born 1908); Sarah (born 1910); Lily (born 1912) and Florence (born 1916).

George Griffith Griffiths was the husband of Isobel Griffiths of Bangor (possibly *Windmill Cottage*) and, during the Second World War, George served with the 7th Battalion, the King's Regiment (Liverpool), Royal Tank Regiment, Royal Armoured Corps. He fought in the Middle East Theatre of War and was taken prisoner. On 13 November 1942 at Tripoli in Libya a large number of Allied Prisoners-of-War were ordered into the cargo hold of the SS *Scillin* – many more than could comfortably be accommodated. The ship was bound for Sicily and on the night of 14 November, in the Tyrrhenian Sea, the SS *Scillin* was ordered to stop by the British submarine HMS *Sahib*. When the SS *Scillin* did not respond, the HMS *Sahib* fired a torpedo. The torpedo hit the hold and the ship sank rapidly. Very few of the prisoners were rescued and only when they were heard speaking English was it realized that the ship had been carrying British Prisoners-of-War. At a subsequent inquiry into this 'friendly fire' tragedy the Commander of HMS *Sahib* was cleared of any wrongdoing because the SS *Scillin* was unmarked and at the time he believed that she was carrying Italian troops.

The SS *Scillin* was a cargo ship built in 1903 by Russell and Company Ltd., Greenock. Originally named the SS *H M Pellatt*, this ship was operated by

British and Canadian companies until 1920, including service in the Great War. After that, under a succession of names, she was operated by Belgian, French and Italian companies. It was as the Italian cargo ship SS *Scillin* that she was torpedoed and sunk on 14 November 1942 and controversy surrounded the sinking.

Trooper George Griffiths was 37 years old when he died and he is commemorated on the Alamein Memorial in Egypt; on Bangor and District War Memorial and in Ballyholme Presbyterian Church.

Grondowski, Stanislaw
St. Sierz (Starszy Sierzant, equivalent to Flight Sergeant)
No. P782063, 315 (City of Deblin) Polish Fighter Squadron
Killed in an aircraft accident on Saturday 11 September 1943 (aged 34)
Ballycranbeg (Mount St. Joseph) Roman Catholic Churchyard, Co. Down

Stanislaw Grondowski was born on 11 September 1909 and during the Second World War he served with 315 (City of Deblin) Polish Fighter Squadron. Saturday 11 September 1943 was described as 'a black day for 315 Squadron' which was based at RAF Ballyhalbert. Two pilots and three aircraft were lost. In the late afternoon, during adverse weather, three pilots took off in Supermarine Spitfire Mark V aircraft to practise formation flying. Flight Sergeant Stanislaw Grondowski was a very experienced pilot and he was leading the formation flight in W3427 (PK-J). The other two pilots – Sergeant E. Zygmund in AR338 (PK-P) and **Sergeant Wladyslaw Kolek** in BL469 (PK-F) – were undergoing training. For some reason the three aircraft left the prescribed training area and in the bad weather they became separated. Within a short space of time, all three aircraft crashed in the hills west and north of Belfast. Flight Sergeant Stanislaw Grondowski was killed near Plantation House, Lisburn and Sergeant Wladyslaw Kolek was killed near Ballyutoag. Sergeant Zygmund was knocked unconscious when his aircraft crashed near Glengormley and then, after he regained consciousness, he climbed out of the wreckage (both wings of his aircraft had been ripped off) and walked to the nearest road.

Flight Sergeant Stanislaw Grondowski died on his 34th birthday and, in accordance with Polish custom, burial took place three days after his death. Tuesday 14 September 1943 was described as a bright, warm day but 'no-

G

one felt very cheerful'. After High Mass in Ballyhalbert Hangar Church, Flight Sergeant Grondowski and Sergeant Kolek were buried in Ballycranbeg (Mount St. Joseph) Roman Catholic Churchyard. In addition to the official representatives and guards of honour there were many mourners from the local community. Flight Sergeant Grondowski was well known in the area; Sergeant Kolek died just two days after arriving from the Operational Training Unit (OTU). Flight Sergeant Stanislaw Grondowski is commemorated on Panel 20 of the Polish War Memorial at Northolt in London.

Hadow, Terence Michael Scott (Terence)
Lieutenant
No. 172204, 1st Battalion, Royal Welch Fusiliers
Killed in action on Thursday 18 March 1943 (aged 21)
Rangoon Memorial, Myanmar (Face 9)

G
II

In the CWGC Debt of Honour it is recorded that Terence Michael Scott Hadow was a son of Patrick Hadow and Monica E. Hadow of Kensington, London. In the 22 May 1943 edition of the *County Down Spectator* under the headline *Young Bangor Officer Reported Killed* it was reported that Lieutenant Terence Michael Scott Hadow, who was the only son of Mrs Murray Forbes, Ava Cottages, Ballyvernott, Bangor had been killed in action. Previously Lieutenant Hadow had been posted as missing in action.

Terence Michael Scott Hadow's birth was registered in the third quarter of 1921 in Kensington, London and he was a son of Douglas Patrick Hadow and Dorothy Monica Evelyn Hadow (nee Cox). During the First World War Douglas Patrick Hadow served as a Lieutenant with the Northumberland Fusiliers and later with the Royal Air Force. In 1916 he was awarded the Military Cross for conspicuous gallantry in action when he led a raid against the enemy with great courage and determination. Other members of the Hadow family fought with distinction in the Indian Mutiny and in the South African War. After the Great War ended Douglas Patrick Hadow was a merchant and he and Dorothy Monica Evelyn Cox were married on 29 January 1920 in Paddington Parish Church of England Church, London. Douglas was 23, Dorothy was 21 and the ceremony was performed by Dorothy's father, the Revd Alfred Peachey Cox, Canon of Gloucester Cathedral.

On 6 February 1920 Douglas and Dorothy Hadow travelled aboard RMS *Avon* from Southampton to Rio de Janeiro in Brazil and on 15 February 1921 Dorothy arrived in Liverpool aboard RMS *Darro* having boarded in Rio de Janeiro. On that trip she described herself as a housewife and she gave as her address in England: 10 The Avenue, Clifton, Bristol (where her father lived). In February 1923 Douglas Hadow travelled from Barbados to Plymouth aboard the Dutch mail ship *Van Rensselaer*. He had been visiting members of his mother's family.

The death of Terence Michael Scott Hadow's parental grandfather, Norman Patrick Mellier Hadow, was registered in the first quarter of 1927 in Islington, London. Norman Patrick Mellier Hadow was born in Bangalore, India and he served as a Captain in the Indian Army. In civilian life he worked as a dressmaker and he was assisted by his wife Helen Furlong Hadow (nee Haynes). Helen was born in Barbados, West Indies and her only child was Douglas Patrick Hadow (Terence Michael Scott Hadow's father).

There were times during the 1920s when Dorothy Monica Evelyn Hadow dropped the Dorothy from her name and used either Monica or Monica E. For example, in November 1928 Monica Hadow described herself as a secretary aged 30 of 11 Cornwall Garden Stables, London when she travelled first class aboard the *Herengaria* from Southampton to New York. Dorothy Monica Evelyn Hadow and Douglas Patrick Hadow divorced and both subsequently remarried. The marriage of Dorothy M.E. Hadow and Murray Forbes was registered in the fourth quarter of 1929 in Chelsea, London and they lived in Ava Cottages, Ballyvernott, Bangor. Terence Hadow came to live there for a time with his mother and step-father. Subsequently his mother married for a third time. The marriage of Dorothy M.E. Forbes (previously Hadow, nee Cox) and Howard A. Ross was registered in the second quarter of 1949 in Kensington, London.

Douglas Patrick Hadow (Terence Michael Scott Hadow's father) moved to Australia where he married Florence Lyndall Stuart of Kalgoorlie, Western Australia. Florence and her brother Donald Stuart were both novelists. Douglas Patrick Hadow worked for Texas Oil and during the Second World War he served with the Royal Australian Air Force. For a time the Hadow family lived at 93 North Road, Bassendean, Perth in Western Australia and Douglas Patrick Hadow died in August 1948; Florence Lyndall Hadow died in 1976.

Terence Michael Scott Hadow received at least part of his education in London and in the preface to the book *Minor and Major* the author George Mills acknowledges the help he received from 12-year old Terence Hadow 'whose criticisms have been invaluable'. During the Second World War

Lieutenant Terence Michael Scott Hadow served with the Royal Welch Fusiliers. On 15 February 1941 he was promoted from a Cadet in the 142nd Officer Cadet Training Unit (OCTU) to a Second Lieutenant in the Royal Welch Fusiliers and subsequently to Lieutenant. He was killed in action against Japanese Forces on 18 March 1943 during the Battle of Donbaik and he is commemorated on the Rangoon Memorial.

Lieutenant Terence Michael Scott Hadow has a further connection with Bangor. Captain James Samuel Davidson who was a son of Sir Samuel Cleland Davidson, founder of the Sirocco Works in Belfast, was killed in action during the First World War and he is commemorated on Page 131 in the Book of Honour *Remembering Their Sacrifice in the Great War – North Down* compiled by Barry Niblock. In August 1914 Captain Davidson's sister, Kathleen Davidson, married Douglas Scott Hadow of the Indian Police. Douglas Scott Hadow was the younger brother of Norman Patrick Mellier Hadow and so he was Douglas Patrick Hadow's uncle and Terence Michael Scott Hadow's great uncle.

H

Kathleen Davidson and Douglas Scott Hadow had first met in India in 1912/13 and then again while Douglas was in Edinburgh to be best man at a friend's wedding at which Kathleen was a bridesmaid. They were married three days later. Douglas returned to India almost immediately after their wedding because his leave was short and there was a war on. Kathleen followed Douglas to India in November 1914 but returned to Bangor in 1915 for the birth of her daughter Kathleen Nancy Hadow. Douglas Scott Hadow and Kathleen Hadow subsequently divorced and Douglas Scott Hadow, who had remarried (Maud Violet Walthew), retired from the police in May 1929 after 32 years service. He moved to Sussex in England where he died on 25 August 1954 in Pendyne Nursing Home Bexhill and he bequeathed his effects to his widow, Maud Violet Hadow. Nancy Hadow recalled once meeting her distant cousin Terence. Kathleen Nancy Hadow married John Bleakley whose brothers **Robert James Bleakley** and **Deryk Jay Bleakley** both died during the Second World War.

Hall, John Corbett
Junior Engineer Officer
SS *Khedive Ismail* (London), Merchant Navy
Died as a result of enemy action on Saturday 12 February 1944 (aged 29)
Tower Hill Memorial, London, England (Panel 60)

John Corbett Hall was born on 10 May 1913 and he was the second son of John and Sarah Hall (nee Harrison) who lived at 10 Irwell Street, Belfast.

They were married on 7 August 1909 in St. Anne's Church of Ireland Cathedral, Belfast and they had at least four children – Elizabeth (born 4 February 1910); John Corbett (born 10 May 1913); Sadie (born 1922, died 29 February 1924) and Sadie (born 30 April 1927, died 14 May 1927).

John Hall Senior served with the Royal Irish Rifles during the Great War and he died aged 55 on 17 August 1936 in the UVF Hospital, Belfast. He was buried in Grave L 435 in Belfast City Cemetery (Glenalina Extension) alongside his two daughters (both named Sadie) who had died in infancy. John Corbett Hall's mother Sarah was 73 years old when she died on 22 September 1959 and she was living at 5 Summerhill Gardens, Bangor. Before that she lived in Bellevue Road, Carnalea. Sarah Hall was buried in the same grave as her husband and two daughters. At the time of writing her name is not inscribed on the headstone.

Carnalea Officer's Death.—Official intimation has come to hand that Engineer Officer J. C. Hall, Merchant Navy, has been lost at sea through enemy action. His wife and two-year-old baby son reside at 38 Roslyn Street, Belfast. Engineer Officer Hall, who was 28, was the second son of Mrs. Sarah Hall and the late Mr. John Hall, Bellevue Road, Carnalea. He was educated at Grosvenor P.E. School, Belfast, and the Belfast

John Corbett Hall was educated at Grosvenor Public Elementary School, Belfast and the Belfast College of Technology. He served his apprenticeship with Messrs James Adams and Company, Donegall Road, Belfast and later he held an appointment with Messrs Short and Harland before becoming an engineer with the Royal Mail Line. He was the husband of Annie Hall, 38 Roslyn Street, Woodstock Road, Belfast and they had a two-year old son.

During the Second World War Junior Engineer Officer John Corbett Hall served aboard the steamship SS *Khedive Ismail*. This ship was launched as the *Aconcagua* by Scotts of Greenock in 1922 and then in 1935 the ship was renamed *Khedive Ismail* when it passed into Egyptian ownership. In 1940 the *Khedive Ismail* was requisitioned as a British troopship. On 6 February 1944 Convoy KR-8 sailed from Kilindini Harbour, Mombasa, Kenya to Colombo, Ceylon (now Sri Lanka). The convoy comprised five troop transport ships escorted by one heavy cruiser, HMS *Hawkins*, and two destroyers, HMS *Paladin* and HMS *Petard*.

In the early afternoon of 12 February 1944 the convoy was attacked in the One and a Half Degree Channel in the Maldive Islands (also known as the Suvadiva Channel) by the Japanese submarine *I-27*. After being hit by two torpedoes, the *Khedive Ismail* sank in less than two minutes with the loss of almost 1,300 lives, including about 80 women, most of whom were nursing

343

sisters. Among them was Sister **Muriel Emily Leckey** from Holywood. Efforts were made to rescue survivors who were floundering in the sea, while at the same time depth charges were released to force the Japanese submarine back to the surface. When it surfaced, *I-27* was rammed by HMS *Paladin* and then sunk by a torpedo fired from HMS *Petard*. Junior Engineer Officer John Corbett Hall was one of those who died and under the headline *Carnalea Officer's Death* his death was reported in the 18 March 1944 edition of the *County Down Spectator*. He was 29 years old when he died and he is commemorated on the Tower Hill Memorial in London.

Hamilton, George Desmond
Flying Officer (Pilot)
No. 150802, Royal Air Force Volunteer Reserve
Died in service on Monday 14 August 1944 (aged 24)
Belfast (Dundonald) Cemetery, Co. Down (Section B 5 Grave 243)

H

George Desmond Hamilton was born on 31 March 1920 in Elham, Kent and he was the younger son of George and Florence Hamilton (nee Parker). When George Hamilton and Florence Parker were married on 24 October 1910 in Newtownards Parish Church of Ireland Church (St. Mark's) George was a soldier serving with the Royal Irish Rifles. George's father William and Florence's father John were both soldiers. George and Florence Hamilton had three children – Raymond (born 13 August 1911); Florence (born 2 February 1914) and George Desmond (born 31 March 1920) – and they had addresses in both Belfast (94 Earlswood Road, Knock and 22 Belmont Park) and Newtownards (Regent Street). George Desmond Hamilton attended Strandtown Public Elementary School, the Model School, Newtownards and then Regent House School, Newtownards from 1933 until 1936. After leaving school he served his apprenticeship in the engine rooms and drawing office of Messrs Harland and Wolff. His father George saw active service in the First World War and George Senior, together with his two sons, took an active interest in the Boy Scout movement. Raymond Hamilton was ordained as a Church of Ireland clergyman and appointed Chaplain to the Royal Fleet Auxiliary.

From the outbreak of war in 1939 George Desmond Hamilton worked at the First Aid Post, Spiers Place, Shankill Road, Belfast. At the beginning of 1942 he joined the Royal Air Force Volunteer Reserve and went to England, Canada and the USA for training. He obtained his wings in December 1943 and then his commission before returning to England for further training. George Desmond Hamilton and Patricia Marie Parker of Wingham, Ontario were married in February 1944 in Toronto.

> **KILLED ON ACTIVE SERVICE.**
> HAMILTON—August, 1944, on Active Service, George Desmond (Pilot-Officer, R.A.F.), beloved husband of Patricia Hamilton, Toronto, Canada, and younger son of Mr. and Mrs. G. Hamilton, 22, Belmont Park, Belfast (formerly of Newtownards). 'Service in St. Mark's, Dundela, Belfast, to-day (Saturday), at 2 p.m., after which funeral to Dundonald Cemetery.

Flying Officer George Desmond Hamilton was 24 years old when he died on 14 August 1944 and after a service on Saturday 19 August 1944 in St. Mark's Church of Ireland Church, Dundela he was buried in Dundonald Cemetery. At the time of writing there are no family details inscribed on the Hamilton family grave headstone but on his CWGC headstone which lies flat in the grave there is an inscription:

Killed on Active Service

In the burial register his last place of residence was recorded as Little Green, Shocklach-Oviatt, Cheshire. Flying Officer George Desmond Hamilton is commemorated in Regent House School, Newtownards. His father George died on 2 August 1951 and was buried in Belfast (Dundonald) Cemetery (Grave B5 244).

Hamilton, John Herbert
Flight Sergeant (Flight Engineer)
No. 1796564, 570 Squadron, Royal Air Force Volunteer Reserve
Killed on active service on Monday 23 April 1945 (aged 24)
Aarhus West Cemetery, Denmark (Row G Collective Grave 311)

John Herbert Hamilton was born on 18 February 1921 and he was the only son of Thompson Hamilton (born in 1883) and Edith Carlisle Hamilton (nee Boal, born 4 September 1884). They lived at 77 Kansas Avenue, Belfast and later 76 Southwell Road, Bangor. Thompson Hamilton was an engineering secretary and he and Edith Boal were married on 15 September 1915 in Fitzwilliam Presbyterian Church, Belfast. They had three children – Edith, Eileen Mary and John Herbert. John Herbert Hamilton was educated at Skegoneill Public Elementary School, Belfast and then Royal Belfast Academical Institution from 1933 until 1936. Prior to joining the Royal Air Force he served an apprenticeship with Short and Harland Ltd., and he was a member of the

H

Ards Motor Cycle Club. He served as a despatch rider attached to the ARP Report Centre in Bangor.

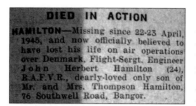

DIED IN ACTION

HAMILTON—Missing since 22-23 April, 1945, and now officially believed to have lost his life on air operations over Denmark, Flight-Sergt. Engineer John Herbert Hamilton (24), R.A.F.V.R., dearly-loved only son of Mr. and Mrs. Thompson Hamilton, 76 Southwell Road, Bangor.

Initially John Herbert Hamilton (aged 24) was reported as missing in action and then his parents placed a *Died in Action* notice in the 25 August 1945 edition of the *County Down Spectator* when he was officially presumed to have lost his life on air operations over Denmark. It was reported in the press that he was dropping supplies over Denmark when his plane was shot down. Of the six crew members on board only two survived. They were aboard a Short Stirling Mark IV aircraft (LJ 645) which took off from RAF Rivenhall in Essex on an air-drop operation to the Danish Resistance. Their plane crashed at Skaering, Aarhus after being hit by German flak (**Flugzeugabwehrkanone**) and soon afterwards exploded in flames. Three men escaped from the burning plane but John Herbert Hamilton was one of the three who were locked in their seat belts and perished in the flames. The pilot, Flying Officer Geoff Adrian Mombrun aged 21 from London, was one of the three who escaped but he was so badly burned that he died in a German field hospital three days later. The other two crew members who died were:

- Flying Officer W G H Hunt (aged 26) from Burton-on-Trent, Staffordshire
- FS Kenneth Ernest Johnson (aged 22) from Wisbech, Cambridgeshire

All four men were buried in Aarhus West Cemetery and there is an inscription on John Herbert Hamilton's CWGC headstone:

Pass not this stone in sorrow but in pride
And may you live as nobly as they died

The two men who survived the crash were Flight Sergeant (Wireless Operator) Frank Rawlings and Flight Sergeant (Air Bomber) C. Flannigan. Both men were captured and held as prisoners until the end of the war. In air-drop operations to the Danish Resistance during the Nazi occupation of Denmark, 69 Allied airmen lost their lives and they are all commemorated in Rebild Hills, Denmark and in the Anglican Church of St. Clement Danes, London:

They defied the perils of darkness and evil in the fight for freedom and peace

Flight Sergeant (Flight Engineer) John Herbert Hamilton is also commemorated on Bangor and District War Memorial; in RBAI and in First Bangor Presbyterian Church. His mother Edith was 81 years old when she died on 26 September 1965 in Southport, Lancashire.

Hamilton, John Nelson (Jack)
Second Lieutenant
No. 183105, Pioneer Corps
Died as a result of enemy action on Monday 5 May 1941 (aged 36)
Bangor Cemetery (Section 4 V Grave 41)

John Nelson (Jack) Hamilton was born on 19 March 1905 and he was the only surviving son of Thomas David Hamilton JP and Maude Caroline Hamilton (nee Nelson) of *Highcliffe*, 31 Clifton Road, Bangor and before that 5 Waverley Drive, Bangor. They were married on 8 June 1904 in Seymour Street Methodist Church, Lisburn. Thomas David Hamilton was a linen manufacturer and he and Maude had at least four children – John Nelson (born 19 March 1905); twins James and Georgina Margaret (born 12 June 1908, James died 13 June 1908) and Gay. During the Second World War Gay Hamilton served with the ATS. Jack Hamilton's mother Maude died on 4 June 1937.

H

Jack Hamilton was educated at Main Street Bangor Public Elementary School and Bangor Grammar School from 1917 until 1921. There his school friends elected him to receive the medal awarded annually to the most popular boy in the school. He played cricket and rugby for the school and then he played for Bangor Rugby Club 1st XV. He played golf at the Fortwilliam Club and he was a member of their Ulster Cup team.

On 6 July 1933 Jack Hamilton and Muriel L. Byford from Belfast were married in St. Peter's Church of Ireland Church, Antrim Road, Belfast and they had two children. The Hamilton family lived at 4 Coolmoyne Park, Belfast. John Nelson (Jack) Hamilton joined the Army and after training was gazetted to the Pioneer Corps. He was 36 years old when he was killed by falling masonry in Belfast during the Blitz on 5 May 1941 and he was buried in Bangor Cemetery. His effects amounted to some £3,086 and probate was granted to J.V.S. Mills, Solicitor.

Second Lieutenant John Nelson (Jack) Hamilton is commemorated on Bangor and District War Memorial; in Wesley Centenary Methodist Church Bangor; in Bangor Grammar School and on the family grave headstone

in Bangor Cemetery. Also buried there was his sister, Georgina Margaret McNeill, and also his brother-in-law, George Herbert McNeill.

Hamilton, Robert George (Bobby)
Able Seaman
No. P/SSX 19719, HMS *Eagle*, Royal Navy
Died as a result of an explosion on Thursday 14 March 1940 (aged 21)
Portsmouth Naval Memorial, Hampshire, England (Panel 38 Column 3)

Robert George Hamilton was born on 9 May 1918 in Newtownards and he was the only son of George and Elizabeth Hamilton (nee McClure) of Cronstown, Newtownards. George Hamilton from Ballyalicock worked as a labourer and he and Elizabeth McClure from Bowtown were married on 2 October 1911 in Second Newtownards Presbyterian Church. They had three children – Robert George, Matilda and Agnes. Robert George Hamilton was educated at Loughriscouse and Movilla Public Elementary Schools and he joined the Royal Navy when he was 17. Before that he worked as a labourer in Dickson's Rose Gardens, Newtownards. It was reported in the press that he was a school-mate of Marine **William Thomas Anderson** of Newtownards who was lost in the sinking of the *Royal Oak* on 14 October 1939 and who was described in the press as 'the first Ards casualty of the war'.

Robert George Hamilton served aboard the aircraft carrier HMS *Eagle* which was built by Armstrong Whitworth, Newcastle-on-Tyne and commissioned in February 1924. She had originally been ordered by Chile as the battleship *Almirante Cochrane* and was later purchased by Britain for conversion to an aircraft carrier. At the outbreak of the Second World War HMS *Eagle* was at Singapore and in October 1939 she was part of the force searching for the German Deutschland-class cruiser (pocket battleship) *Admiral Graf Spee*. As a result of damage sustained during the Battle of the River Plate on 13 December 1939 the *Graf Spee* had to be scuttled at Montevideo, Uruguay. For the first two months of 1940 HMS *Eagle* was escorting troop transports in the Indian Ocean and on 14 March 1940 she was damaged by an internal explosion in her forward bomb room. Able Seaman Robert George Hamilton was among 13 ratings who were killed by the explosion and HMS *Eagle* returned to Singapore for repairs. On 11 August 1942 HMS *Eagle* was

H

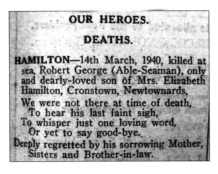

OUR HEROES.

DEATHS.

HAMILTON—14th March, 1940, killed at sea, Robert George (Able-Seaman), only and dearly-loved son of Mrs. Elizabeth Hamilton, Cronstown, Newtownards. We were not there at time of death, To hear his last faint sigh, To whisper just one loving word, Or yet to say good-bye. Deeply regretted by his sorrowing Mother, Sisters and Brother-in-law.

torpedoed and sunk by the German submarine *U-73* in the Mediterranean Sea, some 70 miles south of Cape Salinas, Majorca.

After Robert George Hamilton was killed, the Captain of HMS *Eagle* wrote in a letter to his mother, 'he died as he would have wished – on duty'. His mother placed a *Death Notice* in the 13 April 1940 edition of the *Newtownards Chronicle* and it contained the verse:

We were not there at time of death to hear his last faint sigh,
To whisper just one loving word, or yet to say good-bye

Able Seaman Robert George Hamilton was 21 years old when he died and he is commemorated on the Portsmouth Naval Memorial and on Newtownards and District War Memorial.

Hamilton-Temple-Blackwood, Basil Sheridan (Sheridan)
4th Marquess of Dufferin and Ava
Captain
No. 141136, Royal Horse Guards
Killed on active service on Sunday 25 March 1945 (aged 35)
Rangoon Memorial, Myanmar (Face 1)

H

Basil Sheridan Hamilton-Temple-Blackwood, 4th Marquess of Dufferin and Ava, was born on 6 April 1909 and he was the eldest child and only son of Captain Frederick Temple Hamilton-Temple-Blackwood DSO, 3rd Marquess of Dufferin and Ava and Brenda, Marchioness of Dufferin and Ava of Clandeboye (nee Woodhouse). His sister Veronica Brenda Hamilton-Temple-Blackwood was born on 13 December 1910 and when his father succeeded to the Marquessate on 7 February 1918 Basil Sheridan Hamilton-Temple-Blackwood was known as the Earl of Ava.

Basil Sheridan Hamilton-Temple-Blackwood was educated at Eton (where he won the Rosebery Prize for history) and Balliol College, Oxford (where he had a close friendship with the poet John Betjeman). He and Maureen Constance Guinness were married on 3 July 1930 in St. Margaret's, Westminster and 18 days later, on 21 July 1930, Basil succeeded to the Marquessate when his father was killed in an air crash near Meopham, Kent. His father was buried in the family burying ground at Clandeboye.

Basil Sheridan Hamilton-Temple-Blackwood and Maureen Constance Guinness had three children – Lady Caroline Maureen Hamilton-Temple-Blackwood (born 16 July 1931, died 15 February 1996); Lady Perdita Maureen Hamilton-Temple-Blackwood (born 17 July 1934) and Sheridan Frederick Terence Hamilton-Temple-Blackwood (born 9 July 1938, died 29 May 1988). Sheridan Frederick Terence Hamilton-Temple-Blackwood succeeded to the Marquessate at the age of six when his father died on 25 March 1945, thus becoming the 5th Marquess of Dufferin and Ava. In 1964 he married his cousin Serena Belinda (Lindy) Rosemary Guinness in St. Margaret's Westminster. With the death of Sheridan Frederick Terence Hamilton-Temple-Blackwood in 1988 the Marquessate became extinct.

After succeeding to the Marquessate in 1930 Basil Sheridan Hamilton-Temple-Blackwood followed a political career. He made his maiden speech in the House of Lords in December 1931 during a debate on India. He was appointed Parliamentary Under-Secretary of State for the Colonies in 1937 and in 1940 he joined the Army. In July that year he received a commission as a Captain in the Royal Horse Guards and in 1941 he was released from the Army to become Director of the Empire Division of the Ministry of Information from 1941 to 1942. He rejoined the Army in 1944 and when he was killed on 25 March 1945 he was serving on the Headquarters staff of the Mandalay Section in Burma (now Myanmar). He was shot at point blank range during a surprise attack by Japanese soldiers on 25 March 1945 while he was broadcasting a message to the Japanese in the Letse area, 32 miles south west of Pakkoku in Burma. After his death, the bells of Bangor Parish Church of Ireland Church (St. Comgall's) were tolled and a vote of sympathy to his family was passed at the annual general vestry meeting in Bangor Abbey. The Revd James Hamilton conducted his memorial service.

The 4th Marquess of Dufferin and Ava was 35 years old when he died in Burma (the 1st Marquess took the Ava part of his title from Ava, the ancient capital of Burma). Lord Ian Basil Gawaine Hamilton-Temple-Blackwood, third son of the 1st Marquess was killed in action on 4 July 1917 during the First World War and he is commemorated on Page 166 in the Book of Honour *Remembering Their Sacrifice in the Great War – North Down* compiled by Barry Niblock. During the South African War, Lord Basil's eldest brother, Archibald James Leofric Temple Hamilton-Temple-Blackwood, Earl of Ava, (eldest son of the 1st Marquess), served as a Lieutenant with the 17th Lancers and he died of wounds sustained on 6 January 1900 at Ladysmith.

Basil Sheridan Hamilton-Temple-Blackwood, 4th Marquess of Dufferin and Ava, is commemorated on Bangor and District War Memorial (as Sheriden B.); in Ballygilbert Presbyterian Church (as The Marquis of Dufferin and Ava); in Bangor Parish Church (St. Comgall's); in Royal County Down Golf Clubhouse; by a Celtic Cross in the family burial plot on the Clandeboye Estate and on a memorial scroll in Clandeboye Chapel. The scroll bears the following inscription:

This scroll commemorates Captain the Marquis of Dufferin and Ava, Royal Horse Guards, held in honour as one who served King and Country in the World War of 1939 – 1945 and gave his life to save mankind from tyranny. May his sacrifice help to bring peace and freedom for which he died.

In his memory, John Betjeman wrote the poem *In memory of Basil, Marquess of Dufferin and Ava*. After Basil died, his widow Maureen married twice more, first Major Harry Alexander Desmond Buchanan and then John Cyril Maude QC. She continued to use the title acquired from her first marriage and Maureen Lady Dufferin died on 3 May 1998. She was buried at Clandeboye.

Hancock, Charles Ronald
Officer of the Most Excellent Order of the British Empire (OBE)
Distinguished Flying Cross (DFC)
Wing Commander
No. 05112, 303 (Polish) Squadron, Royal Air Force
Killed in an aircraft accident on Wednesday 29 December 1943 (aged 40)
Runnymede Memorial, Surrey, England (Panel 118)

H

Charles Ronald Hancock's birth was registered in the second quarter of 1903 in Bath, Somerset and he was a son of Charles Edward and Constance Mary Hancock (nee Cox). Charles Edward Hancock was a merchant and his home was in Corfu, Greece when he and Constance Mary Cox were married on 21 August 1899 in the Parish Church of St. Bride, London. Both were 34 years old and, at the time, Constance's father was dead and she was staying at the Vicarage with the Revd Hawkins and his family.

In 1911 Charles Ronald Hancock aged 8 was a boarder at Edgeborough Private School, Epsom Road, Guildford which was run by Arthur Henry James, his wife Emily Pricilla James and his wife's brother, John Herbert Stokoe. Charles Ronald Hancock joined the Royal Air Force and in 1929 he was promoted from the rank of Flying Officer to Flight Lieutenant. He served in the North West Frontier of India and it was there that he was awarded the Distinguished Flying Cross in recognition of gallant and distinguished service between April and September 1930. The marriage of Charles Ronald Hancock and Louise Purshouse of Chelston, Devon was registered in the third quarter of 1933 in Elham, Kent. In 1936 he was promoted to the rank of Squadron Leader and in 1940 to the rank of Wing Commander. In 1941 he was awarded the OBE.

HANCOCK C.R., O.B.E., D.F.C. On 27 August 1943 Wing Commander Charles Ronald Hancock assumed command of RAF Ballyhabert. Before that he was in charge of RAF Eglinton in County Londonderry. On 29 December 1943 Wing Commander Hancock went missing after taking up a Supermarine Spitfire for local flying. His body was never recovered. Temporary command of RAF Ballyhalbert was taken over by Wing Commander Kirkpatrick and on 11 January 1944 Group Captain Richardson assumed full command. Wing Commander Charles Ronald Hancock's effects amounted to some £12,015 and probate was granted to Ronald William Hamilton, solicitor's managing clerk. He is commemorated on the Runnymede Memorial in Surrey.

Hanna, Norman Edmond (Norman)
Flying Officer
No. J/14348, 201 Squadron, Royal Canadian Air Force
Died as a result of enemy action on Saturday 18 December 1943 (aged 22)
Runnymede Memorial, Surrey, England (Panel 173)

Norman Edmond Hanna was born on 15 November 1921 and he was the youngest son of Samuel and Elizabeth Hanna (nee Hardy) of 20 Rosewood Street, Belfast and later 6 Hazeldene Park, Bangor. Samuel Hanna was a bespoke tailor and he and Elizabeth Hardy were married on 31 March 1902 in Ballysillan Presbyterian Church, Belfast. They had four children – Margaretta (Madge, born 10 February 1903); Victor Lewis (born 7 April 1905); Samuel (born 21 August 1907) and Norman Edmond (born 15 November 1921).

Described by the Headmaster as a 'good all-round scholar', Norman Edmond Hanna attended Bangor Grammar School from 1934 until 1939 and he left after gaining his Senior Certificate. He had entered the school with a Junior Down Regional Scholarship. He was a strong swimmer, he played rugby and he excelled at drawing. At school he and **William Francis Ernest Gault** were close friends.

At the age of 17 Norman Hanna set sail from Belfast on 1 September 1939 aboard the SS *Athenia* to go to Canada and work in Montreal. The SS *Athenia* was torpedoed and sunk on 3 September by the German submarine *U-30*, just a few hours after the declaration of war. At the time Norman was on deck recovering from seasickness and he got away in a lifeboat that he had helped to launch. More than 100 people, including Civilian **Margaret Lennon**, lost their lives. After being rescued by the American freighter, SS *City of Flint* Norman turned down the offer of returning to Britain on a British destroyer and instead opted to carry on to Halifax aboard the SS *City of Flint* (this ship was torpedoed and sunk on 23 January 1943 by the German submarine *U-575*). Norman Hanna arrived in Canada in 1939 with just the clothes he was wearing and he went to stay with his brother Victor in Montreal.

It was in Montreal that Norman joined the Royal Canadian Air Force in 1941. On 17 December 1943 he was one of 19 Air Force personnel (including the crew) aboard a Short Sunderland Mark III aircraft (DW106) that took off from Pembroke Dock at 11.45 pm bound for Jui in Gambia, West Africa (via Gibraltar). They were on a transfer operation when their aircraft disappeared without trace. Norman Hanna and nine of the other men on the plane that was lost were being transferred from 201 Squadron to 270 Squadron (both Squadrons operated anti-submarine patrols). 201 Squadron was based in Castle Archdale in County Fermanagh and they flew their patrols out to sea over the Donegal Corridor.

Another Sunderland aircraft following DW106 received a distress signal near Cape St. Vincent, Portugal. No trace of the aircraft, or of the people on board, was ever found and it has been surmised that the aircraft was shot down by a German fighter plane – although the possibility of a lightening strike or mechanical failure being the cause of the crash could not be ruled out. In addition to Flying Officer Norman Edmond Hanna, the other 18 airmen who lost their lives that day were:

- Flight Lieutenant John Eric Wood aged 22 from Sheffield
- FO Reginald Robert T. Crump aged 24 from Short Heath, Staffordshire
- Pilot Officer Neil Procter Chapman aged 23 (RAAF)
- WO Frederic Raymond Brown DFM aged 27 from Ilkley, Yorkshire
- Flying Officer Edward James Jay aged 23 from Morden, Surrey
- Flight Sergeant Francis McPhee from Glasgow
- Flight Sergeant Charles Albert Mark Barber aged 28 (RAAF)
- FS Eric Piggott Botting aged 24 from Haywards Heath, Sussex
- FS Leslie Robinson aged 23 from Whitehaven, Cumberland
- Flying Officer Vernon Maurice Sparkes aged 25 from Barry, Glamorgan
- FO Raymond John Elderfield aged 26 from Reading, Berkshire
- FS Maurice Robert Hunt aged 20 from Rampton, Nottinghamshire

- Sergeant Samuel Hughes aged 22 from Wolverhampton
- Sergeant Edmund Albert Hooker aged 27 from Pinner, Middlesex
- Sergeant William Henry Cryer from Gloucester
- Sergeant Henry Leonard Thompson aged 23 from Brockley, London
- Sgt William Peter Houston aged 21 from Newton-by-Chester, Cheshire
- Flying Officer Stanley Kidd aged 20 from Newcastle-on-Tyne

KILLED ON ACTIVE SERVICE.

HANNA—Reported missing on air operations on December, 1943, now presumed killed, Flying Officer Norman E. Hanna, R.C.A.F., youngest and dearly-loved son of Samuel and Elizabeth Hanna, 6 Hazeldene Park, Bangor.

Very deeply regretted.

Having been initially reported as missing in action it was later officially confirmed that he must be presumed killed in action on 18 December 1943. His body was never recovered. In subsequent years his parents placed *Roll of Honour* notices in the *County Down Spectator* as did his sister and brother-in-law Madge and Alex Walker who lived at 20 Sandringham Drive, Bangor. (During the First World War Alexander Stewart Walker served with the 16th Battalion, Royal Scots and he was wounded, temporarily blinded by gas and taken prisoner in April 1918. During the Second World War he served with the Home Guard). One of the newspaper notices about Norman Edmond Hanna contained the text:

So dearly loved, so sadly missed

Flying Officer Norman Edmond Hanna was 22 years old when he died and he is commemorated on the Runnymede Memorial in Surrey; on the Canadian Virtual War Memorial (Internet); on Page 167 in the Canadian Second World War Book of Remembrance; on Bangor and District War Memorial; in First Bangor Presbyterian Church and in Bangor Grammar School.

Hannay, Herbert (Bertie)
Mentioned in Despatches
Flight Sergeant (Pilot)
No. 754380, 51 Squadron, Royal Air Force Volunteer Reserve
Killed in action on Thursday 12 June 1941 (aged 21)
Eindhoven (Woensel) General Cemetery, Noord-Brabant, Netherlands
(Plot JJ Grave 12)

Herbert (Bertie) Hannay was born on 28 February 1920 in Bangor and he was the younger son of William Herbert and Rosa Hannay (nee Curragh) of 39 Prospect Road, Bangor. They were married on 31 October 1911 in First Donaghadee Presbyterian Church. Bertie's father was an official in Bangor

Gasworks, as was his elder brother William before William joined the Royal Air Force Volunteer Reserve. Bertie had two sisters – Sadie who married William Cresswell and Jean who married Bangor auctioneer George Matthews and who lived in Fourth Avenue, Baylands, Bangor. Herbert Hannay attended Main Street Boys' Public Elementary School and Bangor Grammar School from 1932 until 1936 and then he worked for the Century Insurance Company in Belfast. Before the war Bertie trained with the RAFVR and was called up when hostilities began.

On 10 June 1940 Herbert Hannay and Ena Weir of 5 Farnham Street, Belfast were married by special licence in Whitewaltham Parish Church, Maidenhead, Berkshire. Two days after his first wedding anniversary he was killed in action. Initially he was reported as missing in action over Holland and then in November 1941 his family was officially informed that Bertie was presumed to have been killed in action. On 11 June 1941 Bertie Hannay was one of a crew of five aboard an Armstrong Whitworth Whitley Mark V aircraft (Z6657) that took off from RAF Dishforth in Yorkshire at 11.06 pm on a mission to bomb Duisburg. They were shot down at 3.16 am on 12 June by a German night-fighter and their plane crashed at Borkel, Noord-Brabant, Netherlands. All five were buried in Eindhoven (Woensel) General Cemetery. The other crew members who died that night were:

- Pilot Officer Paul Edward Snyder aged 25 (RCAF)
- Sergeant James Edward Gittins
- Sergeant Cyril Gerrard Humble aged 20 from Carlisle
- Sergeant John Bradshaw aged 21 from Sheffield

Various members of Bertie Hannay's immediate and extended family placed *Roll of Honour* notices in the 12 June 1942 edition of the *County Down Spectator* and the one from his parents contained the verse:

> *We think of him in silence and oft repeat his name,*
> *What would we give to hear his voice and see his smile again?*

His brother, Sergeant-Observer William Hannay, was hospitalised in November 1940, initially in Luton Hospital and later in Halton General Hospital after he sustained a broken right arm and other injuries when his aircraft crashed over London. Unable to write personal letters, William was grateful to the editor of the *County Down Spectator* for publishing an open letter thanking local people for all their good wishes and Christmas presents.

About Herbert Hannay and Geoffrey Bowman the Headmaster of Bangor Grammar School wrote, 'they were together in their work and play; together in their love of fun and abounding vitality; together in their examination successes, in their time of leaving school and choice of a career; together in their voluntary self-dedication to the hazards of air-warfare and now, beyond death's mystery, together they wear the crowns of immortality'. Flying Officer **Geoffrey Bowman** was killed in action on 21 May 1944.

Flight Sergeant Herbert Hannay was 21 years old when he died and he is commemorated on Bangor and District War Memorial; in First Bangor Presbyterian Church; in Bangor Grammar School and on the family grave headstone in Bangor Cemetery. His mother Rosa died on 10 July 1967 and his father William Herbert died on 20 May 1969. The silver Hannay Memorial Bowl was presented to Bangor Grammar School by his parents to be awarded annually for the best performance in the Ulster Schools Sports competition.

Hardy, John
Corporal
No. 567646, Royal Air Force
Killed in an aircraft accident on Thursday 29 March 1945 (aged 26)
Peterborough (Eastfield) Cemetery, Northamptonshire
(Division 4 Block 16 Cons Grave 6370)

John Hardy's death was reported in the 14 April 1945 edition of the *Newtownards Chronicle* under the headline *Former Ards Footballer Killed*. It

> **Former Ards Footballer Killed.**—News has been received that John Hardy, who played some sterling games for Ards Football Club while stationed in our area, has been killed in a flying accident in England. Hardy has been playing for a club in the Oxford district for some time past, and he was about to have a trial with Clapton Orient.

was reported that John Hardy had died in a flying accident in England and that, when he was stationed in Newtownards, he had played some 'sterling games' for Ards Football Club. For some time before his death John Hardy had been playing for a club in Oxfordshire and he was about to have a trial with Clapton Orient (now Leyton Orient).

During the Second World War John Hardy served with the Royal Air Force and he was 26 years old when he died on 29 March 1945. He was a passenger

aboard an Operational and Refresher Training Unit (ORTU) Short Stirling Mark IV aircraft (PW391) which was returning to base when it crashed at 2.55 pm at Knarr Cross Farm, Thorney Toll, Peterborough after a mid-air collision with a solo-trainer Miles Master Mark II aircraft piloted by Corporal Robert de Bienkewicz of the Free French Air Force. Corporal de Bienkewicz and all seven aboard the Stirling were killed. In addition to John Hardy the other six Stirling crew members who died were:

- Warrant Officer Frederick Charles Aldersley aged 23
- Flt Lt Walter John Howes aged 22 from Lampeter, Cardiganshire
- Flying Officer Kenneth Rhodes Inger aged 21 from Wallasey, Cheshire
- Flight Sergeant Robert Henry McAlpine aged 37
- FS Frederick William Rees aged 33 from Weymouth, Dorset
- Sergeant Kenneth Slee aged 19 from Harrowgate, Yorkshire

Corporal John Hardy was 26 years old when he died, his death was registered in Whittlesey, Cambridgeshire and he was buried in Peterborough (Eastfield) Cemetery, Northamptonshire.

H

Harper, Robert Henry
Sergeant (Air Gunner)
No. R/85966, Royal Canadian Air Force
Killed in action on Tuesday 25 August 1942 (aged 24)
Stratford-on-Avon Cemetery, Warwickshire, England (Grave 4149)

Robert Henry Harper was born on 23 June 1918 in Ballywalter and he was a son of Robert Henry and Agnes Harper (formerly Beggs, nee Murphy). Robert Henry Harper Senior was a soldier who served with the Royal Irish Rifles during the First World War and he was stationed at Ballykinlar when he and Agnes Beggs (both of them widowed) were married on 19 February 1916 in Newtownards Parish Church of Ireland Church (St. Mark's). After the war Robert Henry Harper Senior worked as a labourer.

Agnes Harper (formerly Beggs, nee Murphy) was born on 11 May 1888 and she was a daughter of William John and Susanna Murphy (nee McClement) of Ballywalter. William John Murphy worked as a fisherman, Susanna Murphy worked at home as an embroiderer and they had at least 14 children including

William John, Hugh, Charles (died), Robert, Charles, David, Agnes, James and Andrew. Agnes Murphy aged 21 and James Beggs aged 18 were married on 4 December 1908 in Ballywalter Parish Church of Ireland Church (Holy Trinity). They had three children – twins Ellen and James (born 8 February 1909, James died 9 February 1909) and Dorothy (born 10 July 1911). James Beggs was 21 years old when he died on 18 April 1912.

Robert Henry and Agnes Harper (formerly Beggs, nee Murphy) had at least eight children, some of whom were born in Ballywalter and some in Canada – Robert Henry (born in Ballywalter on 23 June 1918 and baptised in Ballywalter Parish Church of Ireland Church); William John (born in Waterdown, Ontario on 1 May 1920 and baptised in Ballywalter Parish Church); Annie (born on 14 January 1922 and baptised in Ballywalter Parish Church); Herbert; David; Maureen; Dorothy and Ellen.

Robert Henry Harper Junior moved to Canada where he worked on a dairy farm before he enlisted. He married Winifred Evans, they lived in Port Credit, Ontario and they had one daughter whose name was Sandra Joan Harper. During the Second World War Robert Henry Harper served with the Royal Canadian Air Force and he was based at RAF Wellesbourne Mountford in Warwickshire. He was 24 years old when he was killed in action with 22 Operational Training Unit on 25 August 1942 and he is buried in Stratford-on-Avon Cemetery. His brothers William and Herbert Harper served with the Royal Canadian Naval Volunteer Reserve during the Second World War.

Sergeant (Air Gunner) Robert Henry Harper is commemorated on the Canadian Virtual War Memorial (Internet) and on Page 80 in the Canadian Second World War Book of Remembrance. There is an inscription on his CWGC headstone:

In loving memory of my darling husband
Dear father of Sandra

During the First World War Robert Henry Harper's uncle, Robert Murphy, served with the Mercantile Marine and he was Master of the SS *Lough Fisher*. Robert Murphy was one of 13 men killed on 30 March 1918 when this ship was shelled and sunk by the German submarine *U-101* and he is commemorated on Page 475 in the Book of Honour *Remembering Their Sacrifice in the Great War – Ards* compiled by Barry Niblock. During the Great War Robert Henry Harper's uncle David Murphy (Robert's brother) was a Leading Stoker in the Royal Navy and he served aboard HMS *Princess Royal* during the Battle of Jutland.

Harper, William John (Willie)
Able Seaman
SS *Marcella* (London), Merchant Navy
Died as a result of enemy action on Saturday 13 March 1943 (aged 25)
Tower Hill Memorial, London, England (Panel 68)

William John (Willie) Harper was born on 27 January 1917, his birth was registered in Newtownards and he was a son of John Walker Harper and Jane Harper (nee Moderate) of 107 Moat Street, Donaghadee. John Harper was a postman and he and Jane Moderate were married on 8 October 1913 in Ballygrainey Presbyterian Church. They had at least six children, three of whom died in infancy. Willie Harper had a sister named Sophia whose married name was Richards; Sophia died on 12 May 2003.

During the Second World War Willie Harper served with the Merchant Navy and when he died he was serving aboard the SS *Marcella*. Before that he had served aboard the SS *Orlock Head* and the SS *Atheltemplar*. In his papers it is noted that he was 5 feet 6 inches tall with grey eyes, brown hair, medium complexion and no distinguishing marks. The SS *Marcella* was a cargo ship built in 1928 by Lithgows Ltd., Port Glasgow and she was owned by Kaye and Son, London. She was on route from the Clyde to Capetown, South Africa via Freetown in Sierra Leone. At 5.30 am on 13 March 1943 the German submarine *U-107* attacked Convoy OS-44 some 190 miles west of Cape Finisterre, Spain. Four ships were torpedoed and sunk by *U-107* – the SS *Clan Alpine*, the SS *Marcella*, the SS *Oporto* and the SS *Sembilangan*. Able Seaman William Harper aged 25 was one of 44 men aboard the SS *Marcella* who were killed. Another SS *Marcella* casualty that morning was **John (Jack) White** from Donaghadee.

ROLL OF HONOUR
HARPER—Cherished memories of our dearly-loved son, Willie, lost at sea through enemy action, March 13th, 1943.
"Parted hands will clasp again."
Lovingly remembered by his Father, Mother, Sister and Brother, 107 Moat Street, Donaghadee.

Able Seaman William Harper is commemorated on the Tower Hill Memorial in London; on Donaghadee and District War Memorial; in Shore Street Presbyterian Church, Donaghadee and on the family grave headstone in Donaghadee Parish Church of Ireland Graveyard. His father, John W. Harper died on 3 August 1957 and his mother Jane died on 19 January 1973.

Harris, John Cecil Beresford (John)
Gunner
No. 989366, 71 Anti-Tank Regiment, Royal Artillery
Died in service on Monday 9 December 1940 (aged 27)
Donaghadee Parish Church of Ireland Graveyard, Co. Down

John Cecil Beresford Harris was a son of Henry Kingsford Harris MA, MIEE, FRSA and Cecile Blanche Kingsford Harris (nee Simms) of Notting Hill Gate, London. Their marriage was registered in the third quarter of 1912 in Marylebone, London and John's birth was registered there in the fourth quarter of 1913.

Gunner John Cecil Beresford Harris served with 71 Anti-Tank Regiment, Royal Artillery and he died on 9 December 1940 (aged 27) when the Regiment was based in Northern Ireland. He was single and unmarried. Gunner John Cecil Beresford Harris was buried in Donaghadee Parish Church of Ireland Graveyard and his CWGC headstone bears the inscription:

H

> *In ever loving and grateful memory of our darling son*
> *One of the truest and best*

Harrison Brothers, Geoffrey Austin and Hugh Raymond

Geoffrey Austin (in some records spelt Austen) Harrison and Hugh Raymond Harrison were sons of George Geoffrey Harrison (born 23 March 1890) and Charlotte Harrison (nee Coldwell). George Geoffrey Harrison was an Army Sergeant when he and Charlotte Coldwell were married on 21 July 1915 in Wrangthorn Parish Church, York. They had at least three children whose births were registered in Leeds, Yorkshire – Geoffrey Austin (first quarter of 1920); Muriel I. (first quarter of 1921) and Hugh Raymond (second quarter of 1922). In the CWGC Debt of Honour the Harrison family address is recorded as Marino, Co. Down. Geoffrey Austin Harrison was the first of the two brothers to die in war.

Harrison, Geoffrey Austin
Flight Lieutenant (Pilot)
No. 60102, 616 Squadron, Royal Air Force Volunteer Reserve
Killed in action on Monday 12 June 1944 (aged 24)
La Pellerine Communal Cemetery, Mayenne, France

During the Second World War Geoffrey Austin Harrison served with the Royal Air Force Volunteer Reserve and he was 24 years old when he died on active service in France on 12 June 1944. He was killed when his Supermarine Spitfire Mark VII aircraft collided with a Messerschmitt Bf 109 aircraft and crashed near Laval in France. His effects amounted to some £891, his home address was recorded as Lismore, Southfield Drive, Roundhay in Leeds and probate was granted to his father, George Geoffrey Harrison, who was at that time a company manager. Flight Lieutenant Geoffrey Austin Harrison was buried in La Pellerine Communal Cemetery, Mayenne, France.

Harrison, Hugh Raymond
Distinguished Flying Cross
Flight Lieutenant
No. 110412, 625 Squadron, Royal Air Force Volunteer Reserve
Killed on active service on Monday 24 July 1944 (aged 22)
Runnymede Memorial, Surrey, England (Panel 202)

During the Second World War Hugh Raymond Harrison served with the Royal Air Force Volunteer Reserve in Bomber Command and he was one of a seven man crew aboard an Avro Lancaster Mark I aircraft (LM174) that took off at 11.03 pm on 24 July 1944 from RAF Kelstern in Lincolnshire on a mission to bomb Kiel in Germany. The aircraft was lost without trace and the other six crew members who died that night were:

H

- Sergeant Roy Joseph Davies aged 21 from Leicester
- Flight Sergeant Kenneth Welland Dewey (RCAF)
- Flight Sergeant Lorne Albert Morfoot aged 19 (RCAF)
- Sergeant Alfred James Newell aged 22 from Cardonald, Renfrewshire
- Sergeant Frank Alfred Powell aged 20
- Pilot Officer Harold Alexander Smith (RCAF)

HARRISON H.R.D.F.C. Flight Lieutenant Hugh Raymond Harrison and his comrades are commemorated on the Runnymede Memorial in Surrey. Hugh Raymond Harrison was 22 years old when he died, exactly six weeks after his brother died, and his effects amounted to some £544. His home address was also recorded as Lismore, Southfield Drive, Roundhay in Leeds and probate was granted to his father, George Geoffrey Harrison. George Geoffrey Harrison was 84 when he died in 1974. Charlotte Harrison pre-deceased her husband; she died on 1 September 1958 (aged 66) and prior to her death she had been living at 6 Hazeldene Avenue, Bangor.

Harrison, Richard John Michael (Michael)
Lieutenant
No. 320633, 4th Battalion, Coldstream Guards
Killed on active service on Thursday 1 March 1945 (aged 20)
Reichwald Forest War Cemetery, Kleve, Nordrhein-Westfalen, Germany
(Grave 43 B 7)

Richard John Michael Harrison was born on 6 September 1924 and he was the elder son of Major General Desmond Harrison CB, DSO and Kathleen Frances Harrison (nee Hazley) who lived at *Shalom*, 52 Bryansburn Road, Bangor. Desmond Harrison was born in County Kilkenny and he served in France and Palestine during the First World War. Desmond Harrison and Kathleen Hazley were married in Bangor Parish Church of Ireland Church (St. Comgall's) on 8 December 1920 and they had four children – Richard John Michael; Desmond Roger Wingate; Patricia (Patsy) and Felicity Mary, all of whom attended Rockport School, Craigavad. The two girls attended this boys' school because their friend Mercy Bing, daughter of the then Headmaster Geoffrey Bing, was being educated there. Michael Harrison was Head Boy at Rockport and then Head of his House at Rugby School. He was a keen bird watcher and a skilled fisherman. Michael Harrison had a classical scholarship to Worcester College, Oxford but instead of going there to read Japanese (he was a skilled linguist) he went straight into the Army and entered Sandhurst in May 1943.

H

During the Second World War, Michael's father, Major General Desmond Harrison CB DSO was Chief Engineer in Lord Louis Mountbatten's South East Asia Command; his mother Kathleen was the Personnel Officer in the Short and Harland Glen Works in Newtownards; his maternal grandfather, William Hazley, owned a linen business in Belfast and his maternal grandmother was a sister of Canon Bradley of Bangor Parish Church; his uncle Richard (Dick) Harrison was Police Commissioner in Belfast; his sister Felicity Harrison (later Preedy) served with the Women's Royal Naval Service (WRNS) in Sydenham, Belfast and also in Leeds and then in Donibristle, Dunfermline; his sister Patsy Harrison was a Land Girl in England. For a time the Harrison family lived in Alresford, Hampshire.

KILLED IN ACTION

HARRISON—March 1945, killed in action in Western Europe, Richard John Michael Harrison (aged 20) Lieutenant, Coldstream Guards, dearly-loved elder son of Major-General Desmond Harrison, D.S.O., South East Asia Command, and Mrs. Harrison, Shalom, Bangor, Co. Down.

Lieutenant Richard John Michael Harrison served in the Coldstream

Guards and was posted to the Independent Tank Brigade which was part of the Guards Armoured Division. He was 20 years old when he was killed by a sniper on 1 March 1945 when taking part in a heavily resisted tank advance on Kervenheim in North Germany. He is commemorated in Bangor Parish Church (St. Comgall's) and in Rockport School. His father Desmond died in 1984 and his mother Kathleen died in 1993.

Harrison, Robert Lyttle (Bertie)
Marine
No. PLY/X 3783, HMS *Neptune,* Royal Marines
Killed in action on Friday 19 December 1941 (aged 19)
Plymouth Naval Memorial, Devon, England (Panel 59 Column 3)

> HARRISON—To the glorious and ever-lasting memory of my only beloved son and our dearly-beloved brother, Bertie, Royal Marines, presumed killed on board H.M.S. "Neptune," December 1941.
> "Time cannot dim the face we loved." Will always be remembered by his Father and Sisters.—13 Arras Park, and 40 Gransha Road, Bangor.

Robert Lyttle Harrison was the only son of David and Florence Irene Harrison (nee Campbell) of 13 Arras Park, Bangor. Both of his parents were originally from Jordanstown in County Antrim. David Harrison worked as a rigger/diver and he and Florence Irene Campbell were married on 13 July 1920 in Whiteabbey Presbyterian Church.

During the Second World War Marine Robert Lyttle Harrison served with the Royal Navy aboard the light cruiser HMS *Neptune*. In the early hours of 19 December 1941 HMS *Neptune* entered an unmarked minefield in the Mediterranean Sea and sank after hitting a total of four mines. Marine Robert Lyttle Harrison aged 19 was one of more than 760 men who died. Seaman Norman Walton from Gateshead was the only survivor and he spent some 15 months in various Prisoner-of-War camps before being repatriated in 1943.

Marine Robert Lyttle Harrison's sisters lived at 40 Gransha Road, Bangor and in the *Roll of Honour* notice that his family placed in the 22 December 1945 edition of the *County Down Spectator* they included the text:

Time cannot dim the face we loved

Marine Robert Lyttle Harrison is commemorated on Plymouth Naval Memorial in Devon and on Bangor and District War Memorial.

Haslett, Colin William Horner
Sub-Lieutenant
HMS *Quebec,* Royal Naval Volunteer Reserve
Killed in action on Wednesday 19 August 1942 (aged 21)
Portsmouth Naval Memorial, Hampshire, England (Panel 71 Column 1)

Colin William Horner Haslett was born on 8 May 1921 and he was a son of James Ross Haslett and Ethel Margaret Haslett (nee Rea) of Killeague, Greenisland, Co. Antrim. James Ross Haslett was a merchant and he and Ethel Margaret Rea were married on 17 February 1909 in Whitehouse Presbyterian Church, Newtownabbey. Colin William Horner Haslett was a grandson of Sir James Horner Haslett, an Irish Conservative politician who sat in the House of Commons from 1885 until 1886. Sir James Horner Haslett was Mayor of Belfast in 1887 (the year he was knighted) and again in 1888; his statue stands outside Belfast City Hall.

Colin William Horner Haslett and his brother, James Desmond Rea Haslett (born 4 October 1914) were educated at Rockport School, Craigavad. Colin William Horner Haslett also attended Sedbergh School in Cumbria from 1936 until 1939 and then he joined the Royal Naval Volunteer Reserve. Initially he was with HMS *King Alfred,* the RNVR officers' training establishment at Hove in Sussex and from there he went to HMS *Prosperine* at Scapa Flow.

Sub-Lieutenant Colin William Horner Haslett went to HMS *Quebec* which was part of the No. 1 Combined Training Centre (CTC) situated at Inveraray. The Royal Navy presence at Inveraray took the form of a Naval Staff, under a Captain RN, working directly to the Commandant. A few miles to the south was the large naval establishment called HMS *Quebec,* also under a Naval Captain who, by virtue of his seniority, was also Naval Officer in Charge (NOIC) Inveraray. The primary role of HMS *Quebec* was to provide and maintain craft for training operations and to accommodate personnel drafted in for the training of units at the CTC.

Sub-Lieutenant Colin William Horner Haslett was 21 years old when he was killed by a sniper on 19 August 1942 during *Operation Jubilee,* the raid on Dieppe. He is commemorated on Portsmouth Naval Memorial in Hampshire and in Rockport School, Craigavad.

Hawkins, Henry Victor (Harry)
Sergeant
No. 658138, 467 (RAAF) Squadron, Royal Air Force Volunteer Reserve
Killed in action on Wednesday 28 July 1943 (aged 25)
Hamburg Cemetery, Germany (Grave 5A L 12)

Henry Victor (Harry) Hawkins was born on 4 August 1917 and he was the second son of William James and Henrietta Hawkins (nee Kerr) of *Downshire*, Ballystrudder, Islandmagee. William James Hawkins was a railway clerk and he and Henrietta Kerr were married on 23 April 1913 in Comber Non-Subscribing Presbyterian Church. They had four sons – Jack, Harry, Billy and Bertie. The Hawkins family lived in Islandmagee where, in addition to his work with the Ulster Transport Authority (UTA), William James ran a retail business and dancehall called *The Rinkha*.

Harry Hawkins attended Royal Belfast Academical Institution from 1930 until 1933 and for a time he played soccer for Ards Football Club. In the 7 August 1943 edition of the *County Down Spectator* it was reported under the headline *Former Ards Footballer Missing* that Harry Hawkins was missing in action. Prior to the outbreak of the Second World War he was in the Territorials and at the outbreak of hostilities was posted to France where he served with an Anti-Aircraft Battery.

> **Former Ards Footballer Missing.—** Sergeant Harry Victor Hawkins, R.A.F., second son of Mr. W. J. Hawkins, Islandmagee, who is reported missing, was in the Territorials prior to the war and served in France with an A.A. Battery. This got away in the last boat to leave Cherbourg and brought its guns back. At Easter, 1941, he was home on leave and was at a dance in Belfast when the big air raid took place. This decided him to join the R.A.F. and help to repay some of Ulster's sufferings. He has taken part in many raids over Germany and Italy, and in one on the latter in July he took a bunch of Orange lilies with him in his plane. A well-known footballer, he assisted Larne and Ards, as well as the 41st Old Boys. His wife resides in London.

During the evacuation of France in June 1940 he was aboard the last boat to leave Cherbourg and his Battery brought all its guns back. At Easter 1941 he was home on leave and he was at a dance in Belfast on 15 April when the German Luftwaffe carried out a large-scale air raid on the city. After that he successfully applied for a transfer to the Royal Air Force and took part in raids over Germany and Italy. On 28 July 1943 he was one of a crew of seven aboard an Avro Lancaster Mark III aircraft (W5003) that took off from RAF Bottesford on the Leicestershire-Lincolnshire border on a mission to bomb Hamburg. Their aircraft was shot down by a German night fighter and five of the crew were killed. Sergeants E.C. Brookes and S. Drake were captured and held as Prisoners-of-War. In addition to Sergeant Henry Victor Hawkins aged 25 the other four crew members who died that night were:

- Pilot Officer James Llewellyn Carrington aged 25 (RAAF)
- FS Michael Rodney Warr King aged 20 from Careby, Lincolnshire
- Sergeant William Green aged 34 from Bryn, Lancashire
- Sergeant Herbert Bradley aged 27 from Brompton, Yorkshire

At the time of Sergeant Henry Victor Hawkins's death, his wife Jean lived in London and she later moved to Australia; they had no family. Sergeant Henry Victor Hawkins is commemorated in RBAI and in St. Anne's Cathedral Belfast.

Hawthorne, John (Jack)
Boatswain
SS *Glen Head* (Belfast), Merchant Navy
Died as a result of enemy action on Friday 6 June 1941 (aged 34)
Tower Hill Memorial, London (Panel 52)

H

John (Jack) Hawthorne was a son of John and Margaret Hawthorne (nee McCrudden) of Tattybrack, Rockcorry, Co. Monaghan and he was born on 12 August 1906 on the family farm. John Hawthorne and Margaret McCrudden (daughter of farmer Samuel McCrudden, Limavady) were married on 14 June 1905 in Magilligan Presbyterian Church, Limavady, Co. Londonderry and they had three children – Jack (born 12 August 1906); Wilfred (born 1910) and Mary Frances (Frances, born 1912). Jack Hawthorne followed a seafaring career and on 1 May 1937 he and Gertrude Wilhelmina (Queenie) O'Flaherty were married in Bangor Parish Church of Ireland Church (St. Comgall's). Queenie O'Flaherty was a schoolteacher from the town of Antrim where her father owned a draper's shop. Queenie's father was killed in a road accident when he was knocked off his bicycle by a car. Jack and Queenie Hawthorne lived at 24 Princetown Road, Bangor.

Frances Hawthorne (Jack's sister) moved from County Monaghan to County Antrim and on 22 September 1933 she married James Niblock from Islandmagee. James Niblock was also a seafarer and both he and Jack Hawthorne worked for the Head Line Shipping Company. They often sailed together on the same ship. Frances and James Niblock had six children – Billy, Andy, Jimmy, Margaret, Betty and Audrey. During the Second World War James Niblock served with the Merchant Navy and he was 41 years old when he died on 18 October 1945. Captain James Niblock was a son of James and Mary Niblock and when he died he had been Captain of the SS *Stramore* (Belfast). Captain James Niblock was buried in Islandmagee (Ballyharry) Cemetery, Co.

Antrim. During the Second World War Chief Officer John Niblock, also from Islandmagee, served with the Merchant Navy aboard the SS *Inver* (Belfast) and he died on 17 December 1940 (aged 52). His body was never recovered and he is commemorated on the Tower Hill Memorial in London.

During the Second World War John Hawthorne served with the Merchant Navy and he died on 6 June 1941 when the SS *Glen Head* was bombed 100 miles southwest of Cape St. Vincent, Portugal. Built in Glasgow in 1909, the SS *Glen Head* was owned by the Headline Shipping Company. After being bombed, the ship sank within three minutes and 27 of the 36 crew members were lost, including the Master, Robert Dick from Islandmagee. Third Engineer Officer **James Skillen** and Chief Steward **William McKinley Rae** also died that day. Boatswain John Hawthorne was 34 years old when he died and he is commemorated on Bangor and District War Memorial and in Bangor Parish Church (St. Comgall's). Jack and Queenie Hawthorne's son, John O'Flaherty Hawthorne, was born on 19 January 1942 (baptised 15 March 1942 in Bangor Abbey). Jack Hawthorne died on 6 June 1941 not knowing that his wife was expecting a baby. When Queenie Hawthorne died she was buried in the O'Flaherty family grave in Antrim Cemetery.

Hayes, Alfred
Private
No. D/24602, 6th (HD) Battalion, Royal Ulster Rifles
Died of illness on Tuesday 6 February 1940 (aged 51)
Holywood Cemetery, Co. Down (Grave 341)

Alfred Hayes was born on 8 May 1888 in Cookstown, Co. Tyrone and he was a son of William and Sarah Ann Hayes (nee Mitchell). William Hayes was a Recruiting Sergeant for the Royal Inniskilling Fusiliers and Sarah Ann Mitchell was 17 years old when they were married on 27 May 1871 in Colchester, England. They had twelve children – Henry and William (born in England); Isabella (born 8 March 1874, died in infancy); Catherine (born 16 May 1876); James (born 13 May 1877); George (born 5 July 1879) and Mabel Jane (born 6 November 1881) born in Co.

Londonderry; Andrew (born 14 February 1884); John (born 26 February 1886); Alfred (born 8 May 1888); Adeline Lucy (born 23 June 1892) and Dudley (born 7 August 1896) born in Co. Tyrone. In 1901 the widowed Sarah Ann (her husband William died of exposure on 12 December 1896 in Cookstown) was living at 120 Canmore Street, Belfast and in 1911 she was living at 4 Bracken Street, Belfast with her widowed son George and his three surviving children William, Jemima and Georgina. Sarah Ann Hayes was 67 years old when she died of cancer on 26 June 1921 in Belfast.

Alfred Hayes enlisted in Belfast on 4 January 1907 and served with the Royal Inniskilling Fusiliers (No. 8908) in Malta, China and India. During the First World War he served in France and in 1917 he was awarded the Military Medal (London Gazette 9 July 1917). He was wounded in action and suffered gunshot wounds to his back, left hip and left leg. After he recovered, pieces of shrapnel remained in his body. In 1918 in France he was transferred to the Royal Irish Fusiliers (No. 49793) and attached to 108th Trench Mortar Battery (Ulster Division). Lance Corporal Alfred Hayes and Annie Smith of 79 Tennant Street, Belfast were married on 8 April 1919 in St. Silas's Church of Ireland Church, Belfast. Alfred was discharged from the Army on 15 September 1919 and awarded the 1914-15 Star, the British War Medal and the Victory Medal. On 16 September 1919 he re-enlisted and joined the Royal Army Medical Corps (No. 206461). It was noted that he was 5 feet 5 inches tall and as a result of the shrapnel in his body he was discharged as being medically unfit on 22 September 1919.

In 1934 Alfred Hayes wrote to the War Office from his home in 38 Moltke Street, Belfast. The Army had never given him a copy of his discharge papers and they could not locate his papers in any of their offices. Alfred Hayes was unemployed and he said that he needed the papers to get a job. He said that he was 'finding things getting hard'.

During the Second World War Alfred Hayes served with the 6th (Home Defence) Battalion, Royal Ulster Rifles. He was 51 years old when he died of septicaemia on 6 February 1940 in Knocknagoney Military Hospital and he was buried two days later in Holywood Cemetery.

Heaven, Henry (Harry)
Corporal
No. 3596449, 1st Battalion, Border Regiment
Died in service on Tuesday 21 May 1940 (aged 27)
Froyennes Communal Cemetery, Hainaut, Belgium (Row 3 Grave 30)

Henry (Harry) Heaven's birth was registered in the second quarter of 1914

in Salford, Lancashire and he was a son Sydney and Amy Heaven (nee Blease). Their marriage was registered in the first quarter of 1912 in Bury, Lancashire. Harry Heaven joined the Army and in 1933 he was stationed at Palace Barracks, Holywood. On 20 December 1933 he and Georgina Herron of Hill Street, Holywood were married in Holywood Non-Subscribing Presbyterian Church. Corporal Harry Heaven served with the 1st Battalion, Border Regiment and in September 1939 the Battalion was posted with the British Expeditionary Force to fight in the France and Belgium Campaign. Harry Heaven was 27 years old when he died on 21 May 1940 during the retreat of Allied Forces to Dunkirk. He was buried in Froyennes Communal Cemetery, Hainaut, Belgium.

Corporal Henry (Harry) Heaven is commemorated on Holywood and District War Memorial and in Holywood Non-Subscribing Presbyterian Church. Harry Heaven was a brother-in-law of **Thomas Anthoney** who died on 7 February 1944.

H

Hegan, Robert Stanley (Robert)
Leading Aircraftman
No. 816245, 502 Squadron, Royal Air Force (Auxillary Air Force)
Died in service on Wednesday 6 January 1943 (aged 24)
Belfast (Dundonald Cemetery), Co Down (Section F 5 Grave 175)

Robert Stanley Hegan's birth was registered in the third quarter of 1919 in Belfast and he was the youngest son of Robert and Sarah Jane Hegan (previously Carberry, nee French) of 137 Ainsworth Avenue, Belfast. Robert Hegan Senior served in India during the Great War and after the war he worked in the Messengers' Department of the Belfast Post Office. Robert Hegan and Sarah Carberry (nee French) were married on 26 October 1910 in Albert Street Presbyterian Church, Belfast.

At the beginning of the Second World War Robert Hegan Junior joined the Royal Air Force and for a time he was attached to the Ulster Bomber Squadron. His wife, Ethel Doris Hegan, lived at 59 Donaghadee Road, Bangor and they had two children – twins born in March 1941. The twins were 22 months old in January 1943 when their father died.

Leading Aircraftman Robert Stanley Hegan was based at RAF Eval in Cornwall and he died there on 6 January 1943. He was buried in Belfast (Dundonald Cemetery), Co. Down (Section F 5 Grave 175). Also buried in that grave were Ethel Doris Ellis who died on 13 April 1987 aged 77 and John (Jack) Ellis who died on 25 December 1981 aged 79. In January 1963 the engagement of Robert Stanley Hegan's son, Mervyn S. Hegan, to Eleanor Brookes of Grafton, New York was announced.

Heller, Wladyslaw Eugeniusz
Wing Commander (Pulkownik Nawig)
No. P0989, No. 3 General Reconnaissance School
Killed in an aircraft accident on Monday 18 October 1943 (aged 48)
Newtownards (Movilla) Cemetery, Co. Down (Plot RC Section 18 Grave 22)

H

Wladyslaw Eugeniusz Heller was born on 27 June 1895 in Stanislawów, Poland and during the First World War he served with the Austrian Army. After the war he served with the Polish Army and during the Second World War he was assigned to the Polish air staff. Wing Commander Heller, who was based at RAF Jurby in the Isle of Man, was one of four men aboard an Avro Anson aircraft (N5372) being flown by Flying Officer Cooper from No. 3 General Reconnaissance School at RAF Squires Gate (Blackpool) on a navigation exercise. In adverse weather the aircraft struck Knocklayd Mountain near Ballycastle in County Antrim, hit a tree and crashed into a house owned by Charles Blaney. Charles Blaney's wife and their five children were at home, as was 22 year old Josephine McGroarty from Frosses in County Donegal who was staying there at the time. Josephine McGroarty was standing outside the house with her boyfriend John Greer from Ballycastle. John Greer was thrown clear as the aircraft crashed into the house but Josephine McGroarty was killed, as were two of those on board the aircraft. In addition to Wing Commander Heller, Warrant Officer Eric George Clarke was also killed. Warrant Officer Clarke was buried in Drumachose (Christ Church) Church of Ireland Churchyard, Co. Londonderry.

The pilot, Flying Officer Cooper, was thrown from the aircraft and he landed in the children's room, none of whom was injured, nor were their parents. Later he was taken to Limavady where he made a statement. He said that he had taken off at approximately 8.40 pm on a navigation exercise with two pupils. Wing Commander Heller was first navigator; Flight Lieutenant J.N. Down (or Dunn) was the second navigator and E.G. Clarke was the wireless operator/ air gunner. The planned route was 15 miles beyond the Mull of

Kintyre direct from Squires Gate, plus a short leg (in the nature of a wide turn to avoid aircraft on a similar trip) and return direct to Squires Gate. Having ascertained before take-off that the highest ground to be encountered was 1,860 feet (including the Isle of Man), the pre-flight plan was to fly at a height of 2,400 feet. On the outward leg the pilot identified RAF West Freugh in Wigtownshire and at that point the cloud base was 2,500 feet reducing, with the result that the plane was flying intermittently in cloud and, as a result, the Mull of Kintyre was not seen.

After the pilot instructed the first navigator to turn for base he observed that they were extremely close to another aircraft on a similar course and at the same height, slightly to starboard and behind. To avoid a possible collision with the other aircraft he increased airspeed by means of a shallow dive to 2,200 feet and temporarily altered course. They resumed their original course and airspeed and soon after the pilot sighted a white flashing marine light the aircraft crashed. The official Accident Report from RAF Squires Gate stated that the aircraft had set course for Squires Gate on the last leg of a navigation exercise, flying at a height of 2,400 feet. Unknown to the crew, the plane was 11 miles to starboard of track. The night was dark with broken cloud and it was not raining. Contributory factors to the accident were noted: The pilot descended to 2,200 feet to avoid another aircraft. Barometric pressure was 4 millibars less at Knocklayd than at Squires Gate and had decreased by a further millibar between the time of take-off and the time of the accident. This brought the plane's true height to about 2,050 feet. As the aircraft approached Knocklayd Mountain from the downwind side it experienced very strong down draughts.

The official report concluded that the accident was the result of a combination of circumstances including broken cloud, a dark night, an error in navigation, proximity of other aircraft, difference in pressure and down draughts. The report also concluded that the pilot had maintained control of the aircraft under very difficult conditions, after striking Knocklayd. Wing Commander Wladyslaw Eugeniusz Heller was 48 years old when he died, he was buried on 20 October 1943 in Movilla Cemetery, Newtownards and he is commemorated on Panel 21 of the Polish War Memorial at Northolt in London.

Henderson, Crawford

Able Seaman
No. D/JX 143656, HM Submarine *Perseus*, Royal Navy
Killed on active service on Friday 19 December 1941 (aged 22)
Plymouth Naval Memorial, Devon, England (Panel 47 Column 2)

KILLED ON ACTIVE SERVICE.
HENDERSON—Killed in Action at Sea
on Submarine Service, 19th December,
1941, Able Seaman Crawford Henderson.
He never shunned his country's call,
But gladly gave his life—his all;
He died, the helpers to defend,
An Ulster sailor's noble end.
Deeply regretted by his sorrowing Father,
Mother, Sisters and Brothers,
Brothers-in-law and Sisters-in-law;
also his Nephews and Nieces.
2, Main Road, Conlig.

Crawford Henderson's birth was registered in the second quarter of 1919 in Newtownards and he was a son of John and Margaret (Maggie) Henderson (nee Lynn) who lived at 2 Main Road, Conlig. John Henderson worked as a general labourer and he and Maggie Lynn were married on 17 May 1899 in Second Newtownards Presbyterian Church. They had at least eleven children including John (born 27 November 1899); William John (born 11 December 1900); Elizabeth (born 8 March 1903); Maggie (born 25 September 1905); Robert (born 17 July 1907); Ernest (born 25 October 1909); Mary (May, born 15 December 1910); Lewis (born 20 July 1913) and Crawford (born 1919).

Crawford Henderson joined the Royal Navy and in November 1938 he travelled aboard the SS *Rajputana* with other Navy personnel from Malta to the Royal Navy Barracks in Devonport. (The SS *Rajputana* was requisitioned by the Admiralty in September 1939 and, on 13 April 1941, she sank west of Reykjavik in Iceland after being hit by a torpedo fired from the German submarine *U-108*). Crawford Henderson's marriage to Elsie Hutchings was registered in the third quarter of 1939 in Plymouth, Devon and they lived in St. Austell, Cornwall.

During the Second World War Able Seaman Crawford Henderson served with the Royal Navy aboard HM Submarine *Perseus*. This Parthian class submarine was built in 1929 by Vickers Armstrong, Barrow-In-Furness. At 10.00 pm on 6 December 1941 (the date in some records whilst in the CWGC Debt of Honour the date of Crawford's death is recorded as 19 December 1941) HM Submarine *Perseus* sank after striking an Italian mine off the island of Cephalonia (Kefalonia), seven miles north of the island of Zakinthos in the Ionian Sea. At the time she was at the surface recharging her batteries under cover of darkness. One man out of the 61 men on board survived – John Capes used Davis Submarine Escape Apparatus to reach the surface from a depth of 171 feet and then he swam five miles to Cephalonia. He was hidden by islanders for 18 months before being smuggled out. The HM Submarine *Perseus* Memorial on Cephalonia is located just outside the town of Poros.

After Crawford Henderson died his family placed a *Killed on Active Service* notice in the 20 June 1942 edition of the *County Down Spectator*. His death was deeply regretted by his father, mother, sisters, brothers, brothers-in-law, sisters-in-law, nephews and nieces and the death notice contained the verse:

He never shunned his country's call, but gladly gave his life – his all;
He died, the helpers to defend, an Ulster sailor's noble end

 Able Seaman Crawford Henderson was 22 years old when he died and he is commemorated on Plymouth Naval Memorial in Devon; in Conlig Presbyterian Church (the organ was dedicated to his memory) and on the family grave headstone in Bangor Cemetery. His mother Margaret died on 9 January 1951 aged 73 and his father John died on 10 October 1953 aged 84. His sister Margaret died on 5 August 1938; his brother Ernest died on 21 July 1941 and his brother Lewis died on 7 October 1983.

Henderson, David Francis (Dai)
Sergeant
No. 978536, 218 Squadron, Royal Air Force Volunteer Reserve
Killed in action on Thursday 10 April 1941 (aged 18)
Runnymede Memorial, Surrey, England (Panel 45)

H

 David Francis (Dai) Henderson was born on 17 October 1922 and he was a son of Mr and Mrs Thomas Henderson. Thomas Henderson was a member of Bangor Borough Council and the Henderson family lived at 18 Hazeldene Gardens, Bangor. Later they moved to *Egremont*, Demesne Avenue, Holywood where Dai's father held the post of Air Raid Precautions (ARP) Officer. Later the Henderson family returned to Bangor and they lived at 19 Southwell Road. Both Dai and his elder brother Roy were confirmed in Bangor Parish Church of Ireland Church (St. Comgall's). During the Second World War Roy Henderson served as a Lieutenant in the Indian Army.

Dai Henderson attended Bangor Grammar School from 1935 until 1940 and he went straight from school to the Royal Air Force Volunteer Reserve in February 1940 at the age of 17 years and 4 months. In sixth form he was a prefect and the Headmaster commented when he was studying for his Senior Certificate that 'he had a distinguished record behind him and the promise of a brilliant career before him'. At school he won prizes for historic modelling and the Headmaster said, 'we never had anyone equal to him in that form of art: his skill, originality and attention to detail were beyond praise.' Several examples of his work were placed in the school history museum, including a miniature bust of the late King George V. He obtained two honours certificates in the Royal Drawing Society's examinations. Dai Henderson had a talent for 'humorous impersonation' in Dramatic Society productions and he also played rugby for the school.

ROLL OF HONOUR.

HENDERSON — In proud and loving memory of our dear son, Sergeant D. F. (Dai) Henderson, R.A.F.V.R., reported missing 10th April, 1941.
Ever remembered by his loving Father, Mother and Brother (Roy), 19 Southwell Road, Bangor.

Sergeant Dai Henderson served as a wireless operator and air gunner in 218 Squadron and on 10 April 1941 he was one of a crew of six aboard a Vickers Wellington Mark IC aircraft (R1442) that took off from RAF Marham in Norfolk at 7.30 pm on a mission to bomb Brest in France where the Germans had a submarine base. After sending a message for help, the aircraft crashed into the sea. The other crew members who died that night were:

- Sergeant Arthur George Plumb
- Sergeant John Donald Brown aged 21 from Dundee
- Flight Sergeant Robert Edward Venning Anderson (RCAF)
- Sergeant George Stewartson Snoddon aged 24 from Liverpool
- Sergeant Tahu William Dabinette aged 21 (RNZAF)

Only Flight Sergeant Anderson's body was recovered and he was buried in Brest (Kerfautras) Cemetery; the others have no known grave and are commemorated on the Runnymede Memorial. Sergeant Dai Henderson was 18 years old when he died and he is commemorated on Bangor and District War Memorial; in Bangor Parish Church (St. Comgall's) and in Bangor Grammar School.

Henderson, Hubert
Captain
No. 137933, 2nd Battalion, the London Irish Rifles, Royal Ulster Rifles
Killed in action on Thursday 21 January 1943 (aged 34)
Medjez-el-Bab Memorial, Tunisia (Face 30)

Hubert Henderson was born on 20 October 1908 in Blyth, Northumberland and his birth was registered in Tynemouth. He was a son of Ephraim McMurtrie Henderson (born in Ayr) and Sarah Henderson (nee Steel) who were married on 31 January 1907 in St. Leonard's Church of

Scotland, Ayr. Sarah was a daughter of Gilbert Steel who worked as a horse trainer. Ephraim Henderson was a medical practitioner and he was 35 years old when he died on 18 March 1909 at Newsham, Northumberland. Dr Ephraim Henderson was buried in Alloway Parish Church Graveyard in Ayr (Hubert was less than five months old when his father died). Sarah Henderson married Robert James Adams who was a linen manufacturer and they lived at *Moyola*, 21 Adelaide Park, Belfast. Hubert Henderson was educated at Rockport School, Craigavad and after he left school he worked as a linen salesman. Between 1930 and 1932 he travelled regularly in that capacity between Belfast and New York, USA.

Hubert Henderson's marriage to Eila P. Bryce was registered in the second quarter of 1934 in Kensington, London and they lived at 49 Godfrey Street, Chelsea in London. During the Second World War Captain Hubert Henderson served with the London Irish Rifles, Royal Ulster Rifles and in November 1942 the London Irish Rifles left Glasgow on route for North Africa. When they entered Tunisia heavy rain turned the ground into a quagmire and conditions were atrocious. Tanks got stuck in the mud and 'H' Company was involved in the task of retrieving them. Subsequently 'H' Company was ordered forward to take Hill 286 and Captain Hubert Henderson was second in command of 'H' Company when he was killed during fighting on Hill 286. His effects amounted to some £1,141 and probate was granted to his widow Eila Henderson and his mother Sarah Adams. Captain Hubert Henderson was 34 years old when he died and he is commemorated on the Medjez-el-Bab Memorial in Tunisia; in Rockport School and on his father's headstone in Alloway Parish Church Graveyard in Ayr.

Henry, William Maxwell (Max)
Pilot Officer
No. 173906, Royal Air Force Volunteer Reserve
Killed in an aircraft accident on Friday 7 July 1944 (aged 21)
Liverpool (Anfield) Cemetery, Lancashire, England
(Section 15 C. of E. Grave 1234)

William Maxwell Henry's birth was registered in the first quarter of 1923 in Cookstown, Co. Tyrone and he was the eldest son of Ernest Hamilton Henry and Susan Hazelton Henry (nee Watters) of Cookstown; later Ballygrangee, Greyabbey; later Whitechurch, Ballywalter and later Cherryvalley, Comber.

375

Ernest Hamilton Henry (son of Silas Henry) was a farmer from Killycurragh, Cookstown when he and Susan Hazelton Watters from Coalisland were married on 9 June 1920 in Albany Presbyterian Church, Ardboe. After William Maxwell Henry was born, the Henry family moved to Ballygrangee and five of their children were baptised in Carrowdore Presbyterian Church – Wilson McLeod (born 29 March 1926); Ernest Hamilton (born 25 July 1927); Mary Patricia Houston (born 26 March 1929); Dorothy Maud (born 18 February 1932) and John Lawrence (born 2 August 1934).

William Maxwell Henry and Phyllis Marguerite Lunt were married on 19 April 1944 and they lived at 134 Stanley Park Avenue, Anfield, Liverpool. Less than three months later Pilot Officer William Maxwell Henry was killed.

KILLED ON ACTIVE SERVICE.

HENRY—July, 1944, Killed in Action, Pilot Officer William Maxwell Henry, R.A.F., eldest son of Mr. and Mrs. Henry, Whitechurch, Ballywalter, and dearly-loved husband of Phyllis Henry, 134, Stanley Park Avenue, Liverpool. "We who loved him will never forget."
Deeply regretted by his sorrowing Father, Mother, Brothers and Sisters.

In the 15 July 1944 edition of the *County Down Spectator* it was reported that Pilot Officer William Maxwell Henry had served in North Africa for 18 months and that when he qualified as a pilot he topped the list in the examination results at the end of his course. He was serving with 53 OTU when he died on 7 July 1944 and the very next day news came through of his promotion to the rank of Flying Officer. There is evidence from the RAF Museum to suggest that Pilot Officer William Maxwell Henry aged 21 was aboard a Vickers Wellington aircraft (LP314) piloted by Flight Sergeant John Phillip Sinclair Dalton aged 21 from Caulfield, Victoria in Australia and they were doing circuits and landing practice. On one approach to land the starboard engine failed and when the aircraft stalled it crashed to the ground. Both men were killed and William Maxwell Henry's death was registered in Aylesbury, Buckinghamshire.

H

Pilot Officer William Maxwell Henry's funeral took place on 13 July 1944 and the chief mourners were his wife and his father. His remains were conveyed to the Church of St. Jude in Liverpool and eight men of the RAF acted as pall-bearers. He was buried in Liverpool (Anfield) Cemetery. Pilot Officer William Maxwell Henry is commemorated in Carrowdore Presbyterian Church.

Hewitt, Ernest Basil Snell (Basil)
Military Cross
Lieutenant
No. 180163, Royal Inniskilling Fusiliers
Killed in action on Wednesday 3 November 1943 (aged 23)
Sangro River War Cemetery, Italy (Grave VIII E 28)

Ernest Basil Snell Hewitt was born in Wallasey, Cheshire and his birth was registered in the second quarter of 1920 in Birkenhead. He was the only son of the Revd James Marshall Hewitt and Alice Evadne Louise Hewitt (nee Snell) of Eastbourne in Sussex. Their marriage was registered in the second quarter of 1919 in Birkenhead and they had three children – Ernest Basil Snell (born 1920); Mary M. (born 1923) and Moyra D. (born 1926).

The Revd Hewitt was the eldest son of James Henry and Jeannie Denby Hewitt (nee Marshall) who were married on 25 June 1879 in Knockbreda Parish Church of Ireland Church, Belfast. They had five children – James Marshall (born 8 September 1880), Edith Mary, Ernest Henry, Holt Montgomery and William Arthur. The Revd Hewitt's three brothers were all killed on active service in the Great War and they are commemorated on Page 180 in the Book of Honour *Remembering Their Sacrifice in the Great War – North Down* compiled by Barry Niblock. James Henry Hewitt died on 4 January 1928 aged 77 and Jeannie Denby Hewitt died on 5 June 1935 aged 80. The Revd Hewitt's only sister, Edith Mary Hewitt, lived in Bangor and she died on 23 November 1966.

H

SON OF BANGOR MAN FALLS IN ACTION.

Official information has been received that Lieut. Basil Ernest Snell Hewitt, M.C., only son of Rev. Marshall Hewitt, M.A., vicar of Islington, London, has been killed on active service with the 8th Army.

UNCLES KILLED AT SOMME.

Lieut. Hewitt's father is the eldest son of the late Mr. James Hewitt, Bangor, who was manager of the Workshops of the Blind, Belfast, for many years. Three of Mr. Hewitt's sons, Lieuts. Hoit M., Ernest and Wm. Hewitt, were killed while serving with the Ulster Division on the Somme in the last war.

Lieut. Basil Hewitt, who was a graduate of Oxford University, served in North Africa, Sicily and Italy, and was awarded the M.C. for his gallantry in the Sicilian Campaign.

Ernest Basil Snell Hewitt was a graduate of Oxford University and during the Second World War he served with the Royal Inniskilling Fusiliers in North Africa, Sicily and Italy. He was awarded the Military Cross in August 1943 for his gallantry in the Sicilian campaign. His Battalion marched overnight on 30/31 July 1943 to a position overlooking Catenanuova and from there they advanced towards Centuripe. There was very heavy fighting and 'in the midst of this confusion a very junior officer, Lieutenant E.B.S. Hewitt, found himself in command of his Company, which, having succeeded in fighting its way against opposition into the centre of the town had established itself in the main square. At 2030 hours the Officer Commanding went off to carry out a reconnaissance and to co-ordinate a plan with a second Company now in the town. During this he was wounded and Lieutenant Hewitt took over command of the Company. Throughout the evening and night the enemy counter-attacked and pressed forward their attack with great determination. Although access to the houses could not be gained, Lieutenant Hewitt, regardless of personal danger and with an example of courage which was an inspiration to all, succeeded in repelling all attacks and later organised patrols further into the town until his Company Commander returned. Had it not been for this officer's devotion to duty and power of leadership it is improbable that the hold on the town could have been maintained during the night'.

It was during the Battle of San Salvo that Lieutenant Ernest Basil Snell Hewitt aged 23 was killed and he was described as 'the best Subaltern in the Brigade with a long record of gallant service'. His death was reported in the 27 November 1943 edition of the *County Down Spectator* and at that time his parents were living at *The Vicarage*, Islington, London. His effects amounted to some £458 and probate was granted to his father. The Revd James Marshall Hewitt died on 18 August 1967.

H

Hewitt, Hugh Robert (Hugh)
Private
No. 5382304, 2ⁿᵈ (Airborne) Battalion, Oxford and Bucks Light Infantry
Killed in action on Saturday 24 March 1945 (aged 28)
Reichswald Forest War Cemetery, Kleve, Nordrhein-Westfalen,
Germany (Grave 35 A 9)

Ards Lady's Brother Killed.—Mrs. M'Ilroy, 11 Scrabo View Terrace, Newtownards, has been officially notified that her brother, Paratrooper Hugh Hewitt, of the Oxford and Bucks Regiment (Airborne) has been killed in action. He was previously wounded on "D" day.

Hugh Robert Hewitt's birth was registered in the fourth quarter of 1917 in Newtownards and he was a son of William and Mary Jane Brown Logan Hewitt (nee Carlisle) of Tullymagee, Newtownards. William Hewitt worked as a labourer and he and Mary Carlisle were married on 27 November 1907 in Kilmood Church of Ireland Church, Killinchy, Co. Down. They had at least two children, a daughter named Anna Spread Wilson (Nan) Hewitt (born 24 December 1913) and Hugh Robert Hewitt (born 1917).

Hugh Robert Hewitt was a career soldier and he served with the Oxfordshire and Buckinghamshire Light Infantry. His marriage to Hilda Ellen Heard of Sheldon, Birmingham was registered in the third quarter of 1943 in Lambeth, London. Private Hugh Robert Hewitt's death was reported in the

21 April 1945 edition of the *Newtownards Chronicle* under the headline *Ards Lady's Brother Killed*. It was reported that Mrs Nan McIlroy of 11 Scrabo View Terrace, Comber Road, Newtownards had been officially notified that her brother, Hugh Hewitt aged 28, had been killed in action during the Allied invasion of Nazi Germany. He had previously been wounded on D-Day.

Private Hugh Robert Hewitt's sister and brother-in-law Anna (Nan) and William McIlroy and their son Arnold placed an *Our Heroes – In Memoriam* notice in the 22 March 1947 edition of the *Newtownards Chronicle* and it contained the verse:

> *It's sweet to think of a brother so dear,*
> *Though absent from me, yet ever so near;*
> *Unseen by the world he stands by my side,*
> *And whispers, Dear sister, death cannot divide.*

Heyes, Eric Joseph
Driver (Despatch Rider)
No. 2004479, 676 General Construction Company,
Corps of Royal Engineers
Died as a result of an accident on Thursday 17 October 1940 (aged 23)
St. Helens Cemetery, Lancashire, England (Section 30 Grave 106)

H

> **Soldier Killed at Kirkistown.**—A fatal accident occurred at Kirkistown on Thursday evening, the victim of which was Eric Joseph Hayes, one of the military stationed in the district. Hayes was riding a motor cycle, and he was thrown from the machine and sustained such injuries that he succumbed shortly afterwards. An inquest was held on Friday, a full report of which will appear in next week's issue.

The death of Despatch Rider Eric Joseph Heyes on 17 October 1940 was reported in the 19 October 1940 edition of the *Newtownards Chronicle*. In the newspaper report his surname was spelt Hayes. A native of St. Helens in Lancashire, he was fatally injured in an accident at Kirkistown, Co. Down. He was riding towards Mageean's Corner and as he attempted to negotiate the bend he was thrown from his machine and crashed into a wall on the opposite side of the road. He was taken to Ards District Hospital but was pronounced dead on arrival. Coroner Dr R.A.McC. Wallace presided at an inquest which was held in the hospital the following day. After hearing medical, police and witness testimonies the Coroner returned a verdict that death was due to laceration of the brain and shock following multiple injuries received when the deceased collided with a wall. He was 23 years old when he died and he was buried in St. Helens Cemetery, Lancashire.

There is evidence that Eric Joseph Heyes's parents were Ernest and Marcella Heyes (nee McCoy) and that their marriage was registered in the fourth quarter of 1916 in Prescot, Lancashire. Eric Joseph Heyes's birth was registered there in the fourth quarter of 1917.

Higgins, Daniel
Fusilier
No. 6980100, 70th Battalion, Royal Inniskilling Fusiliers
Died as a result of enemy action on Wednesday 16 April 1941 (aged 25)
Newtownards (Movilla) Cemetery, Co. Down (Section 28 Prot Plot Grave 81)

Between 10.45 pm on Easter Tuesday 15 April and 4.30 am on Wednesday 16 April 1941 there was a large-scale German Luftwaffe air raid on the City of Belfast. Other nearby towns and villages, including Bangor and Newtownards, were also attacked. Areas of Bangor where bombs fell included Ashley Gardens, Bangor Golf Clubhouse, Baylands, Farnham Road, Hazeldene Gardens and Ranfurly Avenue. Fires blazed on Scrabo Hill, Newtownards and bombs fell on Green Road, Conlig and Comber Road, Newtownards. At least 28 people with North Down and Ards connections were killed, including the following 14 civilians:

- **Matilda Grattan** together with her daughters **Angeline Grattan** and **Shelagh Grattan** who died at 40 Ashley Gardens in Bangor.
- **Margaret Byers Watt** who died at 5 Hazeldene Gardens in Bangor.
- **Robert Wright** of 32 Baylands, Bangor who died of his injuries in Bangor Hospital.
- **Edith, Henry, Isabella and William Dunwoody;**
  Nancy Simms Gribbin; Thomas Morton; Bessie, Ellen Ogle and Evelyn Tate who all died in Belfast.

That night the aerodrome at Newtownards, which was the Headquarters of 231 Squadron, Royal Air Force was attacked. The aerodrome was guarded by soldiers of the 70th (Young Soldiers) Battalion, Royal Inniskilling Fusiliers, some of whom were too young for front line service and were deployed instead on the Home Front. Newtownards aerodrome was attacked with a considerable number of incendiary bombs and some high explosive bombs. One high explosive bomb that fell on the hutments of 'A' Company Headquarters killed 13 men, all of whom served with the 70th Battalion, Royal Inniskilling Fusiliers. Most were killed instantly and the remainder died the following day as a result of their injuries:

- Fusilier **William Bellamy** aged 28
- Fusilier **Samuel Burke** aged 18

- Lance Corporal **Alexander Carlisle** aged 19
- Fusilier **Andrew Copling** aged 16
- Fusilier **Hugh Fulton** aged 17
- Fusilier **George Graham** aged 24
- Fusilier **Daniel Higgins** aged 25
- Fusilier **Leslie Love** aged 34
- Fusilier **Samuel McFarland** aged 19
- Company Quartermaster Sergeant **William McMurray** aged 27
- Fusilier **Ernest McNeill** aged 17
- Warrant Officer Class II **Alfred Penfold** aged 36
- Fusilier **Matthew Wright** aged 18

The casualties were all taken to Ards District Hospital in Newtownards.

(On Monday 5 March 2012 a memorial to the 13 soldiers of the 70th Battalion Royal Inniskilling Fusiliers who were killed during the air raid on Newtownards aerodrome was unveiled and dedicated in the War Memorial Garden, Newtownards).

There was another casualty with an Ards connection who died during the night of 15/16 April 1941. Flight Lieutenant **Wilfrid Mark Hamilton Brookes** (aged 23) of 231 Squadron who was in Belfast at the time was killed during the air raid.

Fusilier Daniel Higgins was born in County Antrim (his birth was registered in the second quarter of 1916 in Larne) and he was a career soldier. His home address at the time of his death was 83 Eskdial Gardens, Belfast. The funeral of Fusilier Daniel Higgins aged 25 to Movilla Cemetery in Newtownards was reported in the 26 April 1941 edition of the *County Down Spectator* under the headline *Military Honours for Raid Victim*. The funeral took place on Saturday 19 April in the morning and the coffin, draped with the Union Jack, was drawn on an Army carriage. The Lord Lieutenant of County Down, Lord Londonderry, together with the Mayor of Newtownards, Alderman Robert Edgar, attended.

Hill, John Stewart (Stewart)
Flight Sergeant
No. 1062419 ,103 Squadron, Royal Air Force Volunteer Reserve
Killed in action on Thursday 21 January 1943 (aged 31)
Runnymede Memorial, Surrey, England (Panel 137)

Image shows plaque text:

TO THE GLORY OF GOD AND IN GRATEFUL
REMEMBRANCE OF THOSE OF THIS
CONGREGATION WHO GAVE THEIR LIVES FOR KING
AND COUNTRY IN WORLD WAR 1939–1945
THE RAIL AND MARBLE STEP ARE ERECTED BY
THE PARISHIONERS OF HOLYWOOD

CAPT. THOS. O. CORRIN, R.A.
F/SGT J. STEWART HILL, R.A.F.
CAPT. JOHN F. SMELLIE, GLIDER PILOT REGT.

John Stewart Hill was born on 11 October 1911 and he was a son of Joseph and Jane Hill (nee Stewart) of *Glenside*, Holywood. Joseph Hill was a commercial traveller and he and Jane Stewart were married on 20 December 1899 in Windsor Presbyterian Church, Belfast. They had at least four children – Dorothy (born 10 July 1901); Alice Kathleen (born 29 August 1907); John Stewart (born 11 October 1911) and Elizabeth Patricia (born 18 April 1914). The last three of these children were baptised in Holywood Parish Church of Ireland Church (St. Philip and St. James).

During the Second World War Flight Sergeant John Stewart Hill served with the Royal Air Force Volunteer Reserve and on 21 January 1943 he was one of a seven man crew aboard an Avro Lancaster Mark I aircraft (W4340) that took off at 5.17 pm from RAF Elsham Wolds in Lincolnshire on a mission to bomb Essen in Germany. The aircraft was lost without trace and all seven crew members are commemorated on the Runnymede Memorial. Along with Flight Sergeant John Stewart Hill the other six crew members who died that evening were:

- PO Edgar H. Burgess aged 23 from Ashton-under-Lyme, Lancashire
- Flight Lieutenant Torkel Torkelsson Lundberg (RCAF)
- Flight Sergeant Kenneth George Curtis (RCAF)
- Sergeant George Henry Anderson aged 20 from Streatham, London
- Sergeant Sidney Edward Perry aged 20 from Bedford
- Sgt Douglas Paterson Kerr aged 20 from Cambuslang, Lanarkshire

Flight Sergeant John Stewart Hill was 31 years old when he died and he is commemorated on Holywood and District War Memorial and in Holywood Parish Church (St. Philip and St. James).

Hodgett, David Alexander Hynes (David)
Mentioned in Despatches
Captain
No. EC/477, 2nd Battalion, 9th Gurkha Rifles
Killed in action on Thursday 29 January 1942 (aged 29)
Singapore Memorial, Singapore (Column 307)

David Alexander Hynes Hodgett was born in Dublin on 12 September 1913 and he was the elder son of the Revd Richard Hodgett who was a Baptist

H

Minister and Mary Elizabeth Hodgett (nee Kerr) who lived at 37 St. Peter's Road, Dublin. Later the Hodgett family moved to 16 Ashley Gardens, Bangor. They were married on 6 August 1912 in Derrylee Methodist Church, Tartaraghan in County Armagh and they had at least five children. The birth of David's sister, Mary Leslie Hodgett, was registered in the first quarter of 1915 in Belfast. At one time the Revd Richard Hodgett was the Minister in Ballymena Baptist Church.

CAPTAIN HODGETT D. A. H.

David Alexander Hynes Hodgett was educated at Ballymena Academy, the Irish Baptist College and Trinity College, Dublin. He volunteered in October 1939 and served with the Royal Ulster Rifles. He gained his commission and was posted to India in August 1940 where he was attached to the Gurkha Rifles. Captain David Alexander Hynes Hodgett was killed in action in Malaya on 29 January 1942. His sister Mary Leslie Hodgett was the welfare officer in a local aircraft factory (in June 1944 she and William Carlyle Rea were married in Bangor Baptist Church). His youngest sister, Marienne Elizabeth Hodgett, and Captain Ernest Edward Harrington RIASC were married on 23 March 1946 in Ballyholme Methodist Church, Bangor (her brother, Signalman Richard Hodgett, was groomsman). Captain David Alexander Hynes Hodgett was 29 years old when he died and he is commemorated on the Singapore Memorial and on Bangor and District War Memorial.

H

Hodgson, Raymond
Flying Officer (Pilot)
No. 171815, Royal Air Force Volunteer Reserve
Killed in an aircraft accident on Sunday 20 August 1944 (aged 23)
Heworth (St. Mary) Churchyard, Durham, England
(New Yard Plot G Grave 95)

Raymond Hodgson was a son of Frederick and Elizabeth Hodgson of Heworth and the husband of Patricia Jane Hodgson (nee McKie) of Felling, Gateshead (their marriage was registered in the first quarter of 1944 in Durham). During the Second World War Raymond served with the Royal Air Force Volunteer Reserve. On 20 August 1944 an Avro Anson aircraft (LT658) from No. 12 Air Gunners School based at Bishops Court was on an air gunnery exercise when it broke up in mid-air as a result of a structural failure. Wreckage fell to the ground over a wide area centred on Ballygalget Roman Catholic Church and all five crew members on board were killed – Flying Officer (Pilot) Raymond Hodgson, Sergeant (Flight Engineer) **Kennedy Boyd Black**, Sergeant (Flight Engineer) **Frank Bennett Bloor**, Flight Sergeant (Flight Engineer) **Thomas Charles Crisp** and Sergeant (Air Gunner) **George William Thomas Walker**. All five deaths were registered in Downpatrick.

Flying Officer Raymond Hodgson was 23 years old when he died and he was buried in Heworth (St. Mary) Churchyard, Durham and his name on the headstone is spelt *Raymund*. Also buried in the grave were Jane McKie who died on 31 March 1970 aged 71 and Henry McKie who died on 14 December 1974 aged 78.

Hodgson, Ronald
Aircraftman Second Class
No. 1495177, 153 Squadron, Royal Air Force Volunteer Reserve
Killed as a result of an accident on Monday 11 May 1942 (aged 19)
Huddersfield (Edgerton) Cemetery, Yorkshire, England
(Section 7G Grave 73)

H

AIRMAN'S TRAGIC END.

CRUSHED UNDER TRACTOR.

The manner in which a nineteen years old member of the Royal Air Force met his death was related at an inquest held by Dr. R. A. Mc. Wallace, Coroner, on Wednesday, 13th May, when District-Inspector M'Neill conducted the proceedings on behalf of the police. The deceased was A/C2 Ronald Hodgson, and his home address was given as Springfield Place, Luck Lane, March, Huddersfield, Yorkshire.

Ronald Hodgson was born on 17 November 1922 and he was a son of Arthur and Hilda L. Hodgson (nee Groom) of Springfield Place, Luck Lane, Marsh, Huddersfield in Yorkshire. Their marriage was registered in the fourth quarter of 1916 in Salford, Lancashire. Prior to the outbreak of the Second World War Ronald worked in a greengrocer's shop. Aged 18, he enlisted on 5 May 1941 and served with 153 Squadron, Royal Air Force Volunteer Reserve. A year later, on 11 May 1942, he was accidentally killed while 153 Squadron was based at RAF Ballyhalbert in County Down. His death was reported in the 23 May 1942 edition of the *Newtownards Chronicle* under the headline *Airman's Tragic End, Crushed Under Tractor*. An inquest was held on 13 May 1942 under the Coroner, Dr R.A.Mc. Wallace, and Aircraftman Second Class (AC2) Leslie Seale gave evidence.

AC2 Seale said that he had been dragging two large chocks across the grass to place in position at an aircraft when AC2 Ronald Hodgson, who was driving a tractor, volunteered to tow the chocks. When the job was done AC2 Hodgson executed a sharp right-hand turn and the tractor rolled

384

over pinning him underneath. By the time help arrived and the tractor was righted, Hodgson was dead. His neck was broken and fractured ribs had penetrated his lungs. The Coroner returned a verdict that Aircraftman Second Class Ronald Hodgson met his death as a result of multiple injuries caused by his accidentally overturning the tractor which he was driving. He was buried in Huddersfield (Edgerton) Cemetery in Yorkshire and there is an inscription on his CWGC headstone (his age is given as 18):

In memory a constant thought, in heart a silent sorrow, sadly missed

Hoey, Robert (Bobbie)
Private
No. 7012466, Army Catering Corps *attached* **Royal Ulster Rifles**
Died of wounds on Sunday 9 July 1944 (aged 28)
Ranville War Cemetery, Calvados, France (Grave IVA C 19)

H

Robert Hoey was born on 5 June 1916 and when he died on 9 July 1944 it was reported in the press that he was the eldest surviving son of Robert and Elizabeth Hoey (nee Nelson) who lived at 28 Station Road, Carnalea. Before that the Hoey family lived for a time in the townland of Craigdunloof, Newtown Crommelin, Co. Antrim. Robert Hoey Senior was a coachman, groom and gardener and he and Elizabeth Nelson were married on 18 May 1910 in Groomsport Presbyterian Church. During the First World War Robert Hoey Senior served with the Royal Irish Rifles. Robert and Elizabeth Hoey had at least eleven children – Ellen (Nellie, born 23 July 1910); William (born 11 July 1911, died in infancy); Kathleen (born 7 July 1912); Sarah Bothwell (Sadie, born 27 July 1913); Molly Carver (born 27 November 1914); Robert (born 5 June 1916); Eveline Doris (born 13 August 1917); Frederick (Fred, born 5 September 1923); Pauline Gwynne Ruddell (born 24 December 1924); Margaret (born 5 January 1926) and Desmond (born 9 June 1927).

Robert Hoey Junior operated a coal business in the Bangor area before he joined the Army in 1932 and he served in various parts of the world including India. Robert Hoey and Elizabeth Telford were married on 20 March 1943 in Ballygilbert Presbyterian Church and it is recorded that, for a time, Elizabeth lived in Inverness, Scotland. During the Second World War Robert Hoey

served with the Army Catering Corps *attached to* the Royal Ulster Rifles and on 9 July 1944 he died of wounds sustained during the Allied advance in Europe. In the 29 July 1944 edition of the *County Down Spectator* there were *Killed in Action* notices from his wife and mother-in-law, his parents, his sister and brother-in-law Nellie and Bertie Robinson of 22 Bingham Street, Bangor; his sister and brother-in-law Sadie and William Clarke of 94 High Street, Bangor; his sister and brother-in-law Kathleen and Jim Jackson of 83 Elmwood Drive, Bangor; his sister and brother-in-law Molly and Hugh Boal of 5 Downhill Avenue, Carnalea. Robert's brother Fred was serving with the RAF and his brother Desmond was engaged in 'war work'. In one of the *Roll of Honour* notices published in 1946 there was the text:

No morning dawns, no night returns but we'll remember

Private Robert Hoey was 28 years old when he died and he is commemorated on Bangor and District War Memorial and in Ballygilbert Presbyterian Church. Robert's twin sons, John and Robert, were born on 17 September 1944 – two months after their father died – and they were baptised in Ballygilbert Presbyterian Church.

Holland, Charles Julius Chennell (Julius)
Sergeant (Observer)
No. 745631, 107 Squadron, Royal Air Force Volunteer Reserve
Killed on active service on Tuesday 23 July 1940 (aged 19)
Tangmere (St. Andrew) Churchyard, Sussex, England
(Plot E Row 1 Grave 460)

Charles Julius Chennell Holland was born on 20 January 1920 in India and he was a son of Julius Alfred and Beryl Ethyl de la Hoyde Holland of 8 Hazeldene Park, Bangor. Julius Holland Junior had a sister called Phyllis who was a local table-tennis champion. The Holland family moved to Bangor in 1933 when Julius's father transferred from the Imperial Civil Service to the Northern Ireland Ministry of Finance. When Julius Holland was a boy he sang in the choir of Bangor Parish Church of Ireland Church (St. Comgall's). Educated at Bangor Central Public Elementary School and Bangor Grammar School from 1933 until 1936, Julius Holland had 'pronounced literary ability'. He was an active member of both the Debating and Dramatic Societies and he took part in several public performances. The Headmaster of Bangor Grammar School said of Julius Holland that he was 'a boy one could not easily forget, of lovable character, undoubted ability and with an urge towards leadership'. After leaving school Julius Holland entered the Ordnance Survey Department of the Northern Ireland Civil Service. In 1939 he joined the Royal Air Force Volunteer Reserve and he commenced his training in 24 Elementary & Reserve Flying Training School at Sydenham. In 1940 he had further training in Monkton, Ayrshire; RAF Upwood in Cambridgeshire and RAF West Raynham in Norfolk.

It was reported in the 3 August 1940 edition of the *County Down Spectator* that Sergeant Observer Julius Holland had been killed on active service. He lost his life returning to RAF Wattisham in Suffolk after a raid on the airfield at Criel in Northern France. His Bristol Blenheim Mark IV (L9414) aircraft was shot down by a German night fighter and crashed into the sea. His body was washed ashore at Littlehampton on the Sussex coast and he was buried with full military honours in Tangmere Churchyard. There is an inscription on his CWGC headstone:

He wrote: What greater cause is there than that of Right, Freedom and God

Charles Julius Chennell Holland was one of a three man crew and the others who lost their lives were:

- Pilot Officer Peter George Anthony Watson aged 19 from Leeds
- Sergeant William Patrick O'Heney

Their bodies were never recovered and they are commemorated on the Runnymede Memorial.

Julius Holland was a prolific letter writer and the last letter that he wrote to his mother was dated 20 July 1940. The telegram reporting that he was missing was dated 23 July 1940 and the telegram reporting his death arrived with his mother one week later. After his death, extensive extracts from many of the letters written to his mother were published in the local press. When he got his Flying Badge he wrote, 'Today is the grandest day of my life; it ranks with my scholarship examination and my Civil Service examination'. In another letter he wrote,

'You have heard often that old proverb – one good moment is enough for any man. My moment will come I know and I am sure I shall be ready and do the right thing before it passes'.

Julius Holland was 19 years of age when he died and he is commemorated on Bangor and District War Memorial; in Bangor Parish Church (St. Comgall's); in Bangor Grammar School and on the family grave headstone in Bangor Cemetery. His father, Julius Alfred Holland, died on 2 April 1934 and his mother, Beryl Ethel de la Hoyde Holland, died on 23 April 1999 aged 96.

Hollywood, David Francis Apperson (Frank)
Sub-Lieutenant (A)
HMS *Goldcrest*, Royal Naval Volunteer Reserve
Died in service on Wednesday 15 September 1943 (aged 20)
Bangor Cemetery, Co. Down (Section 7 Q Grave 25)

David Francis Apperson (Frank) Hollywood was born on 21 March 1923 and he was the younger son of David and Eileen Hollywood (nee Apperson) of 16 Maxwell Road, Bangor. David Hollywood was a senior partner in his father's firm – Messrs James Hollywood and Sons, House Agents, Albertbridge Road, Belfast and he and Eileen Apperson were married on 4 June 1919 in Holywood Parish Church of Ireland Church (St. Philip and St. James). Three of Frank's uncles (his father's brothers) served in the Great War – Arthur, Gerald and James – and two of them were killed in action. Arthur and James Hollywood are commemorated on Page 186 in the Book of Honour *Remembering Their Sacrifice in the Great War – North Down* compiled by Barry Niblock.

David Francis Apperson Hollywood's paternal grandfather, James Hollywood, had a brother named William Johnston Hollywood who worked as a fireman and he and Jane Henderson were married on 20 April 1896 in St. Anne's Church of Ireland Church, Belfast. They had at least four children before Jane died – Jane (born 1898); Eva (born 20 June 1899); Hilda (born 31 December 1900) and David (born 16 September 1903). William Johnston Hollywood and Jane's sister Sarah were married on 2 October 1907 in Ballysillan Presbyterian Church, Belfast and they had at least one child – James (born 21 February 1909). Eva Hollywood and Frederick William Ferguson were married on 5 January 1921 in Knock Methodist Church, Belfast and their son **Clifford Samuel Ferguson** (Frank's second cousin) died on 21 May 1941. Arthur and James Hollywood who were killed in the First World War were Eva Ferguson's cousins.

KILLED ON ACTIVE SERVICE

HOLLYWOOD—September, 1943, Sub-Lieut. (A) David Francis Apperson Hollywood, dearly-loved younger son of Mr. and Mrs. David Hollywood, 16 Maxwell Road, Bangor. Interred in Bangor New Cemetery.

Frank Hollywood attended Campbell College, Belfast from 1936 until 1940. He was a member of the school shooting team and he played hockey for the school. He was a Lance Corporal in the Officers' Training Corps. He was called up in the Fleet Air Arm in November 1941 and after training in Canada he was granted his commission. HMS *Goldcrest* was a shore establishment of the Royal Navy formed on 1 May 1943 at Angle, Pembrokeshire.

During the Second World War Frank's elder brother Arthur James Hollywood (born 1920) served as a Sub-Lieutenant in the Fleet Air Arm and he and Mabel Catherine Liken of 440 Ormeau Road, Belfast were married on 2 November 1943 in Newtownbreda Presbyterian Church.

Sub-Lieutenant David Francis Apperson Hollywood's funeral took place on 19 September 1943 and military honours attended. His parents placed a *Roll of Honour* notice in the 16 September 1944 edition of the *County Down Spectator* and it contained the verse:

To have, to love, to lose, and when God wills – to find

Sub-Lieutenant David Francis Apperson Hollywood was 20 years old when he died and he is commemorated on Bangor and District War Memorial; in Bangor Golf Club; in First Bangor Presbyterian Church; in Campbell College and on the family grave headstone in Bangor Cemetery. A short tribute was published in the December 1943 edition of *The Campbellian*:

'We regret to announce the death on active service of Frank Hollywood. When he was here his cheery disposition made him many friends. He was a good athlete who, if he had stayed at school, would almost certainly have gained his colours in the three main games of the school. We offer our sincere sympathy to the members of his family'.

Frank Hollywood's father David died on 1 June 1953.

Holt, Archibald Joseph Adolphus
Private
No. 7586012, Royal Army Ordnance Corps
Died as a result of enemy action on Monday 5 May 1941 (aged 32)
Holywood Cemetery, Co. Down (RC Ground Collective Grave 1042)

Archibald Joseph Adolphus Holt was born on 8 February 1909 in Malta and he was a son of Alfred George Holt who was born in October 1878 in Murree Hills, North West Province, India and Mary Josephine Holt (nee Donnelly) who was born in 1880 in County Kildare. They were married on 18 February 1904 in St. Michael's Roman Catholic Church, Chatham. They had at least four children – Mary Ellen Joseph (born 12 December 1904 in Chatham, Kent); Alfred George (born 1906 in Malta; died 25 July 1906 in infancy); Evelyn Florence Violet (born 1907 in Malta; died 19 January 1908 in infancy); Archibald Joseph Adolphus (born 8 February 1909 in Malta).

Alfred George Holt was a career soldier and he enlisted as a Boy Soldier on 26 October 1892 at Devonport when he was 14 years old. At that time he was 4 feet 8¼ inches tall and he signed up for 12 years with the colours. He served with the 4th Battalion, Rifle Brigade (No. 2553) and then on 26 October 1896, when he was 18, he was appointed Private. He was promoted to the rank of Corporal in 1901 and to the rank of Sergeant in 1905. His sequence of service was Home, South Africa, Home, Malta, Egypt (he was stationed in the Citadel, Cairo) and Home. Sergeant Alfred George Holt transferred to the 3rd Battalion and he was discharged from the Army on 25 October 1913 in Cork. His intended place of residence was 42 Montpelier Street, Dublin. At that time he was 5 feet 8½ inches tall and he had the Queen's South Africa Medal with three clasps.

During the Second World War Archibald Joseph Adolphus Holt served with the Royal Army Ordnance Corps. He was 32 years old when he died on 5 May 1941 at 23 Witham Street in Belfast as a result of enemy action and he was buried in Holywood Cemetery. Around 150 people in Belfast died on 4/5 May 1941 as a result of a German Luftwaffe air raid.

Hornby, John Samuel
Sub-Lieutenant (A)
HMS *Corncrake*, Royal New Zealand Naval Volunteer Reserve
Killed in an aircraft accident on Wednesday 10 October 1945 (aged 21)
Ballyhalbert (St. Andrew's) Church of Ireland Churchyard, Co. Down
(Grave 5)

John Samuel Hornby was born on 9 October 1924 and he was a son of William Henry and Priscilla Muriel Hornby (nee Addenbrooke) who were

married in 1923. William Henry Hornby died in 1942 when he was 55 years old. John Samuel Hornby was a stepson of Allan Noble Campbell whom his mother married after his father died. Allan Noble Campbell was the manager of the Sports Department in a store in Wanganui, Wellington, New Zealand and the Campbell family lived at 9 Selwyn Street, Wanganui and later 86 North Street, Timaru. During the Second World War Allan Noble Campbell served as a Sergeant in Infantry Reinforcements.

From 1939 until 1942 John Samuel Hornby was educated at Wanganui Collegiate School where he was a member of Marris House, a school prefect and he played rugby for the school. On leaving school he joined No. 9 (Wanganui) Squadron of the Air Training Corps. During the Second World War he served with the Royal New Zealand Naval Volunteer Reserve and he died at 2.15 pm on 10 October 1945 in a flying accident when he was stationed in Ballyhalbert at HMS *Corncrake*. It was the day after his 21st birthday.

(On 24 April 1945 Ballyhalbert Airfield transferred to the Admiralty and became a Royal Naval Air Station. It was commissioned as HMS *Corncrake* and in July 1945 Kirkistown Airfield was commissioned as HMS *Corncrake II*. Ballyhalbert Airfield was closed on 13 November 1945).

Sub-Lieutenant John Samuel Hornby died when his Supermarine Seafire Mark III aircraft (NN631) of No. 718 Squadron Fleet Air Arm based at Ballyhalbert, crashed at Crockagarran, south-south-east of Carrickmore, Co. Tyrone while on a cross-country training exercise.

Sub-Lieutenant John Samuel Hornby was buried in Ballyhalbert (St. Andrew's) Church of Ireland Churchyard at Ballyeasborough and there is a memorial plaque in the field where he crashed. His second cousin, Pilot Officer **Frederick Hugh Anderson**, was killed on 19 November 1941 and he too was buried in Ballyhalbert (St. Andrew's) Church of Ireland Churchyard. Both men are commemorated in Wanganui Collegiate School. In the School Museum there is a 1:48 scale model of John Samuel Hornby's aircraft. Made by Robin Ruddock from a piece of aluminium fuselage wreckage from his aircraft, it was presented to the school by Aviation historians Gary McFarland and Robin Ruddock.

Hossack, Ian Milne (Ian)
Pilot Officer (Pilot)
No. 33568, 144 Squadron, Royal Air Force
Killed in action on Thursday 11 July 1940 (aged 19)
Jonkerbos War Cemetery, Gelderland, Netherlands (Grave 12 G 5)

Ian Milne Hossack was born in 1920 in Surbiton, Surrey and he was a son of James Davidson Hossack who came from Banff in Scotland and Eileen Inez Hossack (nee Rogers) from Bangor. During the First World War, James Davidson Hossack served with the Seaforth Highlanders and then as a Captain with the Royal Engineers. James Davidson Hossack and Eileen Inez Rogers were married on 19 February 1919 in Glencraig Parish Church of Ireland Church, Craigavad. Ian Hossack's younger brother Patrick (Pat) was born in 1926 and, as children, the boys enjoyed holidays at their maternal grandmother's house, *Innisfail*, Princetown Road, Bangor. Their mother Eileen was born on 29 March 1889, she died on 12 May 1929 when Ian was nine years old (Pat was three) and she was buried in Bangor Cemetery. Their grandmother died in 1944.

H

Ian Milne Hossack attended Imperial Service College, Windsor and during the Second World War he served with the Royal Air Force in Bomber Command. He was killed in action on 11 July 1940 when returning from a bombing mission over Wanne-Eickel in Germany. He was one of a crew of four aboard a Handley Page Hampden Mark I aircraft (P4366) that took off from RAF Hemswell in Lincolnshire. The aircraft was hit by flak and crashed near Kessel in the Netherlands. The other three crew members who died that day were:

- Sergeant Eric Basil Hartley France
- Sergeant Edward Dennis Leamy aged 20 from Canterbury
- Sergeant Clarence Rose

All four were buried in Jonkerbos War Cemetery, Netherlands.

Ian's younger brother, Patrick (Pat) Hossack, served with the Royal Air Force from 1944 until 1947 and during the war he flew Spitfire fighter aircraft in the Far East. Pilot Officer Ian Milne Hossack was 19 years old when he died and he is commemorated on Bangor and District War Memorial (as Hossuck I.M.); in Bangor Parish Church (St. Comgall's) and on the family grave headstone in Bangor Cemetery. There are two inscriptions:

Superna Petimus
(This is the motto of the Royal Air Force College Cranwell and means)
We seek higher things

The Spirit Hath Returned Unto God Who Gave It

Houghton, Henry
Sapper
No. 1914295, Royal Engineers
Killed in a motor-cycle accident on Wednesday 9 October 1940 (aged 26)
Old Leake (St. Mary) Churchyard, Lincolnshire, England

Newtownards Tragedy
MILITARY MOTOR CYCLIST KILLED
THE INQUEST

A verdict of accidental death, in accordance with the medical testimony, was returned at an inquest held in the Ards District Hospital on Thursday on Sapper Henry Houghton, 25 years of age, of Boston, Lincolnshire, who died on Wednesday from injuries sustained when his motor cycle was involved in a collision on the Comber Road, Newtownards, with a mineral water lorry, driven by W. J. Eardley, Eblana Street, Belfast.

Henry Houghton's birth was registered in the first quarter of 1914 in Boston, Lincolnshire and he was a son of Arthur Francis Houghton and Rebecca Burr Houghton (nee Duchars) of Old Leake, Lincolnshire. His name was registered as Henry Duchars. Arthur Francis Houghton was a soldier and he and Rebecca Burr Duchars were married on 6 October 1914 in Wrangle Parish Church, Lincolnshire. Their marriage was registered in Boston, Lincolnshire and they had three children – Henry; Gladys whose birth was registered in the third quarter of 1915 in Spilsby, Lincolnshire and Sidney whose birth was registered in the second quarter of 1919, also in Spilsby.

In October 1930 Rebecca Burr Houghton (nee Duchars) married Thomas Cropley and she died on 11 May 1977 aged 84.

During the Second World War Sapper Henry Houghton served with the Royal Engineers and he was 26 years old and stationed in Northern Ireland when he died as a result of an accident on 9 October 1940. A verdict of accidental death was returned at an inquest held in Ards District Hospital. Sapper Houghton died from head injuries sustained when his motor-cycle was involved in a collision with a mineral water lorry on

H

Comber Road, Newtownards. The lorry was being driven by James Eardley of Eblana Street, Belfast. Sapper Henry Houghton was buried in Old Leake (St. Mary) Churchyard in Lincolnshire and there is an inscription on his CWGC headstone:

Remembrance is a golden chain that binds us till we meet again

Houston, Thomas McMahon (Thomas)
Fifth Engineer Officer
SS *Empire Attendant* (Glasgow), Merchant Navy
Died as a result of enemy action on Wednesday 15 July 1942 (aged 20)
Tower Hill Memorial, London, England (Panel 38)

H

Bangor Seaman Presumed Lost.—The parents of a gallant young Bangor merchant seaman have been informed officially that their son is presumed lost as the result of enemy action. He is 5th Engineer Thomas M'Mahon Houston, elder son of Mr. and Mrs. Thos. Houston, Newtownards Road. With his apprenticeship in the engineering department of Messrs. Harland and Wolff, Belfast, three months from completion, he joined the Merchant Navy a few months ago at the age of 21. He received his education at Bangor Central P. E. School and at Belfast Technical. His family are members of First Bangor Presbyterian Church.

Thomas McMahon Houston was the elder son of Thomas and Mary Houston (nee McMahon) of Newtownards Road, Bangor. They were married on 6 October 1920 in Trinity Presbyterian Church, Bangor. Thomas Houston Junior was educated at Bangor Central Public Elementary School and Belfast Technical School and he was just three months away from completing his apprenticeship in the Engineering Department of Messrs Harland and Wolff, Belfast when he joined the Merchant Navy. He served aboard the SS *Empire Attendant*. This passenger cargo vessel was launched in December 1920 as *Magnava* and completed as *Domala* in 1921 by Barclay, Curle and Company, Whiteinch, Glasgow. She was owned by the British India Steam Navigation Company. Following damage sustained in an air attack in 1940, *Domala* was requisitioned by the Ministry of War Transport, rebuilt and renamed SS *Empire Attendant*. She was placed under the management of Andrew Weir and Company (Bank Line). On 1 July 1942 she sailed from Liverpool as part of Convoy OS-33 with a cargo of stores, vehicles and a quantity of explosives bound for Freetown in Sierra Leone. On 10 July 1942 the escort vessel, HMS *Pelican*, signalled the Admiralty that SS *Empire Attendant* had broken down for the seventh time and was out of contact. At 3.30 am on 15 July 1942, when she was south of the Canary Islands and off the west coast of Africa, she sank after being torpedoed by the

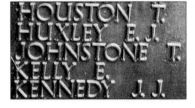

German submarine *U-582*. All 59 men aboard the SS *Empire Attendant* died; there were no survivors.

Able Seaman **John Joseph Kennedy** from Holywood was another one of the

casualties. Fifth Engineer Officer Thomas McMahon Houston's mother, father and brother placed a *Roll of Honour* notice in the 20 July 1946 edition of the *County Down Spectator* and it included the text:

Unknown to the world he walks by my side

Fifth Engineer Officer Thomas McMahon Houston was 20 years old when he died and he is commemorated on Tower Hill Memorial in London; on Bangor and District War Memorial and in First Bangor Presbyterian Church.

Hoy, Edmund John
Sub-Lieutenant (A)
No. 67572, South African Naval Forces
Killed in an aircraft accident on Tuesday 10 April 1945 (aged 27)
Belfast City Cemetery (Glenalina Extension Section D Grave 103)

Edmund John Hoy was a son of Alfred E. Hoy and Catherina M. Hoy of 42 Musgrave Road, Durban, Natal in South Africa and during the Second World War he served with the South African Naval Forces.

On 10 April 1945 he was the pilot aboard a Grumman Hellcat (JW879) aircraft of 892 Squadron, Fleet Air Arm based at RNAS Eglinton that took off from RAF Sydenham. Immediately after take-off the aircraft made a steep turn and dived into the ground at Gillespie's Plant Nursery, killing a child who had been playing there. Sub-Lieutenant (A) Edmund John Hoy was taken to Campbell College Military Hospital, Belfast where he died later that day as a result of his multiple injuries. He was buried on 14 April 1945 in the Glenalina Extension of Belfast City Cemetery and there is an inscription on his CWGC headstone:

Many a lonely heartache, often a silent tear
Always a beautiful memory of one we loved so dear

Sub-Lieutenant (A) Edmund John Hoy was 27 years old and unmarried when he died.

Hoy, Robert James (Robert)
Stoker 1st Class
No. D/KX 95518, HMS *Albatross*, Royal Navy
Killed in action on Friday 11 August 1944 (aged 23)
Plymouth Naval Memorial, Devon, England (Panel 90 Column 1)

H

Robert James Hoy's birth was registered in the third quarter of 1920 in Devonport and he was the eldest son of Robert James Hoy and Daisy Elizabeth Ada Hoy (formerly Richardson, formerly Morris nee Heath) of Plymouth, Devon. Daisy Elizabeth Ada Heath and Herbert Richard M. Morris were married in 1908 and she and Fred Richardson were married in 1917. This marriage ended in 1919 when Fred Richardson was convicted of bigamy. Robert James Hoy Senior and Daisy Elizabeth Ada Richardson were married on 8 May 1920 in St. Paul's Parish Church, Devonport and they had three children – Robert James (born 1920); James (Jim, born 1924) and John A.A. (born 1931). Robert James Hoy Senior spent more than 25 years in the Royal Navy and then 12 years as a Customs Officer before he retired. Daisy Elizabeth Ada Hoy was 54 years old when she died in Plymouth on 10 December 1939. When Robert James Hoy Junior died, his father was living at 48 South Street, Newtownards.

In 1932 Robert James Hoy Junior was living in Belfast and he completed his education in Park Parade Public Elementary School. An all-round athlete, he was associated with the Salvation Army Young People's Band and the Boy Scouts. As a boy of 15 he joined the crew of a Danish barque on which he travelled to Australia, South Africa and the United States of America. He left the barque in New York and stayed there for a time before returning to England where he worked for the Grand Canal Company on a barge trading between London and Birmingham.

ROLL OF HONOUR.

HOY—Proud and loving memories of Stoker 1st Class R. J. Hoy, killed in action August 9; 1944.

"At the going down of the sun, and in the morning, we will remember him."

Dad and Brother Jim (in Far East).— 48 South Street, Newtownards.

In 1938 Robert James Hoy joined the Royal Navy and he was killed in action aboard HMS *Albatross* on 11 August 1944. HMS *Albatross* was built by the Royal Australian Navy Dockyard at Cockatoo Island, Sydney and launched in 1928. She was transferred to the Royal Navy in 1939. In July and August 1944 she was engaged in Repair Ship duty off Juno beach, Normandy and on 11 August she was hit by a torpedo. HMS *Albatross* sustained major structural damage and Stoker 1st Class Robert James Hoy was one of more than sixty men who were killed. HMS *Albatross* was repaired and after the war she went into mercantile service. She was broken up in Hong Kong in 1954.

Stoker 1st Class Robert James Hoy was 23 years old when he died, his body was never recovered and he is commemorated on Plymouth Naval Memorial in Devon and on Newtownards and District War Memorial. His last visit home to visit his father in Newtownards was in January 1942 and during the Second World War his younger brother Jim also served with the Royal Navy.

Hubbard, James Walter
Driver
No. T/185541, 4 Bridge Company, Royal Army Service Corps
Accidentally drowned on Sunday 24 August 1941 (aged 29)
Newtownards (Movilla) Cemetery, Co. Down (Section 23 Grave 109)

James Walter Hubbard's birth was registered in the fourth quarter of 1911 in Barnet, Middlesex and he was a son of Thornton Hubbard (born in Norfolk) and Annie Gertrude Hubbard (nee Rowe, born in London). They were married on 11 September 1897 in St. Luke's Church, Hackney in London and they lived at 8 Brownlow Road, Boreham Wood in Hertfordshire. Thornton Hubbard worked as a house painter and he and Gertrude had at least seven children including Thornton Robert, Elizabeth, Ernest Albert, Donald, Henry and James Walter. Their eldest son, Thornton Robert Hubbard was on active service during the First World War.

James Walter Hubbard was the husband of Edith Mary Hubbard (nee Muller) and they lived in Boreham Wood, Hertfordshire. Their marriage was registered in the first quarter of 1940 in East Ham, Essex. During the Second World War James Walter Hubbard served with the Royal Army Service Corps and he was accidentally drowned on 24 August 1941.

Soldier Drowned.—J. W. Hubbard, a soldier, stationed in the Newtownards district, was drowned in a boating accident in Carlingford Lough on Sunday afternoon. It appears that the deceased and six other passengers were crossing from Warrenpoint to Omeath, when the motor boat capsized in mid-channel. Several motor-boats put out from the shore and saved the other passengers. Mrs. Ada Stewart (wife of another soldier), who resides in Greenwell Street, Newtownards, was brought ashore in an unconscious condition, but she revived after treatment, and she was taken to Newry Hospital. The wife of the deceased soldier was at Warrenpoint at the time of the accident.

Driver James Walter Hubbard's death was reported in the 30 August 1941 edition of the *Newtownards Chronicle*. He was stationed in the Newtownards district and he died in a boating accident in Carlingford Lough. James Walter Hubbard and six other passengers were crossing from Warrenpoint to Omeath when their motorboat capsized in mid-channel. All six of the other passengers were picked up and survived the incident. Edith Mary Hubbard was in Warrenpoint at the time of the accident. Driver James Walter Hubbard was buried in Movilla Cemetery, Newtownards and his wife placed an inscription on his CWGC headstone:

They never fail who died in a great cause

James Walter Hubbard's father Thornton died on 14 April 1956 (aged 83) and his mother Gertrude died in December 1957 (aged 79).

Hughes, Robert
First Officer
MV *Mamutu* (Hong Kong), Australian Merchant Navy
Died as a result of enemy action on Friday 7 August 1942 (aged 51)
Port Moresby Memorial, Papua New Guinea (Panel 10)

Robert Hughes was born on 9 July 1891 and he was a son of Robert and Ann Hughes (nee Palmer) of Portavogie. They were married on 9 January 1880 in Ballycopeland Presbyterian Church, Millisle. Robert Hughes was a fisherman and he and Ann had at least seven children – Mary Elizabeth (born 29 October 1880); James Mahood (born 11 November 1882); Margaret (born 25 August 1884); Hugh (born 29 November 1886); Ellen (Nellie, born 11 September 1888); Robert (born 9 July 1891) and John (born 1 July 1894). All of the children were baptised in Glastry Presbyterian Church.

During the Second World War Robert Hughes served with the Australian Merchant Navy aboard the MV *Mamutu*. Built in Hong Kong in 1938 this wooden motor vessel merchant ship was operated by Burns, Philip and Company as an inter-island trader. At the outbreak of war she was engaged in the evacuation of civilians ahead of the advancing Japanese Forces. She operated as a supply ship for the Royal Australian Navy and on 7 August 1942 she was shelled and sunk by the Japanese submarine *RO-33* in the Gulf of Papua, near Murray Island in the Torres Strait. First Officer Robert Hughes was one of more than 100 men, women and children (many of them natives) who lost their lives during the shelling and follow-up machine gun fire.

First Officer Robert Hughes was 51 years old when he died and he is commemorated in the Commemorative Roll of the Australian War Memorial. This Roll takes the form of a Commemorative Book located in the Memorial's Commemorative Area and it 'commemorates Australians who died during or as a result of wars or warlike operations in which Australians have been on active service but who were not eligible for inclusion on the Roll of Honour (not serving in the Australian Armed Forces)'. The official commencement and cut-off dates for the Second World War were 3 September 1939 to 30 June 1947 (the date of disbandment of the Australian Imperial Force). First

Officer Robert Hughes is also commemorated on the family grave headstone in Glastry Presbyterian Church graveyard:

In loving memory of
Robert Hughes, Portavogie who died 21ˢᵗ February 1923 aged 71 years
Also his wife Ann Hughes who died 29ᵗʰ October 1922 aged 75 years
Also Robert son of above lost at sea August 1942 aged 51 years
Mary Elizabeth daughter of above died 1ˢᵗ April 1968 aged 87 years
Margaret daughter of above died 17ᵗʰ April 1970 aged 86 years
Ellen Hughes died 4ᵗʰ December 1981 aged 93 years
I know that my Redeemer liveth
and that he shall stand at the latter day upon the earth

Hull, Desmond
Rifleman
No. 7021412, 2ⁿᵈ Battalion, the London Irish Rifles, Royal Ulster Rifles
Killed on active service on Thursday 2 December 1943 (aged 20)
Sangro River War Cemetery, Italy (Grave XI C 21)

Desmond Hull was born in 1923 in Saintfield and he was a son of Thomas Hull (son of Thomas Hull, a boot maker of 14 Eastland Street, Belfast) and a stepson of Elizabeth Hull (nee Hull, daughter of John Hull, a house repairer of 51 Argyle Street, Belfast) who later lived in Comber. Desmond's father, Thomas Hull, was 37 years old and a hackle maker when he and Elizabeth Hull (aged 20) were married on 13 May 1926 in St. Anne's Church of Ireland Cathedral, Belfast. Desmond Hull had fifteen siblings – Thomas, Sidney, David, Annie, John, Mary, Georgina, Jessie, Edward, Cecil, William, Barbara, Pearl, Gerald and Alice.

H

During the Second World War Desmond Hull served with the Royal Ulster Rifles and in 1942 he and Barbara Daniels were married in Plympton, Devonshire. Later that year they had a son named Desmond and they lived in Ivybridge, Devonshire. A little over a year later, on 2 December 1943, Rifleman Desmond Hull died during the Allied advance up the Adriatic Coast in Italy and he was buried in Sangro River War Cemetery.

Rifleman Desmond Hull is commemorated on the family grave headstone in Comber Cemetery. His father Thomas died on 17 July 1951 (aged 62) and his mother Elizabeth died on 17 August 1980 (aged 73).

Hunter, William James (James)
Corporal
No. 540459, Royal Air Force
Died as a result of enemy action on Saturday 12 September 1942 (aged 23)
Alamein Memorial, Egypt (Column 263)

H

William James Hunter was a son of Mr and Mrs W. Hunter of 8 James Street, Newtownards and he died in what has come to be known as the *Laconia Incident* about which much has been written. Built by Swan, Hunter and Wigham Richardson, Newcastle-upon-Tyne and launched in 1921 this passenger liner was operated by the Cunard White Star Line. In 1939 she was drafted in for war service and converted into an Armed Merchant Cruiser. On 12 September 1942 and on route from Cape Town to Freetown the RMS *Laconia* had a crew of about 460. She was carrying some 80 civilians, around 280 British service personnel, about 1,800 Italian prisoners of war and more than 100 Polish service personnel. In the evening the ship was struck and sunk off the west coast of Africa by a torpedo fired from the German submarine *U-156*. The U-boat commander, Korvettenkapitän Werner Hartenstein and his crew immediately commenced rescue operations and were joined by the crews of other U-boats in the area. On 13 September 1942 the U-boats were attacked by a US Army B-24 Liberator bomber and it was after the sinking of RMS *Laconia* that German fleet commanders were ordered by Admiral Karl Donitz to stop trying to rescue civilian survivors. Known as the Laconia Order this led to the introduction of unrestricted submarine warfare by the Kriegsmarine – the Nazi German Navy.

Corporal William James Hunter was one of more than 1,000 people who died and he is commemorated on the Alamein Memorial in Egypt and on Newtownards and District War Memorial.

Hutchinson, John

Driver
No. T/214847, Royal Army Service Corps
Died on active service on Saturday 24 January 1942 (aged 33)
Benghazi War Cemetery, Libya (Grave 4 E 10)

John Hutchinson was born on 28 October 1908 and he was a son of John and Eleanor (Ellen) Hutchinson (nee Magowan) of 7 George Street, Newtownards. They were married on 24 September 1906 in Newtownards Parish Church of Ireland Church (St. Mark's) and they had at least three children – John (born 28 October 1908); William (born 21 April 1911) and Ellis (born 11 December 1912).

Driver John Hutchinson's death was reported in the 14 February 1942 edition of the *Newtownards Chronicle*. The report stated that he had served with the Royal Artillery since the outbreak of war and before that he had worked for some 19 years (since he was 12 years old) for Messrs Robert Christie and Sons, Newtownards. He had been a keen supporter of Ards Football Club. There were *Killed in Action* notices in the 28 February 1942 edition of the *Newtownards Chronicle* from his father and mother and his brother William (on active service) and sister-in-law Winnie Hutchinson of 32 James Street, Newtownards; his sister Mary and brother-in-law Thomas Armstrong (Prisoner-of-War) and his nephews and nieces of 6 West Street, Newtownards; his aunt Maria and cousins at 25 George's Street; his aunt Maggie and cousins at 27 George's Street, Newtownards.

H

HUTCHINSON—Killed in Action, in the Middle East, Driver John Hutchinson, R.A.S.C.
Sleep on, dear son, in your foreign grave,
A grave we may never see,
But as long as life and memory last,
We will remember thee.
Deeply regretted by his sorrowing Father and Mother.
JOHN and ELEANOR HUTCHINSON.
7, George Street, Newtownards.

John Hutchinson and Jane Foster were married on 24 March 1932 in Ulsterville Presbyterian Church, Belfast. They had one child and they lived at 32 James Street, Newtownards and later at 19 Donegall Avenue, Belfast. Jane Hutchinson received the news of her husband's death while she was in hospital recovering from a serious operation. Driver John Hutchinson was 33 years old when he died and he is commemorated on Newtownards and District War Memorial and in Newtownards Parish Church (St. Mark's).

Hynds, Patrick (Patsy)
Driver
No. T/64009, Royal Army Service Corps
Died in service on Friday 14 March 1941 (aged 27)
Alexandria (Chatby) Military and War Memorial Cemetery, Egypt
(Grave N 131)

Portaferry Soldier's Death.—It was learned recently with great regret that Driver Patsy Hynds of Portaferry lost his life while on active service in the East. The late Driver Hynds' friendly disposition and genial aspect won for him many friends in the Lower Ards. Aged 25 or 26 years, he had been a serving soldier for three years with the R.A.S.C., and his death comes as a great shock to all who knew him and deep sympathy must be accorded his parents, Mr. and Mrs. Frank Hynds, of Mill Street, Portaferry, who received a telegram stating their son had died in a general hospital from injuries not received as a result of enemy action. Mr. Hynds is well known and respected in Portaferry, and was also a soldier in the last war. He is one of the most enthusiastic members of the Portaferry Branch of the British Legion, and takes a deep interest in all its activities.

Patsy Hynds was born in Portaferry on 2 July 1913 and he was a son of Francis (Frank) Hynds (sometimes Hinds) and Catherine Hynds (nee Walsh, sometimes Welsh). Frank Hynds worked as a labourer and he and Catherine Walsh were married on 26 November 1911 in Portaferry (Ballyphilip) Roman Catholic Church. They lived in Mill Street, Portaferry and their first son, James, was born in 1912.

Frank Hynds served during the First World War and, after the war, he was an active member of the Portaferry Branch of the British Legion. During the Second World War Patsy Hynds served with the Royal Army Service Corps and he was 27 years old when he died in a general hospital from injuries that were 'not received as a result of enemy action'. The death of Driver Patsy Hynds was reported in the 5 April 1941 edition of the *Newtownards Chronicle*. It was reported that he had been a serving soldier for three years and his 'friendly and genial aspect won him many friends in the Lower Ards'.

Ievers, Robert Valentine (Bob)
Sergeant
No. 1126184, 418 Squadron, Royal Air Force Volunteer Reserve
Killed on active service on Monday 30 November 1942 (aged 21)
Runnymede Memorial, Surrey, England (Panel 86)

Robert Valentine (Bob) Ievers was born on 16 October 1921 and he was a son of John and Ellen Campbell Ievers (nee Adair). John Ievers (from County Wexford) served during the First World War and in civilian life he worked as a gardener. It was when he was working for Lord Dunleath in Ballywalter Park that he met Ellen Adair. John Ievers and Ellen Adair were married in Ballywalter

Parish Church of Ireland Church on 10 July 1920 and they had seven children – Robert Valentine (Bob); George; Ella (Anne); Sheila; Edwin John (died of diphtheria on 23 April 1933 aged 4); Thomas (Tom) and Walter. Robert Valentine Ievers was baptised in Ballywalter Parish Church. The family moved from Ballywalter to Belfast when John Ievers was appointed Head Gardener at Forster Green Hospital.

During the Second World War Robert Valentine (Bob) Ievers served with the Royal Air Force Volunteer Reserve in Fighter Command and on 30 November 1942 he was one of a three man crew aboard a Douglas Boston Mark III aircraft (Z2165) that took off from RAF Bradwell Bay in Essex on a Nickel (leaflet dropping) operation and crashed in Belgium. Their bodies were never recovered and the other two crew members who died that day were:

- Warrant Officer Class II Merton Ralph Lockwood aged 21 (RCAF)
- Warrant Officer Class II John Joseph Graham Chabot aged 25 (RCAF)

When Bob Ievers was initially reported as missing in action his girlfriend Eileen, who was serving in the WAAF, came to Belfast to visit Bob's parents. Sergeant Robert Valentine Ievers is commemorated on the Runnymede Memorial in Surrey and on the RAF Bradwell Bay Memorial which was 'erected in memory of the 121 members of the Allied Air Forces who, in answer to the call of duty, left this airfield to fly into the blue forever'. He is also commemorated on a headstone in Whitechurch Cemetery, Ballywalter. There are two headstones on the grave, one commemorating members of the Adair family and the other commemorating members of the Ievers family. Commemorated on the Adair headstone is Lance Corporal John Adair who died of wounds on 14 November 1916 and is commemorated on Page 84 in the Book of Honour *Remembering Their Sacrifice in the Great War – Ards* compiled by Barry Niblock. John Adair was a brother of Ellen Campbell Ievers. The Ievers headstone bears the following inscriptions:

In loving memory of Edwin John
Beloved son of John and Ellen Ievers, died 23 April 1933 aged 4 years
Also the above Ellen Campbell Ievers, died 17 April 1972

Also their eldest son Robert Valentine, Sergeant Observer RAF
Missing on operations 30 November 1942 aged 21 years
2 Samuel 12. 23

This Biblical verse reads:

But now he is dead, wherefore should I fast? Can I bring him back again?
I shall go to him, but he shall not return to me. (King James Version)

Ireland, Sydney

Sergeant
No. 745103, 610 Squadron, Royal Air Force Volunteer Reserve
Killed in a aircraft accident on Friday 12 July 1940 (aged 22)
Knockbreda Cemetery, Co. Down (Section E Grave 78)

Sydney Ireland was born on 28 May 1918 and he was a son of Robert and Sarah (Sadie) Ireland (nee Smyth) of 17 Prince Edward Park, Stranmillis, Belfast and then 2 Castle Hill, Ballywalter. Robert Ireland worked as a tailor and he and Sarah Smyth were married on 12 July 1906 in St. Anne's Church of Ireland Cathedral, Belfast. They had at least three children – Dorothy (Doris, born 25 April 1907); Henry (born 7 May 1911) and Sydney (born 28 May 1918). Sydney Ireland attended Royal Belfast Academical Institution (RBAI) from 1930 until 1936 and he was a member of the RBAI Scout Troop which camped regularly at Baronscourt in County Tyrone in the 1930s.

Sydney Ireland joined the Royal Air Force Volunteer Reserve in 1938 and began his training in de Havilland Tiger Moth aircraft at 24 Elementary & Reserve Flying Training School, Sydenham. He was an accomplished guitar player and in November 1939 when he was going to England for further training, Sydney Ireland and 26 other trainees inscribed their names on a guitar that they purchased to take with them on the journey. In addition to Sydney Ireland, nine others who inscribed their names died in the Second World War. These included Pilot Officer **Thomas Andrew McCann**, Sergeant **Herbert Reginald Megarry** and Sergeant **Victor Hall Skillen**.

Sergeant Sydney Ireland's death was reported in the 20 July 1940 edition of the *Newtownards Chronicle* under the headline *Ballywalter People Bereaved*: 'The parents of Pilot-Sergeant Sydney Ireland, RAF, of Castle Hill, Ballywalter have been officially notified that he has been killed in a flying accident. Pilot-Sergeant Ireland was an old Instonian who had played scrum half for the

BALLYWALTER PEOPLE BEREAVED.

The parents of Pilot-Sergeant Sydney Ireland, R.A.F., of Castle Hill, Bally-walter, have been officially notified that he has been killed in a flying accident. Pilot-Sergeant Ireland was an old Instonian who had played scrum half for the first XV.

He had been successively on the staffs of the Belfast Steamship Company and Victor Robb, Ltd., motor dealers, before he joined the Royal Air Force a year ago. He was a noted athlete and swimmer and took a leading part in the Instonian Dramatic Society.

1st XV. He had been successively on the staffs of the Belfast Steamship Company and Victor H. Robb and Company, Automobile and Electrical Engineers, before he joined the Royal Air Force a year ago. He was a noted athlete and swimmer and took a leading part in the Instonian Dramatic Society'.

Sergeant Sydney Ireland was based at RAF Biggin Hill and on the morning of 12 July 1940 he died while taking part in a dog fight practice when his Supermarine Spitfire aircraft (P9502) crashed at Titsey Park in Surrey. He was 22 years old when he was killed – on his parents' 34th wedding anniversary. His remains were brought home for burial and he is commemorated in St. George's RAF Memorial Chapel, Biggin Hill; in RBAI; in Baronscourt Parish Church of Ireland Church and on the family grave headstone in Knockbreda Cemetery:

Ireland
In memory of our loved son Sydney
Pilot RAF Killed 12 July 1940
Also his dear father Robert Ireland died 19 November 1959
And his dear mother Sarah died 7 May 1960

His father Robert was 78 years old when he died and his mother Sadie was 76.

On Sunday 2 September 2011 a commemorative church service was held in Baronscourt Parish Church to dedicate a plaque to the memory of the eighteen scouts from 74th Belfast (RBAI) Scout Group who lost their lives in the Second World War, many of whom had camped on the Baronscourt Estate in the years immediately prior to the outbreak of hostilities. The plaque commemorated the 70th anniversary of the first building of a memorial cairn by RBAI scouts on the nearby hill known as Bessy Bell. In addition to Sergeant Sydney Ireland, the plaque also bears the names of Warrant Officer **Samuel Nicholl Beckett**, Captain **Samuel David Corry** and Bombardier **Francis Eric Sheals**.

Irvine, Annie
Leading Aircraftwoman
No. 2165476, Women's Auxiliary Air Force
Died of illness on Monday 24 December 1945 (aged 33)
Newtownards (Movilla) Cemetery, Co. Down (Section 2 Grave 120)

Annie Irvine was born on 25 March 1912 and she was the only daughter of

Alfred Norwood Irvine and Gertrude Helen Irvine (nee McClean) of 162 Ravenhill Avenue, Belfast and previously, Newtownards. Alfred Irvine was a factory engineer and he and Gertrude Helen McClean were married on 28 June 1911 in Dundela Presbyterian Church, Belfast. Annie and her brother Ernest Norwood Irvine (born 28 April 1913) were baptised in May Street Presbyterian Church, Belfast. Their brother Harold Nelson Irvine (born 11 October 1915) was baptised in First Newtownards Presbyterian Church.

> Deep regret was felt in New-townards at the news of the death of Miss Annie Irvine, only daughter of Mr. and Mrs. Alfred Irvine, 162 Ravenhill Avenue, Belfast, and formerly of Newtownards, which took place in a R.A.F. hospital

During the Second World War Annie Irvine served with the Women's Auxiliary Air Force (WAAF) and she was attached to the medical staff in Wroughton Royal Air Force Hospital near Swindon in Wiltshire. In November 1945 she became seriously ill and relatives were called to her bedside. She began to recover but suffered a relapse before Christmas and died on Christmas Eve 1945 in Wroughton RAF Hospital. She was 33 years old. Her remains were brought to her parents' home and at her funeral the service in the house was conducted by the Revd Dr Wylie Blue. It was reported that her father Alfred, her uncles Samuel Irvine, Arwood Irvine and Charles McClean were amongst the mourners. Leading Aircraftwoman Annie Irvine was buried in Newtownards (Movilla) Cemetery and there is an inscription on her CWGC headstone:

In devoted service to the wounded she gave her life

Irwin Brothers, John Cecil Brandon and William Thomas

John Cecil Brandon Irwin and William Thomas Irwin were sons of George and Lucinda Ann Irwin (nee Brandon) of Kathleen Place, Craigavad. They were married on 6 August 1918 in Hamilton Road Presbyterian Church, Bangor. George Irwin died on 8 May 1950 (aged 64) and Lucinda Ann Irwin died on 16 July 1975 (aged 84). Both were buried in Holywood Cemetery.

Irwin, John Cecil Brandon (Cecil)
Sergeant (Pilot)
No. 951459, 57 Squadron, Royal Air Force Volunteer Reserve
Killed in an aircraft accident on Friday 4 July 1941 (aged 21)
Holywood Cemetery, Co. Down (Grave 1213)

John Cecil Brandon Irwin was born on 13 October 1919 and he attended Sullivan Upper School, Holywood from 1932 until 1938. After leaving school he worked for the Northern Banking Company (now Danske Bank). He joined the Royal Air Force Volunteer Reserve, he served with Bomber Command and he died on 4 July 1941. Sergeant Cecil Brandon Irwin was one of a six man crew aboard a Vickers Wellington Mark IC aircraft (R1589) that took off from RAF Feltwell in Norfolk around midnight on 3 July 1941 on a mission to bomb Essen in Germany. At eight minutes past midnight the aircraft crashed at Larman's Fen off Southery Road, Feltwell and the cause was attributed to instrument failure. Sergeant Poulton was the only survivor and the other four crew members who died that night were:

- Sgt William Joseph Harry Hoskins aged 22 from Paddington, London
- FS Evan David Evans aged 30 from Erdington, Birmingham
- Sergeant Robert Simeon Sparkes
- Sergeant Philip Herbert Reay aged 21 from Monkseaton, Tyneside

Southery Road remained closed for several days after the crash while unexploded bombs were removed from the wreckage.

Irwin, William Thomas (William)
Flight Lieutenant
No. 127920, 51 Squadron, Royal Air Force Volunteer Reserve
Killed on active service on Sunday 3 October 1943 (aged 22)
Rheinberg War Cemetery, Kamp Lintford, Nordrhein-Westfal, Germany (Grave 3 K 9)

William Thomas Irwin was born on 1 September 1921 and he attended Glencraig Public Elementary School and then Sullivan Upper School, Holywood from 1934 until 1937. William worked in Messrs Short and Harland before he joined the Royal Air Force Volunteer Reserve and he was 22 years old when he died on 3 October 1943. He was one of an eight man crew aboard a Handley Page Halifax Mark II aircraft (HR728) that took off at 6.10 pm from RAF

Snaith in Yorkshire on a mission to bomb Kassel in Germany. Their aircraft crashed near the German town of Petershagen, all aboard were killed and they were buried in Rheinberg War Cemetery. The other seven crew members who died that night were:

- Flt Lt James Alfred Grundy aged 31 from Oxenholme, Westmorland
- Pilot Officer William Joshua Watson
- FO James Jeremiah Dawkins aged 21 from Cupernham, Hampshire
- FO Reginald Thomas Watkinson aged 20 from Wallasey, Cheshire
- Warrant Officer Stanley Woolhouse aged 25 from Walkley, Sheffield
- Sergeant John Dixon from West Ealing, Middlesex
- Sergeant James Frederick Gordon aged 19 from Chryston, Lanarkshire

Both Sergeant (Pilot) John Cecil Brandon Irwin and Flight Lieutenant William Thomas Irwin are commemorated on Holywood and District War Memorial; in Glencraig Parish Church of Ireland Church (as C. Irwin and W. Irwin); on the family grave headstone in Holywood Cemetery and in Sullivan Upper School. Sergeant (Pilot) John Cecil Brandon Irwin is also commemorated on the Northern Banking Company Second World War Memorial Plaque (now in Danske Bank, Donegall Square West, Belfast).

I

Irwin, Robert George Wylie (Roy)
First Radio Officer
SS *Carlton* (Newcastle-on-Tyne), Merchant Navy
Died as a result of enemy action on Friday 20 December 1940 (aged 23)
Tower Hill Memorial, London, England (Panel 23)

Robert George Wylie (Roy) Irwin was born on 19 November 1917 and he was a son of John and Margaret Helena Irwin (nee Holmes) of Cavehill Drive, Belfast then 29 Victoria Gardens, Belfast and later 8 Brooklyn Avenue, Bangor. John Irwin worked as a commercial traveller in the meal and flour trade and he and Margaret Helena Irwin were married on 18 November 1903 in Clonfeacle (St. Patrick's) Church of Ireland Church, Benburb, Co. Tyrone. They had at least six children – William John Roland (born 7 July 1905); Margaret Helen (born 25 October 1908); Lilian H.C. (born 1912); Letitia Doreen (born 7 April 1913); Robert George Wylie (born 19 November 1917); Desmond Millar (born 1919) and Joseph (born 1919).

Roy Irwin was educated at Skegoniell Public Elementary School, Belfast and Royal Belfast Academical Institution from 1930 until 1935. He was a member of the Boy's Brigade and he went to sea in 1937. During the Second World War Roy served with the Merchant Navy aboard the SS *Carlton* and his brother Joseph served with the Royal Air Force. Roy Irwin was home on leave in November 1940 and he died a month later on 20 December 1940. It was the Marconi Radio Company that informed Roy's family of his death.

Memorial Service in Ballyholme Presbyterian Church.—Tribute to the memory of Mr. Robert G. W. (Roy) Irwin, an officer in the Merchant Navy, who made the supreme sacrifice, will be paid at a special service which is to be held on Sunday at 11.30 a.m. in Ballyholme Presbyterian Church (Ashley Drive). A memorial pulpit, presented by Mr. and Mrs. John Irwin, will also be dedicated. A consecration service will take place at 7 p.m. when the preacher will be the Very Rev. A. F. Moody, M.A., D.D. The special soloists are: morning, Mr. Albert Jackson; evening, Miss Kathleen Morrow.

Built in 1924 by Short Brothers Ltd., Pallion, Sunderland, the SS *Carlton* was owned by the Carlton Steamship Company, Newcastle-upon-Tyne. On 20 December 1940 when on route from Newport to Buenos Aires in Convoy OB-260 she was torpedoed and sunk in the Atlantic Ocean (west of Ireland) by the Italian submarine *Pietro Calvi*. The entire crew abandoned ship in two lifeboats but one capsized. The second lifeboat was found 18 days later with only four survivors. First Radio Officer Robert George Wylie (Roy) Irwin aged 23 was one of more than 30 men who died.

First Radio Officer Robert George Wylie (Roy) Irwin is commemorated on the Tower Hill Memorial in London; on Bangor and District War Memorial (as Irwin R.G.) and in Ballyholme Presbyterian Church, Bangor. On Sunday 27 July 1941 there were special services in Ballyholme Presbyterian Church when a memorial pulpit presented by his parents was dedicated. He is also commemorated in RBAI.

Irwin, William Duncan (Willie)
Sergeant
No. 4459560, 2nd Battalion, Royal Inniskilling Fusiliers
Died of illness on Thursday 16 March 1944 (aged 50)
Alexandria (Hadra) War Memorial Cemetery, Egypt (Grave 6 B 9)

William Duncan Irwin was born in Belfast on 25 June 1893 and he was the third son of William Henry and Annie Elizabeth Irwin (nee Mathers). They were married on 19 March 1883 in St. Anne's Church of Ireland Church, Belfast. The Irwin family lived at 17 Upper Frank Street, Belfast before moving to Bangor where they lived at 54 Victoria Road, 90 Seacliff Road and later at Brooklyn Villas, 124 Groomsport Road. William Henry and Annie Irwin had at least ten children including Robert Gordon (born 1 February 1885); Charles Wesley (born 31 January 1887); Florence (Florrie, born 20 December 1888); Mabel (born 20 April 1891); William Duncan (Willie, born 25 June 1893); John Stanley (born 5 April 1895); Caroline (Carrie, born 3 June 1897); Arthur P. (Artie, born 17 March 1901) and Norman (born 14 April 1905).

Willie Irwin's father worked as a tailor; he was known locally as Tailor Irwin and his customers remembered that he sat cross-legged on the floor as he worked. Willie Irwin's mother died on 17 February 1935 aged 73 and his father was 79 years old when he died on 7 February 1940. Both were buried in Bangor Cemetery. Originally from County Kildare, Willie Irwin's father had travelled extensively in India and the Far East and it was reported in the press that he was a pioneer member of Distillery Football Club.

It was reported in the 15 April 1944 edition of the *County Down Spectator* that Willie Irwin had served as a Lieutenant in the Royal Inniskilling Fusiliers during the First World War and that he had been Mentioned in Despatches. He was an Assistant Steward and his address was 43 Southwell Road, Bangor when he joined up as a Cadet (No. 2867) in the 4th Battalion Royal Inniskilling Fusiliers on 23 November 1912 in Belfast. He was demobilised in 1919 and after the war he spent some time working in business in the United States of America. On 4 September 1923 Willie Irwin (then living at 8 Queen's Parade, Bangor) and Ethel Maud Irwin (daughter of Samuel George Irwin, 116 Seacliff Road, Bangor) were married in Ballygilbert Presbyterian Church.

In 1935 Willie Irwin was the Head Waiter in Hotel Pickie, Mount Royal, Bangor. When he was leaving that job the hotel manager gave him a reference which included the sentence, 'His ability has always been of the highest standard and we can thoroughly recommend him to anyone requiring his services in any capacity of trust'. Prior to the outbreak of the Second World War, Willie Irwin worked as a Steward on the Union Castle Line in the Mediterranean. At the outbreak of war Willie rejoined his old Regiment and served as an instructor to a native regiment in East Africa.

During the Second World War Sergeant Willie Irwin served in the Middle East with the Royal Inniskilling Fusiliers and he died of spastic paraplegia in No. 64 General Hospital, Alexandria on 16 March 1944 after having been ill for some months. He was buried the following day with military honours and the Chaplain, Revd H.E.S. Newbold, wrote to Willie's mother and also to Willie's wife to express his condolences. He assured them that Willie had died at 6.30 pm 'in peace with God and man'. He said, 'I don't think he suffered terrible pain as the morphine deadened it'.

Willie's wife Ethel, who was a Corporal in the ATC, lived in High Street, Bangor and later in *Whitten House*, William Street, Portadown in County Armagh. It was reported in the press that Willie Irwin was survived by five brothers – Charles, Arthur, Norman, Stanley and Gordon – and three sisters – Florence Irwin, Mrs Mabel Naye in California and Mrs Carrie Burrowes in Bangor. Charles Irwin was a film actor in Hollywood, California and a well-known figure in American vaudeville. Arthur Irwin served with the US Army and Norman worked in the insurance business in California.

Sergeant William Duncan Irwin is commemorated on Bangor and District War Memorial; in Bangor Parish Church of Ireland Church (St. Comgall's) and on the family grave headstone in Bangor Cemetery.

James, Robert Keith (Keith)
Flying Officer (Navigator/Bomber)
No. 162485, Royal Air Force Volunteer Reserve
Died in service on Thursday 16 November 1944 (aged 21)
Nicosia War Cemetery, Cyprus (Grave 3 A 6)

Robert Keith James was born on 29 November 1922 in Stockton, Durham and he was a son of Robert and Edith Gertrude James (nee Forster). Robert James worked as a marine engineering draughtsman and their marriage was registered in the first quarter of 1921 in Stockton. The James family moved to Belfast and they lived at 7 Wingrove Gardens, Bloomfield and later at 7 Kilhorne Gardens, Knock.

Robert Keith James attended Norton Boys' School and then Regent House School, Newtownards from 1934 until 1940. After leaving school he went to Queen's University Belfast to study medicine. He joined the Royal Air Force Volunteer Reserve and he was 21 years old when he died on 16 November 1944 in Cyprus. His effects amounted to some £49 and probate was granted to his father.

Flying Officer Robert Keith James is commemorated in Regent House School; in Queen's University Belfast and on the Forster family grave headstone in the graveyard of St. Mary the Virgin Church, Norton, Durham. His maternal grandfather, William Forster, died on 7 March 1910 (aged 64) and his maternal grandmother, Martha Forster, died on 26 May 1934 (aged 79).

Jamfrey, James
Mentioned in Despatches
Petty Officer Stoker
No. C/K 17091, HMS *Curacoa*, Royal Navy
Died as a result of an accident at sea on Friday 2 October 1942 (aged 49)
Chatham Naval Memorial, Kent, England (Panel 61 1)

James Jamfrey was born in the townland of Coolnafranky, Cookstown, Co. Tyrone on 17 September 1893 and he was a son of Thomas Jeffers (later Jamfrey) from Omagh and Elizabeth Jamfrey (nee Cardwell) from Coalisland. They were married on 21 April 1887 in Brackaville Church of Ireland Church, Coalisland, Co. Tyrone. Before they moved to Cookstown, Thomas and Elizabeth Jeffers lived at 97 Victoria Street, Lurgan and they changed their surname from Jeffers to Jamfrey. Thomas Jamfrey worked as a railway porter and he and Elizabeth had eight children – William (born 10 April 1888); May (born 18 April 1890); James (born 17 September 1893); male child (born 26 March 1896); Sarah (born 9 April 1897); Ethel (born 11 September 1899); Margaret (born 14 August 1902) and Elizabeth (born 24 September 1907). James Jamfrey and his brother William also worked as railway porters. William retained the surname Jeffers.

During the First World War Private William Jeffers (S/2127) served with the 2nd Battalion, Seaforth Highlanders. He enlisted on 7 August 1914, he went to France on 17 January 1915 and he was wounded three times. He died on 2 November 1918 as a result of wounds received in action and he was buried in St. Souplet British Cemetery, France (Grave I C 29). Born on 10 April 1888 and educated in Derryloran School, Cookstown, William Jeffers was 30 years old when he died.

James Jamfrey joined the Royal Navy and he was in uniform when he and Winifred Mary Owen were married in Chatham, Kent. Their first child, Thomas Edward James (Eddie), was born in England in 1925. Twins William (Billy) and Winifred (Winnie) were born on 5 September 1932 after the family had moved to Lurgan in County Armagh. In 1936 James Jamfrey, his wife and their three children moved from Lurgan to Bangor and they lived at 53 Groomsport Road. Two more children were born in Bangor, James on 17 September 1937 (his father's 44th birthday) and Rosemary on 29 January 1939. James Jamfrey's five sisters, May, Sarah, Ethel, Margaret and Elizabeth – known locally as the Misses Jamfrey – lived at 17 Springfield Road, Bangor.

James Jamfrey left the Royal Navy after 23 years of service and he worked as a lorry driver in a quarry at Conlig. At the start of the Second World War he was called up from the Reserve and rejoined the Royal Navy. When his eldest son died in a road accident in Belfast, James was unable to get leave to attend the funeral. Thomas Edward James (Eddie) Jamfrey aged 15¾ was killed on 8 October 1940 after being struck by a lorry on Queen's Road, Belfast on route to the train station on his way home from work. Since June 1939 Eddie had been serving his time as a sheet metal worker at Messrs Short and Harland in Belfast. Eddie Jamfrey was a choirboy in Bangor Abbey and he was also a member of the Second (Parish) Scout Troop. Eddie Jamfrey was a King's Scout and he was given Scout Honours at his funeral from 17 Springfield Road to Bangor Cemetery. Eddie was buried in his scout uniform.

DIED ON ACTIVE SERVICE.

JAMFREY—October, 1942, Stoker Petty Officer James Jamfrey, R.N., beloved husband of Winifred Mary Jamfrey, 53 Groomsport Road, Bangor, and brother of the Misses Jamfrey, 17 Springfield Road, Bangor—formerly reported missing, now presumed dead.

When James Jamfrey was lost at sea on 2 October 1942 he was serving as a Petty Officer Stoker aboard HMS *Curacoa*. Built as a Ceres Class light cruiser in 1918 by the Pembroke Dockyard in Wales and Harland and Wolff in Belfast, HMS *Curacoa* was rearmed as an anti-aircraft cruiser at the beginning of the Second World War. Initially reported as missing in action, James Jamfrey's body was never recovered and two weeks later, in November 1942, he was officially presumed dead. At the time, HMS *Curacoa* was escorting the ocean liner RMS *Queen Mary*, with more than 10,000 American troops on board, in a convoy from USA to Europe. Both ships were following evasive zigzagging courses about 60 kilometres north of the coast of Donegal when HMS *Curacoa* was struck amidships and cut in half by RMS *Queen Mary*. HMS *Curacoa* sank immediately and, because of the risk of U-Boat attack, RMS *Queen Mary* steamed on. Some time later, the Convoy's lead escort ship returned to the scene and less than 100 men from HMS *Curacoa* were rescued. More than 300 men died. The circumstances of the loss were not reported until after the war ended and a protracted case for compensation ended in 1949 with a final appeal to the House of Lords. Two-thirds of the blame for the loss was attributed to the Admiralty and one-third to Cunard White Star Line.

Petty Officer Stoker James Jamfrey had been Mentioned in Despatches in January 1942 and, after his death some ten months later in October 1942, the Admiralty paid tribute to his outstanding service in a letter to his widow Winifred. James Jamfrey was 49 years old when he died and he is commemorated on Bangor and District War Memorial and in Bangor Parish Church of Ireland Church (St. Comgall's).

Jefferson family, John Frazer and Thomas Francis (father and son)

John Frazer Jefferson was born on 19 October 1896 and he was a son of Jonathan and Agnes Jefferson (nee Frazer) of 45 High Street, Holywood. They were married on 12 December 1885 in the Mariner's Church of Ireland Church, Belfast. Jonathan Jefferson was a spirit merchant and he and Agnes had four children – Sarah (born 12 June 1887, died 14 April 1888); Jonathan (born 12 September 1891); Richard Sinclair (born 19 October 1893) and John Frazer (born 19 October 1896). The last three children were baptised in Holywood Parish Church of Ireland Church (St. Philip and St. James). Agnes Jefferson was 42 years old when she died on 3 October 1901 and Jonathan married Mary Jane Frazer on 24 March 1903 in Ballysillan Presbyterian Church, Belfast. They had at least two children, both of whom were baptised in Holywood Parish Church – Albert Edward (born 2 March 1905, died in infancy) and Albert Edward (born 16 July 1909). Jonathan Jefferson was 79 years old when he died on 29 October 1933.

John Frazer Jefferson and Margaret Anne Rea Valentine Cowan of 19 High Street, Holywood were married on 29 July 1918 in First Holywood Presbyterian Church. John Frazer Jefferson was a mercantile officer and they lived at 2 Walmer Terrace, Holywood. They had at least two children both of whom were baptised in First Holywood Presbyterian Church – Kenneth Frazer (born 15 August 1919) and Thomas Francis (born 17 October 1920).

Thomas Francis Jefferson was a son of John Frazer Jefferson and Margaret Anne Rea Valentine Jefferson and he was a grandson of Francis J. and Eleanor Jane Cowan of Holywood.

Jefferson, John Frazer
Master
SS *Cadillac* (Newcastle-on-Tyne), Merchant Navy
Died as a result of enemy action on Saturday 1 March 1941 (aged 44)
Tower Hill Memorial, London, England (Panel 22)

During the Second World War John Frazer Jefferson served with the

REMEMBERING THEIR SACRIFICE

Merchant Navy aboard the British Steam Tanker SS *Cadillac*. Built in 1917 by Palmer's Shipbuilding and Iron Company Ltd., Newcastle-upon-Tyne she was owned by the Anglo-American Oil Company Ltd., London. Around midnight on 1 March 1941, in Convoy HX-109, the SS *Cadillac* was on route from Aruba, Lesser Antilles in the Caribbean Sea to Avonmouth, Bristol carrying a cargo of some 17,000 tons of aviation fuel when she was torpedoed and sunk by the German submarine *U-552* about 170 miles northwest of the Outer Hebrides. Captain John Frazer Jefferson and Ordinary Seaman **Robert Joseph Shaw** from Portaferry were among more than 30 men who died.

Captain John Frazer Jefferson is commemorated on the Tower Hill Memorial in London; on Holywood and District War Memorial; in First Holywood Presbyterian Church and on the Cowan family grave headstone in Holywood Cemetery. Two years and eight months later, John Frazer Jefferson's son, Warrant Officer **Thomas Francis Jefferson** serving with the RAFVR died in an aircraft accident.

Jefferson, Thomas Francis

Warrant Officer (Pilot)
No. 1062362, Royal Air Force Volunteer Reserve
Killed in an aircraft accident on Friday 5 November 1943 (aged 23)
Holywood Cemetery, Co. Down (Grave 561)

Thomas Francis Jefferson attended Sullivan Upper School, Holywood from 1929 until 1936 and then Portora Royal School, Enniskillen. He was a member of 2nd Holywood Boy Scouts and at school he was a member of the Dramatic Society and a keen cricketer and rugby player. He joined the RAF in 1940 and completed his training in Canada. When he was stationed in Northern Ireland he was a member of Holywood Cricket Club and he captained the 2nd XI. He was engaged to be married in December 1943 to Miss Maxine Warner-Watts of London who was serving in the WAAF.

Warrant Officer Thomas Francis Jefferson was 23 years old and unmarried when he died on 5 November 1943. He was the pilot aboard a Miles Martinet aircraft (MS583) from No. 1617 Flight based at Newtownards which was target-towing off St. John's Point, Co. Down when it crashed into the sea just offshore from Ardglass. His body was subsequently recovered and he was buried in Holywood Cemetery on 8 November 1943. He is commemorated on Holywood and District War Memorial; in First Holywood Presbyterian Church and in Sullivan Upper School.

Johnston, Douglas Holden
Warrant Officer Class II (Company Sergeant Major)
No. 6458965, 2ⁿᵈ Battalion, Royal Fusiliers (City of London Regiment)
Died as a result of an accident on Friday 22 December 1939 (aged 24)
Croix Communal Cemetery, Nord, France (Row 16 Grave 5)

Douglas Holden Johnston was born on 22 May 1915 and he was a son of Henry Steer Johnston and Elizabeth Adelaide Johnston (nee Douglas) of 1 Moira Drive, Bangor. Before that the Johnston family lived in Belfast at *Sharrow*, Kensington Gardens, Knock and *Holmwood*, Eastleigh Drive, Ballyhackamore. Henry Steer Johnston was a chartered accountant and he and Elizabeth Douglas were married on 16 July 1912 in St. Mark's Church of Ireland Church, Dundela. Henry Steer Johnston drowned in the River Lagan on 8 September 1937; Elizabeth Adelaide Johnston died on 19 May 1957 (aged 85) and she was buried in Grave Z 97 in the City Cemetery (Glenalina Extension) alongside Commander Montague Gillot Douglas RD, RNR, HMS *Conway* who died on 30 April 1946 (aged 68).

Douglas Holden Johnston was educated at Campbell College, Belfast from 1929 until 1932 and after leaving school he joined the Army. During the Second World War he served with the Royal Fusiliers (City of London Regiment) and he died in France on 22 December 1939. His effects amounted to some £175, his shore address was 7 Wellington Terrace, Folkestone in Kent and probate was granted to his mother. A short tribute was published in the March 1940 edition of *The Campbellian*:

'It is with feelings of deep regret that we announce the death of Douglas Holden Johnston (late 2ⁿᵈ Battalion Royal Fusiliers), Warrant Officer (CSM), Field Security Police, which took place as a result of an accident somewhere in France on Thursday 22 December. After leaving Campbell, he followed for some years the course of training for a Chartered Accountant. Early in 1936 he joined the Regular Army where, from all accounts, his cheerful disposition coupled with a determination to succeed won him a wide circle of friends. Having attained the rank of Corporal he was transferred from the Royal Fusiliers to the Field Security Police with the status of CSM which, for a soldier of only 3½ years' experience was a remarkable achievement, all the more so when one considers the responsibilities attached to this branch of the Service. To his mother and uncle, William Alfred Bathurst Douglas, we offer sincerest sympathy'.

Warrant Officer Class II (CSM) Douglas Holden Johnston was 24 years old when he died and he is commemorated in Campbell College.

Johnston, Harold
Bombardier
**No. 1477283, 5 Battery, 2 Light Anti-Aircraft Regiment, Royal Artillery
Died as a result of an accident on Wednesday 10 June 1942 (aged 27)
Tobruk War Cemetery, Libya (Grave 2 E 13)**

Harold Johnston's birth was registered in the fourth quarter of 1914 in Newtownards and he was the eldest son of Samuel and Elizabeth Johnston of *Cairn View Villa*, Ballybarnes Road, Killearn, Newtownards. Their daughter Rebecca's birth was registered in third quarter of 1917 in Newtownards and Rebecca's marriage to Joseph Kelly was registered in fourth quarter of 1944 in Oldbury, Worcestershire. Joseph and Rebecca (Ruby) Kelly lived in Birmingham before moving to Bennykerry in County Carlow.

Harold Johnston (aged 22) and Mary Robina Flynn (aged 21, daughter of Edward Flynn) both from Marquis Street, Newtownards were married on 24 August 1934 in Newtownards Registry Office. They had a daughter, Mary Elizabeth, and they lived at 15 Belfast Road, Bangor. Harold's brother William (Billy) Johnston was a Sergeant in the Irish Guards.

KILLED ON ACTIVE SERVICE.
JOHNSTON—Killed in Action, Harold, eldest son of Samuel and Elizabeth Johnston, Killearn, Newtownards. Deeply regretted by his sorrowing Wife and little daughter.
ROBINA JOHNSTON.
15, Belfast Road, Bangor.

JOHNSTON—Killed in Action, Harold Johnston, aged 27 years, dearly-loved son of Mr. and Mrs. Samuel Johnston, Ballybarnes Road, Newtownards. Deeply regretted by his sorrowing Father, Mother, Brothers and Sisters; also his Brother, Sergeant W. Johnston, Irish Guards.

Harold Johnston's death in No. 62 General Hospital, Middle East as the result of an accidental gunshot wound was reported in the 27 June 1942 edition of the *Newtownards Chronicle*. He died as a result of a misfire caused by a defective round in his own weapon. On Thursday 18 June (eight days after Harold died) his wife received 'a cheerful letter' from him and the following Monday she received a telegram announcing his death. Ten days after Harold Johnston died, his brother-in-law, Lance Bombardier **Edward James Flynn** of 15 Belfast Road, Bangor was killed in action at Tobruk.

Various members of Harold Johnston's family placed *Killed in Action* notices in the local press in 1942 and *Our Heroes – In Memoriam* notices in subsequent years. Specifically mentioned by name were his wife and daughter, his parents, his sister Ruby and his brother and sister-in-law Billy and Ena Johnston of 180 Greenwell Street, Newtownards and later 65 Brunswick Road, Bangor. In one of these notices there was a verse:

If we could only see the grave where you are laid to rest
But God some day will join your hands with those who loved you best

Bombardier Harold Johnston was 27 years old when he died and he is commemorated on Newtownards and District War Memorial.

Johnston, John*
Ordinary Seaman
No. D/JX 619483, Royal Navy
Died of illness on Thursday 26 June 1947 (aged 20)
Newtownards (Movilla) Cemetery, Co. Down (Section 13 Grave 123)

J

John Johnston was a son of James and Mary Jane Johnston, of 14 Pound Street, Newtownards. Ordinary Seaman John Johnston served with the Royal Navy and he was 20 years old when he died of tuberculosis on 26 June 1947. He was buried in Movilla Cemetery and there is an inscription on his CWGC headstone:

At the going down of the sun and in the morning we will remember

Ordinary Seaman John Johnston is commemorated on Newtownards and District War Memorial.

Johnston, William (Curly)
Rifleman
No. 7018189, 1st (Airborne) Battalion, Royal Ulster Rifles
Killed in action on Monday 19 June 1944 (aged 22)
Ranville War Cemetery, Calvados, France (Grave VA Q 2)

William Johnston's parents lived in Scotch Street, Downpatrick and his wife, Jane D. (Joye) Johnston (nee McGahey) lived with her parents, Mr and Mrs

John McGaghey, at 12 Circular Street, Newtownards. William Johnston and Jane (Joye) McGaghey were married in February 1944 and William was home on leave in May 1944, about a month before he was killed.

Before he enlisted William Johnston worked for Thornton Printers, Cregagh Road, Belfast. His father served with the RAF in England and one of his brothers served with the RAF in North Africa. William Johnston enlisted in 1940, he served with the Royal Ulster Rifles and he was killed in action on 19 June 1944 in Normandy. Initially he was reported as missing in action and then in October 1944 it was officially confirmed that he had been killed. His wife, his parents-in-law and the McBratney family of 69 South Street, Newtownards placed *Killed in Action* notices in the 7 October 1944 edition of the *Newtownards Chronicle* and they contained the texts:

On his soul Sweet Jesus have mercy

Immaculate Heart of Mary pray for him

Rifleman William Johnston was 22 years old when he died and he is commemorated on Downpatrick and District War Memorial.

Jones, Ernest Alfred Raymond Llewellyn (Bubbles)
Aircraftman 2nd Class
No. 654469, 77 Squadron, Royal Air Force
Killed in an aerodrome accident on Sunday 14 April 1940 (aged 19)
Beeston and Stapleford (Chilwell) Cemetery, Nottinghamshire, England (Section A 4 C Grave 10)

Ernest Alfred Raymond Llewellyn (Bubbles) Jones was born on 3 August 1920 and he was a son of Ernest Alfred and Catherine Jones (nee McGarrigle) who lived at 96 Spencer Road, Londonderry. Ernest Alfred Jones Senior was

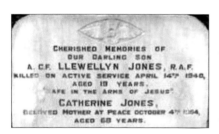

JONES — Ernest Alfred Raymond Llewellyn Jones ("Bubbles"), Aircraftsman, R.A.F., Bearley, dearly-beloved son of Mr. and Mrs. E. A. Jones, late Bingham Street, Bangor, killed in an accident at Aerodrome. Interred at Chilwell Cemetery, Nottingham.

Thy will be done

a soldier when he and Catherine McGarrigle were married on 28 September 1917 in First Londonderry Presbyterian Church. In civilian life after the First World War, Ernest Alfred Jones worked as a painter and decorator and when the Jones family moved to Bangor they lived in Bingham Street. Ernest Alfred Raymond Llewellyn (Bubbles) Jones had two sisters whose names were Thelma and Joy.

From Bangor the Jones family moved to Chilwell in Nottinghamshire and each year after Bubbles's death they placed an *In Memoriam* notice in the *County Down Spectator*. The 1944 notice contained the verse:

We shed many a tear in silence, we breathe many a sigh of regret,
For he is still ours to remember, though the rest of the world forget

J

Aircraftman 2nd Class Ernest Alfred Raymond Llewellyn (Bubbles) Jones was stationed at RAF Snitterfield in Warwickshire when he died in an aerodrome accident on 14 April 1940. His death was registered in Buckrose, Yorkshire and he was buried in Beeston and Stapleford (Chilwell) Cemetery, Nottinghamshire. His mother Catherine died on 4 October 1964 (aged 68) and she was buried in the same grave as her son.

Jones, Spencer
Fusilier
No. 6981965, 2nd Battalion, Royal Inniskilling Fusiliers
Killed in action on Monday 9 October 1944 (aged 31)
Cassino Memorial, Italy (Panel 6)

Spencer Jones was born in 1913 in Glamorganshire, Wales. He was a son of Daniel Jones and for a time he lived in Nottingham. Spencer Jones joined the Royal Inniskilling Fusiliers and it was while Fusilier Jones was stationed in Northern Ireland that he met Emily Gorman of 49 Beatrice Road, Bangor. Emily was a daughter of Alexander and Hannah Gorman and she and Spencer Jones were married on 17 July 1942 in Helen's Bay Presbyterian Church.

ROLL OF HONOUR

JONES—In loving memory of my dearly-beloved husband, Spencer (Royal Inniskilling Fusiliers), killed in action in Italy, October 9, 1944. "He died that we might live." Sadly missed by his loving Wife, Emily Jones — 49 Beatrice Road, Bangor.

Fusilier Spencer Jones was killed in action at Cassino on 9 October 1944 during the Allied advance in Italy and the Revd William George Wimperis, Minister in Trinity Presbyterian Church Bangor, paid tribute to him. The Revd Wimperis described him as 'a bright, devoted and decent young man' who had fought in Tunisia, Sicily and Italy. He had survived a scorpion bite and previously been wounded before being killed in action. The Revd Wimperis referred to a letter written by Fusilier Spencer Jones in which Spencer made reference to Trinity Presbyterian Church Bangor and said that 'by marriage he had become one of its boys'. His wife included the following verse in an *In Memoriam* notice:

His toil is past, his work is done and he is fully blest
He fought the fight, the victory won and entered into rest

Fusilier Spencer Jones was 31 years old when he died and he is commemorated on the Cassino Memorial in Italy.

Keenan, James
Lance Corporal
No. 7012717, Royal Ulster Rifles and No. 4 Commando
Died of wounds on Wednesday 19 August 1942 (aged 24)
Troon Cemetery, Ayrshire, Scotland (Section J 1 Grave 113)

James Keenan's birth was registered in the second quarter of 1918 in Newtownards and he was the second son of James and Annie Keenan (nee McCready) who lived in Greyabbey and later at 24 Corry Street, Newtownards. James Keenan Senior worked as a farm servant and he and Annie McCready were married on 25 June 1909 in Greyabbey Presbyterian Church. They had at least three children – Sarah Jane (born 6 June 1910); Robert (born 13 September 1912) and James (born 1918). During the Great War James Keenan Senior served with the 13th Battalion, Royal Irish Rifles and was wounded in France. At the outbreak of the Second World War he volunteered again for service but was turned down because of his age.

James Keenan Junior joined the Royal Ulster Rifles in 1933 and he volunteered for service in a Commando Battalion. He and Jeanie Jess Barry of Troon in Scotland were married in Troon in April 1942, some four months before James died. In July 1942 James and Jess Keenan spent some time in Newtownards during his last spell of leave. James's sister Sarah married Arthur Eccles on 28 March 1936 in Newtownards Parish Church of Ireland Church (St. Mark's).

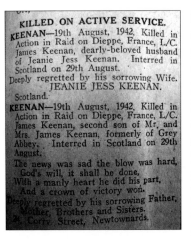

KILLED ON ACTIVE SERVICE.
KEENAN—19th August, 1942, Killed in Action in Raid on Dieppe, France, L/C. James Keenan, dearly-beloved husband of Jeanie Jess Keenan. Interred in Scotland on 29th August.
Deeply regretted by his sorrowing Wife.
JEANIE JESS KEENAN, Scotland.

KEENAN—19th August, 1942, Killed in Action in Raid on Dieppe, France, L/C. James Keenan, second son of Mr. and Mrs. James Keenan, formerly of Grey Abbey. Interred in Scotland on 29th August.
The news was sad the blow was hard, God's will, it shall be done, With a manly heart he did his part, And a crown of victory won.
Deeply regretted by his sorrowing Father, Mother, Brothers and Sisters.
Corry Street, Newtownards.

Lance Corporal James Keenan died of wounds on 19 August 1942 following the raid on Dieppe in France by British, Canadian, American and French forces. Having suffered serious injuries he was found unconscious on the battlefield and conveyed to one of the ships waiting off-shore to bring the raiders back to England. He died on board and his body was taken to Scotland for interment. His parents, James and Annie Keenan, travelled over from Newtownards for the funeral on 29 August 1942.

K

In a letter to Lance Corporal James Keenan's wife, Lieutenant Colonel the Lord Lovat MC wrote, 'I wish to take this opportunity of expressing my deepest sympathy in your bereavement. Your husband behaved magnificently and was a credit to his Commando and his Country. There is little one can say on these occasions, but perhaps it will be of comfort to know that he died in the hour of victory. No man could have done more'.

7012717 L. CPL
J. KEENAN
THE ROYAL ULSTER RIFLES
NO. 4 COMMANDO
19TH AUGUST 1942 AGE 23

Lance Corporal James Keenan's wife and parents placed separate *Killed on Active Service* notices in the 5 September 1942 edition of the *Newtownards Chronicle* and the one from his parents, brothers and sisters contained the verse:

The news was sad, the blow was hard,
God's will, it shall be done,
With a manly heart he did his part,
And a crown of victory won

Lance Corporal James Keenan is commemorated on Newtownards and District War Memorial and in Newtownards Parish Church (St. Mark's). There is an inscription on his CWGC headstone:

To be with us in the same old way would be our dear wish today

Kelly, Angus Campbell (Angus)
Flight Sergeant
No. R/79518, 416 Squadron, Royal Canadian Air Force
Died in service on Wednesday 29 July 1942 (aged 27)
Runnymede Memorial, Surrey, England (Panel 104)

Angus Campbell Kelly was born in 1914 in Canada and he was a son of Hugh Tennant Kelly and Elizabeth Allen (Lily) Kelly (nee Johnston) of Moose Jaw, Saskatchewan. Hugh Tennant Kelly was a teacher and he and Elizabeth Allen Johnston (both of whom were born in County Down) were married on 16 July 1901 in First Ballywalter Presbyterian Church. They moved to Coalisland in County Tyrone where they had five children – John (born 20 April 1904); William (born 22 February 1906); Hugh Tennant (born 30 August 1908); Eileen Florence (born 4 December 1910) and one who died in infancy. In May 1913 they moved to Canada where Angus was born in 1914.

Readers of the " Chronicle " in the Kirkistown district will regret to learn of the death on active service of Flight Sergeant Angus Kelly, who, although born in Canada, was closely associated with the Ards. He was a son of Mr. Hugh Tennant Kelly, who is a brother of Mrs. Hannah Kelly, R.D.C., Kirkistown. His mother was formerly Miss Elizabeth Johnston, of Innishargie, and Miss Carson, of The Glen Farm, Grey Abbey, is his cousin.

During the Second World War Angus Kelly served with the Royal Canadian Air Force and he died on 29 July 1942. His death was reported in the 26 December 1942 edition of the *Newtownards Chronicle* under the headline *Young Airman's Death – His Associations With Ards District*. It was reported that Angus Kelly's father was a brother of Mrs Hannah Kelly of Kirkistown; his mother was from Innishargie, Kircubbin and his cousin, Miss Carson, lived at *Glen Farm*, Greyabbey. Before joining the Royal Canadian Air Force Angus Kelly was a traveller for the Imperial Tobacco Company. In the early part of 1942 Flight Sergeant Angus Campbell Kelly visited his friends in the Cloughey area and he was reported to be planning a further visit 'to see his numerous friends' in the area.

Flight Sergeant Angus Campbell Kelly was 27 years old when he died, his body was never recovered and he is commemorated on the Runymede Memorial in Surrey; on the Canadian Virtual War Memorial (Internet) and on Page 86 in the Canadian Second World War Book of Remembrance.

Kemp, Herbert Walter (Bert)
Mentioned in Despatches during First World War
Gunner
SS *Lady Hawkins* (Halifax), Royal Navy
Died as a result of enemy action on Monday 19 January 1942 (aged 55)
Chatham Naval Memorial, Kent, England (Panel 51, 2)

Herbert Walter Kemp was born on 27 January 1886 in East Dulwich, Camberwell, London and he was a son of Richard Edwin Kemp and Elizabeth Mary Kemp (nee Monshall). Both Richard Edwin Kemp and Elizabeth Mary Monshall (daughter of naval pensioner William Monshall) worked as GPO telegraph clerks and they were married on 15 April 1882 in the Church of St. Peter, Deptford. They lived at 10 Lind Street, Deptford and they had three children – Ernest William (born 22 February 1883); Florence Mary (born 10 February 1884) and Herbert Walter (born 27 January 1886). Elizabeth Mary Kemp was 32 years old when she died at the beginning of 1889 and all three of her children were baptised on 14 October 1891 in the Church of St. John, Deptford. At that time they were living in Deptford with their maternal grandmother, Maureen Monshall. The Kemp family moved to 12 Jerrard Street, Lewisham, London and Richard Edwin Kemp remarried – first to Anne Isabella Florey and later to Ada Louisa Goodchild.

Herbert Walter Kemp was 15 years old when he joined the Royal Navy in 1901. In 1911 he was serving aboard the Cressy-class armoured cruiser HMS *Bacchante*. He served as a Gunner during the First World War and on 13 September 1918 he was Mentioned in Despatches 'for services in action with enemy submarines'. He was demobilised in 1919 but remained on reserve.

Herbert Walter Kemp's marriage to Teresa Stewart was registered in the first quarter of 1922 in Dublin. Bert and Teresa Kemp family moved to Bangor where they lived at 47 Grove Park and they had three children – Betty, Ernie and Reginald. The Kemp children attended Sunday School in St. Columbanus Church Hall, Ballyholme; Ernie and Reginald were baptised in Bangor Parish Church of Ireland Church (St. Comgall's) on 29 November 1927 and 31 March 1935 respectively and Betty was confirmed in Bangor Parish Church in 1938 where she also sang in the choir.

Being on reserve, Bert Kemp was called up again immediately after the outbreak of the Second World War. He was sent initially to Scapa Flow and in 1941 he had a period of home leave in Bangor at Christmas. He was assigned to HMS *Malabar*, the Royal Naval Base in Bermuda, and when he was leaving home to go there at the end of his leave he said to his wife and

K

children that it might be some time before he saw them again. Gunner Bert Kemp was 55 years old when he was killed on passage to Bermuda.

Gunner Bert Kemp was killed on 19 January 1942 when the SS *Lady Hawkins* was torpedoed and sunk by the German submarine *U-66* between Cape Hatteras in North Carolina and Bermuda. At the time there were more than 320 passengers and crew aboard this ocean liner which was built in 1928 by Cammell Laird and Company Ltd., Birkenhead and owned by the Canadian National Steamships Company Ltd. One of the 'Lady Liners', she was on route from Halifax, Nova Scotia to Bermuda and sailing unescorted when she was hit around 1.50 am by two torpedoes. The ship keeled over and burned for 25 minutes before sinking. Three lifeboats were deployed but two were lost. With a capacity for 63 people, the remaining lifeboat had 76 aboard so some had to stand. Five people died and, five days after the sinking, the lifeboat was spotted by the SS *Coamo* and survivors were taken to Puerto Rica. *U-66* was sunk on 6 May 1944 by the USS *Buckley*.

Herbert Walter Kemp's effects amounted to some £883 and probate was granted to his widow Teresa. Teresa moved to 61 Meadowbank Place, Belfast, she was 66 years old when she died on 25 July 1959 and she was buried in Belfast City Cemetery (Glenalina Extension) Grave R1 64.

K

Gunner Herbert Walter Kemp is commemorated on the Chatham Naval Memorial in Kent and in Bangor Parish Church (St. Comgall's).

Kennedy, Hugh
Corporal
No. 7902429, North Irish Horse, Royal Armoured Corps
Died as a result of an accident on Monday 16 December 1940 (aged 31)
Bangor Cemetery, Co. Down (Section 5 W Grave 37)

Hugh Kennedy was born on 16 May 1909 and he was a son of John and Martha Kennedy (nee Dines). John Kennedy from Moneyreagh worked as an agricultural labourer, Martha Dines from Killyleagh was a millworker and they were married on 1 May 1908 in Second Killyleagh Presbyterian Church. Their daughter Mary was born on 15 July 1911. Prior to the outbreak of the First World War the Kennedy family lived at 4 Corporation South, Newtownards and during the war John Kennedy (No. 17/1773) served with the 8th Battalion, Royal Irish Rifles. He died on 2 August 1917 and he is commemorated on Page 313 in the Book of Honour *Remembering Their Sacrifice in the Great War – Ards* compiled by Barry Niblock. Two of Martha's brothers, Alexander and Thomas Dines, were also killed during the Great War and they are commemorated on Page 191 in the same Book of Honour.

Hugh Kennedy's widowed mother Martha married Alexander Thompson Bell on 27 October 1919 in Willowfield Parish Church of Ireland Church, Belfast and they lived at 65 Dam Road in the townland of Cottown, Donaghadee. Hugh's brother Thomas lived at Ballycullen, Newtownards and his sister, Mrs Morgan, lived in Newtownards. Hugh Kennedy and Margaret McDonald of Ballycrochan, Bangor were married on 11 March 1936 in Bangor Abbey and their two children were baptised in Ballygrainey Presbyterian Church – Thomas John (born 8 January 1938) and Margaret (born 14 July 1939). The Kennedy family lived at Ballycrochan, Bangor and, prior to the outbreak of the Second World War, Hugh Kennedy completed a period of service with the Royal Irish Fusiliers. Hugh Kennedy was a member of Schomberg's True Blues Loyal Orange Lodge 589, Groomsport and the Stevenson Memorial Royal Black Preceptory 209, Ballygrainey.

K

KENNEDY—16th December, 1940, at Coleraine Hospital (result of an accident), Corporal Hugh Kennedy, North Irish Horse. Interred Bangor New Cemetery on 19th inst. Deeply regretted by his Mother, Sisters, Brother and W. J. M'Clelland.

KENNEDY—16th December, 1940, at Coleraine Hospital (result of an accident), Corporal Hugh Kennedy, North Irish Horse. Interred Bangor New Cemetery on 19th inst. Will always be remembered by his sorrowing Aunt and Uncle. NELLIE and BERTIE O'LONE.

On the outbreak of war he joined up again in the North Irish Horse and served in Northern Ireland. Corporal Hugh Kennedy was 31 years old when he died in Coleraine Hospital after sustaining multiple injuries in a motoring accident and he was buried in Bangor Cemetery on 19 December 1940. There were two *Died on Active Service* notices in the 21 December 1940 edition of the *Newtownards Chronicle*, one from his mother, sisters, brother and W.J. McClelland and the other from his aunt and uncle, Nellie and Bertie O'Lone of 16 Ann Street, Newtownards. On his CWGC headstone there is the inscription:

Thy word is true, Thy will is just
To Thee we leave him Lord in trust

Corporal Hugh Kennedy is commemorated on Bangor and District War Memorial and in Ballygrainey Presbyterian Church.

Kennedy, John Joseph
Able Seaman
SS *Empire Attendant* (Glasgow), Merchant Navy
Died as a result of enemy action on Wednesday 15 July 1942 (aged 32)
Tower Hill Memorial, London, England (Panel 38)

John Joseph Kennedy was born on 26 November 1909 in the Midnight Mission, 29 Malone Place, Belfast and he was a son of Frances Kennedy who worked as a servant.

John Joseph Kennedy's marriage to Hannah Quigley was registered in the first quarter of 1942 in Belfast and they lived in Glen Cottages, Craigavad. During the Second World War John Joseph Kennedy served with the Merchant Navy aboard the SS *Empire Attendant*. This passenger cargo vessel was launched in December 1920 as *Magnava* and completed as *Domala* in 1921 by Barclay, Curle and Company, Whiteinch, Glasgow. She was owned by the British India Steam Navigation Company. Following damage sustained in an air attack in 1940, *Domala* was requisitioned by the Ministry of War Transport, rebuilt and renamed SS *Empire Attendant*. She was placed under the management of Andrew Weir and Company (Bank Line). On 1 July 1942 she sailed from Liverpool as part of Convoy OS-33 with a cargo of stores, vehicles and a quantity of explosives bound for Freetown in Sierra Leone. On 10 July 1942 the escort vessel, HMS *Pelican*, signalled the Admiralty that SS *Empire Attendant* had broken down for the seventh time and was out of contact. At 3.30 am on 15 July 1942, when she was south of the Canary Islands and off the west coast of Africa, she sank after being torpedoed by the German submarine *U-582*. All 59 men aboard the SS *Empire Attendant* were presumed drowned; there were no survivors. In addition to Able Seaman John Joseph Kennedy, Fifth Engineer Officer **Thomas McMahon Houston** and Sailor **Patrick Joseph Gibson** also died. Able Seaman John Joseph Kennedy was 32 years old when he died and he is commemorated on the Tower Hill Memorial in London.

K

Kerr, James
Private
No. 14261386, Pioneer Corps
Died in service on Friday 25 June 1943 (aged 37)
Newton-le-Willows Cemetery, Lancashire, England
(Section C Grave 1605)

James Kerr was born on 15 April 1906 in Dunmurry and he was a son of Thomas and Elizabeth (Lizzie) Kerr (nee Adamson). Thomas Kerr (son of John Kerr, Blaris) worked as a general labourer and he was a widower when he and Lizzie Adamson (born in Scotland, daughter of Alexander Adamson) were married on 3 May 1898 in Eglantine All Saints Church of Ireland Church, Blaris, Lisburn. Thomas Kerr already had three children – Mary Jane (born about 1886); Thomas (born about 1888) and Elizabeth (born about 1891).

In 1911 the Kerr family was living at 38 Brownlow Street in Comber and before that they lived at 22 Sloan Road in Lisburn. Thomas and Lizzie Kerr had at least six children – Emily; Aggie (born 7 March 1901); William J. (born 7 March 1903); Annie (born 19 December 1904); James (born 15 April 1906) and Samuel (born 17 August 1907).

For a time James Kerr lived in Cheshire and records show that he was the husband of Annie Kerr of Bangor, Co. Down. During the Second World War he served with the Pioneer Corps in the Home Theatre of War and he was 37 years old when he died in service on 25 June 1943. His death was registered in Newton-le-Willows, Lancashire.

Kidd-May, Harold Anthony (Tony)
Flight Lieutenant
No. 81372, 511 Squadron, Royal Air Force Volunteer Reserve
Killed on active service on Tuesday 10 August 1943 (aged 22)
Runnymede Memorial, Surrey, England (Panel 119)

Harold Anthony (Tony) Kidd-May was born in Dublin on 11 October 1920 and he was the elder son of Harold and Cicely Alice Kidd-May (nee Ray). Harold Kidd-May was a Civil Servant and he and Cicely Alice Ray were married on 29 December 1919 in St. Thomas's Church, Oxford. Tony's paternal grandparents, George Alden May (a cotton goods agent) and Isabel May (nee Greenfield) lived at 85 High Street, Holywood. George May and Isabel Greenfield were married on 7 August 1882 in University Road Methodist Church, Belfast.

Tony Kidd-May's father was wounded in action three times during the First

World War. He served with the 5th Battalion, Royal Berkshire Regiment and he was awarded the Military Cross for conspicuous gallantry and devotion to duty when in command of a company in an attack on 30th November 1917. 'He moved about fearlessly under heavy machine gun fire directing the advance. When the advance was held up he went forward to reconnoitre and then directed his platoons to their objectives. He superintended the consolidation with great energy and set his men a splendid example throughout'. He suffered from gas poisoning and was invalided out of front-line service; he was stationed in the Discharge Centre in Dublin until 1922. In 1922 the Kidd-May family moved from Dublin to *Merton*, 25 Osborne Drive, Bangor and Tony's two sisters and his brother were baptised in Bangor Abbey – Cicely Elizabeth (born 24 July 1922, baptised 9 August 1922); Diana Isabel (born 11 March 1926, baptised 28 March 1926) and David James (born 10 September 1931, baptised 11 November 1931). In 1931 Master Tony Kidd-May of *Merton*, 25 Osborne Drive was listed as number six on the Freewill Offering Register for Bangor Abbey.

Harold Kidd-May worked as a civil servant for the Inland Revenue and he died of pneumonia on 6 August 1934 (aged 36). At his father's funeral Tony (then aged 13) wore his father's Military Cross. Tony's mother died on 7 August 1979 and both of his parents were buried in Bangor Cemetery.

K

Tony Kidd-May attended Bangor Grammar School from 1930 until 1934 and it was the custom for the Headmaster, Maurice Wilkins, to write obituary articles for old boys of the school who were killed in action. Of the 39 old boys killed, 36 had attended the school under his headmastership and he wrote *In Memoriam* articles for 30 of them. Later, in relation to Tony Kidd-May, he gave as his reason for not writing an article 'delay in news reaching Bangor where a family had gone away'. After Harold Kidd-May died the family moved to *Greenfield House*, 202 Botley Road, Oxford and Tony attended Oxford High School. There he was renowned for his acting ability and rugby prowess. After leaving school he worked in Barclays Bank.

Tony Kidd-May joined the Royal Air Force Volunteer Reserve, gained his Wings and after completing an Instructors' Course he was based at RAF Kidlington in Oxfordshire. In November 1940, while he was giving instruction to a trainee-pilot in an Airspeed Oxford aircraft (P1094), there was an air raid and the landing lights at Kidlington were extinguished. Tony had to make an emergency landing in a field on Boar's Hill, Oxford. The aircraft ploughed into soft earth and the propeller tip was broken off. Tony and the trainee pilot escaped without injury and the family still has the propeller tip which Tony signed. From there Tony went to Canada to train pilots and whilst there he played rugby for the RAF team. In 1943 he was posted to the New Camp In Gibraltar (there were two RAF camps in Gibraltar, the first was North Front Camp built on a racecourse and the second was New Camp built on reclaimed land next to Montague Bastion). At the end of his tour of duty and whilst waiting for home leave, he volunteered to be the second pilot aboard an Armstrong Whitworth Albermarle GT Mark I transport plane (P1433). Shortly after take-off this aircraft crashed into the sea some 120 miles west of Gibraltar and all 12 airmen aboard the plane were killed. Their bodies were never recovered. In addition to Flight Lieutenant Harold Anthony (Tony) Kidd-May eleven other airmen died that day:

- FO Philip Oscar Davis aged 22 from Ramsey, Huntingdonshire
- FO James Hannan Charnock aged 20 from Leek, Staffordshire
- Flying Officer Douglas Charles Walter Clark (RCAF)
- Flying Officer Albert William Little aged 26 (RCAF)
- Flying Officer Jack Collingridge Valder aged 34 (RAAF)
- Flight Sergeant William Robert McLellan aged 23 (RCAF)
- Flight Sergeant Raymond Douglas Crowley Smith aged 21 (RAAF)
- Sgt William Brownlie Clarkson aged 20 from Glengarnock, Ayrshire
- Sergeant Jack Oxley aged 21 from Morecambe, Lancashire
- Sergeant Desmond Arthur Woods
- Corporal Keith Treffa Alexander

K

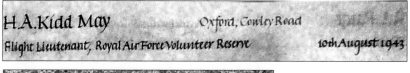

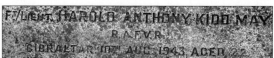

Flight Lieutenant Harold Anthony Kidd-May was 22 years old when he died and he is commemorated on Bangor and District War Memorial; in Bangor Parish Church of Ireland Church (St. Comgall's); in Bangor Grammar School; in Oxford High School (this Memorial Plaque is now located in Oxford University Faculty of History, George Street, Oxford); in St. Lawrence's Church, North Hinksey, Oxford; on the Barclays Bank Memorial Plaque; in the Barclays Bank Book of Remembrance and on the family grave headstone in Bangor Cemetery.

The report of his death published in the May/June 1944 edition (Volume 19, page 85) of *The Spread Eagle*, Barclays Bank staff magazine contained the following: 'Flight Lieutenant H.A. Kidd-May of Cowley Road, Oxford Branch was reported missing from air operations in August 1943 and it is now learned with deep regret that his death has been presumed. Flight Lieutenant Kidd-May entered the Bank on leaving Oxford High School and on his 18th birthday he joined the RAFVR. He spent two years in Canada as an Instructor but volunteered for fighter operations and returned to England in December 1942. An enthusiastic sportsman he won school colours for swimming and also specialised in squash and rugger, playing scrum half for his schools and for the Old Citizens, as well as for the RAF in Canada where he once flew to Winnipeg through a blizzard to take part in a match. Although of a shy nature, he made many friends and his death at the early age of 22 is deeply deplored'.

King, Arthur James
Aircraftman 2nd Class
No. 617525, Royal Air Force
Died of illness on Wednesday 23 April 1941 (aged 20)
Bangor Cemetery, Co. Down (Section 4 V Grave 20)

During the Second World War Aircraftman 2nd Class Arthur James King served with the Royal Air Force and he attended No. 5 Bombing and Gunnery School. He was 20 years old and his address was recorded as Cottown, Donaghadee when he died of meningitis on 23 April 1941. He was buried in Bangor Cemetery on 29 April 1941.

K

King, Desmond Robert (Desmond)
Second Lieutenant
Royal Indian Army Service Corps
Died in service on Tuesday 5 May 1942 (aged 29)
Karachi War Cemetery, Pakistan (Grave 4 D 13)

Desmond Robert King was born on 20 April 1913 in Belfast and he was a son of Robert and Florence King (nee Aird) who lived at 20 Ratcliffe Street. Robert King was a grocer from Moy in County Tyrone and he and Florence Aird from Belfast were married in Great Victoria Street Presbyterian Church, Belfast. Later the King family moved from Belfast to *Kinross*, Sligo Road, Enniskillen, Co. Fermanagh.

During the Second World War Second Lieutenant Desmond Robert King

served with the Royal Indian Army Service Corps (RIASC) in Abbottabad, Pakistan and he died on 5 May 1942 in the British Military Hospital, Abbottabad. His effects amounted to some £209 and probate was granted to his father. Second Lieutenant Desmond Robert King is commemorated on Bangor and District War Memorial and in Wesley Centenary Methodist Church, Bangor. No church records relating to this casualty were available.

King, Margaret Ann (Margaret)
Sergeant
No. NFX139589, AIF 114th General Hospital, Australian Army Medical Corps
Died after a medical operation on Thursday 4 May 1944 (aged 47)
Goulburn General Cemetery, New South Wales, Australia
(Plot G Row A Grave 7)

K

Margaret Ann King was born on 27 December 1896 and she was the younger daughter of James Henry and Margaret Finnegan (nee McMaster) of Ballyridley, Portaferry. They were married in Balligan Church of Ireland Church, Innishargie on 28 February 1892. James Henry Finnegan worked as a farm servant for Francis McDonnell who farmed in the townland of Demesne, Ardquin, Portaferry. James Henry and Margaret Finnegan had five children – Isabella (born 10 April 1893); Thomas (born 28 February 1895); Margaret Ann (born 27 December 1896); William (born 6 July 1889) and James (born 28 December 1906). James Henry Finnegan died on 3 June 1943 (aged 76) and he was buried in the Abbacy Graveyard, Portaferry. Margaret Finnegan died on 27 December 1945 (aged 75) and she was buried in Ballyphilip Graveyard, Portaferry.

Both Isabella Finnegan and her sister Margaret worked as seamstresses and domestic servants before moving to Australia. On 13 September 1912 Isabella sailed from Liverpool to Sydney aboard the White Star liner *Irishman* and on 21 March 1914 Margaret followed her sister to Australia aboard the same ship. On 18 July 1914 Isabella Finnegan married David Murray in Tenterfield, New South Wales and they had nine children. On 28 June 1916 Margaret Finnegan married Arthur James Kong Pow in Killarney Presbyterian Church, Queensland and they had two children, both born in

Killarney, Queensland – Margaret Florence (born 15 February 1917) and Joyce (born 26 June 1919). Arthur Kong Pow's mother (also called Margaret) died on 13 February 1920 (aged 78). Arthur Kong Pow died on 15 June 1960 (aged 64) and he was buried in Killarney General Cemetery, Queensland.

Using the name Margaret King, Margaret Kong Pow enlisted in the Australian Army Nursing Service on 15 October 1942 at Goulburn, New South Wales. In order to enhance her chances of acceptance she declared that she was single and that she was 39 years old (rather than 45). She gave her date of birth as 27 December 1903. Margaret King was allocated service number N437885 and the rank of Private. She was taken on strength of the 114th Australian General Hospital at Goulburn with effect from 15 October 1942. On 15 December 1942 she was transferred to the Australian Imperial Force Nursing Service and allotted army number NFX139589. She was appointed Acting Corporal on 9 March 1943 and, from 15 June 1943 until 26 July 1943, she herself was hospitalised. From 19 October 1943 until 16 November 1943 she attended a Cooking and Catering Course (Australian Womens' Services) at the Cooking and Catering School in Sydney. Known affectionately as Kingy, Margaret King was appointed Acting Sergeant on 20 January 1944.

K

DIED ON ACTIVE SERVICE.

KING—At 114, Australian General Hospital, Sergeant Margaret King, of the Imperial Australian Forces, on the 4th of May, 1944, youngest daughter of Mrs. Margaret Finnegan, Ballyridley, Portaferry; Sister of Wm. Finnegan; also Sergeant James Finnegan (on Active Service, M.E.F.); also her Sister, Mrs. D. Murray, in Australia.
"Resting where no shadows fall."
Sadly missed by her loving Mother and all at Home.
Australian Papers please copy.

On 7 April 1944 Sergeant Margaret King was readmitted to the 114th Australian General Hospital, Goulburn and, following a hysterectomy, she died of cardiac failure on 4 May 1944. That day her sister Isabella, who was living in Bargo, New South Wales, received the news by means of a hand-delivered telegram. Margaret King was buried in Goulburn General Cemetery. During the Second World War, 17 Australian Infantry Training Battalion was located at the Goulburn Showground and in 1942 Kenmore Hospital became the 114th Australian General Hospital (114 AGH). Various supply units were located in Goulburn to support the Battalion and the hospital. Japanese Prisoners-of-War from Cowra, New South Wales were treated at 114 AGH. The Goulburn General Cemetery contains war graves of those who died of wounds, illness or during training.

After she died, Margaret King's family in Australia placed a death notice in the 5 May 1944 edition of the *Goulburn Post*. Her family in Northern Ireland placed a *Died on Active Service* notice in the 20 May 1944 edition of the

Newtownards Chronicle in which she was described as the youngest daughter of Mrs Margaret Finnegan of Ballyridley, Portaferry, a sister of both William Finnegan and James Finnegan (on active service with the Middle East Force) and a sister of Mrs D. Murray in Australia. After the war James Finnegan, along with his wife Emily (nee Reid) and their two sons, Thomas and James Henry (Harry) moved to Australia. The notice in the *Newtownards Chronicle* contained the text:

Resting where no shadows fall

Sergeant Margaret King was awarded the War Medal and the Australia Service Medal and she is commemorated on Panel 96 of the Australian Second World War Roll of Honour, Australian War Memorial. Her age is recorded as 40 on her CWGC headstone.

King, Neville Stuart

K

Flying Officer
No. 112178, 603 Squadron, Royal Air Force Volunteer Reserve
Killed on active service on Wednesday 8 July 1942 (aged 29)
Malta Memorial, Valetta, Malta (Panel 3 Column 1)

Neville Stuart King was born on 24 March 1913, his birth was registered in Rathdown, Dublin and he was a son of Jonas Lowcay King (named as Joseph Lowry King in CWGC records) and Charlotte Mary King (nee Stack, born in County Kerry, daughter of the Revd Thomas Lindsay Stack). Jonas Lowcay King, who was a son of the Revd Robert King, worked as a Local Government auditor and he and Charlotte Mary Stack were married on 4 July 1900 in Langfield Lower Parish Church of Ireland Church, Drumquin, Co. Tyrone (where Charlotte's father served for a time as Rector). They had four children – Nancie Mary Valentine (Nannie, born 14 February 1903); Harriette Doreen (born 3 October 1905, died April 1997); Carlotta Joan Stuart (born 22 November 1910, died September 1996) and Neville Stuart (born 24 March 1913). For a time the King family lived at Martello, Holywood and Neville Stuart King was educated at Rockport School, Craigavad. Jonas Lowcay King was 60 years old when he died at Martello on 2 October 1927.

Neville Stuart King married Brenda Howarth of Leeds, Yorkshire and their marriage was registered in the third quarter of 1939 in Leeds. At that time he was a policeman in the Metropolitan Police. During the Second World War he served with the Royal Air Force Volunteer Reserve and he was 29 years old when he was killed on 8 July 1942. Neville Stuart King was flying a Supermarine Spitfire aircraft in pursuit of German Junkers Ju 88 aircraft over Gozo and, when turning to return to base, he was flying so low that a wing tip touched the water and his aircraft crashed. His body was never recovered. His effects amounted to some £2,593 and probate was granted to his widow.

Flying Officer Neville Stuart King is commemorated on the Malta Memorial and in Rockport School.

Kirham, Samuel (Sam)
Private
No. 4458471, Durham Light Infantry
Died of illness on Saturday 2 March 1940 (aged 20)
Holywood Cemetery, Co. Down (Protestant Ground Joint Grave 1264)

In some records his surname is spelt Kirkham. Samuel Kirham's birth was registered in the fourth quarter of 1919 in Ffestiniog, Merionethshire and his mother's maiden name was Smith. Samuel Kirham lived in Liverpool and during the Second World War he served with the Durham Light Infantry. He was stationed in Palace Barracks, Holywood and he was 20 years old and unmarried when he died on 2 March 1940 in the Military Hospital, Knocknagoney. Private Samuel Kirham died of tuberculous peritonitis and three days later he was buried in Holywood Cemetery.

K

Kirk, Thomas Leonard King (Lennie)
Sergeant
No. 1465494, 5 Battery, 2 Light Anti-Aircraft Regiment, Royal Artillery
Died as a result of enemy action on Friday 5 December 1941 (aged 27)
Alamein Memorial, Egypt (Column 31)

Thomas Leonard King (Lennie) Kirk was born on 7 July 1914 and he was the youngest son of Hugh and Maud Kirk (nee McKellar) of 28 Ann Street and later Chapel View, Newtownards. Hugh Kirk and Maud McKellar (daughter of Sergeant Major James McKellar) were married on 11 December 1902 in Ballygilbert Presbyterian Church. Hugh Kirk declared himself to

be an agnostic and he and Maud Kirk had three children – William (born 13 August 1903); Hugh Gerald (Gerry, born 11 August 1905) and Thomas Leonard (born 7 July 1914). Hugh Kirk owned two shops in Newtownards, one a tobacconist and confectionery shop and the other an antiquarian shop. Locally his nickname was *Anti Que*. Amongst other things, Hugh Kirk collected books, weapons and flint implements and after his death some items from his collection went to museums in Belfast and Dublin. Hugh Kirk was a close friend of the geographer and archaeologist Emyr Estyn Evans and in honour of his friend Hugh gave his son Lennie the forename King (Emyr in Welsh).

Prior to the outbreak of war, Lennie Kirk worked as an engineer and he and Jessie Morrison were married on 9 July 1938 in Helen's Bay Presbyterian Church. They lived at 33 South Street, Newtownards and they had one child – a daughter named Margaret who never saw her father.

K

Ards Soldier Killed.—Official notification has been received by Mrs. Kirk, South Street, Newtownards, that her husband, Sergeant Thomas Leonard Kirk, Royal Artillery, who was reported missing, believed drowned, must now be presumed killed. He was the youngest son of Mr. and Mrs. Hugh Kirk, Chapel View, Newtownards.

Lennie Kirk enlisted before the outbreak of war and he served with 5 Battery, 2 Light Anti-Aircraft Regiment, Royal Artillery. On 5 December 1941 he was posted as 'missing, believed drowned in the Mediterranean Sea' and some six months later it was officially confirmed that he 'must now be presumed killed'. Lennie Kirk had developed a severe case of furuncles (boils) and was being transported out of Tobruk, Libya with other ill and injured soldiers aboard HMS *Chakdina* in Convoy TA.1/M. HMS *Chakdina* was a passenger ship built in 1914 by Ramage and Ferguson, Leith, Scotland and she was owned by the British India Steam Navigation Company. In 1940 she was requisitioned by the Admiralty and used as an Armed Boarding Vessel. At around 9.00 pm on 5 December 1941, HMS *Chakdina* was hit by a torpedo fired from enemy aircraft and she sank inside three minutes. There was a further explosion when her boilers exploded underwater. Sergeant Lennie Kirk was amongst those who died in the attack. Survivors were picked up by the escorting destroyer HMS *Farndale* and taken to Alexandria in Egypt.

There were three *Killed in Action* notices in the 4 July 1942 edition of the *Newtownards Chronicle* – one from Lennie's wife and daughter; one from his father, mother and brother Gerry and one from his brother and sister-in-law William and Nora Kirk (nee Allen) of Donaghadee Road, Newtownards.

Sergeant Thomas Leonard King Kirk was 27 years old when he died and he is commemorated on Newtownards and District War Memorial and in First Newtownards Presbyterian Church.

Kirkham, Samuel (see Kirham, Samuel)

Kolek, Wladyslaw
Plutonwy (Pilot; Sergeant)
No. P783150, 315 (City of Deblin) Polish Fighter Squadron
Killed in an aircraft accident on Saturday 11 September 1943 (aged 26)
Ballycranbeg (Mount St. Joseph) Roman Catholic Churchyard, Co. Down

Sergeant Wladyslaw Kolek was born on 2 July 1917 and during the Second World War he served with 315 (City of Deblin) Polish Fighter Squadron. Saturday 11 September 1943 was described as 'a black day for 315 Squadron' which was based at RAF Ballyhalbert. Two pilots and three aircraft were lost. In the late afternoon, during adverse weather, three pilots took off in Supermarine Spitfire Mark V aircraft to practise formation flying. Flight Sergeant **Stanislaw Grondowski** was a very experienced pilot and he was leading the formation flight in W3427 (PK-J). The other two pilots – Sergeant E Zygmund in AR338 (PK-P) and Sergeant Wladyslaw Kolek in BL469 (PK-F) – were undergoing training. For some reason the three aircraft left the prescribed training area and in the bad weather they became separated. Within a short space of time, all three aircraft crashed in the hills west and north of Belfast. Flight Sergeant Stanislaw Grondowski was killed near Plantation House, Lisburn and Sergeant Wladyslaw Kolek was killed near Ballyutoag. Sergeant Zygmund was knocked unconscious when his aircraft crashed near Glengormley and after he regained consciousness he was able to climb out of the wreckage and walk to the nearest road. Both wings of his aircraft had been ripped off.

K

Sergeant Wladyslaw Kolek was 26 years old when he died and, in accordance with Polish custom, burial took place three days after death. Tuesday 14 September 1943 was described as a bright, warm day but 'no-one felt very cheerful'. After High Mass in Ballyhalbert Hangar Church, Flight Sergeant Grondowski and Sergeant Kolek were buried in Ballycranbeg

(Mount St. Joseph) Roman Catholic Churchyard. In addition to the official representatives and guards of honour there were many mourners from the local community. Flight Sergeant Grondowski was well known in the area; Sergeant Kolek died just two days after arriving from the Operational Training Unit (OTU). Sergeant Wladyslaw Kolek is commemorated on Panel 30 of the Polish War Memorial at Northolt in London.

Komenda Henryk
Kapral (KPL; Leading Aircraftman)
No. P792224, 256 Squadron, Royal Air Force
Killed in an aircraft accident on Thursday 9 July 1942 (aged 20)
Newtownards (Movilla) Cemetery, Co. Down (Plot RC Section 18 Grave 23)

Polish Pilot, Kapral Henryk Komenda was born on 13 January 1922 and he was killed on 9 July 1942 during a training flight when his Boulton Paul Defiant night fighter aircraft (N3402) of 1480 Flight based at RAF Newtownards crashed to the ground to the east of Lough Mourne (the largest of the reservoirs in Woodburn Forest near Carrickfergus). Also killed was Sergeant (Air Gunner) **Peter Charles Hunter Phillips** and both men were buried in Movilla Cemetery, Newtownards. Kapral Henryk Komenda is commemorated on Panel 30 of the Polish War Memorial at Northolt in London.

Kyle, Robert Ernest (Robert)
Master
SS *Texan* (Glasgow), Merchant Navy
Accidentally drowned on Saturday 17 February 1945 (aged 37)

> **DIED ON ACTIVE SERVICE**
> KYLE—February 18, 1945 (lost at sea), Robert E., dearly-beloved husband of Mary Kyle, 6 McDowall Avenue, Ardrossan, and beloved son of the late Wm. Kyle and Mrs. Kyle, Kirkistown.
> Deeply regretted by his Wife, Mother, Brothers and Sisters; also Brothers-in-law and Sisters-in-law and Families.

There was a *Died on Active Service* notice in the 3 March 1945 edition of the *County Down Spectator* indicating that Robert E. Kyle had been lost at sea on 18 February 1945. His date of death was recorded in the Register of Deceased Seamen as 17 February 1945.

Robert Ernest Kyle was born on 2 September 1907 and he was a son of

William and Sarah Kyle (nee McCappin) who lived at Calhame in Cloughey, Co. Down. Robert Ernest's grandfather, Robert Kyle, farmed in the townland of Ballygelagh and Robert Ernest's father, William Kyle, was a seaman. William Kyle's shore address was 13 Bank Road, Bootle when he and Sarah McCappin from Cloughey were married on 16 September 1896 in St. Mary's Church, Bootle. While William Kyle was at sea Sarah lived in Cloughey where she worked as a seamstress. William and Sarah Kyle had at least six children – Annie (born 28 February 1897); Ellen (born 30 January 1900); William (born 12 January 1903); David (born 2 September 1905); Robert Ernest (born 2 September 1907) and Thomas (born 24 April 1909).

After he retired from the sea, Robert Ernest Kyle's father William farmed and he died on 20 March 1933 at Newtownards Union Infirmary. He was buried in Ardkeen (Christ Church) Parish Church of Ireland Graveyard. William's effects amounted to some £66 and probate was granted to his widow Sarah. Sarah Kyle died on 25 December 1946 and she was buried alongside her husband.

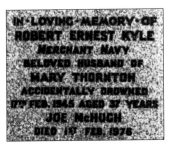

Like his father, Robert Ernest Kyle was a seaman and he and Mary Thornton were married on 7 September 1934 in the Barony Church of Scotland, Ardrossan in Ayrshire. They lived at 6 McDowall Avenue, Ardrossan. During the Second World War Robert Ernest Kyle served with the Merchant Navy and attained the rank of Master. In the Register of Deceased Seamen it is recorded that he drowned in the River Clyde at Renfrew when he was Master of the SS *Texan*. The SS *Texan* was a lighter (a type of flat-bottomed barge used to transport goods and passengers from moored ships). She was built in 1937 by J. and J. Hay, Kirkintilloch and scrapped in 1964. On his death certificate it is recorded that 'on 17 February 1945 he was immersed in water in the River Clyde and his body was found at 6.30 pm on 12 March in Rothesay Dock, Clydebank'.

Captain Robert Ernest Kyle is commemorated on the Second World War Memorial Plaque in the Ardrossan Garden of Remembrance and on the family grave headstone in Ardrossan Cemetery. His wife Mary died on 21 January 1996 (aged 85) and she was buried beside her husband. There is an inscription on their headstone:

Until we meet again

Lacey, Robert Richard
Private
No. 21048946, General Service Corps
Died as a result of an accident on Sunday 19 October 1947 (aged 18)
Holywood Cemetery, Co. Down (Protestant Ground Grave 1265)

Robert Richard Lacey's birth was registered in the first quarter of 1929 in Bishop's Stortford, Hertfordshire and he was a son of Alexander Richard Lacey (born 1888 in London) and Elizabeth Rose Lacey (nee Abraham, born 1885 in London). Both of Elizabeth Rose Abraham's parents were from County Limerick and her father worked as a nurseryman at Dublin Harbour before the Abraham family moved to London. Alexander Richard Lacey worked as a clerk in the London Stock Exchange before the Lacey family moved to Orchard Mead, Haymead's Lane, Bishop's Stortford.

Private Robert Richard Lacey served with the General Service Corps and he was 18 years old and unmarried when he died on 19 October 1947. He was run over by a train and decapitated. Private Lacey was buried in Holywood Cemetery on 22 October and his CWGC headstone bears the inscription:

So he passed over and all the trumpets sounded for him on the other side

Robert Richard Lacey's father, Alexander Richard Lacey, died on 19 May 1962 (aged 74). Alexander Richard Lacey's effects amounted to some £798 and probate was granted to his sisters, Ada Caroline Lacey and Winifred Letitia Lacey. Robert Richard Lacey's mother died in 1972 (aged 87).

Lamb, Harold
Private
No. 14770658, General Service Corps
Died of illness on Sunday 18 June 1944 (aged 37)
Bangor Cemetery, Co. Down (Section 5 X Grave 2)

In the Army Roll of Honour it is recorded that Harold Lamb was born in Perth, Scotland; he lived in Liverpool and, during the Second World War, he served in the North Caribbean Theatre of War. In the CWGC Debt of Honour it is recorded that Private Harold Lamb died on 18 June 1944 and this is confirmed by his death certificate (the Army Roll of Honour gives 11 June 1944 as his date of death). Private Harold Lamb was a 37 year-old bachelor

stationed at the Primary Training Centre (PTC), Ballykinlar Camp, Co. Down when he became ill and was transferred to Bangor Military Hospital. He died there on 18 June 1944 as a result of a perforated duodenal ulcer and was buried on 23 June 1944 in Bangor Cemetery.

Lavender, Anthony Wilson (Anthony)
Sergeant
No. 1157375, 25 Squadron, Royal Air Force Volunteer Reserve
Killed in an aircraft accident on Wednesday 11 February 1942 (aged 25)
Runnymede Memorial, Surrey, England (Panel 87)

Anthony Wilson Lavender was born on 17 August 1916 and his birth was registered in West Bromwich, Staffordshire. He was a son of Thomas Walter Lavender and Gertrude May Lavender (nee Wilson) of 31 Lower High Street, Wednesbury, Staffordshire who were married on 30 October 1915 in West Bromwich. At that time Thomas Lavender was a grocer's assistant and Gertrude Wilson was an assistant school teacher. Thomas Lavender enlisted for service during the First World War and his attestation was on 13 January 1916. He served with the Royal Garrison Artillery (No. 158737) until he was discharged on 8 November 1918 because of valvular heart disease. Thomas and Gertrude Lavender had at least three children – Anthony Wilson (born 17 August 1916); John A. (born 1920) and Tom B. (born 1924). Anthony Wilson Lavender's father Thomas died in 1928 (aged 39) and his mother Gertrude (born 17 February 1888) died in 1988 just a few days short of her 100th birthday.

On 12 February 1942 Sergeant **Nagu Ranganatha** and Sergeant Anthony Wilson Lavender of 25 Squadron based at RAF Ballyhalbert were flying a Bristol Beaufighter aircraft (X7625) which failed to return from a night sector reconnaissance operation. Both Sergeant Nagu Ranganatha and Sergeant Anthony Wilson Lavender were declared missing, their bodies were never recovered and they are commemorated on the Runnymede Memorial in Surrey. Anthony Lavender's estate amounted to some £609 and probate was granted to his widowed mother Gertrude. His last home address was recorded as *Wharfedale House*, Wharfedale Street, Wednesbury, Staffordshire.

L

Leckey Siblings, George McClelland and Muriel Emily

George McClelland Leckey and Muriel Emily Leckey were children of Henry (Harry) and Mary Ann Leckey (nee McClelland, born 22 September 1877 in the townland of Cloven Eden, Co. Armagh). They were married on 20 June 1906 in Loughgall Parish Church of Ireland Church, Co. Armagh. Harry Leckey was a grocer and he and Mary Ann had at least six children – James (born 1 July 1907); Eileen Elizabeth (born 7 June 1909); Muriel Emily (born 26 June 1911); George McClelland (born 8 June 1913); Henry (born 7 April 1918) and William Edward (born 31 July 1919). In 1910 the Leckey family moved from County Armagh to 2 Church Avenue, Holywood and the first four children were baptised in First Holywood Presbyterian Church. The last two children were baptised in Hamilton Road Presbyterian Church, Bangor. George was the first of the two Leckey siblings to die as a result of enemy action during the Second World War.

Leckey, George McClelland (George)
Second Officer
SS *Kenbane Head* (Belfast), Merchant Navy
Died as a result of enemy action on Tuesday 5 November 1940 (aged 27)
Tower Hill Memorial, London, England (Panel 60)

L

George McClelland Leckey was born in Holywood on 8 June 1913 and he was the husband of Susan M. Leckey of *Breezemount*, Park Avenue, Holywood. During the Second World War George McClelland Leckey served with the Merchant Navy as Second Officer aboard the SS *Kenbane Head*. This ship was built in 1919 by Workman, Clark and Company and was owned by G. Heyn and Sons Ltd., who operated the Ulster Steamship Company (Head Line).

In November 1940 the SS *Kenbane Head* was sailing from Halifax in Nova Scotia to Great Britain in Convoy HX-84 with more than 30 other merchant vessels escorted by the armed merchant ship HMS *Jervis Bay*. The convoy was intercepted by the German battle-cruiser *Admiral Scheer* which had been commissioned in November 1934. Hopelessly outgunned, HMS *Jervis Bay* engaged the enemy and was sunk in the process. However, this gave the convoy time to scatter and the *Admiral Scheer* was only able to sink six other ships, five from the convoy (*Beaverford, Fresno City, Kenbane Head, Maidan, Trewellard*) and one sailing independently (*Mopan*). The SS *Kenbane Head* sank off the coast of Greenland with the loss of 23 men. The tanker *San Demetrio* was set on fire by the *Admiral Scheer* but later salvaged. Other local crew members who lost their lives aboard the SS *Kenbane Head* were **James McNeilly Belshaw** from Ballywalter, **Reginald John Primmer** from Portaferry and **David John Pritchard** from Ballyhalbert. (On 9 April 1945 the *Admiral Scheer* was capsized in Kiel harbour, Germany by RAF bombs dropped during a raid).

 Second Officer George McClelland Leckey died on 5 November 1940 and he is commemorated on Holywood and District War Memorial and in Holywood Non-Subscribing Presbyterian Church (as George Leckie MN).

Leckey, Muriel Emily
Sister
No. 208615, Queen Alexandra's Imperial Military Nursing Service
Died as a result of enemy action on Saturday 12 February 1944 (aged 32)
Brookwood Memorial, Surrey, England (Panel 22 Column 2)

Muriel Emily Leckey was born in Holywood on 26 June 1911 and she was a daughter of Harry and Mary Ann Leckey. Muriel Emily Leckey attended Sullivan Upper School in Holywood from 1923 until 1927. She started work in Ards Hospital on 4 July 1934 and qualified as a State Registered Nurse (SRN) in October 1937. She continued working in Ards Hospital until December 1938 and then did private nursing until she joined Queen Alexandra's Imperial Military Nursing Service. In February 1944 she was drafted to the Far East and it was on that voyage that she lost her life. Sister Muriel Emily Leckey was 32 years old when she died aboard the SS *Khedive Ismail*. This ship was launched as the *Aconcagua* by Scotts of Greenock in 1922 and then in 1935 renamed *Khedive Ismail* when she passed into Egyptian ownership. In 1940 the *Khedive Ismail* was requisitioned as a British troopship.

On 6 February 1944 Convoy KR-8 sailed from Kilindini Harbour in Mombasa, Kenya to Colombo, Ceylon (now Sri Lanka). The convoy comprised five troop transport ships escorted by one heavy cruiser, HMS

Hawkins, and two destroyers, HMS *Paladin* and HMS *Petard*. In the early afternoon of 12 February 1944 the convoy was attacked in the One and a Half Degree Channel in the Maldive Islands (also known as the Suvadiva Channel) by the Japanese submarine *I-27*. After being hit by two torpedoes, the *Khedive Ismail* sank in less than two minutes with the loss of almost 1,300 lives, including about 80 women, most of whom were nursing sisters. Among the crew members who died was Junior Engineer Officer **John Corbett Hall** from Carnalea. Efforts were made to rescue survivors who were floundering in the sea, while at the same time depth charges were released to force the Japanese submarine back to the surface. When it surfaced, *I-27* was rammed by HMS *Paladin* and finally sunk by a torpedo fired from HMS *Petard*.

Muriel Emily Leckey's last home address was 14 Marine Parade, Holywood, her effects amounted to some £269 and probate was granted to her father who was described as a coal agent. Sister Muriel Emily Leckey was 32 years old when she died and she is commemorated on Holywood and District War Memorial and on a bronze plaque in Ards Hospital which was unveiled on 8 January 1949.

L

Lee, Edward Elliott (Edward)
Captain
No. 104897, Royal Army Ordnance Corps
Died of illness on Thursday 19 December 1946 (aged 53)
Bangor Cemetery, Co. Down (Section 1 A Grave 114)

In the CWGC Debt of Honour the grave number is recorded as 124. Edward Elliott Lee's birth was registered in the first quarter of 1893 in Dublin and he was the eldest son of Edward Elliott Lee and Eliza (Lillie) Lee (nee Axford) who were married in 1892. Edward Elliott Lee Senior (originally from County Cork) was a wholesale tobacco merchant and he and Eliza (originally from County Mayo) had at least six children – Edward Elliott, Harold, Gwendoline, Alfred, Victor and Mabel.

MILITARY FUNERAL AT BANGOR

THE LATE CAPTAIN E. E. LEE
The funeral of Captain Edward E. Lee, 208, Holywood Road, Belfast, O.C. Returned Stores Depot, Belfast, took place to Bangor Cemetery on Saturday with full military honours. The coffin, covered with a Union Jack, was taken by gun-carriage from Bangor Station to the cemetery, attended by a detachment of the R.A.O.C.

Edward Elliott Lee Junior was a solicitor's clerk and his marriage to Ida Florence Hayes was registered in the third quarter of 1916 in Cork. During the Second World War Edward Lee served with the Royal Army Ordnance Corps and he was 53 years old when he died of a stroke on 19 December 1946. His address was 208 Holywood Road, Belfast and when he died he was Officer Commanding (OC) for the Returned Stores Depot at Kinnegar in Holywood. The chief mourners at his funeral which took place with full military honours were his son, Flight Lieutenant Arthur E. Lee together with his brothers H.F. Lee and Victor Lee. Captain Edward E. Lee was buried in Bangor Cemetery and his coffin was transported from Bangor Station to the cemetery on a gun carriage. The headstone on the Lee family grave in Bangor Cemetery comprises a plain cross set on a four-tiered plinth and bears the inscription:

Lee
In loving memory of
Our dear son Teddie died 2ⁿᵈ August 1923 aged 5½ years
Also his father Edward E. Lee, Captain RAOC died 19ᵗʰ December 1946

Teddie's full name was Edward Hayes Lee and his birth was registered in the first quarter of 1918 in Dublin.

Leebody, Andrew
Private
No. 13053218, Pioneer Corps
Died in service on Sunday 4 October 1942 (aged 32)
Ballygowan Presbyterian Churchyard, Co. Down
(Section G Row 1 Grave 1)

L

Andrew Leebody was born on 28 March 1910 at 28 Cable Street, Belfast. He was a son of Isabella Leebody and a grand-nephew of Hannah Leebody. Hannah, Isabella and Andrew Leebody, along with Andrew's older sister Esther, lived at 46 Cable Street in Belfast. Isabella Leebody worked as a domestic servant and Esther was born on 16 September 1907 in Belfast Workhouse Infirmary at 51 Lisburn Road, Belfast – now the site of Belfast City Hospital.

Isabella, Esther and Andrew Leebody moved to the Ballygowan area when Isabella married Thomas McCrudden from Saintfield. Thomas McCrudden was a soldier who served during the Great War, first with the Royal Inniskilling Fusiliers (No. 28403) and then with the Royal Engineers (No. 130265). After the war he worked as a gardener and he and Isabella Leebody were married on 3 March 1919 in St. Anne's Church of Ireland Cathedral, Belfast.

Andrew Leebody joined the Pioneer Corps, he served in the Home Theatre of War and he was 32 years old when he died on 4 October 1942. His death was registered in Skipton, Yorkshire and he was buried in Ballygowan Presbyterian Churchyard. There is an inscription on his CWGC headstone (where his age is inscribed as 33):

He died that we may live

Leitch, Wilfred
Craftsman
No. 7046457, Royal Electrical and Mechanical Engineers
Died of illness on Saturday 29 June 1946 (aged 40)
Newtownards (Movilla) Cemetery, Co. Down (Section 21 Grave 233)

L

Wilfred Leitch was born on 17 May 1906 in Bessbrook, Co. Armagh and he was a son of Thomas and Mary Jane Leitch (nee McGrath) of 15 College Square West, Bessbrook. They were married on 2 May 1887 in Bessbrook Presbyterian Church. Thomas Leitch was a hawker (pedlar) and he and Mary Jane had at least twelve children including Thomas (born 7 January 1892); Elizabeth (Lizzie, born 1 July 1893); Anabella (born 31 May 1895); Ernest (born 22 July 1897); John (born 25 April 1899); Edward (born 9 May 1901); Victor (born 1902); Violet (born 24 September 1903); Wilfred (born 17 May 1906) and Edith (born 1 December 1908). Wilfred Leitch moved from Bessbrook to Newtownards where he worked for Messrs George Walker and Company (Walkers Mill). Wilfred Leitch was a successful dog breeder and won several rosettes at local dog shows. He and Eileen Cleland (aged 17) from Newtownards were married on 27 October 1934 in Great Victoria Street Presbyterian Church, Belfast and they had five children.

Wilfred Leitch enlisted in Newtownards and during the Second World War he served with the Royal Electrical and Mechanical Engineers. He was 40 years old when he died of cancer on 29 June 1946 at Warrington Military Hospital. His military funeral took place the following Monday and a gun carriage drawn by motor truck conveyed his remains from his home at 15 Movilla Street, Newtownards to Movilla Cemetery. The services at the house and graveside were conducted by the Revd G.M. Glass from Moira. Wilfred Leitch's wife Eileen placed an inscription on his CWGC headstone:

Love's last gift, remembrance
Sadly missed by his loving wife and five little children

Craftsman Wilfred Leitch is commemorated on Newtownards and District War Memorial.

Leland, Francis John
Mentioned in Despatches
Croix de Guerre avec Palme
Lieutenant Colonel
No. 30687, Royal Army Service Corps
Killed in action on Thursday 12 April 1945 (aged 41)
Oldenzaal Protestant Cemetery, Overijssel, Netherlands (Grave 11)

KILLED IN ACTION.

LELAND—April, killed in action, Lt.-Colonel F. J. Leland, R.A.S.C., only son of late Colonel F. W. G. Leland, C.B.E., D.S.O., of Bangor.

Francis John Leland was born in 1904 in Pietermaritzburg, Natal Province, South Africa and he was the only son of Colonel Francis William George Leland CBE, DSO and Ellen Adelaide Leland (nee Woods). They were married on 27 August 1902 in Pietermaritzburg. Francis William George Leland came originally from Drogheda in County Louth and, after attending boarding school in England, he joined the Army Service Corps. He served in the South African War, the First World War and the Second World War until 1941. In civilian life he was a mechanical engineer. After his first wife died, Colonel Francis William George Leland married Ella Houston McIlrath and they lived at 158 Donaghadee Road, Bangor. Colonel Francis William George Leland died suddenly on 22 September 1943 whilst he and his wife were visiting his old family home at Drogheda. His effects in England amounted to some £1,823 and probate was granted to his widow and to his son's wife. When he lived in Bangor, Colonel Leland worshipped in the Church of Ireland Church of St. Columbanus at Ballyholme.

The marriage of Francis John Leland and Violet Ethel Butler of Arborfield Cross, Berkshire was registered in the fourth quarter of 1931 in Marylebone, London. During the Second World War Lieutenant Colonel Francis John Leland served with the Royal Army Service Corps and in 1944 he was awarded the Croix de Guerre with Palm. He was killed in action in Holland on 12 April 1945 during a bombing raid by enemy aircraft. His address in England at the time of his death was 1 Earlsfield, Southampton Street, Farnborough, Hampshire. His effects amounted to some £4,043 and probate was granted to Leonard Arthur Moody, engineer.

Lieutenant Colonel Francis John Leland was 41 years old when he died on 12 April 1945 and he is commemorated in Bangor Parish Church of Ireland Church (St. Comgall's).

Lennon, Margaret
Civilian War Dead
Died as a result of enemy action on Sunday 3 September 1939 (aged 58)

In the CWGC Debt of Honour it is recorded that Margaret Lennon was a daughter of Thomas and Eliza Ann Gunning of Donaghadee and the wife of William Lennon of 2028 Davenport Road, Toronto, Ontario in Canada. Margaret Lennon (nee Gunning) was one of more than 100 people who died when the SS *Athenia* was attacked and sunk on 3 September 1939, some 250 miles west of Inishtrahull Island, Co. Donegal by the German submarine *U-30*. It was on the day that war was declared and the SS *Athenia* was the first British ship to be sunk by enemy action during the Second World War. The SS *Athenia* was built in 1923 by the Fairfield Shipbuilding and Engineering Company at Govan on the Clyde and on 1 September 1939 she left Glasgow for Montreal via Liverpool and Belfast. By the time she left Belfast Lough there were more than 1,400 people aboard and around 1,100 of them were passengers.

Margaret Lennon (nee Gunning) was born on 25 November 1880 in Donaghadee and she was a daughter of Thomas and Eliza Ann Gunning (nee Caughey). Thomas Gunning was a seaman and he and Eliza Ann Caughey were married on 1 September 1868 in Shore Street Presbyterian Church, Donaghadee. They had at least four children – Andrew (born 19 March 1870); Thomas (born 5 January 1874); Mary Ann (born 2 September 1878) and Margaret (born 25 November 1880). Margaret Gunning was baptised in Shore Street Presbyterian Church.

Margaret Gunning and William Lennon were married on 24 July 1902 in Donaghadee Parish Church of Ireland Church and they had two children – Andrew (born 14 January 1903) and James (born 25 February 1905). William Lennon worked with his father, also called William; both men were deep sea divers. Margaret Lennon's sister-in-law, Mary Lennon, married David Nelson from Donaghadee and their son, **William George Nelson**, died on 8 May 1943 in the 'Bangor Bay Disaster'.

William and Margaret Lennon's elder son Andrew worked as a farm labourer and in March 1925 he moved to Canada. He sailed from Belfast to Halifax, Nova Scotia aboard the SS *Canopic* and in his immigration papers he stated that he was going to stay with John Lennon who lived at 61 Osler Avenue, Toronto. In 1927 Andrew Lennon and Martha Miller were married in Canada and they had at least one child, a daughter named Theodora who was born around 1930.

William and Margaret Lennon's younger son James married Theodora Thomas on 25 December 1925. Theodora Thomas was born around 1906 in Eccles, Lancashire and she was a daughter of John Frederick and Elizabeth Thomas. John Frederick Thomas was a calico print salesman and for a time the Thomas family lived in Millisle Road, Donaghadee. In April 1926 James Lennon followed his brother Andrew to Canada. He sailed from Belfast to Quebec aboard the SS *Alaunia* and in his immigration papers he stated that he was going to stay with Andrew Lennon who lived at 61 Osler Avenue, Toronto. He left behind in Donaghadee his wife Theodora who was expecting her first child. In March 1927 Theodora Lennon took her ten-month old son Thomas with her when she followed her husband James to Canada. Theodora and baby Thomas Lennon sailed aboard the SS *Montcalm* from Belfast to St. John, New Brunswick and in her immigration papers Theodora stated that they were going to stay with James Lennon who lived at 85 Edwin Avenue, Toronto. James and Theodora Lennon had at least two more children who were born in Toronto – Theresa (born around 1927) and Margaret (born around 1930).

In May 1928 William and Margaret Lennon (nee Gunning) followed their sons Andrew and James to Canada. They sailed from Belfast to Quebec aboard the SS *Montcalm* and they stated that their home address had been 19 Bow Street, Donaghadee. William described himself as a farmer, and he and Margaret stated that they wanted Canada to be their country of future permanent residence.

From time to time various members of the Lennon family travelled to Britain on holiday and then back home to Canada. For example, in February 1933 James Lennon's wife Theodora and their daughter Margaret sailed from Liverpool to Halifax on their way home to 263 Osler Avenue, Toronto. In 1939 Margaret Lennon and her grand-daughter Theodora (aged nine) spent time in Donaghadee during a visit to the United Kingdom. With rumours of war intensifying, Theodora's father Andrew sent a telegram to his mother urging her to return to Canada immediately. On 1 September 1939 Margaret and Theodora set sail from Glasgow aboard the SS *Athenia* and it was during that voyage that Margaret died as a result of enemy action. Both Margaret and Theodora got into a lifeboat after the ship was torpedoed but the lifeboat capsized and Margaret was drowned; her body was never recovered. Theodora was rescued from the water and taken back to 5 Newall Terrace, Dumfries in Scotland where she and her grandmother had been staying on holiday with the Revd H. Purdie and his family. Theodora Lennon returned to Canada in October 1939 aboard the SS *Duchess of York* which sailed from Liverpool to Quebec.

In his book entitled *Tomorrow Never Came*, Max Caulfield tells the story of the SS *Athenia* and he asserts that 'aboard were people who, but for the irony of fate, ought never to have been on her at all'. One of the examples he cites is Theodora Lennon. Max Caulfield says, 'some time in August 1939, back in Toronto, Mrs Andrew Lennon had dreamed she saw her nine-year old daughter picked up by a lifeboat from the cold black waters. She insisted that her husband should wire his mother who had the child with her on holiday in Britain, telling them to come home at once; they caught the SS *Athenia*'.

Of the many civilians of the Commonwealth whose deaths were due to enemy action in the Second World War, the names of some 67,092 are commemorated in the Civilian War Dead Roll of Honour, located near St. George's Chapel in Westminster Abbey, London. Margaret Lennon's son James died in 1989; her daughter-in-law Theodora died in 1993 and both were buried in St Paul's Cemetery, Innisfil, Ontario – as were her grandson Thomas and grand-daughter Theresa.

Lewandowski, Edward
Sergeant (Kapral Pilot)
No. P783109, No. 6 Anti-Aircraft Co-operation Unit (AACU)
Killed in an aircraft accident on Thursday 30 April 1942 (aged 22)
Belfast (Milltown) Roman Catholic Cemetery (Section A Row Lg Grave 39)

Edward Lewandowski was born on 2 September 1919 and during the Second World War he served with 6 Anti-Aircraft Co-operation Unit (AACU). He was based for a time at RAF Newtownards and he was killed during a training flight on 30 April 1942 when the Westland Lysander Mark II aircraft (P1731) he was piloting collided with a balloon cable at RAF Belfast and spun to the ground. Sergeant Edward Lewandowski was 22 years old when he died, he was buried in Belfast (Milltown) Roman Catholic Cemetery and he is commemorated on Panel 38 of the Polish Air Force Memorial at Northolt in London.

Lindeman, Ross Wellesley (Ross)
Sergeant
No. 403141, 153 Squadron, Royal Australian Air Force
Killed in an aircraft accident on Sunday 25 January 1942 (aged 21)
Ballyhalbert (St. Andrew's) Church of Ireland Churchyard,
Ballyeasborough, Co. Down (Grave 2)

Ross Wellesley Lindeman was born on 4 October 1920 in Burwood, Strathfield, New South Wales, Australia and he was the youngest son of Frederick Harold and Hilda Maud Lindeman (nee Mullens) of Edgecliff, New South Wales. They were married on 12 October 1912 in Homebush, New South Wales and they had at least three children – Colin, Bruce and Ross.

For a time the Lindeman family lived at the Ben Ean Vineyards at Polkolbin, New South Wales and, before he joined the Royal Australian Air Force, Ross was employed at Lysaghts (Galvanized Products) of Newcastle, New South Wales. Ross Wellesley Lindeman's father died on 20 October 1938 and his mother died on 20 October 1981. Ross Lindeman's brother Colin also joined the Royal Australian Air Force and during the Second World War he served in Malaya while Ross served in Europe.

On 25 January 1942, in the afternoon, Sergeant Ross Lindeman of 153 Squadron based at RAF Ballyhalbert was flying a Boulton Paul Defiant aircraft (N1647). He took off from RAF Eglinton in County Londonderry to fly to RAF Ballyhalbert. Before the flight the aircraft had been tested and found to be fully serviceable. There was a gusty wind blowing, the general weather conditions were described as 'fair' and the visibility as 'excellent'.

The accident occurred immediately after take off when the aircraft was seen to bank steeply on take off, turn over on its back and dive into the ground. Both crew members were killed. The other man who died was Flight Sergeant (Air Gunner) **Robert Low** aged 26 (Royal Air Force) and he was buried in Aberdeen (Allenvale) Cemetery in Scotland.

Sergeant Ross Wellesley Lindeman was 21 years old when he was killed and he is commemorated on the Australian War Memorial (Panel 125) and in Ballyhalbert (St. Andrew's) Church of Ireland Church (as R.W. Lineman).

451

Lindsay, David*
Leading Aircraftman
No. 654457, Royal Air Force
Killed in an aircraft accident on Wednesday 14 March 1945 (aged 33)
Lajes War Cemetery, Terceira, Azores (Row E Grave 8)

DIED ON ACTIVE SERVICE.

LINDSAY—March, 1945 (result of flying accident), L.A.C. David Lindsay, much-loved husband of Dorrie Lindsay, 96 Elmwood Drive, Bangor. Deeply regretted by his Wife and Family.

LINDSAY—March, 1945 (result of flying accident), L.A.C. David Lindsay, beloved son of David and Florence Lindsay, 17 Donard Avenue, Bangor. Deeply regretted by his Father, Mother, Sisters and Brother.

David Lindsay was born on 25 November 1911 and he was the elder son of David and Florence Lindsay (nee McMillin) of Alfred Street and later 17 Donard Avenue, Bangor. David Lindsay Senior worked as a bricklayer and he and Florence McMillin were married on 1 November 1909 in Helen's Bay Presbyterian Church. David Lindsay Junior was the husband of Dorothy (Dorrie) Lindsay (nee Rooney) of 96 Elmwood Drive, Bangor. They were married on 14 December 1933 in Newtownards Registry Office.

In the 31 March 1945 edition of the *County Down Spectator* there were four *Died on Active Service* notices, one from his wife Dorrie and family; one from his parents, sisters and brother; one from his sister-in-law and brother-in-law Rubina and Andrew Steele of 96 Elmwood Drive, Bangor and one from his sisters-in-law and brothers-in-law Eileen and William Kennedy and Catherine and James Savage.

LINDSAY—At her uncle's residence, 2 McClure Street, Belfast, August 21, 1946, Yvonne, youngest beloved daughter of Dorothy and the late David Lindsay, 96 Elmwood Drive, Bangor. Deeply regretted by loving Mother and Brother and Sister, Leslie and Vyne.

In the same edition of the *County Down Spectator* it was reported under the headline *Bangor Airman's Death* that, prior to the war, David Lindsay had been employed as a painter by John Jamison of High Street in Bangor. At the outbreak of war he joined the RAF and served in Canada and the Azores. His younger brother John also served in the RAF and was discharged in 1944. His sisters were Mrs Forbes Connor of 122 Donaghadee Road, Bangor and Mrs Raymond Robinson of Hove, Sussex. David Lindsay left a wife and three children – Leslie (aged ten), Vyne (aged seven) and Yvonne (aged six). His daughter Yvonne died on 21 August 1946.

Dorothy's brother, Rifleman Stanley Rooney (No. 3254795) served with the Cameronians (Scottish Rifles) *attached to* Headquarters 157th Infantry Brigade and he was 24 years old when he died suddenly on 7 September 1946. He was buried in Munster Heath War Cemetery, Telgte, Nordrhein-

DIED ON ACTIVE SERVICE

ROONEY—September 7, 1946 (suddenly) in North West Europe, Victor Stanley, beloved brother of Dorothy Lindsay. Deeply regretted by his sorrowing sister, Dorothy; nephew and niece, Leslie and Vyne.—95 Elmwood Drive.
"A loving brother, kind and true."

Westfalen in Germany (Grave 1 C 8). Within a period of 18 months Dorrie Lindsay lost her husband, her youngest child and her brother. Leading Aircraftman David Lindsay is commemorated on Bangor and District War Memorial and in First Bangor Presbyterian Church.

Logan, James Smiley
Able Seaman
SS *Jonathan Holt* (Liverpool), Merchant Navy
Died as a result of enemy action on Monday 24 February 1941 (aged 31)
Tower Hill Memorial, London, England (Panel 59)

Killed by Enemy Action.—Official intimation has been received by Mrs. Hester Logan, 155 Belfast Road, Bangor, of the death by enemy action of her husband, A.B. James Smiley Logan, Merchant Navy, who had previously been reported missing. Aged 31, he had been in the Merchant Service for 15 years; 12 with the Head and Lord Line. He was a son of Mr. and Mrs. Paul Logan, Knockagh, Greenisland.

Able Seaman James Smiley Logan's death was reported in the 20 September 1941 edition of the *County Down Spectator* under the headline *Killed By Enemy Action*. The report indicated that Mrs Hester Logan of 155 Belfast Road, Bangor had been informed that her husband, James Smiley Logan, who had been previously reported as missing, was presumed dead. James Smiley Logan was born on 14 July 1909 and he was a son of Paul and Fanny Logan (nee Smiley) of Knockagh, Greenisland. They were married on 6 November 1901 in First Carrickfergus Presbyterian Church and they had at least eight children – Martha (born 6 June 1902); Sarah (born 3 February 1904); Susan (born 15 December 1905, died 13 May 1906); William (born 11 March 1907); Pauline (born 1 May 1908); James Smiley (born 14 July 1909); John (born 10 June 1911) and Samuel (born 15 July 1912). James Smiley Logan was 16 years old when he went to sea and he served for 12 years with the Ulster Steamship Company.

During the Second World War Able Seaman James Smiley Logan served aboard the SS *Jonathan Holt*. This cargo ship was built in 1938 by Cammell Laird and Company, Birkenhead and was owned by John Holt and Company Ltd., Liverpool. At 2.12 am on 24 February 1941 the *Jonathan Holt* and the *Mansepool* sank southwest of the Faroe Islands after being hit by torpedoes fired by the German submarine *U-97*. Able Seaman James Smiley Logan (aged 31) was among more than 50 men aboard the SS *Jonathan Holt* who were killed and he is commemorated on the Tower Hill Memorial in London.

Logie, David Garfield (David)
Civilian War Dead
Died in a Prisoner-of-War Camp on Sunday 16 January 1944 (aged 60)

David Garfield Logie was born on 13 August 1883 in Dundee and he was a son of James and Mary Logie (nee Cameron) who were married in 1880. James Logie was an engineer and he and Mary had at least seven children – John, Julia, Florence, David Garfield, Harrison, Norman and Christina. Before undertaking a series of mechanical engineering apprenticeships, David Logie was educated at Clepington Public School, Dundee; Dundee High School and Dundee Technical Institute. In 1904 he was appointed Inspector of Works with the Bengal and North Western Railway Company, Gorakhpur in India and in 1908 he took up a similar position in Lagos, West Africa before returning to India in November 1909. On 18 April 1913 he became an Associate Member of the Institution of Mechanical Engineers (AMIME).

David Garfield Logie and Jane (Jennie) Mudie from Birkenhead were married on 17 December 1907 in a Presbyterian Church in Bombay, India and their marriage was registered in the third quarter of 1909 in West Derby, Lancashire. Jennie was the fourth daughter of Alexander and Lillian Mudie; Alexander Mudie was an engine fitter and his death was registered in the first quarter of 1906. David and Jennie Logie's address in England was 25 Thorneycroft Street, Birkenhead and they travelled to many parts of the world in connection with David's work in India, Singapore and Borneo.

Jennie Logie died and, on 25 November 1936, David Garfield Logie and Agnes Sarah Adderley (daughter of the Revd Thomas Adderley) were married in Killeshil Parish Church of Ireland Church, Co. Tyrone. During the Second World War David Garfield Logie was captured by Japanese soldiers and he died of malnutrition in Kuching (Batu Lintang) Prisoner-of-War Camp at Sarawak in Borneo. Conditions in this camp, which housed both Allied PoWs and civilian internees, were very harsh. A high proportion of prisoners held there died. David's effects in England amounted to some £6,996 and probate was granted to his widow, Agnes Sarah. Agnes Sarah Logie of *Armachia*, 32 Seacliff Road, Bangor and later *Kimberley*, Newry Road, Banbridge was 64 years old when she died on 9 April 1951 in Downshire Hospital, Downpatrick.

Of the many civilians of the Commonwealth whose deaths were due to enemy action in the Second World War, the names of some 67,092 are commemorated in the Civilian War Dead Roll of Honour, located near St. George's Chapel in Westminster Abbey, London.

Lorimer, Robert Lawrie (Lawrie)
Flying Officer
No. 37731, 1 Squadron, Royal Air Force
Killed in action on Tuesday 14 May 1940 (aged 25)
Runnymede Memorial, Surrey, England (Panel 6)

Robert Lawrie Lorimer was born on 24 June 1914 in Cleveland, Johannesburg, South Africa and he was baptised in St. Patrick's Church, Cleveland. He was a son of George Hill Lorimer and Jane (Janie) Lorimer (nee Lawrie), both originally from Ireland although they got married on 3 January 1905 in Cleveland, South Africa. George Hill Lorimer was a mining engineer in a goldmine on the Rand and he died of pneumonia on 29 May 1916 in Johannesburg. During the Siege of Kimberley in 1899/1900 George had served as a Private in the Premier Mine Division of Town Guard.

After George Lorimer died, Janie returned to Ireland from South Africa with her two children – Joan (born 24 July 1909, died 10 July 1994) and Lawrie. They lived at *Craig Royston*, Cultra and later in College Gardens, Belfast. Lawrie's sister Joan married Lieutenant **Noel Montgomery Neely** who served with the Royal Naval Volunteer Reserve during the Second World War (aboard HMS *Circe*). Lieutenant Neely was killed on 23 April 1944.

Lawrie Lorimer was educated at Rockport School, Craigavad from 1925 until 1928 and at Campbell College, Belfast from 1928 until 1931. When he left school he worked in insurance from 1932 until 1933. He joined the Royal Ulster Rifles in 1933 and was bought out after three months. He then worked in the motor trade from 1933 until 1935, joined the RAF in 1936 and was commissioned Pilot Officer. He underwent basic flight training at RAF Brough in Yorkshire and from 1937 until 1939 he served in 87 (F) Squadron at RAF Debden in Essex where he flew Gloster Gladiator aircraft. He was part of a three-man aerobatic team that performed with the wing tips of their aircraft tied together with bunting. One of their displays was performed at Villacoublay near Paris.

In 1939 Lawrie Lorimer went to France with 85 Squadron and in 1940 he was with 1 Squadron in Fighter Command when he was killed on 14 May 1940 near Sedan in France. He was flying a Hawker Hurricane Mark 1 aircraft (L1676) on a patrol mission when he was shot down in combat. His body was never recovered and a short tribute was published in the December 1940 edition of *The Campbellian*:

'Lawrie (spelt Laurie in the report) Lorimer as a small boy had an infinite capacity for making a mess of things and getting into scrapes. But he was always eminently likeable. His first few years after leaving school were unsettled: a few months in an insurance office, out of which he walked one afternoon to join the ranks of the Ulster Rifles; two or three months as a private before he was bought out; and then a couple of years as an apprentice in a motor works where, if you believed his own accounts, he spent most of his time dropping irreplaceable nuts into inaccessible places.

Then he obtained a commission in the RAF, and found himself. When he visited Campbell last spring it was difficult to remember the scatterbrained small boy in the self-assured, clearly competent young officer, second in command of a fighter squadron in France. But the new efficiency had not banished the old charm, that charm which made it so hard to strafe him at school and so delightful to spend an afternoon with him in a small boat on his native waters of Belfast Lough'.

LORIMER R.L. Flying Officer Robert Lawrie Lorimer was 25 years old when he was killed and he is commemorated in Rockport School and in Campbell College. His mother Janie lived at 8 Diamond Gardens, Finaghy and she died in the Royal Victoria Hospital, Belfast on 2 June 1943 (aged 72). Janie Lorimer was buried in Belfast City Cemetery (Grave J1 66).

Lough, William
Junior Engineer Officer
MV *Cingalese Prince* (London), Merchant Navy
Died as a result of enemy action on Saturday 20 September 1941 (aged 29)
Tower Hill Memorial, London (Panel 28)

William Lough was born on 26 May 1912 and he was a son of Alexander and Elizabeth Johnston Lough (nee Murdock) who lived in Tomer Street, Belfast and then at 33 Welland Street, Belfast. Alexander was born on 23 June 1869 in Larne and Elizabeth was born in 1869 in Comber. They were married on 16 April 1892 in Clifton Street Presbyterian Church, Belfast and they had thirteen children – Annie (born 25 January 1893); Ellen (born 13 April 1894, her married name was Mollinson and she died in childbirth in Toronto, along with her infant son, on 1 May 1929); Robert (Bob, born 21 April 1896); Mary (born 1 December 1897); Elizabeth (born 27 June 1899, died 21 April 1916 aged 16 and was buried in Comber Cemetery); Alexander (born 3 August 1901); Richard (born 24 March 1903); Jane (born 23 April 1904); Henry (born 3 June 1906); Edward James (born 30 August 1908); Maggie (born 29 May 1910) and twins Charles and William (born 26 May 1912).

During the First World War Robert (Bob) Lough served as a Rifleman (No. 13036) with the 8th Battalion, Royal Irish Rifles and he died of wounds on 2 July 1916. He was buried in Knightsbridge Cemetery, Mesnil-Martinsart, Somme, France and he is commemorated on Page 345 in the *Journey of Remembering – Belfast Book of Honour* compiled by Derek Smyth. Charles Lough (William's twin) moved to England and he died in Bolton in January 1980. Annie, Ellen, Alexander Junior and Edward James all moved to Canada. Margaret Lough moved to England and during the Second World War her husband, Stoker First Class **Thomas Murray**, served with the Royal Navy. He was killed in 1945 when his ship was torpedoed off the coast of Mayo. Alexander Lough Senior worked as a general labourer for Avoniel Irish Distillery in Belfast until his death in the Royal Victoria Hospital, Belfast on 6 September 1922. He was 52 years old when he died as a result of an accident in the distillery and he was buried in Dundonald Cemetery.

LOUGH—William Lough, Merchant Navy, lost at sea. Dearly beloved son of Elizabeth and the late Alexander Lough, formerly of Victoria Road, Bangor. Deeply regretted by his sorrowing Mother, Brothers and Sisters. 72 Upper Newtownards Road, Belfast.

On 8 November 1941 it was reported in the *County Down Spectator* that Junior Engineer William Lough had died on active service. His mother Elizabeth was living at 72 Upper Newtownards Road, Belfast with her daughter Mary and son-in-law William Whiteside. Before that, Elizabeth Lough lived at 54 Victoria Road, Bangor. Elizabeth Lough died on 8 May 1947 (aged 77) and was buried alongside her husband in Dundonald Cemetery.

Junior Engineer William Lough served aboard the motor merchant ship MV *Cingalese Prince* which was built in 1929 by the Blythswood Shipbuilding Company Ltd., Glasgow and owned by Furness, Withy and Company Ltd., Liverpool. She was unescorted on 20 September 1941 when she was torpedoed and sunk by the German submarine *U-111* near St. Paul Rocks off the coast of Brazil. Almost 60 lives were lost. Her scheduled voyage was from Bombay to Capetown to Trinidad to Liverpool and she had on board a general cargo including manganese ore and pig iron.

Junior Engineer Officer William Lough was 29 years of age when he died on 20 September 1941 and he is commemorated on Bangor and District War Memorial; in Bangor Parish Church (St. Comgall's) and on the family grave headstone in Dundonald Cemetery (Grave F4 655).

Love, Leslie
Fusilier
No. 6984566, 70ᵗʰ Battalion, Royal Inniskilling Fusiliers
Died as a result of enemy action on Wednesday 16 April 1941 (aged 34)
Carlton Cemetery, Nottinghamshire, England (Section B Row M 6 Grave 8)

Leslie Love was born in September 1906 and he was a son of Alfred and Annie Love (nee Joyce) who lived at 105 Windmill Row in Carlton, Nottingham. Alfred Love was a chimney sweep and he and Annie has at least seven children including Emily, Lily, Alfred, Leslie and Samuel.

Fusilier Leslie Love was the husband of Frances Gertrude Love (nee Ellis) of Nottingham (they were married in 1933) and he was one of 13 soldiers serving with the 70ᵗʰ Battalion, Royal Inniskilling Fusiliers who died as a result of an air raid on Newtownards aerodrome during the night of 15/16 April 1941. Fusilier **Daniel Higgins** who also died that night was buried in Newtownards (Movilla) Cemetery and under his name in this Book of Honour there is a summary of all those people with North Down or Ards connections who died that night.

It was Frances Gertrude Love who purchased the grave where Fusilier Leslie Love was buried on 22 April 1941 and on it there is an inscription:

With tender love and deep regret, hearts that loved him never forget

Frances Gertrude Love's marriage to Harry Shacklock was registered in the second quarter of 1943 and on 16 January 1950 Delma Wharmby (aged three months, daughter of Frances Wharmby) was buried in the same grave as Fusilier Leslie Love.

Low, Robert
Flight Sergeant (Air Gunner)
No. 817273, Royal Air Force
Killed in an aircraft accident on Sunday 25 January 1942 (aged 26)
Aberdeen (Allenvale) Cemetery, Scotland (Section D Grave 2068)

Robert Low was born on 22 May 1915 and he was a son of Robert and Margaret Singer Low (nee Howitt) of 76 Leslie Terrace, Aberdeen. They were married on 21 June 1905 in Rosemount Place, Aberdeen according to the forms of the Established Church of Scotland and they had two children – John (born 31 July 1906) and Robert (born 22 May 1915). Robert Low Senior worked as a slaughterman in an abattoir and in December 1915 he joined the Royal Army Service Corps. During the First World War he served in France.

Before he joined the Royal Air Force Robert Low Junior worked as a grocer's assistant and he was 25 years old when he and Alexandra Smith Cooper (aged 24, daughter of the late Alexander Smith Cooper) were married on 3 March 1941 in North and Trinity Church of Scotland, Aberdeen. On 25 January 1942 in the afternoon Flight Sergeant Robert Low was aboard a Boulton Paul Defiant aircraft (N1647) being flown by Sergeant **Ross Lindeman** of 153 Squadron based at RAF Ballyhalbert. They took off from RAF Eglinton in County Londonderry to fly to RAF Ballyhalbert. Before the flight the aircraft had been tested and found to be fully serviceable. There was a gusty wind blowing, the general weather conditions were described as 'fair' and the visibility as 'excellent'.

The accident occurred immediately after take off when the aircraft was seen to bank steeply, turn over on its back and dive into the ground. Both crew members were killed. Sergeant Ross Lindeman was buried in Ballyhalbert (St. Andrew's) Church of Ireland Churchyard, Ballyeasborough, Co. Down. Flight Sergeant Robert Low was 26 years old when he died and he was buried in Aberdeen (Allenvale) Cemetery in Scotland. There is an inscription on the Low family headstone:

To the dear memory of my beloved husband Robert Low
Flight Sergeant RAF, died on active service 25 January 1942 aged 26
His dear mother Margaret S. Howitt or Low, died 22 August 1949 aged 69

Our dearly loved mother Jeannie Reid Cooper, died 2 January 1959 aged 77
Beloved wife of Alexander Smith Cooper 1/5 Gordon Highlanders
Fell in action 4 November 1918 aged 40
Interred at Wez-Velvain Cemetery, Belgium
Also Robert Low, father of the first named, died 12 January 1962 aged 82
Also Alexandra Smith Low died 23 October 1994 aged 77
Beloved wife of the late Robert Low Jr
To live in hearts we leave behind is not to die

During the Second World War Alexandra Smith Low (nee Cooper) lost her husband, having already lost her father, Private Alexander Smith Cooper (No. 242212, 5th Battalion, Gordon Highlanders), during the First World War.

Lowden, George Henry Crawford (George)
Sub-Lieutenant (A)
HMS *Venerable*, Royal Naval Volunteer Reserve
Killed in an aircraft accident on Friday 20 April 1945 (aged 22)
Lee-on-Solent Memorial, Hampshire, England (Bay 6 Panel 4)

L

George Henry Crawford Lowden was born on 12 April 1923 and he was the elder son of George and Jeanette Lowden (nee Parker) of 8 First Avenue, Baylands in Bangor. George Lowden Senior (a stationer and merchant with premises at 19/21 Main Street, Bangor) had previously been married to Catherine (Kate) Neely. George Lowden and Kate Neely were married on 10 April 1893 in Newtownards Registry Office and they had two children – Frederick George (born 31 August 1896) and Kathleen May (born 1900). Kate Lowden died at 19 Main Street, Bangor on 24 May 1921 (aged 60). George Lowden Senior was a founder member of the Brethren Assembly in Bangor and he and Jeanette Parker were married on 27 February 1922 in Mourne Street Gospel Hall, Belfast. They had two children – George Henry Crawford (born 12 April 1923) and Noel (born 13 June 1926).

George Lowden Senior (born 31 July 1868) was 64 years old when he died on 8 April 1933 and he was buried in the Lowden family grave in Bangor Abbey Graveyard (his name is not inscribed on the headstone).

George Henry Crawford Lowden was educated at Bangor Public Elementary School and at Bangor Grammar School from 1935 until 1939. He played rugby for the school and excelled at long distance running. The Headmaster described him as 'a boy of robust and manly character who left his mark

460

upon the School'. George's ambition from a young age was to go to sea. He joined the Royal Navy on 6 November 1940 (No. R220731) as a Radio Cadet and undertook training as a wireless operator in Belfast Wireless College. In his papers it was recorded that he was 5 feet 7 inches tall with blue eyes, brown hair, a fresh complexion and no distinguishing marks. He served aboard HMS *Eaglet* (6 November 1940 to 30 November 1940); HMS *Mooltan* (1 December 1940 to 29 January 1941); HMS *Kirriemoor* (30 January 1941 to 12 February 1941); HMS *Mersey* (13 February 1941 to 9 March 1941) and HMS *Aurania* (10 March 1941 to 16 March 1942).

George Lowden transferred to the Fleet Air Arm on 25 February 1942 (No. FX91871) and had training in England, Canada and the USA. After receiving his commission he was engaged in ferrying aircraft in the USA. He served with HMS *Daedalus* (RNAS Lee-on-Solent, 6 April 1942 to 19 April 1942); HMS *St. Vincent*, Gosport (20 April 1942 to 4 April 1943); HMS *Saker* (732 Squadron, Brunswick, Maine, USA, 5 April 1943 to 21 June 1944); HMS *Saker* (Ferry Squadron, Roosevelt Field, USA, 22 June 1944 to 9 January 1945); HMS *Gannet*, Northern Ireland (1851 Squadron, 10 January 1945 to 27 January 1945) and HMS *Venerable* (1851 Squadron, 28 January 1945 to 20 April 1945). HMS *Venerable* was a Colossus-class aircraft carrier.

> **KILLED ON ACTIVE SERVICE**
>
> LOWDEN—April 20, 1945, on active service, Temporary Sub.-Lieut. George H. C. Lowden, R.N.V.R., dearly-loved son of the late George Lowden and of Mrs. J. Lowden, 8 First Avenue, Baylands, Bangor.

The death of Sub-Lieutenant George Henry Crawford Lowden as the result of an aircraft accident was reported in the 28 April 1945 edition of the *County Down Spectator* under the headline *Bangor Officer Missing, Presumed Killed*. On 20 April 1945 he was flying a Chance Vought FG-1D Corsair IV aircraft (KD583) which stalled and crashed into the sea as he was coming in to land on HMS *Venerable* off the coast of Malta. His body was never recovered. It was his brother Noel Lowden who received the news by telephone about George's death and it was Noel who told his mother. Noel was studying at Stranmillis Teacher Training College and his mother was visiting him at the time he received the news.

Sub-Lieutenant George Henry Crawford Lowden was 22 years old when he was killed and he is commemorated on the Lee-on-Solent Memorial in Hampshire; on Bangor and District War Memorial; in Bangor Central Hall and in Bangor Grammar School. His mother Jeanette (born 20 April 1891) was one day short of her 83rd birthday when she died on 19 April 1974 and she was buried in Clandeboye Cemetery.

Lowry, G.E.

 The names G.E. Lowry and G.V. Lowry are both inscribed on Bangor and District War Memorial. Desk studies and public appeals to date have produced no information about G.E. Lowry and it *may* be that G.E. Lowry and G.V. Lowry are one and the same person.

The Second World War Memorial Plaque on Bangor and District War Memorial was not unveiled until November 1967 and this accounts for some of the omissions and inaccuracies in the list of inscribed names. A notice was published in the 1 November 1963 edition of the *County Down Spectator* under the heading *We Will Remember Them Roll of Honour 1935-45 War* (there was a typographical error in the war years – 1935 instead of 1939): 'The British Legion Women's Section, Bangor Branch, with the co-operation of the Men's Branch, schools and churches, has compiled the undernoted list of Bangor people who died in the service of their country during World War II. The object of publishing the names is to ensure that they are accurate and complete before being inscribed on the War Memorial. Relatives or friends who know of any omissions or inaccuracies in the list are asked to get in touch with Councillor J. Halley JP at the British Legion Hall or to supply the necessary information to the Spectator'. A list of 91 names was published.

A revised list of 113 names was published in the 24 December 1963 edition of the *County Down Spectator* and friends and relatives were invited to take this final opportunity to make further corrections. Then, in the 17 November 1967 edition of the *County Down Spectator* it was reported that a plaque bearing 117 names had been unveiled on the War Memorial. The report indicated that Remembrance Sunday in 1967 was unique because a Roman Catholic Priest took part alongside Protestant Clergy for the first time. The plaque was unveiled by Councillor Bertie McConnell who had been blinded whilst on active service in the Second World War and the plaque was dedicated by the Revd W.J. McKinstry Wallace.

At the time of writing it has not been possible to determine whether G.E. Lowry was a casualty of war or if the name G.E. Lowry was inscribed on the plaque in error.

Lowry, George Victor (George)
Able Seaman
No. D/SSX 20899, HMS *Stronghold*, Royal Navy
Killed in action on Monday 2 March 1942 (aged 22)
Plymouth Naval Memorial, Devon, England (Panel 65 Column 3)

George Victor Lowry's birth was registered in the third quarter of 1919 in Newtownards and he was the second son of William and Violet Lowry (nee Watterson) of 7 Railwayview Street, Bangor. William Lowry (whose father was a sailor) worked as a labourer and he and Violet Watterson (whose father was a fisherman) were married on 7 January 1915 in St. Anne's Church of Ireland Cathedral, Belfast. Before joining the Royal Navy around 1937, George Lowry was employed by Messrs Ellis and Company in Main Street, Bangor. He was a member of the Boys' Brigade Company associated with Hamilton Road Methodist Church, Bangor. George's elder brother William served in an infantry regiment in Palestine and his sister Minnie was engaged on munitions work in Scotland.

George Victor Lowry served aboard HMS *Stronghold* which was a Royal Navy destroyer built in 1919 by Scotts Shipbuilding and Engineering Company of Greenock in Scotland. On 2 March 1942 a Japanese task group comprising the heavy cruiser *Maya* and the destroyers *Arashi* and *Nowaki* was operating south of Java when it discovered and sank HMS *Stronghold* at around 7.00 pm. HMS *Stronghold* was on route from the port of Tjilatjap, Java to Australia. Around fifty survivors were picked up by the Dutch ship *Bintoehan* and later they were transferred to the *Maya* after the *Bintoehan* was captured by the Japanese. Thereafter the survivors from HMS *Stronghold* were held as Prisoners-of-War.

L

> LOWRY—Reported missing March 2, 1942, now presumed lost at sea on H.M.S. "Stronghold," George Victor, second and dearly loved son of Wm. and Violet Lowry.
> "Safely, safely gathered in, No more sorrow, no more sin, God has saved, from weary strife, in its dawn this young, fresh life Which awaits us, now, Above, Resting in the Saviour's love."
> Deeply regretted by his sorrowing Father, Mother, Brothers and Sisters, 7 Railway View Street, Bangor; also his Brother, Billie, and Sister-in-law, and little Niece, Bedford House, Essex.

Able Seaman George Victor Lowry was reported missing on 2 March 1942 and it was almost four years before he was officially presumed to have lost his life. In the 15 December 1945 edition of the *County Down Spectator* there were three *Died on Active Service* notices, one from his aunt and uncle Abigail and Hugh Beattie, also his cousin Hugh Beattie and Hugh's wife Ellen of The Hill, Groomsport; one from his parents, brothers and sisters, also his brother Billy, sister-in-law and niece of Bedford House, Essex and one from his cousin Lena, her husband William Hamilton and their little son George Victor Hamilton of *Westbank*, Groomsport. The notice from his parents contained the verse:

Safely, safely gathered in
No more sorrow, no more sin,
God has saved from weary strife,
In its dawn this young, fresh life
Which awaits us, now, Above,
Resting in the Saviour's love

Able Seaman George Victor Lowry was 22 years old when he was killed and he is commemorated on Plymouth Naval Memorial in Devon; on Bangor and District War Memorial; on Groomsport and District War Memorial; in Groomsport Parish Church of Ireland Church and in First Bangor Presbyterian Church.

Lucas, John Robert
Flight Sergeant (Pilot)
No. R/78281, 153 (RAF) Squadron, Royal Canadian Air Force
Killed in an aircraft accident on Wednesday 18 February 1942 (aged 20)
Ballyhalbert (St. Andrew's) Church of Ireland Churchyard,
Ballyeasborough, Co. Down (Grave 3)

L

John Robert Lucas was born in Toronto on 6 July 1921 and he was a son of John Noble Lucas (born in London) and Caroline Lucas (nee Williamson, born in Belfast). During the First World War John Noble Lucas served with the Canadian Overseas Expeditionary Force and after the war he worked as an electrician. John Noble Lucas and Caroline Williamson were married on 20 August 1920 in Toronto and they lived at 833 Sammon Street, Toronto.

In November 1940 John Robert Lucas joined the Royal Canadian Air Force and during the Second World War he served with 153 (RAF) Squadron based at RAF Ballyhalbert. On 18 February 1942 he was the pilot in a Boulton Paul Defiant aircraft (T3914) that crashed into the sea off Kearney, Co. Down. There were reports at the time that he had been attempting to avoid another aircraft. Both crew members were killed and four days later their bodies were recovered from the sea near Burial Island, north of Portavogie. The two men who died were Flight Sergeant (Pilot) John Robert Lucas and Flight Sergeant (Air Gunner) **Cecil Thomas Deane**.

Flight Sergeant John Robert Lucas was buried in Ballyhalbert (St. Andrew's) Church of Ireland Churchyard, Ballyeasborough, Co. Down on 26 February

1942 and his mother added an inscription to his CWGC headstone:

In loving memory of my dear son
To know him was to love him
Till we meet again

Flight Sergeant John Robert Lucas was 20 years old when he died and he is commemorated on the Canadian Virtual War Memorial (Internet); on Page 91 in the Canadian Second World War Book of Remembrance and in Ballyhalbert (St. Andrew's) Church of Ireland Church, Ballyeasborough.

Luke, Samuel John (Samuel)
Sergeant
No. 401438, 223 Squadron, Royal New Zealand Air Force
Drowned on active service on Sunday 17 August 1941 (aged 22)
Suez War Memorial Cemetery, Egypt (Grave 1 B 1)

Samuel John Luke was born in Corboy, Co. Longford on 7 May 1919 and he was the only son of William John and Sarah Elizabeth Kathleen Luke (nee Murray; in some records her surname is spelt Murphy). Their marriage was registered in the third quarter of 1918 in Longford and the Luke family moved to 120 High Street in Bangor. William John Luke was a farmer and a disabled ex-serviceman who had served during the First World War. Samuel Luke attended Bangor Grammar School for one year, from September 1932 until October 1933, before the Luke family moved to Mt. Maunganui, Tauranga, Auckland in New Zealand. Samuel John Luke was 14 years old when they travelled aboard the SS *Orsova* which departed from London on 14 October 1933 bound for Sydney.

SERGEANT OBSERVER S. J. LUKE

Tidings have reached us (Mr. Wilkins continued) also that yet another Old Boy of Bangor Grammar School was lost last September in the Middle East, serving in the Royal New Zealand Air Force—Sergeant Observer Samuel J. Luke, whom we well remember as a junior boy of steady character in Forms III. A and IV. C from September, 1932, to October, 1933. His stay with us was brief, as his father (a disabled ex-Serviceman of the last war) and mother emigrated to New Zealand when he was but fourteen years of age.

Samuel John Luke joined the Royal New Zealand Air Force and served with 223 Squadron in the Egypt campaign. 223 Squadron went to Egypt in April 1941 where it became an Operational Training Unit (OTU). Sergeant Samuel John Luke flew Martin Maryland Mark I aircraft and he was drowned in the Mediterranean Sea on 17 August 1941. He was 22 years old when he died and he was buried in Suez War Memorial Cemetery in Egypt. Sergeant Samuel John Luke is commemorated on the New Zealand National War Memorial in Wellington; on the New Zealand Cenotaph Database in Auckland War Memorial Museum; on Bangor and District War Memorial; in Hamilton Road Presbyterian Church, Bangor and in Bangor Grammar School.

Samuel John Luke's father died in 1961 (aged 82) and his mother died in 1967 (aged 83).

MacCallum, John Evelyn Matier (Lyn)*
Group Captain
No. 26039, Royal Air Force
Died as a result of an accident on Saturday 16 October 1943 (aged 37)
Bangor Cemetery, Co. Down (Section 2 G Grave 76)

The death on active service is announced of Group Captain John Evelyn MacCallum. Lyn MacCallum was born in Lisburn and was educated at Banbridge Academy and Portadown College.

On leaving school in 1923 he joined the R.A.F. and during the last twenty years has seen service in many parts of the Empire

At the time of his death he was the Commanding Officer of an R.A.F. station in Southern England. His parents reside in Portadown.

He is survived by his wife, who is in the W.A.A.F., and two children.

John Evelyn Matier (Lyn) MacCallum was born on 3 October 1906 in Lisburn, Co. Antrim and he was a son of William Henry and Charlotte Mary Christina (Lottie) MacCallum (nee Williams). Henry MacCallum was a school teacher and in 1901 he was teaching in First Bangor Presbyterian Church School. Henry and Lottie were married on 5 August 1903 in Bangor Parish Church of Ireland Church (St. Comgall's) and they had at least four children – James Wallace (born 22 August 1904); Margaret Helena (Madge, born 7 October 1905); John Evelyn Matier (born 3 October 1906) and Henry Cecil Warwick (born 8 May 1908). After leaving Bangor the MacCallum family lived at 152 Longstone Street, Lisburn and later in Portadown. Lyn MacCallum was educated at Banbridge Academy and Portadown College and in 1922/23 he was Captain of the Portadown College 1st XV rugby team.

Lyn MacCallum joined the Royal Air Force in 1923 and in 1931 he and Mollie Patricia Bishop were married in Ismailia, Egypt. Lyn was promoted from Flying Officer to Flight Lieutenant with effect from 1 December 1932 (*London Gazette* 6 December 1932); from Flight Lieutenant to Squadron Leader with effect from 1 August 1937 (*London Gazette* 3 August 1937) and from Squadron Leader to Wing Commander (temporary) with effect from 1 June 1940 (*London Gazette* 7 June 1940). His wife Mollie was serving with the Women's Auxiliary Air Force (WAAF) and they had two children.

Group Captain John Evelyn Matier MacCallum was 37 years old when he died on 16 October 1943 as a result of an accident and he is commemorated

L
Ma

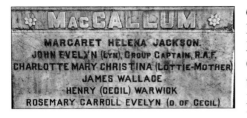

on the family grave headstone in Bangor Cemetery; on Lisburn War Memorial and in Portadown College. In Portadown College there are three Houses – MacCallum, Seale and Shillington. MacCallum House is named in honour of Group Captain Lyn MacCallum. Seale House is named in honour of brothers Squadron Leader W. Terry Seale who was killed on 30 June 1941 and Lieutenant Theo. J. Seale who was killed on 1 June 1944. Shillington House is named in honour of David Graham Shillington who served in the First World War. Two members of the Shillington family died in the First World War – Thomas Graham Shillington and Geoffrey St. George Shillington Cather VC.

MacDonald, William Moody (Billy)
Pilot Officer (Pilot U/T)
No. 102146, Royal Air Force
Died on active service on Thursday 28 August 1941 (aged 20)
Bangor Cemetery, Co. Down (Section 3 K Grave 160)

Ma

William Moody MacDonald was born on 21 February 1921 and he was the younger son of Robert and Sara McCaw MacDonald (nee Robinson) of 47 Bryansburn Road, Bangor. They were married on 22 July 1914 in Killinchy Presbyterian Church. Robert MacDonald was the Headmaster of Bangor Central Public Elementary School and it was there that Billy began his education. He also attended Bangor Grammar School from 1933 until 1937 and Regent House School Newtownards from 1937 until 1938 before going to Queen's University Belfast to study engineering. He was a renowned athlete and played rugby for Bangor Grammar, Regent House and Queen's University. At Regent House he won the trophy awarded to the best senior athlete. He was a member of the First Bangor Company of the Boys' Brigade, of which his father was the President. Billy's uncle, T.H. MacDonald, was Town Clerk in Lisburn Urban Council.

MacDONALD—Killed on Active Service, Pilot Officer William Moody, younger son of Robert and Sara MacDonald, 47 Bryansburn Road, Bangor. Interment notice later.

Billy MacDonald joined the Royal Air Force from Queen's University Officers' Training Corps and he received his commission in June 1941. In early August 1941 he was home on leave and three weeks later, on 28 August 1941, he died on active service. His funeral to Bangor Cemetery on 31 August 1941 was described in the press as 'one of the largest seen in Bangor'. The services in the house and at the graveside were conducted by the Revd Dr Currie and Squadron Leader the Revd A.E. Bothwick, RAF. On 1 November 1941 a cot in the Cripples' Home, now the Northern Ireland Institute for the Disabled (NIID), Downshire Road, Bangor was named in memory of Pilot Officer William Moody MacDonald and an inscribed plaque over the cot was unveiled by his mother Sara. At the time of the unveiling it was reported in the press that 'the crippled child lying in the cot was Norman Campbell'.

Pilot Officer William Moody MacDonald was 20 years old when he was killed and he is commemorated on Bangor and District War Memorial; in First Bangor Presbyterian Church; in Bangor Grammar School; in Regent House School (as W.M. McDonald); on Page 78 in the QUB Book of Remembrance and on the family grave headstone in Bangor Cemetery. In one of the *Roll of Honour* notices published in the *County Down Spectator* there was the text:

His life, our freedom

At Bangor Grammar School Billy MacDonald and **Julius Holland** (killed on 23 July 1940) were close friends. Billy's father, Robert MacDonald, died on 8 December 1942 (aged 55); his mother, Sara MacDonald, died on 30 September 1962 (aged 75) and his elder brother, Robert Mervyn MacDonald, died on 9 September 1985.

MacFarlane, Albert George (Bertie)
Telegraphist
No. D/WRX741, HMS *Drake*, Royal Naval Volunteer (Wireless) Reserve
Died of illness on Thursday 29 January 1942 (aged 28)
Bangor Cemetery, Co. Down (Section 5 O Grave 181; *not Section 5 Q*)

Albert George MacFarlane was born in Belfast on 12 June 1913 and he was the only son of William and Hessie MacFarlane (nee Rodgers) who lived at 30 Glencollyer Street and later at *Shelbourne*, 101 Belfast Road, Bangor. William MacFarlane worked as a plater in the shipyard and he and Hessie Rodgers were married on 9 October 1912 in Alexandra Presbyterian Church, Belfast. They had at least two children, Albert George (Bertie) and a daughter

ROLL OF HONOUR

MACFARLANE — January 29, 1942. Sweet memories of a devoted son and brother, Bertie, late of R.N.V. (W.)R., called to Higher Service.
  "I thank my God upon every remembrance of him."
Bangor and Holywood.

MACFARLANE — January 29, 1942. Everlasting memories of Bertie, late of R.N.V.(W.)R., who sacrificed his life for others.
  "As you did this for the least of mine, you did it for me."
P.J.W.

named Janet who married William Kinkead on 12 September 1938 in Ballygilbert Presbyterian Church. Along with Stewart Templeton, Bertie MacFarlane was joint Assistant Scoutmaster of the First Bangor Company of Boy Scouts. Stewart Templeton (aged 23) died on 10 January 1940 in a road accident during the black-out and Stewart's brother **Moore Templeton** was killed in action on 4 February 1943. Prior to the outbreak of the Second World War, Albert George MacFarlane worked for Messrs Henry Gowan and Company (Shipping Agents), Corporation Street, Belfast. At the outbreak of war he joined the Royal Navy as a Telegraphist and was stationed in British West Africa. There he contracted an infection and was invalided home in the spring of 1941. He recovered sufficiently to resume his business but became seriously ill in October 1941. He was 28 years old when he died of bacterial endocarditis on 29 January 1942 at his parents' residence and his funeral to Bangor Cemetery took place on 31 January 1942.

Ma

Telegraphist Albert George MacFarlane is commemorated on Bangor and District War Memorial; in Trinity Presbyterian Church, Bangor and on the family grave headstone in Bangor Cemetery. In one of the *Roll of Honour* notices published in the *County Down Spectator* there was the text:

I thank my God upon every remembrance of him

MacIlwaine, John Patterson (John)
Sergeant
No. 1114000, Royal Air Force
Killed in an aircraft accident on Tuesday 26 August 1941 (aged 26)
Ardstraw (St. Eugene's) Church of Ireland Churchyard,
Newtownstewart, Co. Tyrone (Section E Grave 445)

John Patterson MacIlwaine was born on 9 September 1914 and he was a son of Robert and Janetta MacIlwaine (nee Tate) of Newtownards. Both Robert and Janetta were National School teachers and they were married on 16 July

1913 in Holywood Presbyterian Church. Later the MacIlwaine family moved to Mill Street, Newtownstewart in County Tyrone and then to *The Bungalow*, Newtownstewart when Robert became Principal of the Model School in Newtownstewart. Robert and Janetta MacIlwaine had five children – John Patterson (born 1914); Robert (Bert, born 1918, died after swallowing a dried pea which 'travelled to his lung' and he was buried on 30 October 1921); Agnes Tate (Nesta, who became a Senior Mistress in Sullivan Upper School, Holywood and was buried on 27 June 1988); Alice (born 1922, buried 25 November 1922) and Roberta Janett (born 1928).

John Patterson MacIlwaine's paternal grandparents were Matthew and Susan MacIlwaine (nee Patterson) who were married on 1 July 1879 in Mountpottinger Presbyterian Church, Belfast. Matthew MacIlwaine was a draper and he moved to the USA where he settled; his wife Susan opted to remain at home.

John Patterson MacIlwaine's maternal grandparents were John and Sarah Jane Tate (nee Kirkpatrick) who were married on 1 August 1884 in St. Stephen's Church of Ireland Church, Belfast. John Tate was a spirit merchant and he had three licensed premises in Newtownards – the Royal, the Corner House and the Ulster Arms. During the First World War their son John (Jack) Tate died of wounds and was buried in France. He is commemorated on Page 628 in the Book of Honour *Remembering Their Sacrifice in the Great War – Ards* compiled by Barry Niblock. John Tate Senior died on 8 February 1917 (aged 61). In addition to losing a son in the First World War Sarah Jane Tate lost her brother, John Kirkpatrick. When John Patterson MacIlwaine joined up to fight in the Second World War his maternal grandmother Sarah Jane Tate predicted that she would never see him alive again. Her prediction proved to be correct.

John Patterson MacIlwaine was a boarder at Methodist College Belfast and in 1936 he obtained a degree in classics from Trinity College Dublin. He taught at Down High School in Downpatrick and was one of three teachers at the school who enlisted around the same time. John Patterson MacIlwaine and Flying Officer William Ernest Norman Maxwell from Belfast, who was killed on 23 January 1943, both served with the Royal Air Force. Ernest Montgomery who served with the Army survived the war and resumed his career as a maths teacher.

John Patterson MacIlwaine travelled to the USA and from there to Moosejaw in Saskatchewan for training. On the journey home the transport ship he

IMPRESSIVE FUNERAL TRIBUTE.

Impressive scenes were witnessed in Newtownstewart on Monday afternoon when the funeral of Sergeant-Pilot John P. MacIlwaine, R.A.F., who died as the result of an accident son of Mr. and Mrs. Robert MacIlwaine of Newtownstewart, and formerly of Newtownards,

was travelling on was torpedoed and he survived but, in a letter home afterwards, he lamented the loss of his golf clubs. Then he served with 'D' Flight, 13 Squadron in No.7 Initial Training Wing (ITW) at RAF Newquay in Cornwall and he was serving with Fighter Command when he died on 26 August 1941. He was due a period of home leave and in a letter to his mother he told her how much he was looking forward to it. But it was not to be. Sergeant John Patterson MacIlwaine's death was reported in the 6 September 1941 edition of the *Newtownards Chronicle*. In the same edition there were *Died on Active Service* notices from his grandmother, Susan MacIlwaine of 26 John Street, Newtownards; his uncle and aunt, John and M. MacIlwaine of 3 Upper Court Street, Newtownards and his maternal grandmother Sarah Jane Tate and family of Frances Street and North Street, Newtownards.

Sergeant John Patterson MacIlwaine was serving with 53 OTU when he died on 26 August 1941 aged 26. His Supermarine Spitfire aircraft ran out of fuel and crashed into the Bristol Channel between Barry in Glamorgan and Weston-super-Mare. He was buried on 1 September 1941 in Ardstraw (St. Eugene's) Church of Ireland Churchyard, Newtownstewart. His effects amounted to some £76 and probate was granted to his father Robert. His father died on 14 July 1948 (aged 67) and his mother Janetta was buried on 1 March 1967.

Sergeant John Patterson MacIlwaine is commemorated on Downpatrick and District War Memorial; in the Trinity College Dublin Roll of Honour; in Methodist College Belfast and in Newtownstewart Presbyterian Church.

Macoun Family, Leslie Stuart and Julie Maude (Husband and Wife)

In the CWGC Debt of Honour Captain (Retired) Leslie Stuart Macoun of 199 Wurtemburg Street, Ottawa, Canada is described as a son of Mary Macoun of Holywood and the late John Macoun. Leslie Stuart Macoun was born on 31 July 1874 and he was a son of linen manufacturer John Robert Macoun (born 1835) of Holywood (previously Malone Park, Belfast) and Wilhelmina Moorehead Macoun (nee Dawson, born 26 October 1845). They were married on 27 February 1872 and they had two children – Leslie Stuart Macoun (born 31 July 1874) and Anita Wilhelmina Macoun (born 1882, died 24 December 1952). Leslie Stuart Macoun was educated in the Isle of Man.

Ma

Leslie Stewart Macoun moved to Canada in 1890 where he secured a position as an accountant at the Horticultural Experimental Station in Ottawa. Later he joined the Princess Louise Dragoon Guards and attained the rank of Captain. His mother, Wilhelmina Macoun, died on 2 January 1898 (aged 51) and his father, John Robert Macoun, died on 2 April 1923 (aged 87).

Macoun, Julie Maude
Civilian War Dead
RMS *Lady Hawkins*
Died as a result of enemy action on Monday 19 January 1942 (aged 63)

In the CWGC Debt of Honour Julie Maude Macoun of 199 Wurtemburg Street, Ottawa in Canada is described as a daughter of Lady Borden of Borden Place, Canning, Nova Scotia and the late Sir Frederick William Borden. She was in fact Lady Borden's step-daughter. Frederick William Borden was born on 14 May 1847 and he obtained an MD degree in 1868 from Harvard Medical School. He practised in Canning, Nova Scotia before entering politics in 1874. The previous year, on 1 October 1873, he and Julia Maude Clarke were married and they had three children – Elizabeth M. (born 1874); Harold Lothrop (born 23 May 1876) and Julie Maude (born 23 March 1879). After Julia Borden died in 1880, Frederick William Borden married Julia's sister, Bessie Blanche Clarke. In 1896 he became Minister for Militia and Defence and his only son, Lieutenant Harold Lothrop Borden, was killed on 16 July 1900 at Witpoort in the South African War. Frederick William Borden was created a Knight Commander of the Most Distinguished Order of St. Michael and St. George (KCMG) in June 1902 and he died in Canning on 6 January 1917 after a short illness. Julie Maude Borden and Leslie Stuart Macoun were married on 22 May 1906 and they had one daughter – Elizabeth Rosamund Macoun (born 1907).

Macoun, Leslie Stuart
Civilian War Dead
RMS *Lady Hawkins*
Died as a result of enemy action on Monday 19 January 1942 (aged 67)

Captain (Retired) Leslie Stuart Macoun and his wife Julie Maude Macoun were travelling together aboard the RMS *Lady Hawkins* when they died as a result of enemy action on 19 January 1942. RMS *Lady Hawkins* was a steam passenger ship owned by Canadian National Steamships

Ltd., Montreal. Built by Cammell Laird and Company, Birkenhead in 1928, she was sailing from Montreal to Bermuda with both passengers and cargo aboard. She was unescorted and blacked out when she was hit by two torpedoes fired from the German submarine *U-66*. More than 250 people were killed when RMS *Lady Hawkins* sank some 150 miles off Cape Hatteras, North Carolina, USA.

Of the many civilians of the Commonwealth whose deaths were due to enemy action in the Second World War, the names of some 67,092 are commemorated in the Civilian War Dead Roll of Honour, located near St. George's Chapel in Westminster Abbey, London.

Madden, John
Gunner
No. 1058272, 1 Battery, 1 Heavy Anti-Aircraft Regiment, Royal Artillery
Died as a result of an accident on Saturday 7 March 1942 (aged 37)
Belfast City Cemetery Glenalina Extension (Section AS Grave 118)

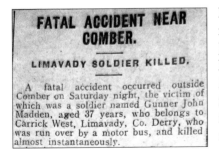

FATAL ACCIDENT NEAR COMBER.

LIMAVADY SOLDIER KILLED.

A fatal accident occurred outside Comber on Saturday night, the victim of which was a soldier named Gunner John Madden, aged 37 years, who belongs to Carrick West, Limavady, Co. Derry, who was run over by a motor bus, and killed almost instantaneously.

In the CWGC Debt of Honour it is recorded that John Madden was a son of J. Madden and Martha Madden and the husband of Martha Madden of Dungiven, Co. Londonderry. John's father's name was John and evidence from another source suggests that his mother's name was Elizabeth.

Ma

John Madden Junior (a labourer from the townland of Bovally, Fruithill, Limavady and a son of John Madden, farm labourer) married Martha Connor (one of 13 children, a daughter of Robert James Connor, a farmer from the townland of Largy, The Highlands, Limavady) on 5 April 1932 in Derramore Presbyterian Church, Drumachose, Limavady. John and Martha Madden lived in Carrick West, Limavady and during the Second World War John served with the Royal Artillery.

Gunner John Madden's death was reported in the 14 March 1942 edition of the *Newtownards Chronicle* under the headline *Fatal Accident near Comber*. At the inquest held in Comber on 9 March 1942 Gunner John Philip gave evidence that he and Gunner John Madden were walking towards Ballystockart along the main Belfast to Comber road at about 10.30 pm on 7 March 1942. Gunner Philip said that shortly after walking under the railway bridge at Ballyloughan they heard a noise and he (Philip) got off the road onto the footpath. When Gunner Philip looked round he saw Gunner Madden lying on the road and he went back to see what had happened to him. As he was about to lift him, a bus ran over Gunner Madden and knocked Gunner Philip down, injuring his toe. Gunner Madden was taken to Mrs Haslett's house where he subsequently died.

Others were called to give evidence too, including Robert Leonard of Church Street, Downpatrick who was the conductor on the bus and John Murray of Bank Row, Shrigley, Killyleagh who was a passenger on the bus. The driver of the bus was James Leo Dalton of Shrigley, Killyleagh. The Coroner recorded a verdict that death was due to shock and multiple injuries received when the deceased was run over by a bus.

Gunner John Madden was 37 years old when he died; he was buried in Belfast City Cemetery and there is an inscription on his CWGC headstone:

Blessed are they that die in the Lord
He will revive us, He will raise us up

Ma
Maginnis, Francis (Frank)
Fireman
SS *River Humber* (Bristol), Merchant Navy
Died as a result of a collision at sea on Tuesday 4 June 1940 (aged 30)
Tower Hill Memorial, London, England (Panel 87)

In different records Frank's surname is spelt Magennis, McGinness, Maginess, Maginness (CWGC) and Maguinness.

> MAGINNIS—In loving memory of my dear son, Frank, who was drowned at sea on June 4, 1940.
> "Your end came sudden, Frank dear,
>   You made us weep and cry,
> But oh the saddest part of all,
>   You could not say 'Good-bye.'"
> Always remembered by his loving Mother, Brothers, Sisters; also his Son and Daughter. — Kirkistown Quarter, Kircubbin.

> MAGINESS—In memory of my dear husband, Frank Maginess, who died 4th June, 1940, through enemy action.
> 'We were not there at time of death
>   To hear his last faint sigh;
> We only know he passed away
>   And never said good-bye."
> Sadly missed by his sorrowing Wife and Family, Kirkistown, Ardkeen, Cloughy.

Francis (Frank) Maginnis was born on 8 March 1909 and he was a son of Francis (Frank) and Mary Maginnis (nee Bryce) who lived in the townland of Kirkistown, Ardkeen, Kircubbin, Co. Down. Frank Maginnis Senior worked as a labourer and he and Mary Bryce were married on 12 May 1905 in Ardkeen Parish Church of Ireland Church. They had at least six children – Robert J. (died 7 November 1954); Francis (born 8 March 1909); Thomas H. (died in infancy); Alexander (Alex, served during the Second World War with the RAF); Jane (died in infancy) and Sarah Ann (died 26 July 1990). Frank Maginnis Senior died on 9 February 1940 (aged 72), some four months before his son, Frank Junior, was killed.

Frank Maginnis Junior worked as a labourer and he and Ellen Thompson (daughter of Andrew Thompson, Ballyhalbert) were married on 3 September 1929 in Glastry Presbyterian Church. Frank and Ellen Maginnis lived in Kirkistown and it was reported in the press that they had six children – named in the press as Thomas (lived with his grandparents), Frances, Ellen, Andrew, Francis Isobel and Cecil. In one of the death notices after Frank died a daughter named Jean was also mentioned.

During the Second World War Frank Maginnis served with the Merchant Navy aboard the SS *River Humber*. Built in 1920 by Hepple and Company Ltd., South Shields and owned by Messrs Charles Neill and Sons Ltd., Bangor, the SS *River Humber* was on passage from Dublin to Preston in ballast when she sank on 4 June 1940 after a collision with HMS *Folkestone* in the Irish Sea east-north-east of Skerries, Dublin. Mate **Jack Cully** and Ordinary Seaman **James McMaster** died in the same incident. The fourth man who died was Chief Engineer Officer John Gibson aged 32 from Gardenstown in Banffshire, Scotland. **John Gibson*** was born in Pennan, Aberdeenshire in Scotland although he did reside for a time at 26 Primrose Street in Bangor. Fireman Frank Maginnis was 30 years old when he died and his body was never recovered. He is commemorated on the Tower Hill Memorial in London and on the family grave headstone in Ardkeen Parish Church of Ireland Graveyard. Frank's mother Mary died on 24 March 1968.

Ma

Mahaffy, William Matchett (Billy)
Sergeant (Air Gunner)
No. 969454, 158 Squadron, Royal Air Force Volunteer Reserve
Killed in action on Monday 13 April 1942 (aged 34)
Reichswald Forest War Cemetery, Kleve, Nordrhein-Westfalen, Germany (Grave 29 E 6)

William Matchett (Billy) Mahaffy was born on 3 March 1908 and he was the younger son of William Irwin Mahaffy and Jeannie Mahaffy (nee Matchett) who lived at Fifth Avenue, Baylands in Bangor and later at 102 Donaghadee

Road, Bangor. Other Bangor addresses associated with the Mahaffy family included *Augustaville*, Princetown Road and *Ward Villa*, Clifton Road. William Irwin Mahaffy (originally from Country Armagh) and his wife Jeannie (born in Bendigo, Victoria, Australia) had six children – Henry Irwin (Harry, born 7 September 1894); Gladys Maureen (born 11 February 1896); Eileen Violet (born 14 April 1898); Beryl (born 15 June 1902); Lorna May (born 28 May 1904) and William Matchett (Billy, born 3 March 1908). Billy Mahaffy's elder brother Harry was baptised in Bangor Parish Church of Ireland Church (St. Comgall's) and his sisters, Gladys Maureen and Lorna May, were married in the same church – Gladys Maureen to Cyril Hugh Mack on 29 April 1925 and Lorna May to Richard Albert Deane on 29 June 1927. Eileen Violet Mahaffy married Balfour Smith and they lived in Calcutta. Beryl Mahaffy married George Cowan and they lived in Liverpool.

William Irwin Mahaffy was a solicitor and his offices were at 25 Callender Street in Belfast. He was Town Solicitor in Bangor for 32 years, from 1901 until 1933, and he was solicitor for the Council during the period when Bangor became a Borough. He died on 1 June 1940 (aged 72) and his wife Jeannie died on 30 December 1951 (aged 84). Billy's elder brother Harry was killed while serving in the First World War and he is commemorated on Page 210 in the Book of Honour *Remembering Their Sacrifice in the Great War – North Down* compiled by Barry Niblock.

> **KILLED IN ACTION.**
> MAHAFFY—Sergeant Gunner William M., R.A.F., dearly-loved son of the late W. Irwin Mahaffy and Mrs. J. Mahaffy, Baylands, Bangor, previously reported missing, now reported killed in action.

Billy Mahaffy attended Bangor Grammar School from 1917 until 1920 and subsequently he attended St. Columba's College in Dublin. During the Second World William Matchett Mahaffy served with the Royal Air Force Volunteer Reserve in Bomber Command and he died on 13 April 1942. He was one of a six man crew (he was the rear gunner) aboard a Vickers Wellington Mark II aircraft (W5525) that took off at 10.08 pm from RAF Driffield in Yorkshire on a mission to bomb Essen in Germany. All six crew members died when their aircraft crashed near Budberg in Germany and they were buried in Reichswald Forest War Cemetery. The other five crew members who died that night were:

- Squadron Leader Wilfred Morgan Protheroe
- Pilot Officer Graham Peter Elliott

- Sergeant Colin Raymond Harper aged 25 (Royal Australian Air Force)
- Sergeant Frank Swinburn aged 23 from Sheffield
- Sergeant Ralph Harry Crews from Leicester

Sergeant Gunner William Matchett Mahaffy was 34 years old when he died on 13 April 1942 and he is commemorated on Bangor and District War Memorial; in Bangor Parish Church (St. Comgall's); in Bangor Grammar School and on the family grave headstone in Bangor Cemetery. His mother Jeannie experienced the loss of both her sons in war, Harry in the First World War and Billy in the Second World War.

Mailey, Richard
Sergeant
No. 1045726, 214 Squadron, Royal Air Force Volunteer Reserve
Killed in action on Sunday 4 July 1943 (aged 20)
Runnymede Memorial, Surrey, England (Panel 158)

Ma

> **MISSING, BELIEVED KILLED**
> MAILEY — Missing, believed killed, July, 1943, Sergeant Richard Mailey, Flight-Engineer, R.A.F., third son of the late John Mailey and of Mrs. Hugh Blakely, 188 Donaghadee Rd., Bangor.

Richard Mailey was the third son of John and Mary Rebecca Mailey (nee Kincaid) of Bangor who were married on 12 July 1915 in Groomsport Presbyterian Church. After Richard's father died on 22 March 1924 (aged 31) his mother married Hugh Blakely on 5 April 1926 in Ballygilbert Presbyterian Church and they lived at 188 Donaghadee Road, Bangor. Richard Mailey was educated at Groomsport Public Elementary School and, before joining up in June 1941, he worked in the Bangor Laundry. Richard's stepfather, Bombardier Hugh Blakely, and Richard's brother-in-law, Company Sergeant Major Ronald Langley were both on active service. Richard's eldest brother, James Mailey, was attached to the Criminal Investigation Department (CID) in Jerusalem.

Sergeant Richard Mailey was 20 years old when he died on 4 July 1943 and his mother placed a *Missing Believed Killed* notice in the 12 February 1944 edition of the *County Down Spectator*. Initially he had been reported as missing in action on 4 July 1943 and then in February 1944 it was officially confirmed that he must be presumed killed in action. Sergeant Richard Mailey was one of a seven man crew aboard a Short Stirling Mark III aircraft (EE882) that took off at 11.10 pm on 3 July 1943 from RAF Chedburgh in

Suffolk on a mission to lay mines in the Nectarines (Frisian Islands) area of the North Sea. The aircraft was lost without trace and all of the crew are commemorated on the Runnymede Memorial. In addition to Sergeant Richard Mailey, the other six crew members who died that night were:

- Sergeant Ronald George Armsworth aged 21 from Goodmayes, Essex
- Sergeant Alan Leonard Warren aged 27 from Ponders End, Middlesex
- Sergeant Francis Elliot Pilkington aged 39 from Henshore, Lancashire
- Sergeant Henry Alan Clark aged 22 from Keswick, Cumberland
- Sergeant Francis William Morrell aged 35
- Flight Sergeant Alfred Ross Dixon aged 20 (Royal Canadian Air Force)

In the 7 July 1945 edition of the *County Down Spectator* his family living at 3 Eden Terrace, Donaghadee Road, Bangor placed a *Roll of Honour* notice and it contained the text:

Not just today, but every day, we remember you

Ma

Sergeant Richard Mailey is commemorated on the Runnymede Memorial in Surrey; on Bangor and District War Memorial; on Groomsport and District War Memorial and in Groomsport Presbyterian Church. On 26 March 1946 his brother Herbert Mailey and Kathleen Irwin of Manor Farm, Donaghadee were married in Donaghadee Parish Church of Ireland Church.

Mair, James Murphy (James)
Lance Bombardier
No. 1811102, 121 (the Leicestershire Regiment) Light Anti-Aircraft Regiment, Royal Artillery
Died of wounds on Wednesday 2 May 1945 (aged 26)
Hamburg Cemetery, Hamburg, Germany (Grave 2A D 3)

Lance Bombardier James Murphy Mair is commemorated on the Mair family grave headstone in Redburn Cemetery, Holywood. Born in 1919 in Govan, Glasgow James Mair was married there in 1941. During the Second World War he served with 121 (the Leicestershire Regiment) Light Anti-Aircraft Regiment, Royal Artillery. He was 26 years old when he died of wounds on 2 May 1945 during the Allied advance through Germany. His wife, Frances Anita Mair, was born on 20 February 1918 and she died on 8 January 1998. On the headstone in Redburn Cemetery she is described as 'an irreplaceable mother and grandma'.

Maitland, Wilfred Ronald (Ronnie)
Distinguished Flying Cross
Flight Lieutenant
No. 111680, 156 Squadron, Royal Air Force Volunteer Reserve
Killed in action on Saturday 30 May 1942 (aged 22)
Viroflay New Communal Cemetery, Yvelines, France (Row A Grave 15)

Wilfred Ronald Maitland was born on 19 May 1920 in Rathdown, Dun Laoghaire and in the CWGC Debt of Honour it is recorded that he was a son of the Revd Walter Maitland BA MSc and Ruby Alice Maitland of Bangor. Walter Maitland and Ruby Alice Lightbown (born in Accrington, Lancashire) were married in 1917 in West Derby, Lancashire. The Revd Maitland was a Church of Ireland clergyman and the Maitland family had also lived in Shillelagh in County Wicklow and Tynan in County Armagh. Wilfred Ronald Maitland attended Campbell College, Belfast from 1936 until 1938 and he played rugby and hockey for the school. In 1937 he played for Ulster on the inter-provincial hockey team. In the *Campbellian* he was described as 'one of those quiet, unobtrusive but nonetheless efficient people, who do their job effectively without any fuss'. He also attended The King's Hospital School in Dublin. After leaving school he worked as an apprentice in the Springfield Dyeing and Finishing Company in Belfast.

Ma

During the Second World War Wilfred Ronald Maitland served with the Royal Air Force Volunteer Reserve in Bomber Command and he was awarded the Distinguished Flying Cross on 17 May 1942. He died on 30 May 1942, eleven days after his 22nd birthday. He was one of a six man crew aboard a Vickers Wellington Mark III aircraft (X3706) that took off from RAF Alconbury in Cambridgeshire at 27 minutes past midnight on a mission to bomb an oil installation and engine factory at Gennevilliers, Paris. The aircraft crashed at Dugny, Paris and all six crew members were killed. Initially they were buried in Dugny and later their bodies were removed to Viroflay New Communal Cemetery. The other five crew members who died that night were:

- Wg Cdr Peter George R. Heath aged 26 from West Ealing, Middlesex
- Sergeant Wilfred George Thomson
- Sergeant Donald Keith Newton Scott
- Sgt F. George Brown aged 23 from Stony Stratford, Buckinghamshire
- Flight Lieutenant Percy Arthur Dalton aged 35 from Leeds, Yorkshire

Three of Wilfred Ronald Maitland's brothers were also on active service during the Second World War – Walter Eric Maitland served with the South Lancashire Regiment; William Norman Maitland served with the Royal Air Force and John Mullin Maitland served with the Royal Naval Volunteer Reserve (Fleet Air Arm). Flight Lieutenant Wilfred Ronald Maitland is commemorated in Campbell College and in The King's Hospital School in Dublin. He was awarded the DFC posthumously and his father Walter died on 13 June 1948 (aged 60) in Tynan, Co. Armagh. His mother, Ruby Alice, died on 23 November 1996 (aged 96) in Carrickfergus, Co. Antrim.

Major, Robert James
Private
No. B/58784, Royal Regiment of Canada, Royal Canadian Infantry Corps
Murdered on Monday 19 June 1944 (aged 24)
Brookwood Military Cemetery, Surrey, England (Grave 54 G 4)

Ma

Robert James Major was born on 16 April 1920 in Newtownards and he was the eldest son of David J. and Sarah (Sadie) Major (nee Hamilton). David J. Major from William Street, Newtownards worked as a barman and he and Sadie Hamilton were married on 23 September 1919 in Newtownards Roman Catholic Church. In 1922 the Major family moved to Canada where David J. Major worked as a salesman. After leaving school Robert James Major worked as a machinist and draftsman and during the Second World War both he and his father David served in the Royal Regiment of Canada.

Robert James Major enlisted in 1942 and was posted to England. In September 1943 he was granted leave which he spent with his grandparents, Robert and Margaret Major of 47 William Street, Newtownards. In 1940 Robert and Margaret had been officially informed that their son, **William Joseph Major**, (Robert James Major's uncle) had been killed in action. *Sorrow Turned to Joy* was the newspaper headline when it was later confirmed that Gunner William Joseph Major was alive and being held as a Prisoner-of-War in Germany.

The death of Private Robert James Major, Royal Regiment of Canada, was reported in the 19 August 1944 edition of the *Newtownards Chronicle* under the headline *Ards Family Bereaved by Death of Canadian Soldier*. The report indicated that he had been accidentally killed in England. On Private Robert James Major's death certificate it is recorded that the cause of death was a perforated bullet wound in his heart; he was the victim of a homicide and the perpetrator was found to be guilty of murder but insane. In the 23 June 1944 edition of the *Dover Express* a detailed account of the circumstances of his death was published, along with details concerning the charge of murder that was preferred against Private Robert Bell Dempster.

Private Robert James Major was 24 years old when he was murdered on 19 June 1944 and he was buried in Brookwood Military Cemetery, Surrey. He is commemorated on the Canadian Virtual War Memorial (Internet) and on Page 377 in the Canadian Second World War Book of Remembrance. His father David travelled to Newtownards in August 1951 and returned to Canada in May 1952.

Major, William Joseph (William)
Gunner
Royal Artillery

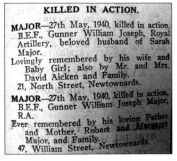

Gunner William Joseph Major's name is included in this Book of Honour as an example of a soldier who was captured and held as a Prisoner-of-War but whose family was initially informed that he had been killed in action on 27 May 1940. His family placed two *Killed in Action* notices in the 13 July 1940 edition of the *Newtownards Chronicle*; one from his wife Sarah, his baby daughter and his parents-in-law Mr and Mrs David Aicken and family of 21 North Street, Newtownards and the other from his father and mother, Robert and Margaret Major and family of 47 William Street, Newtownards. In the same edition of that newspaper his death was reported under the headline *Local Soldier Makes Supreme Sacrifice*.

Then, in the 3 August 1940 edition of the *County Down Spectator* it was reported under the headline *Sorrow Turned To Joy* that Gunner William Joseph Major 'who was previously reported killed in action is now a Prisoner-of-War'. William's wife Sarah was employed by Messrs Webb and

Ma

Company in Newtownards and she was at work on 1 August 1940 when her father David brought her the official notification that William was still alive. A picture of a group of British prisoners in a German Prisoner-of-War Camp was published in the 11 October 1941 edition of the *Newtownards Chronicle* and Gunner William Major was included in the group.

Gunner William Joseph Major's nephew, Private **Robert James Major** was murdered in England on 19 June 1944.

Marr, James Douglas (Jim)
Sergeant
No. 2717958, 1st Battalion, Irish Guards
Died on active service on Tuesday 27 April 1943 (aged 28)
Massicault War Cemetery, Tunisia (Grave II M 1)

James Douglas (Jim) Marr's birth was registered in the fourth quarter of 1916 in Ballymena. He was the youngest son of the late James Douglas Marr and Kathleen (Catherine) Marr (nee McCurdy) who lived at 101 Elmwood Drive, Bangor. James Douglas Marr Senior worked as a boiler maker, Kathleen McCurdy worked as a confectioner and they were married on 31 July 1912 in Kirkinriola Church of Ireland Church, Ballymena.

MARR—May, 1943, in North Africa, Sergt. James Douglas Marr, Irish Guards, youngest son of the late James Douglas Marr and Mrs. Marr, 101 Elmwood Drive, Bangor.
Deeply regretted by his Brother Rover Scouts—R. Drury, R. Gillespie, G. Turnbull, Wm. I. McKinney and P. W. McKinney.

After working for some time in Hooke's Garage in Upper Main Street, Bangor, Jim Marr joined the Irish Guards on 10 April 1934 and before the Second World War he served two periods of duty in Egypt. Jim Marr's marriage to Annie E. Elliott was registered in the fourth quarter of 1939 in Marylebone, London and they had two children whose births were registered in Pontypridd, Wales – Anne Elizabeth E. (third quarter of 1940) and Rachel Catherine E. (first quarter of 1942).

During the war Jim Marr served in Norway and later in North Africa. The 1st Battalion, Irish Guards arrived in Tunisia in March 1943 at a time when Allied Forces were intensifying pressure on the retreating Axis Forces. Sergeant James Douglas (Jim) Marr was 28 years old when he died on 27 April 1943 as Allied Forces made preparations for their final drive to Tunis. There was a death notice in the 29 May 1943 edition of the *County Down Spectator* stating that Jim's death was deeply regretted by his Brother Rover Scouts – R. Drury, R. Gillespie, G. Turnbull, W.I. McKinney and R.W. McKinney.

Ma

Sergeant James Douglas (Jim) Marr is commemorated on Bangor and District War Memorial and in Bangor Parish Church of Ireland Church (St. Comgall's). His brother John served with the Scots Guards and was wounded in action.

Marshall, John Esmond
Sub-Lieutenant (A)
HMS *Ringtail*, Royal New Zealand Naval Volunteer Reserve
Killed in an aircraft accident on Sunday 13 February 1944 (aged 23)
Belfast City Cemetery (Glenalina Extension Section D Grave 30)

Sub-Lieutenant (A) John Esmond Marshall was a son of Henry Horace (Harry) Marshall (born 7 September 1889) and Constance Marshall (nee Hill, born 1889). They were married in 1915 and they lived at 58 The Terrace, Thames in Auckland, New Zealand. They had four children – John Esmond, Owen Harding, Alfred Warwick and Maurice Lane.

John Esmond Marshall was stationed at RNAS Burscough (HMS *Ringtail*) in Lancashire and in February 1944 he was based at Ballyhalbert with 894 Squadron, Fleet Air Arm. On 13 February 1944 he was flying a Supermarine Seafire aircraft (the naval equivalent of the Supermarine Spitfire which was adapted for operation from aircraft carriers) when it crashed into the sea one mile south of Mew Island (one of the Copeland Islands off Donaghadee).

Ma

Sub-Lieutenant (A) John Esmond Marshall (aged 23) was killed and his body was later recovered and brought ashore in a pinnace from 57 Air Sea Rescue Marine Craft Unit (ASRMCU), Donaghadee. He was buried on 17 February 1944 in Belfast City Cemetery (Glenalina Extension). He is commemorated on the New Zealand National War Memorial in Wellington and on the New Zealand Cenotaph Database in Auckland War Memorial Museum. His mother died in 1968 and his father died on 11 August 1975.

Marshall, Robert William Stanley
Squadron Leader
No. 63386, Royal Air Force Volunteer Reserve
Killed in action on Sunday 3 June 1945 (aged 27)
Singapore Memorial, Singapore (Column 445)

In the 23 June 1945 edition of the *County Down Spectator* it was reported

that Squadron Leader Robert William Stanley Marshall was missing. The report cited Elizabeth Stewart Marshall of *Princetown Villa* in Bangor as his maternal grandmother. Robert William Stanley Marshall was a son of Dr Robert Marshall and Evelyn Mary Marshall (nee Marshall) of 9 College Gardens, Belfast. Dr Robert Marshall (son of William John Marshall, a Belfast merchant) and Evelyn Mary Marshall (daughter of William Marshall, a Bangor merchant) were married on 17 October 1916 in May Street Presbyterian Church, Belfast. Robert's sister, Eileen Bertha Marshall, and Evelyn Mary's brother, William Frederick Marshall, were the witnesses.

Ma

Missing Ulster Air Officer.—Squadron-Leader, R. W. S. Marshall, R.A.F., son of Dr. Robert Marshall, 9, College Gardens, Belfast, and a grandson of Mrs. E. S. Marshall, Princeton Villa, Bangor, has been reported missing in Burma. Educated at Methodist College and Queen's University, Belfast, this gallant young officer took his final medical in 1940, and six months later joined the R.A.F. He has served abroad for three and a half years. He was attached to the squadrons of the R.A.F. supporting the operations of the 14th Army in Burma. His wife, a daughter of Professor Crymble, Belfast, is a captain in the R.A.M.C. serving in India.

Robert William Stanley Marshall was educated at Methodist College Belfast and Queen's University Belfast where he took his final medical examinations in 1940. Six months later he joined the Royal Air Force Volunteer Reserve and he was attached to the squadrons supporting the operations of the 14th Army in Burma. His wife, Hilary Marshall (nee Crymble) was a daughter of Professor Percival Templeton Crymble and Norah Isabel Crymble (nee Ireland) who were married on 28 July 1914 in Elmwood Presbyterian Church, Belfast. During the Second World War Hilary Marshall, who qualified as a doctor on 19 July 1940, served in India as a Captain in the Royal Army Medical Corps. Robert and Hilary Marshall had no children.

During the First World War Hilary Crymble's second cousin once removed, John Gordon Crymble, died of wounds and he is commemorated on Page 127 in the Book of Honour *Remembering Their Sacrifice in the Great War – North Down* compiled by Barry Niblock. Lucius Crymble was their 'common' ancestor. Hilary's father was Percival Templeton Crymble who was a son of George Gordon and Agnes Crymble; George Gordon Crymble was a son of Samuel Gordon and Elizabeth Crymble (nee Barry); Samuel Gordon Crymble was a son of Lucius Crymble. John Crymble who died in the Great War was a son of Samuel Gordon and Elizabeth Emily Crymble (nee Agnew); Samuel Gordon Crymble was a son of Matthew and Barbara Crymble; Matthew Crymble was a son of Lucius Crymble.

During the First World War Robert William Stanley Marshall's cousin once removed, Edward Leslie Marshall, died of wounds and he is commemorated on Page 214 in the Book of Honour *Remembering Their Sacrifice in the Great War – North Down* compiled by Barry Niblock. Thomas Marshall was their 'common' ancestor. Robert William Stanley Marshall (son of Evelyn Mary Marshall and grandson of William Marshall) was a great-grandson of Thomas Marshall (on his mother's side); Edward Leslie Marshall (son of Andrew Marshall) was a grandson of Thomas Marshall (on his father's side).

Squadron Leader Robert William Stanley Marshall was initially reported as missing in action and later it was officially confirmed that he must be presumed dead. He is commemorated on the Singapore Memorial; on the Second World War Memorial Plaques in Methodist College and Queen's University, Belfast; in the QUB Book of Remembrance (Page 81); on a Memorial Plaque in Royal County Down Golf Clubhouse and on a Memorial Plaque in the Marshall Room in the Medical Library in the Royal Victoria Hospital Belfast. This room was appointed for the use of students by his parents and there is an inscription on the plaque:

Ma

In perfect honour, perfect truth and gentleness to all mankind
You trod the golden paths of youth, then left the world and youth behind

Martin, Edward
Lance Bombardier
No. 7047144, 1 Maritime Regiment, Royal Artillery
Died of illness contracted in service on Wednesday 20 June 1945
(aged 28)
Bangor Cemetery, Co. Down (Section 3 K Grave 26)

Edward Martin's birth was registered in the second quarter of 1916 in Newtownards and he was the youngest son of James and Jane Martin (nee Ferguson) of Clandeboye Cottages, Bangor. James Martin worked as an agricultural labourer and his marriage to Jane Ferguson was registered in the first quarter of 1897 in Newtownards. They had at least ten children – William (born 26 May 1897); John (born 13 February 1899); Francis (born 9 September 1901); James (born 24 May 1903); Ruth (born 20 June 1906); Alice (born 29 May 1908); Samuel (born 24 July 1910); Campbell (born 2 July 1912); Mary (Molly, born 19 May 1914) and Edward (born 1916).

Edward Martin worked as a gardener on the Clandeboye Estate, he joined the Royal Irish Fusiliers in 1940 and was transferred to the Royal Maritime Artillery. He served as a ship's gunner in many parts of the world including the Malta convoys and the landings in North Africa in 1942 (Operation Torch) during which he served aboard RMS *Orion*. A former passenger liner, RMS *Orion* made two voyages to North Africa carrying more than 5,000 troops each time. It was while he was serving on a tanker off the west coast of Africa that Edward Martin contracted the illness from which he died on 20 June 1945. Full military honours were accorded at his funeral to Bangor Cemetery on 22 June 1945. His coffin, draped with the Union Jack, was conveyed to the cemetery on a gun-carriage and the escort party was furnished by the Artillery at Grey Point Fort, Helen's Bay.

DIED ON ACTIVE SERVICE.

MARTIN—June 20, 1945, at Hospital, Lance-Bombardier Edward Martin, Royal Maritime A.A. Artillery. Funeral, with full military honours, from Clandeboye to-day, Friday, at 3.30 p.m., to Bangor New Cemetery. Thy will be done. Deeply regretted.

Two of Edward Martin's brothers also served during the Second World War – Sergeant Campbell Martin MM served with the Royal Ulster Rifles and Bombardier Samuel Martin served with the Royal Artillery. Campbell Martin attended Edward's funeral, along with their brothers William, John, Frank and James and their brothers-in-law John Jackson and Logan Gray. William Martin had served with the Royal Irish Rifles during the First World War.

Lance Bombardier Edward Martin is commemorated on Bangor and District War Memorial and in First Bangor Presbyterian Church. Edward's sister Ruth died on 18 May 1928 (aged 21); his brother Campbell died on 15 August 1951 (aged 39); his mother Jane died on 15 February 1955 (aged 78); his father James died on 2 March 1960 (aged 87) and his brother Samuel died on 6 April 1986.

Martin, J.W. (see also Martin, Ronald Victor Joseph)

The name J.W. Martin is commemorated on the Second World War Memorial Plaque in Regent House School, Newtownards. Pre-Second World War the only J.W. Martin listed in the Regent House School Register is Joseph Wesley Martin and his details are recorded as follows:

Admission number	957
Date of admission	19 September 1939
Date of birth	4 February 1926

Place of birth	Donaghadee
Address	High Street, Donaghadee
Name of Parent or Guardian	Mrs Stewart, Grandmother, Fruit Merchant
Previous School attended	PES No. II Donaghadee
Class on admission	III B
Examinations passed	None
Class reached	IV C
Date of leaving	31 January 1941
Remarks	Insurance Office

There is compelling evidence to suggest that Joseph Wesley Martin was the name used by Ronald Victor Joseph Martin when he attended Regent House School. Ron Talley (a nephew of Ronald Victor Joseph Martin) has commented that he is 'one hundred percent sure' Joseph Wesley Martin and Ronald Victor Joseph Martin are one and the same person. Why Ronald Victor Joseph Martin would have been enrolled at Regent House as Joseph Wesley Martin is not known.

Martin, Ronald Victor Joseph (Ronald); (see also Martin, J.W.)
Signalman
No. 2602715, 1 Radio Security Company, Royal Corps of Signals
Accidentally drowned on Monday 12 November 1945 (aged 20)
Rangoon Memorial, Myanmar (Face 4)

Ma

Ronald Victor Joseph Martin was born in Donaghadee on 4 February 1925 (not 4 February 1926 as recorded for Joseph Wesley Martin in the Regent House School Register). He was a son of William James Martin of 8 Broadway, Bangor and Florence (Flossie) Martin (nee Stewart) of 14 High Street, Donaghadee who were married on 4 December 1924 in Bangor Abbey. They had two children – Ronald Victor Joseph (born 4 February 1925) and Margaret Elizabeth Stewart (born 28 December 1926).

On 28 January 1927 Flossie Martin died accidentally as a result of a domestic gas-cooker explosion and she was buried in Donaghadee Parish Church of Ireland Graveyard. Baby Margaret Elizabeth, who was just one month old, remained with her father William who moved from Donaghadee to 34 Bingham Street, Bangor. William Martin operated a charabanc service between Bangor and Donaghadee and Baby Margaret Elizabeth was brought up by the Martin family. Margaret Elizabeth Stewart Martin's first marriage was to David McKenna and her second marriage was to William

Calhoun Talley. Margaret Talley (formerly McKenna, nee Martin) died on 24 September 2005 in Bangor.

Ronald Victor Joseph Martin was less than two years old when his mother Flossie died and he was adopted by his maternal grandmother Anna Stewart (nee McCaw) who lived at 2 High Street, Donaghadee. Anna McCaw (originally from Groomsport) and William Stewart were married on 5 October 1898 in Groomsport Parish Church of Ireland Church. Together they ran a fruiterer and florist business in Donaghadee.

There is compelling evidence to suggest that Ronald Victor Joseph Martin was enrolled at Regent House School, Newtownards as Joseph Wesley Martin and he was there from 19 September 1939 until 31 January 1941. After leaving school he went to work in an insurance office and later he studied wireless communications.

Ronald Victor Joseph Martin is remembered as an accomplished boogie-woogie piano player and he joined the Royal Corp of Signals on 10 April 1943. His first posting was to the Special Communications Unit (SCU) at *Whaddon Hall*, Whaddon, Buckinghamshire (now in Milton Keynes). In 1945 he was posted to Colombo in Ceylon (now Sri Lanka) and on 12 November 1945, just a few days after he arrived, he was accidentally drowned in a swimming accident.

Ma

In a letter from his Commanding Officer, which was addressed to Ronald's father, it was initially reported that Ronald was missing believed drowned and later it was officially confirmed that he must be presumed dead. His body was never recovered. On 9 January 1946 Lieutenant-Colonel Pring wrote to Anna Stewart expressing his sympathy on the death of her grandson. In her reply Anna Stewart pointed out that she had adopted her grandson after his mother died and she asked for Ronald's personal belongings to be sent to her so that she could 'treasure them as keepsakes'. She specifically mentioned the gold wrist watch that she had given him and his new cigarette lighter.

Signalman Ronald Victor Joseph Martin is commemorated on Donaghadee and District War Memorial (as Martin, R.); in Regent House School, Newtownards (as Martin J.W.) and on the Stewart family grave headstone in Donaghadee Parish Church of Ireland Graveyard (as Ronald Martin). Ronald's uncle, Wilbert Stewart, died on 26 December 1941 (aged 26); his grandfather, William Stewart, died on 17 January 1955 (aged 77) and his grandmother, Anna Stewart, died on 12 February 1956 (aged 75).

Martin, William

The name William Martin is commemorated in First Bangor Presbyterian Church and the names Martin, W. and Martin, W.J. are both inscribed on Bangor and District War Memorial. **William James (Billy) Martin** who was killed in action on 25 April 1942 was baptised in First Bangor Presbyterian Church. Desk searches and public appeals to date have provided no further information about Martin W. and it *may* be that W. Martin and W.J. Martin are one and the same person. The Second World War Memorial Plaque on Bangor and District War Memorial was not unveiled until November 1967 and this accounts for some of the omissions and inaccuracies in the list of inscribed names. The procedure used to compile the list of names is detailed under the name **Lowry, G.E.** in this Book of Honour.

Martin, William James (Billy)
Gunner
No. 1475556, 5 Battery, 3 Light Anti-Aircraft Regiment, Royal Artillery
Killed in action on Saturday 25 April 1942 (aged 32)
Tobruk War Cemetery, Libya (Grave 2 E 27)

Ma

William James (Billy) Martin was born on 8 September 1909 and he was the eldest son of Samuel and Mary Martin (nee McFarlane) who lived at 4 West Place, Bangor. They were married on 1 March 1909 in Ballygilbert Presbyterian Church. Samuel Martin worked in Scott's fishmonger's shop in Main Street, Bangor and he and Mary had seven children – William James (Billy, born 8 September 1909); Samuel (served with the Merchant Navy); Francis (served in India with the Royal Air Force); Mary Jane (born 20 October 1911); Martha (born 15 October 1922); Alice and Florence. William James, Mary Jane and Martha were baptised in First Bangor Presbyterian Church. Their father Samuel died on 22 December 1947 (aged 63) and their mother Mary died in 1966.

Billy Martin was educated at Ward School and he worked for the Tonic Bus Service, later as a salesman in R.J. Hooke's Garage in Upper Main Street, Bangor. Billy Martin and Patricia Isabel Campbell Crozier were married on 4 June 1935 in Bangor Abbey. Patricia was a daughter of Thomas Crozier who worked as a railway porter and lived at 18 Beatrice Road, Bangor. Billy Martin's wife Patricia was always known as Jean because of her striking resemblance to the film actress Jean Kent. At their wedding, 10-year old Dorothy Adair from Stanley Road, Bangor presented the bride with a horseshoe entwined with silver ribbon and knots of white heather in recognition of Billy Martin's gallantry a few years earlier when he saved Dorothy from drowning. The incident happened on the beach at Queen's Parade, Bangor.

Billy and Jean Martin had one child, a son named William Robert Cochrane (Billy) Martin, who was born on 4 May 1936 and baptised in Bangor Abbey on 10 June 1936. Post-Second World War, Billy Martin Junior served with the Royal Air Force Regiment.

> **KILLED IN ACTION**
>
> MARTIN—William, dearly-loved husband of Jean Martin, 4 Shrewsbury Drive, Bangor, killed in action in the Middle East.
> "He died as he lived, loved by all."
> Deeply regretted by his sorrowing Wife and Son, Billy.

Billy Martin Senior was in the Territorial Army and shortly after the outbreak of the Second World War he was called up for active service with the Royal Artillery. Initially he was posted to Egypt to bolster defence of the Suez Canal against attack by the Italians from Italian-occupied Libya. Gunner Billy Martin saw extensive service in the Middle East, including the siege of Tobruk from 10 April 1941 to 27 November 1941, and he was killed in action on 25 April 1942. Billy's Sergeant was **Alexander Davidson** who died about two months later on 21 June 1942.

Ma

In a letter dated 27 April 1942 to Billy's wife the Revd David L. Rutherford outlined the circumstances of Billy's death. Because of Army regulations the letter could not be posted until a month later. Around 11.00 am on 25 April 1942 Billy and two comrades were travelling between two gun-sites. A raid began and they took shelter in a small stone building which took a direct hit. Billy Martin and one of his comrades, Gunner William Souffham Sands from Fosdyke in Lincolnshire, were killed outright and they were buried side by side in the local cemetery. For security reasons the Revd Rutherford could not divulge the precise location of the cemetery.

Billy's wife and son lived at 4 Shrewsbury Drive in Bangor and in the death notices his brother Sam (serving with the Merchant Navy), his brother Frank (serving with the Royal Air Force), his sister Alice (married to Robert Dobbin) and his sister Mary (married to Joe Miller) were all mentioned. There was also a notice from Mr and Mrs Bruce who lived at 18 Beatrice Road, Bangor. Billy Martin was 32 years of age when he died and one of the tributes paid by his family was:

He died as he lived, loved by all

 Gunner William James Martin is commemorated on Bangor and District War Memorial; in Bangor Parish Church of Ireland Church (St. Comgall's) and *possibly* in First Bangor Presbyterian Church (see **William Martin**).

Mason, Frank
Private
No. 3388489, Gloucestershire Regiment
Died of illness on Sunday 9 February 1941 (aged 21)
Holywood Cemetery, Co. Down (RC Ground Collective Grave 1042)

 Frank Mason was born in Liverpool and he lived at Toll Bar Farm, Claughton near Garstang, Preston, Lancashire. During the Second World War Private Frank Mason served with the Gloucestershire Regiment and he was 21 years old and unmarried when he died of pulmonary tuberculosis in the 24th (London) General Hospital, Belfast (Campbell College) on 9 February 1941. He was buried in Holywood Cemetery, Co. Down.

Ma

Mathers, John Richard
Sub-Lieutenant (A)
HMS *Daedalus*, Royal Naval Volunteer Reserve
Killed in an aircraft accident on Wednesday 25 November 1942 (aged 21)
Belfast City Cemetery (Glenalina Extension Section D Joint Grave 22)

 John Richard Mathers was born in 1921 in Cadder, Lancashire and he was a son of John Alfred Mathers and Maude Machill Mathers (nee Garth). John Alfred Mathers was an electrical engineer and he and Maude Machill Garth were married on 28 June 1913 in the United Free Church, Pollockshields East, Glasgow. In the CWGC Debt of Honour it is recorded that John Alfred Mathers and Maude Machill Mathers lived at 6 The Drive, Orpington in Kent.

During the Second World War, Sub-Lieutenant (A) John Richard Mathers served with the Royal Naval Volunteer Reserve and in November 1942

he was based at RAF Kirkistown, Co. Down. On 24 November 1942 a Fairey Fulmar aircraft (BP821) of 887 Squadron, Fleet Air Arm (based at Kirkistown) made a steep turn when approaching Kirkistown airfield, went out of control and spun to the ground near the airfield. Both crew members were killed. They were the Pilot, Sub-Lieutenant (A) John Richard Mathers who died the following day in Bangor Military Hospital and his Observer, Sub Lieutenant (A) **William Foster** who died on the day of the crash. On 28 November 1942 both men were buried together in Belfast City Cemetery (Glenalina Extension Section D Joint Grave 22).

Matthews, John

Fusilier
No. 6984277, 2nd Battalion, Royal Inniskilling Fusiliers
Killed in action on Sunday 8 August 1943 (aged 23)
Catania War Cemetery, Sicily, Italy (Grave I D 18)

John Matthews was born in Portaferry on 15 April 1920 and he was the eldest son of James and Matilda Boyd (Tillie) Matthews (nee Denvir) who lived at *The Rock* and later in Church Street, Portaferry. James Matthews came from Dromara, Co. Down and in the early 1900s he moved to the United States where he was employed in the steel works at Gary, Indiana. James Matthews subsequently returned to Dromara where he worked as a foreman in a flax mill. In connection with this work he travelled to Portaferry and it was there that he met Matilda Denvir. Matilda was a daughter of James and Mary Denvir (nee Coulter) and she worked as an embroiderer. James Matthews and Matilda Denvir were married on 26 November 1919 in Portaferry Presbyterian Church and while they were living in Portaferry they had three children, all of whom were baptised in Portaferry Presbyterian Church – John (born 15 April 1920); Mary Elizabeth (Lily, born 9 August 1921) and James (born 14 September 1922).

James and Matilda Matthews and their three children moved from Portaferry to the townland of Drumadoney, Dromara where James's parents, John and Isabella Matthews, were farmers. James and Matilda also farmed there and four more children were born – Isabella (born in 1924, died in 1925); Harry (born in 1925, died in 1971); Maud (born in 1928, died in 1994) and Isobel (born in 1932).

John Matthews attended Portaferry No. 2 National School and then Dromara Public Elementary School until he was 13 years old, by which time he was

Ma

Killed in Action.—News has been received that Fusilier John Matthews, Royal Inniskilling Fusiliers, son of Mr. and Mrs. J. Matthews, Dumadoney, Dromara, has been killed in action. Prior to joining the Army three years ago he lived with his grandmother at Portaferry, where he was employed.

proficient in all of the jobs that needed done on the home farm. When he was 13 years old John moved to Portaferry where he lived with Mary Denvir, his maternal grandmother, at 11 High Street. His grandfather James Denvir had died of influenza. John Matthews worked in Portaferry for his uncle Jamie Denvir who operated a milk delivery business. Another of his uncles, John Denvir, worked as a bus driver on the Portaferry to Belfast route. In addition to his work on the milk run, the teenage John Matthews travelled regularly from Portaferry to Dromara by ferry and bicycle to help his father on the home farm.

John Matthews was 20 years old when he joined the Royal Inniskilling Fusiliers in July 1940 and he cited his grandmother as his next of kin. He did his initial training in Omagh and when he had leave he cycled home from there to visit his parents in Drumadoney and help with work on the farm. In the summer of 1941 he helped with the flax pulling. During the Second World War his brother Harry Matthews served with the Home Guard. Aged 14 (he said that he was 17) Harry had tried to enlist for active service but was turned down when it was discovered that he was underage. John's brother, James Matthews, served with the Admiralty Constabulary and then the Ministry of Defence (MOD) Police at Sydenham.

Fusilier John Matthews served initially with the Royal Inniskilling Fusiliers and then as a driver with the Tank Corps. One of the tanks used by the North Irish Horse was named *Lily from Portaferry* after John's sister, Lily Matthews. Lily married Alfie Nichol from Aberdeen who served with the RAF. John Matthews served in Madagascar (*Operation Ironclad*), India, Iraq, Persia (now Iran) and Egypt. He was killed in action in Sicily on 8 August 1943 during the Battle for the Monte Hills (the Battle of the Pimples). Because he had cited his grandmother as his next of kin the telegram bringing news of his death was sent to Portaferry and it was Lily and James who brought it to Drumadoney to tell their parents. On the day they brought the telegram Isobel Smyth (nee Matthews), then aged 11, remembers having had a strong premonition of 'something awful about to happen'. She remembers her mother's terrible sobbing when she heard the news of John's death and her father's utter silence when he came in from working in the fields. Isobel remembers running into Dromara to find her sister Maud.

John Matthews was an accomplished accordion player and a founder member of First Portaferry Accordion Band. In the 24 July 1948 edition of *The Leader* it was reported that a set of drums for the band had been dedicated to John's memory. Mr E.H. Brown JP presided at the dedication ceremony; E.H. Brown's own son, **Ephraim Hugh Brown** had been killed on active service on 25 July 1942.

Fusilier John Matthews is commemorated on the Denvir family grave headstone in Ballymanish Cemetery, Portaferry. His maternal grandmother, Mary Denvir, died on 22 October 1946 (aged 81). He is also commemorated on the family grave headstone in Second Dromara Presbyterian Church Graveyard. His father James died on 14 February 1954 (aged 67) and his mother Matilda died on 1 February 1976. He is also commemorated in Second Dromara Presbyterian Church – as is his great-uncle James Matthews (his grandfather John's brother) who fought in the South African War and in the 36th Ulster Division during the First World War.

Mauger, Leslie Henry Willis
Engineer Commander
HMS *Adamant*, Royal Navy
Died of illness on Saturday 5 April 1941 (aged 43)
Bangor Cemetery, Co. Down (Section 4 V Grave 3)

Leslie Henry Willis Mauger was born in Beckenham, Kent and his birth was registered in the first quarter of 1898 in Bromley, Kent. He was a son of Henry Louis Mauger and Emily Minnie Mauger (nee Neville) whose marriage was registered in the third quarter of 1894 in Islington, London and who subsequently lived in *Rose Villa*, Dendy Road, Paignton, Devon. Henry Louis Mauger was a watchmaker and he and Emily Minnie had at least three children – Elsie Doris, Leslie Henry Willis and Reginald Louis. The marriage of Leslie Henry Willis Mauger and Marjorie C.A. Webber was registered in the second quarter of 1922 in Totnes, Devon.

Leslie Henry Willis Mauger was a career Royal Navy-seaman and during the Second World War he served aboard the submarine depot ship HMS *Adamant*. This ship was built by Harland and Wolff, Belfast; she was launched

in November 1940 and commissioned in February 1942. Eventually HMS *Adamant* was broken up in September 1970 at Inverkeithing, Fife in Scotland. Engineer Commander Leslie Henry Willis Mauger was 43 years old when he died of cancer on 5 April 1941 while he was working on HMS *Adamant* and his wife placed the inscription *In Loving Memory of My Beloved Husband* on his headstone in Bangor Cemetery. He was predeceased by his father who died on 10 February 1941.

Mawhinney, John (Jack)
Lance Corporal
No. 13053095, Royal Irish Fusiliers
Died of wounds on Thursday 2 December 1943 (aged 25)
Moro River Canadian War Cemetery, Italy (Grave XII D 2)

John (Jack) Mawhinney was born on 12 March 1918 in Church Street, Greyabbey and he was baptised on 24 March 1918 in Greyabbey Non-Subscribing Presbyterian Church. He was the only son of John and Margaret Mawhinney (nee Pritchard). John Mawhinney worked as the gravedigger in Greyabbey Old Cemetery and he and Margaret Pritchard were married on 8 September 1916 in Newtownards Non-Subscribing Presbyterian Church. They had two children – Maude and John.

Ma

John (Jack) Mawhinney was educated in Greyabbey Public Elementary School and he was a farm worker before he enlisted. During the Second World War he served with the Royal Irish Fusiliers and in December 1943 he was reported as wounded and taken prisoner. In a letter to Jack's father, Jack's Commanding Officer described what had happened: 'A couple of companies were several miles forward of our own troops doing an important job of work when your son's platoon was cut off by the enemy. Your son was wounded in the left arm and had also what is thought to have been a slight stomach wound. He was taken into a house and left with some civilians, but, before the situation clarified and we were able to get him back, he was carried off by the Germans. I do hope you will have news of him soon, and we too would like to hear he is safe and sound. In the short time he was with us he proved himself thoroughly reliable and an excellent leader. The courage and steadfastness of such men is fast winning the war for us, and all being well you should soon have him home again safe and sound'.

But unfortunately that didn't happen. Lance Corporal John (Jack) Mawhinney died of his wounds and he is commemorated on Greyabbey and District War Memorial which is located on the outside wall of Greyabbey Parish Church of Ireland Church (St. Saviour). He was awarded the 1939/45 Star, the Italy Star, the War Medal and the Defence Medal.

Maxwell, Charles (Charlie)*
Rifleman
No. 7022229, 70th Battalion, Royal Ulster Rifles
Died of illness on Saturday 3 June 1944 (aged 20)
Newtownards (Movilla) Cemetery, Co. Down (Section 16 Grave 146)

Charles (Charlie) Maxwell was a son of William John and Annie Maxwell (nee Smart) of 116 Greenwell Street, Newtownards. William John Maxwell served with the Royal Irish Rifles during the First World War and he and Annie Smart were married on 26 December 1921 in Newtownards Parish Church of Ireland Church (St. Mark's). Charlie Maxwell's brother Tommy served with the Royal Marines in Burma and Charlie wasn't able to get home for his brother's funeral.

Ma

Rifleman Charlie Maxwell was 20 years old when he died of tuberculosis on 3 June 1944. One of the death notices in the 10 June 1944 edition of the *Newtownards Chronicle* was inserted by Peggy Skillen, Mrs Margaret Skillen, Bob and Sheila of Drumawhey, Newtownards.

Rifleman Charlie Maxwell is commemorated on Newtownards and District War Memorial and his parents placed an inscription on his CWGC headstone in Movilla Cemetery:

For ever with the Lord
Deeply regretted by his sorrowing
Father, Mother and Brother

Rifleman Charlie Maxwell's uncle **Charles Smart** was lost at sea on 6 May 1943. Charlie's father, William John Maxwell, died on 12 April 1951 (aged 70) and his mother, Annie Maxwell, died on 31 May 1985.

REMEMBERING THEIR SACRIFICE

Maxwell, John Harold (Harold)
Aircraftman 1st Class
No. 1063559, 968 Balloon Squadron, Royal Air Force Volunteer Reserve
Died as a result of a road accident on Monday 15 September 1941
(aged 31)
Kircubbin Presbyterian Churchyard, Co. Down

John Harold Maxwell was born on 13 April 1910 and he was the youngest son of Thomas James Maxwell and Abigail Maxwell (nee Warnock) of *Rosevale*, Ballygraffin, Kircubbin, Co. Down. Thomas James Maxwell was a farmer and he and Abigail Warnock were married on 25 February 1896 in Greyabbey Presbyterian Church. They had at least eight children, many of whom were baptised in Kircubbin Presbyterian Church – William (born 23 April 1897); Catherine Napier (Cassie, born 20 April 1898); Elizabeth (born 17 February 1900); Thomas Warnock (born 6 March 1902, died 10 January 1980); Robert (born 16 June 1903); Hugh Samuel Mahood (born 5 August 1904); Hilda (born 24 March 1906, died 2001) and John Harold (born 13 April 1910). John Harold Maxwell was 15 years old when his father, Thomas James Maxwell, died on 18 May 1925 (aged 58). His mother Abigail died on 1 September 1946 (aged 79).

Ma

Kircubbin Airman's Death.—At an inquest held by Dr. H. P. Lowe in Belfast on Wednesday, relative to the death of Aircraftsman John H. Maxwell, aged 31 years, a native of Kircubbin, who was killed in a collision between an R.A.F. lorry and a tram car, a verdict was returned that death was due to hæmorrhage following a fracture of the ribs.

John Harold Maxwell attended Campbell College Belfast from 1924 until 1925, the year his father died. He joined up after the outbreak of hostilities and, prior to that, he was employed by Messrs Riddels Ltd., (Hardware Merchants and Ironmongers), Donegall Place, Belfast. He was fatally injured on 15 September 1941 when the lorry in which he was travelling with other airmen collided head-on with a tramcar on the Antrim Road. The lorry was city-bound and he died shortly after being admitted to the Royal Victoria Hospital. At the inquest a verdict was returned that death was due to haemorrhaging following a fracture of the ribs. He was buried in Kircubbin Presbyterian Churchyard on 18 September 1941 after his remains were borne there on a gun carriage from his home in Ballygraffin. The funeral services were conducted by the Revd George Harpur Megaw BA whose brother, Second Lieutenant **William Laurence Megaw** was subsequently killed on 18 February 1943.

L/AC. J. HAROLD MAXWELL. R.A.F. DIED ON ACTIVE SERVICE

Aircraftman 1ˢᵗ Class John Harold Maxwell was 31 years old when he died and he is commemorated in Kircubbin Presbyterian Church.

Maxwell, Victor Edwin (Victor)
Mentioned in Despatches and 2 Bars
Wing Commander
No. 36004, Royal Air Force
Died in service on Wednesday 23 February 1944 (aged 37)
Brookwood Military Cemetery, Surrey, England (Grave 21 C 5)

> **Bangor Family Bereaved**—Wing Commander Victor E. Maxwell, R.A.F., intimation of whose death by enemy action has been received, was the only son of the late Mr. Thomas Maxwell

Wing Commander Victor Edwin Maxwell's death was reported in the 4 March 1944 edition of the *County Down Spectator* under the headline *Bangor Family Bereaved*. Victor Edwin Maxwell was born on 18 August 1906 in Donnybrook, Dublin and he was the only son of Thomas Maxwell (born in Lurgan on 16 January 1870) and Margaret Mary Maxwell (nee Harris, born in 1879). Their marriage was registered in the second quarter of 1903 in Epping, Essex and they lived in *Verona*, Sandycove, Co. Dublin. They had at least three children – Victor Edwin, Ruth Lilian and Margaret. Thomas Maxwell died on 8 June 1940 and his widow, Margaret Mary Maxwell, died on 12 October 1970.

Ma

> **RESULT OF ENEMY ACTION**
> MAXWELL—February, 1944 (result of enemy action), Wing-Commander Victor E. Maxwell, R.A.F., dear husband of Susan Maxwell, beloved only son of the late Thomas Maxwell and of Mrs. Maxwell, Sandycove, Co. Dublin, brother of Mrs. Leslie Smyth, Grove Park, Bangor, and Margaret Maxwell, A.T.S.

Victor Edwin Maxwell was educated at the High School in Dublin and he joined the Royal Air Force in 1924. Early in his career he spent four years in the Middle East. In 1937 he was seconded as Flight Lieutenant to Southern Rhodesia to assist in the formation of an air unit for the Rhodesian Government. On the outbreak of war he was posted to Kenya and later to the Western Desert and Asmara in Eritrea. He was Mentioned in Despatches (2 Bars) and had the Africa Star.

In 1939, in Salisbury, Southern Rhodesia, Victor Edwin Maxwell married Susan Dorothea Fox, daughter of Captain and Mrs Thornton Fox. He returned to service in England in 1943 and the Maxwell family home was at 10 Hart Road, Harlow in Essex. He was a keen sportsman and played rugby for the RAF in inter-Service matches and he also played for the Eastern Counties. He was an expert marksman and had many successes at the National Shooting Centre, Bisley, Surrey. On one occasion he gained top score for Ireland in an inter-Services shoot.

Wing Commander Victor Edwin Maxwell was 37 years old when he died in service on 23 February 1944, his death was registered in Westminster, London and he was buried in Brookwood Military Cemetery in Surrey. There is an inscription on his CWGC headstone:

Greater love hath no man than this that a man lay down his life for his friends

Victor Maxwell's sister, Ruth Lilian Smyth, and his brother-in-law, Leslie Smyth, lived in Grove Park, Bangor and before that they lived at 30 Kimmage Road, Dublin. The marriage of Ruth Lilian Maxwell and Leslie Smyth was registered in the second quarter of 1939 in Rathdown, Dun Laoghaire. Victor Marshall's sister Margaret Maxwell was serving with the ATS. Wing Commander Victor Edwin Maxwell is commemorated on the family grave headstone in Deansgrange Cemetery, Blackrock in Dublin.

McBlain, William
Gunner
No. 1472262, 5 Battery, 2 Light Anti-Aircraft Regiment, Royal Artillery
Died on active service on Saturday 11 September 1943 (aged 38)
Alamein Memorial, Egypt (Column 36)

Ma
McB

William McBlain was born on 9 November 1904 and he was a son of Stewart and Margaret McBlain (nee Shields) who lived at 61 Movilla Street, Newtownards. Stewart McBlain worked as a general labourer and he and Margaret Shields were married on 9 September 1898 in Greenwell Street Presbyterian Church, Newtownards. They had at least eight children all of whom were baptised in Greenwell Street Presbyterian Church – Elizabeth (born 20 October 1899); Stewart (born 2 October 1901); Ellen Jane (born 15 July 1903, married Hugh Adair); William (born 9 November 1904); James (born 5 January 1908, known by the nickname *Big James*); John (born 28 February 1911, known by the nickname *Kill the Weed*); Maggie (born 14 March 1913, later lived in Wolverhampton) and Joseph (born 23 August 1920).

William McBlain's grandfather, James McBlain, was killed in action on 15 November 1914 and he is commemorated on Page 353 in the Book of Honour *Remembering Their Sacrifice in the Great War – Ards* compiled by Barry Niblock. Two of William's brothers were on active service during the Second

World War and a third was attached to the National Fire Service.

William McBlain worked in Donaghadee making concrete breeze blocks and his ambition was to build a bungalow in Donaghadee for his family. He and Rosie Stevenson of 50 Upper Movilla Street, Newtownards were married on 20 October 1926 in Ballygilbert Presbyterian Church and they had four children – Margaret McAuley (born 28 August 1927); Rosaline; Freddie and Jean. Margaret McAuley Hawkins (nee McBlain) wrote a book entitled *An Ards Sparrow – Insights from the Life of Margaret Hawkins* and in it she provided details about her childhood.

Before William McBlain joined the Army the family lived in a two-roomed house; one room was a bedroom where the whole family slept and the other was the kitchen-cum-living room. There was no back door and getting to the outside dry toilet involved going out the front door, walking past the front of the house next door, going down an alley and walking past the back of the house next door to the toilet. The house next door was unoccupied and in it the McBlain family kept goats to provide milk for the family. Margaret McBlain was 16 years old when her father William died and times were very hard. Often her schooling was interrupted when she had to stay at home to nurse her sisters and brother through childhood illnesses while her widowed mother worked full-time.

McB

DIED ON ACTIVE SERVICE.

M'BLAIN—11th September, 1943, died on Active Service, Gunner William M'Blain, R.A.

A loss so great, a shock severe,
To part with one we love so dear;
Though great the loss, we'll not complain,
But trust in Christ to meet again.

Deeply regretted by his sorrowing Wife and Family. Rose M'Blain, 20, Upper Movilla Street, Newtownards.

During the Second World War Gunner William McBlain served with 5 Battery, 2 Light Anti-Aircraft Regiment, Royal Artillery and there is evidence to suggest that he was killed by 'friendly fire' whilst being held in a Prisoner-of-War Camp in Italy. This idea was first mooted during a conversation I had with a survivor of the war and I am indebted to Don Johnston for providing the following information that supports (although it does not prove conclusively) this theory. There were no RAF bombing raids against targets in Germany from 10 to 12 September 1943; the initial destination for most Allied POWs taken in the Desert Campaign was Italy and this is likely to be the place where he died. After the Italian surrender to Allied Forces was announced on 8 September 1943 (three days before his presumed death) German forces moved rapidly to occupy Rome and the situation became even more fluid with the Allied landings at Salerno on 9 September 1943. If there was fighting taking place near his Prisoner-of-War Camp there would likely have been tactical Allied bombing in support of ground forces and the Camp could have taken a hit.

Initially reported as missing in action in June 1942 at Tobruk and then known to have been taken prisoner, it was reported in the press that Gunner William McBlain had escaped in September 1943. It wasn't until April 1946 that his family received official notification that he must be presumed dead.

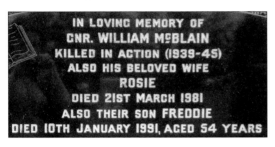

Gunner William McBlain was 38 years old when he died and he is commemorated on the Alamein Memorial in Egypt; on Newtownards and District War Memorial and on the family grave headstone in Movilla Cemetery. His wife Rosie died on 21 March 1981 and their son Freddie died on 10 January 1991 (aged 54). Gunner William McBlain's brother-in-law, **Henry Dougan Sandford**, died as a result of enemy action on 25 October 1940 and his cousin, Fusilier **William John Shields**, was killed in action in Burma on 18 April 1942.

McBride, James (Jim)
Aircraftman 2ⁿᵈ Class
No. 4006295, Royal Air Force Volunteer Reserve
Accidentally drowned on Sunday 1 June 1947 (aged 23, CWGC)
Carrowdore (Christ Church) Church of Ireland Churchyard, Co. Down
(Section N Grave 174)

McB

> McBRIDE—June 1, 1947, (accidental drowning), Aircraftsman James McBride, dearly-loved son of William and Jane McBride, 75, Orby Road, Belfast. Funeral from his parents' residence to Churchill, Carrowdore, to-day (Saturday), at 2 p.m. Deeply regretted by his sorrowing Father, Mother, Brothers and Sisters.
> In the midst of life we are in death.

Aircraftman 2ⁿᵈ Class James McBride was a son of William Thomas and Jane McBride (nee McCutcheon) of 75 Orby Road, Belfast. William Thomas McBride worked as a crane man and he and Jane McCutcheon from Carrowdore were married on 17 February 1919 in Newtownards Parish Church of Ireland Church (St. Mark's). Aircraftman 2ⁿᵈ Class James McBride was accidentally drowned on 1 June 1947 and he was buried on 7 June in Carrowdore (Christ Church) Church of Ireland Churchyard (aged 24, headstone).

There were four death notices in the 7 June 1947 edition of the *Newtownards Chronicle* – one from his father, mother, brothers and sisters; one from his grandmother, uncles, aunts and cousins at Ballyrawer, Carrowdore; one from the residents of Carrowdore village and one from his chums in Carrowdore. The notice from Carrowdore residents contained the text:

He died as he lived – everyone's friend

There were messages of sympathy from Carrowdore LOL 1051, Carrowdore Silver Jubilee Band and Carrowdore United Football Club. James McBride's father William died on 7 February 1954 (aged 61); his mother Jane died on 5 June 1961 (aged 67) and his brother Robert died on 2 January 1991.

McBride, Samuel
Private
No. 4203425, 3rd Battalion, Monmouthshire Regiment
Killed in action on Thursday 3 August 1944 (aged 30)
St. Charles de Percy War Cemetery, Calvados, France (Grave VII B 13)

McB

KILLED IN ACTION.

M'BRIDE—17th May, 1945. Wounded, Missing August, 1944, now believed Killed, 3rd Mons Regiment, Samuel, youngest son of James and the late Jane M'Bride.
Deeply regretted by his Father and Sisters, 23, Mary Street, Newtownards; also his Wife and little Daughter, Sadie Jean, Stockport; also his Brother and Sister-in-law, Bob and Lily, Manchester; also his Brother and Sister-in-law, Hugh and Madge, 32, Greenwell Street, Newtownards.

Samuel McBride was born on 26 January 1914 and he was the youngest son of James and the late Jane McBride (nee Wallace) who were married on 2 November 1900 in Second Newtownards Presbyterian Church. They had at least six children – Elizabeth (born 9 May 1901); Robert (born 7 September 1902); James (born 9 January 1905); Sarah (born 26 May 1907); William Hugh (born 23 September 1909) and Samuel (born 26 January 1914).

Like his father James, Samuel McBride was a laundry worker and he moved to England. He was living at 371 Manchester Road, Heaton Chapel, Stockport when he and Sarah (Sadie) Bennett (aged 20 from 106 Mill Street, Newtownards) were married on 27 March 1937 in Second Newtownards Presbyterian Church. Sadie was a daughter of Hamilton and Elizabeth Bennett (nee Rutherford). Sadie's father worked as a labourer and two of Sadie's cousins, Edward and Hamilton Bennett, were killed in action during the First World War. They are commemorated on Page 109 in the Book of Honour *Remembering Their Sacrifice in the Great War – Ards* compiled by Barry Niblock.

Samuel McBride joined the Army in 1940, he went to France 'on or shortly after D-Day' and on 3 August 1944 he was reported missing in action during heavy fighting centred on Bas Perier Ridge as Allied Forces fought to break out of the Caen bridgehead. In May 1945 it was officially confirmed that he must be presumed dead. There were *Killed in Action* notices in the 19 May 1945 edition of the *Newtownards Chronicle* from his father and two sisters at 23 Mary Street, Newtownards; his wife Sadie and daughter Jean in Stockport; his brother and sister-in-law Bob and Lily in Manchester; his brother and sister-in-law Hugh and Madge at 32 Greenwell Street, Newtownards and also from RBP No. 290 in Newtownards to which his father and brother Hugh belonged. There was an *Our Heroes – In Memoriam* notice in the 4 August 1945 edition of the *Newtownards Chronicle* from his wife and daughter at 106 Mill Street, Newtownards; his father, sisters and brothers and his parents-in-law, Hamilton and Elizabeth Bennett and family.

SAML. McBRIDE Private Samuel McBride was 30 years old when he died and he is commemorated on Newtownards and District War Memorial.

McCaghey, Harold Abraham (Harold)
Flight Lieutenant
No. C/2076, Royal Canadian Air Force
Died in service on Tuesday 9 June 1942 (aged 38)
Ancaster (Bethesda United Church) Cemetery, Ontario, Canada
(Shaver family plot)

McB
McC

Bangor Flying Officer's Death

MEMBER OF CANADIAN AIR FORCE

A wide circle of friends in Northern Ireland have learned with deep regret of the death, on active service, of Flying Officer Harold A. M'Caghey, Royal Canadian Air Force, youngest son of Mr. W. J. M'Caghey, I.S.O., M.B.E., formerly chief inspector of factories for Northen Ireland, and Mrs. M'Caghey, 5 Knockmore Park, Bangor.

Harold Abraham McCaghey was born on 10 June 1903 in Banbridge and he was the youngest son of William John McCaghey ISO MBE and Jennifer (Jeanie) McCaghey (nee Hunter) of 5 Knockmore Park, Bangor. Before that the McCaghey family lived at 7 Glenburn Park, Belfast and before that at 4 Mountainview Terrace, Banbridge. They were married on 5 August 1896 in Magherally Presbyterian Church, Banbridge. William John McCaghey worked as a book-keeper in a linen factory, later becoming an inspector of factories and then Chief Inspector of Factories for Northern Ireland. He and Jeannie had at least four children – Darwin Edward (born 30 May 1897); James Hunter (born 4 January 1900); Harold Abraham (born 10 June 1903) and Annie M. (born 8 November 1906).

Harold Abraham McCaghey was educated at Keighley Grammar School in Yorkshire and Methodist College, Belfast. On leaving school he worked for the Northern Bank in Dublin and Belfast. He had a fine baritone voice

DIED ON ACTIVE SERVICE.

McCAGHEY—June, 1942, in Canada, Flying Officer Harold A. McCaghey, R.C.A.F., youngest son of Mr. W.J. McCaghey, I.S.O., M.B.E., and Mrs. McCaghey, 5 Knockmore Park, Bangor, Co. Down.

and won several singing competitions throughout Ireland. When living in Bangor he sang in the choir of First Bangor Presbyterian Church.

Around 1932 Harold McCaghey moved to Canada where he worked in Toronto and some six years later he married Elva May Shaver of Ancaster, Hamilton, Ontario. They had one daughter. At the outbreak of hostilities Harold joined the Royal Canadian Air Force and he was stationed in Winnipeg, Ontario when he died on 9 June 1942. Elva May Shaver, who was born in 1904, died in 1993.

Flight Lieutenant Harold Abraham McCaghey was 38 years old when he died and he is commemorated on the Canadian Virtual War Memorial (Internet) and on Page 95 in the Canadian Second World War Book of Remembrance.

McC

McCann, Thomas Andrew (Tom)
Pilot Officer
No. 116980, 134 Squadron, Royal Air Force Volunteer Reserve
Killed in action on Monday 27 July 1942 (aged 23)
El Alamein War Cemetery, Egypt (Grave X E 17)

Thomas Andrew (Tom) McCann was born on 9 May 1919 and he was the eldest son of Thomas Andrew Mitchell McCann and Florence McCann (nee Sheppard) who lived at *Mydrum*, 16 Waverley Drive, Ballyholme, Bangor. They were married on 23 June 1918 in Knockbreda Parish Church of Ireland Church and they had five children – Thomas Andrew (born 9 May 1919); John (born 6 July 1920); Joan; Maureen Audrey (born 25 March 1926, baptised in Bangor Parish Church of Ireland Church 25 April 1926) and Michael (born October 1933).

Tom's mother Florence died on 23 October 1933 (aged 36) and on 18 December 1934 his father married Etta Clara Morgan; they had no children. Thomas Andrew Mitchell McCann died on 14 November 1975 and his second wife, Etta Clara McCann died on 8 March 1984.

Tom McCann went to Bangor Grammar School in September 1931 at the age of twelve. He was there for three years and in his final year, at the age of 15, he was the youngest boy ever to win the mile race at the school. After leaving school he worked for Belfast Harbour Commissioners. He joined the Royal Air Force Volunteer Reserve in January 1939 and was called up at the outbreak of war.

ROLL OF HONOUR.

McCANN—In loving memory of my dear husband, Pilot-Officer T. A. McCann, killed in action in Egypt July 27, 1942.—Barbara McCann (née Bradshaw), 6 Dufferin Villas, Bangor.

McCANN—In loving memory of my dear son, Pilot-Officer T. A. McCann, killed in action July 27, 1942.—T. A. McCann and Family, 16 Waverley Drive, Bangor.

Tom McCann and Barbara Bradshaw were married on 8 January 1941 in Groomsport Parish Church of Ireland Church and Tom's brother John, who served as a Junior Engineer in the Merchant Navy, was his best man. Barbara's sister Violet was her bridesmaid and the Revd George Freeman, Rector of Groomsport, performed the ceremony. Barbara's father, Thomas D.O. Bradshaw, was deceased and she was given away by a close family friend – Mr T. Mahood, Manager of the Portaferry Branch of the Belfast Banking Company. The couple spent their honeymoon in Portrush and, after Tom returned to duty in England, Barbara lived in the Bradshaw family home at 6 Dufferin Villas, Bangor – which is where she and Tom had held their wedding reception.

Tom and Barbara's daughter, Felicity Barbara McCann, was born on 17 December 1941 and she was baptised in the Church of Ireland Church of St. Columbanus at Ballyholme on 2 April 1942 – some three months before her father was killed in action.

McC

PILOT OFFICER
T. A. MC CANN.
PILOT
ROYAL AIR FORCE
27TH JULY 1942 AGE 23

During the Second World War Tom McCann saw front line service in several places. In 1940, during the Battle of Britain, he flew with 601 (City of London) Squadron. In September 1941 he was in 134 Squadron which, along with 84 Squadron, formed 151 Wing that was sent to Murmansk. There he provided air support and instruction for Russian pilots and ground crew to enable them to fly and maintain the Hurricanes which they had brought with them from Britain. The book *Hurricanes over Murmansk* by John Golley describes this expedition. Tom McCann returned to England in December 1941. In 1942 Tom McCann was commissioned Pilot Officer and in April 1942 he was sent to Egypt. He was killed near Alexandria in Egypt on 27 July 1942 and was buried in El Alamein War Cemetery. There is an inscription on his CWGC headstone:

With great courage and fortitude he fought against the enemies of liberty

Pilot Officer Tom McCann was 23 years of age when he was killed in the

Middle East and he is commemorated in the RAF Book of Remembrance in St. Anne's Cathedral, Belfast; on Bangor and District War Memorial; in Bangor Parish Church (St. Comgall's); in Bangor Grammar School and on the family grave headstone in Bangor Cemetery.

McCaul, James Charles (James)
Lance Corporal
No. 7011358, 2nd Battalion, Royal Ulster Rifles
Died of wounds on Wednesday 19 June 1940 (aged 28)
Shorne (St. Peter and St. Paul) Churchyard, Kent, England (SE of Church)

ARDS SOLDIER DIES OF WOUNDS.

News has been received that Lance-Corporal J. C. M'Caul, R.U.R., has died of wounds received in action. Corporal M'Caul, who is a son of Mrs. John M'Lean of Ballycastle Road, Ballyblack, was a married man, and his wife and three children live in England, while his sister, Miss Minnie M'Caul, resides at 74 Jamison Street, Belfast.

McC

In some records the surname is spelt McCall. In the CWGC Debt of Honour it is recorded that James Charles McCaul was a son of James Charles McCaul and Mary McCaul and he was 28 years old when he died. His death was reported in the 29 June 1940 edition of the *Newtownards Chronicle* and it was noted that he was a son of Mrs John McLean of Ballycastle Road, Ballyblack, Newtownards; his wife and three children lived in England and his sister Minnie lived at 74 Jamison Street, Belfast. Mrs John McLean's name was Jessie McLean (formerly McCaul, nee Norris). Two of Jessie's stepsons – **James and William McLean** – also died during the Second World War.

Jessie Norris (daughter of Harry Norris, 28 Nelson Street, Belfast) and James Charles McCaul (dock labourer, son of Charles and Sarah McCaul, 12 Ship Street, Belfast) were married on 18 November 1912 in St. Anne's Church of Ireland Cathedral, Belfast. Charles and Sarah McCaul (nee Neill, born Liverpool) were married on 4 February 1875 in St. Patrick's Church of Ireland Church, Newry. In 1901 Charles McCaul, his wife Sarah and their three sons, James Charles (born Ireland), George (born Barrow-in-Furness) and Henry (born Ireland) were living in Barrow-in-Furness, Lancashire. In 1911 the McCaul family was living at 6 Glentoran Street, Belfast.

James Charles and Jessie McCaul (nee Norris) had at least two children – James Charles and Minnie. James Charles McCaul Junior married Gwendolyn Burnige and their marriage was registered in the first quarter of 1934 in Gravesend, Kent. In the CWGC Debt of Honour Gwendolyn

McCaul's address is recorded as Ash Vale, Surrey. James Charles and Gwendolyn McCaul had three children – James Charles (birth registered in the fourth quarter of 1934 in Gravesend); Ivor S. (birth registered in the third quarter of 1936 in Gravesend) and Tanya P. (birth registered in the third quarter of 1939 in Strood, Kent).

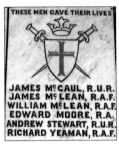

During the Second World War Lance Corporal James Charles McCaul (son of James Charles and Jessie McCaul; grandson of Charles and Sarah McCaul) served with the 2nd Battalion, Royal Ulster Rifles and on 19 June 1940 he died of wounds (three days after D-Day, on 9 June 1940, the 2nd Battalion took Cambes Wood and then held it). Lance Corporal James Charles McCaul's death was registered in the second quarter of 1940 in Watford, Hertfordshire and he is commemorated in Carrowdore Parish Church of Ireland Church.

McClean, Robert Reid (Bobby)*
Leading Aircraftman
No. 627576, 10 Squadron, Royal Air Force
Killed in an accident on Friday 27 February 1942 (aged 22)
El Alamein War Cemetery, Egypt (Grave XVIII G 24)

McC

Robert Reid (Bobby) McClean was born on 18 October 1919 and he was baptised on 26 November 1919 in Bangor Parish Church of Ireland Church (St. Comgall's). He was a son of James Albert and Ellen McClean (nee Reid) who lived at 6 Vimy Ridge, Bangor (previously named The Mount, and New Street and now named Central Street). James Albert McClean (son of William James McClean) was an engine driver employed at Bangor Gasworks when he and Ellen Reid (daughter of Robert Reid, Ballyhackamore) were married on 26 December 1917 in Belmont Presbyterian Church, Belfast.

Bobby McClean was educated at Bangor Central Public Elementary School where he excelled at mathematics. He was a member of Second Bangor

(Hamilton Road Methodist) Boy's Brigade and he was a keen footballer. He was described as 'always dependable and popular with a wide circle of friends'. After leaving school Bobby was employed by aircraft manufacturer Short and Harland in Belfast (in June 1936 Short Brothers collaborated with Harland and Wolff to form Short and Harland). He joined the Royal Air Force in 1938 and after the outbreak of war took part in many operational flights. In 1940 he was in action at the Battles of Narvik and that same year he got married in Scotland.

Leading Aircraftman Bobby McClean served with 10 Squadron RAF and he died on 27 February 1942 following an accidental bomb explosion at El Daba in Egypt. When he died his wife, Elizabeth Ingles McClean, and their 5 month-old son, Robert James McClean, were living in Lossiemouth, Morayshire in Scotland. Leading Aircraftman Bobby McClean was 22 years of age when he died and he is commemorated on Bangor and District War Memorial and in Bangor Parish Church (St. Comgall's).

McClement, Donald

Engine Room Artificer 4th Class

McC

No. P/MX 60352, HMS *Quentin*, Royal Navy
Killed in action on Wednesday 2 December 1942 (aged 23)
Portsmouth Naval Memorial, Hampshire, England (Panel 67 Column 2)

> **Former Kircubbin Engineer Lost.—** Intimation has been received by Mr. Thompson Donald, Townhall Street, Belfast, that his nephew, Donald M'Clement, engineer, R.N., has been lost with the destroyer, Quentin, in the North African operations. Engineer M'Clement was the only son of Mr. and Mrs. H. M'Clement, formerly of Kircubbin and now of Staffordshire.

Donald McClement was born on 16 May 1919 in Wolstanton, Staffordshire and he was the only son of Hugh Henry and Florence (Florrie) Caroline McClement (nee Steele), formerly of Kircubbin and then of Newcastle-under-Lyme in Staffordshire. Donald McClement's uncle and aunt, Thompson and Mary Ann Donald, together with his aunt Lizzie McClement, lived at 41 Adam Street, Belfast. Later they moved to Townhall Street, Belfast. Donald McClement's uncle, John McClement, was drowned on 30 January 1917 and he is commemorated on Page 369 in the Book of Honour *Remembering Their Sacrifice in the Great War – Ards* compiled by Barry Niblock.

During the Second World War Donald McClement served with the Royal Navy aboard the Q-class destroyer HMS *Quentin*. Built by John Samuel White and Company of Cowes in the Isle of Wight she was commissioned on 15 April 1942 and less than eight months later she sank on 2 December 1942.

On 1 December 1942 HMS *Quentin* was part of a British force (Force Q) that

 left Bone Harbour in Algeria with the objective of intercepting an Italian convoy in the Sicilian Narrows. The British ships destroyed the Italian convoy in the Battle of Skerki Bank but the following morning, on the way back to Bone, the ships of Force Q came under attack from German bomber aircraft. At 6.36 am HMS *Quentin* was hit by a 500 kg bomb and sank within four minutes. Engine Room Artificer 4th Class Donald McClement aged 23 was one of around 20 men who died and he is commemorated on Portsmouth Naval Memorial in Hampshire.

McClinton, David
Gunner
No. 1468863, 5 Battery, 2 Light Anti-Aircraft Regiment, Royal Artillery
Died of wounds on Sunday 21 June 1942 (aged 29)
Knightsbridge War Cemetery, Acroma, Libya (Grave 10 C 11)

David McClinton was born on 14 August 1912 in Belfast and he was a son of Andrew and Agnes McClinton (nee Harris) who lived in the townland of Ballywee East in County Antrim and later at 18 Santiago Street, Belfast. Andrew McClinton worked as a yarn dryer and he and Agnes Harris were married on 31 December 1897 in Carnlough Presbyterian Church. They had at least nine children – John (born 23 December 1898); Josephine (born 23 February 1901); Samuel Roland (born 4 May 1903); Thomas James (born 10 May 1905); Sarah Elizabeth (born 18 February 1907); William Andrew (born 30 March 1910); David (born 14 August 1912); Robert Walter (born around 1915) and Francis (born around 1917).

McC

David McClinton's brother John served in the First World War, then in the Royal Ulster Constabulary, then as an Inspector of Police in Vancouver, Canada and then with the Royal Canadian Air Force during the Second World War. His brother James also served with the Royal Canadian Air Force; his brothers William Andrew and Francis served with the Irish Guards and his brother Walter was a Telegraphist in the Royal Navy. Sergeant William Andrew McClinton (No. 2716729; POW No. 4425) was captured and held in the Stalag Prisoner-of-War Camp at Posen in Poland.

David McClinton was the husband of Martha McClinton (nee Graham) of 5 Zion Place, Newtownards. They were married on 27 May 1935 in St. Anne's Church of Ireland Cathedral, Belfast. During the Second World War Gunner David McClinton served with the Royal Artillery and he died of wounds on

M'CLINTON—In loving memory of my dear husband, Gunner David M'Clinton, R.A., killed in action at Tobruk, 20th June, 1942.

Although we're in a far-off land,
And your grave we cannot see,
As long as life and memory last
We shall remember thee.

I do not forget him, nor do I intend,
I think of him always, and will to the end ;
I mourn him in sorrow and silence, unseen,
And dwell on the memory of days that have been.
Ever remembered by his loving Wife.
MARTHA M'CLINTON.
5, Zion Place, Newtownards.

21 June 1942, along with three of his comrades, after being hit by shell-fire at Tobruk. Their gun position was sited some 2¼ miles south of Tobruk docks, on a broad plateau above an escarpment and about a thousand yards east of the road running almost due south out of Tobruk. Their Navy, Army and Air Force Institutes (NAAFI) Building was on the same plateau but slightly further north. The Axis Forces (21 Panzer Division) swept through their gun position some time between 2.30 and 5.00 pm on Saturday 20 June and reached the harbour area shortly afterwards. The other men who died were Lieutenant (Acting Captain) **John Malcolmson Gibson** from Newtownards, Sergeant **Alexander Davidson** from Newtownards and Gunner George Alfred Rayner from Glastonbury in Somerset.

David's wife Martha placed an *Our Heroes – In Memoriam* notice in the 19 June edition of the *Newtownards Chronicle* and it contained the verse:

McC

I do not forget him, nor do I intend,
I think of him always, and will to the end;
I mourn him in sorrow and silence, unseen
And dwell on the memory of days that have been.

Gunner David McClinton was 29 years old when he died and he is commemorated on Newtownards and District War Memorial.

McCloud, Thomas James (Tom)
Sergeant (Observer)
No. 1066739, 18 Squadron, Royal Air Force Volunteer Reserve
Killed in an aircraft accident on Friday 6 November 1942 (aged 24)
Comber Cemetery, Co. Down (Section 7 Grave 86)

Thomas James McCloud was born on 29 March 1918 and he was the only son of Samuel and Martha McCloud (nee McClurg) of 5 Brownlow Street, Comber. Samuel McCloud was a plumber and he and Martha McClurg were married on 14 September 1917 in Second Killyleagh Presbyterian Church. They had two children – Thomas James (Tom) and Johnina (Ina).

Thomas James McCloud attended Comber Public Elementary School and then Regent House School in Newtownards from 1930 until 1935. A keen gymnast and all-round sportsman, he was an active member of First Comber Presbyterian Church. Before joining the Royal Air Force Volunteer Reserve he worked for Messrs G. Cohen and Sons (Scrap Metal Merchants), Sydenham Road, Belfast and also for some time with Messrs W. McCalla (Shipping Agents), Belfast.

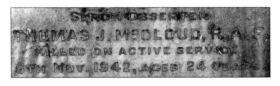

Mr. and Mrs. S. M. M'Cloud, 5 Brownlow Street, Comber, have received official intimation that their son, Sergt.-Observer T. J. M'Cloud, R.A.F., has been killed. Prior to joining he was on the staff of Messrs. G. Cohen and Sons, Sydenham Road, Belfast, and for some time with Messrs. W. M'Calla, shipping agents. He was 23, and the only son. He had been on several operatonal flights over Germany.

During the Second World War Sergeant (Observer) Thomas James McCloud served in Bomber Command and on 6 November 1942 he was one of a three man crew aboard a Bristol Blenheim Mark V aircraft (BA818) that crashed at 3.10 pm at Newton Toney in Wiltshire whilst on a training flight. The other two crew members who died that day were:

- Sergeant Robert Calder Gibson aged 20 from Clarkston, Lanarkshire
- Sergeant Herbert Edward Shaw aged 25 from Kennington, London

McC

Sergeant (Observer) Thomas James McCloud's death was registered in Salisbury, Wiltshire and he is commemorated on Comber and District War Memorial; in First Comber Presbyterian Church; in Regent House School and on the family grave headstone in Comber Cemetery which bears the inscription:

At the going down of the sun and in the morning we will remember thee

McCombe, Albert Ernest
Captain

Captain McCombe's name is included in this Book of Honour to illustrate a point about the interpretation of Roll of Honour data in churches. On the Second World War Roll of Honour in Portaferry Presbyterian Church the name Ernest McCombe, Merchant Navy is listed. This memorial does not differentiate between those who died and those who survived. On the McCombe family grave headstone in Ballymanish Cemetery, Portaferry Captain Albert Ernest McCombe who was lost at sea off Singapore is commemorated. His date of death is not shown and his name was not found in the CWGC Debt of Honour. Family records indicate that Albert Ernest McCombe of Ballywallon, Portaferry was born on 20 June 1914 and he was a career seaman. He obtained his Captain's ticket and he served in the Merchant Navy during the Second World War. He died in the 1960s when he went down with his ship after it was in collision with another ship as it left Singapore Harbour. During the Second World War Ernest's brother, Napier McCombe, served with the Royal Air Force.

McCombe, George Marshall (Marshall)
Pilot Officer
No. 104492, 78 Squadron, Royal Air Force Volunteer Reserve
Killed on active service on Saturday 8 November 1941 (aged 25)
Gaasterland (Nijemirdum) General Cemetery, Friesland, Netherlands
(Plot 1 Row A Grave 4)

George Marshall McCombe was born on 8 March 1916 and he was the only surviving son of George John Marshall McCombe and Mary McCombe (nee Osborne) who lived in Bangor at 35 Moira Drive and, before that, at 8 Donaghadee Road. Before moving to Bangor the McCombe family lived in Belfast at 17 Delhi Street, at 40 College Park Avenue and Cliftonville Road. George John Marshall McCombe was the Chief Clerk in Belfast Tramways Department and he and Mary Osborne were married on 12 June 1906 in Cliftonville Presbyterian Church, Belfast. They had four children – John Osborne (Jackie, born 10 April 1907, died 8 January 1913 aged 5½ years and buried in Grave E3 63, Dundonald Cemetery); Sara Elizabeth (born 29 July 1908, died 31 October 1999); Isobel (born 30 December 1910, died 10 April 1989) and George Marshall (born 8 March 1916).

Marshall McCombe attended the Royal Belfast Academical Institution (RBAI) from 1928 until 1934 where he excelled at rugby and athletics. He won medals in a range of athletics disciplines and held the school record for the long jump – 21 feet 8 inches. He played rugby for the school and later for Instonians and Ulster. He also had an international trial.

Pilot-Officer G. McCombe.—Mrs. Eileen M. McCombe, Cliftonville, Castlerock, has been officially informed that her husband, Pilot-Officer George Marshall McCombe, R.A.F.V.R., is believed killed in action.

An accountant by profession, Marshall McCombe was articled to the firm Messrs Martin Shaw, Leslie and Shaw (Chartered Accountants), Belfast. Marshall McCombe and Eileen Doyle BA were married on 21 October 1941 in Castlerock Presbyterian Church and she was

McC

living at *Cliftonville*, Castlerock, Co. Londonderry when she received the news of Marshall's death. They had been married for less than three weeks.

Marshall McCombe joined the Royal Air Force Volunteer Reserve before the outbreak of war and did his training at Cranwell RAF College. During the Second World War, Pilot Officer George Marshall McCombe served with the Royal Air Force Volunteer Reserve in 78 Squadron, Bomber Command and he died when his plane was shot down by a German night fighter at 6.30 am on 8 November 1941 between Oudemirdum and Nijemirdum in Holland.

He was one of a crew of five aboard an Armstrong Whitworth Whitley Bomber Mark V (Z6948) that took off from RAF Croft (Neasham) Airfield in Yorkshire at 10.31 pm on 7 November 1941 and they were returning after bombing Berlin when their aircraft was shot down. The other four crew members who died that morning were:

- Sergeant John William Bell aged 21 from Carshalton, Surrey
- Sgt Gilbert T. Webb aged 25 from Wheeler End, Buckinghamshire
- Sergeant Donald Cameron aged 29 from Dunoon, Argyllshire
- Sergeant Raymond Boucher aged 20 from Sheffield

McC

Marshall McCombe was 25 years of age when he was killed and he is commemorated in Bangor Parish Church of Ireland Church (St. Comgall's) and in RBAI. After Marshall McCombe died, his parents lived at *Inishowen*, Greenisland and at 4 Mourneview Terrace, Newry Road, Banbridge. Marshall McCombe's father, George John Marshall McCombe, died on 22 December 1953 (aged 80) and his mother, Mary McCombe, died on 4 January 1964 (aged 80). They were buried in Dundonald Cemetery in the same grave as their son John Osborne McCombe. There is an inscription on Pilot Officer George Marshall McCombe's CWGC headstone:

In proud and loving memory of a dear son
The path of duty is the way to glory

McCrory Brothers, John and William James

John and William James McCrory were sons of James and Katherine (Catherine) McCrory (nee Boyd) of Hopefield Avenue, Portrush. James McCrory was a barber and he and Katherine Boyd were married on 12 April

1898 in Ballywillan Presbyterian Church, Coleraine. They had five children – William James (born 11 January 1899, died in infancy); Matilda (born 2 June 1900, died in infancy); William James (born 28 March 1902); John (born 11 August 1908) and Kathleen Marcella (born 4 March 1911). After their mother Katherine died on 24 June 1938 (aged 64) their father James lived at 63 Bryansburn Road, Bangor. William James McCrory was the first of the two brothers to die in war.

McCrory, William James
First Radio Officer
SS *Clan Ferguson* (Glasgow), Merchant Navy
Died as a result of enemy action on Wednesday 12 August 1942 (aged 40)
Tower Hill Memorial, London, England (Panel 30)

During the Second World War First Radio Officer William James McCrory served with the Merchant Navy and he died on 12 August 1942 when the SS *Clan Ferguson* sank some 20 miles north of the Tunisian Zembra Island. She was sunk by a combination of aerial bombs dropped by German Junkers JU88 aircraft, and torpedoes fired by the Italian submarine *Alagi*. The SS *Clan Ferguson* was a British steam cargo ship built in 1938 by the Greenock and Grangemouth Dockyard Company Ltd., Greenock and owned by Clan Line Steamers Ltd., London. The SS *Clan Ferguson* sank when she was in the *Operation Pedestal* Convoy transporting desperately-needed supplies to Malta. William James McCrory was 40 years old when he died; his effects amounted to some £716 and probate was granted to his father. First Radio Officer William James McCrory is commemorated on the Tower Hill Memorial in London and, just over a year after William James was killed, his brother John died.

McCrory, John
Flight Lieutenant
No. 65481, Royal Air Force Volunteer Reserve
Died of illness on Saturday 21 August 1943 (aged 35)
Portrush Cemetery, Co. Antrim (Section C Grave 302)

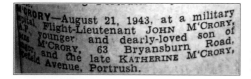

Prior to joining the Royal Air Force Volunteer Reserve John McCrory was a seaman and he held the rank of Second Mate. He was 5 feet 9½ inches tall and had grey eyes, brown hair, a fair complexion and a scar at the base of the second finger on his left hand. At one time he served aboard the SS *Kenbane Head*.

Flight Lieutenant John McCrory was the younger son of James and Katherine McCrory and he was the husband of Elizabeth (Betty) McCrory of *The Grove*, Knockmore, Lisburn. During the Second World War he served with the Royal Air Force Volunteer Reserve and was based at RAF Bishops Court. He died of septicaemia in Bangor Military Hospital on 21 August 1943 and his funeral was at 12 noon the following Tuesday from Lisburn to Ballywillan Cemetery, Portrush. Flight Lieutenant John McCrory was 35 years old when he died and he is commemorated on Lisburn and District War Memorial.

McCullough, Alexander
Private
No. 5949025, 1st Battalion, Bedfordshire and Hertfordshire Regiment
Died of wounds on Thursday 19 November 1942
Ranchi War Cemetery, India (Grave 1 B 7)

McC

Alexander McCullough was born in Belfast and in the 19 December 1942 edition of the *Newtownards Chronicle* it was reported that he was a son of Mrs McCullough of Ballycullen, Newtownards. During the Second World War Alexander served with the Bedfordshire and Hertfordshire Regiment and he died of wounds in India on 19 November 1942. Private Alexander McCullough is commemorated on Newtownards and District War Memorial.

McCullough, Joseph
Rifleman
No. 14442976, 1st (Airborne) Battalion, Royal Ulster Rifles
Died of wounds on Sunday 25 March 1945 (aged 19)
Reichswald Forest War Cemetery, Kleve, Nordrhein-Westfalen, Germany (Grave 40 F 3)

Joseph McCullough was the second son of Joseph and Elizabeth McCullough who lived at 13 Clandeboye Place, Bangor. In civilian life Joseph McCullough Senior worked as a postman and during the First World War he served

 with the Royal Inniskilling Fusiliers and the Machine Gun Corps. During the Second World War Joseph McCullough Senior served with the Royal Warwickshire Regiment

Before the Second World War, Joseph McCullough Junior was employed by Messrs Charles Hurst (Engineers), Belfast. He enlisted in 1943 and served with the 1st (Airborne) Battalion, Royal Ulster Rifles. His elder brother Samuel served as a Paratrooper. Samuel was captured at Arnhem and held as a Prisoner-of-War. His younger brother John served with the Merchant Navy.

Rifleman Joseph McCullough was 19 years old when he died on 25 March 1945 from wounds sustained in action during the crossing of the River Rhine (*Operation Varsity*, the airborne element of *Operation Plunder*) and he is commemorated on Bangor and District War Memorial and in Bangor Parish Church of Ireland Church (St. Comgall's).

McCullough, William Errol Charles (Charlie)
Surgeon
Merchant Navy, RMS *Nova Scotia*
Died at sea on Saturday 24 October 1942 (aged 29)

McC

DIED ON ACTIVE SERVICE.

McCULLOUGH—October, 1942, Dr. W. E. C. McCullough, at sea, second and fondly loved son of Mr. and Mrs. William McCullough, 18 Ward Avenue, Bangor.

William Errol Charles McCullough was born on 25 February 1913 and he was the younger son of William McCormick McCullough and Maria Macdonald McCullough (nee Cleland) of 18 Ward Avenue, Bangor. Before that they lived at 2 Godfrey Avenue, Bangor. William McCullough Senior was a partner in the linen manufacturing firm of Messrs William McCullough and Company, East Bridge Street, Belfast. He and Maria Cleland were married on 26 August 1902 in Cliftonville Presbyterian Church, Belfast and they had three children – Robert Cleland (born 6 March 1904); William Errol Charles (born 25 February 1913) and Marjorie Helen (born 5 January 1915). William Errol Charles and Marjorie Helen were baptised in First Bangor Presbyterian Church.

William Errol Charles McCullough was educated at Mourne Grange, Kilkeel; Bangor Grammar School from 1927 until 1930 and Queen's University Belfast. He took his final medical examinations in 1939 and worked in various hospitals in England before joining the Merchant Navy in 1941. He served aboard the Royal Mail Ship (RMS) *Nova Scotia* which was launched in 1926 and requisitioned as a troop ship during the Second World War. RMS *Nova Scotia* was built by Vickers, Sons and Maxim Ltd., Barrow-in-Furness.

Surgeon William Errol Charles McCullough was 29 years old when he died at sea on 24 October 1942. At the time, RMS *Nova Scotia* was on route from North Africa to Durban, South Africa with more than 700 Italian Prisoners-of-War on board. A little over a month after Surgeon McCullough died at sea, RMS *Nova Scotia* was sunk by torpedoes fired from the German submarine *U-177*. More than 800 people died when she went down on 28 November 1942 in the Indian Ocean some 30 miles off the coast of Natal Province, South Africa.

Surgeon William Errol Charles McCullough is commemorated on Bangor and District War Memorial; in Bangor Grammar School and on the family grave headstone in Bangor Cemetery. His father William died on 11 July 1946 (aged 69); his mother Maria died on 31 July 1958 (aged 80); his brother Robert died on 18 October 1967 and his sister Marjorie died on 10 April 1974.

McC

McCune, Charles Knox
Third Radio Officer
SS *Lalande* (Liverpool), Merchant Navy
Died as a result of enemy action on Saturday 14 November 1942 (aged 22)
Tower Hill Memorial, London, England (Panel 63)

Charles Knox McCune's birth was registered in the third quarter of 1920 in Belfast and he was the third son of Robert Eaton McCune and Margaret Moore McCune (nee Knox) of *Riverside*, Cloughfern, Whiteabbey, Co. Antrim. Robert Eaton McCune was a grocer and general merchant (his father William was a banker) and he and Margaret Moore Knox were married on 11 September 1912 in College Street South Reformed Presbyterian Church, Belfast. They had at least three children including Robert Eaton (born 1918) and Charles Knox (born 1920). Before he went to sea Charles Knox McCune was employed by the Belfast Banking Company and he worked in both the Londonderry and Portaferry Branches.

During the Second World War Charles Knox McCune served with the

Merchant Navy aboard the SS *Lalande*. The SS *Lalande* was a cargo vessel built in 1920 by D. and W. Henderson Ltd., Glasgow and operated by the Lamport and Holt Line Ltd. On 14 November 1942 Charles Knox McCune died in the Mediterranean Sea off Oran in Algeria when the ship was hit at 5.13 am by a torpedo fired from the German submarine *U-73*. In the Register of Deceased Seamen, Cloughfern is spelt Clairghfern. (After the attack the ship made it to port and re-entered service after extensive repairs. In August 1959 she was broken up at Hamburg in Germany). Charles Knox McCune's effects amounted to some £136 and probate was granted to Robert Eaton McCune, merchant. Robert Eaton McCune died on 17 March 1963 (aged 90) and probate was granted to Thomas Strahan McCune general merchant.

Third Radio Officer Charles Knox McCune was 22 years old when he died and he is commemorated on the Tower Hill Memorial in London and on the Belfast Banking Company Second World War Memorial Plaque (now in Danske Bank, Donegall Square West, Belfast).

McC

McCutcheon, Thomas
Bombardier
No. 1467311, 5 Battery, 2 Light Anti-Aircraft Regiment, Royal Artillery
Died in a Prisoner-of-War Camp on Sunday 9 January 1944 (aged 28)
Berlin 1939-1945 War Cemetery, Berlin, Germany (Grave 10 K 1)

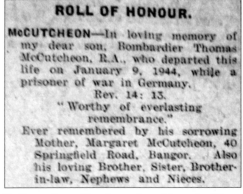

ROLL OF HONOUR.

McCUTCHEON—In loving memory of my dear son, Bombardier Thomas McCutcheon, R.A., who departed this life on January 9, 1944, while a prisoner of war in Germany.
Rev. 14: 13.
"Worthy of everlasting remembrance."
Ever remembered by his sorrowing Mother, Margaret McCutcheon, 40 Springfield Road, Bangor. Also his loving Brother, Sister, Brother-in-law, Nephews and Nieces.

Thomas McCutcheon was a son of William and Margaret McCutcheon (nee Strain) of 45 Springfield Road, Bangor and, before that, the townland of Cottown, Donaghadee. William McCutcheon of Ballyfotherly worked as an agricultural labourer and he and Maggie Strain of Herdstown were married on 11 November 1910 in Ballygrainey Presbyterian Church. Three children were baptised in Shore Street Presbyterian Church Donaghadee – Hugh (born 16 February 1911 at Cottown); Josephine (born 26 April 1913 at Ballyfotherly) and Thomas (born 10 April 1915 at Ballyfotherly). Thomas McCutcheon was educated at Main

Street Public Elementary School in Bangor and he was a keen sportsman. He played soccer for the Rookery Team in Bangor Summer League. He enlisted prior to the outbreak of the Second World War and before that he was employed as an electrician by the Electricity Board in Bangor.

During the war he served with the Royal Artillery and he was held as a Prisoner-of-War after being captured at the fall of Tobruk. After the surrender of Italy to Allied Forces he was transferred to Germany. It was reported in the press that he died of pneumonia in the Lazarett (hospital) beside the German Prisoner-of-War Camp at Stalag 1V B Muhlberg-on-Elbe, Germany. Sympathy was expressed by *County Down Spectator* staff to his widowed mother Margaret, his brother Hugh in Lisburn and his sister, Josephine Carlin of High Street, Donaghadee (Josephine McCutcheon and James Carlin were married on 9 June 1941 in Ballygrainey Presbyterian Church, some six weeks after her father William died on 25 April 1941)

Bombardier Thomas McCutcheon was 28 years old when he died and he is commemorated on Bangor and District War Memorial and on the family grave headstone in Bangor Cemetery. His sister Rose Anna died on 3 April 1929 (aged seven); his sister Amanda died on 25 January 1932 (aged five); his father William died on 25 April 1941 (aged 57) and his mother Margaret died on 26 March 1964 (aged 75). There is an inscription on the headstone:

McC
McD

Safe in the arms of Jesus

McDowell, Alfred George
Ordinary Seaman
No. D/JX 151550, HMS *Glorious*, Royal Navy
Killed in action on Saturday 8 June 1940 (aged 18)
Plymouth Naval Memorial, Devon, England (Panel 39 Column 1)

Alfred George McDowell was a grandson of Charles McDowell (a foreman box maker) and Margaret McDowell (nee Cotter). Margaret Cotter was a daughter of Jane Cotter who died on 21 January 1906. Charles McDowell and Margaret Cotter were married on 11 April 1881 in Carlisle Memorial Methodist Church, Belfast and they had six children – Annie Cotter (born 18 May 1882, married George Henry Sargent on 5 August 1908 in Ballynafeigh Methodist Church, Belfast); William Angus (born 27 September 1884); Alfred Mogey (born 21 January 1887); Mary (born 1 December 1888); Agnes (born 9 May 1891) and Charles (born 3 March 1893, died 11 February 1940).

Alfred George McDowell was a son of Alfred Mogey McDowell and Winifred Catherine McDowell (nee Stott) of 56 University Avenue, Belfast. Alfred Mogey McDowell was a plumber and he and Winifred Catherine Stott were married on 10 July 1915 in Christ Church, Church of Ireland Church, College Square North, Belfast. Winifred's father Samuel was a soldier. Alfred Mogey and Winifred Catherine McDowell had at least two children – Janette Kathleen (born around 1918) and Alfred George (born around 1922).

During the Second World War Alfred George McDowell served with the Royal Navy aboard HMS *Glorious*. HMS *Glorious* was built by Harland and Wolff, Belfast and commissioned in 1917. In the 1920s she was converted from a heavy cruiser to an aircraft carrier. On 8 June 1940 HMS *Glorious* and her two escorting destroyers HMS *Acasta* and HMS *Ardent* were all sunk in the Norwegian Sea by the German battle cruisers *Gneisenau* and *Scharnhorst*. Ordinary Seaman Alfred George McDowell (aged 18) was one of more than 1,200 men from HMS *Glorious* who died. More than 300 from HMS *Acasta* and HMS *Ardent* also died. In total there were around 40 survivors.

McD
McF

The seamen who lost their lives in these three ships are commemorated on a stained glass window to the right of the nave in St. Peter's Church, Martindale, Cumbria and on a Memorial Plaque near the Trondenes Historical Centre in Harstad, Norway.

Along with his brother-in-law, Signalman **Arthur Donald Field**, Ordinary Seaman Alfred George McDowell, is commemorated on the family grave headstone in Holywood Cemetery, Co. Down. On the gravestone both men are described as grandsons of Margaret Cotter McDowell.

McFarland, Samuel
Fusilier
No. 6984390, 70th Battalion, Royal Inniskilling Fusiliers
Died as a result of enemy action on Wednesday 16 April 1941 (aged 19)
Clogherney Church of Ireland Churchyard, Co. Tyrone

Samuel McFarland was a son of Alexander and Elizabeth Margaret McFarland (nee Graham) of Clogherney, Beragh, Co. Tyrone. Alexander McFarland was working as a labourer in Belfast when he and Margaret Graham were married on 1 September 1906 in Berry Street Presbyterian

Church. After their first child was born they moved to Beragh where Alexander's father Robert was a farmer. Alexander and Margaret McFarland had at least five children – Margaret Ellen (born 8 October 1907); Robert (born 27 January 1909); Alexander (born 3 January 1912); William (born 20 March 1914) and Samuel (born 1922).

Fusilier Samuel McFarland aged 19 was one of 13 soldiers serving with the 70th Battalion, Royal Inniskilling Fusiliers who died as a result of an air raid on Newtownards aerodrome during the night of 15/16 April 1941. Fusilier **Daniel Higgins** who also died that night was buried in Newtownards (Movilla) Cemetery and under his name in this Book of Honour there is a summary of all those people with North Down or Ards connections who died that night.

McFarlane, John*
Rifleman
No. 7018909, 70th Battalion, Royal Ulster Rifles
Died as a result of an accident on Thursday 23 October 1941 (aged 18)
Holywood Cemetery, Co. Down (Protestant Ground Collective Grave 1263)

McF
McG

John McFarlane was born in the Republic of Ireland and he lived in Belfast. During the Second World War Rifleman John McFarlane served with the 70th Battalion, Royal Ulster Rifles and he was 18 years old and single when he died of cerebral contusions on 23 October 1941 at Jackson's Field in Holywood. He was buried on 25 October in a collective grave in Holywood Cemetery. The two other men who were buried in this grave are Fusilier **Frederick Bloomfield** and Driver **Sidney John Wren**.

McGarry, Francis Wilfred (Frank)
Lieutenant
Royal Canadian Navy Volunteer Reserve *attached* Royal Navy
Killed in an aircraft accident on Saturday 8 September 1945 (aged 25)
Ballycranbeg (Mount St. Joseph) RC Churchyard, Co. Down (Grave 48)

Francis Wilfred (Frank) McGarry was born in Toronto, Ontario on 30

December 1919 and he was a son of Edward John McGarry (born 20 September 1880) and Agnes McGarry (nee Bailie, born January 1885). They lived in Canada at 12 Alcina Avenue, Toronto. Frank's mother was a daughter of Adam and Sophia Bailie (nee Surgeon) who were married on 26 December 1879 in Rosemary (Ekenhead) Presbyterian Church, Belfast. Edward John McGarry worked as a mailer (he moved newspapers from the printing press to the delivery truck) and he and Agnes Bailie were married in 1907. They had at least four children – Edward; Agnes May (born 28 January 1910); James Maurice (born 18 July 1908, died of meningitis 29 July 1909) and Francis Wilfred (Frank, born 30 December 1919).

Frank McGarry attended De La Salle College (Oaklands) Toronto, he obtained a BA degree and, prior to joining up, he worked for the Otis Fensom Elevator Company in Hamilton, Ontario. He lived at 175 Robinson Street in Hamilton. During the Second World War Frank McGarry served with the Royal Canadian Navy Volunteer Reserve *attached* to the Royal Navy and he died on 8 September 1945 (aged 25). Records show that he was 5 feet 11½ inches tall with brown hair, blue eyes and a fair complexion. It is known that on 4 June 1944 he flew into New York from the Air Force Base in Stephenville in the Dominion of Newfoundland when he was in transit to Ottawa in Canada.

McG

On 8 September 1945 Lieutenant (A) Frank Wilfred McGarry was flying a Chance Vought Corsair aircraft (JT357) of 768 Squadron, Fleet Air Arm based at Ballyhalbert when the engine failed and he crashed five miles south-south-west of the airfield near Ballycranbeg Roman Catholic Church. He was attempting an emergency landing when his aircraft hit a wall and caught fire.

Lieutenant (A) Frank Wilfred McGarry was buried on 12 September 1945 in Ballycranbeg (Mount St. Joseph) Roman Catholic Churchyard and he is commemorated on the Second World War Memorial Plaque for former students in De La Salle College (Oaklands) Toronto; on the Canadian Virtual War Memorial (Internet) and on Page 542 in the Canadian Second World War Book of Remembrance. On his CWGC headstone there is an inscription:

Here I lie, pray for me if you pass by

McGlennon, Hugh Henry (Hugh)
Military Medal
Rifleman
No. 7012171, 2nd Battalion, Royal Ulster Rifles
Killed on active service on Thursday 26 April 1945 (aged 30)
Becklingen War Cemetery, Soltau, Niedersachsen, Germany (Grave 8 G 10)

 Hugh Henry McGlennon was born on 25 June 1914 and he was a son of Patrick and Margaret (Maggie) McGlennon (nee Flynn) of Ballycranbeg, Kircubbin. Patrick McGlennon worked as a farm labourer and he and Maggie Flynn were married on 23 September 1905 in Portaferry Roman Catholic Church. They had at least five children – John (born 2 August 1906); Patrick Anthony (born 8 November 1908); Margaret (born 21 March 1912); Gerard (Gerry) and Hugh Henry (born 25 June 1914).

In the 9 September 1944 edition of the *County Down Spectator* it was reported that Rifleman Hugh Henry McGlennon had been awarded the Military Medal and that his wife lived at Granshaw, Kircubbin. His brother Gerry was also serving with the Forces. In the 23 September 1944 edition of the *County Down Spectator* it was reported that Hugh was unmarried and that he had been in the Forces since 1933.

McG

Newtownards.
Kircubbin Soldier Awarded Military Medal.—Ards people will learn with pride and satisfaction of the award of the Military Medal to Rifleman Hugh McGlennon whose wife resides at Granshaw, Kircubbin. Rifleman McGlennon is a son of Mr. and Mrs. Patrick McGlennon, Ballycranbeg, and another brother, Mr. Gerry McGlennon, is also serving with the Forces.

Rifleman Hugh Henry McGlennon was awarded the Military Medal for gallantry during the Allied invasion of Normandy in June 1944 – in the pre D-day reconnaissance operations, during the landings and in the ensuing advance. The landings took place along a 50-mile stretch of the Normandy coast divided into five sectors: Utah, Omaha, Gold, Juno and Sword. His award was announced in the 31 August 1944 edition of the *London Gazette*.

Rifleman Hugh Henry McGlennon was 30 years old when he was killed on 26 April 1945 during the Allied advance in Nazi Germany. The vehicle he was travelling in activated a magnetic mine and there were no survivors. He is commemorated on the family grave headstone in Ballycranbeg (Mount St. Joseph) Roman Catholic Churchyard, Co. Down.

McGowan, William Thomas and Bertha (Husband and Wife)
Civilian War Dead
Died as a result of enemy action on Tuesday 6 May 1941 (aged 59 and 56)

> M'GOWAN — William and Bertha
> M'Gowan, of 11, Avondale Street,
> Belfast.
> Father, in Thy gracious keeping,
> Leave we now our loved ones sleeping.
> Deeply regretted by their sorrowing
> · Sister and Brother-in-law and Family.
> 49, Mill Street, Newtownards

William Thomas and Bertha McGowan (sometimes Magowan) of 11 Avondale Street, Belfast died on 6 May 1941 as a result of injuries received in a bomb explosion during the Blitz on 4/5 May. Their sister, brother-in-law and family who lived at 49 Mill Street, Newtownards placed a *Result of Enemy Action* death notice in the 10 May 1941 edition of the *Newtownards Chronicle*. William Thomas and Bertha McGowan are commemorated on the Tiger's Bay North Belfast Community Website.

Of the many civilians of the Commonwealth whose deaths were due to enemy action in the 1939-1945 War, the names of some 67,092 are commemorated in the Civilian War Dead Roll of Honour, located near St. George's Chapel in Westminster Abbey, London.

McG

McGowan, Margaret Kate
Civilian War Dead
Died as a result of an accident on Thursday 17 December 1942 (aged 21)

In the CWGC Debt of Honour it is recorded that Margaret Kate McGowan had Air Raid Precautions (ARP) responsibilities; she was a daughter of Charles McGowan of Laughta, Kinlough in Co. Leitrim, Republic of Ireland; she died at Moneyreagh and the Reporting Authority was Newtownards Rural District, Northern Ireland. Margaret Kate McGowan died on ARP duty after fracturing her skull when she alighted from an ambulance while it was in motion.

Of the many civilians of the Commonwealth whose deaths were due to enemy action in the 1939-1945 War, the names of some 67,092 are commemorated in the Civilian War Dead Roll of Honour, located near St. George's Chapel in Westminster Abbey, London.

McGrath, John
Able Seaman
SS *Troutpool* (West Hartlepool), Merchant Navy
Died as a result of enemy action on Saturday 20 July 1940 (aged 53)
Tower Hill Memorial, London, England (Panel 112)

John McGrath was born on 12 August 1886 in Portaferry, he was a son Hugh and Margaret McGrath and he served during the First World War. He lived at 291 Paisley Road, Glasgow with his sister Mrs Margaret Black. During the Second World War, John McGrath served in the Merchant Navy as an Able Seaman aboard the SS *Troutpool* (West Hartlepool). Owned by the Pool Shipping Company, the SS *Troutpool* was built in 1927 by William Gray and Company and in 1940 she was on a voyage from Rosario in Argentina to Great Britain with a cargo of grain when she sank after being struck by two magnetic mines. The SS *Troutpool* had put into Belfast Lough for degaussing – a process involving the passing of an electric current through a cable round the ship's hull (designed to reduce the possibility of magnetic mines in the water being attracted by the ship's hull). After re-starting her engines she was struck by two mines around 2.00 pm on 20 July 1940 and sank about a mile off the coast near Bangor.

> Seaman John M'Grath, whose death as a result of enemy action at sea took place on 20th July last, was well known in the Portaferry district, of which he was a native. He served throughout the last war.
> He resided at 291, Paisley Road, Glasgow, with his sister, Mrs. Margaret Black, who has been notified that his body was recovered and buried in Movilla Cemetery, Newtownards.

Able Seaman John McGrath was one of eleven crew members killed in the explosions. At low tide the superstructure was visible and, because it was a hazard to shipping, the wreckage was dispersed with explosives. At the time it was speculated that the mines which sank the SS *Troutpool* were laid by a long range Focke-Wulf Fw 200 Condor aircraft known to have been operating in the area.

McG
McH

Fireman and Trimmer **Shief Ahmed** was buried in Bangor Cemetery, as was **Thomas Smith Beckett** who was the Ship's Carpenter aboard SS *Troutpool*. Three unidentified sailors from SS *Troutpool* were buried in Movilla Cemetery, Newtownards – one on 1 August 1940, another on 24 August 1940 and the third on 26 August 1940. Able Seaman John McGrath's body was not recovered and he is commemorated on the Tower Hill Memorial in London.

McHugh, John Kavanagh (Jack)
Fusilier
No. 14214477, 11th Battalion, Royal Scots Fusiliers
Killed in action on Sunday 30 July 1944 (aged 21)
Ranville War Cemetery, Calvados, France (Grave I D 9)

John Kavanagh (Jack) McHugh was born in June 1923 in Primrose Street,

Bangor and he was a son of James Kavanagh McHugh (born 10 September 1868) and Margaret McHugh (nee Cookson). James K. McHugh was a bookmaker and during the First World War he worked for the Ministry of Munitions in Gretna, Scotland. During his time there he met Margaret Cookson and their marriage was registered in the third quarter of 1918 in Carlisle, Cumberland. They had three children – Patrick Kavanagh (birth registered first quarter 1919 in Carlisle); Margaret L. (birth registered third quarter 1920 in Carlisle; died in infancy) and John Kavanagh (Jack, born June 1923). Jack's father James died on 5 March 1932 (aged 60) and, after his mother Margaret married William Ferguson on 15 April 1939 in Bangor, they moved to Wigtown in Scotland.

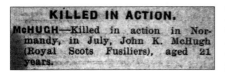

KILLED IN ACTION.

McHUGH—Killed in action in Normandy, in July, John K. McHugh (Royal Scots Fusiliers), aged 21 years.

Jack McHugh's paternal grandparents were Patrick and Selina McHugh (nee Kavanagh). Patrick McHugh worked in the family business started by his father Bernard and his uncle Edward – B. & E. McHugh (Wholesale and Retail Drapery), Rosemary Street, Belfast. Edward McHugh was Member of Parliament for South Armagh from 1892 until 1900.

McH

14214477 FUSILIER
J. K. McHUGH
THE ROYAL SCOTS FUSILIERS
30TH JULY 1944 AGE 21

Jack McHugh was educated at St. Comgall's Public Elementary School, Brunswick Road, Bangor and prior to joining up he worked in a creamery in Scotland. He lived with his mother and step-father and from there he made frequent trips back to Bangor to visit his brother Patrick who lived at 36 Dufferin Avenue. Jack McHugh joined up in June 1942 at the age of 19, he served with the Royal Scots Fusiliers and he was killed in action in Normandy on 30 July 1944. He was buried in Ranville War Cemetery. The Allied offensive in north-western Europe began with the Normandy Landings on 6 June 1944 and Ranville was the first village to be liberated in France when the bridge over the Caen Canal was captured.

Fusilier John Kavanagh (Jack) McHugh was 21 years old when he died and he is commemorated on Bangor and District War Memorial.

McKay, Andrew
Second Officer
SS *Sheaf Mead* (Newcastle-on-Tyne), Merchant Navy
Died as a result of enemy action on Monday 27 May 1940 (aged 61)
Tower Hill Memorial, London, England (Panel 95)

In the CWGC Debt of Honour it is recorded that Andrew McKay was a son of Andrew and Eliza McKay and the husband of Mary McKay of Gransha, Co. Down. Research has shown that Andrew McKay was in fact from Gransha, Islandmagee, Co. Antrim. There are five townlands named Gransha in County Down and two of them are located in the Ards area. There is one townland named Gransha in County Antrim and it is located in Islandmagee.

The 1901 Census shows that the McKay family lived in the townland of Ballytober, Islandmagee. The Head of the family was Elizabeth (Eliza) McKay (aged 54) and she was a widow. Five children were named – Mary (aged 23) was a farmer's daughter; Andrew (aged 21) was a sailor; Robert (aged 18) was a farmer's son; Arthur (aged 15) was a carpenter; Agnes (aged 11) was a scholar, as was Rosina, (aged 9). Andrew McKay Senior died on 1 December 1899 (aged 65) and Eliza died on 10 June 1904 (aged 58). They were buried in Ballypriormore Graveyard in Islandmagee and also commemorated on the family grave headstone is their son Alexander who was lost at sea in 1887 (aged 22) and their son Robert who died on 9 July 1949 (aged 66).

McK

During the Second World War Andrew McKay Junior served with the Merchant Navy aboard the SS *Sheaf Mead* (formerly *Gretaston*). This British Cargo Ship was built in 1924 by Robert Duncan and Company, Glasgow and was owned by the Sheaf Steam Shipping Company, Newcastle-upon-Tyne. On 27 May 1940 she was on route from Swansea to Philadelphia in ballast when she was torpedoed without warning by the German submarine *U-37*. The attack happened around 4.00 pm and SS *Sheaf Mead* sank some 150 miles west of Cape Finisterre in Spain. Second Officer Andrew McKay was one of more than 30 men who lost their lives. The British and German accounts of the sinking of this ship were heard at the Nuremberg War Crimes trials on 14 January 1946. Second Officer Andrew McKay is commemorated as Captain McKay on the family grave headstone in Islandmagee (Ballyharry) Cemetery, Co. Antrim. His wife Mary Johnston

McKay died on 4 March 1961 (aged 79) and their son Charles died on 5 December 1989. During the Second World War Charles McKay (No. 571983) served as a Flight Lieutenant in the Royal Air Force.

McKeag, Robert
Sergeant (Air Gunner)
No. 1522883, 50 Squadron, Royal Air Force Volunteer Reserve
Died on active service on Saturday 4 September 1943 (aged 21)
Berlin 1939-1945 War Cemetery, Berlin, Germany (Grave 7 J 21)

Robert McKeag's birth was registered in the second quarter of 1921 in Newtownards and he was a son of Robert and Agnes Catherine McKeag (nee Scott) who lived in Belfast. Robert McKeag Senior worked as a plater's helper in the shipyard and he and Agnes Scott were married on 11 May 1918 in Belfast Registry Office. Robert McKeag Junior's paternal grandfather, Thomas McKeag was born in Comber and his paternal grandmother, Sarah McKeag was born in Bangor.

McK

Before the outbreak of war in 1939 Robert McKeag Junior worked as a labourer in the Belfast Shipyard and during the Second World War he served with the Royal Air Force Volunteer Reserve. When he died on 4 September 1943 he was one of a seven man crew aboard an Avro Lancaster Mark III aircraft (ED755) that was on a mission to bomb Berlin. They took off at 8.11 pm on 3 September 1943 from RAF Skellingthorpe in Lincolnshire and later crashed at Vielitz, 14 km east-north-east of Neuruppin in Germany. All aboard were killed and they were buried near the crash site on 8 September. Later their bodies were exhumed and reinterred in the 1939-1945 War Cemetery in Berlin. The other six crew members who died that night were:

- Flying Officer Percy Hornby Coates aged 26 (RCAF)
- Sgt George Banks Buchan aged 29 from Tomatin, Inverness-shire
- Flying Officer Jack Morgan Lauder (RCAF)
- Sergeant Rae Warren Buddy Collins (RCAF)
- Sergeant Reginald Gordon Cooper aged 19 from Romford, Essex
- Sergeant Anthony Richard Duncan Bedbrook

Sergeant Robert McKeag was 21 years old when he died and he is commemorated on the family grave headstone in St. Mary's Church of Ireland Graveyard, Comber. His father Robert died on 10 June 1937 (aged 57) and his mother Agnes died on 7 January 1992.

McKee, George

 The name George McKee is inscribed on Newtownards and District War Memorial. In the CWGC Debt of Honour four George McKees who were Second World War casualties are commemorated:

- Lance Corporal George Edward McKee (No. Q28068) was a son of William and Esther McKee, he served with the Australian Infantry and he was 26 years old when he died on 31 December 1941.
- Ordinary Seaman George Robert McKee was a son of James and Mary McKee, he served with the Merchant Navy and he was 21 years old when he died on 8 June 1942.
- Gunner George R. McKee (No. 2977488) was a son of William and Elizabeth Deveney McKee, he served with the Royal Artillery and he was 31 years old when he died on 8 May 1943.
- Sergeant William George McKee (No. C/80113) was a son of William and Charlotte McKee, he served with the Canadian Light Infantry and he was 21 years old when he died on 6 October 1943.

McK

On 9 November 1943 George McKee of 122 Mill Street, Newtownards (a labourer aged 41 who died of Hodgkin's disease in Ards District Hospital) was buried in Movilla Cemetery, Newtownards. His wife Alice remarried and her second husband, David Johnston, died on 13 February 1972. Alice Johnston died on 1 December 1988 and all three are commemorated on a headstone in Movilla Cemetery.

Desk studies and public appeals to date have yielded no further information about the identity of George McKee who is commemorated on Newtownards and District War Memorial.

McKee, Norman Strahan (Norman)
Private
No. S/135409, 8 Petrol Depot, Royal Army Service Corps
Killed in action on Sunday 31 January 1943 (aged 24)
Benghazi War Cemetery, Libya (Grave 7 D 31)

Norman Strahan McKee's birth was registered in the third quarter of 1919 in Ballymoney, Co. Antrim and he was the elder son of Dr Samuel Kenny McKee and Gladys Muriel McKee (nee Frazer, daughter of Methodist Minister, the Revd James Frazer). Dr Samuel McKee was a Captain in the Royal Army Medical Corps when he and Gladys were married on 30 July

> **Son of a Former Bangor Doctor Killed in Action.**—Norman M'Kee, aged 23, elder son of Dr. S. Kenny M'Kee, formerly of Kingscourt, Ballyholme Road, has been killed in action with the Royal Artillery in North Africa. Educated at Glenlola and for five years at Blundell's in Devon, he enlisted at the outbreak of war though in a reserved service, the Great Southern Railway, which he entered in open competition for the three vacancies reserved for public-school boys. He served in North Africa since the beginning of the campaign. His brother, Malcolm, is a Flying-Officer and is now on night patrol over the Continent. Their cousin, Jim (youngest son of the Moderator), who was killed in Tunisia a fortnight after his twentieth birthday, a Lieutenant in the Royal Inniskilling Fusiliers, was born in County Down also.

1918 in Balmoral Methodist Church, Osborne Park, Belfast. The McKee family moved to *Kingscourt*, Ballyholme Road, Bangor and later to 14 Culme Road, Seymour Park, Plymouth. Norman McKee was educated in the preparatory department of Glenlola School, Bangor before going to Blundell's Independent School in Tiverton, Devon.

Norman McKee served with the RASC and he was 24 years old when he was killed in action with the Royal Artillery on 31 January 1943 in Libya. His death was reported in the 12 June 1943 edition of the *County Down Spectator* under the headline *Son of a Former Bangor Doctor Killed in Action*. At the time, Norman's brother Malcolm was serving with the Royal Air Force.

McK

On 4 January 1943, some four weeks before Norman died, one of his distant cousins, Charles James (Jim) McKee, also died. Jim McKee was killed in action in Tunisia and he was the youngest son of the Revd Phineas McKee (Minister of Downshire Road Presbyterian Church, Newry from 1913 until 1943 and Moderator of the Presbyterian Church in Ireland in 1943). Jim McKee was born in County Down, he served as a Lieutenant in the Royal Inniskilling Fusiliers and he is commemorated in Downshire Road Presbyterian Church, Newry. The Revd Phineas McKee died at 1 College Park, Belfast on 9 November 1943 and the death of Private Norman Strahan McKee's father, Samuel Kenny McKee was registered in the first quarter of 1971 in Plymouth.

McKelvey, William Murray
Lance Corporal
**No. 14427503, 1st Battalion, Highland Light Infantry
(City of Glasgow Regiment)
Killed in action on Thursday 2 November 1944 (aged 20)
Bergen-op-Zoom War Cemetery, Noord-Brabant, Netherlands
(Grave 8 C 18)**

William Murray McKelvey was a son of William and Elizabeth McKelvey (nee Harper) of Laurencetown, Co. Down and he was a grandson of Alexander and Mary McKelvey (nee Murray). During the Second World War he served with the 1st Battalion, Highland Light Infantry (City of

Glasgow Regiment) and he was 20 years old when he was killed in action on 2 November 1944 during the Battle of Walcheren Causeway. After he was killed, his sister Edie and brother-in-law Joe Allen, placed a *Killed in Action* notice in the 9 December 1944 edition of the *County Down Spectator*. Edie and Joe Allen lived in Springwell Road, Groomsport.

McKimm, Norman
Guardsman
No. 2719325, 1st Battalion, Irish Guards
Killed in action on Tuesday 30 March 1943 (aged 35)
Medjez-el-Bab Memorial, Tunisia (Face 14)

Norman McKimm was born in Newtownards on 14 December 1907 and he was a son of William and Catherine McKimm (nee Cowell) who were married on 29 September 1896 in Second Newtownards Presbyterian Church. The McKimm family lived at 81 Balfour Street and later at 24 James Street, Newtownards. William McKimm worked as a labourer and he and Catherine (from the Isle of Man) had ten children – Alfred (born 6 February 1897); Ambrose (born 18 May 1898); William (born 14 October 1901); John (born 29 November 1904); Catherine (born 27 January 1906); Norman (born 14 December 1907); Eric (born 7 July 1911); Maurice; Malcolm and Mona.

McK

Ards Soldier Killed in Action.—Mrs. M'Kimm, of 24, James Street, Newtownards, has been notified that her husband, Guardsman Norman M'Kimm, of the Irish Guards, who was reported missing a year ago, has been killed in action. The young Guardsman, who is the third son of the late Mr. and Mrs. Wm. M'Kimm, of 24, James Street, Newtownards, had close on five years' service with the Irish Guards. Much sympathy will be extended to his wife and four young children, the youngest of whom was never seen by Guardsman M'Kimm.

Norman McKimm was a discharged soldier when he married Mary Jane (Jennie) Weir in Newtownards Registry Office. Jennie's father Joe had been on active service during the First World War. Norman and Jennie McKimm lived for a time at 32 Upper Movilla Street, Newtownards and they had four children – Grace Audrey (born 1935); William Norman (born 1939); Eric Desmond (Derek, born 1941) and Noretta (born June 1943, some three months after her father died).

Norman McKimm served with the Royal Scots Fusiliers from 8 January 1930 until 24 August 1936 and after leaving the Army he worked as a general labourer. He enlisted in Belfast on 26 September 1939 and served with the Irish Guards. In his enlistment papers it is recorded that he was 5 feet 9½ inches tall and he had a burn scar on his left forearm. Between periods of service in Britain he was posted to Norway for a short time in 1940 and he went to North Africa on 28 February 1943. One month later, on 30 March 1943, he was reported as missing in action and a year later, in March 1944, it was officially confirmed that he must be presumed killed. In an *Our Heroes – In Memoriam* notice his wife Jennie included the verse:

> *His name is dear to memory, 'tis graven on our hearts*
> *His kindly smile is with us still, lingering, loath to part*

Guardsman Norman McKimm was awarded four service medals – the 1939/45 Star, the Africa Star (1st Army Clasp), the Defence Medal and the War Medal 1939/45. He is commemorated on Newtownards and District War Memorial and in Newtownards Parish Church of Ireland Church (St. Mark's).

McLean Brothers, James and William

McK
McL

It was reported in the 22 December 1945 edition of the *Newtownards Chronicle* that Corporal James McLean, son of John McLean, Ballyblack, Newtownards had died in March 1945 in a Prisoner-of-War Camp in Java. It was also reported that James's brother, Sergeant William McLean, had been killed in action on 7 January 1945. The report continued, 'three members of the family have given their lives in the service of King and Country' and it ended, 'John McLean served in the First and Second World Wars and is at present with the Merchant Navy'. The third family member to die was Lance Corporal **James Charles McCaul**.

In the CWGC Debt of Honour James and William McLean are both described as sons of John and Jessie McLean; they were in fact stepsons of Jessie McLean (formerly McCaul, nee Norris). In some records the surnames are spelt McClean and McCall. John McLean (aged 22, then a sailor from Ballywhiskin) and Ellen McBrier (aged 20 from Carrowdore) were married on 12 November 1909 in Carrowdore Parish Church of Ireland Church (Christ Church) and they had one son – John (born 24 January 1911). Ellen McLean died of tuberculosis on 18 February 1917 and on 6 January 1919 John McLean (then a miner from Ballywhiskin, son of John McCullough) and Mary Campbell (daughter of James Campbell, Ballyblack) were married in Ards Registry Office. They had four children – James (born 3 June 1921); William (born 22 February 1923); Hugh (born 10 February 1925) and Margaret Jane (born 26 July 1926).

Mary McLean died and on 23 June 1933 John McLean and Jessie McCaul (nee Norris) were married in Ballyblack Presbyterian Church. Jessie Norris (daughter of Harry Norris, 28 Nelson Street, Belfast) and Charles McCaul (labourer, son of Charles McCaul, 12 Ship Street, Belfast) were married on 18 November 1912 in St. Anne's Church of Ireland Cathedral, Belfast and they had at least two children – James Charles and Minnie. It was reported in the 29 June 1940 edition of the *Newtownards Chronicle* that Lance Corporal James Charles McCaul, who was a son of Mrs John McLean of Ballycastle Road, Ballyblack, had died of wounds.

John and Jessie McLean had two children both of whom were baptised in Carrowdore Parish Church of Ireland Church – Jamison Johnston Edward (born 26 October 1935) and Frank Orr (born 31 December 1939, died 20 February 1940). John McLean was 81 years old when he died (buried 14 January 1968) and Jessie McLean was 75 years old when she died (buried 2 March 1973). Both were buried in Carrowdore Parish Church Graveyard (Grave G 8) and at the time of writing there is no headstone on the grave.

During the course of my research for this Book of Honour, a lady now living in Australia suggested to me that Leading Stoker Alexander McLean (No. P/KX 97625), who was killed in action aboard HMS *Hood* on 24 May 1941, was a brother of James and William McLean. No evidence has yet been found to substantiate this suggestion. By about two months, William was the first of the two McLean brothers to die in war.

McL

McLean, William
Sergeant (Air Gunner)
No. 1048611, 626 Squadron, Royal Air Force Volunteer Reserve
Killed in an aircraft accident on Sunday 7 January 1945 (aged 21)
Clichy Northern Cemetery, Hauts-de-Seine, France (Plot 16 Row 10 Grave 8)

During the Second World War William McLean (born 22 February 1923) served with the Royal Air Force Volunteer Reserve and on 7 January 1945 he was one of a crew of seven aboard an Avro Lancaster Mark III aircraft (LL961) that took off at 6.44

pm from RAF Wickenby in Lincolnshire on a mission to bomb Munich. On the outward flight the aircraft collided with another Lancaster aircraft and the crew baled out. Sergeant McLean was killed along with the pilot, Flying Officer Robert Marshall Smith of the Royal Canadian Air Force.

> **KILLED ON ACTIVE SERVICE.**
> **M'LEAN** — Sergeant William M'Lean, Killed on Air Operations, third and dearly-beloved son of John M'Lean, Ballyblack.
> Had we but seen him at the last,
> Or raised his drooping head,
> Our hearts would not have been so sore,
> The bitter tears we shed.
> Deeply regretted by his sorrowing Father, Brother and Sister, Brother (Prisoner of War in the Japanese hands), also Brother and Sister-in-law, John and Martha M'Lean, and Family, Ballycopeland, Millisle; also Grandmother and Aunt Margaret, Ballywhisken, Millisle; also Step-mother and Family.

Initially Sergeant William McLean was reported as missing in action and then in March 1945 his father was officially informed that William had been killed. There was a *Killed on Active Service* notice in the 17 March 1945 edition of the *Newtownards Chronicle* from father, brother and sister; brother James (Prisoner-of-War in Japanese hands); brother and sister-in-law John and Martha McLean and family, Ballycopeland, Millisle; grandmother and aunt Margaret, Ballywhiskin, Millisle; also stepmother and family. The *Killed on Active Service* notice contained the verse:

McL

> *Had we but seen him at the last, or raised his drooping head*
> *Our hearts would not have been so sore, the bitter tears we shed*

There is an inscription on his CWGC headstone:

> *His young life he gave that we might live*
> *Loved by Mother*

McLean, James
Corporal
No. 647093, Royal Air Force
Died in a Prisoner-of-War Camp on Saturday 24 March 1945 (aged 23)
Jakarta War Cemetery, Indonesia (Grave 3 L 7)

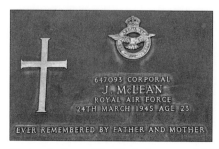

During the Second World War James McLean (born 3 June 1921) served with the Royal Air Force and he was reported missing at the fall of Singapore on 15 February 1942. Then a card arrived from the Red Cross stating that he was 'safe' and being held in a Japanese Prisoner-of-War Camp in Java. He died there on 24 March 1945 (CWGC) but it was not until later in the year that his family received official notification.

News has been received that Temporary Corporal James M'Lean, R.A.F., son of Mr. John M'Lean, Ballyblack, died in a prisoner of war camp in Java on 19th March of this year. The young airman, who was 24 years of age, and had six years' service, had been a prisoner of war in the hands of the Japanese since the fall of Singapore.

DIED ON ACTIVE SERVICE.

M'LEAN—19th March, 1945, in a Prisoner of War Camp in Java, T/Corporal James M'Lean, R.A.F., son of John M'Lean, Ballyblack.
"At the going down of the sun, and in the morning, we will remember him."
Deeply regretted by the entire Family circle.

There was a *Died on Active Service* notice in the 22 December 1945 edition of the *Newtownards Chronicle* from the entire family circle and it contained the verse:

At the going down of the sun, and in the morning, we will remember him.

Both Sergeant William McLean and Corporal James McLean are commemorated in Carrowdore Parish Church of Ireland Church (Christ Church), where Lance Corporal James McCaul is also commemorated.

McManus, John
Newtownards and District War Memorial

JOHN McMANUS The name John McManus is commemorated on Newtownards and District War Memorial and there is evidence to suggest that this casualty was Lance Corporal John McManus (No. 6977788), 1st Battalion, King's Own Royal Regiment (Lancaster) who died on Saturday 14 November 1942 (aged 28) and is commemorated on the Alamein Memorial in Egypt (Column 55). In the Army Roll of Honour 1939-1945 it is recorded that this soldier was born in County Down; he lived in County Down; on 1 September 1939 he was serving with the Royal Irish Fusiliers and during the Second World War he fought in the Middle East Theatre of War.

McL
McM

CORPORAL CHARLES M'MANUS.   LCE. CPL. JOHN M'MANUS.

In the 8 January 1944 edition of the *County Down Spectator* it was reported that Corporal Charles McManus (son of Mr and Mrs John McManus of Ballymacnamee, Portaferry) had been reported missing. The report also referred to Charles's brother Tommy who was serving in Malta and to his brother Lance Corporal John McManus who had been reported missing in June 1943. John McManus joined the Royal Irish Fusiliers in 1935 and served abroad for seven years. His father, John McManus Senior, had served in the First World War.

McManus, Walter Bartholomew Benedict (Walter)
Pilot Officer (Pilot)
No. J/5469, 504 (RAF) Squadron, Royal Canadian Air Force
Killed in an aircraft accident on Wednesday 7 January 1942 (aged 27)
Ballycranbeg (Mount St. Joseph) Roman Catholic Churchyard,
Co. Down (Grave 31)

Walter Bartholomew Benedict McManus was a son of Harold Joseph (Harry) and Rose Ellen McManus of St. Thomas, Ontario, Canada and he had a brother named Joseph who operated a chain of motor service stations in London, Ontario. Walter was a graduate of the University of Western Ontario and Osgoode Hall in Toronto and, prior to the outbreak of the Second World War, he worked as a barrister with the firm Arthur Lebel KC in London, Ontario.

McM

Walter Bartholomew Benedict McManus was the husband of Kathleen Clare McManus (nee Hunt) of Hamilton, Ontario. They were married in May 1941 in St. Patrick's Church, Hamilton and in June 1941 Walter was posted overseas. On 7 January 1942 he was flying a Supermarine Spitfire aircraft (P7823) from St. Angelo Airfield in County Fermanagh to RAF Ballyhalbert when he crashed at Derrymacash near Lurgan. An eye witness reported that, in his opinion, 'the pilot was attempting a forced landing when his plane nose-dived into rising ground'. Walter McManus's plane – named *Down* – was one of a number purchased by the *Belfast Telegraph Spitfire Fund*.

Pilot Officer (Pilot) Walter Bartholomew Benedict McManus was 27 years old when he died and he is commemorated on the Canadian Virtual War Memorial (Internet) and on Page 98 in the Canadian Second World War Book of Remembrance.

McMaster, James
Fusilier
No. 6978240, 2nd Battalion, Royal Irish Fusiliers
Died in service between Monday 15 and Tuesday 16 November 1943 (aged 24)
Athens Memorial, Greece (Face 7)

In the CWGC Debt of Honour it is recorded that James McMaster was a son of Thomas and Maud McMaster of Ballydrain, Co. Down. The townland of

Ballydrain lies between Comber and Killinchy.

James McMaster was born on 29 December 1918 in the townland of Tullybroom, Clogher, Co. Tyrone and he was baptised on 22 January 1919. The McMaster family also lived at different times in the townlands of Eskernabrogue and Eskermore, Co. Tyrone. James McMaster was a son of Thomas and Maud McMaster (nee Gair, sometimes Girr). Thomas (Tom) McMaster worked as a labourer and he and Maud Gair were married on 27 October 1910 in St. Mark's Church of Ireland Church, Augher, Co. Tyrone. Six months later Maud was working as a domestic servant for brothers Robert and John Smyth who farmed in the townland of Tullyvernan, Clogher. Thomas and Maud McMaster had at least four children – Mary (born 12 December 1911); twins Edith and Florence (born 23 July 1914) and James (born 29 December 1918).

During the Second World War James McMaster served with the 2nd Battalion, Royal Irish Fusiliers and he was 24 years old when he died on 15/16 November 1943 on the Greek island of Leros. The Battalion was captured there by German Forces and Fusilier James McMaster is commemorated on the Athens Memorial in Greece.

McM

McMaster, James (Jimmie)
Ordinary Seaman
SS *River Humber* (Bristol), Merchant Navy
Killed in an accident at sea on Tuesday 4 June 1940 (aged 20)
Tower Hill Memorial, London, England (Panel 87)

James McMaster was a son of James (Jim) and Elizabeth (Lizzie) McMaster of Portavogie and during the Second World War he served with the Merchant Navy aboard the SS *River Humber*. Built in 1920 by Hepple and Company Ltd., South Shields and owned by Messrs Charles Neill Ltd., Bangor, the SS *River Humber* was on passage from Dublin to Preston in ballast when she sank after a collision with HMS *Folkestone* in the Irish Sea east-north-east of Skerries, Dublin. Mate **Jack Cully** and Fireman **Frank Maginnis** died in the same incident. The fourth man who died was Chief Engineer Officer John Gibson (aged 32) from Gardenstown in Banffshire, Scotland. **John Gibson*** was born in Pennan, Aberdeenshire in Scotland although he did live for a time at 26 Primrose Street in Bangor.

After James McMaster died, John McMullan, Worshipful Master of Portavogie LOL 552 and W.H. Mawhinney, Secretary placed a notice in the 8 June 1940 edition of the *County Down Spectator*:

'The officers and members of Portavogie LOL 552 desire to tender sincere and heartfelt sympathy to the relatives of Brother Jack Cully and Mr John McMaster who lost their lives in the sinking of the *SS Humber*'.

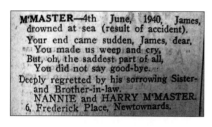

In 1940 and subsequent years there were *Death* and *In Memoriam* notices too from family and friends including his father, mother, brothers and sisters at Ratallagh, Co. Down; his sister and brother-in-law Nannie and Harry McMaster together with niece Elizabeth of 6 Frederick Place, Newtownards; his sister and brother-in-law Netta and Hugh Cardy, together with nieces Betty and May of 43 William Street, Newtownards; his sister and brother-in-law Sadie and David Coffey together with nephew and nieces Hugh, Jean and Jamesina (in some records, Jamisena) of Portavogie; his sister and brother-in-law Cassie and Samuel James Gibson together with niece Belle of 31 Movilla Street, Newtownards; his brother and sister-in-law John and Martha together with nieces Marie and Jeanetta of 30 Church Street, Newtownards; Molly Dunnen of 41 East Street, Donaghadee.

McM

Ordinary Seaman James McMaster is commemorated on Tower Hill Memorial in London and on the family grave headstone in Kirkistown Cemetery. His father Jim died on 31 January 1966; his mother Lizzie died on 7 February 1973 and his brother Bob died on 5 April 1997.

McMeekin, Harold
Ordinary Seaman
No. C/SSX 27721, HMS *Duchess*, Royal Navy
Killed in an accident at sea on Tuesday 12 December 1939 (aged 18)
Chatham Naval Memorial, Kent, England (Panel 33 2)

Harold McMeekin was born in Belfast on 27 April 1921 and he was a son of Mr and Mrs J. McMeekin who lived in Beechwood Gardens, Bangor and later in Hazley's Estate. Described as 'a bright, intelligent youth' Harold McMeekin joined the Royal Navy in November 1938 and was posted to HMS *Duchess* in August 1939.

Ordinary Seaman Harold McMeekin died on 12 December 1939 when his ship, HMS *Duchess*, was in collision with the battleship HMS *Barham* in thick fog some nine miles off the Mull of Kintyre. HMS *Duchess*, a small D-class destroyer, was commissioned in 1933 and built by Palmers Shipbuilding and Iron Company in Jarrow. She was one of four ships assigned

538

Bangor Youth Missing.—Mr. and Mrs. M'Meekin, Beechwood Gardens, Bangor, have been officially notified that their son ordinary seaman Harold M'Meekin, is believed to have been on board H.M.S. Duchess and is missing. H.M.S. Duchess, a small destroyer, was in collision with another vessel of the Fleet and went down with 120 of her crew. Young M'Meekin, who was 18 years of age, joined the Navy in November, 1938, and was posed to H.M.S. Duchess in August.

to escort HMS *Barham* from Gibraltar to Greenock and after the collision HMS *Duchess* capsized, blew up when her depth charges exploded and sank. Ordinary Seaman Harold McMeekin was one of more than 130 crew members who died. The other three ships escorting HMS *Barham* were HMS *Dainty*, HMS *Delight* and HMS *Duncan*.

Ordinary Seaman Harold McMeekin was 18 years old when he died and he is commemorated on Bangor and District War Memorial and in Bangor Parish Church of Ireland Church (St. Comgall's).

McMullan, Malcolm Morgan (Malcolm)
Mentioned in Despatches
Wing Commander
No. 21092, Royal Air Force
Died in service on Friday 17 July 1942 (aged 38)
Hawarden Cemetery, Flintshire, Wales (Section 4G Grave 24)

McM

Malcolm Morgan McMullan was born in Belfast on 24 January 1904 and he was a son of William John McMullan and Alice McMullan (nee Morgan) of 27 Hopefield Avenue, Belfast. William John McMullan worked as a commercial traveller selling tea and he and Alice Morgan were married on 4 June 1888 in May Street Presbyterian Church, Belfast. They had at least seven children, all of whom were baptised in May Street Presbyterian Church – Sarah Mary (born 18 March 1891); Alice (born 30 June 1893); William Edgar (born 1 January 1896); Thomas Alexander (born 28 February 1898); Emily Jane (born 28 June 1901); Malcolm Morgan (born 24 January 1904) and Frederick George (born 17 June 1907).

Malcolm Morgan McMullan attended Royal Belfast Academical Institution (RBAI) from 1918 until 1920 and he was the husband of Elizabeth (Lily) McMullan (nee Wilson) of *Hill Lodge*, Ballycarry, Co. Antrim. They were married on 1 December 1926 in Larne Registry Office.

During the Second World War Malcolm McMullan served with the Royal Air Force and, with effect from 1 December 1940, he was promoted from the rank of Squadron Leader to the rank of Wing Commander (temporary).

Wing Commander Malcolm Morgan McMullan was 38 years old when he died in service on 17 July 1942 and he was buried in Hawarden Cemetery, Flintshire. His home address was Tyn-y-Bryn Farm, Ruthin and he is commemorated in RBAI and on the family grave headstone in Greyabbey New Cemetery where his wife Elizabeth, who died on 14 February 1994 (aged 94) was buried.

McMullan, William Ian Muir (William)
Third Officer
SS *Calabria*, Merchant Navy
Died as a result of enemy action on Sunday 8 December 1940 (aged 34)
Tower Hill Memorial, London, England (Panel 22)

McM

William Ian Muir McMullan was born on 31 October 1906 in Donaghadee and he was a son of William Muir McMullan and Euphemia McMullan (nee Hilton) who were married on 3 June 1902 in Elmwood Avenue Presbyterian Church, Belfast. They lived in the townland of Ballygrot, Crawfordsburn and before that in *Woodaby*, Myrtlefield Park, Belfast. William McMullan Senior was a tea and sugar merchant and he and Euphemia had at least four children – Annie Margaret (born 12 March 1903, died 4 September 1903); Robert (born 16 June 1904); William Ian Muir (born 31 October 1906) and Henry Wallace (born 20 February 1909). William Ian Muir McMullan and Henry Wallace McMullan were baptised in Helen's Bay Presbyterian Church. Four members of William Ian Muir McMullan's family were buried in Belfast City Cemetery (Grave L1/2/23) – his sister Annie Margaret died 4 September 1903 (aged six months), his mother Euphemia died 18 January 1945 (aged 66), his father William died 19 February 1949 (aged 71) and his aunt Florence died 14 June 1949 (aged 56).

In the CWGC Debt of Honour it is recorded that William McMullan Junior was the husband of E. McMullan of Donaghadee and during the Second World War he served with the Merchant Navy aboard the SS *Calabria*. Built in 1923 by Aktein-Gesellschaft Weser, Bremen, Germany for Norddeutscher Lloyd, this German liner was then named SS *Werra*. On 11 June 1940 she was seized by Britain while in dry dock in Calcutta and transferred to the Ministry of War Transport (MoWT).

At 8.58 pm on 8 December 1940 the SS *Calabria* was straggling from Convoy SL-56 (on route from Freetown in Sierra Leone to Britain) when she was torpedoed and sunk off the west coast of Ireland by the German submarine *U-103*. She was carrying a cargo of iron, tea and oil-cake together with hundreds of Indian seamen who were from other ships. Around 400 men, including 22 crew members, were lost. The Indian seamen who were lost are commemorated on the Bombay/Chittagong War Memorial. Third Officer William Ian Muir McMullan was 34 years old when he died and he is commemorated on the Tower Hill Memorial in London.

McMurray, Frederick William (Fred)
Pilot Officer (Observer)
No. 85277, 82 Squadron, Royal Air Force Volunteer Reserve
Killed on active service on Tuesday 10 December 1940 (aged 26)
Schoonselhof Cemetery, Antwerpen, Belgium (Grave II H 32)

Frederick William McMurray was born on 8 February 1914 in South Africa and he was a son of Samuel James McMurray and Anna Louisa McMurray (born 11 September 1877). They had two children – Sylvia Georgina (born 26 December 1907) and Frederick William (born 8 February 1914). On 26 July 1924 the McMurray family arrived in London from South Africa aboard the SS *Garth Castle*. Samuel James McMurray was a retired bank manager and the family's intended place of residence was Lisburn. Samuel James McMurray was born on 28 February 1876 in Lisburn and he was a son of William John and Jane McMurray (nee Brown) who were married on 30 September 1874 in Hillhall Presbyterian Church, Lisburn. In 1901 Samuel James McMurray was working as a bank clerk in Downpatrick.

McM

After moving from South Africa to Lisburn, the McMurray family then moved to Bangor where they lived at 7 Windsor Avenue. Fred McMurray attended Bangor Grammar School from 1924 until 1932 where he excelled in sport. Described by the Headmaster, Maurice Wilkins, as 'an all-round

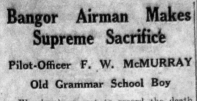

Bangor Airman Makes Supreme Sacrifice

Pilot-Officer F. W. McMURRAY

Old Grammar School Boy

We deeply regret to record the death on active service of Pilot-Officer Frederick William M'Murray, Royal Air Force, aged not quite 27.

sportsman and athlete' Fred captained both the 1st XI cricket team and the 1st XV rugby team. He was 'twelfth man' on the Ulster Schools Inter-Provincial cricket XI.

During the Second World War Fred McMurray served with the Royal Air

Force Volunteer Reserve in Bomber Command and he was one of a three man crew aboard a Bristol Blenheim Mark IV aircraft (T2225) when he was killed on 10 December 1940. They took of from RAF Bodney in Norfolk on a mission to bomb Antwerp and their aircraft crashed in the target area. The others who died were:

- Flight Lieutenant John Rankin Rathbone aged 30 and Member of Parliament for the Bodmin Division of Cornwall
- Sergeant Allan Maurice Birt aged 25 from Marsh Baldon, Oxfordshire

All three casualties were buried in Schoonselhof Cemetery, Belgium.

After Fred McMurray died his widowed mother Anna (then living at 34 Norfolk House Road, Streatham, London) wrote to Maurice Wilkins and her letter was published in the 4 January 1941 edition of the *County Down Spectator*:

McM

'Dear Mr Wilkins – You will be sorry that another of your 'Old Boys' has lost his life in the service of his country. Fred joined the RAF on the outbreak of war and enjoyed every day of his work, eventually gaining a commission as Pilot Officer. He was first reported missing but after a week I got a wire from the Air Ministry on Christmas Eve saying that he had been killed on active service. And only then did I realise how I had been hoping against hope that he was a Prisoner-of-War. Fred was never a good scholar, as you know, but he was a good sport and always a very dear and loving companion to me. He would not wait to be called up, as he said he couldn't expect the other fellow to fight for *his* mother!'

Pilot Officer Frederick William McMurray was 26 years old when he died and he is commemorated on Lisburn War Memorial; on Bangor and District War Memorial; in First Bangor Presbyterian Church and in Bangor Grammar School. His mother Anna died in 1970 and his sister Sylvia died in 1996, both in London.

McMurray, William
Company Quartermaster Sergeant
No. 6983653, 70th Battalion, Royal Inniskilling Fusiliers
Died as a result of enemy action on Thursday 17 April 1941 (aged 27)
Bessbrook Methodist Cemetery, Co. Armagh

William McMurray was born on 1 July 1913 and he was a son of George Albert Ernest and Annie McMurray (nee Sterritt) of Bessbrook, Co. Armagh. George Albert Ernest McMurray (son of William McMurray, master tailor and life assurance agent) worked as a foundry mechanic and he and Annie Sterritt were married on 19 September 1912 in Bessbrook Presbyterian Church. They had two children – William and Albert.

William McMurray was the husband of Susan Elizabeth McMurray (nee Taylor) of Bessbrook, Co. Armagh. They were married on 27 April 1934 in St. Patrick's Church of Ireland Church, Newry and they had three children – Eleanor, Meta and George who was just five months old when his father died. Susan Elizabeth McMurray died on 26 July 1989.

Company Quartermaster Sergeant William McMurray was one of 13 soldiers serving with the 70th Battalion, Royal Inniskilling Fusiliers who died as a result of an air raid on Newtownards aerodrome during the night of 15/16 April 1941. Fusilier **Daniel Higgins** who also died that night was buried in Newtownards (Movilla) Cemetery and under his name in this Book of Honour there is a summary of all those people with North Down or Ards connections who died that night.

McM
McN

Company Quartermaster Sergeant William McMurray is commemorated on Bessbrook War Memorial; in Bessbrook Methodist Church and in the Bessbrook Second World War Roll of Honour Dead.

McNally, Hugh
Petty Officer
No. D/JX 191475, HMS *President III*, Royal Navy
Drowned at sea on Wednesday 11 April 1945 (aged 43)
Plymouth Naval Memorial, Devon, England (Panel 93 Column 3)

In Loving Memory Of
OUR DEAR PARENTS
P.O. HUGH McNALLY (R.N.)
LOST AT SEA 11TH APRIL 1945 AGED 44
BRIDGET
DIED 8TH DECEMBER 1984 AGED 76

Hugh McNally was born on 24 July 1901 and he was a son of James and Mary McNally (nee Maginness, in some records McGuinness) who lived in Little Georges Street, Belfast. They were married on 31 March 1888 in St. Patrick's Roman Catholic Church, Belfast. James McNally worked as a flax dresser and he and Mary had at least six children – Ellen; Mary Ann (born 7 January 1893); James (born 29 July 1894); John (born 1 September 1896); Margaret and Hugh (born 24 July 1901).

Hugh McNally (a mill worker from 21 Artillery Street, Belfast) and Bridget Rock (a spinner, daughter of Richard Rock from 11 Legmore Street, Belfast) were married on 30 March 1929 in St. Vincent de Paul Roman Catholic Church, Ligoniel, Belfast and they lived in Castlereagh, Co. Down. During the Second World War Petty Officer Hugh McNally served with the Royal Navy aboard the MV *Panama* and he was 43 years old when he died on 11 April 1945. He was supposed drowned and his last shore address was 113 Alliance Avenue, Belfast. The diesel-powered MV *Panama* was built in 1915 in Copenhagen and was on route from Cardiff to Philadelphia when she perished. In heavy weather her engines broke down, her ballast shifted and she capsized and sank in mid-North Atlantic. More than forty men died and there were only five survivors.

Petty Officer Hugh McNally is commemorated on the Plymouth Naval Memorial in Devon and on the family grave headstone in Redburn Cemetery, Holywood. Bridget McNally died on 8 December 1984 (aged 76) and their son John died on 17 December 2010.

McN

McNeilance, John Alexander (John)
Carpenter
SS *Empress of Canada* (London), Merchant Navy
Died as a result of enemy action on Sunday 14 March 1943 (aged 49)
Tower Hill Memorial, London, England (Panel 47)

John Alexander McNeilance was born at 4.30 am on 26 May 1893 in Leith, Scotland and he was the youngest son of Alexander and Elizabeth (Eliza) McNeilance (nee Howatson) who lived at 13 Henderson Street, Leith. Alexander McNeilance worked as a marine engineer and the McNeilance family moved from Leith to Belfast where they lived in Mountcollyer Street and later at 39 Greenmount Street. Alexander and Elizabeth McNeilance had seven children including Elizabeth, Anne (Annie), Samuel and John Alexander. Their other three children died young.

When John Alexander McNeilance left school he worked as an apprentice shipwright and qualified as a carpenter. On 2 March 1915 he and Elizabeth (Lily) Robinson were married in Newington Presbyterian Church, Belfast and their daughter Elizabeth Howatson McNeilance was born in Belfast on 29 December 1915. They lived at 110 Nelson Street, Belfast and in his identity papers it was recorded that John Alexander McNeilance was 5 feet 10½ inches tall and he had tattoos on both forearms. His wife Lily died and his marriage to Rowena Crawford was registered in the second quarter of 1925 in Salford, Lancashire. The birth of their son Roy Howatson McNeilance was registered in the third quarter of 1927 in Salford.

During the Second World War John Alexander McNeilance served as a carpenter aboard the SS *Empress of Canada*. The Royal Mail Ship (RMS) *Empress of Canada* was an ocean liner built in 1920 for Canadian Pacific Steamships by the Fairfield Shipbuilding and Engineering Company at Govan on the Clyde in Scotland. Based in Vancouver, she sailed between the west coast of Canada and the Far East until 1939. Following the outbreak of the Second World War the SS *Empress of Canada* was converted for use as a troopship and she carried ANZAC troops from Australia and New Zealand to the war zones in Europe.

On 14 March 1943 while on route from Durban in South Africa to Takoradi in Ghana, carrying Italian Prisoners-of-War along with Polish and Greek refugees, the SS *Empress of Canada* was torpedoed and sunk by the Italian submarine *Leonardo Da Vinci* approximately 400 miles south of Cape Palmas in Liberia. There were about 1,800 people aboard and around 400 died; many of them were Italian Prisoners-of-War.

McN

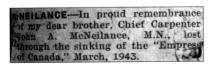

After Carpenter John Alexander McNeilance died on 14 March 1943 his sister Annie Houston and her family who lived at 2 Church Street, Bangor placed a *Roll of Honour* notice in the 18 March 1944 edition of the *County Down Spectator* and it contained the text:

No stone to mark his resting place

Annie McNeilance and Alexander Houston were married in 1905 in St. Anne's Church of Ireland Church, Belfast.

At the time of Carpenter John Alexander McNeilance's death the family address was 124 Church Lane, Marple, Greater Manchester. His effects amounted to some £425 and probate was granted to his widow Rowena who was then living at 39 Burnside Avenue, Salford. Carpenter John Alexander McNeilance was 49 years old when he died and he is commemorated on the Tower Hill Memorial in London.

McNeill, Ernest
Fusilier
No. 6982560, 70th Battalion, Royal Inniskilling Fusiliers
Died as a result of enemy action on Wednesday 16 April 1941 (aged 17)
Mullaghglass (St. Luke) Church of Ireland Churchyard, Co. Armagh
(Grave 4B)

Fusilier Ernest McNeill was a son of John McNeill (a railway linesman) and Margaret McNeill of Craigmore, Co. Armagh. Local sources have indicated that Ernest had at least two brothers, Edward and Lawrence, and two sisters one of whom was called True Elizabeth McNeill (she and William Booth were married on 10 July 1939 in Mullaghglass Church of Ireland Church, Co. Armagh).

McN

Ernest McNeill was one of 13 soldiers serving with the 70th Battalion, Royal Inniskilling Fusiliers who died as a result of an air raid on Newtownards aerodrome during the night of 15/16 April 1941. Fusilier **Daniel Higgins** who also died that night was buried in Newtownards (Movilla) Cemetery and under his name in this Book of Honour there is a summary of all those people with North Down or Ards connections who died that night. Fusilier Ernest McNeill was 17 years old when he died and he is commemorated on Bessbrook War Memorial. There is an inscription on his CWGC headstone:

Safe in the arms of Jesus

McNeilly, John Gracie (Johnnie)
Private
No. 2979791, 2nd Battalion, Seaforth Highlanders
Killed in action between Thursday 6 June and Saturday 8 June 1940 (aged 21)
Blangy-sur-Bresle Communal Cemetery, Seine-Maritime, France (Grave 1)

John Gracie (in some records Gracey) McNeilly was a son of Robert and Mary Jane McNeilly (nee Gracie) and in the 31 October 1942 edition of the *Newtownards Chronicle* there was a *Killed on Active Service* notice announcing that, some 16 months after he had been reported missing in action in June 1940, Private John Gracie McNeilly must now be presumed dead. It contained the verse:

There the buds from earth transplanted,
For our coming watch and wait,
In that Upper Garden growing
Just within the Golden Gate.
Though our hearts may break with sorrow
By the grief so hard to bear,
We shall meet them some glad morning
In the Upper Garden there.

At the rising and the setting of the sun we will remember

KILLED ON ACTIVE SERVICE.

M'NEILLY—Reported Missing June, 1940, now presumed dead, Private John Gracey M'Neilly, Seaforth Highlanders, eldest and dearly-loved son of Robert and Mary M'Neilly.
There the buds from earth transplanted, For our coming watch and wait, In that Upper Garden growing Just within the Golden Gate.
Though our hearts may break with sorrow.
By the grief so hard to bear, We shall meet them some glad morning In the Upper Garden there.
At the rising and setting of the Sun we will remember.
Will always be remembered by his loving Father, Mother, Sisters and Brothers. 201, Earl Street, Scotstoun, Glasgow.

In 1942 Johnnie McNeilly's father and mother (Robert and Mary Jane McNeilly), his sisters (Gretta and Isa) and his brothers were living at 201 Earl Street, Scotstoun, Glasgow and each year thereafter – in the month of June – they placed an *Our Heroes – In Memoriam* notice in the *Newtownards Chronicle*. John Gracie McNeilly's uncle John Gracie (his mother Mary Jane's brother) was killed in action on 26 October 1916 during the First World War and Mary Jane and Robert McNeilly placed an *Our Heroes – In Memoriam* notice in the 1 November 1941 edition of the *Newtownards Chronicle*.

McN

Born in 1882, John Gracie was a son of John and Margaret Mary Gracie (nee Keenan) who were married on 30 May 1874 in Newtownards Parish Church of Ireland Church (St. Mark's). They lived in Greenwell Street, Newtownards before moving in the 1880s to Barony in Lanarkshire. John Gracie Senior worked as a dock labourer and he and Mary had at least six children including Samuel (born 1877); Andrew (born 1879); John (born 1882); Joseph (born 1886); Maggie (born 1890) and Mary Jane (born 1893).

John Gracie Junior and his wife Mary had five children including Maggie, Annie, Isabella and Mollie. It was John Gracie Junior who was killed in action on 26 October 1916 and he is commemorated on Page 250 in the Book of Honour *Remembering Their Sacrifice in the Great War – Ards* compiled by Barry Niblock. John Gracie Junior's brother Samuel married Margaret Hughes and they moved back to Newtownards with their son John, as did John Junior's brother Joseph and his wife Rachel.

Mary Jane Gracie (John Gracie Junior's sister) worked as a sewing machine needle straightener and, on 20 December 1916, she and Robert McNeilly from Newtownards (a son of Alexander and Isabella McNeilly) were married in the Church of Scotland, Bridgeton, Glasgow. At the time, Robert McNeilly was a Bugler in the Royal Irish Rifles and before the outbreak of the First World War he served in Burma. Robert and Mary Jane McNeilly had at least five children including John Gracie (Johnnie), Gretta and Isa.

John Gracie (Johnnie) McNeilly joined up before the outbreak of the Second World War and during 1939/40 he served with the Seaforth Highlanders (Ross-shire Buffs, Duke of Albany's) in the France and Belgium Campaign. The 2nd Battalion, Seaforth Highlanders was part of 51st (Highland) Division in the British Expeditionary Force and Private John Gracie McNeilly was 21 years old when he was killed in action in France sometime between Thursday 6 June and Saturday 8 June 1940. This was just a few days after the Dunkirk evacuation when the 51st Division suffered heavy casualties trying to hold their line along the River Somme; (the 51st Division was forced to surrender to German Forces on 12 June 1940).

McN
McNeilly, William John
Bombardier
No. 7007543, 5 Battery, 2 Light Anti-Aircraft Regiment, Royal Artillery
Killed in action on Thursday 25 September 1941 (aged 39)
Tobruk War Cemetery, Libya (6 K 12)

William John McNeilly was born on 13 July 1902 and he was a son of William John and Ellen McNeilly (nee Taylor) of Greenwell Street, Newtownards. William John McNeilly (a labourer, son of John McNeilly, Ballysallagh, Newtownards) and Ellen Taylor (daughter of James Taylor, a shoe maker of Georges Street, Newtownards) were married on 6 April 1885 in Newtownards Parish Church of Ireland Church (St. Mark's) and they had three children – Ellen (born 1 December 1899); William John (born 13 July 1902) and Margaret (Maggie, born 15 June 1904, died of bronchitis 2 March 1905). The death of William John Junior's mother Ellen (aged 40) was registered in Newtownards in the first quarter of 1907 when William John was around four years old. William John McNeilly Senior worked as a railway porter and then as a carter and on 5 June 1907 he and Anne (Annie) Beale (nee Collins, a charwoman) were married in Newtownards Parish Church of Ireland Church (St. Mark's). Annie Beale had at least seven children including Maggie, John, William James, Henry, Lizzie and Alexander. William John and Annie McNeilly lived at 124 East Street, Newtownards with William John's two surviving children and four of Annie's – William James, Henry, Lizzie and Alexander.

M'NEILLY—Killed on Active Service, Sergeant William John M'Neilly, R.A., beloved husband of Kathleen M'Neilly, 3, Pound Street, Newtownards.

We little thought when he left home, That he would ne'er return; That he so soon in death would sleep, And leave us here to mourn.

Deeply regretted by his sorrowing Wife; also his two children, Wilmer and Maureen.

William John McNeilly Junior joined the Royal Ulster Rifles pre-war and had extensive service in Mesopotamia. Before that he worked as a railway plate layer and he and Margaret Kathleen McRoberts were married on 22 August 1934 in Ballyblack Presbyterian Church. William John and Kathleen McNeilly lived at 3 Pound Street, Newtownards and they had two children – Wilmer and Maureen.

During the Second World War William John McNeilly served with the Royal Artillery and he was killed in action on 25 September 1941 during the siege of Tobruk. There were five *Killed in Action* notices in the 18 October 1941 edition of the *Newtownards Chronicle*: from his wife and two children; from his sister Ella Hawkins and family of 54 Mark Street, Newtownards; from his brother James and his sister and brother-in-law Mary and Isaac Dorrian of 3 John Street Lane, Newtownards; from Unity Masonic Lodge No. 443 and from Royal Arch Chapter No. 443, Newtownards.

McN
McQ

Bombardier William John McNeilly was 39 years old when he was killed in action along with three other men from Newtownards – **Joseph Dalzell**, **Samuel Graham** and **James Meredith**. Bombardier McNeilly is commemorated on Newtownards and District War Memorial and in Newtownards Parish Church (St. Mark's).

McQueen, Terence John (Terence)
Sergeant
No. 7897810, Royal Armoured Corps, North Irish Horse
Killed in action on Saturday 22 July 1944 (aged 30)
Arezzo War Cemetery, Italy (Grave II B 3)

One of two children, Terence John McQueen was born on 23 August 1913 and baptised on 18 October 1913 in Ballygilbert Presbyterian Church. His older sister, Violet Jane Elizabeth McQueen, was born on 24 January 1910. Terence was the only son of John McQueen (originally from County Donegal) and Mary Jane McQueen (nee Wright) of Ballysallagh, Bangor. Terence's parents were married on 23 July 1902 in Ballygilbert Presbyterian Church and they lived at Clandeboye before moving to 58 Moira Drive, Bangor. John McQueen was for many years the Land Steward on the Marquess of Dufferin and Ava's estate. Terence's sister Violet married Henry Ogle on 14 April 1936 in Ballygilbert Presbyterian Church and they lived in Chester-le-Street, Durham where Henry was on the staff of Barclay's Bank.

KILLED IN ACTION.

McQUEEN—July, 1944; killed in action overseas, Sergeant Terence J. McQueen, only son of Mr. and Mrs. John McQueen, 58 Moira Park, Bangor (formerly of Clandeboye).

Terence John McQueen attended Bangor Grammar School for eight years, from 1924 until 1932, and in Sixth Form he was appointed Prefect. He played rugby for the school, he excelled at history and the Headmaster described him as 'one of the gentlest and kindliest, and yet one of the manliest of boys'. For many years he was a Sunday School Teacher in Ballygilbert Presbyterian Church and Secretary of the League of Church Loyalty. It was reported in the 19 August 1944 edition of the *County Down Spectator* that, after leaving school, he was on the staff of the Electricity Board and was stationed in Downpatrick. He joined up at the outbreak of hostilities and served throughout the North African Campaign.

McQ
McR

TERENCE McQUEEN

Sergeant Terence John McQueen was 30 years old when he was killed on 22 July 1944 during the Allied advance northwards in Italy and he is commemorated on Downpatrick and District War Memorial; on Bangor and District War Memorial; in Ballygilbert Presbyterian Church; on the family grave headstone in Bangor Cemetery and in Bangor Grammar School (as T.J. MacQueen). His father John died on 9 October 1949 (aged 71) and his mother Mary died on 15 October 1958 (aged 84).

McReynolds, Norman
Leading Aircraftman
No. 522965, 269 Squadron, Royal Air Force
Killed in action on Monday 8 April 1940 (aged 23)
Runnymede Memorial, Surrey, England (Panel 23)

Norman McReynolds's birth was registered in the second quarter of 1917 in South Shields, Durham and he was the younger son of Andrew Thomas and Hannah McReynolds (nee Gray) of Portadown. Hannah came from Rockwallace in County Monaghan and it was in Monaghan that they were married in 1912. Andrew McReynolds worked as a barman and he and Hannah had a daughter and two sons – Annie Eleanor May ('born 1913); Leslie Oswald (born 2 May 1915 in Portadown) and Norman (born 1917). After Andrew McReynolds died, Hannah moved to County Down and when Norman was killed on 8 April 1940 she was living in High Street, Bangor. Before he joined the Royal Air Force around 1935 Norman lived in Frances Street, Newtownards. He was a member of 1st Newtownards Boys' Brigade and was actively associated with local sport and social activities.

DEATHS.

ON ACTIVE SERVICE.

McREYNOLDS — Leading Aircraftman McReynolds, younger son of the late Andrew McReynolds, Portadown, and Mrs. McReynolds, High Street, Bangor.

Norman McReynolds was a wireless operator and he had his gunner's badge. During the Second World War he served with the Royal Air Force in Coastal Command and on 8 April 1940 he was one of a crew of four aboard an Avro Anson Mark I aircraft (N9678). They took off at 10.55 am on patrol from Wick in Scotland and it is believed that their aeroplane crashed into the sea off Shetland. Wreckage and a dinghy were found later. The other crew members who died that day were:

- PO Peter Duncan Aldous aged 20 from Victoria in British Columbia
- Sgt Gilbert Hunter Scott aged 23 from Slough in Buckinghamshire
- Cpl George Adolphus Verlaque aged 23 from Paisley in Renfrewshire

McR
McS

Each year after Norman's death his mother placed an *In Memoriam* notice in the *County Down Spectator*. These notices included the verses:

In memory a constant thought, in heart a silent sorrow
Precious memories to cherish in an aching heart, like fadeless flowers
A memory may be a wound, but what is life without wounds? They are sacred

Leading Aircraftman Norman McReynolds was 23 years old when he died and he is commemorated on the Runnymede Memorial in Surrey; on Bangor and District War Memorial and on Newtownards and District War Memorial.

McSweeney, Eugene Hector (Eugene)
Able Seaman
No. D/SSX 31967, HMS *Moira*, Royal Navy
Died of illness on Thursday 22 May 1947 (aged 29)
Whitechurch Cemetery, Ballywalter, Co. Down

Eugene Hector McSweeney's birth was registered in the first quarter of 1918 in Merthyr Tydfil, Glamorganshire and he was a son of Morgan and

Elizabeth M. McSweeney (nee Esling). Their marriage was registered in the second quarter of 1917 in Merthyr Tydfil.

The marriage of Eugene Hector McSweeney and Jean (Jane) Eccles was registered in the second quarter of 1945 in Pontypridd, Glamorganshire. Jane Eccles was from Ballywalter and she and Eugene lived in the townland of Ballyatwood, Ballywalter. During the Second World War Eugene McSweeney served with the Royal Navy (HMS *Moira*) and he died of illness on 22 May 1947. It is recalled by people who knew him that, during the war he spent a protracted period of time in the sea after an enemy attack and this had a detrimental effect on his health. Able Seaman Eugene Hector McSweeney died of pyelonephritis on 22 May 1947 and he was buried in Whitechurch Cemetery, Ballywalter on Saturday 24 May 1947. There is an inscription on his CWGC headstone:

He heard the voice of Jesus say 'Come unto me and rest'

McS
McV

During the Second World War Jane Eccles served with the WAAF and she drove an ambulance on the front line. Eugene and Jane McSweeney had one child, a daughter named Elizabeth.

McVea, Alexander Magowan
Flight Sergeant (Pilot)
No. 590584, 216 Squadron, Royal Air Force
Died on active service on Monday 14 April 1941 (aged 25)
Ikoyi No. 2 Cemetery, Nigeria (Grave 363)

Alexander Magowan McVea's birth was registered in the fourth quarter of 1915 in Newtownards. He was a son of David (a postman) and Sarah McVea (nee Magowan) of Portavogie, Co. Down and a grandson of David (a sailmaker) and Agnes Isabella McVea (nee Tennant) of Portavogie. David and Agnes Isabella McVea had at least eight children including Margaret (born 30 April 1871 in Greyabbey) and David (born around 1876).

Alexander McVea's father David was 38 when he and Sarah Magowan were married on 27 January 1914 in Great Victoria Street Presbyterian Church, Belfast and at that time Sarah's father Alexander was deceased. In 1915

David and Sarah named their son Alexander Magowan McVea in memory of Sarah's father.

Pre-war, Alexander Magowan McVea served with the Royal Air Force in Malaya and in November 1938 he returned to Britain where he was stationed at the RAF Depot in Uxbridge, Middlesex. During the Second World War he served with 216 Squadron and he died in service on 14 April 1941 in Nigeria.

Flight Sergeant Alexander Magowan McVea was 25 years old when he died and he is commemorated on the family grave headstone in Cloughey Presbyterian Graveyard. His father David died on 11 September 1963 (aged 87) and his mother Sarah died on 2 February 1979 (aged 93).

McVeigh, Andrew
Lance Corporal
No. 7020231, 6th Battalion, Royal Inniskilling Fusiliers
Killed in action on Wednesday 3 November 1943
Sangro River War Cemetery, Italy (Grave VIII E 9)

Andrew McVeigh was the only son of Robert James and Catherine McVeigh and the brother of Sarah McVeigh of 51 Mark Street, Newtownards. His wife Elizabeth and daughter Shirley lived at 31 Bangor Road, Newtownards. Prior to the outbreak of hostilities Andrew McVeigh worked for newsagent Samuel Ferguson in High Street, Newtownards.

KILLED IN ACTION.

M'VEIGH—Killed in Action, November, 1943 Lance-Corporal Andrew M'Veigh, R.U.R., only son of Robert James and the late Catherine M'Veigh, and brother of Sarah M'Veigh, 51, Mark Street, Newtownards.

Andrew McVeigh joined the Royal Ulster Rifles in October 1940 and was later transferred to the Royal Inniskilling Fusiliers. Having been home on leave in May 1943, he was killed in action some six months later – on 3 November 1943 – as Allied Forces fought their way up the Adriatic Coast in Italy. Lance Corporal Andrew McVeigh is commemorated on Newtownards and District War Memorial and in Newtownards Parish Church of Ireland Church (St. Mark's).

McVitty, Trevor Maynard Watt
Gunner
No. 1488507, 87 Battery, 24 Light Anti-Aircraft Regiment, Royal Artillery
Died as a result of an accident on Saturday 18 May 1940 (aged 33)
Netley Military Cemetery, Hampshire, England (Grave 446)

The death of Gunner Trevor Maynard Watt McVitty was reported in the 25

McV

ULSTER SOLDIER'S FATAL FALL.

FRACTURED SKULL WHILE SLEEPWALKING.

Gunner Trevor Maynard Watt M'Vitty (32), a clergyman's son, whose home was at Millisle Road, Donaghadee, met his death while sleep-walking in East Hampshire, falling out of a window into the roadway and fracturing his skull.

At the inquest at Southampton on Tuesday it was stated that M'Vitty recently, while on leave, was found standing by his bed at night, and said he thought reveille had sounded.

A verdict of accidental death was recorded.

Deceased was son of the Rev. William M'Vitty, a retired Methodist minister.

McV
Me

May 1940 edition of the *Newtownards Chronicle* under the headline *Ulster Soldier's Fatal Fall*. Gunner McVitty was born in County Armagh and he was a son of retired Methodist Minister, the Revd William Presley McVitty (born County Fermanagh) and Margaretta Charlotte Augusta (Gretta) McVitty (nee Moore, born County Tyrone) who lived in Millisle Road, Donaghadee. William McVitty and Gretta Moore were married in 1889 in Dublin and they had at least two children – Reginald Leopold (Rex, born 18 August 1899) and Trevor Maynard Watt (born 20 July 1907).

Gunner Trevor Maynard Watt McVitty was 33 years old when he died on 18 May 1940 in East Hampshire while he was sleep-walking. He fell out of a window into the roadway and fractured his skull. At the inquest in Southampton it was stated that on a recent previous occasion, while on leave, he had been found standing by his bed at night thinking that Reveille had been sounded. A verdict of accidental death was recorded and his death was registered in Winchester, Hampshire. Gunner McVitty's father William died on 3 March 1956 (aged 89) in Donaghadee.

Measday, Leslie Tom (Leslie)
Sergeant
No. 10545608, Royal Army Ordnance Corps
Died of illness on Wednesday 5 December 1945 (aged 41)
Holywood Cemetery, Co. Down (Grave 1487)

Leslie Tom Measday was born on 18 September 1904 in Thorley, Hertfordshire and he was baptised on 1 January 1905 in Thorley Parish Church of England Church. He was the son of William Henry and Ada Mary Measday (nee Collins) who were married on 27 February 1904 in Thorley. William Henry Measday worked as a coachman and groom and he and Ada Mary had three children – Leslie Tom (born 18 September 1904);

Cyril William (born 7 May 1914) and Kenneth (born 17 March 1916).

Sergeant Leslie Tom Measday was the husband of Florence Louisa Measday and during the Second World War he served with the Royal Army Ordnance Corps. He was 41 years old when he died of heart failure on 5 December 1945 at Kinnegar Barracks, Holywood and he was buried in Holywood Cemetery. His effects amounted to some £851 and probate was granted to his widow and to Kenneth Measday, Registrar. Sergeant Measday's address was *Palmyra*, Belfast Road, Holywood.

Mee, Edward George (Edward)
Radio Officer
SS *Kayeson* (London), Merchant Navy
Died as a result of enemy action on Wednesday 2 October 1940 (aged 37)
Tower Hill Memorial, London (Panel 60)

ON ACTIVE SERVICE.

MEE—October 3, 1940, lost at sea through enemy action, Edward, dearly-loved son of the late Mr. R. G. Mee and Mrs. Mee.

Deeply regretted by his sorrowing Mother and Sisters.

15 Hamilton Road, Bangor.

Edward George Mee was born on 2 December 1902 in Belfast and he was a son of Robert George Mee (born in County Londonderry) and Agnes Hannah Mee (nee Taylor). Their marriage was registered in the fourth quarter of 1894 in St. Pancras, London. They lived at 390 Beersbridge Road, Belfast and they had three children – Elizabeth Agnes (born in England); Annie Louise (born 30 May 1899 in Londonderry) and Edward George (born 2 December 1902 in Belfast). Robert George Mee worked as a civil engineer and surveyor with Belfast Corporation and, after he died, Edward's mother and two sisters lived at 15 Hamilton Road, Bangor. They worshipped in Bangor Parish Church of Ireland Church (St. Comgall's).

Me

The marriage of Edward George Mee and Doris Male was registered in the fourth quarter of 1930 in Birkenhead, Cheshire. For a time Edward and Doris Mee (nee Male) lived in Glasgow. During the Second World War, Edward Mee served as a Radio Officer in the Merchant Navy aboard SS *Kayeson*. SS *Kayeson* was a cargo steamer built in 1929 by Hawthorn Leslie and Company Ltd., Hebburn-on-Tyne, Newcastle and owned by the Kaye Steamship Company Ltd. On 2 October 1940 when on route from Liverpool to Montevideo in Uruguay with a 6,700-ton cargo of coal and general goods she sank in the North Atlantic after being torpedoed by the German submarine *U-32*. Some 38 crew members died.

Radio Officer Edward Mee was 37 years old when he died and his wife and two children were living in Wallasey, Cheshire. His mother and two sisters placed a *Died on Active Service* notice in the 30 November 1940 edition of the *County Down Spectator* and he is commemorated on the Tower Hill Memorial in London and in Bangor Parish Church (St. Comgall's).

Meek, William Johnston (William)
Master
SS *Hatasu* (Liverpool), Merchant Navy
Died as a result of enemy action on Thursday 2 October 1941 (aged 48)
Tower Hill Memorial, London, England (Panel 56)

William Johnston Meek was born on 13 January 1893 and he was a son of David and Anna Stewart Meek (nee Johnston) who lived at 71 Clifton Road, Bangor with Anna's widowed father, William Johnston. David Meek and Anna Johnston were married on 16 October 1890 in First Bangor Presbyterian Church. William Johnston was a retired master mariner and David Meek worked as a clothier. David Meek (originally from Portadown) and Anna Meek (nee Johnston) had at least nine children – Helen Johnston (baptised 7 February 1892 in Trinity Presbyterian Church, Bangor, died 30 August 1904 aged 12); William Johnston (born 13 January 1893, baptised in Regent Street Presbyterian Church, Newtownards); the next two children were baptised in Trinity Presbyterian Church, Bangor – Edith Mary (born 14 December 1894, baptised 27 February 1895) and Vida Stewart (born 15 August 1896, baptised 20 January 1897); the next five children were baptised in First Bangor Presbyterian Church – Eileen Stewart (born 16 October 1898), John McCracken Locke (Jack, born 4 August 1900), Mabel Gertrude (born 5 February 1903) and twins Estelle Stewart (Stella) and Caroline Johnston (Lena), both born 29 October 1908. William Johnston Meek attended Bangor Grammar School from 1907 until 1909.

Me

William Johnston Meek was the husband of Elizabeth Johnston Meek of Killinchy and during the Second World War he was Master aboard the SS *Hatasu*. The SS *Hatasu* was a cargo ship built in 1921 by John Bulmer and Company, Sunderland and owned by Moss Hutchison Ltd., London. On 2 October 1941 when she was on route from Manchester to

New York in ballast she was torpedoed by the German submarine *U-431* and sank some 600 miles east of Cape Race, Newfoundland. Captain William Johnston Meek was one of around 40 men who died. His effects amounted to some £1,361 and probate was granted to his widow who was living at 50 Leamington Road, Ainsdale, Southport, Lancashire.

Captain William Johnston Meek was 48 years old when he died and he is commemorated on the Tower Hill Memorial in London; on Bangor and District War Memorial; in First Bangor Presbyterian Church; on the family grave headstone in Bangor Cemetery and in Bangor Grammar School. There is an inscription on the family grave headstone:

He shall gather the lambs in His arms and carry them in His bosom

William Johnston Meek's maternal grandfather William Johnston died on 5 September 1912 (aged 87). His father David died on 18 February 1933 and his mother Anna died on 4 May 1946 (aged 77).

Megarry, Herbert Reginald (Herbert)
Sergeant (Pilot)
No. 745111, No. 6 Service Flying Training School,
Royal Air Force Volunteer Reserve
Killed in an aircraft accident on Saturday 18 May 1940 (aged 20)
Bangor Cemetery, Co. Down (Section 4 V Grave 175)

Herbert Reginald Megarry was born in 1920 and he was the second son of James Herbert and Harriett Megarry (nee Bailie) who were married on 12 August 1914 in Belfast (Christ Church) Church of Ireland Church. James Herbert Megarry worked as a stationer, he and Harriett lived at 74 Ravenhill Avenue, Belfast and they had two children – Harold Charles (born 15 June 1915, died 1998 in South East Surrey) and Herbert Reginald (birth registered in the second quarter of 1920 in Belfast). Harriett Megarry was 40 years old when she died on 3 December 1923 in the Royal Victoria Hospital, Belfast after she contracted pneumonia following an ectopic pregnancy. James Herbert Megarry and Sarah Todd Gilmore were married on 20 November 1930 in St. James's Church of Ireland Church, Belfast and they lived at 1 Brunswick Road, Bangor.

Before joining the Royal Air Force Volunteer Reserve, Herbert Reginald Megarry worked in the Engineering Department of Messrs Gallagher Ltd., and his father worked for W. and G. Baird Ltd. While he was on a training flight in a North American Harvard aircraft (P5842) Sergeant Pilot Herbert Reginald Megarry was killed in a flying accident in Oxfordshire on 18 May 1940. The aircraft spun to the ground after the engine stalled following a steep turn and his death was registered in Ploughley, Oxfordshire. Herbert Megarry's Group Captain said that Herbert was showing excellent promise as a pilot and that he had passed all his ground examinations with good results.

> MEGARRY—In fond memory of Sergt.-Pilot Herbert R. Megarry, killed on Active Service, 18th May, 1940.
> " As long as we are blest with a memory we shall remember him."
> Sadly missed by Dad, Mam and only Brother, Harold, R.A.F.
> 1 Brunswick Road, Bangor.

Herbert Megarry's funeral took place on 25 May 1940 from his parents' residence to Bangor Cemetery. The service was conducted by the Revd James Hamilton, Bangor Abbey. Amongst the mourners were his father Herbert, his only brother Harold (serving with the Royal Air Force), and his uncle and step-uncles Thomas Megarry, Robert Gilmore and Edward Gilmore. One of the tributes paid by his family was:

Me

> *As long as we are blest with a memory, we shall remember him*

Sergeant Pilot Herbert Reginald Megarry was 20 years old when he died and he is commemorated on Bangor and District War Memorial and in Bangor Parish Church of Ireland Church (St. Comgall's). There is an inscription on his CWGC headstone:

> *What peaceful hours we once enjoyed, how sweet their memory still*

Megaw, William Laurence (Laurie)
Second Lieutenant
No. 269264, Somerset Light Infantry *seconded to*
1st Battalion, Royal Inniskilling Fusiliers
Killed in action on Thursday 18 February 1943 (aged 18)
Rangoon Memorial, Myanmar (Face 7)

The death of Second Lieutenant William Laurence Megaw was reported in the 27 March edition of the *Newtownards Chronicle* under the headline *Kircubbin Minister Bereaved*. William Laurence Megaw was the third son of the Revd William Rutledge Megaw and Mabel Megaw (nee Harpur) who were married on 30 June 1910 in College Square Presbyterian Church, Belfast. At that time the Revd Megaw was Minister in Ahoghill Presbyterian Church, Co.

Antrim and their daughter Kathleen was born on 6 August 1912. When Laurie Megaw died his father was Minister in Newtownbreda Presbyterian Church, Belfast. William Laurence Megaw was born on 11 December 1914, he attended Campbell College from 1936 until 1940 and he played rugby and hockey for the school. He joined the 70th YS Battalion, Royal Ulster Rifles on 11 December 1942 – his 18th birthday – and was posted to India. After getting a commission he served with the Somerset Light Infantry *seconded to* 1st Battalion, Royal Inniskilling Fusiliers.

Kircubbin Minister Bereaved.—Second Lieutenant Wm. Laurence Megaw, son of the Rev. W. R. Megaw, M.R.I.A.I., minister of Newtownbreda Presbyterian Church, Belfast, has been killed in action in Burma. He was not yet 20. He joined up as a private in the Royal Ulster Rifles on his 18th birthday, and received a commission in the Royal Inniskilling Fusiliers after going to India. His brother Alan is a captain in the Royal Artillery. Second Lieutenant Megaw was a brother of Rev. George H Megaw, B.A., minister of Kircubbin Presbyterian Church.

Second Lieutenant William Laurence Megaw was 18 years old when he was killed in action in Burma on 18 February 1943. His brother, Alan Robert Megaw, was a Captain in the Royal Artillery; his brother, Colin Rutledge Megaw, worked for the Canada Life Assurance Company and his brother, the Revd George Harpur Megaw BA, was Minister in Kircubbin Presbyterian Church. There was a short tribute in the April 1943 edition of *The Campbellian*:

Me

'We regret to announce the death of Laurie Megaw which took place in the Far East. He is the first of those who have been with us in our exile to Portrush to meet his death in the field of battle. He was under 20 years of age. Laurie was one of those perpetually cheerful fellows, not of the scholarship type, but ever ready to oblige when called on and gifted with a fund of commonsense beyond his years. We offer our sincere sympathy to the members of his family'. Basil White, a fellow Campbellian, wrote:

'Megaw and I both joined 70th YS Battalion RUR but then went our separate ways. In 1944 I was in command of a road convoy en route from the Bombay area to Calcutta when, on entering Cawnpore, I was stopped by a Regimental Policeman of the Inniskillings. He directed me to the convoy park and, on the way, I asked him if he knew Second Lieutenant Megaw. I was surprised to learn that he was Laurie Megaw's batman (personal servant) and was close behind him when he was killed by a Japanese grenade in the Arakan district of Burma'.

Second Lieutenant William Laurence Megaw is commemorated in Campbell College, Belfast.

Mehigan, William Joseph (William)
Sailor
SS *Maritima* (London), Merchant Navy
Died as a result of enemy action on Monday 2 November 1942 (aged 48)
Tower Hill Memorial, London, England (Panel 68)

MEHEGAN. W. In some records the Mehigan surname is spelt Mihegan and in others Mehegan. It is as Mehegan, W. that William Joseph Mehigan is commemorated on Donaghadee and District War Memorial.

William Joseph Mehigan was born on 4 July 1894 and he was a son of James and Ellen Doyle (Helen) Mehigan (nee Quigley). James Mehigan (born around 1857) worked as an electrical wireman and he also served in the Royal Navy. James and Ellen (Helen) Doyle Quigley were married on 5 May 1892 in Newtownards Roman Catholic Church and they had at least three children – William Joseph (born 4 July 1894); Ellen (Helen, born 29 August 1896) and Timothy. The first two children were born in Newtownards and Timothy was born after the Mehigan family moved to 38 Greenfield Street, Govan in Lanarkshire. Timothy was born there at 5.30 am on 26 March 1900 and he died of cerebral convulsions at the same address at 8.15 am on 9 July 1902 (aged 2 years and 3 months). William Joseph Mehigan's sister Ellen (Helen) was living at 6 Victoria Terrace, Donaghadee when she and John McVeigh of 54 McCleery Street, Belfast were married on 29 April 1919 in Newtownards Roman Catholic Church. John McVeigh was a soldier.

Successive generations of Mehigan men were seafarers, both Mercantile Marine and Royal Navy. Some of them served with HM Coastguard and in the 1800s there were Mehigan families living in Cork, Wexford, Donaghadee and Portaferry. The following Mehigan men were related to William Joseph Mehigan who was killed in the Second World War – Timothy Mehigan (born 16 July 1826 in Coolmore, Co. Cork) served with HM Navy (No. 30151) and was the father of Timothy Mehigan (born 13 December 1855 in Donaghadee). Jeremiah and James Mehigan (born in County Cork in the 1830s) also served with HM Navy. Jeremiah Mehigan (born in the 1860s in County Wexford) served with HM Navy (Coastguard) and was a brother of William Joseph Mehigan's father James.

William Joseph Mehigan's uncle, Timothy Mehigan (born 13 December 1855) and Hannah Reilly (in some records spelt Riley) were married on 10 May 1883 in Newtownards Roman Catholic Church. Hannah Reilly was

Me

born in County Cork, her father was a coastguard and the Reilly family moved to Donaghadee where Hannah worked as a dressmaker. Timothy Mehigan served with HM Navy and he and Hannah had at least three children – James Francis (born 4 September 1888 in Newtownards); Guy (born 25 November 1890) and Daniel Reilly Mehigan (born 14 June 1895 in Portaferry). In 1911 James Francis Mehigan was a leading signalman aboard HMS *Colleen* in Queenstown (now Cobh), Co. Cork. After her husband Timothy died, Hannah Mehigan moved to Downpatrick Street, Crossgar.

William Joseph Mehigan was a career seaman and there are records outlining his many voyages. For example, on 5 July 1926 he sailed from Birkenhead to New York via Havana aboard the ship *San Leopold*. On 23 January 1929 he sailed from Liverpool aboard the ship *Ocean Prince* and arrived in New York on 6 February 1929. On 17 June 1941 he sailed from Belfast aboard the ship *Karabagh* and arrived in New York on 9 July 1941. On the ship's manifest it was noted that he was 5 feet 8 inches tall, he weighed 150 lbs and he had no physical marks, peculiarities or disease.

In 1942 William Joseph Mehigan was a sailor aboard the SS *Maritima*. This was a British Cargo Steamer built in 1912 by Hawthorn, Leslie and Company Ltd., Hebburn-on-Tyne, Newcastle. Originally named SS *Port Lincoln*, she was renamed SS *Cambrian Baroness* in 1927, SS *Clan Graham* in 1930 and SS *Maritima* in 1938 for Neill and Pandelis Ltd., London. At around 8.00 am on 2 November 1942 she was in Convoy SC-107 on route from New York to Glasgow via Sydney, Nova Scotia with a cargo that included explosives when she was torpedoed by the German submarine *U-522* about 500 miles northeast of St. John's, Newfoundland. Fifteen ships in the convoy were sunk by the German submarine wolf-pack *Veilchen* – the heaviest loss in any trans-Atlantic convoy during the winter of 1942/43.

Sailor William Joseph Mehigan (aged 48) was among more than 30 men who died that morning on the SS *Maritima*. In the Register of Deceased Seamen his last recorded place of abode was 66 Glenalmond Street, Glasgow. Sailor William Joseph Mehigan is commemorated on the Tower Hill Memorial in London and on Donaghadee and District War Memorial (as Mehegan W.).

Mercer, Joseph
Sergeant
No. 987916, 62 Squadron, Royal Air Force Volunteer Reserve
Killed in action on Tuesday 24 February 1942 (aged 28)
Singapore Memorial, Singapore (Column 415)

Bangor Airman Missing.—Official information has been received by Mrs. Mercer, 19 Manse Road, Bangor, that her son, Sergeant Wireless Gunner Joseph Mercer, R.A.F., is reported missing from operations. Sergeant Mercer served his apprenticeship to the estate agency with Messrs. S. M. Claney & Co., Bangor, and was afterwards on the staff of Mr. Alex. Devon, Estate Agent, Wellington Place, Belfast. He studied for the Fellowship of the Auctioneers' Institute and qualified with honours. Educated at Bangor Central P.E. School and Bangor Technical School, he was an enthusiastic member of Hamilton Road Methodist Church Boys' Brigade. He joined the R.A.F. some 18 months ago, and had a fine record of operational flights to his credit. His father died some years ago. Sympathy is tendered to his mother and his sister,

Me

Joseph Mercer's birth was registered in the third quarter of 1914 in Belfast and he was a son of Joseph Stewart Mercer and Mary Jane Mercer (nee Morton) who lived at 19 Manse Road, Bangor. Joseph Mercer Senior was an iron moulder and he and Mary Jane Morton were married on 9 July 1912 in Albertbridge Congregational Church, Belfast. Joseph Mercer Junior was a grandson of Joseph (a brass finisher) and Mary Mercer who lived in Derwent Street, Belfast.

Joseph Mercer was a member of the Boys' Brigade and he was educated at Bangor Central Public Elementary School and Bangor Technical School. When he left school he served his apprenticeship in estate agency with Messrs S.M. Claney and Company in Bangor. Afterwards he worked for Alex Devon (Estate Agent) Wellington Place, Belfast and he qualified with honours after studying for the Fellowship of the Auctioneers' Institute (FAI). He joined the Royal Air Force Volunteer Reserve in 1940 and in the 7 March 1942 edition of the *County Down Spectator* it was reported that he was missing in action. Sympathy was expressed to his mother and to his sister, Mrs Compton. Later it was officially confirmed that Joseph Mercer must be presumed killed in action.

MERCER - J.

Sergeant Joseph Mercer was 28 years old when he died and he is commemorated on the Singapore Memorial; on Bangor and District War Memorial; on the family grave headstone in Bangor Cemetery (Section 4N Grave 78) and in Wesley Centenary Methodist Church, Bangor. Joseph's father died on 4 May 1932 (aged 51) and his mother died on 28 March 1964 (aged 82). His brother James Harold died on 27 November 1929 (aged 10).

Meredith Brothers, Francis and John

Francis and John Meredith were sons of James Gardiner Meredith and Mary Jane Meredith (nee Bennett) of 5 Church Street, Newtownards. James Gardiner Meredith worked as a labourer and he and Mary Jane Bennett were both minors when they were married on 18 March 1901 in Greenwell Street Presbyterian Church, Newtownards. At the time of his marriage James Gardiner Meredith described himself as a soldier. James and Mary Jane Meredith had at least eleven children, most of whom were baptised in Greenwell Street Presbyterian Church – William; Harriet (born 17 November 1906); Wilhelmina Gibson (Mina, born 9 June 1908); James Gardiner (born 5 August 1909); David George (born 1 April 1911); Richard (born 4 November 1912); Sarah (born 14 March 1914); Francis (Frank, born 1 March 1916); Albert (born 1917); John (born 23 July 1918, died in infancy) and John (born 15 July 1921). James Gardiner Meredith Senior served with the Royal Inniskilling Fusiliers in both the South African and First World Wars and he died on 10 May 1941 (aged 60). During the Second World War, Francis was the first of the two Meredith brothers to die.

Meredith, Francis (Frank)
Aircraftman 1ˢᵗ Class
No. 972615, Royal Air Force Volunteer Reserve
Died in a Prisoner-of-War Camp on Thursday 3 December 1942 (aged 26)
Yokohama Cremation Memorial, Japan (Panel 6)

Me

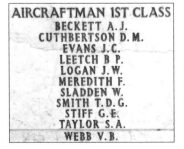

DIED ON ACTIVE SERVICE.
MEREDITH—Previously reported missing, now officially known to have died while a prisoner in the hands of the Japanese, on 3rd December, 1942, A.C.1 Francis Meredith dearly-beloved husband of Madge Meredith.
Deeply regretted by his sorrowing Wife, also all at 15, West Street, Newtownards.

AIRCRAFTMAN 1ST CLASS
BECKETT A. J.
CUTHBERTSON D. M.
EVANS J. C.
LEETCH B P.
LOGAN J. W.
MEREDITH F.
SLADDEN W.
SMITH T. D. G.
STIFF G. E.
TAYLOR S. A.
WEBB V. B.

Francis Meredith was born on 1 March 1916 and he was the husband of Margaret (Madge) Meredith (nee Sloan) of Newtownards. Their marriage was registered in the fourth quarter of 1940 in Newtownards. Frank Meredith joined the Royal Air Force Volunteer Reserve and he fought in the South-East Asian Theatre of War.

Aircraftman 1ˢᵗ Class Francis Meredith was captured by the Japanese and died of acute colitis on 3 December 1942 at Fukuoka No. 4 Branch Camp in Moji, Japan where he was assigned prison number 5062. There is evidence to suggest that he arrived at Moji on 28 November 1942 having been transported on the Japanese 'hell ship' *Dainichi Maru*.

Flight Sergeant **George Francis Grattan** also died at Fukuoka No. 4 Branch Camp in Moji.

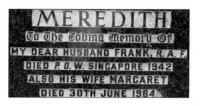

Aircraftman 1st Class Francis Meredith was 26 years old when he died and he is commemorated on the Yokohama Cremation Memorial in Japan; on Newtownards and District War Memorial and on the family grave headstone in Movilla Cemetery, Newtownards. His wife Margaret died on 30 June 1984.

Meredith, John (Johnnie)
Lance Sergeant
No. 6984401, 2nd Battalion, Royal Inniskilling Fusiliers
Killed on active service on Wednesday 18 April 1945 (aged 23)
Argenta Gap War Cemetery, Italy (Grave I B 17)

KILLED ON ACTIVE SERVICE.
MEREDITH—Killed in Action in Italy, April, 1945, Sergeant Johnnie Meredith, loved son of Mary and the late James G. Meredith, and much loved brother of Dick Meredith.
"Manly and brave, his young life he gave."
Deeply regretted by his sorrowing Brother and Sister-in-law and Family, 13, Church Street, Newtownards.

John (Johnnie) Meredith was born on 15 July 1921 and named in memory of his brother John who was born on 23 July 1918 and died in infancy. During the Second World War Johnnie served with the 2nd Battalion, Royal Inniskilling Fusiliers and he was 23 years old when he was killed in Italy on 18 April 1945 during the final Allied offensive. There were *Killed on Active Service* notices from his family in the 5 May 1945 edition of the *Newtownards Chronicle* and they included the texts:

> *Manly and brave his young life he gave*
> *He lies in a hero's grave*

Lance Sergeant John Meredith is commemorated on Newtownards and District War Memorial.

Meredith, James (Jim)
Gunner
No. 1467261, 5 Battery, 2 Light Anti-Aircraft Regiment, Royal Artillery
Killed in action on Thursday 25 September 1941 (aged 40)
Tobruk War Cemetery, Libya (Grave 6 K 4)

James Meredith was born on 8 May 1901 and he was a son of William and

Me

Bridget Meredith (nee Morrison) of 18 Ann Street, Newtownards. Bridget Morrison was born in India and she and William Meredith were married on 7 October 1899 in Second Newtownards Presbyterian Church. William Meredith served with the Royal Irish Rifles in both the South African War and the Great War. In civilian life William Meredith worked as a labourer and for a time he, Bridget and their son William boarded with James and Margaret Gardiner in Newtownards. William and Bridget Meredith had at least seven children – William (born 13 January 1900); James (born 8 May 1901); Harry (born 25 December 1902); Hugh (born 3 January 1905); Roseann (born 2 April 1907); Bridget (born 8 May 1909) and Edward (born 5 May 1911). James Meredith was an active member of St. Patrick's Amateur Dramatic Society in Newtownards, later known as Ards Players. He was also a member of St. Patrick's Billiard Club in Newtownards.

> MEREDITH—Killed on Active Service, Gunner James Meredith, R.A., beloved husband of Sarah Meredith, 65, Mark Street, Newtownards—R.I.P.
> "On his soul, Sweet Jesus, have mercy."
> Deeply regretted by his sorrowing Wife and Family; also his Father, Mother and Sisters, Ann Street, Newtownards; his Father-in-law, Mother-in-law and Family, Mark Street, Newtownards; also his Sister-in-law, Portaferry; Cousin James and Agnes Sweeney and Family, 61. Mark Street, Newtownards; and his two Brothers and Brother-in-law on Active Service.

Gunner James Meredith was the husband of Sarah Meredith (nee McKibben) of 65 Mark Street, Newtownards. They were married on 2 December 1924 in Newtownards Roman Catholic Church and they had three children – Eddie, Olive and James (Jamesy). During the Second World War James (Jim) Meredith served with the Royal Artillery, as did his brothers William and Harry. His brother-in-law John Cardy, husband of Bridget and father of Norma and Brendan, was also on active service. Harry Meredith was a Prisoner-of-War in Italy and his wife Nellie and daughters Breeda, Pat and Mary lived at The Shore, Portaferry. William Meredith was discharged from the army when he became unfit for active service. His brother-in-law Samuel Kerr (Sarah's sister Lizzie's husband) was also on active service. James Meredith's brother-in-law John McKibben (his wife Sarah's brother) was killed in action during the First World War and he is commemorated on Page 416 in the Book of Honour *Remembering Their Sacrifice in the Great War – Ards* compiled by Barry Niblock.

Gunner James Meredith was killed in action on 25 September 1941 during the siege of Tobruk along with three other men from Newtownards – **Joseph Dalzell**, **Samuel Graham** and **William John McNeilly**. His family placed a *Killed on Active Service* notice in the 18 October 1941 edition of the

Me

Newtownards Chronicle and it contained the verse:

> *Immaculate Heart of Mary*
> *Your prayers on him extol;*
> *Most Sacred Heart of Jesus*
> *Have mercy on his soul.*
> *When last we saw him smile*
> *He looked so strong and brave,*
> *We little thought how soon he'd be*
> *Laid in a hero's grave.*

Gunner James Meredith was 40 years old when he died and he is commemorated on Newtownards and District War Memorial.

Merrison Family, Joseph Frederick and Gladys Noreen (Husband and Wife)

Joseph Frederick Merrison was the only surviving son of Joseph Adams Merrison (whose birth was registered in the third quarter of 1893) and Clarissa Hovells Merrison (nee Hanton) of Great Yarmouth, Norfolk. Joseph Adams Merrison was a baker and his marriage to Clarissa Hanton was registered in the fourth quarter of 1913. They had at least four children, births registered as indicated – Joseph (first quarter 1913, died in infancy), Clarissa Jessie Margaret (first quarter 1918), Joseph Frederick (second quarter 1920) and Ethel Joan (third quarter 1928).

Gladys Noreen Merrison (nee Conway) was the third daughter of George Herbert Ewart Conway and Isabella Conway (formerly Savage, nee Thompson) of 21 Croft Street, Bangor, Co. Down. Isabella Thompson and Robert Savage were married on 8 July 1907 and Robert died on 23 May 1908 (aged 26). Herbert Conway was on the staff of Bangor Gas Works and he and Isabella Savage (nee Thompson) were married on 23 January 1911 in St. Anne's Church of Ireland Cathedral, Belfast. They had at least six children – Ruby, Gretta, Violet, Gladys Noreen, Pearl and Bertie.

Both Joseph Frederick and Gladys Noreen Merrison (nee Conway) were killed in the same incident at 14 Higham Place, St. Nicholas Road, Great Yarmouth. They were among eight people who lost their lives when a lone German aircraft dropped a stick of bombs on a residential area. During the Second World War more than 200 Great Yarmouth townspeople were killed in air raids between 1940 and 1944.

Me

Merrison, Joseph Frederick (Joe)
Leading Aircraftman
No. 928709, 995 Balloon Squadron, Royal Air Force Volunteer Reserve
Died as a result of enemy action on Tuesday 22 December 1942 (aged 22)
Great Yarmouth (Caister) Cemetery, Norfolk, England (Section J Grave 178)

After a period of service in Northern Ireland, Leading Aircraftman Joseph Frederick Merrison was posted to England. He was granted leave in December 1942 and he and his wife Gladys went to visit Joe's mother Clarissa in Great Yarmouth. Clarissa Merrison was engaged in war work and the bombs fell on 22 December 1942 after she had left for work. Joe and Gladys were alone in the house at 14 Higham Place when the bombs fell. Gladys Merrison was killed instantaneously and Joe was very severely injured; he died five hours later in hospital.

The tragedy had added poignancy because Joe's mother, Clarissa Merrison, had already lost her two daughters (Clarissa Jessie Margaret and Ethel Joan), a grand-daughter (Margaret) and a niece in earlier German air raids. The marriage of Clarissa Jessie Margaret Merrison and Robert H. Wilson was registered in the first quarter of 1940. Robert H. Wilson was a Gunner in the Royal Artillery and he and Clarissa had one child, a daughter named Margaret (born February 1941). They lived at 59 North Quay, Great Yarmouth. On 11 April 1941 Clarissa Jessie Margaret Wilson, her daughter Margaret (aged two months) and her sister Ethel Joan Merrison (aged 12) died at the George Street Shelter in Great Yarmouth during an air raid.

Me

In 1949 Clarissa Merrison (nee Hanton) married Alfred Davison and she died in 1953 (aged 58). Joseph Adams Merrison died in 1966 (aged 73).

Merrison, Gladys Noreen (Gladys)
Civilian
Civilian War Dead
Died as a result of enemy action on Tuesday 22 December 1942 (aged 22)
Great Yarmouth (Caister) Cemetery, Norfolk, England (Section J Grave 178)

Gladys Noreen Conway met Joseph Frederick Merrison when he was stationed in Northern Ireland and they were married in Bangor Abbey in March 1942. Before her marriage Gladys Noreen Conway was engaged in war work and some years previously she was one of the prize-winners in a local beauty competition. In the 2 January 1943 edition of the *County Down*

Spectator it was reported that she and her husband had shared in many social activities in Bangor and District.

Gladys Merrison was survived by her parents; her sister, Mrs Ruby McGlennon (Ruby's husband, Robert W. McGlennon, died on 18 August 1938); her sisters Gretta, Violet and Pearl Conway and her brother Bertie Conway who was serving with the Royal Air Force. One of her sisters was married to Harry Butler who served with the RASC.

RESULT OF ENEMY ACTION

MERRISON — Cherished memories of our dear daughter, Gladys (née Conway) and her devoted husband, L.A.C. Joseph Merrison, whom God called Home, through enemy action, December, 1942. Both laid to rest in Caister Cemetery, Norfolk, England.
    " Thy will be done."
Sadly missed by her loving Parents, Sisters, Brother, Bertie, in the R.A.F., Brother-in-law, Harry Butler, R.A.S.C. 21 Croft Street, Bangor.

Both Joe and Gladys Merrison (both aged 22) are commemorated on the Conway family headstone in Bangor Cemetery. They had only been married for nine months when they were killed. Of the many civilians of the Commonwealth whose deaths were due to enemy action in the Second World War, the names of some 67,092 are commemorated in the Civilian War Dead Roll of Honour, located near St. George's Chapel in Westminster Abbey, London. Gladys Merrison's father, Herbert Conway, died on 14 July 1963 (aged 76) and her mother, Isabella Conway, died on 22 February 1978.

Me
Mi

Miley, Frederick James (Fred)
Leading Aircraftman
No. 1056802, Royal Air Force Volunteer Reserve
Died of illness on Monday 26 January 1942 (aged 28)
Bangor Cemetery, Co. Down (Section 1 C Grave 86)

Frederick James (Fred) Miley was born on 29 August 1913 in County Kildare and he was a son of Robert Miley (born in County Wicklow) and Margaret Miley (nee Mansfield, born in Enniscorthy, County Wexford). Robert Miley and Margaret Mansfield were married on 29 September 1909 in Clone (Solsboro) St. Paul's Church of Ireland Church, Enniscorthy and they had three children – Robert Harman (Bertie, born 20 February 1911); Frederick James (Fred, born 29 August 1913) and William Mansfield (Billy, born 8 June 1915). Robert Miley and his brother William ran a general merchandise store in Duke Street, Athy, Co. Kildare selling amongst other things groceries, hardware, china and seeds. Margaret Miley died on 8 June

1915 in childbirth and she was buried in Athy Church of Ireland Graveyard.

Robert Miley married May Fitzell on 5 April 1920 in Ballyheigue Parish Church of Ireland Church, Co. Kerry. Robert and May Miley had five children – Gladys (born 20 December 1920, died 6 May 1937 aged 16); Evelyn (born 21 November 1921); Edward (Eddie, born 14 April 1923); twins Norman and Leslie (born 15 June 1925, Leslie died 29 September 1925 aged 3 months). It was in August 1924, after the Miley business had been burned out for the third time, that the Miley families left Athy. William Miley established a grocery business at 717 Lisburn Road, Belfast and Robert Miley established a grocery business – the Mayflower Dairy – in Upper Main Street, Bangor. Robert Miley and his family lived above the shop.

Fred Miley was educated at Main Street Public Elementary School in Bangor and at Bangor Grammar School from 1926 until 1928. Fred and his brother Willie both won Entrance Scholarships to BGS in 1926. At school Fred excelled in all subjects and when he left school he managed the Prospect Branch of the Mayflower Dairy for his father. In 1936 Robert Miley acquired *Prospect House*, at the corner of Prospect and Donaghadee Roads, Bangor. After that Fred worked as a junior representative in Belfast for Messrs R.S. Hudson Ltd.

Mi

Before the war Fred Miley was a Sunday School teacher in Bangor Parish Church of Ireland Church (St. Comgall's) and, along with three of his brothers, he was a member of the church choir under Dr Heathcote Emery. Fred was also a member of Ward Park Lawn Tennis Club and a member of the Bangor Men's Detachment of the British Red Cross Society.

Shortly after the outbreak of the Second World War Fred Miley joined the Medical Branch of the Royal Air Force Volunteer Reserve and he served for a considerable time in the Middle East. He volunteered to participate in tests designed to examine the effects of heat and cold on the human body. This involved immersion up to the neck in ice-cold water for varying lengths of time. In 1941 he contracted an illness in Egypt and, after a protracted period of travelling, he was repatriated by Service Ambulance some three weeks before his death. Fred Miley was shipped home via the Red Sea, Durban, Cape Town, the West Indies, the North Atlantic and Scotland. The journey took more than six weeks.

FRED ... R.A.F. DIED 26TH JAN. 1942, AGED 28

Leading Aircraftman Fred Miley was 28 years old when he died during the afternoon of 26 January 1942 at his parent's home – *Risdale*, 98 Donaghadee

Road, Bangor. His funeral to Bangor Cemetery was conducted by the Revd Walter Horatio Good and mourners included his brothers Bertie (an officer in the ATC in Bushmills), Willie (a Leading Aircraftman in the RAF stationed at Ballyhalbert), Eddie (on the staff of the Bank of Ireland) and Norman (a schoolboy) together with his sister Mrs Evelyn Thompson. On 20 February 1942, less than a month after Fred's death, his eldest brother, Bertie Miley, died in Bushmills after a short illness. Bertie Miley was on the staff of Bushmills Secondary School. Eddie Miley was Captain of the 6th Bangor Company of the Boy's Brigade from 1950 until his death in 1972 and he is commemorated on a stained glass window in Bangor Parish Church (St. Comgall's).

After the death of Leading Aircraftman Fred Miley the Headmaster of Bangor Grammar School said, 'He had brilliant promise but he sacrificed his strength and youth and his splendid intellect in the cause of world freedom and international justice.' Fred Miley was 28 years of age when he died on 26 January 1942 and he is commemorated on Bangor and District War Memorial; in Bangor Parish Church (St. Comgall's); in Bangor Grammar School and on the family grave headstone in Bangor Cemetery. Fred Miley's father Robert died on 1 November 1955 (aged 76) and his stepmother May died on 1 October 1987 (aged 93).

Mi

Miller, William Watson (Billy)
Distinguished Flying Cross
Flying Officer (Navigator)
No. 151387, 248 Squadron, Royal Air Force Volunteer Reserve
Killed in an aircraft accident on Saturday 24 February 1945 (aged 21)
Bangor Cemetery, Co. Down (Section 4 U Grave 113)

William Watson (Billy) Miller was born on 8 November 1923 and he was baptised in Bangor Parish Church of Ireland Church (St. Comgall's) on 16 December 1923. He was the only son of Robert Conroy Higginson (Bob) Miller and Margaret Miller (nee Watson) who lived at 3 Castle Street, Bangor. Bob Miller worked as a plumber and gas fitter (he had worked on the Titanic) and he was a Bell Ringer in Bangor Parish Church. Bob won numerous individual bowls titles and represented Ireland at bowls for over thirty years. He had the nickname *Golden Miller*. Bob Miller's parents, Samuel and Fanny Miller (nee Robinson) owned a painting and decorating shop on Main Street in Bangor.

Bob Miller and Margaret Watson were married on 28 March 1910 in Bangor

Abbey and they had six children – Ada Peacocke (born 12 March 1912); Ethel (born 1914); Fanny (born 1917); Ellen (Ella born 19 August 1919); May and William Watson (Billy, born 8 November 1923).

Billy Miller was educated at Bangor Central Public Elementary School and at Bangor Grammar School from the autumn of 1936 until the summer of 1941. In 1941 he won Lord Bangor's prize as the school's best all round boy in character, studies and games. At school he excelled in English and History and gained honours in the Royal Drawing Society's examinations. The Headmaster described him as being 'dark eyed and sturdily built; there was no nonsense about him and he stood no nonsense from others.' He also excelled on the cricket and rugby fields. At cricket he captained the 1st XI and he was selected to play for the Ulster Schools in an inter-provincial match against Leinster.

Billy Miller was a graduate of Bangor Flight Air Training Corps (ATC) which he joined in March 1941. A year later, in March 1942, he was called up for service. Billy Miller undertook his navigational training in Canada and he was awarded a commission in 1943. He was the first ex-ATC Cadet in Northern Ireland to be decorated; he was awarded the Distinguished Flying Cross (DFC) on 3 October 1944 and the citation read:

Mi

'This officer has participated in a large number of varied sorties. He is a navigator of great ability and his fine work has contributed materially to the success of the operations in which he has taken part. In August 1944, during a reconnaissance of the Gironde area, his aircraft was hit by anti-aircraft fire. The petrol tanks were pierced and a quantity of the contents was lost. A course was set for home but the petrol became exhausted and the aircraft came down on to the sea. Flying Officer Miller, who had temporarily lost consciousness, recovered to find himself submerged in the cockpit. He released his harness and managed to climb clear. His pilot was apparently still trapped. Although FO Miller had both his ankles fractured and was in great distress he re-entered the cockpit in a vain attempt to find his comrade. He displayed great courage, fortitude and resolution in highly trying circumstances.' Billy Miller's mother Margaret and his sister Ella went to Buckingham Palace on 29 October 1946 to receive Billy's DFC.

Flying Officer Billy Miller served with 248 Squadron in the Royal Air Force Volunteer Reserve and he died as a result of a flying accident on 24 February 1945. At the time, 248 Squadron was based at RAF Banff in Scotland and operated as part of the Banff Strike Wing flying anti-submarine missions off the coast of Norway. He was 21 years old when he was killed and his funeral from the family home in Bangor was to Bangor Cemetery. The services at the house and at the graveside were conducted by the Revd Canon Walter Horatio Good MA, Rector of Bangor Parish.

Amongst the mourners were Billy's brothers-in-law Thomas Beattie (Fanny's husband) and Warren Rainey (May's husband). His sister Ethel's husband, Warrant Officer Gordon Ernest Poulson (No. 3443273), who served with the 2/5th Battalion, Lancashire Fusiliers died on active service on 3 August 1944 and was buried in Fontenay-le-Pesnel War Cemetery, Tessel, Calvados, France (Grave IV B 9). His sister Ada's husband, Rifleman **William Fox** (No. 7015254), who served with the Royal Ulster Rifles died on 31 December 1939 following a hospital operation. Ada Fox died on 15 February 1940 after a short illness and their two children, Margaret Irene Fox and William Fox were brought up by their maternal grandparents at 3 Castle Street, Bangor.

Mi

Flying Officer William Watson Miller DFC is commemorated on Bangor and District War Memorial; in Bangor Parish Church (St. Comgall's) and in Bangor Grammar School. The inscription on his CWGC headstone in Bangor Cemetery is:

We thank our God for every remembrance of you

Billy Miller's father Bob died on 30 March 1965 and his mother Margaret died on 27 December 1965. His sister Ethel died on 6 January 1966.

Minnis, Stanley
Sergeant (Air Gunner)
No. 1796309, 622 Squadron, Royal Air Force Volunteer Reserve
Killed in an aircraft accident on Tuesday 12 September 1944 (aged 19)
Sessenheim Communal Cemetery, Bas-Rhin, France (Grave 9)

Sergeant (Air Gunner) Stanley Minnis from Roughfort in County Antrim was one of a crew of seven aboard an Avro Lancaster Mark I aircraft (NF965) that took off at 6.27 pm from RAF Mildenhall in Suffolk on a mission to bomb Frankfurt. They were involved in a mid-air collision with another Lancaster bomber and all on board were killed when the two aircraft crashed to the ground on the west bank of the Rhine between Stattmatten and Roeschwoog in France. The other six crew members who died were:

- Flying Officer George William Owen aged 25 from Birmingham
- Sergeant Walter Andrew Drewett
- Flying Officer John Robert Umphelby Jamieson aged 20 (RAAF)
- Flying Officer Philip John Tofield aged 21 from Eastleigh, Hampshire
- Flight Sergeant Clifford Alexander Vieritz aged 20 (RAAF)
- Sergeant Douglas Thomas Forrest

Sergeant (Air Gunner) Stanley Minnis was 19 years old when he died and he is commemorated on a headstone in the Sloan family grave in Redburn Cemetery, Holywood. Henry Sloan died on 14 December 1976 and his wife Lucy died on 9 November 1977.

Miskimmin, Robert James (Bob)
Rifleman
No. 7019396, 1st Battalion, Royal Ulster Rifles
Killed in action on Saturday 24 March 1945 (aged 23)
Venray War Cemetery, Limburg, Netherlands (Grave VIII E 2)

Mi

Robert James Miskimmin was a son of Matthew John and Mary Miskimmin (nee Hogg) of Ballyvester Road, Donaghadee. They were married on 2 April 1919 in Newtownards Registry Office and they had six children – Janet; Robert James; Thomas (served with the RAF and suffered from shellshock); Matthew (Matt); Molly (died in infancy) and Harry. Robert James Miskimmin was the husband of Florence Violet Miskimmin (nee Bull), of Ramsbury, Wiltshire.

MISKIMMIN—Killed in action, March 1945, in Western Europe, No. 7019396 Rifleman R. J. Miskimmin, Royal Ulster Rifles (Airborne Division), dearly-loved son of Mrs. Miskimmin, Ballyvester Road, Donaghadee.
He died a hero.
Ever remembered by his sorrowing Brothers and Sisters; also his Wife in Ramsbury, Wiltshire, England.

During the Second World War Bob Miskimmin served with the 1st Battalion, Royal Ulster Rifles and he was killed in action during *Operation Varsity* on 24 March 1945. In this operation more than 16,000 paratroopers were parachuted onto the east bank of the Rhine at Rees, Wesel to support *Operation Plunder* – the crossing of the Rhine. When Rifleman Miskimmin was being parachuted in, he came down accidentally on the west side of the Rhine, in enemy territory, and was shot as he came to ground.

Rifleman Robert James Miskimmin was 23 years old when he died and he is commemorated on Donaghadee and District War Memorial. His daughter Valerie was born in September 1945, six months after her father died, and his mother Mary died on 4 December 1945 (aged 52).

Mitchell, John Finlay
Flying Officer
No. 141580, 969 (Balloon) Squadron, Royal Air Force Volunteer Reserve
Killed accidentally by 'friendly fire' on Thursday 23 March 1944 (aged 40)
Runnymede Memorial, Surrey, England (Panel 208)

> **Flying Officer J. F. Mitchell Killed by Enemy Action.**—Many friends of the family in this neighbourhood will regret deeply to learn that Flying Officer John Finlay Mitchell has been killed by enemy action while engaged in saving one of our aircraft at sea. He is the third son of the late Dr. J. F. Mitchell, who was medical officer of Bangor for many years, and of Mrs. Mitchell, "Sevenoaks." Flying Officer Mitchell, after taking his degree at Cambridge, graduated as a naval architect at which (a reserved occupation) he was working when, seeing an advertisement for officers for the Air Sea Rescue Service, he volunteered.

John Finlay Mitchell MA, BSc (Cantab) was born on 21 March 1904 and he was the third son of Dr John Finlay Mitchell and Anna Elizabeth Mitchell (nee Shaw, daughter of Thomas Shaw, Kircubbin). Dr Mitchell and Anna Shaw were married on 3 September 1894 in Holywood Presbyterian Church and they had four children – William Marcus (born 29 April 1897); Thomas (born 2 May 1899); John Finlay (born 21 March 1904) and Eleanor Mary (born 25 August 1908). Dr Mitchell was medical officer in Bangor for many years and the Mitchell family lived in Queen's Parade, Bangor. After Dr Mitchell died, his widow Anna moved to Sevenoaks in Kent.

After taking his degree at Cambridge, John Finlay Mitchell Junior graduated as a naval architect. This was a reserved occupation but when he saw an advertisement seeking officers for the Air Sea Rescue Service he volunteered and was accepted for service. His death on 23 March 1944 was reported in the 8 April 1944 edition of the *County Down Spectator* where it was intimated that he had been killed as a result of enemy action 'while engaged in saving one of our aircraft at sea'. Official records indicate that he was the victim of 'friendly fire'.

Flying Officer John Finlay Mitchell (aged 40) was the Master (Skipper) aboard the High Speed Launch (HSL) *2706* based at RNAS Calshot, Great Yarmouth. HSL *2706* was an Air Sea Rescue (ASR) launch and it was on its way to a rendezvous position to assist the crews of any ditching RAF aircraft (a string of boats was positioned across the North Sea along the course of returning RAF bombers). HSL *2706* was some 30 miles off the

Mi

Dutch Coast when she was attacked by two United States Army Air Force (USAAF) Republic Aviation P-47 Thunderbolt aircraft from the 356th Fighter Group based at RAF Martlesham Heath. They were returning to base from escort duty when they spotted HSL *2706* and they took her to be an Enemy-boat (E-boat). E-boats were fast attack craft of the Kriegsmarine – the Nazi German Navy.

HSL *2706* went on fire and ten of the crew were killed; Corporal Urban Harold Turner aged 32 from Harrow, Middlesex died ashore later as a result of his injuries; LAC W Smallwood and LAC M E Anderson were injured but survived.

In addition to Flying Officer John Finlay Mitchell and Corporal Turner, the other crew members who died were:

- Corporal Francis Hutchins Taylor aged 38 from Kettering, Northamptonshire (Cox 1st Class)
- AC1 Edward Louis D'Esterre Roberts (Motor Boat Crew)
- LAC Robert Desmond Heath Jones aged 21 from Bath, Somerset (Motor Boat Crew)
- LAC Leslie John Nicholls aged 32 from Lowestoft, Suffolk (Wireless Operator/Mechanic)
- LAC William Roy Russell from Ontario, Canada (Wireless Operator)
- AC2 Robert Edward Harry Regent aged 19 from Thetford, Norfolk (Wireless Operator)
- LAC Eric George Harding from Highgate, Middlesex (Fitter/Marine)
- LAC Jack Rushworth aged 23 from Bradford, Yorkshire (Motor Boat Crew)
- LAC Thomas Vince House aged 27 from Sunderland, Durham (Nursing Orderly)

Mi
Mo

MITCHELL, J. F. Flying Officer John Finlay Mitchell was the husband of Evelyn Frances Mitchell (nee Hammond, daughter of Major Hammond) of Dartington, Devon and 15 Wellington Esplanade South, Lowestoft. Their marriage was registered in the first quarter of 1928 in Hendon, Middlesex and they had three children. John Finlay Mitchell's effects amounted to some £3,968 and probate was granted to his widow.

Moir Family: Sara (Sally) and John (Mother and Son)

Sara (Sally) Moir (nee Glover) was born on 4 September 1882 and she was a daughter of James and Mary Glover (nee Palmer) who lived at 13 Shore Row, Kircubbin. James Glover was a schoolteacher (originally from Groomsport) and he and Mary Palmer were married on 22 April 1864 in Ballyhalbert Parish Church of Ireland Church (St. Andrew's) at Ballyeasborough. They had at least nine children – William (born 23 September 1865, died 22 April 1869); Isabella (born 1 January 1867, died in infancy); unnamed daughter (born 27 February 1868, died in infancy); Mary (born 3 January 1870); Robert (born 15 December 1870, died in infancy); James (born 17 February 1872); Robert (born 10 October 1873); Ruth (born 17 November 1876) and Sara (Sally, born 4 September 1882). Mary Glover died on 15 October 1901 (aged 60), James Glover died on 28 June 1925 (aged 81) and they were buried in Ballyhalbert Parish Church Graveyard.

Sally Glover and Archibald Black Moir (an engineer from Scotland) were married on 12 June 1912 in Kircubbin Presbyterian Church and they had at least two children – John and Kathleen. On 5 March 1946 their daughter Kathleen Glover Moir married John Crichton McDouall who was a son of the Revd Crichton Willoughby McDouall and Florence Charlotte McDouall (nee Cogan). Kathleen and John McDouall had three children – Anne Glover (born 3 April 1948); Heather Crichton (born 11 August 1949) and Brian John (born 26 June 1952).

Mo

Moir, John
Lieutenant (E)
Royal Navy, HMS *Edinburgh*
Killed in action on Thursday 30 April 1942 (aged 22)
Plymouth Naval Memorial, Devon, England (Panel 63 Column 1)

John Moir was the only son of Archibald Black Moir and Sally Moir (nee Glover) of Port Glasgow and Hong Kong and he was a grandson of James and Mary Glover of Kircubbin. In the CWGC Debt of Honour it is noted that John Moir was the husband of Mrs Joan Howdle (formerly Moir) of Hove, Sussex. During the Second World War John Moir served with the Royal Navy aboard HMS *Edinburgh*.

HMS *Edinburgh* was a light cruiser of the Belfast class which was built by Swan Hunter and Wigham Richardson Ltd., Newcastle-on-Tyne. She was laid down on 30 December 1936, launched on 31 March 1938 and completed on 6 July 1939. After the outbreak of the Second World War she patrolled between Iceland and the Faroe Islands. Thereafter she undertook various convoy protection duties and in April 1942 she escorted Convoy PQ-14 from Iceland to Kola Bay, Murmansk, Russia. On 28 April 1942 she left Russia to escort the returning Convoy QP-11 and on 30 April 1942 HMS *Edinburgh* was struck by two torpedoes fired from the German submarine *U-456*. She was taken in tow, but later was able to proceed at slow speed under her own steam. (On 2 May HMS *Edinburgh* was attacked by torpedo aircraft and then by three German destroyers off Bear Island, Norway. Hit by a torpedo fired from the German destroyer *Z 24*, she was abandoned and scuttled by a torpedo fired from HMS *Foresight*; HMS *Foresight* herself had to be scuttled in August 1942). Lieutenant John Moir was one of more than 50 men who died as a result of the attack on HMS *Edinburgh* on 30 April 1942.

Lieutenant John Moir was 22 years old when he died and he is commemorated on Plymouth Naval Memorial in Devon and on the Glover family headstone in Ballyhalbert Parish Church of Ireland Graveyard at Ballyeasborough.

Moir, Sally
Civilian War Dead
Died as a result of enemy action on Friday 22 December 1944 (aged 62)

Sally Moir of Cornhill, Quarry Bay, Hong Kong was a nurse with the Hong Kong Auxiliary Nursing Service. She was 62 years old when she died on 22 December 1944 at Shanghai in China and, like her son John, she is commemorated on the Glover family headstone in Ballyhalbert Parish Church of Ireland Graveyard at Ballyeasborough.

Mo

Of the many civilians of the Commonwealth whose deaths were due to enemy action in the Second World War, the names of some 67,092 are commemorated in the Civilian War Dead Roll of Honour, located near St. George's Chapel in Westminster Abbey, London.

Monard, Donald Stanley Ashton (Donald)
Flying Officer (Pilot)
No. 129380, 241 Squadron, Royal Air Force Volunteer Reserve
Killed in action on Wednesday 23 August 1944 (aged 23)
Padua War Cemetery, Italy (Grave II G 5)

Donald Stanley Ashton Monard was born on 18 August 1921 and he was the elder son of Stanley Hopkirk Monard and Kathleen Sarah Monard (nee McIlroy). Kathleen's father was John McIlroy, an estate agent who lived in *The Warren*, Donaghadee, then *Marion House*, Marino, Co. Down and after that, Cosham in Hampshire. Stanley Hopkirk Monard was in the Army and

his address was the Reform Club Belfast when he and Kathleen McIlroy were married on 28 December 1916 in St. Mary Magdalene Church of Ireland Church, Donegall Pass, Belfast. During the First World War Stanley Hopkirk Monard served as a Captain with the 14th Battalion, Royal Irish Rifles and after the war he worked as a chartered surveyor and estate agent. During the Second World War he served as a Major in the Royal Engineers at Weymouth and Portsmouth and after the war he worked in Local Government.

Donald Stanley Ashton Monard was given the name Ashton after his godfather Edward Albert Ashton Bagley who, sponsored by the Tariff Reform League, was elected in 1918 as the Conservative MP for Farnworth, Lancashire. Donald Stanley Ashton Monard attended Campbell College, Belfast from 1934 until 1938 and during the Second World War he served with the RAFVR. He died on 23 August 1944, just five days after his 23rd birthday. Donald's Commanding Officer informed Donald's father that, when Donald flew in low to strafe a train as the Allies advanced northwards through Italy, a bullet fired by a soldier on the train struck the fuel tank of his aircraft which then crashed in flames. A short tribute was published in the December 1944 edition of *The Campbellian*:

'Donald Monard lost his life while taking part in a 'train busting' raid somewhere on the Continent. That is all the news we have received. To those who took the trouble to understand him he was a most charming character. He was by no means a reed shaken by the wind, but held decided views on things. He will be greatly missed and we offer sincere sympathy to his father and mother'.

Donald Monard's effects amounted to some £2,612 and probate was granted to his father. During the Second World War his younger brother, Patrick Terence Monard, served as a Petty Officer Cadet in the RNVR (Fleet Air Arm). Patrick survived the war and afterwards practised as a doctor.

Flying Officer Donald Stanley Ashton Monard is commemorated in Campbell College and on the family grave headstone in Donaghadee Church of Ireland Graveyard. Donald's mother Kathleen died of pneumonia on 5 June 1941 (aged 50) and there are two inscriptions on the headstone:

Mo

A little while
Fear God and fear naught

Donald's father Stanley remarried and his marriage to Daphne Winifred Dore was registered in the third quarter of 1944 in Portsmouth, Hampshire. They had a son named Stuart. Stanley Hopkirk Monard died on 22 August 1964.

Montgomery, William
Bombardier
No. 1054168, 5 Field Regiment, Royal Artillery
Died in a Prisoner-of-War Camp on Thursday 14 June 1945 (aged 43)
Labuan War Cemetery, Malaysia (Grave M D 7)

William Montgomery was born on 9 April 1902 in Castlemount, Bangor and he was the eldest son of Stoker William Montgomery (in civilian life he worked as a grocer and also as a carter) and Ellen Jane Montgomery (nee Beattie). They were married on 16 September 1901 in Wesley Centenary Methodist Church, Bangor and they had at least six children – William (born 9 April 1902); Robert (born 25 January 1904); Ellen (born 1905); Hugh (born 10 February 1907); John (born 9 March 1909, died 18 March 1909, buried Belfast City Cemetery Public Ground) and Francis James Beattie (born 7 October 1910).

Mo

Ellen Jane Montgomery (nee Beattie, aged 55) and James Edmondson (aged 54) were both widowed when they got married on 15 October 1934 in Newtownards Registry Office. James Edmondson was a boot maker, he had previously been married to Ellen Jane's sister, Maggie Beattie (they were married on 8 April 1912 in Bangor Abbey Church of Ireland Church), and James died on 4 March 1944 (aged 58).

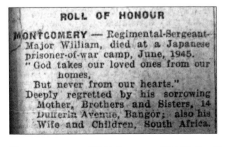

ROLL OF HONOUR
MONTGOMERY — Regimental-Sergeant-Major William, died at a Japanese prisoner-of-war camp, June, 1945.
"God takes our loved ones from our homes,
But never from our hearts."
Deeply regretted by his sorrowing Mother, Brothers and Sisters, 14 Dufferin Avenue, Bangor; also his Wife and Children, South Africa.

Bombardier William Montgomery had an army record of service spanning more than 25 years and he was 43 years old when he died of malaria on 14 June 1945 in a Japanese Prisoner-of-War Camp. (5 Field Regiment, Royal Artillery surrendered to the Japanese in Singapore on 15 February 1942). In the *County Down Spectator* his rank was reported as Regimental Sergeant Major. His brother, Francis James Montgomery, lived at 22A Primrose Street, Bangor and his mother, brothers and sisters lived at 14 Dufferin Avenue, Bangor. William Montgomery's wife and three children lived in Natal, South Africa. His family placed a *Roll of Honour* notice in the 23 February 1946 edition of the *County Down Spectator* and it contained the text:

> *God takes our loved ones from our homes but never from our hearts*

Bombardier William Montgomery is commemorated in Bangor Parish Church of Ireland Church (St. Comgall's).

Moore, Edward Adam Stevenson (Adam)
Gunner
No. 888474, 106 (the Lancashire Hussars) Light Anti-Aircraft Regiment, Royal Artillery
Killed in action between Saturday 26 and Sunday 27 April 1941 (aged 26)
Athens Memorial, Greece (Face 3)

Mo

Edward Adam Stevenson Moore was born on 22 August 1914 and he was a son of George and Margaret Ann Moore (nee McClurg) of Ganaway, Co. Down. George Moore worked as a bricklayer and he and Margaret Ann McClurg (aged 18) were married on 23 September 1909 in Carrowdore Parish Church of Ireland Church (Christ Church). They had two children, both of whom were baptised in Christ Church Carrowdore – Edward Adam Stevenson (born 22 August 1914) and Elizabeth Frances (Eliza, born 27 November 1918, died 29 December 1918). Eliza was buried in Christ Church Graveyard Carrowdore, as were her parents – Margaret Ann Moore (died 15 February 1927, aged 34) and George Moore (died 5 January 1931, aged 53). Adam Moore was 12 years old when his mother died and 16 when his father died.

Edward Adam Stevenson Moore lived for a time in Broadgreen, Liverpool, Lancashire and during the Second World War he served with 106 (the Lancashire Hussars) Light Anti-Aircraft Regiment, Royal Artillery. Gunner Moore was 26 years old when he was killed in action at sea between 26 and 27 April 1941 during the evacuation of Allied Forces from Greece to Crete and Egypt. Edward Adam Stevenson Moore was the husband of Audrey May Moore of Gateacre, Liverpool and he is commemorated in Carrowdore Parish Church of Ireland Church.

Moore, Francis Raymond (Mickey)
Flying Officer
No. 60921, Royal Air Force
Died in a Prisoner-of-War Camp on Thursday 15 July 1943 (aged 36)
Ambon War Cemetery, Indonesia (Grave 6 A 10)

Francis Raymond (Mickey) Moore was born in Bangor on 19 December 1906 and he was baptised in Bangor Parish Church of Ireland Church (St. Comgall's) on 13 March 1907. He was the elder son of Dr Robert Lee (Bob) Moore JP and his second wife, Mrs Frances Moore (nee Gill) who lived at *Redcliffe*, 10-12 Seacliff Road, Bangor (where Dr Moore also had his Surgery) and later at 62 Ward Avenue, Bangor. Dr Bob Moore contributed a regular series of Ulsterisms, riddles and rhymes to the columns of the *County Down Spectator* newspaper.

Dr Bob Moore and his cousin Jemima (Mima) Moore were married on 2 January 1889 in Ballymacarrett Parish Church of Ireland Church (St. Patrick's), Belfast and they had at least five children all of whom were baptised in Bangor Parish Church (St. Comgall's) – James Ernest (Jim, born 12 November 1891, died 8 July 1962); Winifred May (Winnie, born 29 July 1893, died 1 April 1982); Ruby (born 17 February 1895); Alice Isabel (Lallie, born 12 July 1896) and Robert Lee (born 27 February 1898). Mima Moore died on 24 October 1900 (aged 43). Dr Robert Lee Moore remarried in early 1906 (marriage registered in Kendal, Westmorland) and he and his second wife, Frances Moore (nee Gill), had two children – Francis Raymond (Mickey, born 19 December 1906) and Brian Patrick Lee (Paddy, born 18 November 1919). Frances Gill was a daughter of jeweller Dawson Gill from Ambleside in Cumberland (now part of Cumbria).

Mo

Mickey Moore was educated at St. Bee's Grammar School for boys in Copeland, Cumberland. After school he trained as a draughtsman and went on to become a quantity surveyor. After he qualified in 1937 he held an appointment as an Ordnance Survey Assistant Grade III with the Northern Ireland Government Service before he joined the Royal Air Force. Mickey Moore enjoyed racing his motorbike in the Craigantlet hills and he was also a keen photographer and artist. He painted several pictures of Bangor seafront and at one point he spent time living and painting in France and Germany – having travelled from Bangor to Europe on a coal boat. In 1935 he and Agnes Tate (Peggy) Prenter were married in St. Anne's Church of Ireland Cathedral, Belfast. Peggy Prenter was an accomplished seamstress who made all her own gowns and it was in Caproni's Ballroom, Bangor that she and Mickey met. They spent their honeymoon touring Ireland on a motorbike and sidecar. They lived in Belfast for a time and then at *Redcliffe* before moving to Demesne Road, Holywood (where they bred Lakeland Terriers).

Mickey and Peggy Moore had three children: Judith Rosemary (Judi, born 2

June 1936); Frances Brenda Deirdre (Deirdre, born 4 June 1938) and Patricia Michele Lee (Michele, born 22 February 1941). Mickey Moore was a keen golfer and he won the Captain's Day competition at Holywood Golf Club (a silver rose bowl) on the day that Deirdre was born. Mickey Moore last saw his wife Peggy and his daughters Judi and Deirdre in 1940; Mickey never saw his youngest daughter Michele.

FLYING-OFFICER F. R. MOORE

Official intimation has been received that Flying-Officer Francis Raymond ("Mickey") Moore, R.A.F.V.R., has died while a prisoner in Japanese hands.

He is a son of Dr. R. L. Moore, J.P., and Mrs. Moore, Ward Avenue, Bangor, and his wife and three small children reside at Demesne Road, Holywood.

Flying Officer Moore, who was educated at St. Bee's School, Cumberland, was an architect and surveyor by profession and before joining up held an appointment under the Northern Ireland Government.

Flying Officer Mickey Moore served with the Royal Air Force and when he was posted to Singapore he took his golf clubs with him. It was reported in the *County Down Spectator* that he was attached to the Intelligence Branch of the Air Force when Singapore fell to the Japanese in February 1942. He was shot down over Java and initially he was reported as missing in action. Then, in February 1943 it was confirmed that he had been captured by the Japanese and detained in Changi Prisoner-of-War Camp on Haroekoe Island, Singapore. He contracted beri-beri and it was there that he died of dysentery on 15 July 1943. At that time Mickey's wife Peggy and their three young daughters were living in Demesne Road, Holywood.

In 1959 Judi Moore moved to Northern Rhodesia (now Zambia) and she married John Dove. John Dove was killed in a road traffic accident before their daughter Fiona was born. Michele Moore moved to Northern Rhodesia in 1961 to be with Judi and in June 1962 Peggy and Deirdre followed. In July 1964 Peggy Moore married Alex Duff but a month later Peggy was killed in a road traffic accident. She was buried in Lusaka. Mickey Moore's two eldest daughters remained in South Africa and his youngest daughter, Michele, settled in Canada. When Mickey Moore died, his younger brother Paddy was working as a clinical pathologist in the Mater Hospital, Belfast. Paddy had been educated at Campbell College and at St. Mary's Hospital in London where he was a research student under Sir Alexander Fleming and Sir Almroth Wright. Paddy Moore moved to Canada in 1948 where he worked as a haematologist and held a senior position with the Red Cross. He died in Napanee, Ontario on 5 December 2011.

Flying Officer Mickey Moore was 36 years old when he died on 15 July 1943 and he is commemorated in Bangor Parish Church (St. Comgall's) and on the family grave headstone in Bangor Cemetery. There is an inscription on the headstone:

The peace that passeth all understanding

Mickey Moore's father, Robert Lee Moore, died on 30 November 1946 (aged 84) and his mother, Frances Moore, died on 24 May 1962 (aged 81).

Moore, Robert (Bobbie)
Sergeant (Air Gunner)
No. 1040804, 405 (RCAF) Squadron, Royal Air Force Volunteer Reserve
Killed in action on Thursday 11 March 1943
Durnbach War Cemetery, Bad Tolz, Bayern, Germany (Grave 2 K 1)

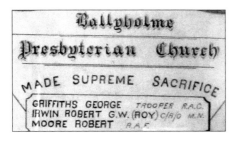

The name Moore, R. is inscribed on Bangor and District War Memorial and the name Moore, Robert RAF is commemorated in Ballyholme Presbyterian Church. Ballyholme Church opened initially on 4 September 1937 as a Church Extension Charge of the Presbyterian Church in Ireland. It was 'erected' to a Congregation on 5 November 1940, and it was only at that stage that Baptismal and Marriage Registers were commenced. Up until his death in 1991 a member of the congregation, Mr Crawford Gourley, kept a scrapbook of items relating to Ballyholme Presbyterian Church. Crawford Gourley recorded that, before he joined the RAF, Bobbie Moore was the leader in charge of Lifeboys in the Church.

Robert (Bobbie) Moore was a son of James and Ellen Moore of Ballymoney, Co. Antrim and during the Second World War he served with 405 (RCAF) Squadron in the Royal Air Force Volunteer Reserve. On 11 March 1943 he was one of a seven man crew aboard a Handley Page Halifax Mark II aircraft (BB212) that took off at 7.03 pm from RAF Topcliffe in Yorkshire on a mission to bomb Stuttgart. They were flying at 17,000 feet when their aircraft was shot down by a Messerschmitt fighter aircraft before they reached their target. Sergeant Bobbie Moore was the rear gunner and he was killed. The other six crew members survived and were held as Prisoners-of-War:

- Pilot — Flight Sergeant G. Chretien
- Flight Engineer — Sergeant A. Collin
- Navigator — Flight Sergeant T. Carlon
- Bomb Aimer — Pilot Officer J. Probert
- Wireless Operator — Sergeant H. Reynolds
- Mid Upper Gunner — Sergeant Arthur Ernest Danes

Sergeant Bobbie Moore was buried in Durnbach War Cemetery in Germany.

Moore, Robert Angus (Bobby)
Flight Sergeant
No. 1074933, 297 Squadron, Royal Air Force Volunteer Reserve
Killed in action on Monday 23 August 1943 (aged 23)
Runnymede Memorial, Surrey, England (Panel 138)

Robert Angus Moore was born on 24 August 1919 and he was the only son of Hugh and Rose Moore (nee Angus), both from Donaghadee. Hugh Moore (son of Alexander Moore) worked as a labourer and he and Rose Angus (daughter of Alexander and Mary Angus) were married on 8 December 1916 in Ballygilbert Presbyterian Church. They lived at 6 Alfred Street, Bangor. During the First World War three of Rose's brothers were killed in action – James, John Blair and Robert Angus – and they are commemorated on Page 76 in the Book of Honour *Remembering Their Sacrifice in the Great War – North Down* compiled by Barry Niblock (and also on Page 93 in the Ards book).

Mo

Robert Angus Moore was educated at Bangor Central Public Elementary School and Bangor Grammar School which he attended from 1932 until 1936. He was a prominent figure in the School's rugby, cricket and athletics teams and he was a Lieutenant in the First Bangor Company of the Boys' Brigade. He left school in 1936 to take up a position in the Ordnance Survey Branch of the Ministry of Finance.

> MOORE—Treasured memories of our dear son, Flight-Sergeant R. A. (Bobby) Moore, missing, presumed killed, August 23, 1943.
> "Thy Will be done."
> Sadly missed by his Mother, Father and Sisters; also Uncles, Aunts and Cousins. — 6 Alfred Street, Bangor.

He joined the Royal Air Force Volunteer Reserve in 1940 and went to Blackpool for initial training. During the war he served with 297 Squadron and when he was killed on 23 August 1943 (the day before his 24th birthday) he was one of a crew of four aboard an Armstrong Whitworth Albemarle aircraft that was shot down and crashed into the sea off the north-east coast of Spain. The other crew members who died that day were:

- WO Herbert Edward Curtis aged 34 from West Wickham, Kent
- Flying Officer John Bruce Bowden aged 23 (RCAF)
- Flight Sgt Albert Edward George Nunn aged 21 from Poplar, London

In the *County Down Spectator* it was reported that Robert Angus Moore was missing 'during special technical operations' and later it was officially confirmed that he must be presumed to have been killed. Robert Angus Moore had two sisters – Mrs Campbell of Grove Hill Gardens, Bangor and Miss Jean Moore.

Flight Sergeant Robert Angus Moore is commemorated on the Runnymede Memorial in Surrey; on Bangor and District War Memorial; in Trinity Presbyterian Church, Bangor; in Bangor Grammar School and on the Moore family grave headstone in Bangor Cemetery. His father Hugh died on 19 December 1972 and his mother Rose died on 13 January 1980. Also commemorated on the Moore headstone is Samuel Campbell, who died on 24 May 1957 (aged 50).

Morrison, Charles Archibald (Charlie)
Leading Stoker
No. C/KX84966
HM Submarine *Swordfish*, Royal Navy
Killed on active service on Saturday 16 November 1940 (aged 29)
Chatham Naval Memorial, Kent, England (Panel 38 1)

Mo

> GRIEVE—MORRISON—In loving remembrance of my dear son, A.V.F. (VICTOR), A.B. R.N.V.R., killed by enemy action at Dunkirk on 28th May, 1940, in H.M.S. Windsor; also his pal, CHARLES F. MORRISON (late of Olive Mount, Bangor), in H.M. Submarine Swordfish, who was lost at sea 23rd December, 1940.—Sadly missed, Mother and Kitty.

Charles Archibald Morrison was born on 17 May 1911 at 96 Castlereagh Road, Belfast and he was a son of Frederick and Ethel Mary Morrison (nee Tuley). Both of his parents were born in Yorkshire and their marriage was registered in Halifax in the second quarter of 1906. Their eldest son, Louis James, was born in Yorkshire in 1910. The Morrison family moved to Belfast where Frederick Morrison worked as an industrial designer and sketcher and for a time the Morrison family lived at *Olive Mount*, Ballymagee, Bangor.

Aged 16 and describing himself as a messenger, Charles Archibald Morrison left London on 22 September 1927 aboard the SS *Beltana* on route to Australia. He gave as his home address 23 Ardgreenan Crescent, Belmont, Belfast. During the Second World War he served with the Royal Navy aboard HM Submarine *Swordfish*. An S-Class submarine with a crew complement of 48, HM Submarine *Swordfish* was completed on 28 November 1932 in

Chatham Dockyard. She left Portsmouth on 7 November 1940 to undertake patrols in the North Sea and was never heard from again. At the time it was believed that she had been sunk by a German destroyer near Brest and in the CWGC Debt of Honour the date of Leading Stoker Charlie Morrison's death is given as 16 November 1940.

Then, in 1983, the wreck of HM Submarine *Swordfish* was discovered 12 miles south of St. Catherine's Point, Isle of Wight at a depth of 150 feet. Her back was broken and it has been surmised that she may have struck a mine shortly after leaving Portsmouth on 7 November 1940. Leading Stoker Charles Archibald Morrison was 29 years old when he died and he is commemorated on the Chatham Naval Memorial in Kent.

Morrison, Frederick Armand (Armand)
Leading Aircraftman
No. 522580, 210 Squadron, Royal Air Force
Killed in action on Tuesday 9 April 1940 (aged 30)
Sylling Churchyard, Norway (Grave 6)

Mo

Frederick Armand Morrison was born on 30 June 1909 and he was the second son of Frederick Armand Morrison and Hannah Maria Morrison (nee Snow) of Mount Stewart, Greyabbey, Co. Down. He was a nephew of Mr and Mrs James Morrison of Greenbank Villas, Newtownards. Hannah Snow was born in County Meath and her marriage to Frederick Armand Morrison was registered in the fourth quarter of 1906. Frederick Armand Morrison Senior was a school teacher in Mount Stewart School until it closed in the 1920s. He and Hannah had at least three children – Roland Haslam (born 19 January 1908); Frederick Armand (born 30 June 1909) and James Victor (born 27 January 1911). Roland Morrison worked for the Ministry of Labour and lived at *The Cliff*, Larne. During the Second World War James Victor Morrison served with the Royal Artillery in the British Expeditionary Force and after the war he worked for the Ministry of Finance. Armand Morrison joined the Royal Air Force around 1935. He was home on leave at Easter 1940 and he spent part of

> **KILLED ON ACTIVE SERVICE.**
>
> MORRISON—Killed on Active Service with R.A.F., Frederick Armand, second son of the late Mr. and Mrs. Fred Morrison, Mount Stewart, and dearly-loved brother of Roland H. Morrison, The Cliff, Larne, and of Victor Morrison, Royal Artillery, B.E.F.

the time at Kiltonga, Newtownards with Mr and Mrs W.C. McRoberts whose daughter was Roland Morrison's wife.

Armand Morrison had his gunner's badge and during the Second World

War he served with the Royal Air Force in Coastal Command. On 9 April 1940 he was one of a crew of ten aboard a Short Sunderland Mark I aircraft (L2167). They took off at 1.00 pm from RAF Invergordon in Scotland and their mission was to carry out reconnaissance in the Oslo area of Norway. Their plane was shot down by a German Messerschmitt aircraft and nine of the crew were killed. Sergeant O.F. George, who was blown out of the aircraft at 3,000 feet without a parachute, fell into deep snow and was taken Prisoner-of-War. In addition to Leading Aircraftman Frederick Armand Morrison the other crew members who died that day were:

- Flight Lieutenant Peter William Hansford Kite aged 20 from Middlesex
- Sergeant Jack Clifford Carpenter aged 28 from Sydney, Australia
- Pilot Officer Arthur Francis le Maistre aged 26 from Winnipeg, Canada
- Sergeant James Alan Llewellyn Barter aged 21
- LAC Douglas William Bailey Upham from Bexley, Kent
- AC1 Graham Herbert Maile
- AC1 Robert Lawrence Millar from Limavady, Co. Londonderry
- AC2 George Eveson aged 29 from Glamorgan, Wales.

All nine were buried in Sylling Churchyard, Norway.

Mo

ALSO THEIR SON FREDERICK ARMAND, R.A.F. KILLED IN ACTION IN NORWAY, 10TH APRIL 1940.

Leading Aircraftman Frederick Armand Morrison was 30 years old when he was killed and he is commemorated on Newtownards and District War Memorial; in Newtownards Parish Church of Ireland Church (St. Mark's) and on the family grave headstone in Movilla Cemetery, Newtownards. His mother died on 22 September 1922 and his father died on 23 March 1932 (aged 57) at 180 Greenwell Street, Newtownards.

Morrison, William John (Billy)
Sergeant (Navigator/Bomber)
No. 1542075, No. 1674 HCU, Royal Air Force Volunteer Reserve
Killed in an aircraft accident on Wednesday 12 April 1944 (aged 21)
Bangor Cemetery, Co. Down (Section 4 U Grave 24)

William John (Billy) Morrison was the younger son of David and Matilda Morrison (nee Cathcart) of 53 Southwell Road, Bangor. They were married on 26 April 1916 in Ballysillan Presbyterian Church, Belfast. William John had two sisters, May and Nana. Nana was married to Jim Gorman who served with the Royal Air Force and they had a daughter named Carole. Billy's elder brother David also served with the Royal Air Force and before the war he was the Assistant Professional at Carnalea Golf Course. David Morrison was reported to be the first member of the Bangor ATC to 'get his wings'.

Billy Morrison was educated at Woodvale Public Elementary School, Belfast and Ballymullen Public Elementary School, Crawfordsburn. He was employed at the Bangor Shipyard Company and later at Messrs Harland and Wolff, Belfast. He joined the Bangor Squadron of the Air Training Corps and was called up for service in the RAF in February 1942 (aged 19). He received his training in Canada and the Bahamas and was then engaged in operational flying with Coastal Command.

At 5.05 pm on 11 April 1944 Billy Morrison was one of a nine man crew aboard a Hanley Page Halifax Mark II aircraft (BB310) that took off from RAF Longtown near Carlisle on a cross country training flight. In the early hours of 12 April 1944 they were on the return leg of the flight and flying in from the north-west coast of England when they overshot their airfield and the aircraft struck the ground. There was low cloud covering the high ground in this area of the country and the aircraft struck Great Dun Fell to the north of Appleby at 1.37 am with the loss of all on board. On 1 May 1994 a memorial was erected at the crash site. The other crew members who died that night were:

- Flying Officer Paul Bevens Stevens aged 25 from Euclid, Ohio, USA
- Flying Officer Sydney Brookes aged 31 from Burtons Green, Essex
- Sgt Robert James Littlefield aged 20 from Bitterne Park, Southampton
- Sergeant Hugh Dunningham aged 22 from Hampstead
- FS William Alan Johnson DFM aged 23 from Gateshead, Durham
- Flight Sergeant Frank Pess aged 28 (RCAF)
- Flight Sergeant Harold Stanley Seabrook aged 20 (RCAF)
- Sergeant Dean Walter Swedberg aged 21 (RCAF)

After Sergeant William John Morrison was killed his family placed a *Killed on Active Service* notice in the 22 April 1944 edition of the *County Down Spectator* and it included the text:

God holds the key of all unknown

The funeral from his parents' residence to Bangor Cemetery was on 19 April 1944 and the casket, draped with the RAF flag, was borne by relays of RAF personnel.

Sergeant William John Morrison was 21 years old when he died and he is commemorated on the Dun Fell Site Memorial Plaque; on Bangor and District War Memorial; in Ballygilbert Presbyterian Church and in the annals of Helen's Bay Presbyterian Church. Billy's mother Matilda died on 16 March 1973 (aged 82) and his father David died on 20 March 1976 (aged 87).

Morrow, David
Second Lieutenant
No. 190209, Royal Inniskilling Fusiliers *attached* 6th Rajputana Rifles
Killed on active service on Wednesday 30 September 1942 (aged 29)
Rawalpindi War Cemetery, Pakistan (Grave 2 E 13)

Mo

David Morrow was born on 28 June 1913 and he was the third and youngest son of Matthew and Agnes Wallace Morrow (nee Moffett) of Ward Avenue, Bangor and before that Ballymagee Street, Bangor. Matthew Morrow was a plumber and he and Agnes Moffett were married on 15 September 1903 in Ballygilbert Presbyterian Church. They had at least four children, all of whom were baptised in First Bangor Presbyterian Church – Olive Hermione (born 23 August 1904); Norman Roderick (born 4 July 1906); Eric (born 19 May 1911) and David (born 28 June 1913).

> **KILLED ON ACTIVE SERVICE.**
> MORROW—September, in India, 2nd-Lieutenant David Morrow, third and youngest son of Mr. and Mrs. Matthew Morrow, Ward Avenue, Bangor.

David Morrow was educated at Main Street Public Elementary School Bangor and Bangor Grammar School from 1924 until 1931. In 1928 he passed the Junior Certificate examination and in 1931 he passed Queen's Matriculation. He played rugby and cricket for the school and was a keen golfer. When he left school he entered the insurance business in Belfast, first with the Eagle Star and British Dominions Insurance Company and later with Messrs R. Martin, Son and Company in Donegall Square South, Belfast. Shortly after the outbreak of hostilities he joined the Royal Inniskilling Fusiliers. He was posted to India where he was attached to the 6th Rajputana Rifles and he was killed on active service in Pakistan on 30 September 1942.

Second Lieutenant David Morrow was 29 years old when he died and he is commemorated on Bangor and District War Memorial; in First Bangor Presbyterian Church; in Bangor Golf Club; in Bangor Grammar School and on the family grave headstone in Bangor Cemetery. His mother Agnes died on 15 July 1948 (aged 67), his father Matthew died on 28 April 1960 and his brother Norman died on 21 May 1964 (aged 57).

Morrow, Hugh Francis (Frank)
Flying Officer (Pilot)
No. J/28294, 432 Squadron, Royal Canadian Air Force
Killed in action on Saturday 17 June 1944 (aged 22)
Gorssel General Cemetery, Gelderland, Netherlands (Row A Grave 19)

Mo

Hugh Francis (Frank) Morrow was born around 1922 in British Columbia, Canada and he was a son of Hugh Morrow (Hugh's father lived in Limavady, Co. Londonderry) and Sarah Morrow (nee McFarlane) who were married on 11 September 1914 in Ballygilbert Presbyterian Church. Hugh Morrow Senior worked as a grocer and in April 1909 he moved to Vancouver, Canada. In the ship's manifest Hugh was described as a merchant when he returned to Ireland in June 1914 in advance of his wedding. In September 1914, after they were married, Hugh and Sarah Morrow travelled to Vancouver aboard the SS *St. Louis*. Hugh and Sarah Morrow had at least three children – Henry (born around 1916); Eileen (born around 1917) and Hugh Francis (Frank, born around 1922).

Frank Morrow joined the Royal Canadian Air Force and during the Second World War he served with 432 Squadron in Bomber Command. On 17 June 1944 Flying Officer (Pilot) Hugh Francis (Frank) Morrow was one of a seven man crew (all RCAF personnel) aboard a Handley Page Halifax aircraft (NA516) that took off from RAF East Moor, Yorkshire on a mission to bomb Sterkrade in Germany. On their way back to base their aircraft was shot down from 18,000 feet by a German night fighter as they approached the Dutch coast and they crashed at Almen in Gelderland. Four crew members were injured (two of them were captured and taken Prisoner-of-War) – Sergeant G. Gelfand, Warrant Officer L.R. McElroy, Sergeant V.R. Herrick (POW) and Flying Officer J.A. Slimmon (POW). Three crew members were killed:

- Flying Officer (Pilot) Hugh Francis Morrow
- Pilot Officer (Air Gunner) John Markey Johnston
- Pilot Officer (Air Gunner) Jack Laverne Shanks

All three were buried in Gorssel General Cemetery, Gelderland, Netherlands (Row A Graves 19, 20 and 21).

Frank Morrow was 22 years old when he was killed and he is commemorated on the Canadian Virtual War Memorial (Internet); on Page 399 in the Canadian Second World War Book of Remembrance; in Ballygilbert Presbyterian Church; on Page 96 in the book *A Light for the Road (Ballygilbert Presbyterian Church 1841-1991)* by John W. McConaghy and Eleanor M. McConaghy and also in the annals of Helen's Bay Presbyterian Church.

Morrow, William James (Billy)
Galley Boy
MV *D L Harper*, Merchant Navy
Drowned at sea on Monday 19 April 1943 (aged 15)

Mo

> **LOST AT SEA.**
>
> MORROW—April, 1943, William James (Billy), M.N., 15½ years, dearly-loved son of the late Elizabeth Morrow and of William James Morrow, 34 North Street, Newtownards.
>
> Deeply regretted by Charlotte and Elizabeth Creelman, also his Brother and Sister-in-law, George and Nancy, 8 Donard Avenue, Bangor.

William James (Billy) Morrow's family placed a *Lost at Sea* notice in the 1 May 1943 edition of the *County Down Spectator*. Billy was described as a son of the late Elizabeth Morrow and of William James Morrow of 34 North Street, Newtownards and he was remembered by Charlotte and Elizabeth Creelman, together with his brother and sister-in-law George and Nancy Morrow, of 8 Donard Avenue, Bangor.

Charlotte Creelman (nee Campbell) was a daughter of James Campbell who farmed in the townland of Ballymacruise, Carrowdore and on 26 October 1893 she and Daniel Creelman were married in First Newtownards Presbyterian Church. Daniel's father Andrew lived in Ballymacruise and he was a linen weaver. Daniel and Charlotte Creelman had one child, a daughter named Elizabeth Sloane Creelman who was born on 23 April 1894 and baptised on 25 June 1894 in Ballyfrenis Presbyterian Church. In both the 1901 and 1911 census returns the Creelman family is recorded as living in the townland of Corporation, Bangor. In the 1911 census Lizzie Beattie (aged 9) is recorded as a boarder living with the Creelmans.

Elizabeth (Lizzie) Beattie and William James Morrow were married on 6 October 1921 in Ballygrainey Presbyterian Church. William James Morrow (aged 20) was a bachelor and a labourer and his father, James Henry Morrow, was a tradesman. Elizabeth Beattie (aged 19) was a spinster and her father was named as Daniel Creelman who was a labourer. William James and Elizabeth Morrow had two children – George Campbell Morrow (born 21 December 1921, baptised 17 March 1922 in First Bangor Presbyterian Church) and William James Morrow (born around 1927/28). George Campbell Morrow (a fitter aged 19) and Agnes Miller (Nancy) McCallum (aged 19, daughter of William McCallum, a welder) were married on 6 September 1941 in Ballygilbert Presbyterian Church.

William James Morrow Junior went to sea and during the Second World War he served as a Galley Boy aboard the petrol tanker MV *D L Harper*. The MV *D L Harper* was built in 1933 by the Deutsche Werft Company in Hamburg, Germany and she was owned by several different oil companies before she was scrapped in 1960 at La Spezia in Italy. Between 1939 and 1950 she was operated by the Anglo-American Oil Company Ltd., London. (During the Second World War the Deutsche Werft Company built U-boats for the Kriegsmarine).

In the Register of Deceased Seamen it is recorded that Galley Boy William James Morrow of 8 Donard Avenue, Bangor serving aboard MV *D L Harper* fell overboard and drowned off the American coast near Boston. He was seen by the ship's cook and also by a gunner shortly before he fell but there was no evidence as to how he came to fall overboard.

ROLL OF HONOUR.

MORROW—In loving memory of our dear Billy, M.N., lost at sea 19th April, 1943.
"God knows best;
He makes no mistakes."
Always remembered by Granny and Mammy, 8 Donard Avenue, Bangor.

MORROW—In loving memory of Billy, M.N., lost at sea 19th April, 1943.
Ever remembered by his Brother and Sister-in-law, George and Nancy, 8 Donard Avenue, Bangor.

There were two *Roll of Honour* notices in the 22 April 1944 edition of the *County Down Spectator*, one from his granny and mammy at 8 Donard Avenue, Bangor and one from his brother and sister-in-law George and Nancy Morrow at the same address.

Galley Boy William James Morrow was 15 years old when he died and he is commemorated on the Creelman family grave headstone in Bangor Cemetery:

Mo

Erected by Daniel Creelman in memory of
Elizabeth Morrow who died 14th Feb 1928 aged 26 yrs
Also the above Daniel Creelman who died 20th Feb 1931 aged 76 yrs
His wife Charlotte died 1st May 1944 aged 82 yrs
William James son of Elizabeth Morrow
Lost at sea 19th April 1943 aged 15 yrs
Elizabeth Creelman daughter of Daniel and Charlotte died 6th Nov 1980

Morton, Thomas
Civilian War Dead
Died as a result of enemy action on Wednesday 16 April 1941 (aged 71)

> **RESULT OF ENEMY ACTION.**
>
> MORTON—TATE—(result of enemy action), Thomas Morton, Nellie Tate and Betty and Evelyn Tate, of Manor Street, Belfast, father, sister and nieces of Thomas G. and Mrs. Morton, 87, South Street, Newtownards.

Thomas Morton was 71 years old and a widower when he died in the Belfast Blitz on 16 April 1941. He worked as a general labourer and after he and his wife Annie (nee McMurray) were married on 11 May 1892 they lived in Mountcollyer Street, Belfast. Thomas and Annie Morton had at least ten children including a female child (born 26 January 1895, died in infancy); Thomas G. (born 29 February 1896); John (born 28 January 1898); William (born 19 July 1901); Alexander (born 11 October 1903); Ellen Ogle (born 18 November 1905); Annie (born 10 May 1908); Evelyn (born 3 July 1910) and Winifred (born 18 January 1914). Thomas Morton Senior died at 174 Manor Street, Belfast along with his married daughter **Ellen Ogle Tate** and his grand-daughters **Bessie (Betty) Tate** (aged 16) and **Evelyn Tate** (aged 14). Thomas Morton Senior's eldest son, Thomas G. Morton, lived at 87 South Street, Newtownards and he placed a *Result of Enemy Action* death notice in the 19 April 1941 edition of the *Newtownards Chronicle*.

The Belfast Blitz comprised high-casualty German Luftwaffe air raids on Belfast in April and May 1941. On the night of Easter Tuesday 15 April 1941 two hundred Luftwaffe bombers attacked the city of Belfast and some 900 people were killed. In another Luftwaffe raid on the night of Saturday 4 May 1941 some 150 people were killed.

Of the many civilians of the Commonwealth whose deaths were due to enemy action in the Second World War, the names of some 67,092 are commemorated in the Civilian War Dead Roll of Honour, located near St. George's Chapel in Westminster Abbey, London.

Mo

Muckle, Thomas Paterson (Tommy)
Corporal
No. 633896, 211 Squadron, Royal Air Force
Died in a Prisoner-of-War Camp on Monday 9 October 1944 (aged 23)
Singapore Memorial, Singapore (Column 437)

Thomas Paterson (Tommy) Muckle was the youngest son of John and Margaret Anna Muckle (nee Small) of Portavoe, Donaghadee. They were married on 8 April 1901 in Ballygrainey Presbyterian Church. John Muckle worked as an agricultural labourer and he and Margaret had at least twelve children – John (born 27 October 1901); David; Mary Small (born 21 April 1904); Elizabeth (born 10 June 1905); Margaret (born 17 September 1906); Jane; Sarah Angus (born 5 June 1909); Annie (born 10 May 1911); Wilhelmina; Robert Cree; James and Thomas Paterson (Tommy).

Before joining the Royal Air Force Tommy was employed as a butcher by Edmund Mills in Windmill Road, Bangor. Tommy Muckle was a well-known amateur boxer and he was a brother-in-law of Ivan Ruddock (or Reddick) of Croft Street, Bangor. In the 21 August 1943 edition of the *County Down Spectator* it was reported that Tommy Muckle was a prisoner in Japanese hands. He had been missing in Java since March 1942. Then, in the 15 December edition of the *County Down Spectator* it was reported that Tommy had died in a Japanese Prisoner-of-War camp in Java.

Corporal Thomas Paterson Muckle was 23 years old when he died and he is commemorated on the Singapore Memorial; on Donaghadee and District War Memorial; in Shore Street Presbyterian Church, Donaghadee and on the family grave headstone in Ballyvester Cemetery, Donaghadee. His father John died on 2 August 1953 (aged 81); his mother Margaret Anna died on 31 January 1957 (aged 78); his eldest brother John died on 1 March 1970; his sister Jane died on 4 October 1973; his brother Robert died on 21 April 1988 and his sister Mary died on 26 May 1988.

Mulligan, Francis Xavier (Francis)
Lance Bombardier
No. 5256357, 179 Field Regiment, Royal Artillery
Killed in action on Monday 30 April 1945 (aged 30)
Becklingen War Cemetery, Soltau, Niedersachsen, Germany (Grave 7 J 7)

Lance Bombardier Francis Xavier Mulligan is commemorated on the Ramsey grave headstone in Redburn Cemetery, Holywood:

Ramsey
In loving memory of
Moira
A loving and much loved wife
Mother and grandmother
Died 7 March 2010
Interred overseas
Francis Xavier (brother of Moira)
1945 (Germany)
Tatiana (infant granddaughter)
2002 (Chile)
Gone to God

Mu

Francis Xavier Mulligan was born in England and he was a son of Peter and Kathleen Mulligan who had at least four children – Francis Xavier, Patrick, Moira and Ann. During the Second World War Lance Bombardier Francis Xavier Mulligan served with the Royal Artillery and his marriage to Ena Maria Springate-Dakens was registered in the second quarter of 1941 in Brentford, Middlesex. Their family home was in Seaford, Sussex and Francis was 30 years old when he was killed in action on 30 April 1945 during the Allied advance through Germany.

Francis Mulligan's sister Moira married Cathal Ramsey and they had five children – Paul, Peter, Colette, John and Michael. They lived in Derryvolgie Avenue, Belfast.

Lance Bombardier Francis Xavier Mulligan is commemorated on Bessbrook War Memorial, Co. Armagh.

Munce, Ian Lindsay (Ian)
Pilot Officer (Pilot)
No. 186936, 220 Squadron, Royal Air Force Volunteer Reserve
Killed on active service on Thursday 8 March 1945 (aged 23)
Lajes War Cemetery, Azores (Row B Grave 8)

Ian Lindsay Munce was born on 30 December 1921 and he was the younger son of James Stillwell Munce and Annie Munce (nee Bearsley) who lived in Marine Parade, Holywood. James Stillwell Munce from Alexandra Park, Holywood was a civil engineer and architect when he and Annie Bearsley from Old Meldrum, Aberdeenshire were married on 20 October 1916 in the Palace Hotel, Castle Street, Edinburgh after Banns according to the form of the United Free Church of Scotland. They had two children – James Frederick (born 1918) and Ian Lindsay (born 1921).

In the early 1900s James Stillwell Munce worked in Belfast before he moved to London where he met Annie Bearsley. She was working as a clerk in the Savings Bank Department of the General Post Office (GPO). He returned to Belfast and set up his own business before entering into partnership to form the company Munce and Kennedy.

Ian Lindsay Munce was educated privately before attending Sullivan Upper School in Holywood from 1930 until 1936. Then he attended Methodist College Belfast. His mother Annie died on 4 June 1940 (aged 56).

During the Second World War Ian Lindsay Munce served with the Royal Air Force Volunteer Reserve and he was 23 years old when he was killed on active service in the Azores on 8 March 1945. He was buried in Lajes War Cemetery. Pilot Officer Ian Lindsay Munce is commemorated on Holywood and District War Memorial; in Sullivan Upper School; in Methodist College; in Queen's University, Belfast and on the family grave headstone in Holywood Cemetery. During the Second World War his brother, James Frederick Munce, served with the Royal Engineers and after the war he joined his father's business. James Frederick Munce carried on the business after his father, James Stillwell Munce, died on 15 July 1952 (aged 74). James Frederick Munce died in 1990.

Murphy, William Hugh (Hugh)
Gunner
No. 1535737, 170 Battery, 57 Light Anti-Aircraft Regiment, Royal Artillery
Died in service on Monday 12 August 1940 (aged 27)
Killysuggan Graveyard, Newtownards, Co. Down (Plot 3 Row 5 Grave 10)

William Hugh Murphy was born on 21 April 1913 in Kircubbin and he was a son of Hugh and Sarah Ellen Murphy (nee Magee, sometimes McGee). Hugh Murphy (son of Patrick Murphy) worked as a labourer and he and Sarah Ellen Magee (a seamstress, daughter of John Magee) were married on 22 April 1912 in St. Mary Star of the Sea Roman Catholic Church, Nunsquarter, Kircubbin. They lived at 68 Court Street, Newtownards and they had at least two children – William Hugh (born 21 April 1913) and a daughter.

Prior to the outbreak of the Second World War William Hugh Murphy worked as a plasterer. He joined the Royal Artillery in December 1939 and saw active service in France. He was based in England when he died on 12 August 1940 and his death was registered in Portsmouth. His remains were brought home to Newtownards for burial and his funeral took place on 19 August 1940.

Mu

There was a service in St. Patrick's Roman Catholic Church, Newtownards before the interment in Killysuggan Graveyard. In a letter to Gunner William Hugh Murphy's parents, one of the officers of his unit wrote, 'His loss is deplored by us all. We all loved him for his cheerfulness and humour and he was always keen and willing. If any member of his section wanted a little help to do a job he was always ready to give a hand'. A sum of money subscribed by the officers, NCOs and men was forwarded to Mrs Murphy to buy a wreath or to be 'used for whatever purpose his parents thought fit'. Gunner William Hugh Murphy was 27 years old when he died and he is commemorated on Newtownards and District War Memorial.

Murray, Sydney
Air Gunner
Royal Air Force
Died of illness on Friday 6 August 1943 (aged 24)
Newtownards (Movilla) Cemetery, Co. Down (Section 24)

Sydney Murray's birth was registered in the first quarter of 1919 in Newtownards and he was a son of Thomas and Mary Ann Murray (nee Graham). Thomas Murray was a soldier and Mary Ann Graham was a servant when they got married on 16 October 1915 in Ballymacarrett (St. Patrick's) Church of Ireland Church, Belfast. Their daughter Agnes was born on 5 July 1920. During the Second World War Sydney Murray served with the Royal Air Force before being discharged on medical grounds. In civilian life Sydney Murray lived at 25 Bangor Road, Newtownards and he worked as a fitter. He was 24 years old when he died of tuberculosis on 6 August 1943.

Air Gunner Sydney Murray is commemorated on the family grave headstone in Movilla Cemetery, Newtownards:

Mu

> MURRAY
> Erected by Thomas and Mary A. Murray
> In loving memory of their son
> Sydney Murray Air Gunner RAF died 6th August 1943
> Also their son Angus died in infancy
> Also the above Mary A. died 14th April 1963
> Also her husband Thomas died 30th January 1978

And on a Brass Plaque:

> In loving memory of
> Agnes Hiller nee Murray 5-7-20 – 11-3-94
> Loving mother of Sydney and Jacqueline and their families
> Home at last

Murray, Thomas (Tom)
Stoker 1st Class
No. D/KX 103032, HMS *Redmill*, Royal Navy
Died as a result of enemy action on Friday 27 April 1945 (aged 35)
Plymouth Naval Memorial, Devon, England (Panel 94 Column 3)

Thomas (Tom) Murray was born on 25 October 1909 in Belfast and he was the third son of Thomas and Sarah Murray (nee Hilditch) of 2 Oban Street,

Belfast and later 57 Southwell Road, Bangor. Thomas Murray Senior worked as a bottle blower and he and Sarah Hilditch were married on 15 December 1901 in St. Anne's Church of Ireland Church, Belfast. They had at least nine children – Annie (born 7 March 1903); William (born 24 November 1904); Mary (born 16 July 1906, died 9 April 1908); unnamed child (born 8 July 1908, died 8 July 1908); Thomas (born 25 October 1909); Sarah (Sadie, born 4 June 1912); Joseph; Ernest and Agnes.

Prior to volunteering on 8 December 1939 Tom Murray worked as a machine operator for Messrs Murray and Sons Ltd., Belfast. He commenced service with the Royal Navy on 28 February 1940 at HMS *Arthur* (a shore establishment at Ingoldmells near Skegness, Lincolnshire). He served aboard a number of ships including HMS *Inglefield*. During the Second World War Tom's brother Joseph served with the RAF and his brother-in-law Denis Pearce (his sister Agnes's husband) served with the 8th Army.

KILLED IN ACTION.

MURRAY—April 1945, missing, presumed killed through enemy action, at sea. 1st Class Stoker Thomas Murray (Tom), third and much-loved son of Mr. and Mrs. T. Murray. A Home at last with Christ, which is far better. Very deeply regretted by his sorrowing Father and Mother, Brothers and Sisters; also his Brother Joseph, R.A.F., S.E.A.C.—57 Southwell Road, Bangor, and 2 Oban Street, Belfast.

Tom Murray (aged 19) and Margaret Lough (aged 18) were married on 29 April 1929 in Belfast Registry Office and they had two daughters, Margaret and Mary Muriel (Muriel). The Murray family lived in Belfast at 23 Crystal Street and 57 Gaffakin Street and in Bangor at 54 Victoria Road and 88 Bryansburn Road. Tom Murray's last posting was aboard HMS *Redmill* which was built in 1943 by the Bethlehem-Hingham Shipyards Inc., Hingham, Massachusetts, USA for the US Navy and commissioned on completion as a frigate in the Royal Navy. On 27 April 1945, about 25 miles west of County Mayo, she was hit by two German Navy Acoustic Torpedoes (GNATS) fired from the German submarine *U-1105*. HMS *Redmill* lost about sixty feet from her stern but remained afloat and was towed to Lisahally on the Foyle. (The ship was declared a total loss and in 1947 the hulk was returned to the US Navy. She was sold for scrap to the Athens Piraeus Electricity Company Ltd., Athens, Greece). Stoker 1st Class Tom Murray (aged 35) was one of more than 20 men who died. His family placed *Killed on Active Service* notices in the 12 and 26 May 1945 editions of the *County Down Spectator* and they contained the texts:

He died that we might live
At home at last with Christ, which is far better

Mu

Tom Murray's daughters were aged 15 and 13 when he died on 27 April 1945. Margaret was working and Muriel was at school. Tom Murray's brother-in-law, Junior Engineer Officer **William Lough**, died on 20 September 1941 when the MV *Cingalese Prince* was torpedoed off the coast of Brazil.

Mynett, Stanley
Leading Aircraftman
No. 1128561, Royal Air Force Volunteer Reserve
Killed in an aircraft accident on Saturday 6 May 1944 (aged 23)
Campsall New Cemetery, Yorkshire, England (Grave B 34)

Mu
My

Stanley Mynett's birth was registered in the fourth quarter of 1920 in Doncaster, Yorkshire and he was a son of Thomas and Sarah Jane Mynett (nee Dey), of Norton, Yorkshire. Their marriage was registered in the fourth quarter of 1911 in Doncaster and they had at least four children including Guy (born 1916); Stanley (born 1920); Clarice (born 1922) and Vera (born 1923). Sarah Jane Mynett died in 1923 (when Stanley was 3) and Thomas Mynett died in 1929 (when Stanley was 9).

During the Second World War Stanley Mynett served with the Royal Air Force Volunteer Reserve. On 6 May 1944 a Miles Martinet aircraft (MS619) from No. 12 Air Gunners School, Bishops Court was low-flying while on drogue-towing duty when it crashed into Strangford Lough about a mile and a half west of the Ards Peninsula coastline and about a mile east of Killyleagh. Both crew members were killed. They were the Pilot, Sergeant **Victor Wadmore** (aged 21) from Sutton, Greater London, and Leading Aircraftman Stanley Mynett from Norton, Yorkshire.

Leading Aircraftman Stanley Mynett was buried in Campsall New Cemetery, Yorkshire and there is an inscription on his CWGC headstone:

His memory is our greatest treasure
In our hearts he will live forever

Stanley Mynett was 23 years old when he died and he is commemorated on the Campsall War Memorial in Doncaster.

600

Neely, Noel Montgomery (Noel)
Lieutenant
HMS *Circe*, Royal Naval Volunteer Reserve
Killed on active service on Sunday 23 April 1944 (aged 33)
Chatham Naval Memorial, Kent, England (Panel 79 2)

Noel Montgomery Neely was born on 27 December 1910, he was baptised in Urney, Sion Mills, Co. Tyrone and he was a son of James and Margaret Neely (nee Irwin). James Neely had previously been married to Fanny Ann (sometimes known as Jane) Montgomery from Belfast. James Neely and Fanny Ann Montgomery were married on 28 July 1880 in Urney and Sion Mills Presbyterian Church and they lived in the townland of Tullyverry, Killyleagh, Co. Down where James worked as a Preparing Master in a local mill. They had seven children – Matthew (born 4 September 1881); James (born 23 May 1884); Andrew (born 28 February 1886, served in the 36th Ulster Division during the First World War); Susan Montgomery (born 22 November 1887); Mary (Mae born 3 October 1891) and twins Elizabeth Dickson (Lilly) and Frances (Fanny Ann) born 15 June 1894.

N

Fanny Ann Neilly was 34 years old when she died in childbirth on 15 June 1894. After Fanny Ann died James Neely moved to Sion Mills and he and Margaret Irwin from Ballykelly, Co. Londonderry were married in Urney and Sion Mills Presbyterian Church on 9 April 1903. James Neely worked as a Preparing Master in Herdman's Mill, Sion Mills and the Neely family lived at 2 Sion Terrace, Sion Mills. James and Margaret Neely had three children – Gerald Irwin (born 5 January 1905, died 5 December 1990); Samuel Stephen (born 26 December 1906, died 14 May 1908) and Noel Montgomery (born 27 December 1910). Noel's parents both died in 1924, his father James on 7 January (aged 67) and his mother Margaret on 11 October (aged 50).

Noel Neely had tutoring from his half-brother James who was a school teacher and, after leaving school, Noel worked as a clerk in the Belfast Banking Company Ltd. His hobbies were amateur dramatics, sailing and rugby. On 1 July 1936 Noel Montgomery Neely married Joan Lorimer from Helen's Bay in Holywood Parish Church of Ireland Church (St. Philip and St. James). They had two children – Peter James (born 16 November 1939, died 1 February 1940) and Patrick Lawrie (born 19 April 1941).

Joan Lorimer was born in Johannesburg and she was a sister of **Robert Lawrie Lorimer** who was killed in action on 14 May 1940, less than four months after Joan's infant son died. When Noel and Joan Neely's second son was born in 1941 they gave him Lawrie as one of his forenames in memory of his uncle Lawrie Lorimer. Patrick Lawrie Neely was just three years old when his father Noel died on 23 April 1944 aboard HMS *Circe*. This Algerine-class minesweeper was built by Harland and Wolff Ltd., Belfast and she was commissioned on 16 October 1942. Along with Radar Operator Gordon Planner, Lieutenant Neely was posted to Belfast to supervise her fitting out and sea trials and, for a time in 1942, the Neely family lived in Groomsport. They also lived at 2 Royal Terrace, Lisburn Road, Belfast; 27 Windmill Road, Bangor and 8 Diamond Gardens, Finaghy, Belfast.

Radar Operator Gordon Planner was injured in the explosion on HMC *Circe* that killed Lieutenant Noel Montgomery Neely and he provided details as to what happened. As well as working together during the fitting out and sea trials they met again on board when, as the officer on watch, Lieutenant Neely visited the radar shack located on the largely open bridge. HMS *Circe* had her first operational deployment in December 1942 as part of the initial escort for Convoy JW51B from Loch Ewe in Scotland to Reykjavik in Iceland (Convoy JW51B continued on to Murmansk in Russia). Following her return from Iceland HMS *Circe* joined the 12th Minesweeping Flotilla (MSF) in the Mediterranean Sea at the beginning of 1943. On 23 April 1944 HMS *Circe* and other ships from the 12th MSF were conducting a sweeping operation north of the Anzio beachhead, near the mouth of the River Tiber. Enemy ships were sighted and emergency retrieval of the sweeping gear was initiated.

KILLED IN ACTION.

NEELY—April, 1944, Lieut. NOEL MONT-
GOMERY NEELY, R.N.V.R., beloved husband
of Joan NEELY, 8 Diamond Gardens, Finaghy, Belfast.

One of Lieutenant Neely's duties was to supervise the sweeping deck during sweeping operations and, during the emergency sweep retrieval, a mine got caught in the gear. It exploded under the stern of the ship. Lieutenant Neely was killed outright and several others, including Gordon Planner, were injured. Lieutenant Neely's remains were transferred to HMS *Espiegle* for burial at sea. HMS *Circe* was badly damaged in the explosion with her stern having been blown off. Two other ships in the flotilla, HMS *Acute* and HMS *Spanker*, were lashed one to either side to keep her afloat and another ship took her in tow. This presented a very big target for enemy aircraft and so the ships were separated again as soon as HMS *Circe* had been made watertight. A tug towed her back to Naples and then to Taranto, for repair. HMS *Circe* rejoined the 12th MSF later in 1944 and eventually returned from the Mediterranean in 1946. In 1966 she was broken up at Dalmuir in Scotland.

Lieutenant Noel Montgomery Neely was 33 years old when he died and he is commemorated on Chatham Naval Memorial in Kent and on the Belfast Banking Company Second World War Memorial Plaque (now in Danske Bank, Donegall Square West, Belfast).

Nelson, Ida May (Ida)
Nursing Sister, Civilian War Dead
SS *Tanjong Pinang*
Died as a result of enemy action on Tuesday 17 February 1942 (aged 35)

Ida May Nelson was born on 19 May 1906 and she was a daughter of Walter and Mary A. Nelson (nee Manson) who lived at 67 Kansas Avenue, Belfast and later at *Thorndale*, Church Road, Helen's Bay. Walter Nelson was a commercial traveller (brewer's agent and spirit merchant) and he and Mary Manson were married on 1 December 1898 in Magheramason Presbyterian Church, Co. Tyrone. They had at least four children – a stillborn child (born April 1900); Emily Elizabeth (born 3 October 1901); Stanley (born 5 August 1903, died 26 September 1904) and Ida May (born 19 May 1906). Their stillborn child was buried on 4 April 1900 in Belfast City Cemetery (Grave L1 304), as was their son Stanley who was buried on 28 September 1904.

N

Also buried in that grave was Sergeant (Flight Engineer) John Frederick Nelson (No. 1796160) aged 21 who served with the RAFVR and was killed in an aircraft accident on 7 February 1944. Based at RAF Pocklington in Yorkshire, he was one of a crew of seven on a training flight aboard a Handley Page Halifax aircraft (DK192) when it crashed into the top of Garrowby Hill at 10.15 am and struck a lorry. All aboard the aircraft, together with the lorry driver, were killed. John Frederick Nelson was a son of John and Dorothy Louie Nelson (nee Attfield) of Belfast. John Nelson worked as a fitter and he and Dorothy Attfield were married on 23 December 1918 in St. Thomas's Church of Ireland Church, Belfast. Dorothy Nelson died on 4 November 1985 (aged 90) and she was buried in Belfast City Cemetery (Grave L1 304). Also buried in that grave was John's brother, Thomas Henry Nelson (born 11 January 1885, died 7 July 1899 in the Royal Victoria Hospital aged 14). John and Thomas Nelson were sons of James Edward and Mary Nelson (nee Buchanan) who were married on 13 March 1884 in Magheragall Church of Ireland Church, Lisburn.

During the Second World War Ida May Nelson was a Nursing Sister in the

General Hospital, Singapore. She worked with the Malayan Nursing Service and was being evacuated from Singapore aboard the SS *Kuala* when this ship was bombed and sunk. Ida managed to reach Pompong Island, some 70 miles south of Singapore and she was taken off the island by the SS *Tanjong Pinang*. Sister Ida May Nelson (aged 35) died when this ship was shelled and sunk in the Banka Straits at 9.30 pm on 17 February 1942. The SS *Tanjong Pinang* was a small ship (length 97 feet, beam width 22 feet) built in the Taikoo Shipyards in Hong Kong in 1936 and owned by the Soon Bee Steamship Company. When the SS *Tanjong Pinang* was shelled she was crowded with women, children and wounded personnel. Sister **Doreen Pedlow** who was also aboard the SS *Tanjong Pinang* died of exposure after clinging to a raft for three days following the shelling.

N

On 1 April 1946 Nursing Sister Ida May Nelson was officially presumed to have lost her life 'on or about 17 February 1942' and she is commemorated in Helen's Bay Presbyterian Church and in Helen's Bay Golf Club where she was an active member. After Ida was presumed dead her father presented a cup to be played for annually in mixed foursomes competition. First won in 1946 the inscription on the cup reads:

Helen's Bay Golf Club
World War 1939 – 1945
Memorial Cup
Presented by Walter Nelson
In memory of Ida May Nelson
Nursing Sister
Colonial Service
Killed by Japanese February 1942

Coincidentally, the cup was supplied by the firm Sharman D. Neill of 22 Donegall Place, Belfast. Sharman D. Neill's sons, James Dermot Neill and Robert Larmour Neill were both killed in action during the First World War and they are commemorated on Page 269 in the Book of Honour *Remembering Their Sacrifice in the Great War – North Down* compiled by Barry Niblock. Ida Nelson's father Walter died on 29 August 1948 (aged 76).

Of the many civilians of the Commonwealth whose deaths were due to enemy action in the Second World War, the names of some 67,092 are commemorated in the Civilian War Dead Roll of Honour, located near St. George's Chapel in Westminster Abbey, London.

Nelson, Ronald (Ronnie)
Flight Sergeant (Air Bomber)
No. 1515342, 106 Squadron, Royal Air Force Volunteer Reserve
Killed on active service on Wednesday 28 June 1944 (aged 21)
Dieppe Canadian War Cemetery, Hautot-sur-Mer, Seine-Maritime, France
(Collective Grave M 8-13)

Former Regent House Boy Killed.— Flight Sergeant Ronald Nelson, R.A.F.-V.R., aged 21, eldest son of Mr. and Mrs. J. A. Nelson, 8 Rathkain, Dundonald, missing, is now reported killed. When he joined in 1941 he was a commerce student at Queen's University, and was previously at Regent House School, Newtownards.

Ronald Nelson was born on 6 December 1922 and he was a grandson of James Aiken Nelson and Emma Nelson (nee Millen). He was a son of James Andrew and Kathleen M. Nelson (nee Holmes) of *Alnwick*, Comber Road, Dundonald. James Andrew Nelson was a draughtsman and he and Kathleen Holmes were married on 26 December 1921 in Bloomfield Presbyterian Church, Belfast.

N

Ronnie Nelson attended Dundonald Public Elementary School and then Regent House School, Newtownards from 2 September 1935 until 27 June 1940. When he left school he went to Queen's University, Belfast to study commerce. During the Second World War he served with the Royal Air Force Volunteer Reserve and he died on 28 June 1944. He was one of a crew of seven aboard an Avro Lancaster Mark I aircraft (LL974) that took off at 10.55 pm from RAF Metheringham in Lincolnshire on a mission to bomb rail facilities at Vitry-le-Francois. The aircraft was shot down by a German night fighter and crashed at Thibie (Marne), west-south-west of Chalons-sur-Marne. All aboard the aircraft died and were buried locally but were later exhumed and reinterred in Dieppe Canadian War Cemetery. The other six crew members who died that night were:

- Flight Sergeant Ernest Clive Fox aged 29 from Hailey, Oxfordshire
- Sergeant C. Henry Southworth aged 20 from Wigan, Lancashire
- Flight Sergeant Arthur Cornelius Croft aged 25 from London
- Sergeant Jack Desmond Pepper aged 19 from Darlington, Durham
- Flight Sergeant Melvin Harold Stoner aged 20 (RCAF)
- Pilot Officer Arthur Evans Cosdett Thomas aged 21 (RCAF)

Flight Sergeant (Air Bomber) Ronald Nelson was 21 years old when he died and he is commemorated in Regent House School and on the Queen's University Second World War Memorial Plaque.

Nelson, William George
Coxswain
Miss Betty, Pilot Launch
Drowned on Saturday 8 May 1943 (aged 28) (Bangor Bay Disaster)
Donaghadee Parish Church of Ireland Graveyard, Donaghadee, Co. Down

Three men from Donaghadee along with one man from Bangor were drowned on Saturday 8 May 1943 in what became known locally as the 'Bangor Bay Disaster'. There were no survivors. The four men died when the Pilot Launch *Miss Betty* capsized and sank while returning to port after responding to a call from a ship entering Belfast Lough. The four men who died worked on the pilot boats that were based in Bangor. These pilot boats were in constant service, not only for merchant shipping coming into Belfast, but also for many of the naval vessels using Belfast Lough. At the outbreak of war *Miss Betty* was requisitioned by the Admiralty from Jim Davidson, Donaghadee.

The three men from Donaghadee who died were **Harry Aiken**, **William George Nelson** and **William White**. The Bangor man who died was **William Anderson**. Aboard *Miss Betty* on the day they died, William White was the pilot and William George Nelson was the coxswain. William Anderson was the engineer and Harry Aiken was the deck hand.

N

William George Nelson was born on 3 November 1917 and he was a son of David and Mary Nelson (nee Lennon) who were married on 11 July 1904 in Millisle Presbyterian Church. David Nelson was a fisherman and he and Mary had seven children (five sons and two daughters) – Martha (known as Rosie, born 8 May 1907, died 1966); John (born 25 June 1909); William (born 24 March 1911, died 2004); Saidie Ferguson (born 3 November 1913, died 2010); Samuel (Sammy, born 3 October 1915, died 15 January 2001); William George (born 3 November 1917); Francis (Frankie, born 3 November 1919, died 12 August 2000). The children were baptised in Donaghadee Parish Church of Ireland Church. Mary Nelson's sister-in-law (her brother William's wife), **Margaret Lennon** was a civilian casualty of war as a result of the sinking of the *SS Athenia*.

William George Nelson was named after his paternal grandfather who was drowned off the coast of Donaghadee on 2 November 1917 (the day before his grandson was born). Grandfather William George Nelson's wife's name was Martha (nee Tollerton) and he was coxswain of the Donaghadee lifeboat from 1910 until his death in 1917. Successive generations of the Nelson family have served aboard Donaghadee lifeboat.

NELSON—In loving memory of my dear husband, William George, accidentally drowned in Bangor Bay on May 8th, 1943. Also my baby son, William George, died 17th October, 1943.

Ever remembered by his loving Wife and little Children.—62 East Street, Donaghadee.

William George Nelson who died in the Bangor Bay Disaster on 8 May 1943 was a member of the crew of Donaghadee lifeboat and his father David was the mechanic. The Nelson family boat was named *The Five Brothers* and she was requisitioned by the Admiralty. She was lost during the war and when David Nelson purchased a replacement boat, *Roberta*, he renamed her *The Brothers*. When the MV *Princess Victoria* sank on 31 January 1953 William George Nelson's uncle, Hugh Nelson Senior, was coxswain on the Donaghadee lifeboat and Hugh's son, Hugh Nelson Junior, was a member of the crew, as were Alex Nelson and William George Nelson's brothers William, Sammy and Frankie. William George Nelson's mother Mary died in 1964 and his father David died in 1967.

The Pilot Launch *Miss Betty* was around 40 feet long and the disaster was witnessed by Bangor Harbour Master John H. Corry and Customs Officer G.A. Coppard. *Miss Betty* was owned by the Admiralty but crewed by civilians under naval direction and she left Bangor in moderate weather conditions at 8.55 am on 8 May 1943. During the trip the weather deteriorated and on the way back to Bangor the crew had to contend with a strong north-easterly gale and a heavy breaking sea. At 11.40 am, when they were only about 60 to 70 yards from the safety of Bangor harbour, the disaster happened. The boat successfully negotiated a number of strong waves before being overwhelmed by a broadside hit on the port side. *Miss Betty* capsized, turned over in the water and remained upside down.

William George Nelson and Isobel Gordon were married on 12 October 1938 in First Donaghadee Presbyterian Church and they lived at 62 East Street, Donaghadee with their two children Audrey (born 28 November 1939) and John Alexander Gordon (born 21 August 1941). It was some time after the sinking of the *Miss Betty* before William George Nelson's body was recovered. It was his uncle Hugh Nelson who found his nephew's body floating face-down in the water when he was fishing off Bangor and he recognised his nephew immediately by his distinctively curly hair.

William George Nelson was 28 years old when he died on 8 May 1943 and he was buried in Donaghadee Parish Church of Ireland Graveyard, near to the grave of Harry Aiken. On 12 August 1943 William George Nelson's widow

ERECTED BY
D. NELSON
IN MEMORY OF HIS SON
W. C. NELSON
LOST IN BANGOR BAY 8TH MAY 1943 AGED 26 YEARS

Isobel gave birth to a son and he was named William George in memory of his father. Isobel Nelson suffered a further bereavement when baby William George died on 17 October 1943 and was buried beside his father.

Along with Pilot William White and Deck Hand Harry Aiken, Coxswain William George Nelson is commemorated on a separate plaque on Donaghadee and District War Memorial.

Newell, Thomas
Private
No. 6976739, 1st Battalion, Worcestershire Regiment
Died on active service on Friday 5 June 1942 (aged 32)
Knightsbridge War Cemetery, Acroma, Libya (Grave 10 A 22)

Thomas Newell was born on 22 May 1910 and he was a son of James A. Newell and Ellen Newell (nee McClung) of Newtownards. They were married on 6 February 1910 in St. Anne's Church of Ireland Church, Belfast. James Newell worked as a labourer and before moving to Newtownards the Newell family lived at 67 Bright Street and then 14 Constance Street, Belfast.

Thomas Newell joined the Army in the 1930s and during the Second World War he served with the 1st Battalion, Worcestershire Regiment in North Africa. He was 32 years old when he died during heavy fighting on 5 June 1942 at Acroma in Libya and he was buried in the Knightsbridge War Cemetery.

Nicholls, James Ernest (Jim)
Sergeant (Air Gunner)
No. 927758, 15 Squadron, Royal Air Force Volunteer Reserve
Killed on active service on Sunday 14 February 1943 (aged 21)
Heverlee War Cemetery, Leuven, Vlaams-Brabant, Belgium
(Collective Grave 10 E 2-8)

James Ernest Nicholls was a son of James Ernest and Hilda Clara Nicholls (formerly Pring, nee Gale). Their marriage was registered in the third quarter of 1918 in Newport, Monmouthshire and Hilda's previous marriage to Police Constable Benjamin Pring was registered in the third quarter of 1906, also in Newport. Benjamin and Hilda Pring had at least two children – Cicely Ivy (born 1908) and Benjamin G. (born 1912). Constable Benjamin

N

Pring died in 1915 (aged 30).

For a time the Nicholls family lived in Canada and there is a record of them returning to Britain in May 1924 when Hilda (aged 40), Benjamin (aged 11) and James (aged 2) arrived in Liverpool having travelled from St. John, New Brunswick aboard the RMS *Montclare*. This ship was requisitioned by the Admiralty in 1939, converted to an Armed Merchant Cruiser and later converted to a Destroyer Depot Ship. She was scrapped in 1958.

James Ernest Nicholls attended Malpas School, Newport and Bassaleg Secondary School, Newport and he worked for A.E. Moss and Sons (Builders and Contractors), Hawarden Road, Newport before joining the Royal Air Force Volunteer Reserve in 1940. He was a member of Newport Harriers and won the Welsh Youths' Cross Country Championship at the age of 15. His half-brother, Sergeant Benjamin G. Pring, also served with the RAF.

James Ernest Nicholls was the husband of Mary E. (Marie) Nicholls of 57 Wallace Street No. 2, Newtownards and they had a son called Ernest.

> **OUR HEROES—IN MEMORIAM.**
> **NICHOLLS**—In proud and loving memory of Sergeant Air-Gunner J. E. Nicholls, R.A.F., Killed in Action 14th February, 1943.
> Ever remembered by his Wife.
> MARIE NICHOLLS.

During the Second World War Sergeant James Ernest Nicholls served with the Royal Air Force Volunteer Reserve and on 14 February 1943 he was one of an eight man crew aboard a Short Stirling Mark I aircraft (BF448) that took off at 6.25 pm from RAF Bourn in Cambridgeshire on a mission to bomb Cologne. The aircraft was shot down at 8.56 pm by a German night-fighter and crashed at Helchteren (Limburg) in Belgium. All of the crew died and they were buried at St. Truiden in Belgium and later reinterred in Heverlee War Cemetery. As well as Sergeant James Ernest Nicholls (aged 21) the other seven crew members who died that evening were:

- Flt Lt Owen Cecil Chave aged 30 from Highfield, Southampton
- Flight Sergeant Lewis Lee Gladwin aged 21 (RCAF)
- Sergeant James Falshaw Cook aged 34 from Hunstanworth, Durham
- Flying Officer William Alexander McLean Archibald
- Sergeant Alfred Arthur Self aged 21 from Rickmansworth, Hertfordshire
- Flying Officer John Neville Macmillan Muir aged 25 from Elham, Kent
- Sgt Thomas Frederick Stocks aged 19 from Penwortham, Lancashire

At least eight other aircraft were shot down that night.

When Sergeant James Ernest Nicholls died, his mother was living at 24 Graig Park Road, Malpas, Newport and his father was living in Manitoba, Canada. He is commemorated on Newport Cenotaph and on a memorial stone at Houthalen Cemetery, Helchteren, Belgium. This memorial commemorates the crews of four RAF aircraft lost over the area. There is an inscription on his CWGC headstone:

In proud and loving remembrance of Jim, dear husband of Marie

Nicholson, John Gilkeson
Chief Engineer
SS *Gatun*, Merchant Navy
Died at sea on Friday 31 December 1943 (aged 74)

N

In the Maritime Register of Deaths of Passengers and Seamen at Sea it is recorded that the ship which reported John Gilkeson Nicholson's death was the SS *Gatun*. John Gilkeson Nicholson was born on 16 October 1869 in Bangor and he was the eldest son of John and Ellen Nicholson (nee Campbell). John Nicholson Senior was also born in Bangor and he and Isabella Neill were married in Bangor on 14 February 1860. After Isabella died, John Nicholson and Ellen Campbell from Cottown were married in Ballygrainey Presbyterian Church on 19 December 1865. They had at least seven children – Sarah (born 27 September 1866); John Gilkeson (born 16 October 1869); James Campbell (born 26 July 1872, studied medicine in Edinburgh and, after qualifying as a doctor, practised in the New Hebridies – now Vanuatu – in the South Pacific, married Anna Isabel Campbell of Bangor on 31 December 1902 in Hamilton Road Presbyterian Church Bangor, lived at 30 Hamilton Road, Bangor and died on 29 October 1934); Louis (born 29 September 1874, worked as a carpenter and with his wife Elizabeth lived at 62 Raby Street, Belfast); William P. (born 3 April 1876, moved to the USA and lived in Los Angeles); Eleanor Mary (born in Conway, Caernarvonshire and married foreign missionary James Bowman Hanna on 22 November 1904 in Helen's Bay Presbyterian Church); Janet Marion (sometimes Maria, born in Conway, Caernarvonshire in 1881 and died on 11 May 1940 aged 59).

John Nicholson Senior was a seaman and he was described as a retired sea captain when he died on 19 April 1918 (aged 88). At the time of his death he was living at *Ellenville*, 106 Princetown Road, Bangor and he also owned

100, 102 and 104 Princetown Road as well as 37/39 Main Street, Bangor. His widow Ellen died on 3 January 1931 (aged 90) and she and John were both buried in Bangor Abbey Graveyard.

NICHOLSON—December 31, 1943 (suddenly), John G. Nicholson (Chief Engineer, Standard Fruit Company), dearly-beloved husband of Jane Nicholson, 37 Ballyholme Esplanade, Bangor (by cable).

John Gilkeson Nicholson was a marine engineer and he and Jane Craig from Bangor were married on 26 July 1905 in Helen's Bay Presbyterian Church. They had two children – Maria Metzeman (born 28 April 1906) and Eleanor (born 17 October 1907). During the Great War John Gilkeson Nicholson served with the British Mercantile Marine and the Nicholson family lived in Bangor at 198 Ballyholme Road before moving to 37 Ballyholme Esplanade.

When John Gilkeson Nicholson died at sea (aged 74) he was Chief Engineer aboard the SS *Gatun*, sailing in Latin American waters while on active service with the United States Navy. His widow Jane died on 14 September 1953 in the Musgrave Clinic Belfast (aged 78). Her home address was 37 Ballyholme Esplanade.

John Gilkeson Nicholson is commemorated on the family grave headstone in Bangor Cemetery (Section 4N Grave 153A):

Nicholson, John Gilkeson
Died at sea on active service, 31st December 1943
Also his wife Jane, died 14th September 1953
And their younger daughter Eleanor, who died 29th March 1999

Sunset and evening star and one clear call for me
And may there be no moaning of the bar when I put out to sea

Nixon, Joseph
Fusilier
No. 6980330, 1st Battalion, Royal Inniskilling Fusiliers
Died on active service on Sunday 25 April 1943 (aged 21)
Rangoon Memorial, Myanmar (Face 11)

In the 29 December 1943 edition of the *Belfast Telegraph* it was reported that

C.S.M. John Nixon, Royal Irish Fusiliers, husband of Mrs. Mary Nixon. 21 Hill Street. Holywood, missing. He has 16 years' service. His younger brother, Joseph, of the Royal Inniskilling Fusiliers, is also missing.

Company Sergeant Major John Nixon (No. 6976429), Royal Irish Fusiliers was missing. CSM John Nixon was the husband of Mary Nixon of 21 Hill Street, Holywood and it was later confirmed that he was being held in the German Prisoner-of-War Camp, Stalag III-A, at Luckenwalde, Brandenburg. At the same time it was reported in the press that John's younger brother Joseph was also missing. Fusilier Joseph Nixon (No. 6980330) who was born in County Tyrone served with the 1st Battalion, Royal Inniskilling Fusiliers and he died on 25 April 1943 in Burma. There is evidence to suggest that Fusilier Joseph Nixon was a brother of CSM John Nixon, Hill Street, Holywood.

Nolan, William
Corporal
No. T/162832, Royal Army Service Corps
Killed in action between Tuesday 28 May and Sunday 02 June 1940 (aged 44)
Dunkirk Memorial, Nord, France (Column 133)

N

William Nolan was born on 21 July 1895 and he was a son of Robert and Frances Nolan (nee Wright) of Unicarville, Ballymaglaff, Comber. Robert Nolan worked as a coachman and he was a widower when he and Frances Wright were married on 3 April 1889 in Dundonald Parish Church of Ireland Church (St. Elizabeth's). Robert and Frances Nolan had ten children – Eva Madeline (born 5 February 1890); Arthur (born 25 September 1891); Lizzie (born 4 August 1893); William (born 21 July 1895); Margaret Ellen (born 2 August 1897); Frances (born 23 December 1899); Amelia Amy (born 23 February 1902); Alice (born 11 October 1904); Robert (born 10 April 1907) and Betty (born 22 March 1912). Their father Robert died on 11 July 1933 (aged 73) and their mother Frances died on 25 December 1943 (aged 74).

During the First World War William Nolan served as a Sergeant (No. 100895) with 25 Battery, Royal Field Artillery. After the war he worked as a horse trainer and he was living in Downpatrick when he and Elizabeth Duffy (daughter of William Duffy) were married on 28 September 1920 in Downpatrick Roman Catholic Church. During the Second World War William Nolan served with the Royal Army Service Corps and he was 44 years old when he was killed in action between 28 May and 2 June 1940 during the evacuation of Allied Forces. His body was never recovered and he is commemorated on the Dunkirk Memorial in France.

Nugent Brothers, John Andrew and Patrick Edmund Charles

IN LOVING MEMORY OF
PATRICK EDMOND CHARLES NUGENT.
LIEUTENANT GRENADIER GUARDS.
BORN NOVEMBER 4TH 1920.
KILLED IN ACTION AT JEBEL BOU-AOUKAZ
TUNISIA APRIL 27TH 1943.
AND OF HIS BROTHER,
JOHN ANDREW NUGENT.
LIEUTENANT GRENADIER GUARDS.
BORN SEPTEMBER 1ST 1925.
KILLED IN ACTION NEAR CASTIGLIONE
NORTHERN ITALY. OCTOBER 7TH 1944.
SONS OF ROLAND AND CYNTHIA NUGENT.
OF PORTAFERRY.
FORTIS ATQUE FIDELIS.

John Andrew Nugent and Patrick Edmund Charles Nugent were sons of Major the Right Honourable Sir Roland Thomas Nugent, Kt., JP, DL and Lady Cynthia Maud Nugent (nee Ramsden) of *Portaferry House*, Portaferry, Co. Down. They were married on 25 September 1917 and they had three children – Elizabeth Anne (born 10 March 1919); Patrick Edmund Charles (born 4 November 1920) and John Andrew (born 1 September 1925). Sir Roland Nugent held a number of different offices including Minister without Portfolio in the Northern Ireland Government and Leader of the Northern Ireland Senate. He died on 18 August 1962. During the Second World War both Nugent brothers served with the 5th Battalion, Grenadier Guards which was raised in 1941, served in North Africa and Italy and disbanded in 1945. Patrick Edmund Charles Nugent was the first of the two brothers to die.

N

Nugent, Patrick Edmund Charles Nugent (Patrick)
Lieutenant
No. 176733, 5th Battalion, Grenadier Guards
Killed in action on Tuesday 27 April 1943 (aged 22)
Massicault War Cemetery, Tunisia (Grave V K 8)

Patrick Edmund Charles Nugent was born on 4 November 1920 and he was educated at Eton College. He joined the Grenadier Guards and was killed in action on 27 April 1943 during the Allied offensive on Axis positions in Tunisia, as the Allies prepared for the final drive towards Tunis. The war in North Africa came to an end in May 1943 with the defeat of the Axis Forces. Lieutenant Patrick Nugent was initially reported as *Missing in Action* and it was some time before his body was recovered. Identified by means of his identity disc, he was buried in Massicault War Cemetery. Lieutenant Patrick Edmund Charles Nugent was 22 years old when he died and he is commemorated in Ballyphilip Parish Church of Ireland Church, Portaferry and in Eton College.

Nugent, John Andrew (John)
Lieutenant
No. 307920, 5th Battalion, Grenadier Guards
Killed in action on Monday 2 October 1944 (aged 19)
Castiglione South African Cemetery, Italy (Grave I D 21)

John Andrew Nugent was born on 1 September 1925 and, like his brother Patrick, was educated at Eton College. He too joined the Grenadier Guards and he was killed in action on 2 October 1944 in Italy as Allied Forces advanced northwards. It was at the end of September 1944 that Allied Forces entered Castiglione and secured their position there. Lieutenant John Andrew Nugent was 19 years old when he died and he is commemorated in Ballyphilip Parish Church of Ireland Church, Portaferry and in Eton College.

Ogram, Joseph William
Sapper
No. 1905427, 585 Corps, Field Park Company, Royal Engineers
Died as a result of enemy action on Thursday 7 January 1943 (aged 24)
Brookwood Memorial, Surrey, England (Panel 6 Column 3)

N
O

> **Donaghadee Lady's Husband Missing.—** Mrs. Ogram, formerly Miss Amelia Moore, Bow Street, Donaghadee, has been notified that her husband, Sapper Joseph Ogram, R.E., is reported missing. Sapper and Mrs. Ogram were married in Donaghadee about a year ago.

Joseph William Ogram's birth was registered in the second quarter of 1918 in York and he was a son of Alexander George and Emma Ogram (nee Clayton). Alexander George Ogram worked as a groom and his marriage to Emma Clayton was registered in the third quarter of 1914 in York. They had at least five children – Lucy (born 1914); Nancy (born 1916); Joseph William (born 1918); Frederick Michael (born 2 January 1920, died 1972) and Eileen P. (born 1930).

During the Second World War Joseph William Ogram served as a Sapper with the Royal Engineers. In the first quarter of 1942 he and Amelia Agnes Moore (born 20 July 1902) were married in Donaghadee. Amelia was a daughter of James Moore (a bricklayer) and Margaret Moore (nee McMahon) of 14 Bow Street, Donaghadee. Less than a year after they were married Sapper Joseph William Ogram died at sea aboard the SS *Benalbanach*.

Built in 1940 by Charles Connell and Company Ltd., Scotstoun, Glasgow for use as a passenger/cargo ship, the SS *Benalbanach* was owned by Ben Line

Steamers Ltd., (William Thomson and Company). In 1941 she was taken over by the Royal Navy as an auxiliary transport ship and in November 1942 she took part in the landing at Oran in the North African campaign. It was on her second trip to the Allied landing area that she sank. The SS *Benalbanach* left the Clyde on 24 December 1942 bound for Bona in North Africa with more than 350 Motor Transport officers and men together with a cargo of tanks, motor vehicles, ammunition, petrol and general military stores. Shortly after 6.00 pm on 7 January 1943 the SS *Benalbanach* sank north-west of Algiers after being hit by two torpedoes fired from an enemy aircraft. The water was very cold and Sapper Joseph William Ogram, along with Convoy Signalman **Hugh Douglas Cole** from Holywood, was among more than 400 men who died.

 Sapper Joseph William Ogram was 24 years old when he died and he is commemorated on the Brookwood Memorial in Surrey.

Oliver, Henry (Harry)
Corporal
No. 5383218, 2ⁿᵈ (Airborne) Battalion, Oxford and Bucks Light Infantry
Died as a result of injuries on Thursday 7 February 1946 (aged 26)
Ault Hucknall (St. John the Baptist) Churchyard Extension (Row 9 Grave 10)

 Henry (Harry) Oliver was a son of George and Eleanor Oliver (nee McAvoy) of 20 Wallaces Street No. 2, Newtownards. George Oliver worked as a weaver and he and Eleanor McAvoy (daughter of Hugh McAvoy) were married on 29 April 1901 in Greenwell Street Presbyterian Church, Newtownards. They had at least ten children – George (born 26 November 1901); James (born 25 June 1903); Kathleen (born 30 October 1904); Jane (Jeannie, born 23 February 1907); Margaret (Madge, born 3 March 1910); Anthony (born 24 August 1912); Hugh; William; Eleanor and Henry (Harry). Harry Oliver's father served in the South African War and was severely wounded. His uncles served with Army and Navy during the First World War and his brother George served with the Royal Ulster Constabulary in Belfast.

Henry (Harry) Oliver and Audrey Lilian Heath from Glapwell, Derbyshire were married in the first quarter of 1943 in the Parish of Ault Hucknall (St. John the Baptist) and they a son named Kenneth whose birth was registered in the third quarter of 1944 in Chesterfield, Derbyshire. After Harry died, Lilian Oliver remarried and became Lilian Wright. Lilian died at the age of 78 and was buried in the same grave as Harry Oliver. Kenneth Oliver married Pauline Caufield and moved to Lincolnshire.

Harry Oliver joined the Oxford and Bucks Light Infantry two years before the outbreak of war and he volunteered for service with the Airborne Battalion. He became an instructor and was severely injured as a result of a parachute jump. After a period in hospital he was discharged from the Army with a disability pension and underwent a series of operations, the last of which was in December 1945. Corporal Harry Oliver was 26 years old when he died in Chesterfield Royal Hospital, Derbyshire on 7 February 1946 and he was survived by his wife and son. He was buried in Ault Hucknall (St. John the Baptist) Churchyard Extension, Derbyshire and there is an inscription on his CWGC headstone:

Sleep on my darling, we're always near
Loving wife Audrey and son Kenneth

O

Corporal Henry Oliver is commemorated on Newtownards and District War Memorial.

Oliver, John Chapman (Jack)
Rifleman
No. 7012565, 1ˢᵗ (Airborne) Battalion, Royal Ulster Rifles
Killed in action on Wednesday 7 June 1944 (aged 31)
Ranville War Cemetery, Calvados, France (Grave IVA O 8)

John Chapman (Jack) Oliver was born on 16 April 1913 and he was the only son of John and Sarah Jane Oliver (formerly Niblock, nee Orr) who lived at 70 Church Street, Bangor. John Oliver (born 20 May 1876) was a sailor and he and Sarah Niblock (nee Orr) were married on 30 August 1906 in Ballygilbert Presbyterian Church. Sarah Niblock's first husband, William Niblock, was also a sailor. Sarah Orr and William Niblock were married on 16 April 1888 in Shore Street Presbyterian Church, Donaghadee and they had five children – Mary Ann (born 4 January 1889); Eleanor Jane (born 8 September 1890, died of measles 16 May 1894 aged 3); William (born 12 October 1892); Eleanor Jane (born 4 December 1894) and Edward (born 8 January 1897). William Niblock Senior died of chronic cystitis on 20 November 1898 (aged 35) and Sarah Jane worked as a charwoman. She and her children lived in Railwayview Street, Bangor. (On 6 October 1913 Mary Ann Niblock married William Chapman Peters who survived the sinking of the *Titanic* on 15 April 1912 and also the sinking of the *Lusitania* on 7 May 1915).

7012565 RIFLEMAN
J. C. OLIVER
THE ROYAL ULSTER RIFLES
AIRBORNE
7TH JUNE 1944 AGE 38

John and Sarah Oliver had three children who were baptised in Hamilton Road Presbyterian Church Bangor – Margaret (born 16 May 1907); Anna Doreen (born 21 August 1909) and John Chapman (born 16 April 1913). John Chapman Oliver's father, who was known locally as *The Admiral*, had served in the Royal Navy for a period of 21 years that included the First World War and he held medals from both the Russian and Boxer campaigns. John Oliver died on 28 July 1938 (aged 61) and Sarah Oliver died on 2 October 1939 (aged 67).

KILLED IN ACTION.

OLIVER—June, 1944, killed in action, Rfm. John Chapman Oliver, R.U.R. (Airborne), only darling brother of Margaret Oliver.
"Divided hands will clasp again."
70 Church Street, Bangor.

OLIVER—June, 1944, killed in action, Rfm. John Chapman Oliver, R.U.R. (Airborne), only loved darling brother of Doreen M'Quillan.
"We loved him in life. Let us not forget him in death."
Very deeply regretted by his sorrowing Sister, Brother-in-law, and two Nephews.—4 Clandeboye Place, Bangor.

The marriage between John Chapman (Jack) Oliver and Frances Nest Lewis was registered in the fourth quarter of 1941 in Carmarthen, Carmarthenshire, Wales. During the Second World War, Rifleman Jack Oliver served with the 1st (Airborne) Battalion of the Royal Ulster Rifles attached to the Intelligence Section and he was killed in action at Longueval in France on 7 June 1944. Jack Oliver had served in the army for twelve years including four in India and one in China. Death notices referred to his sister Margaret, who was single and lived at 70 Church Street, Bangor, and to his sister Doreen McQuillan who lived at 4 Clandeboye Place, Bangor. Family tributes included the verses:

Divided hands will clasp again
We loved him in life; let us not forget him in death

Jack Oliver's wife Frances and their young daughter, Margaret Hannah Marie Oliver, lived in Abergwili, Carmarthenshire, South Wales. Margaret Hannah Marie Oliver was baptised in Bangor Abbey on 30 April 1943. The sons of James and Doreen McQuillan of 4 Clandeboye Place were also baptised in Bangor Abbey: John Chapman (Jackie) McQuillan on 1 June 1943 and Noel

McQuillan on 15 January 1947. Jackie McQuillan became a steeplejack and worked on the spires of both Bangor Parish Church of Ireland Church (St. Comgall's) and Bangor Abbey.

Rifleman John Chapman Oliver was 31 years of age when he died and he is commemorated on Bangor and District War Memorial and in Bangor Parish Church (St. Comgall's).

O'Neill, Robert John
Marine
No. CH/X 3059, HMS *Cornwall*, Royal Marines
Died as a result of enemy action on Sunday 5 April 1942 (aged 20)
Chatham Naval Memorial, Kent, England (Panel 65 2)

Robert John O'Neill was a son of John (worked as a labourer) and Georgina O'Neill (nee Patton) of Ballycopeland, Millisle who were married on 31 March 1920 in Ballyfrenis United Free Church of Scotland. Robert John O'Neill was a grandson of Robert and Mary Ann O'Neill; he was a brother of Georgina O'Neill and a nephew of John and Isabella Myles of Ballycopeland, Millisle.

Robert John O'Neill's mother Georgina died on 8 April 1927 (aged 27) and his father John married Sarah (Cissie) Morrow on 1 January 1930. John and Cissie O'Neill had at least eight children – Jean, David, Lily, Brian, Irene, Leslie, Robert and May.

> **KILLED IN ACTION.**
>
> O'NEILL—Killed in Action at Sea, Marine Robert John O'Neill, beloved grandson of Mary Ann O'Neill, and brother of Georgina O'Neill, Ballycopeland, Millisle.
>
> The news was sad, the blow was hard,
> God's will it shall be done,
> With a manly heart he did his part
> And a crown of victory won.
>
> Deeply regretted by his sorrowing Father, Sister and Grandmother; also his Uncles, Aunts and Cousins.
>
> O'NEILL—Killed in Action at Sea, Marine Robert John O'Neill.
>
> We little thought when he left home,
> That he would ne'er return,
> That he so soon in death would sleep,
> And leave us here to mourn.
>
> Deeply regretted by his sorrowing Uncle and Aunt; also his three little Cousins. John and Isabella Myles. Ballycopeland, Millisle.

During the Second World War Robert John O'Neill served aboard the heavy cruiser HMS *Cornwall*. This ship was built in the 1920s at the Devonport Dockyard in Plymouth for the Royal Navy.

In early April 1942 HMS *Cornwall* and her sister ship HMS *Dorsetshire* were detached from the Pacific fleet to escort the aircraft carrier HMS *Hermes* to Trincomalee in Ceylon (now Sri Lanka) for repairs. On 4 April the Japanese carrier fleet was spotted and the two cruisers left the harbour and, after a hurried refuelling at sea, set out shortly after midnight for Addu Atoll (the southernmost atoll of the Maldives). On 5 April 1942 the two cruisers were sighted about 200 miles southwest of Ceylon by a spotter plane sent up from the Imperial Japanese Navy cruiser *Tone*.

As part of the engagement known as the Easter Sunday Raid (Battle of Ceylon), a wave of dive bombers took off from the Japanese carriers to attack HMS *Cornwall* and HMS *Dorsetshire*. Both ships sank and Marine Robert John O'Neill was one of more than 400 men who died. Family members placed *Killed in Action* notices in the 9 May 1942 edition of the *Newtownards Chronicle* and the one from his father contained the verse:

> *The news was sad, the blow was hard,*
> *God's will it shall be done,*
> *With a manly heart he did his part*
> *And a crown of victory won*

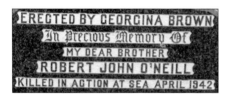

Marine Robert John O'Neill was 20 years old when he died and he is commemorated on Chatham Naval Memorial in Kent; on Donaghadee and District War Memorial; in Millisle Presbyterian Church and on the Brown family headstone in Ballyvester Cemetery, Donaghadee. His sister, Georgina Brown, died on 7 December 2007 (aged 80).

Orr, David
Able Seaman
No. D/SSX 26643, HMS *Farouk*, Royal Navy
Died as a result of enemy action on Saturday 13 June 1942 (aged 22)
Plymouth Naval Memorial, Devon, England (Panel 66 Column 1)

David Orr was the eldest son of John and Margaret Elizabeth Orr (nee Casement) who lived at 3 Central Street, Bangor. John Orr from Groomsport (son of Richard Orr) worked as a labourer and he and Margaret Elizabeth Casement (daughter of John Casement) from Inch were married on 18 September 1916 in Downpatrick Presbyterian Church. They had five children – Eleanor (Ellie), Louise (Louie), David, Hugh and Samuel (Sam). John Orr worked for Neill's of Bangor Coal Merchants and it was Neill's who built the houses in Central Street (originally called Vimy Ridge) in the 1920s and 1930s for their workers.

David Orr was born on 22 March 1920 and he was baptised on 11 April 1920 in Bangor Parish Church of Ireland Church (St. Comgall's). His sister Ellie married David Dowling and they lived at 38 Ashley Gardens, Bangor. David Orr was educated at Bangor Central Public Elementary School and afterwards he was employed for a time in the grocery shop owned by Mr Abraham Millsopp, Main Street, Bangor. David was a member of the 2nd Bangor Company of the Boys' Brigade and his principal hobby was boxing.

On Market Day, 28 September 1932, David Orr's brother Hugh (aged 6) died as a result of an accident. Hugh Orr along with other boys had collected horse-chestnuts and they were playing conkers at the corner of Ruby Street in Bangor when Hugh was knocked down by a farmer's car. Hugh lived for six hours after the accident before he died.

David Orr joined the Royal Navy in 1938 (aged 18). He served aboard HMS *Defiance* and later aboard the destroyer HMS *Jackal* which was torpedoed in May 1942. David was not on board at that time. He then volunteered for special duty on HMS *Farouk*. Requisitioned by the Admiralty in 1940, this two-masted schooner was converted in Alexandria to a Q-ship armed with two hidden guns. She was on route from Beirut in Lebanon to Iskenderum in Turkey when she was sunk off Ramkin Island, Lebanon by the German submarine *U-83*. This submarine never came close enough for fire to be returned and eight of the 18 crew members aboard HMS *Farouk* were killed.

The following verse was included in David Orr's death notice:

He has anchored his soul in that haven of rest
He will sail the wild seas no more
For the tempest may sweep o'er the wild
stormy deep
But in Jesus he is safe evermore

A tribute in the *Roll of Honour* column from his chum, Lexie Hayes, included the verse:

Time rolls on but memory lasts

Lexie Hayes lived in King Street, Bangor before he moved to Australia.

Able Seaman David Orr was 22 years old when he died and he is commemorated on Plymouth Naval Memorial in Devon; on Bangor and District War Memorial; in Bangor Parish Church (St. Comgall's) and on the family grave headstone in Bangor Cemetery. David's father John died on 12

July 1965 and his mother Margaret Elizabeth died on 13 December 1980.

Owen, Edward Francis
Fusilier
No. 4191721, 6th Battalion, Royal Welch Fusiliers
Died of illness on Wednesday 19 February 1941 (aged 24)
Bangor Cemetery, Co. Down (Section 5 X Grave 1A)

It is recorded in the CWGC Debt of Honour that Edward Francis Owen (aged 24) was a son of Robert and Kate Owen and in the Army Roll of Honour it is recorded that he was born in Caernarvonshire, Wales. Up to the time of writing it has not been possible to confirm conclusively any other family details.

- The birth of an Edward Owen was registered in the first quarter of 1915 in Holyhead, Anglesey; his mother's maiden name was Roberts but this birth is too early if the CWGC age is correct.
- The birth of an Edward F. Owen was registered in the first quarter of 1917 in Cardiff, Glamorganshire (his mother's maiden name was transcribed as Thompson).
- An Edward Francis Owen, son of Robert Owen (a boatswain) and Kate Owen (no maiden name recorded) of 17 Amherst Street was baptised on 14 June 1917 in Grangetown, Cardiff.
- The marriage of Robert Owen and Kate Thomas (surname as transcribed) was registered in the third quarter of 1915 in Holyhead, Anglesey.
- The marriage of Robert Owen and Catherine Owen (no maiden name recorded) was registered in the first quarter of 1916 in Anglesey.
- The marriage of Robert Owen and Kate Williams was registered in the first quarter of 1916 in Ffestiniog, Merionethshire.

According to the Army Roll of Honour, Edward Francis Owen joined the Royal Welch Fusiliers before the outbreak of the Second World War and in April 1940 he was posted to Northern Ireland. Fusilier Edward Francis Owen was 24 years old and unmarried when he died of pneumonia on 19 February 1941 in 25th General Hospital, Bangor. He was buried in Bangor Cemetery.

Partridge, William Radcliffe (Bill)
Fusilier
No. 4200499, 7th Battalion, Royal Welch Fusiliers
Killed in action on Monday 17 July 1944 (aged 27)
Bayeux Memorial, Calvados, France (Panel 14 Column 2)

William Radcliffe (Bill) Partridge was born on 20 March 1917 and he was a son of William Daniel and Louisa Alice Maud Partridge (nee Card) of 22 Bridgend Street, Ely, Cardiff, Glamorganshire in South Wales. William Daniel Partridge worked as a stoker and his marriage to Louisa Alice Maud Card was registered in the third quarter of 1914 in Cardiff. They had at least five children – William R. (born 1915); twins William Radcliffe and Thomas James (born 20 March 1917 and baptised in the Church of St. Saviour Roath, Cardiff); Albert George (born 30 March 1920) and Henry Charles (born 1 June 1926).

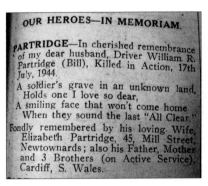

OUR HEROES—IN MEMORIAM.

PARTRIDGE—In cherished remembrance of my dear husband, Driver William R. Partridge (Bill), Killed in Action, 17th July, 1944.
A soldier's grave in an unknown land,
Holds one I love so dear,
A smiling face that won't come home
When they sound the last "All Clear."
Fondly remembered by his loving Wife, Elizabeth Partridge, 45, Mill Street, Newtownards; also his Father, Mother and 3 Brothers (on Active Service), Cardiff, S. Wales.

William Radcliffe (Bill) Partridge enlisted in 1940 and it was while the Royal Welch Fusiliers were stationed in the Ards area that he met Elizabeth McCauley of 45 Mill Street, Newtownards. They were married in October 1941. Three of Bill's brothers were also on active service during the Second World War. Fusilier William Radcliffe Partridge was 27 years old when he was killed in action in France on 17 July 1944, during the Allied advance after the Normandy Landings in June 1944.

Fusilier William Radcliffe Partridge is commemorated on the Bayeux Memorial in France.

Patterson, William Robert
Officer of the Most Excellent Order of the British Empire (OBE)
Distinguished Service Cross
Lieutenant Commander
HMS *Jersey*, Royal Navy
Lost at sea as a result of enemy action on Friday 2 May 1941 (aged 31)
Chatham Naval Memorial, Kent, England (41 1)

Presumed Lost at Sea

LT.-COMMANDER W. R. PATTERSON

Lieut.-Commander William R. Patterson, R.N., who was awarded the O.B.E. in January, 1940, for "undaunted courage, steadfastness, coolness and resource in saving ships and life at sea in the face of peril and adversity," is presumed lost at sea through enemy action. He was reported missing last June. Lieut.-Commander Patterson was the elder son of Mr. and Mrs. C. D. Patterson, Craigavad, and nephew of Captain W. R. Patterson, of H.M.S. King George V. His wife is the daughter of Mr. and Mrs. T. Gordon-Jones, Penylan, Cardiff.

William Robert Patterson was born on 30 January 1910 and he was the elder son of Charles Delamere Patterson and Sarah Haidee Patterson (nee Kennedy) of 124 Eglantine Avenue, Belfast and later *Gulladuff*, Craigavad, Co. Down. They were married on 20 April 1909 in Fitzroy Avenue Presbyterian Church, Belfast and they had at least two children – William Robert (born 30 January 1910) and Charles Delamere (born 1 July 1913; died 23 August 1967).

William Robert Patterson's father and his uncle John Fleming Patterson were directors of the Northern Linen Company (Belfast) Ltd., 27 Wellington Place. Another of his uncles was Captain William Robert Patterson of HMS *King George V*. Captain Patterson was made a Companion of the Order of the Bath in recognition of his part in operations which ended with the sinking of the German battleship *Bismarck* in the North Atlantic on 27 May 1941. Another of his uncles was Vice-Admiral Sir Wilfred Patterson who unveiled the memorial doors in Groomsport Parish Church on 7 November 1948.

William Robert Patterson's paternal grandfather was William Robert Patterson, a linen merchant with homes in Belfast and Bangor. He died on 29 April 1900 at 2 Edenville, Bangor (aged 57) and was buried in Belfast City Cemetery (Grave E1 469). His paternal grandmother was Elizabeth Mary Patterson and she lived in *Dunallen*, Windsor Avenue, Belfast. They had at least twelve children including William Robert, Margaret, John Fleming, Charles Delamere, Grace, Victor, Matthew, Kathleen and Wilfred Rupert. Elizabeth Mary Patterson died on 3 November 1941 (aged 93) at *Newgrove*, Groomsport Road, Bangor. She was buried in Belfast City Cemetery (Grave E1 469).

William Robert Patterson was educated at Inchmarlo and the Royal Belfast Academical Institution (RBAI) from 1921 until 1922. In 1940 William Robert Patterson married Elizabeth Jane Gordon-Jones of Penylan, Cardiff. Their marriage was registered in the second quarter of 1940 in Cardiff, Glamorganshire.

During the Second World War William Robert Patterson served with the Royal Navy aboard HMS *Jersey*. HMS *Jersey* was a J-class destroyer built by

P

J.S. White and Company (Cowes) and commissioned in April 1939. During the night of 6/7 December 1939 HMS *Jersey* and HMS *Juno* were attacked by the German destroyers *Z-10* and *Z-12* off Cromer, Norfolk. HMS *Jersey* was hit by a torpedo fired from *Z-12* and this resulted in a large fire. For his 'undaunted courage, steadfastness, coolness and resource in saving ships and life at sea in the face of peril and adversity' during that incident William Robert Patterson (then Lieutenant) was awarded the OBE (Military Division). He was one of the officers on the bridge at 2.30 am when the torpedo struck. The fuel oil caught fire and all the ship's lights and pumps were put out of action. The magazine was in danger of exploding and several men were marooned in the after part of the ship. The flames were eventually extinguished and the ship brought safely to port. The damage took ten months to repair and HMS *Jersey* was back in action on 23 September 1940. On 2 May 1941 HMS *Jersey* struck a mine and sank off La Valetta, Malta. Lieutenant Commander William Robert Patterson was reported missing and later it was officially confirmed that he must be presumed lost at sea through enemy action.

P

Lieutenant Commander William Robert Patterson was 31 years old when he died and he is commemorated on Chatham Naval Memorial in Kent; on Groomsport and District War Memorial; in Groomsport Parish Church of Ireland Church; in Glencraig Parish Church of Ireland Church (as Patterson W.) and in RBAI. His father Charles died on 15 December 1951 (aged 55); his mother Haidee died on 28 July 1971 (aged 86) and they were buried in Belfast City Cemetery (Grave G1 189).

Patton, William
Sailor
SS *Biela* (Liverpool), Merchant Navy
Died as a result of enemy action on Saturday 14 February 1942 (aged 22)
Tower Hill Memorial, London, England (Panel 17)

William Patton was born in 1920 and he was the eldest son of William Patton (born 11 October 1894, worked as a butcher) and Mary Elizabeth Patton (nee McNeill, born 7 November 1896 in Killinkere, Co. Cavan). William Patton (born 1920) was a grandson of Thomas and Sophia Patton (nee Matier) who were married on 1 March 1893 in Second Newtownards Presbyterian Church and who lived in Donaghadee. William and Mary Elizabeth Patton lived at 5 Church Lane, Donaghadee and two of their children were baptised in First Donaghadee Presbyterian Church – David Matier (born 21 August 1921, baptised 1 September 1921) and Joseph (born 2 September 1923, baptised 3 September 1923).

William Patton's grandfather Thomas and his great-uncle William were farmers and both moved from Donaghadee to Dunedin in New Zealand. William's grandmother Sophia stayed behind in Donaghadee and she subsequently remarried. William Patton's parents moved to Dunedin on 1 September 1926. They sailed from Southampton aboard the SS *Honorata* along with their children David and Joseph. Their son William's name also appears on the original list of ship's intended passengers but there is a note at the end of the list indicating that William did not board and did not travel. Instead, William stayed behind in Donaghadee and he lived with James and Annie Emerson (nee Patton), his uncle and aunt who farmed on Copeland Island. James Emerson and Annie Patton were married on 26 September 1923 in Ballygilbert Presbyterian Church and they had a daughter called Winifred. After James Emerson died on 20 April 1944, Annie and Winifred Emerson moved to New Zealand.

P

After William Patton's parents moved to New Zealand in 1926 they had four more children – Albert Denis (born 24 May 1929); Thomas Arthur (born 16 November 1931, died 28 May 1996); Eileen May (born 28 October 1936, died 19 May 2006) and Patricia Mary (born 4 September 1939). William Patton Senior died on 26 February 1966 in Dunedin and Mary Elizabeth Patton (nee McNeill) died on 31 January 1992, also in Dunedin. Their son David Matier Patton died in a wharf accident on 18 June 1956 in Napier, New Zealand and their son Joseph died on 21 March 1977 in Dunedin.

During the Second World War William Patton served with the Merchant Navy aboard the SS *Biela*. The British steam merchant ship SS *War Mastiff* was built in 1918 by Leslie, Andrew and Company, Hebburn-on-Tyne, Newcastle, and was renamed SS *Biela* in 1919. She was owned by Lamport and Holt Ltd., Liverpool. She left Liverpool on 1 February 1942 on route

for Buenos Aires in Convoy ON-62. She had on board a general cargo and during the voyage she became separated from the convoy. The SS *Biela* was torpedoed and sunk by the German submarine *U-98* on 14 February 1942 about 400 miles southwest of Cape Race, Newfoundland. All 50 crew were lost. Nine months later, on 15

November 1942, *U-98* was sunk with the loss of all hands.

Sailor William Patton was 22 years old when he died and he is commemorated on the Tower Hill Memorial in London; on Donaghadee and District War Memorial; in Shore Street Presbyterian Church Donaghadee and on the Emerson family grave headstone in the Copeland Island Cemetery.

Paul, William Edward David
Second Lieutenant
No. 90305, 4ᵗʰ Battalion, Royal Welch Fusiliers
Accidentally drowned on Saturday 19 October 1940 (aged 24)
Brookwood Memorial, Surrey, England (Panel 11 Column 1)

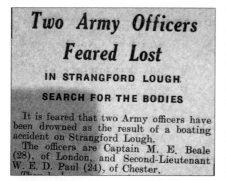

Two Army Officers Feared Lost

IN STRANGFORD LOUGH.

SEARCH FOR THE BODIES

It is feared that two Army officers have been drowned as the result of a boating accident on Strangford Lough.
The officers are Captain M. E. Beale (28), of London, and Second-Lieutenant W. E. D. Paul (24), of Chester.

William Edward David Paul's birth was registered in the third quarter of 1916 in Chester and he was a son of William and Ida Paul (nee Tyrer) of *Hoole House*, Chester. Their marriage was registered in the fourth quarter of 1912 in Chester. William Edward David Paul's father worked as a corn merchant in the Spillers Milling Group of Companies and his grandfather Edward Paul, also a grain merchant, was born in Ireland. His mother was born in 1880 in Knotty Ash, Liverpool and her father was a solicitor. William Edward David Paul's sister, Eileen Patience Paul, married Harold Cunningham and their marriage was registered in the second quarter of 1937 in West Cheshire. Eileen's subsequent marriage to Thomas P.D. Spens was registered in the third quarter of 1947 in Chelsea, London.

Hoole House in Chester was built by William Hamilton in 1760 and in the early 1800s it was the home of Lady Eliza Broughton. The garden was described as 'remarkable'. During the First World War the house was used as a seventy-bed hospital and in the 1930s it became the home of the Paul family. In 1953 the house was converted into flats that were later demolished to make way for homes for the elderly and so the original house and grounds have been lost within the suburban outskirts of Chester.

Second Lieutenant William Edward David Paul was Intelligence Officer in the 4ᵗʰ Battalion, Royal Welch Fusiliers when the Battalion was stationed in Northern Ireland (from December 1939 to November 1941 headquartered at Banbridge and then Keady). At the time of his death he was stationed in Killyleagh, Co. Down. On 19 October 1940, along with Captain **Maurice**

Evelyn Beale of Hammersmith, London, he borrowed a 14-foot centre-board sailing boat from Benjamin Bennett of Killyleagh to go sailing in Strangford Lough. A heavy sea was running as they left Killyleagh harbour and some hours later the boat, badly holed, was washed ashore at Holm Bay. There was no trace of either of the two bodies. Exactly five months later, on 19 March 1941, Captain Beale's body was found floating in the water and brought ashore at Portaferry. At the inquest the Coroner returned a verdict of 'found drowned' and Captain Beale was buried at 10.00 am on Sunday 23 March 1941 in Killyleagh Parish Church of Ireland Churchyard.

Second Lieutenant Paul's body was never found. He was 24 years old when he died and he is commemorated on the Brookwood Memorial in Surrey; on Hoole War Memorial in Cheshire and on the war memorial plaque in All Saint's Church, Hoole. Second Lieutenant William Edward David Paul's effects amounted to some £1,300 and probate was granted to his mother, Ida Paul.

P

Pedlow, Edith Doreen (Doreen)
Mentioned in Despatches
Sister
No. 206391, Queen Alexandra's Imperial Military Nursing Service
Died as a result of enemy action on Friday 20 February 1942 (aged 37)
Singapore Memorial, Singapore (Column 114)

THREE DAYS AND NIGHTS ON RAFT

NEWS has now been received of the death of Sister D. E. Pedlow, Q.A.I.M.N.S., daughter of the late Mrs. Pedlow, 16, Godfrey Avenue, Ballyholme, Bangor. When Sister Pedlow was being evacuated from Singapore the ship was bombed and sunk, but she managed to reach a small island. From this she was later taken off by another ship which was shortly afterwards shelled. Once again she was struggling in the water until she and another Sister managed to reach a small raft. To this they clung for three days and nights. The exposure however, was too severe; Sister Pedlow died before rescue came and her companion died after reaching a prisoner of-war camp in Sumatra.

Edith Doreen Pedlow was born on 29 December 1904 in County Armagh and she was the eldest child of William and Edith Mary Pedlow (nee Ross) who lived at 47 William Street, Lurgan. They were married on 8 January 1903 in Shankhill Parish Church of Ireland Church, Lurgan. William and Edith Mary Pedlow had four children – Edith Doreen (born 29 December 1904); Norah (born 1 November 1906); Kathleen (born 10 January 1908) and William. Doreen's father died in the 1930s and her widowed mother lived at 16

Godfrey Avenue, Bangor. During the Second World War Doreen Pedlow's sister Norah served as a nursing sister with the US Navy; her sister Kathleen Clarke (nee Pedlow) worked in the munitions industry in Great Britain (Kathleen's husband, Captain Raymond Clarke, was on active service) and her brother William served as a Lieutenant with the Royal Navy.

Edith Doreen Pedlow received her nursing training in the Royal Victoria Hospital, Belfast and she had war service at home, in France and in Singapore where she was attached to the Royal Military Hospital. How Doreen died was reported in the 1 December 1945 edition of the *County Down Spectator* – by which time her mother had died. When Sister Pedlow was being evacuated from Singapore aboard the SS *Kuala* this ship was bombed and sunk but she managed to reach Pompong Island, some 70 miles south of Singapore. She was taken off this island by the SS *Tanjong Pinang* which was shelled soon thereafter and once again Sister Pedlow found herself in the water. She and another Sister managed to reach a small raft to which they clung for three days and three nights. Sister Pedlow (aged 37) died of exposure before rescue came and her companion died after being taken to a Prisoner-of-War Camp in Sumatra. Sister **Ida May Nelson** from Helen's Bay who was also aboard the SS *Tanjong Pinang* died in the shelling.

P

Sister Edith Doreen Pedlow is commemorated on the Singapore Memorial; on Bangor and District War Memorial and in First Bangor Presbyterian Church.

Pendlebury, Michael Kenny (Michael)
Second Lieutenant
No. 331902, 1ˢᵗ Battalion, East Lancashire Regiment
Died on active service on Monday 16 April 1945 (aged 19)
Becklingen War Cemetery, Soltau, Niedersachsen, Germany (Grave 6 E 6)

Michael Kenny Pendlebury was born on 21 January 1926 in Wigan, Lancashire and he was a son of Brigadier James William Pendlebury DSO MC and Dorothy Pendlebury (nee Best) of Burley, Hampshire. Their marriage was registered in the third quarter of 1916 in Wigan and they had at least two children – Peter J. (born 1921) and Michael Kenny (born 1926). Michael Pendlebury attended Campbell College, Belfast from September 1939 until April 1940 when Brigadier James William Pendlebury (then Lieutenant Colonel) was in command at Palace Barracks, Holywood.

After leaving school Michael Kenny Pendlebury lived in Cornwall and during the Second World War he served with the East Lancashire Regiment. Second Lieutenant Michael Kenny Pendlebury was 19 years old when he died on 16 April 1945 during the Allied advance through Germany and he is commemorated in Campbell College.

Penfold, Alfred Harold (Alfred)
Warrant Officer Class II (Company Sergeant Major)
No. 6392875, 70th Battalion, Royal Inniskilling Fusiliers
Died as a result of enemy action on Wednesday 16 April 1941 (aged 36)
Glendermott Church of Ireland Churchyard and New Cemetery,
Co. Londonderry (Section H Grave 846B)

Alfred Harold Penfold was baptised on 9 June 1904 in Kensington, London and he was a son of Frank and Caroline (Carrie) Penfold of 6 Edinboro' Terrace. Frank Penfold worked as a carpenter and he and Carrie had at least ten children including Mary, Walter, Carrie, Alfred, George and Hannah. Alfred Penfold (aged 21) was a drummer in the 1st Brigade, Royal Sussex Regiment stationed in Ebrington Barracks, Londonderry when he and Annie Noble (aged 17) of 16 Alfred Street, Londonderry were married on 1 May 1924 in All Saints Clooney Church of Ireland Church, Londonderry. Annie was a daughter of Alexander and Annie Noble. Annie's father worked as a boatman and box maker and she had at least three brothers – Robert, John and Alexander.

Alfred and Annie Penfold lived in the Waterside, Londonderry and during the Second World War Alfred served with the 70th Battalion, Royal Inniskilling Fusiliers. He was one of 13 soldiers who died as a result of an air raid on Newtownards aerodrome during the night of 15/16 April 1941. Fusilier **Daniel Higgins** who also died that night was buried in Newtownards (Movilla) Cemetery and under his name in this Book of Honour there is a summary of all those people with North Down or Ards connections who died that night.

Warrant Officer Class II Alfred Penfold was 36 years old when he died and he was buried in Glendermott Church of Ireland Churchyard and New Cemetery in County Londonderry and there is an inscription on his CWGC headstone:

Peace perfect peace

Pentz, Leland Truesdale (Lee)
Purple Heart
Private
No. 10601871, 301st Infantry Regiment, 94th Infantry Division, US Army
Died of wounds on Friday 9 February 1945 (aged 19)
Luxembourg American Cemetery, Luxembourg City, Luxembourg
(Plot D Row 10 Grave 25)

PENTZ—February 9, 1945, in France (died of wounds), Leland Truesdale (Lee), dearly beloved elder son of Lorne Truesdale and Grace Burke Pentz, 45 Park Drive, Rathmines, Dublin; late of 4a Downshire Road, Bangor.—R.I.P.
(American and Canadian papers please copy).

Leland Truesdale (Lee) Pentz was born on 24 November 1925 in Massachusetts, USA and he was a son of Lorne Truesdale (in some records spelt Truesdell) and Dora Pentz (nee Bell). Lee's father Lorne was born on 8 October 1896 in Nova Scotia, Canada and during the First World War he served with the Canadian Field Artillery (No. 1261179) and then with the Canadian Air Force (a contingent of two squadrons formed in 1918 and stood down in January 1920; the Canadian Air Force was reformed in May 1920 with the prefix 'Royal' added in 1924). Lorne's home address in Nova Scotia in 1916 was 244 Lockman Street, Halifax and in 1918 it was 1076 Barrington Street, Halifax.

Lorne T. Pentz (son of Cecil Lorne Pentz, a railway baggage man, and Ophelia Pentz) married Dora Bell (born in England, daughter of Robert and Janet Bell) on 11 April 1919 in Halifax, Nova Scotia and they moved to Massachusetts, USA. They had two children – Leland Truesdale (Lee) and Roger Lorne and in 1928 the Pentz family was living at 8 Lancaster Street, Cambridge, Massachusetts. Lorne's wife, Dora Pentz (nee Bell), died in Cambridge, Massachusetts in 1929 and his younger son, Roger Lorne Pentz, died there in 1930.

In April 1930 Lorne T. Pentz (a salesman aged 33) travelled from Boston, USA to Liverpool aboard the SS *Antonia*. His proposed address in the UK was 136 Regent Street, London. The marriage of Lorne T. Pentz and Grace O'Malley Burke (born 1899 in Dublin, daughter of Edmund Burke who was a Professor of Elocution) was registered in the third quarter of 1930 in Hampstead, Middlesex. Their son, Warren J.B. Pentz was born in the third quarter of 1931 and his birth was registered in Brentford, Oxfordshire.

In August 1931 Lee Pentz (aged 5) travelled from Halifax, Nova Scotia to Liverpool aboard the SS *Nova Scotia*. The ship's manifest does not show whether Lee was accompanied on his journey or travelled alone; his proposed

P

address in the UK was 29 Park Road, Chiswick, London.

In the 1930s the Pentz family moved to Northern Ireland and they lived at *Dunraven*, 4a Downshire Road, Bangor (they rented this house from Marcus Patton). It was from there that Lee's stepmother ran the Burke School of Elocution and Dramatic Art. In August 1938 Lorne T. Pentz (aged 41) travelled on business from Belfast to Montreal, Canada aboard the SS *Montrose*. The Pentz family left Bangor in April 1941 immediately after the Blitz and moved to Dublin where they lived at 45 Park Drive, Rathmines.

Lee Pentz attended Bangor Grammar School from 1936 until 1941 and after he died the Headmaster said that he was, 'a bright and attractive lad, full of mischief and tricks, compact of fancies and ideas peculiar to himself. He excelled on the stage of the School Dramatic Society. He had the gift of artistic self-expression in the written and the spoken word'. He also said that Lee Pentz had 'inflexible determination and courage, moral and physical; the resolve to play a man's part in this war, cost what it might and in the teeth of uttermost pain and peril. Pentz won his way against odds and across frontiers into the armies of three nations'.

This was a reference to the fact that, after leaving school, Lee Pentz joined the British Army but was discharged when it was discovered that he was underage. Then he joined the Irish Army and this time he disclosed his proper age because the policy of neutrality would not have provided him with the opportunity he wanted for active service. He joined the US Army on 18 November 1944 'for the duration of the war or other emergency, plus six months, subject to the discretion of the President or otherwise according to law'. He purported to be a year older than he was. He was posted to the European Theatre of War and less than three months after enlisting he died of wounds sustained during the Allied advance.

Private Leland Truesdale (Lee) Pentz was 19 years old when he died on 9 February 1945 and he is commemorated on Bangor and District War Memorial and in Bangor Grammar School. Lee Pentz was buried in Luxembourg American Cemetery and the interment notice was sent to his father, Lorne T. Pentz, c/o Burrows Adding Machines Ltd., Rylands Building, 15 Tib Street, Manchester. Lorne T. Pentz's death was registered in the first quarter of 1972 in Westminster, London, England.

Perceval-Maxwell, Robert Patrick (Robin)
Captain
No. 226390, 10th (The Rangers) Battalion, King's Royal Rifle Corps
attached 9th Battalion, Royal Fusiliers (City of London Regiment)
Killed in action on Sunday 5 December 1943 (aged 20)
Cassino War Cemetery, Italy (Grave XIX J 7)

Robert Patrick (Robin) Perceval-Maxwell was born on 9 December 1922 and his birth was registered in Hitchin, Hertfordshire. He was the eldest son of Major John Robert (Jock) Perceval-Maxwell and Phoebe Laura (Phoebe) Perceval-Maxwell (nee Cherry) of Finnebrogue, Downpatrick. Their marriage was registered in the second quarter of 1921 in St. George, Hanover Square, London and they had six children – Robert Patrick (born 9 December 1922); Gavin Richard (born 1924); Andrew John (born 8 February 1927); Peter (born 1928, died in infancy); Selina Imogen Elizabeth Lorraine (born December 1930) and Michael (born September 1933). Major Jock Perceval-Maxwell was a member of the Senate of Northern Ireland from 1935 until 1945, he was Member of Parliament for Ards from 1945 until 1949 and he held the office of Deputy Lieutenant (DL) for County Down.

Two of Robin Perceval-Maxwell's relatives were killed in action during the First World War. Lieutenant Richard Nigel (Nigel) Perceval-Maxwell (born 1896) was 21 years old when he died on 30 March 1918. A son of Stephen and Harriet Mabel Perceval-Maxwell (nee Richardson) of *Ballydugan House*, Downpatrick, he served with the 16th (The Queen's) Lancers. Lieutenant Nigel Perceval-Maxwell was buried in Moreuil Communal Cemetery Allied Extension, Somme, France. Lieutenant Richard H. (Dick) Perceval-Maxwell was 20 when he died on 23 July 1918. A son of Lieutenant Colonel Robert David and Mrs Perceval-Maxwell of Finnebrogue, Downpatrick, he served with the 3rd Battalion *attached* 10th Battalion Cameronians (Scottish Rifles). Lieutenant Dick Perceval-Maxwell was buried in Buzancy Military Cemetery, Aisne, France.

Robin Perceval-Maxwell was educated at Eton College and when he left in 1940 he was commissioned into the King's Royal Rifle Corps. He was killed in action on 5 December 1943 at Mount Camino during the Allied advance in Italy. It was reported in the 15 January 1944 edition of the *County Down Spectator* that a memorial service for Captain Robert Patrick Perceval-Maxwell had been held on 12 January 1944 in Inch Parish Church of Ireland Church. There is an inscription on his memorial plaque in the Church:

Be thou faithful unto death and I will give you a crown of life

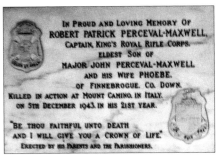

In PROUD AND LOVING MEMORY OF
ROBERT PATRICK PERCEVAL-MAXWELL,
CAPTAIN, KING'S ROYAL RIFLE CORPS.
ELDEST SON OF
MAJOR JOHN PERCEVAL-MAXWELL
AND HIS WIFE PHOEBE.
OF FINNEBROGUE. CO. DOWN.
KILLED IN ACTION AT MOUNT CAMINO, IN ITALY.
ON 5TH DECEMBER 1943, IN HIS 21ST YEAR.

"BE THOU FAITHFUL UNTO DEATH
AND I WILL GIVE YOU A CROWN OF LIFE".
ERECTED BY HIS PARENTS AND THE PARISHIONERS.

Captain Robert Patrick (Robin) Perceval-Maxwell was 20 years old when he died and he is commemorated on Groomsport and District War Memorial (the site for this memorial was donated by Miss Maxwell of Groomsport House and Colonel Robert David Perceval-Maxwell of Finnebrogue, Downpatrick); in Groomsport Parish Church of Ireland Church; in Inch Parish Church of Ireland Church and in Eton College.

Perrott, Robert Dermot Barnes
Distinguished Service Order
Officer of the Most Excellent Order of the British Empire (OBE)
Military Cross
Brigadier
No. 10220, Royal Engineers *attached* X Corps HQ
Died in service on Monday 29 June 1942 (aged 46)
El Alamein War Cemetery, Egypt (Grave XXIII C 24)

P

PERROTT
GABRIELLE FRANCES
DIED 19TH MAY 1984 AGED 88
WIFE OF
BRIGADIER ROBERT DERMOT PERROTT
KILLED EL ALAMEIN 1942
AND BELOVED MOTHER
OF
BILL, HELEN AND MICHAEL

Brigadier Robert Dermot Barnes Perrott is commemorated on the family grave headstone in Redburn Cemetery, Holywood. He was born on 13 January 1896 in Dublin and he was the elder son of William George Perrott (born in Cork) and Margaret Alexandra Perrott (nee McCowen) who was born in Tralee, Co. Kerry. William George Perrott was a civil engineer and he and Margaret Alexandra McCowan were married in 1892 in Tralee. They had two children – Robert Dermot Barnes (born 1896) and Richard Oswald Barnes (born 1898). On the war memorial plaque in St. Philip and St. James Church of Ireland Church, Blackrock, Dublin it is recorded that father and both sons served during the First World War. Margaret Alexandra Perrott died in 1948 and William George Perrott died in 1950.

During the First World War Robert Dermot Barnes Perrott served with the Royal Engineers in France, Belgium and Italy. In 1915 he was a Second Lieutenant; in 1916 he was a Lieutenant and was wounded three times. He was *Mentioned in Despatches* and awarded the Military Cross for gallantry. He was promoted to the rank of Captain in 1918, Major in 1930, Lieutenant Colonel in 1938, Colonel in 1941 and Brigadier in 1941. Between the two world wars he served in Afghanistan, the Northwest Frontier, Waziristan and Palestine. In 1937 he was awarded the OBE and in 1940 he was awarded the DSO. During the Second World War he served with the Royal Engineers.

Robert Dermot Barnes Perrott was the husband of Gabrielle Frances Perrott (nee Webb) who was born in Dublin and they lived at 6 West Avenue, Worthing, West Sussex. They were married on 6 October 1922 in St. Thomas's Cathedral, Bombay, India and they had three children – William (born 1926); Helen (born 1928) and Michael (born 1933). The family address at the time of Brigadier Perrott's death on 29 June 1942 was *The Anchorage*, Cado Hill, Gillingham, Kent. He was 46 years old when he died, his effects amounted to some £7,963 and probate was granted to Lloyds Bank Ltd.

His brother, Richard Oswald Barnes Perrott, also served during the Second World War and in March 1955 it was reported in the press that 57 year-old Retired British Army Colonel Richard Oswald Barnes Perrott, who had been kidnapped on 6 February, had been released on 3 March after friends paid a ransom of 25,000 kyats to the Burmese bandits who had snatched him while he was duck shooting some 42 miles north of Rangoon.

P

Brigadier Robert Dermot Barnes Perrott's wife Gabrielle Frances died on 16 May 1984 (aged 88). She was buried in Redburn Cemetery, Holywood and Brigadier Robert Dermot Barnes Perrott is commemorated on the headstone. There is an inscription on his CWGC headstone in El Alamein War Cemetery:

Asleep in Jesus

Petts, Ritson Finlay (Ritson)
Leading Aircraftman
No. 524461, 100 Squadron, Royal Air Force
Killed on active service on Wednesday 27 September 1939 (aged 25)
Singapore Memorial, Singapore (Column 410)

Ritson Finlay Petts's birth was registered in the fourth quarter of 1914 in Newtownards and he was the youngest son of John and Annie Petts (nee Finlay) of Castle Buildings, Comber. Their marriage was registered in the second quarter of 1895 in Darlington, Co. Durham. John Petts worked as a groom and huntsman with foxhounds and before moving to Comber the Petts family lived at Hurworth Kennels, Hurworth-on-Tees, Darlington. John and Annie Petts had at least 13 children – Alfred William; Alice Finlay; Mary Winnifred; John Edward; Ruth; Idina; Gerard; Neil Finlay; Jessie Finlay; Freda Finlay; Jack; Neville and Ritson Finlay. Ritson Petts joined the Royal Air Force in 1935 and during the Second World War he served with 100 Squadron. At the outbreak of war 100 Squadron was based in Singapore and the air crews were flying Vickers Vildebeest biplanes. Initially three planes from 100 Squadron were deployed to Alor Setar (Alor Star) in Malaysia.

LDG. AIRCRAFTMAN PETTS R.F. Leading Aircraftman Ritson Finlay Petts was 25 years old when he died on 27 September 1939. His aircraft came under attack and crashed into the sea and a survivor of the crash told how he and Ritson Petts had swum for hours together until large waves separated them and the survivor was washed ashore. The name of the survivor was not recorded. Leading Aircraftman Ritson Finlay Petts's body was not recovered and he is commemorated on the Singapore Memorial; on Comber and District War Memorial and in the annals of Comber Non Subscribing Presbyterian Church (there is no Second World War Memorial Plaque in that church).

P

Ritson's father John died on 9 September 1947 (aged 76) and on Friday 27 June 1952, at the opening of Comber's new Garden of Remembrance, John's widow Annie laid a wreath in memory of her husband and son:

In loving memory of my dear son Ritson, RAF, killed in action Singapore. Also in loving memory of my dear husband, died 9 September 1947, result of war service

Annie Petts died on 22 February 1968.

Phillips, Peter Charles Hunter
Sergeant (Air Gunner)
No. 1312411, Royal Air Force Volunteer Reserve
Killed in an aircraft accident on Thursday 9 July 1942 (aged 21)
Newtownards (Movilla) Cemetery, Co. Down
(Section 28 Prot Plot Grave 82)

Peter Charles Hunter Phillips was a son of Hunter and Elsie Phillips of Claremount Street, Finbarrs Road, Fowey, Cornwall. Hunter Phillips was a banker and they had three children – John David Hunter, Neil Seymour Hunter and Peter Charles Hunter. In the 1920s the Phillips family spent

some time in India.

Sergeant (Air Gunner) Peter Charles Hunter Phillips was 21 years old when he was killed on 9 July 1942 during a training flight. His Boulton Paul Defiant night fighter aircraft (N3402) of 1480 Flight based at RAF Newtownards crashed to the ground to the east of Lough Mourne (the largest of the reservoirs in Woodburn Forest near Carrickfergus). Also killed was the Polish Pilot, Kapral **Henryk Komenda**. Both men were buried in Movilla Cemetery, Newtownards.

Peter Charles Hunter Phillips's effects amounted to some £1,987 and probate was granted to Colonel (retired) John Alfred Steele Phillips.

Phillips, William Ward
Lance Bombardier
No. 1535781, 7/4 Maritime Regiment, Royal Artillery
Killed in action at sea on Thursday 11 September 1941 (aged 33)
Plymouth Naval Memorial, Devon, England (Panel 62 Column 2)

P

William Ward Phillips was born on 28 August 1908 and he was a son of William and Josephine Hamilton S. Phillips (nee Ward) of *Mountpleasant*, Victoria Road, Holywood. Before that the Phillips family lived in Belfast at 105 North Road and also at *Tremona*, 27 Knockdene Park. William Phillips Senior was a linen salesman and he and Josephine Ward were married on 11 April 1906 in St. Mary Magdalene Church of Ireland Church, Belfast. They had at least five children – Josephine (born 2 February 1907); William Ward (born 28 August 1908); Noel (born 25 December 1909); Maurice (born 31 July 1911) and John (14 December 1912).

William Ward Phillips attended Campbell College, Belfast from January 1918 until April 1921 and then the King's Hospital Church of Ireland School in Palmerstown, Dublin. His brother Noel also attended Campbell College before going to the Masonic Boy's School in Dublin.

After leaving school William Ward Phillips worked as an apprentice with F. Kirkpatrick and Company (Wholesale Tea Merchants), 27 Oxford Street, Belfast and then as an agent in Belfast with the Sun Life Assurance Company of Canada at which time he lived at 1 Spokane Villas, Knock Road, Belfast.

During the Second World War, William Ward Phillips served with the 7/4

Maritime Regiment, Royal Artillery and he was 33 years old when he was killed in action at sea on Thursday 11 September 1941. There is evidence that he was one of ten RA gunners who were killed while serving aboard four merchant ships (SS *Berury*, SS *Empire Crossbill*, SS *Gypsum Queen* and SS *Stonepool*) that were sunk by German U-boats while on route from Sydney, Nova Scotia to Liverpool in Convoy SC-42. His effects amounted to some £930 and probate was granted to his widowed mother. (Coincidentally, an unrelated family who had lived for a time at *Tremona* lost a son during the First World War. Second Lieutenant Thomas Brignall Elliott who was a son of Thomas and Annie Elliott and who served with the 10th Battalion, Royal Irish Rifles was killed in action on 1 July 1916, the first day of the Battle of the Somme). Lance Bombardier Phillips is commemorated in Campbell College.

Pinkerton, William James Neely
Second Lieutenant
No. SR/598490V, General Service Corps, South African Forces *seconded to* **1st Battalion King's Royal Rifle Corps**
Died of wounds on Wednesday 13 September 1944 (aged 34)
Gradara War Cemetery, Italy (Grave II F 73)

P

Bangor Family Bereaved.— Lieut. Wm. James Neely Pinkerton, e'der son of Mr. W. Pinkerton, J.P., and Mrs. Pinkerton, Thomas Street, Armagh, has died from wounds. In 1939 he took up an appointment under the Southern Rhodesian Government, and in 1940 joined the South African Army. He was married in 1938 to Miss Renee M'Crea, daughter of Mr. and Mrs. M'Crea, Bangor. The Rev. R. H. Pinkerton, Trinity Presbyterian Church, Omagh, is a younger brother.

Second Lieutenant William James Neely Pinkerton's death was reported in the 30 September 1944 edition of the *County Down Spectator* under the headline *Bangor Family Bereaved*.

William James Neely Pinkerton was born on 3 February 1910 and he was the elder son of William and Elizabeth Pinkerton (nee Menary) of Thomas Street, Armagh. William Pinkerton was a merchant and he and Elizabeth Menary were married on 14 April 1909 in Armaghbreague Parish Church of Ireland Church, Lisnadill, Armagh. They had at least three children – William James Neely (born 3 February 1910); Mary (born 23 January 1912) and Robert Harold (born 6 November 1913, later the Revd R. Harry Pinkerton of Trinity Presbyterian Church, Omagh).

William James Neely Pinkerton and Edith Irene (Renee) McCrea of Bangor were married on 7 September 1938 in Ballygilbert Presbyterian Church and in 1939 he took up an appointment with the Government of Southern Rhodesia. In 1940 he joined the South African Army and was seconded to the 1st Battalion, King's Royal Rifle Corps. Second Lieutenant William James

Neely Pinkerton was 34 years old when he died of wounds on 13 September 1944 during the Allied advance northwards in Italy.

Podobinski, Stanislaw
Flying Officer (Poruczenik Pilot)
No. P1691, 303 (Kosciuszko) Polish Fighter Squadron, Royal Air Force
Killed in an aircraft accident on Tuesday 14 December 1943 (aged 25)
Jurby (St. Patrick) Churchyard, Isle of Man (Grave 370)

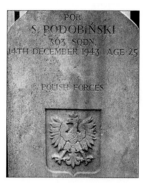

Flying Officer Stanislaw Podobinski was born on 7 July 1918 and he was based at RAF Ballyhalbert when he died. It was reported in the press that on 14 December 1943 Flying Officer Podobinski of 303 Polish Fighter Squadron was lost while returning to Ballyhalbert from Toome in County Antrim. He was on a training flight and off-course in adverse weather when his Supermarine Spitfire aircraft (EN856) crashed into a hillside two miles south of Snaefell Mountain in the Isle of Man. Flying Officer Podobinski was 25 years old when he died and he is commemorated on Panel 55 of the Polish War Memorial at Northolt, London.

Polley, Edward Victor (Victor)
Lieutenant
Royal Canadian Engineers
Killed in an accident on Wednesday 3 March 1943 (aged 22)
Belfast City Cemetery (Glenalina Extension Section J Grave 38)

Edward Victor Polley was born on 26 March 1920 and he was the only son of Robert Victor and Edith Polley (nee Leathem) of Belfast. They were married on 8 June 1918 in All Saints Church of Ireland Church, Belfast. In civilian life Robert Victor Polley was a bank official and he worked for a time in the town of Tipperary. During the First World War Robert Victor Polley served as a Lieutenant with the Royal Irish Fusiliers and he died on 17 February 1921 (aged 31). He was suffering from lung disease caused by gas poisoning. At that time the Polley family was living in University Street, Belfast and they worshipped in St. Jude's Parish Church of Ireland Church. Later Victor Polley and his mother moved to 136 Donaghadee Road, Bangor and they worshipped in Bangor Parish Church of Ireland Church (St. Comgall's).

Victor Polley attended Bangor Grammar School from September 1930 until June 1931 and then Methodist College, Belfast. At Bangor Grammar School

Victor Polley was remembered by the Headmaster as 'a fair haired and attractive boy in the Higher Preparatory'. In 1938 he enrolled in the Faculty of Applied Science at Queen's University Belfast to study engineering and he obtained a B.Sc. degree.

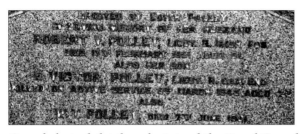

When the Second World War began, Victor Polley was keen to enlist but his mother tried every possible means of dissuading him. She took him to Canada but whilst there he joined the Royal Canadian Engineers and served as a motorcycle dispatch rider. After being posted to England he died on 3 March 1943 in an accident during military exercises. Eight days later he was buried in Belfast City Cemetery (Glenalina Extension) in the same grave as his father, Robert Victor Polley, and his grandfather, William Thomas Polley, who died on 7 June 1931 (aged 82).

Lieutenant Edward Victor Polley was 22 years old when he was killed and he is commemorated on Bangor and District War Memorial; in Bangor Parish Church (St. Comgall's); in Bangor Grammar School; in Methodist College Belfast; in Queen's University Belfast and on the family grave headstone in Belfast City Cemetery.

Polley, James (served as Polly, James)
Private First Class
No. 36715472, 339 Infantry Regiment, 85 Infantry Division, US Army
Died on active service on Friday 12 May 1944 (aged 40)
Body repatriated and interred on 3 December 1948 in Camp Butler National Cemetery, Springfield, Sangamon County, Illinois
(Plot C Grave 214)

James Polley was born on 3 November 1904 in Cloughey, Co. Down and he was a son of William James and Margaret (Maggie) Polley (nee Adair) who were married on 1 December 1885 in Ardkeen Parish Church of Ireland Church and who lived in the townland of Ardkeen. William James Polley (born 8 September 1862) was a mariner and Maggie Polley (born 17 October 1865) was a seamstress. They had at least eight children – Elizabeth (Lizzie, born 21 October 1886);

P

639

Jane (Jeannie, born 5 December 1888); William (born 19 February 1892); Francis (born 3 August 1894); Margaret (Maggie, born 20 December 1896); Thomas David (Tommie, born 9 January 1900); Catherine (born 21 April 1901) and James (born 3 November 1904). James Polley was four years old when his mother Maggie died on 27 July 1909; his sister Jeannie died on 2 November 1911 (the day before James's seventh birthday) and James was nine when his father William was drowned at sea on 10 February 1914. James Polley was brought up by his sister Lizzie. James's brother, Thomas David, moved to the United States of America; he entered the US at Detroit, Michigan on 3 November 1923 and became a naturalised US citizen on 19 February 1930. He and his wife Caroline lived at 7216 South Honore Street, Chicago, Illinois. Thomas David Polley died in May 1985.

> **Cloughey Soldier Killed.**—Mr. James Polley, youngest son of the late Mr. and Mrs. W. J. Polley, Cloughey, who has been killed in action while serving with the United States Army in Italy. Mr. Polley emigrated to America about 17 years ago, has three sisters and two brothers resident in Belfast. They are Mrs. Elizabeth Porter and Mrs. Margaret Lyons, Nendrum Gardens, Bloomfield; Mrs. Catherine M'Ilhagga, Grace Avenue; Mr. William Polley, 23, Jocelyn Gardens, and Mr. Frank Polley, Omeath Street. A third brother is living in Chicago.

P

James Polley was a carpenter and he followed his older brother to the United States. He lived in Chicago from 1927 until 1931 and then he returned to Cloughey for a short time. On 11 April 1932 he re-entered the US from Halifax, Nova Scotia at Detroit, Michigan. He resumed residence in Chicago with his brother Thomas.

Described as 5 feet 3 inches tall with a fair complexion, brown hair and brown eyes, James Polley enlisted on 7 December 1941. He served with 339 Infantry Regiment, 85 Infantry Division in the US Army and he was 40 years old when he died on 12 May 1944 in Carano, Italy during the Allied advance. After the war ended his body was repatriated to the US and on 3 December 1948 he was interred in Camp Butler National Cemetery, Springfield, Sangamon County, Illinois.

James Polley's death was reported in the 1 July 1944 edition of the *Newtownards Chronicle*. He was described as the youngest son of the late William James and Maggie Polley of Cloughey. He was survived by his brother Tommie Polley living in Chicago, USA and by three sisters and two brothers living in Belfast – Mrs Elizabeth Porter of 27 Glenmore Street; Mrs Margaret Lyons of Nendrum Gardens, Bloomfield; Mrs Catherine McIlhagga of Grace Avenue; William Polley of 23 Jocelyn Gardens and Frank Polley of Omeath Street. Private James Polley was 40 years old when he died and he is commemorated on the family grave headstone in Ardkeen Parish Church of Ireland Graveyard, Co. Down

Pollock, William
Guardsman
No. 2718328, 1st Battalion, Irish Guards
Killed on active service on Tuesday 8 February 1944 (aged 26)
Cassino Memorial, Italy (Panel 4)

 There was a report in the 25 November 1944 edition of the *County Down Spectator* that Guardsman Robert Pollock from Ballyrickard, Comber had been severely wounded and had had to have a leg amputated. He had been serving in Italy with the Irish Guards. The report stated that his brother, Guardsman William Pollock, who also served with the Irish Guards, had been posted as missing since February 1944. There is evidence to suggest that Robert's brother William's service number was 2718328. William Pollock's birth was registered in the first quarter of 1918 in Newtownards; he joined the Army in the 1930s and he served with the Irish Guards prior to the outbreak of the Second World War. Guardsman William Pollock died during the Allied advance northwards through Italy and he is commemorated on the Cassino Memorial.

Potts, Edward
Distinguished Conduct Medal
Warrant Officer Class II (Company Sergeant Major)
No. 3384774, 1st Battalion, East Lancashire Regiment
Killed in action on Thursday 12 April 1945 (aged 30)
Becklingen War Cemetery, Niedersachsen, Germany (Grave 1 B 5)

Edward Potts's birth was registered in the second quarter of 1914 in Cockermouth, Cumberland and he was a son of Edward and Agnes Potts (nee Blair) of Parsonby, Aspatria, Allerdale, Cumberland. Their marriage was registered in the first quarter of 1901 in Penrith, Cumberland. Edward Potts Senior worked as a hewer in a coal mine and he and Agnes had at least six children – Maria, James, William, Jane, Robinson and Edward.

Edward Potts joined the East Lancashire Regiment before the outbreak of

the Second World War and he was the husband of Margaret Patricia Potts of Belfast. Edward and Margaret Patricia Potts had two sons, William and Edward. When Edward Potts died on 12 April 1945 his effects amounted to some £290 and probate was granted to his brother Robinson Potts. In early April 1945 the 1st Battalion, East Lancashire Regiment moved through the eastern border areas of Holland, dealing with enemy stragglers, and then on 12 April 1945 they were involved in a heavy engagement when crossing the River Aller. Company Sergeant Major Edward Potts DCM was 30 years old when he died and he is commemorated on the family grave headstone in Movilla Cemetery, Newtownards. Margaret Patricia Potts died on 13 April 1980.

Price, Hugh McKee
(served as Price, Hugh Blackwood; known as Hugh)
Sergeant
No. A/22283, Royal Canadian Army Service Corps
Murdered on Saturday 18 August 1945 (aged 45)
Windsor (Grove) Cemetery, Ontario, Canada (Section 14 Grave 13)

P

Hugh McKee Price was born on 16 December 1899 and he was baptised in First Comber Presbyterian Church. He was the third son of William James and Sarah Ann Price (nee McKee) who lived in *Ashview House*, Lisbarnett, Comber. William James Price was a farmer and he and Sarah Ann McKee were married on 28 April 1893 in Killinchy Presbyterian Church. They had at least nine children – John (born 27 March 1894); Samuel (born 2 September 1895); Mary Elizabeth (born 5 November 1896); Hugh McKee (born 16 December 1899); William James (born 7 August 1902); Sarah Agnes Winifred (born 17 August 1903); Emily Flora (born 21 March 1906); Mabel Isabella (Born 23 November 1910) and Maggie Clawson (born 4 August 1912). During the First World War Hugh's eldest brother John served in 'B' Company, 13th Battalion, Royal Irish Rifles and was killed in action on 10 June 1916. Private John Price is commemorated on Page 523 in the Book of Honour *Remembering Their Sacrifice in the Great War – Ards* compiled by Barry Niblock.

Hugh McKee Price worked as a farm labourer and on 13 March 1926 (aged 26) he moved to Canada. He travelled aboard the Canadian Pacific Steamship *Montnairn* from Belfast to St. John, New Brunswick and from there he went to Winnipeg. In the 1930s he moved to Windsor, Ontario where he lived in Pitt Street West. There he described himself as a psychologist and, dressed in a turban and oriental clothes, he performed an astrology act in restaurants and bars. Using the stage name Professor Cosmo he used a crystal ball to tell fortunes and he also wrote an astrology column for a local newspaper.

During the Second World War Hugh McKee Price served as Hugh Blackwood Price, first with the Essex Scottish Regiment of the Canadian Army and then with the Royal Canadian Army Service Corps. The war in Europe ended and on 7 August 1945 Hugh Price returned to Windsor, Ontario where he rented a room on Church Street and took a job hefting barrels in a cold storage warehouse. On Friday 17 August 1945 he came home from work as usual and his landlady saw him going out again at 8.30 pm. In the early hours of 18 August 1945 his body was found on waste ground. He had been murdered. Sergeant Price died of multiple stab wounds and much was written at the time about his death. Since then at least two books have been written. In his book entitled *The Slasher Killings* Patrick Brode describes a series of murders in Windsor during July and August 1945 and one of the victims was Sergeant Hugh Blackwood Price. In his book entitled *Cold North Killers: Canadian Serial Murder* Lee Mellor addresses the same subject.

P

Sergeant Hugh Blackwood Price was buried on 21 August 1945 in Windsor Grove Cemetery and he is commemorated on the Canadian Virtual War Memorial (Internet) and on Page 556 in the Canadian Second World War Book of Remembrance. Sergeant Price was unmarried and in his service papers he cited as his next of kin his sister Mrs Elizabeth P. Donnan of Brownlow Street, Comber.

Price, Hugh Longueville (Hugh)
Sixth Engineer Officer
MV *Waimarama* (Southampton), Merchant Navy
Died as a result of enemy action on Thursday 13 August 1942 (aged 21)
Tower Hill Memorial, London, England (Panel 116)

Hugh Longueville (Hugh) Price was born in Dublin on 27 August 1920 and he was a son of Francis Longueville (Frank) Price AMIME (Associate Member of the Institute of Mechanical Engineers) and Winifred Olive Price (nee Bushell). They were married in 1919 in Forden, Montgomeryshire. Hugh was baptised on 22 September 1920 in Donnybrook Church of Ireland Church, Dublin. The Price family lived in Merrion Road, Dublin; then

Greenisland, Co. Antrim; then *Gorselands*, Downshire Road, Holywood and then 354 Kilmarnock Road, Newlands, Glasgow. Hugh's father died in 1972 in Claro, Yorkshire.

Hugh Price attended Royal Belfast Academical Institution (RBAI) from 1932 until 1938 and was captain of rowing in 1938. During the Second World War Hugh Price served with the Merchant Navy as Sixth Engineer Officer aboard the MV *Waimarama* and he died on 13 August 1942 when this ship sank as a result of an enemy air attack shortly after 8.00 am. The MV *Waimarama* was in a convoy of 14 merchant ships travelling from Scotland to Malta and she was carrying ammunition and octane spirit in cans. This cargo ship was built in 1938 by Harland and Wolff Ltd., (Belfast and Glasgow) and she was owned by the Shaw, Savill and Albion Company Ltd. The MV *Waimarama* sank in the Mediterranean Sea off Cape Bon, Tunisia after taking a direct hit and exploding in a blazing inferno. Nine of the 14 ships in the convoy were lost. Despite being showered with debris the nearby MV *Melbourne Star* was one of the five ships that reached Malta.

Sixth Engineer Officer Hugh Longueville Price was 21 years old when he died and he is commemorated on the Tower Hill Memorial in London and in RBAI. His effects in Northern Ireland amounted to some £81 and probate was granted to his father.

Primmer, Reginald John (Reggie)
Assistant Steward
SS *Kenbane Head* (Belfast), Merchant Navy
Died as a result of enemy action on Tuesday 5 November 1940 (aged 19)
Tower Hill Memorial, London, England (Panel 60)

Reginald John Primmer was born on 21 February 1921 in Portsmouth, Hampshire and he was a son of John Henry and Violet May Primmer (nee Tanner, born in County Armagh and, before she was married, worked as a Post Office clerk). They were married on 19 March 1919 in St. Patrick's Church of Ireland Church, Coleraine and at that time John Henry Primmer was stationed at HMS *Victory* in Portsmouth. John Henry Primmer served with the Royal Navy in the Coastguard Service and in 1932 the Primmer family moved to The Square, Portaferry with their two children, twins Reginald John and Dorothy Violet (aged 11).

Before the war Reginald John Primmer served as a commis waiter aboard the RMS *Queen Mary* and then the RMS *Franconia*. During the Second World War he served as an Assistant Steward in the Merchant Navy aboard the SS *Kenbane Head*. This ship was built in 1919 by Workman, Clark and Company, Belfast and was owned by G. Heyn and Sons Ltd., who operated the Ulster Steamship Company (Head Line).

> Very sincere sympathy will be extended to Mr. and Mrs. J. H. Primmer, of The Square, Portaferry, who have received notification that their only son, Reginald John Primmer, has been killed on board ship by enemy action. The young seaman, who was only 19 years of age, was, we understand, in the Mercantile Marine, and he had been at sea for three or four years, having served as a boy on the "Queen Mary." He was a most popular young man, and the news of his death has cast a gloom in Portaferry, where his parents are held in the highest respect. The twin sister of the deceased is serving with the A.T.S. in Holywood.

In November 1940 the SS *Kenbane Head* was sailing from Halifax in Nova Scotia to Great Britain in Convoy HX-84 with more than 30 other merchant vessels escorted by the armed merchant ship HMS *Jervis Bay*. The convoy was intercepted by the German battlecruiser *Admiral Scheer* which had been commissioned in November 1934. Hopelessly outgunned, HMS *Jervis Bay* engaged the enemy and was sunk in the process. However, this gave the convoy time to scatter. The Admiral Scheer was only able to sink six other ships, five from the convoy (*Beaverford, Fresno City, Kenbane Head, Maidan, Trewellard*) and one sailing independently (*Mopan*). The SS *Kenbane Head* went down off the coast of Greenland with the loss of 23 men. The tanker *San Demetrio* was set on fire by the *Admiral Scheer* and later salvaged. Other crew members from North Down/Ards who lost their lives aboard the SS *Kenbane Head* were **James McNeilly Belshaw** from Ballywalter, **George McClelland Leckey** from Holywood and **David John Pritchard** from Ballyhalbert. On 9 April 1945 the *Admiral Scheer* was capsized in Kiel harbour, Germany by RAF bombs dropped during a raid.

P

Assistant Steward Reginald John Primmer was 19 years old when he died on 5 November 1940 and he is commemorated on the Tower Hill Memorial in London; in Ballyphilip Parish Church of Ireland Church, Portaferry and on the family grave headstone in Ballyphilip Cemetery. Reggie's twin sister Dorothy was serving with the ATS in Holywood. His effects amounted to some £199 and probate was granted to his father. His father died on 17 December 1951 (aged 62) and his mother died on 26 January 1976.

Pritchard, David John (Dave)
Sailor
SS *Kenbane Head* (Belfast), Merchant Navy
Died as a result of enemy action on Tuesday 5 November 1940 (aged 21)
Tower Hill Memorial, London, England (Panel 60)

David John (Dave) Pritchard was born on 16 April 1919 in Ballyhalbert and

he was baptised on 25 April 1919 in Glastry Methodist Church. He was a son of David and Eliza Jane Pritchard (nee McMaster) who were married on 1 January 1908 in Glastry Methodist Church. David Pritchard Senior was from Church Street, Greyabbey and he worked as a labourer; Eliza Jane McMaster came from Ballyhalbert and they had four children – James (born 26 October 1908); Janet (born 26 June 1911); Lucinda and David John (Dave, born 16 April 1919). During the Second World War Dave Pritchard served as a sailor in the Merchant Navy aboard the SS *Kenbane Head*. This ship was built in 1919 by Workman, Clark and Company, Belfast and was owned by G. Heyn & Sons Ltd., who operated the Ulster Steamship Company (Head Line).

> Mrs. Eliza Jane Pritchard, Ballyhalbert, has received notification that her son, A.B. David Pritchard ("Dave") has been reported missing, probably lost, as a result of enemy action at sea. Aged 21 years, he had been afloat since the start of the war.

In November 1940 the SS *Kenbane Head* was sailing from Halifax in Nova Scotia to Great Britain in Convoy HX-84 with more than 30 other merchant vessels escorted by the armed merchant ship HMS *Jervis Bay*. The convoy was intercepted by the German battlecruiser *Admiral Scheer* which had been commissioned in November 1934. Hopelessly outgunned, HMS *Jervis Bay* engaged the enemy and was sunk in the process. However, this gave the convoy time to scatter and the Admiral Scheer was only able to sink six other ships, five from the convoy (*Beaverford*, *Fresno City*, *Kenbane Head*, *Maidan*, *Trewellard*) and one sailing independently (*Mopan*). The SS *Kenbane Head* sank off the coast of Greenland with the loss of 23 men. The tanker *San Demetrio* was set on fire by the *Admiral Scheer* and later salvaged. Other crew members from North Down/Ards who lost their lives aboard the SS *Kenbane Head* were **James McNeilly Belshaw** from Ballywalter, **George McClelland Leckey** from Holywood and **Reginald John Primmer** from Portaferry. On 9 April 1945 the *Admiral Scheer* was capsized in Kiel harbour, Germany by RAF bombs dropped during a raid.

Each year after Dave Pritchard died his family and friends placed *Roll of Honour* insertions in both the *County Down Spectator* and the *Newtownards Chronicle*. These included his mother, brother and sister of Shore Street, Ballyhalbert; his sister and brother-in-law Janet and Sam Burns of Ballyvester, Donaghadee and his comrade James Thompson of Shore

Street, Ballyhalbert. Some of the verses were:

At the river's crystal brink, Christ shall join each broken link
No morning dawns, no night returns, but we remember thee
He sleeps where all is peace

Sailor David John Pritchard was 21 years old when he died and he is commemorated on the Tower Hill Memorial in London; in Glastry Methodist Church and on the family grave headstone in Ballyhalbert Graveyard. His father David died on 10 November 1935 (aged 50), his mother Eliza Jane died on 20 January 1962 (aged 72) and his sister Janet died on 13 November 1992.

Proctor, Hilton David (Hilton)
Major
Royal Canadian Corps of Signals; First Canadian Parachute Battalion
Killed in an aircraft accident on Monday 7 September 1942 (aged 31)
Ottawa (Pinecrest) Cemetery, Ottawa, Canada (Plot 552 Section D Grave 1)

> **Comber Born Paratroop Chief Killed.—**
> Major Hilton D. Proctor, leader of a Canadian contingent of paratroops, was killed in a jump at Fort Benning, Georgia, when his parachute was struck by a transport plane. Major Proctor, who was 31, was to have returned shortly to Manitoba to direct the training of the first Canadian parachute battalion. Born in Comber, County Down, he leaves a widow and son in their Ottawa home. He was a son of the late Mr. Hugh David Todd, wine and spirit merchant, of Belfast Road, Comber. He changed his name after the marriage of his mother to Mr. Jack Proctor, son of the late Mr. John and Mrs. Proctor, of Killinchy Street, Comber.

Major Hilton David Proctor's death was reported in the 12 September 1942 edition of the *County Down Spectator* under the headline *Comber Born Paratroop Chief Killed.* His appointment as leader of the First Canadian Parachute Battalion had been reported in the 15 August 1942 edition of the same newspaper.

Born in Comber on 20 August 1911, Hilton David Proctor was baptised Hamilton David Todd and he was a son of Hugh David Dugan McCleery Todd who was a wine and spirit merchant with premises on the Belfast Road in Comber. Hugh David Dugan McCleery Todd and Eleanor Whiteside Coulter (daughter of Hamilton Coulter, a cattle dealer) were married on 30 September 1908 in Dunmurry Non-Subscribing Presbyterian Church. They had at least three children – Rachel (born 30 March 1909); Hamilton David (born 20 August 1911) and Eleanor (born 21 June 1914). Hugh David Dugan McCleery Todd was 34 years old when he died on 9 February 1916.

After his father died, Hamilton David Todd's mother married John (Jack) Proctor who was the third son of John and Barbara Proctor of Killinchy Street, Comber. Hamilton David Todd's stepfather, Jack Proctor, was a brother of James Proctor who was killed in action on 16 August 1917. Sergeant

James Proctor served in 'B' Company, 13th Battalion, Royal Irish Rifles and he is commemorated on Page 526 in the Book of Honour *Remembering Their Sacrifice in the Great War – Ards* compiled by Barry Niblock.

After moving to Canada, Hamilton David Todd officially changed his name to Hilton David Proctor and in 1935 he was chosen as a member of the Ottawa team to take part in the shooting competitions at Bisley in Surrey. He worked for the Bell Telephone Company in Montreal where he helped transfer the city's telephone system from the old manual exchange to the new dial system. He enlisted in Montreal and served with the Royal Canadian Corps of Signals.

After his appointment as leader of the First Canadian Parachute Battalion, Major Proctor went to Fort Benning, Georgia in the USA for training and it was there that he was killed. It was reported that he died during a parachute jump when a transport plane sheared into his parachute. Major Proctor had been due to return to Shilo, Manitoba to direct the training of the Canadian Parachute Battalion.

Major Hilton David Proctor was the husband of Dorothy E. Proctor (nee Hutton) who lived with their three-year-old child in Ottawa. Major Proctor is commemorated on the Canadian Virtual War Memorial (Internet) and on Page 108 in the Canadian Second World War Book of Remembrance.

Prosser, David Francis
Fusilier
No. 4193168, Royal Welch Fusiliers
Died of illness on Monday 3 July 1944 (aged 27)
Newtownards (Movilla) Cemetery, Co. Down (Section 29 Grave 86)

PROSSOR—Monday, 3rd July, 1944, at Ards District Hospital, David Francis Prossor, loved husband of Jeannie Prossor. Interred in Movilla Cemetery.
Deeply regretted by his sorrowing Wife and two Children; also Father and Mother, Brothers and Sister, and Father-in-law and Mother-in-law, and Brother and Sister-in-law.

The surname is spelt Prossor in the 8 July edition of the *County Down Spectator*. David Francis Prosser's birth was registered in the second quarter of 1917 in Dolgelly, Merionethshire and he was a son of William Austin Prosser and Annie

Prosser (nee Jones) who was born in Newbridge, Monmouthshire. William (in some records Walter) Austin Prosser worked as a coal miner and his marriage to Annie Jones was registered in the third quarter of 1911 in Pontypridd, Glamorganshire.

David Francis Prosser was the husband of Jeannie Prosser of 55 East Street, Newtownards and they had two children. During the Second World War Fusilier Prosser served with the Royal Welch Fusiliers and he died of a carcinoma in Ards District Hospital on 3 July 1944 after a long illness. There is an inscription on his CWGC headstone:

Worthy of everlasting remembrance

His wife Jeannie died on 30 August 2001 (aged 82).

Pudelko, Josef Antoni
Sergeant (Kapral Pilot)
No. P781015, No. 6 Anti-Aircraft Co-operation Unit (AACU)
Killed in an aircraft accident on Thursday 23 April 1942 (aged 23)
Belfast (Milltown) Roman Catholic Cemetery (Section A Row Lg Grave 38)

P

Jozef Antoni Pudelko was born on 13 December 1918 and during the Second World War he served with No. 6 Anti-Aircraft Co-operation Unit (AACU) and he was based for a time at RAF Newtownards. On 23 April 1942 he was the pilot of a Westland Lysander Mark III communications and target-towing aircraft (V9721) which crashed on take-off from RAF Belfast (now the George Best Belfast City Airport) on a training flight. Also killed that day was Sergeant (Wireless Operator/Air Gunner) **Norman Elcock*** (No. 1112747) aged 21 from Winsford, Cheshire. Norman was a son of Albert Edward and Phyllis Elcock and he was buried in Over Congregational Burial Ground, Cheshire.

Sergeant Jozef Antoni Pudelko was buried in Belfast (Milltown) Roman Catholic Cemetery and he is commemorated on Panel 57 of the Polish Air Force Memorial at Northolt, London.

Quillan, Alexander Louis (Alexander)
Sergeant
No. 359508, Royal Air Force
Died of illness on Friday 4 June 1943 (aged 44)
Holywood Cemetery, Co. Down (Grave 197)

Alexander Quillan was born on 14 January 1899 at 16 Roslea Drive, Glasgow and he was a son of James and Isabella Quillan (nee Todd). After his father James died on 22 August 1901, Alexander Quillan and his younger sister Mary were adopted by Peter and Emily Winn. Emily Winn was a sister of James Quillan's first wife, Roseann.

Alexander Quillan's paternal grandparents, Peter and Elizabeth (Betsy) Quillan (nee Lynch) were both born in County Monaghan and they were married in 1854 in Glasgow. Alexander Quillan's father James was born on 22 June 1855 and he worked as a barrel maker. James Quillan (aged 18) of 6 Low Green Street, Glasgow and Roseann Moore (aged 18, a housekeeper) of 10 Low Green Street, Glasgow were married on 23 April 1874 in St. Andrew's Roman Catholic Chapel, Great Clyde Street, Glasgow.

In 1881 the Quillan family was living at 65 East John Street, Glasgow – James and Roseann, (both of whom were born in Ireland), their three children Elizabeth (aged 3), James (aged 2) and Joseph (aged less than one year) together with Roseann's parents John and Mary Moore (nee Reid) and Roseann's unmarried sister Emily. Emily Moore of 756 Gallowgate, Glasgow worked as a domestic servant and, aged 19, she and Peter Winn, a shale miner aged 22 who was the son of Peter and Sarah Winn (nee Quillan) of 39 Mid Street, Mossend, West Calder were married on 28 July 1882 in St. Mary's Roman Catholic Chapel, Glasgow. Peter Winn Junior was born in County Monaghan and he was educated at Slatefield Roman Catholic Industrial School, St. John, Glasgow.

After Roseann Quillan died, James Quillan (a master cooper aged 42 living at 48 London Street, Glasgow) married Isabella Todd on 28 December 1897 in St. Alphonsus's Roman Catholic Chapel, Glasgow. Isabella Todd (an unmarried school teacher aged 28) was a daughter of basket-maker James Todd and Mary Ann Todd (nee Cameron) of 6 East Campbell Street, Glasgow.

In 1901 James and Isabella Quillan were living at 67 Whitevale Street,

Q

Glasgow with their four young children – Emily, Alexander, Mary and Dominick. James Quillan died of cardiac failure on 22 August 1901 and Peter and Emily Winn, who had no children of their own, adopted Alexander and Mary Quillan.

During the Second World War, Alexander Quillan served with the Royal Air Force and he attended No. 3 School of Technical Training at RAF College Cranwell. He and Louise Harold of Holywood were married on 27 December 1920 in a Belfast Roman Catholic Church. Alexander Quillan was 44 years old when he died of bowel cancer on 4 June 1943 in Westminster Military Hospital in London and he was buried on 9 June 1943 in Holywood Cemetery. His CWGC headstone (in the Stevenson family plot) bears the inscription:

Most merciful Jesus
Grant him eternal rest

Rae, William McKinley (Bill)
Chief Steward
SS *Glen Head* (Belfast), Merchant Navy
Died as a result of enemy action on Friday 6 June 1941 (aged 28)
Tower Hill Memorial, London, England (Panel 52)

Q
R

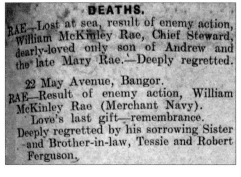

DEATHS.

RAE—Lost at sea, result of enemy action, William McKinley Rae, Chief Steward, dearly-loved only son of Andrew and the late Mary Rae.—Deeply regretted.

22 May Avenue, Bangor.

RAE—Result of enemy action, William McKinley Rae (Merchant Navy).
Love's last gift—remembrance.
Deeply regretted by his sorrowing Sister and Brother-in-law, Tessie and Robert Ferguson.

William McKinley Rae was born on 23 March 1913 in Belfast and he was a son of Andrew and Mary Rae (nee McKinley) who lived in Willowfield Street before they moved to 22 May Avenue, Bangor. Andrew Rae was a cabinet maker and he and Mary McKinley were married on 20 April 1908 in St. Anne's Church of Ireland Cathedral, Belfast. They had three children – Theresa (Tessie, born 31 May 1909); Robert (born 23 September 1911, died in infancy) and William McKinley (born 23 March 1913). Tessie Rae married Robert Ferguson and they too lived at 22 May Avenue, Bangor. Mary Rae died on 25 January 1933 (aged 43) and was buried in Bangor Cemetery.

William McKinley Rae went to sea in 1929 when he was 16 years old. During the Second World War he served with the Merchant Navy and he died on 6 June 1941 when the SS *Glen Head* was bombed some 100 miles southwest of Cape St. Vincent, Portugal. Built in Glasgow in 1909, the SS *Glen Head* was owned by the Headline Shipping Company. After being bombed, the ship sank within three minutes and 27 of the 36 crew members were lost. Boatswain **John Hawthorne** and Third Engineer **James Skillen** also died that day.

After William McKinley Rae died, his father, sister and brother-in-law placed death notices in the *County Down Spectator* and in subsequent years they placed *Roll of Honour* notices. Three such notices contained the texts:

> *Too good in life to be forgotten*
> *A loved one whose memory I cherish*
> *Love's last gift – remembrance*

Chief Steward William McKinley Rae was 28 years old when he died at sea on 6 June 1941 and his effects amounted to some £236. Probate was granted to his sister Theresa Ferguson. Chief Steward William McKinley Rae is commemorated on the Tower Hill Memorial in London and on Bangor and District War Memorial.

R
Ranganatha, Nagu
Sergeant
No. 1291581, 25 Squadron, Royal Air Force Volunteer Reserve
Killed in an aircraft accident on Wednesday 11 February 1942 (aged 20)
Runnymede Memorial, Surrey, England (Panel 92)

Nagu Ranganatha was a son of Colattur Ranganatha Rao Sahib and Manjula Ranganatha of 9 Limes Avenue, Golders Green, Middlesex. (*Rao Sahib* was a title of honour issued during the era of British rule in India to individuals who performed great service to the nation by way of 'visionary leadership'. The title was accompanied by a medal). In 1927 Colattur Ranganatha Rao Sahib held the position of Director of Industries and Commerce in Mysore, Southern India. Later he was based in London when he was appointed Trade Commissioner for Mysore. In that position he made frequent international trips to countries including Canada, USA, Japan and India (in December 1931 he travelled aboard the SS *Berengaria* from Southampton to India).

Colattur and Manjula Ranganatha had at least four children – Nagu, Rama, Semi and Tulali (in some records Tulasi). At times Manjula travelled with

Colattur (in July 1933 they travelled aboard the *Empress of Britain* from Southampton on their way to Japan via Canada and the USA). It was reported in the press that, on 23 February 1935 at the British Industries Fair held at Olympia in London, Tulasi Ranganatha (aged 10) was 'dressed in native Indian costume' when she served 'a steaming cup of coffee' to the British Prime Minister, Ramsay MacDonald.

During the Second World War, Nagu Ranganatha served with the Royal Air Force Volunteer Reserve. On 12 February 1942 Sergeant Nagu Ranganatha and Sergeant **Anthony Wilson Lavender** of 25 Squadron based at RAF Ballyhalbert were flying a Bristol Beaufighter aircraft (X7625) which failed to return from a night sector reconnaissance operation. Both crew members were declared missing, their bodies were never recovered and they are commemorated on the Runnymede Memorial in Surrey.

A little over a year after Nagu Ranganatha died his mother Manjula died (aged 43) and her death was registered in the second quarter of 1943. After the war ended Nagu's father continued to travel internationally on official business and sometimes Tulasi went with him (in December 1947 they travelled aboard the *Empress of Australia* from Liverpool to Bombay). Sometimes Colattur travelled alone (in July 1960 he travelled aboard RMS *Cilicia* from Liverpool to Bombay).

R

Rea, Charles Arthur (Charles)
Captain
No. 184755, 2nd Battalion, Royal Inniskilling Fusiliers
Died on active service on Thursday 4 November 1943 (aged 32)
Cassino War Cemetery, Italy (Grave VII J 14)

Charles Arthur Rea was born on 9 September 1911 in Belfast and he was a son of William Robert Rea and Alice Jane Rea (nee Cowan). There is evidence that in 1901 William Robert Rea (then aged 19) was living in Hilsen Barracks, Cosham in Hampshire where he was a Driver in the Royal Field Artillery. William Robert Rea and Alice Jane Cowan were married on 22 September 1908 in All Souls Non-Subscribing Presbyterian Church, Belfast and their daughter Eileen Gertrude was born at 90 Omeath Street, Belfast on 30 March 1909. At that time William Robert Rea was a Constable in the Royal Irish Constabulary. He was stationed at Mountpottinger RIC Station and the

Rea family was living at 21 Cherryville Street, Belfast when Charles Arthur was born on 9 September 1911.

The marriage of Captain Charles Arthur Rea and Mabel Winifred Wilson (born 5 October 1914) of Shepherd's Bush, London was registered in the first quarter of 1935 in Hammersmith, London. The birth of their son Brian W.D. Rea was registered in the first quarter of 1936, also in Hammersmith.

Charles Arthur Rea was a career soldier who served with the Irish Guards (Foot Guards) prior to the outbreak of the Second World War. During the war he served with the 2nd Battalion, Royal Inniskilling Fusiliers and he was promoted to the rank of Captain. Captain Charles Arthur Rea was 32 years old when he died on 4 November 1943 near Cassino in Italy during the Allied advance northwards and he is commemorated on Bangor and District War Memorial (as Rea C.A.) and in Hamilton Road Presbyterian Church, Bangor. Mabel Winifred Rea's death was registered in March 1994 in Hillingdon, London.

Rea, Edward Douglas
Mentioned in Despatches

R

Major
No. 64505, 14 Anti-Tank Regiment, Royal Artillery
Killed in action on Saturday 21 October 1944 (aged 29)
Cesena War Cemetery, Italy (Grave II E 9)

In the CWGC Debt of Honour it is recorded that Edward Douglas Rea was a son of Thomas Rea MA and Dora Rea of Bangor. In an October 1944 newspaper death notice it was recorded that Major Rea was the younger son of the late Thomas Rea MA and Dora Rea of 39 Myrtlefield Park, Belfast. Thomas Rea was born in County Tyrone, he worked as an Inspector of Intermediate Schools and his marriage to Dora Grace (born in County Carlow) was registered in the third quarter of 1910 in Rathdown, Dun Laoghaire. Thomas and Dora's first son, Henry Maxwell Rea, was born on 30 October 1911 and his birth was registered in Belfast.

Edward Douglas Rea's birth was registered in the second quarter of 1915 in Belfast and after he left school he became a career soldier. As a Gentleman Cadet he moved on 31 January 1935 from the Royal Military Academy Sandhurst to be a Second Lieutenant in the Royal Regiment of Artillery. During the Second World War he served with the Royal Artillery and was promoted to the rank of Major. Major Edward Douglas Rea was 29 years old when he was killed in action in Italy on 21 October 1944 during the Allied advance northwards, During the action he was Mentioned in Despatches and this award was gazetted posthumously in the 19 July 1945 edition of the London Gazette.

His effects amounted to some £971 and probate was granted to his widowed mother Dora. His elder brother, Henry Maxwell Rea, also served during the Second World War.

Reid, Donald Gordon (Don)
Fireman
SS *Empire Lytton* (Middlesbrough), Merchant Navy
Died as a result of enemy action on Saturday 9 January 1943 (aged 23)
Tower Hill Memorial, London (Panel 43)

Donald Gordon (Don) Reid was born in Colchester, Essex on 18 August 1919 and he was a son of William Reid (a butcher) and Margaret Reid (nee Welham) of 14 St. Mary's Road, Colchester. Their marriage was registered in 1913. They had a daughter named Constance whose birth was registered in the first quarter of 1914. In April 1920 the Reid family moved to London, Ontario in Canada (they sailed aboard the SS *Haverford*). After leaving school Don Reid served in the Canadian Army and then he moved to Bangor, Co. Down. During the Second World War he served with the Merchant Navy and his wife, Sadie Reid, lived at 65 Ballymaconnell Road, Bangor.

> **Merchant Navyman Lost at Sea.**—Mrs. Reid, 65, Ballymaconnell Road, Bangor, has been notified her husband, Fireman Donald Gordon Reid, Merchant Navy, has been lost at sea. Aged 23 years, Fireman Reid was a Canadian citizen belonging to London, Ontario, and his home had been at Bangor for the last two years. He served for some years in the Canadian Army and lately rejoined the Merchant Navy.

Don Reid served as a Fireman aboard the SS *Empire Lytton*, a British steam tanker built in 1942 by the Furness Shipbuilding Company Ltd., Middlesbrough for the Ministry of War Transport (MOWT). On 9 January 1943 the SS *Empire Lytton* was in Convoy TM-1 on route from Trinidad to Gibraltar (carrying a cargo of 12,500 tons of benzene) when she was hit by torpedoes fired from the German submarine *U-442*. The SS *Empire Lytton* sank in the North Atlantic to the west of the Canary Islands and around a quarter of the 48 men on board died. Apprentice **William Edward Trimble** who was serving aboard the MV *British Dominion* in the same convoy was killed on 10 January 1943. Of the nine tankers in Convoy TM-1, seven were sunk by a German Wolfpack – MV *Albert L Ellsworth*, MV *British Dominion*, MV *British Vigilance*, SS *Empire Lytton*,

MV *Minister Wedel*, MV *Norvik* and SS *Oltenia II*. Only MV *Cliona* and SS *Vanja* reached port safely.

Fireman Donald Gordon Reid was 23 years of age when he died and he is commemorated on the Tower Hill Memorial in London and in Bangor Parish Church of Ireland Church (St. Comgall's).

Reid, Francis Graham
Sub-Lieutenant (A)
HMS *Landrail*, Royal New Zealand Naval Volunteer Reserve
Killed in an aircraft accident on Sunday 12 March 1944 (aged 24)
New Zealand Naval Memorial, Devonport, Auckland (Panel 9)

Francis Graham Reid was a son of Robert Theodore and Kathleen Lena Reid of 8 Beresford Street, Bayswater, Auckland, New Zealand and he was unmarried. During the Second World War Sub-Lieutenant (A) Francis Graham Reid served with the Royal New Zealand Naval Volunteer Reserve at the Royal Naval Air Station Machrihanish (named HMS *Landrail* on 15 June 1941), which was located on the western side of the Kintyre peninsula in Scotland. Most of the operations from there focused on training.

On 12 March 1944 Sub-Lieutenant (A) Francis Graham Reid was the pilot of a Supermarine Seafire aircraft (LR846) based at RAF Ballyhalbert that crashed into the sea one mile east of Portavogie, following practice dog-fighting. Sub-Lieutenant (A) Francis Graham Reid was 24 years old when he was killed and his body was never recovered.

Sub-Lieutenant (A) Francis Graham Reid is commemorated on the New Zealand Naval Memorial in Devonport, Auckland; on the New Zealand National War Memorial in Wellington; on the New Zealand Cenotaph Database in Auckland War Memorial Museum; on Takapuna War Memorial and in Takapuna Grammar School.

Reid, Frederick John Bartlett
Flying Officer
No. 156648, 125 Squadron, Royal Air Force Volunteer Reserve
Killed in an aircraft accident on Friday 17 March 1944 (aged 23)
Runnymede Memorial, Surrey, England (Panel 243)

Frederick John Bartlett Reid was a son of Frederick Ellis Reid and Hilda K. Reid of Heart's Delight, Trinity Bay, Newfoundland and during the Second

World War he served with the Royal Air Force Volunteer Reserve.

On 17 March 1944 two de Havilland Mosquito aircraft (HK 261 and HK 326) of No. 125 Squadron based at RAF Ballyhalbert were airborne over the Irish Sea on a night practice interception exercise from which they failed to return. Based on Ground Controlled Interception (GCI) radar evidence from Ballywooden, Bishopscourt it was presumed that the two aircraft had collided, resulting in the deaths of both crews. Each crew comprised two men and their bodies were never recovered. They were Flight Lieutenant **Eric Augustus Snow** (pilot of HK261); Flying Officer **Donald Maldwyn Griffiths** (navigator aboard HK261); Flying Officer Frederick John Bartlett Reid (pilot of HK326) and Pilot Officer **Horace James Rich** (navigator aboard HK326).

Flying Officer Frederick John Bartlett Reid was 23 years old when he died and he is commemorated on Page 190 of the Newfoundland Book of Remembrance and on the Canadian Virtual War Memorial (Internet). Newfoundland (now Newfoundland and Labrador) was a former Colony and Dominion of the United Kingdom and it was the tenth Province to enter the Canadian Confederation on 31 March 1949.

R

Reid, Gordon Wemyss (Gordon)
Flight Sergeant
No. 590717, Royal Air Force
Killed in an aircraft accident on Wednesday 14 January 1942 (aged 25)
Bushey (St. James) Churchyard, Hertfordshire, England (Section A Grave 23)

Gordon Wemyss Reid was born on 11 July 1916 and his birth was registered in Birkenhead, Cheshire. He was a son of Thomas Wemyss Reid and Margery Ann Reid (nee Robinson). Gordon's father, Thomas Wemyss Reid (one of eight children) was born on 22 November 1886 in Scotland and he was a son of Alexander Goran Reid and Mary Jane Reid, both of whom were born in England. It is recorded in the 1911 Census that Alexander Goran Reid was working as a railway general manager in Dublin and that Thomas was a student in Dublin.

Thomas Wemyss Reid and his family moved from Birkenhead to Northern Ireland and they lived at 3 Moffett's Terrace, Demesne Road, Holywood, Co. Down. Gordon attended Belmont Public Elementary School and then Sullivan Upper School, Holywood from 1929 until 1932. When he left school Gordon joined the Royal Air Force and his marriage to Dorothy Hilda Lack was registered in the third quarter of 1940 in Watford, Hertfordshire. Dorothy Reid lived in Bushey Heath, Hertfordshire.

Flight Sergeant Gordon Wemyss Reid was 25 years old when he was killed in an aircraft accident in Scotland on 14 January 1942 and he is commemorated in Sullivan Upper School. His father's death was registered in the second quarter of 1971 in Uckfield, Sussex.

Reid, Hugh Erin (Hugh)
Driver
No. 1893526, Royal Engineers
Accidentally drowned on Tuesday 9 April 1940 (aged 33)
Newtownards (Movilla) Cemetery, Co. Down (Section 29 Grave 41)

R

Hugh Erin (spelt Aaron in his baptismal record) Reid was born on 11 September 1906 and he was a son of Hugh and Elizabeth Margaret Reid (nee Smith; in some records spelt Smyth) of 8 Carney Hill, Carrowdore. Hugh Reid Senior worked as an agricultural labourer and he and Elizabeth Smith were married on 3 October 1900 in Carrowdore Presbyterian Church. They had at least eight children all of whom were baptised in Carrowdore Presbyterian Church – Agnes (born 10 July 1901); James (born 11 December 1902); Mary Elizabeth (born 16 January 1905); Hugh Aaron (born 11 September 1906); Jane (born 27 June 1908); Martha (born 8 January 1910, died in infancy); William (born 26 July 1911) and Martha (born 15 August 1915).

REID—Accidentally drowned in England, Motor Driver Hugh Erin Reid, R.E. The remains of my beloved husband will be removed from his late residence, 20, Raceview Terrace, Newtownards, for interment in Movilla Cemetery on Monday, at 2 p.m. Deeply regretted by his sorrowing Wife and Daughter,
ELIZA JANE REID.

Hugh Erin Reid was the husband of Eliza Jane Reid of 20 Raceview Terrace, Newtownards and their daughter Elizabeth was born on 11 February 1929. During the Second World War Hugh Reid served with the Royal Engineers and it was reported in the press that he had been accidentally drowned in the River Ouse in Yorkshire. He was reported missing on 13 March 1940 and his body was recovered from the river on 9 April 1940. He was 33 years old when he died. Hugh's body was brought to Newtownards and he was buried in Movilla Cemetery on 13 April 1940.

There is an inscription on his CWGC headstone:

*If ye then be risen with Christ, seek those things
which are above*

Hugh's wife Eliza Jane died on 9 July 1951 (aged 56) and their daughter Elizabeth Jones died on 9 March 2003 – *brought home by Vanessa and Trefor*. Driver Hugh Erin Reid is commemorated on Newtownards and District War Memorial.

Reid, Leonard Stanley (known to his friends as Basil)
Private
No. 6844158, 2nd Battalion, Northamptonshire Regiment
Died of heart failure on Thursday 28 September 1939 (aged 26)
Holywood Cemetery, Co. Down (Protestant Ground Joint Grave 1264)

Leonard Stanley Reid was born on 14 April 1912 in London and he was a son of Frederick Thomas Andrew Reid and Florence Esther Reid (nee Webb) of 23 Camborne Road, Southfields, London. They were married in Wandsworth Registry Office, London and they had at least three children – Ernest Frederick George (born 3 September 1909); Leonard Stanley (born 14 April 1912) and Violet Winifred (born 10 January 1914). Frederick Thomas Andrew Reid (aged 29) enlisted in February 1915 for service during the First World War but he was discharged on medical grounds after ten days.

R

Before the outbreak of the Second World War Leonard Stanley Reid was a serving soldier in the Northamptonshire Regiment. Stationed in Northern Ireland, he was 26 years old and a married man when he died of heart failure on 28 September 1939 in the Union Hospital, Dundrum. He was buried on 3 October 1939 in Holywood Cemetery, Co. Down.

There is an inscription on Private Leonard Stanley Reid's CWGC headstone (he had been predeceased by his father):

*In loving memory of my dear son
Safe in the arms of Jesus*

Reid, Robert James (Robert)
Second Lieutenant
Royal Artillery
Died of illness on Sunday 28 December 1941 (aged 40)
Newtownards (Movilla) Cemetery, Co. Down (Section 14 Grave 24)

REID—December 28, 1941, at Cuan View, Belfast Road, Newtownards, Second Lieut. Robert J. Reid, B.Com., A.C.I.S. (Royal Artillery), beloved husband of Elizabeth E. Reid. Interred in Movilla Cemetery. Deeply regretted by his loving Wife.

REID—December 28, 1941, at Cuan View, Ballyrogan, Newtownards, Second Lieut. Robert J. Reid, B.Com., A.C.I.S. (Royal Artillery), eldest and dearly-beloved son of Margaret and the late Thomas A. Reid. Interred in Movilla Cemetery. Deeply regretted by his loving Mother, Brothers and Sisters.

The death of Second Lieutenant Robert James Reid B.Com., ACIS was reported in the 3 January 1942 edition of the *County Down Spectator*. He was the eldest son of Thomas Alexander and Margaret M. Reid (nee Stirling) of Cuan View, Ballyrogan, Newtownards; for many years Thomas Alexander Reid was the Principal of Ballyrogan Public Elementary School. Thomas Alexander Reid and Margaret Stirling were married on 31 July 1900 in First Antrim Presbyterian Church. Before the Reid family moved to Newtownards they lived at *Glenravel*, Ballymena and they had at least nine children including Robert James (born 11 November 1901); David C. (born 26 April 1903); John (born 21 June 1904, died in infancy); Thomasina A.M. (born 5 January 1906); George Arnott (born 5 September 1907); Thomas H.B. (born 21 September 1908); Louisa Elizabeth (born 11 April 1910) and Agnes (born 14 December 1913).

Robert Reid was educated at Royal Belfast Academical Institution (RBAI) and he obtained his Bachelor of Commerce degree from London University. Later he became an Associate of the Chartered Institute of Secretaries. For several years he was employed by Belfast Corporation and about a year before the outbreak of the Second World War he joined the Territorials. He was called up for active service at the outbreak of hostilities and he was with the British Expeditionary Force in France until the evacuation in 1940. On return to England he was granted a commission in his own Regiment and, until he became ill, he served with the Royal Artillery in South Wales.

After several months of illness (carcinoma) and a serious operation he died at the family residence in Newtownards (aged 40) and was interred on 30 December 1941 in the Reid family burying ground in Movilla Cemetery. Amongst the mourners at his funeral were his brothers George and Thomas Reid; his brothers-in-law David McAlpine, Frank L. Osborne, Alexander Johnston and Samuel McLaurin; his cousin Captain W. Shaw-Leathem RAOC; Captain G. Boyd Harris, Royal Artillery; Captain S. Currie, Royal

Navy and Mr M.J. Johnston.

Second Lieutenant Robert James Reid was survived by his wife Elizabeth E. Reid and by his mother, four sisters and two brothers. His brother David died on 21 June 1924 (aged 21); his father Thomas died on 23 July 1938 (aged 67) and his mother Margaret died on 28 August 1953 (aged 78). At the time of writing Second Lieutenant Robert James Reid's name is not included on the family grave headstone.

Reuben, Albert Edward (Albert)
Corporal
No. 7212199, Royal Army Ordnance Corps
Died of illness on Sunday 10 June 1945 (aged 46)
Bangor Cemetery, Co. Down (Section 5 W Grave 90)

There is evidence to suggest that Albert Edward Reuben's birth was registered in 1899 in Mandalay, Burma and that he and Sarah Francis Mulholland of Bangor were married in 1939. During the Second World War Corporal Albert Edward Reuben served with the Royal Army Ordnance Corps and he was 46 years old when he died of heart failure on 10 June 1945. His address was recorded as 13 Gransha Road, Bangor and he was buried in Bangor Cemetery. There is an inscription on his CWGC headstone:

R

Come Unto Me and I Will Give You Rest

Rich, Horace James (Horace)
Pilot Officer
No. 170389, 125 Squadron, Royal Air Force Volunteer Reserve
Killed in an aircraft accident on Friday 17 March 1944 (aged 25)
Runnymede Memorial, Surrey, England (Panel 212)

Horace James Rich's birth was registered in the first quarter of 1918 in Dartford, Kent and he was a son of William Leslie Rich and Lilian (Lily) Ada Rich (nee Judd). William Rich worked as a steam wagon driver in a flour mill and his marriage to Lilian Ada Judd was registered in the second quarter of 1908 in Dartford. Their first child, a son named Ernest, was born in 1910.

The marriage of Horace James Rich and Nancy Belle Cole was registered in the first quarter of 1942 in Chippenham, Wiltshire and they lived in Stockley, Wiltshire. During the Second World War, Horace James Rich served with the Royal Air Force Volunteer Reserve.

On 17 March 1944 two de Havilland Mosquito aircraft (HK 261 and HK 326) of No. 125 Squadron based at RAF Ballyhalbert were airborne over the Irish Sea on a night practice interception exercise from which they failed to return. Based on Ground Controlled Interception (GCI) radar evidence from Ballywooden, Bishopscourt it was presumed that the two aircraft had collided, resulting in the deaths of both crews. Each crew comprised two men and their bodies were never recovered. They were Flight Lieutenant **Eric Augustus Snow** (pilot of HK261); Flying Officer **Donald Maldwyn Griffiths** (navigator aboard HK261); Flying Officer **Frederick John Bartlett Reid** (pilot of HK326) and Pilot Officer Horace James Rich (navigator aboard HK326). Pilot Officer Horace James Rich was 25 years old when he died and he is commemorated on the Runnymede Memorial in Surrey.

Richardson, Robert
Sergeant
No. 976613, 10 Squadron, Royal Air Force Volunteer Reserve
Killed in action on Sunday 11 May 1941 (aged 29)
Kiel War Cemetery, Kiel, Schleswig-Holstein, Germany
(Collective Grave 3 J 18-20)

Comber Man's Brother Reported Missing.—Sergeant-Gunner R. Richardson, R.A.F., younger son of Mr. and Mrs. Richardson, "Ramoan," Whitewell, Belfast, has been reported missing. He returned to his unit from leave about a fortnight ago. He is a brother of Mr. C. Richardson, cashier of the Comber branch of the Northern Bank.

In the 17 May 1941 edition of the *Newtownards Chronicle* under the headline *Comber Man's Brother Reported Missing* it was reported that Sergeant Robert Richardson had been reported missing. Robert Richardson was the younger son of Robert and Elizabeth (Eliza) A. Richardson (nee McConaghy) of *Ramoan*, Whitewell, Belfast and he was a brother of Mr C. Richardson who was a cashier in the Comber branch of the Northern Bank. Robert Richardson Senior from Bushmills was a school teacher and he and Eliza McConaghy (daughter of Daniel McConaghy) were married on 14 July 1896 in Second Presbyterian Church, Ballymoney. They had at least six children – Margaret (born 15 June 1897); Sarah Anne (born 2 May 1899); Elizabeth Jane (born 29 January 1901); Charles (born 29 January 1903); Robert (born 2 July 1911) and Martha (born 12 August 1913).

Sergeant Robert Richardson served with the Royal Air Force Volunteer Reserve and on 10 May 1941 he was one of a five man crew aboard an

Armstrong Whitworth Whitley Mark V aircraft (P5048) that took off from RAF Leeming in Yorkshire at 10.25 pm on a mission to bomb Hamburg. At 2.23 am on 11 May they reported that the target had been attacked and after that the aircraft disappeared without trace. After Sergeant Robert Richardson was reported missing on 11 May 1941 it was later confirmed that he must be presumed killed in action. The other crew members who died that night were:

- Flying Officer Peter Beckford Gough aged 23 from Wivenhoe, Essex
- Sergeant Frederick Gordon Stewart aged 27 from Newquay, Cornwall
- Sergeant Leonard Manchip aged 21 from Battersea, London
- Sgt Desmond Frank Fitzwilliam Watson aged 19 from Hounslow, Middlesex

After the war his grave was located and his body was exhumed and reinterred in Kiel War Cemetery, Germany. Sergeant Robert Richardson was 29 years old when he died.

Ridley, Richard Herbert (Dick)
Lieutenant (A)
HMS *Kestrel*, Royal Naval Volunteer Reserve
Killed in an aircraft accident on Wednesday 4 December 1940 (aged 25)
Bridgnorth Cemetery, Shropshire, England (Grave 1064)

R

Richard Herbert (Dick) Ridley was born on 14 February 1914 in Bridgnorth, Shropshire and he was the youngest son of Samuel Ridley JP of Bridgnorth and Lucy Trevethick Ridley (nee Spargo) of Croxteth Road, Liverpool. Samuel Ridley was a maltster and seed merchant and his marriage to Lucy Spargo was registered in the fourth quarter of 1906 in Toxteth Park, Lancashire. Dick's eldest brother was Samuel Edmund Ridley and their father Samuel died in December 1938.

Dick Ridley worked as a motor salesman and he obtained his Great Britain Aero Club Aviator's Certificate on 14 July 1938 at Liverpool and District Aero Club. He was flying a Tiger Moth – Gipsy Major – 130. At that time he was living in Cheshire at *Oak Lea*, Prospect Road, Prenton, Birkenhead.

Prior to the outbreak of the Second World War Dick Ridley and Herbert Victor Armstrong operated a Flying School and Dick gave flying lessons. During the war he was stationed for a time at RAF Aldergrove and then at

HMS *Kestrel* – a Royal Naval Air Station at Worthy Down near Winchester.

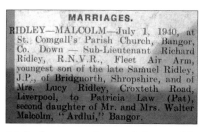

MARRIAGES.

RIDLEY—MALCOLM—July 1, 1940, at St. Comgall's Parish Church, Bangor, Co. Down — Sub-Lieutenant Richard Ridley, R.N.V.R., Fleet Air Arm, youngest son of the late Samuel Ridley, J.P., of Bridgnorth, Shropshire, and of Mrs. Lucy Ridley, Croxteth Road, Liverpool, to Patricia Law (Pat), second daughter of Mr. and Mrs. Walter Malcolm, "Ardlui," Bangor.

Dick Ridley and Patricia Law (Pat) Malcolm were married on 1 July 1940 in Bangor Parish Church of Ireland Church (St. Comgall's). Pat Malcolm was the second daughter of Councillor and Mrs Walter Malcolm who lived at *Ardlui*, 55 Ballyholme Road, Bangor. Walter Malcolm was a former Mayor of Bangor and he died on 9 June 1945 (aged 64).

Lieutenant (A) Richard Herbert (Dick) Ridley was 26 years of age when he was killed in an aircraft accident on 4 December 1940. His aircraft crashed into the side of a mountain in England and afterwards it was reported to have had a faulty altimeter. Lieutenant Ridley had been married for just five months and he is commemorated in Bangor Parish Church (St. Comgall's).

Ritchie, Frederick Watson (Frederick)
Flight Lieutenant (Wireless Operator/Air Gunner)
No. 425506, 279 (RAF) Squadron, Royal New Zealand Air Force
Killed in an aircraft accident on Sunday 7 January 1945 (aged 22)
Harrogate (Stonefall) Cemetery, Yorkshire, England
(Section G Row E Grave 12)

R

Bangor New Zealander's Death.— Flying Officer Frederick W. Ritchie, R.N.Z.A.F., who has been killed in an accident, was a nephew of Mr. and Mrs. Robert Ritchie, 42b Bridge End, Newtownards Road, Belfast. He was aged 22, and joined up at the outbreak of war. His parents, Mr. and Mrs. John Ritchie, reside in Auckland. His father, a native of Bangor, was wounded in the last war. A brother, Flight-Lieut. John Ritchie, is in the R.N.Z.A.F.

The death of Flight Lieutenant Frederick Watson Ritchie was reported in the 20 January 1945 edition of the *County Down Spectator* under the headline *Bangor New Zealander's Death*. He was a nephew of Mr and Mrs Robert Ritchie of 42b Bridge End, Newtownards Road, Belfast and a son of Mr and Mrs John Ritchie who lived in Auckland, New Zealand. John Ritchie was a native of Bangor and he was wounded on active service during the First World War.

During the Second World War Frederick Ritchie and his brother John both served as Flight Lieutenants with the Royal New Zealand Air Force and Frederick was 22 years old when he died on 7 January 1945. He was one of a six man crew that took off at 10.50 am from RAF Thornaby in Yorkshire in a Vickers Warwick B/ASR Mark I aircraft (BV233) on a training exercise. During the exercise, when they were taking evasive action during a simulated attack, the aircraft dived vertically into the ground from 500 feet and it was later concluded that this was probably the result of a high speed stall. In addition to Flight Lieutenant Frederick Watson Ritchie, the other five crew members who died were:

- Flight Lieutenant Harvey Samuel Luck aged 32 (RCAF)
- Flight Lieutenant Ronald Cooper
- Flying Officer Desmond Charles Holland aged 20 (RNZAF)
- Flying Officer Robert Percy Woolfield aged 28 (RNZAF)
- Sergeant James Wiles

Flight Lieutenant Frederick Watson Ritchie was buried in Harrogate (Stonefall) Cemetery, Yorkshire and he is commemorated on the New Zealand National War Memorial in Wellington and on the New Zealand Cenotaph Database in Auckland War Memorial Museum.

Robinson, Francis (Frank)
Able Seaman
No. D/SSX 22722, HMML *466*, Royal Navy
Died as a result of enemy action on Sunday 25 March 1945 (aged 26)
Plymouth Naval Memorial, Devon, England (Panel 80 Column 1)

R

At the time of writing, the date of Able Seaman Francis Robinson's death is incorrectly recorded in the CWGC Debt of Honour as 25 March 1943.

Frank Robinson was born on 28 February 1919 in Newtownards and he was the second son of the late William and Elizabeth (Lizzie) Robinson (nee Johnston) of 31 Greenwell Street, Newtownards. William Robinson worked as a labourer and he and Elizabeth Johnston were married in Newtownards Registry Office on 11 March 1911. They had nine children – Mary (born 1911); Annie (born 23 July 1913); Hugh; Francis (Frank, born 28 February 1919); James (Jimmy); William (Willie); Robert; Agnes and Jane.

Before joining the Royal Navy, Frank Robinson worked as a Rove Boy in Walker's Spinning Mill, Castle Gardens, Newtownards (rove was the name given to the fibres of heckled flax before they were spun into linen thread) and he was a member of Newtownards True Blues Loyal Orange Lodge (LOL) No. 1055 and Royal Arch Purple Chapter (RAPC) No. 1055.

Frank Robinson joined the Royal Navy on 2 September 1937 (aged 18) and

ROBINSON—March, 1945, lost at sea, Frank, dearly-beloved husband of Ivy Robinson, 98A, Greenwell Street, Newtownards.

Why should I weep, when my darling one rests
In the bosom of Jesus supreme,
In the Mansion of Glory prepared for the blest,
Where death is no more than a dream.

"He died that we might live."

Deeply regretted by his sorrowing Wife and two little Children.

he was 5 feet 5 inches tall with brown hair, blue eyes and a fresh complexion. Between 1937 and 1945 he served aboard a number of ships including HMS *Royal Oak*, HMS *Drake*, HMS *Furious*, HMS *Kestrel*, HMS *Ferret* and HMS *Cormorant*. He was serving aboard His Majesty's Motor Launch (HMML) *466* when he died on 25 March 1945. The home base for HMML *466* was HMS *Beehive*, a Royal Naval Coastal Forces Base headquartered at Felixstowe Dock in Suffolk. The War Diary entry for HMML *466* for 25 March 1945 indicates that HMML *466* was mined 3 miles northwest of Walcheren in the Netherlands, caught fire and disintegrated and left no survivors. HMML *466* was a unit of 21st Flotilla based at Ostend at the time.

Frank Robinson and Ivy McLaughlin were married on 14 August 1939 in Greenwell Street Presbyterian Church, Newtownards and they lived at 98a Greenwell Street. Frank and Ivy Robinson had two children, Hugh and Ann, and when their father died they were 3 years old and 3 months old respectively. Initially Frank Robinson was reported as missing and then it was officially confirmed that he must be presumed killed. There were *Lost at Sea* notices in the 14 April 1945 edition of the *Newtownards Chronicle* from his wife and children; his mother, brothers and sisters; his sister Mary and brother-in-law James Boal of 45 Greenwell Street, Newtownards; his sister Annie and brother-in-law George Carlisle of 46 George Street, Newtownards; his sister Jane and brother-in-law Thomas Daye of 43 Greenwell Street, Newtownards and his parents-in-law John and Ann McLaughlin of Ballyhay. The one from his wife Ivy contained the text:

Why should I weep when my darling one rests
In the bosom of Jesus supreme
In the Mansion of Glory prepared for the blest
Where death is no more than a dream

He died that we might live

Ivy Robinson was 28 years old when she died on 1 January 1949 and her parents, John and Ann McLaughlin, were assigned guardians of her two children, Hugh and Ann Robinson. Hugh Robinson is an award-winning writer and radio storyteller.

Able Seaman Francis Robinson is commemorated on Plymouth Naval Memorial in Devon and on Newtownards and District War Memorial.

Rodgers, Thomas George (Thomas)
Flying Officer
No. 126149, Royal Air Force Volunteer Reserve
Killed in an aircraft accident on Sunday 8 August 1943 (aged 25)
Knockbreda Cemetery, Co. Down (Section K Grave 443)

Thomas George Rodgers's birth was registered in the first quarter of 1918 and he was the only son of Edward Rodgers (born in County Louth) and Frances Rodgers (nee Colville). Edward was one of at least ten children and Frances, who was ten years older than Edward, was one of 18 children. Edward Rodgers worked as a grocer's assistant, Frances Colville worked as a linen weaver and they were married on 29 November 1916 in Great Victoria Street Presbyterian Church, Belfast. The Rodgers family lived for a time in Bangor before moving to 15 Orpen Road, Finaghy, Co. Antrim. Thomas George Rodgers was educated in Bangor and he was well known in swimming circles. He was captain of Bangor Amateur Swimming Club and he represented Bangor Boys' Brigade at the BB Jubilee celebrations in 1933 in Glasgow, Scotland.

R

Thomas George Rodgers enlisted at the outbreak of war and was commissioned in May 1942. He was 25 years old when he died in a flying accident on 8 August 1943 and he had been scheduled to be married on his next leave. Flying Officer Thomas George Rodgers was one of a two man crew aboard an Avro Anson aircraft (NS105) from 1510 Flight that was coming in to land at RAF Leuchars in Fife after a non-operational test flight when it was struck by a Mosquito aircraft from No. 333 (Norwegian) Squadron that was coming in to land at the same time. Both aircraft crashed to the ground on the boundary of the airfield and all four airmen aboard the two aircraft were killed. The pilot of the Mosquito was Hakon Offerdal and his navigator was Andres Paulson. In addition to Flying Officer Thomas George Rodgers his co-pilot was also killed:

- Flying Officer Allister Francis Shapcott aged 29 (RAAF)

Military honours were accorded at Flying Officer Rodgers's funeral which took place from his parents' residence to Knockbreda Cemetery. The chief mourners were his father Edward; his uncles Thomas, William and David Colville and his cousins Samuel, Stanley and Jack Colville. At the time, Jack

Colville was serving with the Royal Air Force.

Flying Officer Thomas George Rodgers is commemorated on Bangor and District War Memorial (as Rogers T.) and there is an inscription on his CWGC headstone in Knockbreda Cemetery:

To have, to love, to lose and when God will, to end

In Knockbreda Cemetery his headstone is located beside a Colville headstone commemorating David Colville who died on 8 March 1944 (aged 49) and David's wife Martha who died on 27 August 1962 (aged 65).

Rogerson, Peter Murray
Sergeant
No. 1217612, 501 Squadron, Royal Air Force Volunteer Reserve
Killed in an aircraft accident on Monday 12 April 1943 (aged 20)
Wigtoft (St. Peter and St. Paul) Churchyard, Lincolnshire, England

Peter Murray Rogerson was born on 23 June 1922 in Worcestershire and he was the younger son of Major William Alexander Rogerson MC, MICE and Alison Pagan Rogerson (nee Dinwoodie) of Hoffleet Stow, Lincolnshire. Their marriage was registered in the first quarter of 1916 in Birkenhead, Cheshire. (In the New Year's Honours List for 1952 Major William Alexander Rogerson, then County Surveyor with Holland County Council in Lincolnshire, was awarded the OBE).

Peter Murray Rogerson enlisted on 31 January 1941 and during the Second World War he served with the Royal Air Force Volunteer Reserve. He was 20 years old when he died in a flying accident on 12 April 1943. Two Supermarine Spitfire aircraft out of RAF Ballyhalbert were practising formation flying when they collided over Derry Farm, Ballyrusley, Portaferry. Local men working in the fields ran to help but they could not open the hatch of Sergeant Rogerson's aircraft. The plane caught fire and Sergeant Rogerson perished in the flames. The other pilot survived. It was reported that, following this incident, instruction was provided in Portaferry for local people on how to open an aircraft hatch. It was also reported that discussions after the incident led to a Fire Station being established in Portaferry.

Peter Murray Rogerson's mother died on 21 December 1960 (aged 69) and his father died on 18 October 1961 (aged 72).

Rothwell, Brian Thomas Stewart
Lieutenant
No. 190207, 2nd Battalion, Royal Inniskilling Fusiliers
Killed in action on Monday 19 July 1943 (aged 21)
Cantania War Cemetery, Sicily (Grave II G 17)

Brian Thomas Stewart Rothwell was born in Dublin on 14 October 1921 and he was the third son of Lieutenant Colonel William Edward Rothwell DSO and Frances Violet Rothwell (nee Poole, born in 1887) of Terenure, Dublin and later Ormeau Road, Belfast. They were married in 1915 in Dublin. Brian Thomas Stewart Rothwell was a grandson of Mrs J.C. Poole of 49 Adelaide Park, Belfast. Both Brian Thomas Stewart Rothwell and his brother, John Edward Desmond Rothwell, who was born in 1920 in Sealkote, India, were educated at Rockport School, Craigavad.

During the Second World War, Brian Thomas Stewart Rothwell served with the 2nd Battalion, Royal Inniskilling Fusiliers and he was 21 years old when he died on 19 July 1943 during fighting at the Simento River in Sicily. His effects in England amounted to some £425 and probate was granted to his brother.

R

Lieutenant Brian Thomas Stewart Rothwell is commemorated in Rockport School and in Trinity College, Dublin.

Rowan, James Harvey (Jim)
Corporal
No. 522932, 39 Squadron, Royal Air Force
Killed in an aircraft accident on Friday 4 April 1941 (aged 28)
Cairo War Memorial Cemetery, Egypt (Grave K 3)

James Harvey (Jim) Rowan was born on 11 September 1912 and he was the elder son of William George and Elizabeth Rowan (nee Harvey) of 28 Broadway, Bangor. William George Rowan was born on 15 January 1886 in County Cavan, he worked as a gardener and he and Elizabeth Harvey were married on 11 March 1912 in Trinity Presbyterian Church, Bangor. They had three children – James Harvey (born 11 September 1912); William George (born 21 December 1913) and Sarah Elizabeth (Sally, born 29 December 1918). During the First World War their father, Lance Corporal William George Rowan, served with the 13th Battalion Royal Irish Rifles. He was killed in action on 20 October 1918 and he is commemorated on Page 313 in the Book of Honour

Remembering Their Sacrifice in the Great War – North Down compiled by Barry Niblock. Jim Rowan was six years old when his father died.

Jim Rowan joined Bangor Grammar School in 1929 in fifth form, when he was almost 17 years of age. He studied for the King's Scholarship examination which he passed in 1931. In school he was 'popular with both pupils and masters' and the Headmaster also said that he was 'something of a bohemian with a vein of whimsical originality peculiar to himself.' He was 'a skilled exponent of association football' and he played rugby for the school.

Jim Rowan was confirmed in Bangor Parish Church of Ireland Church (St. Comgall's) in 1929 and he and Sarah Francis were married in Bangor Abbey on 18 April 1938. They had one child, a son named Hugh Harvey Rowan, who was born on 23 August 1939 and who attended Bangor Grammar School from 1950 until 1957. Prior to the outbreak of war Jim Rowan worked as an insurance agent. Jim's sister Sally worked in the Town Clerk's office in Bangor and on 16 November 1943 she and John Clark from Donaghadee were married in the Church of Ireland Church of St. Columbanus at Ballyholme.

R

OUR HEROES—IN MEMORIAM.

ROWAN—In loving memory of my dear husband, Corporal James Rowan, Killed in Middle East, 4th April, 1941. Ever remembered by his loving Wife and little Son.
SARAH ROWAN.
14, Scrabo Road, Newtownards.

ROWAN—In loving remembrance of my dear son, Corporal James Rowan, Killed in Middle East, 4th April, 1941. Lovingly remembered by his Mother and all at 28, Broadway, Bangor.

Corporal Jim Rowan served as a Wireless Operator with 39 Squadron in the Royal Air Force and he was killed near Heliopolis in Egypt on 4 April 1941 as a result of an aircraft accident. He was being transferred from Egypt to Aden but the plane failed to take off and burst into flames on the runway. In the newspaper death notices there were tributes from his wife Sarah, and his son Hugh Harvey, who lived at 14 Scrabo Road, Newtownards and from his widowed mother who lived at 28 Broadway, Bangor. Elizabeth Rowan lost her husband in the First World War and her son in the Second. Harvey Rowan was 19 months old when his father died.

In the 29 May 1943 edition of the *County Down Spectator* there was a *Roll of Honour* tribute from Jim's 'Brother Rover Scouts' – R. Drury, R. Gillespie, G. Turnbull, W.I. McKinney and P.W. McKinney. Corporal Jim Rowan was 28 years of age when he died and he is commemorated on Bangor and District War Memorial; in Bangor Parish Church (St. Comgall's) and in Bangor Grammar School.

Russell, Brian Beven (Brian)
Lieutenant
No. 278612, 3rd Battalion, Irish Guards
Killed in action on Monday 2 April 1945 (aged 20)
Rheinberg War Cemetery, Kamp Lintfort, Nordrhein-Westfal, Germany
(Grave 13 B 23)

Brian Beven Russell was born on 10 April 1924 in Dublin and he was a grandson of George Murray Knox-Peebles and Ailne Mary Knox-Peebles (nee O'Brien), of Westfield Park, Harold's Cross, Dublin. He was the elder son of Wing Commander George Henry Russell DFC and Mary (Molly) Sarah Russell (nee Knox-Peebles). His maternal grandfather, George Murray Knox-Peebles, died on 16 November 1926.

Molly Knox-Peebles and George Russell were married in 1920 in Dublin and, after they divorced, Molly Russell (nee Knox-Peebles) and William Welman were married in 1927 in Dublin. Thus, Brian Beven Russell was a stepson of Major William Herbert Eyre Welman of *Herdstown House*, Donaghadee and, before that, *Innisfree*, Cairnburn Road, Belfast.

R

Brian Beven Russell attended Campbell College, Belfast from 1937 until 1941 and he was a member of the school swimming team. He was an accomplished piper and he also played in the school Band. His younger brother, John Anthony Russell, also attended Campbell College.

During the Second World War Lieutenant Brian Beven Russell served with the Irish Guards and he was killed in action on 2 April 1945, just a few days before his 21st birthday. He was killed during the advance into Germany from Oldenzaal in the Netherlands. Lieutenant Brian Beven Russell is commemorated in Campbell College and there is an inscription on his CWGC headstone:

Loved and remembered always

During the Second World War Brian Beven Russell's uncle, Major William Charles Knox-Peebles, served with the 6th Airborne Division and he was 43 years old when he was killed in action in Germany on 24 March 1945. He was the elder son of George Murray and Ailne Mary Knox-Peebles, *Westfield Park*, Harold's Cross, Dublin; he was the husband of Ann Knox-Peebles (nee O'Reilly) and he was a brother of Molly Welman (formerly Russell, nee

Knox-Peebles). His younger brother, Major George Edward Knox-Peebles, was awarded the DSO in December 1941. Brian Beven Russell's maternal grandmother, Ailne Mary Knox-Peebles, died on 15 June 1945 and his mother, Molly Sarah Welman, died on 22 February 1952 (aged 52). In 1955 his stepfather, William Welman, married Cicely Mildred O'Carroll Smyth (nee Darby). (Within 3 months Molly lost her brother, son and mother.)

Rutherford, Robert Henry (Bobby)*
Flying Officer (Navigator)
No. 133718, Royal Air Force Volunteer Reserve
Killed in an aircraft accident on Thursday 22 July 1943 (aged 20)
Bangor Cemetery, Co. Down (Section 2 H Grave 166)

Robert Henry (Bobby) Rutherford was born on 20 August 1922 in Dublin and he was the younger son of Samuel William and Pauline Anne Rutherford (nee Bryant) of 25 High Street, Bangor. Samuel Rutherford (born in County Cork) was a policeman and his marriage to Pauline Bryant (born in County Longford) was registered in the second quarter of 1910 in Dublin. Bobby's father died in the Royal Victoria Hospital, Belfast on 14 September 1935 (aged 55). Bobby was educated at Bangor Central Public Elementary School, then Bangor Grammar School from 1935 until 1938 and Ardmore College, Belfast. After leaving school he worked in the costing office of Messrs Short and Harland in Belfast before joining the Royal Air Force Volunteer Reserve in 1941. His brother, Samuel W. Rutherford, became a teacher at Bangor Central School and Samuel and his wife Eleanor had at least two children, Lorna and Wendy. Bobby's sister Pauline worked in Bangor Library before moving to Holywood after her marriage to Henry Ballagh.

Bobby Rutherford was described as a 'gifted amateur actor' and he played principal roles with Bangor Drama Club. He had a good singing voice and was a member of First Bangor Presbyterian Church choir. He was also a fine athlete and won both the 100 and 200 yards Northern Ireland Boys' Championships. He played rugby for Bangor Grammar School.

Bobby Rutherford went to Canada for training under the Empire Training Scheme and extracts from a letter that he wrote to friends at home were published in the 9 May 1942 edition of the *County Down Spectator*. He described the camp as 'super, the most up-to-date in Canada'. He said, 'The 'food is marvellous (ham and eggs each morning for breakfast), as are the beds and bathrooms where you may have a shower at any time of the day'.

He described the sea crossing to the United States of America when at times the seas were very rough and how he had volunteered for duty on the anti-submarine look-out post – a swivel-chair on top of the bridge deck – and how he was equipped with special oilskins and powerful binoculars. Then he travelled by train to Canada and he told of his experiences on route in New York and in Bangor, Maine, USA. He was impressed by all the shops 'brim-full of chocolate, cigarettes, fruit (bananas too) and every conceivable product you could think of'.

Bobby Rutherford qualified for his commission as Pilot Officer in December 1942 and he was promoted to the rank of Flying Officer in June 1943. One month later, when he was serving with 1657 Heavy Conversion Unit, he was killed and his death was announced in a *Died on Active Service* notice in the 31 July 1943 edition of the *County Down Spectator*. On 22 July 1943 he was one of a crew of seven aboard a Short Stirling aircraft (W7586) that took off from RAF Stradishall in Suffolk to practise circuits and landings. The starboard outer engine was feathered and they were making a three-engined approach. When the aircraft overshot, the pilot made an attempt to go round again but the aircraft stalled and crashed at 5.46 pm. All the crew on board were killed. In addition to Flying Officer Robert Henry (Bobby) Rutherford (aged 20) the other six crew members who died were:

R

- Pilot Officer Leonard Gerrard Sellars aged 31 (RAAF)
- Sergeant John Archibald Campbell aged 20
- Flight Sergeant Raymond Henry Murdock aged 31 (RCAF)
- Sergeant Richard George Kings aged 27 from Ettington, Warwickshire
- Sergeant George Frank Albert Wix aged 20 from Leytonstone, London
- Flight Sergeant Ernest Henry Benjamin Saker aged 20 (RAAF)

On its way from Belfast to Bangor on 27 July 1943 the funeral cortege stopped at Holywood for a few minutes where the Revd W.G. Wimperis conducted a short family service. The interment in Bangor Cemetery was preceded by a service in First Bangor Presbyterian Church. His CWGC headstone bears the inscription:

At Rest
Greater Love Hath No Man

Flying Officer Robert Henry Rutherford is commemorated on Bangor and District War Memorial; in First Bangor Presbyterian Church and in Bangor Grammar School. His mother, Pauline Anne Rutherford, died on 19 December 1975 (aged 90).

Ryan, Martin
Corporal
No. 3384041, 1st Battalion, East Lancashire Regiment
Killed on active service on Friday 6 April 1945 (aged 35)
Reichswald Forest War Cemetery, Kleve, Nordrhein-Westfalen, Germany (Grave 61 C 10)

Martin Ryan's birth was registered in the first quarter of 1910 in Killarney, Co. Kerry and he was a son of Timothy (Tim) and Annie (Ann) Ryan (nee Buckley) of Duckett's Lane, Killarney. Their marriage was registered in the first quarter of 1909 in Killarney.

Martin Ryan joined the Army before the outbreak of war and in the CWGC Debt of Honour it is recorded that he was the husband of Alice Ryan of Holywood. During the Second World War he served with the East Lancashire Regiment and he was 35 years old when he was killed on 6 April 1945 during the Allied advance through Germany. Corporal Martin Ryan is commemorated on Holywood and District War Memorial.

R
S

Sadd, John Peter
Pilot Officer (Pilot)
No. 106188, 153 Squadron, Royal Air Force Volunteer Reserve
Killed in an aircraft accident on Sunday 19 July 1942 (aged 24)
Idmiston (All Saints) Churchyard, Wiltshire, England (South side of church)

John Peter Sadd was a son of Major John Ambrose Sadd and Doris Sadd (nee Mooney) of Salisbury and his birth was registered in the first quarter of 1918 in Willesden, Middlesex. His parents' marriage was registered in the second quarter of 1916 in Bradford, Yorkshire.

John Peter Sadd joined the Royal Air Force Volunteer Reserve and in July 1942 he was serving with 153 Squadron based at RAF Ballyhalbert. On 19 July 1942 a Bristol Beaufighter aircraft (X7822) of 153 Squadron was returning to Ballyhalbert airfield, having completed a practice night interception and radar calibration exercise, when it flew straight into Shanlieve Mountain in the Mourne Mountains at Grid Reference J250214. It was reported at the time that 'the aircraft appeared to have *homed* on an inappropriate radio beacon'. The aircraft was totally destroyed and both crew members were killed. They were Pilot Officer John Peter Sadd (aged 24) from

Willesden, Middlesex and the Navigator/Radar Operator, Sergeant **Marks Weiner (served as Marks Wayne)** of Maida Vale, London. Pilot Officer John Peter Sadd was buried in Idmiston (All Saints) Churchyard, Wiltshire and there is an inscription on his CWGC headstone:

O valiant heart

Sandfield, Albert
Third Engineer Officer
MV *Larchbank* (Glasgow), Merchant Navy
Died as a result of enemy action on Thursday 9 September 1943 (aged 29)
Tower Hill Memorial, London, England (Panel 64)

Albert Sandfield was born on 21 August 1914 in Holywood, Co. Down and he was the third son of George Benjamin Sandfield and Florence Mabel Sandfield (nee Manning). His parents were married on 28 February 1907 in Billericay, Essex and they had at least five children – Francis (born around 1907); Jessie Augusta (born around 1909); George Alfred (born around 1911); Albert (born 21 August 1914) and Julia Florence (born 1916 in Holywood).

Albert's father worked as a blacksmith before joining the Army's Medical Staff Corps (later the Royal Army Medical Corps) in 1889. He served for 21 years, including a period in South Africa (1896 to 1903) during which he was wounded. In 1911 he was employed as a chef by Lipton's Ltd., and in May 1916 (aged 47) Albert's father rejoined the Army to serve with the Royal Irish Rifles. At that time the Sandfield family was living at 2 Yew Place, Downshire Road, Holywood. Albert's father remained in the Army until January 1920.

During the Second World War Albert Sandfield served in the Merchant Navy aboard MV *Larchbank*. This cargo motor vessel was built in 1925 by Harland and Wolff Ltd., Govan, Glasgow for the Bank Line. Third Engineer Officer Albert Sandfield was among more than 40 men killed on 9 September 1943 when MV *Larchbank* was torpedoed and sunk by the Japanese submarine *I-27* in the Indian Ocean while on route from Baltimore, Maryland, USA to Colombo, Ceylon (now Sri Lanka). A little more than four months earlier, on 28 April 1943, Albert's father had died (aged 75) at 130 Costead Manor Road, Brentwood, Essex. Albert's mother was living at 38 Marconi Road, Chelmsford and before that at 23 Eves Crescent, Chelmsford. His mother died in 1965.

On 29 January 1944 a Mass was held for Albert Sandfield in Our Lady Immaculate Roman Catholic Church, London Road, Chelmsford. Third Engineer Officer Albert Sandfield is commemorated on Tower Hill Memorial in London; on Chelmsford War Memorial and on Holywood and District War Memorial. His sister Julia served as a Corporal in the WAAF and she was *Mentioned in Despatches* for devotion to duty. Julia survived the war. Before the war Julia worked for the Hoffman Manufacturing Company in Belfast.

Sandford, Henry Dougan (Harry)
Leading Aircraftman
No. 537402, Royal Air Force
Died as a result of enemy action on Friday 25 October 1940 (aged 25)
Montrose (Sleepy Hillock) Cemetery, Angus, Scotland
(Section 10 Class A Grave 336)

S

> **OU RHEROES—IN MEMORIAM.**
> SANDFORD—In treasured memory of my darling son, and our dear brother, Leading Aircraftsman H. D. Sandford, who was Killed in Action on 25th October, 1940. and was interred in Sleepy Hillock Cemetery, Montrose, Angus, Scotland.
> Never a day but his name is spoken,
> Never a day but he is in our thoughts,
> A link in the family chain is broken,
> He has gone from our homes—but not from our hearts.
> Some may think he is forgotten,
> When they see us smile,
> But little do they know the heart-ache
> That a smile hides all the while.
> Still sadly missed by his Mother and Dad; also his Brothers, Sisters and Brothers-in-law at Home and Abroad.
> 32, Thorndyke Street, Belfast, and 114, East Street, Newtownards.

Henry Dougan (Harry) Sandford was a son of Henry and Agnes Jane Sandford (nee Bell). They were married on 26 October 1907 in Ballymacarrett Parish Church of Ireland Church (St. Patrick's), Belfast. Henry Sandford was a shipyard labourer and he and Agnes Jane had at least four children – Margaret Ann (born 8 August 1908); Agnes Jane (born 14 April 1910); Sarah (born 18 April 1912) and Henry Dougan (born about 1915).

Henry Dougan (Harry) Sandford was the husband of Margaret Sim Sandford (nee Duncan, daughter of David Duncan) of Graham Street, Montrose, Scotland. They were married in 1939. During the Second World War Leading Aircraftman Henry Dougan (Harry) Sandford served with the Royal Air Force and he died at dusk on 25 October 1940 during a Luftwaffe air raid on RAF Montrose. Harry's family in Belfast and Newtownards placed an *Our Heroes – In Memoriam* notice in the 24 October 1942 edition of the *Newtownards Chronicle* and it contained the verse:

> *Never a day but his name is spoken,*
> *Never a day but he is in our thoughts,*
> *A link in the family chain is broken,*

He has gone from our homes but not from our hearts.
Some may think he is forgotten,
When they see us smile,
But little do they know the heart-ache
That a smile hides all the while.

Harry's sister Agnes and brother-in-law Stewart McBlain (they were married on 1 April 1929 in Ballygilbert Presbyterian Church) lived at 114 East Street, Newtownards and his sister Sadie and brother-in-law Bruce Ross lived at 32 Thorndyke Street, Belfast.

It was Leading Aircraftman Henry Dougan (Harry) Sandford's father-in-law, David Duncan of Myrtlebank Bank, Rosehill Road, Montrose who purchased the lair (grave plot) in which Harry was buried and his widow placed an inscription on Harry's CWGC headstone:

Cherished memories of my beloved husband,
Killed in the service of his country

S

Leading Aircraftman Henry Dougan (Harry) Sandford's brother-in-law **William McBlain** died on active service on 11 September 1943. William McBlain's cousin, Fusilier **William John Shields**, was killed in action in Burma on 18 April 1942.

Scott, David
Ordinary Seaman
D/SSX 30791, HMS *Glorious*, Royal Navy
Killed in action on Saturday 8 June 1940 (aged 18)
Plymouth Naval Memorial, Devon (Panel 39 Column 1)

David Scott was born on 21 November 1921, his birth was registered in Newtownards and he was the second son of Robert and Margaret Stewart Scott (nee Eagleson) who lived at 101 Scrabo Road, Newtownards. Margaret Stewart Eagleson (born 16 November 1900) was a daughter of William Eagleson (son of David Eagleson, Ballyrea) and Margaret Ann Stewart (daughter of Robert Stewart, Ballywatticock) who were married on 3 September 1896 in Ballyblack Presbyterian Church.

Robert Scott (aged 21), a son of William John and Margaret Scott (nee

Hayes), both deceased was a labourer living at 60 Ardeer Square, Stevenston, Ayr when he and Margaret Stewart Eagleson (aged 19), a millworker of 26 Bridgend, Kilwinning, Ayr were married on 18 July 1919 in the Original Secession Manse, Kilwinning after Banns according to the forms of the Original Secession Church. Their first two children were baptised in Greenwell Street Presbyterian Church, Newtownards – Robert (Bobby, born 10 February 1920, later married Hannah) and David (born 21 November 1921). Robert and Margaret Scott had at least five more children – John; Gretta (married David Kelly); another daughter; Desmond (born around 1942) and Wilfred (born 21 April 1943).

During the Second World War David Scott served with the Royal Navy aboard the aircraft carrier HMS *Glorious*. This ship was built as a battle cruiser by Harland and Wolff in Belfast and completed in 1917. During the late 1920s she was converted to an aircraft carrier.

S

SCOTT—Lost at sea, through enemy action, Seaman David Scott, second son of Mr. and Mrs. Robert Scott, 101, Scrabo Road, Newtownards.
To love, to love, and then to part, Is the greatest sorrow of a mother's heart.
Deeply regretted by his Mother, Father (serving with H.M. Forces in England), Brothers and Sisters.

The evacuation of Allied Forces from Norway (*Operation Alphabet*) was carried out between 5 and 8 June 1940. On the afternoon of 8 June 1940 HMS *Glorious* and her escorting destroyers HMS *Acasta* and HMS *Ardent* were proceeding independently to Scapa Flow when they were intercepted in the Norwegian Sea by the German battle cruisers *Gneisenau* and *Scharnhorst*. At around 6.00 pm the three British ships were sunk by sustained and heavy gunfire with the loss of more than 1,500 lives. In addition to Ordinary Seaman David Scott, these included Able Seaman **Alexander Doak** and Able Seaman **Hugh Alexander Eagleson**, both also from Newtownards.

Ordinary Seaman David Scott was 18 years old when he died on 8 June 1940 and his mother, father, brothers and sisters placed a *Killed on Active Service* notice in the *Newtownards Chronicle*. It contained the verse:

To love, to love and then to part
Is the greatest sorrow of a mother's heart

Ordinary Seaman David Scott is commemorated on Plymouth Naval Memorial in Devon; on a stained glass window in the Church of St. Peter, Martindale in Cumbria, on a memorial plaque in Harstad, Norway and on Newtownards and District War Memorial. His father, Robert Scott, was on active service with the Army during the Second World War.

David Scott's brothers, Desmond and Wilfred, were born after David was killed. On Friday 16 April 1954 (five days before Wilfred's 11th birthday) the two brothers were playing together in a quarry at Ballycullen, Newtownards when Wilfred received a shotgun wound to the head. Two young men who were also in the quarry at the time were shooting crows. Wilfred Scott died that evening in Ards Hospital and he was buried in Movilla Cemetery, Newtownards.

David Scott's father Robert died in April 1966 (records vary as to the exact date) and his mother Margaret died on 16 March 2000 in her 100th year. Both were buried in the same grave as their son Wilfred. David Scott's brother Robert (Bobby, Hannah's husband) died on 10 May 1993 (aged 73); Hannah Scott died on 29 January 2004.

Scott, James Gilmore (Gillie)
Lieutenant
No. 258659, 5th Battalion Royal Inniskilling Fusiliers *attached*
45th Regiment Reconnaissance Corps, Royal Armoured Corps
Killed in action on Thursday 13 April 1944 (aged 22)
Taukkyan War Cemetery, Myanmar (Grave 13 F 18)

Killed in Action.—News has come to hand of the death in action of Lieut. James Gilmore Scott, of the Royal Irish Fusiliers (attached Reconnaissance Corps), at the age of 22. He was the only child of Mr. and Mrs. W. Scott, Burn Brae, Ballyrobert, Ballyclare, to whom sympathy is tendered in their bereavement. Lieut. Scott was a popular member of the staff of Bangor Branch of the Ulster Bank when he joined up in 1941.

James Gilmore (Gillie) Scott was born on 30 March 1922 in Wallasey, Cheshire and he was the only child of William James Scott (born in County Antrim) and Ida Mabel Scott (nee Coote, born in County Leitrim). Their marriage was registered in the second quarter of 1921 in Longford and, after the birth of their son, they lived at Burn Brae, Ballyrobert, Ballyclare, Co. Antrim. James Gilmore Scott attended Royal Belfast Academical Institution (RBAI) from 1937 until 1940 and, prior to enlisting in 1941, he worked in the Bangor Branch of the Ulster Bank.

In the CWGC Debt of Honour it is recorded that Lieutenant Scott served with the 5th Battalion, Royal Inniskilling Fusiliers *attached to* the 45th Regiment Reconnaissance Corps, Royal Armoured Corps. It is also recorded there that he served with the Chindits. This was a special force serving in Burma and India and trained to operate behind enemy (Japanese) lines.

Lieutenant James Gilmore Scott died on 13 April 1944, just two weeks after his 22nd birthday, and he is commemorated on the RBAI Memorial Plaque and on the Ulster Bank Memorial Plaque in their Donegall Square East premises.

Scott, Robert Norman Cecil*
Second Lieutenant
No. 89740, 10 Battery, 3 Searchlight Regiment, Royal Artillery
Killed in action on Monday 27 May 1940 (aged 23)
Dunkirk Memorial, Nord, France (Column 7)

Robert Norman Cecil Scott was born on 26 July 1916 and he was a son of Robert Norman Cecil and Alison Scott (nee Vivash). Robert Norman Cecil Scott worked as an oil and hardware merchant in Belfast and he and Alison Vivash were married on 31 July 1915 in St. George's Church of Ireland Church, Belfast. They lived at *Eisleben House*, Stranmillis Road, Belfast. Robert Norman Cecil Scott's uncles worked in the same business as his father and one of them, James Herbert Scott, married Jessie McMullan on 1 June 1910 in Claremont Presbyterian Church, Londonderry.

Robert Norman Cecil Scott was educated at Rockport School, Craigavad and he played hockey for the Lisnagarvey Club. He joined the Royal Artillery before the start of the Second World War and on 1 April 1939 he was commissioned from Sapper to Second Lieutenant. Second Lieutenant Robert Norman Cecil Scott was 23 years old when he was killed on 27 May 1940 during the Dunkirk evacuation and he is commemorated on the Dunkirk Memorial and in Rockport School. Robert Norman Cecil Scott Senior was 63 years old when he died on 23 July 1944.

Shanks, Joseph
Gunner
No. 1465491, 539 Battery, 157 Heavy Anti-Aircraft Regiment, Royal Artillery
Killed in a motor cycle accident on Monday 26 February 1945 (aged 34)
Southend-on-Sea (Sutton Road) Cemetery, Essex, England
(Plot R Grave 12164)

DIED ON ACTIVE SERVICE.

SHANKS—February 26, 1945, Joseph, dearly-loved husband of Emma. "A loving husband, true and kind, He ever was, in heart and mind, A tender parent, too, as well, While he with us on earth did dwell." Deeply regretted by his loving Wife and daughter Patsy, 64 Beatrice Road, Bangor.

Joseph Shanks was born in 1910 and he was a son of Thomas and Susan Shanks of Plymouth where Thomas was the Harbour Constable. Before the war Joseph Shanks lived at 52 Mark Street, Newtownards and he worked as a knitter. He and Emma Mary Couser were married on 12 July 1933 in Donaghadee Roman Catholic Church and they lived at 64 Beatrice Road, Bangor. Emma Mary Couser was a daughter of John Andrew and Margaret Couser (nee Finlay) who were married on 17 April 1911 in Newtownards Parish Church of Ireland

Church (St Mark's); in different records their surname is spelt Carser, Couser and Cowser. John Andrew Couser's brother James served in the Great War as James Carser and he was killed at Gallipoli on 21 November 1915. James Carser is commemorated on Page 152 in the Book of Honour *Remembering Their Sacrifice in the Great War – Ards* compiled by Barry Niblock.

Joseph and Emma Shanks had one child, a daughter named Patsy, who was ten years old when her father died. Joseph had joined up at the outbreak of war and he served with the Royal Artillery in the Middle East before being stationed in England. The death of Joseph Shanks in Southend-on-Sea was reported in the 10 March 1945 edition of the *County Down Spectator*. Working as a despatch rider, Gunner Shanks was killed when his motor cycle was in collision with a motor bus on 26 February 1945. He was 34 years old and he died half an hour after the accident without regaining consciousness. He was buried in Southend-on-Sea (Sutton Road) Cemetery, Essex. His wife and daughter placed a *Died on Active Service* notice in the 17 March 1945 edition of the *County Down Spectator* and it contained the verse:

> *A loving husband, true and kind, he ever was in heart and mind*
> *A tender parent too, as well, while he with us on earth did dwell*

S

Shanks, Owen
Military Medal
Lieutenant
No. 329143, 7th Battalion, Black Watch (Royal Highlanders)
Killed in action on Thursday 8 February 1945 (aged 34)
Jonkerbos War Cemetery, Gelderland, Netherlands (Grave 14 G 3)

BANGOR OFFICER KILLED

18 YEARS' SERVICE

Official intimation has been received that Lieut. Owen Shanks, M.M., Black Watch, aged 35, son of Mrs. M. A. Shanks, 73 Clandeboye Road, has been killed on active service. He had 18 years' service. His late father served with the R.U.R. in the Boer and Great Wars. A brother is serving, and another was recently discharged through illness after 21 years' service. His wife resides in Edinburgh. Sincere sympathy is tendered to the relatives of the gallant officer in their bereavement.

Owen Shanks was born on 5 November 1910 and he was a son of Joseph and Mary Ann Shanks (nee Hamilton) who lived at 57 McTier Street, Belfast. Joseph Shanks (son of William Shanks) worked as a labourer and he and Mary Ann Hamilton (daughter of John Hamilton) were married on 3 April 1899 in Trinity Church of Ireland Church, Belfast. Joseph Shanks served in both the South African and First World Wars. Joseph and Mary Ann Shanks had at least nine children including Jeanie; Martha (born 20 September 1900); Elizabeth (born 28 January 1905); James (born 18 May 1906); Mary (born 18 June 1908); Owen (born 5 November 1910); Letitia (born 22 December 1912) and Margaret (born 15 September 1918). Owen's sister Martha died on 15 September 1923 (aged 23), his father Joseph died on 6 December 1933 (aged 64) and his mother Mary Ann died on 10 April 1954 (aged 76). They were buried in Dundonald Cemetery (Grave E2 94).

Owen Shanks joined the Army on 17 September 1927 and during the Second World War he served with the 7th Battalion Black Watch. His marriage to Grace Darling Clazie (daughter of Henry Clazie) was registered in 1943 in Lasswade, Midlothian, Scotland. Acting Company Sergeant Major Owen Shanks made his will on 9 May 1944 and in it he named his mother Mary Ann (then living at 73 Clandeboye Road, Bangor) as his Executor. He left all of his estate to his wife Darling who was living at *Hillview*, Edgefield Road, Loanhead, Midlothian.

The 7th Battalion Black Watch landed in Normandy in early June 1944 and was heavily involved in the actions leading to the breakout from Caen and the Falaise Gap. Later that year the Battalion took part in the heavy fighting in the low-lying country astride the River Maas in Holland. On 24 July 1944 Sergeant Owen Shanks was granted an Immediate Emergency Commission from the ranks as Second Lieutenant and later he was promoted to the rank of Lieutenant. He was awarded the Military Medal and the announcement was made in the 19 October 1944 Supplement to the *London Gazette*. In the bitter weather of January 1945 the 7th Battalion was employed in operations to stem the last German offensive into the Ardennes and, after that, the Battalion fought on the Dutch-German border in the Battle of Reichswald Forest which commenced on 8 February 1945.

Lieutenant Owen Shanks was killed in action on 8 February 1945 and his death was reported in the 24 February 1945 edition of the *County Down Spectator* under the headline *Bangor Officer Killed*. He was buried in Jonkerbos War Cemetery, and there is an inscription on his CWGC headstone:

Until the day break

Shaw, Edmund Verner (Edmund)
Flight Sergeant (Pilot)
No. 748518, Royal Air Force Volunteer Reserve
Killed in an aircraft accident on Thursday 21 May 1942 (aged 22)
Belfast (Dundonald) Cemetery, Co. Down (Section D 4 Grave 105)

Edmund Verner Shaw was born in September 1919 in Church View,

Holywood and he was a son of Edmund Shaw (born 23 September 1876 in Belfast) and Mary Shaw (nee Clemence). His paternal grandparents were Edmund and Sarah Jane Shaw (nee Dawson) of 168 Parkgate Avenue, Belfast. Edmund Verner Shaw's father was a commercial traveller and he and Mary Clemence were married on 28 January 1916 in St. Barnabas's Episcopal Church, Paisley in Scotland. They had a son who was born on 21 January 1917 but he only lived for 20 minutes and was buried in the Public Ground of Belfast City Cemetery.

Edmund Verner Shaw attended Holywood Public Elementary School, Strandtown Public Elementary School and Royal Belfast Academical Institution (RBAI). When he left school he worked as a clerk for the Belfast Steamship Company. He joined the Royal Air Force Volunteer Reserve in May 1939 and was called up for full time service at the beginning of the Second World War. He went to England for training and on 14 December 1940 he was posted to 218 (Gold Coast) Squadron based at RAF Marham near King's Lynn in Norfolk. In February 1941 he survived when he had to bale out of his Vickers Wellington aircraft which ran out of fuel in fog on the way back to base after a bombing mission over Bremen. In April 1941 he was posted to Egypt and then S Iraq. He returned to Britain in March 1942 and in April he was posted to 20 Operational Training Unit (OTU) as an instructor on Avro Anson aircraft. On 21 May 1942 he was returning with his pupils from a cross country exercise in Anson N5259 when the aircraft struck overhead pylon cables near RAF Little Rissington in Gloucestershire and crashed. Flight Sergeant Edmund Verner Shaw was severely injured and he died in the Station Hospital; his effects amounted to some £187. Everyone on board the aircraft was killed.

Flight Sergeant Edmund Verner Shaw's funeral took place on 27 May 1942 and he is commemorated on the family grave headstone in Belfast (Dundonald) Cemetery. His father Edmund died on 9 August 1960 (aged 83) and his mother Mary died on 31 March 1968 (aged 80).

Shaw, Eric
Sergeant (Air Gunner)
No. 1074934, 101 Squadron, Royal Air Force Volunteer Reserve
Killed in action on Friday 12 March 1943 (aged 22)
Reichswald Forest War Cemetery, Kleve, Nordrhein-Westfalen, Germany (Grave 10 B 10)

Eric Shaw was born on 16 June 1921 and he was a son of John and Margaretta

(Margaret) Shaw (nee Scott) of 15 Ardgreenan Gardens, Strandtown, Belfast. John Shaw was an electrician and he and Margaret Scott were married on 23 August 1920 in Eglinton Street Presbyterian Church, Belfast.

Eric Shaw attended Strandtown Public Elementary School and then Sullivan Upper School, Holywood from September 1934 until June 1937. During the Second World War Eric Shaw served with the Royal Air Force Volunteer Reserve in Bomber Command and he died on 12 March 1943. Sergeant Eric Shaw was one of a seven man crew aboard an Avro Lancaster Mark I aircraft (W4862) that took off from RAF Holme-on-Spalding Moor in Yorkshire on a mission to bomb Essen. Their aircraft crashed in the target area and all aboard were killed. On 16 March 1943 they were all buried in Dusseldorf North Cemetery and later exhumed and reinterred in Reichswald Forest War Cemetery. In addition to Sergeant (Air Gunner) Eric Shaw (aged 22) the other six crew members who died that day were:

- Flying Officer John Richard Kee aged 26 (RCAF)
- Sergeant William Hynd aged 23 from Dunfermline, Fife
- Sergeant Arthur Dennis Slade aged 20 from Wareham, Dorsetshire
- Sergeant Stanley Gordon Smith
- Sgt William Edmund Greasley aged 20 from Wirksworth, Derbyshire
- Sergeant Ernest Alfred Steed aged 24 from Bassett, Hampshire

Sergeant (Air Gunner) Eric Shaw is commemorated in Sullivan Upper School.

Shaw, Robert Joseph (Robert)
Ordinary Seaman
SS *Cadillac* (Newcastle-on-Tyne), Merchant Navy
Died as a result of enemy action on Saturday 1 March 1941 (aged 18)
Tower Hill Memorial, London, England (Panel 22)

Robert Joseph Shaw was born on 15 November 1922 and he was a son of Robert Gordon Shaw and Elizabeth Shaw (nee Bannon) of Portaferry, Co. Down. He was baptised on 20 November 1922 in St. Joseph's Roman Catholic Church, Belfast. During the Second World War, Robert Joseph Shaw served with the Merchant Navy aboard the British Steam Tanker SS *Cadillac*. Built in 1917 by Palmer's Shipbuilding and Iron Company Ltd., Newcastle-upon-Tyne SS *Cadillac* was owned by the Anglo-American Oil Company Ltd., London. Around midnight on 1 March 1941, in Convoy HX-109, the SS *Cadillac* was on route from Aruba, Lesser Antilles in the

Caribbean Sea to Avonmouth, Bristol carrying a cargo of some 17,000 tons of aviation fuel when she was torpedoed and sunk by the German submarine *U-552* about 170 miles northwest of the Outer Hebrides.

Ordinary Seaman Robert Joseph Shaw and Captain **John Frazer Jefferson** from Holywood were among more than 30 men who died. Ordinary Seaman Robert Joseph Shaw was 18 years old when he died and he is commemorated on the Tower Hill Memorial in London.

Shaw, William
Newtownards and District War Memorial

 The name William Shaw is listed on Newtownards and District War Memorial. In the CWGC Debt of Honour 77 William Shaws are commemorated, 54 of them with one or more additional forenames. Two William Shaws from Newtownards were buried in Movilla Cemetery during the war years; both died of tuberculosis:

- 27 July 1941, a school teacher (aged 40) of Bangor Road
- 16 September 1944, a bus conductor (aged 38) of 12 Corry's Street

Desk studies and public appeals to date have yielded no further information about the identity of William Shaw who is commemorated on Newtownards and District War Memorial.

Sheals Brothers, Hubert Stanley and Eric Francis

Hubert Stanley and Eric Francis Sheals were sons of Hugh Townley Sheals and Frances Sheals (nee Timbey) who were married on 10 September 1903 in St. James's Church of Ireland Church, Belfast. Hugh Townley Sheals was a linen merchant and he and Frances had at least three children – Hubert Stanley (born 19 June 1904); Ashley Timbey (born 21 July 1908) and Eric Francis (born 18 July 1912). For a time the Sheals family lived with Frances's widowed mother, Eliza Timbey, in the townland of Ballyfinaghy, Malone, Belfast. Later they lived at *Arden*, Balmoral, Belfast.

Both Hubert and Eric Sheals attended Royal Belfast Academical Institution (RBAI), Hubert from 1918 until 1920 and Eric from 1924 until 1929. Their mother, Frances Sheals, died on 1 January 1945 (aged 65) and their father, Hugh Townley Sheals, died on 25 September 1951 (aged 76). Both parents were buried in Belfast City Cemetery (Grave A2 4). Eric was the first of the two brothers to be killed.

Sheals, Francis Eric (Eric)
Bombardier
No. 1486508, 5 Battery, 2 Light Anti-Aircraft Regiment, Royal Artillery
Killed in action on Sunday 4 January 1942 (aged 29)
Benghazi War Cemetery, Libya (Grave 7 C 5)

Eric Sheals joined the Royal Artillery and he served with 5 Battery, 2 Light Anti-Aircraft Regiment. Bombardier Francis Eric Sheals was 29 years old when he was killed in action on 4 January 1942 and he was buried in Benghazi War Cemetery, Libya (Grave 7 C 5). He is commemorated in RBAI.

On Sunday 2 September 2011 a commemorative church service was held in Baronscourt Parish Church, Co. Tyrone to dedicate a plaque to the memory of the eighteen scouts from 74th Belfast (RBAI) Scout Group who lost their lives in the Second World War, many of whom had camped on the Baronscourt Estate in the years immediately prior to the outbreak of hostilities. The plaque commemorated the 70th anniversary of the first building of a memorial cairn by RBAI scouts on the nearby hill known as Bessy Bell. In addition to Bombardier Francis Eric Sheals the plaque bears the names of Warrant Officer **Samuel Nicholl Beckett**, Captain **Samuel David Corry** and Sergeant **Sydney Ireland**.

Sheals, Hubert Stanley (Hubert)
Flying Officer
No. 61116, Royal Air Force
Killed on active service on Friday 6 March 1942 (aged 37)
Singapore Memorial, Singapore (Column 413)

SHEALS H.S. Hubert Stanley Sheals joined the Royal Air Force and he was on war service when he and Ethel Winifred Milliken (daughter of Samuel Milliken) were married on 17 April 1941 in Helen's Bay Presbyterian Church. Less than a year later Flying Officer Hubert Stanley Sheals died on 6 March 1942 during operations following the fall of Singapore to Japanese Forces on 15 February 1942. Flying Officer Hubert Stanley Sheals was 37 years old when he was killed (just two months after his brother Eric) and he is commemorated on the Singapore Memorial; in Ballygilbert Presbyterian Church (as Hubert Sheals); in the annals of Helen's Bay Presbyterian Church and in RBAI.

Hubert's widow, Ethel Winifred Sheals (nee Milliken), was living at 35 Rosevale (Roseville), Craigavad when she and Wallace Hamilton Robb were married on 30 March 1949 in Ballygilbert Presbyterian Church.

Shepherd, Lambert Charles
(Lambert, known to his friends as Bush)
Ordinary Seaman
No. P/JX 223842, HMS *Hood*, Royal Navy
Killed in action on Saturday 24 May 1941 (aged 30)
Portsmouth Naval Memorial, Hampshire, England (Panel 51 Column 2)

Lambert Charles Shepherd was born on 28 February 1911 in Hale, Cheshire and he was the only son of Major Percy Edward Shepherd (born in Romford Essex) and Ella Shepherd (nee Roome, born in Birmingham which was then in Warwickshire). They were married on 3 February 1907. Major Shepherd worked as a civil engineer for a railway company and the Shepherd family came to Northern Ireland around 1922 when Major Shepherd became Director of Works for the Government of Northern Ireland. The Shepherd family lived at 21 Knockmore Park, Bangor. Lambert's mother Ella died on 24 September 1944 (aged 66). His father Percy remarried and Percy died on 2 March 1948 (aged 69). Sir Percy Shepherd was buried in Bangor Cemetery after a service in Bangor Abbey at which the Revd James Hamilton officiated.

Lambert Charles Shepherd was educated at Oakfield Preparatory School, Rugby; at Shrewsbury School and at Jesus College Cambridge, where he graduated in 1933 with a first class honours degree in Classics and a second class honours degree in English Literature. He was an accomplished rower.

In 1934 he joined the staff of the Newsletter in Belfast, later moving to Allied Newspapers in Manchester and then to the *London Daily Mirror* and the *London Evening Standard*. In June 1939 he married Iris Eunice Henry of Woolaston, Sutton, Surrey and in the same year he joined the London Fire Service as an auxiliary fireman. In 1940 he was a volunteer member of a ship's crew that went to Dunkirk to help with the evacuation. In April 1941 he joined the Royal Navy and was posted to HMS *Hood* for probationary service prior to sitting his final examinations for commissioned rank. Nicknamed the *Mighty Hood*, HMS *Hood* was an Admiral-class battle cruiser built by John Brown & Company, Clydebank and she was commissioned in May 1920. On 24 May 1941 HMS *Hood* and HMS *Prince of Wales* were in the Denmark Strait between Greenland and Iceland when they intercepted the German warships *Prinz Eugen* and *Bismarck*. HMS *Hood* was hit by shells fired from both ships but it was a shell fired from *Bismarck* which triggered the magazine explosion that destroyed the aft part of the ship. With her back broken she sank in less than three minutes. More than 1,410 men lost

S

their lives including Lambert Charles Shepherd and **John Gordon Morrison Erskine** (Holywood).

Ordinary Seaman Lambert Charles Shepherd's death was reported in the 31 May 1941 edition of the *County Down Spectator*. He was 30 years old when he died and his wife lived at 16 Unwin Mansions, Queen's Club Gardens, West Kensington, London. His effects amounted to some £1,274 and probate was granted to his widow. In 1944 Iris Eunice Shepherd married John Cameron and in 1969, at the request of the British Government, her husband – by then Lord Cameron – undertook an inquiry into civil unrest in Northern Ireland. Lady Cameron was 94 years old when she died on 7 June 2009 in Edinburgh Royal Infirmary.

Ordinary Seaman Lambert Charles Shepherd is commemorated on Portsmouth Naval Memorial in Hampshire; in the HMS *Hood* Book of Remembrance in St. John the Baptist Parish Church, Boldre in Hampshire; in Bangor Parish Church of Ireland Church (St. Comgall's) and on the family grave headstone in Bangor Cemetery. Sir Percy Shepherd established a scholarship (Classics and English Triposes) at Jesus College in memory of his son.

Shields, James
Sergeant (Air Gunner)
No. 1795770, 192 Squadron, Royal Air Force Volunteer Reserve
Killed on active service on Thursday 25 May 1944 (aged 21)
Heverlee War Cemetery, Leuven, Vlaams-Brabant, Belgium (Grave 5 C 5)

James Shields was a son of Alexander (Sandy) and Bridget (Bridie) Shields (nee Flanagan) of Cullintra, Comber. Alexander Shields worked as a labourer and he and Bridie Flanagan were married on 29 November 1916 in Ballymacarrett Church of Ireland Church (St. Patrick's), Belfast. They had at least six children including Alec, Mary and James. During the Second World War, Alec Shields served in the Royal Air Force as a Flight Mechanic. Mary Shields married William Munn and they lived at Castle Espie, Comber. James Shields was educated at Ballydrain Public Elementary School and after leaving school he worked for Messrs Short and Harland in Belfast.

KILLED ON ACTIVE SERVICE

SHIELDS—James, Sgt. Air-Gunner, R.A.F.V.R., missing since May 25th, now presumed killed on that date. Manly and brave, His young life he gave. Deeply regretted by his loving Father and Mother, Brothers and Sisters.—Alex. and Bridie Shields, Cullintra, Comber.

In 1942 James Shields joined the Royal Air Force Volunteer Reserve and he was reported missing in May 1944. He was one of a crew of nine aboard a Handley Page Halifax Mark III aircraft (MZ501) which flew out of RAF Foulsham in Norfolk and crashed at 11.44 pm in Limburg, Netherlands. Only Flying Officer D.B. Gaunt survived the crash and he was taken Prisoner-of-War. Sergeant James Shields (aged 21) was killed and the other seven men who died that night were:

- Pilot Officer Philip Hicken aged 29 from Langwith, Nottinghamshire
- Flying Officer John Daniel Hurley aged 22 from London
- Sergeant Philip John Jeffs
- Flight Sergeant Arthur Clarence MacGillivray aged 22 (RCAF)
- Sergeant Ronald Rook aged 21 from Sheffield
- Pilot Officer Eugene Preston Sabine aged 26 (RCAF)
- Sergeant Claire Douglas Stroud aged 22 (RCAF)

They were all buried south of Limburg at Sint-Truiden (St. Tront) where there was a major Luftwaffe air base and later reinterred in Heverlee War Cemetery.

In November 1944 it was officially reported that Sergeant (Air Gunner) James Shields must be presumed dead and his father, mother, brothers and sisters placed a *Killed on Active Service* notice in the 18 November 1944 edition of the *County Down Spectator*.

Sergeant James Shields is commemorated on Comber and District War Memorial; in Second Comber Presbyterian Church and on the family grave headstone in Comber Cemetery. His father Sandy died on 11 September 1965; his brother Alec died on 18 May 1987 and his mother Bridie died on 20 October 1989.

Shields, William John
Fusilier
No. 3129613, 1st Battalion, Royal Inniskilling Fusiliers
Killed in action on Saturday 18 April 1942 (aged 27)
Rangoon Memorial, Myanmar (Face 11)

William John Shields was the elder son of William John and Jane Shields of 12 George Street, Newtownards and he was a member of Greenwell Street LOL No. 1948 in Newtownards. During the First World War William John Shields Senior served with the 2nd Battalion, Royal Irish Rifles and he was a Prisoner-of-War in Germany for four years. During the Second World War William John Shields Junior served with the Royal Inniskilling Fusiliers (and before that the Royal Air Force) and in the 17 October 1942 edition of the *Newtownards Chronicle* it was reported that he was missing in action. Then, in the 8 September 1945 edition of the same newspaper, it was reported that he was still missing. The report indicated that he had 16 years service to his credit and that he had served in India, China and Burma. His younger brother Stewart was serving with the Royal Irish Fusiliers in Burma.

S

In the 2 March 1946 edition of the *Newtownards Chronicle* under the headline *Ards Soldier's Death Presumed After Four Years* it was reported that Fusilier William John Shields must be presumed killed in action. This report indicated that on the night of 18/19 April 1942 the 1st Battalion, Royal Inniskilling Fusiliers was engaged in fierce fighting in Burma and when roll was called many men, including Fusilier Shields, were missing. Since then there had been no news of his fate and now, some four years later, he must be presumed dead. Family members placed *Killed on Active Service* notices in the same edition of that newspaper and then *Our Heroes – In Memoriam* notices in the 20 April 1946 edition. These included one from his sister Lizzie and brother-in-law Sandy Smyth and their children Bill and Jean Smyth of 5 Zion Place, Newtownards.

Fusilier William John Shields is commemorated on the Rangoon Memorial; on Newtownards and District War Memorial; in

Newtownards Parish Church of Ireland Church (St. Mark's) and on the family grave headstone in Movilla Cemetery. His father William John died on 26 August 1955 (aged 66) and his sister Margaret died on 10 November 1978. Fusilier William John Shields's cousin, Gunner **William McBlain**, was killed in action on 11 September 1943.

Shillington, Thomas (Tom)
Trooper
No. 7942895, 8th Royal Tank Regiment, Royal Armoured Corps
Died on active service on Tuesday 3 November 1942 (aged 26)
Alamein Memorial, Egypt (Column 24)

Thomas Shillington was born on 27 September 1916 and he was a son of Thomas Averell Shillington (a linen manufacturer and merchant, born in County Armagh) and Margaret Shillington (nee McDougall, born in England). Their marriage was registered in the second quarter of 1908 in Woolwich, London and they lived at *Greenoge*, Deramore Drive, Belfast; later at *Ardkeen*, Craigavad, Co. Down.

S

Both Thomas and his brother, James Averell Shillington (born 14 August 1910) were educated at Rockport School, Craigavad. After obtaining a degree from Trinity College, Dublin Thomas Shillington dedicated his life to moral rearmament through the Oxford Group founded by Frank Buchman. His brother James was a solicitor's apprentice when he (James) obtained his pilot's licence on 14 August 1937 (his 27th birthday).

During the Second World War Thomas Shillington served with the 8th Royal Tank Regiment, Royal Armoured Corps and he died on active service in the Western Desert on 3 November 1942. Trooper Thomas Shillington's effects amounted to some £697 and probate was granted to his brother James who was a Lieutenant in the Royal Irish Fusiliers.

Trooper Thomas Shillington is commemorated on the Alamein Memorial; in Glencraig Parish Church of Ireland Church and in Rockport School. His mother Margaret (born 29 October 1874) died on 19 February 1951 (aged 76) and was buried in Bangor Cemetery. His father Thomas died on 14 September 1951 (aged 77). Trooper Thomas Shillington was related to Flying Officer **Anthony Alexander Talbot Bulloch** who was killed in action on 24 April 1940.

Shipcott, Henry Hanna (Harry)
Seaman First Class
No. 8882442, USS *Morrison*, United States Naval Reserve
Died as a result of enemy action on Saturday 4/Sunday 5 May 1945 (aged 36)
Honolulu Memorial (Court 2), Hawaii

Henry Hanna (Harry) Shipcott was born on 20 April 1909 in Belfast and he was a son of William Bradford Shipcott (a tinsmith, son of William Shipcott, a millwright) and Elizabeth Shipcott (nee McMillen, born 15 December 1873, daughter of William John McMillen, a painter). They were married on 2 April 1896 in St. Enoch's Church of Ireland Church, Belfast (witnessed by Henry Hanna and Elizabeth's sister, Sarah Lyttle McMillen). Henry Hanna and Sarah McMillen were married later the same day in the same church. William and Elizabeth Shipcott had five children – Eleanor (born 18 December 1896); Sarah Beatrice (born 24 March 1898); Mabel Logan (born 8 October 1901); William Bradford (born 6 September 1905) and Henry Hanna (born 20 April 1909). William Bradford Shipcott Senior had previously been married to Annie Cain (sometimes Cean, married 27 March 1886 in Mariner's Church of Ireland Church, Belfast) and they had a daughter called Annie Ethel (born 27 November 1887). In 1901 the Shipcott family (it was the only Shipcott family in Ireland) was living at 22 Howe Street, Belfast and in 1911 the Shipcott family was living at 11 Stranmillis Road, Belfast. In 1911 William Bradford Shipcott was the manager of a soup factory and on 10 July 1911 his eldest daughter, Annie Ethel Shipcott, married Samuel McMillen (sometimes McMillan) in Fisherwick Presbyterian Church, Belfast

William Bradford Shipcott Senior of 2 Lockview Road, Belfast died in the Royal Victoria Hospital, Belfast on 24 October 1914 (aged 48) and he was buried in Belfast City Cemetery (Grave M 62). After William's death his widow Elizabeth and her five children moved to Bangor where they worshipped in Hamilton Road Presbyterian Church. They were living at 29 Alfred Street when Eleanor died on 1 July 1915 (aged 18), and at 12 May Avenue when Beatrice Sarah died on 25 March 1917 (aged 19). Eleanor and Beatrice Sarah Shipcott were both buried in Belfast City Cemetery (Grave M 62) alongside their father.

After Beatrice died, Elizabeth and her three surviving children moved to Canada; in April 1921 Mabel Logan Shipcott travelled from Liverpool to St. John, New Brunswick aboard the *Empress of France* and records also show Elizabeth Shipcott (aged 43) travelling to Niagara Falls, Ontario with her three children – Mabel Logan (aged 18), William Bradford (aged 15) and Henry Hanna (aged 9). Mabel Logan Shipcott died of tuberculosis on

S

12 March 1923 (aged 21) in Toronto Free Hospital and she was buried in Prospect Cemetery, Toronto. At the time her mother Elizabeth was living at 159 Campbell Ave, Toronto.

After Mabel died, Elizabeth and her two sons – William Bradford Shipcott and Henry Hanna (Harry) Shipcott – moved to the USA. Harry completed his education at Biola Bible Institute and College, Los Angeles, California where his mother did clerical work. In the archives of Hamilton Road Presbyterian Church, Bangor it is recorded that Harry Shipcott, a former member of the Congregation, was 'engaged in active full-time Christian service in connection with Dr Torrey's work in the USA'. Dr Reuben Archer Torrey conducted evangelistic campaigns throughout the world before being appointed Dean of the Biola Bible Institute in Los Angeles.

Both William Bradford Shipcott and Henry Hanna (Harry) Shipcott had fine singing voices and they were part of a Men's Quartet that gave performances up and down the coast of California. Both men became naturalised US citizens in California. During the Second World War Seaman First Class Harry Shipcott served aboard USS *Morrison* with the United States Naval Reserve. USS *Morrison* was a Fletcher-class destroyer built by the Seattle-Tacoma Shipbuilding Corporation in Washington State, USA and launched in 1943. She was engaged in the Central Pacific Campaigns, the Philippines Campaign and the Battle of Okinawa. USS *Morrison* sank on 4/5 May 1945 after being struck by four Japanese kamikaze aircraft and Seaman First Class Harry Shipcott (aged 36) was one of more than 150 men who were killed.

Seaman First Class Harry Shipcott is commemorated in the Courts of the Missing (Court 2) and on the Tablets of the Missing, Honolulu Memorial, Hawaii. Harry Shipcott's wife Viola (in some records Clara nee Anderson) lived at 163 16th Street, Richmond, Contra Costa County, California and she and Harry had one son, Harry Clifford (born 1931).

In 1930 William Bradford Shipcott was working as a farm labourer and living in Turlock, Stanislaus County, California. He and Florence Idamae Rodman (born in Sweden) were married on 1 January 1928 in the Swedish Free Church, Turlock. In 1940 they and their five children were living in Eden, California – William (aged 11); Ronald (aged 8); Florence (aged 5); Stanley (aged 4) and Robert (aged 2).

William Bradford Shipcott joined the US Army Transportation Corps and during the Second World War he served on various ships in both the South Pacific and European Theatres of War. He remained at sea after the war ended (in 1951 he was serving aboard USNS *Cardinal O'Connell*) and his last appointment was as First Mate on the *Puerto Del Sol*, William Bradford Shipcott of 508 North Rama Street, Puente, California died at 8.55 am on 8 September 1955 (aged 50). He died of cirrhosis of the liver in a hospital in Buenos Aires, Peru and his remains were shipped to Schanel Mortuary, 444 South Tyler Avenue, El Monte, California. In the archives of Hamilton Road Presbyterian Church, Bangor it is recorded that 'W.B. Shipcott from the Congregation served with the US Navy'.

Shipcott, Thomas
Bangor and District War Memorial
Hamilton Road Presbyterian Church Bangor

The name Thomas Shipcott is listed on Bangor and District War Memorial and on the Second World War Memorial Plaque in Hamilton Road Presbyterian Church, Bangor. Desk searches and public appeals to date have yielded no further information about Thomas Shipcott and there is strong evidence to suggest that Thomas Shipcott and **Harry Shipcott** are one and the same person.

Simpson, Raymond Farquhar
Flight Sergeant (Wireless Operator/Air Gunner)
No. 410530, Royal New Zealand Air Force
Killed in an aircraft accident on Thursday 18 November 1943 (aged 23)
Newtownards (Movilla) Cemetery, Co. Down (Section 28 Prot Plot Grave 99)

Raymond Farquhar Simpson was a son of Robert Farquhar Simpson and May Simpson (nee Dodd) of Papanui, Canterbury, New Zealand. During the Second World War Flight Sergeant Raymond Farquhar Simpson served with the Royal New Zealand Air Force and he died on 18 November 1943 along with the other three members of crew when their Lockheed Hudson Mark V aircraft (AE653) of No 5. (Coastal) Operational Training Unit, based at RAF Long Kesh, crashed into Strangford Lough just south of Chapel Island (off Greyabbey). They were on a rocket-firing exercise using the submarine target at South Island in Strangford Lough.

The other three men who died in the crash were the pilot, Sergeant **Walter Edward Fern**; Flight Sergeant **William Barraclough** and Flight Sergeant

Andrew Greenwell Gibbison. Flight Sergeant Raymond Farquhar Simpson's body was recovered from Strangford Lough in January 1944 and he was buried on 18 January in Newtownards (Movilla) Cemetery, Co. Down. He is commemorated on the New Zealand National War Memorial in Wellington and on the New Zealand Cenotaph Database in Auckland War Memorial Museum.

Sinton, Arthur Buckby
Flying Officer
No. 119279, 515 Squadron, Royal Air Force Volunteer Reserve
Killed on active service on Saturday 26 June 1943 (aged 28)
Runnymede Memorial, Surrey, England (Panel 129)

Arthur Buckby Sinton was born on 3 August 1914 and he was a son of Frederick Buckby Sinton (born 27 July 1870, died 25 June 1943) and Hannah Maria Sinton (nee Woods, born 1 April 1884, died 23 May 1968) who lived in *Banford House*, Knockagore, Gilford, Co. Down. They were married on 6 November 1912 in Friends Meeting House, Churchtown, Dublin and they had three children – Thomas Tertius (born 13 January 1913, died 16 August 1963); Arthur Buckby (born 3 August 1914, died 26 June 1943); Margaret Greville (born 12 June 1917, died 29 March 1999).

Frederick Buckby Sinton had previously been married to Edith Uprichard Woods. They were married on 8 March 1899 in Friends Meeting House, Churchtown, Dublin and they had five children – Annie Dorothy (born 14 January 1900, died 4 December 1988); Elizabeth Maud (born 17 February 1901, died 6 February 1971); Edith Marjorie (born 13 June 1902, died 1997); Frederick Maynard (born April 1904, died 16 May 1936) and Rosemary Buckby (born 8 August 1907, died 20 September 2005).

Arthur Buckby Sinton was educated at Rockport School, Craigavad and he was a keen golfer. He was the husband of Vera Wilson Sinton (nee Woods, born 1 April 1916, died 18 August 2006) and they lived in Gilford, Co. Down. They had two children – David Frederick Sinton and Vera May Sinton.

During the Second World War Arthur Buckby Sinton served with the Royal Air Force Volunteer Reserve in 515 Squadron. From October 1942 this Squadron used Electronic Countermeasures (ECM) to jam enemy radar installations. Flying Officer Arthur Buckby Sinton was one of a two man crew aboard a Boulton Paul Defiant Mark II aircraft (AA572) that took off from RAF Coltishall in Norfolk and was shot down over Zeeland in the Netherlands by a German night fighter. Flying Officer Sinton was the pilot and the other crew member who died that night was the air gunner:

- PO Leonard Arthur Johnson aged 31 from West Bergholt, Essex

Pilot Officer Johnson's body was recovered and buried in Amsterdam New Eastern Cemetery. Flying Officer Arthur Buckby Sinton was 28 years old when he died on 26 June 1943 and his body was never recovered. He is commemorated on the Runnymede Memorial in Surrey; in Rockport School; in Royal County Down Golf Clubhouse and on the family grave headstone in Friends Burial Ground, Moyallan, Co. Down.

Skillen, James
Third Engineer Officer
SS *Glen Head* (Belfast), Merchant Navy
Died as a result of enemy action on Friday 6 June 1941 (aged 49)
Tower Hill Memorial, London, England (Panel 52)

S

> **LOST AT SEA.**
> SKILLEN—Previously reported missing, now reported lost at sea, result of enemy action, James Skillen, Engineer, loved husband of Alberta Skillen.
> Sadly missed by his sorrowing Wife and Sons, Hugh, William and Albert, Ingleheim, 434 Upper Newtownards Road, Belfast.
>
> SKILLEN—Lost at sea, result of enemy action, James Skillen, Engineer.
> Deeply regretted by his Brother, H. A. Skillen, M.B., Duncairn Gdns., Belfast.
>
> SKILLEN—Lost at sea, as the result of enemy action, James Skillen, Engineer.
> Deeply regretted by his Father-in-law and Mother-in-law,
> W. J. & E. BAILIE.
> 2 Ward Avenue, Bangor.
>
> SKILLEN—Lost at sea, result of enemy action, James Skillen, Engineer.
> Deeply regretted by his loving Sister, Hannah, and Brother-in-law, John Aiken, 28 Brixton Road, London.
>
> SKILLEN—Lost at sea as the result of enemy action, James Skillen, Engineer.
> Deeply regretted by his Sister-in-law, Brother-in-law and Family.
> M. & J. FERGUSON.
> 24 College Avenue, Bangor.
>
> SKILLEN—Lost at sea as the result of enemy action, James Skillen, Engineer.
> Deeply regretted by his Sister-in-law, Brother-in-law and Family.
> S. & W. AGNEW & FAMILY.
> 165 Belfast Road, Bangor.
>
> SKILLEN—Lost at sea, result of enemy action, James Skillen, Engineer.
> Deeply regretted by his sorrowing Cousin, Dr. G. Miller, 434 Upper Newtownards Road, Belfast.

James Skillen was born on 1 March 1892 and he was a son of James and Margaret Jane Skillen (nee Skillen) of Ballymaconnell, Bangor. James Skillen (son of William and Sarah Skillen) and Margaret Skillen (daughter of William and Hannah Skillen) were married on 26 March 1880 at 21 Abbotsford Place, Glasgow (according to the forms of the Church of Scotland) in the district of Gorbals, Lanarkshire. James Skillen Senior was a carpenter; Margaret Jane Skillen was a school teacher and when the Skillen family moved to Bangor she taught in the National School at Ballymaconnell. James and Margaret Jane Skillen had three children – Hugh Andrew (born 2 August 1881); Hannah (born 24 April 1884) and James (born 1 March 1892). James Skillen Senior (aged 50) was found drowned at Groomsport on 28 November 1902. He had been missing for about a month and there was no evidence as to how he had come to be in the water.

During the First World War James Skillen Junior served with the Merchant Navy and his elder brother, Hugh Andrew (a school teacher), also served. James Skillen and Ann (Nannie) Alberta Bailie of *Ingleheim*, 434 Upper Newtownards Road, Belfast were married on 7 April 1917 in Helen's Bay Presbyterian Church and they had three sons, all of whom were baptised in Trinity Presbyterian Church, Bangor – Hugh Andrew (baptised 10 February 1918); William James Bailie (baptised 18 March 1921) and James Albert (baptised 9 April 1925). During the Second World War James Skillen's son Hugh served in the Merchant Navy as an engineer and his son William was a wireless operator. James Skillen's father-in-law, W.J. Bailie was a JP, a member of Bangor Borough Council, a member of Newtownards Rural Council and a member of the Board of Guardians and Hospital Governors.

During the Second World War James Skillen served in the Merchant Navy and he died on 6 June 1941 when the SS *Glen Head* was bombed 100 miles southwest of Cape St. Vincent, Portugal. Built in Glasgow in 1909, the SS *Glen Head* was owned by the Head Line Shipping Company. After being bombed the ship sank within three minutes and 27 of the 36 crew members were lost. Boatswain **John Hawthorne** and Chief Steward **William McKinley Rae** also died that day.

S

Initially James Skillen was reported as missing and, after it was officially confirmed that he must be presumed dead, his immediate and extended family placed *Lost at Sea* notices in the 19 July 1941 edition of the *County Down Spectator*. The notices were from his wife and sons; his parents-in-law W.J. and E. Bailie of 2 Ward Avenue, Bangor; his brother Dr H.A. Skillen of Duncairn Gardens, Belfast; his sister Hannah and brother-in-law John Aiken of 28 Brixton Road, London; the Ferguson family of 24 College Avenue, Bangor; the Agnew family of 165 Belfast Road, Bangor and his cousin Dr G. Millar of 434 Upper Newtownards Road, Belfast.

Third Engineer Officer James Skillen is commemorated on the Tower Hill Memorial in London and on the family grave headstone in Bangor Abbey Graveyard. His father James died on 8 November 1902 (aged 50); his mother Margaret Jane died on 25 August 1937 (aged 80) and his sister Hannah died on 19 December 1941 (aged 58) – six months after James was killed.

Skillen, Victor Hall (Victor)
Sergeant (Pilot)
No. 745460, 23 Squadron, Royal Air Force Volunteer Reserve
Killed on active service on Tuesday 11 March 1941 (aged 24)
St. Pierre Cemetery, Amiens, Somme, France (Plot 1 Row A Grave 12)

Victor Hall Skillen was born on 11 August 1917 and he was a son of William

Robert and Margaret Skillen (nee Hall) of 45 Halliday's Road, Belfast and later 174 Upper Newtownards Road, Belfast. William Robert Skillen from Holywood was a widower and a pawnbroker when he and Margaret Hall were married on 5 September 1916 in Portadown Parish Church of Ireland Church. Victor Hall Skillen attended Holywood Parochial School and then Sullivan Upper School in Holywood from 1930 until 1935. He was a keen sportsman and played rugby for the school. After leaving school he joined the Civil Service as a clerk in January 1936. In 1939 he joined the Royal Air Force Volunteer Reserve and learned to fly at 24 Elementary & Reserve Flying School, Sydenham. At the outbreak of war he was called up for full time service and went to England for training.

In May 1940 he was posted to No. 5 Operational Training Unit (OTU) at RAF Aston Down in Gloucestershire and then in June 1940 to 29 Squadron at RAF Digby in Lincolnshire. He was a night fighter pilot during the Battle of Britain and in December 1940 he was posted to 23 Squadron at RAF Ford in Sussex. Victor Hall Skillen (aged 24) was killed on 11 March 1941 when the Bristol Blenheim aircraft (L1507) he was piloting collided with a German Heinkel He 111 aircraft and crashed during a night intruder patrol over France. He was buried in St. Pierre Cemetery, Amiens. Buried on either side of him were Sergeant (Navigator) Francis Hibbs Abbott and Sergeant (Air Gunner) Romilly Ronald James Nute. There is an inscription on his CWGC headstone:

Glory to God in the highest, and on earth peace, good will toward men

Sergeant (Pilot) Victor Hall Skillen is commemorated in Sullivan Upper School, Holywood. His effects amounted to some £186 and probate was granted to his father.

Sloss, Francis Neville (Frank)
Corporal
No. 1544915, 83 (Pathfinder) Squadron, Royal Air Force Volunteer Reserve
Killed in an aircraft accident on Friday 18 June 1943 (aged 19)
Bangor Cemetery, Co. Down (Section 1 D Grave 17)

Francis Neville (Frank) Sloss was born on 15 July 1923 and he was the elder son of Francis Alexander Sloss and Alice Mary Frances Violet Sloss (nee Patchell) who lived at 50 Central Avenue, Bangor. They were married

on 25 November 1918 in Bangor Parish Church of Ireland Church (St. Comgall's) and they had three children – Alice Violet (born 7 May 1922); Francis Neville (born 15 July 1923) and Joseph William Alexander (born 16 November 1926). Frank's father, Francis Alexander Sloss, was a solicitor and Frank's late paternal grandfather, Joseph Sloss MD, was a staff surgeon in the Royal Navy.

In the First World War, Frank's uncle, William Neville Patchell, served as a Private in the Royal Fusiliers and was killed in action on 16 July 1916. Private Patchell is commemorated on Page 286 in the Book of Honour *Remembering Their Sacrifice in the Great War – North Down* compiled by Barry Niblock.

Francis Neville Sloss was baptised on 6 January 1924 in Bangor Parish Church (St. Comgall's). He was educated at Sligo Grammar School where he was Honorary Secretary of the Debating Society. Frank was a member of Second Bangor Scout Troop and a chorister in the choir of Bangor Abbey.

DIED ON ACTIVE SERVICE.

SLOSS—June, 1943, Corporal Francis Neville Sloss, R.A.F.V.R., age 19 years, elder son of Francis A. Sloss, LL.B., Solicitor, Bangor, Co. Down, and grandson of the late Joseph Sloss, M.D., Staff Surgeon, Royal Navy, and of William A. Patchell, Belfast. Interred in Bangor New Cemetery.

Frank Sloss joined the Royal Air Force Volunteer Reserve in 1941 and, after training as a Wireless Mechanic, he was promoted to the rank of Corporal and appointed as a Wireless Instructor. After Corporal Frank Sloss was killed in an aircraft accident on 18 June 1943 his Commanding Officer wrote, 'He will be greatly missed as an instructor as he was very popular with both trainees and his colleagues.'

Corporal Frank Sloss was killed along with eight other men when their Avro Lancaster aircraft (ED439) crashed at Highgate Farm, Scredington, Nr Sleaford, Lincolnshire during a training (practice bombing) flight. They had taken off at 10.10 am from RAF Wyton in Cambridgeshire. The other men who died in the crash were:

- Pilot Officer Max Keiran Cummings aged 30 (RAAF)
- Sergeant Henry Whitfield Luker aged 24 (RAAF)
- Sergeant John Roughley aged 21 from Lathom, Lancashire
- Sergeant Harry William Cheshire aged 22
- Sergeant Francis William Wilcox aged 24 from Gorton, Manchester
- Sergeant Norman Woodcock aged 19 from Whitchurch, Shropshire
- Flight Sergeant Robert Allan Taylor aged 25 (RCAF)
- Corporal Thomas John Bond aged 30 from Blaenavon, Monmouthshire

In the absence of a crash report it is not known why the aircraft crashed but it may have been due to airframe failure. It is known that, prior to the crash, this aircraft had been out of action for a time following damage sustained

in a previous raid. Both Corporals on board were wireless mechanics/instructors.

Frank Sloss's funeral on Wednesday 23 June 1943 to Bangor Cemetery was preceded by a service in Bangor Abbey at which the Revd James Hamilton officiated. The Rector's Prayer Desk in Bangor Abbey was donated in memory of Frank Sloss by his mother. The desk has a plaque with the following inscription:

In memory of Francis Neville Sloss, Corporal Royal Air Force (V.R.)
A chorister of this Church
Killed on Active Service 18 June 1943, aged 19 years

Corporal Francis Neville Sloss is commemorated on Bangor and District War Memorial; in Bangor Parish Church (St. Comgall's) and in St. Andrew's Church, Scredington, Lincolnshire. Frank's sister, Alice Violet, served with the WRNS and she married Captain William Henry Crosson of Dorchester, New Jersey who served with the US Army. Frank's brother Joseph served with the Royal Navy and he married Ann Elizabeth Oldfield Havers (later Baroness and DBE). Frank's father died on 14 January 1952 (aged 86) and his mother died on 26 May 1981.

Smallman, Denis Harold (Denis)
Lieutenant
No. 247203, 7th Battalion, South Staffordshire Regiment
Killed in action on Saturday 8 July 1944 (aged 26)
Cambes-en-Plaine War Cemetery, Calvados, France (Row G 2)

Denis Harold Smallman's birth was registered in the first quarter of 1917 in Edmonton, Middlesex and he was a son of James and Mary Alice Smallman (nee Sarchfield) whose marriage was registered in the first quarter of 1908 in Holburn, London. In the 1911 census James Smallman described himself as a Naval Policeman and during the First World War he served as a Master-at-Arms in the Royal Navy.

James and Mary Alice Smallman had four children – James Leslie (born 1911 in St. Pancras, London, served with the Royal Indian Navy); Eileen H. (born

1915); Denis Harold (born 1917) and Ronald David Reginald (born 1921, served with the Royal Artillery). In the 1920s the Smallman family moved to Belfast and they lived at 24 Knutsford Drive (off the Cliftonville Road) when James was employed as a Head Warder in Crumlin Road Gaol. Later they moved to 1 Kingsdale Park, Cherryvalley and Denis Smallman worked as a coachbuilder with Belfast Corporation Transport (BCT). He was also a Boys' Brigade Captain in Belfast and a Lay Reader in the Church of Ireland.

In 1939 Denis Smallman married Emelia Lavinia Millicent Robst. Emelia Robst was born in 1908 in Colchester and before the Second World War she held the position of Lady's Companion – for a time in the British Embassy in Berlin and also in Portland Castle, Dorset. It was while she was living in Portland Castle that she met Leslie Smallman and they planned to marry but these plans came to naught and instead Emelia Robst married Leslie's brother Denis. Denis and Emelia Smallman had two sons – Michael (Mike, born 8 April 1941) and John (born September 1942). Mike Smallman was born in Sutton-in-Ashfield, Nottinghamshire and he was baptised in St. James's Church of Ireland Church, Antrim Road, Belfast.

In the 1940s Denis, Emelia, Mike and John Smallman moved to Ballywalter where they lived in Strand Park. Denis joined the Army and served with the 6th Airborne Division. He was wounded in action in France and taken home to Northern Ireland to recuperate. He returned to France with the South Staffordshire Regiment and was killed in action during the Battle of Charnwood. His Chaplain was the Revd Alan Alexander Buchanan who was *Mentioned In Despatches* during the Battle of Arnhem in September 1944. In 1955 the Revd Buchanan became Rector of Bangor Parish Church of Ireland Church (St. Comgall's) and later Archbishop of Dublin and Primate of Ireland.

Lieutenant Denis Harold Smallman was 26 years old when he was killed in action during *Operation Charnwood*, the objective of which was to capture the German occupied French city of Caen. He was buried in Cambes-en-Plaine War Cemetery and he is commemorated in the Roll of Honour for the South Staffordshire Regiment in Lichfield Cathedral and on the Roll of Honour in Holy Trinity and St. Silas with Immanuel Church of Ireland Church, Belfast. After Denis Smallman died, his widow and two sons, Mike and John, continued to live in Strand Park, Ballywalter. Later, Mike Smallman served with the Royal Air Force and John served with the Army.

Denis Harold Smallman's mother, Mary Alice Smallman, died on 11 February 1959 (aged 72) and she was buried in Belfast City Cemetery (Glenalina Extension Grave U 221). His father, James Smallman, was living at 19 Sunningdale Grove, Belfast when he died on 27 December 1967. James Smallman was 87 years old and he was buried in the same grave as his wife.

Denis Harold Smallman's widow Emelia died on 28 July 1990 and on 24 September 1990 her ashes were interred in the Garden of Remembrance at Ballywalter (Trinity) Church of Ireland Church.

Smart, Charles
Rifleman
No. 7019390, 2nd Battalion the London Irish Rifles, Royal Ulster Rifles
Lost at sea on Thursday 6 May 1943 (aged 33)
Medjez-el-Bab Memorial, Tunisia (Face 31)

Charles Smart was born on 4 August 1909 and he was a son of Charles and Kathleen (or Catherine) Smart (nee McChesney) of Kiltonga, Newtownards. Charles Smart Senior worked as a general labourer and he and Kathleen McChesney were married on 22 January 1894 in Greenwell Street Presbyterian Church, Newtownards. They had at least eleven children, the first four of whom were baptised in Greenwell Street Church – Eleanor (Ellen) McChesney (born 5 August 1894); Maggie (born 21 April 1896); Annie (born 13 November 1897); Thomas George (born 8 May 1899, died in infancy); Jane (born 16 May 1902); John (born 14 January 1905, died in infancy); George (born 23 December 1905); Charles (born 7 January 1908, died in infancy); Charles (born 4 August 1909); Rachel (born 9 March 1911) and Mary (born 1 January 1913).

> LOST AT SEA ON ACTIVE SERVICE.
> SMART—Lost at Sea, on Active Service, in May, 1943. Rifleman Charles Smart, second son of Charles and the late Kathleen Smart, Kiltonga, Newtownards.
> Sleep on, dear son, in your foreign grave,
> A grave we may never see,
> But as long as life and memory last,
> We will remember thee.
> Deeply regretted by his sorrowing Father; also his Three Children, Elizabeth, William and Charles.

In May 1943 Charles Smart Senior was officially informed that his son, Rifleman Charles Smart, had been reported missing and was believed to have accidentally drowned. In the 4 September 1943 edition of the *Newtownards Chronicle* there were six *Lost at Sea on Active Service* notices – one from his widowed father and also his three children Elizabeth, William and Charles; one from his brother George and sister-in-law Jean Smart of Milecross, Newtownards; one from his sister Maggie and brother-in-law Willie Stevenson of 167 Greenwell Street, Newtownards; one from his sister Annie and brother-in-law Willie Maxwell and their sons Thomas and Charlie of 116 Greenwell Street, Newtownards; one from his sister Rachel and brother-in-law William Gunning of 114 John Street, Newtownards and one from his sister Nellie and brother-in-law Charles Dorrian of 163 Mill Street, Newtownards.

 Rifleman Charles Smart was 33 years old when he died on 6 May 1943 and he is commemorated on the Medjez-el-Bab Memorial in Tunisia and on Newtownards and District War Memorial. His nephew **Charlie Maxwell** died on 3 June 1944.

Smellie, John Frederick (Jack)
Captain
No. 158421, 1st Wing, the Glider Pilot Regiment, Army Air Corps
Died on active service on Saturday 23 September 1944 (aged 30)
Arnhem Oosterbeek War Cemetery, Gelderland, Netherlands (Grave 6 A 4)

 John Frederick (Jack) Smellie was born on 21 January 1914 and he was a son of Nicholas Sarens Herbert Smellie (born 1883) and Ileen Mary Smellie (nee McLean) of *Plasmerdyn*, Holywood, Co. Down. Herbert Smellie (son of Herbert and Anna Smellie) was a bank official and he and Ileen McLean (daughter of John McLean of Rose Bank Terrace, Tramore, Co. Waterford) were married on 4 October 1910 in Drumcannon Parish Church of Ireland Church, Co. Waterford. After their marriage they lived in Dundanion, Blackrock, Co. Cork. They had two sons, both of whom attended Campbell College, Belfast – John Frederick (Jack) Smellie and Herbert Wilkin James Smellie. In school records they are recorded as being sons of Mrs Wood (Nicholas Sarens Herbert Smellie died on 25 March 1922 at King Edward VII Hospital, Ealing, Middlesex).

John Frederick (Jack) Smellie attended Campbell College from April 1924 until July 1932 and he played rugby for the school. In his last term he was acting Head Prefect and Pipe Major in the school's Officers' Training Corps (OTC). He was a senior member of the School Scout Troop and later he became Scoutmaster of the Holywood Troop. John Frederick (Jack) Smellie studied at Queen's University Belfast where he qualified as a solicitor.

During the Second World War John Frederick (Jack) Smellie served in the 6th Airborne Division with the Glider Pilot Regiment, Army Air Corps and he died on 23 September 1944 at Arnhem. Two tributes were published in *The Campbellain*, Volume 11 No. 3 (July 1945) and Volume 11 No. 4 (December 1945). One included the sentence, 'He was endowed with a great personal

S

charm and though modest and self-effacing he was able to get things done and done well.'

Captain John Frederick (Jack) Smellie was 30 years old when he died and he is commemorated on Holywood and District War Memorial; in Queen's University Belfast; in the Royal Courts of Justice Belfast; on the McLean family grave headstone in Holywood Cemetery (where he is described as a grandson of John McLean) and in Holywood Parish Church of Ireland Church (St. Philip and St. James).

Smith, Nathaniel Robert (Nathaniel)
Colour Sergeant
No. D/24698, 30th (HD) Battalion, Royal Ulster Rifles
Died of illness on Sunday 14 June 1942 (aged 46)
Bangor Cemetery, Co. Down (Section 4 V Grave 27)

S

Nathaniel Robert Smith was born on 5 November 1895 and he was a son of Nathaniel Robert and Sarah Smith (nee Munce) who were married on 7 February 1895 in Regent Street Presbyterian Church, Newtownards. Nathaniel Robert Smith Senior was a policeman and the Smith family lived in Court Street, Newtownards. After Nathaniel's father died on 24 May 1902 (aged 66) his mother Sarah married Robert Nevin on 28 August 1902 in Ballygilbert Presbyterian Church. Robert Nevin lived in West Street, Newtownards and he was a shoemaker. Robert and Sarah Nevin's daughter Sarah was born on 10 December 1905.

Nathaniel Robert Smith Junior was also a policeman and he was the husband of Mary (Maimie) Smith (nee Conway) who lived at 24 King Street, Bangor. Nathaniel Robert Smith and Mary Conway were married on 4 June 1924 in Ballygilbert Presbyterian Church and they had two daughters – Eileen and Anna. Eileen Smith married Lieutenant E.T.G. Cole in Bangor Abbey.

The death in service of Colour Sergeant Nathaniel Smith was reported in the 20 June 1942 edition of the *County Down Spectator*. He died of a stroke on 14 June 1942 in the Military Hospital in Belfast. Originally from Newtownards, Nathaniel Robert Smith served with the 13th Battalion, Royal Irish Rifles

SMITH—June 14, 1942 (suddenly), at a Military Hospital, Belfast, Nathaniel Robert Smith, C.Q.M.S., R.U.R., 24 King Street, Bangor, dearly-beloved husband of Maimie Smith. Interred in Bangor New Cemetery.
Deeply regretted by his sorrowing Wife and Family.

during the First World War and was wounded in France.

Colour Sergeant Nathaniel Robert Smith's military funeral was to Bangor Cemetery and the services were conducted by the Revd Walter Horatio Good. Volleys were fired over the open grave and *The Last Post* was sounded by buglers. Mourners included his son-in-law Lieutenant E.T.G. Cole (RNR), his stepbrother Norman Nevin, his father-in-law John Conway and his brothers-in-law John Conway, Hugh Conway and John Boal. Colour Sergeant Nathaniel Robert Smith was 46 years old when he died and he is commemorated in Bangor Parish Church of Ireland Church (St. Comgall's). There is an inscription on his CWGC headstone in Bangor Cemetery:

'Abide with me'
Also his dear wife Mary
Died 27 May 1988 aged 87

Smith, Peter Tristan
Sergeant (Navigator)
No. 1290933, 61 Squadron, Royal Air Force Volunteer Reserve
Killed on active service on Wednesday 21 April 1943 (aged 21)
Berlin 1939 – 1945 War Cemetery, Berlin, Germany (Grave 2 L 19)

S

Peter Tristan Smith was born on 31 March 1922 in Romford, Essex and he was a son of Leonard Francis Sampson Smith (born 4 June 1895, died 8 May 1961) and Lilian Elizabeth Smith (nee Brooker, born 7 August 1894, died 5 December 1974). Their marriage was registered in the second quarter of 1921 and they had four children including Peter Tristan (born 31 March 1922) and Pamela (born 6 May 1924, died 20 December 2008). It is recorded in the CWGC Debt of Honour that the Smith family moved to Northern Ireland and they lived in Bangor, Co. Down.

During the Second World War Sergeant Peter Tristan Smith served with the Royal Air Force Volunteer Reserve in Bomber Command and on 20 April 1943 he was one of a crew of seven aboard an Avro Lancaster Mark I aircraft (W4795) that took off at 9.27 pm from RAF Syerston in Nottinghamshire on a mission to bomb Stettin (then in Germany). The aircraft crashed at 2.30 am on 21 April and all on board were killed. One casualty (Sergeant Jackson) has no known grave and the others were buried in Berlin 1939 – 1945 War Cemetery. In addition to Sergeant Peter Tristan Smith the other six crew members who died that night were:

- Pilot Officer James Louis Rossignol aged 21 from Florida, USA (RCAF)
- Sergeant William John Jackson aged 23 from Tankerton, Kent
- Sergeant Graham Fellows aged 20 from Walton, Derbyshire
- FS Thomas Charles James Grist aged 28 from Dagenham, Essex
- Sergeant Joseph Francis McNeill
- Sergeant Michael Charles Burgoine aged 20 from Eaton Hill, Norwich

Sergeant Peter Tristan Smith was 21 years old when he died.

Smith, Samuel
Able Seaman
No. D/JX 198146, HMS *Prince of Wales*, Royal Navy
Killed in action on Wednesday 10 December 1941 (aged 21)
Plymouth Naval Memorial, Devon, England (Panel 48 Column 2)

Samuel Smith was the eldest son of Hamilton and Margaret Smith (nee Rowley) of 10 Thomas Street, Newtownards. They were married on 17 April 1919 in Newtownards Parish Church of Ireland Church (St. Mark's). Hamilton Smith served for 9½ years with the Connaught Rangers and was wounded during the Great War.

During the Second World War Samuel Smith served with the Royal Navy aboard the battleship HMS *Prince of Wales* and, after that ship was sunk on 10 December 1941, he was reported missing. In May 1942 his parents were informed that their son must now be presumed killed. His parents, brothers and sisters placed an *Our Heroes – In Memoriam* notice in the 12 December 1942 edition of the *Newtownards Chronicle* and it contained the verse:

> *May the heavenly winds blow softly*
> *O'er that sweet and hallowed spot,*
> *Though the sea divides us from your grave,*
> *You will never be forgot.*

Built at the Cammel Laird shipyard in Birkenhead and launched in May 1939, HMS *Prince of Wales* was damaged by German bomber aircraft in August 1940 while still being fitted out. She suffered further damage in May 1941 when she and HMS *Hood* fought the German battleship *Bismarck* in the Battle of the Denmark Strait.

On 25 October 1941 HMS *Prince of Wales* departed for Singapore to join Force Z, a British naval detachment that also included the battle cruiser

S

HMS *Repulse*. HMS *Prince of Wales* docked in Singapore on 2 December with the rest of the force and, at 2.11 am on 10 December, Force Z was dispatched to investigate reports of Japanese Forces landing at Kuantan, Malaysia. They found the reports to be false. At 11.00 am Japanese bombers and torpedo aircraft began an assault on Force Z. In a second attack at 11.30 am torpedoes struck the *Prince of Wales* on the port side, wrecking the outer propeller shaft and causing the ship to take on a heavy list. HMS *Repulse* was also hit and sank at 12.33 pm.

SMITH—Reported Killed on Active Service, Samuel Smith, Able Seaman, eldest and dearly-loved son of Hamilton and Margaret Smith, 10, Thomas Street, Newtownards.
Deeply regretted by his sorrowing Father, Mother, Brothers and Sisters; also his Grandfather, Uncles, Aunts, Nephews and Nieces.

More torpedoes hit HMS *Prince of Wales* and then a 500 kg bomb hit the catapult deck, penetrated through to the main deck and when it exploded it tore a hole in the port side of the hull. At 1.15 pm the order was given to abandon ship and at 1.20 pm HMS *Prince of Wales* sank. Able Seaman Samuel Smith was among more than 320 men who died. Able Seaman **David Cowan** from Holywood who was aboard HMS *Repulse* was also killed.

Able Seaman Samuel Smith is commemorated on Plymouth Naval Memorial in Devon; on Newtownards and District War Memorial and in Newtownards Parish Church (St. Mark's).

Smith, Walter Stanley
Warrant Officer Class III
No. 1065147, 27 Field Regiment, Royal Artillery
Killed in action on Saturday 1 June 1940 (aged 29)
Dunkirk Memorial, Nord, France (Column 7)

Walter Stanley Smith's birth was registered in the fourth quarter of 1910 in Portsmouth, Hampshire and he was a son of Edward Henry and Edith Annie Smith. They had at least four children – Albert, Frederick, Edward and Walter. Walter Stanley Smith's marriage to Lilian Whitaker of Portaferry, Co. Down was registered in the third quarter of 1938 in Colchester, Essex.

Walter Stanley Smith joined the Royal Artillery before the outbreak of war and fought in the 1939/40 France and Belgium Campaign. He was 29 years old when he was killed on 1 June 1940 during the evacuation of Allied Forces from Dunkirk. His body was never recovered and he is commemorated on the Dunkirk Memorial.

Smyth, Aaron
Trooper
No. 7018785, Reconnaissance Corps, Royal Armoured Corps,
49th (West Riding) Regiment
Died in service on Tuesday 3 October 1944 (aged 23)
Belfast (Dundonald) Cemetery, Co. Down (Section A 3 Grave 586)

Aaron Smyth was a son of Aaron and Sarah Ann Smyth (nee Thornton) of 44 Derwent Street, Belfast. They were married on 25 December 1914 in Seagoe Parish Church of Ireland Church, Lurgan, Co. Armagh; (interestingly, an Aaron Smith married Hannah McCune on 25 December 1903 in the same church). Aaron Smyth who died in the Second World War was the husband of Margaret Smyth of Newtownards and he served with the Reconnaissance Corps, Royal Armoured Corps, 49th (West Riding) Regiment.

Trooper Aaron Smyth died on 3 October 1944 in the Royal Hospital, Chester and he was buried on 10 October 1944 in Belfast (Dundonald) Cemetery. Subsequently buried in the same grave were his father Aaron Smyth of 44 Derwent Street who died on 21 February 1949 (aged 71, he had served with the Royal Inniskilling Fusiliers from 1892 until 1908); his sister Margaret McMeekin of 70 Templemore Avenue, Belfast (died 28 January 1973 aged 58) and his mother Sarah Ann Smyth of 70 Templemore Avenue (died 7 April 1976 aged 80). The inscription on Trooper Aaron Smyth's CWGC headstone records his father's age at death as 75 (rather than 71).

Smyth, John Stanley (Stanley)
Pilot Officer
No. 139301, 51 Squadron, Royal Air Force Volunteer Reserve
Killed on active service on Monday 26 July 1943 (aged 29)
Castricum Protestant Churchyard, Noord-Holland, Netherlands
(Plot J Collective Grave 7)

John Stanley Smyth was born on 18 April 1914 and he was the second son of John and Sarah Smyth (nee McClean) of 20 Hamilton Road, Bangor. John Smyth was a grocer (his father Jeremiah was a weaver) and he and Sarah McClean (her father William was a butcher) were married on 16 September 1909 in Hamilton Road Presbyterian Church, Bangor. They had three

children who were baptised in Hamilton Road Presbyterian Church – Karl Kamon (born 2 September 1910); John Stanley (born 18 April 1914) and Robert McClean (Bertie, born 30 December 1916). John Stanley Smyth was educated at Main Street Public Elementary School in Bangor and then at Bangor Grammar School from 1925 until 1931 when he gained the Queen's University Belfast Matriculation. He played rugby for the school and later for Bangor Rugby Club.

Stanley Smyth was apprenticed to the pharmacy business with Mr R. McCutcheon in Bangor and he qualified as a Member of the Pharmaceutical Society of Northern Ireland. He was employed by Mr R. Morrow, Conway Square, Newtownards. In August 1941 Stanley Smyth and Olive Maude McKay Perry of 78 Beechwood Avenue, Londonderry were married and their baby son was born on 9 December 1942. Stanley's younger brother Bertie served with the Royal Artillery and was captured at Tobruk in June 1942.

KILLED ON ACTIVE SERVICE

SMYTH — Pilot-Officer John Stanley Smyth, R.A.F.V.R., second son of the late John Smyth and of Mrs. Smyth Finlay, 20 Hamilton Road, Bangor, and beloved husband of Olive M. Smyth, 78 Beechwood Avenue, Londonderry. Buried Castrium, N. Holland, August, 1943.

John Stanley Smyth enlisted in July 1942 and on completing his training in England and the USA he received his commission as a Pilot Officer in March 1943. On 25 July 1943 Pilot Officer John Stanley Smyth was one of a seven man crew aboard a Handley Page Halifax Mark II aircraft (HR934) that took off at 10.26 pm from RAF Snaith in Yorkshire on a mission to bomb Essen. The aircraft was 'presumed lost off the Netherlands coast' because the bodies of all seven crew members were later recovered from the sea. In addition to Pilot Officer John Stanley Smyth the other six crew members who died that night were:

- Flying Officer John Stuart Cole aged 23 from Wembley, Middlesex
- Sergeant Leslie Alfred Taylor aged 32 from Cardiff
- Pilot Officer Charles Edwin Parkin aged 28
- Sgt Frederick Arthur James Edwards aged 29 from Watchet, Somerset
- Pilot Officer John Sarginson aged 23 from Marske, Yorkshire
- Sgt George Clark Thompson aged 32 from West Hampstead, London

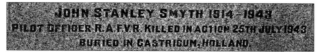

JOHN STANLEY SMYTH 1914 - 1943
PILOT OFFICER R.A.F.V.R. KILLED IN ACTION 25TH JULY 1943
BURIED IN CASTRICUM, HOLLAND.

Pilot Officer John Stanley Smyth was 29 years old when he died and he is commemorated on Bangor and District War Memorial; in Hamilton Road Presbyterian Church, Bangor; in Bangor Grammar School and on the family grave headstone in Bangor Cemetery. His father John died in 1923, his mother Sarah died in 1962 and his brother Karl died in 1983; Karl's ashes were scattered on the waters of Donaghadee Sound.

Smyth, Joseph (Joe)
Rifleman
No. 7020056, 2nd Battalion the London Irish Rifles, Royal Ulster Rifles
Killed in action between Wednesday 20 and Thursday 21 January 1943 (aged 21)
Medjez-el-Bab War Cemetery, Tunisia (Grave 2 C 8)

Joseph Smyth was the eldest son of William John and Mary Smyth (nee Hawthorne) of 112 East Street and then 24 Mary Street, Newtownards. They were married on 24 October 1919 in First Newtownards Presbyterian Church and they had at least five children – Joseph, Hugh, Isaac, William and another son. During the Second World War Joseph Smyth served with the Royal Ulster Rifles. His brother Hugh also served with the Royal Ulster Rifles and in 1945 Hugh was hospitalised in Belfast Emergency Hospital. During the Great War their father, William John Smyth, served with the Royal Engineers and the Durham Light Infantry.

> **KILLED ON ACTIVE SERVICE.**
>
> SMYTH—January, 1943, Killed in Action at Bou Arada, Tunisia, Rifleman Joseph Smyth. Loving Grandson of Mrs. Gregory, 5, George's Street, Newtownards.

Joseph Smyth joined up in 1940 and he was 21 years old when he was killed in action in January 1943 at Bou Arada in Tunisia. He had landed at Algiers in November 1942 and from there gone into the Allied front line in Tunisia where there was heavy fighting during January 1943. Rifleman Joseph Smyth is commemorated on Newtownards and District War Memorial and on the family grave headstone in Movilla Cemetery, Newtownards. Joseph Smyth had a brother who died in infancy and his brother Isaac died on 12 August 1944 (aged 18). His brother William and sister-in-law Hetty Smyth lived in Craigantlet Cottages, Newtownards.

Smyth, Wallace Robert
Pilot Officer (Navigator)
No. 149676, 57 Squadron, Royal Air Force Volunteer Reserve
Killed in action on Friday 30 July 1943 (aged 21)
Hamburg Cemetery, Hamburg, Germany (Grave 10 A C 7)

Wallace Robert Smyth was born on 15 May 1922 and he was the eldest son of Henry Percy and Maude Adelaide Smyth (nee Wallace) of Demesne Road,

 Holywood. Henry Percy Smyth was a Lieutenant in the Army when he and Maude Wallace were married on 29 May 1919 in Horley Parish Church, Surrey.

Wallace Robert Smyth attended Sullivan Upper School in Holywood from 1930 until 1938. Actively involved in the Boy Scout movement, he attended the 5th World Jamboree in Bloemendaal, Holland in 1937. After leaving school he was employed in the Holywood office of the Belfast Corporation Gas Department. He joined the Royal Air Force Volunteer Reserve in 1940 and received his training in Canada and the USA. His death was reported in the 29 December 1943 edition of the *Belfast Telegraph* where his surname was spelt Smythe. It was reported that he had a younger brother in the RAF.

Wallace Robert Smyth was one of a seven man crew aboard an Avro Lancaster Mark III aircraft (ED616) that took off at 11.25 pm from RAF Scampton in Lincolnshire on a mission to bomb Hamburg. The aircraft was hit by flak and crashed in the Fuhlsbuttel quarter of Hamburg. In addition to Pilot Officer Wallace Robert Smyth the other six crew members who died that night were:

- PO Geoffrey Albert Norris Parker aged 22 from Farnworth, Lancashire
- Sergeant Thomas Lancaster aged 36 from Colne, Lancashire
- Flying Officer Gerard Mathews aged 23 from Stockport, Cheshire
- Sgt Louis Edward Walters aged 21 from Mountsorrel, Leicestershire
- Sergeant James Clement Carpenter
- Sergeant George Samuel Maddocks

Pilot Officer Wallace Robert Smyth was 21 years old when he died and he is commemorated on Holywood and District War Memorial; in First Holywood Presbyterian Church and in Sullivan Upper School.

Snow, Eric Augustus
Flight Lieutenant
No. 41878, 125 Squadron, Royal Air Force Volunteer Reserve
Killed in an aircraft accident on Friday 17 March 1944
Runnymede Memorial, Surrey, England (Panel 203)

Whilst it has not been possible to confirm conclusively the family circumstances of Eric Augustus Snow there is evidence to suggest that he was born in 1914 and that he was a son of Alexander Augustus Snow and Lizzie Snow of Topsail, Avalon Peninsula, Conception Bay, Newfoundland. Alexander and Lizzie Snow had at least six children – William, Edna, Charles, Clarence, Eric A. and Edith.

SNOW E. A. On 17 March 1944 two de Havilland Mosquito aircraft (HK 261 and HK 326) of No. 125 Squadron based at RAF Ballyhalbert were airborne over the Irish Sea on a night practice interception exercise from which they failed to return. Based on Ground Controlled Interception (GCI) radar evidence from Ballywooden, Bishopscourt it was presumed that the two aircraft had collided, resulting in the deaths of both crews. Each crew comprised two men and their bodies were never recovered. They were Flight Lieutenant Eric Augustus Snow from Newfoundland who enlisted on 1 April 1939 and was the pilot of HK261; Flying Officer **Donald Maldwyn Griffiths** (navigator aboard HK261); Flying Officer **Frederick John Bartlett Reid** (pilot of HK326) and Pilot Officer **Horace James Rich** (navigator aboard HK326).

Flight Lieutenant Eric Augustus Snow is commemorated on the Runnymede Memorial in Surrey; in the Memorial University of Newfoundland; on Page 198 in the Newfoundland Book of Remembrance and on the Canadian Virtual War Memorial (Internet). Newfoundland (now Newfoundland and Labrador) was a former Colony and Dominion of the United Kingdom and it was the tenth Province to enter the Canadian Confederation on 31 March 1949.

S

Stanley, Henry Walter (Henry)
Sergeant (Pilot)
No. 1330743, 501 Squadron, Royal Air Force Volunteer Reserve
Killed in an aircraft accident on Wednesday 17 February 1943 (aged 20)
Ightham (St. Peter) Churchyard, Kent

Henry Walter Stanley's birth was registered in the first quarter of 1923 in Malling, Kent and he was a son of Henry Leslie and Margaret Stanley (nee Terry) of Ightham, Kent. His parents' marriage was registered in the first quarter of 1914 and the birth of his sister, Vera D. Stanley, was registered in the first quarter of 1921, both also in Malling, Kent. His father, Henry Leslie Stanley, was a blacksmith and his grandparents, Gordon and Keturah Stanley, owned an ironmongery shop in Ightham.

During the Second World War Henry Walter Stanley served with the Royal Air Force Volunteer Reserve and on 17 February 1943 a Supermarine Spitfire aircraft (AB960) of 501 Squadron Royal Air Force based at RAF Ballyhalbert flew into Slieve Croob near Dromara, Co. Down during a night flying exercise. The pilot, Sergeant Henry Walter Stanley, was killed and his death was registered in Downpatrick. He was 20 years old and single when he died and he was buried in Ightham (St. Peter) Churchyard, Kent.

Sergeant (Pilot) Henry Walter Stanley is commemorated on Ightham War Memorial and in Ightham (St. Peter) Church.

Steavenson, Alexander Arthur Fenwich Towry (Towry)
Flying Officer
No. 85756, Royal Air Force Volunteer Reserve
Died in service on Monday 1 September 1941 (aged 55)
Kirk Maughold (St. Maughold) Churchyard, Isle of Man (East Boundary)

FLYING OFFICER A. F. T. STEAVENSON, BANGOR

The death has occurred, on active service, of Flying Officer A. F. T. Steavenson, who in the Great War was a captain in the Royal Irish Rifles. Flying Officer Steavenson, who was 52, was born in India. His father was Registrar of the High Court, Madras. He engaged in tea planting in India until 1914, when he went to France with the Royal Irish Rifles and served throughout the war, attaining the rank of captain. In 1917 he married Miss Violet Rea, daughter of the late Mr. Henry Tighe Rea, of Bangor, former secretary of the Lagan Navigation Company. After the last war he and his wife returned to India. Flying Officer Steavenson joined the R.A.F. at the outbreak of the present conflict, and Mrs. Steavenson returned to Ireland and, with her daughter, now resides in Bangor. Sincere sympathy is tendered to Mrs. Steavenson and her daughter in their bereavement.

Alexander Arthur Fenwich Towry Steavenson was born on 17 September 1885 in Madras, India and he was the only son of Joseph and Jeannie Steavenson (nee Weir). His mother Jeannie was born in Lisnabreeny, Castlereagh and his father Joseph (born in Liverpool) was appointed Registrar, Taxing Master, Receiver and Commissioner of the High Court in Madras. In 1912 his sister Elizabeth Dorothy Patricia Steavenson (1885 -1981) married Lieutenant Edmund de Warenne Waller, 1st Battalion Royal Irish Rifles.

S

In 1901 Towry Steavenson was a pupil at Malew, Isle of Man and after leaving school he joined the 6th Battalion Royal Irish Rifles (Louth Militia) as a Second Lieutenant. He was promoted to Lieutenant in 1905 and when the old 6th RIR was disbanded in 1908 under the Haldane Scheme he transferred to the 3rd Battalion Royal Irish Rifles. He moved to the 4th Royal Irish Rifles and then to the 1st Royal Irish Fusiliers. In January 1915 he completed a course of musketry in Dublin and went to France on 2 May 1915. He was promoted to Captain on 13 October 1915 and *attached to* the 1st Battalion Royal Irish Rifles. On 12 April 1916 he was placed on the sick list and on 23 April 1916 he was taken off the strength of the Battalion. Later he served with the 3rd Echelon, General Headquarters (GHQ), Egyptian Expeditionary Force (EEF).

In 1917 Alexander Arthur Fenwich Towry Steavenson and Violet Carmen

Tighe Rea were married. Violet's brother, Lieutenant Vivian Trevor Tighe Rea, died of wounds sustained on active service during the Great War and he is commemorated on Page 299 in the Book of Honour *Remembering Their Sacrifice in the Great War – North Down* compiled by Barry Niblock. After the Great War ended Towry Steavenson and his wife went to India where he worked on a tea plantation and on 31 May 1921 his war medals were sent to Sondura, Kalain PO, Cachar, Assam. Their daughter, Joy E. Steavenson, was born in 1926 and the family spent time in the United Kingdom as well as in India. They lived at *Mendoza*, 69 Marlborough Park South, Malone Road, Belfast (1924); 76 Clifton Road, Bangor (1936); 128 Seacliff Road, Bangor (1938); 15 Ballymaconnell Road, Bangor and Highgate, Middlesex.

At the outbreak of the Second World War Alexander Arthur Fenwich Towry Steavenson joined the Royal Air Force Volunteer Reserve and on 1 September 1941 he died at Noble's Hospital, Maughold in the Isle of Man. His English effects were valued at £4,166. Flying Officer Alexander Arthur Fenwich Towry Steavenson was 55 years old when he died and he was buried in Kirk Maughold (St. Maughold) Churchyard, Isle of Man in the same grave as his parents. His father Joseph died on 3 September 1910 (aged 68) and his mother Jeannie died on 24 December 1934 (aged 88). Flying Officer Steavenson is commemorated on Groomsport and District War Memorial and in Groomsport Parish Church of Ireland Church.

Steele-Nicholson, John Edwin Charles Averell (John)
Sergeant (Air Gunner)
No. 1591275, Royal Air Force Volunteer Reserve
Killed in an aircraft accident on Monday 14 September 1942 (aged 20)
Kirkinner Cemetery, Wigtownshire, Scotland (Grave 604)

John Edwin Charles Averell (John) Steele-Nicholson was born in India on 1 August 1922 and he was a son of Robert Charles Henry (Charles) and Lydia Mary Noel Amelia (Ivy) Steele-Nicholson (nee Lloyd) of *Balloo House*, Bangor. John's uncles, Alfred Francis James Steele-Nicholson and William Herbert Hamilton Steele-Nicholson, were killed on active service during the First World War and both are commemorated on Page 329 in the

Book of Honour *Remembering Their Sacrifice in the Great War – North Down* compiled by Barry Niblock.

John's father, Charles Steele-Nicholson, was a Tea Planter in India (on the Jamirah Tea Estate in Dibrugarh, Assam) and in March 1920 he sailed from Calcutta to London aboard the *City of Marseilles* to prepare for his wedding. Charles Steele-Nicholson (son of James Steele-Nicholson) and Ivy Lloyd (daughter of Averell Lloyd) were married on 18 August 1920 in Killyman Parish Church of Ireland Church (St. Andrew's), Dungannon, Co. Tyrone and in September 1920 the newly-weds travelled from Liverpool to Calcutta aboard the *City of Exeter*. Charles was 41 and Ivy was 26. In May 1924 Ivy, Kathleen (aged 2) and John (aged 1) sailed from Calcutta to London aboard the *Margha*.

John Edwin Charles Averell (John) Steele-Nicholson was educated at Rockport School, Craigavad and during the time that he was there the Steele-Nicholson family had an address at 8 Raglan Road, Bangor. The Steele-Nicholson family travelled regularly between India and Britain; in 1925/1926 Charles and Ivy with Charles (aged 8), Ivy (aged 8) and Lily (aged 2) sailed from London to Calcutta aboard the *Dumana*. In November 1929 Charles and Ivy with Elfreda (aged 3) sailed from London to Bombay aboard the *Rajputana* and in February 1932 Ivy and Elfreda (aged 7) sailed from London to Bombay aboard the *Ranchi*. John's father, Robert Charles Henry (Charles) Steele-Nicholson died on 16 November 1937.

During the Second World War Sergeant John Edwin Charles Averell Steele-Nicholson served with the Royal Air Force Volunteer Reserve and he died on 14 September 1942. He was one of an eight man crew aboard a Consolidated B-24 Liberator Mark II aircraft (AL624) in 1653 Heavy Conversion Unit that took off at 11.00 am from RAF Burn in Yorkshire on a cross country navigation exercise. The aircraft crashed on Drigmorn Hill, Millfore near Newton Stewart in Dumfries and Galloway and the other seven crew members who were killed that day were:

- Pilot Officer Ivan Harold Betts aged 31 from Radipole, Dorsetshire
- Sergeant Derek Eaton Warner aged 20 from Bromley, Kent
- Sergeant John Churley Freestone aged 29 from Stanmore, Winchester
- Sergeant George Douglas Calder aged 24 (RAAF)
- Sergeant Geoffrey Crisp Boar aged 27 from Ealing, Middlesex
- Sergeant Victor Frederick Talley
- Sergeant James Bowrey from Hanham, Gloucestershire

Sergeant John Edwin Charles Averell Steele-Nicholson was 20 years old when he died, he was buried in Kirkinner Cemetery, Wigtownshire and he is commemorated in Rockport School and on Dungannon and District War Memorial, Co. Tyrone.

Stewart, Andrew Robert (Andrew)*
Lance Sergeant
No. 7012091, 2nd Battalion, Royal Ulster Rifles
Died of wounds on Monday 19 June 1944 (aged 30)
Hermanville War Cemetery, Calvados, France (Grave 1 U 9)

Andrew Robert Stewart was born on 27 May 1914 and he was the youngest son of Robert and Mary Jane Stewart (nee Rebby) who lived in the townland of Grangee, Carrowdore. Robert Stewart worked as a labourer and he and Mary Jane Rebby were married on 9 July 1908 in Carrowdore Parish Church of Ireland Church (Christ Church). They had six children – William Rusk (born 1 August 1908); Annie (born 29 August 1909); Thomas (born 11 February 1911); James (born 18 May 1913); Andrew Robert (born 27 May 1914) and Violet Maureen (born 25 April 1917).

Carrowdore Soldier Dies from Wounds.—Very sincere sympathy will be tendered to Mr. and Mrs. R. Stewart, Grangee, Carrowdore, on the death of their youngest son, L./Sergt. Andrew Robert Stewart. The sad news came in the form of a telegram from the War Office to the effect that he had died from wounds received in "North West Europe." L./Sergt. Stewart saw service in Hong Kong and Egypt and was mentioned, for gallantry on the Indian North West Frontier. Two of his brothers also joined the colours. Mr. Wm. R. Stewart is serving with the Royal Ulster Rifles, and Mr. Thomas Stewart, who also joined the Royal Ulster Rifles, has been a prisoner-of-war in Germany for the past four years.

During the Second World War Andrew Robert Stewart served with the Royal Ulster Rifles and in the 8 July edition of the *County Down Spectator* it was reported that he had died of wounds on 19 June 1944. The news came to his parents by means of a telegram from the War Office. The newspaper report stated that Andrew Stewart had been with the Rifles for twelve years and he had seen service in Hong Kong, Egypt and India. While he was in Hong Kong he obtained a second class Army Certificate of Education in English, Army and Empire, Map Reading and Mathematics. As a result of his foreign service he wore the North-West Frontier ribbon. Two of his brothers, William and Thomas, also served with the Royal Ulster Rifles during the Second World War. Thomas was held as a Prisoner-of-War in Germany for more than four years. One of his sisters worked as a manageress in the firm of

Messrs A.K. Beattie and Son (Shirt Manufacturers), Queen Street, Newtownards.

Lance Sergeant Andrew Robert Stewart was 30 years old when he died and he is commemorated in Carrowdore Parish Church (Christ Church).

Stewart, Thomas
Private
No. 34156, Corps of Military Police
Died of illness in service on Saturday 16 December 1944 (aged 54)
Bangor Cemetery, Co. Down (Section 4 V Grave 151 A)

Thomas Stewart was born on 13 July 1889 and he was a son of Robert and Sarah Jane (Jane) Stewart (nee Craney) who lived at 29 Church Street, Bangor. Robert Stewart was a minor when he and Jane Craney were married in Willowfield Church of Ireland Church, Belfast. Thomas was born in the family home and he was baptised in Bangor Abbey. Robert Stewart worked as a lamplighter and he and Jane had ten children – Thomas (born 13 July 1889); Maria (born 24 January 1892); Mary Elizabeth (born 12 November 1893); Robert (born 17 October 1895); Charles Hiram (born 26 February 1898); Sarah Jane (born 25 June 1900); Albert Edward (born 25 May 1902); Donald (born 31 May 1904); Don Carlos (born 2 April 1908) and Olive (born 24 April 1909).

S

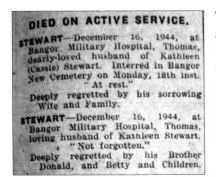

DIED ON ACTIVE SERVICE.

STEWART—December 16, 1944, at Bangor Military Hospital, Thomas, dearly-loved husband of Kathleen (Cassie) Stewart. Interred in Bangor New Cemetery on Monday, 18th inst.
" At rest."
Deeply regretted by his sorrowing Wife and Family.

STEWART—December 16, 1944, at Bangor Military Hospital, Thomas, loving husband of Kathleen Stewart.
" Not forgotten."
Deeply regretted by his Brother Donald, and Betty and Children.

Thomas Stewart went to school in Conlig and after leaving school he joined the Royal Navy as a youth. He served during the First World War and attained the rank of Stoker Petty Officer. Thomas Stewart and Kathleen (Cassie) Mulholland from Conlig (born 5 November 1898) were married on 27 July 1918 in Conlig Presbyterian Church and after the war Thomas worked for the Bangor Gas Undertaking. Thomas and Cassie Stewart had four children – Thomas Arthur (born 12 January 1920); James Warwick (born 22 February 1929); Robert (born 16 December 1932) and Rose Ann (born 27 August 1934).

In December 1939 Thomas Stewart enlisted for service in the Second World War and he joined the Royal Ulster Rifles, subsequently transferring to the Corps of Military Police in England. Private Thomas Stewart died of cancer on 16 December 1944 at Bangor Military Hospital (Bangor High School). His wife Kathleen (Cassie) lived at 44 Railwayview Street, Bangor. The officiating minister at his funeral was the Revd R.W. Williams of Bangor Abbey. Thomas

Stewart was survived by his wife Cassie; his three sons Thomas A., Warwick and Robert; his daughter Ann; his mother Sarah Jane and his brothers and sisters. Cassie Stewart placed a *Roll of Honour* notice in the 15 December 1945 edition of the *County Down Spectator* and it contained the text:

Resting where no shadows fall

Private Thomas Stewart was 54 years old when he died and he is commemorated in Bangor Parish Church of Ireland Church (St. Comgall's). There is an inscription on his CWGC headstone:

At Rest
Deeply Regretted By His Wife And Family
Kathleen

Kathleen (Cassie) Stewart died on 3 August 1975.

S

Stockdale, Thomas Norman (Norman)
Pilot Officer (Wireless Operator/Air Gunner)
No. 52486, Royal Air Force
Died in service on Saturday 28 August 1943 (aged 21)
Belfast (Dundonald) Cemetery, Co. Down (Section D1 Joint Grave 306)

Thomas Norman Stockdale was born in 1922 and he was a son of Thomas and Hanna Stockdale (nee Coey). Thomas Stockdale of 5 Geoffrey Street, Belfast worked as a labourer and Hannah Coey of 1 Keswick Street, Belfast worked as a reeler when they were married on 14 December 1913 in St. Silas's Church of Ireland Church, Belfast. They had at least four children – Elsie, Molly, Iris and Thomas Norman. They lived at Clonfin, Ballymaconnell, Bangor and Hannah Stockdale died there on 8 February 1926. Hannah Stockdale was buried in Belfast City Cemetery – Glenalina Extension (Grave J 120). Also buried in that grave were Ellen Stockdale of 16 Harrybrook Street, Belfast who died on 2 March 1946 and Mary Stockdale of 107 Clandeboye Road, Bangor who died on 18 February 1970. Ellen Stockdale was Thomas Stockdale Senior's mother and Mary Stockdale was his second wife. After Hannah died, Thomas Stockdale Senior married Mary Brown (nee Scott). Mary's son, Squadron Quartermaster Sergeant **Alexander Scott Brown**, was killed in action on 21 March 1943 –

five months before Thomas Norman Stockdale died.

DIED ON ACTIVE SERVICE

STOCKDALE—August, 1943, killed on active service, Pilot-Officer T. Norman Stockdale, R.A.F., beloved son of Mr. and Mrs. Stockdale, 107 Clandeboye Road, late of 33 Princetown Road, Bangor. Funeral on Saturday, at 3 p.m., from above address to Dundonald Cemetery.

After leaving Ballymaconnell, the Stockdale family lived at 33 Princetown Road and then 107 Clandeboye Road, Bangor. Thomas Norman Stockdale joined the Royal Air Force at the age of 16 and at the time of his death he had taken part in 112 operational flights. His death was reported in the 11 September 1943 edition of the *County Down Spectator* and the article described how RAF officers acted as pallbearers at his funeral and how his chum, Pilot Officer Geoffrey Bowman, was in charge of the bearer party. Some nine months later, on 21 May 1944, **Geoffrey Bowman** was killed in action. It was also reported that Thomas's sister Molly was a Sergeant in the ATS; Molly's husband John Thomson was a Lance Bombardier in the Royal Artillery and Thomas's sister Iris was a Private in the ATS.

Thomas Norman Stockdale's brother-in-law **John Thomson** died on 28 June 1945 at Palace Barracks, Holywood and he was buried in Belfast (Dundonald) Cemetery alongside his brother-in-law. Pilot Officer Thomas Norman Stockdale was 21 years old when he died and he is commemorated on Bangor and District War Memorial; in Wesley Centenary Methodist Church, Bangor and on the Scott family grave headstone in Belfast (Dundonald) Cemetery. Thomas Norman Stockdale and Alexander Scott Brown were both grandsons of John and Mary Duff Scott. Mary Duff Scott died on 10 April 1933 (aged 66) and John Scott died on 11 November 1942 (aged 79).

Stone, Gerald Cecil William (Gerald)
Mentioned in Despatches
Pilot Officer (Wireless Operator/Air Gunner)
No. 49988, 156 Squadron, Royal Air Force
Killed on active service on Thursday 27 August 1942 (aged 25)
Reichswald Forest War Cemetery, Kleve, Nordrhein-Westfalen, Germany (Collective Grave 24 C 12-18)

Gerald Cecil William Stone was a son of Leonard William and Daisy

Stone of Ipswich and he was the husband of Mary Mather (Maimie) Stone (nee Whittaker) of 31 Victoria Avenue, Newtownards. Gerald Stone and Maimie Whittaker were married in 1939 in Strean Presbyterian Church, Newtownards. Maimie's brother, John Whittaker, served with the RAF in the Middle East.

ARDS AIRMAN MISSING.

NEWS RECEIVED BY WIFE.

News has been received by Mrs. M. Stone of Newtownards that her husband, Flight Sergeant G. C. W. Stone has been reported missing on active service. Flight Sergeant Stone has had several years service with the R.A.F., and early in the war he received a "mention" for his good work. He has participated in over thirty operational flights against the enemy, and is stated to have shown exceptional ability as a gunner and bomb aimer.

KILLED ON ACTIVE SERVICE.

STONE—August, 1942, formerly reported missing, now reported Killed on Active Service, Pilot Officer Gerald Cecil William Stone, R.A.F., husband of Maimie Stone, 31, Victoria Avenue, Newtownards. Interred in the Protestant Cemetery, Konigeschstrasse, Rheine-on-River Ems, North West Germany, September, 1942.

During the Second World War Gerald Stone served with the Royal Air Force in Bomber Command and in the 5 September 1942 edition of the *Newtownards Chronicle* it was reported that he was missing in action over Germany. He was said to have shown exceptional ability as a gunner and bomb aimer and had taken part in 33 operational flights. Later it was confirmed that he had been killed in action along with his five comrades. Pilot Officer Gerald Cecil William Stone was one of a six man crew aboard a Vickers Wellington Mark III aircraft (X3367) that took off from RAF Warboys in Cambridgeshire at 8.26 pm on 27 August 1942 on a mission to bomb the Fiesler aircraft works at Kassel in Germany. They were shot down at 11.23 pm by a German night fighter and crashed into the Laurenz Textile Factory at Epe. They were buried in the Evangelical Cemetery at Rheine and later their bodies were exhumed and moved to Reichswald Forest War Cemetery. The other five crew members who died that night were:

- FS Michael Gordon Savage aged 20 from Eastbourne, Sussex
- Sergeant Gilbert Hebblethwaite aged 24 from Huddersfield
- Pilot Officer Peter Hayes aged 20 (RNZAF)
- Pilot Officer Jack Leewarden aged 25 from Hampstead Heath, London
- Sergeant Frederick Valentine Herbert Shepherd

Pilot Officer Gerald Cecil William Stone was 25 years old when he died.

S

Stronge, Frederick Eustace (Frederick)
Pilot Officer
No. 79997, Royal Air Force Volunteer Reserve
Killed in an aircraft accident on Wednesday 23 October 1940 (aged 32)
Donaghadee Parish Church of Ireland Graveyard, Co. Down

Frederick Eustace (Frederick) Stronge was born on 25 October 1907 and he was a son of James Taylor Stronge and Mary Helen Stronge (nee McClaughlin or McLoughlin, daughter of James McClaughlin of 48 Brougham Street, Belfast). They were married on 17 March 1904 in St. James's Church of Ireland Church, Belfast and they had at least three surviving children – Frederick Eustace (born 25 October 1907); Winifred (born 29 May 1910) and Eileen (born 8 September 1912). James Taylor Stronge JP died on 21 October 1945 at 22 Hartington Street, Belfast and he was a former chairman of Donaghadee Urban District Council

Frederick Eustace Stronge and Mary Rankin were married on 27 October 1931 in Donaghadee Parish Church of Ireland Church. Mary was a daughter of William Rankin, proprietor of the Railway Hotel, Donaghadee and she and Frederick had two children, Gladys Mary and Taylor. During the Second World War, Frederick Stronge served with the Royal Air Force Volunteer Reserve and on 23 October 1940 he was a passenger aboard an Avro Anson aircraft (R2510) which hit barrage balloon cables and crashed into houses at Woodlands Way, Mill Hill, London. The aircraft was on route from Hendon Aerodrome to Belfast with a crew of five and there were six passengers on board. There were no survivors and the others who died were:

- Flight Lieutenant Edward Charles Norman Jeffries
- Flying Officer William Ledlie aged 46 from Loughbrickland, Co. Down
- Cpl Alexander Hamilton Knighton Robertson aged 20 from Highgate, Middlesex
- Leading Aircraftman Leslie Donald Rudling aged 24 from Penge, Kent
- LAC Walter John Wynne-Harley aged 29 from New Zealand
- Air Vice Marshal Charles Hubert Boulby CB OBE MC aged 46
- Lieutenant Commander Michael Joseph Toole aged 42 (Royal Navy)
- Lieutenant (E) Thomas Gwyn James Mathias aged 40 (Royal Navy)
- Pilot Officer George Grant aged 40 from Canada
- Warrant Officer Alfred Berry aged 38 from Gillingham, Kent

Pilot Officer Frederick Eustace Stronge's death was registered at Hendon, Middlesex. He died two days before his 33rd birthday. His daughter Gladys Mary Stronge died on 14 May 1948 (aged 15) and his wife Mary died on 18

February 1983. A James Taylor Stronge (aged eight weeks) died at 49 Sunnyside Street, Belfast on 4 March 1922 and was buried in Belfast City Cemetery (Grave A 515). Also buried in the same grave were Eliza Devlina of 46 Hill Street who died on 6 April 1903 (aged 30); James Scott McClaughlin of 48 Brougham Street who died on 13 July 1906 (aged 62); Florence Muriel Stronge of 22 Whitehall Parade who died on 3 September 1906 (aged six weeks) and Helen Jones of 12 McClure Street who died on 30 April 1928 (aged 81).

Pilot Officer Frederick Eustace Stronge is commemorated on Donaghadee and District War Memorial and his headstone bears the inscription:

> *In loving memory of Frederick E. Stronge Pilot Officer RAF*
> *Dearly beloved husband of Mary Stronge*
> *Killed on active service 23 October 1940 aged 32 years*

Strutt, Frederick
Civilian War Dead
Killed accidentally on Wednesday 4 November 1942 (aged 31)

S

Frederick Strutt was a son of Frederick and Charlotte Strutt, of 14 Conliffe Gardens, Clonliffe Road, Dublin and he was the husband of Catherine Strutt of 21 Fleming Road, Drumcondra, Dublin. He was a civilian working on the lighting at Ballyhalbert Airfield and he was fatally injured on 4 November 1942 when a Bristol Beaufort aircraft piloted by Sergeant G.B. Swift of 153 Squadron ran off the runway and knocked him down.

Of the many civilians of the Commonwealth whose deaths were due to enemy action in the Second World War, the names of some 67,092 are commemorated in the Civilian War Dead Roll of Honour, located near St. George's Chapel in Westminster Abbey, London.

Stubbings, Barry John (Barry)
Private
No. 5392025, Oxford and Bucks Light Infantry
Died of illness in service on Saturday 14 March 1942 (aged 15)
Bangor Cemetery, Co. Down (Section 5 X Grave 20)

On Barry John Stubbings's CWGC headstone in Bangor Cemetery it is recorded that he was 16 years old when he died. His birth was registered in the third quarter of 1926 in Woolwich, London and so he had not yet reached his 16th birthday when he died.

Barry John Stubbings's paternal grandfather, James Stubbings, worked as a carpenter and he came from Chelmsford in Essex. Barry's father, Allan John Stubbings, who was born on 27 March 1897 was one of eleven children. The marriage of Allan John Stubbings and Kathleen M. Hughes was registered in the second quarter of 1918 in Woolwich, London. Kathleen's death was registered in the third quarter of 1926 in Woolwich, London – the same quarter as Barry's birth. Kathleen Stubbings was 28 years old when she died and three years later Barry's father remarried. The marriage of Allan John Stubbings and Violet Ivy Rose Fisher (born 31 March 1903) was registered in the fourth quarter of 1929 in Amersham, Buckinghamshire.

Allan John Stubbings was an engineer and Violet Ivy Rose Stubbings was a secretary and they made frequent trips across the Atlantic. In December 1937 Allan (described then as an engraver) sailed on his own from Southampton to the USA aboard the SS *Washington*; in April 1945 both Allan and Violet arrived at Southampton from New York aboard the *John Ericsson* and at that time their address was 2 Orchard Park, Dartington, Totnes, Devon; in December 1945 both sailed from Avonmouth, Bristol to New York aboard the *Loreto*; Allan flew from San Francisco to Sydney in October 1947; in January 1957 Allan sailed to New York aboard the *Queen Elizabeth* and in March 1957 he returned to Southampton aboard RMS *Ivernia*; in September 1960 Allan sailed from Southampton to New York aboard the SS *Liberte*. Violet Ivy Rose Stubbings's death was registered in the fourth quarter of 1981 in Exeter, Devon.

Barry John Stubbings joined the Oxford and Bucks Light Infantry and he was just 15 years old when he died of diphtheria on 14 March 1942 in Purdysburn Fever Hospital, Belfast. His home address at the time of his death was 5 Orchard Street, Dartington, Totnes, Devon.

Sturgeon, John
Able Seaman
No. D/JX 148794, HMS *Courageous*, Royal Navy
Died as a result of enemy action on Sunday 17 September 1939 (aged 28)
Plymouth Naval Memorial, Devon, England (Panel 33 Column 3)

In the CWGC Debt of Honour John Sturgeon's date of death is recorded as

7 September 1939. John Sturgeon was born on 13 May 1911 and he was a son of James and Isabella Sturgeon (nee Hedley) of Mill Street, Comber. James Sturgeon worked as a bread server and he and Isabella Hedley were married on 16 November 1909 in First Comber Presbyterian Church. They had eight children all of whom were baptised in First Comber Presbyterian Church – Joseph Hedley (born 11 June 1910); twins William and John (born 13 May 1911, William died in infancy); James (born 29 December 1912); William (born 2 January 1915); Agnes (born 14 June 1916); Isabella (born 31 July 1918) and Samuel (born 29 December 1923).

John Sturgeon joined the Royal Navy and in September 1939 he was serving aboard the aircraft carrier HMS *Courageous*. Built as a battle cruiser in 1916 by Armstrong Whitworth in Newcastle-Upon-Tyne, HMS *Courageous* was reconstructed as an aircraft carrier in the 1920s. On 17 September 1939 she was being escorted by four destroyers when she was sunk by the German submarine *U-29* about 190 miles south-west of Dursey Head, Co. Cork. At around 7.50 pm she was struck on the port side by two torpedoes and she sank 17 minutes later. Able Seaman John Sturgeon was one of around 520 men who died (her complement was around 750 naval ratings and 470 RAF personnel). The entire crew of *U-29* was awarded the Iron Cross 2nd Class. (*U-29* was scuttled on 4 May 1945 in Kupfermuhlen Bay, east of Flensberg in Germany).

Able Seaman John Sturgeon was 28 years old when he died and he is commemorated on Plymouth Naval Memorial in Devon; on Comber and District War Memorial and in First Comber Presbyterian Church (as Gunner John Sturgeon).

Swift, Derek Rodney
Private
No. T/88493, Royal Army Service Corps
Died as a result of an accident on Thursday 21 November 1940 (aged 24)
Blackpool (Carleton) Cemetery, Lancashire, England (Section B Grave 1130)

Derek Rodney Swift was born in August 1916 and he was a son of Thomas Whittham Swift (born October 1883) and Agnes Swift (nee Young) of 3 Canterbury Avenue, Blackpool, Lancashire. Thomas Whittham Swift worked as an electrician and he and Agnes Young were married on 30 March 1903 in St. John's Church, Blackpool. They had at least three children – Frank George, Charles Victor and Derek Rodney. Thomas Whittham Swift enlisted on 15 March 1915 and during the First World War he served with the Army

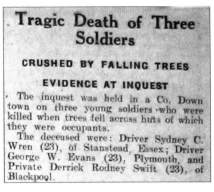

Tragic Death of Three Soldiers

CRUSHED BY FALLING TREES

EVIDENCE AT INQUEST

The inquest was held in a Co. Down town on three young soldiers who were killed when trees fell across huts of which they were occupants.

The deceased were: Driver Sydney C. Wren (23), of Stanstead, Essex; Driver George W. Evans (23), Plymouth, and Private Derrick Rodney Swift (23), of Blackpool.

Service Corps.

During the Second World War Private Derek Rodney Swift served with the Royal Army Service Corps and his death was reported in the 30 November 1940 edition of the *County Down Spectator* under the headline *Tragic Death of Three Soldiers*. Three young soldiers were killed in Clandeboye Camp, Ballyleidy when trees fell across huts in which they were sleeping. They were Driver **George William Evens** (aged 23) from Plymouth; Private Derek Rodney Swift (aged 24) from Blackpool and Driver **Sydney John Wren** (aged 23) from Stansted in Essex. The roof of the hut in which Private Swift was sleeping caved in and pinned him to the bed. To release him his comrades used a heavy jack to raise the fallen roof and hacksaws to cut down the bed. Private Swift suffered severe head injuries and was dead when his comrades got him out. Driver Wren and Driver Evens were crushed by fallen debris and both died from 'asphyxia due to crushing'.

Private Derek Rodney Swift was buried in Blackpool (Carleton) Cemetery, Lancashire, England.

Tait Family; John James (father) and John McCalla (son)

John McCalla Tait (the son) was the first of the two men to die.

Tait, John McCalla (Jack)
Flight Sergeant (Pilot)
No. 1063628, 78 Squadron, Royal Air Force Volunteer Reserve
Killed on active service on Friday 26 March 1943 (aged 21)
Doetinchem (Loolaan) General Cemetery, Gelderland, Netherlands
(Row 1 Grave 10)

John McCalla (Jack) Tait was born on 4 August 1921 and he was the only son of **John James Tait** and Jane Cowan McCalla Tait (nee Brown) of Bellevue, Holywood. John James Tait was a marine engineer and he and Jane Cowan McCalla Brown were married on 5 January 1921 in Ballygilbert Presbyterian Church. Jane Cowan McCalla Brown's father, Nathaniel McCalla Brown, was an iron merchant.

John McCalla Tait was educated privately before attending Sullivan Upper School, Holywood from 1930 until 1939. He joined the Royal Air Force Volunteer Reserve in 1940 and during the Second World War he served in Bomber Command. He took part in 33 operational flights before he died on 26 March 1943. He was one of an eight man crew aboard a Handley Page Halifax Mark II aircraft (W7931) that took off at 7.02 pm on 26 March 1943 from RAF Linton-on-Ouse in Yorkshire on a mission to bomb Duisburg. On the outward flight their aircraft was crippled by flak and crashed at Gaanderen-Pinnedijk in Holland. Five crew members survived the crash and were taken Prisoner-of-War – Sergeant F.E. Lemon, Warrant Officer S. Hauxwell, Sergeant G.R. Johnston, Pilot Officer R.W. Keen and Sergeant R.R.H. Huleatt. In addition to Flight Sergeant John McCalla Tait, the other two crew members who died that night were:

- Sergeant James Archibald Wilson aged 21 (RNZAF)
- Sergeant Andrew Wilson

Flight Sergeant (Pilot) John McCalla Tait was 21 years old when he died on 26 March 1943 and he is commemorated on Holywood and District War Memorial; in First Holywood Presbyterian Church and in Sullivan Upper School. Less than eight months later his father died.

Tait, John James
Chief Engineer (Marine)
Died of illness in service on Saturday 13 November 1943 (aged 59)
Holywood Cemetery, Co. Down (Grave 877)

ALSO THE FOLLOWING WHO GAVE THEIR LIVES IN THE WORLD WAR 1939 — 1945

JAMES HAMILTON GORDON	25TH MAY 1940
JOHN FRAZER JEFFERSON	1ST MARCH 1941
DAVID COWAN	10TH DECEMBER 1941
JOHN McCALLA TAIT	26TH MARCH 1943
WALLACE ROBERT SMYTH	29TH JULY 1943
THOMAS FRANCIS JEFFERSON	5TH NOVEMBER 1943
JOHN JAMES TAIT	13TH NOVEMBER 1943

"GREATER LOVE HATH NO MAN THAN THIS, THAT A MAN LAY DOWN HIS LIFE FOR HIS FRIENDS"

John James Tait was a son of James Fowler Tait (born in County Down) and Jean Tait (born in Scotland). James Fowler Tait worked as a commercial traveller for the Craigmillar Creamery in Edinburgh and he and Jane had four children – John James (born 1884); Joseph S. (born 1885); Marian (born 1887) and Douglas (born 1890). All four children were born in England before the Tait family moved to Belfast. They lived in Halcombe Street, Belfast before moving to Holywood.

John James Tait was a Chief Engineer (Marine) and he was 59 years old when he died of toxaemia on 13 November 1943. Two days later he was buried in Holywood Cemetery and he is commemorated on Holywood and District War Memorial and in First Holywood Presbyterian Church. His son, **John McCalla Tait**, was killed less than eight months earlier, on 26 March 1943.

Tate Family; Ellen Ogle, Bessie and Evelyn

> **RESULT OF ENEMY ACTION.**
>
> **MORTON—TATE**—(result of enemy action), Thomas Morton, Nellie Tate and Betty and Evelyn Tate, of Manor Street, Belfast, father, sister and nieces of Thomas G. and Mrs. Morton, 87, South Street, Newtownards.

Ellen Ogle (Nellie) Tate (nee Morton) was a daughter of Thomas and Annie Morton (nee McMurray) who were married on 11 May 1892 and lived in Mountcollyer Street, Belfast. Thomas Morton worked as a general labourer and he and Annie McMurray had at least ten children including a female child (born 26 January 1895, died in infancy); Thomas G. (born 29 February 1896); John (born 28 January 1898); William (born 19 July 1901); Alexander (born 11 October 1903); Ellen Ogle (born 18 November 1905); Annie (born 10 May 1908); Evelyn (born 3 July 1910) and Winifred (born 18 January 1914).

Ellen Ogle Morton (aged 18) and George Linden Tate (aged 19) were married on 22 March 1924 in Belfast Domestic Mission for the Poor and they lived at 174 Manor Street, Belfast. On 16 April 1941 four members of the family died at 174 Manor Street – Ellen Ogle Tate (nee Morton), her daughters Bessie and Evelyn and her father **Thomas Morton**. Ellen Ogle Tate's brother, Thomas G. Morton, lived at 87 South Street, Newtownards and he placed a *Result of Enemy Action* death notice in the 19 April 1941 edition of the *Newtownards Chronicle* in memory of his father, sister and nieces.

The Belfast Blitz comprised high-casualty German Luftwaffe air raids on Belfast in April and May 1941. On the night of Easter Tuesday 15 April 1941 two hundred Luftwaffe bombers attacked the city of Belfast and some 900 people were killed. In another Luftwaffe raid on the night of Saturday 4 May 1941 some 150 people were killed.

Tate, Ellen Ogle (Nellie)
Civilian War Dead
Died as a result of enemy action on Wednesday 16 April 1941 (aged 35)
Buried on 21 April 1941 in Dundonald Cemetery, Co. Down (Grave D2 392)

Tate, Elizabeth (Bessie, sometimes Betty)
Civilian War Dead
Died as a result of enemy action on Wednesday 16 April 1941 (aged 16)
Buried on 21 April 1941 in Dundonald Cemetery, Co. Down (Grave D2 392)

Tate, Evelyn
Civilian War Dead
Died as a result of enemy action on Wednesday 16 April 1941 (aged 14)
Buried on 21 April 1941 in Dundonald Cemetery, Co. Down (Grave D2 392)

Of the many civilians of the Commonwealth whose deaths were due to enemy action in the Second World War, the names of some 67,092 are commemorated in the Civilian War Dead Roll of Honour, located near St. George's Chapel in Westminster Abbey, London.

George Linden Tate died on 28 June 1969 and he was buried in Dundonald Cemetery, Co. Down (Grave F3 1033)

Taylor, Samuel Irwin (Irwin)
Pilot Officer (Wireless Operator/Air Gunner)
No. 195102, 114 Squadron, Royal Air Force Volunteer Reserve
Killed in action on Monday 19 February 1945 (aged 26)
Udine War Cemetery, Italy (Collective Grave 1 C 3-5)

Samuel Irwin Taylor was born on 24 July 1918 and he was a son of William John and Elizabeth Taylor (nee Templeton) of *Ashleigh*, Comber and later 141 Orby Drive, Belfast. William John Taylor came from Bellaghy in County Londonderry, he worked as a Public Elementary School teacher and he and Elizabeth Templeton from Jordanstown were married on 7 February 1912 in Carnmoney Presbyterian Church, Newtownabbey. Their daughter Mary was born on 14 November 1912.

Samuel Irwin Taylor attended Royal Belfast Academical Institution (RBAI) from 1931 until 1936 and during that time the Taylor family lived in Comber. During the Second World War Irwin Taylor served with the Royal Air Force

MADE THE SUPREME SACRIFICE

Signalman Hans Calvert

Sgt. James Shields

Pilot Officer Irwin Taylor

Ldg. Cook Thomas Wilson

Volunteer Reserve and on 19 February 1945 he was reported missing in action. Later it was officially confirmed that he must be presumed killed.

Pilot Officer (Wireless Operator/Air Gunner) Samuel Irwin Taylor was 26 years old when he died and he is commemorated on Comber and District War Memorial (as LAC Irwin Taylor) and in Second Comber Presbyterian Church (as Pilot Officer Irwin Taylor). There is evidence to suggest that Flight Lieutenant J. W. Robb DFC survived the crash and that Wing Commander Ronald Roumieu Thomson DFC (aged 30) of Kelso, Roxburghshire together with Pilot Officer James Spalding Cameron (aged 32) of Kelday Castle, Yorkshire were killed.

Templeton, Arthur Moore (Moore)
Sergeant (Wireless Operator/Air Gunner)
No. 1071533, 427 (RCAF) Squadron, Royal Air Force Volunteer Reserve
Killed in action on Thursday 4 February 1943 (aged 30)
Guidel Communal Cemetery, Morbihan, France (Row 3 Grave 14)

T

Arthur Moore Templeton was born at 59 Brunswick Road, Bangor on 28 July 1912 and he was the second son of James and Mary Colville Templeton (nee Dugan) who lived in Osborne Park, Bangor. James Templeton worked as a commercial traveller (drapery) and he was a widower when he and Mary Colville Dugan were married on 10 January 1900 in Cliftonville (Donegal Street) Presbyterian Church, Belfast. James Templeton's first wife was Margaret (Maggie) Suffern and they were married on 25 December 1894 in Fitzroy Presbyterian Church, Belfast. They had two children – Elizabeth Suffern (born 13 April 1895) and Margaret Scott (born 8 January 1897) and they lived at 27 Shankill Road, Belfast. Maggie Templeton died there on 31 October 1897 (aged 27) and she was buried in Belfast City Cemetery (Grave F1 154). James and Mary Colville Templeton had at least four children – Mary Colville (born 15 May 1904); James Stanley (born 24 January 1906); Arthur Moore (born 28 July 1912) and William Stewart (born 1916).

Prior to joining the Royal Air Force Volunteer Reserve in 1940 Arthur Moore Templeton was on the staff at the Head Office of the Belfast Banking Company and he was prominently identified with the Scout Movement in Bangor – as was his brother William Stewart Templeton. On 10 January 1940 William Stewart Templeton was killed in Bangor 'in a black-out accident'. It was reported in the 13 January 1940 edition of the *County Down Spectator* that 'death was caused by fracture of the base of the skull and laceration of the brain, the result of deceased being accidentally thrown from his push bicycle when he collided with a pedestrian'. Stewart Templeton (aged 23) was returning home from a Boy Scout meeting in Bangor. He was buried in his scout uniform in Bangor Cemetery and his brother Moore attended the funeral. Not long after Stewart's death Moore joined the Royal Air Force Volunteer Reserve.

On 14 November 1942 Moore Templeton and Esme Joan Dawson were married in Harehills Lane Methodist Church, Leeds. She was a member of the WAAF and her sister Audrey was her bridesmaid. The duties of best man were performed by Moore's RAF comrade, Harry Megarry from Bangor. Harry Megarry's brother **Herbert Reginald Megarry** had been killed in a flying accident on 18 May 1940.

T

 Less than three months after his wedding, Sergeant Arthur Moore Templeton was killed in action on 4 February 1943. He was one of a five man crew aboard a Vickers Wellington Mark III aircraft (BJ668) that took off at 6.26 pm from RAF Croft in Durham on a mission to bomb the Keroman Submarine Base (German U-boats) in Lorient, France. The aircraft was hit by flak and crashed at Ploemeur in Morbihan. Pilot Officer A.J.B. Thompson was the only survivor and he was taken Prisoner-of-War. In addition to Sergeant Arthur Moore Templeton the other three crew members who died and were buried in Guidel Communal Cemetery were:

- Flying Officer Cuthbert Michael Parsons aged 22 from Guildford, Surrey (his brother, Peter Francis Parsons, also died on active service)
- Sergeant Peter Sandover aged 20 from Ivybridge, Devon
- Sergeant Hughie Francis Davies aged 19 from Tregayan, Anglesey

 Sergeant Arthur Moore Templeton was 30 years old when he died and he is commemorated on Bangor and District War Memorial; in Trinity Presbyterian Church, Bangor (as A. Moore Templeton); on the Belfast Banking Company Second World War Memorial Plaque (now in Danske Bank, Donegall

Square West, Belfast) and on the family grave headstone in Bangor Cemetery. His father James died on 14 August 1956 and his mother Mary died on 21 June 1965.

Thompson, Edward Carson (Teddy)
Flight Sergeant
No. 748054, 101 Squadron, Royal Air Force Volunteer Reserve
Killed in action on Friday 8 August 1941 (aged 27)
Sage War Cemetery, Oldenburg, Niedersachsen, Germany (Grave 7 E 10)

> **KILLED IN ACTION.**
>
> THOMPSON—Flight Sergeant Edward Carson Thompson (Teddy), R.A.F.V.R., killed in action, August, 1941.
> He died that we might live.
> Severed only "till He come."
> Deeply regretted by his Wife, Father, Mother, Brother and Sisters.
> 4 Lancaster Avenue, Bangor.

Edward Carson (Teddy) Thompson was born on 21 February 1914 and he was the younger son of Alexander and Annie Thompson (nee Young) who lived at 15 Jerusalem Street, Belfast. Alexander Thompson was working as a joiner when he and Annie Young (born County Londonderry, daughter of William and Margaret Young) were married on 19 April 1897 in Ballygilbert Presbyterian Church. They had at least six children including Mary (born 24 January 1898); Henrietta (born 4 May 1899); William (born 15 October 1902; Florence (born 18 September 1904) and Edward Carson (Teddy, born 21 February 1914). When Teddy was eight years old, the Thompson family moved from Belfast to Bangor. Teddy was educated in Ward School and Bangor Technical School. He worshipped in Bangor Parish Church of Ireland Church (St. Comgall's) and belonged to the Parish Badminton Club. After Teddy left school he worked with his father Alexander in the family building and contracting business. Teddy was a member of the British Order of Ancient Free Gardeners' Friendly Society and on 26 August 1939 he and Olga Mencarelli (daughter of confectioner Andrew Mencarelli, 11 Bridge Street, Bangor) were married in St. Polycarp's Church of Ireland Church, Belfast.

Teddy joined the Royal Air Force Volunteer Reserve and completed his training before the Second World War. He was called to service when hostilities commenced and he was 27 years old when he was killed in action on 8 August 1941. There is evidence that he baled out of a Vickers Wellington aircraft (X9601) over the North Sea when under attack from a German night fighter and that the pilot, Flight Lieutenant L. A. Rickinson, brought the aircraft back to base and was awarded the DFC.

Death notices expressed deep regret from his wife Olga, who was living in married quarters in Coventry and from his father, mother, brother and sisters who lived at 4 Lancaster Avenue, Bangor. Tributes included the verses:

Not just today but every day,
In silence we remember

He died that we might live,
Severed only 'till He come

His effects amounted to some £393 and probate was granted to his widow. Flight Sergeant Edward Carson Thompson is commemorated on Bangor and District War Memorial and in Bangor Parish Church (St. Comgall's).

Thompson Family, Ernest Oscar (son) and William Oscar (father)

Both father and son were accidentally drowned and William Oscar Thompson was the first of the two men to die.

Thompson, William Oscar (Bill)
Constable
Royal Marine Police
Accidentally drowned on Thursday 22 August 1940 (aged 49)
Douglas Bank Cemetery, Rosyth, Scotland

William Oscar (Bill) Thompson was born on 20 July 1890 in Derrygonnelly, Co. Fermanagh and he was a son of Frederick Thompson (born in Dublin) and Margaret Ellen Thompson (nee Griffith, born in England). Frederick Thompson and Margaret Ellen Griffith were married on 4 December 1887 in Fivemiletown Parish Church of Ireland Church, Co. Tyrone. Frederick Thompson was a Constable in the Royal Irish Constabulary and after he retired he worked as a gamekeeper. Margaret Ellen Griffith was an Upper House-Maid in *Blessingbourne House* near Fivemiletown. This manor house on an 8,000 acre estate overlooked Lough Fadda and was owned by Hugh de Fellenberg Montgomery.

Frederick and Margaret Ellen Thompson had seven children – Robert (born 1889); William Oscar (born 20 July 1890); Ryland George (born 26 August 1891; died 1913); twins Frederick Charles and Reuben Harold (born 13 February 1893); Joseph Percival (born 25 September 1894) and Lillian Maude Mary (born 14 March 1897). Robert was born in England and the rest were born in County Fermanagh. The Thompson family moved to Bangor where they lived at 76 Castle Street. Frederick Thompson died around 1904 and Margaret Ellen worked as a gatekeeper.

ROLL OF HONOUR.

THOMPSON—In loving remembrance of my dear husband, and our dear father, William Oscar (Bill), who lost his life on August 22, 1940, while serving with the Royal Marine Police, and interred in Douglas Bank Cemetery, Rosyth.
" At the going down of the sun, and in the morning, we will remember him."
Always remembered by his loving Wife, Margaret, and Daughters, Winnie and Maureen, 42 Railway View Street, Bangor; also his Sons, Ernie and Clarence, on active service.

William Oscar (Bill) Thompson and Margaret Stockdale were married on 2 April 1910 in Bangor Abbey and they lived at 42 Railwayview Street, Bangor. Bill Thompson served throughout the First World War with the Royal Field Artillery and he joined up again in May 1940. Between the two world wars he operated a window cleaning business in Bangor. Constable Bill Thompson served as a member of the Royal Marine Police at Rosyth Dockyard, Fife in Scotland and on 22 August 1940 he was accidentally drowned. That was the date when he was last seen alive and his body was not found until 5 September 1940. He was interred in Douglas Bank Cemetery, Rosyth on 7 September 1940.

T

Bill Thompson was survived by his wife Margaret; his four sons: William Thompson (a member of Bangor Golf Club's senior team), Clarence Thompson (a Rangefinder in the Royal Field Artillery), **Ernest Oscar Thompson** (a Rifleman who drowned on active service on 17 November 1943) and Cecil Thompson (who died on 9 November 1940 aged 15½); his three daughters: Essie (Mrs Bertie McMillan), Winnie and Maureen Doris; his two brothers Reuben and Fred and his sister Lily Thompson. His wife Margaret placed a *Death Notice* in the 14 September 1940 edition of the *County Down Spectator* and it included the following verse:

Short and sudden was the call
His sudden death surprised us all
Only those who have lost can tell
The sorrow of parting without farewell

733

Constable William Oscar Thompson was 49 years old when he died and he is commemorated on Bangor and District War Memorial; in Bangor Parish Church of Ireland Church (St. Comgall's) and on the family grave headstone in Bangor Cemetery. His wife Margaret died on 20 March 1965. There is an inscription on his headstone:

Resting where no shadows fall

Thompson, Ernest Oscar (Ernie)
Rifleman
No. 7020212, 7th Battalion, Royal Ulster Rifles *attached* 5th Battalion, Royal Inniskilling Fusiliers
Accidentally drowned on Wednesday 17 November 1943 (aged 21)
Bangor Cemetery, Co. Down (Section 4 U Grave 25)

T

DIED ON ACTIVE SERVICE

THOMPSON—Accidentally drowned in Boston, England, November 17, 1943. Ernest O., aged 21, dearly-beloved husband of Anna Thompson. Interred in Bangor New Cemetery, November 24th.
"Absent but not forgotten."
Sadly missed by his sorrowing Wife and two children, 45 King Street, Bangor.

THOMPSON—Accidentally drowned on Active Service, Boston, England, on November 17th, 1943, Ernest O. (age 21), third and beloved son of Margaret and the late William O. Thompson. Interred in Bangor New Cemetery, 24th November.
"His battle's fought,
His victory won."
Sadly missed by his sorrowing Mother, 42 Railway View Street, Bangor.

Ernest Oscar (Ernie) Thompson was the third son of Margaret and the late William Oscar Thompson who lived at 42 Railwayview Street, Bangor and he was baptised in Bangor Abbey on 11 October 1922. Before he enlisted in September 1940 Ernie was working in his father's window cleaning business. Ernie was the husband of Anna Thompson, 45 King Street, Bangor and they had two children.

Rifleman Ernie Thompson was accidentally drowned on 17 November 1943 while on active service in Boston, Lincolnshire. His father, **William Oscar Thompson**, was drowned on 22 August 1940 while on active service with the Military Police in Scotland and his brother Cecil (aged 15½) died on 9 November 1940. His brother Clarence (Clarrie) was on active service in Italy.

Rifleman Ernie Thompson was 21 years old when he died and he was buried in Bangor Cemetery on 24 November 1943 and the services were conducted by the Revd James Hamilton of Bangor Abbey. Rifleman Ernest Oscar Thompson is commemorated on Bangor and District War Memorial; in Bangor Parish Church of Ireland Church (St. Comgall's) and on the family grave headstone in Bangor Cemetery.

Thompson, Hugh Conn (Hugo)
Pilot Officer
No. 52755, 44 Squadron, Royal Air Force
Killed in action on Tuesday 22 June 1943 (aged 21)
Runnymede Memorial, Surrey, England (Panel 133)

Hugh Conn (Hugo) Thompson was born on 23 May 1922 and he was the only son of Annie Thompson (nee Conn) and the late Hugh Thompson who lived at *Penlee*, Bellevue Road, Carnalea. They were married on 15 January 1918 in St. Thomas's Church of Ireland Church, Shankill, Belfast. Hugo Thompson's father had been a coastguard officer stationed at Donaghadee. Coastguard archives indicate that Hugo's father was born in 1892 and that he joined the coastguard on 27 November 1935. He went first to Killough, Co. Down and transferred to Donaghadee on 1 February 1937.

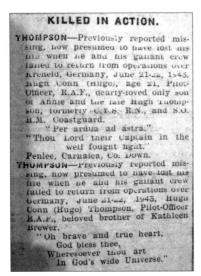

KILLED IN ACTION.

THOMPSON—Previously reported missing, now presumed to have lost his life when he and his gallant crew failed to return from operations over Krefeld, Germany, June 21-22, 1943. Hugh Conn (Hugo), age 21, Pilot Officer, R.A.F., dearly-loved only son of Annie and the late Hugh Thompson, formerly C.Y.S. R.N., and S.O. H.M. Coastguard.
 " Per ardua ad astra."
" Thou Lord their Captain in the well fought fight."
Penlee, Carnalea, Co. Down.
THOMPSON—Previously reported missing, now presumed to have lost his life when he and his gallant crew failed to return from operations over Germany, June 21-22, 1943, Hugh Conn (Hugo) Thompson, Pilot-Officer R.A.F., beloved brother of Kathleen Brewer.
 " Oh brave and true heart,
  God bless thee,
  Wheresoever thou art
   In God's wide Universe."

Hugo Thompson was educated at Bangor Central Public Elementary School and Bangor Grammar School from 1934 until 1938 (except for a few months when he attended Down High School, Downpatrick). He was remembered by the headmaster as 'a simple, steady, sturdy, unassuming boy who worked hard at his books and played hard on the sports field.' His ambition was to join the Royal Air Force and he passed his Apprentice Clerkship Examination (RAF) in April 1938.

During the Second World War Pilot Officer Hugo Thompson served with the Royal Air Force in Bomber Command and he was killed during the night of 21/22 June 1943. He was one of an eight man crew aboard an Avro Lancaster Mark III aircraft (LM330) that took off at 11.50 pm on 21 June 1943 from RAF Dunholme Lodge in Lincolnshire on a mission to bomb Krefeld in Germany. Their aircraft was lost without trace and all aboard are commemorated on the Runnymede Memorial. In addition to Pilot Officer Hugh Conn Thompson the other seven crew members who died that night were:

- Pilot Officer Lawrence Sinclair Welsh aged 21 from Edinburgh

- Sergeant Louis Renton McGrath from Belfast
- Sergeant Samuel David Mindel aged 24
- Sergeant Leonard Arthur Harrison aged 21 from Sydenham, London
- Sergeant Norman Nicholas England aged 24 from Belfast
- Sergeant Norman Metcalfe aged 20 from Nelson, Lancashire
- Sergeant James Henry Arlow aged 23 from Cleveland, Ohio, USA

Hugo Thompson's sister, Kathleen Elizabeth Thompson, married George Paul Richard Brewer. Their son who was born on 4 June 1944 and baptised in Bangor Abbey on 26 July 1944 was named after his uncle Hugo Thompson – Hugo Kenneth George Brewer. They too lived at *Penlee*, Bellevue Road, Carnalea.

THOMPSON H.C. Pilot Officer Hugh Conn Thompson was 21 years old when he died and he is commemorated on Bangor and District War Memorial (as Thompson J.C.); in Bangor Parish Church of Ireland Church (St. Comgall's) and in Bangor Grammar School.

Thompson, James

T

Civilian War Dead

Died as a result of enemy action on Monday 5 May 1941 (aged 36)

THOMPSON—Cherished memories of my dear brother, James, killed by enemy action May 5th, 1941. "Gone to be with other loved ones." Always remembered by a loving Sister.—K. Lennon, 16 Belfast Road, Bangor.

James Thompson was born in Donaghadee on 14 June 1904 and he was a son of Andrew and Elizabeth (Lizzie) Thompson (nee Gunning) who lived at 41 Moat Street. Andrew Thompson worked as a labourer and he and Lizzie Gunning were married on 12 April 1893 in Donaghadee Parish Church of Ireland Church. Andrew and Lizzie Thompson had at least nine children – Catherine (sometimes Katherine, born 16 January 1895); John (born 19 October 1896); Mary (born 28 December 1898, died in infancy); James (born 29 April 1901, died in infancy); Andrew (born 28 April 1902); James (born 14 June 1904); Isabella (born 14 April 1906); Robert (born 26 August 1908) and Albert (born 3 August 1912).

James Thompson and Margaret Spratt (daughter of George Spratt, builder, 5 Ava Terrace, Donaghadee) were married on 19 September 1934 in Donaghadee Parish Church. James Thompson was a Special Constable in the RUC and he and Margaret lived at 158 Upper Greenville Road, Bloomfield, Belfast. Their son James Gunning Thompson was born in 1938.

Special Constable James Thompson died on 5 May 1941 at Dunraven Avenue, Belfast during a German Luftwaffe air raid and his sister, Katherine Lennon, who lived at 16 Belfast Road, Bangor placed a *Roll of Honour* notice in the 6 May edition of the *County Down Spectator*. Of the many civilians of the Commonwealth whose deaths were due to enemy action in the Second World War, the names of some 67,092 are commemorated in the Civilian War Dead Roll of Honour, located near St. George's Chapel in Westminster Abbey, London.

Some 19 months after her husband's death Margaret Thompson suffered a further bereavement. Her son, James Gunning Thompson, (aged 5½) died of tuberculous meningitis on 14 December 1943 in the Childrens' Hospital, Belfast and he was buried the following day in Dundonald Cemetery (Grave A3 165). Also buried in that grave was his maternal grandmother Margaret Spratt (died 5 February 1961 aged 86); his mother Margaret Thompson (died 29 April 1995 aged 88) was subsequently buried there. At the time of writing there is no headstone on the grave.

Thompson, Robert Arnold
Second Lieutenant
No. 121604, East Lancashire Regiment
Died as a result of an accident on Sunday 14 April 1940 (aged 27)
Belfast (Dundonald) Cemetery, Co. Down (Section C 1 Grave 9)

T

Robert Arnold Thompson was a grandson of John Thompson who was born in 1847, raised on a farm near Ahoghill and in 1870 opened his first grain mill in Belfast. The company motto was *Pioneers of Better Feeding Stuffs*. The company mill was destroyed in 1941 during the Blitz and subsequently rebuilt. Robert Arnold Thompson was born on 7 February 1913 and he was a son of William and Florence Olivia Thompson (nee McClure) of *Lauriston*, 15 Derryvolgie Avenue, Belfast and before that 264 Seacliff Road, Bangor. William Thompson worked as a grain mill manager and director in the family business and he and Florence McClure were married on 18 September 1907 in Trinity Presbyterian Church, Bangor. Robert Arnold Thompson attended Rockport School, Craigavad and then Campbell College, Belfast from September 1926 until July 1930. After leaving school he worked in the Sun Insurance Office and he was also a director of the family firm Messrs John Thompson and Sons Ltd., Donegall Quay Mills, Belfast. Two of his brothers also attended Campbell College – Raymond Emerson Thompson (born 30 October 1909) and William Stafford Thompson (born 21 April 1918).

During the Second World War Robert Arnold Thompson served with the East Lancashire Regiment and he was 27 years old when he died in Victoria Hospital, Blackpool on Sunday 14 April 1940. His effects amounted to some £145 and probate was granted to his widowed mother, Florence Olivia Thompson, then living at 41 Myrtlefield Park, Belfast.

Second Lieutenant Robert Arnold Thompson is commemorated in Rockport School; in Campbell College (there was a tribute published in *The Campbellian* Vol. 9, No. 12, July 1940) and on the family grave headstone in Dundonald Cemetery. His father died on 27 January 1938 and his mother died on 3 April 1970. His brother Raymond died on 8 March 2002 and Raymond's wife Maureen died on 27 November 1995.

During the Second World War Leading Aircraftwoman Hilda Marjorie Thompson (No. 2097973) served with the Women's Auxiliary Air Force (WAAF). Related to Second Lieutenant Robert Arnold Thompson, Hilda was 21 when she died on 28 July 1945 and she was buried in Heliopolis War Cemetery, Cairo, Egypt (Grave 4 F 18).

Thompson, Robert Orr (Bobby)
Lance Bombardier
No. 876648, 3 Regiment, Royal Horse Artillery
Killed in action on Thursday 1 May 1941 (aged 22)
Tobruk War Cemetery, Libya (Grave 3 Q 2)

KILLED IN ACTION.

THOMPSON—May, 1941, Lance-Bombardier Robert Orr Thompson, R.A., dearly-loved elder son of Samuel and Anna Thompson, 133, Greenwell Street, Newtownards.
Deeply regretted by his sorrowing Father, Mother, Brother and Sisters.

LORD LONDONDERRY C.L.B. FLUTE BAND, NEWTOWNARDS.

THOMPSON—The Members of the above Band deeply regret to learn of the death of their esteemed Member, Lance-Bombardier Robert O. Thompson, and tender to his parents and to the members of his family their sincere sympathy.
    JOHN DICKSON, Chairman.
    THOS. CAUGHERS, Hon. Secty.

Robert Orr Thompson was the elder son of Samuel and Anna Thompson (nee Orr) of 133 Greenwell Street, Newtownards. They were married on 30 October 1918 in Ballygilbert Presbyterian Church. Samuel Thompson worked as a fowl dealer and he and Anna had at least four children including Robert Orr and Walter S.

Robert Orr Thompson was educated in Castle Gardens Public Elementary School in Newtownards. He joined the Life Boys and later the Boy Scouts. After leaving school he was employed by William McConnell, rate collector, Newtownards and subsequently worked for the firm of Messrs Webb and Company, Newtownards. He was an accomplished pianist and a member

of Lord Londonderry's Own CLB Flute Band in Newtownards. Robert Orr Thompson joined the Royal Artillery in February 1938 and he was killed in action on 1 May 1941. Poignantly, on the day before his mother received the telegram informing her that her son had died, she received a cheerful letter from him assuring her that he was well. Lance Bombardier Robert Orr Thompson was 22 years old when he died and he is commemorated on Newtownards and District War Memorial and on the family grave headstone in Movilla Cemetery, Newtownards. His brother Walter died on 23 November 1933; his father Samuel died on 6 March 1962 and his mother Anna died on 19 March 1977.

Thomson, Humphrey Barron (Humphrey)
Captain
No. 128238, Royal Army Medical Corps *attached* East Surrey Regiment
Died as a result of enemy action on Sunday 14 December 1941 (aged 25)
Singapore Memorial, Singapore (Column 103)

Humphrey Barron Thomson was born on 25 January 1916 and he was the only child of Sir William Willis Dalziel Thomson MD FRCP and Lady Thomson (nee Josephine Hunter Barron) of Annahilt, Hillsborough, Co. Down. They were married on 22 October 1914 in Duncairn Presbyterian Church, Belfast and they lived at 25 University Square, Belfast. Sir William Thomson was professor of medicine at Queen's University, Belfast for 27 years and he died on 26 November 1950 (aged 65). He had a country residence – *Seven Tides* – in Donaghadee where he enjoyed gardening. During the First World War he served as Captain with the RAMC in No. 13 General Hospital at Boulogne.

Humphrey Barron Thomson attended Campbell College, Belfast from September 1929 until July 1933 and he studied medicine at Queen's University, Belfast, graduating in 1939. On 19 April 1940 Humphrey Thomson and Mary Graham (Mary) Glendinning of Island Reagh, Comber were married in Fitzroy Presbyterian Church, Belfast and they lived for a time at Malone, Belfast. Mary Glendenning was the youngest daughter of Acheson Harden Glendinning who was a director of William Coates and Sons, Belfast.

COMBER LADY'S LOSS.

HUSBAND MISSING IN FAR EAST.

Professor W .W. D. Thomson, University Square, Belfast, has received official notification from the War Office that his son, Captain Humphrey D. Thomson, R.A.M.C., is missing. Captain Thomson had been serving in Singapore. Captain Thompson married, in April, 1940, Miss Mary Graham Glendinning, youngest daughter of Mr. and Mrs. A. H. Glendinning, Island Reagh, Comber.

After graduating in medicine from Queen's University Humphrey Thomson worked for a short time as a house surgeon in the Royal Victoria Hospital, Belfast. He joined the Royal Army Medical Corps and went to Malaya with the East Surrey Regiment. His Battalion was holding part of the border between Kedah (in the northwest Malay Peninsula) and Thailand. The regimental aid-post of the East Surreys, established near Alor Star, was attacked and wiped out by the Japanese in the early days of the invasion of Malaya. The Sergeant of the unit escaped and reported that Captain Thomson had been killed in this assault. Before his death was confirmed he was reported as missing by the War Office and this news was reported in the 14 February 1942 edition of the *Newtownards Chronicle* under the headline *Comber Lady's Loss*.

THOMSON. H. B.

T

Captain Humphrey Thomson is commemorated on the Singapore Memorial; in Campbell College and on the Queen's University War Memorial. The Thomson Room in the Medical Library at Queen's University, Belfast was furnished 'to keep alive the memory of Captain Humphrey Thomson'. A tribute published in the Campbellian (Vol. 10, No. 10, December 1943) contained the following, 'Humphrey was full of the joy of life and his wit and keen sense of humour, his high ideals of honour, his straightforward nature, his outspoken championship of what he considered right won the regard and affection of his contemporaries, while his innate kindness of heart and his old-world courtesy endeared him to the older generation'.

Thomson, John
Gunner
No. 1560614, Royal Artillery
Died in service on Thursday 28 June 1945 (aged 28)
Belfast (Dundonald) Cemetery, Co. Down (Section D 1 Joint Grave 306)

John Thomson's birth was registered in the first quarter of 1917 in West Ham, Essex and he was a son of Henry and Minnie Margaret Thomson (nee Stirk) of Penge, Kent; John had a twin sister whose name was Minnie. Henry Thomson worked as a dyer and cleaner and he and

Minnie Margaret Stirk were married on 7 August 1909 in St. Mary of Eton Parish Church, Middlesex. Their first child, Irene Florence, was born in 1910. John Thomson was the husband of Mary (Molly) Thomson (nee Stockdale) and they lived with Molly's parents at 107 Clandeboye Road, Bangor.

John Thomson was a brother-in-law of Squadron Quartermaster Sergeant **Alexander Scott Brown** who was killed in action on 21 March 1943 and of Pilot Officer **Thomas Norman Stockdale** who died on 28 August 1943. Gunner John Thomson died at Palace Barracks, Holywood on 28 June 1945 and he was buried in the same grave as Thomas Norman Stockdale. Also buried in that grave were Thomas Norman Stockdale's grandparents, Mary Duff Scott who died on 10 April 1933 (aged 66) and John Scott who died on 11 November 1942 (aged 79).

Torney, Thomas (Tommy)
Sergeant (Air Gunner)
No. 1799465, 61 Squadron, Royal Air Force Volunteer Reserve
Killed in action on Wednesday 21 March 1945 (aged 19)
Durnbach War Cemetery, Bad Tolz, Bayern, Germany (Joint grave 5 C 22-23)

Thomas Torney was born on 6 June 1925 and he was a son of George and Isabella Torney (nee Moore) of Ballyvester, Donaghadee. Both came from Hogstown, Donaghadee and they were married on 10 March 1905 in Millisle Presbyterian Church. George Torney was a farmer and he and Isabella had eleven children – Eliza J. (Lila, born 1905); Agnes (born 9 December 1906); George (born 3 December 1908, served with the Home Guard); Anna (Annie, born 16 February 1911); James Adair (born 30 August 1913, he served with the Irish Guards); Hugh Moore (born 8 February 1916, served with the Royal Navy); Isabella (born 4 September 1918); William (Billy, born 4 March 1921, served with the Royal Navy); John (served with the Royal Ulster Rifles); Thomas (Tommy, born 6 June 1925) and Joseph (Joe, born 9 June 1928). Joe Torney married Phyllis Gardner whose uncle, Robert Gardner, served with the West Yorkshire Regiment (Prince of Wales's Own) and was killed in Burma on 24 June 1945 (aged 34).

Thomas Torney joined the Royal Ulster Rifles when he was 15 years of age (he had falsified his age) and went for training. At one point he was granted leave of absence but he stayed at home for longer than he had been authorised to stay and, on a Sunday morning at 2.00 am, the Military Police came to the Torney home to pick him up. His father told the police that Tommy was only 15 years old but they took him back to the barracks and his parents had to bring documentary evidence of his date of birth to Palace Barracks, Holywood to have him discharged. After his discharge he worked for Short Brothers in Belfast and while he was serving his time there he joined the

Royal Air Force Volunteer Reserve on 6 June 1943, his 18th birthday.

On 20 March 1945 Thomas Torney was one of a seven man crew aboard an Avro Lancaster Mark I aircraft (RA560) that took off at 11.34 pm from RAF Skellingthorpe in Lincolnshire on a mission to bomb a synthetic oil plant at Bohlen in Germany. Their aircraft was shot down and the other six airmen who died that night were:

- Flying Officer John Frederick Swales aged 23 (RAAF)
- Sgt Anthony J. Maxwell Davies aged 19 from Kingsland, Herefordshire
- FO Charles Henry Saunders aged 32 from West Chiltington Common, Sussex
- Flight Sergeant Ralph Taylor
- Flight Sergeant Donald Murray Easton aged 20 (RAAF)
- Sergeant William Lane aged 22 from Sheffield

Sergeant (Air Gunner) Thomas Torney was 19 years old when he died and he is commemorated on Donaghadee and District War Memorial and in Shore Street Presbyterian Church Donaghadee.

Totton Family, Robert (father) and Robert (son)

Robert Totton Junior was the first of the two men to die.

Totton, Robert Junior (Bobby)
Marine
No. PO/X 4901, Royal Marines
Killed in action on Saturday 16 December 1944 (aged 22)
Portsmouth Naval Memorial, Hampshire, England (Panel 93)

Robert Totton Junior was born in July 1922 and he was the eldest son of Robert and Mary Totton (nee Steele) of 46 Shaftesbury Road, Bangor. Robert Totton Senior (born in County Armagh) of 13 Howe Street, Belfast worked as a labourer and he and Mary Steele of 82 Dover Street, Belfast were married on 23 December 1918 in St Anne's Church of Ireland Cathedral, Belfast.

BIRTHDAY MEMORIES
TOTTON—Birthday memories of our darling son, Bobby, Royal Marines, on his 23rd birthday.
Loved and longed for always, Dad, Mums, John, Reggie, Terry and Denny—46 Shaftesbury Ave., Bangor.

Robert Totton Junior served for five years with the Royal Marines and he was reported missing in action on 16 December 1944. Less than a month later it was officially confirmed that he must be presumed killed on active service. Robert Totton Junior's brother John served with the Royal Navy.

TOTTON R.

Robert Totton Junior's family placed a *Birthday Memories* notice in the 21 July 1945 edition of the *County Down Spectator* and it contained the message:

Loved and longed for always, Dad, Mum, John, Reggie, Terry and Denny.

Robert Totton Junior was 22 years old when he was killed and he is commemorated on Portsmouth Naval Memorial in Hampshire; on Bangor and District War Memorial; on the family grave headstone in Bangor Cemetery and in Wesley Centenary Methodist Church, Bangor (as Robert Totton Junior, Royal Marines). His father, **Robert Totton Senior**, died on 27 October 1948 and his mother Mary died on 19 November 1975.

Totton, Robert Senior
Royal Irish (in some reports Inniskilling) Fusiliers (discharged)
Died of illness on Wednesday 27 October 1948 (aged 61)
Bangor Cemetery, Co. Down (Section 5 X Grave 74)

TOTTON
ROBERT
DEARLY LOVED HUSBAND OF MARY
DIED 27TH OCT. 1948
ALSO THEIR SON BOBBY
KILLED IN ACTION 16TH DEC. 1944
ALSO THE ABOVE
MARY
DIED 19TH NOV. 1975

Robert Totton Senior was born on 12 December 1886 and he was a son of David and Annie Totton (nee Hanan, daughter of John Hanan, a butcher) who were married on 2 May 1875 in Lurgan Methodist Church, Co. Armagh. David Totton worked as a chandler (as did his father John) and he and Annie had six children – John (born 2 February 1877); David (born 6 March 1879); Isabella (born 5 September 1881); Jane (born 25 July 1884); Robert (born 12 December 1886) and Margaret (born 3 June 1891).

Robert Totton Senior was the father of **Robert Totton Junior** who was killed in action on 16 December 1944. During the Second World War Robert Totton Senior served for three years with the Royal Irish Fusiliers (church records) Royal Inniskilling Fusiliers (newspaper report) before being invalided out of the Army in August 1943. Robert Totton Senior died of a

T

cerebral haemorrhage on 27 October 1948 (aged 61). He died at his home, 46 Shaftesbury Road, Bangor and, having been invalided out of the Army in 1943, his Church decided that he should be commemorated as a casualty of war. Robert Totton Senior is commemorated in Wesley Centenary Methodist Church (as Robert Totton Senior, Royal Irish Fusiliers) and on Bangor and District War Memorial.

Treanor, Alan Lancelot
Pilot Officer
No. 41965, 245 Squadron, Royal Air Force
Killed in action on Saturday 1 June 1940 (aged 19)
Runnymede Memorial, Surrey, England (Panel 10)

In the CWGC Debt of Honour it is recorded that Pilot Officer Alan Lancelot Treanor was a son of Sydney A.R. Treanor and Ena Treanor of Bangor, Co. Down. His parents, Sydney Allen Robinson Treanor and Marthena (Ena) Mary Henderson, were married on 29 July 1918 in Fitzroy Avenue Presbyterian Church, Belfast.

T

Born in 1891 in Cork, Sydney Treanor grew up in Belfast where his family lived at 32 Burmah Street and then at 16 Fitzwilliam Avenue. During the First World War Sydney Treanor served as a Lieutenant with the Royal Irish Rifles and he went to France in September 1916. After the war Sydney and Ena Treanor lived in Waterford and Alan Lancelot Treanor's birth was registered there in the third quarter of 1920.

Alan Lancelot Treanor joined the Royal Air Force and on 15 April 1939 he was granted a short service commission as an Acting Pilot Officer on probation. On 6 November 1939 he was graded as a Pilot Officer on probation and this appointment was confirmed on 6 February 1940. On 1 June 1940 he was piloting a single-seater Hawker Hurricane Mark I aircraft on a patrol operation over Dunkirk. Pilot Officer Robert Alan West was piloting another Hawker Hurricane Mark I aircraft on the same mission and both aircraft were lost without trace.

Pilot Officer Alan Lancelot Treanor is commemorated on Dungannon and District War Memorial and in Dungannon Parish Church of Ireland Church (St. Anne's).

Trimble, William Edward (Billy)
Apprentice
MV *British Dominion* (London), Merchant Navy
Died as a result of enemy action on Sunday 10 January 1943 (aged 17)
Tower Hill Memorial, London, England (Panel 19)

TRIMBLE—Cadet William Edward Trimble, M.N., aged 17½, elder and beloved Son of Mr. and Mrs. G. Grant Trimble, 60 Grove Park Bangor, and Grandson of the late Mr. and Mrs Edward Trimble, Portadown, and the late Wm. Wilson, A.I.M.C.E., Town Clerk and Surveyor, Portadown, and Mrs. Wm. Wilson, Ben-Hurst, Brunswick Road, Bangor.
"Greater love hath no boy than this, that he lay down his life for that of his friends."

William Edward Trimble was born in 1925 and baptised in Bangor Parish Church of Ireland Church (St. Comgall's) on 27 September 1925. He was the elder son of George Grant Trimble, a civil servant, and Elizabeth Trimble (nee Wilson) who lived at 60 Grove Park, Bangor. His paternal grandparents were Edward and Mary Jane Trimble of Portadown and his maternal grandparents were William Wilson AIMCE who had been Town Clerk and Surveyor in Portadown and Mrs Wilson who lived at *Ben-Hurst*, Brunswick Road, Bangor. George Grant Trimble and Elizabeth Wilson were married on 25 February 1923 in Portadown Parish Church of Ireland Church (St. Mark's). William Edward Trimble's sister, Sheila Wilson Trimble, married Cameron Stuart Malcolm on 24 February 1945 in the Church of Ireland Church of St. Columbanus at Ballyholme, Bangor (they later moved to Berkeley, California, USA). Billy's brother George moved to Australia in 1963 with his wife Muriel and their four children.

During the Second World War Apprentice William Edward Trimble served with the Merchant Navy aboard the ship SS *British Dominion*. This British Motor Tanker was built in 1928 by Swan, Hunter and Wigham Richardson Ltd., Wallsend-on-Tyne and was owned by the British Tanker Company Ltd. On 10 January 1943 the MV *British Dominion* was on route from Curacao (Lesser Antilles) to Gibraltar via Trinidad. Carrying 9,000 tons of aviation spirit, she and eight other tankers were in Convoy TM-1 when she was torpedoed and damaged by the German submarine *U-522*. Thirty-seven men were killed and 16 survivors were picked up by HMS *Godetia*. The abandoned wreck was sunk by the German submarine *U-620*. Of the nine tankers in Convoy TM-1, seven were sunk – MV *Albert L Ellsworth*, MV *British Dominion*, MV *British Vigilance*, SS *Empire Lytton*, MV *Minister Wedel*, MV *Norvik* and SS *Oltenia II*. Only MV *Cliona* and SS *Vanja* reached port safely.

Fireman **Donald Gordon Reid** aboard the SS *Empire Lytton* in the same convoy was killed on 9 January 1943.

Apprentice William Edward Trimble was 17 years old when he died and his body was never recovered. He is commemorated on the Tower Hill Memorial in London; on Bangor and District War Memorial and in Bangor Parish Church of Ireland Church (St. Comgall's). A text was included with the *Death Notice* published in the 1 May 1943 edition of the *County Down Spectator*:

> *Greater love hath no boy than this*
> *That he lay down his life for that of his friends*

Tuczemski, Jerzy Ryszard
PPOR (Podporucznik, equivalent to Pilot Officer)
No. P2124, 315 (City of Deblin) Polish Fighter Squadron, Royal Air Force
Killed in an aircraft accident on Sunday 22 August 1943 (aged 24)
Ballycranbeg (Mount St. Joseph) Roman Catholic Churchyard, Co. Down

Pilot Officer Jerzy Ryszard Tuczemski was born on 7 April 1919 and he was killed on 22 August 1943 when his Supermarine Spitfire Mark V aircraft (AB245) crashed during a low-flying navigational training exercise. He had joined 315 Squadron less than six weeks before the crash. His aircraft was observed to be experiencing engine trouble prior to flying into the ground on Long Mountain, north-north-east of Rasharkin in County Antrim.

In accordance with Polish custom he was interred on the third day after his death. His funeral took place at Ballycranbeg (Mount St. Joseph) Roman Catholic Churchyard and was attended by all of his Squadron. An escort party of British personnel was also provided and Wing Commander Charles Ronald Hancock deputised for the Ballyhalbert Station Commander who was absent on duty. Full military honours were accorded. In December 1943 Wing Commander **Charles Ronald Hancock** was killed in a flying accident.

Pilot Officer Jerzy Ryszard Tuczemski was 24 years old when he died and he is commemorated on Panel 73 of the Polish War Memorial at Northolt in London.

Tweed, William James (William)
Ordinary Seaman
No. D/JX 253909, HMS *Audacity*, Royal Navy
Killed on active service on Monday 22 December 1941 (aged 22)
Plymouth Naval Memorial, Devon, England (Panel 49 Column 3)

William James Tweed's birth was registered in the first quarter of 1919 in Newtownards and he was the eldest son of David John and Agnes Mary Tweed (nee Moore) who were married on 4 March 1918 in Newtownards Parish Church of Ireland Church (St. Mark's). At that time David John Tweed (aged 19) was a soldier with the 12th Battalion, Royal Irish Rifles stationed at Clandeboye Camp. His parents, William and Hessie Tweed, together with his brothers and sisters lived in Rodenfoot Street, Ballymoney, Co. Antrim. Agnes Mary Moore of 154 Greenwell Street, Newtownards was a daughter of Lance Corporal William Moore who was killed in action at Gallipoli on 11 August 1915 and is commemorated on Page 460 in the Book of Honour *Remembering Their Sacrifice in the Great War – Ards* compiled by Barry Niblock. David John and Agnes Mary Tweed lived at 23 North Street, Newtownards and they had at least eight children – William James, Vina, Anna, Maud, Wilson, Isabel, Hessie and Harry.

William James Tweed joined the Royal Navy in 1939 and during the Second World War he served aboard HMS *Audacity*. HMS *Audacity* was a British escort carrier and the first of her kind. Launched in March 1939 she was originally the German merchant ship MV *Hannover*. The MV *Hannover* was captured by the Royal Navy in the West Indies in March 1940 and renamed *Sinbad*. She was converted and commissioned as HMS *Empire Audacity*, then renamed HMS *Audacity*.

Convoy HG-76 (bound for the UK) left Gibraltar on 14 December 1941 and HMS *Audacity* had only four serviceable Grumman Martlet aircraft aboard. On the night of 21 December 1941 HMS *Audacity* was hit in the engine room by a torpedo fired from the German submarine *U-751*. Two more torpedoes caused the aviation fuel to explode, blowing off her bow. HMS *Audacity* sank some 500 miles west of Cape Finisterre on the west coast of Spain and Ordinary Seaman William James Tweed was one of the men who died that night.

TWEED—Killed in Action at Sea, Wm. James, eldest and dearly-loved son of David and Agnes Mary Tweed, 23. North Street, Newtownards.

There were *Killed in Action* notices in the 24 and 31 January 1942 editions of the *Newtownards Chronicle* from his parents, brothers and sisters at 23 North Street, Newtownards; his sister

Hessie and brother-in-law Alex Ferguson of 147 Greenwell Street, Newtownards; his sister Isabel and brother-in-law William Briggs of 103 Broom Street, Woodvale, Belfast; his grandmother Ann Jane Moore of 143 Greenwell Street, Newtownards; his aunt Winnie and uncle Jim Robinson and cousins Belle and Ann of 143 Greenwell Street, Newtownards; his aunt Eleanor Maxwell, Maisie and Billy of 168 Greenwell Street, Newtownards; his aunt Maud and uncle Hugh Coffey (on active service in the Middle East, subsequently wounded and held Prisoner-of-War) of 18 Upper Movilla Street, Newtownards; his aunt Emma and uncle James Bell and cousins Jean and Billy of 32 Thomas Street, Newtownards; the directors and workmates of the Strangford Knitting Company, Newtownards and from Loughries True Blues Loyal Orange Lodge No. 1948.

Ordinary Seaman William James Tweed was 22 years old when he died and he is commemorated on Plymouth Naval Memorial in Devon and on Newtownards and District War Memorial.

Tyler, Albert Charles
Corporal
No. 405992
'B' Squadron, Queen's Own Yorkshire Dragoons, Royal Armoured Corps
Killed in action on Wednesday 28 October 1942 (aged 27)
Alamein Memorial, Egypt (Column 30)

Corporal Albert Charles Tyler and Caroline Mabel Beattie (daughter of photographer William Beattie and Sarah Beattie of 21 William Street, Newtownards) were married about 1937. Corporal Tyler's death was reported in the 21 November 1942 edition of the *Newtownards Chronicle* under the headline *Ards Soldier Killed in Middle East Fighting*.

Corporal Tyler was born in Portsmouth and he had about six years service when he was recalled shortly after the outbreak of the Second World War. He was killed in action on 28 October 1942 in the Middle East. For 60 years following the end of the Second World War the only memorial to the men and women of Portsmouth who died was a low stone wall at the rear of the Cenotaph with the inscription:

ARDS SOLDIER KILLED.

IN MIDDLE EAST FIGHTING.

Mrs. Tyler, of William Street, Newtownards, has been officially notified that her husband, Corporal Albert Charles Tyler, of the Yorkshire Dragoons, has been killed in action during the fighting in the Middle East.

In memory of those who lost their lives in World War II.

748

On 8 November 2005 a memorial to those who died was unveiled by Princess Alexandra. In 2007 a campaign was launched in Portsmouth to raise money to inscribe the names of an estimated 3,500 local people killed during the Second World War onto the town's war memorial. Efforts to compile a list of names are ongoing and the names collected are being added to a touch-screen computer in the Cathedral Church of St. Thomas of Canterbury in Old Portsmouth. I contacted the Civic Offices in Portsmouth and, as a result, Corporal Albert Charles Tyler's name has been added to the list. In the Cathedral there is also a Second World War Book of Remembrance.

Vance, Gordon Elgin (Gordon)
Flying Officer (Pilot)
No. J/24133, 290 (RAF) Squadron, Royal Canadian Air Force
Killed in an aircraft accident on Saturday 15 April 1944 (aged 22)
Eglantine Church of Ireland Cemetery, Co. Down (Section E Grave 41)

Gordon Elgin Vance was a son of Samuel and Beatrice Emily Vance of Winnipeg, Manitoba, Canada. On 15 April 1944 an Airspeed Oxford aircraft (BG601) of 290 (RAF) Squadron based at RAF Long Kesh crashed into the sea near the Copeland Islands and both crew-members were killed. They were Squadron Leader **Thomas George Westlake** and Flying Officer Gordon Elgin Vance.

Squadron Leader Westlake was leading a formation of three Oxfords in a naval exercise involving simulated torpedo attacks on ships. The Oxfords were being escorted by five Martinet aircraft forming fighter cover above them. At around 10.15 pm Squadron Leader Westlake called up the other aircraft and instructed them to return to Ballyhalbert and shortly afterwards his Oxford's propeller was seen to touch the sea. Then his aircraft hit the water and broke up on impact. RAF high speed launches were dispatched from Donaghadee and they picked up Squadron Leader Westlake who died later of his injuries.

KILLED ON ACTIVE SERVICE.

VANCE—Killed on Active Service in April, 1944, Flying Officer Gordon E. Vance (Royal Canadian Air Force), of Vancouver, B.C.
    Very deeply regretted.
                    VIOLET MOORE,
Ballyalicock, Newtownards.

After Flying Officer Gordon Elgin Vance was killed, Violet Moore of Ballyalicock, Newtownards placed a *Killed on Active Service* notice in the 22 April 1944 edition of the *Newtownards Chronicle*. He was buried in Eglantine Church of Ireland Cemetery, Co. Down (CWGC designation) and there is an inscription on his CWGC headstone:

> *He is not dead*
> *He is just away*

Flying Officer Gordon Elgin Vance is commemorated on the Canadian Virtual War Memorial (Internet) and on Page 467 in the Canadian Second World War Book of Remembrance.

Vinycomb, Alexander Richard Day (Richard)
Military Medal
Lance Corporal
No. 1942414, 185 (S) Tunnelling Company, Royal Engineers
Died as a result of an accident on Saturday 24 April 1943 (aged 49)
Towcester Cemetery, Northamptonshire, England (Row G Grave 7)

V

Alexander Richard Day Vinycomb was born on 9 December 1893 in Holywood and his birth was registered in the first quarter of 1894 in Belfast. He was the youngest son of John Vinycomb (born 1834 in Newcastle-on-Tyne; died in London, 1928) and Dorothea Vinycomb (nee Thorpe; born 1852 in Cork; died in London, December 1923). John Vinycomb worked as an artist, designer and illuminator and Dorothea Thorpe was his second wife. They lived in Church Road, Holywood until 1909. John Vinycomb was a member of the Royal Irish Academy; Vice-President of the Royal Society of Antiquaries of Ireland; Vice-President of the Ex-libra Society of London and founder and past President of the Belfast Art Society and the Ulster Arts Club. He also served as President of Belfast Naturalists' Field Club. He was a recognised authority on heraldry and illuminating, and he published books, notably on the illustration of bookplates. The City Hall in Belfast has an example of his scroll, and the Belfast Harbour Office and the Victoria and Albert Museum also have examples of his work.

John Vinycomb (son of Andrew Vinycomb) and Sarah Swinburn (born 1843, daughter of Joseph Swinburn) were married on 14 July 1860 in Knockbreda

Parish Church of Ireland Church (St. Andrew's) and they had one child, William Andrew Vinycomb, who was born in 1862 and died on 7 December 1880. Sarah Vinycomb was 23 years old when she died on 28 January 1866. John and Dorothea Vinycomb (nee Thorpe) had ten children, all of whom were born in Holywood – Frances Dorothea (born 13 April 1877); Thomas Bernard (born 2 November 1878; died in June 1943 in Brighton, Sussex); John Knox (born 14 June 1880); Robert Knox (born 21 March 1882); Sarah (born 23 May1884); Andrew (born 3 April 1886; died 1916); Violet Jane (born 13 April 1888; died 1963); Vera (born 16 April 1890); Marcus (born 8 February 1892) and Alexander Richard Day (born 9 December 1893).

During the First World War Andrew Vinycomb served with the Royal Medical Corps and he was the husband of Frances Anna Wilkinson. He died on 5 August 1916 and was buried in St. Peter's Cemetery, Sherbrooke, Quebec, Canada. During the First World War Marcus Vinycomb served with the Irish Guards.

During the First World War Thomas Bernard Vinycomb served with the Royal Army Ordnance Corps (he attained the rank of Captain) and in 1918 he was awarded the Military Cross 'for conspicuous gallantry and devotion to duty while in charge of an ammunition depot. The depot had been under heavy shell fire all day, and as the enemy approached in the afternoon it was considered necessary to blow up the dumps. This officer gave the necessary orders, and after destroying all records personally fired the dumps until he was severely wounded by a bursting grenade' (Page 8852, Supplement to the *London Gazette* 26 July 1918).

V

Thomas Bernard Vinycomb was the husband of Emily Katharine Adams (born 14 January 1875 in Omagh, Co. Tyrone; died 25 January 1973 in Brighton Sussex). They were married on 24 December 1907 in First Omagh Presbyterian Church and at that time Bernard was a lecturer in physics. They had three children – Dora Katharine (born 1908 in Woolwich, Kent; died 2005 in Dunoon, Argyll); Godfrey Bernard (born 1910 in Woolwich; died 2000 in Edinburgh) and William Anthony MBE (born 1914 in Wandsworth; died 1999 in New Forest, Hampshire).

During the First World War Alexander Richard Day Vinycomb served with 185 (S) Tunnelling Company, Royal Engineers and he was awarded the Military Medal. In the autumn of 1921 Alexander Richard Day Vinycomb married Alice A. Herrd de Nordwall (born 6 June 1897 in Germany; died 1970 in Horley, Surrey) and they had two children, Richard and Heather. After the war Alexander Richard Day Vinycomb worked as a mining engineer (and for a short time as a journalist) and on 20 February 1926 he and his family moved from England to British Guiana in South America. Alexander Richard Day Vinycomb served again during the Second World War and his commemorative entry in the CWGC Debt of Honour records his war service with 185 (S) Tunnelling Company, Royal Engineers – which operated during the First World War. (Some Tunnelling Companies were formed early in the Second World War on the assumption that there was going to be a similar kind of trench warfare on the Western Front as there was in the First World War and then, later in the Second World War, Tunnelling Companies were deployed in Gibraltar to dig tunnels there). Lance Corporal Alexander Richard Day Vinycomb died on 24 April 1943 following a road accident in which he sustained multiple injuries including a fractured skull.

Vivash, Bernard Christopher (Christopher)
Chief Engine Room Artificer
No. P/272124, HMS *Greenwich*, Royal Navy
Died of illness in service on Saturday 1 April 1944 (aged 54)
Glasgow (Cardonald) Cemetery, Glasgow, Scotland
(Section E Joint grave 25)

V

Bernard Christopher Vivash was born in 1890 in Brooklyn, New York, USA and he was a son of Robert Duncan Vivash (born 7 June 1855, Edinburgh) and Emily Vivash (nee Stewart) of *Fairy Knowe*, Cannyreagh, Donaghadee. They were married on 27 June 1885 in Belfast Registry Office and they had three children – Stewart (born 20 October 1885 in Belfast); Alice Demaus (born 30 September 1887 in Belfast, married Robert Scott on 31 July 1915) and Bernard Christopher (born around 1890 in Brooklyn, New York). Robert Duncan Vivash was a son of William Vivash who, in partnership with his son-in-law, Charles Mavius, ran the photographic business 'Mavius and Vivash' in Ann Street, Belfast. Robert Duncan Vivash was a seaman and he drowned in Barry Dock, Wales on 8 May 1914.

In 1901 Stewart Vivash (an apprentice druggist, aged 15) and Bernard Christopher Vivash (a schoolboy, aged 11) were lodging with Joseph and Sophia Mary Carothers at 138 Fitzroy Avenue, Belfast and in 1911 Bernard Christopher Vivash was an Engine Room Artificer (ERA) 5th Class in the Royal Navy. He served with the Royal Navy during the First World War and afterwards he was in Australia for a time (his war medals were sent to him there). In 1922 he arrived in London from Brisbane aboard the *Ormonde*.

The following year, on 10 May 1923, Stewart Vivash (aged 38) arrived in Quebec, Canada after sailing from Belfast aboard the *Regina*.

During the Second World War Bernard Christopher Vivash served aboard the destroyer depot ship HMS *Greenwich*. Ordered by the Greek Navy from Swan Hunter who sub-contracted the hull to W. Dobson and Company, Wallsend-on-Tyne, this ship was launched in 1915 and taken over on the stocks by the Admiralty. During the Second World War she was at Scapa Flow from 1939 until 1941 and then at Canada and Iceland in 1942 before returning to home waters; in 1947 she was sold into mercantile service.

Chief Engine Room Artificer Bernard Christopher Vivash was 54 years old when he died of bronchial carcinoma on 1 April 1944 in Mearnskirk Hospital, Glasgow and he is commemorated on Donaghadee and District War Memorial. His nephew, 2nd Lt. **R.N.C. Scott**, died on 27 May 1940.

V
W

Wadmore, Victor
Sergeant (Pilot)
No. 1585841, Royal Air Force Volunteer Reserve
Killed in an aircraft accident on Saturday 6 May 1944 (aged 21)
Benhilton (All Saints Churchyard), Surrey, England (South of Church)

Victor Wadmore's birth was registered in the fourth quarter of 1922 in Mutford, Suffolk and he was a son of William and Begonia Wadmore (nee Fisk), of Sutton, Surrey. Their marriage was registered in the fourth quarter of 1921 in Croyden, Surrey and they had at least two children – Victor (born 1922) and Raymond (born 1924).

During the Second World War Victor Wadmore served with the Royal Air Force Volunteer Reserve. On 6 May 1944 a Miles Martinet aircraft (MS619) of No. 12 Air Gunners School, Bishops Court was low-flying while on drogue-towing duty when it crashed into Strangford Lough about a mile and a half west of the Ards Peninsula coastline and about a mile east of Killyleagh. Both crew members were killed. They were the Pilot, Sergeant Victor Wadmore (aged 21) from Sutton, Greater London, and

Leading Aircraftman **Stanley Mynett** (aged 23) from Norton, Yorkshire.

Sergeant Victor Wadmore was buried in Benhilton (All Saints Churchyard), Surrey.

Waite, Leslie
Private
No. 3385342, 1st Battalion, East Lancashire Regiment
Killed in action on Saturday 1 June 1940 (aged 23)
Pihen-les-Guines War Cemetery, Pas de Calais, France (Grave 2 B 8)

Leslie Waite was born in Treorchy in the Rhondda Fawr Valley in South Wales and his birth was registered in the fourth quarter of 1917 in Pontypridd. He was a son of Edwin and Mary Elizabeth (Ellen) Waite (nee Whittaker) who were married on 25 October 1911 in the Registry Office in Bridgend, Glamorganshire. Edwin Waite was a coal miner and he and Mary Ellen had eight children – Albert Edwin (died aged 7); Reginald George; Doris (died in infancy); Edith (died in infancy); Leslie; Ada; Ethel and Lucie (died in infancy). Edwin Waite enlisted in Wrexham on 27 October 1914; he joined the Royal Welch Fusiliers but was discharged soon thereafter on medical grounds. Mary Ellen Waite died in 1952 and Edwin died in 1970.

W

In the 1930s Leslie Waite joined the East Lancashire Regiment and he was posted to Palace Barracks in Holywood. It was while he was stationed there that he met Maureen Harriet Elizabeth Marshall from Holywood. She was a daughter of Basil and Lizzie Marshall and she had four brothers. Leslie Waite and Maureen Marshall were married on 20 December 1938 in Holywood Parish Church of Ireland Church (St. Philip and St. James). Their son, Leslie Edwin Marshall Waite, was born on 19 July 1939 and less than one year later his father was killed in action. Maureen Waite later remarried and she had three daughters – Victoria, Margaret and Heather.

During the Second World War Leslie Waite served with the 1st Battalion, East Lancashire Regiment and he was 23 years old when he was killed in action in France on 1 June 1940 during the evacuation of Allied Forces at Dunkirk (*Operation Dynamo*, 27 May to 4 June 1940). Private Leslie Waite is commemorated on Holywood and District War Memorial.

Wakeford, Bernard

Second Lieutenant

No. 226993, Royal Army Service Corps

Died as a result of an accident on Sunday 20 September 1942 (aged 26)

Eltham Cemetery, Woolwich, London (Section B Grave 206)

YOUNG OFFICER KILLED ON BANGOR ROAD

Car Skids and Overturns

FOUR OTHERS INJURED

How Second Lieutenant Bernard Wakeford was fatally injured when a car he was driving overturned on the Crawfordsburn Road near Bangor last Saturday night was described by a young lady passenger in her evidence to Dr. Wallace, Coroner for North Down, at an inquest in Bangor on Monday.

Bernard Wakeford's birth was registered in the second quarter of 1916 in Cardiff and he was a son of Leonard Ernest and Sarah Ann Wakeford (nee Work). Leonard Ernest Wakeford was Deputy Superintendent in the Mercantile Marine Office, Board of Trade and he and Sarah Ann Work were married on 3 June 1914 in All Saints' Parish Church, Penarth, Glamorganshire. Bernard Wakeford was the husband of Elizabeth Mary Wakeford (nee Green) of 5 Penrhyn Avenue, Rhos-on-Sea, Denbighshire (their marriage was registered in the third quarter of 1939 in Woolwich, London).

W

The inquest on Second Lieutenant Wakeford's death was reported in the 26 September 1942 edition of the *County Down Spectator*. He died after being fatally injured when the car he was driving overturned on the Crawfordsburn Road near Bangor. There were four passengers in the car – Second Lieutenant John Ruane, Driver William Thomas Hodges, Miss Lila Millar and Miss Ena Houston. The car was travelling down Carson's Hill on the Crawfordsburn Road when the vehicle skidded, struck a footpath and overturned. All five occupants were pinned beneath the vehicle and Second Lieutenant Bernard Wakeford died before reaching hospital.

Ena Houston gave evidence before Dr Wallace, the Coroner for North Down, in which she stated that she, Lila Millar and the two officers had been dancing at Crawfordsburn Country Club on Saturday 19 September 1942. At 11.45 pm, when the taxi they had booked did not arrive, Second Lieutenant Wakeford rang for a military vehicle and when it arrived he told the soldier in charge of the car that he would drive. Lila Millar was the front seat passenger. The Coroner returned as his verdict that death was due to the injuries caused by the deceased being pinned underneath a motor car which he was driving and which developed a skid at the time of the accident. Bernard Wakeford's effects amounted to some £311 and probate was granted to his father.

Second Lieutenant Bernard Wakeford was buried in Eltham Cemetery, Woolwich, London and it was his wife Elizabeth Mary who purchased the exclusive right of burial. Bernard is the only interment in the grave and she placed an inscription on the headstone:

> *Treasured Memories of my Beloved Husband*
> *2nd Lieut, Bernard Wakeford RASC*
> *Who Died 20th September 1942 aged 26 Years*

At the time of Bernard's death his wife was living at 7 Philippa Gardens, Eltham.

Walker, George William Thomas
Sergeant (Air Gunner)
No. 1876569, Royal Air Force Volunteer Reserve
Killed in an aircraft accident on Sunday 20 August 1944 (aged 19)
Ardglass (St. Nicholas) Church of Ireland Churchyard, Co. Down (Grave 2)

W

George William Thomas Walker's birth was registered in the third quarter of 1924 in Freebridge Lynn, Norfolk and he was a son of Walter William and Elizabeth Walker (nee Church) of Weasenham, Norfolk. During the Second World War he served with the Royal Air Force Volunteer Reserve.

On 20 August 1944 an Avro Anson aircraft (LT658) from No. 12 Air Gunners School based at Bishops Court was on an air gunnery exercise when it broke up in mid-air as a result of a structural failure. Wreckage fell to the ground over a wide area centred on Ballygalget Roman Catholic Church and all five crew members on board were killed – Flying Officer (Pilot) **Raymond Hodgson**, Sergeant (Flight Engineer) **Kennedy Boyd Black**, Sergeant (Flight Engineer) **Frank Bennett Bloor**, Flight Sergeant (Flight Engineer) **Thomas Charles Crisp** and Sergeant (Air Gunner) George William Thomas Walker. All five deaths were registered in Downpatrick.

Sergeant George William Thomas Walker was 19 years old when he died and he was buried in Ardglass (St. Nicholas) Church of Ireland Churchyard. There is an inscription on his CWGC headstone:

> *We thank our God for every remembrance of thee*

Wallace, Herbert Noel (Herbert)
Military Cross
Major
No. 63581, 5th Battalion, East Yorkshire Regiment
Killed in action on Tuesday 6 April 1943 (aged 28)
Sfax War Cemetery, Tunisia (Grave II D 20)

Herbert Noel Wallace was born on 20 December 1914 and he was the youngest son of Jeremiah Thomas Wallace and Elizabeth Wallace (nee Taylor) of 129 Cavehill Road, Belfast, then 3 Thirlmere Gardens, Belfast, then *Glenburn*, 25 Ballyholme Road, Bangor and then 29 Knockmore Park, Bangor. Their marriage was registered in the second quarter of 1906 in Dublin South and they had at least four children – Frederick Ingram (born 2 September 1907 at 47 Oakley Road, Dublin); Ethel Harriett (born 28 August 1910 in the RIC Depot, Dublin); Thomas Victor (born 12 October 1912 in the RIC Depot, Dublin) and Herbert Noel (born 20 December 1914).

Jeremiah Thomas Wallace was a former District Inspector in the Royal Irish Constabulary and he died on 2 February 1945 (aged 76). It was reported at the time that severe shock caused by the death of his son Herbert had contributed to an illness which led to his death. Jeremiah Thomas Wallace was buried in Dundonald Cemetery (Grave A3 391) and his funeral service was conducted by the Revd Walter Horatio Good of Bangor Parish Church of Ireland Church (St. Comgall's). Jeremiah Wallace was survived by his wife Elizabeth; his two sons – Lieutenant Colonel Frederick Ingram Wallace then serving in Burma and Gunner Thomas Victor Wallace who had worked in the Ulster Bank before the war and his daughter Ethel Harriett Wallace who was married to Dr H.P. Lowe the City Coroner in Belfast.

W

Bangor Officer Awarded M.C.—Major H. N. Wallace, The East Yorkshire Regiment, has been awarded the Military Cross posthumously for gallant and distinguished services in the Middle East. He was killed at Wadi Akarit on April 6 last. He was the youngest son of Mr. and Mrs. J. T. Wallace, 29 Knockmore Park, Bangor, and was educated at Royal Belfast Academical Institution and Sandhurst. Two brothers are also serving, one in Burma and the other with the Central Mediterranean Forces. His only sister is the wife of Dr. H. P. Lowe, City Coroner.

Herbert Noel Wallace was educated at Royal Belfast Academical Institution (RBAI) from 1925 until 1932 where he excelled at swimming, and then at Sandhurst, from which he received his commission in 1934. In the 7 August 1943 edition of the *County Down Spectator* it was reported that Major Herbert Wallace, serving with the East Yorkshire Regiment, had been killed in action at the Battle of Wadi Akarit in Southern Tunisia on 6 April 1943. He

757

was awarded the Military Cross posthumously for gallant and distinguished services in the Middle East. This was announced in the 17 June 1943 edition of the *London Gazette*. His effects in England amounted to some £420 and probate was granted to his father Jeremiah.

Major Herbert Noel Wallace was 28 years old when he died and he is commemorated in Bangor Parish Church (St. Comgall's) and in RBAI. His brother, Thomas Victor Wallace, died on 1 July 1962 (aged 49) and his mother Elizabeth died on 22 September 1962 (aged 80). Both were buried in Dundonald Cemetery in the same grave as Jeremiah Thomas Wallace.

Warden, Robert
Rifleman
No. 7046535, 2ⁿᵈ Battalion the London Irish Rifles, Royal Ulster Rifles
Died of wounds on Sunday 12 November 1944 (aged 22)
Arezzo War Cemetery, Italy (Grave V D 5)

W

Robert Warden was the youngest son of John and Sarah Warden (nee McNeilly) of 70 Greenwell Street, Newtownards. John Warden worked as a labourer and he and Sarah McNeilly were married on 30 September 1914 in Newtownards Parish Church of Ireland Church (St. Mark's). They had at least five children – Robert, Margaret, David, Eleanor and Ann. Robert Warden enlisted after the outbreak of the Second World War and in the press it was reported that he had service with the Royal Irish Fusiliers before being posted to the London Irish Rifles. He served through the North African campaign before going to Italy. Initially his father was informed that Robert had been seriously wounded and then it was officially confirmed that he had died of his wounds on 12 November 1944.

> **DIED OF WOUNDS IN ACTION.**
> WARDEN—November, 1944, Died of Wounds received in Action, Fusilier Robert Warden, London Irish Rifles, youngest and dearly-loved son of John and the late Sarah Warden, 70, Greenwell Street, Newtownards.
> Deeply regretted by his sorrowing Father, Brother and Sister.

There were four *Died of Wounds* notices in the 25 November 1944 edition of the *Newtownards Chronicle* – one from his widowed father, brother and sister; one from his sister Margaret and brother-in-law Jim Martin of 59 East Street, Newtownards; one from his brother David and sister-in-law Peggy Warden of 58 William Street, Newtownards and one from his sister Eleanor and brother-in-law James McCracken (RAF) of 70 Greenwell Street, Newtownards. On 3 January 1945 his sister Ann married Chief Petty Officer Frederick Victor Ewles, Fleet Air Arm (his parents lived at 51 Cockayne

Street, Derby) in Newtownards Parish Church (St. Mark's).

Rifleman Robert Warden was 22 years old when he died and he is commemorated on Newtownards and District War Memorial and in Newtownards Parish Church (St. Mark's).

Warden, Robert John (Bobbie)
Able Seaman
No. D/SSX 15810, HMS *Matabele*, Royal Navy
Killed on active service on Saturday 17 January 1942 (aged 26)
Plymouth Naval Memorial, Devon, England (Panel 66 Column 3)

Robert John (Bobbie) Warden was the eldest son of Robert John and Elizabeth Warden (nee Hyles) of 62 Greenwell Street, Newtownards. Robert John Warden Senior worked as a yarn carrier and he and Elizabeth Hyles were married on 27 September 1913 in Newtownards Parish Church of Ireland Church (St. Mark). They had at least five children – Eleanor (born 23 February 1914); Robert John; Margaret; John and Thomas.

W

Robert John (Bobbie) Warden was the husband of Josephine Sarah Warden of 61 Gordon Terrace, Scrabo Road, Newtownards (they were married around 1940) and they had a son named Roy. Roy was about a year-old when his father died. It was noted in the press that Robert John (Bobbie) Warden was a keen supporter of Ards Football Club.

Robert John Warden joined the Royal Navy around 1935 and two of his brothers (John and Thomas) served with the Royal Ulster Rifles. During the Second World War Able Seaman Robert John Warden served

WARDEN—Killed in Action at Sea, Able Seaman Robert John Warden, dearly-loved husband of Josephine Warden, 61, Scrabo Road, Newtownards.
Sleep on; there is nought now on earth that can wake thee,
No cruel guns' roar can disturb thy repose,
Nor bursting of shells can now overtake thee,
Save the call of the Trumpet when night draws to a close.
Until that morn dawns we are patiently waiting,
While the past happy memories ever-green shall remain,
And as years grow in number the anchor holds firmer,
Till hand shall clasp hand, for to part ne'er again.
Deeply regretted by his sorrowing Wife and little Son Roy; also his Mother-in-law.

aboard HMS *Matabele*. This ship was a Tribal-class destroyer built by the Scotts Shipbuilding and Engineering Company, Greenock, Scotland and commissioned in January 1939.

In January 1942, along with HMS *Somali*, HMS *Matabele* formed a screen for the cruiser HMS *Trinidad* in Convoy PQ-8 sailing from Iceland to Murmansk in Russia. On 17 January 1942 HMS *Matabele* was hit by a torpedo fired from the German submarine *U-454* and she sank almost immediately. Only two of around 240 men aboard survived; they were picked up by the minesweeper HMS *Harrier*. Many who were able to leave the ship died in the ice-cold water before rescue was possible and Able Seaman Robert John Warden was one of those who died.

Various family members placed *Killed in Action* notices in the *Newtownards Chronicle* – his wife and son; his father, mother, brothers and sisters; his aunts Jane Shields and Minnie McCullough; his sister and brother-in-law Margaret and John Montgomery and nephew John of 66 Castlereagh Street, Belfast and his aunt Letitia Hyles of 92 Movilla Street, Newtownards. There was a notice too from the officers and members of Greenwell Street Loyal Orange Lodge No. 1363, Newtownards.

Able Seaman Robert John Warden was 26 years old when he died and he is commemorated on the Plymouth Naval Memorial in Devon and on Newtownards and District War Memorial.

Waterson, Arthur Hill Coates (Arthur)
Master
SS *Atheltemplar* (Liverpool), Merchant Navy
Died as a result of enemy action on Saturday 1 March 1941 (aged 37)
Tower Hill Memorial, London, England (Panel 12)

W

Arthur Hill Coates Waterson was born on 13 May 1903 and he was a son of Robert and Annie Waterson (nee Graham) who lived at 24 The Hill, Groomsport. Robert Waterson worked as a fisherman and he and Annie Graham were married on 15 October 1901 in Ballygilbert Presbyterian Church. They had four children – Arthur Hill Coates (born 13 May 1903); Fanny (born 22 October 1907); John (born 1 December 1911) and Ellen (Nellie, born 9 November 1912). Arthur Waterson attended Groomsport National School and the family worshipped in Groomsport Parish Church of Ireland Church.

When Arthur left school he worked with his father for two years before leaving Groomsport to join the Ulster Steamship Company (Headline Shipping Company). He worked aboard the SS *Kenbane Head* and the SS *Rathlin Head* and he obtained his Master's ticket at the age of 21.

Arthur Waterson and Aileen Alexandra (Eileen) Montgomery were married in 1934 in Dartford, Kent and when they lived at 2 Braemar Park, Bangor they worshipped in Bangor Parish Church of Ireland Church (St. Comgall's). Their son, Brian Vigers Waterson was born in 1937 and he too became a seaman. He worked on the dredging boats in Belfast Lough. Brian Waterson died in a car accident in the early 1960s when he was returning home after watching a rugby match in Dublin.

During the Second World War Captain Arthur Waterson served with the Merchant Navy and in the 8 March 1941 edition of the *County Down Spectator* it was reported that he had played a gallant part in the Dunkirk evacuation. In 1941 he captained the SS *Atheltemplar* which was a molasses tanker built by Lithgows, Port Glasgow, Scotland and launched in April 1930. Initially operated by the United Molasses Company Ltd., the SS *Atheltemplar* transferred to the Athel Line in 1940.

WATERSON—On Active Service, Captain Arthur Hill Coates Waterson, dearly-loved and elder son of Robert and Annie Waterson, 24, The Hill, Groomsport.

WATERSON—On Active Service, Captain Arthur Hill Coates Waterson, dearly-loved husband of Eileen Waterson, 2 Braemar Park, Bangor.

On 14 December 1939 the SS *Atheltemplar* struck a mine off the Tyne Estuary and after repairs she returned to service on 9 April 1940. Following a refit during the winter of 1940/1941 she sailed northwards in ballast on 1 March 1941 from Methil in Scotland at the head of the starboard column of vessels in Convoy EN-79. As darkness fell, the convoy was attacked off the Aberdeenshire coast by Heinkel He 111 bombers operating from their base in Denmark and the SS *Atheltemplar* was struck on the navigation bridge by two 250 kg bombs. Fire swept through the vessel and survivors were forced to abandon ship. At least twelve men, including Captain Waterson, died during the incident (five unidentified members of the crew were buried in New Calton Burial Ground, Edinburgh). Survivors were taken aboard HMS *Leda* and the SS *Atheltemplar* was taken in tow by HMS *Speedwell* to the Imperial Dock at Leith. After extensive repairs the SS *Atheltemplar* returned to service in June 1941 and she sank on 14 September 1942 after being torpedoed by the German submarine *U-457*.

Captain Arthur Hill Coates Waterson was 37 years old when he died and he is commemorated on the Tower Hill Memorial in London; on Groomsport and District War Memorial; in Bangor Parish Church (St. Comgall's) and in Groomsport Parish Church. His father Robert died on 17 November 1948 (aged 75), his mother Annie died on 28 April 1968, his sister Fanny died on 30 June 1997 and they are buried in Bangor Cemetery. When Arthur Hill Coates Waterson died his effects amounted to some £1,918 and probate was granted to his widow.

Watson, Edwin Appleby Record (Edwin)
Fusilier
No. 7046510, 1st Battalion, Royal Inniskilling Fusiliers
Killed in action on Thursday 18 February 1943 (aged 25)
Rangoon Memorial, Myanmar (Face 12)

Killed in Action.—The many friends of Mr. Cowan Watson, who was formerly a member of the "Spectator" Editorial staff and is now serving with a tank corps in Africa, will learn with regret that his youngest brother, Fusilier Edwin Appleby Watson, has been killed in action in the Far East. We extend our deepest sympathy to the bereaved parents, Mr. and Mrs. H. C. Watson, Cliftonville Road, Belfast, and the members of the family. Mr. Cowan Watson's elder brother, Mr. Harry Watson, is serving with the King's Own Scottish Borders.

Edwin Appleby Record Watson was born on 9 May 1917 and he was the youngest son of Henry Cowan Watson (born in Scotland) and Mary Watson (nee Dewar) of 31 Cliftonville Road, Belfast. Henry Cowan Watson worked as a linen merchant and yarn agent and he and Mary Dewar were married on 16 October 1902 in the Queen's Hotel Dundee (after Banns according to the forms of the Established Church of Scotland). They had at least four children – Henry (Harry, born 4 July 1904); David (born 14 June 1906); Cowan (born 4 June 1913) and Edwin (born 1917). Before the outbreak of the Second World War Cowan Watson was a member of the *County Down Spectator* editorial staff. During the war Cowan Watson served with the Tank Corps in Africa and his brother Harry served with the King's Own Scottish Borderers.

W

Fusilier Edwin Appleby Record Watson served with the 1st Battalion, Royal Inniskilling Fusiliers and his death was reported in the 13 March 1943 edition of the *County Down Spectator*. He was 25 years old when he died and he is commemorated on the Rangoon Memorial, Myanmar.

Watson, Ernest (Ernie)
Sergeant (Observer)
No. 1073521, 218 (Gold Coast) Squadron, Royal Air Force Volunteer Reserve
Killed in an aircraft accident on Tuesday 15 September 1942 (aged 32)
Bangor Cemetery, Co. Down (Section 5 O Grave 82)

Ernest Watson was born on 29 November 1909 and he was the youngest son of William and Maria Watson (nee Parkhill) of 24 Donnybrook Street, Belfast. Wiliam Watson worked as a coachman and he and Maria Parkhill were married on 3 October 1898 in Donegall Street Congregational Church, Belfast. They had three children – William (born 5 September 1899); Norman (born 15 June 1902) and Ernest (born 29 November 1909). After his mother died on 2 July 1923 (aged 47), Ernest Watson lived with his aunt Ellen and

uncle John Robinson, in Alfred Street, Bangor.

Ernest Watson joined the Royal Air Force Volunteer Reserve and during the Second World War he served with 218 (Gold Coast) Squadron in Bomber Command. (218 Squadron got its name after the Governor and people of the Gold Coast in West Africa officially adopted the Squadron). Sergeant Observer Ernest Watson was one of an eight man crew aboard a Short Stirling Mark I aircraft (N3725) that took off at 7.55 pm on 14 September 1942 from RAF Downham Market in Norfolk on a mission to bomb Wilhelmshaven. When they were over the target area the starboard inner engine failed and they returned to base on three engines. As they came in to land the outer starboard engine lost power and just before 1.00 am the aircraft spun to the ground east of Stoke Ferry, Norfolk. Sergeant Observer Ernest Watson and five other members of the crew were killed while Sergeant E.N. Bell and Sergeant W.W. Marshall were injured. The other five crew members who died were:

- Flying Officer John Clarence Frankcomb aged 28 (RAAF)
- Flight Sergeant Donald Ivor Pearce aged 30 from Bristol
- Sergeant Valentine Picken aged 19 from South Elmsall, Yorkshire
- Sergeant Ernest Trevor Pellow aged 24 (RNZAF)
- Sergeant Sidney Horace Ives aged 23 (RNZAF)

W

KILLED ON ACTIVE SERVICE.
WATSON—September, 1942, killed in air operations, Ernest Watson, Sergeant-Observer, R.A.F., youngest son of the late William and Maria Watson, Belfast. Interred in Bangor New Cemetery on Sunday, 20th September.
Deeply regretted by his sorrowing Brother, William, Uncle, Aunt and Cousin, 12 Alfred Street, Bangor.

After Sergeant Observer Ernest Watson died on 15 September 1942, family members placed *Killed on Active Service* notices in the 19 and 26 September 1942 editions of the *County Down Spectator* – deeply regretted by his sorrowing brother William, uncle John, aunt Ellen and cousin Isobel of 12 Alfred Street, Bangor; deeply regretted by his sorrowing brother Norman, sister-in-law Rose and family of 6 Summerhill Park, Bangor (Norman died in 1966 and Rose died in 1994).

Ernest Watson's funeral to Bangor Cemetery on 20 September 1942 was reported in the 26 September 1942 edition of the *County Down Spectator*. It was conducted by the Revd John Pedlow who was a personal friend of the deceased. In his tribute the Revd Pedlow referred to Ernie's faithful service in First Bangor Presbyterian Church as a Sabbath School teacher and ardent worker in the

Christian Endeavour. Ernest Watson was also an amateur football international. Chief mourners included his brothers William and Norman Watson, his uncle John Robinson and his cousins Jack and Bertie Robinson.

Sergeant Ernest Watson was 32 years old when he died and he is commemorated on Bangor and District War Memorial and in First Bangor Presbyterian Church. His CWGC headstone in Bangor Cemetery bears the inscription:

Called to a higher service

Ernest's mother, Maria Parkhill Watson, who died on 2 July 1923 (aged 47), is commemorated on her son's CWGC headstone.

Watson, Thomas Henderson
Leading Aircraftman
No. 636354, 231 Squadron, Royal Air Force
Died as a result of an accident on Wednesday 11 December 1940 (aged 19)
Cadder Cemetery, Lanarkshire, Scotland (Section C Grave 127)

W

Thomas Henderson Watson was born at 6.45 am on 9 August 1921 at 30 Hill Street, Glasgow. He was a son of John and Jeanie Wright Galbraith Watson (nee Henderson) who were married on 31 December 1919 in Glasgow. John Watson worked as an engineer's machineman. The death of Leading Aircraftman Thomas Henderson Watson of Maryhill, Glasgow was reported in the 14 December 1940 edition of the *County Down Spectator* under the headline *Poignant Shooting Fatality*. An inquest held in the Ards District Hospital heard that when Leading Aircraftman Watson was admitted between 1.30 am and 2.00 am on 11 December 1940 he was already dead.

POIGNANT SHOOTING FATALITY

VERDICT OF ACCIDENTAL DEATH

The circumstances of a very distressing accident, resulting in the death of a young aircraftsman, Thomas Henderson Watson, 19 years of age and a native of Maryhill, Glasgow, were investigated at an inquest held in the Ards District Hospital on Wednesday.

Aircraftman E.H. Evans gave evidence at the inquest. He said that, upon taking up guard, he was handed a rifle but did not notice the position of the safety catch or ascertain what ammunition the rifle contained. Upon coming off guard he went to waken Watson. He had the rifle on his shoulder but had to take it down to enter the tent. He put it under his right arm and, with his left hand, shook Watson to waken him. The rifle went off. What caused it to go off he did not know. He saw that the deceased had been wounded and rushed off to inform the orderly officer. A verdict of death from gunshot wounds caused by the accidental discharge of a rifle was returned. Leading Aircraftman Thomas Henderson Watson was 19 years old when he died and he was buried in Cadder Cemetery, Lanarkshire.

Watson, William Ernest
Lieutenant
No. 245394, 145th (8th Battalion The Duke of Wellington's Regiment) Regiment, Royal Armoured Corps
Killed in action on Thursday 31 August 1944 (aged 24)
Coriano Ridge War Cemetery, Italy (Grave XII C 5)

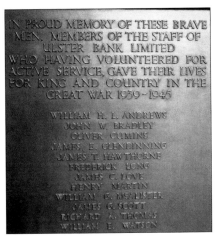

William Ernest Watson was born on 4 October 1919 and he was a son of Thomas Edward and Jane Watson (nee Moffatt) who lived at 13 Wingrove Gardens, Belfast. Thomas Watson was a shipwright and he and Jane Moffatt were married on 14 April 1914 in Macrory Memorial Presbyterian Church, Duncairn Gardens, Belfast. William Ernest Watson attended St. Donard's School, Belfast before going to Sullivan Upper School, Holywood on 5 September 1932. He left Sullivan in 1938 and he worked for the Ulster Banking Company before joining the Army.

W

During the Second World War William Ernest Watson served with the 145th (8th Battalion The Duke of Wellington's Regiment) Regiment, Royal Armoured Corps and he was 24 years old when he was killed in action on 31 August 1944. Coriano Ridge was the last important ridge in the way of the Allied advance in the Adriatic Sector and Nazi German Forces put up fierce resistance. Lieutenant William Ernest Watson is commemorated in Sullivan Upper School and on the Ulster Bank Memorial Plaque (this plaque was unveiled on 19 November 1948 and is now located in Ulster Bank Head Office, Donegall Square East, Belfast).

Watt, Margaret Byers
Civilian War Dead
Died as a result of enemy action on Wednesday 16 April 1941 (aged 64)

Margaret Byers Watt was born on 11 February 1877 and she was a daughter of

William and Eliza Orr Watt (nee Legate, daughter of Presbyterian Minister George Legate who served for 50 years in the Presbyterian Congregation of Kilkinamurry, Banbridge). William Watt worked as a grocer in Belfast and he and Eliza Legate were married on 30 September 1862 in Kilkinamurry Presbyterian Church. They had at least six childen – George Legate (born 25 June 1867); Jane Macready (born 2 August 1869); John Wilfrid (born 5 May 1871, he became a Church of Ireland minister); William Ernest (born 29 June 1873); Charles Williams (born 1 October 1874) and Margaret Byers (born 11 February 1877).

Margaret Byers Watt was a 64 year old spinster living at 5 Hazeldene Gardens in Bangor when a bomb fell on her house during a German Luftwaffe air attack. She died on 16 April 1941, her effects amounted to some £4,926 and probate was granted to Jane Allen, her married sister.

Between 2245 hours and 0430 hours during the night of Easter Tuesday 15 April and Wednesday 16 April 1941 there was a large-scale German air raid on the City of Belfast. Other nearby towns and villages, including Bangor and Newtownards, were also attacked. Areas of Bangor where bombs fell included Ashley Gardens, Bangor Golf Clubhouse, Baylands, Farnham Road, Hazeldene Gardens and Ranfurly Avenue. Fires blazed on Scrabo Hill, Newtownards and bombs fell on Green Road, Conlig and Comber Road, Newtownards. At least 28 people with North Down and Ards connections were killed, including 14 civilians.

Matilda Grattan (aged 54), together with her daughters **Angeline** (aged 18) and **Shelagh** (aged 20), died at 40 Ashley Gardens, Bangor. Margaret Byers Watt (aged 64) died at 5 Hazeldene Gardens Bangor. **Robert Wright** (aged 41) of 32 Baylands, Bangor died of injuries in Bangor Hospital.

That night the aerodrome at Newtownards, which was the Headquarters of 231 Squadron, Royal Air Force, was attacked and 13 soldiers serving with the Royal Inniskilling Fusiliers were killed. Fusilier **Daniel Higgins** was buried in Newtownards (Movilla) Cemetery and under his name in this Book of Honour there is a summary of all those people with North Down or Ards connections who died that night.

Of the many civilians of the Commonwealth whose deaths were due to enemy action in the Second World War, the names of some 67,092 are commemorated in the Civilian War Dead Roll of Honour, located near St. George's Chapel in Westminster Abbey, London.

Wayne, Marks (see Weinberg, Marks)

Webb, John Cameron Keith
Flight Sergeant (Pilot)
No. 1498781, 35 Squadron, Royal Air Force Volunteer Reserve
Killed on active service on Wednesday 22 March 1944 (aged 20)
Durnbach War Cemetery, Bad Tolz, Bayern, Germany
(Collective Grave 7 K 14-19)

 John Cameron Keith Webb was the only son of John Alexander Webb and Anne Hull Webb (nee Stewart) of Belfast. John Alexander Webb was a travelling salesman from the Woodstock Road in Belfast and he and Anne Hull Stewart were married on 5 February 1918 in Donegall Square East Methodist Church, Belfast.

During the Second World War John Cameron Keith Webb served with the Royal Air Force Volunteer Reserve and he was 20 years old when he died on active service on 22 March 1944. He was one of a crew of seven aboard an Avro Lancaster Mark III aircraft (ND649) that took off at 6.55 pm from RAF Graveley in Cambridgeshire on a mission to bomb Frankfurt. The aircraft crashed at Eschborn, all aboard were killed and they were buried in Durnbach War Cemetery. The other six crew members who died that night were:

- Sergeant Kenneth Ephraim Harris
- Sergeant Edwin Gordon Fidler from Edmonton, Middlesex
- Flight Sergeant Wallace Rose aged 31 from Shipley, Yorkshire
- FS William Frederick Martin aged 23 from Trimdon, Durham
- FS Frederick James Marriott aged 31 from Houndslow, Middlesex
- Sergeant William McKenna Smith.

Flight Sergeant (Pilot) John Cameron Keith Webb is commemorated on the family grave headstone in Comber Cemetery. His mother, Anne Hull Webb, died in January 1945 (aged 51) and his father, John Alexander Webb, died in February 1945 (aged 52). There is an inscription at the base of the headstone taken from St. John's Gospel Chapter 10 Verse 10:

That they might have life and have it more abundantly

Weinberg, Marks (served as Wayne, Marks)
Sergeant (Observer/Wireless Operator)
No. 657189, 153 Squadron, Royal Air Force
Killed in a flying accident on Sunday 19 July 1942 (aged 26)
East Ham (Marlow Road) Jewish Cemetery, Essex, England
(Block I Grave 276)

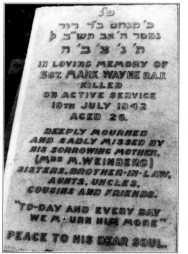

Marks Weinberg's birth was registered in the first quarter of 1916 in Mile End Old Town, London and he was a son of David and Amelia (Millie) Weinberg (nee Coots) of Maida Vale, London. David Weinberg worked as a dental mechanic and his marriage to Millie Coots was registered in the third quarter of 1907 in London City. David and Millie Weinberg had at least three children – Isidore, Minnie and Marks.

W

Marks Weinberg joined the Royal Air Force (he served as Marks Wayne) and in July 1942 he was serving with 153 Squadron based at RAF Ballyhalbert. On 19 July 1942 a Bristol Beaufighter aircraft (X7822) of 153 Squadron was returning to Ballyhalbert airfield, having completed a practice night interception and radar calibration exercise, when it flew straight into Shanlieve Mountain in the Mourne Mountains at Grid Reference J250214. It was reported at the time that 'the aircraft appeared to have *homed* on an inappropriate radio beacon'. The aircraft was totally destroyed and both crew members were killed. They were Pilot Officer **John Peter Sadd** from Willesden, Middlesex and the Navigator/Radar Operator, Sergeant Marks Weinberg (who served as Marks Wayne) of Maida Vale, London. On his headstone his forename is inscribed as Mark and there is an inscription from his family:

Today and every day we mourn him more

Weir, D.R.
Bangor and District War Memorial
Trinity Presbyterian Church Bangor

The name D.R. Weir is inscribed on Bangor and District War Memorial and on the Memorial Plaque in Trinity Presbyterian Church Bangor. There is

only one D.R. Weir commemorated in the CWGC Debt of Honour; Sapper David Ross Weir (No. 2003878) was a son of David Ross Weir and Elizabeth Helen Weir of Glasgow and during the Second World War he served with 255 Field Company, Royal Engineers. He was 24 years old when he died on 12 July 1944 and he was buried in Cambes-en-Plaine War Cemetery, Calvados, France (Row F Grave 19). David Ross Weir Senior (a grocer's salesman aged 24 from 197 Garrioch Road, Glasgow) and Elizabeth Helen Bowie (aged 26 from 68 Doncaster Street, Glasgow) were married on 25 July 1911 at 68 Doncaster Street after Banns according to the Forms of the United Free Church.

Sapper David Ross Weir who died on 12 July 1944 was born in Glasgow in 1919. Desk studies and public appeals to date have not confirmed a connection between this Second World War casualty and the D.R. Weir who is commemorated on Bangor and District War Memorial and in Trinity Presbyterian Church Bangor. No reference to this casualty has been found in any Trinity Church records – including minutes of meetings and the registers of births, marriages and deaths.

W

Weir, James Kenneth
Flying Officer
No. 133093, 15 Squadron, Royal Air Force Volunteer Reserve
Killed on active service on Thursday 15 June 1944 (aged 31)
Runnymede Memorial, Surrey, England (Panel 209)

James Kenneth Weir was born on 20 July 1912 and he was a son of William and Mabel Florence Weir (nee Edwards) of *Roseneath*, Cranmore Gardens, Malone Road, Belfast and then *The Cottage*, Glenavy, Co. Antrim. They were married on 23 February 1911 in Belmont Presbyterian Church, Belfast. William Weir was one of the first pupils to attend Campbell College, Belfast in 1894 and he worked as a master cotton spinner before becoming Managing Director of the Springfield Spinning Company Ltd., Belfast and later the Standard Finishing Company Ltd. James Kenneth Weir's mother, Mabel Florence, died in the Royal Victoria Hospital, Belfast on 12 July 1936 (aged 51) and his father William died in Whiteabbey Sanatorium on 7 January 1944 (aged 64). Both were buried in Dundonald Cemetery (Grave D3 414).

James Kenneth Weir was educated at Rockport School, Craigavad and Campbell College and after he left school he worked as an inspector for the Beacon Insurance Company, Belfast. James Kenneth Weir joined the Royal Air Force Volunteer Reserve and in 1943 he visited Campbell College at Portrush. He served with Bomber Command and he died on 15 June 1944. He was one of a seven man crew aboard an Avro Lancaster Mark I aircraft (LL889) that took off at 11.31 pm from RAF Mildenhall in Suffolk on a mission to bomb E-boat facilities in le Havre. E (Enemy) boats were fast attack craft of the Kriegsmarine (Nazi German Navy). Their aircraft crashed and all but one were killed. Flight Sergeant R.M. Gilleade survived and managed to evade capture. In addition to Flying Officer James Kenneth Weir the other five crew members who died that night were:

- Flight Lieutenant Ronald Leonard Purry aged 21 (RAAF)
- Sergeant Ronald John Rolfe aged 21 from Slough, Buckinghamshire
- Pilot Officer Noel Goodridge aged 20 (RAAF)
- FS Thomas Lowry Nixon aged 19 from Omagh, Co. Tyrone
- Sergeant Christopher Felix Cantwell aged 24 from Liverpool

W WEIR J. K. Flying Officer James Kenneth Weir was 31 years old when he died and he is commemorated on the Runnymede Memorial in Surrey; in Rockport School and in Campbell College. In a tribute published in the July 1945 edition of *The Campbellian* (Vol. 11, No. 3) he was described as 'a boy of unassuming character and pleasant disposition'.

Werts, George Leslie
Lieutenant (A)
HMS *Daedalus*, Royal Naval Volunteer Reserve
Killed in an aircraft accident on Saturday 12 June 1943 (aged 37)
Belfast City Cemetery (Glenalina Extension Section D Grave 24)

George Leslie Werts was a son of Charles Jerome Werts and Gertrude Sarah Werts (nee Juby) and his birth was registered in the third quarter of 1905 in Ipswich, Suffolk. His parents' marriage was registered in the second quarter of 1903, also in Ipswich. Charles Jerome Werts worked as a motor car engineer and he and Gertrude had at least one other child – Reginald Charles Werts (born 1904).

The marriage of George Leslie Werts and

Winifred Edith Miles of Ealing, Middlesex was registered in the second quarter of 1935 in Brentford, Middlesex. During the Second World War George Leslie Werts served with the Royal Naval Volunteer Reserve. In the *GRO War Death Naval Officers Indices* Lieutenant (A) George Leslie Werts is recorded as serving with HMS *Caroline* whilst in the CWGC Debt of Honour he is recorded as serving with HMS *Daedalus*. From 1939 HMS *Daedalus* (previously RNAS Lee-on-Solent) was under the control of the Fleet Air Arm; Fleet Air Arm personnel based at RAF Sydenham, Belfast came under HMS *Caroline*.

On 12 June 1943 a de Havilland Tiger Moth aircraft (X5045) of Queen's University Air Squadron based at RAF Sydenham crashed in the grounds of the Stormont Estate close to the Massey Avenue entrance, killing the two men on board. They were Flying Officer **Douglas Williams** from Hamilton, Ontario, Canada and his passenger, Lieutenant (A) George Leslie Werts from Middlesex. Flying Officer Williams from 410 Squadron was on attachment to RAF Belfast (Sydenham) from 1480 Flight based at Newtownards.

Westlake, Thomas George (Tommy)
Squadron Leader (Pilot)
No. 89387, 290 (RAF) Squadron, Royal Air Force
Killed in an aircraft accident on Saturday 15 April 1944 (aged 27)
Bristol (Greenbank) Cemetery, Gloucestershire, England (Screen Wall PP 94)

W

Thomas George (Tommy) Westlake's birth was registered in the third quarter of 1916 and he was a son of Richard Hill Westlake and Annie Matilda Westlake (nee Amos). Richard Hill Westlake worked as a warehouse labourer and his marriage to Annie Amos was registered in the second quarter of 1899 in Bristol, Gloucestershire. They had four children – Annie Vaughan (born 1900); Richard B. (Dick, born 1914); Thomas George (Tommy, born 1916) and Alienor L.U. (born 1918).

Annie Matilda Westlake was 52 years old when she died on 21 February 1929 and Richard Hill Westlake remarried. The marriage between Richard Hill Westlake and Winifred May Holvey was registered in the third quarter of 1930 in Bristol. Richard Hill Westlake was 71 years old when he died on 26 February 1942 at Southmead Hospital in Bristol. His effects amounted to some £630 and probate was granted to his widow Winifred who was living at 19 Stadium Road, Westbury Park, Bristol.

During the Second World War Tommy Weslake served with 290 (RAF) Squadron. On 15 April 1944 an Airspeed Oxford aircraft (BG601) of 290

(RAF) Squadron based at RAF Long Kesh crashed into the sea near the Copeland Islands and both crew-members were killed. They were Squadron Leader Thomas George Westlake and Flying Officer **Gordon Elgin Vance**.

Squadron Leader Westlake was leading a formation of three Oxfords in a naval exercise involving simulated torpedo attacks on ships. The Oxfords were being escorted by five Martinet aircraft forming fighter cover above them. At around 10.15 pm Squadron Leader Westlake called up the other aircraft and instructed them to return to Ballyhalbert and shortly afterwards his propeller was seen to touch the sea. His aircraft hit the water and broke up on impact. RAF high speed launches were dispatched from Donaghadee and they picked up Squadron Leader Westlake who later died of his injuries.

Squadron Leader Thomas George (Tommy) Westlake was buried in Bristol (Greenbank) Cemetery, Gloucestershire, England alongside his mother and father. His stepmother died on 25 January 1958 (aged 75) and she was buried in the same grave. Squadron Leader Thomas George (Tommy) Westlake is not named on the headstone. There is an inscription on the headstone:

I love them that love me, and those that seek me early shall find me

Squadron Leader Thomas George (Tommy) Westlake was 27 years old when he died.

Whelan, James H.
Corporal
No. 527885, Royal Air Force
Killed in action on Monday 31 July 1944 (aged 34)
Alamein Memorial, Egypt (Column 281)

Former Ardsman Killed in Action.— Readers of the "Chronicle" will regret to learn that Cpl. James H. Whelan of the R.A.F., eldest son of Mrs. C. Whelan and the late Constable James Whelan, R.U.C., of 95 Westmoreland Street, Belfast, and formerly of Wallace Street No. 2, Newtownards, and William Street Road, Newtownards, has been killed in action. Cpl. Whelan, who had almost ten years' service, four of which were overseas, was a former pupil of Londonderry P.E. School. His mother was formerly Miss Charlotte Graham of Zion Place, Newtownards, while his father, prior to the last war, was for some years in the employment of Messrs. Webb and Co., Newtownards. He joined the Royal Engineers in the Ulster Division and was awarded the Military Medal for gallantry in France, and following demobilisation he joined the R.U.C.

Corporal James H. Whelan's death was reported in the 19 August 1944 edition of the *Newtownards Chronicle*. James H. Whelan was born on 21 March 1910 in Newtownards and he was a son of Charlotte Whelan (nee Graham) of 95 Westmoreland Street, Belfast and the late Constable James Whelan, Royal Ulster Constabulary. James Whelan Senior and Charlotte Graham of Zion Place, Newtownards were married on 5 October 1905 in St. Anne's Church of Ireland Cathedral,

Belfast and they had at least five children – Christina Eleanor (born 3 May 1906); Mary Agnes (born 13 March 1908); James H. (born 21 March 1910); Charlotte (born 2 April 1911) and John (born 21 September 1913).

Prior to the outbreak of the Great War the Whelan family lived in Newtownards at addresses including 5 Glen Road, Wallace Street No. 2 and Red Row, William Street. James Whelan Senior worked as a fireman for Messrs Webb and Company in Newtownards and during the Great War he served in the Ulster Division with the Royal Engineers. He was awarded the Military Medal for gallantry in France and following demobilisation he joined the RUC

 James Whelan Junior was educated at Londonderry Public Elementary School, Newtownards and he joined the RAF around 1934. During the Second World War he served in Egypt and he was killed in action on 31 July 1944. He was 34 years old when he died and he is commemorated on the Alamein Memorial (aged 36 in the CWGC Debt of Honour).

Whiston, Leonard (Len)
Second Officer
SS *Testbank* (Glasgow), Merchant Navy
Died as a result of enemy action on Thursday 2 December 1943 (aged 24)
Tower Hill Memorial, London, England (Panel 107)

 Leonard Whiston was born on 25 February 1919 in Cromer, Norfolk and he was the youngest son of Thomas and Mabel Whiston (nee Harvey) who were married on 2 January 1909 in Grangetown Parish Church (St. Paul's), Cardiff. Thomas Whiston was a Coastguard Officer and for a time he was stationed in Donaghadee before being transferred to Cornwall in 1941. There the Whiston family lived in Bude. Leonard Whiston attended Newcastle Public Elementary School and then Regent House School, Newtownards from 1932 until 1935 before going to sea at the age of 15. He joined the Bank Line Ltd. as an apprentice and his first ship was the MV *Lossie Bank*. Leonard's brothers, Thomas and Arthur Whiston, also joined the Merchant Navy.

Leonard Whiston and Patricia Margaret Cochrane were married on 17 March 1942 in Shore Street Presbyterian Church, Donaghadee and they lived at 6 Manse Road, Bangor. Their son, Robin Leonard Whiston, was born on 7 April 1943 and he was baptised on 16 May 1943 in the Church of Ireland Church of St. Columbanus at Ballyholme. Children of Thomas and Arthur

Second Officer L. WHISTON, M.N.

Official intimation has been received that Second Officer Leanord Whiston, Merchant Navy, of 6 Manse Road, Bangor, has been lost at sea by enemy action. He is the youngest son of Mr. Thomas Whiston who was district officer of Coastguard, stationed at Donaghadee for a number of years being transferred to Cornwall three years ago. Second Officer Whiston who went to sea at the age of 15 has been serving with the Merchant Navy since the outbreak of war, and had a splendid record as an officer. He belongs to a family which has a notable war record. both his brothers, Captain Thomas Whiston, and Chief Officer Arthur Whiston, being in the Merchant Navy and the latter having twice undergone the ordeal of being torpedoed. Second Officer Whiston was married to Miss Patricia Cochrane (grand-daughter of the late Mr. and Mrs. Laird, Manse Road, Bangor) and there is a baby son of one year.

Whiston were also baptised in that church – Rosemary Ann (daughter of Thomas and Kathleen, born 10 May 1941, baptised 29 June 1941); Thomas Hamilton (son of Thomas and Kathleen, born 17 March 1944, baptised 7 May 1944) and Maureen Alexandra (daughter of Arthur and Jean, born 22 June 1944, baptised 7 January 1945).

During the Second World War Second Officer Leonard Whiston served with the Merchant Navy aboard the SS *Testbank*. This cargo ship was built in 1937 by Readhead, John and Sons, South Shields and was owned by Andrew Weir's Bank Line Ltd., Glasgow. On 2 December 1943 there was a massive German air attack on the port of Bari in Italy with bombers hitting merchant ships unloading supplies for the Allied Forces engaged in the battle for Rome. Seventeen merchant ships laden with nearly 35,000 tons of cargo were destroyed in the attack (five American, five British, three Norwegian, two Italian and two Polish). Another seven vessels were severely damaged. Direct hits by bombs and subsequent fires on the American ammunition ships *John Harvey* and *John L. Motley* caused massive detonations that severed a bulk gasoline pipeline. The escaping fuel ignited and fire engulfed other ships moored close by. The *John Harvey* was also carrying 60 tons of mustard gas bombs and many people suffered gas poisoning when these bombs detonated and this gas was released. (During investigations in the aftermath of the disaster it was discovered that mustard gas kills white blood cells which, like cancer cells, divide very quickly. This discovery led to the use of chemotherapy in the treatment of cancer).

Second Officer Len Whiston's death was reported in the 27 May 1944 edition of the *County Down Spectator* and after he died his widow Patricia and son Robin emigrated to Australia. Second Officer Leonard Whiston was 24 years old when he died and he is commemorated on Bangor and District War Memorial; in Bangor Parish Church of Ireland Church (St. Comgall's) and in Regent House School.

White, Alfred
Sergeant (Wireless Operator U/T)
No. 540565, Royal Air Force
Killed in an aircraft accident on Tuesday 1 October 1940 (aged 22)
Newtownards (Movilla) Cemetery, Co. Down
(Section 28 Protestant Plot Grave 92)

Funeral of R.A.F. Sergeant.—The body of the young airman washed ashore at Ballyhalbert on Thursday last was later identified as that of Sergeant Alfred White, aged 22, a native of England. The remains were removed to the morgue at the Ards District Hospital and the funeral took place to Movilla Cemetery on Wednesday afternoon. Comrades of the R.A.F. joined in a farewell tribute to one of their number who had made the supreme sacrifice and the coffin was draped with the Union Jack. The funeral service was conducted by an R.A.F. chaplain

Alfred White was a son of Alfred James White and Ada Beatrice H. White (nee Woods) of Heanor, Derbyshire. Their marriage was registered in the first quarter of 1903 in Norwich, Norfolk where Alfred James White worked as a school teacher. Alfred James and Ada Beatrice White had at least four children including Reginald, Dorothy and Alfred.

During the Second World War Alfred White served with the Royal Air Force and he was 22 years old when he died on 1 October 1940. Initially posted as missing, Sergeant Alfred White was killed when his Avro Anson aircraft ditched in the Irish Sea during an exercise over Cardigan Bay. His body was washed ashore at Ballyhalbert on 24 October 1940 and removed to the morgue at Ards District Hospital.

W

His funeral to Movilla Cemetery on 1 November 1940 was reported in the 2 November 1940 edition of the *County Down Spectator* under the headline *Funeral of RAF Sergeant*. RAF comrades attended his funeral which was conducted by an RAF Chaplain and RAF Buglers sounded the *Last Post* at the graveside. There were wreaths from 10th Operational Training Unit (OTU) and 231 Squadron. His parents placed an inscription on his CWGC headstone:

Beloved son of A.J. and A.B.H. White of Heanor, Derbyshire
His life for his comrades

White Brothers, John and William

John (Jack) and William (Willie) White were born in Donaghadee and they were sons of Andrew (Andy, son of William White) and Martha White (nee Moore, a minor, daughter of Hugh Moore) who lived at 25 Mount Street, Donaghadee. Andy White was a seaman, he was Coxswain of the Donaghadee lifeboat and he and Martha Moore were married on 28 December 1907 in Ballygrainey Presbyterian Church. They had at least eight children – Isabella (Isabel, born 13 March 1909); William (born 19 August 1910, died 15 May 1912); Margaret (Maggie born 26 December 1911, died 5 January 1916); William (born 14 February 1914); John (Jack, born 1916); Andrew; Norman D. (born January 1926, died 14 February 1926) and Victor (born 1929, died 20 March 1930). Jack was the first of the two brothers to die in war.

White, John (Jack)
Able Seaman
SS *Marcella* (London), Merchant Navy
Died as a result of enemy action on Saturday 13 March 1943 (aged 27)
Tower Hill Memorial, London, England (Panel 68)

W

WHITE—Cherished memories of our dearly-loved son, Jack, lost at sea through enemy action, March 13th, 1943.
"Abide with me."
Lovingly remembered by his Father, Mother, Sisters and Brothers, 25 Mount Street, Donaghadee.

During the Second World War Jack White served with the Merchant Navy aboard the cargo vessel SS *Marcella*. The SS *Marcella* was a cargo ship built by Lithgows Ltd., Port Glasgow in 1928 and was owned by Kaye and Son, London. She was on route from the Clyde to Capetown, South Africa via Freetown in Sierra Leone when she sank. At 5.30 am on 13 March 1943 the German submarine *U-107* attacked Convoy OS-44 some 190 miles west of Cape Finisterre, Spain. Four ships were torpedoed and sunk by *U-107* – the SS *Clan Alpine*, the SS *Marcella*, the SS *Oporto* and the SS *Sembilangan*. Able Seaman John White was one of 44 men aboard the SS *Marcella* who were killed that morning. Another casualty was **William John (Willie) Harper** from Donaghadee.

MARCELLA LONDON
DOWNIE R., MASTER
WHITE J.

Able Seaman Jack White is commemorated on the Tower Hill Memorial in London; on Donaghadee and District War Memorial and on the family grave headstone in Donaghadee Parish Church of Ireland Graveyard. Less than two months after Jack died his brother **William (Willie) White** also died.

White, William (Willie)
Pilot
Miss Betty, Pilot Launch
Drowned on Saturday 8 May 1943 (aged 29) (Bangor Bay Disaster)
Donaghadee Parish Church of Ireland Graveyard, Co. Down

Three men from Donaghadee along with one man from Bangor were drowned on Saturday 8 May 1943 in what became known locally as the 'Bangor Bay Disaster'. There were no survivors. The four men died when the Pilot Launch *Miss Betty* capsized and sank while returning to port after responding to a call from a ship entering Belfast Lough. The four men who died worked on the pilot boats that were based in Bangor. These pilot boats were in constant service, not only for merchant shipping coming into Belfast, but also for many of the naval vessels using Belfast Lough. At the outbreak of war *Miss Betty* was requisitioned by the Admiralty from Jim Davidson, Donaghadee.

The three men from Donaghadee who died were **Harry Aicken**, **William George Nelson** and **William White**. The Bangor man who died was **William Anderson**. Aboard *Miss Betty* on the day they died, William White was the pilot and William George Nelson was the coxswain. William Anderson was the engineer and Harry Aicken was a deck hand. William White was also a member of the crew of Donaghadee lifeboat.

W

WHITE—Cherished and loving memories of our dearly-loved son, Willie, who lost his life in Bangor Bay, May 8, 1943.
"Silent memories bring silent tears." Ever remembered by his Father, Mother, Brothers and Sisters; also his Brother-in-law (on active service).—25 Mount Street, Donaghadee.

The Pilot Launch *Miss Betty* was around 40 feet long and the disaster was witnessed by Bangor Harbour Master John H. Corry and Customs Officer G.A. Coppard. *Miss Betty* was owned by the Admiralty but crewed by civilians under naval direction and she left Bangor in moderate weather at 8.55 am on 8 May 1943. During the trip the weather deteriorated and on the way back to Bangor the crew had to contend with a strong north-easterly gale and a heavy breaking sea. At 11.40 am, when they were only about 60 to 70 yards from the safety of Bangor harbour, the disaster happened. The boat successfully negotiated a number of strong waves before being overwhelmed by a broadside hit on the port side. *Miss Betty* capsized, turned over in the water and remained upside down.

William White's body was washed ashore at Seacliff Road, Bangor on Thursday 3 June 1943 and he was buried in Donaghadee Parish Church of Ireland Graveyard. He is commemorated along with the other two Donaghadee men on a separate plaque on Donaghadee and District War Memorial. He is also commemorated on the family grave headstone in Donaghadee Parish Church of Ireland Graveyard. Less than two months before Willie died his brother **John (Jack) White** was killed. Their father Andrew died on 4 October 1969 (aged 83) and their mother Martha died on 22 October 1973. Their brother Andrew served during the Second World War and their sister Isabel married Herbert Tiffany of Cheswick, Northumberland.

White, Herbert Anthony (Herbert)
Private
**No. B/46807, Perth Regiment, Royal Canadian Infantry Corps
Killed in action on Wednesday 13 September 1944 (aged 26)
Coriano Ridge War Cemetery, Italy (Grave II C 2)**

W

Herbert Anthony White was born in Newtownards and he was a son of James and Ellen White (nee McGuinness) of 48 South Street, Newtownards. James White from Glastry worked as an agricultural labourer and he and Ellen McGuinness were married on 13 March 1901 in Innishargie (Balligan) Church of Ireland Church. They had at least ten children – Ellen (Nellie, born 2 June 1901); Annie (born 18 April 1904); Isabella (born 29 April 1906); James (born 3 October 1911); Charles (born 14 December 1912); John; Hessie; Herbert; Vera and Vincent.

In 1927 the White family moved to Canada where they lived in Sarah Street, Orangeville, Ontario. Herbert was eight when the family set sail from Belfast on 9 April 1927 on route for St. John in New Brunswick. After leaving school Herbert Anthony White worked in Orangeville Conservatories and at the Dale and Calvert Greenhouses in Brampton, Ontario. In 1942 he joined the Lorne Scots (Peel, Dufferin and Halton Regiment) which was a Reserve Infantry Regiment of the Canadian Army and after training he was posted overseas. He was transferred to the Perth Regiment and was wounded in action. When he recovered he rejoined his unit and he was 26 years old when he was killed on 13 September 1944 during the Allied advance northwards in Italy.

His death was reported in the 18 November 1944 edition of the *Newtownards Chronicle* where details were given about family members. He was survived by his parents; his five sisters – Mrs E. Gaw of 16 Court Street, Newtownards; Vera of Orangeville, Ontario; Mrs Vincent McCormick of Caledon, Co.

News has been received by Mrs. E. Gaw of 16 Court Street, Newtownards, that her brother, Private Herbert Anthony White, has been killed in action while serving with a Canadian regiment in Italy. Aged 26 years, Pte. White was a son of Mr. and Mrs. James White, who lived at 48 South Street, Newtownards, before going to Canada, where they have been residing at Sarah Street, Orangeville, Ontario. Pte. White was born in Newtownards, and he went abroad with his parents in 1927.

Tyrone; Mrs Thomas Kaene of Brampton, Ontario; Mrs George Chadwick of New Toronto; his four brothers – Private John White (serving with the RCASC in Italy); James White and Vincent White of Orangeville and Charles White of Hamilton, Ontario.

White, James
Able Seaman
SS *San Gerardo* (London), Merchant Navy
Died as a result of enemy action on Tuesday 31 March 1942 (aged 19)
Tower Hill Memorial, London, England (Panel 92)

James White was born on 23 February 1923 and he was a son of William and Mary Jane White (nee Drysdale) who lived at Gransha, Kircubbin. William White (aged 22) worked as a labourer and he and Mary Jane Drysdale (aged 19) were married on 30 April 1909 in Ardkeen Parish Church of Ireland Church. Mary Jane from Ratallagh was a daughter of Robert Drysdale who worked as a fisherman. William and Mary Jane named their eldest son Adam after his paternal grandfather. James White went to sea in April 1938 (aged 15) and he worked as a Deck Hand aboard the Royal Mail Motor Vessel (RMMV) *Winchester Castle* which was built by Harland and Wolff and operated by the Union-Castle Mail Steamship Company.

During the Second World War James White served with the Merchant Navy aboard the British tanker SS *San Gerardo*. This ship was built in 1922 by Palmer's Shipbuilding and Iron Company Ltd., Newcastle-upon-Tyne and owned by the Eagle Oil and Shipping Company, London. On 31 March 1942 she was some 700 miles off Cape Hatteras, North Carolina and not in convoy when she was torpedoed and sunk by the German submarine *U-71*.

Able Seaman James White was one of around 50 men who died and his death was reported in the 5 September 1942 edition of the *Newtownards Chronicle* under the headline *Kircubbin Seaman Killed*.

Able Seaman James White was 19 years old when he died and he is commemorated on the Tower Hill Memorial in London and in Kircubbin

779

Parish Church of Ireland Church (Holy Trinity).

White, John
Gunner
No. 1839643, 356 Battery (Heavy Anti-Aircraft) Regiment Royal Artillery
Died of illness on Monday 2 November 1942 (aged 39)
Bangor Cemetery, Co. Down (Section 5 X Grave 10)

During the Second World War Gunner John White served with 356 Battery (Heavy Anti-Aircraft) Regiment Royal Artillery and he was 39 years old and a widower when he died of cardiac failure in Bangor Military Hospital (also known as 25th General Hospital) on 2 November 1942. He was buried on 4 November 1942 in Bangor Cemetery.

W

Whitehouse, Patrick Leslie
Sergeant
No. 3383453, 1st Battalion, East Lancashire Regiment
Killed in action on Friday 22 September 1944 (aged 30)
Valkenswaard War Cemetery, Noord-Brabant, Netherlands (Grave I F 6)

Patrick Leslie Whitehouse was born in the Republic of Ireland and he was the husband of Maud Whitehouse of Holywood. During the Second World War he served with the East Lancashire Regiment and he was 30 years old when he died on 22 September 1944 at Valkenswaard in the Netherlands. Valkenswaard was the first village to be liberated on the main line of the Allied advance into Holland in September 1944 and Sergeant Patrick Leslie Whitehouse was buried in Valkenswaard War Cemetery.

Williams, Douglas
Flying Officer (Pilot)
No. J/15206, 410 Squadron, Royal Canadian Air Force
Killed in an aircraft accident on Saturday 12 June 1943 (aged 22)
Belfast City Cemetery (Glenalina Extension Section A S Grave 21)

Douglas Williams was born on 20 March 1921 in Ontario, Canada and he was a son of Henry Ernest Williams (born Plymouth, England) and Christina

Williams (née Campbell) of 390 Main Street West, Hamilton, Ontario. They were married on 5 November 1918 in Hamilton, Ontario and they had at least three children – Kenneth, Stanley and Douglas. Henry Ernest Williams was a soldier and during the First World War he served with the Canadian Overseas Expeditionary Force (he enlisted on 31 January 1916).

In 1940 Douglas Williams joined the Royal Canadian Air Force. On 12 June 1943 a de Havilland Tiger Moth (X5045) aircraft of Queen's University Air Squadron based at RAF Sydenham crashed in the grounds of the Stormont Estate close to the Massey Avenue entrance, killing the two men on board. They were Flying Officer Douglas Williams from Hamilton, Ontario and his passenger, Lieutenant (A) **George Leslie Werts** from Middlesex. Flying Officer Williams from 410 Squadron was on attachment to RAF Belfast (Sydenham) from 1480 Flight based at Newtownards. In his certificate of death registration it was noted that he was 22 years 2 months and 23 days old when he died and he was buried in Belfast City Cemetery. There is an inscription on his CWGC headstone:

W

His memory is as dear today as in the hour he passed away

Flying Officer Douglas Williams is commemorated on the Canadian Virtual War Memorial (Internet) and on Page 226 in the Canadian Second World War Book of Remembrance.

Williams, John
Corporal
No. 6981913, Royal Inniskilling Fusiliers
Killed in action on Wednesday 17 May 1944 (aged 30)
Cassino War Cemetery, Italy (Grave XI A 7)

> **KILLED ON ACTIVE SERVICE.**
> **WILLIAMS**—May, 1944, reported Killed in Action, Corporal John Williams, Royal Inniskilling Fusiliers, dearly-loved husband of Annie Williams, 74, Balfour Street, Newtownards.
> Very deeply regretted.

The death of Corporal John Williams was reported in the 3 June 1944 edition of the *Newtownards Chronicle*. John Williams was a son of William and Alice Williams of Derbyshire and he was the husband of Annie Williams (nee Rogan, daughter of Hugh Rogan) of 74 Balfour Street, Newtownards. John Williams and Annie Rogan were married in 1943.

During the Second World War Corporal John Williams served with the Royal

Inniskilling Fusiliers and he was 30 years old when he was killed in action on 17 May 1944 during fierce fighting at Cassino in Italy. Cassino was finally taken on 18 May 1944 – the day after Corporal John Williams was killed.

Williams, Leslie Frederick (Leslie)
Leading Aircraftman
No. 1281889, Royal Air Force Volunteer Reserve
Accidentally drowned on Saturday 30 May 1942 (aged 22)
Wandsworth (Streatham) Cemetery, London
(Block 12 Grave 596 Screen Wall Panel 6)

AIRMAN'S FATAL BATHE.

The manner in which a twenty-two yeears old member of the R.A.F. met his death was described at an inquest held on Saturday by Rr R. A. McC. Wallace, Coroner for the district. District-Inspector S. M'Neill conducted the proceedings on behalf of the police.

The deceased was a native of London, L.A.C. Leslie H. Williams, and while bathing in Lough Cowie on Saturday he got into difficulties, and in spite of the efforts of fellow airmen, the body was not recovered until half-an-hour after it submerged.

W

Leslie Frederick Williams's birth was registered in the second quarter of 1920 in Wandsworth, London and his mother's maiden name was Cole. The death of Leading Aircraftman Leslie Frederick Williams was reported in the 6 June 1942 edition of the *Newtownards Chronicle* under the headline *Ards Drowning Tragedy – Airman's Fatal Bathe*. The deceased was a native of London and while bathing in Lough Cowie (Cowey) between Kircubbin and Portaferry he got into difficulties. He and two other airmen had gone out in a small boat and Leslie Williams was the first to jump in. When he got into difficulties LAC Sam Reilly jumped in to help him. Sam was unable to hold him and Leslie disappeared from view. His two friends called for help and a local man, William Sheridan, used a grappling hook to recover Leslie Williams's body, some half-an-hour after he submerged.

Leading Aircraftman Leslie Frederick Williams was buried in Wandsworth (Streatham) Cemetery, London and his name is commemorated on a Second World War memorial panel in the Cemetery.

Williams, Newtown Hunter Middleton (Tony)
Sergeant
No. 1490507, Royal Air Force Volunteer Reserve
Killed in an aircraft accident on Monday 23 August 1943 (aged 19)
Watford North Cemetery, Hertfordshire, England
(Section B Cons Grave 1373)

Newtown Hunter Middleton (Tony) Williams was born on 4 December 1923 and he was a son of Newtown Middleton Williams and Eleanor Purdon

 Williams (nee Payne). Newtown Middleton Williams of 114 Tollington Park, London who served as a Captain with the Gloucestershire Regiment and Eleanor Purdon Payne from Marino, Holywood were married on 7 May 1919 in Holywood Parish Church of Ireland Church (St. Philip and St. James).

Tony Williams attended Campbell College, Belfast from 1937 until 1941 and he was a Lance Corporal in the Officers' Training Corps. His brother Brian Middleton Williams, who was born on 18 October 1925, also attended Campbell College and during the Second World War Brian served in Europe and the Far East.

During the Second World War Tony Williams served with the Royal Air Force Volunteer Reserve and early in 1942, when he was on home leave, he visited Campbell College when it was at the Northern Counties Hotel in Portrush. Tony Williams was 19 years old when he died in a flying accident on 23 August 1943 at RAF Lulsgate Bottom in Somerset and his death was registered in Weston-Super-Mare. His mother's address was *Iva Craig Cottage*, Craigavad, Co. Down.

Sergeant Newtown Hunter Middleton Williams was buried in Watford North Cemetery, Hertfordshire on 27 August 1943 and four others were buried in the same plot:

W

- Sergeant Williams's aunt, Ann Emily Hazel Payne who died on 28 May 1941 (aged 41) and was interred on 3 June 1941; she lived at 27 Conduit Street, London; she was a daughter of Katharine Payne of Marino, Holywood and the late George Whateley Payne; she served in Westminster Division ARP; she was injured in Conduit Street during a German air raid on 10 May 1941; she died 18 days later at Leavesden Emergency Hospital and there is an inscription on the headstone below her name:
  She loved London and died in its defence

- Sergeant Williams's father, Newton Middleton Williams who died on 7 May 1945 (aged 55) and was interred on 11 May 1945
- Sergeant Williams's mother, Eleanor Purdon Williams (aged 92) who was interred on 24 June 1985
- Sergeant Williams's brother, Brian Middleton Williams (aged 70) who was interred on 27 November 1996

Sergeant Newtown Hunter Middleton Williams is commemorated in Campbell College and in Queen's University, Belfast.

Willis, William Richard
Sergeant (Observer/Radar)
No. 1212906, 153 Squadron, Royal Air Force Volunteer Reserve
Killed in an aircraft accident on Tuesday 26 May 1942 (aged 22)
Ballycranbeg (Mount St. Joseph) Roman Catholic Churchyard, Co. Down
(Grave 34)

Sergeant Observer William Richard Willis was killed when his Bristol Beaufighter aircraft (X7573) crashed in the townland of Moneyneagh near Loughguile in County Antrim on 26 May 1942 during a training flight. The crew of three on board were all killed.

The Pilot was **Stanley Donald Wills** (aged 20, Royal Australian Air Force) who was buried in Ballyhalbert (St. Andrew's) Church of Ireland Churchyard, Ballyeasborough, Co. Down. The other Sergeant Observer aboard was **Gordon Charles Edwards** (aged 25, Royal Air Force Volunteer Reserve) who was buried in Harbledown (St. Michael's) Churchyard, Kent.

W

Wills, Stanley Donald
Flight Sergeant (Pilot)
No. 400746, 153 Squadron RAF, Royal Australian Air Force
Killed in an aircraft accident on Tuesday 26 May 1942 (aged 20)
Ballyhalbert (St. Andrew's) Church of Ireland Churchyard,
Ballyeasborough, Co. Down (Grave 4)

Flight Sergeant Stanley Donald Wills who served with the Royal Australian Air Force during the Second World War was a son of Korah Stanley Wills and Helen Pearson Wills of East St. Kilda, Victoria, Australia.

Flight Sergeant Stanley Donald Wills was killed when his Bristol Beaufighter aircraft (X7573) crashed in the townland of Moneyneagh near Loughguile in County Antrim on 26 May 1942 during a training flight. The crew of three on board were all killed. In addition to Flight Sergeant Wills there were two Sergeant Observers (both RAFVR) aboard – **William Richard Willis** who was buried in Ballycranbeg (Mount St. Joseph) Roman Catholic Churchyard, Co. Down and **Gordon**

Charles Edwards (aged 25) who was buried in Harbledown (St. Michael's) Churchyard, Kent.

Flight Sergeant Stanley Donald Wills is commemorated on the Australian War Memorial (Panel 132); in Ballyhalbert (St. Andrew's) Church of Ireland Church and on his CWGC headstone there is the inscription:

His duty nobly done
We will remember him

Wilson, Alan McDonald (Alan)*
Flight Sergeant (Navigator/Bomber)
**No. 1126225, 356 Squadron, Royal Air Force Volunteer Reserve
Killed on active service on Saturday 16 September 1944 (aged 21)
Taukkyan War Cemetery, Myanmar (Collective Grave 28 F 8-17)**

Alan McDonald Wilson was the elder son of James and Mary I. Wilson of 92 Seacliff Road, Bangor. Before the war he worked as a clerk and he enlisted in October 1940 (he overstated his age). He had training in England before going to the USA (via Canada) for further training under the Arnold Scheme. He transferred from pilot to navigation training and was posted to South Africa. He returned to England before being posted to India in December 1943 (he arrived in February 1944) to serve with 356 Squadron. This Squadron was formed on 15 January 1944 at Salbani, Bengal, India as a long range bomber unit equipped with Consolidator B-24 Liberator aircraft. The squadron developed techniques for low-level bombing relatively small, dispersed targets in Burma (Myanmar) and Siam (Thailand).

W

DIED ON ACTIVE SERVICE.
WILSON—Missing since September, 1944, now officially presumed to have lost his life while on operations in Burma, Flight-Sergt. Alan McDonald Wilson, aged 21, R.A.F.V.R., elder and dearly-loved son of Mr. and Mrs. James Wilson, 92 Seacliffe Road, Bangor, Co. Down.

Initially Flight Sergeant Alan McDonald Wilson was posted as missing in action on 16 September 1944 and some ten months later, in July 1945, it was officially confirmed that he had been killed while on operations in Burma. He was one of a crew of ten aboard a Consolidator B-24 Liberator aircraft (EW114) that took off from RAF Salbani at 6.05 am on a mission to bomb Maymyo Railway Station. Over the target area his aircraft and another Liberator aircraft (EV902 of 355 Squadron) collided while they were flying in formation and crashed. In addition to Flight Sergeant Alan McDonald Wilson the other nine crew members aboard EW114 who died were:

- Flight Sergeant John Edward Carr
- FS Raymond Henry Chapman aged 21 from Peterborough, Northamptonshire
- Flight Sergeant John James Collins
- FS William Henry Dobson aged 22 from Bermondsey, London
- Sergeant Charles Gilbert Griffiths aged 19 from Newmarket, Suffolk
- FS Douglas Desmond Holmes aged 21 from Abergavenny, Monmouthshire
- Flight Sergeant Stanley Mason aged 23 from Wingate, Co. Durham
- Sergeant Victor John Vallin aged 30 from Camelford, Cornwall
- Sergeant Peter George Waghorn aged 19 from Shirley, Southampton

Seven of the ten crew members aboard EV902 were also killed. The three survivors were taken Prisoner-of-War and held in Rangoon Jail. Flight Sergeant Alan McDonald Wilson was 21 years old when he died and he was buried in Taukkyan War Cemetery. He is commemorated on Bangor and District War Memorial and in Wesley Centenary Methodist Church, Bangor.

Wilson, Garner McCartney (Garner)*
Fireman
SS *Empire Heritage* (Cardiff), Merchant Navy
Died as a result of enemy action on Friday 8 September 1944 (aged 37)
Tower Hill Memorial, London, England (Panel 42)

GARNER WILSON Garner McCartney Wilson was born on 17 March 1907 at 26 Whitestar Street, Belfast and he was the younger son of William Reid Wilson and Minnie Wilson (nee McMahon). William Reid Wilson was born on 16 November 1874 and he was a son of Joseph and Frances Wilson (nee McCartney) who were married on 30 July 1866 in Moira Presbyterian Church. Garner's older brother, Joseph John Wilson, was born on 13 June 1899. Garner Wilson went to sea and during the Second World War he served with the Merchant Navy. In 1942 he served aboard the SS *Empire Coral* and the SS *Empire Fletcher*. On 24 August 1944 he signed on as one of the crew of the SS *Empire Heritage* sailing from New York to Liverpool. All of the *Empire* ships were owned by the Ministry of War Transport and in the Register of Deceased Seamen his last place of abode is recorded as 73 Mark Street, Newtownards.

The SS *Empire Heritage* was completed in 1930 by Armstrong Whitworth and Company Ltd., Newcastle-upon-Tyne as the SS *Tafelberg* – a South African whale factory ship built for the Kerguelen Sealing and Whaling Company Ltd., Capetown, South Africa. On 28 January 1941 the *Tafelberg* was damaged by a mine and beached at Porthkerry in Wales. A year later the ship was refloated and taken to Whitmore Bay. She was rebuilt as the steam tanker *Empire Heritage* by the Ministry of War Transport and returned to service in February 1943. The SS *Empire Heritage* was torpedoed and sunk about 15 miles northwest of Malin Head, Co. Donegal when on route from New York to Liverpool in Convoy HX-305. At around 6.00 am on 8 September 1944 she was struck by a torpedo fired by the German submarine *U-482* and an hour later she was hit by a German Navy Acoustic Torpedo (GNAT). On board the SS *Empire Heritage* were 73 'Distressed British Seamen' (DBS) – these were survivors of previous sinkings or men discharged from ships abroad because of illness and being given passage back to Britain. The rescue ship *Pinto* stopped to pick up survivors and at around 6.40 am the *Pinto* was torpedoed and sunk by *U-482*. *Pinto* survivors were picked up by the trawler HMS *Northern Wave* and taken to Londonderry. Thus it was that some of the DBS who had been aboard the SS *Empire Heritage* survived three separate sinkings during one crossing of the Atlantic. In addition to its passengers, the *Empire Heritage* was carrying a cargo of 16,000 tons of fuel oil and almost 2,000 tons of deck cargo. The deck cargo included a number of Sherman tanks that are now strewn over the seabed around the wreck site.

Fireman Garner Wilson (aged 37) and Cabin Boy **Thomas Crawford Barbour** from Bangor were two of those aboard the SS *Empire Heritage* who were presumed drowned. Fireman Garner Wilson is commemorated on the Tower Hill Memorial in London and on Newtownards and District War Memorial.

Wilson, George*
Flight Sergeant
No. 522964, 156 Squadron, Royal Air Force
Killed on active service on Friday 3 September 1943 (aged 29)
Runnymede Memorial, Surrey, England (Panel 140)

Ards Airman Missing.—News has been received by Mrs. Wilson of Mill Street, Newtownards, that her husband, Sergeant Air-Gunner George Wilson, R.A.F., is missing in recent operations. Sergeant Wison, whose mother resides in Frederick Street, Newtownards, has had altogether nine years' service with the R.A.F. Before joining up, Sergeant Wilson was prominently identified with the Newtownards Company of the Boys Brigade.

George Wilson was a son of Robert and Martha Wilson (nee McConnell) and he was born on 2 August 1914 in his parents' house at 48 Frederick Street, Newtownards. Martha McConnell (born in Aberdeen) and Robert Wilson

787

were married on 4 July 1897 in St Anne's Church of Ireland Church, Belfast.

Robert Wilson worked as a butter and egg dealer and he and Martha had at least five children – Minnie (born 1 August 1900 at 39 Keswick Street, Belfast, married William McNamee); David (born 3 December 1902 at Ballysallagh); Robert (born 17 March 1905 at Ballysallagh); Helen (born 1 March 1909) and George (born 2 August 1914). Also living with them was Richard John Wilson (born 13 May 1891), Robert's son by a previous marriage. Before he joined the Royal Air Force around 1934 George Wilson was associated with the Newtownards Company of the Boys' Brigade. He was the husband of Annie Wilson of Mill Street, Newtownards.

During the Second World War George Wilson served with the Royal Air Force. On 3 September 1943 he was the Rear Gunner aboard an Avro Lancaster aircraft (JA681) that took off at 7.48 pm from RAF Warboys in Huntingdonshire (now Cambridgeshire) on a mission to bomb Berlin. Nothing was heard from the aircraft after takeoff and no trace of it was ever found. Initially the crew members were reported as missing in action and later it was officially confirmed that they must be presumed dead. The other crew members who died that night were:

- Flying Officer Michael O'Meara Shanahan aged 30 (RAAF)
- Flight Lieutenant Hume Melville Stafford aged 32 (RAAF)
- Pilot Officer John Cyril Collins aged 25 (RAAF; champion surfer)
- Flight Sergeant Tom Hoyle aged 23 from Catford, London
- Pilot Officer Neil Howard Denyer aged 22 (RAAF)
- Pilot Officer David Laing Dodds aged 23 (RAAF)

That night 316 Lancaster aircraft left Britain to bomb Berlin; 22 aircraft and 130 airmen were lost.

Flight Sergeant George Wilson was 29 years old when he died and he is commemorated on the Runnymede Memorial in Surrey and on Newtownards and District War Memorial.

Wilson, Hugh
Pilot Officer (Wirless Operator/Air Gunner)
No. 178769, 90 Squadron, Royal Air Force Volunteer Reserve
Killed in action on Saturday 26 August 1944 (aged 22)
Durnbach War Cemetery, Bayern, Germany (Grave 6 A 2)

Hugh Wilson was born on 2 June 1922 and he was a son of William and Jemima Wilson (nee Maddock) who were married on 23 March 1916 in

Newtownards Parish Church of Ireland Church (St. Mark's). William Wilson was a soldier and during the First World War he served with the Royal Horse Artillery in India. William and Jemima Wilson lived at 59 Balfour Street, Newtownards and they had four children – Jane Maddock, Elizabeth Larmour, Hugh and Isabel Darragh.

Hugh Wilson's aunt (his mother Jemima's sister), Jeannie Maddock, was married to Private Archibald Nisbett who died on 13 January 1919. Private Archibald Nisbet is commemorated on Page 483 in the Book of Honour *Remembering Their Sacrifice in the Great War – Ards* compiled by Barry Niblock. Hugh Wilson was a member of the First Newtownards Company of the Boys' Brigade and, prior to enlisting on 22 March 1941, he was a member of the Ulster Home Guard while he worked as a grocer's assistant.

During the Second World War Pilot Officer Hugh Wilson served with the Royal Air Force and on 26 June 1944 he was appointed to a temporary commission. Just two months later, on 26 August 1944, he was killed in action. Hugh Wilson was one of a crew of seven aboard an Avro Lancaster Mark I aircraft (ME802) that took off at 8.23 pm on 25 August from RAF Tuddenham in Suffolk on a mission to bomb Russelsheim in Germany. Their aircraft crashed and all aboard were killed. The other six crew members who died that night were:

W

- Squadron Leader Henry Philip Lee-Warner DFC AFC aged 31 from Kilburn, Middlesex
- Sergeant John Stanley Holdcroft
- Flying Officer Francis Edward Good (RCAF)
- Flight Sergeant James Ross Court aged 22 (RNZAF)
- Pilot Officer William John Hope DFC aged 20 (RCAF)
- Flight Sergeant Maurice Kieff aged 20

That night the RAF sent 116 Lancasters to bomb Russelsheim and they dropped a great many bombs and incendiaries. On 26 August 1944, a war crime was committed in Russelsheim. In reprisal for the intensive Allied bombing, townspeople killed six American airmen who parachuted to the ground after their Consolidated B-24 Liberator aircraft was shot down. Initially Pilot Officer Hugh

Wilson was reported missing presumed killed and it wasn't until October 1945 that his death was confirmed. His grave was located and his remains were exhumed and reinterred in Durnbach War Cemetery.

Pilot Officer Hugh Wilson was 22 years old when he died on 26 August 1944 and he is commemorated in the Books of Remembrance held in the RAF Central Church, St. Clement Danes, The Strand, London; on Newtownards and District War Memorial; on the family grave headstone in Movilla Cemetery and in Newtownards Parish Church (St. Mark's). His mother Jemima died on 20 March 1943 (aged 58) and his father William died on 20 February 1951 (aged 75).

Wilson, Matthew (Matt)
Mentioned in Despatches
Corporal
No. 522495, 233 Squadron, Royal Air Force
Killed in action on Friday 12 April 1940 (aged 25)
Runnymede Memorial, Surrey, England (Panel 22)

W

Matthew Wilson's birth was registered in the second quarter of 1915 in Newtownards and he was a son of Matthew and Margaret (Maggie) Wilson (nee Mason) of 21 Brownlow Street, Comber and before that The Cattogs, Comber. They were married on 12 July 1893 in Killyleagh Parish Church of Ireland Church. Matthew Wilson Senior worked as a labourer and he and Maggie had at least nine children including Annie (born 24 October 1894); James (born 27 February 1897, died in infancy); Lizzie (born 2 April 1899); Samuel (born 28 June 1900); William (born 20 July 1902); James (born 18 January 1905); Matthew (born 20 June 1907, died 8 February 1912); David (born 2 December 1909); Margaret (born 7 September 1912) and Matthew (born 1915).

Matthew Wilson was educated at Comber Public Elementary School and he was a member of the Unity Players connected with Comber Non-Subscribing Presbyterian Church. He joined the Royal Air Force around 1936 and became a Wireless Operator, later earning his Air Gunner's Badge. Before the outbreak of the Second World War he had been recommended for appointment as an Observer.

In the 24 February 1940 edition of the *Newtownards Chronicle* it was reported that Matthew Wilson had been Mentioned in Despatches 'for wisdom shown in an emergency when the wireless apparatus of the plane was put out of order whilst in action'. During a North Sea reconnaissance flight,

COMBER AIRMAN MISSING.

WAS IN RECENT HONOURS LIST.

News was received an Monday morning that Corporal Matthew Wilson, R.A.F., son of Mr. Mathew Wilson, sen., of Brownlow Street, Comber, has been officially reported missing.

machine gun fire from an enemy aircraft damaged the petrol tank and put the wireless apparatus out of order. Wireless Operator Wilson, himself a non-smoker, asked one of his comrades for some silver foil from a cigarette packet, repaired the defect and re-established contact with the home station which then guided the plane back to base. After this action he was promoted to the rank of Corporal and in March 1940 he was home in Comber for a period of leave. His brother Thomas also served with the Royal Air Force.

Corporal Matthew Wilson served in Coastal Command and on 12 April 1940 he was one of a crew of four aboard a Lockheed Hudson Mark I aircraft (N7258). They took off from RAF Leuchars in Scotland at 7.28 am to intercept and shadow a convoy of enemy ships and it was during this operation that their plane was shot down by enemy aircraft at 1.55 pm. The other crew members who died that day were:

- PO George James Denzil Yorke aged 25 from Wellington, New Zealand
- Flt Lt Andrew Hood McLaren DFC aged 21 from Lochee, Dundee
- Leading Aircraftman James Alexander Milne aged 19 from Glasgow

W

Corporal Matthew Wilson died on 12 April 1940 (aged 25) and he is commemorated on the Runnymede Memorial in Surrey; on Comber and District War Memorial; in Comber Non Subscribing Presbyterian Church and on the family grave headstone in Comber Cemetery. Matthew's brother David died on 16 November 1924 (aged 15); his mother Margaret died on 21 March 1938 (aged 62) and his father Matthew died on 16 September 1962 (aged 91).

Wilson, Robert Logan (Bobby)
Aircraftman 1st Class
No. 995972, Royal Air Force Volunteer Reserve
Killed in an aircraft accident on Sunday 28 June 1942 (aged 23)
Bangor Cemetery, Co. Down (Section 4 R Grave 147)

Robert Logan (Bobby) Wilson was born on 28 January 1919 in Lurgan and he was the third son of William Ogilvie Wilson (born 1861) and Mary Wilson (nee Logan). William Ogilvie Wilson was a farmer's son from Bright

 near Downpatrick and he worked as a landscape gardener. Mary Logan was William Ogilvie Wilson's second wife. William Ogilvie Wilson (then living in Ballycarry, County Antrim) and Isabella Orr were married on 11 March 1903 in Christ Church Church of Ireland Church in Belfast and they had two children, Kathleen Eugenie Elizabeth (born 17 March 1906) and William John (Jack, born 1907) before Isabella died.

William Ogilvie Wilson and Mary Logan from Muckamore were married on 3 September 1915 in Antrim Parish Church of Ireland Church. When the Wilson family moved to Bangor they lived in Springhill Cottages and they worshipped in Bangor Abbey. William Ogilvie Wilson worked for Sir Robert Kennedy of Cultra who lived where the Ulster Folk and Transport Museum is now located. William and Mary Wilson had five children – twins James (known as Roger) and Dorothy (born 1916); Robert Logan; Ogilvie Ennis (born 1921) and Mary (Molly).

W

William Ogilvie Wilson died before the outbreak of the Second World War and Mary suffered from rheumatoid arthritis. During her illness Mary was looked after by her daughters Dorothy and Molly; Mary died on 27 September 1941 (aged 56). Both William Ogilvie and Mary Wilson were buried in Bangor Cemetery. After their mother died, Dorothy and Molly Wilson both worked in F.W. Woolworth's Bangor store. Dorothy died on 29 July 1973.

Bobby Wilson worked in the Grocery Department of Hugh Furey Ltd., Bangor for four years before he enlisted. He was educated at Bangor Central Public Elementary School and Bangor Technical School. From an early age he was interested in aircraft and astronomy and he was a renowned storyteller. He is remembered for his striking appearance – almost 6 feet 5 inches tall with curly, ginger hair. His other great interest was music and he would have liked to pursue this interest further. Regularly he went to the Tonic Cinema in Bangor for organ lessons from the organist Stendel Todd. Bobby Wilson joined the Royal Air Force Volunteer Reserve in 1940.

WILSON—June, 1942. A.C.1. Robert Logan Wilson, R.A.F. Interment in Bangor New Cemetery to-day (Friday) at 3 o'clock.
  Deeply regretted by his sorrowing Brothers and Sisters.

The death of Aircraftman First Class Bobby Wilson was reported in the 4 July 1942 edition of the *County Down Spectator*. A member of ground staff, Bobby Wilson was one of two people aboard a Vickers Wellington Mark IC aircraft (R1445) that took off at 5.30 pm on 28 June 1942 from RAF Steeple Morden in Hertfordshire on a night flying test. RAF Steeple Morden was a grass satellite dispersal airfield of RAF Bassingbourn used by No. 11 Operational

Training Unit (OTU) of Bomber Command. The aircraft lost power in one engine, stalled off a tight turn, crashed into a house at Ashwell, Hertfordshire (around two miles southwest of the airfield) and burst into flames. The pilot, who had 450 hours of experience flying Wellingtons, was also killed:

- Pilot Officer John Edwin Casey DFC aged 23 (RNZAF)

The funeral of Aircraftman First Class Bobby Wilson to Bangor Cemetery took place on Friday 3 July 1942 and the Revd James Hamilton of Bangor Abbey officiated. At the time of Bobby's death, his brother James (known as Roger) was serving as a gunner with the Royal Artillery and he was a Prisoner-of-War in Italian hands. Roger later escaped and was on the run for 28 days before he reached the safety of an American base. Roger was a keen swimmer and golfer and he played golf at Carnalea. He died on Carnalea Golf-course in November 1989. Bobby's brother Jack worked as a gardener for Mr and Mrs R.W. Lindsay of *Glen House*, Crawfordsburn and his brother Ogilvie was an engineer on war work in England.

W

Aircraftman First Class Robert Logan Wilson was 23 years old when he died and he is commemorated on Bangor and District War Memorial and in Bangor Parish Church of Ireland Church (St. Comgall's).

Wilson, Thomas
Leading Cook (S)
No. D/MX 61660, HMS *Hermes*, Royal Navy
Died as a result of enemy action on Thursday 9 April 1942 (aged 29)
Plymouth Naval Memorial, Devon, England (Panel 72 Column 1)

Comber Man Missing.—Miss Sarah Wilson, 20 Railway Street, Comber, has received official notification that her brother, Thomas Wilson (Leading Cook) is reported missing presumed killed. He was serving on board H.M.S. Hermes. Ldg. Cook Wilson was 29 years of age and joined the Royal Navy at the outbreak of war. Before joining he was an employe of Messrs. J. M. Andrews and Co., Ltd., Comber.

Thomas Wilson was born on 19 April 1913 and he was a son of Samuel and Elizabeth Wilson (Lizzie, nee Warnock) of 20 Railway Street, Comber. They were married on 1 May 1893 in First Newtownards Presbyterian Church and they had at least nine children – Sarah (born 8 February 1894); Eliza (born 12 July 1895, died in infancy); James (born 20 April 1898); Matthew (born 9 July 1900); Martha (born 17 October 1902, died in infancy); Samuel (born 14 July 1905); Martha (born 8 September 1906); Mary (born 12 January 1909) and Thomas (born 19 April 1913).

Prior to the outbreak of war Thomas Wilson was employed by Messrs J.M. Andrews and Company, Ltd., Comber. He joined the Royal Navy at the outbreak of war and served aboard HMS *Hermes*. He was reported missing in action on 9 April 1942 and about a month later his sister Sarah was officially informed that he must be presumed killed.

HMS *Hermes* was an aircraft carrier built by Armstrong Whitworth for the Royal Navy. She was laid down in 1918 and commissioned in 1923. After a brief refit in August 1939 HMS *Hermes* then conducted anti-submarine patrols in the Western Approaches before going to Dakar in French West Africa (now Senegal). In December she escorted a convoy to Britain and after another refit in January 1940 she returned to Dakar. In July 1940 HMS *Hermes* collided with HMS *Corfu* and, after temporary repairs in Freetown, she sailed to Simonstown in South Africa for more permanent repairs and further refitting.

In February 1941 HMS *Hermes* gave support to the British offensive against Italian Somaliland before proceeding to the Persian Gulf and then the Indian Ocean. In December 1941 she returned to Simonstown for further refitting. After sea trials she was transferred to the Eastern Fleet based at Ceylon (now Sri Lanka). On 8 April the Japanese Carrier Fleet was sighted approaching Trincomalee, Ceylon and the British ships were ordered to withdraw. The following day HMS *Hermes* and her escorting Australian destroyer HMAS *Vampire* were attacked by some 80 Japanese bombers and fighters. Both ships were sunk southeast of Trincomalee and Leading Cook Thomas Wilson was one of more than 300 men aboard HMS *Hermes* who died. Survivors were picked up by the hospital ship HMHS *Vita*.

Leading Cook Thomas Wilson was 29 years old when he died and he is commemorated on Plymouth Naval Memorial in Devon; on Comber and District War Memorial and in Second Comber Presbyterian Church.

Winter, Ralph Henry John (Ralph)
Sergeant
No. 1386870, 153 Squadron, Royal Air Force Volunteer Reserve
Killed on active service on Saturday 10 January 1942 (aged 20)
Runnymede Memorial, Surrey, England (Panel 97)

Ralph Henry John Winter's birth was registered in the first quarter of 1922 in Barnet, Middlesex and he was a son of Frank and Ellen H. Winter (nee Lavis). Their marriage was registered in the third quarter of 1912 in Hackney, London and they had at least two children

– Dorothy E. (born 1913) and Ralph Henry John (born 1922).

During the Second World War Sergeant Ralph Henry John Winter served in the Royal Air Force Volunteer Reserve with 153 Squadron based at RAF Ballyhalbert. He died on 10 January 1942 when his Boulton Paul Defiant aircraft (T3931) failed to return from a night patrol over the Irish Sea. The two crew members were declared missing and their bodies were never recovered. They were the pilot, Sergeant **Robert Wilkinson Foreman** aged 20 from Corbridge in Northumberland and his air gunner, Sergeant Ralph Henry John Winter. Sergeant Ralph Henry John Winter was 20 years old when he died and both men are commemorated on the Runnymede Memorial in Surrey.

Woods, Frederick James (Fred)*
Royal Marines Police Officer
Royal Marines Police
Died as a result of an accident on Thursday 28 December 1939 (aged 46)
Belfast (Dundonald) Cemetery, Co. Down (Grave D1 477)

> **GALLANT SELF-SACRIFICE**
> A former Comber man, Mr. Fred J. Woods, lost his life on active service on Thursday night, 28th December, in a gallant, if futile, attempt to save the life of a badly injured boy at Devonport Dockyard.

Frederick James Woods and Hester Lunn were married on 18 August 1917 in St. Anne's Church of Ireland Cathedral, Belfast and the death of Fred Woods was reported in the 13 January 1940 edition of the *County Down Spectator* under the headline *Gallant Self-Sacrifice*. Described in the report as a former Comber man, it was reported that Fred Woods had 'lost his life on active service in a gallant, if futile, attempt to save the life of a badly injured boy at Devonport Dockyard. On hearing the cries for help coming from the depths of a dry dock Mr Woods, after telephoning headquarters, proceeded to clamber down the side of the dock, but in the inky darkness must have missed his footing and was, as far as is known, killed instantaneously by the fall. The boy who was 16 years of age, died from injuries received, on the following Saturday'.

Fred Woods served for twelve years in the Royal Marines and for four years as an A Special in the Ulster Special Constabulary. At the outbreak of the Second World War he volunteered his services and became a member of the Royal Marines Police at Devonport Dockyard. He was 46 years old when he died on 28 December 1939 and he was buried in Belfast (Dundonald) Cemetery on 5 January 1940.

Interestingly, the date of death for Frederick J. Woods has been inscribed as 2 January 1939 on the headstone. The full inscription on the headstone is:

LUNN – In loving memory of Duncan died 7 January 1933
WOODS – Frederick J. died 2 January 1939

Duncan Lunn (aged 42) lived at 35 Lorton Street, Belfast. Two other men are buried in the same grave – William John Clarke (aged 58) of 163 Cupar Street, Belfast who died on 18 May 1939 and Albert Victor Moorehead (aged 72) of 11 Beverley Street, Belfast who died on 12 January 1965.

Woods, Morrison*
Sapper
No. 153284, Royal Engineers
Died of illness on Monday 19 August 1946 (aged 30)
Bangor Cemetery, Co. Down (Section Wall West Grave 369)

W

Morrison Woods (born 1916) was the third son of Morrison Woods (an engineer in a shipbuilding yard) and Margaret Woods (nee Smith) of 985 or 1014 Govan Road, Glasgow. They had at least four children including James, Elizabeth and Morrison. Morrison Woods Junior was the husband of Phyllis Marguerite Woods of 4 Beechwood Avenue, Bangor and during the Second World War he served with the Royal Engineers. Sapper Morrison Woods was 30 years old when he died of cancer on 19 August at his residence, 4 Beechwood Avenue, Bangor. On his CWGC headstone in Bangor Cemetery his wife Phyllis included the inscription:

Worthy of Everlasting Remembrance
His Loving Wife

WOODS—August 19, 1946, at his residence, 4 Beechwood Avenue, Bangor, Morrison, dearly-loved husband of Phyllis Woods. Interred in Bangor Cemetery on Wednesday, 21st inst. Deeply regretted by his sorrowing Wife and little Son, Morris.

WOODS—August 19, 1946, at his residence, 4 Beechwood Avenue, Bangor, Morrison, dearly-loved third son of Margaret and the late Morrison Woods, 1014 Govan Road, Glasgow. Deeply regretted by his sorrowing Mother, Brothers and Sister.

Morrison and Phyllis Woods had a son called Morrison (known as Morris) and on an adjacent headstone there is another inscription:

Silcock
In loving memory of Phyllis
Beloved wife of Charles and mother of
Morrison Woods
Died 18 February 1999

Woods, William Charles (Willie)*
Able Seaman
No. D/JX 181588, HMS *President III*, Royal Navy
Died of illness on Monday 9 February 1942 (aged 32)
Donaghadee Parish Church of Ireland Graveyard, Co. Down

WOODS—In loving memory of my dear son, and our dear brother, Seaman Gunner William Charles Woods, Royal Navy, died 9th February, 1942, youngest son of Thomas and the late Matilda Woods. Ever remembered by his loving father, Sister, Mother-in-law and Nephew. Also my dear wife, and our dear mother, Matilda Woods, died 28th April, 1938.

"Deep in our hearts lies a picture
More precious than silver or gold:
It's a picture of our dear Willie,
Whose memory will never grow
old."

Thomas Woods; Francis, Mary and Ronald Kirk, 26 Castle Street, Donaghadee.

William Charles Woods was the youngest son of Thomas and Matilda Woods (nee Miskimmins) of Moat Street and later 26 Castle Street, Donaghadee. They were married on 22 December 1887 in Newtownards Registry Office. Thomas Woods worked as a railway labourer and he and Matilda had at least twelve children including John (baptised 6 January 1889); Eliza Jane (born November 1890); James (baptised 28 August 1892); Isabella (born March 1894); Martha Smith (born 14 April 1896); William Charles (died); Francis (born 3 April 1899); Hugh; Mary (married Francis Kirk on 25 June 1930 and they had a son named Ronald) and William Charles (named after his brother who died). The first four children were baptised in Millisle & Ballycopeland Presbyterian Church and the next two in Shore Street Presbyterian Church Donaghadee. Matilda Woods died on 28 April 1938.

During the Second World War Willie Woods served with the Royal Navy. HMS *President III* was the shore-based accounting base for the naval gunners on Defensively Armed Merchant Ships (DEMS) and Able Seaman William Charles Woods died of illness on 9 February 1942. His father placed a *Death Notice* in the 13 February 1943 edition of the *County Down Spectator* and it contained the verse:

> *Deep in our hearts lies a picture*
> *More precious than silver or gold*
> *It's a picture of our dear Willie*
> *Whose memory will never grow old*

Able Seaman William Charles Woods was 32 years old when he died and he is commemorated on Donaghadee and District War Memorial and on the Woods family grave headstone in Donaghadee Parish Church of Ireland Graveyard.

W

Woodsend, Philip Kenneth (Ken)
Flying Officer
No. 62692, 501 Squadron, Royal Air Force Volunteer Reserve
Killed in an aircraft accident on Sunday 17 January 1943 (aged 21)
Paisley (Hawkhead) Cemetery, Renfrewshire, Scotland
(Section H Grave 776-779)

Philip Kenneth Woodsend was born on 4 June 1921 and he was a son of Philip Duncan Woodsend and Norah Agnes Woodsend (nee Eadie) and a grandson of John Scott Eadie and Agnes Ferguson Eadie (nee Wilson) of Paisley. His great-grandfather, Peter Eadie was Provost of Paisley from 1905 until 1908. Philip Duncan Woodsend (aged 24) was a Second Lieutenant in Horse Transport, Army Service Corps when he and Norah Agnes Eadie (born 29 October 1891) were married on 4 June 1915 in the Abbey Church, Paisley.

Philip Kenneth Woodsend was just seven months old when his mother Norah died on 18 December 1921. From 1935 until 1939 he attended Loretto School near Edinbugh where he was a House Prefect and a Corporal in the OTC. He was on the school hockey and swimming teams. He joined the Royal Air Force Volunteer Reserve in 1940 and after training he served as a fighter pilot in Malta. Seriously injured, he was invalided home in 1941 and the following year he resumed operational duties. Flying Officer Philip Kenneth Woodsend was based at RAF Ballyhalbert when he died on 17 January 1943. He was piloting a Supermarine Spitfire aircraft (BL615) when it collided with another Spitfire during a practice dog fight at 29,000 feet and crashed close to RAF Kirkistown. Flying Officer Woodsend baled out but his parachute failed to open and he plummeted onto the shore at Portavogie, close to the spot where Portavogie couple Dave and Hannah Donnan were standing watching the practice dogfight. The other aircraft landed safely.

PETER EADIE, PROVOST OF PAISLEY 1905-1908 BORN 6TH JULY 1837 DIED 21ST MARCH 1919
NORAH, BELOVED WIFE OF PHILIP D. WOODSEND
AND VERY DEAR DAUGHTER OF JOHN AND AGNES SCOTT EADIE,
BORN 29TH OCTOBER 1891, DIED 18TH DECEMBER 1921.
PHILIP KENNETH WOODSEND, FLYING OFFICER R.A.F. V.R.,
BORN 4TH JUNE 1921, KILLED ON ACTIVE SERVICE 17TH JANUARY 1943.

Flying Officer Philip Kenneth Woodsend was 21 years old when he died and he was buried in Paisley (Hawkhead) Cemetery, Renfrewshire. His maternal grandmother died on 31 January 1954 (aged 87) and his parental grandfather died on 2 December 1954 (aged 91).

Wray, John
Private
No. 6979739, 1st Battalion, Argyll and Sutherland Highlanders
Killed on active service on Friday 6 October 1944 (aged 32)
Faenza War Cemetery, Italy (Grave V D 21)

John Wray was born on 22 March 1912 and he was baptised in Donegal Presbyterian Church, Donegal Town. He was the eldest son of John and Mary (May) Wray (nee Wilson) of Tullyearl, Laghey, Co. Donegal. Their marriage was registered in the second quarter of 1910 in Donegal. John Wray Senior was a farmer and he and May had at least nine children – Sarah Anne (born 17 March 1911); John (born 22 March 1912); Isobel (born 11 September 1913); Francis (Frank, born 21 August 1915); Mary Jane (born 12 September 1917); George (born 3 August 1919); Margaret (born 3 March 1921); Alexander (born 24 February 1922) and Henry (born 18 February 1924).

> WRAY—Killed in action in Italy, October, 1944, Private John Wray, R.I.F., eldest son of John Wray and the late May Wray, Tullyearl, Co. Donegal, and loved brother of Frank and Nan Wray, Ivy Cottage, Newtownards Road, Bangor, Co. Down.

Prior to the start of the Second World War, John Wray served with the Royal Inniskilling Fusiliers and during the war he served with the Argyll and Sutherland Highlanders (Princess Louise's). His marriage to Winifred May Richards was registered in the fourth quarter of 1940 in Newtown, Montgomeryshire in Wales and Winifred lived in Abermule, Montgomeryshire. The 1st Battalion Argyll and Sutherland Highlanders landed on Sicily during *Operation Husky* in 1943 and from February 1944 fought during the Italian Campaign. After Private John Wray was killed on Friday 6 October 1944, his brother Frank and sister-in-law Nan who lived in *Ivy Cottage*, Newtownards Road, Bangor placed a *Killed on Active Service* notice in the 18 November edition of the *County Down Spectator*.

Wren, Sidney John
Driver
No. T/169758, Royal Army Service Corps
Died as a result of an accident on Thursday 21 November 1940 (aged 23)
Holywood Cemetery, Co. Down (Protestant Ground Collective Grave 1263)

Driver Sidney John Wren was a son of George and Annie Wren (nee Brand) of Stansted, Essex. Their marriage was registered in the second quarter of 1913 in Bishops Stortford, Hertfordshire and Sidney's birth was registered there in the first quarter of 1917. George Wren worked as a farm labourer and he and Annie had at least three children – Cyril G. (born 1914); Sidney

T/69758 DRIVER
S J WREN
ROYAL ARMY SERVICE CORPS
21ST NOVEMBER 1940 AGE 23

Tragic Death of Three Soldiers

CRUSHED BY FALLING TREES

EVIDENCE AT INQUEST

The inquest was held in a Co. Down town on three young soldiers who were killed when trees fell across huts of which they were occupants.

The deceased were: Driver Sydney C. Wren (23), of Stanstead, Essex; Driver George W. Evans (23), Plymouth, and Private Derrick Rodney Swift (23), of Blackpool.

J. (born 1917) and Dorothy M. (born 1920).

The death of Driver Sidney John Wren who was unmarried was reported in the 30 November 1940 edition of the *County Down Spectator* under the headline *Tragic Death of Three Soldiers*. Three young soldiers were killed in Clandeboye Camp, Ballyleidy when trees fell across huts in which they were sleeping. They were Driver **George William Evens** (aged 23) from Plymouth; Private **Derek Rodney Swift** (aged 24) from Blackpool and Driver Sydney John Wren (aged 23) from Stansted in Essex. The roof of the hut in which Private Swift was sleeping caved in and pinned him to the bed. To release him his comrades used a heavy jack to raise the fallen roof and hacksaws to cut down the bed. He suffered severe head injuries and was dead when his comrades got him out. Driver Wren and Driver Evens were crushed by fallen debris and both were asphyxiated. Driver Sydney John Wren was 23 years old when he died and he was buried in Holywood Cemetery. His CWGC headstone bears the inscription:

W

Rest in Peace

Two other men were buried in this collective grave – Fusilier **Frederick Bloomfield** and Rifleman **John McFarlane**.

Wright, Frederick George
Private
No. 4923019, 2nd Battalion, Essex Regiment
Died on active service on Sunday 18 June 1944 (aged 30)
Ryes War Cemetery, Bazenville, Calvados, France (Grave V C 5)

Frederick George Wright was a son of David and Mary Ann Wright (nee Price) whose marriage was registered in the second quarter of 1905 in Hackney, London. Frederick George Wright's birth was registered there in

the third quarter of 1913. David Wright worked as a hewer in a coal mine and he and Mary Ann had at least four children – David (born 1907); Clara (born 1908); Olive (born 1910) and Frederick George (born 1913).

Frederick George Wright was the husband of Ellen Wright of Comber, Co. Down and during the Second World War he served with the Essex Regiment. Private Frederick George Wright was 30 years old when he died on 18 June 1944 during the Allied offensive in France – less than two weeks after the Normandy Landings on 6 June.

Wright, Jean Dibby
Aircraftwoman 2nd Class
No. 2002675, Women's Auxiliary Air Force
Died of illness on Sunday 8 February 1942 (aged 17)
Nottingham Crematorium, Nottinghamshire, England (Panel 5)

W

It is recorded in the CWGC Debt of Honour that Jean Dibby Wright was a daughter of William Grant Wright and Mary Victoria Wright of Portaferry, Co. Down. The death of Jean Dibby (in some records Dibbey) Wright was registered in the first quarter of 1942 in Newark, Nottinghamshire. She died on 8 February 1942 in St. Ann's War Emergency Hospital, Newark and was cremated on 11 February 1942 in Nottingham Crematorium. The applicant was William R.G. Wright who lived at 19 Mayfield Terrace, Edinburgh and in the Crematorium records it is noted that 'her ashes were taken away for burial at Victoria Falls in Canada' (the Victoria Falls are in fact located in Zimbabwe but there is a Victoria Park in Canada at the Niagara Falls).

Wright, Matthew
Fusilier
No. 6984533, 70th Battalion, Royal Inniskilling Fusiliers
Died as a result of enemy action on Thursday 17 April 1941 (aged 18)
Macosquin (St. Mary's) Church of Ireland Churchyard, Co. Londonderry (Grave 462)

Fusilier Matthew Wright was a son of Matthew and Mary Anne Wright (nee Dinsmore) of Cross Lane, Coleraine. Matthew Wright Senior (son of James

Wright) was a bricklayer and a widower when he and Mary Anne Dinsmore were married on 2 August 1920 in Macosquin (St. Mary's) Church of Ireland Church, Co. Londonderry. Mary Anne Dinsmore was a daughter of John Wilson Dinsmore who in turn was a son of Harrison and Rebecca Dinsmore (nee Douthert). Matthew Wright Senior and Agnes Laverty were married on 31 January 1918 and Agnes was 23 years old when she died of puerperal fever on 28 January 1920 at her home in Society Street, Coleraine.

Fusilier Matthew Wright was one of 13 soldiers serving with the 70th Battalion, Royal Inniskilling Fusiliers who died as a result of an air raid on Newtownards aerodrome during the night of 15/16 April 1941. Fusilier **Daniel Higgins** who also died that night was buried in Newtownards (Movilla) Cemetery and under his name in this Book of Honour there is a summary of all those people with North Down or Ards connections who died that night.

W

Fusilier Matthew Wright was wounded in the attack and he was 18 years old when he died of his wounds on 17 April 1941. He was buried in Macosquin (St. Mary's) Church of Ireland Churchyard, Co. Londonderry and there is an inscription on his CWGC headstone:

He gave his young life for freedom

His headstone stands in a Dinsmore family plot where the following people are also commemorated:

John Wilson Dinsmore died 22 January 1955
And his son John died 17 May 1989
Rebecca Dinsmore died 30 December 1950
And her son Samuel died 28 December 1918
Also her daughter Hannah died 27 February 1972

During the First World War, Private John Dinsmore (No. 595456) died on 29 October 1918 and he was buried in Macosquin (St. Mary's) Church of Ireland Churchyard. He was a son of James Dinsmore, Englishtown and a grandson of John Dinsmore, Farranseer and he is commemorated on Page 373 in the Book of Honour *Coleraine Heroes* compiled by Robert Thompson.

Wright, Robert Ebenezer (Robert)*
Civilian War Dead
Died as a result of enemy action on Thursday 17 April 1941 (aged 41)
Bangor Cemetery, Co. Down (Section 1 C Grave 11)

Between 10.45 pm and 4.30 am during the night of Easter Tuesday 15 April and Wednesday 16 April 1941 there was a large-scale German Luftwaffe air raid on the City of Belfast. Other nearby towns and villages, including Bangor and Newtownards, were also attacked. Areas of Bangor where bombs fell included Ashley Gardens, Bangor Golf Clubhouse, Baylands, Farnham Road, Hazeldene Gardens and Ranfurly Avenue. Fires blazed on Scrabo Hill, Newtownards and bombs fell on Green Road, Conlig and Comber Road, Newtownards. At least 28 people with North Down and Ards connections were killed, including 14 civilians

Matilda Grattan (aged 54) together with her daughters **Angeline** (aged 18) and **Shelagh** (aged 20), died at 40 Ashley Gardens, Bangor. **Margaret Byers Watt** (aged 60) died at 5 Hazeldene Gardens Bangor. **Robert Wright** (aged 41) of 32 Baylands, Bangor died of injuries in Bangor Hospital on 17 April 1941.

That night the aerodrome at Newtownards, which was the Headquarters of 231 Squadron, Royal Air Force, was attacked and 13 soldiers serving with the Royal Inniskilling Fusiliers were killed. Fusilier **Daniel Higgins** was buried in Newtownards (Movilla) Cemetery and under his name in this Book of Honour there is a summary of all those people with North Down or Ards connections who died that night.

Robert Ebenezer Wright was born on 22 June 1900 and he was a son of Robert and Jane Wright (nee Cairns) of Drumgath, Newry, Co. Down. Jane was a daughter of Ebenezer Cairns. Robert Wright was a farmer and he and Jane Cairns were married on 14 July 1899 in Newry (Plymouth Brethren) Church. They had three children – Robert Ebenezer (born 22 June 1900); Samuel Joseph (born 3 August 1901) and John (born 17 February 1903).

FUNERAL OF MR. R. WRIGHT
There was a large attendance at the funeral to Bangor New Cemetery on Sunday of Mr. Robert Wright, who died as a result of enemy action.
Prior to the interment an impressive service was held in connection with the Plymouth Brethren congregation of which Mr. Wright was a member.

The funeral of Robert Wright was reported in the 26 April 1941 edition of the *County Down Spectator*. Prior to the

W

interment in Bangor Cemetery on 20 April 'an impressive service was held in connection with the Plymouth Brethren congregation of which Mr Wright was a member'.

Robert Ebenezer Wright of *Ashvale House*, Carryduff and 9 Hazeldene Gardens, Bangor worked as an estate agent and his effects amounted to some £1,665. Probate was granted to his widow Louise.

Of the many civilians of the Commonwealth whose deaths were due to enemy action in the Second World War, the names of some 67,092 are commemorated in the Civilian War Dead Roll of Honour, located near St. George's Chapel in Westminster Abbey, London.

Robert Wright is commemorated on the family grave headstone in Bangor Cemetery as is his wife Louise who died on 8 December 1969. There is an inscription on the headstone:

I know that my Redeemer liveth

Yeaman, Richard George (Richard)
Leading Aircraftman
No. 1350724, 2957 Squadron, RAF Regiment,
Royal Air Force Volunteer Reserve
Killed by an accidental gunshot on Thursday 27 April 1944 (aged 27)
Carrowdore (Christ Church) Churchyard, Co. Down (Section N Grave 122)

W
Y

Richard George Yeaman was born on 30 July 1916 in Carrowdore and he was the second son of William James and Sarah Ann Yeaman (nee Coulter). William James Yeaman worked as a labourer and during the Great War he served with the 11th Battalion, Royal Irish Rifles. He was awarded the Military Medal. William James Yeaman and Sarah Ann Coulter were married on 23 February 1912 in Ballygrainey Presbyterian Church and at least six of their children were baptised in that church – Richard George (born 30 July 1916); Michael Francis (born 4 November 1917); Eliza Jane (born 7 September 1919); Samuel (born 16 January 1921); Eleanor Sarah (born 11 June 1922) and Albert Noel (born 24 December 1924, died 23 March 1940). The Yeaman family moved from Carrowdore to 6 Patricia Gardens, Donaghadee Road, Newtownards.

During the Second World War, Richard Yeaman served with the Royal Air

DIED ON ACTIVE SERVICE.

YEAMAN—April, 1944, accidentally killed, L.A.C. Richard George Yeaman, R.A.F. His remains were interred in family burying-ground, Church Hill, Carrowdore, on Wednesday, 3rd May.

Trust ye in the Lord, for He is everlasting strength.

Some day we'll meet and we will understand.

Deeply regretted by his sorrowing Father, Mother and Sister Ella.
6, Patricia Gardens,
Donaghadee Road, Newtownards.

Force and it was reported in the 6 May 1944 edition of the *Newtownards Chronicle* that he died on 27 April 1944 as the result of a bullet wound. After a short service in the house he was buried in Carrowdore Parish Church of Ireland (Christ Church) Churchyard on 3 May 1944 and RAF personnel formed a guard of honour. There is an inscription on his CWGC headstone:

We will remember him
Help me Lord to bear my cross

Various members of the Yeaman family placed *Died on Active Service* notices in the 6 May 1944 edition of the *Newtownards Chronicle*: there was one from his father, mother and sister Ella of 6 Patricia Gardens, Donaghadee Road, Newtownards; one from his sister Elizabeth (Betty), brother-in-law William John Pritchard and family of 1 Rosedene Gardens, Donaghadee Road, Newtownards; one from his sister Catherine, brother-in-law William Carson and family (William was serving with the Royal Navy); one from his sister Agnes and brother-in-law Henry Robson of 128 Mill Street, Newtownards; one from his brother Thomas Henry (he was serving with the RAF) and sister-in-law Dorothy Yeaman of 6 Patricia Gardens and one from his brother Michael, sister-in-law Josephine Yeaman and family of Carrowdore (and before that 17 Frederick Street, Newtownards). The notice inserted by his parents included the verse:

Trust ye in the Lord, for He is everlasting strength
Some day we'll meet and we will understand

Leading Aircraftman Richard George Yeaman was 27 years old when he died and he is commemorated on Newtownards and District War Memorial; in Carrowdore Parish Church (Christ Church) and in Newtownards Parish Church (St. Mark's). His father William James died on 7 March 1955 (aged 72) and his mother Sarah Ann died on 21 October 1961 (aged 69).

Young Brothers, Albert John and George Henry

In the CWGC Debt of Honour it is recorded that Albert John Young and George Henry Young were sons of Edward and Margaret Young and nephews of Robert Maguire of Holywood, Co. Down. During the Second World War both brothers served with the 1st Battalion, Royal Inniskilling Fusiliers. Early in 1942 the 1st Battalion was flown to Burma to help stem the

Japanese advance. British Forces were compelled to retreat and both brothers were killed during very heavy fighting on 18 and 19 April. They were killed in Burma on successive days – Lance Corporal George Henry Young on 18 April 1942 and Fusilier Albert John Young on 19 April 1942.

Young, George Henry
Lance Corporal
No. 6976947, 1ˢᵗ Battalion, Royal Inniskilling Fusiliers
Killed in action on Saturday 18 April 1942 (aged 26)
Rangoon Memorial, Myanmar (Face 11)

George Henry Young was born in County Down, his birth was registered in the first quarter of 1916 in Belfast and he lived in Belfast. He was 26 years old when he was killed and he is commemorated on the Rangoon Memorial.

Young Albert John
Fusilier
No. 6977675, 1ˢᵗ Battalion, Royal Inniskilling Fusiliers
Killed in action on Sunday 19 April 1942 (aged 27)
Rangoon Memorial, Myanmar (Face 12)

Albert John Young was born in County Down, his birth was registered in the second quarter of 1915 in Belfast and he lived in County Tyrone. He was 27 years old when he was killed and he is commemorated on the Rangoon Memorial.

Young, George Burch (George)
Fusilier
No. 3128307, 2ⁿᵈ Battalion, Royal Scots Fusiliers
Killed in action on Wednesday 29 May 1940 (aged 28)
Bedford House Cemetery, Ieper, West-Vlaanderen, Belgium
(Enclosure No. 6 V C 9)

George Burch Young was born on 23 April 1912 and he was the third son of James (Jim) and Annie Young (nee Wilson) of Corry Street, Newtownards and later 20 Frederick Street, Newtownards. During the Great War Jim Young served with the 13ᵗʰ Battalion, Royal Irish Rifles and he was killed in action at Thiepval on 1 July 1916. He is commemorated on Page 667 in the Book of Honour *Remembering Their Sacrifice in the Great War – Ards* compiled by Barry Niblock. James Young and Annie Wilson were married on 20 December 1907 in Greenwell Street Presbyterian

3128307 FUSILIER
G. YOUNG
THE ROYAL SCOTS FUSILIERS
29TH MAY 1940 AGE 34

Church, Newtownards and they had five sons, four of whom were baptised in the same church (no record for James) – Andrew (born 26 October 1908); James (born 2 July 1910); George Burch (born 23 April 1912); Robert (born 17 August 1914) and Elliott Thiepval (born 12 October 1916). Annie Young named her newborn son Elliott after his late father's Captain, Elliott Johnston, and Thiepval after the place where his father Jim died. (Captain Elliott Johnston MC is commemorated on Page 296 in the Book of Honour *Remembering Their Sacrifice in the Great War – Ards* compiled by Barry Niblock.)

ROLL OF HONOUR.

YOUNG—29th May, 1940, died on active service, George, 2nd Battalion The Royal Scots Fusiliers, third and dearly-loved son of Mrs. Young, 20, Frederick Street, Newtownards, and the late James Young (died in action at Thiepval 1st July, 1916). His remains were interred near Victory Monument at Zilleborks, Ypern.

God is good, He gives us grace
To bear our heavy cross;
He is the only One Who knows
How bitter is our loss.

Deeply regretted by his sorrowing Mother, Brothers, Sister-in-law and Nieces; also his Uncles, Aunts and Grandmother.

In the early 1930s George Young joined the Royal Scots Fusiliers and he served abroad in Egypt, Palestine and India. An Army Reservist, George Young was called up at the outbreak of hostilities and he was 28 years old when he was killed in action at Zillebeke in Belgium on 29 May 1940 (his age was inscribed as 34 on his CWGC headstone). In the 20 July 1940 edition of the *Newtownards Chronicle* there were three *Roll of Honour* notices – one from his mother, brothers, sister-in-law, nieces Maureen and Georgina, uncles, aunts and grandmother; one from his grandma, uncles, aunts and cousins and one from the officers and members of the Temple of Loyalty LOL No. 481 and RAPC Newtownards. The notice from his mother contained the verse:

God is good, He gives us grace
To bear our heavy cross;
He is the only One who knows
How bitter is our loss

Fusilier George Young is commemorated on Newtownards and District War Memorial. His brother Robert was also on active service.

Y

Young, Hugh
Private
No. WX14050, 2/5 Battalion, Australian Infantry, AIF
Killed on active service on Saturday 6 February 1943 (aged 42)
Lae War Cemetery, Papua New Guinea (Grave G B 1)

> **KILLED ON ACTIVE SERVICE.**
>
> YOUNG—Killed in Action, 6th February, 1943, in New Guinea, Hugh, second son of the late Hugh Young, Ballyskeagh, and Sarah Young, Whitespots, Newtownards.
>
> Sunshine passes, shadows fall,
> But loving memories outshine all.
>
> Deeply regretted by his sorrowing Mother, Brother John and Sister Lizzie; also his Sister-in-law.

Hugh Young was born on 3 November 1900 and he was the second son of Hugh and Sarah Boyd Young (nee Gibson) of Ballyskeagh, Newtownards. Hugh Young Senior was a farmer and he and Sarah Boyd Gibson (from Whitespots, Newtownards) were married on 6 January 1886 in Regent Street Presbyterian Church, Newtownards. They had eight children – William James (born 4 December 1886); Anna (born 23 December 1888, died 5 January 1893); Mary Ellenor (born 1 March 1891); Andrew (born 5 May 1893, died in infancy); Sarah (born 27 September 1894, died 22 May 1928); Elizabeth (Lizzie born 17 June 1897, died 26 November 1978); Hugh (born 3 November 1900) and John Andrew (born 21 December 1903, died 21 June 1991). The first three children were baptised in Regent Street Presbyterian Church.

Hugh Young was 22 years old when he moved to Australia where he intended to farm. On 26 April 1923 he sailed on his own from London to Adelaide aboard the SS *Borta*. During the Second World War, Hugh Young served with 2/5th Battalion, Australian Infantry. He was the husband of Jessie Young of Maylands, Western Australia and he was 42 years old when he was killed on 6 February 1942 in Papua New Guinea. His family in Newtownards placed a *Killed on Active Service* notice in the 15 May 1943 edition of the *Newtownards Chronicle* and it contained the verse:

> *Sunshine passes, shadows fall,*
> *But loving memories outshine all*

Private Hugh Young is commemorated on the Australian War Memorial (Panel 31). His father Hugh died on 13 August 1937 (aged 82) and his mother Sarah died on 28 May 1956 (aged 90). Both were buried in Movilla Cemetery, Newtownards.

Y

Young, James Frederick
Corporal
No. 6844553, 2ⁿᵈ Battalion, King's Royal Rifle Corps
Killed in action between 23 and 26 May 1940 (aged 31)
Dunkirk Memorial, Nord, France (Column 117)

James Frederick Young was born in London and he was a son of James F. and Elizabeth Young. He was a soldier living in Corry's Quarter, Newtownards and his father, also a soldier, was deceased when he and Jane Robb of 123 Mark Street, Newtownards were married on 22 December 1930 in Ballygilbert Presbyterian Church.

During the Second World War James Frederick Young served with the King's Royal Rifle Corps and he was 31 years old when he was killed during the fall-back of Allied Forces to Dunkirk where the evacuation began on 27 May. His body was never recovered and he is commemorated on the Dunkirk Memorial in France. At that time Jane Young was living in Millisle, Co. Down.

Young, Maurice Edward (Maurice)
Lieutenant
No. 296607, 2ⁿᵈ Battalion, Royal Inniskilling Fusiliers
Killed in action on Tuesday 20 March 1945 (aged 24)
Faenza War Cemetery, Italy (Grave II A 15)

Y

Maurice Edward Young was born on 2 December 1920 and he was the only son of Edward Anderson Young and Matilda Elizabeth Young (nee Spratt) of 15 Windmill Road, Bangor. Edward Anderson Young was a company secretary and he and Matilda Elizabeth Spratt were married on 14 January 1920 in Newington Presbyterian Church, Belfast.

Maurice Edward Young attended Bangor Grammar School from 1930 until 1939 and he played both rugby and cricket for the school. He was prominent too in athletics and represented the school at the Ulster School Sports where he won several trophies. The Headmaster said that he was 'one of those who by their personal qualities, athletic prowess and simple-hearted manliness draw to themselves the love of comrades and the respect of superiors'.

KILLED IN ACTION.

YOUNG—Killed in action in Italy, March, 1945, Lieutenant Maurice E. Young, Royal Inniskilling Fusiliers, only and dearly-loved son of Mr. and Mrs. E. A. Young, Windmill Road, Bangor.

Under the care of the Ards Presbytery he completed two years of study for church ministry at Magee University College, Londonderry before he enlisted as a Private in the Royal Artillery in April 1942. After being commissioned he was transferred to the Royal Inniskilling Fusiliers and was posted to Italy in April 1944. The Royal Inniskilling Fusiliers formed part of the Irish Brigade which was honoured with a Papal Reception in St. Peter's Basilica, Rome for St. Patrick's Day 1945. Lieutenant Maurice Young was killed in action three days later on 20 March 1945. He was leading a patrol near the Senio River when they came under heavy enemy fire. In a letter to Maurice's parents the Battalion CO wrote, 'Maurice was a first rate officer who more than once showed himself to be a brave and inspiring leader. I spoke to Maurice the evening before he met his death; he was cheerful and brimful of confidence which inspired the whole platoon. He had volunteered for a job the next morning, which was the wiping out of an enemy post. He died in front leading his men into the position'.

Lieutenant Maurice Edward Young is commemorated on Bangor and District War Memorial; in Hamilton Road Presbyterian Church, Bangor (where his father was for a time the Clerk of Session) and in Bangor Grammar School. His parents presented the Maurice Young Cup (House Athletics Trophy) to Bangor Grammar School to be competed for annually.

Y

Young, Robert Neville Desmond (Desmond)
Mentioned in Despatches
Captain
No. 137409, 1st Battalion, Irish Guards
Killed in action on Wednesday 23 February 1944 (aged 27)
Beach Head War Cemetery, Anzio, Italy (Grave XX C 1)

Robert Neville Desmond Young was born on 16 August 1916 and he was a son of Robert Chichester Young and Amy Isabel Young (nee Stuart) from Culdaff, Co. Donegal who later lived at *Millmount*, Randalstown, Co. Antrim. Successive generations of the Young family lived in *Culdaff House* from about 1608. Robert Chichester Young was a Barrister-at-Law and he and Amy Isabel Stuart were married on 30 September 1913. They had at least four children – George Stuart (born 23 September 1914, died 1971); twins Robert Neville Desmond and Olive Margaret Lawrence (born 16 August 1916, Olive died 1982) and Mary Vivien Barbara (known as Kinna, born 31 January 1922, died 1990). Amy Isabel Young was the author of *Three Hundred Years in Inishowen*. Robert Chichester Young died on 25 December 1941 (aged 54) and Amy Isabel Young died on 17 October 1949 (aged 64).

Desmond's twin sister, Olive Margaret Young, and Thomas Stanley Winton were married on 2 December 1942 and their home address was Culdaff, Co. Donegal. During the Second World War Lieutenant Winton served with the Royal Naval Volunteer Reserve aboard HMS *Harvester* and he was killed in action on 11 March 1943. During the Second World War Vivien Young served with the WRNS.

Robert Neville Desmond Young was educated at Rockport School, Craigavad and Tonbridge School in Kent before he went to London to train to be a solicitor. When war broke out he joined the Army and was gazetted Second Lieutenant in the Irish Guards in 1940. He and Mary Cunningham were married on 19 February 1941, he was promoted to the rank of Captain in 1943 and their home address was Sanderstead in Surrey. Desmond and Mary Young had one child, a daughter named Jane.

From March 1943 the 1st Battalion, Irish Guards fought in North Africa where they suffered heavy casualties. Early in 1944 the Battalion moved to Italy and again suffered heavy losses in the bitter fighting at Anzio. Captain Robert Neville Desmond Young was killed by machine-gun fire on 23 February 1944 and he was buried in the Beach Head War Cemetery at Anzio. In the 11 January 1945 *Supplement to the London Gazette* it is recorded that Captain Young had been Mentioned in Despatches. He is commemorated on a memorial window in Culdaff Church of Ireland Church and in Rockport School, Craigavad.

Y

Names by Centre of Population

In this Section, the names of servicemen, servicewomen, nursing personnel and civilians with North Down/Ards family or work connections who died in the Second World War are presented alphabetically by surname, in relation to the centre of population they are associated with. Because families and individuals moved around within the North Down/Ards area, some of those who died had a demonstrable association with more than one population centre. Casualties who died in the North Down/Ards area have also been included – as have those who died while they were stationed in the area, together with those who were buried in the area.

BALLYGILBERT, CARNALEA, CRAWFORDSBURN, HELEN'S BAY AND DISTRICT

Commander **Eduard Bakker DFC**	Royal Air Force
Flt Lt **Desmond Wallace Ferguson Barker DFC**	Royal Air Force
Pilot Officer **Richard Percival William Barker**	RNZAF
Warrant Officer **Samuel Nicholl Beckett**	RAFVR
Flight Sergeant **George Johnston Cheatley**	RAFVR
Chaplain 4th Class **James Arthur Douglas MID**	RAChD
Third Engineer Officer **Joseph Gerald Foster**	Merchant Navy
Flight Sergeant **David Harrison Freeland**	RAFVR
Sergeant (Pilot) **David John Goodchild**	RAFVR
Junior Engineer Officer **John Corbett Hall**	Merchant Navy
Private **Robert Hoey**	Army Catering Corps
Flying Officer **Hugh Francis Morrow**	RCAF
Lieutenant **Noel Montgomery Neely**	RNVR
Nursing Sister **Ida May Nelson**	Civilian War Dead
Bombardier **Francis Eric Sheals**	Royal Artillery
Flying Officer **Hubert Stanley Sheals**	Royal Air Force
Pilot Officer **Hugh Conn Thompson**	Royal Air Force

BALLYGOWAN AND DISTRICT

Gunner **Hector Black**	Royal Artillery
Aircraftman First Class **Hugh Craig**	RAFVR
Private **Andrew Leebody**	Pioneer Corps

BALLYHALBERT AND DISTRICT

Sub-Lieutenant (A) **Frederick Robert Akister**	RNVR
Pilot Officer (Pilot) **Frederick Hugh Anderson**	RNZAF
Captain **David Martin Bailie**	US Merchant Marine
Lance Sergeant **John Boocock**	Royal Artillery
Sub-Lieutenant (E) **Samuel McMaster Boyd**	Royal Naval Reserve
Flight Sergeant (Pilot) **Edward Dennis Cannon**	RNZAF
Leading Aircraftman **John Connell Cowan**	RAFVR
Mate **John Hughes Cully**	Merchant Navy
Flight Sergeant **Cecil Thomas Deane**	RAFVR
Corporal **Andrew Eccles**	Border Regiment
Flight Sergeant **Gordon Charles Edwards**	RAFVR
Sergeant **Robert Wilkinson Foreman**	RAFVR
Flight Sergeant (Pilot) **William Benjamin Fry**	RCAF
Sergeant (Pilot) **William Des Brisay Gilmour**	RAFVR
Flying Officer **Donald Maldwyn Griffiths**	RAFVR
Wg Cdr **Charles Ronald Hancock OBE DFC**	Royal Air Force
Aircraftman Second Class **Ronald Hodgson**	RAFVR
Sub-Lieutenant (A) **John Samuel Hornby**	RNZNVR
Sergeant **Anthony Wilson Lavender**	RAFVR
Sergeant **Ross Wellesley Lindeman**	RAAF
Flight Sergeant (Air Gunner) **Robert Low**	Royal Air Force
Flight Sergeant (Pilot) **John Robert Lucas**	RCAF
Sub-Lieutenant (A) **John Esmond Marshall**	RNZNVR
Lieutenant (E) **John Moir**	Royal Navy
Civilian **Sally Moir**	Civilian War Dead
Flying Officer **Stanislaw Podobinski**	Polish Forces
Sailor **David John Pritchard**	Merchant Navy
Sergeant **Nagu Ranganatha**	RAFVR
Sub-Lieutenant (A) **Francis Graham Reid**	RNZNVR
Flying Officer **Frederick John Bartlett Reid**	RAFVR
Pilot Officer **Horace James Rich**	RAFVR
Sergeant (Pilot) **Peter Murray Rogerson**	RAFVR
Pilot Officer (Pilot) **John Peter Sadd**	RAFVR
Flight Lieutenant **Eric Augustus Snow**	RAFVR
Sergeant (Pilot) **Henry Walter Stanley**	RAFVR
Civilian **Frederick Strutt**	Civilian War Dead
Sergeant **Marks Weinberg (Marks Wayne)**	Royal Air Force
Flight Sergeant **Stanley Donald Wills**	RAAF
Sergeant **Ralph Henry John Winter**	RAFVR

Ballyhalbert and District continued...

Flying Officer (Pilot) **Philip Kenneth Woodsend**   RAFVR

BALLYWALTER AND DISTRICT

Carpenter **James McNeilly Belshaw**	Merchant Navy
Captain **Hugh Conway Campbell**	Merchant Navy
Stoker First Class **David Cromie**	Royal Navy
Lance Corporal **Henry Cromie**	Royal Engineers
Gunner **Robert Cromie**	Royal Artillery
Sergeant (Air Gunner) **Robert Henry Harper**	RCAF
Sergeant **Robert Valentine Ievers**	RAFVR
Sergeant **Sydney Ireland**	RAFVR
Able Seaman **Eugene Hector McSweeney**	Royal Navy
Lieutenant **Denis Harold Smallman**	South Staffs Regt

BANGOR AND DISTRICT

Fireman and Trimmer **Shief Ahmed**	Merchant Navy
Corporal **Campbell Allen**	RASC
Engineer **William Anderson**	Pilot Launch
Driver **Kenneth Herbert Andow**	RASC
Lieutenant **William Henry Lowry Andrews**	Royal Artillery
Civilian **George Holden Baird**	Civilian War Dead
Commander **Eduard Bakker DFC**	Royal Air Force
Cabin Boy **Thomas Crawford Barbour**	Merchant Navy
Sergeant **Ernest Henry Mackenzie Barr**	RAFVR
Sub-Lieutenant (E) **James Gordon Barre**	RNVR
Lt Cdr (E) **Robert Pollock Beattie**	Royal Naval Reserve
Warrant Officer **Samuel Nicholl Beckett**	RAFVR
Carpenter **Thomas Smith Beckett**	Merchant Navy
Private **Gerald Mavor Bell**	Australian Infantry
3rd Radio Officer **George Barry Neville Bewley**	Canadian MN
PO (Flying Instructor) **Deryk Jay Bleakley**	RAFVR
Captain **Robert James Bleakley**	Straits Settlements VF
Sergeant (Pilot) **Eric Ritchie Bowman**	RAFVR
Flying Officer **Geoffrey Alexander Bowman**	RAFVR
Private **George Boyling**	KSLI
Private **Frank William Braisher**	Dorsetshire Regiment
SQMS **Alexander Scott Brown**	North Irish Horse

Bangor and District continued...

Driver **Ronald James Buckingham**	RASC
Private **Harold William Calvert**	VGofC
Aircraftman 2nd Class **Cyril Charles Cameron**	RAFVR
Flight Sergeant **Ian (John) Gordon Campbell**	RAFVR
Sergeant **Robert Samuel Carson**	RAFVR
Leading Seaman **Frederick Caulfield**	RN Patrol Service
Sapper **William Coffin**	Royal Engineers
Petty Officer Stoker **Albert Parr Cole**	Royal Navy
Able Seaman **Douglas Collister**	Merchant Navy
Private **Robert Conway**	Pioneer Corps
Pilot Officer (Pilot) **Derek Alfred Cook**	RAFVR
Third Radio Officer **James McMurtry Corbett**	Merchant Navy
Flying Officer (Pilot) **George Stanley Corry**	Royal Air Force
Captain **Samuel David Corry MID**	RAMC
Telegraphist **Jacob Walter Coulter**	Royal Navy
Private **Stewart Courtney**	Parachute Regt, AAC
Cook **Robert Crone**	Merchant Navy
ERA 4th Class **Norman Crothers**	Royal Navy
Private **Archibald Crozier**	Pioneer Corps
Sergeant **Cyril Johnson Crozier**	RAFVR
Sergeant **William Cummins**	RAFVR
Corporal **James Darragh**	RAMC
Able Seaman **John Ferris Deveney**	Merchant Navy
Private **Thomas Charles Deville**	Pioneer Corps
Lance Corporal **Thomas Dickson**	Royal Ulster Rifles
LAC **Alexander James Donaghy**	Royal Air Force
Civilian **Patrick Edward Doran**	Civilian War Dead
Leading Stoker **Robert Heyburn Duff**	Royal Navy
Sergeant **Joseph Gerald Earley**	RAFVR
Lieutenant-Commander (S) **George Ellis**	Royal Navy
Driver **George William Evens**	RASC
Civilian **Thomas Gardiner Ferguson**	Civilian War Dead
Lieutenant **Simon Denis St. Ledger Fleming**	Royal Artillery
Third Engineer Officer **Joseph Gerald Foster**	Merchant Navy
Rifleman **William Fox**	Royal Ulster Rifles
Surgeon **William Elliot Fraser**	Merchant Navy
Flight Lieutenant **Brian Kenneth Levinge Fuge**	Royal Air Force
Sergeant (Pilot) **William Francis Ernest Gault**	RAFVR
Able Seaman **Stanley Geddis**	Royal Navy
Sergeant **David Burrows George**	RAFVR

Bangor and District continued...

Sailor **Patrick Joseph Gibson**	Merchant Navy
R G Gibson	Bangor War Memorial
Sergeant **Robert Trevor Gibson**	RAFVR
Lieutenant **John Lyle Taggart Glass**	Royal Naval Reserve
Sergeant (Pilot) **David John Goodchild**	RAFVR
LAC **Francis John Noel Gorman**	Royal Air Force
Flight Sergeant **John Thompson Graham**	RAFVR
Lieutenant **William Harold Graham**	RIASC
Civilian **Angeline Grattan**	Civilian War Dead
Flight Sergeant **George Francis Grattan**	Royal Air Force
Civilian **Matilda Grattan**	Civilian War Dead
Civilian **Shelagh Grattan**	Civilian War Dead
Trooper **George Griffith Griffiths**	Royal Tank Regiment
Lieutenant **Terence Michael Scott Hadow**	Royal Welch Fusiliers
FS (Flight Engineer) **John Herbert Hamilton**	RAFVR
Second Lieutenant **John Nelson Hamilton**	Pioneer Corps
Captain **Basil Hamilton-Temple-Blackwood**	Royal Horse Guards
Flying Officer **Norman Edmond Hanna**	RCAF
Flight Sergeant (Pilot) **Herbert Hannay MID**	RAFVR
Lieutenant **Richard John Michael Harrison**	Coldstream Guards
Marine **Robert Lyttle Harrison**	Royal Marines
Boatswain **John Hawthorne**	Merchant Navy
Leading Aircraftman **Robert Stanley Hegan**	Royal Air Force
Sergeant **David Francis Henderson**	RAFVR
Lieutenant **Ernest Basil Snell Hewitt MC**	R Innis Fus
Captain **David Alexander Hynes Hodgett MID**	Gurkha Rifles
Private **Robert Hoey**	Army Catering Corps
Sergeant (Observer) **Charles Julius Holland**	RAFVR
Sub-Lieutenant (A) **David Francis A Hollywood**	RNVR
Pilot Officer (Pilot) **Ian Milne Hossack**	Royal Air Force
5th Engineer Officer **Thomas McM Houston**	Merchant Navy
First Radio Officer **Robert George Wylie Irwin**	Merchant Navy
Sergeant **William Duncan Irwin**	R Innis Fus
Petty Officer Stoker **James Jamfrey MID**	Royal Navy
WO Class II (CSM) **Douglas Holden Johnston**	Royal Fusiliers
AC2 **Ernest Alfred Raymond Llewellyn Jones**	Royal Air Force
Fusilier **Spencer Jones**	R Innis Fus
Gunner **Herbert Walter Kemp**	Royal Navy
Corporal **Hugh Kennedy**	North Irish Horse
Private **James Kerr**	Pioneer Corps

Bangor and District continued...

Flight Lieutenant **Harold Anthony Kidd-May**	RAFVR
Aircraftman Second Class **Arthur James King**	Royal Air Force
Second Lieutenant **Desmond Robert King**	RIASC
Private **Harold Lamb**	General Service Corps
Captain **Edward E Lee**	RAOC
Lt Col **Francis J Leland MID Croix de Guerre**	RASC
Leading Aircraftman **David Lindsay**	Royal Air Force
Able Seaman **James Smiley Logan**	Merchant Navy
Civilian **David Garfield Logie**	Civilian War Dead
Junior Engineer Officer **William Lough**	Merchant Navy
Sub-Lt (A) **George Henry Crawford Lowden**	RNVR
George E Lowry	Bangor War Memorial
Able Seaman **George Victor Lowry**	Royal Navy
Sergeant **Samuel John Luke**	RNZAF
Grp Cpt **John Evelyn Matier MacCallum**	Royal Air Force
Pilot Officer **William Moody MacDonald**	Royal Air Force
Telegraphist **Albert George MacFarlane**	RNVR
Sergeant **William Matchett Mahaffy**	RAFVR
Sergeant **Richard Mailey**	RAFVR
Flight Lieutenant **Wilfred Ronald Maitland DFC**	RAFVR
Sergeant **James Douglas Marr**	Irish Guards
Sqn Ldr **Robert William Stanley Marshall**	RAFVR
Lance Bombardier **Edward Martin**	Royal Artillery
William Martin	Bangor War Memorial
Gunner **William James Martin**	Royal Artillery
Engineer Commander **Leslie Henry W Mauger**	Royal Navy
Wg Cdr **Victor Edwin Maxwell MID and 2 bars**	Royal Air Force
Flight Lieutenant **Harold Abraham McCaghey**	RCAF
Pilot Officer **Thomas Andrew McCann**	RAFVR
Leading Aircraftman **Robert Reid McClean**	Royal Air Force
Pilot Officer **George Marshall McCombe**	RAFVR
Flight Lieutenant **John McCrory**	RAFVR
First Radio Officer **William James McCrory**	Merchant Navy
Rifleman **Joseph McCullough**	Royal Ulster Rifles
Surgeon **William Errol Charles McCullough**	Merchant Navy
Bombardier **Thomas McCutcheon**	Royal Artillery
Fusilier **John Kavanagh McHugh**	Royal Scots Fusiliers
Private **Norman Strahan McKee**	RASC
Ordinary Seaman **Harold McMeekin**	Royal Navy
Pilot Officer **Frederick William McMurray**	RAFVR

Bangor and District continued...

Carpenter **John Alexander McNeilance**	Merchant Navy
Sergeant **Terence John McQueen**	North Irish Horse
Leading Aircraftman **Norman McReynolds**	Royal Air Force
Radio Officer **Edward George Mee**	Merchant Navy
Master **William Johnston Meek**	Merchant Navy
Sergeant (Pilot) **Herbert Reginald Megarry**	RAFVR
Sergeant **Joseph Mercer**	RAFVR
Civilian **Gladys Doreen Merrison**	Civilian War Dead
LAC **Joseph Frederick Merrison**	RAFVR
Leading Aircraftman **Frederick James Miley**	RAFVR
FO (Navigator) **William Watson Miller DFC**	RAFVR
Flying Officer **John Finlay Mitchell**	RAFVR
Bombardier **William Montgomery**	Royal Artillery
Flying Officer **Francis Raymond Moore**	Royal Air Force
Sergeant **Robert Moore**	RAFVR
Flight Sergeant **Robert Angus Moore**	RAFVR
Leading Stoker **Charles Archibald Morrison**	Royal Navy
Sgt (Navigator/Bomber) **William John Morrison**	RAFVR
Second Lieutenant **David Morrow**	R Innis Fus
Galley Boy **William James Morrow**	Merchant Navy
Stoker First Class **Thomas Murray**	Royal Navy
Chief Engineer **John Gilkenson Nicholson**	Merchant Navy
Rifleman **John Chapman Oliver**	Royal Ulster Rifles
Able Seaman **David Orr**	Royal Navy
Fusilier **Edward Francis Owen**	Royal Welch Fusiliers
Sister **Edith Doreen Pedlow MID**	QAIMNS
Private **Leland Truesdale Pentz Purple Heart**	US Army
2nd Lieutenant **William James Neely Pinkerton**	South African Forces
Lieutenant **Edward Victor Polley**	RCE
Chief Steward **William McKinley Rae**	Merchant Navy
Captain **Charles Arthur Rea**	R Innis Fus
Major **Edward Douglas Rea MID**	Royal Artillery
Fireman **Donald Gordon Reid**	Merchant Navy
Corporal **Albert Edward Reuben**	RAOC
Lieutenant (A) **Richard Herbert Ridley**	RNVR
Flight Lieutenant **Frederick Watson Ritchie**	RNZAF
Flying Officer **Thomas George Rodgers**	RAFVR
Corporal **James Harvey Rowan**	Royal Air Force
FO (Navigator) **Robert Henry Rutherford**	RAFVR
Lieutenant **James Gilmore Scott**	R Innis Fus

Bangor and District continued...

Lieutenant **Owen Shanks MM**	Black Watch
Ordinary Seaman **Lambert Charles Shepherd**	Royal Navy
Seaman First Class **Henry Hanna Shipcott**	US Navy
Thomas Shipcott	Bangor War Memorial
Third Engineer Officer **James Skillen**	Merchant Navy
Corporal **Francis Neville Sloss**	RAFVR
Colour Sergeant **Nathaniel Robert Smith**	Royal Ulster Rifles
Sergeant (Navigator) **Peter Tristan Smith**	RAFVR
Pilot Officer **John Stanley Smyth**	RAFVR
Sgt **John Edwin Charles A Steele-Nicholson**	RAFVR
Private **Thomas Stewart**	Military Police
Pilot Officer **Thomas Norman Stockdale**	Royal Air Force
Private **Barry John Stubbings**	OBLI
Private **Derek Rodney Swift**	RASC
Sergeant **Arthur Moore Templeton**	RAFVR
Flight Sergeant **Edward Carson Thompson**	RAFVR
Rifleman **Ernest Oscar Thompson**	Royal Ulster Rifles
Pilot Officer **Hugh Conn Thompson**	Royal Air Force
Civilian **James Thompson**	Civilian War Dead
Constable **William Oscar Thompson**	Royal Marine Police
Gunner **John Thomson**	Royal Artillery
Marine **Robert Totton**	Royal Marines
Robert Totton	Royal Irish Fusiliers
Pilot Officer **Alan Lancelot Treanor**	Royal Air Force
Apprentice **William Edward Trimble**	Merchant Navy
Second Lieutenant **Bernard Wakeford**	RASC
Major **Herbert Noel Wallace MC**	East Yorkshire Regt
Master **Arthur Hill Coates Waterson**	Merchant Navy
Fusilier **Edwin Appleby Record Watson**	R Innis Fus
Sergeant (Observer) **Ernest Watson**	RAFVR
Civilian **Margaret Byers Watt**	Civilian War Dead
D R Weir	Bangor War Memorial
Second Officer **Leonard Whiston**	Merchant Navy
Gunner **John White**	Royal Artillery
Flight Sergeant **Alan McDonald Wilson**	RAFVR
Aircraftman First Class **Robert Logan Wilson**	RAFVR
Sapper **Morrison Woods**	Royal Engineers
Private **John Wray**	A&SH
Civilian **Robert Ebenezer Wright**	Civilian War Dead
Lieutenant **Maurice Edward Young**	R Innis Fus

CARROWDORE, MILLISLE AND DISTRICT

Flt Lt Patrick Joseph Anthony Byers	Royal Air Force
Pilot Officer William Maxwell Henry	RAFVR
Aircraftman Second Class James McBride	RAFVR
Lance Corporal James Charles McCaul	Royal Ulster Rifles
Corporal James McLean	Royal Air Force
Sergeant (Air Gunner) William McLean	RAFVR
Gunner Edward Adam Moore	Royal Artillery
Marine Robert John O'Neill	Royal Marines
Lance Sergeant Andrew Robert Stewart	Royal Ulster Rifles
Leading Aircraftman Richard George Yeaman	RAFVR
Corporal James Frederick Young	KRRC

CLOUGHEY, KIRKISTOWN, PORTAVOGIE AND DISTRICT

Chief Officer Hugh Bell	Merchant Navy
Mate John Hughes Cully	Merchant Navy
Sub-Lieutenant (A) William Foster	RNVR
Driver Eric Joseph Heyes	Royal Engineers
First Officer Robert Hughes	Australian MN
Flight Sergeant Angus Campbell Kelly	RCAF
Master Robert Ernest Kyle	Merchant Navy
Fireman Francis Maginnis (Maginness)	Merchant Navy
Sub-Lieutenant (A) John Richard Mathers	RNVR
Ordinary Seaman James McMaster	Merchant Navy
Flight Sergeant Alexander Magowan McVea	Royal Air Force
Private First Class James Polley (Polly)	US Army

COMBER AND DISTRICT

Assistant Steward Ronald Wilson Baker	Merchant Navy
Signalman Hans Calvert	Royal Navy
Sergeant Alexander Campbell	RAFVR
Sergeant James Campbell	Canadian Army
Able Seaman William Jordan Cooke	Royal Navy
Fusilier George Leslie Gell	Royal Welch Fusiliers
Lieutenant John Malcomson Gibson	Royal Artillery
Rifleman Desmond Hull	Royal Ulster Rifles

Comber and District continued...

Gunner **John Madden**	Royal Artillery
Sergeant (Observer) **Thomas James McCloud**	RAFVR
Sergeant (Air Gunner) **Robert McKeag**	RAFVR
Fusilier **James McMaster**	Royal Irish Fusiliers
Corporal **William Nolan**	RASC
Leading Aircraftman **Ritson Finlay Petts**	Royal Air Force
Guardsman **William Pollock**	Irish Guards
Sergeant **Hugh Blackwood Price**	RCASC
Major **Hilton David Proctor**	RCCS
Sergeant **Robert Richardson**	RAFVR
Sergeant (Air Gunner) **James Shields**	RAFVR
Able Seaman **John Sturgeon**	Royal Navy
Pilot Officer **Samuel Irwin Taylor**	RAFVR
Captain **Humphrey Barron Thomson**	RAMC
Flight Sergeant **John Cameron Keith Webb**	RAFVR
Corporal **Matthew Wilson MID**	Royal Air Force
Leading Cook (S) **Thomas Wilson**	Royal Navy
RM Police Officer **Frederick James Woods**	Royal Marines Police
Private **Frederick George Wright**	Essex Regiment

CONLIG AND DISTRICT

Able Seaman **Thomas Gould**	Royal Navy
Able Seaman **Crawford Henderson**	Royal Navy

CRAIGAVAD, CULTRA, MARINO AND DISTRICT

Pilot Officer **Kenneth Duncan Adams**	RAFVR
FO **Anthony Alexander Talbot Bulloch**	Royal Air Force
FO **Ian Alexander Calthrop Campbell**	RAFVR
Lieutenant (A) **John Carr**	RNVR
Lieutenant **James Craig MID and 2 Bars**	Royal Ulster Rifles
Squadron Leader **George Crawford DFC AFC**	RAFVR
Major **Robert Henry Cutler**	King's African Rifles
Rifleman **John Robert Gilpin**	Royal Ulster Rifles
Sergeant **Albert Abraham Goldstone**	RAFVR
PO **Alexander William Valentine Green**	RAFVR
Flt Lt **Geoffrey Austin Harrison**	RAFVR

Craigavad, Cultra, Marino and District continued...

Flt Lt **Hugh Raymond Harrison DFC**	RAFVR
Sub-Lieutenant **Colin William Horner Haslett**	RNVR
Captain **Hubert Henderson**	Royal Ulster Rifles
Sergeant (Pilot) **John Cecil Brandon Irwin**	RAFVR
Flight Lieutenant **William Thomas Irwin**	RAFVR
Able Seaman **John Joseph Kennedy**	Merchant Navy
Flying Officer **Neville Stuart King**	RAFVR
Flying Officer **Robert Lawrie Lorimer**	Royal Air Force
Lt Cdr **William Robert Patterson OBE DSC**	Royal Navy
Lieutenant **Brian Thomas Stewart Rothwell**	R Innis Fus
Second Lieutenant **Robert Norman Cecil Scott**	Royal Artillery
Trooper **Thomas Shillington**	Royal Armoured Corps
Flying Officer **Arthur Buckby Sinton**	RAFVR
Second Lieutenant **Robert Arnold Thompson**	East Lancashire Regt
Flying Officer **James Kenneth Weir**	RAFVR
Sergeant **Newtown Hunter Middleton Williams**	RAFVR
Captain **Robert Neville Desmond Young MID**	Irish Guards

DONAGHADEE AND DISTRICT

Lieutenant **James Sinclair Adair**	Royal Ulster Rifles
Sergeant **Thomas Adair**	RAFVR
Deck Hand **Harry Aiken**	Pilot Launch
Leading Aircraftman **Alan Brown**	RAFVR
Lance Corporal **William Young Brown**	Intelligence Corps
Fireman **James Clegg**	Merchant Navy
Sergeant **Richard Sweet Cruise**	Royal Air Force
Corporal **Edward Dempster**	Royal Ulster Rifles
Gunner **Hugh Gamble**	Royal Artillery
Lieutenant **Anthony Godby**	Royal Armoured Corps
Able Seaman **William John Harper**	Merchant Navy
Gunner **John Cecil Beresford Harris**	Royal Artillery
Civilian **Margaret Lennon**	Civilian War Dead
Signalman **Ronald Victor Joseph Martin**	Royal Corps of Signals
Third Officer **William Ian Muir McMullan**	Merchant Navy
Gunner **Trevor Maynard Watt McVitty**	Royal Artillery
Sailor **William Joseph Mehigan**	Merchant Navy
Rifleman **Robert James Miskimmin**	Royal Ulster Rifles
Flying Officer **Donald Stanley Ashton Monard**	RAFVR

Donaghadee and District continued...

Corporal **Thomas Paterson Muckle**	Royal Air Force
Coxwain **William George Nelson**	Pilot Launch
Sapper **Joseph William Ogram**	Royal Engineers
Marine **Robert John O'Neill**	Royal Marines
Sailor **William Patton**	Merchant Navy
Lieutenant **Brian Beven Russell**	Irish Guards
Pilot Officer **Frederick Eustace Stronge**	RAFVR
Sergeant (Air Gunner) **Thomas Torney**	RAFVR
Flying Officer (Pilot) **Gordon Elgin Vance**	RCAF
Chief ERA **Christopher Vivash**	Royal Navy
Squadron Leader **Thomas George Westlake**	Royal Air Force
Able Seaman **John White**	Merchant Navy
Pilot **William White**	Pilot Launch
Able Seaman **William Charles Woods**	Royal Navy

GREYABBEY AND DISTRICT

Able Seaman **James Francis Bailie**	Royal Navy
Flight Sergeant **Hugh Baird**	RNZAF
Flight Sergeant **William Barraclough**	RAFVR
Sergeant **Walter Edward Fern**	RAFVR
Flight Sergeant **Andrew Greenwell Gibbison**	RNZAF
Lance Corporal **John Mawhinney**	Royal Irish Fusiliers
Wg Cdr **Malcolm Morgan McMullan MID**	Royal Air Force
Flight Sergeant **Raymond Farquhar Simpson**	RNZAF

GROOMSPORT AND DISTRICT

Major **Robert Henry Cutler**	King's African Rifles
Leading Stoker **Robert Heyburn Duff**	Royal Navy
Able Seaman **George Victor Lowry**	Royal Navy
Sergeant **Richard Mailey**	RAFVR
Lance Corporal **William Murray McKelvey**	Highland Light Infantry
Lt Cdr **William Robert Patterson OBE DSC**	Royal Navy
Captain **Robert Patrick Perceval-Maxwell**	KRRC
FO **Alexander Arthur Fenwich T Steavenson**	RAFVR
Master **Arthur Hill Coates Waterson**	Merchant Navy

HOLYWOOD AND DISTRICT

Staff Sergeant **Thomas Anthoney**	RAMC
Sergeant **Benjamin Beeby**	Royal Scots Fusiliers
Sergeant **Reginald Austin Bigger**	Royal Air Force
Fusilier **Frederick Bloomfield**	R Innis Fus
Bombardier **Thomas Wesley Boyd**	Royal Artillery
Lance Sergeant **Ronald Chapman**	East Lancashire Regt
Marine **Samuel Clydesdale**	Royal Marines
Convoy Signalman **Hugh Douglas Cole**	Royal Navy
Captain **Thomas Oswald Corrin**	Royal Artillery
Able Seaman **David Cowan**	RNVR
Sergeant **George Stewart Crossan**	Royal Air Force
Gunner **James Cartner Dixon**	Royal Artillery
Major **Walter Raleigh Draper**	RAOC
Civilian **Edith Dunwoody**	Civilian War Dead
Civilian **Henry Dunwoody**	Civilian War Dead
Civilian **Isabella Dunwoody**	Civilian War Dead
Civilian **William Dunwoody**	Civilian War Dead
Pilot Officer (Pilot) **Basil Pollock Erskine**	Royal Air Force
Lt Cdr (E) **John Gordon Morrison Erskine**	Royal Navy
Lt (E) **Thomas Hugh Cecil Hickland Fee**	Royal Naval Reserve
LAC **Clifford Samuel Ferguson**	RAFVR
Signalman **Arthur Donald Field MID**	RNVR
Private **John Matthew Forshaw**	East Lancashire Regt
Fusilier **William Fox**	R Innis Fus
Flight Sergeant **David Harrison Freeland**	RAFVR
2nd Engineer Officer **Reginald William D Gibbs**	Merchant Navy
Pilot Officer **James Hamilton Gordon**	Royal Air Force
Civilian **Nancy Simms Gribbin**	Civilian War Dead
Private **Alfred Hayes**	Royal Ulster Rifles
Corporal **Henry Heaven**	Border Regiment
Flight Sergeant **John Stewart Hill**	RAFVR
Private **Archibald Joseph Adolphus Holt**	RAOC
Sub-Lieutenant (A) **Edmund John Hoy**	South African Forces
Sergeant (Pilot) **John Cecil Brandon Irwin**	RAFVR
Flight Lieutenant **William Thomas Irwin**	RAFVR
Master **John Frazer Jefferson**	Merchant Navy
Warrant Officer **Thomas Francis Jefferson**	RAFVR
Private **Samuel Kirham**	Durham Light Infantry
Private **Robert Richard Lacey**	General Service Corps

Holywood and District continued...

Second Officer **George McClelland Leckey**	Merchant Navy
Sister **Muriel Emily Leckey**	QAIMNS
Civilian **Julie Maude Macoun**	Civilian War Dead
Civilian **Leslie Stuart Macoun**	Civilian War Dead
Lance Bombardier **James Murphy Mair**	Royal Artillery
Private **Frank Mason**	Gloucestershire Regt
Ordinary Seaman **Alfred George McDowell**	Royal Navy
Rifleman **John McFarlane**	Royal Ulster Rifles
Petty Officer **Hugh McNally**	Royal Navy
Sergeant **Leslie Tom Measday**	RAOC
Sergeant (Air Gunner) **Stanley Minnis**	RAFVR
Flying Officer **Francis Raymond Moore**	Royal Air Force
Lance Bombardier **Francis Xavier Mulligan**	Royal Artillery
Pilot Officer (Pilot) **Ian Lindsay Munce**	RAFVR
Fusilier **Joseph Nixon**	R Innis Fus
Second Lieutenant **Michael Kenny Pendlebury**	East Lancashire Regt
Brigadier **Robert D B Perrott DSO OBE MC**	Royal Engineers
Lance Bombardier **William Ward Phillips**	Royal Artillery
6th Engineer Officer **Hugh Longueville Price**	Merchant Navy
Sergeant **Alexander L Quillan**	Royal Air Force
Flight Sergeant **Gordon Wemyss Reid**	Royal Air Force
Private **Leonard Stanley Reid**	Northamptonshire Regt
Corporal **Martin Ryan**	East Lancashire Regt
Third Engineer Officer **Albert Sandfield**	Merchant Navy
Flight Sergeant (Pilot) **Edmund Verner Shaw**	RAFVR
Sergeant (Air Gunner) **Eric Shaw**	RAFVR
Sergeant (Pilot) **Victor Hall Skillen**	RAFVR
Captain **John Frederick Smellie**	Army Air Corps
Pilot Officer **Wallace Robert Smyth**	RAFVR
Chief Engineer (Marine) **John James Tait**	Holywood War Mem
Flight Sergeant (Pilot) **John McCalla Tait**	RAFVR
L/Cpl **Alexander Richard Day Vinycomb MM**	Royal Engineers
Private **Leslie Waite**	East Lancashire Regt
Lieutenant **William Ernest Watson**	Royal Armoured Corps
Sergeant **Patrick Leslie Whitehouse**	East Lancashire Regt
Driver **Sidney John Wren**	RASC
Fusilier **Albert John Young**	R Innis Fus
Lance Corporal **George Henry Young**	R Innis Fus

KILLINCHY AND DISTRICT

Sub-Lieutenant **Samuel Jamieson Fitchie**	Royal Navy
Master **William Johnston Meek**	Merchant Navy

KIRCUBBIN, GRANSHA, BALLYCRANBEG AND DISTRICT

Corporal **Andrew Ennis**	Royal Armoured Corps
Flight Sergeant **Stanislaw Grondowski**	Polish Forces
Sergeant **Wladyslaw Kolek**	Polish Forces
Fireman **Francis Maginnis (Maginness)**	Merchant Navy
Aircraftman First Class **John Harold Maxwell**	RAFVR
ERA Fourth Class **Donald McClement**	Royal Navy
Lieutenant (A) **Frank Wilfred McGarry**	RCNVR
Rifleman **Hugh Henry McGlennon MM**	Royal Ulster Rifles
Pilot Officer **Walter Bartholomew McManus**	RCAF
Second Lieutenant **William Laurence Megaw**	R Innis Fus
Pilot Officer **Jerzy Ryszard Tuczemski**	Polish Forces
Able Seaman **James White**	Merchant Navy
Leading Aircraftman **Leslie Frederick Williams**	RAFVR
Sergeant **William Richard Willis**	RAFVR

MONEYREAGH AND DISTRICT

Able Seaman **William Jordan Cooke**	Royal Navy
Civilian **Margaret Kate McGowan**	Civilian War Dead

NEWTOWNARDS AND DISTRICT

Corporal **John Ancham**	Hampshire Regiment
Sergeant **William Anderson**	Royal Scots Fusiliers
Marine **William Thomas Anderson MID**	Royal Marines
Sergeant **Maxwell Warnock Apperson**	Royal Air Force
Gunner **William Robert Bailie**	Royal Artillery
Flight Sergeant **Alex Joseph Bell**	RAFVR
Fusilier **William Bellamy**	R Innis Fus
Private **John George Benson**	Pioneer Corps
Rifleman **John Harold Blythe**	Royal Ulster Rifles

Newtownards and District continued...

Private Hugh Brown Boal	RCIC
Flt Lt Wilfrid Mark Hamilton Brookes	Royal Air Force
Gunner John Brown	Royal Artillery
Fusilier Samuel Burke	R Innis Fus
Sergeant Henry Garrett Burrows	RCAC
Private Robert Byers	Royal Berkshire Regt
Trooper John Bennett Campbell	Royal Armoured Corps
Lance Corporal Alexander Carlisle	R Innis Fus
Sergeant Thomas Carnduff	RAFVR
Sergeant Robert Clarke	Royal Air Force
Able Seaman Thomas John Cochrane	Royal Navy
Fusilier Andrew Copling	R Innis Fus
Flying Officer William Howard Corbett	RAFVR
Sergeant David Corry	Royal Scots Fusiliers
Gunner Henry Corry	Royal Artillery
Captain Samuel David Corry MID	RAMC
Gunner Joseph Dalzell	Royal Artillery
Sergeant Alexander Davidson	Royal Artillery
Able Seaman Alexander Doak	Royal Navy
Flight Sergeant Thomas Watters Doggart	RAFVR
Flt Lt Robert Aubrey Alexander Doherty DFC	RAFVR
Sergeant Thomas Ernest Victor Doherty	RAFVR
Sergeant David Stuart Donaldson	RAFVR
Sergeant Thomas Norman Dunlop	RAFVR
Able Seaman Hugh Alexander Eagleson	Royal Navy
Gunner John Edmonds	Royal Artillery
Sergeant Robert Keith Eston	Royal Armoured Corps
Sergeant Henryk Andrzej Flegier	Polish Forces
Lance Bombardier Edward James Flynn	Royal Artillery
Sergeant Rudolph Angel Antonio Forte	RAFVR
Fusilier Hugh Fulton	R Innis Fus
Gunner Hugh Gamble	Royal Artillery
Lieutenant John Malcomson Gibson	Royal Artillery
Warrant Officer William Gallagher Gordon	RAFVR
Fusilier George Graham	R Innis Fus
Fusilier James Graham	Royal Scots Fusiliers
Flight Sergeant John Thompson Graham	RAFVR
Gunner Samuel Graham	Royal Artillery
Driver William Graham	RASC
Gunner William Graham	Royal Artillery

Newtownards and District continued...

Flying Officer George Desmond Hamilton	RAFVR
Able Seaman Robert George Hamilton	Royal Navy
Corporal John Hardy	Royal Air Force
Sergeant Henry Victor Hawkins	RAFVR
Wg Cdr Wladyslaw Eugeniusz Heller	Polish Forces
Private Hugh Robert Hewitt	OBLI
Fusilier Daniel Higgins	R Innis Fus
Sapper Henry Houghton	Royal Engineers
Stoker First Class Robert James Hoy	Royal Navy
Driver James Walter Hubbard	RASC
Corporal William James Hunter	Royal Air Force
Driver John Hutchinson	RASC
Leading Aircraftwoman Annie Irvine	WAAF
Flying Officer Robert Keith James	RAFVR
Bombardier Harold Johnston	Royal Artillery
Ordinary Seaman John Johnston	Royal Navy
Rifleman William Johnston	Royal Ulster Rifles
Lance Corporal James Keenan	Royal Ulster Rifles
Sergeant Thomas Leonard Kirk	Royal Artillery
Kapral (LAC) Henryk Komenda	Polish Forces
Craftsman Wilfred Leitch	REME
Sergeant (Kapral Pilot) Edward Lewandowski	Polish Forces
Fusilier Leslie Love	R Innis Fus
Pilot Officer William Moody MacDonald	Royal Air Force
Sergeant John Patterson MacIlwaine	Royal Air Force
Private Robert James Major	RCIC
J W Martin	RHS Newtownards
Rifleman Charles Maxwell	Royal Ulster Rifles
Gunner William McBlain	Royal Artillery
Private Samuel McBride	Monmouthshire Regt
Gunner David McClinton	Royal Artillery
Private Alexander McCullough	Beds and Herts Regt
Fusilier Samuel McFarland	R Innis Fus
Civilian Bertha McGowan	Civilian War Dead
Civilian William McGowan	Civilian War Dead
Civilian Margaret Kate McGowan	Civilian War Dead
George McKee	Newtownards War Mem
Guardsman Norman McKimm	Irish Guards
John McManus	Newtownards War Mem
CQMS William McMurray	R Innis Fus

Newtownards and District continued...

Fusilier **Ernest McNeill**	R Innis Fus
Private **John Gracie McNeilly**	Seaforth Highlanders
Bombardier **William John McNeilly**	Royal Artillery
Leading Aircraftman **Norman McReynolds**	Royal Air Force
Lance Corporal **Andrew McVeigh**	R Innis Fus
Gunner **James Meredith**	Royal Artillery
Aircraftman First Class **Francis Meredith**	RAFVR
Lance Sergeant **John Meredith**	R Innis Fus
LAC **Frederick Armand Morrison**	Royal Air Force
Galley Boy **William James Morrow**	Merchant Navy
Civilian **Thomas Morton**	Civilian War Dead
Gunner **William Hugh Murphy**	Royal Artillery
Air Gunner **Sydney Murray**	Royal Air Force
Flight Sergeant (Air Bomber) **Ronald Nelson**	RAFVR
Private **Thomas Newell**	Worcestershire Regt
Sergeant (Air Gunner) **James Ernest Nicholls**	RAFVR
Corporal **Henry Oliver**	OBLI
Fusilier **William Radcliffe Partridge**	Royal Welch Fusiliers
Warrant Officer Class II (CSM) **Alfred Penfold**	R Innis Fus
Sergeant **Peter Charles Hunter Phillips**	RAFVR
WO Class II (CSM) **Edward Potts DCM**	East Lancashire Regt
Fusilier **David Francis Prosser**	Royal Welch Fusiliers
Driver **Hugh Erin Reid**	Royal Engineers
Second Lieutenant **Robert James Reid**	Royal Artillery
Able Seaman **Francis Robinson**	Royal Navy
Leading Aircraftman **Henry Dougan Sandford**	Royal Air Force
Ordinary Seaman **David Scott**	Royal Navy
Gunner **Joseph Shanks**	Royal Artillery
William Shaw	Newtownards War Mem
Fusilier **William John Shields**	R Innis Fus
Rifleman **Charles Smart**	Royal Ulster Rifles
Able Seaman **Samuel Smith**	Royal Navy
Trooper **Aaron Smyth**	Royal Armoured Corps
Rifleman **Joseph Smyth**	Royal Ulster Rifles
Pilot Officer **Gerald Cecil William Stone MID**	Royal Air Force
Civilian **Ellen Ogle Tate**	Civilian War Dead
Civilian **Elizabeth Tate**	Civilian War Dead
Civilian **Evelyn Tate**	Civilian War Dead
Lance Bombardier **Robert Orr Thompson**	Royal Horse Artillery
Ordinary Seaman **William James Tweed**	Royal Navy

Newtownards and District continued...

Corporal **Albert Charles Tyler**	Royal Armoured Corps
Rifleman **Robert Warden**	Royal Ulster Rifles
Able Seaman **Robert John Warden**	Royal Navy
LAC **Thomas Henderson Watson**	Royal Air Force
Lieutenant (A) **George Leslie Werts**	RNVR
Corporal **James H Whelan**	Royal Air Force
Second Officer **Leonard Whiston**	Merchant Navy
Sergeant **Alfred White**	Royal Air Force
Private **Herbert Anthony White**	RCIC
Flying Officer (Pilot) **Douglas Williams**	RCAF
Corporal **John Williams**	R Innis Fus
Fireman **Garner McCartney Wilson**	Merchant Navy
Flight Sergeant **George Wilson**	Royal Air Force
Pilot Officer **Hugh Wilson**	RAFVR
Fusilier **Matthew Wright**	R Innis Fus
LAC **Richard George Yeaman**	RAFVR
Fusilier **George Burch Young**	Royal Scots Fusiliers
Private **Hugh Young**	Australian Infantry

PORTAFERRY AND DISTRICT
(including BALLYGALGET)

3rd Engineer Officer **John George B Baxter**	Merchant Navy
Sergeant **Kennedy Boyd Black**	RAFVR
Sergeant **Frank Bennett Bloor**	RAFVR
Sapper **John Bowen**	Royal Engineers
Flight Lieutenant **Ephraim Hugh Brown**	RAFVR
Private **Robert Byers**	Royal Berkshire Regt
Barber **William James Canavan**	Merchant Navy
Flight Sergeant **Thomas Charles Crisp**	RAFVR
Fusilier **Edward Graham**	Royal Irish Fusiliers
Flying Officer (Pilot) **Raymond Hodgson**	RAFVR
Driver **Patrick Hynds**	RASC
Sergeant **Margaret Ann King**	AAMC
Fusilier **John Matthews**	R Innis Fus
Third Radio Officer **Charles Knox McCune**	Merchant Navy
Able Seaman **John McGrath**	Merchant Navy
Lieutenant **John Andrew Nugent**	Grenadier Guards
Lieutenant **Patrick Edmund Charles Nugent**	Grenadier Guards

Portaferry and District (including Ballygalget) continued...

Assistant Steward **Reginald John Primmer**	Merchant Navy
Sergeant (Pilot) **Peter Murray Rogerson**	RAFVR
Ordinary Seaman **Robert Joseph Shaw**	Merchant Navy
Warrant Officer Class III **Walter Stanley Smith**	Royal Artillery
Sergeant **George William Thomas Walker**	RAFVR
ACW2 **Jean Dibby Wright**	WAAF

STRANGFORD LOUGH

Captain **Maurice Evelyn Beale**	Royal Welch Fusiliers
Leading Aircraftman **Stanley Mynett**	RAFVR
2nd Lieutenant **William Edward David Paul**	Royal Welch Fusiliers
Sergeant (Pilot) **Victor Wadmore**	RAFVR

Cemeteries/Memorials by Country

In this Section, the names of the Cemeteries and CWGC Memorials where Second World War casualties with North Down/Ards connections are buried or commemorated are listed alphabetically by Country.

Algeria
> Bone War Cemetery, Annaba

Australia
> Goulburn General Cemetery, New South Wales

Belgium
> Bedford House Cemetery, Ieper, West-Vlaanderen
> Froyennes Communal Cemetery, Hainaut
> Heverlee War Cemetery, Leuven, Vlaams-Brabant
> Schoonselhof Cemetery, Antwerpen

Bermuda
> Bermuda Royal Naval Cemetery

Canada
> Ancaster (Bethesda United Church) Cemetery, Ontario
> Halifax Memorial, Nova Scotia
> Ottawa (Pinecrest) Cemetery, Ottawa
> Somenos (St. Mary's) Church Cemetery, British Columbia
> Toronto (St. James') Cemetery, Ontario
> Windsor (Grove) Cemetery, Ontario

Cyprus
> Nicosia War Cemetery

Denmark
> Aarhus West Cemetery

Egypt
> Alamein Memorial
> Alexandria (Chatby) Military and War Memorial Cemetery
> Alexandria (Hadra) War Memorial Cemetery
> Cairo War Memorial Cemetery
> El Alamein War Cemetery
> Suez War Memorial Cemetery

England – Derbyshire
> Ault Hucknall (St. John the Baptist) Churchyard Extension

England – Devon
    Plymouth Naval Memorial

England – Durham
    Gateshead (Saltwell) Cemetery
    Heworth (St. Mary) Churchyard

England – Essex
    East Ham (Marlow Road) Jewish Cemetery
    Southend-on-Sea (Sutton Road) Cemetery

England – Gloucestershire
    Bristol (Greenbank) Cemetery

England – Hampshire
    Gosport (Ann's Hill) Cemetery
    Lee-on-Solent Memorial
    Netley Military Cemetery
    Portsmouth Naval Memorial

England – Hertfordshire
    Bushey (St. James) Churchyard
    Watford North Cemetery

England – Kent
    Chatham Naval Memorial
    Chislehurst Cemetery
    Harbledown (St. Michael) Churchyard
    Ightham (St. Peter) Churchyard
    Shorne (St. Peter and St. Paul) Churchyard

England – Lancashire
    Blackpool (Carleton) Cemetery
    Chorley Cemetery
    Liverpool (Anfield) Cemetery
    Liverpool Naval Memorial
    Nelson Cemetery
    Newton-le-Willows Cemetery
    St. Helens Cemetery

England – Lincolnshire
    Grantham Cemetery
    Old Leake (St. Mary) Churchyard
    Wigtoft (St. Peter and St. Paul) Churchyard

England – London
     Eltham Cemetery, Woolwich
     Tower Hill Memorial
     Wandsworth (Streatham) Cemetery

England – Norfolk
     Great Yarmouth (Caister) Cemetery

England – Northamptonshire
     Peterborough (Eastfield) Cemetery
     Towcester Cemetery
     Wellingborough (Doddington Road) Cemetery

England – Nottinghamshire
     Beeston and Stapleford (Chilwell) Cemetery
     Carlton Cemetery
     Finningley (Holy Trinity and St. Oswald) Churchyard Extension
     Kingsway New Cemetery
     Nottingham Crematorium
     Sutton-in-Ashfield Cemetery

England – Oxfordshire
     Upper Heyford Cemetery

England – Shropshire
     Bridgnorth Cemetery

England – Suffolk
     Lowestoft Naval Memorial

England – Surrey
     Benhilton (All Saints Churchyard)
     Brookwood Memorial
     Mortlake Crematorium
     Runnymede Memorial
     Streatham Park Cemetery

England – Sussex
     Tangmere (St. Andrew) Churchyard

England – Warwickshire
     Stratford-on-Avon Cemetery

England – Wiltshire
     Idmiston (All Saints) Churchyard

England – Yorkshire
  Barmby-on-the-Moor (St. Catherine) Churchyard
  Campsall New Cemetery
  Harrogate (Stonefall) Cemetery
  Hatfield (Woodhouse) Cemetery
  Huddersfield (Edgerton) Cemetery
  Rawdon (St. Peter) Churchyard

France – Bas-Rhin
  Sessenheim Communal Cemetery

France – Calvados
  Banneville-La-Campagne War Cemetery
  Bayeux Memorial
  Bretteville-sur-Laize Canadian War Cemetery
  Cambes-en-Plaine War Cemetery
  Hermanville War Cemetery
  La Bigne Churchyard
  Ranville War Cemetery
  Ryes War Cemetery, Bazenville
  St. Charles de Percy War Cemetery
  Tilly-sur-Seulles War Cemetery

France – Hauts-de-Seine
  Clichy Northern Cemetery

France – Mayenne
  La Pellerine Communal Cemetery

France – Morbihan
  Guidel Communal Cemetery

France – Nord
  Croix Communal Cemetery
  Dunkirk Memorial
  Merville Communal Cemetery Extension

France – Oise
  Orry-la-Ville Dutch War Cemetery

France – Pas de Calais
  Pihen-les-Guines War Cemetery
  St. Inglevert Churchyard

France – Seine-Maritime
  Blangy-sur-Bresle Communal Cemetery

France – Seine-Maritime continued...

Dieppe Canadian War Cemetery, Hautot-sur-Mer
St. Sever Cemetery Extension, Rouen

France – Somme
St. Pierre Cemetery, Amiens

France – Yvelines
Viroflay New Communal Cemetery

Germany
Becklingen War Cemetery, Soltau, Niedersachsen
Berlin 1939-1945 War Cemetery
Durnbach War Cemetery, Bad Tolz, Bayern
Hamburg Cemetery
Kiel War Cemetery, Kiel, Schleswig-Holstein
Reichswald Forest War Cemetery, Kleve, Nordrhein-Westfalen
Rheinberg War Cemetery, Kamp Lintford, Nordrhein-Westfalen
Sage War Cemetery, Oldenburg, Niedersachsen

Greece
Athens Memorial

India
Kirkee War Cemetery
Madras War Cemetery, Chennai
Ranchi War Cemetery

Indonesia
Ambon War Cemetery
Jakarta War Cemetery

Isle of Man
Jurby (St. Patrick) Churchyard
Kirk Maughold (St. Maughold) Churchyard

Israel and Palestine (including Gaza)
Ramleh War Cemetery

Italy
Arezzo War Cemetery, Tuscany
Argenta Gap War Cemetery, Ferrara
Assisi War Cemetery, Perugia
Bari War Cemetery, Carbonara
Beach Head War Cemetery, Anzio

Italy continued...

Cassino War Cemetery, Cassino
Castiglione South African Cemetery, Bologna
Catania War Cemetery, Sicily
Cesena War Cemetery, Forli
Coriano Ridge War Cemetery, Romagna
Faenza War Cemetery, Romagna
Florence War Cemetery, Tuscany
Foiano Della Chiana War Cemetery, Tuscany
Gradara War Cemetery, Pesaro
Moro River Canadian War Cemetery, Abruzzo
Padua War Cemetery, Veneto
Sangro River War Cemetery, Abruzzo
Staglieno Cemetery, Liguria
Udine War Cemetery, Friuli-Venezia Giulia

Japan
Yokohama Cremation Memorial

Kenya
City Park Cemetery, Nairobi
Mombasa (Mbaraki) Cemetery

Libya
Benghazi War Cemetery
Knightsbridge War Cemetery, Acroma
Tobruk War Cemetery

Luxembourg
Luxembourg American Cemetery, Luxembourg City

Malaysia
Labuan War Cemetery

Malta
Malta Memorial, Floriana

Myanmar (Burma)
Rangoon Memorial
Taukkyan War Cemetery

Netherlands
Arnhem Oosterbeek War Cemetery, Gelderland
Bergen-op-Zoom War Cemetery, Noord-Brabant
Castricum Protestant Churchyard, Noord-Holland

Netherlands continued...

Doetinchem (Loolaan) General Cemetery, Gelderland
Eindhoven (Woensel) General Cemetery, Noord-Brabant
Gaasterland (Nijemirdum) General Cemetery, Friesland
Gorssel General Cemetery, Gelderland
Jonkerbos War Cemetery, Gelderland
Oldenzaal Protestant Cemetery, Overijssel
Valkenswaard War Cemetery, Noord-Brabant
Venray War Cemetery, Limburg

New Zealand
New Zealand Naval Memorial, Devonport, Auckland

Nigeria
Ikoyi No. 2 Cemetery

Northern Ireland – Antrim
Belfast City Cemetery
Belfast City Cemetery (Glenalina Extension)
Portrush Cemetery

Northern Ireland – Armagh
Belleek (St. Luke) Church of Ireland Churchyard
Bessbrook Methodist Cemetery
Drumcree Church of Ireland Churchyard
Mullaghglass (St. Luke) Church of Ireland Churchyard

Northern Ireland – Down
Ardglass (St. Nicholas) Church of Ireland Churchyard
Ballycranbeg (Mount St. Joseph) Roman Catholic Churchyard
Ballygowan Presbyterian Churchyard
Ballyhalbert (St. Andrew) Church of Ireland Churchyard
Bangor Cemetery
Belfast (Dundonald) Cemetery
Carrowdore (Christ Church) Church of Ireland Churchyard
Comber Cemetery
Donaghadee Church of Ireland Churchyard
Dromore Cathedral Churchyard
Eglantine Church of Ireland Cemetery, Lisburn (CWGC)
Holywood Cemetery
Killinchy Non Subscribing Presbyterian Churchyard
Killyleagh Church of Ireland Churchyard
Killysuggan Graveyard, Newtownards

Northern Ireland – Down continued...

Kircubbin Presbyterian Churchyard
Knockbreda Cemetery
Newtownards (Movilla) Cemetery
Whitechurch Cemetery Ballywalter

Northern Ireland – Londonderry

Drumachose Church of Ireland Churchyard
Glendermott Church of Ireland Churchyard
Londonderry City Cemetery
Macosquin (St. Mary) Church of Ireland Churchyard

Northern Ireland – Tyrone

Ardstraw Church of Ireland Churchyard, Newtownstewart
Cappagh (St. Eugenius) Church of Ireland Churchyard
Clogherney Church of Ireland Churchyard
Omagh (Dublin Road) Cemetery

Norway

Sola Churchyard
Sylling Churchyard

Pakistan

Karachi War Cemetery
Rawalpindi War Cemetery

Papua New Guinea

Lae War Cemetery
Port Moresby Memorial

Portugal

Lajes War Cemetery, Terceirs, Azores
Lisbon (St. George) British Churchyard

Scotland

Aberdeen (Allenvale) Cemetery, Aberdeenshire
Ardrossan Cemetery, Ayrshire
Arngask New Cemetery, Perthshire
Cadder Cemetery, Lanarkshire
Douglas Bank Cemetery, Rosyth
Glasgow (Cardonald) Cemetery
Kirkinner Cemetery, Wigtownshire
Montrose (Sleepy Hillock) Cemetery, Angus
Paisley (Hawkhead) Cemetery, Renfrewshire

Scotland continued...

Sannox Old Churchyard, Kilbride, Isle of Arran
Stoneykirk Cemetery, Wigtownshire
Troon Cemetery, Ayrshire

Singapore
Kranji War Cemetery
Singapore Memorial

South Africa
Bloemfontein (Hamilton) War Cemetery

Tunisia
Massicault War Cemetery
Medjez-el-Bab Memorial
Medjez-el-Bab War Cemetery
Sfax War Cemetery

United States of America
Miami (Grand Army of the Republic) Cemetery, Oklahoma
National Memorial Cemetery of the Pacific, Honolulu, Hawaii
Camp Butler National Cemetery, Illinois

Wales
Hawarden Cemetery, Flintshire

Names by Cemetery and/or CWGC Memorial

In this Section, the names of servicemen, servicewomen, nursing personnel and civilians with North Down/Ards connections who died in the Second World War are presented alphabetically by surname, in relation to the Cemetery and/or CWGC Memorial where they are buried and/or commemorated. Where there is a specific CWGC grave or memorial reference this is shown beside the casualty's name.

Aarhus West Cemetery, Denmark

Flight Sergeant **John Herbert Hamilton**   Row G Collective Grave 311

Aberdeen (Allenvale) Cemetery, Aberdeenshire, Scotland

Flight Sergeant **Robert Low**   Section D Grave 2068

Alamein Memorial, Alamein, Egypt

The campaign in the Western Desert was fought between the Commonwealth Forces based in Egypt (joined later by French, Greek and Polish forces) and the Axis Forces based in Libya. The battlefield comprised the 1,000 kilometres of desert between Alexandria in Egypt and Benghazi in Libya and the objectives included control of the Mediterranean, control of the link with the East through the Suez Canal, control of the Middle East oil supplies and control of the supply route to Russia through Persia (Iran).

The Alamein Memorial forms the entrance to the El Alamein War Cemetery and those commemorated include Commonwealth soldiers who died in various campaigns in Egypt, Iraq, Lebanon, Libya, Persia, Syria and Tunisia. Also commemorated are Commonwealth airmen who died in various campaigns in Aden, the Aegean, Crete, East Africa, Egypt, Eritrea, Ethiopia, Greece, Iraq, Lebanon, Libya, Madagascar, Somalia, Sudan and Syria.

Flight Lieutenant **Ephraim Hugh Brown**	Column 247
Lance Bombardier **Edward James Flynn**	Column 33
Trooper **George Griffith Griffiths**	Column 24
Corporal **William James Hunter**	Column 263
Sergeant **Thomas Leonard Kirk**	Column 31
Gunner **William McBlain**	Column 36
Lance Corporal **John McManus**	Column 55
Trooper **Thomas Shillington**	Column 24
Corporal **Albert Charles Tyler**	Column 30
Corporal **James Whelan**	Column 281

Alexandria (Chatby) Military and War Memorial Cemetery, Egypt

Like Hadra (see immediately below), Chatby is a district on the eastern side of the city of Alexandria. The cemetery at Chatby was used during the First World War until 1916 when a new cemetery was opened at Hadra. During the Second World War Alexandria was again an important Hospital Centre and casualties were brought from various campaigns in the Aegean Islands, Crete, Greece, the Mediterranean and the Western Desert. Also in Alexandria there were rest camps, an anti-aircraft base, a communications base and a Military Police headquarters.

Driver **Patrick Hynds** Grave N 131

Alexandria (Hadra) War Memorial Cemetery, Egypt

Like Chatby (see immediately above), Hadra is a district on the eastern side of the city of Alexandria. The cemetery at Hadra was extended for Second World War burials and was used from 1941.

Sergeant **William Duncan Irwin** Grave 6 B 9

Ambon War Cemetery, Indonesia

Ambon Island lies close to the south west coast of Seram (Ceram) in the Maluka (Molucca or Spice) Islands. During the Second World War, Ambon was the site of a Dutch military base which was captured from the Allied Forces by the Japanese Forces in the Battle of Ambon (February 1942). The base was used by the Japanese as a Prisoner-of-War Camp where many prisoners died of overwork, malnutrition, disease and the brutality of the camp regime.

Flying Officer **Francis Raymond Moore** Grave 6 A 10

Ancaster (Bethesda United Church) Cemetery, Ontario, Canada
Flight Lieutenant **Harold Abraham McCaghey** Shaver Family Plot

Ardglass (St. Nicholas) Church of Ireland Churchyard, Co. Down
Sergeant **George William Thomas Walker** Grave 2

Ardrossan Cemetery, Ayrshire, Scotland
Captain **Robert Ernest Kyle**

Ardstraw Church of Ireland Churchyard, Newtownstewart, Co. Tyrone
Sergeant **John Patterson MacIlwaine** Section E Grave 445

Arezzo War Cemetery, Tuscany, Italy

The Allied invasion of the Italian mainland began on 3 September 1943 near Reggio Calabria in the south followed by the Gulf of Salerno. The invasion coincided with an armistice made with the Italians who then re-entered the war on the Allied side. Progress through southern Italy was rapid but, by the end of October 1943, the Allies were facing the German winter defensive position known as the Gustav Line. This stretched from the river Garigliano in the west to the Sangro in the east. Initial attempts to breach the western end of the line were unsuccessful and the Allied advance halted. Allied operations in January 1944 landed troops behind the German lines at Anzio but defences were well organised and a breakthrough was not achieved until 18 May 1944 when Cassino was finally taken. Rome was taken on 3 June 1944. The Germans made a stand at Arezzo and there was fierce fighting before Arezzo was taken on 16 July 1944. Arezzo War Cemetery was established in November 1944 and burials were brought in from the surrounding area.

Sergeant **Terence John McQueen**	Grave II B 3
Rifleman **Robert Warden**	Grave V D 5

Argenta Gap War Cemetery, Ferrara, Italy

As the Germans retreated after Arezzo (see immediately above) they made successive stands in a series of defensive lines. In the northern Apennine Mountains the Gothic Line was breached by the Allies during the 1944 Autumn Campaign and the battle front moved forward to Ravenna in the Adriatic sector. There the Allied advance halted again as winter set in. At the beginning of April 1945 the Allies launched their final offensive against the German positions spread out in a line across Italy, south of Bologna. German resistance was by then diminishing and the Allies were able to fan out rapidly across the Po Valley. The Argenta Gap War Cemetery marks the final stages of the fighting in Italy.

Lance Sergeant **John Meredith**	Grave I B 17

Arngask New Cemetery, Perthshire, Scotland

Leading Aircraftman **John Connell Cowan**	Section 4 Grave 342

Arnhem Oosterbeek War Cemetery, Gelderland, Netherlands

Following the Normandy Landings of June 1944, the Allied Forces advanced through northern Europe and on 11 September 1944 the Second Army entered the Netherlands just south of Eindhoven. The next objective was to secure bridges at various places such as Grave, Nijmegan and Arnhem with a view to crossing the Rhine. In September 1944 the Commonwealth First

Airborne Division landed west of Arnhem and in the midst of fierce fighting formed a perimeter at Oosterbeek. Arnhem Oosterbeek War Cemetery contains the graves of many of those killed during the September landings together with those killed in later fighting in the area.

Captain **John Frederick Smellie**   Grave 6 A 4

Assisi War Cemetery, Perugia, Italy

In January 1944 Allied troops landed behind the German lines at Anzio in Italy but defences were well organised and a breakthrough was not achieved until 18 May 1944 when Cassino was finally taken. Rome was taken on 3 June 1944. Many of the burials in Assisi War Cemetery date from June and July 1944 when the Germans were trying to stop the Allied advance. The site for the cemetery was selected in September 1944 and burials were brought in from the surrounding battlefields.

Driver **Ronald James Buckingham**   Grave III C 12

Athens Memorial, Greece

The Athens Memorial stands within Phaleron War Cemetery and commemorates Commonwealth land forces with no known grave who lost their lives during the campaigns in Greece and Crete in 1941 and 1944/1945, the campaigns in the Dodecanese Islands in 1943/45 and the campaigns in Yugoslavia in 1943/1945.

Gunner **Hugh Gamble**   Face 2
Gunner **William Graham**   Face 2
Fusilier **James McMaster**   Face 7
Gunner **Edward Adam Moore**   Face 3

Ault Hucknall (St. John the Baptist) Churchyard Extn, Derbyshire, England
Corporal **Henry Oliver**   Row 9 Grave 10

Ballycranbeg (Mount St. Joseph) Roman Catholic Churchyard, Co. Down
Corporal **Andrew Ennis**   Plot 3 Row D Grave 4
Flight Sergeant **Stanislaw Grondowski**
Sergeant **Wladyslaw Kolek**
Lieutenant (A) **Frank Wilfred McGarry**   Grave 48
Pilot Officer **Walter Bartholomew McManus**   Grave 31
Pilot Officer **Jerzy Ryszard Tuczemski**
Sergeant **William Richard Willis**   Grave 34

Ballygowan Presbyterian Churchyard, Co. Down
Gunner **Hector Black**   Section E Row 6 Grave 63
Private **Andrew Leebody**   Section G Row 1 Grave 1

Ballyhalbert (St. Andrew's) Church of Ireland Churchyard, Co. Down
Pilot Officer **Frederick Hugh Anderson**   Grave 1
Sub-Lieutenant (A) **John Samuel Hornby**   Grave 5
Sergeant **Ross Wellesley Lindeman**   Grave 2
Flight Sergeant **John Robert Lucas**   Grave 3
Flight Sergeant **Stanley Donald Wills**   Grave 4

Balteagh Presbyterian Churchyard, Co. Londonderry
Sergeant **Kennedy Boyd Black**

Bangor Cemetery (formerly known as Bangor New Cemetery), Co. Down
Fireman and Trimmer **Shief Ahmed**   Section 5 X Grave 23 B
Engineer **William Anderson**   Section 4 U Grave 12
Carpenter **Thomas Smith Beckett**   Section 5 X Grave 21
Sergeant **Eric Ritchie Bowman**   Section 4 V Grave 82
Aircraftman 2nd Class **Cyril Charles Cameron**   Section 4 V Grave 86
Sapper **William Coffin**   Section 5 W Grave 95
Private **Robert Conway**   Section 6 P Grave 21 C
Pilot Officer **Derek Alfred Cook**   Section 3 L Grave 1 B
Corporal **James Darragh**   Section 5 X Grave 9
Private **Thomas Charles Deville**   Section 5 X Grave 1
Lance Corporal **Thomas Dickson**   Section 5 W Grave 79
Civilian **Patrick Edward Doran**   Section 1 A Grave 33
Leading Stoker **Robert Duff**   Section 5 X Grave 35
Lieutenant Commander (S) **George Ellis**   Section 4 U Grave 112
Surgeon **William Elliot Fraser**   Section 4 R Grave 158
Sergeant **William Francis Ernest Gault**   Section 4 V Grave 39
Civilian **Angeline Grattan**   Section 1 A Grave 164
Civilian **Matilda Grattan**   Section 1 A Grave 164
Civilian **Shelagh Grattan**   Section 1 A Grave 164
Second Lieutenant **John Nelson Hamilton**   Section 4 V Grave 41
Sub-Lieut (A) **David Francis Apperson Hollywood**   Section 7 Q Grave 25
Corporal **Hugh Kennedy**   Section 5 W Grave 37
Aircraftman Second Class **Arthur James King**   Section 4 V Grave 20
Private **Harold Lamb**   Section 5 X Grave 2
Captain **Edward E Lee**   Section 1 A Grave 124
Group Captain **John Evelyn Matier MacCallum**   Section 2 G Grave 76

Bangor Cemetery continued...

Pilot Officer **William Moody MacDonald**	Section 3 K Grave 160
Telegraphist **Albert George MacFarlane**	Section 5 Q Grave 181
Lance Bombardier **Edward Martin**	Section 3 K Grave 26
Engineer Commander **Leslie Henry Willis Mauger**	Section 4 V Grave 3
Sergeant **Herbert Reginald Megarry**	Section 4 V Grave 175
Leading Aircraftman **Frederick James Miley**	Section 1 C Grave 86
Flying Officer **William Watson Miller DFC**	Section 4 U Grave 113
Sergeant **William John Morrison**	Section 4 U Grave 24
Chief Engineer **John Gilkeson Nicholson**	Section 4 N Grave 153 A
Fusilier **Edward Francis Owen**	Section 5 X Grave 1 A
Corporal **Albert Edward Reuben**	Section 5 W Grave 90
Flying Officer **Robert Henry Rutherford**	Section 2 H Grave 166
Corporal **Francis Neville Sloss**	Section 1 D Grave 17
Colour Sergeant **Nathaniel Robert Smith**	Section 4 V Grave 27
Private **Thomas Stewart**	Section 4 V Grave 151 A
Private **Barry John Stubbings**	Section 5 X Grave 20
Rifleman **Ernest Oscar Thompson**	Section 4 U Grave 25
Robert Totton (Senior)	Section 5 X Grave 74
Sergeant **Ernest Watson**	Section 5 O Grave 82
Gunner **John White**	Section 5 X Grave 10
Aircraftman First Class **Robert Logan Wilson**	Section 4 R Grave 147
Sapper **Morrison Woods**	Section Wall Grave 369
Civilian **Robert Wright**	Section 1 C Grave 11

Banneville-La-Campagne War Cemetery, Calvados, Normandy, France

The Allied offensive in north-western Europe began with the Normandy Landings on 6 June 1944. Most of those buried in the Banneville-la-Campagne War Cemetery were killed in the fighting which took place between the second week of July 1944 when Caen was captured and the last week in August when the Falaise Gap had been closed and the Allied Forces were preparing their advance beyond the Seine towards Paris.

Lance Sergeant **Ronald Chapman**	Grave IV E 23

Bari War Cemetery, Carbonara, Italy

The Allied invasion of the Italian mainland began on 3 September 1943 near Reggio Calabria in the south followed by the Gulf of Salerno. The invasion coincided with an armistice made with the Italians who then re-entered the war on the Allied side. The town of Bari was an important supply base and hospital centre.

Bari War Cemetery, Carbonara, Italy continued...

Private **Stewart Courtney**   Grave VI D 20

Barmby-on-the-Moor (St. Catherine) Churchyard, Yorkshire, England
The Parish Church of St. Catherine in the village of Barmby-on-the-Moor was used by personnel on the RAF base at nearby Pocklington.

Sergeant **Maxwell Warnock Apperson**   Row F Grave 1

Bayeux Memorial, Calvados, Normandy, France
The Allied offensive in north-western Europe began with the Normandy Landings on 6 June 1944. The Bayeux Memorial bears the names of men who died in the early stages of the campaign and have no known grave. They died during the landings in Normandy, during the intense fighting in Normandy and during the advance to the River Seine in August 1944.

Private **George Boyling**   Panel 16 Column 2
Fusilier **William Radcliffe Partridge**   Panel 14 Column 2

Beach Head War Cemetery, Anzio, Italy
In January 1944 Allied troops landed behind the German lines at Anzio (a coastal town 70 kilometres south of Rome) but defences were well organised and a breakthrough was not achieved until May 1944. Rome was taken on 3 June 1944. The site chosen for Beach Head War Cemetery lay close to a casualty clearing station. Burials were made direct from the battlefield after the landings at Anzio and later, after the Army had moved forward, many burials were brought in from the surrounding country.

Captain **Robert Neville Desmond Young MID**   Grave XX C 1

Becklingen War Cemetery, Soltau, Niedersachsen, Germany
Becklingen War Cemetery is located on a hillside overlooking Luneburg Heath which is where Field-Marshal Montgomery accepted the German surrender from Admiral Doenitz on 4 May 1945. Most of those buried in Becklingen War Cemetery died during the last two months of the war.

Corporal **John Ancham**   Grave 4 K 11
Rifleman **Hugh Henry McGlennon MM**   Grave 8 G 10
Lance Bombardier **Francis Xavier Mulligan**   Grave 7 J 7
Second Lieutenant **Michael Kenny Pendlebury**   Grave 6 E 6
Warrant Officer Class II (CSM) **Edward Potts DCM**   Grave 1 B 5

Bedford House Cemetery, Ieper, West-Vlaanderen, Belgium

Bedford House Cemetery contains the graves of British Expeditionary Force soldiers who died in the defence of the Ypres-Comines canal and railway at the end of May 1940.

Fusilier **George Young**   Enclosure 6 V C 9

Beeston and Stapleford (Chilwell) Cemetery, Nottinghamshire, England

Aircraftman 2nd Class **Ernest Alfred Llewellyn Jones**   Section A 4 C Grave 10

Belfast Cemeteries (City, Dundonald and Milltown)

During the Second World War Belfast was a Naval Base of the Western Approaches Command, Fighter Command Headquarters for the defence of naval anchorages in Northern Ireland and a Hospital Centre. There was a Royal Air Force station at the airport; Victoria Barracks in Belfast was the Headquarters of Northern Ireland District; there was a Prisoner-of-War Camp at Holywood and a Prisoner-of-War Military Hospital at Orangefield.

Belfast City Cemetery, Co. Antrim

Lieutenant **James Sinclair Adair**	Section H Grave 471
Lieutenant **James Craig** MID (2 bars)	Section G 2 Grave 593
Civilian **Thomas Gardiner Ferguson**	Section K2 Grave 145

Belfast City Cemetery (Glenalina Extension), Co. Antrim

Sub-Lieutenant (A) **William Foster**	Section D Joint Grave 22
Rifleman **William Fox**	Section U 1 Grave 214
Sergeant **Robert Trevor Gibson**	Section B Grave 68
Sub-Lieutenant (A) **Edmund John Hoy**	Section D Grave 103
Gunner **John Madden**	Section AS Grave 118
Sub-Lieutenant (A) **John Esmond Marshall**	Section D Grave 30
Sub-Lieutenant (A) **John Richard Mathers**	Section D Joint Grave 22
Lieutenant **Edward Victor Polley**	Section J Grave 38
Lieutenant (A) **George Leslie Werts**	Section D Grave 24
Flying Officer **Douglas Williams**	Section A S Grave 21

Belfast (Dundonald Cemetery), Co. Down

Fusilier **George Graham**	Section E 1 Grave 490
Flying Officer **George Desmond Hamilton**	Section B 5 Grave 243
Leading Aircraftman **Robert Stanley Hegan**	Section F 5 Grave 175
Flight Sergeant **Edmund Verner Shaw**	Section D 4 Grave 105
Trooper **Aaron Smyth**	Section A 3 Grave 586
Pilot Officer **Thomas Norman Stockdale**	Section D 1 Joint Grave 306

Belfast (Dundonald Cemetery), Co. Down continued...

Civilian **Ellen Ogle Tate**	Section D 2 Grave 392
Civilian **Elizabeth Tate**	Section D 2 Grave 392
Civilian **Evelyn Tate**	Section D 2 Grave 392
Second Lieutenant **Robert Arnold Thompson**	Section C 1 Grave 9
Gunner **John Thomson**	Section D 1 Joint Grave 306
Military Policeman **Frederick James Woods**	Section D 1 Grave 477

Belfast (Milltown Cemetery)

Sergeant **Edward Lewandowski**	Section A Row Lg Grave 39
Sergeant **Josef Antoni Pudelko**	Section A Row Lg Grave 38

Belleek (St. Luke) Church of Ireland Churchyard, Co. Armagh
Fusilier **Hugh Fulton**

Benghazi War Cemetery, Libya
Benghazi in Libya was an important objective for both Allied and Axis Forces during the Western Desert campaigns of 1942 and 1943.

Flight Lieutenant **Patrick Joseph Anthony Byers**	Grave 8 E 17
Driver **John Hutchinson**	Grave 4 E 10
Private **Norman Strahan McKee**	Grave 7 D 31
Bombardier **Francis Eric Sheals**	Grave 7 C 5

Benhilton (All Saints Churchyard), Surrey, England

Sergeant **Victor Wadmore**	Grave South of Church

Bergen-op-Zoom War Cemetery, Noord-Brabant, Netherlands
Bergen-op-Zoom is a town in the Dutch Province of Noord-Brabant, about 40 kilometres north-west of Antwerp in Belgium. Many of the casualties buried in this cemetery fell during the Battle for Walcheren at the beginning of November 1944. Dominating the entrance to the River Scheldt, Walcheren was an island which the Germans fortified to prevent the Allies gaining access to the vital deep water port at Antwerp. After a hard fought battle the island was secured by the Allies on 8 November 1944.

Lance Corporal **William Murray McKelvey**	Grave 8 C 18

Berlin 1939-1945 War Cemetery, Berlin, Germany
The site for the Berlin 1939-1945 War Cemetery was chosen jointly by the British Occupation Authorities and War Grave Commission officials in

1945, soon after hostilities ended.

Flight Sergeant Ian (John) Gordon Campbell	Collective Grave 8 J 11-12
Sergeant Rudolph Angel Antonio Forte	Collective Grave 6 A 13-16
Bombardier Thomas McCutcheon	Grave 10 K 1
Sergeant Robert McKeag	Grave 7 J 21
Sergeant Peter Tristan Smith	Grave 2 L 19

Bermuda Royal Naval Cemetery, Bermuda

Bermuda had significant dockyards and naval establishments and during the Second World War, the United States established naval and air bases on land leased by the British Government. The Royal Air Force base on Darrell's Island was used for the ferrying of aircraft from the United States to Africa across the 'South Atlantic Bridge'.

Sub-Lieutenant (E) Samuel McMaster Boyd	Grave 427

Bessbrook Methodist Cemetery, Co. Armagh
Company Quartermaster Sergeant William McMurray

Blackpool (Carleton) Cemetery, Lancashire, England

Private Derek Rodney Swift	Section B Grave 1130

Blangy-sur-Bresle Communal Cemetery, Seine-Maritime, France

Private John Gracey McNeilly	Grave 1

Bloemfontein (Hamilton) War Cemetery, South Africa

During the Second World War, a military hospital was established in the Tempe Military Camp, which also housed the headquarters of the Orange Free State Command. Numbers 27 and 62 Air Schools were operated from the Bloemspruit Aerodrome very close to the city, where training was carried out under the Empire Air Training Scheme.

Pilot Officer (Flying Instructor) Deryk Jay Bleakley	European Block Grave 7

Bone War Cemetery, Annaba, Algeria

Allied troops made a series of landings on the Algerian coast in early November 1942. From there they advanced into Tunisia where the North African campaign came to an end in May 1943 with the surrender of the Axis Forces. Bone was occupied by the Allied Forces on 12 November 1942 and became an important supply port, airfield and hospital base.

Driver Kenneth Herbert Andow	Grave VIII B 3

Bretteville-sur-Laize Canadian War Cemetery, Calvados, France

Most of those buried in this cemetery died during the later stages of the Battle of Normandy, the capture of Caen and the thrust southwards to close the Falaise Gap (led initially by the 4th Canadian and 1st Polish Armoured Divisions).

Sergeant **James Campbell**	Grave X D 4

Bridgnorth Cemetery, Shropshire, England

Lieutenant (A) **Richard Herbert Ridley**	Grave 1064

Bristol (Greenbank) Cemetery, Gloucestershire, England

Squadron Leader **Thomas George Westlake**	Screen Wall PP 94

Brookwood Memorial, Surrey, England

The Brookwood Memorial in Brookwood Military Cemetery commemorates almost 3,500 men and women of the Commonwealth land forces who died during the Second World War and have no known grave. The circumstances of their deaths are such that they could not be commemorated on any of the campaign memorials in the various Theatres of War.

Lance Corporal **William Young Brown**	Panel 21 Column 1
Lance Corporal **Alexander Carlisle**	Panel 11 Column 2
Private **Archibald Crozier**	Panel 20 Column 3
Driver **George William Evens**	Panel 16 Column 2
Sister **Muriel Emily Leckey**	Panel 22 Column 2
Sapper **Joseph William Ogram**	Panel 6 Column 3
Second Lieutenant **William Edward David Paul**	Panel 11 Column 1

Brookwood Military Cemetery, Surrey, England

Brookwood Military Cemetery is owned by the Commonwealth War Graves Commission and is the largest Commonwealth war cemetery in the United Kingdom, covering approximately 37 acres.

Private **Robert James Major**	Grave 54 G 4
Wing Commander **Victor Edwin Maxwell MID (2 bars)**	Grave 21 C 5

Bushey (St. James) Churchyard, Hertfordshire, England

Flight Sergeant **Gordon Wemyss Reid**	Section A Grave 23

Cadder Cemetery, Lanarkshire, Scotland

Leading Aircraftman **Thomas Henderson Watson**	Section C Grave 127

Cairo War Memorial Cemetery, Egypt

General Headquarters, Middle East Command, was established in Cairo shortly before the start of the Second World War and it remained there for the duration of the war. In January 1941, a Royal Air Force Sector Headquarters for Fighter Defence Canal Zone was established in Cairo. Cairo was an important hospital centre during the Second World War.

Corporal **James Rowan**   Grave K 3

Cambes-en-Plaine War Cemetery, Calvados, France

The Allied offensive in north-western Europe began with the Normandy Landings on 6 June 1944. A unit of the East Riding Yeomanry RAC in support of the 3rd British Infantry Division reached the northern outskirts of Cambes-en-Plaine on 9 June. They found the Germans well dug in and the advance to Caen was halted. The original burials date from 8 to 12 July 1944, when the final attack on Caen (*Operation Charnwood*) was in progress. By noon on 9 July, most of Caen, north of the river Orne, had been captured. More than half of the burials here belong to the 59th (Staffordshire) Division, in particular units of The South and North Staffordshire Regiments which were involved in this battle.

Lieutenant **Denis Harold Smallman**   Row G 2

Camp Butler National Cemetery, Illinois, USA

Private First Class **James Polley**   Plot C Grave 214

Campsall New Cemetery, Yorkshire, England

Leading Aircraftman **Stanley Mynett**   Grave B 34

Cappagh (St. Eugenius) Church of Ireland Churchyard, Co. Tyrone

Sergeant **William Des Brisay Gilmour**

Carlton Cemetery, Nottinghamshire, England

Sergeant **Frank Bennett Bloor**   Section A Row M 6 Grave 190
Fusilier **Leslie Love**   Section B Row M 6 Grave 8

Carrowdore (Christ Church) Churchyard, Co. Down

Aircraftman Second Class **James McBride**   Section N Grave 174
Leading Aircraftman **Richard George Yeaman**   Section N Grave 122

Cassino Memorial and Cassino War Cemetery, Cassino, Italy

Arezzo War Cemetery has details about the war in Italy up until 18 May

1944 when Cassino was finally taken. The site for Cassino War Cemetery was originally selected in January 1944, but the development of the battle during the first five months of that year made it impossible to use it until after the Germans had withdrawn from Cassino. During these early months of 1944, Cassino saw some of the fiercest fighting of the Italian campaign, the town itself and the dominating Monastery Hill proving the most stubborn obstacles encountered in the advance towards Rome. The majority of those buried in the war cemetery died in the battles during these months. Within the cemetery stands the Cassino Memorial which commemorates over 4,000 Commonwealth servicemen who took part in the Italian campaign and whose graves are not known.

Cassino Memorial, Italy

Corporal **Andrew Eccles**	Panel 7
Fusilier **Edward Graham**	Panel 11
Fusilier **Spencer Jones**	Panel 6
Guardsman **William Pollock**	Panel 4

Cassino War Cemetery, Italy

Captain **Robert Patrick Perceval-Maxwell**	Grave XIX J 7
Captain **Charles Arthur Rea**	Grave VII J 14
Corporal **John Williams**	Grave XI A 7

Castiglione South African Cemetery, Bologna, Italy

Following the fall of Rome to the Allies in June 1944, the German retreat was ordered and successive stands were made on a series of defensive lines. In the northern Apennine Mountains the last of these, the Gothic Line, was breached by the Allied Forces during the autumn campaign and the front inched forward as far as Ravenna in the Adriatic Sector. After Allied Divisions were transferred to support the new offensive in France, and the Germans dug in to a number of key defensive positions, the advance stalled as winter set in. Castiglione South African Cemetery was started in November 1944 by the 6th South African Armoured Division, which had entered Castiglione at the end of September and remained in the area until the following April. Many of the burials were made direct from the battlefields of the Apennines, where during that winter South African troops held positions some 8 kilometres north of Castiglione. The majority of those buried in this cemetery were South Africans, the remainder belonging mostly to the 24th Guards Brigade, which was under command of the 6th South African Armoured Division.

Lieutenant **John Andrew Nugent**	Grave I D 21

Castricum Protestant Churchyard, Noord-Holland, Netherlands

Commonwealth Forces suffered casualties when the Netherlands fell to the Germans on 14 May 1940 and more when the Allied Forces returned between September 1944 and April 1945. In the intervening years, many airmen were shot down or crashed in raids on strategic objectives in the Netherlands, or while returning from missions over Germany.

Pilot Officer **John Stanley Smyth**   Plot J Collective Grave 7

Catania War Cemetery, Sicily, Italy

Following the successful conclusion of the North African Campaign in mid May 1943, a combined Allied force of Commonwealth and American troops invaded Sicily on 10 July 1943. This was a prelude to the assault on mainland Italy. German opposition was intense but the Italians offered little resistance and shortly thereafter the Italians made peace with the Allies and re-entered the war on their side. The campaign in Sicily came to an end on 17 August 1943 when the two Allied Forces came together at Messina, but failed to cut off the retreating Axis Forces. Catania War Cemetery contains burials from the later stages of the campaign, from Lentini northwards. Many died in the heavy fighting just short of the town of Catania, taken on 5 August, and in the battle for the Simeto River bridgehead.

Sapper **John Bowen**   Grave I E 34
Fusilier **John Matthews**   Grave I D 18
Lieutenant **Brian Thomas Stewart Rothwell**   Grave II G 17

Cesena War Cemetery, Forli, Italy

In January 1944 Allied troops landed behind the German lines at Anzio in Italy but defences were well organised and a breakthrough was not achieved until 18 May 1944 when Cassino was finally taken. As the Germans retreated, they made successive stands in a series of defensive lines. In the northern Apennine Mountains the Gothic line was breached by the Allies during the 1944 Autumn Campaign and the battle front moved forward to Ravenna in the Adriatic Sector. There the Allied advance halted again as winter set in. Most of those buried in Cesena War Cemetery died during the advance from Rimini to Forli and beyond in September to November 1944, an advance across one flooded river after another in atrocious autumn weather. The cemetery site was selected in November 1944 and burials were brought in from the surrounding battlefields.

Major **Edward Douglas Rea MID**   Grave II E 9

Chatham Naval Memorial, Kent, England

After the First World War there were discussions to find an appropriate way of commemorating those members of the Royal Navy who had no known grave. An Admiralty Committee recommendation was accepted that the three manning ports in Great Britain – Chatham, Plymouth and Portsmouth – should each have an identical memorial in the form of an obelisk. The Chatham Naval Memorial was unveiled by the Prince of Wales (the future King Edward VIII) on 26 April 1924. After the Second World War the three naval memorials were extended, each site with a different architectural treatment. The Chatham Naval Memorial Extension was unveiled by the Duke of Edinburgh on 15 October 1952.

Able Seaman **Thomas John Cochrane**	75, 1
Convoy Signalman **Hugh Douglas Cole**	70, 3
Engine Room Artificer 4th Class **Norman Crothers**	60, 2
Gunner **James Cartner Dixon**	67, 2
Petty Officer Stoker **James Jamfrey MID**	61, 1
Gunner **Herbert Walter Kemp**	51, 2
Ordinary Seaman **Harold McMeekin**	33, 2
Leading Stoker **Charles Archibald Morrison**	38, 1
Lieutenant **Noel Montgomery Neely**	79, 2
Marine **Robert John O'Neill**	65, 2
Lieutenant-Commander **William Robert Patterson OBE DSC**	41, 1

Chislehurst Cemetery, Kent, England
Lieutenant **Anthony Godby**	Section A Grave 128

Chorley Cemetery, Lancashire, England
Flight Sergeant **William Barraclough**	Section E E C Grave 921

City Park Cemetery, Nairobi, Kenya
Major **Robert Henry Cutler**	Section 3 Lot 75

Clichy Northern Cemetery, Hauts-de-Seine, France

Clichy is a town adjoining the northern boundary of Paris.

Sergeant **William McLean**	Plot 16 Row 10 Grave 8

Clogherney Church of Ireland Churchyard, Co. Tyrone
Fusilier **Samuel McFarland**

Comber Cemetery, Comber, Co. Down
Sergeant **Thomas James McCloud**   Section 7 Grave 86

Coriano Ridge War Cemetery, Emilia Romagna, Italy
In January 1944 Allied troops landed behind the German lines at Anzio in Italy but defences were well organised and a breakthrough was not achieved until 18 May 1944 when Cassino was finally taken. As the Germans retreated, they made successive stands in a series of defensive lines. In the northern Apennine Mountains the Gothic Line was breached by the Allies during the 1944 Autumn Campaign and the battle front moved forward to Ravenna in the Adriatic sector. There the Allied advance halted again as winter set in.

Coriano Ridge was the last important ridge in the way of the Allied advance in the Adriatic sector in the autumn of 1944. Its capture was the key to Rimini and eventually to the River Po. German parachute and panzer troops, aided by bad weather, resisted all attacks on their positions between 4 and 12 September 1944. On the night of 12 September the Eighth Army reopened its attack on the Ridge, with the 1st British and 5th Canadian Armoured Divisions. This attack was successful in taking the Ridge, but marked the beginning of a week of the heaviest fighting experienced since Cassino in May, with daily losses for the Eighth Army of some 150 killed.

Lieutenant **William Ernest Watson**   Grave XII C 5
Private **Herbert Anthony White**   Grave II C 2

Croix Communal Cemetery, Nord, France
Croix is a small town some ten kilometres north-east of Lille.

Warrant Officer Class II (CSM) **Douglas Holden Johnston** Row 16 Grave 5

Dieppe Canadian War Cemetery, Hautot-sur-Mer, Seine-Maritime, France
The Dieppe Raid of 18-19 August 1942 had as its objectives: destruction of the Dieppe defences and neighbouring radar and aerodrome installations; the raiding of a German divisional headquarters close by and the capture of prisoners. A largely Canadian military force undertook the main assault on Dieppe itself, with flanking assaults by Commando units and additional Canadian battalions to the east and west of the town. These were intended to neutralise batteries that defended the direct approach. Support was provided by more than 250 naval vessels and 69 air squadrons. Only the assaulting parties on the extreme flanks came within reasonable reach of their ambitious objectives and casualties were very heavy, with more than 3,600 of the military force of 6,100 killed, wounded, missing or captured.

Naval casualties numbered 550.

Private **Hugh Boal**	Special Memorial No. 7
Flight Sergeant (Air Bomber) **Ronald Nelson**	Collective Grave M 8-13

Doetinchem (Loolaan) General Cemetery, Gelderland, Netherlands
Doetinchem is a small town about thirty kilometres east of Arnhem.

Flight Sergeant **John McCalla Tait**   Row 1 Grave 10

Donaghadee Church of Ireland Churchyard, Donaghadee, Co. Down
Deck Hand **Harry Aiken**
Gunner **John Cecil Beresford Harris**
Coxswain **William George Nelson**
Pilot Officer **Frederick Eustace Stronge**
Pilot Launch Pilot **William White**
Able Seaman **William Charles Woods**

Douglas Bank Cemetery, Rosyth, Scotland
Military Policeman **William Oscar Thompson**

Dromore Cathedral Churchyard, Co. Down
Fusilier **Andrew Copling**   Grave 26

Drumachose Church of Ireland Churchyard, Co. Londonderry
Flight Sergeant **William Benjamin Fry**   Grave 8

Drumcree Church of Ireland Churchyard, Co. Armagh
Private **John George Benson**   New Ground Grave 325

Dunkirk Memorial, Nord, France
During the Second World War, Dunkirk was the scene of the historic evacuation of the British Expeditionary Force from France in May 1940. The Dunkirk Memorial stands at the entrance to the Commonwealth War Graves section of Dunkirk Town Cemetery. It commemorates more than 4,500 casualties of the British Expeditionary Force with no known grave who died in the campaign of 1939-40 or who were captured during this campaign and died in captivity.

Rifleman **John Robert Gilpin**	Column 129
Corporal **William Nolan**	Column 133
Second Lieutenant **Robert Norman Cecil Scott**	Column 7

Dunkirk Memorial, Nord, France continued...

Warrant Officer Class III Walter Stanley Smith	Column 7
Corporal James Frederick Young	Column 117

Durnbach War Cemetery, Bad Tolz, Bayern, Germany

The village of Durnbach lies approximately 45 kilometres south of Munich. The site for Durnbach War Cemetery was chosen, after hostilities had ceased, by officers of the British Army and Air Force, in conjunction with officers of the American Occupation Forces in whose zone Durnbach was located. The majority of those buried in this cemetery were airmen shot down over Bavaria, Wurtemberg, Austria, Hessen and Thuringia; they were brought in from their scattered graves by the Army Graves Service. The remainder are men who were killed while escaping from Prisoner-of-War camps in the same areas, or who died towards the end of the War on forced marches from the camps to more remote areas.

Sergeant Ernest Henry Mackenzie Barr	Grave 5 D 20
Sergeant Robert Moore	Grave 2 K 1
Sergeant Thomas Torney	Joint Grave 5 C 22-23
Flight Sergeant John Cameron Keith Webb	Collective Grave 7K 14-19
Pilot Officer Hugh Wilson	Grave 6 A 2

East Ham (Marlow Road) Jewish Cemetery, Essex, England

Sergeant Marks Wayne (Weinberg)	Block I Grave 276

Eglantine Church of Ireland Cemetery, Co. Down (CWGC designation)

Flight Sergeant Andrew Greenwell Gibbison	Section E Grave 36
Flying Officer Gordon Elgin Vance	Section E Grave 41

Eindhoven (Woensel) General Cemetery, Noord-Brabant, Netherlands

Most of the men buried in this cemetery belonged to the air forces, and they lost their lives in raids over this part of Holland or in returning from Germany between 1941 and 1944.

Flight Sergeant Herbert Hannay MID	Plot JJ Grave 12

El Alamein War Cemetery, Alamein, Egypt

Alamein Memorial has details about the Western Desert Campaigns. El Alamein War Cemetery contains the graves of men who died at all stages of the Western Desert Campaigns and who were brought in from a wide area, especially those who died in the Battle of El Alamein at the end of October

1942 and in the period immediately before that.

Lieutenant **William Henry Lowry Andrews**	Grave XXIX A 9
Leading Aircraftman **Francis John Noel Gorman**	Grave XXXI D 17
Pilot Officer **Thomas Andrew McCann**	Grave X E 17
Leading Aircraftman **Robert Reid McClean**	Grave XVIII G 24
Brigadier **Robert Dermot Barnes Perrott DSO OBE MC**	Grave XXIII C 24

Eltham Cemetery, Woolwich, London
Second Lieutenant **Bernard Wakeford** Section B Grave 206

Faenza War Cemetery, Romagna, Italy
As the Germans retreated in 1944, they made successive stands in a series of defensive lines. In the northern Apennine Mountains the Gothic line was breached by the Allies during the 1944 Autumn Campaign and the battle front moved forward to Ravenna in the Adriatic sector. There the Allied advance halted again as winter set in. The war cemetery at Faenza was formed for the burial of those who were killed in the static fighting line before the Allied advance was renewed in April 1945.

Private **John Wray**	Grave V D 21
Lieutenant **Maurice Edward Young**	Grave II A 15

Finningley (Holy Trinity & St. Oswald) Chyd Ext Nottinghamshire, England
There was a Royal Air Force station at Finningley during the Second World War and only a hedge separated the aerodrome from the churchyard extension. During the early part of the war, ground in the churchyard was set aside for Air Force burials.

Flight Lieutenant **Desmond Wallace Ferguson Barker DFC** Row H Grave 1

Florence War Cemetery, Tuscany, Italy
As the Germans retreated in 1944, they made successive stands in a series of defensive lines – the Trasimene, Arezzo, Arno and Gothic lines. Florence, which was taken by the Allied Forces on 13 August 1944, was the centre of the Arno Line and the point from which the attack on the German Gothic Line defences in the Apennines was launched. The site for Florence War Cemetery was selected in November 1944 for burials from the hospitals established in and around Florence but the greater part of those buried there lost their lives in the fighting in this area from July to September 1944.

Flying Officer **George Stanley Corry** Grave XII E 4

Foiano Della Chiana War Cemetery, Tuscany, Italy

Early in July 1944 there was heavy fighting in the Chiana Valley where the Germans made their last stand in front of Arezzo and the Arno. The Foiano Della Chiana War Cemetery is a battlefield cemetery originally formed by the 4th Division and later increased when burials were brought in from the surrounding area.

Lieutenant **Simon Denis St. Ledger Fleming**   Grave I G 1

Froyennes Communal Cemetery, Hainaut, Belgium

The British Expeditionary Force was involved in the later stages of the defence of Belgium (following the German invasion in May 1940) and suffered many casualties in covering the withdrawal to Dunkirk.

Corporal **Henry Heaven**   Row 3 Grave 30

Gaasterland (Nijemirdum) General Cemetery, Friesland, Netherlands
Pilot Officer **George Marshall McCombe**   Plot 1 Row A Grave 4

Gateshead (Saltwell) Cemetery, Durham, England
Lance Sergeant **John Boocock**   Division 1 Grave 381

Glasgow (Cardonald) Cemetery, Glasgow, Scotland

Battalions of a number of Scottish regiments had their headquarters at Glasgow during the Second World War and the Clydeside shipyards were targeted by German bombers during the Blitz. Glasgow suffered a particularly ferocious attack on the night of 13/14 March 1941 when many civilians and servicemen were killed.

Chief Engine Room Artificer **Christopher Vivash**   Section E Joint Grave 25

Glendermott Church of Ireland Chyd and New Cemetery, Co. Londonderry
Warrant Officer Class II (CSM) **Alfred Penfold**   Section H Grave 846B

Gorssel General Cemetery, Gelderland, Netherlands
Flying Officer (Pilot) **Hugh Francis Morrow**   Row A Grave 19

Gosport (Ann's Hill) Cemetery, Hampshire, England
Second Engineer Officer **Reginald William Dudley Gibbs** Plot 189 Grave 13

Goulburn General Cemetery, New South Wales, Australia
Sergeant **Margaret Ann King**   Plot G Row A Grave 7

Gradara War Cemetery, Pesaro, Italy

As the Germans retreated in 1944, they made successive stands in a series of defensive lines – the Trasimene, Arezzo, Arno and Gothic lines. Florence, which was taken by the Allied Forces on 13 August 1944, was the centre of the Arno Line and the point from which the attack on the German Gothic Line defences in the Apennines was launched. The site for the Gradara War Cemetery was chosen in November 1944 and it contains the graves of casualties incurred during the advance from Ancona to Rimini, which broke the German's heavily defended Gothic Line, and in the heavy fighting around Rimini, which was taken by the Allies on 21 September 1944.

Second Lieutenant **William James Neely Pinkerton**   Grave II F 73

Grantham Cemetery, Lincolnshire, England

During the Second World War there was a Royal Air Force station at Grantham and there is a small group of RAF graves is Section 17.

Pilot Officer **Richard Percival William Barker**   Section 17 Row M Grave 11

Great Yarmouth (Caister) Cemetery, Norfolk, England

Civilian **Gladys Doreen Merrison**

Leading Aircraftman **Joseph Frederick Merrison**   Section J Grave 178

Guidel Communal Cemetery, Morbihan, France

Sergeant **Arthur Moore Templeton**   Row 3 Grave 14

Halifax Memorial, Nova Scotia, Canada

The Halifax Memorial commemorates men and women of the Commonwealth Forces who died in both world wars and have no known grave, in particular those Canadian sailors, merchant seamen, soldiers and nursing sisters who lost their lives at sea. It also bears the names of men of the Canadian Army stationed in Canada who have no known grave.

Third Radio Officer **George Barry Neville Bewley**   Panel 23

Hamburg Cemetery, Hamburg, Germany

The Commonwealth section of Hamburg Cemetery contains more than 1,400 Second World War burials, mostly of servicemen who died with the occupying forces, or airmen lost in bombing raids over Germany.

Sergeant **Henry Victor Hawkins**   Grave 5A L 12

Lance Bombardier **James Murphy Mair**   Grave 2A D 3

Pilot Officer **Wallace Robert Smyth**   Grave 10A C 7

Harbledown (St. Michael) Churchyard, Kent, England
Flight Sergeant **Gordon Charles Edwards**   **North of Church**

Harrogate (Stonefall) Cemetery, Yorkshire
Many airfields were established in Yorkshire during the Second World War including Harrogate, Linton-on-Ouse, Tockwith, Rufforth and Marston Moor. Most of the Second World War burials in Harrogate (Stonefall) Cemetery are of airmen, some of whom died in the military wing of Harrogate General Hospital.

Flight Lieutenant **Frederick Watson Ritchie**   **Section G Row E Grave 12**

Hatfield (Woodhouse) Cemetery, Yorkshire, England
Sergeant **Alexander Campbell**   **Row EE Grave 20**

Hawarden Cemetery, Flintshire, Wales
Wing Commander **Malcolm Morgan McMullan MID**   **Section 4G Grave 24**

Hermanville War Cemetery, Calvados, France
The Allied offensive in north-western Europe began with the Normandy Landings of 6 June 1944. The village of Hermanville lay behind Sword Beach and was occupied early on 6 June by men of the South Lancashire Regiment. Many of those buried in Hermanville War Cemetery died on 6 June or during the first days of the drive towards Caen.

Corporal **Edward Dempster**   **Grave 2 A 3**
Lance Sergeant **Andrew Robert Stewart**   **Grave 1 U 9**

Heverlee War Cemetery, Leuven, Vlaams-Brabant, Belgium
The British Expeditionary Force (BEF) was involved in the later stages of the defence of Belgium following the German invasion in May 1940, and the BEF suffered many casualties in covering the withdrawal to Dunkirk. Commonwealth Forces did not return until September 1944, but in the intervening years, many airmen were shot down or crashed in raids on strategic objectives in Belgium, or while returning from missions over Germany.

Sergeant **James Ernest Nicholls**   **Collective Grave 10 E 2-8**
Sergeant **James Shields**   **Grave 5 C 5**

Heworth (St. Mary) Churchyard, Durham, England
Flying Officer **Raymond Hodgson**   **New Yard Plot G Grave 95**

Holywood Cemetery, Co. Down

Sergeant Benjamin Beeby	Protestant Ground Grave 1393
Fusilier Frederick Bloomfield	Protestant Ground Collective Grave 1263
Bombardier Thomas Wesley Boyd	Grave 1397
Major Walter Raleigh Draper	Grave 1189
Civilian Edith Dunwoody	Grave 1372
Civilian Henry Dunwoody	Grave 1371
Civilian Isabella Dunwoody	Grave 1372
Civilian William Dunwoody	Grave 1371
Leading Aircraftman Clifford Samuel Ferguson	Grave 1217
Private John Matthew Forshaw	Grave 1264
Fusilier William Fox	Roman Catholic Ground Collective Grave 1042
Civilian Nancy Simms Gribbin	Grave 479
Private Alfred Hayes	Grave 341
Pte Archibald Joseph A Holt	Roman Catholic Ground Collective Grave 1042
Sergeant (Pilot) John Cecil Brandon Irwin	Grave 1213
Warrant Officer (Pilot) Thomas Francis Jefferson	Grave 561
Private Samuel Kirham	Protestant Ground Joint Grave 1264
Private Robert Richard Lacey	Protestant Ground Grave 1265
Private Frank Mason	Roman Catholic Ground Collective Grave 1042
Rifleman John McFarlane	Protestant Ground Collective Grave 1263
Sergeant Leslie Tom Measday	Grave 1487
Sergeant Alexander L Quillan	Grave 197
Private Leonard Stanley Reid	Protestant Ground Collective Grave 1264
Chief Engineer (Marine) John James Tait	Grave 877
Driver Sidney John Wren	Protestant Ground Collective Grave 1263

Huddersfield (Edgerton) Cemetery, Yorkshire, England

Aircraftman Second Class Ronald Hodgson	Section 7G Grave 73

Idmiston (All Saints) Churchyard, Wiltshire, England

Pilot Officer John Peter Sadd	South side of Church

Ightham (St. Peter) Churchyard, Kent

Sergeant (Pilot) Henry Walter Stanley

Ikoyi No. 2 Cemetery, Nigeria

Flight Sergeant Alexander Magowan McVea	Grave 363

Jakarta War Cemetery, Java, Indonesia

Jakarta, capital of the Republic of Indonesia and located on the north-west coast of the island of Java, was the administrative capital of the former Dutch East Indies. It was known as Batavia and that was the name used in the records of the Second World War. Batavia was the port by which British and Commonwealth servicemen entered Java in February 1942 from Singapore and Sumatra, shortly before the Japanese invasion of the island. Most of the Allied Prisoners-of-War captured in Java were later concentrated in a number of prison camps around Batavia.

Corporal **James McLean**   Grave 3 L 7

Jonkerbos War Cemetery, Nijmegan, Gelderland, Netherlands
The Netherlands fell to the Germans in May 1940 and was not re-entered by Allied Forces until September 1944. Nijmegen was a front line town from 17 September 1944 until February 1945. Jonkerbos War Cemetery, which was created by No. 3 Casualty Clearing Station, is in a wooded area known as Jonkers Bosch, from which it took its name.

Pilot Officer **Ian Milne Hossack**   Grave 12 G 5
Lieutenant **Owen Shanks MM**   Grave 14 G 3

Jurby (St. Patrick) Churchyard, Isle of Man
Flying Officer **Stanislaw Podobinski**   Grave 370

Karachi War Cemetery, Pakistan
Second Lieutenant **Desmond Robert King**   Grave 4 D 13

Kiel War Cemetery, Kiel, Schleswig-Holstein, Germany
Most of those buried in Kiel War Cemetery were airmen lost in bombing raids over northern Europe, whose graves were brought in from cemeteries and churchyards throughout Schleswig-Holstein, the Frisian Islands and other parts of north-western Germany.

Sergeant **Robert Richardson**   Collective Grave 3 J 18-20

Killinchy Non Subscribing Presbyterian Churchyard, Co. Down
Sub-Lieutenant **Samuel Jamieson Fitchie**   Row 2 Grave 22

Killyleagh Church of Ireland Churchyard, Co. Down
Captain **Maurice Evelyn Beale**   Section A Grave 470

Killysuggan Graveyard, Newtownards, Co. Down
Gunner **William Hugh Murphy**   Plot 3 Row 5 Grave 10

Kingsway New Cemetery, Nottinghamshire
Fusilier **George Leslie Gell**   Section A Row L Grave 1254

Kircubbin Presbyterian Churchyard, Kircubbin, Co. Down
Aircraftman First Class **John Harold Maxwell**

Kirk Maughold (St. Maughold) Churchyard, Isle of Man
Flying Officer **Alexander Arthur Fenwich Towry Steavenson**   East Boundary

Kirkee War Cemetery, India
Kirkee War Cemetery was created to receive Second World War graves from the western and central parts of India where their permanent maintenance could not be assured.

Private **Robert Byers**   Grave 7 B 8

Kirkinner Cemetery, Wigtownshire, Scotland
A plot in the south-western part of the burial ground was acquired by the Royal Air Force, which had a station at Wigtown during the Second World War.

Sergeant **John Edwin Charles Averell Steele-Nicholson**   Grave 604

Knightsbridge War Cemetery, Acroma, Libya
The defence against Rommel's drive across Cyrenaica towards Suez consisted of a number of irregularly spaced strong points known as 'boxes' linked by deep minefields. Those nearest the Axis Forces were held by infantry, while those further back served as reserve static positions and as bases from which the armour could operate. The chief 'box', known as Knightsbridge, was round a junction of tracks about 20 kilometres west of Tobruk and 16 kilometres south of Acroma, commanding all the tracks by which supplies came up to the front. The Eighth Army's advance fuelling stations and airfields were at Acroma, El Adem, El Duda, Sidi Rezegh and Gambut, while by February 1941, Gazala Aerodrome, taken from the Italians early in the campaign, housed two Commonwealth squadrons. Knightsbridge was thus a key position, and the pivot on which the armies manoeuvred during the heavy fighting which commenced in late May 1942. Fierce actions were fought at all these places, and a battlefield cemetery was created at each for the burial of the dead.

Gunner **William Robert Bailie**	Grave 1 D 16
Lance Corporal **Harry Cromie**	Collective grave 8 C 12-14
Sergeant **Alexander Davidson**	Grave 2 F 5
Lieutenant **John Malcomson Gibson**	Grave 2 F 1

Knightsbridge War Cemetery, Acroma, Libya continued...

Gunner **David McClinton**   **Grave 10 C 11**
Private **Thomas Newell**   **Grave 10 A 22**

Knockbreda Cemetery, Co. Down
Sergeant **Sydney Ireland**   **Section E Grave 78**
Flying Officer **Thomas George Rodgers**   **Section K Grave 443**

Kranji War Cemetery, Singapore

Before 1939 the Kranji area was a military camp and at the time of the Japanese invasion of Malaya, it was the site of a large ammunition magazine. On 8 February 1942, the Japanese crossed the Johore Straits in strength, landing at the mouth of the Kranji River within two miles of the place where the war cemetery now stands. On the evening of 9 February, they launched an attack between the river and the causeway. During the next few days there was fierce hand to hand fighting until the superior Japanese numbers and air strength forced a withdrawal. After the fall of the island, the Japanese established a Prisoner-of-War Camp at Kranji and a hospital was set up nearby at Woodlands. After the reoccupation of Singapore, Kranji War Cemetery was developed by the Army Graves Service from a small cemetery started by the prisoners at Kranji. Other burials from all parts of the island were transferred to Kranji together with all Second World War burials from Saigon Military Cemetery in French Indo-China (now Vietnam).

Corporal **Campbell Allen**   **Special Memorial 24 E 16**

La Bigne Churchyard, Calvados, France
Trooper **John Bennett Campbell**

La Pellerine Communal Cemetery, Mayenne, France
Flight Lieutenant **Geoffrey Austin Harrison**

Labuan War Cemetery, Malaysia

Labuan (part of Sabah, Malaysia) is a small island in Brunei Bay, off the coast of north-west Borneo.

Bombardier **William Montgomery**   **Grave M D 7**

Lae War Cemetery, Papua New Guinea

In the early months of 1942 Japan had superiority in the air and it was Lae and its neighbouring airfields that were the objects of the first Japanese attack on New Guinea. Lae and Salamaua were bombed on 21 January 1942 by 100 Japanese planes but land forces did not enter the territory until 7 March, when 3,000 Japanese troops landed at Lae. There were landings too at Salamaua, followed on 21 July by further landings at Buna and Gona on the east coast in preparation for a drive through the Owen Stanley Mountains across the Papuan peninsula to Port Moresby. The vital stage of the New Guinea campaign dates from that time. Lae became one of the bases from which the southward Japanese drive was launched and maintained until it was stopped by Allied Forces at Ioribaiwa Ridge, a point within 60 kilometres of Port Moresby.

Private **Hugh Young**   Grave G B 1

Lajes War Cemetery, Azores
Located on the island of Terceira, Lajes War Cemetery was established during the Second World War when Commonwealth Forces were stationed on the island and the aerodrome was used by the Commonwealth and American Air Forces.

Leading Aircraftman **David Lindsay**   Row E Grave 8
Pilot Officer **Ian Lindsay Munce**   Row B Grave 8

Lee-on-Solent Memorial, Hampshire, England
During the Second World War the Fleet Air Arm served in almost every Theatre of War. In a reconnaissance role they supported land operations in France, the Netherlands, North Africa, Italy, and the Far East. Operating from aircraft carriers (seven of which were lost during the war) they were one of the chief weapons against the U-boats in the Atlantic and in support of the Russian convoys.

In November 1940, Fleet Air Arm Fairey Swordfish biplanes carrying torpedoes undertook a night raid on the harbour at Taranto, resulting in disaster for the Italian Navy. Aircraft from HMS *Victorious* and *Ark Royal* took part in the sinking of the German battleship *Bismark* in May 1941 and in February 1942, when the *Scharnhorst, Gneisenau* and *Prinz Eugen* attempted to sail via the English Channel from the Atlantic Ocean to the relative safety of the North Sea, they were attacked by Fairey Swordfish of the Fleet Air Arm. The principal base of the Fleet Air Arm, Lee-on-the-Solent, Hampshire, was chosen as the site for the memorial to almost 2,000 men of that service who died during the Second World War and who have no known grave.

Lieutenant (A) **John Carr**   Bay 2 Panel 6
Sub-Lieutenant (A) **George Henry Crawford Lowden**   Bay 6 Panel 4

Lisbon (St. George) British Churchyard, Portugal

Pilot Officer **Kenneth Duncan Adams**   **Plot G1 Front Row Grave 16**

Liverpool (Anfield) Cemetery, Lancashire, England

During the Second World War, Liverpool was headquarters of Western Approaches Command and a manning depot for officers and men of the Merchant Navy who agreed to serve with the Royal Navy for the duration of the war.

Pilot Officer **William Maxwell Henry**   **Section 15 C of E Grave 1234**

Liverpool Naval Memorial, Lancashire, England

At the outbreak of the Second World War, it was clear that the Royal Navy would not be able to man all the auxiliary vessels that would serve with it. To deal with the shortfall in manpower, a number of officers and men of the Merchant Navy agreed to serve with the Royal Navy under the terms of a 'T.124 agreement', which made them subject to Naval discipline while generally retaining their Merchant Navy rates of pay and other conditions. The manning port established to administer these men was at Liverpool.

More than 13,000 seamen served under these conditions in various types of auxiliary vessels, at first mainly in armed merchant cruisers, but also in armed boarding vessels, cable ships, rescue tugs, and other craft on special service.

The Liverpool Naval Memorial commemorates 1,400 of these officers and men, who died on active service aboard more than 120 ships, and who have no grave but the sea.

Sub-Lieutenant (E) **James Gordon Barre**   **Panel 4 Column 1**
Lieutenant Commander **Robert Pollock Beattie**   **Panel 1 Column 2**
Lieutenant (E) **Thomas Hugh Cecil Hickland Fee**   **Panel 2 Column 1**

Londonderry City Cemetery, Co. Londonderry

Fusilier **Samuel Burke**   **Section S Class B Grave 1218**

Lowestoft Naval Memorial, Suffolk, England

The Depot for the Royal Naval Patrol Service, developed from the pre-war Royal Naval Reserve Trawler Section was at Lowestoft during the Second World War. At the outset of the war the men of this service were mainly the fishermen of the requisitioned trawlers and drifters used on patrol work, but later it included men from all walks of life and various types of small craft. In the spring of 1944 the Royal Naval Patrol Service reached its maximum strength of some 57,000 men.

Between 1942 and 1946 more than 1,600 newly constructed ships and craft were manned by the Service, among them minesweepers of various kinds, corvettes, fuel carriers, motor launches and naval seaplane tenders. Their objective was to maintain wartime patrols and safeguard the coasts of Britain. Lowestoft was chosen as the site for the Memorial to those men of the Royal Naval Patrol Service who have no grave but the sea.

Leading Seaman **Frederick Caulfield**   Panel 14 Column 1

Luxembourg American Cemetery, Luxembourg City, Luxembourg
Private **Leland Truesdale Pentz, Purple Heart**   Plot D Row 10 Grave 25

Macosquin (St. Mary) Church of Ireland Churchyard, Co. Londonderry
Fusilier **Matthew Wright**   Grave 462

Madras War Cemetery, Chennai, India
Madras War Cemetery was created to receive Second World War burials from many civil and cantonment cemeteries in the south and east of India where their permanent maintenance could not be assured.

Sergeant **Robert Clarke**   Grave 5 C 13

Malta Memorial, Floriana, Malta
The Malta Memorial commemorates almost 2,300 airmen who lost their lives during the Second World War whilst serving with the Commonwealth Air Forces flying from bases in Austria, Italy, Sicily, Islands of the Adriatic and Mediterranean, Malta, Tunisia, Algeria, Morocco, West Africa, Yugoslavia and Gibraltar, and who have no known grave.

Sergeant **Thomas Adair**   Panel 14 Column 2
Flying Officer **Neville Stuart King**   Panel 3 Column 1

Massicault War Cemetery, Tunisia
In May 1943, the war in North Africa came to an end in Tunisia with the defeat of the Axis Powers by a combined Allied Force. The North African campaign began on 8 November 1942 when Commonwealth and American troops made a series of landings in Algeria and Morocco. The Germans responded by sending a force from Sicily to northern Tunisia and in early December this checked the Allied advance eastwards. In the south, the Axis Forces who were defeated at El Alamein withdrew into Tunisia along the coast through Libya, pursued by the Allied Eighth Army. By mid April 1943, the combined Axis Force was confined to a small part of north-eastern Tunisia and the Allies prepared for their final offensive. Many of those buried at Massicault War

Cemetery died in the preparation for the final drive to Tunis in April 1943 and in that advance at the beginning of May 1943.

Sergeant **James Douglas Marr**   Grave II M 1
Lieutenant **Patrick Edmund Charles Nugent**   Grave V K 8

Medjez-el-Bab Memorial and Medjez-el-Bab War Cemetery, Tunisia

See the information under Massicault War Cemetery immediately above. Medjez-el-Bab was at the limit of the Allied advance in December 1942 and remained on the front line until the decisive Allied advances during April and May 1943. The Medjez-el-Bab Memorial which stands within Medjez-el-Bab War Cemetery commemorates almost 2,000 men of the First Army who died during the operations in Algeria and Tunisia between 8 November 1942 and 19 February 1943, and those of the First and Eighth Armies who died in operations in the same areas between 20 February 1943 and 13 May 1943, and who have no known graves.

Medjez-el-Bab Memorial, Tunisia

Squadron QMS **Alexander Scott Brown**   Face 4
Captain **Hubert Henderson**   Face 30
Guardsman **Norman McKimm**   Face 14
Rifleman **Charles Smart**   Face 31

Medjez-el-Bab War Cemetery, Tunisia

Rifleman **Joseph Smyth**   Grave 2 C 8

Merville Communal Cemetery Extension, Nord, France

During the Second World War the river Lys was the southern end of an area held by British Forces at the end of May 1940. Merville is on the territory over which intense rearguard actions were fought during the withdrawal of the British Expeditionary Force to the coast for evacuation from Dunkirk.

Flight Sergeant **David Harrison Freeland**   Plot 2 Row B Grave 15

Miami (Grand Army of the Republic) Cemetery, Oklahoma, USA

Leading Aircraftman **Alan Brown**   Block 14 Row 1 Grave 3

Mombasa (Mbaraki) Cemetery, Kenya

During the First World War, Mombasa was where No.1 Base Hospital was located. In addition to hospital facilities, numerous other wartime activities were centred at Mombasa during the Second World War, including its use as a naval base.

Mombasa (Mbaraki) Cemetery, Kenya continued...

Lieutenant **John Lyle Taggart Glass** **Protestant Service Plot Row D Grave 22**

Montrose (Sleepy Hillock) Cemetery, Angus, Scotland
Leading Aircraftman **Henry Dougan Sandford** **Section 10 Class A Grave 336**

Moro River Canadian War Cemetery, Abruzzo, Italy
Arezzo War Cemetery has details about the war in Italy up until October 1943 when the Allies were facing the German winter defensive position known as the Gustav Line. This stretched from the river Garigliano in the west to the Sangro in the east. The Allied force that had fought its way up the Adriatic took the Sangro River positions by 30 November 1943. The 1st Canadian Division went on to cross the Moro River on 6 December 1943 and to take Ortona on 28 December. The site of the cemetery was chosen by the Canadian Corps in January 1944. It contains the graves of those who died during that fighting at Moro River and Ortona, and during the weeks that preceded and followed it.

Lance Corporal **John Mawhinney** **Grave XII D 2**

Mortlake Crematorium, Surrey, England
Flight Sergeant **Cecil Thomas Deane** **Panel 4**

Mullaghglass (St. Luke) Church of Ireland Churchyard, Co. Armagh
Fusilier **Ernest McNeill** **Grave 4B**

National Memorial Cemetery of the Pacific, Honolulu, Hawaii
Captain **David Martin Bailie** **Plot P Row O Grave 509**
Seaman First Class **Henry Hanna Shipcott** **Court 2**

Nelson Cemetery, Lancashire, England
Captain **Thomas Oswald Corrin** **Special Memorial**

Netley Military Cemetery, Hampshire, England
Netley Military Cemetery is a permanent military cemetery and is the property of the Ministry of Defence. The cemetery was at the back of the Royal Victoria Military Hospital and was used during both wars for burials from the hospital.

Gunner **Trevor Maynard Watt McVitty** **Grave 446**

New Zealand Naval Memorial, Devonport, Auckland, New Zealand

This memorial commemorates 352 officers and men of the Royal New Zealand Navy, Royal New Zealand Naval Reserve and the Royal New Zealand Naval Volunteer Reserve who died in all parts of the world during the Second World War and who have no known grave.

Sub-Lieutenant (A) **Francis Graham Reid**   Panel 9

Newton-le-Willows Cemetery, Lancashire, England
Private **James Kerr**   Section C Grave 1605

Newtownards (Movilla) Cemetery, Newtownards, Co. Down

The CWGC list of Second World War burials in Movilla Cemetery includes seven that are unidentified.

Gunner **John Brown**	Section 23 Grave 111
Sergeant **David Corry**	Section 23 Grave 131
Gunner **Henry Corry**	Section 23 Grave 40
Gunner **John Edmonds**	Section 24 Grave 158
Sergeant **Henryk Andrzej Flegier**	Section 18 RC Plot Grave 24
Warrant Officer **William Gallagher Gordon**	Section 1 Grave 6
Fusilier **James Graham**	Section 12 Grave 127
Wg Cdr **Waldyslaw Eugeniusz Heller**	Section 18 RC Plot Grave 22
Fusilier **Daniel Higgins**	Section 28 Protestant Plot Grave 81
Driver **James W Hubbard**	Section 23 Grave 109
Leading Aircraftwoman **Annie Irvine**	Section 2 Grave 120
Ordinary Seaman **John Johnston**	Section 13 Grave 123
Sergeant **Henryk Komenda**	Section 18 RC Plot Grave 23
Craftsman **Wilfred Leitch**	Section 21 Grave 233
Rifleman **Charles Maxwell**	Section 16 Grave 146
Air Gunner **Sydney Murray**	Section 24
Sgt **Peter Charles Hunter Phillips**	Section 28 Protestant Plot Grave 82
Fusilier **David Francis Prosser**	Section 29 Grave 86
Driver **Hugh Erin Reid**	Section 29 Grave 41
Second Lieutenant **Robert J. Reid**	Section 14 Grave 24
Flt Sgt **Raymond Farquhar Simpson**	Section 28 Protestant Plot Grave 99
Sergeant **Alfred White**	Section 28 Protestant Plot Grave 92

Nicosia War Cemetery, Cyprus

Nicosia War Cemetery was established by the military authorities during the Second World War for the burial of servicemen who died while on duty in Cyprus. A number of graves were also moved in from small civilian cemeteries in villages in different parts of the island.

Flying Officer **Robert Keith James**   Grave 3 A 6

Nottingham Crematorium, Nottinghamshire, England
The Crematorium Memorial is within Nottingham Southern Cemetery.

Aircraftwoman Second Class **Jean Dibby Wright**   Panel 5

Nunhead (All Saints) Cemetery, London, England
FS **Thomas Charles Crisp** Screen Wall Panel 5 Square 5 Collective Grave 41286

Old Leake (St. Mary) Churchyard, Lincolnshire, England
Sapper **Henry Houghton**

Oldenzaal Protestant Cemetery, Overijssel, Netherlands
Oldenzaal Protestant Cemetery contains 13 Commonwealth burials of the Second World War, all members of the land forces who died in the latter stages of the war in the Netherlands.

Lt Col **Francis John Leland MID Croix de Guerre avec Palme**   Grave 11

Omagh (Dublin Road) Cemetery, Omagh, Co. Tyrone
Sergeant **Robert Samuel Carson**   Section B Grave 444

Orry-la-Ville Dutch War Cemetery, Senlis, Oise, France
Commander **Eduard Bakker DFC**   Section C Row 1 Grave 9

Ottawa (Pinecrest) Cemetery, Ottawa, Canada
Major **Hilton David Proctor**   Plot 552 Section D Grave 1

Padua War Cemetery, Veneto, Italy
At the beginning of April 1945 the Allies launched their final offensive against the German positions spread out in a line across Italy, south of Bologna. German resistance was by then diminishing and the Allies were able to fan out rapidly across the Po Valley. Padua War Cemetery lies in the zone of the Allied breakthrough in the spring of 1945 when, despite some resistance, the town was captured.

Flying Officer **Donald Stanley Ashton Monard**   Grave II G 5

Paisley (Hawkhead) Cemetery, Renfrewshire, Scotland
Flying Officer **Philip Kenneth Woodsend**   Section H Grave 776-779

Peterborough (Eastfield) Cemetery, Northamptonshire
Corporal **John Hardy**   Division 4 Block 16 Cons Grave 6370

Pihen-les-Guines War Cemetery, Pas de Calais, France
The land on which Pihen-les-Guines War Cemetery is situated was requisitioned from a private owner by the Germans in 1943, and was set apart for the burial of Allied servicemen.

Private **Leslie Waite**   Grave 2 B 8

Plymouth Naval Memorial, Devon, England
After the First World War there were discussions to find an appropriate way of commemorating those members of the Royal Navy who had no known grave. An Admiralty Committee recommendation was accepted that the three manning ports in Great Britain – Chatham, Plymouth and Portsmouth – should each have an identical memorial in the form of an obelisk. The Plymouth Naval Memorial was unveiled by the HRH Prince George on 29 July 1924. After the Second World War the three naval memorials were extended, each site with a different architectural treatment. The Plymouth Naval Memorial Extension was unveiled by HRH Princess Margaret on 20 May 1954.

Able Seaman **James Francis Bailie**	Panel 46 Column 2
Signalman **Hans Calvert**	Panel 67 Column 3
Marine **Samuel Clydesdale**	Panel 43 Column 1
Petty Officer Stoker **Albert Parr Cole**	Panel 51 Column 3
Able Seaman **William Jordan Cooke**	Panel 33 Column 2
Telegraphist **Jacob Walter Coulter**	Panel 39 Column 3
Stoker First Class **David Cromie**	Panel 82 Column 1
Able Seaman **Alexander Doak**	Panel 37 Column 2
Able Seaman **Hugh Alexander Eagleson**	Panel 37 Column 2
Able Seaman **Stanley Geddis**	Panel 86 Column 2
Marine **Robert Lyttle Harrison**	Panel 59 Column 3
Able Seaman **Crawford Henderson**	Panel 47 Column 2
Stoker First Class **Robert James Hoy**	Panel 90 Column 1
Able Seaman **George Victor Lowry**	Panel 65 Column 3
Ordinary Seaman **Alfred George McDowell**	Panel 39 Column 1
Petty Officer **Hugh McNally**	Panel 93 Column 3
Lieutenant (E) **John Moir**	Panel 63 Column 1
Stoker First Class **Thomas Murray**	Panel 94 Column 3
Able Seaman **David Orr**	Panel 66 Column 1
Lance Bombardier **William Ward Phillips**	Panel 62 Column 2

Plymouth Naval Memorial, Devon, England continued...

Able Seaman **Francis Robinson**	Panel 80 Column 1
Ordinary Seaman **David Scott**	Panel 39 Column 1
Able Seaman **Samuel Smith**	Panel 48 Column 2
Able Seaman **John Sturgeon**	Panel 33 Column 3
Ordinary Seaman **William James Tweed**	Panel 49 Column 3
Able Seaman **Robert John Warden**	Panel 66 Column 3
Leading Cook (S) **Thomas Wilson**	Panel 72 Column 1

Port Moresby Memorial, Papua New Guinea

Port Moresby has a good harbour on the Gulf of Papua and its situation close to the Australian mainland made it suitable as a naval and military base for operations in the south-west Pacific.

First Officer **Robert Hughes**	Panel 10

Portrush Cemetery, Co. Antrim

Flight Lieutenant **John McCrory**	Section C Grave 302

Portsmouth Naval Memorial, Hampshire, England

After the First World War there were discussions to find an appropriate way of commemorating those members of the Royal Navy who had no known grave. An Admiralty Committee recommendation was accepted that the three manning ports in Great Britain – Chatham, Plymouth and Portsmouth – should each have an identical memorial in the form of an obelisk. The Portsmouth Naval Memorial was unveiled by the Duke of York (the future King George VI) on 15 October 1924. After the Second World War the three naval memorials were extended, each site with a different architectural treatment. The Portsmouth Naval Memorial Extension was unveiled by Queen Elizabeth the Queen Mother on 29 April 1953.

Marine **William Thomas Anderson MID**	Panel 36 Column 1
Able Seaman **David Cowan**	Panel 60 Column 3
Lt Cdr (E) **John Gordon Morrison Erskine**	Panel 45 Column 2
Signalman **Arthur Donald Field MID**	Panel 80 Column 2
Able Seaman **Thomas Gould**	Panel 82 Column 2
Able Seaman **Robert George Hamilton**	Panel 38 Column 3
Sub-Lieutenant **Colin William Horner Haslett**	Panel 71 Column 1
Engine Room Artificer 4th Class **Donald McClement**	Panel 67 Column 2
Ordinary Seaman **Lambert Charles Shepherd**	Panel 51 Column 2
Marine **Robert Totton**	Panel 93

Ramleh War Cemetery, Israel and Palestine (including Gaza)

The cemetery dates from the First World War, when Ramleh (now Ramla) was occupied by the 1st Australian Light Horse Brigade on 1 November 1917. During the Second World War, this cemetery was used by the Ramla Royal Air Force Station and by various Commonwealth hospitals posted in turn to this area.

Sergeant **Thomas Carnduff**   Grave 5 H 13

Ranchi War Cemetery, India

After the fall of Rangoon in March 1942 to the Japanese, the possibility that Japanese Forces would occupy the whole of Burma posed a threat to India and Ceylon. Further British Forces were deployed and Ranchi became an important base. The cemetery was begun on 1 June 1942 by the Army, and used until the end of the war. Afterwards burials from isolated positions and small inaccessible cemeteries were brought in.

Private **Alexander McCullough**   Grave 1 B 7

Rangoon Memorial, Myanmar

The Rangoon Memorial is located in Taukkyan War Cemetery, about 35 kilometres north of Yangon (formerly Rangoon). It bears the names of almost 27,000 men of the Commonwealth Land Forces who died during the campaigns in Burma (now Myanmar) and who have no known grave.

Lieutenant **Terence Michael Scott Hadow**	Face 9
Captain **Basil Sheridan Hamilton-Temple-Blackwood**	Face 1
Signalman **Ronald Victor Joseph Martin**	Face 4
Second Lieutenant **William Laurence Megaw**	Face 7
Fusilier **Joseph Nixon**	Face 11
Fusilier **William John Shields**	Face 11
Fusilier **Edwin Appleby Record Watson**	Face 12
Fusilier **Albert John Young**	Face 12
Lance Corporal **George Henry Young**	Face 11

Ranville War Cemetery, Calvados, France

The Allied offensive in north-western Europe began with the Normandy Landings of 6 June 1944. Ranville was the first village to be liberated in France when the bridge over the Caen Canal was captured intact in the early hours of 6 June by troops of the Sixth Airborne Division, who were landed nearby by parachute and glider.

Rifleman **John Blythe**	Grave IVA B 19
Private **Robert Hoey**	Grave IVA C 19

Ranville War Cemetery, Calvados, France continued...

Rifleman **William Johnston**	Grave VA Q 2
Fusilier **John Kavanagh McHugh**	Grave I D 9
Rifleman **John Chapman Oliver**	Grave IVA O 8

Rawalpindi War Cemetery, Pakistan
Rawalpindi War Cemetery is part of the Protestant Cemetery known as *Gorah Qabrastaan* (The Foreign Cemetery).

| Second Lieutenant **David Morrow** | Grave 2 E 13 |

Rawdon (St. Peter) Churchyard, Yorkshire, England
| Sub-Lieutenant (A) **Frederick Robert Akister** | Section D Grave 578 |

Reichswald Forest War Cemetery, Kleve, Nordrhein-Westfalen, Germany
Reichswald Forest War Cemetery was created after the Second World War when burials were brought in from all over western Germany and it is the largest Commonwealth cemetery in the country. Some members of the land forces buried there died in the advance through Reichswald Forest in February 1945. Others died crossing the Rhine, among them members of the airborne forces whose bodies were brought from Hamminkeln, where landings were made by the Sixth Airborne Division from bases in England. Some of the airmen buried in the cemetery lost their lives in supporting the advance into Germany, but many died earlier in the war in the intensive air attacks over Germany. Their graves were brought in from cemeteries and isolated sites in the surrounding area.

Private **Frank William Braisher**	Grave 57 A 7
Sergeant **Richard Sweet Cruise**	Collective Grave 14F 7-14
Lieutenant **Richard John Michael Harrison**	Grave 43 B 7
Private **Hugh Robert Hewitt**	Grave 35 A 9
Sergeant **William Matchett Mahaffy**	Grave 29 E 6
Rifleman **Joseph McCullough**	Grave 40 F 3
Corporal **Martin Ryan**	Grave 61 C 10
Sergeant **Eric Shaw**	Grave 10 B 10
Pilot Officer **Gerald Cecil William Stone MID**	Collective Grave 24C 12-18

Rheinberg War Cemetery, Kamp Lintfort, Nordrhein-Westfal, Germany
The site of Rheinberg War Cemetery was chosen in April 1946 by the Army Graves Service for the burial of Commonwealth graves recovered from numerous German cemeteries in the area. The majority of those now buried

in the cemetery were airmen, whose graves were brought in from Dusseldorf, Krefeld, Munchen-Gladbach, Essen, Aachen, Dortmund and Cologne. Men of the other fighting services buried in Rheinberg mostly lost their lives during the Battle of the Rhineland, or in the advance from the Rhine to the Elbe.

Sergeant **William Anderson**	Grave 13 C 7
Warrant Officer **Samuel Nicholl Beckett**	Collective Grave 8 K 12-17
Sergeant **William Cummins**	Grave 6 D 7
Flight Lieutenant **William Thomas Irwin**	Grave 3 K 9
Lieutenant **Brian Beven Russell**	Grave 13 B 23

Runnymede Memorial, Surrey, England

The Air Forces Memorial at Runnymede commemorates by name over 20,000 airmen who were lost in the Second World War during operations from bases in the United Kingdom and North and Western Europe, and who have no known graves. They served in Bomber, Fighter, Coastal, Transport, Flying Training and Maintenance Commands, and came from all parts of the Commonwealth. Some were from countries in continental Europe which had been overrun but whose airmen continued to fight in the ranks of the Royal Air Force.

Flight Sergeant **Hugh Baird**	Panel 263
Sergeant **Reginald Austin Bigger**	Panel 1
Flying Officer **Geoffrey Alexander Bowman**	Panel 204
Flying Officer **Anthony Alexander Talbot Bulloch**	Panel 5
Flight Sergeant **George Johnston Cheatley**	Panel 73
Squadron Leader **George Crawford DFC AFC**	Panel 200
Sergeant **George Stewart Crossan**	Panel 80
Flight Sergeant **Thomas Watters Doggart**	Panel 270
Flight Lieutenant **Robert Aubrey Alexander Doherty DFC**	Panel 265
Sergeant **Thomas Ernest Victor Doherty**	Panel 147
Leading Aircraftman **Alexander James Donaghy**	Panel 22
Sergeant **David Stuart Donaldson**	Panel 147
Sergeant **Thomas Norman Dunlop**	Panel 274
Sergeant **Joseph Gerald Earley**	Panel 42
Sergeant **Walter Edward Fern**	Panel 149
Sergeant **Robert Wilkinson Foreman**	Panel 83
Flight Lieutenant **Brian Kenneth Levinge Fuge**	Panel 265
Sergeant **Albert Abraham Goldstone**	Panel 150
Flight Sergeant **John Thompson Graham**	Panel 74
Pilot Officer **Alexander William Valentine Green**	Panel 8
Flying Officer **Donald Maldwyn Griffiths**	Panel 206

Runnymede Memorial, Surrey, England continued...

Wing Commander **Charles Ronald Hancock OBE DFC**	Panel 118
Flying Officer **Norman Edmond Hanna**	Panel 173
Flight Lieutenant **Hugh Raymond Harrison DFC**	Panel 202
Sergeant **David Francis Henderson**	Panel 45
Flight Sergeant **John Stewart Hill**	Panel 137
Sergeant **Robert Valentine Ievers**	Panel 86
Flight Sergeant **Angus Campbell Kelly**	Panel 104
Flight Lieutenant **Harold Anthony Kidd-May**	Panel 119
Sergeant **Anthony Wilson Lavender**	Panel 87
Flying Officer **Robert Lawrie Lorimer**	Panel 6
Sergeant **Richard Mailey**	Panel 158
Leading Aircraftman **Norman McReynolds**	Panel 23
Flying Officer **John Finlay Mitchell**	Panel 208
Flight Sergeant **Robert Angus Moore**	Panel 138
Sergeant **Nagu Ranganatha**	Panel 92
Flying Officer **Frederick John Reid**	Panel 243
Pilot Officer **Horace James Rich**	Panel 212
Flying Officer **Arthur Buckby Sinton**	Panel 129
Flight Lieutenant **Eric Augustus Snow**	Panel 203
Pilot Officer **Hugh Conn Thompson**	Panel 133
Pilot Officer **Alan Lancelot Treanor**	Panel 10
Flying Officer **James Kenneth Weir**	Panel 209
Flight Sergeant **George Wilson**	Panel 140
Corporal **Matthew Wilson MID**	Panel 22
Sergeant **Ralph Henry John Winter**	Panel 97

Ryes War Cemetery, Bazenville, Calvados, France

Bazenville is a village 8 kilometres east of Bayeux. The Allied offensive in north-western Europe began with the Normandy Landings of 6 June 1944. Ryes War Cemetery is not far inland from the beaches at Arromanches, where the 50th Division landed on 6 June. The first burials were made there just two days after the landings.

Private **Frederick George Wright**	Grave V C 5

Sage War Cemetery, Oldenburg, Niedersachsen, Germany

Sage is a village in the north of Germany around 56 kilometres west of Bremen. Sage was on the line of the Allied advance across northern Germany in 1945 but most of those buried at Sage War Cemetery were airmen lost in bombing raids over northern Europe whose graves were brought in from cemeteries in the Frisian Islands and other parts of north-west Germany.

Flight Sergeant **Edward Carson Thompson**   **Grave 7 E 10**

Sangro River War Cemetery, Chieti, Abruzzo, Italy
In November 1943 the Allied force that had fought its way up the Adriatic Coast attacked German positions on the Sangro River positions. A bridgehead was established and by nightfall on 30 November the ridge overlooking the river was in Allied hands. The site for this cemetery was selected by the 5th Corps and many graves were brought in, including men who had died in the fighting on the Adriatic sector of the front in November and December 1943, and during the static period that followed. In addition, the cemetery contains the graves of a number of escaped Prisoners-of-War who died while trying to reach the Allied Lines.

Flying Officer **Ian Alexander Calthrop Campbell**   **Grave XI C 7**
Lieutenant **Ernest Basil Snell Hewitt MC**   **Grave VIII E 28**
Rifleman **Desmond Hull**   **Grave XI C 21**
Lance Corporal **Andrew McVeigh**   **Grave VIII E 9**

Sannox Old Churchyard, Kilbride, Isle of Arran, Scotland
Flight Lieutenant **Wilfrid Mark Hamilton Brookes**   **West extension**

Schoonselhof Cemetery, Antwerpen, Belgium
Antwerp was the seat of the Belgian Government from 17 August to 7 October 1914 and then from 10 October 1914 to the Armistice the city was in German hands. German Forces returned to Belgium in May 1940 and occupied Antwerp until its liberation by the Allies on 4 September 1944.

Pilot Officer **Frederick William McMurray**   **Grave II H 32**

Sessenheim Communal Cemetery, Bas-Rhin, France
Sessenheim is a commune some 38 kilometres north-east of Strasbourg.

Sergeant **Stanley Minnis**   **Grave 9**

Sfax War Cemetery, Tunisia
Sfax is a town about 270 kilometres south of Tunis. In May 1943, the war in North Africa came to an end in Tunisia with the defeat of the Axis powers by a combined Allied Force. In the south, the Axis Forces defeated in Egypt at El Alamein withdrew into Tunisia along the coast through Libya, pursued by the Allied Eighth Army. Most of those buried in Sfax War Cemetery died in attacks on successive Axis positions at Medenine, the Marith Line and Wadi

Akarit during March and April 1943.

Major **Herbert Noel Wallace MC**   Grave II D 20

Shorne (St. Peter and St. Paul) Churchyard, Kent, England
Lance Corporal **James Charles McCaul**   SE of Church

Singapore Memorial, Singapore
The Singapore Memorial stands in the Kranji War Cemetery and bears the names of over 24,000 casualties of the Commonwealth land and air forces who have no known grave. The land forces commemorated by the memorial died during the campaigns in Malaya and Indonesia or in subsequent captivity, many of them during the construction of the Burma-Thailand railway, or at sea while being transported into imprisonment elsewhere. The Memorial also commemorates airmen who died during operations over the whole of southern and eastern Asia and the surrounding seas and oceans.

Private **Gerald Mavor Bell**	Column 119
Captain **Robert James Bleakley**	Column 391
Aircraftman First Class **Hugh Craig**	Column 417
Captain **David Alexander Hynes Hodgett MID**	Column 307
Squadron Leader **Robert William Stanley Marshall**	Column 445
Sergeant **Joseph Mercer**	Column 415
Corporal **Thomas Paterson Muckle**	Column 437
Sister **Edith Doreen Pedlow MID**	Column 114
Leading Aircraftman **Ritson Finlay Petts**	Column 410
Flying Officer **Hubert Stanley Sheals**	Column 413
Captain **Humphrey Barron Thomson**	Column 103

Sola Churchyard, Norway
During the Second World War, Norway was of strategic importance to the Germans. Their invasion on 9 April 1940 was sudden and widespread and despite Allied intervention, the entire country was under German occupation by early June. Thereafter, Allied activity in Norway was confined to raids and special operations, with the Commonwealth Air Forces providing support to Norwegian resistance groups until the German capitulation in May 1945. There are no Commonwealth war cemeteries in Norway, those who died there being buried in civil cemeteries and churchyards. Sola, the site of Stavanger airport, was captured by the Germans on 9 April 1940 and was raided constantly thereafter by the Commonwealth Air Forces, being the nearest aerodrome in Norway to the home bases in Scotland. It was heavily defended and many of the crews were shot down.

Sola Churchyard, Norway continued...

Sergeant **Cyril Johnson Crozier**	**British Plot E 9**
Pilot Officer **Basil Pollock Erskine**	**British Plot B 4**

Somenos (St. Mary's) Church Cemetery, British Columbia, Canada
Private **Harold William Calvert**

Southend-on-Sea (Sutton Road) Cemetery, Essex, England
Gunner **Joseph Shanks**   **Plot R Grave 12164**

St. Charles de Percy War Cemetery, Calvados, France
Private **Samuel McBride**   **Grave VII B 13**

St. Helens Cemetery, Lancashire, England
Driver **Eric Joseph Heyes**   **Section 30 Grave 106**

St. Inglevert Churchyard, Pas de Calais, France
Pilot Officer (Air Gunner) **James Hamilton Gordon**   **Collective Grave**

St. Pierre Cemetery, Amiens, Somme, France
During the Second World War, Amiens was an important British base and GHQ Reserve was accommodated in the area south-west of the town. There was heavy fighting in and around Amiens when the Germans broke through the Somme line and took the town on 18 May 1940. Much damage was done, but although all the houses to the west of the cathedral were completely destroyed by the bombardment, the cathedral itself and the Church of St. Germain l'Ecossais survived. Amiens was retaken by the British Second Army on 31 August 1944. Numbers 25 and 121 General Hospitals were posted there in October 1944, remaining until April 1945.

Sergeant (Pilot) **Victor Hall Skillen**   **Plot 1 Row A Grave 12**

St. Sever Cemetery Extension, Rouen, Seine-Maritime, France
This cemetery extension was created in 1916 when Rouen was an important hospital base during the Great War. During the Second World War, Rouen was a hospital centre once more and the cemetery extension was used again for the burial of Commonwealth servicemen, many of whom died as Prisoners-of-War during the German occupation.

Captain **Samuel David Corry MID**   **Block S Plot 4 Row R Grave 14**

Staglieno Cemetery, Genoa, Liguria, Italy

Most of the Second World War graves were garrison burials; others were brought in from the surrounding countryside.

Sergeant **Robert Keith Eston**   Grave III A 28

Stoneykirk Cemetery, Wigtownshire, Scotland
Flight Sergeant **Edward Dennis Cannon**   Section C Grave 134

Stratford-on-Avon Cemetery, Warwickshire, England
Sergeant **Robert Henry Harper**   Grave 4149

Streatham Park Cemetery, Surrey, England
Sergeant (Pilot) **David John Goodchild**   Square 6B Grave 19215

Suez War Memorial Cemetery, Egypt

Suez was an important hospital centre during the First World War and the War Memorial Cemetery was established in 1918. The Second World War burials were from the large garrison based in and around Suez.

Driver **William Graham**   Grave 2 G 12
Lieutenant **William Harold Graham**   Grave 3 B 6
Sergeant **Samuel John Luke**   Grave 1 B 1

Sutton-in-Ashfield Cemetery, Nottinghamshire, England
Fusilier **William Bellamy**   Section C Grave 7629

Sylling Churchyard, Norway

Sola Churchyard has details about the war in Norway; Sylling Churchyard is 27 kilometres west of Oslo.

Leading Aircraftman **Frederick Armand Morrison**   Grave 6

Tangmere (St. Andrew) Churchyard, Sussex, England

The churchyard of St. Andrew adjoins the RAF Aerodrome at Tangmere and it has been used for the burial of airmen from this station who died before, during and since the Second World War.

Sergeant (Observer) **Charles Julius Holland**   Plot E Row 1 Grave 460

Taukkyan War Cemetery, Myanmar

Taukkyan War Cemetery is the largest of the three war cemeteries in Burma (now Myanmar). It was begun in 1951 for the reception of graves from four battlefield cemeteries at Akyab, Mandalay, Meiktila and Sahmaw which were difficult to access and could not be maintained. The last was an original Chindit cemetery containing many of those who died in the battle for Myitkyina in August 1944. Burials were also transferred from civil and cantonment cemeteries and from a number of isolated jungle and roadside sites. Because of prolonged post-war unrest there was delay in completing this work.

Staff Sergeant **Thomas Anthoney**   Grave 12 K 17
Lieutenant **James Gilmore Scott**   Grave 13 F 18
Flight Sergeant **Alan McDonald Wilson**   Collective Grave 28 F 8-17

Tilly-sur-Seulles War Cemetery, Calvados, France
The Allied offensive in north-western Europe began with the Normandy Landings of 6 June 1944 and there was heavy fighting in the vicinity of Tilly-sur-Seulles immediately after the landings. Tilly-sur-Seulles itself was captured by the Allies on 18 June 1944 and fighting continued nearby.

Chaplain 4th Class **The Revd James Douglas MID**   Grave VII C 3

Tobruk War Cemetery, Libya
Tobruk is a Mediterranean port with an excellent deep water harbour. During the Second World War it was important to both Allied and Axis Forces for the reception of supplies and reinforcements. In January 1941 it was captured by Allied Forces from the Italians and, after the harbour was cleared, the port was extensively used. When Rommel commenced his drive across Cyrenaica towards Suez it was decided that Tobruk should be held, and the resulting siege lasted from 11 April to 10 December 1941, when the Axis Forces were driven back. They recovered more quickly than was expected and by early February 1942 the Allies were forced to fall back towards a line running southwards from Gazala to Bir Hakeim. Again orders were given to hold Tobruk, but it fell to Rommel on 21 June. Tobruk was retaken five months later by the Eighth Army in their final sweep along the North African coast into Tunisia. Tobruk War Cemetery incorporates the burial ground used during the siege and many battlefield graves in the desert were brought into the cemetery.

Gunner **Robert Cromie**   Grave 10 D 6
Gunner **Joseph Dalzell**   Grave 6 K 9
Gunner **Samuel Graham**   Grave 6 K 11
Bombardier **Harold Johnston**   Grave 2 E 13
Gunner **William James Martin**   Grave 2 E 27
Bombardier **William John McNeilly**   Grave 6 K 12

Tobruk War Cemetery, Libya continued...

Gunner **James Meredith**	Grave 6 K 4
Lance Bombardier **Robert Orr Thompson**	Grave 3 Q 2

Toronto (St. James) Cemetery, Ontario, Canada
Sergeant **Henry Garrett Burrows** — Block T Lot 181 North

Towcester Cemetery, Northamptonshire, England
Lance Corporal **Alexander Richard Day Vinycomb MM** — Row G Grave 7

Tower Hill Memorial, London, England

The Tower Hill Memorial commemorates men and women of the Merchant Navy and Fishing Fleets who died in both World Wars and who have no known grave but the sea. It stands on the south side of the garden of Trinity Square, London, close to the Tower of London. During the Second World War losses were high in the early years, reaching a peak in 1942. The heaviest losses were suffered in the Atlantic, but convoys making their way to Russia around the North Cape, and those supplying Malta in the Mediterranean were also particularly vulnerable to attack. The Second World War extension to the Tower Hill Memorial was unveiled by Queen Elizabeth II on 5 November 1955.

Assistant Steward **Ronald Wilson Baker**	Panel 66
Cabin Boy **Thomas Crawford Barbour**	Panel 42
Third Engineer Officer **John George Briggs Baxter**	Panel 15
Chief Officer **Hugh Bell**	Panel 27
Carpenter **James McNeilly Belshaw**	Panel 60
Barber **William James Canavan**	Panel 19
Fireman **James Clegg**	Panel 44
Able Seaman **Douglas Collister**	Panel 114
Third Radio Officer **James McMurtry Corbett**	Panel 21
Cook **Robert Crone**	Panel 69
Mate **John Cully**	Panel 87
Able Seaman **John Ferris Deveney**	Panel 114
Third Engineer Officer **Joseph Gerald Foster**	Panel 36
Chief Engineer Officer **John Gibson**	Panel 87
Sailor **Patrick Joseph Gibson**	Panel 38
Junior Engineer Officer **John Corbett Hall**	Panel 60
Able Seaman **William Harper**	Panel 68
Boatswain **John Hawthorne**	Panel 52
Fifth Engineer Officer **Thomas McMahon Houston**	Panel 38

Tower Hill Memorial, London, England continued...

First Radio Officer **Robert George Wylie Irwin**	**Panel 23**
Master **John Frazer Jefferson**	**Panel 22**
Able Seaman **John Joseph Kennedy**	**Panel 38**
Second Officer **George McClelland Leckey**	**Panel 60**
Able Seaman **James Smiley Logan**	**Panel 59**
Junior Engineer Officer **William Lough**	**Panel 28**
Fireman **Francis Maginness**	**Panel 87**
First Radio Officer **William James McCrory**	**Panel 30**
Third Radio Officer **Charles Knox McCune**	**Panel 63**
Able Seaman **John McGrath**	**Panel 112**
Second Officer **Andrew McKay**	**Panel 95**
Ordinary Seaman **James McMaster**	**Panel 87**
Third Officer **William Ian Muir McMullan**	**Panel 22**
Carpenter **John Alexander McNeilance**	**Panel 47**
Radio Officer **Edward George Mee**	**Panel 60**
Master **William Johnston Meek**	**Panel 56**
Sailor **William Joseph Mehigan**	**Panel 68**
Sailor **William Patton**	**Panel 17**
Sixth Engineer Officer **Hugh Longueville Price**	**Panel 116**
Assistant Steward **Reginald John Primmer**	**Panel 60**
Sailor **David John Pritchard**	**Panel 60**
Chief Steward **William McKinley Rae**	**Panel 52**
Fireman **Donald Gordon Reid**	**Panel 43**
Third Engineer Officer **Albert Sandfield**	**Panel 64**
Ordinary Seaman **Robert Joseph Shaw**	**Panel 22**
Third Engineer Officer **James Skillen**	**Panel 52**
Apprentice **William Edward Trimble**	**Panel 19**
Master **Arthur Hill Coates Waterson**	**Panel 12**
Second Officer **Leonard Whiston**	**Panel 107**
Able Seaman **James White**	**Panel 92**
Able Seaman **John White**	**Panel 68**
Fireman **Garner Wilson**	**Panel 42**

Troon Cemetery, Ayrshire, Scotland

Lance Corporal **James Keenan**	**Section J 1 Grave 113**

Udine War Cemetery, Friuli-Venezia Giulia, Italy

Udine was entered by Allied troops on 1 May 1945, the day before the German surrender in Italy. Burials in Udine War Cemetery include casualties from the last few days of the war in Italy, some earlier prisoner-of-war and air force casualties, later garrison burials and some made from 70 British General Hospital which was at Udine for several months from May 1945.

Pilot Officer **Samuel Irwin Taylor**   Collective Grave I C 3-5

Upper Heyford Cemetery, Oxfordshire, England
During the early part of the Second World War ground in the south-western corner of this cemetery was set aside for service war burials and was used by the RAF Station at Upper Heyford.

Flying Officer **William Howard Corbett**   Section B Grave 87

Valkenswaard War Cemetery, Noord-Brabant, Netherlands
The town of Valkenswaard is located in the south of the Netherlands, around 10 kilometres south of Eindhoven and close to the Belgian border. Valkenswaard was the first village to be liberated on the main line of the British advance into Holland in September 1944. The cemetery which lies in a pine wood contains over 220 graves and most of them are of men who fell during the fighting in the woods around Valkenswaard that month.

Sergeant **Patrick Leslie Whitehouse**   Grave I F 6

Venray War Cemetery, Limburg, Netherlands
The town of Venray lies in the south of the Netherlands approx 40 kilometres to the east of Eindhoven. The Netherlands fell to the Germans in May 1940 and was not re-entered by Allied Forces until September 1944. The town of Venray was liberated by Allied troops in the middle of October 1944 and the burials in this cemetery date from October 1944 to March 1945.

Sergeant (Flight Engineer) **David Burrows George**   Grave VII B 4
Rifleman **Robert James Miskimmin**   Grave VIII E 2

Viroflay New Communal Cemetery, Yvelines, France
Viroflay is a small town 4 kilometres east of Versailles.

Flight Lieutenant **Wilfred Ronald Maitland DFC**   Row A Grave 15

Wandsworth (Streatham) Cemetery, London
The cemetery is in Garratt Lane, mid way between Upper and Lower Tooting.

LAC **Leslie Frederick Williams**   Block 12 Grave 596 Screen Wall Panel 6

Watford North Cemetery, Hertfordshire, England
Sergeant **Newtown Hunter Middleton Williams** Section B Cons Grave 1373

Wellingborough (Doddington Road) Cemetery, Northamptonshire, England
Flight Sergeant **Alex Joseph Bell**   Section N Grave 65

Whitechurch Cemetery, Ballywalter, Co. Down
Able Seaman **Eugene Hector McSweeney**

Wigtoft (St. Peter and St. Paul) Churchyard, Lincolnshire, England
Sergeant **Peter Murray Rogerson**

Windsor (Grove) Cemetery, Ontario, Canada
This cemetery is on the corner of Giles Boulevard and Howard Avenue.

Sergeant **Hugh Blackwood Price**   Section 14 Grave 13

Yokohama Cremation Memorial, Japan
This Memorial is located in Yokohama War Cemetery and takes the form of a shrine which houses an urn containing the ashes of 335 soldiers, sailors and airmen of the Commonwealth, the United States of America and the Kingdom of the Netherlands who died as Prisoners-of-War in Japan. Their names (apart from 51 who were not identified) are inscribed on the walls of the shrine.

Flight Sergeant **George Francis Grattan**   Panel 5
Aircraftman First Class **Francis Meredith**   Panel 6

Abbreviations and Glossary of Terms

This is not an exhaustive list of all the abbreviations and terms used in this book; some abbreviations and terms are explained at the point in the text where they are used.

A&SH	Argyll and Sutherland Highlanders
AAC	Army Air Corps
	The AAC was formed in 1942 and comprised the Glider Pilot Regiment, the Parachute Regiment and, from 1944, the SAS Regiment.
AACU	Anti-Aircraft Co-operation Unit
AAMC	Australian Army Medical Corps
ABMC	American Battle Monuments Commission
ABV	Armed Boarding Vessel
AC1	Aircraftman 1st Class
AC2	Aircraftman 2nd Class
ACIS	Associate of the Chartered Institute of Secretaries
Ack-ack	Anti-aircraft fire
ACT	Australian Capital Territory
ACW	Aircraftwoman
AFC	Air Force Cross
AIF	Australian Imperial Force
AMC	Armed Merchant Cruiser
AMES	Air Ministry Experimental Stations
AMIME	Associate Member of the Institute of Mechanical Engineers
AOP	Air Observation Post
ARP	Air Raid Precautions
	ARP was an organisation in the UK formed in 1924 and dedicated to the protection of civilians from the dangers of air raids. During the Second World War it was responsible for the issuing of gas masks, pre-fabricated air-raid shelters, the upkeep of public shelters and the maintenance of the blackout.
ASR	Air Sea Rescue
ASRMCU	Air Sea Rescue Marine Craft Unit
ASW	Anti-Submarine Warfare
ATC	Air Training Corps
ATS	Auxiliary Territorial Service
	The ATS was the women's branch of the British Army

during the Second World War. It was formed on 9 September 1938 and existed until 1 February 1949 when it was merged into the Women's Royal Army Corps (WRAC). The ATS had its roots in the Women's Auxiliary Army Corps (WAAC) which was formed in 1917 as a voluntary service and disbanded in 1921.

attd	attached
B&GS	Bombing & Gunnery School
BB	Boys' Brigade
Bde	Brigade
BEF	British Expeditionary Force
BGS	Bangor Grammar School
Bn	Battalion
BS	Boundary Stone
CAM	Catapult Armed Merchantmen
CB	Companion of the Order of the Bath
Chyd	Churchyard
Chindits	British special force that served during the Burma Campaign. *They were trained to operate deep behind the enemy (Japanese) lines in Burma and India.*
CID	Criminal Investigation Department
CIE	Companion of the Order of the Indian Empire
CIYMS	Church of Ireland Young Men's Society
CLB	Church Lads' Brigade
Cmdr	Commander
CO	Commanding Officer
C of E	Church of England
C of I	Church of Ireland
Cons	Consecrated
Coy	Company
Cpl	Corporal
CQMS	Company Quartermaster Sergeant
CSM	Company Sergeant Major (the senior NCO in an Army Company)
CTC	Combined Training Centre
CVWM	Canadian Virtual War Memorial
CWGC	Commonwealth War Graves Commission
DAP	Deutsche Arbeiterpartei (German Workers' Party). *Formed in January 1919, Hitler joined the Party in September that year. In 1920 the party name was changed to: **Na**tionalso**zi**alistische Deutsche Arbeiterpartei (National*

Socialist German Workers' Party or Nazi Party).

DBE	Dame Commander of the Most Excellent Order of the British Empire
DBS	Distressed British Seamen
DCM	Distinguished Conduct Medal
DEMS	Defensively Equipped Merchant Ships
DF	Direction Finding
DFC	Distinguished Flying Cross
DL	Deputy Lieutenant
Div	Division
DOW	Died of wounds
DSC	Distinguished Service Cross
DSO	Distinguished Service Order
(E)	Engineer
ECM	Electronic Countermeasures
EFTS	Elementary Flying Training School
ERA	Engine Room Artificer
Ext	Extension
FAI	Fellowship of the Auctioneers' Institute
FAFL	Forces Aeriennes Francaises Libres (Free French Air Force)
FFAF	Free French Air Force
Flak	**Fl**ugzeug**a**bweh**rk**anone
Flt Lt	Flight Lieutenant
FO	Flying Officer
FS	Flight Sergeant
FWW	First World War (also World War One or Great War)
GCI	Ground Controlled Interception
Gestapo	**Ge**heime **Sta**at**spo**lizei (Secret State Police)
	The Gestapo was formed in 1933 by Herman Goring and from 1934 it was led by Heinrich Himmler.
GHQ	General Headquarters
GNAT	German Navy Acoustic Torpedo
GPO	General Post Office
GRO	General Register Office
Grp Cpt	Group Captain
GRT	Gross Register Tonnage
HAA	Heavy Anti-Aircraft
HCU	Heavy Conversion Unit
HD	Home Defence
HLI	Highland Light Infantry
HQ	Headquarters

HMHS	His Majesty's Hospital Ship
HMLCT (A)	His Majesty's Landing Craft Tank (Armoured)
HMML	His Majesty's Motor Launch
HMMM	His Majesty's Motor Minesweeper
HMRT	His Majesty's Rescue Tug
HMS	His Majesty's Ship
HMT	His Majesty's Transport or His Majesty's Troopship
HSL	High Speed Launch
HWM	High Water Mark
ISO	Imperial Service Order
ITW	Initial Training Wing
Jnr	Junior
KCMG	Knight Commander of the Order of St. Michael and St. George
KIA	Killed in Action
Kriegsmarine	Nazi German Navy
KRRC	King's Royal Rifle Corps
KSLI	King's Shropshire Light Infantry
LAA	Light Anti-Aircraft
LAC	Leading Aircraftman
L/Cpl	Lance Corporal
LOL	Loyal Orange Lodge
Lt	Lieutenant
Lt Cdr	Lieutenant Commander
Lt Col	Lieutenant Colonel
Maj	Major
MBE	Member of the Order of the British Empire
MC	Military Cross
MCB	Methodist College Belfast
MF	Medium Frequency
MFP	Military Foot Police
MIA	Missing in Action
MICE	Member of the Institute of Civil Engineers
MID	Mentioned in Despatches
MLD	Marine-Luchtvaartdienst (Netherlands Naval Aviation Service)
MM	Military Medal
MOWT	Ministry of War Transport
MSF	Minesweeping Flotilla
MU	Maintenance Unit
MV	Motor Vessel

NAAFI	Navy, Army and Air Force Institutes
Nazi	**Na**tionalso**zi**alist
NCO	Non-Commissioned Officer
NOIC	Naval Officer in Charge
NSDAP	**Na**tionalso**zi**alistische Deutsche Arbeiterpartei *(National Socialist German Workers' Party or Nazi Party)*
NZ	New Zealand
NZEF	New Zealand Expeditionary Force
OBE	Officer of the Most Excellent Order of the British Empire
OBLI	Oxford and Bucks Light infantry
Obs	Observer
OCTU	Officer Cadet Training Unit
ORTU	Operational and Refresher Training Unit
OTC	Officers' Training Corps
OTU	Operational Training Unit
PCI	Presbyterian Church in Ireland
PFC	Private First Class
PO	Pilot Officer
POW	Prisoner-of-War
Prot	Protestant
PTC	Primary Training Centre
Pte	Private
QAIMNS	Queen Alexandra's Imperial Military Nursing Service
QL	Quick Light
QMS	Quartermaster Sergeant
Q-ship	Armed merchant ship with concealed weaponry
QUB	Queen's University Belfast
RA	Royal Artillery
RAAF	Royal Australian Air Force
RAC	Royal Armoured Corps
RAChD	Royal Army Chaplains' Department
RAF	Royal Air Force
RAFO	Reserve of Air Force Officers
RAFVR	Royal Air Force Volunteer Reserve *(formed in July 1936)*
RAMC	Royal Army Medical Corps
RAOC	Royal Army Ordnance Corps
RAPC	Royal Arch Purple Chapter
RASC	Royal Army Service Corps *(Army Service Corps until 1918)*
RBAI	Royal Belfast Academical Institution (Inst)
RBL	Royal British Legion
RBP	Royal Black Preceptory

RC	Roman Catholic
RCAC	Royal Canadian Armoured Corps
RCAF	Royal Canadian Air Force
RCASC	Royal Canadian Army Service Corps
RCCS	Royal Canadian Corps of Signals
RCE	Royal Canadian Engineers
RCIC	Royal Canadian Infantry Corps
RCM	Refugee Children Movement
RCNVR	Royal Canadian Navy Volunteer Reserve
RE	Royal Engineers
	The Corps of Royal Engineers is commonly referred to as the Royal Engineers or the Sappers. The Royal Corps of Signals is commonly referred to as the Royal Signals.
Red Army	National military service of the Soviet Union
	The Workers' and Peasants' Red Army was the national military service of the Soviet Union until 1946 when it was renamed the Soviet Army.
Regt/Rgt	Regiment
REME	Royal Electrical and Mechanical Engineers
Revd	Reverend
RHA	Royal Horse Artillery
RHS	Regent House School (Newtownards)
RIASC	Royal Indian Army Service Corps
R Innis Fus	Royal Inniskilling Fusiliers
RIC	Royal Irish Constabulary
RIP	Requiescat in Pace (Rest in Peace)
RAOC	Royal Army Ordnance Corps
RM	Royal Marines
RMS	Royal Mail Ship
RNAS	Royal Naval Air Station
RNPS	Royal Naval Patrol Service
RNVR	Royal Naval Volunteer Reserve
RNZAF	Royal New Zealand Air Force
RNZNVR	Royal New Zealand Naval Volunteer Reserve
RSM	Regimental Sergeant Major (the most senior NCO)
RUC	Royal Ulster Constabulary
RUR	Royal Ulster Rifles
SA	South African
SA	Sturmabteilung (Stormtroopers or Brownshirts)
	The SA formed the paramilitary wing of the Nazi Party and from 1921 to 1934 provided protection at Nazi rallies.

In June/July 1934 the Nazi regime carried out a purge and many SA leaders were murdered by the SS and the Gestapo during the 'night of the long knives'.

SAC	Senior Aircraftman
SAS	Special Air Service
SAS Regiment	Founded by Colonel David Stirling and later commanded by Lieutenant Colonel Blair 'Paddy' Mayne after Stirling was captured.
Sgt	Sergeant
SLG	Satellite Landing Ground
Snr	Senior
SQMS	Squadron Quartermaster Sergeant
Sqn Ldr	Squadron Leader
SS	Steamship
SS	**S**chutz**s**taffel
	The SS was Hitler's personal bodyguard and from 1929 Heinrich Himmler was its leader.
SSV	Special Service Vessel
Stalag	Stammlager (German Prisoner-of-War Camp)
SUS	Sullivan Upper School (Holywood)
SWW	Second World War (also World War Two)
TB	Tuberculosis
transfd	transferred
TSM	Troop Sergeant Major (the senior NCO in a Royal Artillery Troop)
U-boat	Unterseeboot (Undersea Boat); German submarine
UK	United Kingdom (England, Scotland, Wales and Northern Ireland)
UKSF	United Kingdom Special Forces
US/USA	United States of America
USAAF	United States Army Air Force
USNS	United States Naval Ship
USS	United States Ship
USSR	Union of Soviet Socialist Republics (Soviet Union)
	This union existed from 1922 until 1991
U/T	Under training
UTA	Ulster Transport Authority
VF	Volunteer Force
VGofC	Veterans Guard of Canada
WAAC	Women's Auxiliary Army Corps
WAAF	Women's Auxiliary Air Force

WD	War Department
Wg Cdr	Wing Commander
WO	Warrant Officer
WRAC	Women's Royal Army Corps
WRAF	Women's Royal Air Force
WRNS	Women's Royal Naval Service
WW1	World War One (also First World War or Great War)
WW2	World War Two (also Second World War)
YS Bn	Young Soldiers' Battalion
YMCA	Young Men's Christian Association
YWCA	Young Women's Christian Association

Rank Equivalents across the Services

Army	Navy	Air Force
Field Marshal	Admiral of the Fleet	Marshal of the Air Force
General	Admiral	Air Chief Marshal
Brigadier	Commodore	Air Commodore
Colonel	Captain	Group Captain
Lieutenant Colonel	Commander	Wing Commander
Major	Lieutenant Commander	Squadron Leader
Captain	Lieutenant	Flight Lieutenant
Lieutenant	Sub-Lieutenant	Flying Officer
Second Lieutenant	Ensign	Pilot Officer
Officer Cadet	Midshipman	Officer Cadet
Sergeant Major	Warrant Officer	Warrant Officer
Sergeant	Petty Officer	Sergeant
Corporal	Leading Seaman	Corporal
Private	Seaman	Aircraftman

Adjutant	*Officer in charge of Battalion administration*
Ordinary Seaman	*Apprenticeship to becoming an Able Seaman*
Quartermaster	*Sergeant responsible for stores and transport*
Subaltern	*Commissioned Officer below the rank of Captain*

Additional Information

In this Section there is additional information about some of the people with North Down/Ards connections who died in the Second World War.

Anderson, Frederick Hugh
Pilot Officer (Pilot)
No. 404880, 153 (RAF) Squadron, Royal New Zealand Air Force

His parents, Hugh Alexander Anderson and Ruby Eleanor Anderson (nee Pemberton), were married in 1916 in New Zealand.

Blythe, John Harold (known as Jack, sometimes as Norris)
Rifleman
No. 7019887, 1st (Airborne) Battalion, Royal Ulster Rifles

Rifleman Blythe died of wounds sustained in a mortar attack at Le Mesnil.

Cheatley, George Johnston (George)
Flight Sergeant
No. 748222, 269 Squadron Royal Air Force Volunteer Reserve

David Johnston Cheatley, son of George Johnston Cheatley and Hughedna Doreen Cheatley (nee Shanks), was born on 8 July 1940.

Crozier, Archibald
Private
No. 13011578, Pioneer Corps

Archibald's brother, Samuel Finlay Kitchener Crozier, was born on 9 November 1914.

Cutler, Robert Henry (Tabby)
Major (demobilised)
King's African Rifles

His parents' marriage was registered in the second quarter of 1903 in Cork.

Dickson, Thomas (Tommy)
Lance Corporal
No. 7019627, 2nd Battalion, Royal Ulster Rifles

Lance Corporal Dickson died as a result of a fractured skull in Peel Hospital, Clovenfords, Scotland.

Elcock, Norman M.
Sergeant (Wireless Operator/Air Gunner)
No. 1112747, Royal Air Force Volunteer Reserve
Killed in an aircraft accident on Thursday 23 April 1942 (aged 21)
Over Congregational Burial Ground, Winsford, Cheshire (Grave 258)

Norman M. Elcock's birth was registered in the fourth quarter of 1920 in Conway, Merionethshire, Wales and he was a son of Albert Edward and Phyllis Elcock (nee Templar). Their marriage was registered in the third quarter of 1914 in Conway and they had at least two children – Louise Vivienne (born 3 January 1917, married Thomas Hough in the fourth quarter of 1939, died December 1988) and Norman M. (born 1920). Norman's paternal grandparents were Richard and Hannah Elcock.

During the Second World War Sergeant Norman Elcock served with the Royal Air Force Volunteer Reserve. On 23 April 1942 he was the wireless operator/air gunner aboard a Westland Lysander Mark III communications and target-towing aircraft (V9721) which crashed on take-off from RAF Belfast (now the George Best Belfast City Airport) on a training flight. Also killed that day was the pilot, Sergeant **Jozef Antoni Pudelko**. Sergeant Norman Elcock was buried in Over Congregational Burial Ground, Winsford, Cheshire and he is commemorated on the War Memorial sited in front of the United Reformed Church, Over, Cheshire. Norman's father, Albert Edward Elcock, of 425 High Street, Winsford died on 18 March 1950.

Gibson, John
Chief Engineer Officer
SS *River Humber* (Bristol), Merchant Navy
Died as a result of a collision at sea on Tuesday 4 June 1940 (aged 32)
Tower Hill Memorial, London, England (Panel 87)

John Gibson was born around 1908 in Pennan, Aberdeenshire and he was a son of Alexander Pratt Gibson and Mary Jane Gibson (nee West) of Aberdour, Aberdeenshire. Alexander Gibson was an oatmeal miller and he and Mary West were married around 1895. They had at least ten children including Barbara (born around 1897); Alexander W. (born around 1898); Baden P. (born around 1902); Bertie (born around 1904); John (born around 1908) and Charlotte (born around 1910).

John Gibson (aged 24) was the driver on a drifter when he and Christina Wiseman (a fishworker aged 17), daughter of James Wiseman (a fisherman) and Christine Ann Wiseman (nee Webster) of Gardenstown, Banffshire were married on 22 December 1932 in The Manse, Aberdour (according to the forms of the Church of Scotland).

During the Second World War John Gibson served with the Merchant Navy aboard the SS *River Humber*. Built in 1920 by Hepple and Company Ltd., South Shields and owned by Charles Neill Ltd., Bangor, the SS *River Humber* was on passage from Dublin to Preston in ballast when she sank after a collision with HMS *Folkestone* in the Irish Sea east-north-east of Skerries, Dublin. Chief Engineer Officer John Gibson was 32 years old when he died; Mate **Jack Cully**, Ordinary Seaman **James McMaster** and Fireman **Frank Maginnis** died in the same incident.

In the Register of Deceased Seamen it is recorded that Chief Engineer Officer John Gibson lived for a time at 26 Primrose Street, Bangor. He is commemorated on the Tower Hill Memorial in London.

Gilpin, John Robert
Rifleman
No. 7013792, 2nd Battalion, Royal Ulster Rifles

Rifleman Gilpin was killed at Bray Dunes during the Dunkirk evacuation.

Johnston, John
Ordinary Seaman
No. D/JX 619483, Royal Navy

John Johnston was born in 1927 and he was a son of James and Mary Jane Johnston (nee Brown, from Londonderry). The Johnston family came from Ballymagee Street, Bangor and James joined the Royal Inniskilling Fusiliers in 1904. He was demobilised in 1913, rejoined the Colours in 1914 and was demobilised in France in 1919. James and Mary Jane Johnston lived in Newtownards at 34B South Street (later at 14 Pound Street) and they had four children – Harold, Agnes Jane, Jim and John. Mary Jane Johnston died of Bright's Disease on 19 July 1927 when John was a baby.

John Johnston attended Castle Gardens National School, Newtownards and during the Second World War he served with the Royal Navy. During the First World War his uncle Samuel Johnston also served with the Royal Navy and Samuel was killed in action on 1 November 1914; Able Seaman Samuel Johnston is commemorated on Page 301 in the Book of Honour *Remembering Their Sacrifice in the Great War – Ards* compiled by Barry Niblock.

Lindsay, David
Leading Aircraftman
No. 654457,Royal Air Force

Leading Aircraftman David Lindsay was killed in an aircraft accident on 14 March 1945 when he was on his way home after being given compassionate posting due to his son's illness (his son Leslie suffered from asthma).

Rifleman Victor Stanley Rooney (Leading Aircraftman David Lindsay's brother-in-law) was a son of Hugh Henry Rooney, 39 Skegoniell Avenue, Belfast and the late Mrs Rooney of Colebrooke, Co. Fermanagh. Rifleman Rooney was wounded in action in the Black Forest in April 1945 and was due for demobilisation when he died suddenly in Germany on 7 September 1946.

MacCallum, John Evelyn Matier (Lyn)
Group Captain
No. 26039, Royal Air Force

In 1922/23 Lyn MacCallum was Captain of the Portadown College 1st XV rugby team.

Maxwell, Charles (Charlie)
Rifleman
No. 7022229, 70th Battalion, Royal Ulster Rifles

Rifleman Maxwell was discharged from the Army on 18 May 1943.

McClean, Robert Reid (Bobby)
Leading Aircraftman
No. 627576, 10 Squadron, Royal Air Force

Robert Reid (Bobby) McClean (aged 20, Aircraftman 1ˢᵗ Class based at RAF Lossiemouth, son of Albert and Ellen McClean) and Elizabeth Inglis (in some records spelt Ingles) Main (aged 19, daughter of fisherman James Main and Elizabeth Inglis Main nee MacLeod of 5 Argyle Street, Lossiemouth) were married on 23 August 1940 at St. James's Manse in Draine, Moray, Scotland according to the forms of the Church of Scotland.

McFarlane, John
Rifleman
No. 7018909, 10th Battalion, Royal Ulster Rifles

Rifleman McFarlane was knocked down by an Army utility vehicle.

Rutherford, Robert Henry (Bobby)
Flying Officer (Navigator)
No. 133718, Royal Air Force Volunteer Reserve

Flying Officer Rutherford was buried in Bangor Cemetery.

Scott, Robert Norman Cecil
Second Lieutenant
No. 89740, 10 Battery, 3 Searchlight Regiment, Royal Artillery

Second Lieutenant Scott's uncle (his mother's brother), Chief Engine Room Artificer **Bernard Christopher Vivash**, died on 1 April 1944.

Stewart, Andrew Robert (Andrew)
Lance Sergeant
No. 7012091, 2ⁿᵈ Battalion, Royal Ulster Rifles

Lance Sergeant Stewart died on 19 June 1944 after being wounded in the abdomen by shrapnel on 9 June 1944 at Cambes-en-Plaine.

Wilson, Alan McDonald (Alan)
Flight Sergeant (Navigator/Bomber)
No. 1126225, 356 Squadron, Royal Air Force Volunteer Reserve

Flight Sergeant Alan McDonald Wilson was born on 16 October 1922 and he was the elder son of Wesley James Havergal Wilson and Mary (May) Isabelle Wilson (nee Ferris) who were married on 6 January 1920 in Ballinderry Parish Church of Ireland Church, Co. Antrim. Wesley James Havergal Wilson was a grain merchant and he and May had three children – Alan McDonald (born 16 October 1922); David (born 31 March 1924) and Moyra Dorothy (born 29 October 1928). The Wilsons were active members of Duncairn Gardens Methodist Church, Belfast before they moved to Bangor.

Alan McDonald Wilson attended Bangor Technical College and afterwards worked as a clerk before he enlisted. Alan's mother died in 1959, his father died in 1963 and both were buried in Clandeboye Cemetery, Bangor.

Wilson, Garner McCartney (Garner)
Fireman
SS *Empire Heritage* (Cardiff), Merchant Navy

Garner Wilson's father, William Reid Wilson of 51 Central Street, Belfast died on 19 October 1911 (aged 38) and was buried in Belfast City Cemetery (Public Ground).

Wilson, George
Flight Sergeant
No. 522964, 156 Squadron, Royal Air Force

George Wilson (aged 23, an aircraftman, son of Robert Wilson, general merchant of 48 Frederick Street, Newtownards) and Annie Wilson (aged 22, a weaver, daughter of William John Wilson, compositor of 120 Mill Street, Newtownards) were married on 16 July 1937 in Newtownards Baptist Church.

Woods, Frederick James (Fred)
Royal Marines Police Officer
Royal Marines Police

Frederick James Woods aged 20 (son of Robert James Woods, a labourer) was a Private in the Royal Marine Light Infantry when he and Hester (Hessie) Lunn aged 20 (daughter of John Lunn, a gamekeeper) were married on 18 August 1917.

Woods, Morrison
Sapper
No. 153284, Royal Engineers

Morrison Woods was born on 17 May 1916; his parents, Morrison and Margaret Woods (nee Smith) were married on 7 December 1906.

Woods, William Charles (Willie)
Able Seaman
No. D/JX 181588, HMS *President III*, Royal Navy

William Charles Woods was born on 4 September 1909 and he was a son of Thomas and Matilda Woods who had at least twelve children – John (born 6 November 1888); Eliza Jane (born 5 October 1890); James (born 15 May 1892); Isabella (born 21 March 1894); Martha Smith (born 14 April 1896); William Charles (born 6 August 1897, died 16 November 1908); Francis (born 3 April 1899); Hugh (born 25 March 1901); Thomas (born 29 October 1902, died 31 July 1903); Mary (born 17 September 1904, married Francis Kirk on 25 June 1930 and they had a son named Ronald); Thomas (born 21 January 1907, died 25 October 1907) and William Charles (born 4 September 1909, named after his brother who died in 1908 aged 11).

Wright, Robert Ebenezer (Robert)
Civilian War Dead

Robert Wright (son of Robert Wright, a farmer then living at Ballysallagh, Newtownards) and Louise Maxwell (daughter of Thomas Maxwell, a farmer then living at *Ashvale House*, Carryduff) were married on 25 June 1929 in Lisburn Registry Office.

Acknowledgements

A great many people have contributed in different ways to the production of this book and their contributions are all gratefully acknowledged. The author extends his apologies to anyone who has been omitted from the following list. Some people have helped in more ways than one and in addition to **Heather Lyons** whose help I acknowledged at the outset I want to thank **Lester Morrow** for his military expertise and advice; **Doreen Walker** for the family history information she provided and **Wesley Johnston** of April Sky Design for his customer-care, professional advice and attention to detail.

Family details, letters from the Front, photographs and memorabilia contributed by relatives of those who died;

Assistance from other people in gathering information (including Council, Cemetery, Regimental Museum and Church representatives throughout the United Kingdom and further afield) together with members of the North of Ireland Family History Society (www.nifhs.org) and the Ulster Aviation Society (www.ulsteraviationsociety.org);

Information, photographs, photographic enhancements and advice from experts, including the authors and compilers of other Books of Honour:

George Abbs, Josie Adair, Angus Adamson, Tiffany Allen, Jane Amin, Amy Anderson, Louise Anderson, Louise Angus, Rebecca Arnott, Samuel Bailie, John Ballard, Jane Barkham, John Barnett, Susan Barr, Gerald Mavor Bell, Rosslyn Bell, Jean and Sheila (nee Belshaw), Elsie Berner, Joyce Bewley, Charlotte Bingham, Leonie Bingham, Cathleen Black, Gilbert Black, Lady Perdita Blackwood, Sean Blake, Kathleen Blayney, Bob Bleakley, Tom Boal, Doug Boreham, Richard Bourne, Terence Bowman, Sue Boyce, Des Briggs, Eleanor Brown, Kevin Browne, Louise Buffham, Ian Burnett, Valerie Burns, Charlie Burrowes, Ina Busby, Joseph Butler-Sloss, Olive Byers, Leanne Briggs, Caroline Campbell, Scott Caputo, Billy Carlile, Glynne Carse, Kevin Carter, Jean Caughey, George Cheatley, Derek Clegg, Shirley Cochrane, Gloria Colwell, Jenny Connor, Andy Copling, Fiona Cotton-Betteridge, John Craggs, Heather Craig, Christine Crockett, Ernie Cromie, Willie Cromie, Angela Crutchley, Joyce Cudworth, Will Cudworth, Joe Davidson, Rob Davidson, Wayne Davies, Peter Davis, Ian Dawson, Tom Deacon, Andrew Dennis, Sharon Deveney, Karen Dews, Ivan Dinsmore, David Donnan, Bernie Doran, Sandy Dorrian, Fiona Dove, Jane Downing, Donald Drage, Jayne Draper, Tony Dunlop, Audrey Dwyer, Vincent Elliott,

Roy Elvins, Claire Evans, Christine Ewing, Gordon Fallowfield, Ann Fee, Ann Fell, Roddy Fisher, Anne Forbes, Edwin Franklin, Erwin Franzen, Laura Fretwell, Richard Fretwell, Joanna Friel, Joanna Fuller, Ella Fulton, David Gabbie, Lynn Gardner, Jack Gault, Jim Getty, Katrina Forrest Giebels, Gavin Glass, Andy Glenfield, Dave Goble, Lorna Goudie, Edward Graham, Robert Graham, Thomas Graham, Barry Greenaway, Jack Goodman, Mary Goodman, Julie Green, Nellie Green, Richard Gun-Cuninghame, Tommy Halliday, Phyllis Hancox, Mark Hanmer, Alice Harland, Peter Harnden, Diane Harriman, Alan Harris, Roger Harrison, Colette Hawkins, William Hawkins, John Hawthorne, Andy Heber, Nigel Henderson, David Henry, John C. Hewitt, Linda Hewitt, June Heyburn, Carol Hill, Peter Hine, Ben Hodge, Raymond Hoey, Desmond Hull, Florence Hull, Alfie Hunter, Cathy Ievers, Walter Ievers, Jim Jamieson, Irene Jennings, Laura Jerome, Don Johnston, Katrina Johnston, Tracey Jolliffe, George Jones, Paddy Kelly, Joyce Kermeen, Stewart Kermeen, Julie Kessler, Barbara Kinghan, Celia Kinsella, Bill Kirk, Russ Lamb, Derick Lamond, Karen Latimer, Derek Lawson, Cyril Leathers, Jenny Lee, Michelle Lee, Bryan Legate, Gerard Lennon, Gerrard Lennon, Julia Llewellyn, Margie Love, George Lowden, Noel Lowden, Christopher Lowdon, Julie Lowe, Paul Lynas, Margaret Lyle, Heather Lyons, Gail Mack, Terence Mack, Rachel Magowan, Eileen Mann, Billy Martin, Joan Martin, Patricia Martin, Ronnie Matthews, Jemima Maxwell, Ray Maxwell, Stella Maxwell, Tom McCombe, Hazel McConnell, Jim McCormick, Brian McDonald, Christine McDowell, Norman McGimpsey, Edmund McGregor, Jack McHugh, Patrick McHugh, Derek McKimm, Kaye McKinnie, Ralph McLean, Sharon McLean-Bromley, Shirley McLoughlin, George McMurray, Bill McNee, Bill McVicker, Claire McWhirter, Heather McWilliams, David Measday, Andrew Melville, Hazel Menzies, James Meredith, Ursula Mezza, Pamela Miley, George Mills, Stuart Monard, Wendy Monson, Anne Moore, Colin Moore, Michelle Moore, Vernon Moore, Rosie Moorehead, Jonathan Morris, Michael Morris, Lester Morrow, Pauline Mossey, Byron Mullett, Kathleen Munce, Marjorie Munroe, Shirley Murphy, Zena Murphy-Hinch, Carol Murray, Charlotte Murtagh, Patrick Neely, John Neill, Tom Neill, Gordon Nelson, Margie Nelson, Hugh Nelson, Elizabeth Nesbitt, Norman Nesbitt, Anne Niblock, Mark Niblock, John Noble, Cayte Norman, Gaynor Norris, Rosemary Notley, Felicity O'Neill, Wesley O'Neill, Jean Orr, Raymond Orr, Ruth Patterson, Winnie Patterson, Ian Pearson, Molly Pearson, Michael Peck, Richard Perceval-Maxwell, Roberta Janett Phillips, Steven Pillar, Colin Pilling, Matt Poole, Fiona Porter, Anne Pringle, Rachel Quirey, Neil Redeyoff, Amanda Rhodes, Dorothy Ritchie, Judy K. Roberts, Hugh Robinson, Karen Robson, Glenda Rodgers, Simon Rogers, Ann Russell, Pat Russell, Muriel Sandford, Deirdre Sarnitz, Mick Saunders, John Savage, Kerry Savage, Shane

Savage, Yvonne Savage, Victor Sharman, Len Shear, Wayne Shepheard, Clare Sheridan, Alex Shooter, Maria Sienkiewicz, Bob Sinton, Michael Smallman, Donna Smith, Isabel Smith, Jane Smith, Paul Smith, Derek Smyth, Kannaya Somu, Pete Southern, Tommy Stevenson, Ivan Strahan, Ken Stronge, Phyllis Stuart, Jane Studholme, Michelle Sweeney, Glen Swemmer, Maureen Sykes, Alison Symington, Ron Talley, Derek Taylor, Helen Taylor, Johan Teeuwisse, Dave Telford, Alan Thompson, Helen Thompson, Mark Thompson, Joe Torney, Jane Turner, Christine Tyrrell, George Vance, Pierre Vandervelden, Claire Vinycomb, Leslie Waite, Alastair Walker, Colin Walker, Doreen Walker, Tony Walsh, Donald Ward, Andrea Waterhouse, Donald Watt, Brian Whiston, Alwyn Whitehouse, Andrew Whiteside, Kim Whitfield, Elma Wickens, Steve Williamson, Bill Wilsdon, Donna Wilson, Muriel Wilson, Meg Winters, Ken Wood, Shelagh Wright, Sue Wright, Teena Wright, Lesley Young

Permission to reproduce photographs and/or previously published information from individuals and organisations including the CWGC, the *Belfast Telegraph, Newtownards Chronicle* and *County Down Spectator* Newspapers, Danske Bank, Ulster Bank, Bangor Grammar School, Belfast Royal Academy, Campbell College Belfast, Coleraine Academical Institution, Methodist College Belfast, Portadown College, Regent House School Newtownards, Rockport School Craigavad, Royal Belfast Academical Institution, Sullivan Upper School Holywood, Ards Borough Council, North Down Borough Council, Regimental Museums and Military Archives in the United Kingdom, Australia, Canada, South Africa, New Zealand and the United States of America:

Rodney Brown, Jim Carolan, Joe Cassells, Norma Crooks, Bernie Crossan, Ian Duddy, Paul Flowers, David Gabbie, Andy Glenfield, Barry Greenaway, Malcolm Guy, Keith Haines, Nigel Henderson, Gary Knox, Norman McGimpsey, Darlene Middleton, Lester Morrow, Tom Neill, Guy Revel, Alison Symington, Brian Todd, George Vance, Alison Weir, Jackie Withers

Financial support from Ards Borough Council and North Down Borough Council

Development and maintenance of the *War Dead of North Down and Ards Website* (www.barryniblock.co.uk) by Austen Lennon of Austen Lennon Web Design (www.austenlennon.co.uk)

Professional and customer-focused publishing service from all the team at April Sky Design (www.aprilsky.co.uk)